International Business

Fourth Edition

International Business

Fourth Edition

Michael R. Czinkota *Georgetown University*

Ilkka A. Ronkainen *Georgetown University*

Michael H. Moffett *The American Graduate School of International Management (Thunderbird)*

THE DRYDEN PRESS
Harcourt Brace College Publishers

Fort Worth Philadelphia San Diego New York Orlando Austin San Antonio
Toronto Montreal London Sydney Tokyo

Acquisitions Editor   Ruth Rominger
Developmental Editor   Traci Keller
Project Editor   Kathryn Stewart
Production Manager   Eddie Dawson
Product Manager   Lisé Johnson
Art Director   Brian Salisbury
Project Management   Elm Street Publishing Services, Inc.
Compositor   York Graphic Services, Inc.
Text Type   10/12 Garamond

Address for Editorial Correspondence
The Dryden Press, 301 Commerce Street, Suite 3700, Fort Worth, TX 76102

Address for Orders
The Dryden Press, 6277 Sea Harbor Drive, Orlando FL 32887
1-800-782-4479, or 1-800-433-0001 (in Florida)

ISBN: 0-03-012888-9

Library of Congress Catalog Card Number: 95-70001

Printed in the United States of America

5 6 7 8 9 0 1 2 3 4   048   9 8 7 6 5 4 3 2 1

The Dryden Press
Harcourt Brace College Publishers

To all the Czinkotas: Ilona, Ursula, Mihaly, and Thomas—MRC
To Sirkka and Alpo Ronkainen—IAR
To Bennie Ruth and Hoy Moffett—MHM

THE DRYDEN PRESS SERIES IN MANAGEMENT

Preface

In a highly competitive market, few textbooks progress to a fourth edition. You have made that progress possible, and we are grateful for the encouragement. By the same token, we are taking the mandate from the market very seriously by further concentrating our energies on strengthening our leadership position. We present this fourth edition as another step up in our continuing effort to successfully address the realities of educational and marketplace needs in the teaching and learning of international business.

There are several reasons why this textbook is unique in its approach to international business. It goes beyond a discussion of the glamorous operations of the multinational corporation and includes the operational concerns of smaller and medium-sized firms. International business is examined from a truly global perspective rather than just the view from the United States. The reality of the interplay between business and government is specifically addressed by presenting business as well as policy concerns. The text retains a strong theory base but at the same time reflects the managerial concerns of those who work on the front lines of the business world. To enhance the "tool" value of the text, improvements in pedagogy, presentation, and writing continue to make this book fun to teach with and learn from.

CHANGES IN THE FOURTH EDITION

In preparing this edition we followed the proven corporate strategy of incremental improvement to develop and deliver a superior product. Our ultimate goal was to make the task of the instructor easier and to make the learning experience more efficient, relevant, and fun for the student.

In terms of overall content, we have added new sections in almost every chapter and further increased the focus on ethics, the environment, and diversity by fully integrating these important societal dimensions into the text. The global orientation of the book was enhanced by drawing less on U.S.-specific examples and focusing more on relevant international vignettes. In addition, during the formulation of all data, charts, and graphs, worldwide trends rather than just U.S. trends were considered. To fully incorporate global diversity into text discussion, we made a conscientious effort to eliminate the use of the term "foreign" when possible. We further increased the focus of the book on smaller and medium-sized firms by specifically addressing the issue of "what does all this mean for the smaller and medium-sized firms in terms of implementation."

Key efforts were also concentrated on improving the business relevance of the material, increasing the timeliness of the information provided, and enhancing the reader friendliness of the book. Chapter content reflects cutting edge advances in both research and practice. All tables, figures, and maps were updated to present the latest available data. The Global Perspectives featured in each chapter present the most recent business activities and the best business practices. More than half of the cases are either new or revised and now reflect more diverse coverage both in terms of geography and firm size.

Part 1 has been extensively updated with new data. More worldwide trends rather than country-specific changes are now presented, together with a new appendix that focuses on the linkages between geography and international business.

In addition, a newly expanded discussion of the evolving theories of imperfect trade, together with a comparison to the continuing work of Michael Porter, is included.

Part 2 now offers added emphasis on how the balance of payments and subaccount balances differ among diverse countries, cultures, levels, and types of industrial development. New sections discuss the continuing turmoil within the European Monetary System (EMS), the recent developments in the Central African "CFA-Zone," and the implications of the changing values of the dollar, deutschemark, and yen. Furthermore, a complete update of regional agreement is presented, the NAFTA discussion has been significantly expanded, and a section on the implications of economic integration for international managers has been added.

Part 3 discusses the shifts in political relationships with a new in-depth exposition on export controls. A completely revised section focuses on world religions and their impact on international business. Emerging market economies are treated in more detail to also include China, India, Southeast Asia, and Latin America.

In Part 4, the area of international business preparation and market entry now places more emphasis on the research issues that confront today's firms. A new section focusing on the use of computers and on-line databases for research highlights the effects of the information revolution and the most advanced research techniques in the business world. In addition, a section on manufacturing that addresses the foreign direct investment perspective, as well as the increase in intra-firm cooperation, is included.

Part 5 now concentrates even more on the phenomenon of increasing globalization and its impact on firms, governments, and individuals. New ways of cash flows across borders, particularly within the system of multinational corporations, are presented. The development of the truly global manager is discussed, together with the implementation of global programs within firms, which now increasingly include an overarching perspective that fully includes suppliers and customers in the planning and implementation process.

SPECIAL FEATURES

Art and Photo Program

In order to inspire the student's imagination, many color photographs are presented in this edition. Throughout the text, concepts are visually depicted through tables, figures, and graphics. Artwork is designed to reiterate key concepts as well as provide a pleasing format for student learning.

Organization

The text is divided into five parts. The first part introduces the basic concepts of international business activity and theory. The second focuses on the economic and financial environment, reviews institutions and markets, and delineates trade policy issues. Part 3 concentrates on the business-government interface, with special attention given to emerging market economies and state-owned enterprises. Part 4 is devoted to the preparation for international business and market entry. Part 5 covers strategic management issues.

Coverage

The text covers the international business activities of small and medium-sized firms that are new to the international arena as well as those of giant multinational corporations. It also provides thorough coverage of the policy aspects of international business, reflecting the concerns of the U.S. government, foreign governments, and international institutions.

The text consistently adopts a truly global approach. Attention is given to topics that are critical to the international manager yet so far have eluded other international texts. This coverage includes chapters on countertrade, logistics, international service trade, and doing business with newly emerging market economies under conditions of privatization.

Geography

To increase the geographic literacy of students, the specific color maps have been redesigned and updated. They provide the instructor with the means visually to demonstrate concepts such as political blocs, socioeconomic variables, and transportation routes. In addition, a unique appendix focuses specifically on the topic of geography and international business. A list of maps appears on page xxx.

Contemporary Realism

Each chapter offers a number of Global Perspectives that describe actual contemporary business situations. They are intended to serve as reinforcing examples, or mini-cases. As such, they will assist the instructor in stimulating class discussion and aid the student in understanding and absorbing the text material.

Research Emphasis

A special effort has been made to provide current research information. Chapter notes are augmented by lists of relevant recommended readings. These materials will enable the instructor and the student to go beyond the text whenever time permits.

Cases and Video Support

All sections of the text are followed by cases, many written especially for this book. Five cases are also supported by video materials available to the instructor. Challenging questions accompany each case. They encourage in-depth discussion of the material covered in the chapters and allow students to apply the knowledge they have gained. In addition, two videos from the acclaimed "Challenge to America" series by Hedrick Smith are available for purchase by students.

Pedagogy

A textbook is about teaching and we have made a major effort to strengthen the pedagogical value of this book.

- The use of color makes it easier to differentiate sections and improves the presentation of graphs and figures.
- The design of maps specific to chapters adds a visual dimension to the verbal explanation.
- The Global Perspectives bring concrete examples from the business world into the classroom.

- The video support materials enable better and more efficient instruction.
- A glossary has been provided for the student's benefit. Each key term is bold-faced and defined in the text where it first appears. A complete glossary has also been provided at the end of the text.

COMPREHENSIVE LEARNING PACKAGE

Instructor's Manual, Test Bank, and Transparency Masters

The text is accompanied by a completely revised *Instructor's Manual* designed to provide in-depth assistance to the professor. For this edition, this manual has been thoroughly updated and expanded with assistance from Myron Miller, Carol Cirulli, and Amit Shah. For each chapter of the text, the manual provides suggested teaching notes, possible group projects, an overview of the chapter's objectives, and answers to all end-of-chapter Review and Discussion Questions. Answers are provided for all the questions that follow the end-of-part cases, and video teaching notes are provided for each video case that appears in the text. In addition, an annotated list of suggested films and videos is provided. The *Test Bank* portion of the manual provides a range of over 1,000 incisive multiple choice, short answer, and essay questions for each chapter.

Computerized Test Bank and RequesTest

All the questions in the printed Test Bank are available on computer diskette in IBM- and Macintosh-compatible form. Adopters also can request customized tests with Dryden's special service, RequesTest. By simply calling our toll-free number, Dryden will compile test questions according to a requestor's criteria and then either mail or fax the test master to the user within 48 hours. The number to call is 1-800-447-9457.

Acetate Package

Transparency acetates are now available on disk from the text art and maps. Acetates are accompanied by detailed teaching notes that include summaries of key concepts.

Computerized Instructor's Manual

A computer disk that contains most elements of the *Instructor's Manual* will be available to text adopters.

The Dryden Press will provide complimentary supplements or supplement packages to those adopters qualified under our adoption policy. Please contact your sales representative to learn how you may qualify. If as an adopter or potential user you receive supplements you do not need, please return them to your sales representative or send them to:

Attn: Returns Department
Troy Warehouse
465 South Lincoln Drive
Troy, MO 63379

ACKNOWLEDG-MENTS

We are grateful to a number of reviewers for their imaginative comments and criticisms and for showing us how to get it even more right:

Kamal M. Abouzeid
Lynchburg College
Yaur Aharoni
Duke University
Riad Ajami
Rensselaer Polytechnic Institute
Joe Anderson
Northern Arizona University
Robert Aubey
University of Wisconsin-Madison
David Aviel
California State University
Bharat B. Bhalla
Fairfield University
Julius M. Blum
University of South Alabama
Sharon Browning
Northwest Missouri State University
Peggy E. Chaudhry
Villanova University
Ellen Cook
University of San Diego
Luther Trey Denton
Georgia Southern University
Gary N. Dicer
The University of Tennessee
Massoud Farahbaksh
Salem State College
Anne-Marie Francesco
Pace University-New York
Esra F. Gencturk
University of Texas-Austin
Debra Glassman
University of Washington-Seattle
Raul de Gouvea Neto
University of New Mexico
Antonio Grimaldi
Rutgers, The State University of New Jersey
John H. Hallaq
University of Idaho
Veronica Horton
Middle Tennessee State University
Basil J. Janavaras
Mankato State University
Michael Kublin
University of New Haven

Diana Lawson
University of Maine
Jan B. Luytjes
Florida International University
David McCalman
Indiana University-Bloomington
James Neelankavil
Hofstra University
Moonsong David Oh
California State University-Los Angeles
Sam C. Okoroafo
University of Toledo
Diane Parente
State University of New York-Fredonia
Jesus Ponce de Leon
Southern Illinois University-Carbondale
Jerry Ralston
University of Washington-Seattle
Peter V. Raven
Eastern Washington University
William Renforth
Florida International University
Martin E. Rosenfeldt
The University of North Texas
Tagi Sagafi-nejad
Loyola College
Rajib N. Sanyal
Trenton State College
Ulrike Schaede
University of California-Berkeley
John Stanbury
Indiana University-Kokomo
John Thanopoulos
University of Akron
Douglas Tseng
Portland State University
Heidi Vernon-Wortzel
Northeastern University
Steven C. Walters
Davenport College
James O. Watson
Millikin University
George H. Westacott
SUNY-Binghamton
Jerry Wheat
Indiana University Southeast

Many thanks to those faculty members and students who helped us in sharpening our thinking by cheerfully providing challenging comments and questions. Several individuals had particular long-term impact on our thinking. These are Professor Bernard LaLonde, of the Ohio State University, a true academic mentor; the late Professor Robert Bartels, also of Ohio State; Professor Arthur Stonehill, of Oregon State University; Professor James H. Sood, of American University; Professor Arch G. Woodside, of Tulane University; Professor David Ricks, of Thunderbird; Professor Brian Toyne, of St. Mary's University; and Professor John Darling, of Mississippi State University. They are our academic ancestors.

Many colleagues, friends, and business associates graciously gave their time and knowledge to clarify concepts; provide us with ideas, comments, and suggestions; and deepen our understanding of issues. Without the direct links to business and policy that you have provided, this book could not offer its refreshing realism. In particular, we are grateful to Secretaries Malcolm Baldrige, C. William Verity, Clayton Yeutter, and William Brock for the opportunity to gain international business policy experience and to William Morris, Paul Freedenberg, H. P. Goldfield, and J. Michael Farrell for enabling its implementation. We also thank William Casselman, Lew Cramer of US WEST, Joseph Lynch of ADI, and Reijo Luostarinen of HSE.

Valuable research assistance was provided by Peter Fitzmaurice and Kristin Sharp, as well as LuAnn Hartley, all of Georgetown University. We appreciate all of your work!

A very special word of thanks to the people at The Dryden Press. Ruth Rominger and Traci Keller made the lengthy process of writing a text bearable with their enthusiasm, creativity, and constructive feedback. Major assistance was also provided by the friendliness, expertise, and help of Michele Heinz of Elm Street Publishing Services.

Foremost, we are grateful to our families, who have had to tolerate late-night computer noises, weekend library absences, and curtailed vacations. The support and love of Ilona Vigh-Czinkota, Susan and Sanna Ronkainen, and Megan Murphy, gave us the energy, stamina, and inspiration to write this book.

Michael R. Czinkota
Ilkka A. Ronkainen
Michael H. Moffett
September 1995

About the Authors

MICHAEL R. CZINKOTA

Michael R. Czinkota is on the faculty of marketing and international business of the Graduate School and the School of Business Administration at Georgetown University. From 1981 to 1986 he was the Chairman of the National Center for Export-Import Studies at the university.

From 1986 to 1989 Dr. Czinkota served in the U.S. government as Deputy Assistant Secretary of Commerce. He was responsible for macro trade analysis, departmental support of international trade negotiations and retaliatory actions, and policy coordination for international finance, investment, and monetary affairs. He also served as Head of the U.S. Delegation to the OECD Industry Committee in Paris and as Senior Trade Advisor for Export Controls.

Dr. Czinkota's background includes eight years of private sector business experience as a partner in an export-import firm and in an advertising agency and seventeen years of research and teaching in the academic world. He has been the recipient of research grants from various organizations, including the National Science Foundation, the National Commission of Jobs and Small Business, and the Organization of American States. He was listed as one of the three most prolific contributors to international business research in the *Journal of International Business Studies* and has written several books including *International Marketing, Export Policy,* and *The Global Market Imperative.*

Dr. Czinkota served on the Board of Directors of the American Marketing Association and is on the Board of Governors of the Academy of Marketing Science and the editorial boards of the *Journal of Business Research, Journal of International Business Studies, International Marketing Review* and *Asian Journal of Marketing.* In 1991, he was named a Distinguished Fellow of the Academy of Marketing Science.

Dr. Czinkota has served as advisor to a wide range of individuals and institutions in the United States and abroad. He has worked with corporations such as AT&T, IBM, GE, Nestlé, and US WEST and has assisted various governmental organizations in the structuring of effective trade promotion policies.

Dr. Czinkota was born and raised in Germany and educated in Austria, Scotland, Spain, and the United States. He studied law and business administration at the University of Erlangen-Nürnberg and was awarded a two-year Fulbright Scholarship. He holds an MBA in international business and a Ph.D. in marketing from The Ohio State University. He and his wife, Ilona, live in Luray, located in Virginia's Shenandoah Valley.

ILKKA A. RONKAINEN

Ilkka A. Ronkainen is a member of the faculty of marketing and international business at the School of Business Administration at Georgetown University. From 1981 to 1986 he served as Associate Director and from 1986 to 1987 as Chairman of the National Center for Export-Import Studies.

Dr. Ronkainen serves as docent of international marketing at the Helsinki School of Economics. He was visiting professor at HSE during the 1987–1988 and 1991–1992 academic years and continues to teach in its Executive MBA, International MBA, and International BBA programs. Dr. Ronkainen holds a Ph.D. and a master's degree from the University of South Carolina as well as an M.S. (Economics) degree from the Helsinki School of Economics.

Dr. Ronkainen has published extensively in academic journals and the trade press. He is a co-author of *International Marketing.* He serves on the review boards of the *Journal of Business Research, International Marketing Review,* and *Journal of International Business Studies.* He served as the North American coordinator for the European Marketing Academy 1986–1990. He was a member of the board of the Washington International Trade Association from 1981 to 1986 and started the association's newsletter, Trade Trends.

Dr. Ronkainen has served as a consultant to a wide range of U.S. and international institutions. He has worked with entities such as IBM, the Rand Organization, and the Organization of American States. He maintains close relations with a number of Finnish companies and their internationalization and educational efforts.

MICHAEL H. MOFFETT

Michael H. Moffett is currently Associate Professor of Finance and International Business at the American Graduate School of International Management (Thunderbird). Dr. Moffett has a B.A. in Economics from the University of Texas at Austin (1977), an M.S. in Resource Economics from Colorado State University (1979), and M.A. and Ph.D. in International Economics from the University of Colorado, Boulder (1985).

Dr. Moffett has lectured at a number of universities around the world, including the Aarhus School of Business (Denmark), the Helsinki School of Economics and Business Administration (Finland), the Norwegian School of Economics (Norway), and the University of Ljubljana (Slovenia). Dr. Moffett has also lectured at a number of universities in the United States including Trinity College, Washington D.C., and the University of Colorado, Boulder. He is a former visiting research fellow at the Brookings Institution and he recently completed a two-year visiting professorship in the Department of International Business at the University of Michigan, Ann Arbor.

Michael Moffett's research publications have appeared in a number of academic journals, including the *Journal of International Money and Finance,* the *Journal of Financial and Quantitative Analysis, Contemporary Policy Issues,* and the *Journal of International Financial Management and Accounting.* He is co-author of *Multinational Business Finance,* sixth edition, 1992 with David Eiteman and Arthur Stonehill, as well as co-editor with Arthur Stonehill of *Transnational Financial Management* for the United Nations Centre for Transnational Corporations, 1993. He is a continuing contributor to numerous collective works in the fields of international finance and international business. Dr. Moffett has also consulted with a number of private firms both in the United States and Europe.

Brief Contents

Contents

PART 2
The International Business Environment and Institutions   77

Chapter 3   The International Economic Activity of the Nation: The Balance of Payments   78

Chapter 4   The International Monetary System: Principles and History   104

Chapter 5   International Financial Markets   138

P A R T   4
International Business Preparation and Market Entry   367

Chapter 11   International Business Research   368

PART 5
International Business Strategy and Operations   501

Chapter 14   International Marketing   502

Chapter 15   International Services   538

Chapter 16   International Logistics   564

Chapter 17   International Financial Management   596

Maps

P A R T 1

Introduction to International Business Theory and Practice

Changes in the world environment are bringing totally new opportunities and threats to firms and individuals. The challenge is to compete successfully in the global marketplace as it exists today and develops tomorrow.

Part 1 sets the stage and then provides theoretical background for international trade and investment activities. Key classical concepts such as absolute and comparative advantage are explained and expanded to include modern-day realities. The intent is to enable the reader to understand both the theoretical and practical rationale for international business activities.

CHAPTER 1

The International Business Imperative

Learning Objectives

1. To understand the history and importance of international business.

2. To learn the definition of international business.

3. To recognize the growth of global linkages today.

4. To understand the U.S. position in world trade and the impact international business has on the country.

5. To appreciate the opportunity offered by international business.

Looking for Work? Try the World

In growing numbers, students in U.S. colleges and professional schools are looking to go abroad. Traveling and working abroad traditionally has been a way to let off steam after school and gain experience before going home to the serious business of life. The difference today is that younger people are leaving the United States not for pleasure but for the "serious business of life."

U.S. business schools have noticed a quiet brain drain as of late. Fourteen percent of Stanford's class of 1994 elected to work abroad, compared to 6 percent in 1989. Business schools across the country—from UCLA to the University of Chicago to Harvard—report similar numbers. At New York University's Stern School of Business, the number of American graduates taking jobs overseas jumped 20 percent in 1994 compared to a year earlier.

Undergraduates are likewise increasing their international interests. Student applications for the University of Michigan's overseas study programs in 20 countries have shot up 70 percent during 1993 and 1994. At Duke, 9.2 percent of 1993's graduating seniors said they planned to work abroad, in contrast to 3.2 percent a year earlier.

In Buenos Aires, Martin Porcel, spokesman for the American Chamber of Commerce in Argentina, receives between 8 and 10 resumes per month. Some 19 Americans arrive in Hong Kong each day to take up jobs. In 1994, the Japanese government's Japan Exchange and Teaching Program, which offers one-year contracts to foreigners to work with local municipalities or as assistant language teachers, attracted 4,100 U.S. applicants, up fourfold since 1989. This whole phenomenon even has its own magazine, *Transitions Abroad,* targeted at American college students who want to work overseas.

Are young people venturing abroad completely out of entrepreneurial zeal, or does it also have something to do with the squeezed and stymied U.S. job market? One observer says the twentysomethings she listens to express frustration at the "logjam caused by baby boomers, so many of whom are ahead of them in management jobs and won't retire for another 20 years."

Michael Kahan is a political science professor at Brooklyn College of the City University of New York. He tells his students, all within a subway ride of Wall Street, to think globally if they can't find work at home. "Their skills could be put to better use in less developed places like Mexico and the former Soviet Union. If my students ask me where they should look for jobs, I say, 'Learn Spanish and go to Mexico. Try the unconventional. Don't just look in the *New York Times* for a job; look in *The Economist*.' " Kahan thinks worldwide career searches are likely to be commonplace in the future. "It is going to be a life choice, not a vacation or a lark like the Peace Corps, where the purpose was always to come back."

Three areas are attracting the majority of U.S. graduates: the Pacific Rim, including Tokyo and Hong Kong, but also places such as China, Vietnam, and Cambodia; Latin America, especially Mexico; and Eastern Europe and countries of the former U.S.S.R., where capitalism is breaking out all over.

Should this temporary or permanent loss of such ambitious and energetic talents be a cause of concern? William Glavin, former vice chairman of Xerox and now the president of Babson College, says, "It is not a brain drain but an enhancement of the brain power of the U.S." Glavin believes the new expatriates are receiving—and will return with—invaluable training they cannot now get at home: "A major problem in corporate America is a lack of global management knowledge. They are not going to learn much from managers in the U.S."

The dean of the Haas School of Business at the University of California, Berkeley, William Hasler, finds the current outflux of young business people "very positive, because most of these people will end up working for American companies and will be able to make those companies more successful and globalized." Even those who don't return, Hasler argues, will benefit American businesses by providing advice to their foreign employers on how to deal most productively and profitably in the United States.

Jameson Firestone is 27 and works in Moscow. He says, "Here the work is like being a doctor in an emergency room—everything is critical." What could be next for Firestone? "Jakarta, maybe. I hear that's a pretty interesting place."

Source: Paul Gray, "Looking for Work? Try the World," *Time,* September 19, 1994: 44

THE NEED FOR INTERNATIONAL BUSINESS

You are about to begin an exciting, important, and necessary task: the exploration of international business. International business is exciting because it combines the science and the art of business with many other disciplines, such as economics, anthropology, geography, history, language, jurisprudence, statistics, and demography. International business is important and necessary because economic isolationism has become impossible. Failure to become a part of the global market assures a nation of declining economic influence and a deteriorating standard of living for its citizens. Successful participation in international business, however, holds the promise of improved quality of life and a better society, even leading, some believe, to a more peaceful world.

International business offers companies new markets. Since the 1950s, growth of international trade and investment has been substantially larger than the growth of domestic economies. International business, therefore, presents more opportunities for expansion, growth, and income than does domestic business alone. International business causes the flow of ideas, services, and capital across the world. As a result, innovations can be developed and disseminated more rapidly, human capital can be used better, and financing can take place more quickly. International business also offers consumers new choices. It can permit the acquisition of a wider variety of products, both in terms of quantity and quality, and do so at prices that are reduced through international competition. International business facilitates the mobility of factors of production—except land—and, as the opening vignette has shown, provides challenging employment opportunities to individuals with professional and entrepreneurial skills. Therefore, both as an opportunity and a challenge, international business is important to countries, companies, and individuals.

A DEFINITION OF INTERNATIONAL BUSINESS

International business consists of transactions that are devised and carried out across national borders to satisfy the objectives of individuals and organizations. These transactions take on various forms, which are often interrelated. Primary types of international business are export-import trade and direct foreign investment. The latter is carried out in varied forms including wholly owned subsidiaries and joint ventures. Additional types of international business are licensing, franchising, and management contracts.

As the definition indicates, and as for any kind of domestic business, "satisfaction" remains a key tenet of international business. The fact that the transactions are *across national borders* highlights the difference between domestic and international business. The international executive is subject to a new set of macroenvironmental factors, to different constraints, and to quite frequent conflicts resulting from different laws, cultures, and societies. The basic principles of business still apply, but their application, complexity, and intensity may vary substantially.

The definition also focuses on international *transactions*. The use of this term recognizes that doing business internationally is an activity. Subject to constant change, international business is as much an art as a science. Yet success in the art depends on a firm grounding in the scientific aspects. Individual consumers, policymakers, and business executives with an understanding of both aspects will be able to incorporate international business considerations into their thinking and planning. They will be able to consider international issues and repercussions and make decisions related to questions such as these:

- How will our idea, product, or service fit into the international market?
- Should we enter the market through trade or through investment?
- What adjustments are or will be necessary?
- What threats from global competition should be expected?
- How can these threats be counteracted?
- What are the strategic global alternatives?

A Vietnamese woman walks in front of a billboard advertising Pepsi. U.S. companies were free to begin trade with Vietnam in February 1994.

Source: Reuters/Bettmann.

When management integrates these issues into each decision, international markets can provide growth, profit, and needs satisfaction not available to firms that limit their activities to the domestic marketplace. To aid in this decision process is the purpose of this book.

A Brief History

Ever since the first national borders were formed, international business has been conducted by nations and individuals. In many instances, international business itself has been a major force in shaping borders and changing world history.

As an example, international business played a vital role in the formation and decline of the Roman Empire, whose impact on thought, knowledge, and development can still be felt today. Although we read about the marching of the Roman legions, it was not through military might that the empire came about. The Romans used as a major stimulus the **Pax Romana,** or Roman peace. This ensured that merchants were able to travel safely on roads built, maintained, and protected by the Roman legions and their affiliated troops. A second stimulus was the use of common coinage, which enabled business transactions to be carried out and easily compared throughout the empire. In addition, Rome developed a systematic law, central market locations through the founding of cities, and an effective communication system; all of these actions contributed to the functioning of the marketplace and a reduction of business uncertainty.

International business flourished within the empire, and the improved standard of living within the empire became apparent to those outside. Soon city-nations and tribes that were not part of the empire decided to join as allies. They agreed to pay tribute and taxes because the benefits were greater than the drawbacks.

Thus the immense growth of the Roman Empire occurred mainly through the linkages of business. Of course, substantial effort was needed to preserve this favorable environment. When pirates threatened the seaways, for example, Pompeius sent out a large fleet to subdue them. Once this was accomplished, the cost of international distribution within the empire dropped substantially because fewer shipments were lost at sea. Goods could be made available at lower prices, which in turn translated into larger demand.

The fact that international business was one of the primary factors that held the empire together can also be seen in the decline of Rome. When "barbaric" tribes overran the empire, again it was not mainly through war and prolonged battles that Rome lost ground. Rather, outside tribes were attacking an empire that was already substantially weakened at its foundations because of infighting and increasing decadence. The Roman peace was no longer enforced, the use and acceptance of the common coinage had declined, and communications no longer worked as well. Therefore, affiliation with the empire no longer offered the benefits of the past. Former allies, no longer seeing any benefits in their association with Rome, willingly cooperated with invaders rather than face prolonged battles.

Similar patterns also can be seen during later cycles of history. The British Empire grew mainly through its effective international business policy, which provided for efficient transportation, intensive trade, and an insistence on open markets.[1] More recently, the United States developed a world leadership position largely due to its championship of market-based business transactions in the Western world, the broad flow of ideas, products, and services across national borders, and an encouragement of international communication and transportation. One could say the period from 1945 to 1990 was, for Western countries, characterized by a **Pax Americana,** an American peace.

The withholding of the benefits of international business has also long been seen as a national policy tool. The use of economic coercion by nations or groups of nations, for example, can be traced back to the time of the Greek city-states and the Peloponnesian War. In the Napoleonic wars, combatants used naval blockades to achieve their goal of "bringing about commercial ruin and shortage of food by dislocating trade."[2] Similarly, during the Civil War period in the United States, the North consistently pursued a strategy of denying international business opportunities to the South in order to deprive it of needed export revenues. More recently, the United Nations imposed a trade embargo against Iraq for its invasion and subsequent occupation of Kuwait in an attempt to force it back to its original national boundaries. Even though the measure itself was not effective in achieving withdrawal, the fact that Iraq's isolation from the trade community was seen as a major policy action demonstrates the importance of international business.

The importance of international business was also highlighted during the 1930s. At that time, the **Smoot-Hawley Act** raised import duties to reduce the volume of goods coming into the United States. The act was passed in the hope that it would restore domestic employment. The result, however, was retaliation by most trading partners. The ensuing worldwide depression and the collapse of the world financial system were instrumental in bringing about the events that led to World War II.

World trade and investment have assumed a heretofore unknown importance to the global community. In past centuries, trade was conducted internationally but not at the level or with the impact on nations, firms, and individuals that it has recently achieved. In the past 20 years alone, the volume of international trade has expanded from $200 billion to more than $4 trillion. As Figure 1.1 shows, the growth in both the volume and value of trade has greatly exceeded the level of overall world growth.

During the same time, foreign direct investment grew tenfold, from $211 billion to more than $2.13 trillion in 1993.[3] **Multinational corporations** have invested in

FIGURE 1.1
World Merchandise Exports (Value and Volume) and World Gross Domestic Product (GDP), 1980–1993

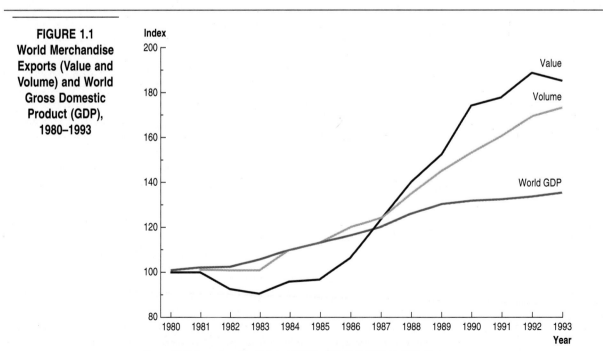

Source: World Economic and Social Survey 1994 (New York: United Nations, 1994): 64.

Global Perspective

1.1
Free Trade Needs a Dominant Champion

The whole notion of reducing trade barriers is in serious trouble. Some of the sources of this trouble include the slow growth of most of the world's economies, increased competition from developing countries, global excess capacity in most industries and, as a result of all of these forces, the politically disruptive weakness of job markets around the world. A little-noted problem may also undermine further attempts to negotiate trade pacts and even to keep commerce as open as it is now. No one is in a dominant position to impose free trade.

Only twice in history has free trade had such a powerful advocate, according to Susan B. Stanton, an economist at A. Gary Shilling & Co. She first cites the mid-nineteenth century, when Britain took advantage of its industrial head start and began liberalizing its trade in a search for markets for its greatly increased production. After a while, other industrializing nations followed Britain's path to prosperity and negotiated liberal trade agreements.

After World War II, Ms. Stanton writes, "The U.S., like 19th century Britain, was in a unique position to push for liberal trade." It had vastly expanded its industrial base during the war years and it bore the cost of free trade to help rebuild other nations' economies and fortify Cold War allies.

But in the 1970s, the Bretton Woods monetary agreement and stable currency rates collapsed. Oil shocks and surging inflation further rattled financial markets. As other industrial nations, notably Japan, grew stronger, international competition sharpened. The ending of the Soviet threat weakened the Western alliance. And developing nations stepped up exports of manufactured goods. Now, the world's economies are facing this startling array of changes without a dominant nation able to uphold free trade.

"The sudden entry of three billion people from low-wage economies such as China, Mexico, and India into the global marketplace for goods, industries, and services is provoking new concerns among workers in the old industrial countries about their living standards," said David Hale, chief economist at Kemper Financial Companies. "Demographers project that practically all the growth in the world labor supply during the next half century will occur in developing nations." New technology will play a major role, too. The invasion of developing-world competitors into the marketplace will be facilitated by continuing improvements in worldwide communications. Almost across the board, technological change will keep wiping out old jobs while creating new ones.

Many people will blame the resulting turmoil in various industries and job markets on foreign competition. Without a dominant nation with the economic power and self-interest to demand free trade, these pressures, Ms. Stanton writes, will encourage protectionism and "the formation of inward-looking trade blocs" as "the individual domestic needs of countries overwhelm their international outlook." If protectionism spreads, unchecked by a strong, persistent free trade champion, the growth of international trade could slow down in coming decades and the world's economies would pay a heavy price.

Source: Henry F. Myers, "Free Trade Idea Needs a Dominant Champion," *The Wall Street Journal,* November 22, 1993, A1.

countries around the globe, with more than 800 of them having sales of more than $1 billion. Countries that have never been thought of as major participants have emerged as major economic powers. Individuals and firms have come to recognize that they are competing not only domestically but in a global marketplace. As a result, the international market has taken on a new dynamic, characterized by major change. Global Perspective 1.1 explains how this change offers both an opportunity and a threat.

GLOBAL LINKAGES TODAY

International business has forged a network of **global linkages** around the world that binds us all—countries, institutions, and individuals—much closer than ever before. These linkages tie together trade, financial markets, technology, and living stan-

Global Perspective

1.2
Free Markets and the Environment

As trade barriers fall and large areas of the ex-communist and developing worlds move to rejoin global trade after years of isolation, the world economy is becoming swiftly intertwined—but so are its environmental problems. Global warming, greenhouse gases, and ocean dumping all are familiar ecological challenges that transcend national borders. A less familiar and less manageable problem is waste.

The tremendous increase in the exploitation of natural resources in countries that were previously closed to world markets has created new mountains of waste byproducts. Waste accumulates during the mining of raw materials as well as after their consumption. The growth of waste in these emerging markets is also a consequence of growth in manufacturing.

One of the keys to understanding the global problem of waste and pollution, however, is that much of its incidence in the developing world is due to developed nations' illegal shipment of their own waste to these regions. In effect, what has been created is world trade in environmental waste. Half a million trucks, carrying $27 billion in annual trade, now roar between Germany and Eastern Europe each year. Some of the trucks entering Eastern Europe export hundreds of thousands of tons of waste that Westerners find too expensive or too inconvenient to dispose of themselves.

The pressure is mainly financial. Under U.S. and European environmental laws today, the cost of disposing of hazardous industrial and mining waste can be as high as several thousand dollars per ton, depending on its content. Shipping such materials abroad is often much cheaper. For instance, administrators at hospitals in the Polish region of Katowice no longer open the truckloads of unsolicited, supposed medical charity shipped from the West. If they did they'd likely find soiled hospital wastes.

Even less harmful wastes, such as plastics, can cause major problems. The state of Washington sends about two-thirds of the plastic it collects from individual recyclers to

Asia, where low wage laborers go through the process of recycling or disposal without strict environmental laws. Under the massive "Green Dot" program, German consumers recycle so much plastic that the government is now paying overseas customers to accept the material. "The damage that worries me is the damage to other countries' recycling systems from having a lot of waste dumped on them . . . particularly in poor countries where recycling is often carried out by the poorest in society," said author Frances Cairncross.

Economists, traders, and multinational corporations see waste as an emerging global resource because it has value and often can be traded like a commodity. Businesses involved with the most fungible wastes, such as paper, plastics, and glass, already are planning formal commodity and futures exchanges.

The global waste management market in 1991 was worth more than $90 billion and some economic forecasters see the figure rising to $500 billion by the year 2000. However, these forecasts need to be tempered by the fact that many of the countries that would host such waste projects possess sharply varied financial resources. For instance, in Eastern Europe, earlier forecasts of a $300 billion waste management market by the year 2000 are deflating as Western businesses realize there is simply not enough money in the region to fund such an industry. Firms offering advanced but expensive waste management technology find that their "competition is the river."

Western public opinion has reached the point where even waste incinerators and landfills boasting state-of-the-art technologies—reducing pollution to miniscule amounts compared with years past—nonetheless take decades to build because of regulatory and political objections. The trouble is that if the West will not dispose of its own wastes somehow, then its incentives to export rise, even as such waste trade becomes increasingly illegal and unpopular overseas.

Source: Steve Coll, "Free Market Intensifies Waste Problem," *The Washington Post,* March 23, 1994,. A1.

dards in an unprecedented way. They were first widely recognized during the worldwide oil shock of the 1970s and have been apparent since then. A freeze in Brazil and its effect on coffee production are felt around the world. The sudden decline in the Mexican peso affected financial markets in the United States and in all emerging economies and reverberated throughout Poland, Hungary, and the Czech

Republic. Iraq's invasion of Kuwait and the subsequent Persian Gulf War affected oil prices, stock markets, trade, and travel flows in all corners of the earth.

These linkages have also become more intense on an individual level. Communication has built new international bridges, be it through music or the watching of international programs transmitted by CNN. New products have attained international appeal and encouraged similar activities around the world—we wear denims, we dance the same dances, we eat pizzas and tacos.[4] Transportation linkages let individuals from different countries see and meet each other with unprecedented ease. Common cultural pressures result in similar social phenomena and behavior—for example, more dual-income families are emerging around the world, which leads to more frequent, but also more stressful, shopping.[5]

International business has also brought a global reorientation in production strategies. Only a few decades ago, for example, it would have been thought impossible to produce parts for a car in more than one country, assemble it in another, and sell it in yet other countries around the world. Yet such global strategies, coupled with production and distribution sharing, are common today. Firms are also linked to each other through global supply agreements and joint undertakings in research and development.

Firms and governments also are recognizing production's worldwide effects on the environment common to all. For example, high acid production in one area may cause acid rain in another. Pollution in one country may result in water contamination in another. As Global Perspective 1.2 shows, the accumulation of waste itself results in more trade, often to the detriment of developing countries.

Not only the production of products has become global. Increasingly, service firms are part of the international scene. Banks, insurance companies, software firms, and universities are participating to a growing degree in the international marketplace. Figure 1.2 illustrates the global activities of a service firm.

The level of **international investment** is at an unprecedented high. Multinational corporations conducting such investments have become corporate giants which, in terms of sales, can be bigger than entire nations. Ford's sales are greater than Saudi Arabia's and Norway's economies. Philip Morris's annual sales exceed New Zealand's gross domestic product.[6] Global investment strategies have had major effects on the patterns of trade. For example, many export and import flows are the result of multinational corporations shipping products to or from their subsidiaries. Such global investment also forces companies to recognize and play by new rules in areas such as business practices, legal requirements, and **ethics.** Global Perspective 1.3 explains some of this increase in complexity.

The United States, after having been a net creditor to the world for many decades, has been a world debtor since 1985. This means that the United States owes more to foreign institutions and individuals than they owe to U.S. entities. The shifts in financial flows have had major effects on international direct investment into plants as well. While U.S. direct investment abroad in 1994 was more than $607 billion, foreign investment in the United States had grown to $505 billion.[7] As Table 1.1 shows, currently more than two-fifths of the workers in the U.S. chemical industry toil for foreign owners. Many U.S. office buildings are held by foreign landlords. The opening of plants abroad and in the United States increasingly takes the place of trade. All of these developments make us more and more dependent on one another.

This interdependence, however, is not stable. On an ongoing basis, realignments take place on both micro and macro levels that make past orientations at least partially obsolete. For example, for its first 200 years, the United States looked to Europe for markets and sources of supply. Despite the maintenance of this orientation by many individuals, firms, and policymakers, the reality of trade relationships is

International Trade as a Percentage of Gross Domestic Product

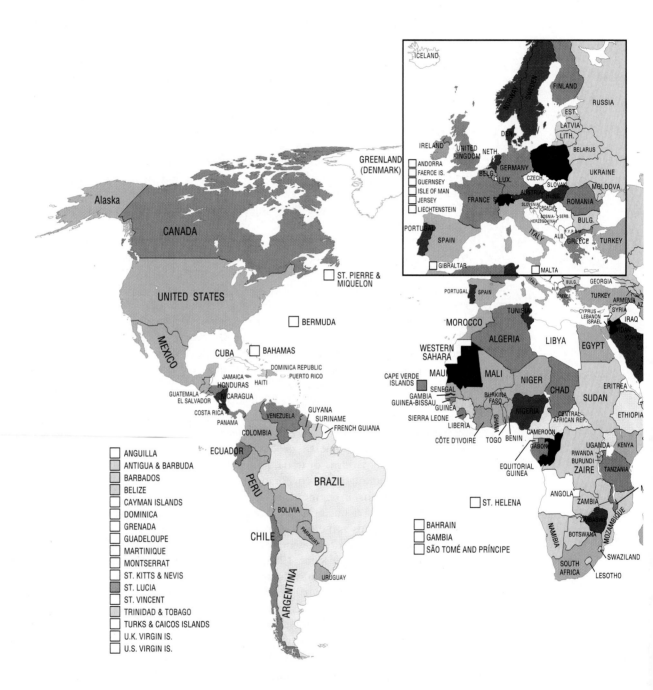

Note: $\dfrac{\text{Exports} + \text{Imports}}{\text{GDP}}$ = International Trade Percentage

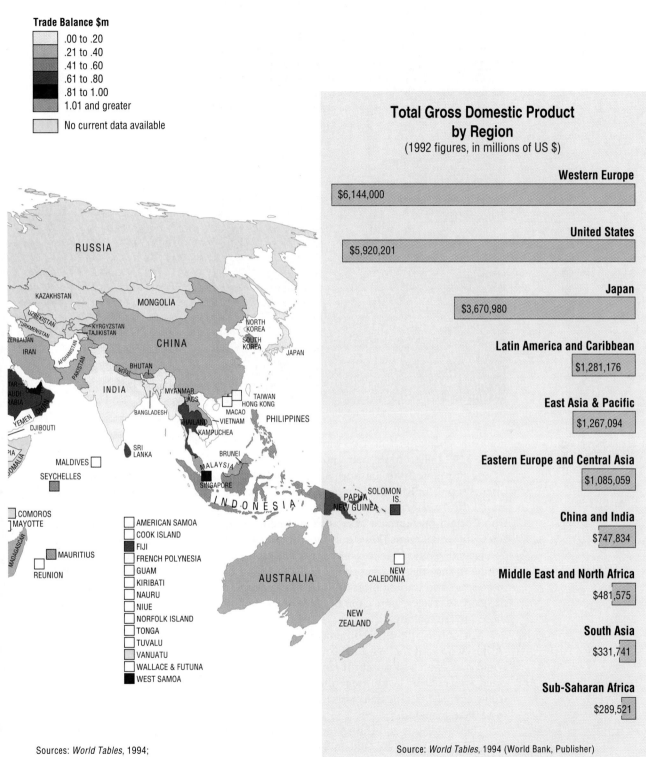

Trade Balance $m

- .00 to .20
- .21 to .40
- .41 to .60
- .61 to .80
- .81 to 1.00
- 1.01 and greater

No current data available

RUSSIA

KAZAKHSTAN

UZBEKISTAN

TURKMENISTAN

ZERBAIJAN

IRAN

MONGOLIA

KYRGYZSTAN
TAJIKISTAN

AFGHANISTAN

PAKISTAN

NEPAL

BHUTAN

CHINA

NORTH
KOREA

SOUTH
KOREA

JAPAN

INDIA

MYANMAR
LAOS

BANGLADESH

AUDI
ARABIA

YEMEN
OMAN

DJIBOUTI

SRI
LANKA

MACAO
VIETNAM
KAMPUCHEA

THAILAND

TAIWAN
HONG KONG

PHILIPPINES

PIA

SOMALIA

MADAGASCAR

MALDIVES

SEYCHELLES

COMOROS
MAYOTTE

MAURITIUS

REUNION

BRUNEI

MALAYSIA

SINGAPORE

I N D O N E S I A

PAPUA
NEW GUINEA

SOLOMON
IS.

AMERICAN SAMOA
COOK ISLAND
FIJI
FRENCH POLYNESIA
GUAM
KIRIBATI
NAURU
NIUE
NORFOLK ISLAND
TONGA
TUVALU
VANUATU
WALLACE & FUTUNA
WEST SAMOA

AUSTRALIA

NEW
CALEDONIA

NEW
ZEALAND

Sources: *World Tables*, 1994;
World Almanac, 1995, Houghton Mifflin (publisher)

Total Gross Domestic Product by Region
(1992 figures, in millions of US $)

Western Europe

$6,144,000

United States

$5,920,201

Japan

$3,670,980

Latin America and Caribbean

$1,281,176

East Asia & Pacific

$1,267,094

Eastern Europe and Central Asia

$1,085,059

China and India

$747,834

Middle East and North Africa

$481,575

South Asia

$331,741

Sub-Saharan Africa

$289,521

Source: *World Tables*, 1994 (World Bank, Publisher)

FIGURE 1.2
An Example of a Global
Services Firm

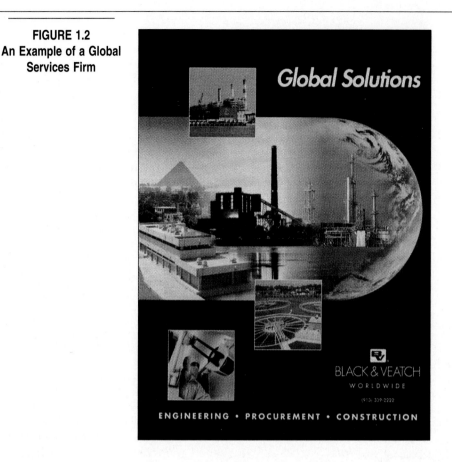

gradually changing. U.S. two-way trade across the Pacific totalled $420 billion in 1994, $177 billion more than trade across the Atlantic.

At the same time, entirely new areas for international business activities have opened up. The East-West juxtaposition had for more than 40 years effectively separated the "Western" economies from the centrally planned ones. The lifting of the Iron Curtain presented a new array of trading and investment partners. As a result, trade and investment flows may again be realigned in different directions.

Concurrently, an increasing regionalization is taking place around the world, resulting in the split up of countries in some areas of the world and the development of country and trading blocs in others. Over time, firms may find that the free flow of goods, services, and capital encounters more impediments as regions become more inward-looking.

Not only is the environment changing, but the pace of change is accelerating. "A boy who saw the Wright brothers fly for a few seconds at Kitty Hawk in 1903 could have watched Apollo II land on the moon in 1969. The first electronic computer was built in 1946; today the world rushes from the mechanical into the electronic age. The double helix was first unveiled in 1953; today biotechnology threatens to remake mankind."[8]

These changes and the speed with which they come about significantly affect countries, corporations, and individuals. For example, the relative participation of countries in world trade is shifting. As Figure 1.3 shows, the relative market share of Western Europe in trade has been declining. For the United States, the export

Global Perspective

1.3
Ethics and International Business

As the global economy becomes increasingly interdependent, cultural conflict becomes more prevalent. At the same time, societal concern for ethical corporate behavior is on the rise. These two forces intersect to highlight a particular problem of multinational businesses and any company involved in international trade or business. It is the problem of making ethical decisions when cultures have contradictory or inconsistent ethical perspectives.

Alternatives for responding to cross-cultural ethical conflict form a continuum, from complete adaptation to the host country's ethical standards to complete insistence on the application of home-country standards.

The view of adaptation encourages managers to become more familiar with a host culture, to avoid offending native sensibilities, and to build effective working relationships based on respect for the way things are done in the host country. Adaptation is also supported by the ethical stance of cultural relativism, which claims that the standards of each culture determine what is right in that culture.

On the other hand, many serious students of ethics are dissatisfied with any kind of relativism. They maintain that ethical standards are universal, and that cultural behavior that does not meet those standards should be identified as unethical. Thus, supporting governments that oppress their people or supporting ways of doing business that do not respect human life or that depend on deception are unacceptable, no matter what the culture.

In fact, neither adaptation nor relativism is satisfactory by itself. As managers face ethical conflicts, the appropriate strategies for dealing with them will depend on the nature of the specific ethical situation. The following is a range of possible responses to cross-cultural ethical conflict.

Avoiding—When a party simply chooses to ignore or not deal with the conflict; this response is often employed when the costs of dealing with the problem are high, due to, for example, massive legal fees or prolonged publicity.

Forcing—When one party forces its will upon another; often used when one party is stronger than the other, such as a host country requiring payoffs.

Education and Persuasion—An attempt to convert others to one's position by providing information and through reasoning; for example, extolling the virtues of free enterprise.

Infiltration—Deliberately or not, by introducing values to another society an appealing idea may be spread.

Negotiation and Compromise—Both parties give up something yet one or both feel dissatisfied; for example, current U.S.–Japan trade negotiations.

Accommodation—One party adapts to the ethic of the other; for instance, an American business executive might learn to drink sake to do business in Japan.

Collaboration and Problem Solving—The parties work together to achieve a mutually satisfying solution, a win-win outcome, in which both their needs are met.

The appropriate response depends on the centrality of the values at stake, the degree of social consensus regarding the ethical issue, the decision maker's ability to influence the outcome, and the level of urgency surrounding the situation. Appropriate occasions exist for the use of each of these strategies.

Source: John Kohls and Paul Buller, "Resolving Cross-Cultural Ethical Conflict: Exploring Alternative Strategies," *Journal of Business Ethics* (1994): 31.

share has declined while the import share has increased. Concurrent with these shifts, the market shares of Japan, Southeast Asian countries, and China have increased.

The **composition of trade** also has been changing. Figure 1.4 demonstrates the shift for some countries over two decades. In all instances, the role of primary commodities has dropped precipitously while the importance of manufactured goods has increased.

TABLE 1.1 **Total Assets of U.S.** **Affiliates of Foreign** **Corporations and of All** **U.S. Business in** **Manufacturing (1992)**	**Product Categories**	**Affiliates*** **($ millions)**	**All Business** **($ millions)**	**Affiliate as a Percentage of** **All Business**
	Stone, clay, glass products	$ 27,727	$ 59,359	46.7%
	Chemicals and allied products	161,181	384,491	41.9
	Rubber and plastics	17,751	61,321	28.9
	Primary metals	33,036	105,038	31.4
	Petroleum and coal	66,661	324,173	20.5
	Fabricated metals	19,370	95,915	20.1
	Electric and electronic equip.	48,635	223,677	21.7
	Printing and publishing	22,369	163,368	13.6
	Machinery (excluding electrical)	34,515	269,043	12.8
	Paper and allied products	11,420	138,036	8.2
	Instruments and related products	16,119	124,683	12.9
	Textile products	7,314	42,621	17.1
	Transportation equipment	17,224	357,567	4.8
	All manufacturing	$473,047	$2,790,910	16.9%

*Affiliates are U.S. companies owned 10 percent or more by foreigners.
Source: U.S. Department of Commerce *Survey of Current Business,* (Washington, D.C.: Government Printing Office, July 1994), 180.

FIGURE 1.3   **Merchandise Trade Flows**

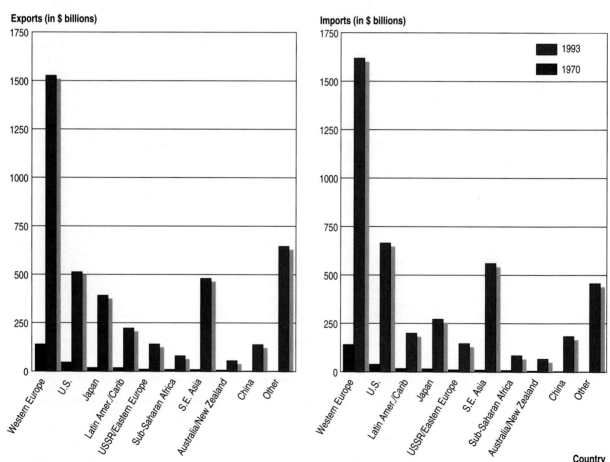

Note: Western Europe includes EU, Austria, Norway, Sweden, Switzerland, Finland;
S.E. Asia includes Singapore, Hong Kong, Thailand, Malaysia, Indonesia, Philippines.

Source: Direction of Trade Statistics (Washington D.C.: IMF, March 1995): Annual 1969–1975.

**FIGURE 1.4
The Changing
Composition of
Merchandise Exports
(1992)**

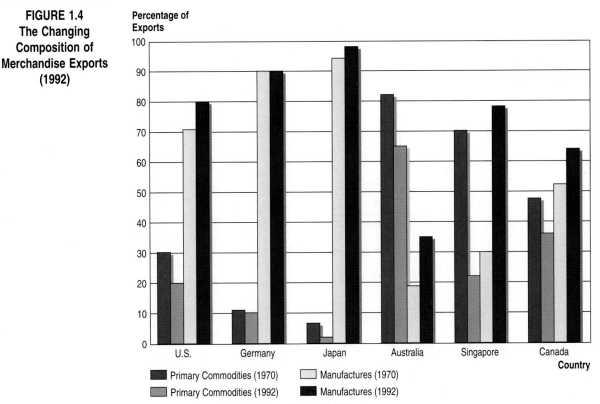

Source: The World Bank, *World Development Report 1995*, 1995.

THE CURRENT U.S. INTERNATIONAL TRADE POSITION

From a global perspective, the United States has lost some of its importance as a supplier to the world but has gained in prominence as a market for the world. In spite of the decline in the global market share of U.S. exports, the international activities of the United States have not been reduced. On the contrary, exports have grown rapidly and successfully. However, many new participants have entered the international market. In Europe, firms in countries with war-torn economies following World War II have reestablished themselves. In Asia, new competitors have aggressively obtained a share of the growing world trade. U.S. export growth was not able to keep pace with total growth of world exports.

U.S. exports as a share of the GNP have grown substantially in recent years. However, this increase pales when compared with the international trade performance of other nations. Germany, for example, has consistently maintained an export share of more than 20 percent of GNP. Japan, in turn, which so often is maligned as the export problem child in the international trade arena, exports less than 10 percent of its GNP. Exports across countries in terms of percentage of GNP can be seen in Figure 1.5.

A Diagnosis of the U.S. Trade Position

The lack of international business participation by the United States immediately fosters the question, "How did this happen?" Merely citing temporary factors such as the value of exchange rates or unfair trade barriers abroad is not enough. A further

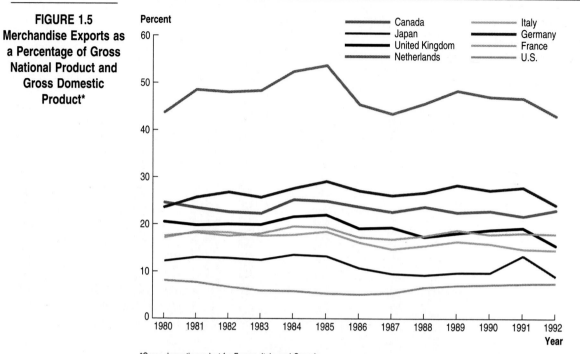

FIGURE 1.5
Merchandise Exports as
a Percentage of Gross
National Product and
Gross Domestic
Product*

*Gross domestic product for France, Italy, and Canada.
Sources: U.S. Department of Commerce, *International Economic Indicators,* March 1995, 35; IMF, *International Financial Statistics,* January 1995; *Quarterly National Accounts,* OECD, No. 2, 1995; *Bank of Canada Review,* January 1995; *Japan Economic Statistics Monthly,* November 1995; Reihe 4, *Saisonbereinigte Wirtschaftszahlen,* December 1995 (Statistische Beihette zu den Monatsberichten der Deutschen Bundesbank). Economic Intelligence Unit Country Reports.

search is needed to find the root causes of the decline in U.S. international competitiveness.

Since World War II, it had been ingrained in the minds of U.S. policymakers that their country led in world power and world business. This perception was accompanied by the belief that the United States had an obligation to help other countries with their trade performance because, without American assistance, they would not be able to play a meaningful role in the world economy. At the same time, due to strong domestic growth, the importance of international business and its impact on jobs available to U.S. workers could be overlooked in the effort to achieve other major national policy goals. Many of these goals grew out of national security concerns related to a continuing struggle against political adversaries.

The measures taken seemed reasonable in light of continuous worldwide admiration for "Yankee ingenuity." U.S. firms were viewed as the most entrepreneurial, the most innovative, and the most aggressive in the world. U.S. policymakers firmly believed that the U.S. private sector did not need any help in its international business efforts.

Because the policies established were so successful, no one wanted to tamper with them. They continued, even though the global environment changed. U.S. encouragement in the 1950s and 1960s succeeded in making other nations again full partners in the world economy. The same policies, when continued into the late 1970s, placed U.S. firms at a distinct disadvantage.

U.S. governmental actions were accompanied by assurances to U.S. firms that "because of its size and the diversity of its resources the American economy can satisfy consumer wants and national needs with a minimum of reliance on foreign

	Country	Exports per Capita	Imports per Capita
TABLE 1.2 **Exports and Imports** **per Capita for Selected** **Countries** **(1994)**	United States	$1,965	$2,546
	Canada	5,898	5,258
	France	4,037	3,953
	Germany	5,204	4,630
	Netherlands	8,765	7,938
	United Kingdom	3,596	3,989
	Japan	3,162	2,193

Source: CIA, *The World Fact Book,* 1994; Statistics Directorate, OECD, *Monthly Statistics of Foreign Trade,* April 1995.

trade."[9] U.S. firms simply did not feel a compelling need to seek business beyond national borders. Subsequently, the perception emerged within the private sector that doing business abroad was "too risky, complicated, and [therefore] not worth it."[10]

As a result of delayed adjustments in policy outlook, inadequate information, ignorance of where and how to do business internationally, unfamiliarity with foreign market conditions, and complicated trade regulations, the U.S. private sector became unwilling to participate in and fearful of international business. Table 1.2 shows the degree to which the United States comparatively "underparticipates" in international business on a per capita basis, particularly on the export side.

The Impact of International Business on the United States

Why should we worry about all of this unwillingness and fear? Why not simply concentrate on the large domestic market and get on with it? Why should it bother us that the largest portion of U.S. exports is attributed to only 2,500 companies? Why should it be of concern that the Department of Commerce estimates that tens of thousands of U.S. manufacturing firms are believed to be capable of exporting but do not do so?

U.S. international business outflows are important on the **macroeconomic level** in terms of balancing the trade account. Lack of U.S. export growth has resulted in long-term trade deficits. In 1983, imports of products into the United States exceeded exports by more than $70 billion. This deficit rose to a record $171 billion in 1987. While in the ensuing years exports increased at a rapid rate, import growth also continued. As a result, in 1994, the U.S. merchandise trade deficit was again $166.3 billion.[11] Ongoing annual trade deficits in this range are still unsupportable in the long run. Such deficits add to the U.S. international debt, which must be serviced and eventually repaid. Exports therefore continue to be a major concern, particularly since one billion dollars' worth of exports creates, on average, 20,000 jobs.[12] Exporting is not only good for the international trade picture but also a key factor in increasing employment. Imports, in turn, bring a wider variety of products and services into a country. They exert competitive pressure for domestic firms to improve. Imports, therefore, expand the choices of consumers and improve their standard of living.

On the **microeconomic level,** participation in international business can help firms achieve economies of scale that cannot be achieved in domestic markets. Addressing a global market simply adds to the number of potential customers. Increasing production also lets firms ride the learning curve more quickly and therefore makes goods available more cheaply at home. Finally, and perhaps most important, international business permits firms to hone their competitive skills abroad by meeting the challenge of foreign products. By going abroad, U.S. firms can learn from their

Global Perspective

1.4
Small U.S. Firms Are Moving Forward in the Global Marketplace

A report by the United Nations confirms what the U.S. business community is all too aware of: Small and medium-sized companies in the United States are far behind their counterparts in other countries in setting up foreign operations. Compared with Japan and Western Europe, the United States has a relatively small percentage of corporate direct investment abroad from companies with fewer than 500 employees at their home sites. Small and medium-sized U.S. companies have $15 billion in foreign direct investments, 3 percent of the U.S. total. Similar size Japanese companies had $40 billion (15 percent) and developed European countries had about $43 billion (7.5 percent), according to the report.

Hopes are, however, that this tendency within the United States will shift as global business accelerates. There are some encouraging signs. The larger size of the U.S. marketplace was the main reason so many smaller companies tended to stay home, according to one of the authors of the report. Now, U.S. overseas presence has taken a big jump since the early 1980s because even small

and medium-sized companies are beginning to feel competition from less developed countries. In addition, more firms are finding it easier to manage foreign operations or a joint venture because "recent technological developments in communications, transportation, and financial services have enabled firms of all sizes to better exploit international opportunities."

The growth in exports by U.S. companies of all sizes may well accelerate the pace of direct investments, according to John Williams, chief global economist of Bankers Trust Company. The weakness of the dollar, which makes U.S. goods cheaper for foreign customers, is giving many companies their first taste of foreign sales, he noted. "In the mid-1980s, when the dollar was much stronger, far fewer U.S. companies could compete."

Adds John Endean, vice president of the American Business Conference, "What we found with our members was that they start as exporters and move very quickly to rolling out direct investments to enhance or supplant their export strategy."

Source: Fred R. Bleakley, "Smaller Firms In U.S. Avoid Business Abroad," *The Wall Street Journal,* August 24, 1993, A7.

foreign competitors, challenge them on their ground, and translate the absorbed knowledge into productivity improvements back home. Research has shown that U.S. multinationals of all sizes and in all industries outperformed their strictly domestic counterparts—growing more than twice as fast in sales and earning significantly higher returns on equity and assets.[13] Firms that operate only in the domestic market are at risk of being surprised by the onslaught of foreign competition and thus seeing their domestic market share threatened.

The United States as a nation and as individuals must therefore seek more involvement in the global market. The degree to which Americans can successfully do business internationally will be indicative of their competitiveness and so help to determine their future standard of living.

As Global Perspective 1.4 shows, individual firms and entire industries are coming to recognize that in today's trade environment isolation is no longer possible. Both the willing and unwilling are becoming participants in global business affairs. Most U.S. firms are affected directly or indirectly by economic and political developments in the international marketplace. Firms that refuse to participate actively are relegated to reacting to the global economy. Consider how the industrial landscape in the United States has been restructured in the past decade as a result of international business.

McDonald's is one example of a U.S. service business that realized early on the opportunities available through international activities. McDonald's actively continues expansion. The company has restaurants in 79 countries with more than 15,000 restaurants worldwide; 9,750 domestically and 5,460 internationally. McDonald's opens between 900 and 1,200 new restaurants every year, two-thirds of them outside of the United States.

Source: Business Today, Spring 1995.

Some industries are beginning to experience the need for international adjustments. U.S. farmers, because of high prices, increased international competition, trade-restricting government actions, and unfair foreign trade practices, have increasingly lost world market share. U.S. firms in technologically advanced industries, such as semiconductor producers, saw the prices of their products drop precipitously and their sales volumes shrink by half in a two-year period because of foreign competition.

Other industries that were exposed early to foreign competition have partially adjusted, but with great pain. Examples abound in the steel, automotive, and textile sectors of the U.S. economy.

Still other U.S. industries never fully recognized what had happened and, therefore, in spite of attempts to adjust, were not successful and have ceased to exist. VCRs are no longer produced domestically. Only a small percentage of motorcycles are produced in the United States. The shoe industry is in its death throes.

These developments demonstrate that it has become virtually impossible to disregard the powerful impact that international business now has on all of us. Temporary isolation may be possible and delay tactics may work for a while, but the old adage applies: You can run, but you cannot hide. Participation in the world market has become truly imperative.

Global activities offer many additional opportunities to business firms. Market saturation can be delayed by lengthening or rejuvenating the life of products in other countries. Sourcing policies that once were inflexible have become variable, because plants can be shifted from one country to another and suppliers can be found on every continent. Cooperative agreements can be formed that enable each party to bring its major strength to the table and emerge with better products, services, and ideas than it could on its own. Consumers all over the world can select from among a greater variety of products at lower prices, which enables them to improve their choices and lifestyles, as Global Perspective 1.5 shows.

All of these opportunities need careful exploration if they are to be realized. What is needed is an awareness of global developments, an understanding of their meaning, and a development of the capability to adjust to change. Judging by the global linkages found in today's market and the rapid changes taking place, a

5. With wages in some countries at one-tenth of U.S. wages, how can America compete?

6. Compare and contrast domestic and international business.

7. Why do more firms in other countries enter international markets than do firms in the United States?

8. What is needed to maintain U.S. competitiveness?

Recommended Readings

Czinkota, Michael R., Ilkka A. Ronkainen, and John J. Tarrant. *The Global Marketing Imperative.* Chicago: NTC, 1995.

Hassan, Salah S., and Erdener Kaynak. *Globalization of Consumer Markets: Structures and Strategies.* New York: International Business Press, 1994.

Marquardt, Michael J., and Angus Reynolds. *The Global Learning Organization.* Burr Ridge, Ill.: Irwin, 1994.

Naisbitt, John. *Global Paradox.* New York: William Morrow, 1994.

Porter, Michael E. *The Competitive Advantage of Nations.* New York: The Free Press, 1990.

Reich, Robert B. *The Work of Nations: Preparing Ourselves for 21st-Century Capitalism.* New York: Random House, 1992.

Tyson, Laura D. *Who's Bashing Whom? Trade Conflict in High-Technology Industries.* Washington, D.C.: Institute of International Economics, 1992.

Wolf, Charles, Jr. *Linking Economic Policy and Foreign Policy.* New Brunswick, N.J.: Transaction Publishers, 1991.

Notes

1. Paul R. Krugman, "What Do Undergraduates Need to Know about Trade?" AEA Papers and Proceedings, May 1993: 23–26.

2. Margaret P. Doxey, *Economic Sanctions and International Enforcement* (New York: Oxford University Press, 1980), 10.

3. John Rutter, *Recent Trends in International Direct Investment* (Washington, D.C.: U.S. Department of Commerce), 1992.

4. Michael Marquardt and Angus Reynolds, *The Global Learning Organization* (Burr Ridge, Ill.: Irwin, 1994), vi.

5. Eugene H. Fram and Riad Ajami, "Globalization of Markets and Shopping Stress: Cross-Country Comparisons," *Business Horizons,* January–February 1994, 17–23.

6. Richard J. Barnet and John Cavanagh, *Global Dreams: Imperial Corporations and the New World Order* (New York: Simon and Schuster, 1994), 14.

7. *Survey of Current Business* (Washington, D.C.: U.S. Department of Commerce), August 1992.

8. Arthur M. Schlesinger, Jr., *The Cycles of American History* (Boston: Houghton Mifflin, 1986), XI.

9. Mordechai E. Kreinin, *International Economics: A Policy Approach* (New York: Harcourt Brace Jovanovich, 1971), 142.

10. House Subcommittee of the Committee on Government Operations, hearings on *Commerce and State Department's Export Promotion Programs,* March 22–23, 1977, 66.

11. U.S. Department of Commerce News, Economics and Statistics Administration, February 17, 1995, 1.

12. *U.S.-Latin Trade,* January 1995, 8.

13. Charles Taylor and Witold Henisz, *U.S. Manufacturers in the Global Market Place,* Report 1058, The Conference Board, 1994.

14. "Management Education," *The Economist,* March 2, 1991, 7.

The authors hope that upon finishing the book, you will not only have completed another academic subject, but also will be well versed in the theoretical, policy, and strategic aspects of international business and therefore will be able to contribute to the attainment of improved international competitiveness.

SUMMARY

International business has been conducted ever since national borders were formed and has played a major role in shaping world history. Growing in importance over the past three decades, it has shaped an environment that, due to economic linkages, today presents us with a global marketplace.

In the past two decades, world trade has expanded from $200 billion to more than $4 trillion while international direct investment has grown from $211 billion to $2.13 trillion. The growth of both has been more rapid than the growth of most domestic economies. As a result, nations are much more affected by international business than in the past. Global linkages have made possible investment strategies and business alternatives that offer tremendous opportunities. Yet these changes and the speed of change also can represent threats to nations and firms.

Over the past 30 years, the dominance of the U.S. international trade position has gradually eroded. Increasingly, new participants in international business compete fiercely for world market share, and U.S. firms have fallen behind in their global competitiveness. Apart from changes in the world environment, this development is mainly the result of delays in policy adjustments and an unwillingness by the U.S. private sector to participate in international business.

Yet times are changing. Individuals, corporations, and policymakers have awakened to the fact that international business is a major imperative and opportunity for future growth and prosperity. International business offers access to new customers, affords economies of scale, and permits the honing of competitive skills. Performing well in global markets is the key to improved standards of living, higher profits, and the continued leadership of the United States in the world. Knowledge about international business is therefore important to everyone, whether it is used to compete with foreign firms or simply to add to an understanding of the world around us.

Key Terms and Concepts

Pax Romana

Smoot-Hawley Act

multinational corporation

global linkages

macroeconomic level

microeconomic level

Pax Americana

international investment

ethics

composition of trade

globalization

Questions for Discussion

1. Will future expansion of international business be similar to that in the past?
2. Discuss the reasons for the decline in the U.S. world trade market share.
3. Does increased international business mean increased risk?
4. Is it beneficial for nations to become dependent on one another?

5. With wages in some countries at one-tenth of U.S. wages, how can America compete?

6. Compare and contrast domestic and international business.

7. Why do more firms in other countries enter international markets than do firms in the United States?

8. What is needed to maintain U.S. competitiveness?

Recommended Readings

Czinkota, Michael R., Ilkka A. Ronkainen, and John J. Tarrant. *The Global Marketing Imperative.* Chicago: NTC, 1995.

Hassan, Salah S., and Erdener Kaynak. *Globalization of Consumer Markets: Structures and Strategies.* New York: International Business Press, 1994.

Marquardt, Michael J., and Angus Reynolds. *The Global Learning Organization.* Burr Ridge, Ill.: Irwin, 1994.

Naisbitt, John. *Global Paradox.* New York: William Morrow, 1994.

Porter, Michael E. *The Competitive Advantage of Nations.* New York: The Free Press, 1990.

Reich, Robert B. *The Work of Nations: Preparing Ourselves for 21st-Century Capitalism.* New York: Random House, 1992.

Tyson, Laura D. *Who's Bashing Whom? Trade Conflict in High-Technology Industries.* Washington, D.C.: Institute of International Economics, 1992.

Wolf, Charles, Jr. *Linking Economic Policy and Foreign Policy.* New Brunswick, N.J.: Transaction Publishers, 1991.

Notes

1. Paul R. Krugman, "What Do Undergraduates Need to Know about Trade?" AEA Papers and Proceedings, May 1993: 23–26.

2. Margaret P. Doxey, *Economic Sanctions and International Enforcement* (New York: Oxford University Press, 1980), 10.

3. John Rutter, *Recent Trends in International Direct Investment* (Washington, D.C.: U.S. Department of Commerce), 1992.

4. Michael Marquardt and Angus Reynolds, *The Global Learning Organization* (Burr Ridge, Ill.: Irwin, 1994), vi.

5. Eugene H. Fram and Riad Ajami, "Globalization of Markets and Shopping Stress: Cross-Country Comparisons," *Business Horizons,* January–February 1994, 17–23.

6. Richard J. Barnet and John Cavanagh, *Global Dreams: Imperial Corporations and the New World Order* (New York: Simon and Schuster, 1994), 14.

7. *Survey of Current Business* (Washington, D.C.: U.S. Department of Commerce), August 1992.

8. Arthur M. Schlesinger, Jr., *The Cycles of American History* (Boston: Houghton Mifflin, 1986), XI.

9. Mordechai E. Kreinin, *International Economics: A Policy Approach* (New York: Harcourt Brace Jovanovich, 1971), 142.

10. House Subcommittee of the Committee on Government Operations, hearings on *Commerce and State Department's Export Promotion Programs,* March 22–23, 1977, 66.

11. U.S. Department of Commerce News, Economics and Statistics Administration, February 17, 1995, 1.

12. *U.S.–Latin Trade,* January 1995, 8.

13. Charles Taylor and Witold Henisz, *U.S. Manufacturers in the Global Market Place,* Report 1058, The Conference Board, 1994.

14. "Management Education," *The Economist,* March 2, 1991, 7.

McDonald's is one example of a U.S. service business that realized early on the opportunities available through international activities. McDonald's actively continues expansion. The company has restaurants in 79 countries with more than 15,000 restaurants worldwide; 9,750 domestically and 5,460 internationally. McDonald's opens between 900 and 1,200 new restaurants every year, two-thirds of them outside of the United States.

Source: Business Today, Spring 1995.

Some industries are beginning to experience the need for international adjustments. U.S. farmers, because of high prices, increased international competition, trade-restricting government actions, and unfair foreign trade practices, have increasingly lost world market share. U.S. firms in technologically advanced industries, such as semiconductor producers, saw the prices of their products drop precipitously and their sales volumes shrink by half in a two-year period because of foreign competition.

Other industries that were exposed early to foreign competition have partially adjusted, but with great pain. Examples abound in the steel, automotive, and textile sectors of the U.S. economy.

Still other U.S. industries never fully recognized what had happened and, therefore, in spite of attempts to adjust, were not successful and have ceased to exist. VCRs are no longer produced domestically. Only a small percentage of motorcycles are produced in the United States. The shoe industry is in its death throes.

These developments demonstrate that it has become virtually impossible to disregard the powerful impact that international business now has on all of us. Temporary isolation may be possible and delay tactics may work for a while, but the old adage applies: You can run, but you cannot hide. Participation in the world market has become truly imperative.

Global activities offer many additional opportunities to business firms. Market saturation can be delayed by lengthening or rejuvenating the life of products in other countries. Sourcing policies that once were inflexible have become variable, because plants can be shifted from one country to another and suppliers can be found on every continent. Cooperative agreements can be formed that enable each party to bring its major strength to the table and emerge with better products, services, and ideas than it could on its own. Consumers all over the world can select from among a greater variety of products at lower prices, which enables them to improve their choices and lifestyles, as Global Perspective 1.5 shows.

All of these opportunities need careful exploration if they are to be realized. What is needed is an awareness of global developments, an understanding of their meaning, and a development of the capability to adjust to change. Judging by the global linkages found in today's market and the rapid changes taking place, a

Global Perspective

1.5
Affluence through Global Business

Consumers in advanced nations are learning how to be affluent. Consider this example of an affluent person living in Asia: He wears Ferragamo-designed shirts and Hermes ties, sports a Rolex or Cartier watch, has a Louis Vuitton attaché case, signs his signature with a Montblanc pen, goes to work in his flashy BMW, endlessly talks on a mobile Motorola cellular phone, puts all his charges on an American Express card, and travels Singapore Airlines. He uses Giorgio Armani aftershave and buys Poison perfume for his girlfriend. As a career woman, the girlfriend's wardrobe is filled with Christian Dior and Nina Ricci clothes, her dressing table is congested with makeup and skin-care products from Guerlain, YSL, and Estée Lauder, her shoes are from Bruno Magli, and she wears Chanel No. 5 and jewelry from Tiffany. They both listen to Beethoven's Ninth Symphony on their Sony compact disc player in her Mazda sports car.

Source: Adapted from John Naisbitt, *Global Paradox* (New York: Morrow and Co., 1994), 31.

background in international business is highly desirable for business students seeking employment. **Globalization** is the watchword that "describes the need for companies and their employees, if they are to prosper, to treat the world as their stage."[14]

THE STRUCTURE OF THE BOOK

This book is intended to enable you to become a better, more successful participant in the global business place. It is written for both those who want to attain more information about what is going on in international markets in order to be more well-rounded and better educated and for those who want to translate their knowledge into successful business transactions. The text melds theory and practice in order to provide a balance between conceptual understanding and knowledge of day-to-day realities. The book therefore addresses the international concerns of both beginning internationalists and multinational corporations.

The beginning international manager will need to know the answers to basic, yet important, questions: How can I find out whether demand for my product exists abroad? What must I do to get ready to market internationally? These issues are also relevant for managers in multinational corporations, but the questions they consider are often much more sophisticated. Of course, the resources available to address them are also much greater.

Throughout the book, public policy concerns are included in discussions of business activities. In this way, you are exposed to both macro and micro issues. Part 1 of the book serves as an introduction to the field of international business, stressing its importance and theoretical foundation. Part 2 focuses on the international business environment and institutions, with particular emphasis on the financial dimensions. Part 3 discusses the interaction between international business and the nation–state and addresses policy, political, legal, and cultural issues. Part 4 presents the research activities required to properly prepare for international business and the options for market entry. Part 5 reviews international business management issues from a strategic perspective.

Geographical Perspectives on International Business[1]

The dramatic changes in the world of business have made geography indispensable for the study of international business. Without significant attention to the study of geography, critical ideas and information about the world in which business occurs will be missing.

Just as the study of business has changed significantly in recent decades, so has the study of geography. Once considered by many to be simply a descriptive inventory that filled in blank spots on maps, geography has emerged as an analytic approach that uses scientific methods to answer important questions.

Geography focuses on answering "Where?" questions. Where are things located? What is their distribution across the surface of the earth? An old aphorism holds, "If you can map it, it's geography." That statement is true, because one uses maps to gather, store, analyze, and present information that answers "Where?" questions. But identifying where things are located is only the first phase of geographic inquiry. Once locations have been determined, "Why?" and "How?" questions can be asked. Why are things located where they are? How do different things relate to one another at a specific place? How do different places relate to each other? How have geographic patterns and relationships changed over time? These are the questions that take geography beyond mere description and make it a powerful approach for analyzing and explaining geographical aspects of a wide range of different kinds of problems faced by those engaged in international business.

Geography answers questions related to the location of different kinds of economic activity and the transactions that flow across national boundaries. It provides insights into the natural and human factors that influence patterns of production and consumption in different parts of the world. It explains why patterns of trade and exchange evolve over time. And because a geographic perspective emphasizes the analysis of processes that result in different geographic patterns, it provides a means for assessing how patterns might change in the future.

Geography has a rich tradition. Classical Greeks, medieval Arabs, enlightened European explorers, and twentieth-century scholars in the United States and elsewhere have organized geographic knowledge in many different ways. In recent decades, however, geography has become more familiar and more relevant to many people because emphasis has been placed on five fundamental themes as ways to structure geographic questions and to provide answers for those questions. Those themes are (1) location, (2) place, (3) interaction, (4) movement, and (5) region. The five themes are neither exclusive nor exhaustive. They complement other disciplinary approaches for organizing information, some of which are better suited to addressing specific kinds of questions. Other questions require insights related to two or more of the themes. Experience has shown, however, that the five themes provide a powerful means for introducing students to the geographic perspective. As a result, they provide the structure for this discussion.

---

1. This appendix was contributed by Thomas J. Baerwald. Dr. Baerwald is deputy assistant director for the geosciences at the National Science Foundation in Arlington, Virginia. He is co-author of *Prentice Hall World Geography*—a best selling geography textbook.

LOCATION

For decades, people engaged in real estate development have said that the value of a place is a product of three factors: location, location, and location. This statement also highlights the importance of location for international business. Learning the location and characteristics of other places has always been important to those interested in conducting business outside their local areas. The drive to learn about other kinds of places, and especially their resources and potential as markets, has stimulated geographic exploration throughout history. Explorations of the Mediterranean by the Phoenicians, Marco Polo's journey to China, and voyages undertaken by Christopher Columbus, Vasco da Gama, Henry Hudson, and James Cook not only improved general knowledge of the world but also expanded business opportunities.

Assessing the role of location requires more than simply determining specific locations where certain activities take place. Latitude and longitude often are used to fix the exact location of features on the Earth's surface, but to simply describe a place's coordinates provides relatively little information about that place. Of much greater significance is its location relative to other features. The city of Singapore, for example, is between 1 and 2 degrees North latitude and is just west of 104 degrees East longitude. Its most pertinent locational characteristics, however, include its being at the southern tip of the Malay Peninsula near the eastern end of the Strait of Malacca, a critical shipping route connecting the Indian Ocean with the South China Sea. For nearly 150 years, this location made Singapore an important center for trade in the British Empire. After attaining independence in 1965, Singapore's leaders diversified its economy and complemented trade in its bustling port with numerous manufacturing plants that export products to nations around the world.

An understanding of how location influences business therefore is critical for the international business executive. Without clear knowledge of an enterprise's location relative to its suppliers, to its market, and to its competitors, an executive operates like the captain of a fog-bound vessel that has lost all navigational instruments and is heading for dangerous shoals.

PLACE

In addition to its location, each place has a diverse set of characteristics. Although many of those characteristics are present in other places, the ensemble makes each place unique. The characteristics of places—both natural and human—profoundly influence the ways that business executives in different places participate in international economic transactions.

Natural Features

Many of the characteristics of a place relate to its natural attributes. **Geologic characteristics** can be especially important, as the presence of critical minerals or energy resources may make a place a world-renowned supplier of valuable products. Gold and diamonds help make South Africa's economy the most prosperous on that continent. Rich deposits of iron ore in southern parts of the Amazon Basin have made Brazil the world's leading exporter of that commodity, while Chile remains a preeminent exporter of copper. Coal deposits provided the foundation for massive industrial development in the eastern United States, the Rhein River Basin of Europe, in western Russia, and in northeastern China. Because of abundant pools of petroleum beneath desert sands, standards of living in Saudi Arabia and nearby nations have risen rapidly to be among the highest in the world.

The geology of places also shapes its **terrain.** People traditionally have clustered in lower, flatter areas, because valleys and plains have permitted the agricultural development necessary to feed the local population and to generate surpluses that can be traded. Hilly and mountainous areas may support some people, but their population densities invariably are lower. Terrain also plays a critical role in focusing and inhibiting the movement of people and goods. Business leaders throughout the centuries have capitalized on this fact. Just as feudal masters sought control of mountain passes in order to collect tolls and other duties from traders who traversed an area, modern executives maintain stores and offer services near bridges and at other points where terrain focuses travel.

The terrain of a place is related to its **hydrology.** Rivers, lakes, and other bodies of water influence the kinds of economic activities that occur in a place. In general, abundant supplies of water boost economic development, because water is necessary for the sustenance of people and for both agricultural and industrial production. Locations like Los Angeles and Saudi Arabia have prospered despite having little local water, because other features offer advantages that more than exceed the additional costs incurred in delivering water supplies from elsewhere. While sufficient water must be available to meet local needs, overabundance of water may pose serious problems, such as in Bangladesh, where development has been inhibited by frequent flooding. The character of a place's water bodies also is important. Smooth-flowing streams and placid lakes can stimulate transportation within a place and connect it more easily with other places, while waterfalls and rapids can prevent navigation on streams. The rapid drop in elevation of such streams may boost their potential for hydroelectric power generation, however, thereby stimulating development of industries requiring considerable amounts of electricity. Large plants producing aluminum, for example, are found in the Tennessee and Columbia river valleys of the United States and in Quebec and British Columbia in Canada. These plants refine materials that originally were extracted elsewhere, especially bauxite and alumina from Caribbean nations like Jamaica and the Dominican Republic. Although the transport costs incurred in delivery of these materials to the plants is high, those costs are more than offset by the presence of abundant and inexpensive electricity.

Climate is another natural feature that has profound impact on economic activity within a place. Many activities are directly affected by climate. Locales blessed with pleasant climates, such as the Cote d'Azur of France, the Crimean Peninsula of Ukraine, Florida, and the "Gold Coast" of northeastern Australia, have become popular recreational havens, attracting tourists whose spending fuels the local economy. Agricultural production also is influenced by climate. The average daily and evening temperatures, the amount and timing of precipitation, the timing of frosts and freezing weather, and the variability of weather from one year to the next all influence the kinds of crops grown in an area. Plants producing bananas and sugar cane flourish in moist tropical areas, while cooler climates are more conducive for crops such as wheat and potatoes. Climate influences other industries, as well. The aircraft manufacturing industry in the United States developed largely in warmer, drier areas where conditions for test and delivery flights were more beneficial throughout the year. In a similar way, major rocket-launching facilities have been placed in locations where climatic conditions are most favorable. As a result, the primary launch site of the European Space Agency is not in Europe at all, but rather in the South American territory of French Guiana. Climate also affects the length of the work day and the length of economic seasons. For example, in some regions of the world, the construction industry can build only during a few months of the year because permafrost makes construction prohibitively expensive the rest of the year.

Variations in **soils** have a profound impact on agricultural production. The world's great grain-exporting regions, including the central United States, the Prairie Provinces of Canada, the "Fertile Triangle" stretching from central Ukraine through southern Russia into northern Kazakhstan, and the Pampas of northern Argentina, all have been blessed with mineral-rich soils made even more fertile by humus from natural grasslands that once dominated the landscape. Soils are less fertile in much of the Amazon Basin of Brazil and in central Africa, where heavy rains leave few nutrients in upper layers of the soil. As a result, few commercial crops are grown.

The **interplay between climate and soils** is especially evident in the production of wines. Hundreds of varieties of grapes have been bred in order to take advantage of the different physical characteristics of various places. The wines fermented from these grapes are shipped around the world to consumers, who differentiate among various wines based not only on the grapes but also on the places where they were grown and the conditions during which they matured.

Human Features

The physical features of a place provide natural resources and influence the types of economic activities in which people engage, but its human characteristics also are critical. The **population** of a place is important because farm production may require intensive labor to be successful, as is true in rice-growing areas of eastern Asia. The skills and qualifications of the population also play a role in determining how a place fits into global economic affairs. Although blessed with few mineral resources and a terrain and climate that limit agricultural production, the Swiss have emphasized high levels of education and training in order to maintain a labor force that manufactures sophisticated products for export around the world. In recent decades, Japan and smaller nations such as South Korea and Taiwan have increased the productivity of their workers to become major industrial exporters.

As people live in a place, they modify it, creating a **built environment** that can be as or more important than the natural environment in economic terms. The most pronounced areas of human activity and their associated structures are in cities. In nations around the world, cities have grown dramatically during the twentieth century. Much of the growth of cities has resulted from the migration of people from rural areas. This influx of new residents broadens the labor pool and creates vast new demand for goods and services. As urban populations have grown, residences and other facilities have replaced rural land uses. Executives seeking to conduct business in foreign cities need to be aware that the geographic patterns found in their home cities are not evident in many other nations. For example, in the United States, wealthier residents generally have moved outward and as they established their residences, stores and services followed. Residential patterns in the major cities of Latin America and other developing nations tend to be reversed, with the wealthy remaining close to the city center while poorer residents are consigned to the outskirts of town. A store location strategy that is successful in the United States therefore may fail miserably if transferred directly to another nation without knowledge of the different geographic patterns of that nation's cities.

INTERACTION

The international business professional seeking to take advantage of opportunities present in different places learns not to view each place separately. How a place functions depends not only on the presence and form of certain characteristics but also on interactions among those characteristics. Fortuitous combinations of features can spur a region's economic development. The presence of high-grade supplies of iron ore, coal, and limestone powered the growth of Germany's Ruhr Valley as one of Europe's foremost steel-producing regions, just as the proximity of the fertile Pampas and the deep channel of the Rio de la Plata combine to make Buenos Aires the leading economic center in southern South America.

Interactions among different features change over time within places, and as they do, so does that place's character and its economic activities. Human activities can have profound impacts on natural features. The courses of rivers and streams are changed, as dams are erected and meanders are straightened. Soil fertility can be improved through fertilization. Vegetation is changed, with naturally growing plants replaced by crops and other varieties that require careful management.

Many human modifications have been successful. For centuries, the Dutch have constructed dikes and drainage systems, slowly creating polders—land that once was covered by the North Sea but that now is used for agricultural production. But other human activities have had disastrous impacts on natural features. A large area in Ukraine and Belarus was rendered uninhabitable by radioactive materials leaked from the Chernobyl reactor in 1986. In countless other places around the globe, improper disposal of wastes has seriously harmed land and water resources. In some places, damage can be repaired, as has happened in rivers and lakes of the United States following the passage of measures to curb water pollution in the last three decades, but in other locales, restoration may be impossible.

Growing concerns about environmental quality have led many people in more economically advanced nations to call for changes in economic systems that harm the natural environment. Concerted efforts are under way, for example, to halt destruction of forests in the Amazon Basin, thereby preserving the vast array of different plant and animal species in the region and saving vegetation that can help moderate the world's climate. Cooperative ventures have been established to promote selective harvesting of nuts, hardwoods, and other products taken from natural forests. Furthermore, an increasing number of restaurants and grocers are refusing to purchase beef raised on pastures that are established by clearing forests.

Like so many other geographical relationships, the nature of human–environmental interaction changes over time. With technological advances, people have been able to modify and adapt to natural features in increasingly sophisticated ways. The development of air conditioning has permitted people to function more effectively in torrid tropical environments, thereby enabling the populations of cities such as Houston, Rio de Janeiro, and Jakarta to multiply many times over in recent decades. Owners of winter resorts now can generate snow artificially to ensure favorable conditions for skiers. Advanced irrigation systems now permit crops to be grown in places such as the southwestern United States, northern Africa, and Israel. The use of new technologies may cause serious problems over the long run, however. Extensive irrigation in large parts of the U.S. Great Plains has seriously depleted ground water supplies. In central Asia, the diversion of river water to irrigate cotton fields in Kazakhstan and Uzbekistan has reduced the size of the Aral Sea by more than one-half since 1960. In future years, business leaders may need to factor into their decisions additional costs associated with the restoration of environmental quality after they have finished using a place's resources.

MOVEMENT

Whereas the theme of interaction encourages consideration of different characteristics within a place, movement provides a structure for considering how different places relate to each other. International business exists because movement permits the transportation of people and goods and communication of information and ideas among different places. No matter how much people in one place want something found elsewhere, they cannot have it unless transportation systems permit the good to be brought to them or allow them to move to the location of the good.

The location and character of transportation and communication systems long have had powerful influences on the economic standing of places. Especially significant have been places on which transportation routes have focused. Many ports have become prosperous cities because they channeled the movement of goods and people between ocean and inland waterways. New York became the largest city in North America because its harbor provided sheltered anchorage for ships crossing the Atlantic; the Hudson River provided access leading into the interior of the continent. In eastern Asia, Hong Kong grew under similar circumstances, as British traders used its splendid harbor as an exchange point for goods moving in and out of southern China.

Businesses also have succeeded at well-situated places along overland routes. The fabled oasis of Tombouctou has been an important trading center for centuries because it had one of the few dependable sources of water in the Sahara. Chicago's ascendancy as the premier city of the U.S. heartland came when its early leaders engineered its selection as the termination point for a dozen railroad lines converging from all directions. Not only did much of the rail traffic moving through the region have to pass through Chicago, but passengers and freight passing through the city had to be transferred from one line to another, a process that generated numerous jobs and added considerably to the wealth of many businesses in the city.

In addition to the business associated directly with the movement of people and goods, other forms of economic activity have become concentrated at critical points in the transportation network. Places where transfers from one mode of transportation to another were required often were chosen as sites for manufacturing activities. Buffalo was the most active flour-milling center in the United States for much of the twentieth century because it was the point where Great Lakes freighters carrying wheat from the northern Great Plains and Canadian prairies were unloaded. Rather than simply transfer the wheat into rail cars for shipment to the large urban markets of the northeastern United States, millers transformed the wheat into flour in Buffalo, thereby reducing the additional handling of the commodity.

Global patterns of resource refining also demonstrate the wisdom of careful selection of sites with respect to transportation systems. Some of the world's largest oil refineries are located at places like Bahrain and Houston, where pipelines bring oil to points where it is processed and loaded onto ships in the form of gasoline or other distillates for transport to other locales. Massive refinery complexes also have been built in the Tokyo and Nagoya areas of Japan and near Rotterdam in the Netherlands to process crude oil brought by giant tankers from the Middle East and other oil-exporting regions. For similar reasons, the largest new steel mills in the United States are near Baltimore and Philadelphia, where iron ore shipped from Canada and Brazil is processed. Some of the most active aluminum works in Europe are beside Norwegian fjords, where abundant local hydroelectric power is used to process imported alumina.

Favorable location along transportation lines is beneficial for a place. Conversely, an absence of good transportation severely limits the potential for firms to succeed in a specific place. Transportation patterns change over time, however, and so does their impact on places. Some places maintain themselves because their business leaders use their size and economic power to become critical nodes in newly evolving transportation networks. New York's experience provides a good example of this process. New York became the United States's foremost business center in the early nineteenth century because it was ideally situated for water transportation. As railroad networks evolved later in that century, they sought New York connections in order to serve its massive market. During the twentieth century, a complex web of roadways and major airports reinforced New York's supremacy in the eastern United States. In similar ways, London, Moscow, and Tokyo reasserted themselves as transportation hubs for their nations through successive advances in transport technology.

Failure to adapt to changing transportation patterns can have deleterious impacts on a place. During the middle of the nineteenth century, business leaders in St. Louis discouraged railroad construction, seeking instead to maintain the supremacy of river transportation. Only after it became clear that railroads were the mode of preference did St. Louis officials seek to develop rail connections for the city, but by then it was too late; Chicago had ascended to a dominant position in the region. For about 30 years during the middle part of the twentieth century, airports at Gander, Newfoundland, Canada, and Shannon, Ireland, became important refueling points for trans-Atlantic flights. The development of planes that could travel nonstop for much longer distances returned those places to sleepy oblivion.

Continuing advances in transportation technology effectively have "shrunk" the world. Just a few centuries ago, travel across an ocean took harrowing months. As late as 1873, readers marveled when Jules Verne wrote of a hectic journey around the world in 80 days. Today's travelers can fly around the globe in less than 80 hours, and the speed and dependability of modern modes of transport have transformed the ways in which business is conducted. Modern manufacturers have transformed the notion of relationships among suppliers, manufacturers, and markets. Automobile manufacturers, for example, once maintained large stockpiles of parts in assembly plants that were located near the parts plants or close to the places where the cars would be sold. Contemporary auto assembly plants now are built in places where labor costs and worker productivity are favorable and where governments have offered attractive inducements. They keep relatively few parts on hand, calling on suppliers for rapid delivery of parts as they are needed when orders for new cars are received. This "just-in-time" system of production leaves manufacturers subject to disruptions caused by work stoppages at supply plants and to weather-related delays in the transportation system, but losses associated with these infrequent events are more than offset by reduced operating costs under normal conditions.

The role of advanced technology as a factor affecting international business is even more apparent with respect to advances in communications systems. Sophisticated forms of telecommunication that began more than 150 years ago with the telegraph have advanced through the telephone to facsimile transmissions and electronic mail networks. As a result, distance has practically ceased to be a consideration with respect to the transmission of information. Whereas information once moved only as rapidly as the person carrying the paper on which the information was written, data and ideas now can be sent instantaneously almost anywhere in the world.

These communication advances have had a staggering impact on the way that international business is conducted. They have fostered the growth of multinational corporations, which operate in diverse sites around the globe while maintaining effective links with headquarters and regional control centers. International financial operations also have been transformed because of communication advances. Money and stock markets in New York, London, Tokyo, and secondary markets such as Los Angeles, Frankfurt, and Hong Kong now are connected by computer systems that process transactions around the clock. As much as any other factor, the increasingly mobile forms of money have enabled modern business executives to engage in activities around the world.

REGIONS

In addition to considering places by themselves or how they relate to other places, regions provide alternative ways to organize groups of places in more meaningful ways. A region is a set of places that share certain characteristics. Many regions are defined by characteristics that all of the places in the group have in common. When economic characteristics are used, the delimited regions include places with similar kinds of economic activity. Agricultural regions include areas where certain farm products dominate. Corn is grown throughout the "Corn Belt" of the central United States, for example, although many farmers in the region also plant soybeans and many raise hogs. Regions where intensive industrial production is a prominent part of local economic activity include the manufacturing belts of the northeastern United States, southern Canada, northwestern Europe, and southern Japan.

Regions can also be defined by patterns of movement. Transportation or communication linkages among places may draw them together into configurations that differentiate them from other locales. Studies by economic geographers of the locational tendencies of modern high-technology industries have identified complex networks of firms that provide products and services to each other. Because of their linkages, these firms cluster together into well-defined regions. The "Silicon Valley" of northern California, the "Western Crescent" on the outskirts of London, and "Technopolis" of the Tokyo region all are distinguished as much by connections among firms as by the economic landscapes they have established.

Economic aspects of movement may help define functional regions by establishing areas where certain types of economic activity are more profitable than others. In the early nineteenth century, German landowner Johann Heinrich von Thünen demonstrated how different costs for transporting various agricultural goods to market helped to define regions where certain forms of farming would occur. Although theoretically simple, patterns predicted by von Thünen can still be found in the world today. Goods such as vegetables and dairy products that require more intensive production and are more expensive to ship are produced closer to markets, while less demanding goods and commodities that can be transported at lower costs come from more remote production areas. Advances in transportation have dramatically altered such regional patterns, however. Whereas a New York City native once enjoyed fresh vegetables and fruit only in the summer and early autumn when New Jersey, upstate New York, and New England producers brought their goods to market, New Yorkers today buy fresh produce year-round, with new shipments flown in daily from Florida, California, Chile, and even more remote locations during the colder months.

Governments have a strong impact on the conduct of business, and the formal borders of government jurisdictions often coincide with the functional boundaries of economic regions. The divisive character of these lines on the map has been altered in many parts of the world in recent decades, however. The formation of common markets and free trade areas in Western Europe and North America has dramatically changed the patterns and flows of economic activity, and similar kinds of formal restructuring of relationships among nations likely will continue into the next century. As a result, business analysts increasingly need to consider regions that cross international boundaries.

Some of the most innovative views of regional organization essentially have ignored existing national boundaries. In 1981, Joel Garreau published a book titled *The Nine Nations of North America,* which subdivided the continent into a set of regions based on economic activities and cultural outlooks. Seven of Garreau's nine regions include territory in at least two nations. In the Southwest, "Mexamerica" recognized the bicultural heritage of Anglo and Hispanic groups and the increasingly close economic ties across the U.S.–Mexican border that were spurred by the *maquiladora* and other export-oriented programs. The evolution of this region as a distinctive collection of places has been accelerated by the passage of the North American Free Trade Agreement (NAFTA). Another cross-national region identified by Garreau is "The Islands," a collection of nations in the Caribbean for which Miami has become the functional "capital." Many business leaders seeking to tap into this rapidly growing area have become knowledgeable of the laws and customs of those nations. They often have done so by employing émigrés from those nations who may now be U.S. citizens but whose primary language is not English and whose outlook on the region is multinational.

In a similar vein, Darrell Delamaide's 1994 book entitled *The New Superregions of Europe* divides the continent into ten regions based on economic, cultural, and social affinities that have evolved over centuries. His vision of Europe challenges regional structures that persist from earlier times. Seen by many as a single region known as Eastern Europe, the formerly communist nations west of what once was the Soviet Union are seen by Delamaide as being part of five different "superregions": "The Baltic League," a group of nations clustered around the Baltic Sea; "Mitteleuropa," the economic heartland of northern Europe; "The Slavic Federation," a region dominated by Russia with a common Slavic heritage; "The Danube Basin," a melange of places along and near Europe's longest river; and "The Balkan Peninsula," a region characterized by political turmoil and less advanced economies.

Delamaide's book has been as controversial as Garreau's was a decade earlier. In both cases, however, the value of the ideas they presented was not measured in terms of the "accuracy" of the regional structures they presented, but rather by their ability to lead more people to take a geographic perspective of the modern world and how it functions. The regions defined by Garreau and Delamaide are not those described by traditional geographers, but they reflect the views of many business leaders who have learned to look across national boundaries in their search for opportunities. As business increasingly becomes international, the most successful entrepreneurs will be the ones who complement their business acumen with effective application of geographic information and principles.

References Cited

Darrell Delamaide. *The New Superregions of Europe.* New York: Dutton, a division of Penguin Books, 1994.

Joel Garreau. *The Nine Nations of North America.* New York: Houghton Mifflin Co., 1981.

CHAPTER 2

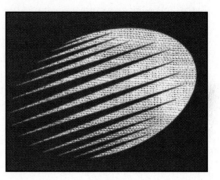

The Theory of International Trade and Investment

Learning Objectives

1. To understand the traditional arguments as to how and why international trade improves the welfare of all countries.

2. To review the history and compare the implications of trade theory from the original work of Adam Smith to the contemporary theories of Michael Porter.

3. To examine the criticisms of classical trade theory and examine alternative viewpoints of what business and economic forces determine trade patterns between countries.

4. To explore the similarities and distinctions between international trade and international investment.

Trade Booming under NAFTA

Despite continuing uncertainty south of the border, the North American Free Trade Agreement spurred a boom in trade among the United States, Mexico, and Canada during its first year in effect.

The U.S. Department of Commerce reported that U.S. companies were selling more high-dollar products—automobiles, agricultural equipment, computers, other electronics and consumer goods—than they had in the past, thanks, in part, to NAFTA's reduction of Mexican and Canadian tariffs and non-tariff barriers.

"Ross Perot has a little hearing problem," U.S. Treasury Secretary Lloyd Bentsen said. "That sucking sound is really products going south."

Figures for 1994 will probably set new records in U.S. exports to Mexico. A record 17 percent increase ($24.5 billion) was recorded during the first six months. The current annualized rate is $48.9 billion compared to $41.6 billion in 1993.

Trade with Canada is soaring, also. Exports to Canada during this same period showed a 10 percent jump, or a $4.8 billion increase, over the 1993 figures of $55.6 billion. The Commerce Department estimated the increase in exports to Mexico and Canada could boost U.S. employment by as many as 100,000 new jobs in 1994 in manufacturing, autos, machinery, and computers.

Bentsen had pointed out in an earlier interview that the United Automobile Workers Union lobbied hard against NAFTA when it came up for a vote in Congress in 1993, but government figures showed that in the first five months of 1994, the U.S. automobile industry exported 12,380 passenger vehicles to Mexico, nearly 4,000 more than in the comparable 1993 period, and more than the total passenger vehicles exported in 1993 (10,910). Chrysler, Ford, and GM expected to export a combined 55,000 cars and trucks to Mexico in 1994.

Source: Adapted from "Trade Booming under NAFTA," by David Bennett, *Twin Plant News/The Mexico Option,* 1995, 19–22.

The debates, the costs, the benefits, and the dilemmas of international trade have in many ways not changed significantly from the time when Marco Polo crossed the barren wastelands of Eurasia to the time of the expansion of U.S. and Canadian firms across the Rio Grande into Mexico under the North American Free Trade Agreement. At the heart of the issue is what the gains—and the risks—are to the firm and the country as a result of a seller from one country servicing the needs of a buyer in a different country. If a Spanish firm wants to sell its product to the enormous market of mainland China, whether it produces at home and ships the product from Cadiz to Shanghai (international trade) or actually builds a factory in Shanghai (international investment), the goal is still the same: To sell a product for profit in the foreign market.

This chapter provides a directed path through centuries of thought on why and how trade and investment across borders occurs. Although theories and theorists come and go with time, a few basic questions have dominated this intellectual adventure:

- Why do countries trade?
- Do countries trade or do firms trade?
- Do the elements that give rise to the competitiveness of a firm, an industry, or a country as a whole, arise from some inherent endowment of the country itself, or do they change with time and circumstance?
- Once identified, can these sources of competitiveness be manipulated or managed by firms or governments to the benefit of the traders?

International trade is expected to improve the productivity of industry and the welfare of consumers. Let us learn how and why we still seek the exotic silks of the Far East.

THE AGE OF MERCANTILISM

The evolution of trade into the form we see today reflects three particular events: the collapse of feudal society, the emergence of the mercantilist philosophy, and the life cycle of the colonial systems of the European nation-states. Feudal society was a state of **autarky,** a society that did not trade because all of its needs were met internally. The feudal estate was self-sufficient (although hardly "sufficient" in more modern terms, given the limits of providing entirely for oneself). Needs literally were those of food and shelter, and all available human labor was devoted to the task of fulfilling those basic needs. As merchants began meeting in the marketplace, as travelers began exchanging goods from faraway places at the water's edge, the attractiveness of trade became evident.

In the centuries leading up to the Industrial Revolution, international commerce was largely conducted under the authority of governments. The goals of trade were, therefore, the goals of governments. As early as 1500 the benefits of trade were clearly established in Europe as nation-states expanded their influence across the globe in the creation of colonial systems. To maintain and expand their control over these colonial possessions, the European nations needed fleets, armies, food, and all other resources the nations could muster. They needed wealth. Trade was therefore conducted in a fashion that would fill the governments' coffers, their treasuries, at minimum expense to themselves and to the detriment of their captive trade partners. Although colonialism normally is associated with the exploitation of those captive societies, it went hand in hand with the evolving exchange of goods among the European countries themselves, **mercantilism.**

Mercantilism mixed exchange through trade with accumulation of wealth. Since government controlled the patterns of commerce, it identified strength with the accumulation of **specie** (gold and silver) and the general policy of exports dominating imports. Trade across borders—exports—was considered preferable to domestic trade in that an excess of exports would earn gold. Import duties, tariffs, subsidization of exports, and outright restriction on the importation of many agricultural products and other goods actually wanted by the people (but not the government), were used to maximize the gains from exports over the costs of imports. Laws were passed making it illegal to take gold or silver out of the country, even if, as was argued by merchants, such specie was needed to purchase imports to produce their own goods for domestic or foreign sale. This was one-way trade, the trade of greed and power.

The demise of mercantilism was inevitable given class structure and the distribution of society's product. As the Industrial Revolution introduced the benefits of mass production to the people, lowering prices and increasing the supplies of goods to all, the exploitation of colonies and trading partners came to an end. The eighteenth century saw the development of new types of production and exchange that are more familiar to us today, but the limbs and branches of the international trade tree have never spread very far from its roots. Governments still exercise considerable power and influence on the conduct of trade. Countries such as Taiwan even today follow policies that are termed neo-mercantilist, attempting to maintain net trade surpluses in all products while accumulating massive amounts of foreign currency reserves and gold.

CLASSICAL TRADE THEORY

The question of why countries trade appears simple to answer but has proven to be quite complex. Since the second half of the eighteenth century, academicians have tried to understand not only the motivations and benefits of international trade, but

FIGURE 2.1   The Evolution of International Trade Theory

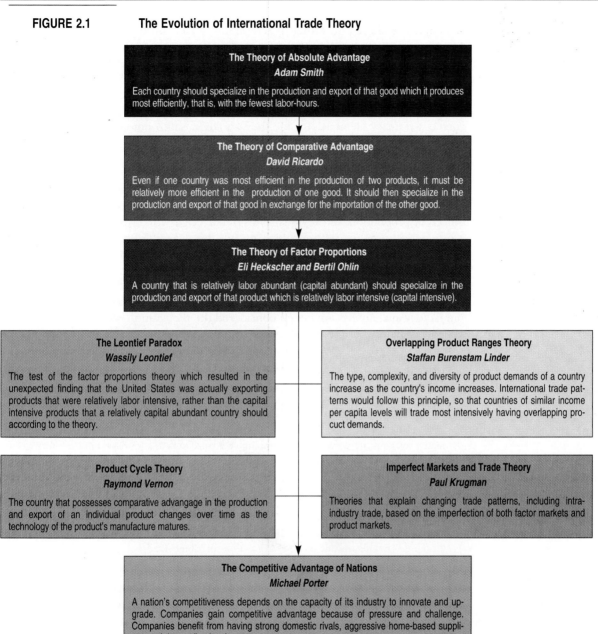

also why some countries grow faster and wealthier than others through trade. Figure 2.1 provides an overview of the evolutionary path of international trade theory since the fall of mercantilism. Although somewhat simplified, it shows the line of development of the major theories put forward over the past two centuries. It also serves as an early indication of the path of modern theory: the shifting focus from the country to the firm, from cost of production to the market as a whole, and from the perfect to the imperfect.

The Theory of Absolute Advantage

Generally considered the father of economics, Adam Smith published *The Wealth of Nations* in 1776 in London. In this book, Smith attempted to explain the process by which markets and production actually operate in society. His studies led him to a number of striking results. Smith's two main areas of contribution, *absolute advantage* and the *division of labor,* were fundamental to trade theory.

Production, the creation of a product for exchange, always requires the use of society's primary element of value, human labor. Smith noted that some countries, owing to the skills of their workers or the quality of their natural resources, could produce the same products as others with fewer labor-hours. He termed this efficiency **absolute advantage.**

Adam Smith observed the production processes of the early stages of the Industrial Revolution in England and recognized the fundamental change that had occurred in production. In previous states of society, a worker performed all stages of a production process, with resulting output that was little more than sufficient for the worker's own needs. The factories of the industrializing world were, however, separating the production process into distinct stages, in which each stage would be performed exclusively by one individual. Smith termed this the **division of labor.** This specialization increased the production of workers and industries. Smith's pin factory analogy has long been considered the recognition of one of the most significant principles of the industrial age.

> To take an example, therefore, from a very trifling manufacture; but one in which the division of labour has been very often taken notice of the trade of the pin-maker; a workman not educated to this business . . . could scarce, perhaps, with his utmost industry, make one pin in a day, and certainly could not make twenty. But in a way in which this business is now carried on, not only the whole work is a peculiar trade, but it is divided in to a number of branches, of which the greater part are likewise peculiar trades. One man draws out the wire, another straights it, a third cuts it, a fourth points it, a fifth grinds it at the top for receiving the head; to make the head requires two or three distinct operations; to put it on is a peculiar business . . . I have seen a small manufactory of this kind where ten men only were employed, and where some of them consequently performed two or three distinct operations. But though they were very poor, and therefore but indifferently accommodated with the necessary machine, they could, when they exerted themselves, make among them about twelve pounds of pins in a day. There are in a pound upwards of four thousand pins of a middling size.[1]

Adam Smith then extended his division of labor in the production process to a division of labor and specialized product across countries. Each country would specialize in a product for which it was uniquely suited. More would be produced for less. Thus, by each country specializing in products for which it possessed absolute advantage, countries could produce more in total and exchange products—trade— for goods that were cheaper in price than those produced at home.

The Theory of Comparative Advantage

Although Smith's work was instrumental in the development of economic theories about trade and production, it did not answer some fundamental questions about trade. First, Smith's trade relied on a country possessing absolute advantage in production, but did not explain what caused the production advantages. Second, if a country did not possess absolute advantage in any product, could it (or would it) trade?

David Ricardo, in his 1819 work entitled *On the Principles of Political Economy and Taxation,* sought to take the basic ideas set down by Smith a few steps further. Ricardo noted that even if a country possessed absolute advantage in the production of two products, it still must be relatively more efficient than the other country in one good's product than the other. Ricardo termed this the **comparative advantage.** Each country would then possess comparative advantage in the production of one of the two products, and both countries would then benefit by specializing completely in one product and trading for the other.

A Numerical Example of Classical Trade

To fully understand the theories of absolute advantage and comparative advantage, consider the following example. Two countries, France and England, produce only two products, wheat and cloth (or beer and pizza, guns and butter, and so forth). The relative efficiency of each country in the production of the two products is measured by comparing the number of labor-hours needed to produce one unit of each product. Table 2.1 provides an efficiency comparison of the two countries.

England is obviously more efficient in the production of wheat. Whereas it takes France four labor-hours to produce one unit of wheat, it takes England only two hours to produce the same unit of wheat. France takes twice as many labor-hours to produce the same output. England has absolute advantage in the production of wheat. France needs two labor-hours to produce a unit of cloth that it takes England four labor-hours to produce. England therefore requires two more labor-hours than France to produce the same unit of cloth. France has absolute advantage in the production of cloth. The two countries are exactly opposite in relative efficiency of production.

David Ricardo took the logic of absolute advantages in production one step further to explain how countries could exploit their own advantages and gain from international trade. Comparative advantage, according to Ricardo, was based on what was given up or traded off in producing one product instead of the other. In this

---

TABLE 2.1
Absolute Advantage and Comparative Advantage*

Country	Wheat	Cloth
England	2	4
France	4	2

- England has absolute advantage in the production of wheat. It requires fewer labor-hours (2 being less than 4) for England to produce one unit of wheat.
- France has absolute advantage in the production of cloth. It requires fewer labor-hours (2 being less than 4) for France to produce one unit of cloth.
- England has comparative advantage in the production of wheat. If England produces one unit of wheat, it is foregoing the production of 2/4 (0.50) of a unit of cloth. If France produces one unit of wheat, it is foregoing the production of 4/2 (2.00) of a unit of cloth. England therefore has the lower opportunity cost of producing wheat.
- France has comparative advantage in the production of cloth. If England produces one unit of cloth, it is foregoing the production of 4/2 (2.00) of a unit of wheat. If France produces one unit of cloth, it is foregoing the production of 2/4 (0.50) of a unit of wheat. France therefore has the lower opportunity cost of producing cloth.

*Labor-hours per unit of output.

numerical example England needs only two-fourths as many labor-hours to produce a unit of wheat as France, while France needs only two-fourths as many labor-hours to produce a unit of cloth. England therefore has comparative advantage in the production of wheat, while France has comparative advantage in the production of cloth. A country cannot possess comparative advantage in the production of both products, so each country has an economic role to play in international trade.

National Production Possibilities

If the total labor-hours available for production within a nation were devoted to the full production of either product, wheat or cloth, the **production possibilities frontiers** of each country can be constructed. Assuming both countries possess the same number of labor-hours, for example 100, the production possibilities frontiers for each country can be graphed, as in Figure 2.2. If England devotes all labor-hours (100) to the production of wheat (which requires 2 labor-hours per unit produced), it can produce a maximum of 50 units of wheat. If England devotes all labor to the production of cloth instead, the same 100 labor-hours can produce a maximum of 25 units of cloth (100 hours/4 hours per unit of cloth). If England did not trade with any other country, it could only consume the products that it produced itself. England would therefore probably produce and consume some combination of wheat and cloth such as point A in Figure 2.2 (15 units of cloth, 20 units of wheat).

France's production possibilities frontier is constructed in the same way. If France devotes all 100 labor-hours to the production of wheat, it can produce a maximum of 25 units (100 labor hours/4 hours per unit of wheat). If France devotes all 100 labor-hours to cloth, the same 100 labor-hours can produce a maximum of 50 units of cloth (100 labor hours/2 hours per unit of cloth). If France did not trade with other countries, it would produce and consume at some point such as point D in Figure 2.2 (20 units of cloth, 15 units of wheat).

These frontiers depict what each country could produce in isolation—without trade (sometimes referred to as *autarky*). The slope of the production possibility frontier of a nation is a measure of how one product is traded off in production with the other (moving up the frontier, England is choosing to produce more wheat and less cloth). The slope of the frontier reflects the "trade-off" of producing one product over the other; the trade-offs represent prices, or opportunity costs. **Opportunity cost** is the foregone value of a factor of production in its next-best use. If England chooses to produce more units of wheat (in fact, produce only wheat), moving from point A to point B along the production possibilities frontier, it is giving up producing cloth to produce only wheat. The "cost" of the additional wheat is the loss of cloth. The slope of the production possibilities frontier is the ratio of product prices (opportunity costs). The slope of the production possibilities frontier for England is −50/25, or −2.00. The slope of the production possibilities frontier for France is flatter, −25/50, or −0.50.

The relative prices of products also provide an alternative way of seeing comparative advantage. The flatter slope of the French production possibilities frontier means that to produce more wheat (move up the frontier), France would have to give up the production of relatively more units of cloth than would England, with its steeper sloped production possibilities frontier.

FIGURE 2.2   Production Possibility Frontiers, Specialization of Production, and the Benefits of Trade

England

1. Initially produces and consumes at point A.
2. England chooses to specialize in the production of wheat, and shifts production from point A to point B.
3. England now exports the unwanted wheat (30 units) in exchange for imports of cloth (30 units) from France.
4. England is now consuming at point C, where it is consuming the same amount of wheat, but 15 more units of cloth than at original point A.

France

1. Initially produces and consumes at point D.
2. France chooses to specialize in the production of cloth, and shifts production from point D to point E.
3. France now exports the unwanted cloth (30 units) in exchange for imports of wheat (30 units) from England.
4. France is now consuming at point F, where it is consuming the same amount of cloth, but 15 more units of wheat than at original point D.

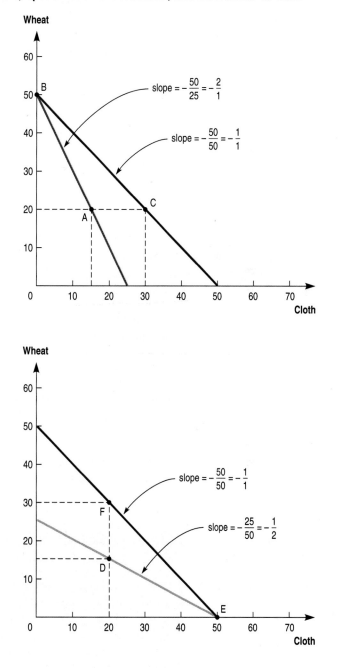

The Gains from International Trade

Continuing with Figure 2.2, if England were originally not trading with France (the only other country) and it was producing at its own maximum possibilities (on the frontier and not inside the line), it would probably be producing at point A. Since it was not trading with another country, whatever it was producing it must be using itself—consuming. So England could be said to be consuming at point A also. Therefore, without trade, you consume what you produce.

If, however, England recognized that it has comparative advantage in the production of wheat, it should, according to the theory of comparative advantage, move production from point A to point B. England should specialize completely in the product it produces best. It does not want to consume only wheat, however, so it would take the wheat it has produced and does not want to consume and trade with France. For example, England may only want to consume 20 units of wheat, as it did at point A. It is now producing 50 units, and therefore has 30 units of wheat it can sell or export to France. If England could export 30 units of wheat in exchange for imports of 30 units of cloth (a 1:1 ratio of prices), England would clearly be better off than before. The new consumption point would be point C, where it is consuming the same amount of wheat as point A, but is now consuming 30 units of cloth instead of just 15. More is better; England has benefited from international trade.

France, following the same principle of completely specializing in the product of its comparative production advantage, moves production from point D to point E, producing 50 units of cloth. If France now exported the unwanted cloth, for example 30 units, and exchanged the cloth with England for imports of 30 units of wheat (note that England's exports are France's imports), France too is better off as a result of international trade. Each country would do what it does best, exclusively, and then trade for the other product.

But at what prices will the two countries trade? Since each country's production possibilities frontier has a different slope (different relative product prices), the two countries can determine a set of prices between the two domestic prices. In the above example, England's price ratio was $-2:1$, while France's domestic price ratio was $-1:2$. Trading 30 units of wheat for 30 units of cloth is a price ratio of

Heckscher and Ohlin noted that countries are endowed with varying degrees of productive resources and contended that the production of goods is a function of the most intensive use of those resources. DeKalb Genetics Corporation, an international marketer of seed products, is the leading supplier of corn, grain sorghum, and sunflower seeds to Argentina, where the growing season is the opposite of the United States'. Seasonal conditions are a significant factor in the high volume of corn production in Argentina.

Source: Courtesy of DeKalb Genetics Corporation

Current Account Balances as a Percentage of Gross Domestic Product (1993)

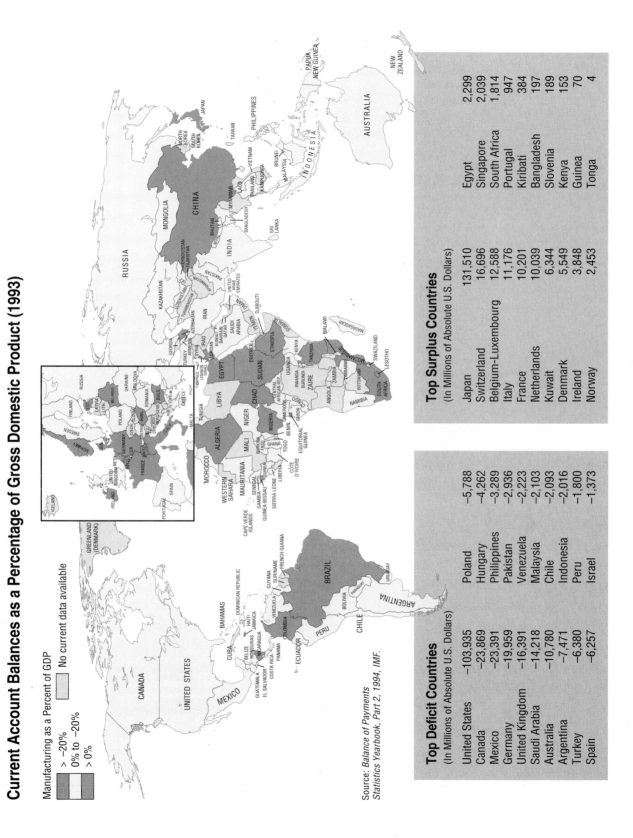

Manufacturing as a Percent of GDP

> −20%

0% to −20%

> 0%

No current data available

Source: *Balance of Payments Statistics Yearbook, Part 2, 1994, IMF.*

Top Deficit Countries
(In Millions of Absolute U.S. Dollars)

United States	−103,935
Canada	−23,869
Mexico	−23,391
Germany	−19,959
United Kingdom	−16,391
Saudi Arabia	−14,218
Australia	−10,780
Argentina	−7,471
Turkey	−6,380
Spain	−6,257
Poland	−5,788
Hungary	−4,262
Philippines	−3,289
Pakistan	−2,936
Venezuela	−2,223
Malaysia	−2,103
Chile	−2,093
Indonesia	−2,016
Peru	−1,800
Israel	−1,373

Top Surplus Countries
(In Millions of Absolute U.S. Dollars)

Japan	131,510
Switzerland	16,696
Belgium–Luxembourg	12,588
Italy	11,176
France	10,201
Netherlands	10,039
Kuwait	6,344
Denmark	5,549
Ireland	3,848
Norway	2,453
Egypt	2,299
Singapore	2,039
South Africa	1,814
Portugal	947
Kiribati	384
Bangladesh	197
Slovenia	189
Kenya	153
Guinea	70
Tonga	4

−1:1, a slope or set or prices between the two domestic price ratios. The dashed line in Figure 2.2 illustrates this set of trade prices.

Are both countries better off as a result of trade? Yes. The final step to understanding the benefits of classical trade is to note that the point where a country produces (point B for England and point E for France in Figure 2.2) and the point where it consumes are now different. This allows each country to consume beyond their own production possibilities frontier.

This final point concerns what the work of Adam Smith and David Ricardo was in many ways all about. Society's welfare, which is normally measured in its ability to consume more wheat, cloth, or any other goods or services is increased through trade.

Concluding Points about Classical Trade Theory

Classical trade theory contributed much to the understanding of how production and trade operates in the world economy. Although like all economic theories they are often criticized for being unrealistic or out of date, the purpose of a theory is to simplify reality so that the basic elements of the logic can be seen. Several of these simplifications have continued to provide insight in understanding international business.

- **Division of Labor.** Adam Smith's explanation of how industrial societies can increase output using the same labor-hours as in pre-industrial society is fundamental to our thinking even today. Smith extended this specialization of the efforts of a worker to the specialization of a nation.
- **Comparative Advantage.** David Ricardo's extension of Smith's work explained for the first time how countries that seemingly had no obvious reason for trade could individually specialize in producing what they did best, and trade for products they did not produce.
- **Gains from Trade.** The theory of comparative advantage argued that nations could improve the welfare of their populations through international trade. A nation could actually achieve consumption levels beyond what it could produce by itself. To this day this is one of the fundamental principles underlying the arguments for all countries to strive to expand and "free" world trade.

FACTOR PROPORTIONS TRADE THEORY

Trade theory changed drastically in the first half of the twentieth century. The theory developed by the Swedish economist Eli Heckscher and later expanded by his former graduate student Bertil Ohlin formed the major theory of international trade that is still widely accepted today, **factor proportions theory.** Factor proportions theory, also termed Heckscher-Ohlin theory, was based on a more modern concept of production, one that raised capital to the same level of importance as labor.

Factor Intensity in Production

The Heckscher-Ohlin theory considered two **factors of production,** labor and capital. Technology determines the way they combine to form a product. Different products required different proportions of the two factors of production.

Figure 2.3 illustrates what it means to describe a product by its factor proportions. The production of one unit of good X requires 4 units of labor and 1 unit of capital. At the same time, to produce 1 unit of good Y requires 4 units of labor and

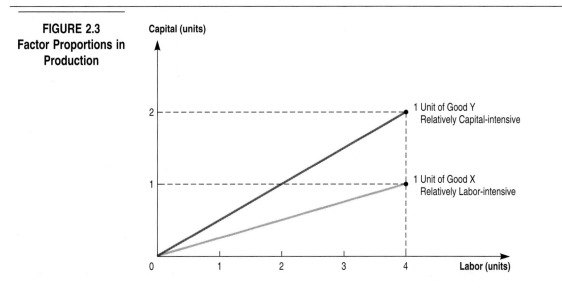

FIGURE 2.3
Factor Proportions in
Production

2 units of capital. Good X therefore requires more units of labor per unit of capital (4 to 1) relative to Y (4 to 2). X is therefore classified as a relatively labor-intensive product, and Y is relatively capital-intensive. These **factor intensities** or **proportions** are truly relative and are determined only on the basis of what product X requires relative to product Y and not to the specific numbers of labor to capital.

It is easy to see how the factor proportions of production differ substantially across goods. For example, the manufacturing of leather footwear is still a relatively labor-intensive process, even with the most sophisticated leather treatment and patterning machinery. Other goods, such as computer memory chips, however, although requiring some highly skilled labor, require massive quantities of capital for production. These large capital requirements include the enormous sums needed for research and development and the manufacturing facilities needed for clean production to ensure the extremely high quality demanded in the industry.

According to factor proportions theory, factor intensities depend on the state of technology, the current method of manufacturing a product. The theory assumed that the same technology of production would be used for the same goods in all countries. It is not, therefore, differences in the efficiency of production that will determine trade between countries as it did in classical theory. Classical theory implicitly assumed that technology or the productivity of labor is different across countries. Otherwise, there would be no logical explanation as to why one country requires more units of labor to produce a unit of output than another country. Factor proportions theory assumes no such productivity differences.

Factor Endowments, Factor Prices, and Comparative Advantage

If there is no difference in technology or productivity of factors across the countries, what then determines comparative advantage in production and export? The answer is that factor prices determine cost differences. And these prices are determined by the endowments of labor and capital the country possesses. The theory assumes that labor and capital are immobile, meaning they cannot move across country borders. Therefore, the country's endowment determines the relative costs of labor and capital as compared to other countries.

For example, a country such as China possesses a relatively large endowment of labor and a relatively smaller endowment of capital. At the same time, Japan is a relatively capital-abundant country, with a relatively smaller endowment of labor. China possesses relatively cheaper labor and should therefore specialize in the production and export of labor-intensive products (such as good X in Figure 2.3). Japan possesses relatively cheap capital and should specialize in the production and export of capital-intensive products (such as good Y in Figure 2.3). Comparative advantage is derived not from the productivity of a country, but from the relative abundance of its factors of production.

Using these assumptions, factor proportions theory stated that a country should specialize in the production and export of those products that use intensively its relatively abundant factor.

- A country that is relatively labor-abundant should specialize in the production of relatively labor-intensive goods. It should then export those labor-intensive goods in exchange for capital-intensive goods.
- A country that is relatively capital-abundant should specialize in the production of relatively capital-intensive goods. It should then export those capital-intensive goods in exchange for labor-intensive goods.

Assumptions of the Factor Proportions Theory

The increasing level of theoretical complexity of the factor proportions theory, as compared with the classical trade theory, increased the number of assumptions necessary for the theory to "hold." It is important to take a last look at the assumptions before proceeding further.

1. The theory assumes two countries, two products, and two factors of production, the so-called $2 \times 2 \times 2$ assumption. Note that if both countries were producing all of the output they could and trading only between themselves (only two countries), both countries would have to have balances in trade!

2. The markets for the inputs and the outputs are perfectly competitive. The factors of production, labor, and capital were exchanged in markets that paid them only what they were worth. Similarly, the trade of the outputs (the international trade between the two countries) was competitive so that one country had no market power over the other.

3. Increasing production of a product experiences diminishing returns. This meant that as a country increasingly specialized in the production of one of the two outputs, it eventually would require more and more inputs per unit of output. For example there would no longer be the constant "labor-hours per unit of output" as assumed under the classical theory. This means that the production possibilities frontiers would no longer be straight lines, but concave in shape. The result was that complete specialization would no longer occur under factor proportions theory.

4. Both countries were using identical technologies. Each product was produced in the same way in both countries. This meant the only way that a good could be produced more cheaply in one country than in the other was if the factors of production used (labor and capital) were cheaper.

Although there were a number of additional technical assumptions necessary, these four highlight the very specialized set of conditions needed in order to explain international trade with factor proportions theory. Much of the international trade theory developed since has focused on how trade changes when one or more of these assumptions is not found in the real world.

The Leontief Paradox

One of the most famous tests of any economic or business theory occurred in 1950, when economist Wassily Leontief tested whether the factor proportions theory could be used to explain the types of goods the United States imported and exported. Leontief's premise was the following.

> A widely shared view on the nature of the trade between the United States and the rest of the world is derived from what appears to be a common sense assumption that this country has a comparative advantage in the production of commodities which require for their manufacture large quantities of capital and relatively small amounts of labor. Our economic relationships with other countries are supposed to be based mainly on the export of such "capital intensive" goods in exchange for foregoing products which—if we were to make them at home—would require little capital but large quantities of American labor. Since the United States possesses a relatively large amount of capital—so goes this oft repeated argument—and a comparatively small amount of labor, direct domestic production of such "labor intensive" products would be uneconomical; we can much more advantageously obtain them from abroad in exchange for our capital intensive products.[2]

Leontief first had to devise a method to determine the relative amounts of labor and capital in a product. His solution, known as **input-output analysis,** was an accomplishment on its own. Input-output analysis is a technique of decomposing a product into the values and quantities of the labor, capital, and other potential factors employed in the product's manufacture. Leontief then used this methodology to analyze the labor and capital content of all U.S. merchandise imports and exports. The hypothesis was relatively straightforward: U.S. exports should be relatively capital-intensive (use more units of capital relative to labor) than U.S. imports. Leontief's results were, however, a bit of a shock.

Leontief found that the products that U.S. firms exported were relatively more labor-intensive than the products the United States imported.[3] It seemed that if the factor proportions theory were true, the United States is a relatively labor-abundant country! Alternatively, the theory could be wrong. Neither interpretation of the results was acceptable to many in the field of international trade.

A variety of explanations and continuing studies have attempted to solve what has become known as the **Leontief Paradox.** At first, it was thought to have been simply a result of the specific year (1947) of the data. However, the same results were found with different years and data sets. Second, it was noted that Leontief did not really analyze the labor and capital contents of imports, but rather the labor and capital contents of the domestic equivalents of these imports. It was possible that the United States was actually producing the products in a more capital-intensive fashion than were the countries from which it also imported the manufactured goods.[4] Finally, the debate turned to the need to distinguish different types of labor and capital. For example, several studies attempted to separate labor factors into skilled labor and unskilled labor. These studies have continued to show results more consistent with what the factor proportions theory would predict for country trade patterns.

Linder's Overlapping Product Ranges Theory

The difficulties in empirically validating the factor proportions theory led many in the 1960s and 1970s to search for new explanations of the determinants of trade between countries. The work of Staffan Burenstam Linder focused not on the production or supply side, but instead on the preferences of consumers, the demand side. Linder acknowledged that in the natural resource-based industries, trade was indeed determined by relative costs of production and factor endowments. This was consistent with the previous factor proportions theory.

However, Linder argued, trade in manufactured goods was dictated not by cost concerns but rather by the similarity in product demands across countries. Linder's was a significant departure from previous theory. His theory was based on two principles:

1. As income, or more precisely per capita income, rises, the complexity and quality level of the products demanded by the country's residents also rises. The total range of product sophistication demanded by a country's residents is largely determined by its level of income.
2. The entrepreneurs directing the firms that produce society's needs are more knowledgeable about their own domestic market than about foreign markets. An entrepreneur could not be expected to effectively service a foreign market that is significantly different from the domestic market because competitiveness comes from experience. A logical pattern would be for an entrepreneur to gain success and market share at home first, then expand to foreign markets that are similar in their demands or tastes.

International trade in manufactured goods would then be influenced by similarity of demands. The countries that would see the most intensive trade are those with similar per capita income levels for they would possess a greater likelihood of overlapping product demands.

So where does trade come in? According to Linder, the overlapping ranges of product sophistication represent the products that entrepreneurs would know well from their home markets and could therefore potentially export and compete in foreign markets. For example, the United States and Canada have almost parallel sophistication ranges, implying they would have a lot of common ground, overlapping product ranges, for intensive international trade and competition. They are quite similar in their per capita income levels. But Mexico and the United States, or Mexico and Canada, would not. Mexico has a significantly different product sophistication range as a result of a different per capita income level.

The conclusions drawn from Linder's overlapping product ranges are strikingly different from the traditional cost-oriented trade theory preceding it. First, the most intensive trade, according to Linder, would exist between countries of the same income or industrialization levels, not dissimilar levels as often concluded from previous theory. Second, the theory implied a large part of international trade would consist of the exchange of similar or slightly differentiated goods. Commonly referred to as intra-industry trade, the exchange of essentially identical goods between countries raised questions as to why consumers would import a product seemingly identical to the one they were often working to produce and export from their own country.

The overlapping product ranges described by Linder would today be termed market segments. Linder's work was not only instrumental in extending trade theory beyond cost considerations, but it has also found a place in the field of international marketing. As illustrated in the theories following the work of Linder, many of the questions that his work raised were the focus of considerable attention in the following decades.

INTERNATIONAL INVESTMENT AND PRODUCT CYCLE THEORY

A very different path was taken by Raymond Vernon in 1966 concerning what is now termed **product cycle theory.** Diverging significantly from traditional approaches, Vernon focused on the product (rather than the country and the technology of its manufacture), not its factor proportions. Most striking was the appreciation of the role of information, knowledge, and the costs and power that go hand in hand with knowledge.

> . . . we abandon the powerful simplifying notion that knowledge is a universal free good, and introduce it as an independent variable in the decision to trade or to invest.

Using many of the same basic tools and assumptions of factor proportions theory, Vernon added two technology-based premises to the factor-cost emphasis of existing theory:

1. Technical innovations leading to new and profitable products require large quantities of capital and highly skilled labor. These factors of production are predominantly available in highly industrialized capital-intensive countries.

2. These same technical innovations, both the product itself and more importantly the methods for its manufacture, go through three stages of maturation as the product becomes increasingly commercialized. As the manufacturing process becomes more standardized and low-skill labor-intensive, the comparative advantage in its production and export shifts across countries.

The Stages of the Product Cycle

Product cycle theory is both supply-side (cost of production) and demand-side (income levels of consumers) in its orientation. Each of these three stages that Vernon described combines differing elements of each.

Stage I: The New Product   Innovation requires highly skilled labor and large quantities of capital for research and development. The product will normally be most effectively designed and initially manufactured near the parent firm and therefore is a highly industrialized market due to the need for proximity to information; the need for communication among the many different skilled-labor components required.

In this development stage, the product is nonstandardized. The production process requires a high degree of flexibility (meaning continued use of highly skilled labor). Costs of production are therefore quite high.

The innovator at this stage is a monopolist and therefore enjoys all of the benefits of monopoly power, including the high profit margins required to repay the high development costs and expensive production process. Price elasticity of demand at this stage is low; high-income consumers buy it regardless of cost.

Stage II: The Maturing Product   As production expands, its process becomes increasingly standardized. The need for flexibility in design and manufacturing declines, and therefore the demand for highly skilled labor declines. The innovating country increases its sales to other countries. Competitors with slight variations develop, putting downward pressure on prices and profit margins. Production costs are an increasing concern.

As competitors increase, as well as their pressures on price, the innovating firm faces critical decisions as to how to maintain market share. Vernon argues that the firm faces a critical decision at this stage, to either lose market share to foreign-based manufacturers using lower-cost labor or for the firm itself to invest abroad to maintain its market share by exploiting the comparative advantages of factor costs in other countries. This is one of the first theoretical explanations of how trade and investment become increasingly intertwined.

Stage III: The Standardized Product   In this final stage, the product is completely standardized in its manufacture. Thus, with access to capital on world capital markets, the country of production is simply the one with the cheapest unskilled labor. Profit margins are thin, and competition is fierce. The product has largely run its course in terms of profitability for the innovating firm.

The country of comparative advantage has therefore shifted as the technology of the product's manufacture has matured. The same product shifts in its location of production. The country possessing the product during that stage enjoys the benefits of net trade surpluses. But such advantages are fleeting, according to Vernon. As knowledge and technology continually change, so does the country of that product's comparative advantage.

Trade Implications of the Product Cycle

Product cycle theory shows how specific products were first produced and exported from one country but, through product and competitive evolution, shifted their location of production and export to other countries over time. Figure 2.4 illustrates the trade patterns that Vernon visualized as resulting from the maturing stages of a specific product's cycle. As the product and the market for the product mature and change, the countries of its production and export shift.

The product is initially designed and manufactured in the United States. In its early stages (from time t_0 to t_1), the United States is the only country producing and consuming the product. Production is highly capital-intensive and skilled labor-intensive at this time. At time t_1 the United States begins exporting the product to Other Advanced Countries, as Vernon classified them. These countries possessed the income to purchase the product in its still New Product Stage, in which it was relatively high priced. These Other Advanced Countries also commence their own production at time t_1, but continue to be net importers. A few exports, however, do find their way to the Less Developed Countries at this time as well.

As product moves into the second stage, the Maturing Product Stage, production capability expands rapidly in the Other Advanced Countries. Competitive variations begin to appear as the basic technology of the product becomes more widely known, and the need for skilled labor in its production declines. These countries eventually also become net exporters of the product near the end of the stage (time t_3). At time t_2 the Less Developed Countries begin their own production, although they continue to be net importers. Meanwhile, the lower cost production from these growing competitors turns the United States into a net importer by time t_4. The competitive advantage for production and export is clearly shifting across countries at this time.

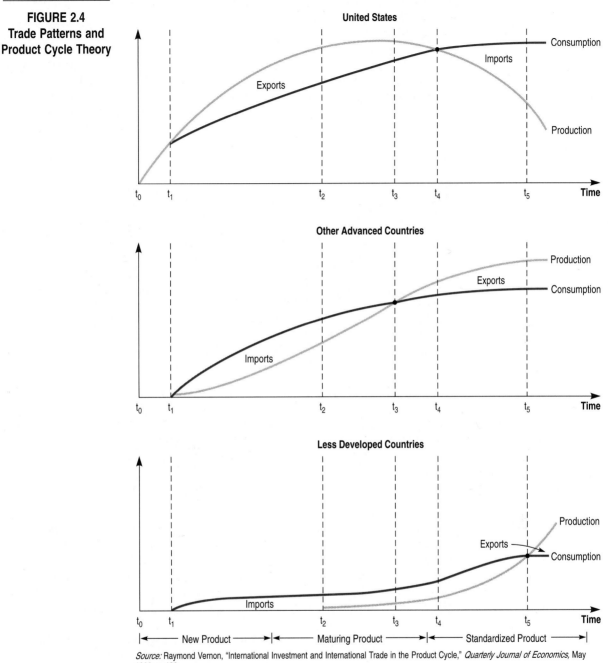

FIGURE 2.4
Trade Patterns and Product Cycle Theory

Source: Raymond Vernon, "International Investment and International Trade in the Product Cycle," *Quarterly Journal of Economics,* May 1966, p. 199.

The third and final stage, the Standardized Product Stage, sees the comparative advantage of production and export now shifting to the Less Developed Countries. The product is now a relatively mass-produced product that can be made with increasingly less-skilled labor. The United States continues to reduce domestic production and increase imports. The Other Advanced Countries continue to produce and export, although exports peak as the Less Developed Countries expand production and become net exporters themselves. The product has run its course or life cycle in reaching time t_5.

A final point: Note that throughout this product cycle, the countries of production, consumption, export, and import are identified by their labor and capital levels, not firms. Vernon noted that it could very well be the same firms that are moving production from the United States to Other Advanced Countries to Less Developed Countries. The shifting location of production was instrumental in the changing patterns of trade, but not necessarily in the loss of market share, profitability, or competitiveness of the firms. The country of comparative advantage changes.

The Contributions of Product Cycle Theory

Although interesting in its own right for increasing emphasis on technology's impact on production costs, product cycle theory was most important because it explained international investment. Not only did the theory recognize the mobility of capital across countries (breaking the traditional assumption of factor immobility), it shifted the focus from the country to the product. This made it important to match the product by its maturity stage with its production location to examine competitiveness.

Product cycle theory has many limitations. It is obviously most appropriate for technology-based products. These are the products that are most likely to experience the changes in production process as they grow and mature. Other products, either resource-based (such as minerals and other commodities) or services (which employ capital but mostly in the form of human capital), are not so easily characterized by stages of maturity. And product cycle theory is most relevant to products that eventually fall victim to mass production and therefore cheap labor forces. But, all things considered, product cycle theory served to breach a wide gap between the trade theories of old and the intellectual challenges of a new, more globally competitive market in which capital, technology, information, and firms themselves were more mobile.

THE NEW TRADE THEORY

Global trade developments in the 1980s led to much criticism of the existing theories of trade. First, although there was rapid growth in trade, much of it was not explained by current theory. Secondly, the massive size of the merchandise trade deficit of the United States—and the associated decline of many U.S. firms in terms of international competitiveness—served as something of a country-sized lab experiment demonstrating what some critics termed the "bankruptcy of trade theory." Academics and policymakers alike now looked for new explanations that would help them help economies.

Two new contributions to trade theory were met with great interest. Paul Krugman, along with several colleagues in the mid-1980s, developed a theory of how trade is altered when markets are not perfectly competitive, or when production of specific products possess economies of scale. A second and very influential development was the growing work of Michael Porter, who examined the competitiveness of industries on a global basis, rather than relying on country-specific factors to determine competitiveness.

Economies of Scale and Imperfect Competition

Paul Krugman's theoretical developments once again focused on cost of production and how cost and price drive international trade. Using theoretical developments from microeconomics and market structure analysis, Krugman focused on two types of economics of scale, *internal economies of scale* and *external economies of scale.*[5]

Internal Economies of Scale

When the cost per unit of output depends on the size of an individual firm, the larger the firm the greater the scale benefits, and the lower the cost per unit. A firm possessing internal economies of scale could potentially monopolize an industry (creating an *imperfect market*), both domestically and internationally. If it produces more, lowering the cost per unit, it can lower the market price and sell more products, because it *sets* market prices.

The link between dominating a domestic industry and influencing international trade comes from taking this assumption of imperfect markets back to the original concept of comparative advantage. For this firm to expand sufficiently to enjoy its economies of scale, it must take resources away from other domestic industries in order to expand. A country then sees its own range of products in which it specializes narrowing, providing an opportunity for other countries to specialize in these so-called abandoned product ranges. Countries again search out and exploit comparative advantage.

A particularly powerful implication of internal economies of scale is that it provides an explanation of intra-industry trade, one area in which traditional trade theory had indeed seemed bankrupt. **Intra-industry trade** is when a country seemingly imports and exports the same product, an idea that is obviously inconsistent with any of the trade theories put forward in the past three centuries. According to Krugman, internal economies of scale may lead a firm to specialize in a narrow product line (to produce the volume necessary for economies of scale cost benefits); other firms in other countries may produce products that are similarly narrow, yet extremely similar: *product differentiation.* If consumers in either country wish to buy both products, they will be importing and exporting products that are, for all intents and purposes, the same.[6]

Intra-industry trade has been studied in detail in the past decade. Intra-industry trade is measured with the Grubel-Lloyd Index, the ratio of imports and exports of the same product occurring between two trading nations. It is calculated as follows:

$$\text{Intra-Industry Trade Index}_i = \frac{|X_i - M_i|}{(X_i + M_i)},$$

where i is the product category and $|X - M|$ is the absolute value of net exports of that product (exports − imports). For example, if Sweden imports 100 heavy machines for its forest products industry from Finland, and at the same time exports to Finland 80 of the same type of equipment, the intra-industry trade (IIT) index would be:

$$\text{IIT}_i = \frac{|80 - 100|}{(80 + 100)} = 1 - .1111 = .89.$$

The closer the index value to 1, the higher the level of intra-industry trade in that product category. The closer the index is to 0, the more one-way the trade between the countries exists, as traditional trade theory would predict.

External Economies of Scale

When the cost per unit of output depends on the size of an industry, not the size of the individual firm, the industry of that country may produce at lower costs than the same industry that is smaller in size in other countries. A country can potentially dominate world markets in a particular product, not because it has one massive firm producing enormous quantities (for example, Boeing), but rather because it has many small firms that interact to create a large, competitive, critical mass (for example, fine crystal glassware in eastern Germany). No one firm need be all that large, but all small firms in total may create such a competitive industry that firms in other countries cannot ever break into the industry on a competitive basis.[7]

Unlike internal economies of scale, external economies of scale may not necessarily lead to imperfect markets, but they may result in an industry maintaining its dominance in its field in world markets. This provides an explanation as to why all industries do not necessarily always move to the country with the lowest-cost energy, resources, or labor. What gives rise to this critical mass of small firms and their interrelationships is a much more complex question. The work of Michael Porter provides a partial explanation of how these critical masses are sustained.

The Competitive Advantage of Nations

In many ways, the study of international trade has come full circle. The focus of early trade theory was on the country or nation and its inherent, natural, or endowment characteristics that may give rise to increasing competitiveness. As trade theory evolved, it shifted its focus to the industry and product level, leaving the national-level competitiveness question somewhat behind. Recently, many have turned their attention to the question of how countries, governments, and even private industry can alter the conditions within a country to aid the competitiveness of its firms.

The leader in this area of research has been Michael Porter of Harvard. As he states:

> National prosperity is created, not inherited. It does not grow out of a country's natural endowments, its labor pool, its interest rates, or its currency's values, as classical economics insists.
>
> A nation's competitiveness depends on the capacity of its industry to innovate and upgrade. Companies gain advantage against the world's best competitors because of pressure and challenge. They benefit from having strong domestic rivals, aggressive home-based suppliers, and demanding local customers.
>
> In a world of increasingly global competition, nations have become more, not less, important. As the basis of competition has shifted more and more to the creation and assimilation of knowledge, the role of the nation has grown. Competitive advantage is created and sustained through a highly localized process. Differences in national values, culture, economic structures, institutions, and histories all contribute to competitive success. There are striking differences in the patterns of competitiveness in every country; no nation can or will be competitive in every or even most industries. Ultimately, nations succeed in particular industries because their home environment is most forward-looking, dynamic, and challenging.[8]

Porter argued innovation is what drives and sustains competitiveness. A firm must avail itself of all dimensions of competition, which he categorized into four major components of "the diamond of national advantage":

1. **Factor Conditions:** The appropriateness of the nation's factors of production to compete successfully in a specific industry. Porter notes that although these factor conditions are very important in the determination of trade, they are not the only source of competitiveness as suggested by the classical or factor proportions theories of trade. Most importantly for Porter, it is the ability of a nation to continually create, upgrade, and deploy its factors (such as skilled labor) that is important, not the initial endowment.

2. **Demand Conditions:** The degree of health and competition the firm must face in its original home market. Firms that can survive and flourish in highly competitive and demanding local markets are much more likely to gain the competitive edge. Porter notes that it is the character of the market, not its size, that is paramount in promoting the continual competitiveness of the firm. And Porter translates *character* as demanding customers.

3. **Related and Supporting Industries:** The competitiveness of all related industries and suppliers to the firm. A firm that is operating within a mass of related firms and industries gains and maintains advantages through close working relationships, proximity to suppliers, and timeliness of product and information flows. The constant and close interaction is successful if it occurs not only in terms of physical proximity but also through the willingness of firms to work at it.

4. **Firm Strategy, Structure, and Rivalry:** The conditions in the home-nation that either hinder or aid in the firm's creation and sustaining of international competitiveness. Porter notes that no one managerial, ownership, or operational strategy is universally appropriate. It depends on the fit and flexibility of what works for that industry in that country at that time.

These four, as illustrated in Figure 2.5, constitute what nations and firms must strive to "create and sustain through a highly localized process" to ensure their success.

The work of Porter is in many ways a synthesis of all that came before it. The emphasis on innovation as the source of competitiveness reflects the increased focus on the industry and product that we have seen in the past three decades. The acknowledgement that the nation is "more, not less, important" is to many eyes a welcome return to a positive role for government and even national-level private industry in encouraging international competitiveness. Including factor conditions as a cost component, demand conditions as a motivator of firm actions, and competitiveness all combine to include the elements of classical, factor proportions, product cycle, and imperfect competition theories in a pragmatic approach to the challenges that the global markets of the twenty-first century present to the firms of today.

**FIGURE 2.5
Determinants of
National Competitive
Advantage: Porter's
Diamond**

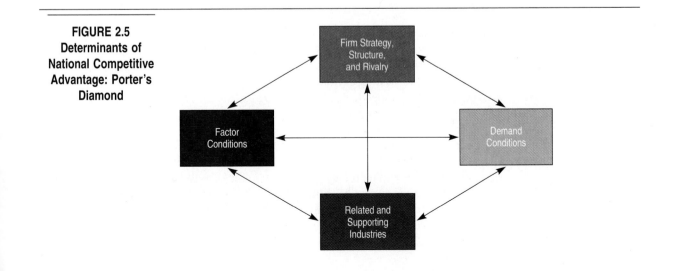

THE THEORY OF INTERNATIONAL INVESTMENT

To understand international investment, its motivation, process, and implications, we return to the basic premise of international trade.[9] Trade is the production of a good or service in one country and its sale to a buyer in another country. In fact, we specifically note that it is a firm (not a country) and a buyer (not a country) that are the subjects of trade, domestically or internationally. A firm therefore is attempting to access a market and its buyers. The producing firm wants to utilize its competitive advantage for growth and profit.

Although this sounds easy enough, consider any of the following potholes on this freeway to investment success. Any of the following potholes may be avoided by producing within another country.

- Sales to some countries are difficult because of tariffs imposed on your product when it is entering. If you were producing within the country, your product would no longer be an import.
- Your product requires natural resources that are available only in certain areas of the world. It is therefore imperative that you have access to the natural resources. You can buy them from that country and bring them to your production process (import) or simply take the production to them.
- Competition is constantly pushing you to improve efficiency and decrease the costs of producing your product. You therefore may want to produce where it will be cheaper—cheaper capital, cheaper energy, cheaper natural resources, or cheaper labor. Many of these factors are still not mobile, and therefore you will go to them instead of bringing them to you.

There are thousands of reasons why a firm may want to produce in another country, and not necessarily in the country that is cheapest for production or the country where the final product is sold. And there are many shades of gray between the black and white of exporting or investing directly in the foreign country.

The subject of international investment arises from one basic idea: the mobility of capital. Although many of the traditional trade theories assumed the immobility of the factors of production, it is the movement of capital that has allowed **foreign direct investments** across the globe. If there is a competitive advantage to be gained, capital can get there.

The Foreign Direct Investment Decision

Consider a firm that wants to exploit its competitive advantage by accessing foreign markets as illustrated in the decision-sequence tree of Figure 2.6.

The first choice is whether to exploit the existing competitive advantage in new foreign markets or to concentrate resources in the development of new competitive advantages in the domestic market. Although many firms may choose to do both as resources will allow, more and more firms are choosing to go international as at least part of their expansion strategies.

Second, should the firm produce at home and export to the foreign markets or produce abroad? Customarily, the firm will choose the path that will allow it to access the resources and markets it needs to exploit its existing competitive advantage. That is the minimum requirement. But it also should consider two additional dimensions of each foreign investment decision: (1) the degree of control over assets, technology, information, and operations, and (2) the magnitude of capital that the firm must risk. Each decision increases the firm's control at the cost of increased capital outlays.

For some reason, possibly one of the potholes described previously, the firm decides to produce abroad. There are, however, many different ways to produce abroad. The distinctions among different kinds of foreign direct investment (branch 3 and downward in Figure 2.6), licensing agreements to greenfield construction (building a new facility from the ground up), vary by degrees of ownership. The licensing management contract is by far the simplest and cheapest way to produce abroad; another firm is actually doing the production, but with your firm's technology and know-how. The question for most firms is whether the reduced capital investment of simply licensing the product to another manufacturer is worth the risk of loss of control over the product and technology.

FIGURE 2.6   **The Direct Foreign Investment Decision Sequence**

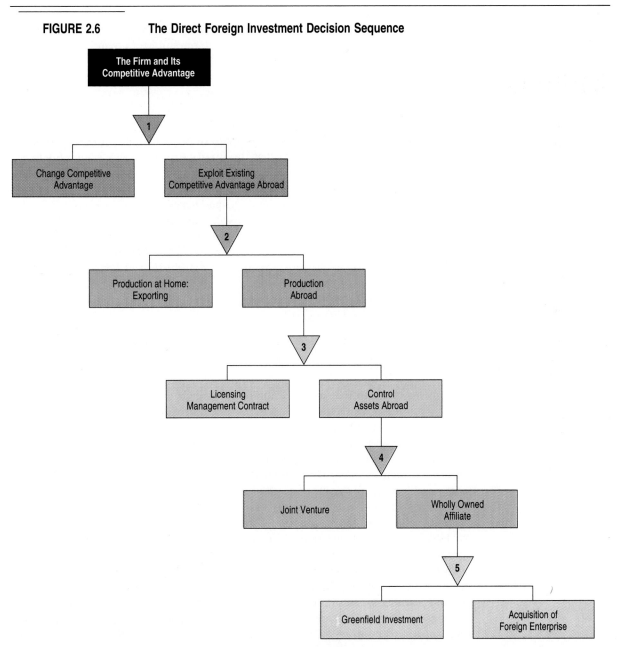

Source: Adapted from Gunter Dufey and R. Mirus, "Foreign Direct Investment: Theory and Strategic Considerations," unpublished, University of Michigan, May 1985.

The firm that wants direct control over the foreign production process next determines the degree of equity control, to own the firm outright or as a joint investment with another firm. Trade-offs with shared ownership continue the debate over control of assets and other sources of the firm's original competitive advantage. Many countries, trying to ensure the continued growth of local firms and investors, may require that foreign firms operate jointly with local firms.

The final decision branch between a "greenfield investment"—building a firm from the ground up—and the purchase of an existing firm, is often a question of cost. A greenfield investment is usually the most expensive of all foreign investment alternatives. The acquisition of an existing firm is often lower in initial cost but may also contain a number of customizing and adjustment costs that are not apparent at the initial purchase. The purchase of a going concern may also have substantial benefits if the existing business possesses substantial customer and supplier relationships that can be used by the new owner in the pursuit of its own business line.

The Theory of Foreign Direct Investment

What motivates a firm to go beyond exporting or licensing? What benefits does the multinational firm expect to achieve by establishing a physical presence in other countries? These are the questions that the theory of foreign direct investment has sought to answer. As with trade theory, the questions have remained largely the same over time while the answers have continued to change. With hundreds of countries, thousands of firms, and millions of products and services, there is no question that the answer to such an enormous question will likely get messy.

The following overview of investment theory has many similarities to the preceding discussion of international trade. The theme is a global business environment that continues to attempt to satisfy increasingly sophisticated consumer demands, while the means of production, resources, skills, and technology needed become more complex and competitive. A more detailed analysis of foreign direct investment theory is presented in Chapter 12.

Firms as Seekers

There is no question that much of the initial foreign direct investment of the eighteenth and nineteenth centuries was the result of firms seeking unique and valuable natural resources for their products. Whether it be the copper resources of Chile, the linseed oils of Indonesia, or the petroleum resources spanning the Middle East, firms established permanent presences around the world to get access to the resources at the core of their business. The twentieth century has seen the expansion of this activity combined with a number of other objectives sought by multinationals.

The resources needed for production are often combined with other advantages that may be inherent in the country of production. The same low-cost labor that was used as the source of international competitiveness in labor-intensive products according to factor proportions trade theory provides incentives for firms to move production to countries possessing those factor advantages. And, consistent with the principles of Vernon's product cycle, the same firms may move their own production to locations of factor advantages as the products and markets mature.

Seeking may also include the search for knowledge. Firms may attempt to acquire firms in other countries for the technical or competitive skills they may possess.

Alternatively, companies may locate in and around centers of industrial enterprise unique to their specific industry, such as the footwear industry of Milan or the semi-conductor industry of the Silicon Valley of California.

Firms continue to move internationally as they seek political stability or security. The massive outflow of capital and industry now occurring from Hong Kong is a striking example of how firms attempt to find new locations that will allow them to continue to operate and grow unfettered by the Chinese takeover of Hong Kong scheduled for 1997. Mexico has experienced a significant increase in the level of foreign direct investment as a result of the increasing political stability of the post-1985 government and the tacit support of the United States and Canada reflected by the North American Free Trade Agreement.

Finally, firms may seek markets. The ability to gain and maintain access to markets is of paramount importance to multinational firms. The need to grow beyond the domestic market is central to all of international trade and business theory (see Global Perspective 2.1). Whether following the principles of Linder, in which firms learn from their domestic market and use that information to go international, or the principles of Porter, which emphasized the character of the domestic market as dictating international competitiveness, foreign-market access is necessary. As governments have become more intertwined in the business affairs of their constituents, multinational firms have often been forced to position themselves against the potential loss of market access by establishing permanent physical presence. The reaction of North American and East Asian firms to the Single European Market pushed forward in 1986 was to increase their level of investment in the European Union to ensure that they would not fall victim to a "Fortress Europe" if it were to arise (it did not).

Firms as Exploiters of Imperfections

Much of the investment theory developed in the past three decades has focused on the efforts of multinational firms to exploit the imperfections in factor and product markets created by governments. The work of Stephen Hymer (1960), Charles Kindle-berger (1969), and Richard Caves (1971) noted that many of the policies of governments create imperfections. These market imperfections cover the entire range of supply- and demand-related principles of the market: trade policy (tariffs and quotas), tax policies and incentives, preferential purchasing arrangements established by the governments themselves, and financial restrictions on the access of foreign firms to domestic capital markets. As illustrated in Global Perspective 2.2, government policies are currently used to manipulate foreign investment.

For example, many of the world's developing countries long have sought to create domestic industry by restricting imports of competitive products in order to allow smaller, less competitive domestic firms to grow and prosper—so-called **import substitution** policies. Multinational firms have sought to maintain their access to these markets by establishing their own production presence within the country, effectively bypassing the tariff restriction but at the same time fulfilling the country's desire to stimulate domestic industrial production (and employment) in that area.

Other multinational firms have exploited the same sources of comparative advantage identified throughout this chapter: the low cost resources or factors often located in less developed countries or countries with restrictions in place on the mobility of labor and capital. It should once again be noted that it is mobility of capital, international investment and foreign direct investment, that is the topic.

Global Perspective

2.1
Investment Destinations

The rapidly growing economies of Asia are the favourite destinations for emerging-market investments by multinational companies, according to a survey by Ernst & Young, an accounting firm. Four-fifths of the firms polled had investments in emerging markets. Of these, almost 90 percent had invested in Asia and just under 70 percent in Latin America. For American firms, Latin America and Asia were almost equally popular. Japanese companies, however, have focused much more on Asia. Europeans, too, prefer Asia, though they have been keener than Americans and Japanese to invest in Eastern Europe and southern Africa.

Future Plans Asia is expected to stay the star attraction. Companies from Europe, America, and Japan all regard it as easily their most important target. American firms, however, are also keen to invest in Latin America, particularly in Mexico and Brazil. Surprisingly, only 16 percent of West European companies said Eastern Europe was a priority.

Many countries actively advertise and promote themselves as attractive locations for foreign investment. The Netherlands' Foreign Investment Agency is seen here highlighting the locational advantages of Holland for doing business in Europe.

Source: *The Economist*, back cover, Sept. 17, 1994.

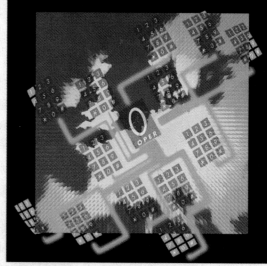

IF YOU'RE LOOKING AT EUROPE

American companies operating in Europe are opening centralized call centers. They are introducing the techniques that have made their domestic operations competitive and responsive to customers.

It's not just because of new capabilities from European telecom carriers. Rather, borders — telephonic, regulatory and attitudinal — are relaxing. Demographic trends are creating crossborder niches of consumers with common needs.

No wonder companies can centralize telephone-based functions like technical support, customer service, reservations, order fulfillment, research and sales.

And no wonder Holland has attracted so many toll-free call centers.

The Netherlands is known for its advanced and flexible telecom facilities and infrastructure. The most multilingual of populations. Highly competitive utility and phone tariffs. A neutral reputation that makes it a preferred base for pan-European activity.

With unsurpassed distribution facilities — required for order fulfillment linked to telemarketing — the Netherlands can be described as either a value-added logistics center or a value-added telemarketing hub.

That's why companies like Holiday Inn, Sun, Hewlett-Packard, Azerty and Packard Bell have established call centers in the Netherlands. **THEY KNOW: YOU CAN MAKE IT IN HOLLAND.**

Netherlands Foreign Investment Agency

Source: *The Economist*, Emerging Market Indicators, November 26, 1994, p. 120.

Global Perspective

2.2
Beijing Imposes Substantial New Taxes and Duties on Imports by Foreigners

China has imposed hefty new duties and taxes on goods frequently imported by foreign enterprises and individuals, adding to the already soaring costs of doing business here.

In a quiet policy change effective Jan. 1, China has begun to require almost all enterprises and individuals to pay customs duties and value-added tax on 20 so-called luxury imports that weren't previously taxed, Chinese tax officials and Western accountants say.

While the new charges are unlikely to stop foreign companies from flocking to do business in China, they will further raise foreign businesses' operating costs. The new measure also appears to be part of a general, tougher policy taken by Beijing toward overseas investors after the country saw record levels of foreign-capital inflows over the past few years.

Although Beijing has termed them luxury items, the products affected include furniture and basic electrical appliances such as TV sets, personal computers, and refrigerators that are frequently brought in by companies and individual business people when they set up shop in China. Duties range from 14 percent for pagers to 100 percent for furniture and as much as 130 percent for air conditioners. The value-added tax, which must be paid in addition to the duties, is a uniform 17 percent.

Western accountants quoted Chinese customs officials as saying that the new taxes wouldn't be implemented for companies that signed joint-venture contracts or obtained import permits before Jan. 1. But some companies say they have been asked to pay the taxes despite having met this condition.

In the past, foreign enterprises engaging in joint ventures in China could import such products duty-free as part of their capital contribution. Foreign individuals could import personal effects, including a limited number of electrical appliances, without paying taxes. Under the new policy, ethnic Chinese abroad, including from Taiwan, are still allowed such tax-free status.

Paying More: New Chinese Customs Duties and Taxes on Imports

Product	Customs Duty	Total Payment*
Black & white TV sets	100%	177%
Color TV sets	130	147
Video cameras/VCRs	130	147
Stereo equipment	80–130	97–147
Air conditioners	90–130	107–147
Refrigerators	50–130	67–147
Washing machines	80–130	97–147
Cameras	17–100	34–117
Photocopiers	40	57
Telephone systems	14–40	31–57
Personal computers	70	87
Telephones	30	47
Fax machines	14–17	31–34
Calculators	80	97
Word processors	40	57
Furniture	100	117

*Includes 17% VAT tax
Source: People's Republic of China Customs Notice, courtesy of Coopers & Lybrand China

One tax official at the State General Administration of Taxation said Wednesday that the main reason for the new policy is that in the past, China couldn't guarantee supplies of some office equipment. "Now this problem doesn't exist," he says. "Locally made products are cheap, and the quality is good."

Western accountants think other factors could be driving the decision, such as the poor results last year in the collection of customs duties and taxes or Beijing's desire to sell more domestically made products. With foreign investments pouring into China in record volume, Chinese officials have increasingly started to set terms for doing business, as well as taking steps to protect local industries.

The combining of the mobility of capital with the immobility of low-cost labor has characterized much of the foreign investment seen throughout the developing world over the past 30 years.

The ability of multinational firms to exploit or at least manage these imperfections will still rely on their ability to gain an advantage. Market advantages or powers are seen in international markets in the same way as in domestic markets: cost advantages, economies of scale and scope, product differentiation, managerial or marketing technique and knowledge, and financial resources and strength. All are the things of which competitive dreams are made. The multinational firm needs to find these in some form or another to justify the added complexities and costs of international investments.

Firms as Internalizers

The question that has plagued the field of foreign direct investment is why can't all of the advantages mentioned above be achieved through management contracts or licensing agreements (the choice available to the international investor at step 3 in Figure 2.6). Why is it necessary for the firm itself to establish a presence in the country? What pushes the multinational firm farther down the investment-decision tree?

The research and writings of Peter Buckley and Mark Casson (1976) and John Dunning (1977) have attempted to answer these questions by focusing on nontransferable sources of competitive advantage—proprietary information possessed by the firm and its people. Many of the true advantages possessed by firms center on their hands-on knowledge of producing a product or providing a service. By establishing their own multinational operations, they can internalize the production, thus keeping within the firm the information that is at the core of the firm's competitiveness. **Internalization** is preferable to the use of arm's-length investment arrangements, such as management contracts or licensing agreements. They either do not allow the effective transmission of the knowledge or represent too serious a threat to the loss of the knowledge to allow the firm to achieve the benefits of international investment.

As stated, these are theories. The synthesis of motivations provided by Dunning and others has only sought to partially explain, in the manner of Porter, many of the facts and forces leading firms to pursue international investment. To date, there is scant empirical evidence to support or refute these theories.

SUMMARY

The theory of international trade has changed drastically from that first put forward by Adam Smith. The classical theories of Adam Smith and David Ricardo focused on the abilities of countries to produce goods more cheaply than other countries. The earliest production and trade theories saw labor as the major factor expense that went into any product. If a country could pay that labor less, and if that labor could produce more physically than labor in other countries, the country might obtain an absolute or comparative advantage in trade.

Subsequent theoretical development led to a more detailed understanding of production and its costs. Factors of production are now believed to include labor (skilled and unskilled), capital, natural resources, and other potentially significant commodities that are difficult to reproduce or replace, such as energy. Technology, once assumed to be the same across all countries, is now seen as one of the premier driving forces in determining who holds the competitive edge or advantage. International trade is now seen as a complex combination of thousands of products, technologies, and firms that are constantly innovating to either keep up with or get ahead of the competition.

Modern trade theory has looked beyond production cost to analyze how the demands of the marketplace alter who trades with whom and which firms survive domestically and internationally. The abilities of firms to adapt to foreign markets, both in the demands and the competitors that form the foreign markets, have required much of international trade and investment theory to search out new and innovative approaches to what determines success and failure.

Finally, as world economies grew and the magnitude of world trade increased, the simplistic ideas that guided international trade and investment theory have had to grow with them. The choices that many firms face today require them to directly move their capital, technology, and know-how to countries that possess other unique factors or market advantages that will help the firm keep pace with market demands.

Key Terms and Concepts

mercantilism

specie

absolute advantage

division of labor

comparative advantage

production possibilities frontier

autarky

opportunity cost

factor proportions theory

factors of production

factor intensities

input-output analysis

Leontief Paradox

product cycle theory

intra-industry trade

competitive advantage

product differentiation

economies of scale

foreign direct investment

import substitution

internalization

Questions for Discussion

1. According to the theory of comparative advantage as explained by Ricardo, why is trade always possible between two countries, even when one is absolutely inefficient compared to the other?

2. The factor proportions theory of international trade assumes that all countries produce the same product the same way. Would international competition cause or prevent this from happening?

3. What, in your opinion, were the constructive impacts on trade theory resulting from the empirical research of Wassily Leontief?

4. Product cycle theory has always been a very "attractive theory" to many students. Why do you think that is?

5. If the product cycle theory were accepted for the basis of policy-making in the United States, what should the U.S. government do to help U.S. firms exploit the principles of the theory?

6. Many trade theorists argue that the primary contribution of Michael Porter has been to repopularize old ideas, in new, more applicable ways. To what degree do you think Porter's ideas are new or old?

7. How would you analyze the statement that "international investment is simply a modern extension of classical trade"?

8. Why would a country like the Netherlands try to convince firms to locate in its country?

Recommended Readings

Buckley, Peter J., and Mark Casson. *The Future of the Multinational Enterprise.* London: Macmillan, 1976.

Caves, Richard E. "International Corporations: The Industrial Economics of Foreign Investment." *Economica* (February 1971): 1–27.

Dunning, John H. "Trade Location of Economic Activity and the MNE: A Search for an Eclectic Approach," in *The International Allocation of Economic Activity.* Bertil Ohlin, Per-Ove Hesselborn, and Per Magnus Wijkman, editors. New York: Homes and Meier, 1977, 395–418.

Heckscher, Eli. "The Effect of Foreign Trade on the Distribution of Income," in *Readings in International Trade.* Howard S. Ellis and Lloyd A. Metzler, editors. Philadelphia: The Blakiston Company, 1949.

Helpman, Elhaman, and Paul Krugman. *Market Structure and Foreign Trade.* Cambridge, Mass.: MIT Press, 1985.

Husted, Steven, and Michael Melvin. *International Economics.* New York: Harper & Row, 1990.

Hymer, Stephen H. *The International Operations of National Firms: A Study of Direct Foreign Investment.* Cambridge, Mass.: MIT Press, 1976.

Linder, Staffan Burenstam. *An Essay on Trade and Transformation.* New York: John Wiley & Sons, 1961.

Maskus, Keith E., Deborah Battles, and Michael H. Moffett. "Determinants of the Structure of U.S. Manufacturing Trade with Japan and Korea, 1970-1984," in *The Internationalization of U.S. Markets.* David B. Audretch and Michael P. Claudon, editors. New York: New York University Press, 1989, 97–122.

Ohlin, Bertil. *Interregional and International Trade.* Boston: Harvard University Press, 1933.

Porter, Michael. "The Competitive Advantage of Nations." *Harvard Business Review* (March–April 1990).

Ricardo, David. *The Principles of Political Economy and Taxation.* Cambridge, United Kingdom: Cambridge University Press, 1981.

Root, Franklin R. *International Trade and Investment,* sixth edition. Chicago: South-Western Publishing, 1990.

Smith, Adam. *The Wealth of Nations.* New York: The Modern Library, 1937.

Vernon, Raymond. "International Investment and International Trade in the Product Cycle." *Quarterly Journal of Economics* (1966): 190–207.

Wells, Louis T., Jr. "A Product Life Cycle for International Trade?" *Journal of Marketing* 22 (July 1968): 1–6.

Notes

1. Adam Smith, *An Inquiry into the Nature and Causes of the Wealth of Nations,* (New York: E.P. Dutton & Company, 1937), 4–5.

2. Wassily Leontief, "Domestic Production and Foreign Trade: the American Capital Position Re-Examined," *Proceedings of the American Philosophical Society,* vol. 97, no. 4, September 1953, as reprinted in Wassily Leontief, *Input-Output Economics* (New York: Oxford University Press, 1966), 69–70.

3. In Leontief's own words: "These figures show that an average million dollars' worth of our exports embodies considerably less capital and somewhat more labor than would be required to replace from domestic production an equivalent amount of our competitive imports. . . . The widely held opinion that—as compared with the rest of the world—the United States' economy is characterized by a relative surplus of capital and a relative shortage of labor proves to be wrong. As a matter of fact, the opposite is true." Leontief, 1953, 86.

4. If this were true, it would defy one of the basic assumptions of the factor proportions theory, that all products are manufactured with the same technology (and therefore same proportions of labor and capital) across countries.

However, continuing studies have found this to be quite possible in our imperfect world.

5. For a detailed description of these theories see Elhanan Helpman and Paul Krugman, *Market Structure and Foreign Trade,* (Cambridge: MIT Press, 1985).

6. This leads to the obvious debate as to what constitutes a "different product" and what is simply a cosmetic difference. The most obvious answer is found in the field of marketing: If the consumer believes the products are different, then they are different.

7. There are a variety of potential outcomes from external economies of scale. For additional details see Paul R. Krugman and Maurice Obstfeld, *International Economics: Theory and Policy,* 3rd ed. (Harper-Collins, 1994).

8. Michael E. Porter, "The Competitive Advantage of Nations," *Harvard Business Review* (March–April 1990): 73–74.

9. The term "international investment" will be used in this chapter to refer to all nonfinancial investment. International financial investment includes a number of forms beyond the concerns of this chapter, such as the purchase of bonds, stocks, or other securities issued outside the domestic economy.

P A R T 1

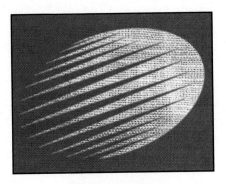

Cases

America for Sale—and Returned

During the late 1980s and early 1990s, it appeared that the United States had become a country for sale. For the first time in decades, total foreign direct investment in the United States exceeded U.S. direct investment abroad. Purchases by foreign investors included Columbia Pictures, Carnation Foods, Allied Stores, Chesebrough-Ponds, Firestone Tire and Rubber, Exxon's headquarters in Manhattan's Rockefeller Center, and a major portion of the Watergate complex in Washington, D.C.

By the end of the 1980s, foreign investors owned more than half of the commercial real estate in downtown Los Angeles, more than one-third of Alaska's $680 million seafood-packaging industry, more than half of the hotels along Hawaii's Waikiki Beach, and four of the ten largest banks in California.

Japanese foreign direct investment has increased more than investment by any other country. Although Britain holds approximately twice as many investments in the United States as Japan, the Japanese increased their foreign direct investment in the United States more than 18-fold during the 1980s, by far the largest increase. Furthermore, American direct investment in Japan is only one-fourth of Japanese investment in the United States.

There are a number of reasons behind the rapid growth in foreign investment in the United States. First, U.S. businesses and properties are selling for low prices because of the plunge in the value of the dollar during the middle and late 1980s.

Sources: Hobart Rowen, "Dispelling Some Myths about Foreign Investment," *The Washington Post,* March 18, 1990, H1; John Burgess, "Foreigners Keep Investing in the U.S.—But with American Loans," *The Washington Post,* January 22, 1991, D1; "For Sale: America," *Time,* September 14, 1987, 52–62; "Unwelcome Mat," *The Wall Street Journal,* July 24, 1987, 1; "Distant Deals," *The Wall Street Journal,* February 24, 1988, 1; "The Selling of America," *Fortune,* December 22, 1986, 43–56; "As Foreign Investment Increases, So Do Concerns about Its Impact," *The Washington Post,* February 21, 1988, H1; "Most Americans Favor Laws to Limit Foreign Investment in U.S., Poll Finds," *The Wall Street Journal,* March 8, 1988, 60; Mitchell Pacelle, "Japan's U.S. Property Deals: A Poor Report Card," *The Wall Street Journal,* June 9, 1995, B1.

A Japanese real estate investor visiting Manhattan noted, "Everything here is so cheap!" While prices seemed high to Americans, they seemed enticingly low to an investor holding yen or marks, both of which appreciated by about 40 percent relative to the dollar during the mid-1980s. Second, many foreign investors were flush with cash to invest. This was the result of both high savings rates in many other countries and the persistent U.S. current account deficits, which had transferred billions of dollars abroad. A third factor is that foreign investors were attracted to America's stable political climate and the open nature of its economy and capital markets.

Historically, the United States has allowed capital to flow freely across its borders, and many argue that this is how it should be. "This is in everybody's interests, just as trade is in everybody's interests," said Robert Ortner, undersecretary for economic affairs at the Commerce Department. Proponents argue that the world is in the process of integration, and the United States should not stand in the way. Freedom of investment promotes efficiency in allocation of capital, according to most economists. "We get the jobs, we get the production," argues Ortner. "And for that matter, we are beginning to get the exports," he says, referring to an announcement by Japanese companies that they planned to export some of their U.S.-made cars to Japan.

Other benefits of foreign direct investment in the United States have also been apparent. Many industrial cities in the United States have been unable to attract American investors. For these cities, foreign investment that has come in to reopen plants has resulted in employment and growth. Foreign investment is also likely to reduce the United States's reliance on imports, because many of the goods previously imported are now manufactured in the United States. Another benefit is that foreign investment brings not only money but managerial talent, innovation, and technology.

Despite the obvious benefits, however, a number of observers have pointed out that there are corresponding costs. Lawrence Brainard, chief international economist for Bankers Trust, said, "By the end of the century the United States will have the most modern manufacturing sector in the world, but it won't own it." A Texas congressman has said, "America has been selling its family jewels to pay for a night on the town, and we don't know enough about the proud new owners."

Some observers are skeptical about that claim that foreign investment increases employment. A study by the United Auto Workers concluded the opposite: For every job created, the study claimed, three are destroyed because the foreign-owned operations import so many of their components. Further, because many foreign companies are nonunion, they may have cost advantages over their American competitors. Other studies, however, have disputed the claim that foreign investment reduces employment.

Some of the opposition to growth in direct investment in the United States is rooted in issues of national pride and security. In fighting to prevent a takeover by a British firm, a major textbook publisher argued that foreigners were unfit to publish textbooks for American schoolchildren. The Pentagon has objected to proposed purchases of defense contractors, such as Fairchild Semiconductors, arguing that national security interests were at stake.

Foreign ownership in America raised a number of questions. How does foreign investment affect America's ability to compete? What, if any, controls should be placed on foreign investment? What are the economic effects of the growth in foreign direct investment? Finally, there are social and cultural implications of the growth in direct investment. Said a Japanese banker in Tokyo: "We are amazed at the way Americans are willing to sell out. In Japan, owners of companies hold on for life."

Surveys found the general public to be alarmed about the extent of foreign investment in the United States. Some people believed that (1) foreign investment causes America to have less control over the economy, (2) foreign investors might pull their money out at any time, and (3) laws should limit the extent of foreign ownership of American business and real estate.

Within a few years, however, the concerns changed. Suddenly, Japanese firms were not investing and buying, but rather selling—and often at a loss. For example, the Pebble Beach Golf Links, bought by Japanese developer Minoru Isutani in 1990 for $841 million, was sold in 1992 for about $500 million. Rockefeller Center, 80 percent of which was bought by Mitsubishi Estate Co., had to seek bankruptcy protection in May of 1995. Overdevelopment and a real estate market drop accounted for some of the problems. But Japanese investors were hit even harder by the rise of the yen, which further reduced the amount they received after a sale.

Questions for Discussion

1. Do you think foreign investors should be limited in their ability to acquire (a) U.S. farmland or (b) majority ownership in defense-related industries? Why or why not?

2. Direct foreign investment may take place through either the acquisition of existing facilities or the building of new ones. From the perspective of the host country, which do you think is preferable? Why?

3. Some observers have argued that foreign direct investment in developing countries should be limited so that the countries may develop their own industries. What is your opinion?

4. Given the yen's increase against the dollar, how likely is it that any Japanese investor in U.S. real estate made money?

Vanport Manufacturing, Incorporated

In early 1990 Adolf Hertrich, president of Vanport Manufacturing, Inc. (Vanport) located in Boring, Oregon, was examining the latest old-growth timber compromise reported by the U.S. Congress. The compromise was only a short-term truce in the war between environmentalists and timber companies in the Pacific Northwest. As more and more timber was removed from harvesting, Vanport's main business of exporting finished lumber to Japan was placed in increasing jeopardy.

BACKGROUND

Vanport started business 20 years ago as an exporter to Japan of raw logs from predominantly national forest lands in Oregon and Washington. The firm was organized by G. Adolf Hertrich, a German immigrant, and several associates who had extensive forestry experience.[1] The first 10 years of the log export enterprise were relatively successful. The future of Vanport was first threatened in 1974, however, with the passage of federal legislation prohibiting the export of unprocessed logs from U.S. federal lands.[2] Vanport faced two alternatives for its future viability: (1) to focus exclusively on domestic sales of raw logs and forest products; (2) to attempt to enter the processed log markets of the Pacific Rim, specifically Japan.

Vanport first assessed the U.S. domestic market potential. In the middle to late 1970s the general forecast for the U.S. housing industry was very strong. The consensus among private and public agencies in the housing industry was for rapid and continual growth of the residential construction sector for the whole of the 1980s. Vanport, however, did not share this optimism. Analysis of several factors, such as the volatility of the domestic housing industry, the rapid increase in domestic lumber production capacity, the growth of the forest products industries in and around the major residential construction growth areas in the southeastern United States, and the high transportation costs in the domestic market led Vanport to view the general optimism about the immediate housing markets with skepticism. It then assessed their second alternative, the Japanese lumber market.

Hertrich and his associates examined the Japanese market in detail to determine if there were potential markets in which they could utilize the high quality old-growth resources of the Northwest. Japan at that time imported over 70 percent of its softwood needs. The Japanese had also shown a strong and growing demand for the high-quality old-growth timber of the northwestern United States, and were willing to pay a premium for it (particularly the Cascade Mountain variety). The prices paid by Japanese sawmills at that time for lumber were considerably higher at current

---

Source: Adolf Hertrich, Michael H. Moffett, and Arthur Stonehill; President, Vanport Manufacturing, Inc., Associate Professor, and Professor, Oregon State University, 1991. This case is for the purpose of class discussion only, and not to portray either effective or ineffective business or financial management practices.

[1] Hertrich had worked for the U.S. Forest Service for over a decade when he realized that, in his own words, "he had left one bureaucratic system only to move to another"; he soon after resigned and organized fellow investors to form Vanport.

[2] Although the Morse Amendment in 1968 established a quota of 350 mbf per year on logs harvested for export from federal lands in the West, it had not proved a major restriction to the date of the 1974 Act. Although the majority of forest lands in the West are privately held, what concerned Vanport was that the logs valued by Japanese importers were of the old-growth variety, and most of the old growth was on federal lands.

exchange rates than those paid by U.S. mills for the same quality and quantities of old-growth softwood lumber. An additional factor of considerable promise was the apparent stability of demand for lumber by the residential housing construction industry in Japan. This translated into more stable lumber prices paid by the Japanese buyers. Although the additional distance Vanport would be required to go to compete with the domestic Japanese timber mills was considerable, trans-Pacific transportation costs were considerably lower than domestic costs due to the impacts of the Jones Act on domestic ocean-freight expenses.[3] Contrary to public opinion, there were no tariffs or other measures that affected an American lumber producer selling douglas fir, hemlock, or noble fir lumber in Japan.

THE TRADITIONAL JAPANESE LUMBER MARKET

Vanport believed that the export market to Japan would continue to be a strong and growing market if it could somehow succeed in penetrating the market. The costs of production for the Japanese firms were considered to be—in principle—higher than those for an American mill. Most of their imported logs traveled substantial distances, and the majority of the ships were carrying cargo only one-way. This was largely a result of the special design of the log-carrying cargo ships used. Energy costs were substantially higher in Japan (importing nearly 100 percent of their petroleum needs), and other expenses such as real estate were considered exorbitant. Vanport felt that it could produce at a lower cost, at least match the transportation costs, and provide a higher quality old-growth timber product that was superior to the lower quality products available from second-growth logs on private industry lands.

The Japanese market did constitute some serious problems. It was very different from that of the United States, utilizing a different grading of woods and different sizes (metric) and forms (many different cuts, little standardization) than that of the American market.[4] There were no firms (mills) outside of Japan that had been approved or licensed as being capable of cutting lumber to the traditional Japanese standards, including the use of the JAS stamp signifying acceptability for Japanese residential construction.

The differences between the U.S. and Japanese housing industries are considerable. The lumber used in the construction of residential housing in the United States has fewer quality demands than its Japanese counterpart. The framing and internal wood construction of U.S. houses is not visible from the outside, all beams and rafters being covered and hidden by typical American housing construction methods. The Japanese style of housing construction, however, utilizes the wood beams and lumber as part of the actual visible interior, and the quality, color, grain, and even degree of dirt in the lumber are critical to its usefulness.

---

[3] The Jones Act of 1920 reserves trade between U.S. ports to U.S.-operated and U.S. owned ships, manned by U.S. crews. This did not require that the ships be built in the United States, but rather owned and operated and registered by U.S. parties. The law has been broadened over time to include all intercoastal trade, and trade between the mainland United States and its noncontiguous areas of Alaska, Hawaii, Puerto Rico, and all other U.S. territories and possessions.

[4] Approximately 3 percent of the Japanese lumber market consisted of U.S. lumber products (traditional American cellular 2" by 4" construction) at that time, with the rest consisting of traditional Japanese metric size and quality. The percentage of American lumber products has grown from 3 to 7 percent since that time, but that still means that nearly 93 percent of all lumber consumption in Japan is of the traditional Japanese product.

The lumber needs of the Japanese industry are also much more complex by U.S. standards. The wood is to be cut by metric measurements, and in many different sizes and shapes uncommon to U.S. lumber mill experience. Knowledge of the Japanese industry was also considered critical given the varying construction requirements by cities and regions. For example, the roof rafter (the *taruki*) standards vary by city: Tokyo, 36 by 45 millimeters; Nagoya, 45 by 45 millimeters; and Osaka, 42 by 42 millimeters. Traditional domestic Japanese lumber producers know these standards and adjust their products by the source of the lumber order without undue contractual specifications and requirements. Gaining knowledge of these market needs and specifications was considered critical if Vanport was to be able to compete effectively.

The business relations between lumber producers and buyers was also different. American lumber mills traditionally sell to the open market at the going price, and are rarely "linked" to any particular buyer for any length of time. The Japanese industry stressed long-term relationships over price, and it was considered mandatory that in order to be an effective competitor the mill would have to be willing to commit its products to the markets even in the face of uncertain market conditions. Japanese buyers needed to believe that the American producers would be providing a steady product for a long time and would not divert their lumber to other markets due to short term changes in market conditions, either in the United States or Japan. It was also clear from the beginning that in order for Vanport to gain the trust of the buyers—buyers who had serious doubts as to whether a non-Japanese producer could consistently provide lumber of Japanese high quality and standards—that they would have to not only meet but surpass the standards of their Japanese competition.

Transportation costs were often considered prohibitive for an American mill's ability to compete in the Asian-Pacific market. Vanport contacted shipping agents in the Northwest and found that there were a large number of container ships which were delivering Japanese products to Northwest ports but were then returning to Japan empty. Vanport found it very easy and reasonable to negotiate relatively affordable rates for shipping to Japan. Vanport loaded its own lumber, and the containers were then not opened again until arriving at the destination, allowing the firm to insure the quality and prevent damage to the specialized product.

THE TRADITIONAL JAPANESE LUMBER PRODUCT

The critical factors in producing for the Japanese market were both proper grading and proper packaging of the lumber for the various regional markets. Vanport first brought in two Japanese lumber graders for a half-year to train its own staff in the Japanese standards of lumber grading. At the same time it also sent one of its graders to train in Japan. In order for Vanport to receive the JAS stamp of lumber quality, its graders studied for the examination given by the Japanese Ministry of Agriculture. After two comprehensive training periods, all Vanport staff passed the examination. Vanport became the only lumber mill outside of Japan to receive the JAS stamp approval for traditional Japanese lumber products.

The Japanese method of grading and cutting lumber is somewhat more judgmental than is common in U.S. lumber milling. The wood grain, color, and positioning of knotholes must be considered prior to any individual cuts, requiring the mill workers often to be cross-trained in order to perform job responsibilities correctly. This cross-training would be counter to the policies of many wood-worker union guidelines, and is one reason Vanport has worked to pay its workers well to avoid unionization. The production process is definitely more labor-intensive, and requires more highly skilled workers than is typical of U.S. domestic lumber milling. All told, these requirements make automation of the production of these lumber products extremely difficult.

In order to aid in the marketing of the lumber products, Vanport felt it would be desirable to construct a "model home" at its mill site in Boring, Oregon. This would demonstrate its ability to produce the high-quality and specific cuts necessary for Japanese home-building needs. The construction and use of such a model—which also serves as a guesthouse—were helpful in providing visiting Japanese buyers with a demonstration of Vanport's product quality. It was also helpful in providing a more traditional Japanese environment in which to conduct business (for example, the use of a traditional Japanese tea room). Finally, it provided familiar housing for the comfort of visiting Japanese business executives.

FINANCIAL ASPECTS

Vanport was confronted with significant transactions and payments problems from the beginning. In order to acquire letters of credit, it was necessary to insure (by a third party) the shipments. Vanport felt that the high cost of insurance would make it more difficult to compete in the Japanese market. In addition, although it is typical for Japanese industry to utilize letters of credit in international transactions, the exclusive domestic nature of the traditional lumber products industry in Japan made the use of letters a significant barrier to Vanport's ability to compete on an equal footing with the Japanese producers. After evaluating the ocean-going freight history in the Pacific, Vanport concluded that there was little risk of loss at sea, and that the letters of credit would make them uncompetitive in the eyes of the Japanese lumber buyers. It was decided to conduct all transactions on an open-account basis and self-insure all shipments.

FIGURE 1
The Spot and 90-Day Forward Exchange Rates of the Yen/U.S. $, June 1984–May 1985

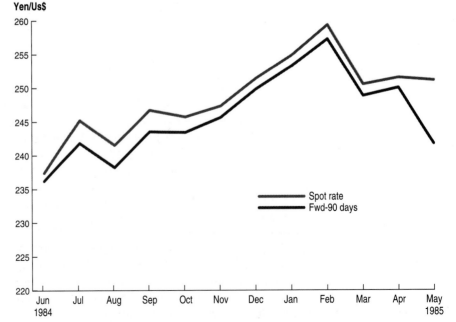

FIGURE 2
Vanport
Manufacturing's
Revenue Squeeze and
the Benefits and Costs
of Hedging

Date	Current Spot[1]	90 Days Out (¥/$) Forward Rate	Actual Spot	Gain/Loss[2]
6/84	237.4	236.2	246.7	$ −180.19
7/84	245.2	241.8	245.7	−91.98
8/84	241.5	238.2	247.3	−154.48
9/84	246.7	243.5	251.4	−129.06
10/84	245.7	243.4	254.8	−183.81
11/84	247.3	245.6	259.3	−215.12
12/84	251.4	249.8	250.5	−11.18
1/85	254.8	253.2	251.5	26.69
2/85	259.3	257.2	251.1	94.46
3/85	250.5	248.8	248.3	8.10
4/85	251.5	250.0	236.2	233.70
5/85	251.1	241.7	238.8	50.24

[1]Spot and 90-day forward exchange rates, yen per U.S. dollar, last trading day of month, Bankers Trust Company of New York, *The Wall Street Journal.*
[2]Gains and losses on a 1 million yen payment received 90 days from the date of the contract or order; value equals the actual spot rate at the payment date less the amount potentially earned if all orders were hedged with forward contracts.

Since Vanport had worked for some time in establishing a business-trust relationship with Japanese buyers, it felt that it was not accepting any undue risk in conducting most transactions on a handshake basis. Communication by facsimile machine, which could reproduce documents in Japanese, eliminated the need to establish a Japanese sales office. Several staff members located in Boring were fluent in Japanese.

Vanport's export of lumber to Japan was increasingly successful in the early 1980s. Vanport priced its product in Japanese yen in the Japanese market to present a product as acceptable as possible to the Japanese wholesalers and builders. The yen earnings, however, presented Vanport with two immediate problems:

1. The increasing appreciation of the dollar versus the yen between 1980 and 1985 was "squeezing" dollar margins significantly (see Figure 1).
2. The constant movement of the exchange rate (against Vanport), particularly on an open-account basis with no hedging, was exposing Vanport to increasingly uncertain dollar revenues.

Because Vanport was still highly conscious of being a relatively small producer, attempting to control overhead and other expenses, Hertrich wished to avoid forward contracts and other relatively expensive currency hedges. Vanport was aware of the fact that although its dollar products yielded fewer and fewer dollars back home when invoiced in yen, yen assets simultaneously would yield higher and higher returns in yen when sold in the United States for dollars. Vanport considered the use of yen earnings for the purchase of yen-denominated assets, and the subsequent sale (import) of those Japanese assets back to the United States, yielding dollars. (For spot exchange rates and forward rates available during this period, see Figure 2.)

Vanport considered the prospect of purchasing merchandise in Japan and reselling it in the United States as a hedge against the rising dollar. It reasoned that although its lumber exports might continue to earn fewer and fewer dollars when repatriated, if the yen earnings were used to buy Japanese goods for resale in the United States, Vanport could recoup the losses. The problem was that this venture put Vanport into an entirely new business.

MARKET GROWTH, EXPANSION, AND COMPETITIVE STRATEGIES

In early 1989 new environmental concerns over the possible threats to the survival of the spotted owl led to preservation of increasing proportions of old-growth timber resources on federal lands. Although this did not pose an immediate threat to Vanport's ability to meet its customers' needs, it was clear that it could pose a long-term limitation to its ability to expand its production for the specialized Japanese industry. If the old-growth timber supply was cut by up to 50 percent, the price competition for supplies in the Northwest would cause losses across all producers. Vanport felt that although it was dependent on old-growth, it had the capital resources ("deep pockets") that would allow it to weather the storm and wait out other producers until they exited the industry. Although this was thought to be a Vanport strength, there was still considerable concern that forest product producers with operations across the United States could also sustain losses in the Northwest, constituting much of the competitive threat in the long run to Vanport's access to its needed old-growth resources.

Coincident with the old-growth—spotted owl issue were increasing trade frictions between the United States and Japan. As a result of the Omnibus Trade Act of 1988 and its "Super 301" provisions, the United States labeled Japan as an "unfair trader" in May of 1989.[5] The classification of Japan as an unfair trader heightened existing trade tensions between the two countries, much of it arising as a result of the United States's bilateral merchandise deficit of over $50 billion at that time. In the event of retaliatory actions by Japan or other more aggressive protectionist measures by the United States, Vanport feared it might find itself excluded from its Japanese markets, markets that by early 1989 constituted over 90 percent of its sales volume.

Adolf Hertrich wondered what alternative strategies Vanport might employ to meet the new environmental challenges. He also wanted to reevaluate Vanport's foreign exchange hedging strategy in light of the continuing long-run strength of the yen.

Questions for Discussion

1. How did the market penetration strategy used by Adolf Hertrich to target the Japanese market differ from that employed by many other U.S. firms?

2. Why did the United States continue to restrict trade related to the use of timber harvested from public lands?

3. How effective was Vanport's hedging strategy? Was it better than simply buying forward contracts?

4. What do you think Vanport should do to protect itself against the increasing threat of a trade war and the loss of its major revenue-producing business from protection of spotted owl habitat?

---

[5] The Super 301 referred to Article 301 of the 1974 Trade Adjustment Act which stated that the United States could take actions against other countries deemed as practicing unfair trade toward U.S. exporters. The Omnibus Trade Act of 1988 had added strength to the clause in requiring the U.S. Trade Representative to determine annually which countries were trading unfairly, and then to work toward the opening of these markets and the elimination of the unfair practices. It was known that such actions might result in retaliatory restrictions against U.S. exports.

The Global Car Market: The European Battleground

Cars are as essential to people as the clothes they wear; after a home, a car is the second-largest purchase for many. The car provides more than just instant and convenient personal transportation: it can be a revered design or a sign of success. Developers estimate that 200 yards is the maximum distance an American is prepared to walk before getting into a car. When the Berlin Wall came down, one of the first exercises of a newfound freedom for the former East Germans was to exchange their Trabants and Wartburgs for Volkswagens and Opels.

Western Europe is the largest car market in the world (see Figure 1). But while the car markets of Western Europe, North America, and Japan account for 90 percent of the vehicles sold, these markets are quite saturated. By the year 2000, for example, there will probably be one car per person aged 20–64 in North America.

FIGURE 1
World Car Sales by Region, 1992–2002 (in Millions of Cars)

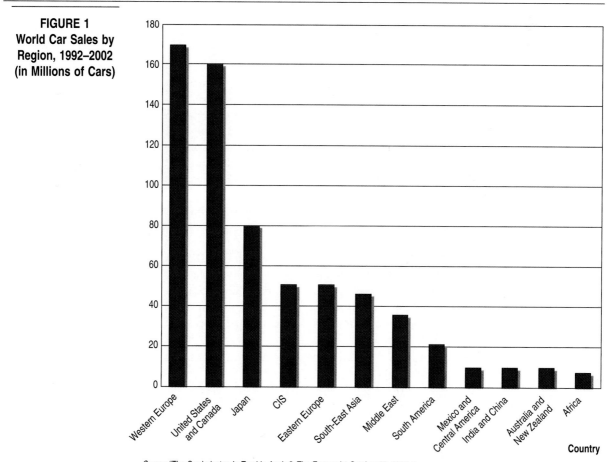

Source: "The Car Industry: In Trouble Again," *The Economist,* October 17, 1992, 4.

Sources: This case was prepared by Ilkka A. Ronkainen. It is largely based on "The Endless Road," *The Economist,* October 17, 1992, 1–18; "On Guard, Europe," *Business Week,* December 14, 1992, 54–55; Carla Rapoport, "Europe Takes on the Japanese," *Fortune,* January 11, 1993, 14–18; "Back to the Way We Were," *The Economist,* November 6, 1993, 83–84; and Louis Kraar, "Korea's Automakers," *Fortune,* March 6, 1995, 152–164.

	Average* for car plants in:		
FIGURE 2 Differences in Car Manufacturing	**Japan**	**United States**	**Europe**
Performance			
Productivity (hours per car)	16.8	25.1	36.2
Quality (defects per 100 cars)	60	82	97
Layout			
Factory space (per sq ft per car per year)	5.7	7.8	7.8
Size of repair area (as % of assembly space)	4.1	12.9	14.4
Stocks**	0.2	2.9	2
Employees			
Workforce in teams (%)	69.3	17.3	0.6
Suggestions (per employee per year)	61.6	0.4	0.4
Number of job classifications	12	67	15
Training of new workers (hours)	380	46	173
Automation (% of process automated)			
Welding	86	76	77
Painting	55	34	38
Assembly	2	1	3

*1989
**for eight sample parts
Source: "The Secrets of the Production Line," *The Economist,* October 17, 1992, 6.

Two general approaches will become evident. First, car manufacturers need to sell fewer cars, but more profitably. Secondly, they need to look for new markets. In the coming decades market growth will come from Asia, Eastern and Central Europe, and Latin America. China and India will eventually provide millions of new drivers. These new realities will have a profound impact on the car market and its players in the future.

In 1986, the Massachusetts Institute of Technology started a study that was published in a book, *The Machine that Changed the World.* The results showed that the Japanese took less time to make a car with fewer defects than the Americans or the Europeans. The main differences were due to the way factories were organized as shown in Figure 2. The higher productivity of the Japanese has given them an overwhelming advantage: though they have not used it to cut prices, it has given them more profit per car than competitors get. As earnings mount, they can spend more to develop better cars or build the sales networks they need to expand sales.

THE EUROPEAN CAR MARKET

The "1992" process was to have opened up European car market to competition by December 31, 1992. However, largely due to the performance gap between the Europeans and the Japanese producers, the European Commission has pushed the dismantling of trade barriers to the end of 1999. This has taken the form of voluntary quotas which for 1994 was 993,000 cars. The Europeans fear that while all the Japanese car makers together just barely equal the share of no. 2 General Motors, things could change rapidly in a market where no one company has even 20 percent market share (see Figure 3).

Japanese car manufacturers are also hindered in Europe due to exclusive dealerships; i.e., dealers are not allowed to sell competing brands. Car manufacturers argue that such arrangements are critical in protecting the character, quality and service

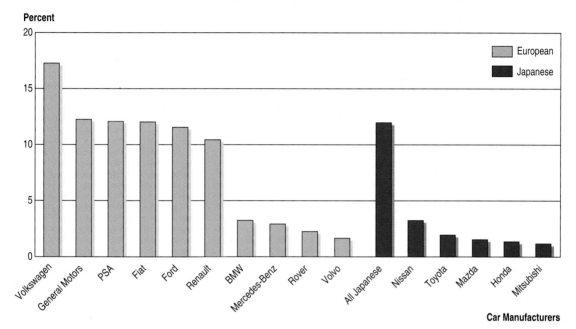

FIGURE 3   **Europe's Fiercely Contested Car Market**

Source: Carla Rapoport, "Europe Takes on the Japanese," *Fortune,* January 11, 1993, 14.

of their cars. In practice, this means that outsiders would have to develop distribution systems from scratch. The European Commission has granted a block exemption for this practice from the antitrust provisions of the Treaty of Rome.

Behind the protectionism is that European car makers want to avoid the fate of their American counterparts a decade earlier, when Japanese market share jumped from 20 percent to 32 percent in the United States. By the end of the 1990s, the Japanese could be producing more than 1.5 million cars in Europe. Added to growing imports from Japan, Japanese market share could grow to 18 percent of the market from 12 percent in 1993. The prospect has stirred both protectionist impulses, especially in France and Italy, and new competitiveness by the European producers.

Both in France and in Italy the car industry is one of the national champions that have fared well in protected markets but are relative weaklings in the global marketplace. Italy's Fiat, for example, produces about 4 percent of the country's GNP, which makes it impossible for the government to let it go down. In France, Jacques Calvet, the chairman of PSA (producer of Peugeot and Citroen) has repeatedly called for prohibiting new Japanese transplant factories in Europe, strict quotas, and freezing Japanese market share within the European Union.

More alarming for the Europeans is their loss of share outside of Europe. France's Renault and PSA have completely written off the U.S. market, believing that they can prosper with a strong European base while holding off the Japanese. Even some of the European specialists, such as Mercedes Benz and Volvo, have been steadily losing share in the growing luxury segment of the U.S. market. Some have faith in their own markets. One auto executive forecast by saying: "The French are, well, so French. I don't think foreign cars, especially Japanese cars will do well in France. Not in our lifetime."

Questions for Discussion

1. The CEO of BMW Eberhard von Kuenheim commented on the Japanese threat by saying: "Where is the rule that the Japanese must win? The story of their endless success just may be ending." Is he realistic?

2. What must the European car manufacturers do to face the global realities of their industry to survive and succeed?

3. Two of the largest car manufacturers in Europe are General Motors and Ford. Neither has been targeted by European Commission moves and are not generally seen as a threat. Why?

P A R T 2

The International Business Environment and Institutions

Operating internationally requires both firms and managers to be aware of a highly complex environment. Domestic and international environmental factors and their interaction have to be recognized and understood. In addition, ongoing changes in these environments have to be appreciated. Furthermore, the international manager must be acquainted with the purpose and activities of major international institutions.

Part 2 delineates the macroenvironmental factors and institutions affecting international business. It also highlights the increasing trend toward economic integration and its effect on international business operations. Finally, it discusses the policy concerns raised by today's changing international environment and institutions.

CHAPTER 3

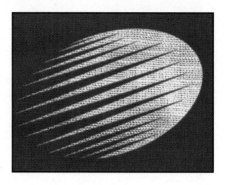

The International Economic Activity of the Nation: The Balance of Payments

Learning Objectives

1. To understand the fundamental principles of how countries measure international business activity, the balance of payments.

2. To examine the similarities of the current and capital accounts of the balance of payments.

3. To understand the critical differences between trade in merchandise and services, and why international investment activity has recently been controversial in the United States.

4. To review the mechanical steps of how exchange rate changes are transmitted into altered trade prices and eventually trade volumes.

5. To understand how countries with different government policies toward international trade and investment, or different levels of economic development, differ in their balance of payments.

Emerging Market Firms Innovate to Raise Funds

Raising capital used to be a cinch for emerging-market companies, as foreign investors couldn't seem to buy enough of their stocks and bonds. Then U.S. rates skyrocketed in the last year and the Mexican peso fell, and suddenly the flush days were gone.

Today's hard times mean "portfolio investment is out and direct investment is in," said Roberto Danino, chairman of the Latin American practice group at the law firm Rogers & Wells in Washington. There are two basic routes to direct investing. First, there's "securitization," or buying securities that are backed by specific company assets. Alternatively, there is ven

ture capital, which involves taking a direct stake in a company through a privately negotiated transaction.

Throughout the world's emerging markets, "it's cheaper to get deals" today, said Joseph Fogg, head of the venture capital firm JG Fogg & Co. in Westbury, Conn. A former executive at Morgan Stanley & Co., Mr. Fogg has already launched two $50 million venture funds, one to invest exclusively in Peru, the other in Vietnam. In both funds, he is focusing on "very simple basic stuff, appropriate to economies at early stages of development like bottled water and real estate."

Source: Thomas T. Vogel, Jr., and Jose de Cordoba, "Emerging Market Firms Innovate to Raise Funds," *The Wall Street Journal,* February 13, 1995, C1, C17.

International business transactions occur in many different forms over the course of a year. The measurement of all international economic transactions between the residents of a country and foreign residents is called the **balance of payments (BOP).**[1] Government policymakers need such measures of economic activity to evaluate the general competitiveness of domestic industry, set exchange-rate or interest-rate policies or goals, and for many other purposes. Individuals and businesses use various BOP measures to gauge the growth and health of specific types of trade or financial transactions by country and regions of the world with the home country.

International transactions take many forms. Each of the following examples is an international economic transaction that is counted and captured in the U.S. balance of payments.

- U.S imports of Honda automobiles, which are manufactured in Japan.
- A U.S.-based firm, Bechtel, is hired to manage the construction of a major water treatment facility in the Middle East.
- The U.S. subsidiary of a French firm, Saint Gobain, pays profits (dividends) back to the parent firm in Paris.
- Daimler-Benz, the well-known German automobile manufacturer, purchases a small automotive parts manufacturer outside Chicago, Illinois.
- An American tourist purchases a hand-blown glass figurine in Venice, Italy.
- The U.S. government provides grant financing of military equipment for its NATO (North Atlantic Treaty Organization) military ally, Turkey.
- A Canadian dentist purchases a U.S. Treasury bill through an investment broker in Cleveland, Ohio.

These are just a small sample of the hundreds of thousands of international transactions that occur each year. The balance of payments provides a systematic method for the classification of all of these transactions. There is one rule of thumb that will always aid in the understanding of BOP accounting: Watch the direction of the movement of money.

The balance of payments is composed of a number of subaccounts that are watched quite closely by investors on Wall Street, farmers in Iowa, politicians on Capitol Hill, and in boardrooms across America. These groups track and analyze the two major subaccounts, the **current account** and the **capital account,** on a continuing basis. Before describing these two subaccounts and the balance of payments as a whole, it is necessary to understand the rather unusual features of how balance of payments accounting is conducted.

FUNDAMENTALS OF BALANCE OF PAYMENTS ACCOUNTING

The balance of payments must balance. If it does not, something has not been counted or counted properly. It is therefore improper to state that the BOP is in disequilibrium. It cannot be. The supply and demand for a country's currency may be imbalanced, but that is not the same thing. Subaccounts of the BOP, such as the merchandise trade balance, may be imbalanced, but the entire BOP of a single country is always balanced.

There are three main elements to the process of measuring international economic activity: (1) identifying what is and is not an international economic transaction; (2) understanding how the flow of goods, services, assets, and money creates debits and credits to the overall BOP; and (3) understanding the bookkeeping procedures for BOP accounting, called double-entry.

Defining International Economic Transactions

Identifying international transactions ordinarily is not difficult. The export of merchandise, goods such as trucks, machinery, computers, telecommunications equipment, and so forth, is obviously an international transaction. Imports such as French wine, Japanese cameras, and German automobiles are also clearly international transactions. But this merchandise trade is only a portion of the thousands of different international transactions that occur in the United States or any other country each year.

Many international transactions are not so obvious. The purchase of a glass figure in Venice, Italy, by an American tourist is classified as a U.S. merchandise import. In fact, all expenditures made by American tourists around the globe that are for goods or services (meals, hotel accommodations, and so forth) are recorded in the U.S. balance of payments as imports of travel services in the current account. The purchase of a U.S. Treasury bill by a foreign resident is an international financial transaction and is dutifully recorded in the capital account of the U.S. balance of payments.

The BOP as a Flow Statement

The BOP is often misunderstood because many people believe it to be a balance sheet, rather than a cash flow statement. By recording all international transactions over a period of time, it is tracking the continuing flow of purchases and payments between a country and all other countries. It does not add up the value of all assets and liabilities of a country like a balance sheet does for an individual firm.

There are two types of business transactions that dominate the balance of payments:

1. **Real Assets.** The exchange of goods (for example, automobiles, computers, watches, textiles) and services (for example, banking services, consulting services, travel services) for other goods and services (barter) or for the more common type of payment, money.

2. **Financial Assets.** The exchange of financial claims (for example, stocks, bonds, loans, purchases or sales of companies) in exchange for other financial claims or money.

Although assets can be separated as to whether they are real or financial, it is often easier to simply think of all assets as being goods that can be bought and sold. An American tourist's purchase of a hand-woven area rug in a shop in Bangkok is not all that different from a Wall Street banker buying a British government bond for investment purposes.

BOP Accounting: Double-Entry Bookkeeping

The balance of payments employs an accounting technique called **double-entry bookkeeping.** Double-entry bookkeeping is the age-old method of accounting in which every transaction produces a debit and a credit of the same amount. Simultaneously. It has to. A debit is created whenever an asset is increased, a liability is decreased, or an expense is increased. Similarly, a credit is created whenever an asset is decreased, a liability is increased, or an expense is decreased.

An example clarifies this process. A U.S. retail store imports from Japan $2 million worth of consumer electronics. A negative entry is made in the merchandise-import subcategory of the current account in the amount of $2 million. Simultaneously, a positive entry of the same $2 million is made in the capital account for the transfer of a $2 million bank account to the Japanese manufacturer. Obviously, the result of hundreds of thousands of such transactions and entries should theoretically result in a perfect balance.

That said, it is now a problem of application, and a problem it is. The measurement of all international transactions in and out of a country over a year is a daunting task. Mistakes, errors, and statistical discrepancies will occur. The primary problem is that although double-entry bookkeeping is employed in theory, the individual transactions are recorded independently. Current and capital account entries are recorded independently of one another, not together as double-entry bookkeeping would prescribe. It must then be recognized that there will be serious discrepancies (to use a nice term for it) between debits and credits, and the possibility in total that the balance of payments may not balance!

The following section describes the various balance of payment accounts, their meanings, and their relationships, using the United States as the example. The chapter then concludes with a discussion—and a number of examples—of how different countries with different policies or levels of economic development may differ markedly in their balance of payment accounts.

THE ACCOUNTS OF THE BALANCE OF PAYMENTS

In addition to the BOP's two primary subaccounts, the current account and the capital account, the official reserves account tracks government currency transactions, and a fourth statistical subaccount is produced to preserve the balance in the BOP, the net errors and omissions account.

The Current Account

The current account includes all international economic transactions with income or payment flows occurring within the year, the current period.[2] The current account consists of four subcategories:

1. **Merchandise Trade.** This is the export and import of goods. **Merchandise trade** is the oldest and most traditional form of international economic activity. Although many countries depend on imports of many goods (as they should, according to the theory of comparative advantage), they also normally work to preserve either a balance of merchandise trade or even a surplus. As illustrated in Table 3.1, the United States had a deficit of more than $166 billion in merchandise trade in 1993.

2. **Service Trade.** This is the export and import of services. Common international services include financial services provided by banks to foreign importers and exporters, travel services of airlines, and construction services of U.S. firms building pipelines or bridges in other countries. For the major industrial countries, this subaccount has shown the fastest growth in the past decade. The United States had gross exports of **service trade** of $164 billion in 1993, service imports of $122 billion, with a balance on service trade of a surplus of $42 billion. The service sector, both in domestic trade and international trade, continues to be a major growth sector for the U.S. economy.

3. **Investment Income.** This is the current income associated with investments that were made in previous periods. If a U.S. firm created a subsidiary in South Korea to produce metal parts in a previous year, the proportion of net income that is paid back to the parent company this year (the dividend) constitutes current **investment income.** The United States experienced a $18 billion surplus in income receipts on prior investments in 1993.

4. **Unilateral Transfers.** Any transfer between countries which is one-way, a gift or grant, is termed a **unilateral transfer.** A common example of a unilateral transfer would be funds provided by the U.S. government to aid in the development of a less-developed nation. The United States incurred a deficit in unilateral transfers of $32 billion in 1993.

TABLE 3.1 **The U.S. Current** **Account, 1993 (billions** **of U.S. dollars)**	

Current Account	1993
Exports of merchandise	456.87
Imports of merchandise	−589.44
Trade balance	−132.57
Exports of services	164.21
Imports of services	121.79
Service trade balance	42.42
Income receipts on investments	134.60
Income payments on investments	−116.06
Income balance	18.34
Net unilateral transfers (private and official)	−32.12
Balance on current account	−103.93

Source: The International Monetary Fund, *Balance of Payments Statistics Yearbook,* 1994, p. 744.

All countries possess some amount of trade, most of which is merchandise. Many smaller and less-developed countries have little service trade and may also have very few international financial transactions that would be classified under the capital account.

The current account is typically dominated by the first component described, the export and import of merchandise. For this reason, the balance of trade (BOT), which is so widely quoted in the business press in most countries, refers specifically to the balance of exports and imports of merchandise trade only. For larger industrialized countries, however, the BOT is somewhat misleading in that service trade is not included, and that trade may actually be fairly large as well. Although the merchandise trade deficit has been a continuing source of concern for the United States since the early 1980s, the other three major subaccounts of the current account should not be ignored.

Merchandise Trade   Figure 3.1 places the current account values of 1994 in perspective over time by dividing the current account into its two major components: (1) merchandise trade and (2) services trade and investment income. The first and most striking message is the magnitude of the merchandise trade deficit throughout the 1980s and early 1990s. The balance on services and income, although not large in comparison to net merchandise trade, has with few exceptions run a surplus over the past two decades. The merchandise trade deficit of the United States hit then all-time high of $160 billion in 1987, improved consistently until 1991, then expanded once again beginning in 1992.

FIGURE 3.1
The U.S. Merchandise Trade Deficit and Services/Income Surplus, 1985–1993 (billions of U.S. dollars)

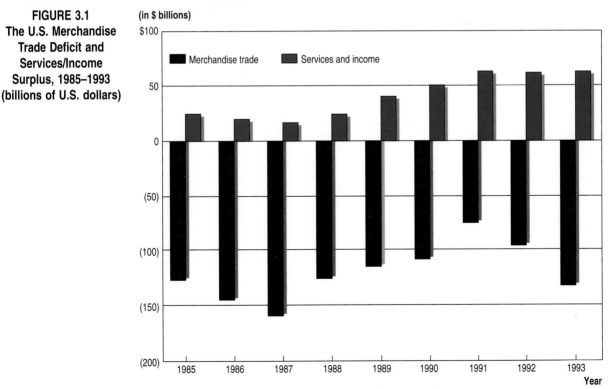

Manufacturing: A Major Factor in Gross Domestic Product

ICELAND
NORWAY
SWEDEN
FINLAND
RUSSIA
IRELAND
UNITED KINGDOM
DEN.
EST.
LATVIA
LITH.
BELARUS
NETH.
GERMANY
POLAND
UKRAINE
BELG.
LUX.
CZECH.
SLOVAK.
MOLDOVA
FRANCE
SWITZ.
AUSTRIA
HUNG.
ROMANIA
SLO.
CRO.
BOS.
HERZ.
SERB.
BULG.
PORTUGAL
SPAIN
ITALY
ALB.
F.Y.R.O.M.
TURKEY
GREECE
TURKE

CANADA

UNITED STATES

MEXICO

CUBA
BAHAMAS
DOMINICAN REPUBLIC
PUERTO RICO
BELIZE
HAITI
HONDURAS
JAMAICA
GUATEMALA
NICARAGUA
EL SALVADOR
COSTA RICA
PANAMA
COLOMBIA

CAPE VERDE ISLANDS

CYPRUS
LEBANON
ISRAEL

MOROCCO
TUNISIA
ALGERIA
LIBYA
EGYPT
WESTERN SAHARA
MAURITANIA
MALI
NIGER
CHAD
SUDAN
SENEGAL
GAMBIA
GUINEA-BISSAU
GUINEA
BURKINA FASO
NIGERIA
SIERRA LEONE
LIBERIA
GHANA
CENTRAL AFRICAN REP.
TOGO
BENIN
CAMEROON
UGANDA
CÔTE D'IVOIRE
EQUITORIAL GUINEA
GABON
CONGO
RWANDA
BURUNDI
ZAIRE

VENEZUELA
GUYANA
SURINAME
FRENCH GUIANA

ECUADOR
PERU
BRAZIL
BOLIVIA
PARAGUAY
CHILE
URUGUAY
ARGENTINA

ST. HELENA

ANGOLA
ZAMBIA
ZIMBABWE
NAMIBIA
BOTSWANA
SOUTH AFRICA

ANGUILLA
ANTIGUA & BARBUDA
BARBADOS
BELIZE
CAYMAN ISLANDS
DOMINICA
GRENADA
GUADELOUPE
MARTINIQUE
MONTSERRAT
ST. KITTS & NEVIS
ST. LUCIA
ST. VINCENT
TRINIDAD & TOBAGO
TURKS & CAICOS ISLANDS
U.K. VIRGIN IS.
U.S. VIRGIN IS.

BAHRAIN
GAMBIA
SÃO TOMÉ AND PRÍNCIPE

Source: *Europa World Yearbook, 35 Ed.*, 1994; *World Factbook*, 1994; *Statistical Abstract of the United States*, 1994.

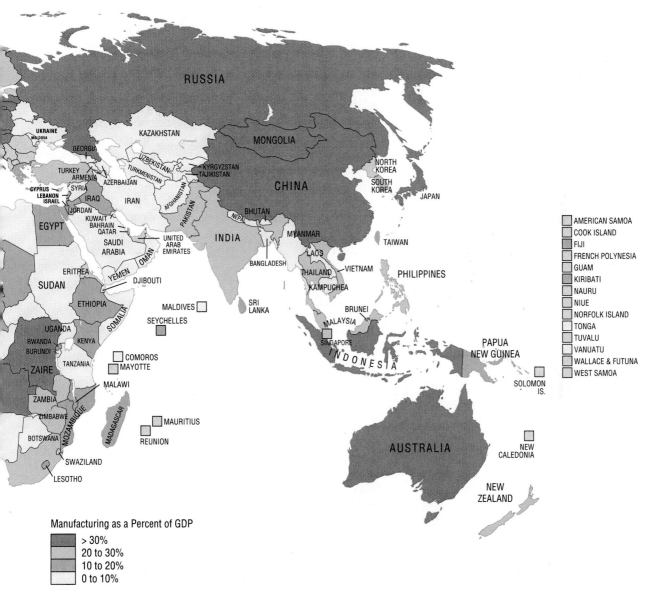

RUSSIA

UKRAINE
MOLDOVA

GEORGIA

KAZAKHSTAN

MONGOLIA

TURKEY
ARMENIA

UZBEKISTAN
TURKMENISTAN

KYRGYZSTAN
TAJIKISTAN

CYPRUS
LEBANON
ISRAEL

SYRIA

IRAQ

JORDAN

KUWAIT
BAHRAIN
QATAR

SAUDI
ARABIA

AZERBAIJAN

IRAN

AFGHANISTAN

PAKISTAN

CHINA

NORTH
KOREA

SOUTH
KOREA

JAPAN

EGYPT

UNITED
ARAB
EMIRATES

OMAN

INDIA

BHUTAN

NEPAL

MYANMAR

TAIWAN

ERITREA

YEMEN

DJIBOUTI

BANGLADESH

LAOS

THAILAND

VIETNAM

PHILIPPINES

SUDAN

ETHIOPIA

SOMALIA

MALDIVES

SRI
LANKA

KAMPUCHEA

SEYCHELLES

BRUNEI

MALAYSIA

UGANDA

KENYA

SINGAPORE

PAPUA
NEW GUINEA

RWANDA
BURUNDI

TANZANIA

COMOROS
MAYOTTE

INDONESIA

ZAIRE

MALAWI

ZAMBIA

ZIMBABWE

MOZAMBIQUE

MADAGASCAR

MAURITIUS

SOLOMON
IS.

BOTSWANA

REUNION

SWAZILAND

LESOTHO

AUSTRALIA

NEW
CALEDONIA

NEW
ZEALAND

AMERICAN SAMOA
COOK ISLAND
FIJI
FRENCH POLYNESIA
GUAM
KIRIBATI
NAURU
NIUE
NORFOLK ISLAND
TONGA
TUVALU
VANUATU
WALLACE & FUTUNA
WEST SAMOA

Manufacturing as a Percent of GDP

> 30%
20 to 30%
10 to 20%
0 to 10%

No current data available

The merchandise trade deficits of the past decade have been an area of considerable concern for the United States, in both the public and private sectors. Merchandise trade is the original core of international trade. The manufacturing of goods was the basis of the Industrial Revolution and the focus of the theory of international trade described in the previous chapter. Manufacturing is traditionally the sector of the economy that employs most of a country's workers. The merchandise trade deficit of the 1980s saw the decline in traditional heavy industries in the United States, industries that have historically employed many of America's workers. Declines in the net trade balance in areas such as steel, automobiles, automotive parts, textiles, shoe manufacturing, and others have caused massive economic and social disruption. The problems of dealing with these shifting trade balances will be discussed in detail in a later chapter.

The most encouraging news for U.S. manufacturing trade is the growth of exports in the latter half of the 1980s and early years of the 1990s as shown in Figure 3.2. A number of factors contributed to the growth of U.S. exports, such as the weaker dollar (which made U.S. manufactured goods cheaper in terms of the currencies of other countries) and more rapid economic growth in Europe in the latter part of the 1980s. Understanding merchandise import and export performance is much like analyzing the market for any single product. The demand factors that drive both imports and exports are income, the economic growth rate of the buyer, and the price of the product in the eyes of the consumer after passing through an exchange rate. For example, U.S. merchandise imports reflect the income level and growth of American consumers and industry. As income rises, so does the demand for imports. As shown in Figure 3.2, when the United States came out of the

FIGURE 3.2   **U.S. Merchandise Exports and Imports, 1985–1993**

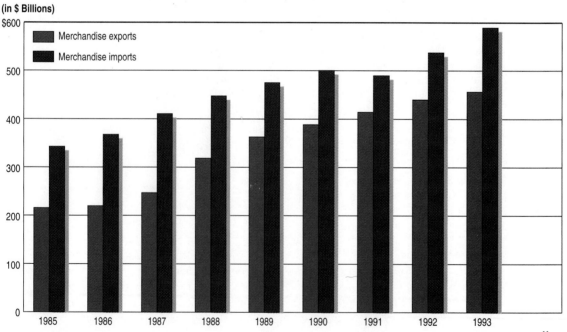

1981–1982 recession, imports rose dramatically as the U.S. economy recovered. Of course supply side factors, such as the cost of production and the eventual cost of the product, are also important. Many experts argue that in the early to middle 1980s the U.S. economy had no reasonably priced competitive products for much of the merchandise that was imported in larger and larger volumes.

Exports follow the same principles but in the reversed position. U.S. manufacturing exports depend not on the incomes of U.S. residents, but on the incomes of buyers of U.S. products in all other countries. The major markets for U.S. exports are the industrialized nations such as Canada, Japan, and western Europe. When these economies are growing, the demand for U.S. products rises. The rapid growth of the western European economies in the later 1980s, as well as the falling dollar making U.S. products relatively cheaper to European consumers, aided greatly in the growth of U.S. merchandise exports beginning in 1987.

The merchandise exports of the United States are normally subdivided into agricultural products and nonagricultural products. In 1994, more than $43.7 billion worth of exports, almost 10 percent, were agricultural products. Agricultural and nonagricultural exports are separated for a variety of reasons. First, agricultural exports have been a strength of the U.S. economy for a very long time. The agricultural sector was probably the most "internationalized" sector of the U.S. economy. Second, because agricultural products are subject to random supply side disturbances, such as the impact of weather on crop production, these products experience very volatile price movements from year to year, month to month, and even day to day. Non-agricultural merchandise exports are industrial and consumer goods. This sector has suffered the majority of the declines in relative competitiveness and trade balance in the past decade.

U.S. merchandise imports are subdivided into petroleum products and non-petroleum products. For example, in 1993 the United States imported $51.5 billion worth of petroleum products (9 percent of total merchandise imports) while non-petroleum products totalled $538 billion. Petroleum imports are kept track of separately because of the impact this one commodity has on U.S. imports as a whole. The fact that U.S. consumption of petroleum and petroleum products is insensitive to price changes, its so-called **price inelasticity,** makes the distinction between petroleum imports and all other imports important for government policymakers.

The service component of the U.S. current account is one of mystery to many. As noted in Table 3.1, the United States enjoyed a $42 billion surplus in service trade in 1993. The major categories of services include travel and passenger fares, transportation services, expenditures by U.S. students abroad and foreign students pursuing studies in the United States, telecommunications services, and financial services.

Global Perspective 3.1 presents a current account of a strikingly different character—Finland in the 1990s.

The Capital Account

The capital account of the balance of payments measures all international transactions of financial assets. Financial assets can be classified in a number of ways, including the length of the life of the asset (its maturity), by nature of the ownership (public or private), or by the degree of control over assets or operations that the claim represents (portfolio, with no control, or direct investment, with some degree of control).

Global Perspective

3.1
The Current Account and Finland

Although many users of the balance of payments equate the current account with the trade balance, they are clearly not the same. A case in point is the country of Finland. As shown in the figure below, Finland has consistently run a surplus in merchandise trade—reaching more than $6 billion in the black in 1993. But Finland still suffers from a deficit in its overall current account balance.

The problem is services and income—specifically income. Because the current account includes all current payments on previous investments and loans, if a country has borrowed heavily from other countries in years past, the current interest payments on that debt may be quite large. In the case of Finland, the net deficit on the services and income subaccounts of the current account are greater than the net surplus on merchandise trade; hence, a country with a deficit on current account due to the excessive borrowing of the past.

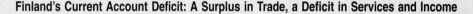

Finland's Current Account Deficit: A Surplus in Trade, a Deficit in Services and Income

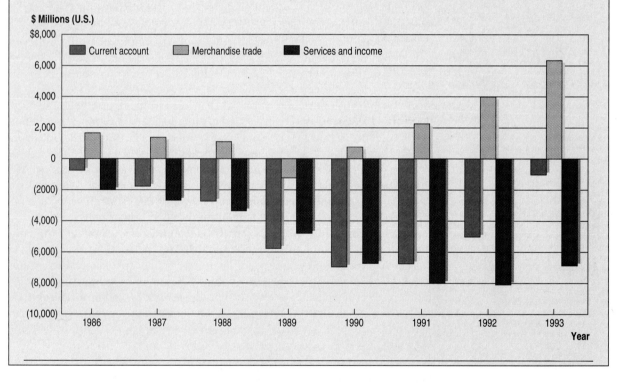

Table 3.2 shows the major subcategories of the U.S. capital account balance for 1993, **direct investment, portfolio investment,** and other long-term and short-term capital.

1. **Direct Investment.** This is the net balance of capital that flows out of and into the country for the purpose of exerting control over assets. For example, if a U.S. firm either builds a new automotive parts facility in another country (Ford built a fuel-handling-part facility in Hungary) or purchases a

Capital Account	1993
Direct investment in United States	21.37
Direct investment abroad	−57.87
Net direct investment	−36.51
Net portfolio investment	−17.55
Other long-term capital	4.33
Other short-term capital	63.87
Balance on capital account	+14.14

TABLE 3.2
The U.S. Capital Account, 1993 (billions of U.S. dollars)

Source: The International Monetary Fund, *Balance of Payments Statistics Yearbook*, 1994, p. 744.

company in another country, this would fall under direct investment in the U.S. balance of payments accounts. When the capital flows out of the United States, as in the two examples just used, it enters the balance of payments as a negative cash flow. If, however, foreign firms purchase firms in the United States (for example, Sony of Japan purchased Columbia Pictures in 1989), it is a capital inflow and enters the balance of payments positively. Whenever 10 percent or more of the voting shares in a U.S. company are held by foreign investors, the company is classified as the U.S. affiliate of a foreign company and a foreign direct investment. Similarly, if U.S. investors hold 10 percent or more of the control in a company outside the United States, that company is considered the foreign affiliate of a U.S. company. The United States experienced a deficit of $36.51 billion in direct investment in 1993.

2. **Portfolio Investment.** This is net balance of capital that flows in and out of the United States but that does not reach the 10 percent ownership threshold of direct investment. If a U.S. resident purchases shares in a Japanese firm but does not attain the 10 percent threshold, it is considered a portfolio investment (and in this case an outflow of capital). The purchase or sale of debt securities (such as U.S. Treasury bills or bonds) across borders is always classified as portfolio investment because debt securities by definition do not provide the buyer with ownership or control. Net portfolio investment for the United States was a negative $17.55 billion in 1993.

3. **Other Long-Term and Short-Term Capital.** This category consists of various bank loans extended by U.S. resident banking operations as well as net borrowing by U.S. firms from financial institutions outside the United States. The net balance on other long-term capital in 1993 was $4.33 billion, with net gain on other short-term capital of $63.87 billion.

Direct Investment   Figure 3.3 shows how the two major subaccounts of the U.S. capital account, net direct investment and portfolio investment, have changed since 1980. Net direct investment started the 1980s with a slight deficit in 1980 but showed a surplus every year between 1981 and 1990. The balance on net direct investment went negative in 1991 for the first time in a decade. It appears the world's enthusiasm for the acquisition of U.S. firms and other foreign-controlled investment (direct investment) in the United States has waned.

The boom in foreign investment in the United States during the 1980s was, however, extremely controversial. Historically, it has typically been the case that U.S.

firms invested abroad. The rapid growth of the U.S. economy and the expansion of many U.S. firms to build manufacturing, mining, refining, and many other industrial facilities around the world had become the norm. With the 1980s came a complete reversal in the direction of these net capital flows. Foreign investors were pouring more long-term capital into the United States than U.S. firms invested abroad. Many Americans worried about this increasing foreign presence in the U.S. marketplace, not just in selling products to U.S. consumers as has become so common with merchandise imports, but with foreign investors actually exercising significant control over U.S. firms, U.S. workers, and U.S. assets.

The source of concern over foreign investment in any country, including the United States, normally focuses on one of two major topics, control and profit. Most countries have restrictions on what foreigners may own. This is based on the premise that domestic land, assets, and industry in general should be held by residents of the country. For example, until 1990 it was not possible for a foreign firm to own more than 20 percent of any company in Finland. And this is the norm, rather than the exception. The United States has traditionally had few restrictions on what foreign residents or firms can own or control in the United States, with most restrictions remaining today being related to national-security concerns as Global Perspective 3.2 shows. As opposed to many of the traditional debates over whether international trade should be free or not, there is not the same consensus for unrestricted international investment. This is a question that is still very much a domestic political concern first and an international economic issue second.

The second major source of concern over foreign direct investment is who receives the profits from the enterprise. Foreign companies owning firms in the United

FIGURE 3.3   **U.S. Capital Account Components, 1974–1993: Net Direct Investment and Net Portfolio Investment**

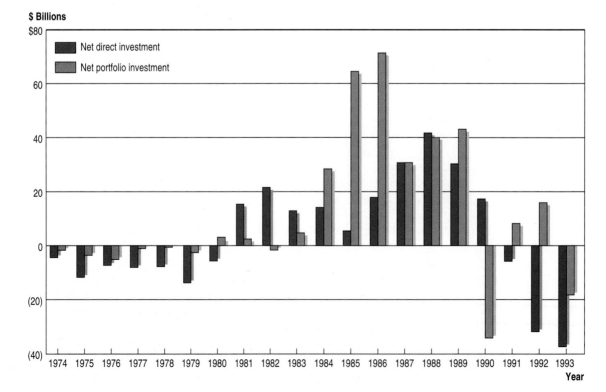

Global Perspective

3.2
"They Don't Let Just Anyone Buy a Defense Contractor"

Alain Gomez, the dapper chairman of France's Thomson-CSF, lined up some of the best string-pullers money can buy to help acquire bankrupt LTV Corp.'s missile business. The defense-electronics giant, 58 percent-owned by the French government, joined with the Carlyle Group, a well-connected Washington investment bank whose vice chairman is former Defense Secretary Frank C. Carlucci. For public relations, Gomez tapped Carter Administration Press Secretary Jody Powell's high-powered spin-ship, Powell Tate, as well as a legion of K Street lawyers.

But the pricey talent couldn't overcome the volatile politics of selling sensitive U.S. defense assets to foreigners, particularly in an election year. On July 5, Thomson withdrew its $450 million joint bid with Carlyle to buy LTV's missile and aircraft businesses. Small wonder. The U.S. defense establishment carried out a blistering behind-the-scenes assault on Thomson over its status as a French government holding and its past business dealings with Iraq.

Even if Thomson can pull together a new proposal, it will still face heated opposition from Martin Marietta Corp. and Lockheed Corp., whose rival $385 million offer lost out to the French in April. Martin Marietta Chairman Norman R. Augustine objects to Thomson's taking even a minority stake. Augustine has friends in high places: He was on Bush's short list of potential defense secretaries back in 1988.

Ironically, Thomson's association with the Carlyle Group also hurt the deal. Roughly one-third of the $150 million Carlyle planned to put up for LTV's aircraft unit was bankrolled by state-backed Credit Lyonnais. So the group was viewed as "a front" for the French government, says an administration source. Such rough treatment speaks volumes about the U.S. defense industry's inevitable post-cold-war consolidation. Foreigners serious about buying their way in had better be combat-ready.

Source: Brian Bremner, Seth Payne, and Jonathan B. Levine, "They Don't Let Just Anyone Buy A Defense Contractor," *Business Week,* July 20, 1992, 41–42.

States will ultimately profit from the activities of the firms, or put another way, from the efforts of American workers. In spite of evidence that indicates foreign firms in the United States reinvest most of the profits in the United States (in fact, at a higher rate than domestic firms), the debate has continued on possible profit drains. Regardless of the choices made, workers of any nation usually feel the profits of their work should remain in the hands of their own countrymen. Once again, this is in many ways a political and emotional concern more than an economic one.

A final note regarding the massive capital inflows into the United States in the 1980s. The choice of which words are used to describe this increasing foreign investment can alone influence public opinion. If these massive capital inflows are described as "capital investments from all over the world showing their faith in the future of American industry," the net capital surplus is represented as decidedly positive. If, however, the net capital surplus is described as resulting in "the United States as the world's largest debtor nation," the negative connotation is obvious. But which, if either, is correct? The answer is actually quite simple. Capital, whether short-term or long-term, flows to where it believes it can earn the greatest return for the level of risk. And although in an accounting sense this is "international debt," when the majority of the capital inflow is in the form of direct investment, a long-term commitment to jobs, production, services, technological, and other competitive investments, the competitiveness of American industry (industry located within the United

States) is increased. The "net debtor" label is also misleading in that it invites comparison with large "debtor-nations" such as Mexico and Brazil. But unlike Mexico and Brazil, the majority of this foreign investment is not bank loans that will have to be paid back in regular installments over eight to ten years, and it is not bank loans denominated in a currency that is foreign. Mexico and Brazil owe U.S. dollars; the United States "owes" U.S. dollars. Therefore, the profitability of the industry and the economy in the United States will be the source of repaying the investors.

Portfolio Investment   Portfolio investment is capital that is invested in activities that are purely profit-motivated (return), rather than ones made in the prospect of controlling or managing or directing the investment. Investments that are purchases of debt securities, bonds, interest-bearing bank accounts, and the like are only intended to earn a return. They provide no vote or control over the party issuing the debt. Purchase of debt issued by the U.S. government, U.S. Treasury bills, notes, and bonds, by foreign investors constitute net portfolio investment in the United States.

As illustrated in Figure 3.3, portfolio investment has shown a similar pattern to net direct investment over the past decade. Many U.S. debt securities, such as U.S. Treasury securities and corporate bonds, were in high demand throughout the 1980s. The primary reason for the surge in net portfolio investment resulted from two different forces, return and risk.

In the early 1980s, interest rates were quite high in the United States, the result of high inflation in the late 1970s and the "tight money policy" (slow money-supply growth) of the U.S. Federal Reserve. The rate of inflation fell rapidly in the early 1980s, while interest rates did not. This resulted in very high "real rates" of interest (interest less inflation), which was much higher than what could be earned in many other nations. Capital flowed into the U.S. economy in order to take advantage of these relatively high **real returns.**

At the same time, many of the major industrial countries were suffering prolonged recessions or very slow economic growth. This meant that profitable investments for capital were hard to find. And many of the major borrower countries, such as Mexico and Brazil, were turning out to be bad borrowers, unable to repay their debts. Capital was therefore looking for a **safe haven,** a place where the political and economic systems were dependable and secure. The safe haven for world capital in the early to middle 1980s was the United States.

As shown in Figure 3.3, the balance on portfolio investment was positive for every year between 1980 and 1989, except for a slight deficit in 1982. The net surplus of portfolio investment peaked in 1986 at more than $70 billion. By 1990, however, interest rates and other motivations for portfolio investment in the United States had waned, as did the flow of portfolio investment. The balance on portfolio investment in 1993 saw a massive shift to the negative, with a net outflow of capital of over $17 billion.

Current and Capital Account Balance Relationships

Figure 3.4 illustrates the recent current and capital account balances for Germany, Japan, and the United States. What the figure shows is one of the basic economic and accounting relationships of the balance of payments: the inverse relation between the current and capital accounts. This inverse relationship is not accidental. The methodology of the balance of payments, double-entry bookkeeping, requires that the current and capital accounts be offsetting.

FIGURE 3.4
Current and Capital
Account Balances for
Germany, Japan, and
the United States

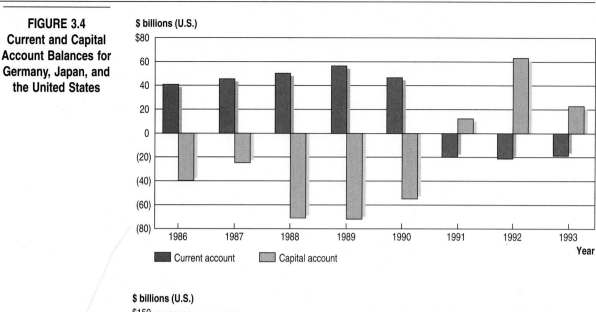

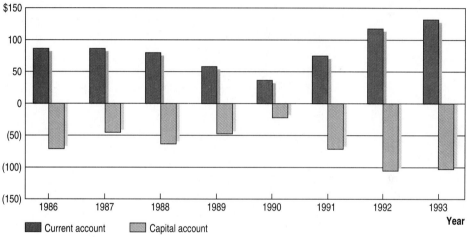

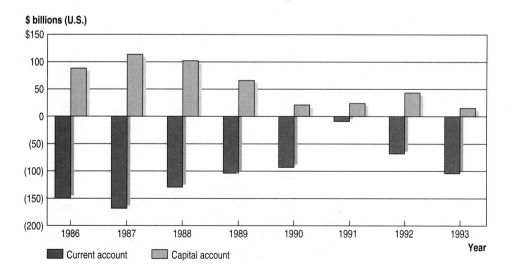

These three countries in many ways show three classic examples of how trade and capital work together. For the United States, the current account deficits of the late 1980s were "financed" by equally large surpluses in the capital account. Basically, current account activities in this case cause capital account entries. Many experts, however, argue that it could very well be the other way around, with capital account activities inducing the current account activities. The truth most likely is that economic forces cause simultaneous actions in both accounts.

Japan during this same period demonstrated the opposite situation as the United States: it ran a surplus on current account while suffering a deficit in the capital account. This is often described as recycling excess currency earned through foreign trade. Japan's current account surplus generates excess capital which is then recycled into increased levels of foreign investment in other countries—the capital account deficit.

Germany demonstrates two different eras of current account/capital account relations. In the period prior to reunification, the German economy ran consistent current account surpluses and capital account deficits. The period after reunification, however, demonstrates the burdens on the economy in meeting the rapid expansion in consumer needs as imports surged in 1991 forcing a current account deficit and a very uncharacteristic capital account surplus.

Net Errors and Omissions

As noted before, because current account and capital account entries are collected and recorded separately, errors or statistical discrepancies will occur. The net errors and omissions account (the title used by the International Monetary Fund) makes sure that the BOP actually balances.

For the United States the size of the net errors and omissions account has varied substantially over recent times. The United States recorded surpluses in "errors" of $53 billion and $40 billion in 1989 and 1990, but in the years following turned negative. However, 1994 saw a sudden net surplus again in "errors" of more than $33 billion. There are a variety of potential explanations for this, including underreporting of exports and the underground or illegal economy's impacts on the flows of asset values across borders.

Official Reserves Account

The **official reserves account** is the total currency and metallic reserves held by official monetary authorities within the country. These reserves are normally composed of the major currencies used in international trade and financial transactions (so-called "hard currencies" such as the U.S. dollar, German mark, Japanese yen, British pound, Swiss franc, French franc, and Canadian dollar) and gold.

The significance of official reserves depends generally on whether the country is operating under a fixed exchange rate regime or a floating exchange rate system. If a country's currency is fixed, this means that the government of the country officially declares that the currency is convertible into a fixed amount of some other currency. For example, for many years the South Korean won was fixed to the U.S. dollar at 484 won equal to 1 U.S. dollar. If the exchange rate is fixed, the government accepts responsibility for maintaining this fixed rate (also called parity rate). If for some reason there is an excess of Korean won on the currency market, to prevent the value of the won from falling, the South Korean government must "support the won." Supporting a currency is identical to supporting any price; to push a price up you must increase demand. Under such conditions, the South Korean government would go to the currency markets and purchase its own currency until it eliminated the excess supply. But what does the South Korean government use to purchase South Korean won? Other major currencies such as the dollar, the mark, the yen, or even gold. Therefore, in order for a country with a fixed exchange rate to be able to support its own currency, the country needs to maintain substantial reserves of foreign currencies and gold, official reserves.

As will be discussed in Chapters 4 and 5, many countries still use fixed exchange rate systems. For them it is still critically important to maintain official reserves in sufficient quantity to support their own currencies in case of need. However, many of the major industrial countries, such as the United States and Japan, no longer operate under fixed exchange rates. For these countries, holdings of official reserves are not as critically important and have, in fact, declined substantially over the past two decades in proportion to the volume of international trade and investment.

THE BALANCE OF PAYMENTS IN TOTAL

Table 3.3 provides the official balance of payments for the United States as presented by the International Monetary Fund (IMF), the multinational organization that collects those statistics for more than 160 countries. Now that the individual accounts and the relationships among the accounts have been discussed, Table 3.3 allows an overview of how the individual accounts are combined to create useful summary measures.

The current account (line A in Table 3.3) and the long-term capital account (line B in Table 3.3) together constitute the **basic balance.** This is one of the most frequently used summary measures of the BOP to describe the international economic activity of the nation which is determined by market forces, and not by government decisions (such as currency market intervention). The U.S. basic balance deficit totalled $153.66 billion in 1993, the largest ever experienced by the United States. Compared to the basic balances of 1991 (a surplus of $10.12 billion) and 1992 (a deficit of $81.89 billion), this was a remarkable deterioration.

A second summary measure is the **overall balance,** or **official settlements balance** as it is often termed. The overall balance is the sum of the current account (line A in Table 3.3), capital accounts (short-term and long-term, lines B and C), and net errors and omissions accounts (line D). The United States's overall balance in 1993 was a deficit of $68.65 billion.

The remaining accounts of the balance of payments—exceptional financing ("E"), liabilities constituting foreign authorities' reserves ("F"), and U.S. reserves ("G")—are largely measures of official government transactions. Because these balances and values are largely a result of public policy, and do not necessarily reflect the economic forces at work upon a nation's international economic activity, they are not used as frequently to characterize a country's BOP.

The meaning of "the balance of payments" has changed over the past 25 years. As long as most of the major industrial countries were still operating under fixed exchange rates, the interpretation of the BOP was relatively straightforward. A surplus in the BOP implied that the demand for the country's currency exceeded the supply, and the government should either allow the currency value to increase (revalue) or intervene and accumulate additional foreign currency reserves in the official reserves account. This would occur as the government sold its own currency in exchange for other currencies, thus building up its stores of hard currencies. A deficit

	TABLE 3.3	The U.S. Balance of Payments: Aggregated Presentation, Transactions Data, 1986–1993*							
		1986	**1987**	**1988**	**1989**	**1990**	**1991**	**1992**	**1993**
A.	**Current Account, excl. Group E**...............	−145.42	−160.20	−126.37	−101.20	−90.46	−3.69	−67.85	−103.94
	Merchandise: exports f.o.b..........................	223.36	250.28	320.34	361.67	388.71	415.96	440.36	456.87
	Agricultural products..............................	27.36	29.55	38.25	42.19	40.18	40.13	44.05	43.70
	Other..	196.00	220.73	282.09	319.48	348.53	375.83	396.31	413.17
	Merchandise: imports f.o.b........................	−368.41	−409.77	−447.31	−477.38	−497.55	−489.40	−536.46	−589.44
	Petroleum and related products...............	−34.39	−42.94	−39.63	−50.92	−62.30	−51.18	−51.58	−51.48
	Other..	−334.02	−366.83	−407.68	−426.46	−435.25	−438.22	−484.88	−537.97
	Trade balance.....................................	−145.05	−159.49	−126.97	−115.71	−108.84	−73.44	−96.10	−132.57
	Services: credit..	72.26	81.81	91.50	113.91	132.02	145.71	156.50	164.21
	Services: debit...	−73.20	−82.66	−89.06	−97.69	−112.35	−113.21	−114.66	−121.79
	Income: credit..	88.34	99.71	121.63	153.88	160.15	143.25	134.53	134.40
	Reinvested earnings..............................	10.02	19.71	13.33	14.77	19.48	17.89	14.48	29.57
	Other investment income.......................	70.95	70.82	97.32	125.93	124.08	107.44	99.97	84.28
	Other..	7.37	9.18	10.98	13.18	16.59	17.92	20.08	20.56
	Income: debit...	−71.88	−85.24	−108.42	−129.98	−128.50	−113.99	−116.08	−116.06
	Reinvested earnings..............................	2.30	.86	−2.82	8.52	16.28	20.05	11.65	9.40
	Other investment income.......................	−72.30	−83.79	−102.51	−134..87	−140.54	−128.92	−121.56	−119.31
	Other..	−1.88	−2.31	−3.09	−3.63	−4.24	−5.12	−6.17	−6.15
	Total: goods, services, and income........	−129.53	−145.87	−111.32	−75.59	−57.52	−11.68	−35.81	−71.82
	Private unrequited transfers........................	−1.86	−1.84	−1.76	−12.32	−12.39	−12.99	−13.29	−13.72
	Total: excl. official unrequited transfers	−131.39	−147.71	−113.08	−87.91	−69.91	−24.67	−49.10	−85.54
	Official unrequited transfers........................	−14.03	−12.49	−13.29	−13.29	−20.55	20.98	−18.75	−18.40
	Grants (excluding military)......................	11.87	−10.28	−10.74	−10.77	−21.86	−18.08	−16.31	−14.61
	Other..	−2.16	−2.21	−2.55	−2.52	1.31	39.06	−2.44	−3.79
B.	**Direct Investment and Other Long-Term**.....								
	Capital, excl. Groups E through G............	81.86	57.52	93.48	85.58	2.00	2.94	−14.04	−49.73
	Direct investment.....................................	15.39	27.10	41.54	38.87	12.45	−15.65	−31.12	−36.51
	In United States....................................	34.08	58.14	59.42	67.87	45.14	11.50	9.89	21.37
	Abroad...	−18.69	−31.04	−17.88	−29.00	−32.69	−27.15	−41.01	−57.87
	Portfolio investment..................................	−71.60	31.06	40.31	43.50	−33.00	5.44	16.63	−17.55
	Other long-term capital..............................								
	Resident official sector..........................	−.47	−1.26	1.05	2.43	3.70	6.45	−.51	1.26
	Disbursements on loans extended........	−7.14	−4.85	−5.82	−3.93	−6.65	−10.11	−5.46	−4.36
	Repayments on loans extended............	5.65	7.19	9.92	6.29	10.36	16.04	5.28	5.47
	Other..	1.02	−3.60	−3.05	.07	−.01	.52	−.33	.15
	Deposit money banks.............................	−4.66	.62	10.58	.78	18.85	6.70	.95	3.07
	Other sectors..	—	—	—	—	—	—	—	—
	Total, Groups A plus B...................	−63.56	−102.68	−32.89	−15.62	−88.46	−.75	−81.89	−153.66
C.	**Other Short-Term Capital, excl. Groups E**								
	through G...	13.92	52.54	5.75	30.12	11.19	−20.71	56.90	63.87
	Resident official sector..............................	−.52	−1.96	−.15	1.80	3.77	−.71	6.44	2.57
	Deposit money banks.................................	26.76	45.88	5.49	10.91	−1.05	−14.81	36.24	21.91
	Other sectors...	−12.32	8.62	.41	17.41	8.47	−5.19	14.23	39.39
D.	**Net Errors and Omissions**...........................	15.86	−6.72	−9.13	2.43	47.46	−1.12	−17.20	21.14
	Total, Groups A through D...................	−33.78	−56.86	−36.27	16.93	−29.81	−22.58	−42.20	−68.65
E.	**Exceptional Financing**.................................	—	—	—	—	—	—	—	—
	Total, Groups A through E.................	−33.78	−56.86	−36.27	16.93	−29.81	−22.58	−42.20	−68.65
F.	**Liabilities Constituting Foreign Authorities'**								
	Reserves..	33.46	47.72	40.19	8.34	32.04	16.82	38.27	70.02
	Total, Groups A through F...................	−.32	−9.14	3.92	25.27	2.23	−5.76	−3.92	1.37
G.	**Reserves**...	.32	9.14	−3.92	−25.27	−2.23	5.76	3.92	−1.37
	Monetary gold..	.01	—	—	.01	—	—	—	.01
	SDRs...	−.25	−.51	.13	−.53	−.20	−.18	2.32	−.54
	Reserve position in the Fund......................	1.50	2.07	1.02	.47	.66	−.37	−2.66	−.04
	Foreign exchange assets...........................	−.94	7.58	−5.07	−25.22	−2.70	6.31	4.27	−.80
	Other claims...	—	—	—	—	—	—	—	—
	Use of Fund credit and loans.....................	—	—	—	—	—	—	—	—
	Memorandum items....................................								
	Total change in reserves........................	−5.11	2.58	−1.79	−26.81	−8.68	5.61	6.38	−2.08
	of which: revaluations............................	−5.43	−6.56	2.13	−1.55	−6.45	−.15	2.46	−.71

*In billions of U.S. dollars   *Source:* The International Monetary Fund, Balance of Payments Statistics Yearbook, 1994, p. 742.

in the BOP implied an excess supply of the country's currency on world markets, and the government would then either devalue the currency or expend its official reserves to support its value.

But the major industrial nations such as Japan, the United States, and Germany are no longer operating in a world of fixed exchange rates. Now major industrial governments and other authorities no longer refer to the balance of payments for their country, but instead monitor and measure balances on trade, current account, net direct and portfolio investments, and sometimes basic balances.

THE BALANCE OF PAYMENTS AS A REFLECTION OF ECONOMIC OPENNESS AND DEVELOPMENT

Although the United States serves as a good example of the various component accounts of the balance of payments, it is not necessarily typical of the balance of payments of all countries. Many countries choose to restrict the degreee or level of international commerce in their country, whether it be trade or investment. It should also be obvious that countries are at different levels of economic development. Many countries, for example, are not yet large enough in their industrial development to possess domestic financial markets that would be able to handle short-term capital flows as would be seen in the balance of payment account "C" as listed in Table 3.3. In this section, we provide a series of examples of how specific national policies and economic development levels are reflected in various countries' balances of payments.

The Case of Mexico

Mexico is a country that, unfortunately, is often in the balance of payments news. The debt crises of the early 1980s (see Chapter 5) and the recent devaluation of the Mexican peso (December 1994) have focused much attention on the trade and capital accounts of Mexico. But Mexico is also an example of how investment capital can find its way quickly and efficiently to countries representing good long-term development prospects.

Figure 3.5 illustrates the massive and sudden infusion of long-term investment, particularly portfolio investment, accompanying the negotiation and initiation of the North American Free Trade Agreement (NAFTA) in the early 1990s. Net portfolio investment in Mexico rose to more than $27 billion in 1993 from a net deficit of $4 billion as recently as 1990. This is indeed a miraculous movement of capital, capital which may be put to use in building additional infrastructure, buying firms that previously were owned by the state (privatization), and building new industry from the ground up.

The infusion of capital into Mexico is the result of two fundamental changes: first, the willingness of the Mexican government and people to open Mexico to foreign investors and foreign ownership; second, the willingness of foreign investors to put large quantities of capital at risk in a country with a less than sterling investment history. If there is a source of concern in the numbers depicted in Figure 3.5, it is the dominance of portfolio investment, in which the degree of foreign ownership is less than 10 percent of the enterprise (and often represents only the purchase of stock or bonds traded on financial markets). The long-term outcome is impossible to foresee, particularly given the recent crisis with the Mexican peso. It will be interesting to see what the final investment figures illustrated in Figure 3.5 will look like for 1994 and 1995.

FIGURE 3.5
Mexico's Long-Term
Capital: Direct
Investment versus
Portfolio Investment

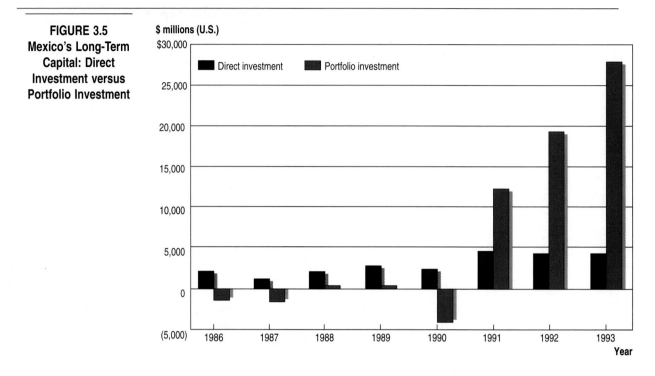

The Case of Nepal

Nepal serves as an example of a country with only one account—the current account. The Nepal government does not allow long-term private investment in any form, direct or portfolio, so the only capital investment that occurs in or out of the country is by official authorities. The official authorities contributed a net inflow of long-term capital amounting to $126 million in 1993, all of it in the official residential sector. This is mostly investment spending by foreign governments building and expanding foreign embassies in Nepal. Nepal itself is not all that unusual in that a number of other countries, for example India, currently allow little if any direct ownership of their enterprises by foreigners. Thus, direct investment and portfolio investment hover near zero year after year.

The Case of Malaysia

Malaysia is like Mexico in that it has recently been the recipient of major net inflows of capital. But, as illustrated in Figure 3.6, the capital is predominately long-term direct investment, in which foreign investors control more than 10 percent of the stock or ownership of the investments. Long-term direct investment is generally thought to have much more beneficial impacts on the economy, as opposed to the short-term/portfolio capital flows experienced recently by Mexico. The negative side of this is the consideration discussed previously in reference to the United States: the idea that foreign investors control domestic resources, domestic workers, and make profits that may in turn be returned to the investor's own home country.

**FIGURE 3.6
Malaysia's Direct
Investment and
Portfolio Growth**

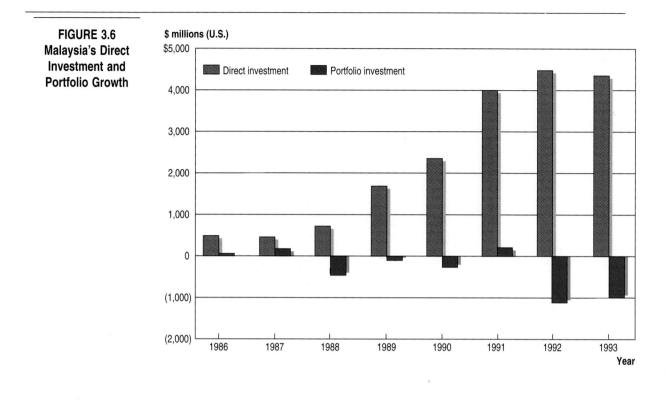

BALANCE OF
PAYMENTS
DYNAMICS

The two major subaccounts of the BOP, the current and capital accounts, are watched individually for the magnitude of their imbalances, if imbalanced. However, it is not at all clear that they should be balanced individually or that a balance in either (actually, if one is balanced the other must be) is desirable.

Although economists do not really agree on what is best or what is sustainable, the bilateral relationship between the United States and Japan serves to demonstrate the trade-offs. The United States ran substantial current account deficits and capital account surpluses throughout the 1980s. Japan ran sizable current account surpluses and capital account deficits over the same period. And much of these respective imbalances were with each other (bilateral). But which is better off? There is no clear answer to this. Many have argued that the U.S. current account deficit, more specifically the U.S. merchandise trade deficit, was unsustainable. But this also allowed massive capital inflows into the United States aiding in the expansion and modernization of many industries.

Merchandise Trade and Exchange Rate Dynamics

Merchandise trade—exports and imports—is sensitive to exchange rate changes. Many countries in the not too distant past have intentionally devalued their currencies to make their export products more competitive on world markets. These competitive devaluations, however, are normally considered self-destructive because although they do make export products relatively cheaper, they also make imports

relatively more expensive. So what is the logic of intentionally devaluing the domestic currency to improve the trade balance?

A country typically devalues its currency as a result of persistent and sizable trade deficits. Economic analysis has usually characterized the trade balance adjustment process as occurring in three stages: (1) the currency contract period, (2) the pass-through period, and (3) the quantity adjustment period.

In the first period, a sudden unexpected devaluation of the domestic currency has a somewhat uncertain impact, simply because all of the contracts for exports and imports are already in effect. Firms operating under these agreements are required to fulfill their obligations, regardless of whether they profit or suffer losses. If the United States experienced a sudden fall in the value of the U.S. dollar (as occurred in the 1985–1987 period) and most exports were priced in U.S. dollars but most imports were contracts denominated in foreign currency, the result of a sudden depreciation would be an increase in the size of the trade deficit. This is because the cost to U.S. importers of "paying their bills" would rise (as they spent more and more dollars to buy the foreign currency they needed), while the revenues earned by U.S. exporters would remain unchanged. Although this is the commonly cited scenario regarding trade balance adjustment, there is little reason to believe that most U.S. imports are denominated in foreign currency and most exports in U.S. dollars.

The second period of the trade balance adjustment process is termed the pass-through period. As exchange rates change, importers and exporters eventually must **pass** these exchange rate changes **through** to their own product prices. For example, a foreign producer selling to the U.S. market after a major fall in the value of the U.S. dollar will have to cover its own domestic costs of production. This will require that the firm charge higher dollar prices in order to earn its own local currency in large enough quantities. The firm must raise its prices in the U.S. market. Import prices rise substantially, eventually passing through the full exchange rate changes into prices. American consumers see higher prices for imported products on the shelf. Similarly, the U.S. export prices are now cheaper compared to foreign competitors' because the dollar is cheaper. Unfortunately for U.S. exporters, many of their inputs may be imported, causing them also to suffer slightly rising prices after the fall of the dollar.

The third and final period, the quantity adjustment period, achieves the balance of trade adjustment that is expected from a domestic currency devaluation or de-

Global Perspective

3.3
A Rose by Any Other Name: The Terminology of the BOP

Measures of the international economic activity of the nation have been known to go by a variety of aliases. The two major institutions that measure the international transactions of the United States are the International Monetary Fund and the U.S. Department of Commerce, which each use very different names for the same measurements.

International Monetary Fund	**U.S. Department of Commerce**
Balance of Payments	Balance on International Transactions
Errors and Omissions	Statistical Discrepancy
Balance on International Indebtness	International Investment Position of the U.S.

preciation. As the import and export prices change as a result of the pass-through period, consumers both in the United States and in the U.S. export markets adjust their demands to the new prices. Imports are relatively more expensive, therefore the quantity demanded decreases. Exports are relatively cheaper, and therefore the quantity of exports rises. The balance of trade, the expenditures on exports less the expenditures on imports, improves.

Unfortunately, these three adjustment periods do not occur overnight. Countries such as the United States that have experienced major exchange rate changes also have seen this adjustment take place over a prolonged period. Often, before the adjustment is completed, new exchange rate changes occur, frustrating the total adjustment process. Trade adjustment to exchange rate changes does not occur in a sterile laboratory environment, but in the messy and complex world of international business and economic events. And as detailed in Global Perspective 3.3, even the terminology of BOP accounting is a mess.

SUMMARY

The balance of payments is the summary statement of all international transactions between one country and all other countries. The balance of payments is a flow statement, summarizing all the international transactions that occur across the geographic boundaries of the nation over a period of time, typically a year. Because of its use of double-entry bookkeeping, the BOP must always balance in theory, though in practice there are substantial imbalances as a result of statistical errors and misreporting of current account and capital account flows.

The two major subaccounts of the balance of payments, the current account and the capital account, summarize the current trade and international capital flows of the country. Due to the double-entry bookkeeping method of accounting, the current account and capital account are always inverse on balance, one in surplus while the other experiences deficit. Although most nations strive for current account surpluses, it is not clear that a balance on current or capital account, or a surplus on current account, is either sustainable or desirable. The monitoring of the various subaccounts of a country's balance of payments activity is helpful to decision makers and policymakers at all levels of government and industry in detecting the underlying trends and movements of fundamental economic forces driving a country's international economic activity.

Key Terms and Concepts

balance of payments (BOP)	price inelasticity
current account	direct investment account
capital account	portfolio investment account
double-entry bookkeeping	real returns
merchandise trade	safe haven
service trade	official reserves account
investment income	basic balance
unilateral transfer	official settlements balance

Questions for Discussion

1. Why must a country's balance of payments always be balanced in theory?
2. What is the difference between the merchandise trade balance (BOT) and the current account balance?
3. What is service trade?
4. Why is foreign direct investment so much more controversial than foreign portfolio investment? How does this relate to Mexico in the 1990s?
5. Should the fact that the United States may be the world's largest net debtor nation be a source of concern for government policymakers? Is the United States like Finland?
6. While the United States "suffered" a current account deficit and a capital account surplus in the 1980s, what were the respective balances of Japan doing?
7. What does it mean for the United States to be one of the world's largest indebted countries?
8. How do exchange rate changes alter trade so that the trade balance actually improves when the domestic currency depreciates?

Recommended Readings

Agenor, Pierre-Richard, Jagdeep S. Bhandari, and Robert P. Flood. "Speculative Attacks and Models of Balance of Payments Crises." *International Monetary Fund Staff Papers*, 39, 2 (June 1992) 357–394.

Bergsten, C. Fred, editor. *International Adjustment and Financing: The Lessons of 1985–1991*. Washington, D.C.: Institute for International Economics, 1991.

Evans, John S. *International Finance: A Markets Approach*. New York: Dryden Press, 1992.

Grabbe, J. Orlin. *International Financial Markets*. 2d edition. New York: Elsevier, 1991.

Handbook of International Trade and Development Statistics, New York: United Nations, 1989.

Husted, Steven, and Michael Melvin. *International Economics.* New York: Harper & Row, 1990.

IMF Balance of Payments Yearbook, Washington, D.C.: International Monetary Fund, annually.

Root, Franklin R. *International Trade and Investment.* 6th edition. Chicago: South-Western Publishing, 1990.

62nd Annual Report. Basle, Switzerland: Bank for International Settlements, June 15, 1992.

Notes

1. The official terminology used throughout this chapter, unless otherwise noted, is that of the International Monetary Fund (IMF). Since the IMF is the primary source of similar statistics for balance of payments and economic performance worldwide, it is more general than other terminology forms, such as that employed by the U.S. Department of Commerce.

2. All balance of payment data used in this chapter is drawn from the International Monetary Fund's *Balance of Payments Statistics Yearbook.* This source is used because the IMF presents the balance of payments statistics for all member countries on the same basis and in the same format allowing comparison across countries. The U.S. Department of Commerce also publishes the balance of payments and other international transaction statistics for the United States alone in the *Survey of Current Business.* Unfortunately, the U.S. Department of Commerce uses a different organization for the various sub-accounts than that used by the IMF. Also—unfortunately—the U.S. Department of Commerce is much quicker in its publication of statistics (for the United States alone) than the IMF is (for the hundreds of member countries). When this book went to press in September 1995, the most recent *Balance of Payments Statistics Yearbook* had been published in December 1994 and included data ending 1993.

   This results in a dilemma for textbook authors: to use the most recent data for whichever country is the subject of discussion from whatever sources, or to use a single consistent source across all countries. We have chosen to stay with the single source, the IMF, and risk appearing one year out of data statistically on publication. For the purposes of edification and consistency, we feel the IMF's balance of payments statistics are preferable. For those readers interested in the most recent data for any specific country, the central bank bulletin of most countries reports balance of payments statistics typically four to six months previous to those of the IMF. But, the reader must also be forewarned of the varying formats of statistical presentation.

CHAPTER 4

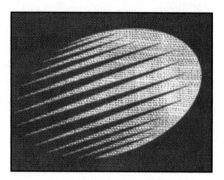

The International Monetary System: Principles and History

Learning Objectives

1. To define what an exchange rate is and what its value should be.

2. To review the history of the international monetary system of the twentieth century in order to understand why the major world currencies are floating today.

3. To compare fixed and floating exchange rates.

4. To understand the purpose, mechanics, and future ambitions of the European Monetary System.

5. To understand the prime economic forces that will drive exchange rates in the future.

104

A Matter of Exchange Rates

The American manufacturing sector has been getting some pretty good press lately, even from those who were busy writing its obituary just a few years ago. Yes, the numbers are pretty good. But there's a case to be made for at least a second look at this newly acclaimed supremacy of American manufacturing.

Exhibit A is the currency situation. In 1985, the yen was 270 to the dollar. Today, it's roughly 150 percent stronger, at 105. In 1985, the mark was 3.30 to the dollar. It's now about 50 percent stronger, 1.65. How much would we be selling; how bold and innovative would we American managers be; how envious would the world be of our manufacturing prowess if that yen and that mark were at the same strength they were not nine years ago, but only three—about 140 yen to the dollar?

The annual report of Toyota Motor, one of the world's greatest manufacturers, lays out very clearly solution number one to the problem of the yen: "We will cut costs like we have never cut costs before." The Japanese are grimly determined to achieve not incremental performance improvements, but what they call "bullet train," or order-of-magnitude improvements. They put no stock in predictions of a weaker yen, and are preparing themselves to compete at 90 yen to the dollar. I could make the case that the powerful yen is the best thing that ever happened to Japanese competitiveness.

Global competitors are taking actions today that could push U.S. manufacturers from the deceptive tranquility of the eye back into the turbulence of the hurricane, a hurricane that this time will come with a ferocity that could be intensified should the currency go the wrong way. What happens if the yen swings back over 130, as it was just two years ago, or the mark moves toward 2?

We should not wait that long. There are things that can be done now. If the Japanese are preparing to compete at 90 yen, the U.S. must be ready to compete at 130. Until we are, we delude ourselves if we think we are in control of our own fate.

Source: Excerpts from John F. Welch, "A Matter of Exchange Rates," *The Wall Street Journal,* June 21, 1994, editorial page. Mr. Welch is chairman and CEO of General Electric Co. This is an adaptation of a talk to the Economic Club of Detroit.

What is a currency worth? Answer: Whatever it will buy. A currency can buy goods, services, assets, or even other currencies. Actually, the larger problem is not really what it will buy today, but what a currency will buy tomorrow.

If exchange rates are set by market forces, and market forces are thought to be efficient, how can exchange rates change over such wide ranges? Exchange rates and currency markets have long been a mystery to many people. This chapter provides an overview of the basic economic principles of exchange rates and a brief history of the recent **international monetary system.** Chapter 5 provides a more detailed description of the mechanics of exchange rate markets today. The first problem, however, is to understand what purpose these exchange rates have for people and firms in international business.

THE PURPOSE OF EXCHANGE RATES

If countries are to trade, they must be able to exchange currencies. To buy wheat, or corn, or videocassette recorders, the buyer must first have the currency in which the product is sold. An American firm purchasing consumer electronic products manufactured in Japan must first exchange its U.S. dollars for Japanese yen, then purchase the products. And each country has its own currency.[1] The exchange of one country's currency for another should be a relatively simple transaction, but it's not.

What Is a Currency Worth?

At what rate should one currency be exchanged for another currency? For example, what should the exchange rate be between the U.S. dollar and the Japanese yen?

The simplest answer is that the exchange rate should equalize purchasing power. For example, if the price of a movie ticket in the United States is $6, the "correct" exchange rate would be one that exchanges $6 for the amount of Japanese yen it would take to purchase a movie ticket in Japan. If ticket prices are ¥540 (a common symbol for the yen is ¥) in Japan, then the exchange rate that would equalize purchasing power would be:

$$\frac{¥540}{$6} = ¥90/$.$$

Therefore, if the exchange rate between the two currencies is ¥90/$, regardless of which country the movie-goer is in, he or she can purchase a ticket. This is the theory of **purchasing power parity (PPP),** generally considered the definition of what exchange rates ideally should be. The purchasing power parity exchange rate is simply the rate that equalizes the price of the identical product or service in two different currencies:

$$\text{Price in Japan} = \text{Exchange rate} \times \text{Price in U.S.}$$

If the price of the same product in each currency is $P^¥$ and $P^$$, and the spot exchange rate between the Japanese yen and the U.S. dollar is $S^{¥/$}$, the price in yen is simply the price in dollars multiplied by the spot exchange rate,

$$P^¥ = S^{¥/$} \times P^$.$$

If this is rearranged (dividing both sides by $P^$$), the spot exchange rate between the Japanese yen and the U.S. dollar is the ratio of the two product prices,

$$S^{¥/$} = \frac{P^¥}{P^$}.$$

These prices could be the price of just one good or service, such as the movie ticket mentioned previously, or they could be price indices for each country that cover many different goods and services. Either form is an attempt to find comparable products in different countries (and currencies) in order to determine an exchange rate based on purchasing power parity. The question then is whether this logical approach to exchange rates actually works in practice.

The Law of One Price

The version of purchasing power parity that estimates the exchange rate between two currencies using just one good or service as a measure of the proper exchange for all goods and services is called the **Law of One Price.** To apply the theory to actual prices across countries, we need to select a product that is identical in quality and content in every country. To be truly theoretically correct, we would want such a product to be produced entirely domestically, so that there are no imported factors in its construction.

Where would one find such a perfect product? McDonald's. Table 4.1 presents what *The Economist* magazine calls the "Big Mac Index of Currencies." What it provides is a product that is essentially the same the world over and is produced and consumed entirely domestically.

The Big Mac Index compares the actual exchange rate with the exchange rate implied by the purchasing power parity measurement of comparing Big Mac prices across countries. For example, say the average price of a Big Mac in the United States on a given date is $2.30. On the same date, the price of a Big Mac in Canada, in

TABLE 4.1		(1) Big Mac	(2) Actual	(3) Big Mac	(4) Implied	(5) Local Currency
The Law of One Price: The Big Mac Hamburger Standard		Price in Local Currency	Exchange Rate 4/5/94	Prices in Dollars	PPP of the Dollar	under (−)/over (+) Valuation
	Country					
	United States	$2.30	—	2.30	—	—
	Argentina	Peso 3.60	1.00	3.60	1.57	+ 57
	Australia	A$ 2.45	1.42	1.72	1.07	− 25
	Austria	Sch 34.00	12.0	2.84	14.8	+ 23
	Belgium	BFr 109	35.2	3.10	47.39	+ 35
	Brazil	Cr 1,500	949	1.58	652	− 31
	Britain	£ 1.81	1.46	2.65	1.27	+ 15
	Canada	C$ 2.86	1.39	2.06	1.24	− 10
	Chile	Peso 948	414	2.28	412	− 1
	China	Yuan 9.00	8.70	1.03	3.91	− 55
	Czech Rep	CKr 50	29.7	1.71	21.7	− 27
	Denmark	DKr 25.75	6.69	3.85	11.2	+ 67
	France	FFr 18.50	5.83	3.17	8.04	+ 38
	Germany	DM 4.60	1.71	2.69	2.00	+ 17
	Greece	Dr 620	251	2.47	270	+ 8
	Holland	Fl 5.45	1.91	2.85	2.37	+ 24
	Hong Kong	HK$ 9.20	7.73	1.19	4.00	− 48
	Hungary	Forint 169	103	1.66	73.48	− 29
	Italy	Lire 4,550	1,641	2.77	1,978	+ 21
	Japan	¥ 391	104	3.77	170	+ 64
	Malaysia	M$ 3.77	2.69	1.40	1.64	− 39
	Mexico	Peso 8.10	3.36	2.41	3.52	+ 5
	Poland	Zloty 31,000	22,433	1.40	13,478	− 40
	Portugal	Esc 440	174	2.53	191	+ 10
	Russia	Rouble 2,900	1,775	1.66	1,261	− 29
	Singapore	$ 2.98	1.57	1.90	1.30	− 17
	S. Korea	Won 2,300	810	2.84	1,000	+ 24
	Spain	Ptas 345	138	2.50	150	+ 9
	Sweden	SKr 25.50	7.97	3.20	11.1	+ 39
	Switzerland	SwFr 5.70	1.44	3.96	2.48	+ 72
	Taiwan	NT$ 62	26.4	2.35	26.96	+ 2
	Thailand	Baht 48	25.3	1.90	20.87	− 17

Column (1): Prices in local currency; may vary by location.
Column (2): Actual exchange rate on April 5, 1994 (London quotes).
Column (3): column (1) ÷ column (2)
Column (4): column (1) ÷ $2.3028 (price of Big Mac in United States).
Column (5): column (4) ÷ column (2)

Source: Adapted from "Big MacCurrencies," *The Economist*, April 9, 1994, p. 88. Original quotations courtesy of McDonald's. United States Big Mac price is the average of New York, Chicago, San Francisco, and Atlanta. British exchange rate and implied PPP rates quoted in U.S. dollar per pound.

Canadian dollars, is C$2.86. This then is used to calculate the PPP exchange rate as before:

$$\frac{\text{C\$2.86 per Big Mac}}{\text{\$2.30 per Big Mac}} = \text{C\$1.24/\$}.$$

The exchange rate between the Canadian dollar and the U.S. dollar should be C$1.24/$, according to a PPP comparison of Big Mac prices. The actual exchange rate on the date of comparison (April 5, 1994) was C$1.39/$. This means that each U.S. dollar was actually worth 1.39 Canadian dollars, when the index indicates that each U.S. dollar should have been worth 1.24 Canadian dollars. Therefore, if one is to believe in the Big Mac index, the U.S. dollar was being "overvalued" on the markets by about 10 percent (or the Canadian dollar was undervalued by 10 percent— take your pick).

Not simply entertaining, the Big Mac index is actually an excellent example of how purchasing power parity should work in determining exchange rates. There are few products that are not only identical across so many countries, but also produced completely within that country. Note that for most currencies listed, the Big Mac index implies an exchange rate that is not that distant from the actual rate.

What should one conclude from this example of purchasing power parity? Although there are many valid criticisms of the Big Mac index (for example, local taxes, property values, tariffs, and so forth, all affecting the prices in each country), it does serve as a measure of what currencies should be worth. Any single product could be similarly criticized, and the alternative method of comparing consumer or producer price indices across countries may actually be worse, considering how few products actually meet the requirements so clearly fulfilled by the Big Mac. In conclusion, one could do worse!

Qualities Desired in an Exchange Rate

The theory of purchasing power parity provides a measure of the goal in the exchange of currencies between countries. It provides a focus for the value desired. But what other qualities are desired in an exchange rate?

First and foremost, stability. Currencies are only a medium of exchange, a store of value, a unit of account. They are money. The purpose of money is to facilitate business and commerce. Prices play a critical role in how goods are allocated be-

Global Perspective

4.1
"It Pays to Be Jailed in Switzerland"

ZURICH, Switzerland—Drug smugglers have discovered a novel and lucrative form of employment—getting themselves arrested and imprisoned in Switzerland.

Swiss jails have long been held up as models of progressive enlightenment where prisoners are paid for their labors. While the rate is low by Swiss standards—around 23 Swiss francs ($15) per day—it's attractive to South American drug couriers.

During the average 3 1/2-year sentence, a smuggler can earn about 28,000 francs ($18,480). Convicts can send checks to support their families or take lump sums on release.

The jails are clean, modern, and furnished with one-man cells. They provide three meals a day and health care. Despite the forced confinement, some offenders find the environment preferable to drug-running. Officials said one smuggler flew back to Switzerland after having been deported to poverty in Colombia, asking to be returned to his cell.

Prosecutor Marcel Bebie, who feels the prison system is being abused, wants prison pay linked to the cost of living in the offender's country. "Drug smugglers earn far more in a Swiss jail than a policeman in Colombia or Bolivia," he said. "To earn 20 or 25 francs a day may be punishment for the Swiss, but it is heaven on earth for these people."

Bebie's district handles drug-runners caught at or near Zurich Airport. Regensdorf Prison now houses 120 men arrested for smuggling at the airport last year.

An Interior Ministry spokesman defended the prison-pay policy. "Eventually these people have to reintegrate into society, so it is better to give them something to do while they are in jail," he said. He added that many Third World drug-runners were pushed into crime because they had families.

"If they have young children, it is very beneficial that they are able to send some money back home."

Source: Birna Helgadottir, "It Pays to Be Jailed in Switzerland," *The European,* distributed by Insight News.

tween buyers and sellers, consumers and producers. If the prices of products across borders are more volatile or unpredictable than the prices within borders, international trade and commerce is more difficult and the benefits of trade pointed out in Chapter 2 are not fully realized. Regardless of how it is achieved, a stable and predictable currency value is conducive to international trade. Trade is easier when the price of a foreign product or asset, at least as affected by exchange rates, will be the same tomorrow and the day after as it is today. As Global Perspective 4.1 shows, even a prison sentence may be lucrative if the exchange rate is favorable.

Second, a system or regime (as exchange rate systems are often referred to) is generally more dependable if it is "self-directing." This means a system or device that operates properly and dependably on its own, without the interference or direction of authorities such as governments or groups of governments. The self-correcting properties of markets is one of the dominant features of the market economy as opposed to other forms, such as directed economies.

The major exchange rate regimes discussed in the following sections all employ slightly different methods, rules, and agreements in attempting to achieve these goals. Some have worked better than others, but much of what has worked in the past will not work in the future because, literally, times change.

INTERNATIONAL MONETARY SYSTEMS OF THE TWENTIETH CENTURY

The exchange rate system we see today is the latest stage in a world of continuing change. The systems that have preceded the present floating exchange rate system varied between gold-based standards, in which currencies were nothing other than lightweight replacements for gold, and complex systems, in which the U.S. dollar was considered "good as gold." To understand why major world currencies such as the dollar and yen are floating today, it is necessary to return to the (pardon the pun) "golden oldies."

A few words of caution are in order, however, before proceeding with a discussion of the modern history of exchange rates.

- History as conveyed in books tends to focus on outcomes, not processes. Very often the outcome is more a combination of principles or procedures or both, rather than the dominance of one idea or set of ideas. The most important lesson is the cause of change, not the result.

- Agreements between participants such as governments can be either formal or informal. The procedures or rules of a system may be laid down specifically in written articles, which are then signed and confirmed by all members, or totally informal in structure where all participants play by the same rules—they are just not written down or stated in an agreed-upon document or setting. An agreement is only as good as the adherence of all parties to it and not to the level of detail spelled out in its formalized rules. It is actions that count most.

- Finally, times change. The political and economic powers of the world change and evolve, and some systems or rules of markets may have to change with them.

The following discussion of the major international monetary systems of the twentieth century will continually return to these three points: the causes of change, the actions of participants rather than the stated rules of the system, and finally the changing world economic conditions that have driven the global trading system from a standard based on gold to one based on faith.

THE GOLD STANDARD

Although there is no official starting date, the **gold standard** as we know it extended from the 1880s to the outbreak of World War I in 1914. History has looked on the gold standard with generally favorable recollections, although its success may be attributed to the relatively simpler economic world in which it existed and the fact that this era was one of few international wars or crises. The gold standard had three major features that are helpful in understanding why it did work and also why it may never work again.

1. It established a system of fixed exchange rates between participating countries. Stable exchange rates were considered a necessary ingredient to increase trade among nations.

2. The gold standard limited the rate of growth in a country's money supply. This was due to the fact that all "money" had to be backed by gold, and the supply of gold in the world increased quite slowly during this period in history.

3. Gold served as an automatic adjustment tool for countries experiencing balance of payments problems. If a country was running a balance of payments deficit, gold would, by market forces, flow out of the country, decreasing economic activity and pushing the balance of payments back toward balance.

See Global Perspective 4.2 for an example of how Eurotunnel fares are affected by exchange rates.

Fixed Exchange Parity Rates

The mechanics of the gold standard system were actually quite simple. Each country's currency was set in value per ounce of gold. For example, the U.S. dollar was defined as being $20.67/oz. of gold,[2] while the British pound sterling, the dominant world currency at the time, was £4.2474/oz. The obvious benefit of this fixing to gold weight was that if each currency maintained its value relative to gold, then each currency was in effect fixed to every other currency. For example, with the dollar and the pound fixed at $20.67/oz. and £4.2474/oz., the dollar–pound exchange rate was fixed at:

$$\frac{\$20.67/oz. \text{ of gold}}{£4.2474/oz. \text{ of gold}} = \$4.8665/£.$$

Although most countries followed the same basic set of principles, the "system" was not formalized to any great degree among countries. It worked because most governments followed, of their own accord, the same sets of rules. But, first and foremost, the gold standard established relatively fixed exchange rates.

These **par values,** or parity rates as they were known, were established on the basis of purchasing power parity, similar to that described in the previous section (although obviously not on the basis of the Big Mac). The selection of gold as the core element was more a result of historical tradition rather than anything particularly unique about gold itself. Gold was durable and divisible, although gold itself is a relatively soft metal. The most significant factor in favor of the use of gold was that it had been in relatively short supply for most of human history. Gold was generally accepted in all countries as a means of payment.

Establishing the system was only the first step. For the gold standard to work, the countries participating in such a system had to follow certain rules. The first and

Global Perspective

4.2
Purchasing Power Parity and "Le Shuttle"

The Eurotunnel, the tunnel that connects the United Kingdom and France underneath the English Channel, poses a classic problem of purchasing power parity. Also nicknamed *Le Shuttle* and the *Chunnel,* the tube provides two-way transportation for people and products between two different currency markets.

On December 17, 1994, the Eurotunnel announced the fare structure for passenger cars. A one-day return (round-trip ticket) will cost £49, or $76.59 at the exchange rate in effect on that date ($1.5630/£). At a spot exchange rate of FF8.4637/£ between the British pound and the French franc—the currency at the other end of the tunnel—the same

return ticket will cost FF414.72. Now every time the spot rate changes between the pound and the franc, a potential passenger on one side of the channel will *win* and one on the other side will *lose*.

Although this is not a unique problem—after all, planes, trains, and automobiles have been crossing borders and paying tolls on both sides for many years—this case poses a particularly tricky problem given that the Eurotunnel is a joint project of investors, private and public, in both countries. For now, with primary administration lying with the United Kingdom, it seems the *fixed price* will be the pound-price.

foremost **"rule of the game"** was that a currency was indeed valued as its parity rate with gold. The only way this could be proven was if the government stood ready, willing, and able to buy or sell gold at the stated parity rate. For example, the Bank of England assured both the British public and foreign public that the pound sterling was worth £4.2474 per ounce of gold by selling gold to anyone wanting it at that price. Whenever there was doubt in the minds of the public, the government would sell gold in return for the paper pounds. If for some reason the public believed that the pound sterling was worth more, again, the British government and the Bank of England would buy gold on the open market at the stated price of £4.2474 per ounce and stabilize the price.

Second, governments had to "let the gold flow." This meant that countries had to allow gold to move freely in and out of the country to earn the continued faith in the currency's worth. For example, a British citizen holding Federal Reserve notes issued by the U.S. Treasury was assured by the U.S. government that 20.67 one dollar bills were worth one ounce of gold. If the British citizen or anyone else outside the United States holding U.S. dollar bills had doubts, the U.S. Treasury assured all such people that they could exchange the paper for gold. If everyone believed it, no one really needed to exchange the paper for the more unwieldy gold. In the case of doubt, however, and there are always doubters, the governments had to be able to convert paper for gold to maintain the integrity of the system.

The origins of money are listed in Global Perspective 4.3.

Restriction on Money Supply Growth

In addition to implicitly establishing fixed exchange rates, the gold standard had a very powerful impact on the monetary policy of the participating countries. Each unit of currency was backed by gold so the supply of money in the country could

Global Perspective

4.3
The Origins of Monies

Currency Name	Representative Currencies	Origins
Krona	Czech Republic koruna Danish krone Icelandic krona Norwegian krone Slovak Republic koruna Swedish krona	From the word meaning "crown" and simultaneously that of "gold" from the Latin word *aureus*.
Dollar	Australian dollar Canadian dollar Hong Kong dollar Singapore dollar Taiwanese dollar United States dollar	From the old German *Daler* or *Taler*, an abbreviation of the name given the silver coin—*joachimsthaler*—a coin with the likeness of St. Joachim imprinted upon it and first minted in 1519.
Franc	French franc Swiss franc Belgian franc Luxembourg franc Liechtenstein franc	From the Latin inscription of the coin first minted in 1360 by order of King John II of France which read, *Johannes Dei Gracia Francorum Rex* (John by the Grace of God King of the Franks).
Mark	German mark (Deutschemark) Finnish markka	From an old Norse term for a unit of measure, a mark, used as early as the third century A.D. It was first employed by the Goths and later by the Germans.
Peso	Argentina peso Chilean peso Mexican peso Philippines peso Spanish peseta Uruguay new peso	From the word meaning "weight." The *peso* was established in Spain in 1497 by King Ferdinand and Queen Isabella. The Spanish *peseta* was introduced as a companion coin to the *full peso*, the famous "piece of eight," referring to its value of eight *reales*.
Pound	British pound sterling Italian lira Maltese lira Turkish lira	Pound is from the Roman *libra* or pound, money of account from early medieval times. The British pound is from the eighth century in Anglo-Saxon Britain when the basic monetary unit called the *sterling* was defined as 1/240 of a *pound of sterling silver*. The Italian lira from *libra* was first minted in 1472 by the Doge Nicolas Tron of Venice (also being known as the *testone* or "head" because it depicted the head of Doge Nicolas).
Yen	Japanese yen Chinese yuan	From Japanese meaning "round," and basically borrowed from the Chinese term *yuan* also meaning round.

Source: Adapted by authors from Leslie Dunkling and Adrian Room, *The Guinness Book of Money,* Facts on File Publishing, New York, 1990.

not increase faster than the amount of gold, and the supply of gold in the world was expanding quite slowly at that time. This meant that government authorities in charge of monetary policy were restricted in how fast they could increase the money supply.

This automatic restraint was distinctly anti-inflationary, and historical evidence, although inconclusive, suggests that average inflation rates were lower during the time of the gold standard than they have been since. However, this system prevents governments from deciding their own independent monetary policies. Some scholars have argued that it is illogical to allow the world supply of a metal to dictate policy as important as the quantity of money available to society.

Automatic Balance of Payments Adjustment

The third and final feature of the gold standard also relied on the ability of the gold to flow. Rapid growth, particularly in imports, could push the balance of payments into deficit (outflows of money and currency exceeding inflows). The system relied on fixed exchange rates and **convertibility** of currencies to gold, so anyone not wanting to be paid in paper currency could essentially demand gold bullion. Thus, if there was reason to doubt the value of the currency, the government would allow gold to flow, even out of the country.

The gold flow out of the country reduced the supply of money (remember the fixed link of paper money to gold), pushing the system back into balance. Having less money in the country's economy would slow business and economic activity. The slowed activity would return the country to a balance of payments.

Regardless of the strengths of the gold standard, the first world war effectively halted the free flow of gold across borders, and the world's currency markets were in substantial turmoil until 1919. The United States returned to the gold standard in June 1919. Great Britain did not return to the standard until 1925, and its term even then proved short-lived.

The London financial district flourished during the decades prior to World War I when the British pound sterling was the dominant world currency and when most currencies were based on the gold standard.

Source: The Bettmann Archive.

THE INTERWAR YEARS, 1919–1939

The 1920s and 1930s were a tumultuous period for the international monetary system. The British pound sterling, the world's dominant currency prior to World War I, survived the war but was greatly weakened. Inflation in England during and after the war threatened the stability of the British economy. In a desperate move to return to times of relative calm, the Bank of England once more established the British pound at its prewar parity of £4.2474 per ounce of gold.

It should be noted that one of Britain's leading economists of the time, John Maynard Keynes, vehemently opposed the return of the pound sterling to the gold standard. The advocates of the gold standard were led by Winston Churchill, then chancellor of the exchequer, and they held the day. But the pound was not what it had been, and continued runs on the stock of gold held by the Bank of England finally forced the abandonment of the gold standard again in 1931. As seen in Figure 4.1, this caused an enormous fall in the value of the pound in 1931 and 1932.

The U.S. dollar returned to the gold standard at the end of the war in June 1919. For the United States, which had suffered none of the physical destruction of the war and which also had not experienced many of the inflationary pressures, the return to gold was much simpler. It was not until the bank runs and subsequent "holidays" of 1933 that the United States was forced again to abandon gold convertibility.

There is no question that the decade of the 1930s was a dark period for world trade and currency markets. With the onslaught of depression, many countries, including the United States, resorted to isolationist policies and protectionism. Markets were closed to foreign producers. In the international markets that did remain open, exporting countries tried to undercut each other through continual currency devaluations. These **competitive devaluations** only succeeded in pushing many of the world's currencies below their true values and increasing the pressures for further nationalistic protectionist policies to shield domestic firms from unfair for-

FIGURE 4.1
The Dollar–Pound Exchange Rate

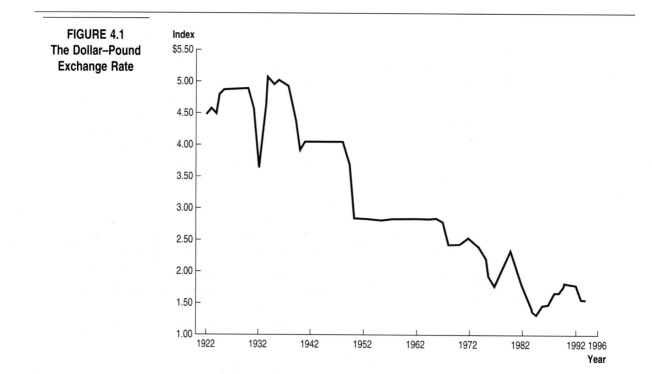

eign competition. By the early days of World War II, international trade had ground to a halt.

| THE BRETTON WOODS AGREEMENT | The governments of the Allied powers knew that the devastating impacts of World War II would require swift and decisive policies. Therefore, a full year before the end of the war, representatives of 44 nations met in the summer of 1944 in Bretton Woods, New Hampshire. Their purpose was to plan the postwar international monetary system. It was a difficult process, and the final synthesis of viewpoints was shaded by pragmatism and significant doubt.[3] |

Although the conference was attended by more than 40 nations, the leading policymakers at Bretton Woods were the British and the Americans. The British delegation was led by Lord John Maynard Keynes, termed "Britain's economic heavyweight."[4] The British argued for a postwar system that would be decidedly more flexible than the various gold standards used before the second world war. Keynes argued, as he had after World War I, that attempts to tie currency values to gold would create pressures for deflation (a general fall in the level of prices in a country) in many of the war-ravaged economies. And these economies were faced with enormous reindustrialization needs that would likely cause inflation, not deflation.

The American delegation was led by the director of the U.S. Treasury's monetary research department, Harry D. White, and the U.S. Secretary of the Treasury, Henry Morgenthau, Jr. The American delegation argued for the need for stability (fixed rates) but not a return to the gold standard itself. In fact, although the United States at that time held most of the gold of the Allied powers, the U.S. delegates argued that currencies should be fixed in parities but redemption of gold should occur only between official authorities (central banks of governments).

On the more pragmatic side, all parties agreed that a postwar system would be stable and sustainable only if there was sufficient credit available for countries to defend their currencies in the event of balance of payments imbalances, which they knew to be inevitable in a reconstructing world order.

The conference divided up into three commissions for weeks of negotiation. One commission, led by U.S. Treasury Secretary Henry Morgenthau, was charged with the organization of a fund of capital to be used for exchange rate stabilization. A second commission, chaired by Britain's Lord Keynes, was charged with the organization of a second "bank" whose purpose would be for long-term reconstruction and development. The third commission was to hammer out details such as what role silver would have in any new system.

The Agreement

After weeks of meetings, the participants finally came to a three-part **Bretton Woods Agreement** for the structure of the postwar international monetary system. The plan called for:

1. Fixed exchange rates, termed an "adjustable peg" among members;
2. A fund of gold and constituent currencies available to members for stabilization of their respective currencies, called the **International Monetary Fund (IMF); and**
3. A bank for financing long-term development projects.

Although the third component, which became known as the World Bank, was not integral to the operation of the system, the adjustable peg and the stabilization fund were to work hand in hand.

The Adjustable Peg

All currencies were to establish par values defined in terms of gold. However, unlike the gold standard prior to World War I, there was little if any convertibility of currencies for gold. Each government was responsible for monitoring its currency value to ensure that it varied by less than 1 percent from its par value. If a country experienced a **fundamental disequilibrium** in its balance of payments, it could alter its peg by up to 10 percent from its initial par value without approval from the IMF. But, as with any fixed price system, the goal of the system was not to change the par value. The "adjustment" part of the peg was to be kept to a minimum.[5] A country experiencing significant problems could therefore apply to the IMF for temporary loans of gold or convertible currencies for the purpose of defending its par value and adjusting the balance of payments back toward equilibrium.

The one currency that was convertible to gold was the U.S. dollar. The dollar was pegged at $1 = 1/35 ounce of gold, or $35 per ounce. The U.S. Treasury would, however, convert U.S. dollars for gold only with foreign governments, not with private individuals, domestic or foreign. This was a significant reduction in convertibility compared to that of the old gold standard. But with all currencies pegged to gold, and the dollar convertible to gold, even if only with official authorities, the dollar was considered "good as gold." This was the feature of the system that brought 25 years of success, as well as its eventual collapse.

For example, a country experiencing a balance of payments deficit would normally experience devaluation pressure on its currency value. The country's authorities, normally the central bank, would defend its currency by using its foreign currency reserves, primarily U.S. dollars, to purchase its own currency on the open market to push its value back up and preserve its par value. Once a country used up a large proportion of its currency reserves, it could apply to the IMF for additional funds to stabilize its currency value. Similarly, if the country was experiencing a balance of payments surplus and associated upward pressure on its currency, it could sell additional currency on the open market and accept payment in major convertible currencies such as the U.S. dollar. Since the dollar was convertible for gold, the U.S. dollar was quite acceptable.

The International Monetary Fund

The International Monetary Fund was created to provide funds to countries in need of additional assistance for economic stabilization. It was initially funded through contributions from all members. Each country was given a quota in the original agreement at Bretton Woods. Quotas were established on the basis of the size and estimated strengths at the end of the second world war, in addition to the size of foreign trade the country demonstrated prior to the war.[6] Table 4.2 lists the agreed-upon quotas of the original members. Once paid, the quotas would establish the pool of capital available to the IMF for its economic stabilization lending.

Each quota was payable at 25 percent in gold and 75 percent in the country's own currency.[7] Since most countries possessed currencies that were obviously not convertible and therefore of little value, it was the gold portion of the quota that was considered the true source of the IMF's lending capabilities.

	Country	Quota
TABLE 4.2 **Initial IMF Quotas**	United States	$2,750,000,000
	Great Britain	1,300,000,000
	Russia	1,200,000,000
	China	550,000,000
	France	450,000,000
	Total	$8,500,000,000

Source: "Rivalries Beset Monetary Pact," *Business Week,* Number 776, July 15, 1944, 15–16.

A final feature of the IMF, not added until the mid-1960s, was the creation of an index of currencies, the **Special Drawing Right (SDR).** The SDR was intended as an artificial reserve asset for member countries, representing the resources available to each member in the event it were to draw upon IMF funds. The fund of SDRs would represent currency credits among central banks and would aid a country in the management of temporary balance of payments problems. The value of the SDR was originally calculated as the average of 16 different world currencies but was later reduced to five major currencies.

The International Bank for Reconstruction and Development

The third and final part of the Bretton Woods Agreement was the formation of the **International Bank for Reconstruction and Development,** or World Bank. As opposed to the other two elements, which were focused on exchange rate stabilization, the World Bank was intended for reconstruction and development. Although initially focused on lending for the reconstruction of the war-torn member countries, the World Bank quickly found its focus shifting toward the developing countries of Africa, Asia, the Middle East, and South America.

Even in the early stages of the Bretton Woods negotiations, the World Bank was considered the most politically acceptable portion of the three-part agreement. As noted by *Business Week* in July 1944, "the process of lending money is a fairly simple operation. Congress and the country find it easier to understand than currency stabilization. Hence, the bank might get approval as a rehabilitation measure when the currency plan would be smothered in economic debate."[8]

The Experience under Bretton Woods, 1946–1971

The best indication of the success or failure of the Bretton Woods Agreement is the flat line in Figure 4.1 between 1949 and 1967. Although this is the U.S. dollar–British pound exchange rate only, the stability of the rate and the length of time of such stability is unparalleled before or after Bretton Woods. The U.S. economy was the foundation for the system. The fact that the U.S. economy had survived the war physically unscathed allowed the United States to emerge in the postwar world as the dominant economic power.

The 1950s were characterized by a dollar shortage on world markets as the United States ran balance of payments surpluses, primarily as a result of the strength of U.S. exports, as opposed to predicted deficits. As countries struggled to obtain the U.S. dollars needed for their currency reserves, the balances on trade and capital accounts slowly shifted as the European and Japanese economies recuperated from the devastation of World War II.

By the late 1960s, the adjustable peg exchange rate system was showing signs of stress. As the United States continued to run larger and larger balance of payments deficits, many countries were being forced to intervene to preserve fixed parities. They bought dollars to keep the dollar from falling and their own currencies from rising. But imbalances on world currency markets persisted, and the fixed parities of member nations started changing at an alarming rate: on November 19, 1967, the British pound sterling was devalued 14.3 percent; on August 8, 1969, the French franc was devalued 11.1 percent; on October 24, 1969, the West German mark was revalued 9.3 percent. Canada simply allowed the Canadian dollar to float on May 31, 1970, with no specific plans to return to a fixed parity. By May 1971, the system was in turmoil. The major European currency exchanges closed the week of May 5, 1971. The German mark and Dutch guilder were floated and revalued, the Swiss franc was revalued 7.1 percent, and even the Austrian shilling was revalued 5.05 percent against the dollar.

The continued defense of the dollar left central banks around the world with massive quantities of U.S. dollars. These countries, knowing that the dollars they held were in fact convertible into gold with the U.S. Treasury, attempted to hold back demanding gold in exchange. The central banks knew that if they demanded gold in exchange for the paper balances they held it could send the international monetary system into a tailspin. It became painfully clear in 1971 that the U.S. dollar was overvalued and that devaluation of the dollar versus gold was inevitable. More and more central banks began presenting U.S. dollar balances to the U.S. Treasury for conversion to gold. The United States allowed the gold to flow, and it flowed out of the Treasury coffers at an alarming rate.

Collapse and Transition, 1971–1973

On August 15, 1971, President Richard M. Nixon announced that "I have instructed [Treasury] Secretary [John B.] Connally to suspend temporarily the convertibility of the dollar into gold or other assets." With this simple statement, President Nixon effectively ended the fixed exchange rates established at Bretton Woods, New Hampshire, more than 25 years earlier.

The closing of the "gold window" by President Nixon was in fact not a major surprise to world currency markets. The events of the previous months and years had foretold the need for the dollar to fall. The real question was what would come next? What would the international monetary system look like now? In September 1970, almost a full year previous, the International Monetary Fund had completed an in-depth study of the possibility that the world monetary system would move to a full and permanent floating rate basis. The report had been met with a deafening silence.

In the weeks and months following the August announcement, world currency markets devalued the dollar, although the United States had only ended gold convertibility, not officially declared the dollar's value to be less. The **Group of Ten** finance ministers met at the Smithsonian Institution in Washington, D.C., in December 1971 to patch the faltering system.[9] The resulting **Smithsonian Agreement** attempted to preserve the fixed parities without gold convertibility with three principal actions. First, the U.S. dollar was officially devalued to $38 an ounce of gold (although this was on paper only). Second, other major Group of Ten currencies were revalued versus the dollar in varying percentages. And third, the percentage by which a currency would be allowed to deviate from its fixed parity rate was expanded to 2.25 percent, a sizable increase from the previous 1 percent.

Gold flowed out of the U.S. Treasury coffers in 1970 when international central banks converted their U.S.dollar balances to gold.

Source: Courtesy of the Federal Reserve Bank

Without convertibility of one of the member currencies to gold, the system was doomed from the start. Currencies continually surpassed their allotted plus-2.25 percent versus the dollar, so that by mid-1972, the central banks simply gave up. The British pound was floated in June 1972, the Swiss franc in January 1973. On February 12, 1973, the U.S. dollar was once again officially devalued versus gold, this time to $42.22 per ounce. After the system ground to a complete halt in March 1973, when major currency markets were closed for more than two weeks, most major currencies were simply allowed to float. The last vestiges of fixed rates sank with this final float.

In January 1976, the members of the Group of Ten met in Jamaica to formalize the new floating system. The **Jamaica Agreement** freed countries to float their currencies "legally," managing their currencies' values through various forms of intervention if they deemed it appropriate. Gold was officially demonetized as a reserve asset. This meant that the original gold quotas used in the financing of the International Monetary Fund were returned to members. The resources of the IMF itself, however, were increased to provide additional aid to countries needing assistance in the management of their balance of payments. The IMF, an original institution of the Bretton Woods Agreement, was not to die with the agreement. In fact, the IMF's role in the international monetary system would only grow over the coming decade.

FLOATING EXCHANGE RATES, 1973–PRESENT

A floating exchange rate system poses many new and different problems for participants. The biggest is the most obvious: the lack of certainty as to at what rate currencies will be exchanged a year, a month, or a day from now. However, firms worldwide have learned relatively quickly to live and deal with these price-risk issues. A larger crisis in the eyes of many major countries is that floating exchange rates do not allow the same degree of economic policy isolation that they previously enjoyed.

Under the previous fixed exchange rate regime, governments could conduct relatively independent monetary policy. The central bank of a country would normally increase the country's money supply at rates consistent with domestic economic policy goals. If interest rates rose or fell, although they might attract capital into or cause it to flow out of the country, government intervention in the foreign exchange markets could offset negative exchange rate effects. Governments enjoyed this degree of independence; the ability to self-determine domestic economic policy is one of the ways a country might define sovereignty. Floating exchange rates changed all of that. A country's domestic economic policies now translated into immediate impacts on its external relations, its currency's exchange value. There is no better example of this than the events in the United States beginning in 1979.

The Rise of the Dollar, 1980–1985

The United States suffered increasing rates of inflation throughout the 1970s. By 1979, the annual rate of inflation was approaching 12 percent, and the U.S. economy was continuing to suffer both inflation and stagnant economic growth. Paul Volker, the newly named chairman of the U.S. Federal Reserve system, implemented a strict new monetary policy in the late summer of 1979.[10] The policy was intended to end, once and for all, the inflationary expectations imbedded in the U.S. economy. Volker instituted a tight monetary growth rule. This meant the Federal Reserve would increase the money supply of the United States at a steady, but slow rate, regardless of economic conditions. Interest rates would, therefore, not be the focus of monetary policy and within weeks interest rates in the United States rose precipitously. Over the following years the United States suffered a modest recession (1980) and a severe recession (1981–1982). Inflation was purged slowly from the U.S. economy, but at the cost of increased unemployment and slow economic growth.

The eventual rebound of the U.S. economy in 1983 and 1984 was also characterized by a rapidly rising dollar. The relatively rapid economic growth of the United States compared to other industrial countries, the falling rate of inflation, the still extremely high real rates of interest available in the United States, and the role of the country as a "safe haven" in a world of increasing risk all contributed to the rise of the dollar. Depending on which currencies are used for measurement, the dollar rose roughly 45 percent against currencies of other major industrial countries between the spring of 1980 and early 1985. As illustrated in Figure 4.2, the rate of the dollar's rise was matched by the speed of its fall.

Although the dollar rose as a result of many forces, many of which were signs of relative economic health, the degree of the dollar's rise was not healthy for anyone inside or out of the United States. The strong dollar resulted in extreme U.S. purchasing power abroad, which led to rising import bills, while U.S. exports languished. American product prices were increasingly uncompetitive on world markets as a result of the dollar. Before you could buy an American product, you had to buy a dollar. And dollars were very expensive.

The single most powerful argument against freely floating exchange rates has always been the uncertainty it introduces into international commerce. Although the dollar had floated relatively freely throughout the 1970s, the volatility of its movements had not been an insurmountable problem for firms or governments. The first half of the 1980s, however, confronted policymakers around the world with the very thing they had always feared: massive exchange rate movement over a very short period of time. Someone needed to do something.

FIGURE 4.2
The U.S. Dollar under Floating Rates

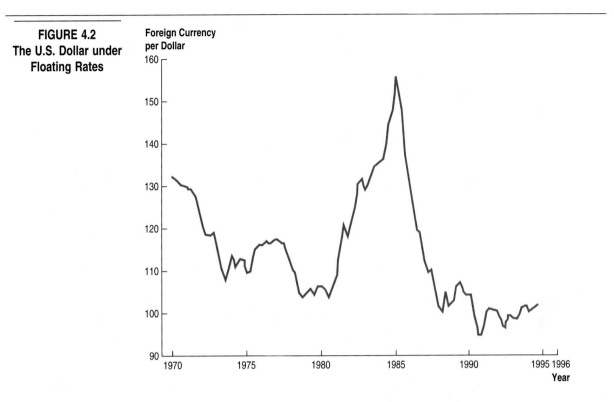

Intervention in the 1980s: Expectations and Coordination

The intervention of a government in a foreign exchange market has traditionally referred to the actual buying and selling of the country's own currency on the open market. If the magnitude of government sales or purchases relative to the total size of the market at the time of the trades is substantial, the government can literally alter the exchange rate on its own. However, while the world's currency markets grew in size during the 1960s, 1970s, and into the 1980s, the amount of official reserves (major currencies and gold) held by governments did not. It therefore became increasingly difficult for an individual government to intervene successfully.

A government attempt to move its currency in the opposite direction of its current trend is termed "leaning into the wind," while an attempt to accelerate or perpetuate the current trend is termed "leaning with the wind." Leaning into the wind, as it implies, is very difficult to do successfully. When major industrial countries attempted to move their own exchange rates, they found their efforts increasingly futile and quite expensive.

By the mid-1980s, it was clear that major world currencies such as the U.S. dollar, the German mark, or the Japanese yen could only be managed by the coordination of policies among the industrial countries. Successful policy would also include much more than simply direct intervention. Coordination also would have to include the monetary and interest rate policies of the individual countries, as well as general economic beliefs of the countries themselves. It became necessary to act on the factors causing currency movements. Intervention through simply buying and selling, acting as part of the market, was no longer enough.

Governments realized that one of their most powerful tools was their ability to influence the expectations of the market. Currency traders, international speculators, and investors all are moving the world's capital into currencies and assets that they expect to yield relatively higher returns. Therefore, government economic policies with respect to monetary policy, anti-inflationary measures, stimulus measures, and so forth alter the actual yields that these investors pursue. If a government can alter what investors believe, it may successfully influence the supply and demand forces for its currency—in theory.

The countries meeting at the Plaza Hotel in New York in 1985 were well aware of the inability of any individual country to "talk the dollar down," so they proposed to do it as a group.

The Plaza Agreement, September 1985

Although the U.S. dollar peaked in its rise against most currencies in February 1985, it was September before the **Group of Five,** or G5 countries (United States, Japan, West Germany, United Kingdom, France), could meet to discuss the issue. Meeting at the Plaza Hotel in New York, the members convened to discuss the recent declines in the dollar, to reach some consensus on to where they might like the dollar to fall, and to decide what actions they might take to move the dollar. The rapidly deteriorating U.S. trade balance had caused a surge of protectionist sentiment in the United States. This renewed call for protection from imports—imports from Japan and Germany—prompted the meeting to aid in the dollar's fall to competitiveness.

The meeting of the G5 on Sunday, September 22, 1985, was a complex one. Although preliminary and background studies had been circulated before the meeting, there was little agreement going in. After all was said and done, the communiqué issued stated that "some further orderly appreciation of the main non-dollar currencies is desirable." The message to the world's financial markets was clear: The G5 countries wanted the dollar to fall, and they intended to work cooperatively toward that end. What the communiqué of the **Plaza Agreement** did not state was what measures would actually be taken or how far the dollar was intended to fall versus the Japanese yen and German mark.[11] In fact, after the finance ministers returned home, continuing statements and actions indicated little real action. It was generally concluded that the countries other than the United States needed to stimulate their own economies (and possibly raise their interest rates relative to dollar rates), and the United States in turn needed to work toward lowering interest rates through concerted efforts to reduce the ballooning U.S. government budget deficit. Although it is difficult to find true coordination of the policies following the Plaza meeting, the dollar did fall considerably over the following 18 months.

The Louvre Accord, February 1987

By February 1987 the dollar was thought to have fallen far enough. A meeting of the **Group of Seven,** or G7, was held February 21 and 22 at the Louvre Museum in Paris to consider the immediate prospects of the international monetary system.[12] The U.S. representative, Treasury Secretary James Baker, proposed the establishment of **reference zones,** in which exchange rates would be allowed to fluctuate over a specified range. If the dollar, mark, and yen were to move out of these ranges, coordinated intervention and macroeconomic policies would be utilized to push them back in line.

The response to Secretary Baker's proposal was noncommittal. West Germany's finance minister, Gerhard Stoltenberg, was interested only in short-term agreements on desirable currency values. Germany was not interested in any longer-term commitments on coordinated intervention or policies. Japanese Finance Minister Kiichi Miyazawa, when asked about reference zones, responded only that "the word is unfamiliar to me." The results of the Louvre meeting were obviously weak, with the concluding communiqué stating that the dollar's present level against the Japanese yen and German mark was "about right." There was also an informal agreement, the details of which were not made public, that coordinated intervention (buying and selling) would be forthcoming if the dollar were to fall significantly further. After all, the Louvre meetings were intended to put a floor under the dollar, to stop its precipitous fall.

Less than a month later, the dollar was indeed falling further. By the end of March 1987, the U.S. dollar was hitting record lows against the Japanese yen (approximately ¥148/$). Coordinated intervention by all major central banks did succeed in stabilizing the dollar's value over the next few months. Although the degree of coordinated policy was relatively short-lived, the events following the **Louvre Accord** demonstrated that coordinated policy among industrial countries could gain some degree of success in managing exchange rates. The real question was whether domestically oriented macroeconomic policies (such as government spending, taxation, monetary policy) would be subservient to international policies in controlling exchange rates.

Endaka

Not all major currencies experienced the fluctuations that the U.S. dollar did during the 1980s. The Japanese yen, as illustrated in Figure 4.3, saw only momentary pauses in its continual appreciation in value versus the dollar over the past two decades. Although the dollar did rise dramatically against all major European currencies between 1980 and 1985, it gained relatively little over this same period against the yen. Yet, the dollar fell like a rock against the yen after February 1985. As illustrated in Figure 4.3, the dollar fell in value from ¥250/$ to ¥125/$ in a two-year period, termed **Endaka** in Japan.

There are many different reasons given for the astounding rise in the Japanese yen in the middle to late 1980s. The continued rapid growth of the Japanese economy, the continuing doubts regarding the prospects for growth in the American and European economies, the deregulation of the Japanese financial markets, and the rapid growth in Japanese land values and share prices all are considered to have contributed to the rapidly growing demand for Japanese yen on world currency markets. The yen resumed its appreciation against the dollar in 1994 and 1995, hovering just above ¥80/$ throughout 1995.

FIXED AND FLOATING CURRENCIES

The exchange rate regimes in use around the world today cover the full spectrum from rigidly fixed to freely floating. The statement that we live in a world of floating exchange rates is, however, a misrepresentation of the world currency markets in general.

Table 4.3 summarizes world currency arrangements as of September 30, 1994, as categorized by the International Monetary Fund. All currencies listed are first classified in general categories of "currency pegged to," "flexibility limited in terms of a single currency or group of currencies," and "more flexible." The results are quite striking. Of the 177 currencies listed, 23 were pegged to the U.S. dollar, 14 were pegged to the French franc, and 37 currencies were pegged to another currency or a currency composite of their choosing (an index). The European Monetary System (EMS), an exchange rate system composed of nine countries that

FIGURE 4.3
Endaka: The Rise of the
Japanese Yen

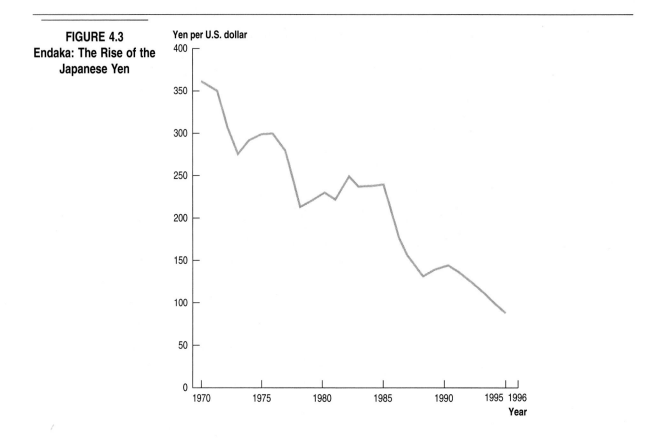

currently are members of the European Union, was classified by the IMF as a "cooperative agreement." There were 31 countries whose currencies were "managed floating" and 57 that were classified as truly "independently floating."

In the following section we provide a sample of the different types of currency regimes that are operating in the world today. The CFA franc zone, the Argentine peso, and the European Monetary System make up just a sample of the way that currencies are valued and managed in the world today; they demonstrate how countries "make money out of money."

The CFA Franc Zone

Although it is one of the least-known exchange rate systems, the Communaute Financiere Africaine (CFA) is one of the oldest and most successful. This group of 14 African nations (Benin, Burkina Faso, Cameroon, Central African Republic, Chad, Comoros, Congo, Cote d'Ivoire, Equatorial Guinea, Gabon, Mali, Niger, Senegal, and Togo), 13 of which are former French colonies, maintained its common currency at a fixed rate with the French franc from 1948 until 1993. In 1993, the CFA franc was devalued by a massive 50 percent, one of the most radical currency write-downs observed in modern history. The story of the economic health of these countries illustrates the negative and the positive of fixed exchange rate systems.

For more than 40 years, the fixed CFA franc provided a strong measure of stability to the economies of these central African nations. Fixed exchange rates provide stable prices for international trade and commerce, and also serve to restrain governments from following overly expansive economic policies that may lead to in-

TABLE 4.3   **Exchange Rate Arrangements as of September 30, 1994[1]**

Currency Pegged To:				Flexibility Limited in Terms of a Single Currency or Group of Currencies				More Flexible	
U.S. Dollar	French Franc	Other Currency	SDR	Other Composite[2]	Single Currency[3]	Cooperative Arrangements[4]	Adjusted According to a Set of Indicators[5]	Other Managed Floating	Independently Floating
Antigua & Barbuda	Benin	Bhutan (Indian rupee)	Libya	Algeria	Bahrain	Belgium	Chile	Angola	Afghanistan, Islamic State of
Argentina	Burkina Faso	Estonia	Myanmar	Austria	Qatar	Denmark	Nicaragua	Belarus	Albania
Bahamas	Cameroon	(deutsche-	Rwanda	Bangladesh	Saudi Arabia	France		Cambodia	Armenia
Barbados	C. African Rep.	mark)	Seychelles	Botswana	United Arab	Germany		China, P.R.	Australia
Belize	Chad	Kiribati		Burundi	Emirates	Ireland		Colombia	Azerbaijan
Djibouti	Comoros	(Australian		Cape Verde		Luxembourg		Ecuador	Bolivia
Dominica	Congo	dollar)		Cyprus		Netherlands		Egypt	Brazil
Grenada	Côte d'Ivoire	Lesotho		Czech Republic		Portugal		Greece	Bulgaria
Iraq	Equatorial	(South African		Fiji		Spain		Guinea	Canada
Liberia	Guinea	rand)		Hungary				Guinea-Bissau	Costa Rica
Lithuania	Gabon	Namibia		Iceland				Honduras	Croatia
Marshall	Mali	(South African		Jordan				Indonesia	Dominican Rep.
Islands	Niger	rand)		Kuwait				Israel	El Salvador
Micronesia,	Senegal	San Marino		Malta				Korea	Ethiopia
Fed. States of	Togo	(Italian lira)		Mauritania				Lao P.D. Rep.	Finland
Nigeria		Swaziland		Mauritius				Malaysia	Gambia, The
Oman		(South African		Morocco				Maldives	Georgia
Panama		rand)		Nepal				Mexico	Ghana
St. Kitts &		Tajikistan,		Papua New				Pakistan	Guatemala
Nevis		Rep. of		Guinea				Poland	Guyana
St. Lucia		(Russian		Slovak				Sao Tome &	Haiti
St. Vincent and		ruble)		Republic				Principe	India
the				Solomon				Singapore	Iran, I. R. of
Grenadines				Islands				Slovenia	Italy
Syrian Arab				Thailand				Somalia	Jamaica
Rep.				Tonga				Sri Lanka	Japan
Turkmenistan				Vanuatu				Sudan	Kazakhstan
Venezuela				Western				Suriname	Kenya
Yemen,				Samoa				Tunisia	Kyrgyz Rep.
Republic of								Turkey	Latvia
								Uruguay	Lebanon
								Viet Nam	Macedonia, FYR of
									Madagascar
									Malawi
									Moldova
									Mongolia
									Mozambique
									New Zealand
									Norway
									Paraguay
									Peru
									Philippines
									Romania
									Russia
									Sierra Leone
									South Africa
									Sweden
									Switzerland
									Tanzania
									Trinidad and Tobago
									Uganda
									Ukraine
									United Kingdom
									United States
									Zaire
									Zambia
									Zimbabwe

TABLE 4.3 (Cont.)   **Exchange Rate Arrangements as of September 30, 1994[1]**

Classification Status[1]	1988	1989	1990	1991	1992 QI	1992 QII	1992 QIII	1992 QIV	1993 QI	1993 QII	1993 QIII	1993 QIV	1994 QI	1994 QII	1994 QIII
Currency pegged to															
U.S. dollar	36	32	25	24	23	24	26	24	23	20	20	21	24	23	23
French franc	14	14	14	14	14	14	14	14	14	14	14	14	14	14	14
Russian ruble	—	—	—	—	—	—	5	6	7	7	5	—	—	—	—[6]
Other currency	5	5	5	4	4	5	6	6	6	6	7	8	8	8	8
SDR	7	7	6	6	6	5	5	5	4	4	4	4	4	4	4
Other currency composite	31	35	35	33	32	32	31	29	27	27	26	26	25	25	25
Flexibility limited vis-à-vis															
a single currency	4	4	4	4	4	4	4	4	4	4	4	4	4	4	4
Cooperative arrangements	8	9	9	10	10	10	11	9	9	9	9	9	9	9	9
Adjusted according to a															
set of indicators	5	5	3	5	5	4	4	3	4	4	4	4	3	2	2
Managed floating	22	21	23	27	25	23	22	23	21	27	27	29	29	31	31
Independently floating	17	20	25	29	33	36	41	44	48	49	52	56	55	57	57
Total[7]	151	152	154	156	156	158	167	167	167	171	172	175	175	177	177

[1]For members with dual or multiple exchange markets, the arrangement shown is that in the major market.
[2]Comprises currencies which are pegged to various "baskets" of currencies of the members' own choice, as distinct from the SDR basket.
[3]Exchange rates of all currencies have shown limited flexibility in terms of the U.S. dollar.
[4]Refers to the cooperative arrangement maintained under the European Monetary System.
[5]Includes exchange arrangements under which the exchange rate is adjusted at relatively frequent intervals, on the basis of indicators determined by the respective member countries.
[6]Starting May 24, 1994, the Azerbaijan authorities ceased to peg the manat to the Russian ruble and the exchange arrangement was reclassified to "independently floating."
[7]Excluding the following two countries which as of end-June 1994 have not yet formally notified the Fund of their exchange rate arrangements: Eritrea and Uzbekistan.

Source: International Financial Statistics, International Monetary Fund, December 1994, p. 8.

flation. The maintenance of the fixed rate regime among neighboring countries fostered internal trade, trade that most likely would have been constantly distorted or disrupted if conducted with 14 different currencies in varying degrees of independent movement.

The CFA franc was not an island alone, however, and the currencies of non-member countries in the region such as Ghana and Nigeria—competitors in export markets for commodities such as coffee and cocoa—had continually weakened over the previous decade against major western European and other industrial nations' currencies. Such competitors were winning the export wars through cheaper prices, and the members of the CFA zone experienced continual declines in export revenues and falling export market shares. The CFA franc had indeed become overvalued against the major world currencies, as well as the currencies of the African continent.

The export competitiveness of the Communaute returned after the 50 percent devaluation of 1993. Much in the same way as American manufacturers found themselves suddenly more cost competitive following the rise of the Japanese yen in the late 1980s and mid-1990s, the members of the CFA zone of Central Africa have now found that they, too, can once again compete in the sale of their products.

The Argentine Peso (or Dollar?)

Argentina has constructed its own currency regime, a *currency-board system,* which is much more rigid than a simple fixed exchange rate system such as the CFA. The

Argentine peso is fixed at one peso per one U.S. dollar, a fixed rate. Yet this alone has not been sufficient to preserve the stability of many currencies worldwide, and the Argentines know this better than most (having suffered inflation rates rising above 100 percent per annum in the recent past). So, under the currency-board system, the government of Argentina cannot issue an additional peso unless the government gains an additional dollar (or other hard currency equivalent) in foreign reserves.

Argentina's system is a more extreme form of the Bretton Woods system described previously, in which the rules of the currency system serve to restrain the government's ability to "print money" and inflate the economy. One of the major benefits of this is the creation of confidence among both domestic and international investors. They trust in the system, its rules, and its transparency; they are not reliant on the good faith of the governing political party of the time.

One of the unusual attributes of the Argentina currency-board system is the ability of Argentines to hold their money in bank accounts in either pesos or dollars (this is essentially unheard of in most countries today). Any failure in the confidence of the populace in the value of the peso results in a sudden and massive shift from peso holdings to dollar holdings. In January 1995, the Argentine government held $17.8 billion in currency reserves, more than enough to exchange a dollar for every single peso outstanding—an amount that stood at $16.2 billion!

The European Monetary System

In the week following the suspension of dollar convertibility to gold in 1971, the finance ministers of a number of the major countries of western Europe discussed how they might maintain the fixed parities of their currencies independently of the U.S. dollar. By April 1972, they had concluded an agreement that was termed the "snake within the tunnel." The member countries agreed to fix parity rates between currencies with allowable trading bands of 2.25 percent variance. As a group they would allow themselves to vary by 4.5 percent versus the U.S. dollar. Although the effort was well intentioned, the various pressures and crises that rocked international economic order in the 1970s, such as the OPEC price shock of 1974, resulted in a relatively short life for the "snake."

In 1979 a much more formalized structure was put in place among many of the major members of the European Community. The **European Monetary System (EMS)** officially began operation in March 1979 and once again established a grid of fixed parity rates among member currencies. The EMS was a much more elaborate system for the management of exchange rates than its predecessor "snake." The EMS consisted of three different components that would work in concert to preserve fixed parities (also termed central rates).

First, all countries that were committing their currencies and their efforts to the preservation of fixed exchange rates entered the **Exchange-Rate Mechanism (ERM).** Although all the currencies of the countries of the European Union would be used in the calculation of important indices for management purposes, several countries chose not to be ERM participants. Participation meant the country would commit itself to the preservation of the agreed-upon grid of fixed rates, and several of the member countries were not yet willing to do so. Participation in the ERM technically required that countries accept bilateral responsibility of maintaining the fixed rates.

The second element of the European Monetary System was the actual grid of bilateral exchange rates with their specified band limits. As under the Smithsonian Agreement and the former snake, member currencies were allowed to deviate

FIGURE 4.4
The Composition of the
European Currency Unit

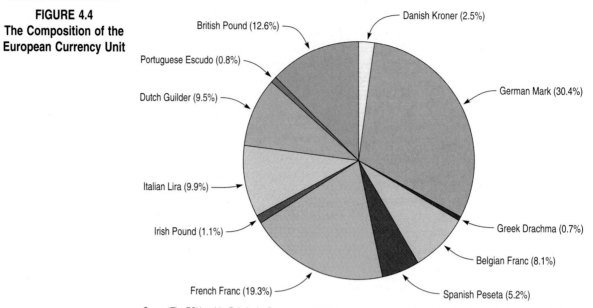

Source: "The ECU and Its Role in the Process towards Monetary Union," *European Economy*, No. 48, September 1991, p. 125.

± 2.25 percent from their parity rate. Some currencies, however, such as the Italian lira, were originally allowed larger bands (± 10 percent variance) due to their more characteristic volatility.

The third and final element of the European Monetary System was the creation of the European Currency Unit (ECU). As illustrated in Figure 4.4, the ECU is a weighted average index of the currencies that are part of the EMS. Each currency is weighted by a value reflecting the relative size of that country's trade and gross domestic product. This allows each currency to be defined in units per ECU. The ECU can also serve as a method of value accounting among EMS members without showing preference by using one individual currency.

Events and Performance of the EMS   The need for fixed exchange rates within Europe is clear. The countries of western Europe trade among themselves to a degree approaching interstate commerce in the United States. It is therefore critical to the economies and businesses of Europe that exchange rates be as stable as possible. Although it has its critics, the EMS generally has been successful in providing exchange rate stability.

The EMS, however, has recently experienced several setbacks. A number of the political and economic forces that have driven European economies in the past decade have started to put new and exceptional pressures on the EMS.

- **Deutschemark dominance.** Most EMS realignments have resulted in the revaluation of the German mark and the devaluation of most other member currencies. The rapid growth of German industry and trade has resulted in the deutschemark growing in its proportion of world currency trading. The EMS is often now referred to as the "DMZ" or "DM Zone."

- **EMS membership expansion.** Although not formally a part of the European Union, the EMS is a parallel organization in terms of membership. As the EU has expanded to include Greece (1981) and Portugal and Spain

(1986), so has the EMS. The British pound has long been included in the calculation of the ECU, but it was not until the autumn of 1990 that Great Britain joined the ERM. Although all countries are not ERM participants, the expansion of more countries, economies, and their currencies into the EMS has introduced considerable pressure on the system.

- **German reunification.** The merging of West Germany and East Germany in 1989 increased inflationary and budgetary pressures in Germany significantly. The West German currency, the deutschemark, was exchanged for the East German currency, the ostmark, at fixed rates that were artificially high for the ostmark. This caused major monetary policy actions that threatened the internal stability of the EMS as the dominance of the deutschemark within the EMS was only seen to increase.

- **Maastricht and a single currency for Europe.** The continuing movements toward European integration (the **Maastricht Treaty**) have resulted in a specific time schedule for the eventual creation of a single currency to replace the individual currencies of the EMS/EU members.

The Maastricht Treaty

In an attempt to maintain the momentum of European integration, the members of the European Union in December 1991 concluded the Maastricht Treaty. The treaty, besides laying out long-term goals of harmonized social and welfare policies in the Union, specified a timetable for the adoption of a single currency to replace all individual currencies. This was a very ambitious move. The Maastricht Treaty called for the integration and coordination of economic and monetary policy so that few financial differences would exist by the time of currency unification in 1997. For a single currency to work, there could be only one monetary policy across all countries. Otherwise, different monetary policies would lead to different interest rates. Differences in interest rates often lead to large capital flows. In fact, not even Germany would at the time of the signing of the treaty have met all the required criteria for economic performance.

The first major hurdle for the single currency was the acceptance of the treaty. Denmark had been successful in gaining the right to conduct a popular vote of its citizens to determine whether the degree of integration described by Maastricht was indeed desirable. In May 1992, the Danes voted "nej" (no). The Irish and French immediately scheduled popular votes in their own countries. The Irish vote resulted in a relatively strong show of support, while the French vote conducted on September 20 was an extremely narrow yes vote. The French result was immediately dubbed "le petit oui."

Recent Crises in the EMS

The inflationary pressures of absorbing, employing, and redeveloping the former East Germany led the German central bank, the Bundesbank, to tighten monetary policy in 1992. As interest rates rose in Germany over the summer of 1992, capital continued to flow out of other major European currencies into deutschemarks. Several EMS currencies experienced pressure to the point they were hitting their allowed bands versus the deutschemark. Although the Bundesbank was well aware of its impact on the exchange markets, its primary responsibility was preserving price stability in Germany—not exchange rate stability.

Even after raising interest rates several times in attempts to defend their currencies (equivalent to trying to "bribe" capital to stay at home), both Italy and Great Britain withdrew their currencies from the ERM the week of September 14, 1992. The Spanish peseta and Portuguese escudo were devalued officially at the same time,

Total External Debt by Country

(millions of United States dollars)

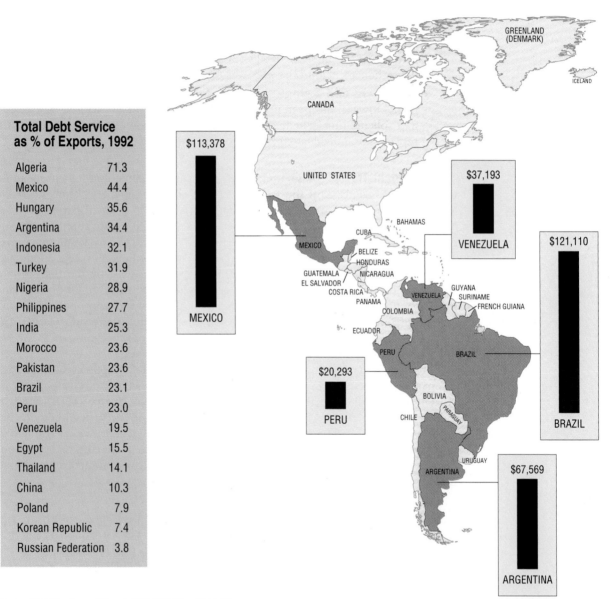

Total Debt Service as % of Exports, 1992	
Algeria	71.3
Mexico	44.4
Hungary	35.6
Argentina	34.4
Indonesia	32.1
Turkey	31.9
Nigeria	28.9
Philippines	27.7
India	25.3
Morocco	23.6
Pakistan	23.6
Brazil	23.1
Peru	23.0
Venezuela	19.5
Egypt	15.5
Thailand	14.1
China	10.3
Poland	7.9
Korean Republic	7.4
Russian Federation	3.8

MEXICO $113,378

VENEZUELA $37,193

BRAZIL $121,110

PERU $20,293

ARGENTINA $67,569

Source: *World Development Report, 1994, Table 20 and Table 23.*

Note: *External debt* includes all debt provided by both public and private lenders to all public and private borrowers in the subject country.

Total debt service as a % of exports is a relative measure of the ability of a country to earn the hard currency from exports necessary to make total principal and interest payments due on external debt in that year. As the percentage of exports needed for debt service rises, the greater the burden debt service is of the country's foreign currency earnings, and the riskier the country is considered as a borrower on international financial markets.

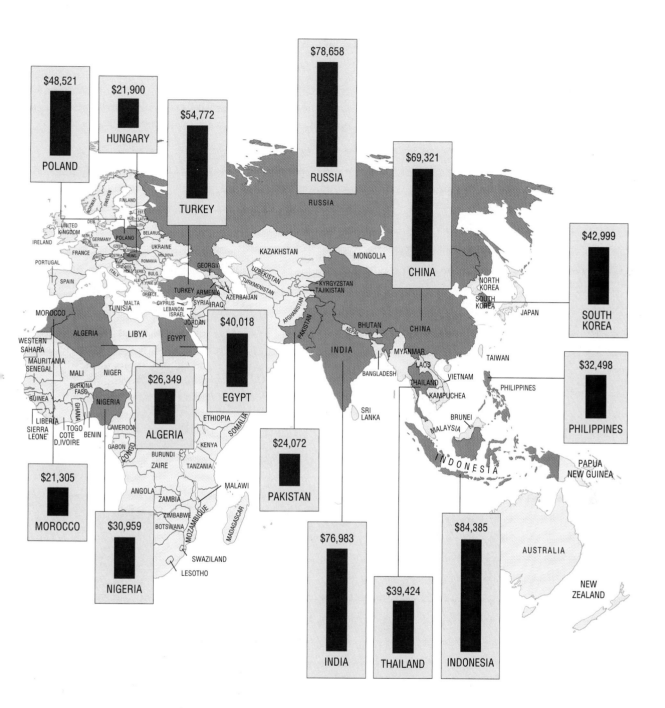

although remaining within the ERM. This was a serious setback to the European Union's plans for a single currency.

In 1993, the problems only worsened. In the summer of 1993, a number of non-EMS currencies were hit with speculative attacks (Norway, Sweden, and Finland). Finally, on July 31, the French monetary authorities were unable to defend the franc any longer. The EMS, knowing that the devaluation of the franc was probably only a temporary solution, made a drastic change in the entire system: all currencies would be allowed to vary by 15 percent, not 2.25 percent (the Netherlands was the sole exception, maintaining the 2.25 percent range).

The goal of a single currency for Europe appears—at least for the moment—to be a distant dream. As the following section describes, the fundamental financial forces that drive exchange rate movements are known, but the inherent conflict between domestic economic goals and international economic goals continues to plague the world's monetary system.

EXCHANGE RATES, INTEREST RATES, AND ECONOMIC POLICY

The international monetary system of the 1990s is a significantly different one than any of the past. The capital markets of major industrialized countries are now linked so closely that significant economic or financial events that used to be isolated can now affect capital flows worldwide in minutes. For those who believe in the efficiency of unregulated markets, the trend toward more open financial markets worldwide is a good one. But open markets and freely flowing markets also come at a cost. The cost is the ability of a country to define and determine its domestic economic and monetary policies independently of world markets. An additional factor is that many present and former government policymakers do not always approve of what the markets do or think.

As noted in the previous section, currencies respond to interest rate movements. Assuming all markets and currencies are relatively stable and secure, a country that can lower its domestic interest rates to encourage growth may at the same time find its currency under downward pressure as capital flows out in search of higher interest. This poses a serious problem for the country. If it believes in open and free markets, government policymakers do not want to restrict capital flows. Yet, most countries prefer stable exchange rates. So what is the government to do?

This is the problem now confronting the members of the European Union. Simply put, internal goals and external goals are in direct conflict. The conflict arises from the following three financial policies:

1. **Fixed Exchange Rates.** A fixed exchange rate is best for the conduct of international commerce. The stability it provides in pricing helps a country's importers and exporters to manage sourcing and sales without dealing with large currency risks.

2. **Freedom of Capital Flows.** Not only within the European Union, but throughout the world, countries are deregulating financial markets. Capital flows among countries and major financial markets are increasing. As capital moves more freely, it can move in larger quantities and more quickly to take advantage of higher returns (such as higher interest rates). If economic and monetary policies are roughly the same across countries, there is little reason to exchange currency in an attempt to escape inflation or seek out higher interest rates.

3. **Independent Monetary Policies.** Every country wants to conduct its own economic policy. This means the ability to utilize fiscal policy measures (government spending and taxation) and monetary policy measures

(money supply growth, interest rate restricting or **pegging**) to manage domestic economic needs.

The result is that a country can have two of these, but not all three. If capital is allowed to move freely and monetary policy is used for domestic goals regardless of how it compares to other economies, fixed exchange rates are difficult to achieve (or maintain in the recent EMS crisis). The authors of the Maastricht Treaty recognized this when they designed a system that would have fixed exchange rates, free capital flows, but one single monetary policy for all countries. It seems that the internal-versus-external crisis hit the system in its early stages of transition. Exchange rates were fixed, but capital flow freedom moved forward much faster than any harmonization of monetary policy.

SUMMARY

The exchange of currency is necessary for international trade and commerce. The purpose of exchange rate systems is to provide a free and liquid market for the world's currencies while providing some degree of stability and predictability to currency values. The modern history of the international monetary system has seen periods of success and failure in the accomplishments of this purpose.

The gold standard, which was in wide use during the early years of the twentieth century, was a highly restrictive system. The ability to convert currency to gold imposed restrictions on the ability of countries to run inflationary monetary policies or conduct imbalanced trade for substantial periods of time. But the gold standard was also inflexible, and many have argued that it slowed economic growth unduly by limiting the amount of money that could be put into growing economies.

The Bretton Woods Agreement signed in 1944, in anticipation of the reconstruction of the world economy after World War II, was an international monetary system in which the U.S. dollar was the centerpiece and literally "good as gold." Although it worked well for 25 years, it saw its natural decline as the world economy changed and world currency markets needed to change with it. The result, the floating exchange rate system in use today, reflects the dominance of market economies, market forces, and the growth in international commerce. Two of the most influential multilateral institutions in operation today, the International Monetary Fund and the World Bank, arose from the Bretton Woods Agreement.

Key Terms and Concepts

international monetary system	International Monetary Fund (IMF)
purchasing power parity (PPP)	fundamental disequilibrium
Law of One Price	Special Drawing Right (SDR)
gold standard	Group of Ten
par value	Smithsonian Agreement
rules of the game	Jamaica Agreement
convertibility	Group of Five
competitive devaluation	Plaza Agreement
Bretton Woods Agreement	Group of Seven
	reference zone

Louvre Accord

European Monetary
    System (EMS)

Exchange Rate
    Mechanism (ERM)

International Bank for
    Reconstruction and
    Development (World Bank)

Maastricht Treaty

pegging

Questions for Discussion

1. Why has the gold standard always been considered such a solid and dependable system?

2. Why was it so important that the U.S. dollar be convertible to gold for the Bretton Woods system to operate effectively?

3. Why did the major world currencies move from a fixed to a floating exchange rate system in the 1970s?

4. How has foreign exchange market intervention changed in the past two decades? Why is it that direct intervention no longer works?

5. Why have the currencies of the European Union countries remained relatively fixed, while the U.S. and Japanese currencies have continued to float?

6. Why is it necessary for the European Union to form a single banking system with a single monetary policy before it can adopt a single currency?

7. What caused the British pound to be withdrawn from the ERM in September 1992?

8. Why, if it is so difficult to accomplish, do countries still try to "fix" exchange rates?

Recommended Readings

"Black Wednesday: The Campaign for Sterling." *The Economist,* January 9, 1993, 52, 54.

Commission of the European Communities. "The ECU and Its Role in the Process Towards Monetary Union." *European Economy* 48 (September 1991): 121-138.

Dewey, Davis Rich. *Financial History of the United States.* 2d Edition. New York: Longmans, Green, and Company, 1903.

Driscoll, David D. *What Is the International Monetary Fund?* Washington, D.C.: External Relations Department, International Monetary Fund, November 1992.

Evans, John S. *International Finance.* Fort Worth, Tex.: Dryden Press, 1992.

Funabashi, Yuichi. *Managing the Dollar: From the Plaza to the Louvre.* Washington, D.C.: Institute of International Economics, 1988.

Morgan Guaranty. *World Financial Markets,* New York, various issues.

"The New Trade Strategy." *Business Week,* October 7, 1985, 90-93.

O'Cleireacain, Seamus. *Third World Debt and International Public Policy.* New York: Praeger, 1990.

"The Paris Pact May Not Buoy the Dollar for Long," *Business Week,* March 9, 1987, 40-41.

"Treasury and Federal Reserve Foreign Exchange Operations," *Federal Reserve Bulletin,* October 1971, 783-814.

"Rivalries Beset Monetary Pact." *Business Week,* Number 776, July 15, 1944, 15-16.

Ungerer, Horst, Jouko J. Hauvonen, Augusto Lopez-Claros, and Thomas Mayer. *The European Monetary System: Developments and Perspectives.* Washington, D.C.: International Monetary Fund, 1990.

Van Dormael, Armand. *Bretton Woods.* New York: Holmes & Meier, 1978.

The World Bank. *World Debt Tables, 1991-92.* Washington, D.C., 1992.

Notes

1. Actually there are a few exceptions. Panama has used the U.S. dollar as its currency for many years.

2. The U.S. dollar was actually stated as being officially worth $20.67 per ounce of gold from 1837 to 1914, although there were many periods in which the United States backed its money with both gold and silver and many periods in which it was very difficult to say that the paper currency was indeed redeemable for gold.

3. The student is often led in the study of historical events to believe that policies or laws or decisions were achieved so clearly or with little question or doubt. *Business Week*'s issue of July 8, 1944, in its regular "The War and Business Abroad" report led with the following statement:

   > The world is watching the monetary conference at Bretton Woods for the first clews to the way the United Nations are prepared to cooperate in shaping the peace—and the results inevitably will be disappointing.

   Although the Bretton Woods Agreement eventually worked well for more than 20 years, there was considerable debate regarding its prospects in 1944. And yes, the word was spelled "clews" and not "clues."

4. *Business Week,* July 15, 1944, 15.

5. The participants at Bretton Woods specifically wanted to avoid the devaluation problems experienced on world markets in the 1930s. The competitive devaluations that dominated that period proved disastrous to world trade and economic stability as governments continually attempted to devalue to keep exports cheaper than foreign competitors'. The point of the adjustable peg was ultimately not to have to adjust it.

6. The meetings at Bretton Woods had hardly begun when the delegation from the Soviet Union objected to its preliminary quota as being too small. Soviet delegates argued that prewar trade was not representative of the true size and strength of the Soviet economy, and the postwar era would see a much more powerful trading nation. The quotas were readjusted, with the Soviet quota rising from about $800 million to $1.2 billion.

7. The original proposal was to contribute 25 percent of its quota in gold or 10 percent of its domestic gold stock, whichever the country chose. The Soviet Union, as well as a number of other countries, opposed this. Everyone was actually quite happy to eliminate the choice and choose the 25 percent of quota approach since it generally required a significantly smaller contribution of gold.

8. "Rivalries Beset Monetary Pact," *Business Week,* July 15, 1944, 16.

9. The Group of Ten, or G-10 Countries, consists of the United States, Canada, Great Britain, France, Germany, Italy, Belgium, the Netherlands, Sweden, and Japan.

10. Paul Volker was not new to the Federal Reserve or to world currency markets. It was Paul Volker, then Under Secretary of the U.S. Treasury, who had flown to London in August 1971 to explain President Nixon's closing of the gold window to European currency authorities.

11. Yuichi Funabashi, in *Managing the Dollar: From the Plaza to the Louvre,* provides an enlightening discussion of the rounds of private negotiation regarding the level of intervention each individual G5 member would be committed to under the Plaza Agreement. Although each country is believed to have committed itself to significant intervention, it is not believed that the actual levels were ever discussed.

12. The Group of Seven is composed of the United States, Japan, Germany, France, Great Britain, Canada, and Italy. The Italian delegation withdrew from the meetings the first day, however, in protest over being excluded from a G5 (G7 less Canada and Italy) state dinner the evening before. So the meetings may actually have been classified as the G6.

CHAPTER 5

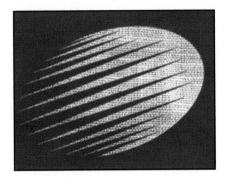

International Financial Markets

Learning Objectives

1. To understand how currencies are traded and quoted on world financial markets.

2. To examine the linkages between interest rates and exchange rates.

3. To understand the similarities and differences between domestic sources of capital and international sources of capital.

4. To examine how the needs of individual borrowers have changed the nature of the instruments traded on world financial markets in the past decade.

5. To understand how the debt crises of the 1980s and 1990s are linked to the international financial markets and exchange rates.

Who's Making the Most?

Wall Street's chief executives get the corporate perks—but not always the biggest paychecks. Consider Salomon Brothers, Inc. The Salomon Inc. unit paid Deryck C. Maughan, its chairman and chief executive officer, a 1993 pay package of $7 million amid record profit at the big investment bank, according to the firm's proxy statement. But Salomon's fattest 1993 pay package went to its foreign exchange head, people familiar with the firm said. Hans U. Hufschmid, 38, received $28 million in salary, bonus, and other compensation amid record currency-trading revenue at Salomon, the people said.

Mr. Hufschmid didn't take home the entire paycheck last year. As much as half his 1993 pay package is in the form of Salomon common stock that can't be cashed in for five years. Still, to put it in perspective, his pay rivals the $34.2 million salary cap for an entire National Football League team next season.

Source: Michael Siconolfi, "Salomon's Fattest Pay Didn't Go to CEO," *The Wall Street Journal,* March 29, 1994, p. C1.

International financial markets serve as links between the financial markets of each individual country and as independent markets outside the jurisdiction of any one country. The market for currencies is the heart of this international financial market. International trade and investment are often denominated in a foreign currency, so the purchase of the currency precedes the purchase of goods, services, or assets.

This chapter provides a detailed guide to the structure and functions of the foreign currency markets, the international money markets, and the international securities markets. All firms striving to attain or preserve competitiveness will need to work with and within these international financial markets in the 1990s.

THE MARKET FOR CURRENCIES

The price of one country's currency in terms of another country's currency is called a foreign currency exchange rate. For example, the exchange rate between the U.S. dollar (USD) and the German mark (deutschemark, or DEM) may be "1.5 marks per dollar," or simply abbreviated DEM 1.5000/USD. This is the same exchange rate as when stated USD 1.00 = DEM 1.50. Since most international business activities require at least one of the two parties to first purchase the country's currency before purchasing any good, service, or asset, a proper understanding of exchange rates and exchange rate markets is very important to the conduct of international business.

A word on symbols. As already noted, the symbols USD and DEM are often used as the symbols for the U.S. dollar and the German mark. The field of international finance suffers, however, from a lack of agreement when it comes to currency abbreviations. This chapter will use the computer symbols used by the Telerate news service for the sake of consistency (although any other set would work just as well). But as a practitioner of international finance, as with all fields, stay on your toes. Every market, every country, every firm, has its own set of symbols. For example, the symbol for the British pound sterling can be £ (the pound symbol), GBP (Great Britain pound), STG (sterling), or UKL (United Kingdom pound).

FIGURE 5.1   Exchange Rate and Cross Rate Tables

CURRENCY TRADING

EXCHANGE RATES

Friday, January 27, 1995

The New York foreign exchange selling rates below apply to trading among banks in amounts of $1 million and more, as quoted at 3 p.m. Eastern time by Bankers Trust Co., Dow Jones Telerate Inc. and other sources. Retail transactions provide fewer units of foreign currency per dollar.

Country	U.S. $ equiv. Fri.	U.S. $ equiv. Thur.	Currency per U.S. $ Fri.	Currency per U.S. $ Thur.
Argentina (Peso)	1.00	1.00	1.00	1.00
Australia (Dollar)	.7591	.7656	1.3174	1.3063
Austria (Schilling)	.09398	.09373	10.64	10.67
Bahrain (Dinar)	2.6525	2.6525	.3770	.3770
Belgium (Franc)	.03198	.03198	31.27	31.27
Brazil (Real)	1.1841326	1.1855365	.84	.84
Britain (Pound)	1.5890	1.5897	.6293	.6290
30-Day Forward	1.5885	1.5892	.6295	.6292
90-Day Forward	1.5873	1.5882	.6300	.6296
180-Day Forward	1.5855	1.5867	.6307	.6303
Canada (Dollar)	.7069	.7074	1.4146	1.4136
30-Day Forward	.7059	.7063	1.4167	1.4158
90-Day Forward	.7039	.7043	1.4207	1.4198
180-Day Forward	.7013	.7016	1.4260	1.4253
Czech. Rep. (Koruna)				
Commercial rate	.0363003	.0362674	27.5480	27.5730
Chile (Peso)	.002451	.002453	407.96	407.65
China (Renminbi)	.118506	.118502	8.4384	8.4387
Colombia (Peso)	.001168	.001165	855.80	858.25
Denmark (Krone)	.1670	.1670	5.9890	5.9880
Ecuador (Sucre)				
Floating rate	.000420	.000419	2381.52	2384.00
Finland (Markka)	.21129	.21071	4.7329	4.7459
France (Franc)	.18972	.19060	5.2710	5.2465
30-Day Forward	.18978	.19068	5.2692	5.2443
90-Day Forward	.18991	.19085	5.2658	5.2396
180-Day Forward	.19011	.19113	5.2600	5.2320
Germany (Mark)	.6600	.6590	1.5152	1.5173
30-Day Forward	.6606	.6596	1.5139	1.5160
90-Day Forward	.6619	.6610	1.5108	1.5127
180-Day Forward	.6644	.6636	1.5051	1.5068
Greece (Drachma)	.004233	.004232	236.25	236.30
Hong Kong (Dollar)	.12931	.12936	7.7335	7.7305
Hungary (Forint)	.0090096	.0090098	110.8700	110.9900
India (Rupee)	.03187	.03188	31.38	31.37
Indonesia (Rupiah)	.0004505	.0004502	2220.00	2221.00
Ireland (Punt)	1.5711	1.5712	.6365	.6365
Israel (Shekel)	.3325	.3330	3.0079	3.0031
Italy (Lira)	.0006242	.0006246	1602.00	1600.90

Country	U.S. $ equiv. Fri.	U.S. $ equiv. Thurs.	Currency per U.S. $ Fri.	Currency per U.S. $ Thurs.
Japan (Yen)	.010065	.010063	99.36	99.38
30-Day Forward	.010095	.010093	99.06	99.08
90-Day Forward	.010161	.010160	98.42	98.42
180-Day Forward	.010280	.010283	97.27	97.25
Jordan (Dinar)	1.4327	1.4327	.6980	.6980
Kuwait (Dinar)	3.3484	3.3473	.2987	.2987
Lebanon (Pound)	.000608	.000608	1643.50	1643.52
Malaysia (Ringgit)	.3912	.3909	2.5565	2.5583
Malta (Lira)	2.7510	2.7562	.3635	.3628
Mexico (Peso)				
Floating rate	.1754386	.1785714	5.7000	5.6000
Netherland (Guilder) ..	.5887	.5880	1.6987	1.7006
New Zealand (Dollar) .	.6395	.6425	1.5637	1.5565
Norway (Krone)	.1505	.1505	6.6436	6.6460
Pakistan (Rupee)	.0324	.0324	30.83	30.83
Peru (New Sol)	.4588	.4581	2.18	2.18
Philippines (Peso)	.04063	.04049	24.61	24.70
Poland (Zloty)	.41220100	.41220100	2.43	2.43
Portugal (Escudo)	.006378	.006378	156.80	156.80
Saudi Arabia (Riyal) ..	.26663	.26662	3.7506	3.7507
Singapore (Dollar)	.6889	.6883	1.4515	1.4529
Slovak Rep. (Koruna) .	.0325945	.0325945	30.6800	30.6800
South Africa (Rand)				
Commercial rate	.2824	.2827	3.5417	3.5377
Financial rate	.2469	.2439	4.0500	4.1000
South Korea (Won)	.0012668	.0012749	789.40	784.35
Spain (Peseta)	.007587	.007581	131.80	131.90
Sweden (Krona)	.1343	.1335	7.4454	7.4889
Switzerland (Franc) ...	.7848	.7840	1.2743	1.2755
30-Day Forward	.7861	.7854	1.2720	1.2733
90-Day Forward	.7891	.7884	1.2673	1.2685
180-Day Forward	.7941	.7935	1.2593	1.2602
Taiwan (Dollar)	.038033	.038078	26.29	26.26
Thailand (Baht)	.03990	.03987	25.06	25.08
Turkey (Lira)	.0000247	.0000247	40508.79	40508.79
United Arab (Dirham) .	.2723	.2723	3.6727	3.6727
Uruguay (New Peso)				
Financial	.174216	.173913	5.74	5.75
Venezuela (Bolivar) ...	.00589	.00589	169.87	169.87
SDR	1.47251	1.47247	.67911	.67913
ECU	1.24620	1.24570	....	....

Special Drawing Rights (SDR) are based on exchange rates for the U.S., German, British, French and Japanese currencies. Source: International Monetary Fund.

European Currency Unit (ECU) is based on a basket of community currencies.

z-Not quoted.

Key Currency Cross Rates   Late New York Trading Jan. 27, 1995

	Dollar	Pound	SFranc	Guilder	Peso	Yen	Lira	D-Mark	FFranc	CdnDlr
Canada	1.4148	2.2481	1.11008	.83297	.25063	.01423	.00088	.93374	.26886	....
France	5.2622	8.362	4.1288	3.0981	.93219	.05294	.00328	3.4729		3.7194
Germany	1.5152	2.4077	1.1889	.89208	.26841	.01524	.00095		.28794	1.0710
Italy	1602.0	2545.6	1256.96	943.19	283.79	16.117		1057.29	304.44	1132.3
Japan	99.40	157.95	77.991	58.522	17.609		.06205	65.602	18.889	70.26
Mexico	5.6450	8.9699	4.4292	3.3235		.05679	.00352	3.7256	1.0727	3.9900
Netherlands ..	1.6985	2.6989	1.3327		.30089	.01709	.00106	1.1210	.32277	1.2005
Switzerland ..	1.2745	2.0252		.75037	.22578	.01282	.00080	.84114	.24220	.9008
U.K.	.62933		.49378	.37052	.11148	.00633	.00039	.41534	.11959	.44482
U.S.	....	1.5890	.78462	.58875	.17715	.01006	.00062	.65998	.19003	.70681

Source: Dow Jones Telerate Inc.

Source: The Wall Street Journal, January 30, 1995, C15.

Foreign exchange traders, such as these at Republic National Bank of New York, can move millions of dollars, yen, or marks around the world with a few keystrokes on their networked computer terminals. In addition to technological advances in communications and data processing, the deregulation of international capital flows also contributes to faster, cheaper transactions in the currency markets.

Source: Courtesy of Republic National Bank of New York. Photo by William Taufic.

Exchange Rate Quotations and Terminology

The order in which the foreign exchange (FX) rate is stated is sometimes confusing to the uninitiated. For example, when the rate between the U.S. dollar and the German mark was stated above, a **direct quotation** on the German mark was used. This is simultaneously an **indirect quotation** on the U.S. dollar. The direct quote on any currency is the form when that currency is stated first; an indirect quotation refers to when the subject currency is stated second. Figure 5.1 illustrates both forms, direct and indirect quotations, for major world currencies for Friday, January 27, 1995. The daily currency quotations from *The Wall Street Journal* are the most commonly seen set of exchange rate quotations in use today.

Most of the quotations listed in Figure 5.1 are **spot rates.** A spot transaction is the exchange of currencies for immediate delivery. Although it is defined as immediate, in practice settlement actually occurs two business days following the agreed-upon exchange. The other time-related quotations listed in Figure 5.1 are the **forward rates.** Forward exchange rates are contracts that provide for two parties to exchange currencies on a future date at an agreed-upon exchange rate. Forwards are typically traded for the major volume currencies for maturities of 30, 90, 120, 180, and 360 days (from the present date). The forward, like the basic spot exchange, can be for any amount of currency. Forward contracts serve a variety of purposes, but their primary purpose is to allow a firm to lock in a future rate of exchange. This is a valuable tool in a world of continually changing exchange rates.

The quotations listed will also occasionally indicate if the rate is applicable to business trade (the commercial rate) or for financial asset purchases or sales (the financial rate). Countries that have government regulations regarding the exchange of their currency may post official rates, while the markets operating outside their jurisdiction will list a floating rate. In this case, any exchange of currency that is not under the control of its government is interpreted as a better indication of the currency's true market value.

Direct and Indirect Quotations

The Wall Street Journal quotations list the rates of exchange between major currencies, both in direct and indirect forms. The exchange rate for the German mark

FIGURE 5.2

Guide to World Currencies

The table below gives the latest available rates of exchange (rounded) against four key currencies on Friday, January 27, 1995. In some cases the rate is nominal. Market rates are the average of buying and selling rates except where they are shown to be otherwise. In some cases market rates have been calculated from those of foreign currencies to which they are tied.

		£ STG	US $	D-MARK	YEN (X 100)
Afghanistan	(Afghani)	5502.75	3456.5	2286.24	3488.05
Albania	(Lek)	159.68	100.302	66.3425	101.217
Algeria	(Dinar)	67.4054	42.34	28.005	42.7265
Andorra	(Fr Franc)	8.3554	5.2483	3.4714	5.2962
	(Sp Peseta)	209.461	131.571	87.0252	132.772
Angola	(New Kwanza)	817866.3	513735	339801	518424
Antigua	(E Carr $)	4.2903	2.6949	1.7825	2.7195
Argentina	(Peso)	1.5919	0.9999	0.6613	1.009
Armenia	(Dram)	627.000o	393.844	260.501	397.439
Aruba	(Florin)	2.8443	1.7866	1.1817	1.8029
Australia	(Aus $)	2.0880	1.3115	0.8675	1.3235
Austria	(Schilling)	16.932	10.6356	7.0347	10.7327
Azores	(Port Escudo)	248.461	156.068	103.229	157.493
Bahamas	(Bahama $)	1.5920	1	0.6614	1.0091
Bahrain	(Dinar)	0.6002	0.377	0.2493	0.3804
Balearic Is	(Sp Peseta)	209.461	131.571	87.0252	132.772
Bangladesh	(Taka)	63.3596	39.7987	26.3241	40.162
Barbados	(Barb $)	3.1960	2.0075	1.3278	2.0258
Belarus	(Rouble)	18691.3o	11740.8	7765.72	11847.9
Belgium	(Belg Fr)	49.6386	31.18	20.6234	31.4646
Belize	(B $)	3.1780	1.9962	1.3203	2.0144
Benin	(CFA Fr)	835.54	524.837	347.144	529.627
Bermuda	(Bermudian $)	1.5920	1	0.6614	1.0091
Bhutan	(Ngultrum)	49.9495	31.3753	20.7526	31.6617
Bolivia	(Boliviano)	7.5300	4.7298	3.1285	4.773
Botswana	(Pula)	4.2854	2.6918	1.7804	2.7164
Brazil	(Real)	1.3444	0.8444	0.5585	0.8521
Brunei	(Brunei $)	2.3107	1.4514	0.96	1.4646
Bulgaria	(Lev)	106.0244	66.5982	44.0501	67.2061
Burkino Faso	(CFA Fr)	835.54	524.837	347.144	529.627
Burma	(Kyat)	9.1838	5.7687	3.8156	5.8213
Burundi	(Burundi Fr)	385.72	242.286	160.256	244.498
Cambodia	(Riel)	4145.70	2604.08	1722.42	2627.85
Cameroon	(CFA Fr)	835.54	524.837	347.144	529.627
Canada	(Canadian $)	2.2522	1.4146	0.9357	1.4276
Canary Is	(Sp Peseta)	209.461	131.571	87.0252	132.772
Cp. Verde	(CV Escudo)	131.839	82.8134	54.7754	83.5693
Cayman Is	(CI $)	1.3160	0.8266	0.5467	0.8341
Cent.Afr. Rep	(CFA Fr)	835.54	524.837	347.144	529.627
Chad	(CFA Fr)	835.54	524.837	347.144	529.627
Chile	(Chilean Peso)	649.436	407.937	269.823	411.661
China	(Yuan)	13.4336	8.4381	5.5812	8.5152
Colombia	(Col Peso)	1366.13	858.122	567.589	865.955
CIS ‡	(Rouble)	1.0412o	0.654	0.4325	0.6599
		6470.68m	4064.5	2688.39	4101.6
Comoros	(Fr)	626.062	393.255	260.111	396.845
Congo (Brazz)	(CFA Fr)	835.54	524.837	347.144	529.627
Costa Rica	(Colon)	265.093	166.516	110.139	168.036
Côte d'Ivoire	(CFA Fr)	835.54	524.837	347.144	529.627
Croatia	(Kuna)	8.7723	5.5102	3.6446	5.5605
Cuba	(Cuban Peso)	1.5890	0.9981	0.6601	1.0072
Cyprus	(Cyprus £)	0.7448	0.4678	0.3094	0.4721
Czech Rep.	(Koruna)	43.97	27.6193	18.2683	27.8714
Denmark	(Danish Krone)	9.5070	5.9717	3.9498	6.0262
Djibouti Rep	(Djib Fr)	282.907	177.985	117.928	179.004
Dominica	(E Carrib $)	4.2903	2.6949	1.7825	2.7195
Dominican Rep	(D Peso)	21.3403	13.4047	8.8663	13.527
Ecuador	(Sucre)	3701.58o	2325.11	1537.9	2346.34
		3788.18a	2379.51	1573.88	2401.23
Egypt	(Egyptian £)	5.4018	3.393	2.2442	3.424
El Salvador	(Colon)	13.9196	8.7434	5.7832	8.8232
Equat'l Guinea	(CFA Fr)	835.54	524.837	347.144	529.627
Estonia	(Kroon)	19.304	12.1256	8.0202	12.2363
Ethiopia	(Ethiopian Birr)	8.6124	5.4097	3.5782	5.4591
Falkland Is	(Falk £)	1	0.6281	0.4154	0.6338
Faroe Is	(Danish Krone)	9.5070	5.9717	3.9498	6.0262
Fiji Is	(Fiji $)	2.2413	1.4078	0.9311	1.4207
Finland	(Markka)	7.5194	4.7232	3.1241	4.7663
France	(Fr)	8.3554	5.2483	3.4714	5.2962
Fr. Cty/Africa	(CFA Fr)	835.54	524.837	347.144	529.627
Fr. Guiana	(Local Fr)	8.3554	5.2483	3.4714	5.2962
Fr. Pacific Is	(CFP Fr)	151.773	95.3347	63.0574	96.2049
Gabon	(CFA Fr)	835.54	524.837	347.144	529.627

		£ STG	US $	D-MARK	YEN (X 100)
Gambia	(Dalasi)	15.5325	9.7565	6.4533	9.8456
Germany	(D-Mark)	2.4069	1.5118	1	1.5256
Ghana	(Cedi)	1644.62	1033.05	683.294	1042.48
Gibraltar	(Gib £)	1	0.6281	0.4154	0.6338
Greece	(Drachma)	375.621	235.943	156.06	238.096
Greenland	(Danish Krone)	9.5070	5.9717	3.9498	6.0262
Grenada	(E Carr $)	4.2903	2.6949	1.7825	2.7195
Guadaloupe	(Local Fr)	8.3554	5.2483	3.4714	5.2962
Guam	(US $)	1.5920	1	0.6614	1.0091
Guatemala	(Quetzal)	9.1507	5.7479	3.8018	5.8003
Guinea	(Fr)	1592.35	1000.22	661.577	1009.35
Guinea-Bissau	(Peso)	21561.1	13543.4	8958.04	13667
Guyana	(Guyanese $)	225.638	141.732	93.7463	143.026
Haiti	(Gourde)	30.191	18.9641	12.5435	19.1372
Honduras	(Lempira)	14.7459	9.2625	6.1265	9.347
Hong Kong	(HK $)	12.3106	7.7327	5.1147	7.8033
Hungary	(Forint)	178.839	112.336	74.3026	113.361
Iceland	(Icelandic Krona)	107.162	67.3128	44.5228	67.9272
India	(Indian Rupee)	49.9495	31.3753	20.7526	31.6617
Indonesia	(Rupiah)	3534.12	2219.92	1468.33	2240.19
Iran	(Rial)	2732.50	1716.39	1135.28	1732.06
Iraq	(Iraqi Dinar)	0.9534	0.5988	0.3961	0.6043
Irish Rep	(Punt)	1.0116	0.6354	0.4202	0.6412
Israel	(Shekel)	4.7835	3.0047	1.9874	3.0321
Italy	(Lira)	2546.32	1599.45	1057.93	1614.05
Jamaica	(Jamaican $)	50.848	31.9396	21.1259	32.2312
Japan	(Yen)	157.762	99.0967	65.5457	100.001
Jordan	(Jordanian Dinar)	1.1112	0.6979	0.4616	0.7043
Kenya	(Kenya Shilling)	70.7105	44.4161	29.3782	44.8215
Kiribati	(Australian $)	2.0880	1.3115	0.8675	1.3235
Korea North	(Won)	3.4164	2.1459	1.4194	2.1655
Korea South	(Won)	1256.69	789.378	522.12	796.583
Kuwait	(Kuwaiti Dinar)	0.4754	0.2986	0.1975	0.3013
Laos	(New Kip)	1152.03	723.637	478.636	730.242
Latvia	(Lats)	0.8652	0.5434	0.3594	0.5484
Lebanon	(Lebanese £)	2616.37	1643.45	1087.03	1658.45
Lesotho	(Maluti)	5.6343	3.5391	2.3408	3.5714
Liberia	(Liberian $)	1.5920	1	0.6614	1.0091
Libya	(Libyan Dinar)	0.5679	0.3567	0.2359	0.3599
Liechtenstein	(Swiss Fr)	2.0239	1.2712	0.8408	1.2828
Lithuania	(Litas)	6.3560	3.9924	2.6407	4.0289
Luxembourg	(Lux Fr)	49.6386	31.18	20.6234	31.4646
Macao	(Pataca)	12.7044	7.9801	5.2783	8.0529
Madagascar	(MG Fr)	5919.03	3717.98	2459.19	3751.92
Madeira	(Port Escudo)	248.902	156.345	103.412	157.773
Malawi	(Kwacha)	24.3687	15.3069	10.1245	15.4466
Malaysia	(Ringgit)	4.0714	2.5574	1.6915	2.5807
Maldive Is	(Rufiya)	18.7025	11.7478	7.7703	11.855
Mali Rep	(CFA Fr)	835.54	524.837	347.144	529.627
Malta	(Maltese Lira)	0.5769	0.3623	0.2396	0.3656
Martinique	(Local Fr)	8.3554	5.2483	3.4714	5.2962
Mauritania	(Ouguiya)	193.858	121.77	80.5426	122.882
Mauritius	(Maur Rupee)	28.2921	17.7714	11.7545	17.9336
Mexico	(Mexican Peso)	8.9548	5.6248	3.7204	5.6762
Miquelon	(Local Fr)	8.3554	5.2483	3.4714	5.2962
Monaco	(French Fr)	8.3554	5.2483	3.4714	5.2962
Mongolia	(Tugrik)	654.604	411.183	271.97	414.937
Montserrat	(E Carr $)	4.2903	2.6949	1.7825	2.7195
Morocco	(Dirham)	13.9435	8.7584	5.7931	8.8384
Mozambique	(Metical)	10505.67	6599.04	4364.81	6659.27
Namibia	(S A Rand)	5.6343	3.5391	2.3408	3.5714
Nauru Is	(Australian $)	2.0880	1.3115	0.8675	1.3235
Nepal	(Nepalese Rupee)	78.4966	49.3069	32.6131	49.7569
Netherlands	(Guilder)	2.6977	1.6945	1.1208	1.71
N'nd Antilles	(A/Guilder)	2.8443	1.7866	1.1817	1.8029
New Zealand	(NZ $)	2.4865	1.5618	1.033	1.5761
Nicaragua	(Gold Cordoba)	11.3920	7.1557	4.733	7.221
Niger Rep	(CFA Fr)	835.54	524.837	347.144	529.627
Nigeria	(Naira)	35.0229	21.9993	14.551	22.2001
Norway	(Nor. Krone)	10.5467	6.6248	4.3818	6.6852
Oman	(Rial Omani)	0.6129	0.3849	0.2546	0.3885

		£ STG	US $	D-MARK	YEN (X 100)
Pakistan	(Pak. Rupee)	49.0784	30.8281	20.3907	31.1095
Panama	(Balboa)	1.5620	0.9811	0.6489	0.9901
Papua New Guinea	(Kina)	1.8543	1.1647	0.7704	1.1753
Paraguay	(Guarani)	3078.69	1933.85	1279.11	1951.5
Peru	(New Sol)	3.4705	2.1799	1.4418	2.1998
Philippines	(Peso)	39.1779	24.6092	16.2773	24.8338
Pitcairn Is	(£ Sterling)	1	0.6281	0.4154	0.6338
	(NZ $)	2.4865	1.5618	1.033	1.5761
Poland	(Zloty)	3.8374	2.4104	1.5943	2.4324
Portugal	(Escudo)	248.902	156.345	103.412	157.773
Puerto Rico	(US $)	1.5620	0.9811	0.6489	0.9901
Qatar	(Riyal)	5.7832	3.6326	2.4027	3.6658
Reunion Is. de la	(F/Fr)	8.3554	5.2483	3.4714	5.2962
Romania	(Leu)	2785.0	1749.37	1157.09	1765.34
Rwanda	(Fr)	218.53	137.268	90.7931	138.521
St Christopher	(E Carr $)	4.2903	2.6949	1.7825	2.7195
St Helena	(£)	1	0.6281	0.4154	0.6338
St Lucia	(E Carr $)	4.2903	2.6949	1.7825	2.7195
St Pierre	(French Fr)	8.3554	5.2483	3.4714	5.2962
St Vincent	(E Carr $)	4.2903	2.6949	1.7825	2.7195
San Marino	(Italian Lira)	2546.32	1599.45	1057.93	1614.05
Sao Tome	(Dobra)	1923.80	1208.42	799.285	1219.45
Saudi Arabia	(Riyal)	5.9707	3.7504	2.4806	3.7846
Senegal	(CFA Fr)	835.54	524.837	347.144	529.627
Seychelles	(Rupee)	7.7996	4.8992	3.2405	4.9439
Sierra Leone	(Leone)	977.235	613.841	406.014	619.444
Singapore	($)	2.3107	1.4514	0.96	1.4646
Slovakia	(Koruna)	48.371	30.3837	20.0968	30.6611
Slovenia	(Tolar)	193.906	121.8	80.5625	122.912
Solomon Is	($)	5.2685	3.3093	2.1889	3.3395
Somali Rep	(Shilling)	4163.18	2615.06	1729.69	2638.93
South Africa	(Rand)	5.6343c	3.5391	2.3408	3.5714
		6.4474g	4.0498	2.6787	4.0868
Spain	(Peseta)	209.461	131.571	87.0252	132.772
Spanish Ports In N Africa	(Sp Peseta)	209.461	131.571	87.0252	132.772
Sri Lanka	(Rupee)	79.4543	49.9084	33.011	50.364
Sudan Rep	(Dinar)	61.1129	38.3875	25.3907	38.7378
Surinam	(Guilder)	662.613	416.214	275.297	420.013
Swaziland	(Lilangeni)	5.6343	3.5391	2.3408	3.5714
Sweden	(Krona)	11.8539	7.4459	4.9249	7.5138
Switzerland	(Fr)	2.0239	1.2712	0.8408	1.2828
Syria	(£)	66.74	41.9221	27.7286	42.3047
Taiwan	($)	41.8572	26.2922	17.3905	26.5322
Tanzania	(Shilling)	850.115	533.992	353.199	538.866
Thailand	(Baht)	39.8943	25.0592	16.5749	25.2879
Togo Rep	(CFA Fr)	835.54	524.837	347.144	529.627
Tonga Is	(Pa'anga)	2.0880	1.3115	0.8675	1.3235
Trinidad/Tobago	($)	9.0176	5.6643	3.7465	5.716
Tunisia	(Dinar)	1.5563	0.9775	0.6465	0.9864
Turkey	(Lira)	64450.10	40483.7	26777.2	40853.3
Turks & Caicos	(US $)	1.5920	1	0.6614	1.0091
Tuvalu	(Australian $)	2.0880	1.3115	0.8675	1.3235
Uganda	(New Shilling)	1461.88	918.266	607.37	926.648
Ukraine	(Karbovanets)	186230.8	116979	77373.7	118047
U A E	(Dirham)	5.8469	3.6726	2.4292	3.7061
United Kingdom	(£)	1	0.6281	0.4154	0.6338
United States	(US $)	1.5920	1	0.6614	1.0091
Uruguay	(Peso Uruguayo)	9.1209	5.7292	3.7894	5.7815
Vanuatu	(Vatu)	175.751	110.396	73.0196	111.404
Vatican	(Lira)	2546.32	1599.45	1057.93	1614.05
Venezuela	(Bolivar)	270.424	169.864	112.354	171.415
Vietnam	(Dong)	17536.2	11015.2	7285.8	11115.7
Virgin Is-British	(US $)	1.5920	1	0.6614	1.0091
Virgin Is-US	(US $)	1.5920	1	0.6614	1.0091
Western Samoa	(Tala)	3.9361	2.4724	1.6353	2.4949
Yemen (Rep of)	(Rial)	88.30a(2)	55.4648	36.6861	55.971
Yemen (Rep of)	(Dinar)	0.6884(2)	0.4324	0.286	0.4363
Yugoslavia	(New Dinar) (1)				
Zaire Rep	(Zaire)	5012.00	3148.24	2082.35	3176.98
Zambia	(Kwacha)	1088.47	683.712	452.229	689.953
Zimbabwe	($)	13.3158	8.3641	5.5323	8.4405

Special Drawing Rights January 26, 1995 United Kingdom £0.923758 United States $1.47247 Germany DM2.23447 Japan Y146.555 European Currency Unit Rates January 27, 1995 United Kingdom £0.788615 United States $1.25130 Germany DM1.89784 Japan Y124.504

Source: The Financial Times, January 30, 1995.

versus U.S. dollar, in the third column shown, is DEM 1.5152/USD. This is a direct quote on the German mark or indirect quote on the U.S. dollar. The inverse of this spot rate is listed in the first column, the indirect quote on the German mark or direct quote on the U.S. dollar, USD .6600/DEM. The two forms of the exchange rate are of course equal, one being the inverse of the other.[1]

$$\frac{1}{\text{DEM } 1.5152/\text{USD}} = \text{USD } .6600/\text{DEM}$$

Luckily, world currency markets do follow some conventions to minimize confusion. With only a few exceptions, most currencies are quoted in direct quotes versus the U.S. dollar (DEM/USD, YEN/USD, FFR/USD), also known as **European terms.** The major exceptions are currencies at one time or another associated with the British Commonwealth, including the Australian dollar and, of course, the British pound sterling. These are customarily quoted as USD per pound sterling or USD per Australian dollar, known as **American terms.** Once again, it makes no real difference whether one quotes U.S. dollars per Japanese yen or Japanese yen per U.S. dollar, as long as one knows which is being used for the transaction.

Figure 5.2, the foreign currency quotations from the *Financial Times* of London, provides wider coverage of the world's currencies, including many of the lesser known and traded. These quotes are also for Friday, January 27, 1995, the same day as the quotes from *The Wall Street Journal* in Figure 5.1. However, even though the currency quotations are for the same day, they are not necessarily the same, reflecting the differences in the time zones, the local markets, and even the actual banks surveyed for newspaper quotation purposes. For example, the *Financial Times* quotes the spot rate on the deutschemark as DEM 1.5118/USD, while *The Wall Street Journal* lists a quote of DEM 1.5152/USD. Not enormous, but significant if you were buying one million of either currency!

Cross Rates

Although it is common among exchange traders worldwide to quote currency values against the U.S. dollar, it is not necessary. Any currency's value can be stated in terms of any other currency. When the exchange rate for a currency is stated without using the U.S. dollar as a reference, it is referred to as a **cross rate.** For example, the German mark and Japanese yen are both quoted on Friday, January 27, 1995, versus the U.S. dollar: DEM 1.5152/USD and YEN 99.36/USD. But if the YEN/DEM cross rate is needed, it is simply a matter of division:

$$\frac{\text{YEN } 99.36/\text{USD}}{\text{DEM } 1.5152/\text{USD}} = \text{YEN } 65.5755/\text{DEM}$$

The YEN/DEM cross rate of 65.5755 is the third leg of the triangle, which must be true if the first two exchange rates are known. If one of the exchange rates changes due to market forces, the others must adjust for the three exchange rates again to align. If they are out of alignment, it would be possible to make a profit simply by exchanging one currency for a second, the second for a third, and the third back to the first. This is known as **triangular arbitrage.** Besides the potential profitability of arbitrage that may occasionally occur, cross rates have become increasingly common in a world of rapidly expanding trade and investment. The world's financial markets no longer revolve around the U.S. dollar.

Global Perspective

5.1
Yin/Yang Balance with the Yuan

Proving its resolve to become part of the world economy soon, China eliminated its two-tiered exchange rate mechanism on Jan. 1. Instead of an official rate and a swap center rate—the latter normally set at about 45 percent below the former—the swap rate has now become official.

Coming as it did almost a year ahead of schedule, the move is a strong indication of the Chinese government's desire to continue to attract foreign investment. For companies of all sizes, China has become a hotbed of new investment. Currency stability and convertibility are essential to the success of foreign ventures and to the government's efforts to reform the economy.

But the exchange rate realignment has also raised some new concerns for companies with joint ventures in China. The biggest worry: The government continues to hold the reins on the yuan by controlling the supply of hard currency. And just how Beijing will use its discretion is as hard to decipher as the *I Ching.*

Source: "Becoming," *International Business,* March 1994, 120–121.

Percentage Change Calculations

The quotation form is important when calculating the percentage change in an exchange rate. For example, if the spot rate between the Japanese yen and the U.S. dollar changed from YEN 125/USD to YEN 150/USD, the percentage change in the value of the Japanese yen is:

$$\frac{\text{YEN } 125/\text{USD} - \text{YEN } 150/\text{USD}}{\text{YEN } 150/\text{USD}} \times 100 = -16.67\%$$

The Japanese yen has declined in value versus the U.S. dollar by 16.67 percent. This is consistent with the intuition that it now requires more yen (150) to buy a dollar than it used to (125).

The same percentage change result can be achieved by using the inverted forms of the same spot rates (indirect quotes on the Japanese yen), if care is taken to also "invert" the basic percentage change calculation. Using the inverse of YEN 125/USD (USD 0.0080/YEN) and the inverse of YEN 150/USD (USD 0.0067/YEN), the percentage change is still − 16.67 percent:

$$\frac{\text{USD } 0.0067/\text{YEN} - \text{USD } 0.0080/\text{YEN}}{\text{USD } 0.0080/\text{YEN}} \times 100 = -16.67\%$$

If the percentage changes calculated are not identical, it is normally the result of rounding errors introduced when inverting the spot rates. Both methods are identical, however, when calculated properly.

Foreign Currency Market Structure

The market for foreign currencies is a worldwide market that is informal in structure. This means that it has no central place, pit, or floor like the floor of the New York Stock Exchange, where the trading takes place. The "market" is actually

TABLE 5.1
Typical Foreign
Currency Quotations on
a Reuters Screen

13:07	CCY	Page	Name	*Reuters Spot Rates*	CCY	HI* Euro**	Lo FXFX
13.06	DEM	DGXX	DG BANK	FFT	1.8528/33 * DEM	1.8538	1.8440
13.06	GBP	AiBN	AL IRISH	N.Y.	1.7653/63 * GBP	1.7710	1.7630
13.06	CHF	CITX	CITYBANK	ZUR	1.5749/56 * CHF	1.5750	1.5665
13.06	JPY	CHNY	CHEMICAL	N.Y.	128.53/58 * JPY	128.70	128.23
13.07	FRF	MGFX	MORGAN	LDN	6.3030/60 * FRF	6.3080	6.2750
13.06	NLG	MGFX	MORGAN	LDN	2.0920/30 * NLG	2.0925	2.0815
13.00	ITL	MGFX	MORGAN	LDN	1356.45/6.58 * ITL	1356.45	1349.00
13.02	XEV	PRBX	PRIVAT	COP	1.1259/68 * XEV	1.1304	1.1255

Column 1: Time of entry of the latest quote to the nearest minute (British Standard time).
Column 2: Currency of quotation (bilateral with the U.S. dollar); quotes are currency per USD, except for the British pound sterling (dollars per unit of pound) and the European Currency Unit (dollars per unit of XEV). The currency symbols are as follows: DEM—German mark; GBP—British pound sterling; CHF—Swiss franc; JPY—Japanese yen; FRF—French franc; NGL—Netherlands guilder; ITL—Italian lira; XEV—European Currency Unit.
Column 3: Mnemonic of inputting bank. Allows the individual trader to dial up the correct page (by this mnemonic) where the trader could see the full set of spot and forward quotes for this and other currencies being offered by this bank.
Column 4: Name of the inputting bank.
Column 5: Branch location of that bank from which the quote has emanated (so that an inquiring trader can telephone the correct branch); FFT—Frankfurt; N.Y.—New York; ZUR—Zurich; LDN—London; COP—Copenhagen.
Column 6: Spot exchange rate quotation, bid quote, then offer quote.
Column 7: Recent high price for this specific quote.
Column 8: Recent low price for this specific quote.
Source: Adapted from C. A. E. Goodhart and L. Figliuoli, "Every Minute Counts in Financial Markets," *Journal of International Money and Finance,* 10, 1991, pp. 23–52.

the thousands of telecommunications links among financial institutions around the globe, and it is open 24 hours a day. Someone, somewhere, is nearly always open for business.

The structure of the foreign currency market leads to some interesting problems. (Global Perspective 5.1 illustrates how China is changing its structure.) For example, since there is no one exchange, no one floor, no world central bank, is there a single exchange rate? The answer is no, there is no single agreed-upon rate of exchange for all financial institutions. Since all the banks and financial institutions that are trading the currencies are calling and communicating with dozens or hundreds of banks all over the world, they are all seeing or hearing slightly different rates.

For example, Table 5.1 reproduces a computer screen from one of the major international financial information news sources, Reuters. This is the spot exchange screen, called FXFX, which is available to all subscribers to the Reuters news network. The screen serves as a bulletin board, where all financial institutions wanting to buy or sell foreign currencies can post representative prices. Although the rates quoted on these computer screens are indicative of current prices, due to the rapid movement of rates worldwide, the buyer is still referred to the individual bank for the latest quotation. There also are hundreds of banks operating in the markets at any moment that are not listed on the brief sample of Reuters FXFX page.[2] The speed with which this market moves, the multitude of players playing on a field that is open 24 hours a day, and the circumference of the earth with its time and day differences produce many different "single prices." A good example of this lack of one price is to look back at Figure 5.1. The explanation of the exchange rate quotes states:

> The New York foreign exchange selling rates below apply to trading among banks in amounts of $1 million and more, as quoted at 3 p.m. Eastern time by Bankers Trust Co., Telerate and other sources. Retail transactions provide fewer units of foreign currency per dollar.

Those are pretty specific prices! The rates quoted are the FX rates as seen by only one or a few members of the world of participants and at a specific point in time (3 p.m. Eastern time). The rates are obviously "wholesale rates," applicable to large-scale trading, and will therefore be better than one might trade at in an airport when exchanging currencies on international trips.

One way to put this ever-changing market in perspective is to think of the FX market as a never-ending horse race. The winner is the one that is ahead at one point on the track, at one point in time, from the viewpoint of where in the stands the audience is sitting. The markets continue, as would the theoretical horses, forever. The rates quoted by Bankers Trust or Telerate are therefore only daily snapshots of the race, the daily photo finish from the individual bank's seat in the stands.

Currency Bid and Offer Quotes

The individual spot quotes shown in Table 5.1 have both bid and offer quotations for the currencies listed. For example, DG Bank (Deutsche Bank) in Frankfurt, Germany, posted a spot quote on the German mark (DEM) of 1.8528/33 at 13:07 (1:07 p.m. London time). These bid and offer quotes are for either the purchase (bid) or sale (offer) of German marks in exchange for U.S. dollars.

Bid:	DEM 1.8528/USD	The spot rate of exchange at which the bank is willing to purchase U.S. dollars, or sell German marks.
Offer:	DEM 1.8533/USD	The spot rate of exchange at which the bank is willing to sell U.S. dollars, or buy German marks.

The quote is stated with only the last two digits of the offer rate listed separately. Every exchange rate has a customary number of digits used. In the case of the DEM/USD, all quotes are carried to the fourth decimal place. These are referred to as "basis points" or "pips."[3] The individual bank makes its profit on a single trade on the **spread,** the difference between the bid and offer quotes (if it simultaneously bought and sold dollars for marks at the quoted rates).

Market Size and Composition

Until recently there was little data on the actual volume of trading on world foreign currency markets. Starting in the spring of 1986, however, the Federal Reserve Bank of New York, along with other major industrial countries' central banks through the auspices of the Bank for International Settlements (BIS), started surveying the activity of currency trading every three years. Some of the principal results are shown in Figure 5.3.

Growth in foreign currency trading has been nothing less than astronomical. The survey results for the month of April 1992 indicate that daily foreign currency trading on world markets exceeded $1,000,000,000,000 (a trillion with a "t"). In comparison, the annual (not daily) U.S. government budget deficit has never exceeded $300 billion, and the U.S. merchandise trade deficit has never topped $200 billion.

The majority of the world's trading in foreign currencies is still taking place in the cities where international financial activity is centered: London, New York, and Tokyo. The recent survey by the U.S. Federal Reserve of currency trading by finan-

FIGURE 5.3   Daily Foreign Currency Trading on World Markets (billions of U.S. dollars)

Survey year

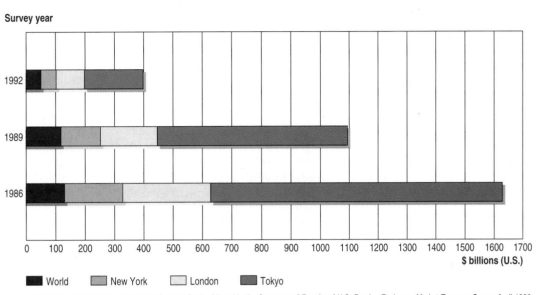

Source: Adapted by authors from the Federal Reserve Bank of New York's *Summary of Results of U.S. Foreign Exchange Market Turnover Survey,* April 1992, and the Bank for International Settlements *60th Annual Report.*

cial institutions and independent brokers in New York reveals additional information of interest. Approximately 66 percent of currency trading occurs in the morning hours (Eastern Standard Time), with 29 percent between noon and 4 p.m., and the remaining 5 percent between 4 p.m. and 8 a.m. the next day. The average size of a single spot currency trade in New York in April 1992 was $4 million.

Three reasons typically given for the enormous growth in foreign currency trading are:

1. **Deregulation of International Capital Flows**—It is easier than ever to move currencies and capital around the world without major governmental restrictions. Much of the deregulation that has characterized government policy over the past 10 to 15 years in the United States, Japan, and the now European Union has focused on financial deregulation.

2. **Gains in Technology and Transaction Cost Efficiency**—It is faster, easier, and cheaper to move millions of dollars, yen, or marks around the world than ever before. Technological advancements in not only the dissemination of information, but also in the conduct of exchange or trading, have added greatly to the ability of individuals working in these markets to conduct instantaneous arbitrage (some would say speculation).

3. **The World Is a Risky Place**—Many argue that the financial markets have become increasingly volatile over recent years, with larger and faster swings in financial variables such as stock values and interest rates adding to the motivations for moving more capital at faster rates.

INTERNATIONAL MONEY MARKETS

A money market traditionally is defined as a market for deposits, accounts, or securities that have maturities of one year or less. The international money markets, often termed the Eurocurrency markets, constitute an enormous financial market that is in many ways outside the jurisdiction and supervision of world financial and governmental authorities.

Eurocurrency Markets

A **Eurocurrency** is any foreign currency–denominated deposit or account at a financial institution outside the country of the currency's issuance. For example, U.S. dollars that are held on account in a bank in London are termed **Eurodollars.** Similarly, Japanese yen held on account in a Parisian financial institution would be classified as Euroyen. The *Euro* prefix does not mean these currencies or accounts are only European, as German marks on account in Singapore would also be classified as a Eurocurrency, a Euromark account.

Eurocurrency Interest Rates

What is the significance of these foreign currency–denominated accounts? Simply put, the purity of value that comes from no governmental interference or restrictions with their use. Eurocurrency accounts are not controlled or managed by governments (for example, the Bank of England has no control over Eurodollar accounts), therefore, the financial institutions pay no deposit insurance, hold no reserve requirements, and normally are not subject to any interest rate restrictions with respect to such accounts. Eurocurrencies are one of the purest indicators of what these currencies should yield in terms of interest. Sample Eurocurrency interest rates for 1995 are shown in Table 5.2.

There are hundreds of different major interest rates around the globe, but the international financial markets focus on a very few, the **interbank interest rates.** Interbank rates charged by banks to banks in the major international financial centers such as London, Frankfurt, Paris, New York, Tokyo, Singapore, and Hong Kong are generally regarded as "the interest rate" in the respective market. The interest rate that is used most often in international loan agreements is the Eurocurrency interest rate on U.S. dollars (Eurodollars) in London between banks: the London Interbank Offer Rate (LIBOR). Because it is a Eurocurrency rate, it floats freely without regard to governmental restrictions on reserves or deposit insurance or any other regulation or restriction that would add expense to transactions using this capital. The interbank rates for other currencies in other markets are often named similarly, PIBOR (Paris interbank offer rate), MIBOR (Madrid interbank offer rate), HIBOR (either Hong Kong or Helsinki interbank offer rate), SIBOR (Singapore interbank offer rate). While **LIBOR** is the offer rate—the cost of funds "offered" to those acquiring a loan—the equivalent deposit rate in the **Euromarkets** is LIBID, the London InterBank Bid Rate, the rate of interest other banks can earn on Eurocurrency deposits.

How do these international Eurocurrency and interbank interest rates differ from domestic rates? Answer: not by much. They generally move up and down in unison, by currency, but often differ by the percentage by which the restrictions alter the rates of interest in the domestic markets. For example, because the Euromarkets have no restrictions, the spread between the offer rate and the bid rate (the loan rate and the deposit rate) is substantially smaller than in domestic markets. This means the loan rates in international markets are a bit lower than domestic market loan rates,

TABLE 5.2 Exchange Rates and Eurocurrency Interest Rates	Exchange/Interest Rate	Maturity	U.S. Dollar (USD)	German Mark (DEM/USD)	Japanese Yen (JAP/USD)
	Spot Exchange Rate		—	1.5496	99.61%
	Eurocurrency Deposit Rate				
	London bid rates;	1 month	5.8750%	5.0625%	2.2813%
	percent per annum	3 months	6.3750%	5.1875%	2.3438%
		6 months	6.8750%	5.3750%	2.3438%
		12 months	7.6250%	5.7500%	2.5938%
	Forward Exchange Rate				
		1 month	—	1.5486	99.36
		3 months	—	1.5451	98.62
		6 months	—	1.5384	97.43
		12 months	—	1.5226	94.95

Source: Adapted from *Harris Bank Foreign Exchange Weekly Review,* Harris Trust and Savings Bank, Chicago, December 30, 1994.

and deposit rates are a bit higher in the international markets than in domestic markets. This is, however, only a big-player market. Only well-known international firms, financial or nonfinancial, have access to the quantities of capital necessary to operate in the Euromarkets. But as described in the following sections on international debt and equity markets, more and more firms are gaining access to the Euromarkets to take advantage of deregulated capital flows.

Linking Eurocurrency Interest Rates and Exchange Rates

Eurocurrency interest rates also play a large role in the foreign exchange markets themselves. They are, in fact, the interest rates used in the calculation of the forward rates we noted earlier (for examples of forward rate quotes refer back to Figure 5.1). Recall that a forward rate is a contract for a specific amount of currency to be exchanged for another currency at a future date, usually 30, 60, 90, 180, or even 360 days in the future. Forward rates are calculated from the spot rate in effect on the day the contract is written along with the respective Eurocurrency interest rates for the two currencies.

For example, to calculate the 90-day forward rate on Friday, December 30, 1994, multiply the spot rate on that date by the ratio of the two Eurocurrency interest rates. Note that it is important to adjust the interest rates for the actual period of time needed, 90 days (3 months) of a 360-day financial year:

$$\text{90-Day Forward} = \text{Spot} \times \left[1 + \left(i_{90}^{\text{DEM}} \times \frac{90}{360} \right) \right]$$

Now, plugging in the spot exchange rate of DEM 1.5496/USD and the two 90-day (3-month) Eurocurrency interest rates from Table 5.2 (5.1875 percent for the DEM and 6.3750 percent for the USD), the 90-day forward exchange rate is:

$$\text{DEM } 1.5496/\text{USD} \times \left[1 + \left(.051875 \times \frac{90}{360} \right) \right] = \text{DEM } 1.5451/\text{USD}$$

The forward rate of DEM 1.5451/USD is a "stronger rate" for the German mark than the current spot rate. This is because it takes 1.5496 marks to buy one dollar spot, but will only take 1.5451 marks to buy one dollar at the forward rate 90 days in the future. The German mark is said to be "**selling forward** at a premium," meaning that the forward rate for purchasing marks is more expensive than the spot rate.

Why is this the case? The reason is that the Eurocurrency interest rate on the German mark for 90 days is lower than the Eurocurrency interest rate on the U.S. dollar. If it were the other way around—if the German mark interest rate were higher than the U.S. dollar interest rate—the German mark would be "selling forward at a discount." The forward rates quoted in the foreign exchange markets, and used so frequently in international business, simply reflect the difference in interest rates between the two currencies.

Businesses frequently use forward exchange-rate contracts to manage their exposure to currency risk. As Chapter 17 will detail, corporations use many other financial instruments and techniques beyond forward contracts to manage currency risk, but forwards are still the mainstay of industry.

INTERNATIONAL CAPITAL MARKETS

Just as with the money markets, the international capital markets serve as links among the capital markets of individual countries, as well as constituting a separate market of its own, the capital that flows into the Euromarkets. Firms can now raise capital, debt or equity, fixed or floating interest rates, in any of a dozen currencies, for maturities ranging from one month to 30 years, in the international capital markets. Although the international capital markets traditionally have been dominated by debt instruments, international equity markets have shown considerable growth in recent years.

The international financial markets can be subdivided in a number of ways. The following sections describe the international debt and equity markets for securitized and nonsecuritized capital. This is capital that is separable and tradable, like a bond or a stock. Nonsecuritized, a fancy term for bank loans, was really the original source of international capital (as well as the international debt crisis).

Defining International Financing

The definition of what constitutes an international financial transaction is dependent on two fundamental characteristics: (1) whether the borrower is domestic or foreign, and (2) whether the borrower is raising capital denominated in the domestic currency or a foreign currency. These two characteristics form four categories of financial transactions, illustrated in Figure 5.4.

- **Category 1: Domestic Borrower/Domestic Currency**—This is a traditional domestic financial market activity. A borrower who is resident within the country raises capital from domestic financial institutions denominated in local currency. All countries with basic market economies have their own domestic financial markets, some large and some quite small. This is still by far the most common type of financial transaction.
- **Category 2: Foreign Borrower/Domestic Currency**—This is when a foreign borrower enters another country's financial market and raises capital denominated in the local currency. The international dimension of this transaction is only who the borrower is. Many borrowers, both public and

FIGURE 5.4
Categorizing International Financial Transactions: Issuing Bonds in London

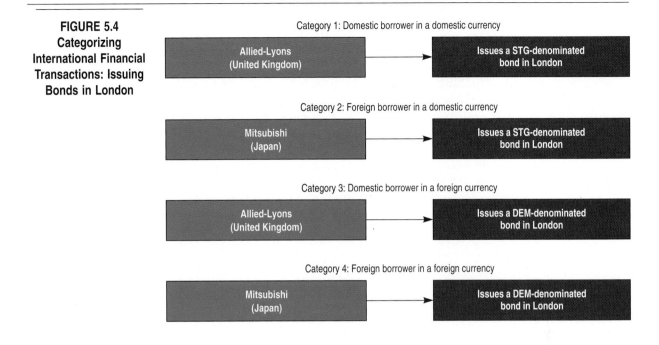

private, increasingly go to the world's largest financial markets to raise capital for their enterprises. The ability of a foreign firm to raise capital in another country's financial market is sometimes limited by government restrictions on who can borrow, as well as the market's willingness to lend to foreign governments and companies that it may not know as well as domestic borrowers.

- **Category 3: Domestic Borrower/Foreign Currency**—Many borrowers in today's international markets need capital denominated in a foreign currency. A domestic firm may actually issue a bond to raise capital in its local market where it is known quite well, but raise the capital in the form of a foreign currency. This type of financial transaction occurs less often than the previous two types because it requires a local market in foreign currencies, a Eurocurrency market. A number of countries, such as the United States, highly restrict the amount and types of financial transactions in foreign currency. International financial centers such as London and Zurich have been the traditional centers of these types of transactions.

- **Category 4: Foreign Borrower/Foreign Currency**—This is the strictest form of the traditional Eurocurrency financial transaction, a foreign firm borrowing foreign currency. Once again, this type of activity may be restricted by which borrowers are allowed into a country's financial markets and which currencies are available. This type of financing dominates the activities of many banking institutions in the **offshore banking** market.

Using this classification system, it is possible to categorize any individual international financial transaction. For example, the distinction between an international bond and a Eurobond is simply that of a Category 2 transaction (foreign borrower in a domestic currency market) and a Category 3 or 4 transaction (foreign currency denominated in a single local market or many markets).

Driving Forces in the International Financial Markets

The rapid growth of the international financial markets over the past 30 years is the result of four different but complementary forces: deregulation, innovation, securitization, and internationalization. Although one normally thinks of the world's largest industrial countries when describing financial markets, all four forces are visible in differing degrees the world over. In fact, the newly opened economies of the former eastern European bloc such as Czechoslovakia (now split into the Czech Republic and Slovakia), Hungary, Poland, and many others are now seeing the impacts of these four forces at something approaching the speed of light.

1. **Deregulation**—Deregulation is the first and most important force in opening financial markets. As governments continue to allow foreign firms to enter their markets for the buying and selling of goods, they have also become more willing to allow foreign firms to participate in their local financial markets. Financial deregulation, however, usually lags behind the deregulation of trade markets by long periods of time. The deregulation of domestic markets for domestic firms itself has been important. For example, the distinction as to which types of financial institutions can undertake which types of financial transactions (accept deposits; pay interest; make consumer, industrial, or mortgage loans; underwrite and syndicate securities, and so forth) is very important to the growth of financial markets.

   One of the major areas still restricted by many governments is the ability to conduct financial transactions in foreign currencies. Only the true international financial centers such as London allow the types of transactions described in Categories 3 and 4, Euromarket transactions. The reason for the slow deregulation of foreign currency transactions is that government authorities are charged with maintaining the security and stability of their own financial institutions. Since the quantities and values of foreign currency are beyond their control, they are hesitant to allow their own financial institutions to undertake significant activity in these currencies. Even in the case of traditional international financial centers such as London or Hong Kong, the government creates regulatory walls between local and foreign currencies.

2. **Innovation**—Innovation has been the second major driving force. While product markets have grown increasingly competitive, so has the market for financial services. Financial institutions worldwide continue to offer new and more efficient and effective services for both their public and private clients. The creation of new types of financial instruments, such as floating rate loans and notes and bonds in the 1970s, was a logical market reaction to a world in which inflation was generally rising across all countries and currencies. Floating interest rates allowed lenders such as banks to shift more of the risk of rising interest rates to the borrowers of capital while still allowing the markets to operate and provide much needed financing for growth.

3. **Securitization**—Securitization has been a remarkably important force in just the past decade. Securitization is the process of turning an illiquid loan

into a tradable, asset-backed security. For example, a bank loan is a highly customized contract between a bank and a borrower. Because each loan is so different, it is difficult for the bank to sell its loans, even though it may want to in order to free up more lending capacity. Securitization is the process of creating new ways to make these types of financial agreements liquid (salable in a secondary market) so that the values of these transactions can more easily be identified.

Many firms have shifted away from traditional bank loan markets to securitized debt markets. Large firms in the United States, for example, used to acquire most of the long- and short-term capital from banks. As bond markets have grown in size, however, corporations have started funding their long-term capital needs through bonds, debt securities. In the past 20 years, many of America's largest firms have acquired more of their short-term capital from securitized markets, such as the commercial paper market. These long-term and short-term securitization forces are now spreading to many national and international markets.

4. **Internationalization**—The fourth and final force of what this book is all about is internationalization. More than a buzzword, internationalization of business activity has forced many firms to acquire capital in many different markets in many different currencies. The growth of the multinational firm, a firm with subsidiaries and affiliates in 10, 20, or 30 countries, has provided an incentive for domestic financial markets to deregulate, innovate, and even securitize financial transactions to compete. Financial services in today's technologically sophisticated information age are considered by many to be more competitive than any product market. Capital today can move around the globe in seconds at practically zero cost.

INTERNATIONAL BANKING AND BANK LENDING

Banks have existed in different forms and roles since the Middle Ages. Bank loans provided nearly all of the debt capital needed by industry since the start of the Industrial Revolution. Even in this age in which securitized debt instruments (bonds, notes, and other types of tradable paper) are growing as sources of capital for firms worldwide, banks still perform a critical role by providing capital for medium-sized and smaller firms, which dominate all economies.

Structure of International Banking

Similar to the direct foreign investment decision sequence discussed in Chapter 2, banks can expand their cross-border activities in a variety of ways. Like all decisions involving exports and direct investment, increasing the level of international activity and capability normally requires placing more capital and knowledge at risk to be able to reap the greater benefits of expanding markets.

A bank that wants to conduct business with clients in other countries but does not want to open a banking operation in that country can do so through correspondent banks or representative offices. A **correspondent bank** is an unrelated bank (by ownership) based in the foreign country. By the nature of its business, it has knowledge of the local market and access to clients, capital, and information, which a foreign bank does not.

A second way that banks may gain access to foreign markets without actually opening a banking operation is through representative offices. A **representative**

The Locations of the World's International Financial Centers (IFCs) and International Offshore Financial Centers (IOFCs)

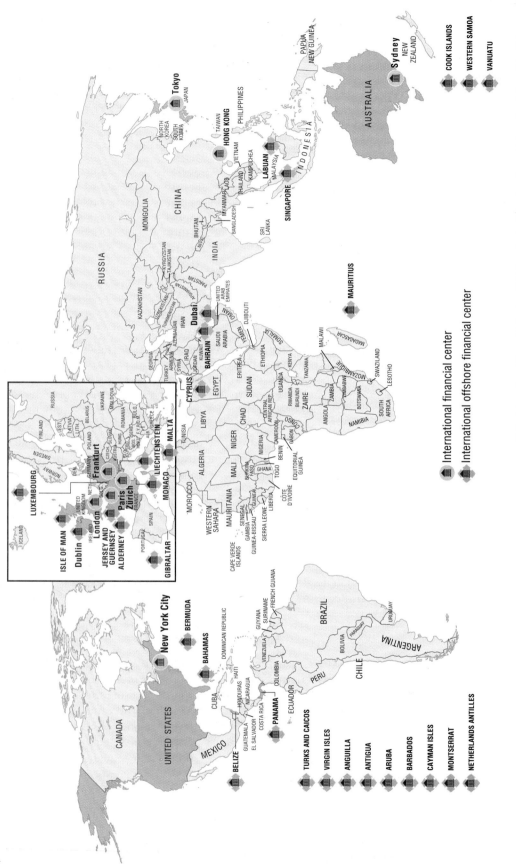

Note: *International Financial Centers (IFCs)* are the traditional centers of international financial activity, and normally include the conduct of both domestic and international financial transactions. *International Offshore Financial Centers (IOFCs)* are centers of offshore financial activities only (no interaction is allowed with the domestic financial or business community), and normally exist because of specific tax

office is basically a sales office for a bank. It provides information regarding the financial services of the bank, but it cannot deliver the services itself. It cannot accept deposits or make loans. The foreign representative office of a U.S. bank will typically sell the bank's services to local firms that may need banking services for trade or other transactions in the United States.

If a bank wants to conduct banking business within the foreign country, it may open a branch banking office, a banking affiliate, or even a wholly owned banking subsidiary. A branch banking office is an extension of the parent bank and is not independently financed from the parent. The branch office is not independently incorporated, and therefore commonly is restricted in the types of banking activities that it may conduct. Branch banking is by far the most common form of international banking structure used by banks, particularly by banks based in the United States.

A foreign banking affiliate or banking subsidiary is a locally and separately incorporated bank from the parent bank. If the local bank is wholly owned by the parent, it is a subsidiary; if only partially owned, it is an affiliate. For all intents and purposes, these are local banks, and they usually can provide the same financial services provided by any other bank in that country. Despite this freedom, many foreign banking subsidiaries find it difficult to compete with true local banks due to long-standing business relationships and corporate–banking ties that may date back decades or longer. Among the major industrial countries today, however, many foreign banking affiliates and subsidiaries are so highly integrated into local financial markets that they are indistinguishable from local banks.

Offshore Banking

Most governments regulate the degree of financial activity in a foreign currency that can take place. This has encouraged the growth of what is generally referred to as offshore banking. Offshore banking is the name given to Category 4 transactions, foreign borrowers of foreign currencies.

The primary motivation of offshore banking is avoiding regulation. Governments do not normally regulate banking activity that does not affect their domestic markets, so countries that have historically allowed unregulated foreign banking activity have been the centers of offshore banking. Many tropical islands, such as the Caymans, the Bahamas, and the Netherlands Antilles, have been the centers of much of offshore banking activity, although countries such as Luxembourg and Switzerland have also provided many of the same services. Although transactions are officially "booked" through the offshore centers, most of the activity is on paper or via telex only; most of the capital never reaches the remote locales.

Most of the appeal of the offshore centers has been avoiding taxes on income earned abroad, thus offshore banking centers have often been referred to as "tax havens." The centers can shield income from taxes because capital can be held unbeknownst to the owner's home country tax authorities. For the most part, these "Wild West" days of international finance are over, and it is generally no longer possible to shield income in tax havens.

International Bank Lending

Bank lending internationally consists of two types of financial credits: (1) loans extended by a single bank, and (2) loans extended by a collection or syndicate of banks.

These loans are international loans if they are extended to a foreign borrower or are denominated in a foreign currency.

International bank lending has grown significantly since the early 1980s when net lending was dominated by syndicated loans extended to developing countries. After the decline of the syndicated loan market in the mid-1980s, the growth in international bank lending was in the more traditional form of a simple loan arranged between a single bank and a corporate (not government) borrower.

Syndicated Loans   A **syndicated loan,** sometimes called a syndicated credit, is an arrangement in which between 20 and 50 banks in many different countries contribute to the funding of a single large loan. Originally a market that transferred capital from the richer industrial countries to the less developed countries in need of development capital, the market has changed to one that recycles capital among the industrial countries. The market now focuses on lending not to less developed country governments, but to corporations. Additionally, the capital no longer is targeted at long-term development projects, but rather for the financing of a large proportion of the merger and acquisition financing needed for corporate takeovers in the United States and the United Kingdom.

INTERNATIONAL SECURITY MARKETS

Although banks continue to provide a large portion of the international financial needs of government and business, it is the international debt securities markets that have experienced the greatest growth in the past decade. The market is composed of the **Euronote** market and the **international bond** market.

The Euronote Market

The Euronote market is a collective term for a variety of short- to medium-term types of financing. The original types of financing were termed note issuance facilities (NIFs) and revolving underwriting facilities (RUFs). These "facilities" were arrangements that would allow a firm to borrow capital as needed but at a predetermined rate of interest through notes that were guaranteed to be purchased by a group of financial institutions.

The true source of sustained financing in the Euronote market came from a financial export of the United States, commercial paper (CP). Commercial paper is a short-term note, typically 30, 60, 90, or 180 days in maturity, sold directly into the financial markets by large corporations. The market originated in the United States in the 1970s when a number of major firms realized they were actually larger and more creditworthy than many of the banks from which they were borrowing. The solution was to sell their own debt notes directly to the market and bypass the costs of banks. These notes were called commercial paper.

The international version, **Euro commercial paper (ECP),** arrived in the European markets with a splash in the early 1980s. One of the primary reasons for its rapid growth was the lack of anything similar in most national financial markets.[4] Although the growth of domestic CP markets has taken a little steam out of the Euro–CP market of late, it has continued to provide the majority of the financing in the general Euronote market since the mid-1980s.

The third and final type of financing available in the Euronote market is the Euro-medium-term note (EMTN). Another export of the rapidly innovating financial markets in the United States, the EMTN is the Euromarket version of a method of selling short- to medium-maturity bonds when needed. Unlike a bond issue, which is the sale of a large quantity of long-term debt all at one time, medium-term notes can be sold gradually into the market as the firm decides it needs additional debt financing. This is the result of having a "shelf-registration," in which the government authorities (the Securities and Exchange Commission in the United States) allow a large quantity of debt (the notes) to be registered but to be held "on the shelf" and sold as needed by the firm.

The International Bond Market

Even with all these strange and innovative ways of raising capital in the international financial markets, it is still the international bond market that provides the bulk of financing.

The four categories of international debt financing discussed previously particularly apply to the international bond markets. Foreign borrowers have been using the large, well-developed capital markets of countries such as the United States and the United Kingdom for many years. These issues are classified generally as **foreign bonds** as opposed to Eurobonds. Each has gained its own pet name for foreign bonds issued in that market. For example, foreign bond issues in the United States are called Yankee bonds, in the United Kingdom Bulldogs, in the Netherlands Rembrandt bonds, and in Japan they are called Samurai bonds. When bonds are issued by foreign borrowers in these markets, they are subject to the same restrictions that apply to all domestic borrowers. If a Japanese firm issues a bond in the United States, it still must comply with all rules of the U.S. Securities and Exchange Commission, including the fact that they must be dollar-denominated.

Bonds that fall into Categories 3 and 4 are termed **Eurobonds.** The primary characteristic of these instruments is that they are denominated in a currency other than that of the country where they are sold. For example, many U.S. firms may issue Euro-yen bonds on world markets. (See Global Perspective 5.2 for a famous case.) These bonds are sold in international financial centers such as London or Frankfurt, but they are denominated in Japanese yen. Because these Eurobonds are scattered about the global markets, most are a type of bond known as a **bearer bond.** A bearer bond is owned officially by whoever is holding it, with no master registration list being held by government authorities who then track who is earning interest income from bond investments.[5] Bearer bonds have a series of small coupons that border the bond itself. On an annual basis, one of the coupons is cut or "clipped" from the bond and taken to a banking institution that is one of the listed paying agents. The bank will pay the holder of the coupon the interest payment due, and usually no official records of payment are kept.

International Equity Markets

Firms are financed with both debt and equity. Although the debt markets have been the center of activity in the international financial markets over the past three decades, there are signs that international equity capital is becoming more popular.

Again using the same categories of international financial activities, the Category 2 transaction of a foreign borrower in a domestic market in local currency is the predominant international equity activity. Foreign firms often issue new shares in foreign markets and list their stock on major stock exchanges such as those in New York, Tokyo, or London. The purpose of foreign issues and listings is to expand the

Global Perspective

5.2
Taxes, Eurobonds, and the Netherlands Antilles

Until 1984, U.S. corporations found themselves at a distinct disadvantage in their ability to sell bonds to the international markets. The U.S. government required taxes of 20 percent be withheld from all interest payments to nonresidents of the United States. This meant that investors outside the United States would have a significant portion of their interest earnings withheld, and they did not intend to file tax returns in the United States in an attempt to have the tax refunded. This effectively shut out U.S. corporations from issuing international bonds and tapping the world's capital markets (at lower rates). That was until the discovery of the Caribbean tax loophole.

It seems that the United States had signed a very unusual tax treaty with a chain of islands in the Caribbean that had formerly been Dutch territories, the Netherlands Antilles. The treaty's primary provision of interest was that subsidiaries of U.S. corporations located in the Netherlands Antilles were free to issue bonds to the international capital markets without withholding taxes. And the proceeds of the issues could then be re-loaned to the parent corporation in the United States.

The results were predictable. Hundreds of U.S. firms incorporated financial subsidiaries in the Netherlands Antilles (usually on Curacao or Aruba). Each of these subsidiaries in turn issued debt to the international markets and then funneled the cheaper capital back to its U.S. parent. It is estimated that by 1984 there was more than $32 billion in debt outstanding that was issued through these islands off the Venezuelan coast. The result was a slight detour in the way capital flowed from the European markets to the United States. The capital would take a legal trip through a few small desert islands in the south Caribbean on its way to the U.S. mainland. Finally in May 1984, the United States repealed the withholding tax on interest payments to foreign investors. The Netherlands Antilles's brief period of time at center stage among the world's financial centers was over.

investor base, in the hope of gaining access to capital markets in which the demand for shares of equity ownership is strong.

A foreign firm that wants to list its shares on an exchange in the United States does so through American Depository Receipts. These are the receipts to bank accounts that hold shares of the foreign firm's stock in that firm's country. The equities are actually in a foreign currency, so by holding them in a bank account and listing the receipt on the account on the American exchange, the shares can be revalued in dollars and redivided so that the price per share is more typical of that of the U.S. equity markets ($20 to $60 per share frequently being the desired range).

Although listing on a multitude of foreign exchanges is quite common among the world's largest multinational corporations, the degree of success achieved to date is debatable. There is evidence that most foreign listings do little more than react to price movements of the stock on its home exchange and with little additional investor appeal other than simple international diversification. In fact, a number of large multinationals have been delisting their stock on exchanges in Europe and particularly Tokyo in recent years.

There has been considerable growth, however, in the Euro-equity markets. A Euro-equity issue is the simultaneous sale of a firm's shares in several different countries, with or without listing the shares on an exchange in that country. The sales take place through investment banks. Once issued, most Euro-equities are listed at least on the computer screen quoting system of the International Stock Exchange

(ISE) in London, the SEAQ. As of late 1994, the Frankfurt stock exchange was the most globalized of major equity exchanges, with more than 45 percent of the firms listed on the exchange being foreign. At the same time, 18.8 percent of the firms on the London exchange were foreign, New York was a distant third with 7.6 percent foreign firms, with Tokyo fourth with less than 6 percent. Figure 5.5 illustrates a recent announcement, a "tombstone" as it is called in the investment banking industry, of a global equity offering by the Italian Ministry of the Treasury.

Private Placements

One of the largest and largely unpublicized capital markets is the **private placement** market. A private placement is the sale of debt or equity to a large investor. The sale is normally a one-time-only transaction in which the buyer of the bond or stock purchases the investment and intends to hold it until maturity (if debt) or until repurchased by the firm (if equity). How does this differ from normal bond and stock sales? The answer is that the securities are not resold on a secondary market such as the domestic bond market or the New York or London stock exchanges. If the security was intended to be publicly traded, the issuing firm would have to meet a number of disclosure and registration requirements with the regulatory authorities. In the United States, this would be the Securities and Exchange Commission.

Historically, much of the volume of private placements of securities occurred in Europe, with a large volume being placed with large Swiss financial institutions and large private investors. But in recent years the market has grown substantially across all countries as the world's financial markets have grown and as large institutional investors (particularly pension funds and insurance firms) have gained control over increasing shares of investment capital.

Gaining Access to International Financial Markets

Although the international markets are large and growing, this does not mean they are for everyone. For many years, only the largest of the world's multinational firms could enter another country's capital markets and find acceptance. The reasons are information and reputation.

Financial markets are by definition risk-averse. This means they are very reluctant to make loans to or buy debt issued by firms that they know little about. Therefore, the ability to gain access to the international markets is dependent on a firm's reputation, its ability to educate the markets about what it does, how successful it has been, and its patience. The firm must in the end be willing to expend the resources and effort required to build a credit reputation in the international markets. If successful, the firm may enjoy the benefits of new, larger, and more diversified sources of the capital it needs.

The individual firm, whether it be a chili dog stand serving the international tastes of office workers at the United Nations Plaza or a major multinational firm such as Honda of Japan is affected by exchange rates and international financial markets. Although the owner of the chili dog stand probably has more important and immediate problems than exchange rates to deal with, it is clear that firms such as Honda see the movements in these markets as critically important to their long-term competitiveness.

FIGURE 5.5
An Advertisement for a
Global Equity Offering

All of these securities having been sold, this announcement appears as a matter of record only.

The Ministry of the Treasury of the Republic of Italy

Global Equity Offering of 1,890,000,000 Shares

INA

Istituto Nazionale delle Assicurazioni S.p.A.

Joint Global Coordinators

Goldman Sachs International   Istituto Mobiliare Italiano S.p.A.

International Institutional Offering
285,981,600 Shares
in the form of Shares or American Depositary Shares

| Goldman Sachs International | Istituto Mobiliare Italiano S.p.A. | Dresdner Bank Aktiengesellschaft |
| Indosuez Capital | NatWest Securities Limited   Schroders/Fox-Pitt, Kelton N.V. | UBS Limited |

ABN AMRO Bank N.V.	Argentaria Bolsa	Banca Commerciale Italiana
James Capel & Co.	Creditanstalt-Bankverein	Credito Italiano
Daiwa Europe Limited	Istituto Bancario San Paolo di Torino S.p.A.	Paribas Capital Markets
Swiss Bank Corporation	S.G.Warburg Securities	Wood Gundy Inc.

Italian Institutional Offering
182,114,600 Shares

| Istituto Mobiliare Italiano S.p.A. | Banca Commerciale Italiana |
| Credito Italiano | Istituto Bancario San Paolo di Torino S.p.A. |

United States Public Offering
131,903,800 Shares
in the form of Shares or American Depositary Shares

Goldman, Sachs & Co.	CS First Boston
Bear, Stearns & Co. Inc.	Fox-Pitt, Kelton Inc./Wertheim Schroder & Co. Incorporated
Mabon Securities Corp. (IMI Banking Group)	Morgan Stanley & Co. Incorporated Salomon Brothers Inc

Italian Public Offering
1,290,000,000 Shares

| Istituto Mobiliare Italiano S.p.A. | Banca Commerciale Italiana |
| Credito Italiano | Istituto Bancario San Paolo di Torino S.p.A. |

July 1994

Source: The Economist, September 17, 1994.

THE DEBT CRISIS AND CURRENCY EARNINGS

The flow of capital across borders and currencies can have a number of positive and negative impacts, some of which were not intended. The difficulty in repayment of much of the capital that flowed into the world's developing countries in the late 1970s and early 1980s created a continuing series of severe problems for borrower and lender alike in the past decade. There have been many different individual "debt crises" over the past 40 years, in which countries could not repay the debt they had borrowed from others, but the difficulties of several major Latin American and South American countries beginning in 1982 are the focus of what is commonly termed the debt crisis.

The "debt" of the debt crisis was capital acquired by government borrowers primarily from large international banking syndicates worldwide. Throughout the 1970s and 1980s, many national governments (and other governmental units, such as states or provinces, national oil companies, railroads, and utilities) borrowed large quantities of capital to aid in the industrialization of their economies. Many of these countries possessed massive quantities of natural resources and other factors that would aid in rapid development, and the access to more capital was thought to constitute a sound policy for more rapid economic growth. At the same time, slower economic growth among the major industrial countries had produced large quantities of capital that could not find profitable uses.[6] The developing countries wanted to borrow, and the international banks wanted to lend. It was thought to be a profitable arrangement for both sides.

Debt, and the ability to repay or "service" debt, usually is not a particularly difficult problem. (Global Perspective 5.3 discusses how debt service affects a country's credit rating.) The proceeds of commerce produce the cash flows necessary for an individual, a firm, or even a country through its taxation to repay the debt. But what if the debt and its repayment are denominated in a foreign currency, such as the U.S. dollar? How does a country such as Mexico acquire U.S. dollars to repay debt in dollars? Simply exchanging the domestic currency such as the Mexico peso for U.S. dollars will not work for the quantities needed. Attempts to exchange massive quantities of pesos for foreign currencies would quickly drive the value of the peso down to virtual worthlessness.

The answer is that a country obtains foreign currency only one way, by exporting. When Mexico or Brazil or Argentina exports products to world markets, it can request payment in a currency that is readily convertible on world markets, such as the U.S. dollar, German mark, or Japanese yen (often referred to as hard currencies). The country must not only export large quantities of goods to earn sufficient currency, but it also must not spend much of what it earns for imports. Only by running a trade surplus can a country such as Mexico hope to earn the hard currency needed for debt repayment.

Friday, August 13, 1982: The Crisis

On Friday, August 13, 1982, the finance minister of Mexico called the U.S. secretary of the Treasury to inform him that Mexico would be unable to meet major debt service payments that were due to banks on the following Monday. Mexico was requesting the aid of the United States and the other major industrial countries in finding solutions to the problem. Although the economic forces that produced this crisis had been in motion for years, it is this date that is often termed the "beginning of the Latin American debt crisis."[7]

Global Perspective

5.3
Sovereign Credit Ratings

Developing countries' desire to gain access to foreign funds has fueled formal rating activity by international rating agencies. The assignment of investment-grade credit ratings to developing countries by rating agencies such as Moody's and Standard & Poor's has allowed these countries to raise resources from institutional investors (such as pension funds and insurance companies). Stipulated portfolio allocation guidelines by the trustees of institutional investors often do not permit investment of asset portfolios in less than investment-grade securities. There were seven first-time sovereign ratings by the two major rating agencies (Moody's and Standard & Poor's) during the year ending September 1994, including a first-ever rating for Slovakia. Several countries saw rating changes during the year: Chile and the Czech Republic received upgrades, but lower ratings were assigned to Turkey and Venezuela. In October, South Africa was assigned credit ratings by the two rating agencies.

An increasing number of developing country borrowers other than sovereigns are also being rated, as established issuers diversify funding sources and gain access to a wider investor base and as new borrowers enter the market. As emerging market issuers shift from the Eurobond market to other international bond markets, demand for ratings is rising. For example, issuers entering the Samurai market have all been required to obtain ratings. Ratings are not formally required in the Yankee market, but because a credit rating provides investors with a standardized benchmark for evaluating bond issues, several developing country borrowers in this market have acquired ratings. In the primary issue market, 18 percent of total bond issues by developing country borrowers were rated by Moody's and Standard & Poor's in 1993, compared with 15 percent in 1992. Despite a falloff in bond issuance this year, the shift toward rated issues is continuing.

Long-Term Ratings of Sovereign Foreign Currency Debt, end-September 1994

Country	Moody's	Standard & Poor's
Investment Grade		
Chile[2]	Baa2	BBB+[1]/AA
China	A3	BBB[2]
Colombia	Ba1	BBB−[2]
Czech Republic	Baa2	BBB+[2]
Greece	Baa3	BBB−[1]
Indonesia	Baa3	BBB−[2]
Korea, Rep.	A1	A+[3]
Malaysia[2]	A2	A[2]/AA+
Malta	A2	A[1]
Portugal[2]	A1	AA−[1]/AAA
South Africa[b]	Baa3	BB[2]
Thailand	A2	A−[1]
Below Investment Grade		
Argentina	B1	BB−[2]/BBB−
Brazil	B2	. .
Hungary	Ba1	BB+[1]
India	Ba2	BB+[1]
Mexico[2]	Ba2/Baa1	BB+[2]/AA−
Philippines	Ba3	BB−[1]
Slovakia	. .	BB−[1]
Trinidad and Tobago	Ba2	. .
Turkey	Ba3	B+[1]
Uruguay	Ba1	BB+[1]
Venezuela	Ba2	B+[3]

Rating systems for investment-grade bonds are as follows:
Moody's   Aaa   Aa1   Aa2   Aa3   A1   A2   A3   Baa1   Baa2   Baa3
Standard
& Poor's   AAA   AA+   AA   AA−   A+   A   A−   BBB+   BBB   BBB−
. . Not rated.
a. The first rating applies to foreign currency debt; the second rating applies to domestic currency debt.
b. Rated in October 1994.
1. Stable outlook.
2. Positive outlook.
3. Negative outlook.
Source: Moody's and Standard & Poor's.

Mexico, like Brazil, Argentina, Peru, Ecuador, and many other Latin American countries, had borrowed large amounts of capital on the assumption that its export earnings would continue to grow rapidly as they had throughout the 1970s. But the worldwide recession of 1980–1982 had slowed economies to the point that no one was buying, and the export earnings of the debtor countries dropped precipitously. The exports of these countries were primarily commodities. More than 70 percent of Mexico's export earnings came from the production and sale of one product, oil. However, oil prices had dropped from more than $30 a barrel in late 1979 to less than $20 a barrel in 1982. Other countries, such as Brazil and Argentina, were heavily dependent on the exports of agricultural and timber products, all of which had experienced substantial declines in price and sales in the depressed world economy.

The debtor countries were unable to obtain the currencies they needed for debt service. It is estimated that more than 90 percent of all Latin American debt was dollar-denominated. It was only a matter of weeks before Mexico's debt service difficulties spread to Brazil and Argentina, the countries with the largest and third-largest debts. The crisis took on epic proportions.

Due to the scale of the problem, both in terms of the magnitude of debt and the number of individual banks and institutions with which renegotiations and debt restructurings needed to take place, the International Monetary Fund took on an increasingly central role in the debt crisis. In addition to providing much of the bailout lending throughout the 1980s, in many cases the IMF also served as chief negotiator and manager. This constituted a significant increase in the power and visibility of the IMF, originally constructed only as a source of lending for countries with short-term balance of payments problems (which of course the debtor countries were experiencing).

Many of the most heavily indebted countries have continued to suffer high rates of inflation and slow or negative economic growth. But, unfortunately, most policies necessary for long-term economic stability (the reduction of inflation, reduced government deficits, and exchange rate stability) cause increases in unemployment and reductions in the standard of living of the lower income groups. The countries that are attempting to manage large international debt burdens today are no longer specific to any one area of the world—debt speaks all languages, as Table 5.3 shows.

Solutions to the Debt Crisis

Solutions to the crisis have been both short- and long-term. First, the debtor countries needed additional capital immediately to avoid defaulting on the existing loans. Additional credit was immediately provided by international organizations such as the International Monetary Fund, the Bank for International Settlements (BIS), and individual loans or advance export purchases by industrial governments such as the United States.[8]

The continuing management of the debt service problems of the heavily indebted countries has gone through four stages of evolution. Each can be seen as a response to the economic pressures of the time, the successes and failures of previous stages, and the philosophy and capabilities of the individuals leading the debate.

- **Stage 1: Bailout Lending**—The immediate liquidity aid provided by the IMF, BIS, and others was only a temporary fix, and all parties knew that true solutions would require the restructuring of the existing debt. This

TABLE 5.3 Debt Service Burdens of and Resource Transfers to SILICs[c] and Selected SIMICs[c], 1993						
Country	Actual Debt Service (U.S.$ millions)	Actual Debt Service to Exports (percent)	Scheduled Debt Service, 1994 (U.S. $ millions)	Scheduled Debt Service to Exports[a] (percent)	Scheduled Debt Service to Exports plus Grants[a] (percent)	Resource Transfers to GDP (percent)
SILICs	6,643	18.2	16,527	44.9	36.8	4.9
Burundi	36	40.9	43	42.2	18.7	19.1
Central African Republic	9	4.7	36	21.3	14.5	11.6
Côte d'Ivoire	964	30.0	1,516	46.8	43.9	0.8
Equatorial Guinea	1	1.6	24	44.4	33.8	33.8
Ethiopia	69	9.0	377	47.4	23.3	24.7
Ghana	277	22.8	197	23.5	18.6	6.3
Guinea	84	12.8	223	29.9	23.8	12.4
Guinea-Bissau	4	11.1	51	127.8	59.8	28.6
Guyana	90	24.5	131	45.2	36.2	11.6
Honduras	360	31.5	415	36.3	29.3	3.8
Kenya	652	28.0	700	29.7	25.5	2.5
Lao PDR	28	9.5	23	10.5	8.1	12.9
Liberia	21	3.4	105	18.1	14.8	—
Madagascar	69	13.9	349	70.8	48.6	9.5
Mali	26	5.0	151	28.3	20.6	8.8
Mauritania	125	27.2	138	27.9	22.4	21.3
Mozambique	77	20.7	308	83.8	27.2	56.1
Myanmar	116	15.0	323	40.5	38.2	0.0
Nicaragua	116	29.3	1,205	323.0	143.9	12.4
Niger	93	31.3	136	41.6	24.9	10.3
Nigeria	1,831	14.9	4,355	32.5	32.2	− 1.2
Rwanda	6	5.0	30	22.3	8.8	16.8
São Tomé and Principe	3	25.0	13	90.9	29.4	146.1
Sierra Leone	20	12.1	53	27.8	20.5	26.4
Somalia	0	0.0	116	175.9	21.2	—
Sudan	20	4.0	397	75.1	41.8	6.3
Tanzania	155	25.1	495	78.8	36.8	29.4
Uganda	302	60.6[b]	162	81.1	34.3	8.6
Vietnam	498	13.6	2,464	78.5	75.2	—
Yemen	120	7.5	385	21.6	20.5	1.1
Zaire	28	1.5	1,280	74.4	66.1	—
Zambia	349	20.7[b]	326	27.6	19.0	18.0
Selected SIMICs						
Angola	153	5.3	1,287	35.6	33.8	—
Bolivia	489	38.6[b]	428	49.5	35.4	11.4
Cameroon	444	21.8	844	34.4	31.3	2.1
Congo	126	10.6	542	42.0	40.6	17.6

— Not available.

[a] 1991–93 average for exports and grants.

[b] Excludes effect of up-front payments for debt reduction operations and arrears clearance.

[c] SILICS: severely indebted lower income countries; SIMICS: severely indebted middle-income countries.

Source: World Debt Tables 1994–1995, Volume 1, The International Bank for Reconstruction and Development/World Bank, Washington, D.C., p. 39.

meant providing grace periods before additional debt service payments were required, lower interest rates, and extended maturities for repayment. Although all agreed these measures were necessary, it was critical that the debtor countries be provided with short-term capital, so-called bailout lending, to see them through the time required for renegotiating the hundreds of loans. Much of the management during this period, 1982 and 1983, was simply the consolidation of debt that was coming due or already in arrears.

- **Stage 2: Multiyear-Restructuring Agreements**—Once consolidation had taken place, immediate concern was to ensure some minimal continuing flow of capital to these heavily indebted countries. In 1983 and 1984 all parties entered into continuing renegotiations to attempt to restructure the debt to alleviate some of the burden on the debtors. Little real progress was made, however, as many of the renegotiations continued to be pursued on an individual basis, each country having to negotiate with the multitude of the banks and organizations holding their debt. It has also been argued that one of the reasons little progress was made in this period was that the burden of blame was concentrated on the borrowers, with little blame and burden accepted by the banking institutions, which, in the eyes of many, had been overly zealous in their lending practices.

- **Stage 3: The Baker Plan**—When James Baker took over as secretary of the Treasury at the start of the second Reagan Administration, major initiatives were put forward to solve the ever-worsening debt crisis. Secretary Baker and the U.S. administration, in a complete reversal of previous policy, now wanted to take a larger and more active hand in solving the crisis. The Baker Plan, as first presented at the IMF meetings in Seoul, Korea, in October 1985, had three elements: (1) recognition of realistic limits to the austerity measures being imposed from outside and inside on the debtor countries; (2) solutions to the continuing crisis required not only debt reduction but positive measures of promoting economic growth in the debtor countries; and (3) the need for renewed lending by private banking institutions to the developing countries.

- **Stage 4: The Brady Plan**—With a new U.S. secretary of the Treasury, Nicholas Brady, came a new plan in March 1989. The Brady Plan differed markedly from previous strategies, given its adoption of ideas promoted the previous year by the Japanese finance minister, Kiichi Miyazawa. Miyazawa's plan was to focus multilateral efforts on debt reduction, not debt service. Debt reduction was to be accomplished by dividing the outstanding debt of several indebted countries into two parts, one part for debt reduction, the other for debt interest payment guarantees. Multilateral institutions such as the IMF and World Bank would guarantee the interest payments on the second portion of the outstanding debt, thus shifting credit risk from the borrower countries to the institutions. Japan itself also served as a major source of the capital necessary for much of this debt reduction policy. In addition, many of the debt–swap programs (debt for equity, debt for environment, debt for development, and so forth) that involve the substitution of local currency debt for dollar debt were pushed forward.

The debt crisis is still far from over. Continued efforts at debt reduction and debt management are ongoing as many of the most severely indebted countries still struggle under the burden of servicing their obligations. But, as illustrated in Table 5.4

TABLE 5.4
External Debt of the Countries of the Former Soviet Union (excluding Russia), 1992–1993 (US\$ millions)

Most countries of the former Soviet Union other than Russia did not initiate international borrowing programs until 1992. That was also the year when these countries started to establish firm legal, administrative, and institutional norms for external borrowing. Over 1992–93 all countries of the former Soviet Union initiated external debt reporting to the World Bank. Their total debt stock had increased almost tenfold, from \$928 million in 1992 to just under \$9 billion (including borrowing among these countries) by 1993. The external debt of this group of countries continued to grow in 1994. Ukraine, Kazakhstan, Belarus, Uzbekistan, and Georgia account for 84 percent of the debt stock of 14 countries of the former Soviet Union (excluding Russia). The other nine countries have smaller loan portfolios. In the coming years, the countries of the former Soviet Union will have to continue to mobilize substantial external resources to sustain imports and stem the fall in production.

| | Total Debt Outstanding and Disbursed | |
Country	1992	1993
Armenia	10	140
Azerbaijan	0	36
Belarus	189	961
Estonia	58	155
Georgia	79	568
Kazakhstan	35	1,640
Kyrgyz Republic	0	308
Latvia	61	231
Lithuania	38	291
Moldova	39	289
Tajikistan	10	42
Turkmenistan	0	9
Ukraine	554	3,584
Uzbekistan	10	739
Total	1,082	8,993

Source: World Debt Tables 1994–1995, Volume 1, the International Bank for Reconstruction and Development/World Bank, Washington,

and Global Perspective 5.4 on Mexico's new crisis, new countries join the list of the indebted each year.

SUMMARY

This chapter has spanned the breadth of the international financial markets from currencies to capital markets. The world's currency markets expanded threefold in only six years, and there is no reason to believe this growth will end. It is estimated that more than \$1 trillion worth of currencies change hands daily, and the majority of it is either U.S. dollars, German marks, or Japanese yen. These are the world's major floating currencies.

But the world's financial markets are much more than currency exchanges. The rapid growth in the international financial markets—both on their own and as linkages between domestic markets—has resulted in the creation of a large and legitimate source of finance for the world's multinational firms. The recent expansion of market economics to more and more of the world's countries and economies sets the stage for further growth for the world's currency and capital markets, but also poses the potential for new external debt crises.

Key Terms and Concepts

direct quotation	Euromarkets
indirect quotation	selling forward

Global Perspective

5.4
Spending at Core of Mexico's Woes

WASHINGTON—Here are answers to some basic questions about the Mexican financial crisis:

QUESTION: How did Mexico get into this mess?

ANSWER: For years, both the Mexican government and the Mexican people have been spending beyond their means. The country's trade deficit is high, and the government relies too much on money borrowed from foreigners. In December, a renewed peasant uprising in Chiapas state made investors nervous, with the result that they dumped pesos and called in their debts, causing the currency's value to begin dropping on international markets. The government did not have enough foreign currency reserves to buy pesos and halt the decline. It had to call on its allies for help.

Q: So why is this a problem for the United States?

A: Sales of U.S. goods in Mexico could plunge because the prices of our products are soaring there. This could cost thousands of U.S. jobs as exports are slowed. Also, with the peso's value plunging, more U.S. jobs could shift to Mexico because wages and production costs would be lower there. And many U.S. investors who purchased Mexican stocks or mutual funds holding Mexican stocks could lose much of their investments. There also could be political problems in the United States if the peso remained weak, because a sharp rise in illegal immigration would be expected as more and more Mexicans tried to get dollar-paying jobs.

Q: What are we going to do to help?

A: Originally, President Clinton wanted to extend loan guarantees of $40 billion to Mexico, much the same way the government bailed out Chrysler Corp. But Congress refused to support the idea because it would impose too much of a financial risk on U.S. taxpayers. Clinton is bypassing Congress and going straight to the U.S. Treasury, using his executive power to commit $20 billion for emergency assistance to Mexico. This is not foreign aid or a grant. Instead, it is expected to take the form of currency swaps: The Treasury will exchange dollars for pesos with an agreement to swap them back in the future as a way of pumping dollars into Mexican coffers.

Q: How much will this cost U.S. taxpayers?

A: There's no direct cost. But there is a risk for the Treasury, which will be committing billions of its reserves to the proposition that the value of the peso will stabilize.

Q: What about Mexico's other allies?

A: The International Monetary Fund and Bank of International Settlements will kick in $27 billion in loans, while the Bank of Canada will provide a $1 billion line of credit.

Q: What will Mexico do with the money?

A: Investor confidence has been so shaken that Mexico needs to be able to commit billions of dollars to cover all its obligations if bondholders decide to take the money and run. Hopefully, that won't be necessary. But the Mexican government has to be prepared for the worst.

Q: Is this a bailout for Wall Street?

A: Many in Congress think so. But unlike a Mexican debt crisis in 1982, when just a few big commercial banks were holding bad loans, this crisis has many more potential victims, including millions of Americans who have invested money in bond funds for "emerging nations." According to some estimates, U.S. investors hold as much as $100 billion in Mexican stocks and bonds.

Q: Did the North American Free Trade Agreement cause this crisis?

A: Indirectly. During debate over the agreement in 1993, President Clinton and Mexico's then-President Carlos Salinas de Gortari emphasized the progress Mexico had made in opening and reforming its economy, not its shortcomings. Salinas could have taken steps to reduce imports and pay Mexico's soaring foreign debt, but that would have meant higher inflation and a recession.

Source: Knight-Ridder Tribune, *The Arizona Republic,* February 1, 1995, p. A7.

spot rates   offshore banking
forward rates   correspondent banks
European terms   representative office
American terms   syndicated loan
cross rates   Euronote
triangular arbitrage   international bond
spread   Euro–commerical paper (ECP)
Eurocurrency   foreign bond
Eurodollars   Eurobond
interbank interest rates   bearer bond
LIBOR   private placement

Questions for Discussion

1. How and where are currencies traded?
2. Does it matter whether a currency is quoted as DEM/USD or USD/DEM?
3. What is a forward rate? How do banks set forward rates?
4. What is a Eurocurrency?
5. What is a Eurocurrency interest rate? Is it different from LIBOR?
6. What makes a currency sell forward at a discount?
7. What is the difference between an international bond and a Eurobond?
8. What is the link between exchange rates and the external debt of a country?
9. How will the heavily indebted countries repay their debt?
10. Was the Mexican crisis of 1994–1995 caused by the same external debt problems Mexico experienced in 1982?

Recommended Readings

Bank for International Settlements. *Annual Report.* Basle, Switzerland, annually.

Eiteman, David, Arthur Stonehill, and Michael H. Moffett. *Multinational Business Finance.* 7th edition. Reading, Mass.: Addison-Wesley, 1995.

Federal Reserve Bank of New York. *Summary of Results of the U.S. Foreign Exchange Market Turnover Survey,* April 1992.

The Financial Times. *FT Guide to World Currencies,* January 30, 1995.

Giddy, Ian. *Global Financial Markets.* Heath, 1993.

Goodhart, C.A.E., and L. Figliuoli. "Every Minute Counts in Financial Markets." *Journal of International Money and Finance* 10 (1991): 23–52.

Grabbe, J. Orlin. *International Financial Markets.* 2d edition. New York: Elsevier, 1991.

International Monetary Fund. *International Financial Statistics.* Washington, D.C., monthly.

The Wall Street Journal. Foreign Exchange Rates, January 30, 1995, C15.

Tran, Hung Q., Larry Anderson, and Ernst-Ludwig Drayss. "Chapter 8: Eurocapital Markets," in *International Finance and Investing.* The Library of Investment Banking, edited by Robert Lawrence Kuhn. Homewood, Ill.: Dow Jones–Irwin, 1990, 129–160.

Notes

1. Rounding errors are solved quite simply with exchange rates. With a few notable exceptions, all active trading takes place using direct quotations on foreign currencies versus the U.S. dollar (DEM 1.5152/USD, YEN 99.36/USD) and for a conventional number of decimal places. These are the base rates that are then used if needed for the calculation of the inverse indirect quotes on the foreign currencies.

2. A currency trader once remarked to the authors that the spot quotes listed on such a screen were no more and no less accurate to the "true price" than the sticker price on a showroom automobile. Of course, this may no longer be true since the introduction of the Saturn, which sells at sticker price only!

3. Exchange rate "basis points" should not be confused with interest rate basis points, where a single basis point is 1/100th of a percent.

4. Domestic commercial paper markets were legalized in many major countries only in the middle to late 1980s: France in 1985, the United Kingdom in 1986, Japan in 1987, Belgium in 1990, and Germany in 1991.

5. Bearer bonds were issued by the U.S. government up until the early 1980s, when discontinued. Even though they were called bearer bonds, a list of bond registration numbers was still kept and recorded in order to tax investors holding the bearer instruments.

6. The large increases in the price of oil instituted by the Organization of Petroleum Exporting Countries (OPEC) in 1974 and 1979 had also resulted in enormous quantities of capital that needed to be invested in profitable ventures. Because oil is priced and sold on world markets in U.S. dollars, this accumulation of capital, OPEC dollars, provided an enormous supply of one specific currency.

7. Mexico was indeed in crisis. In August 1982 Mexico devalued the peso 30 percent versus the U.S. dollar, instituted a two-tier exchange-rate system, froze dollar-denominated bank accounts in Mexico, and on August 12 announced the total embargo of U.S. dollars crossing the U.S.-Mexico border (on their way out). On Wednesday, September 1, President Jose Lopez Portillo announced the nationalization of Mexico's private banks.

8. One example of this is the advance payment to Mexico by the United States (specifically the Department of Energy) for $1 billion worth of oil. The United States purchased the oil for the government's strategic petroleum reserves. At the time of payment, however, the oil was still in the ground in Mexico.

CHAPTER 6

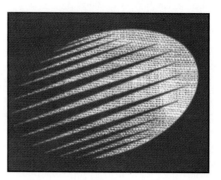

Economic Integration

1. To review types of economic integration among countries.

2. To examine the costs and benefits of integrative arrangements.

3. To understand the structure of the European Union and its implications for firms within and outside Europe.

4. To explore the emergence of other integration agreements, especially the North American Free Trade Agreement.

Building Blocs (or Stumbling Blocs?) of Worldwide Free Trade

Regional groupings based on economics will become increasingly important in the 1990s. Countries around the globe are making efforts to suppress national interests in favor of regional ones. A total of 32 such groupings is estimated to be in existence: three in Europe, four in the Middle East, five in Asia, and ten each in Africa and the Americas. With respect to the three major blocs, the North American, Western European, and Asian, trade inside these blocs has grown at a rapid pace, while trading among these blocs or with outsiders is either declining or growing far more moderately.

Some of these groupings around the world have the superstructure of nation-states (such as the European Union), some (such as the ASEAN Free Trade Area) are multinational agreements that may be more political arrangements than cohesive trading blocs at present. Some arrangements are not trading blocs per se, but work to further them. The Enterprise for the Americas Initiative is a foreign policy initiative designed to further democracy in the region through incentives to capitalistic development and trade liberalization. The Andean Common Market and Mercosur both have indicated an intention to negotiate with the parties of the North American Free Trade Agreement (NAFTA) to create a hemispheric market. Regional economic integration in Asia has been driven more by market forces than by treaties, and by a need to maintain balance in negotiations with Europe and North America. Broader formal agreements are in formative stages; for example, Malaysians have led a move to form the East Asian Economic Group (EAEG) of AFTA countries plus Hong Kong, Japan, South Korea, and Taiwan. The Asia Pacific Economic Cooperation (APEC) initiated in 1988 would bring together partners from multiple continents: AFTA members are joined by such economic powerhouses as China, South Korea, Taiwan, and the United States.

Regional groupings are constantly in a state of development. In 1995, informal proposals were made to create a new bloc between NAFTA and EU members called TAFTA, the Transatlantic Free Trade Area. Since the elimination of the Soviet Union in 1991, 12 former republics have tried to forge common economic policies, but thus far only Belarus, Kazakhstan, and Russia are signatories to a free-trade pact.

Regional groupings will mean that companies are facing ever-intensifying competition and trading difficulties for sales inside a bloc. In the long term, firms will come under pressure to globalize and source locally. Actions of these global companies may also allay fears that regional blocs are nothing but protectionism on a grander scale.

NAFTA
North American Free Trade Agreement
Canada, Mexico, United States
GNP: $6 trillion; 364 million people

EEA
European Economic Area
Total of 18 European nations
GNP: $4.7 trillion; 375 million people

EAEG
East Asian Economic Group
Add Hong Kong, Japan, South Korea, and Taiwan to AFTA
GNP: $4.2 trillion; 413 million people

EAI
Enterprise for the Americas Initiative

MERCOSUR
South Cove Common Market
Argentina, Brazil, Paraguay, Uruguay
GNP: $753 billion; 200 million people

AFTA ASEAN Free Trade Area
Brunei, Indonesia, Malaysia, Philippines, Singapore, Thailand
GNP: $321 billion; 320 million people

Source: Ilkka A. Ronkainen, "Trading Blocs: Opportunity or Demise for International Trade?" *Multinational Business Review* 1(Spring 1993): 1–9; Paivi Vihma, "Gatt Kittuu, Kauppablokit Nousevat," *Talouselama,* number 11, 1992, 42–43; and Joseph L. Brand, "The New World Order," *Vital Speeches of the Day* 58(December): 155–160.

The benefits of free trade and stable exchange rates are available only if nation-states are willing to give up some measure of independence and autonomy. This has resulted in increased economic integration around the world with agreements among countries to establish links through movement of goods, services, capital, and labor across borders. Some predict, however, that the regional **trading blocs** of the new economic world order will divide into a handful of protectionist superstates that, although liberalizing trade among members, may raise barriers to external trade.

Economic integration is best viewed as a spectrum. At one extreme we might envision a truly global economy in which all countries shared a common currency and agreed to free flows of goods, services, and factors of production. At the other extreme would be a number of closed economies, each independent and self-sufficient. The various integrative agreements in effect today lie along the middle of the spectrum. The most striking example of successful integration is the historic economic unification that is taking place around the world today. These developments were discussed in the chapter's opening vignette. Some countries, however, give priority to maintaining economic self-sufficiency and independence. However, their ranks have thinned considerably in the 1990s with countries such as Vietnam becoming heavily involved in international trade and investment. Even North Korea is now considered as a possible future market by companies such as Coca-Cola.

This chapter will begin with an explanation of the various levels of economic integration. The level of integration defines the nature and degree of economic links among countries. Next, major arguments both for and against economic integration will be reviewed. Finally, the European Union, the North American Free Trade Agreement, Asia Pacific Economic Cooperation, and other economic alliances will be discussed.

LEVELS OF ECONOMIC INTEGRATION

A trading bloc is a preferential economic arrangement among a group of countries. The forms it may take are provided in Table 6.1. From least to most integrative, they are the free trade area, the customs union, the common market, and the economic union.[1]

The Free Trade Area

The **free trade area** is the least restrictive and loosest form of economic integration among countries. In a free trade area, all barriers to trade among member countries are removed. Therefore, goods and services are freely traded among member countries in much the same way that they flow freely between, for example, South Carolina and New York. No discriminatory taxes, quotas, tariffs, or other trade barriers are allowed. Sometimes a free trade area is formed only for certain classes of goods and services. An agricultural free trade area, for example, implies the absence of restrictions on the trade of agricultural products only. The most notable feature of a free trade area is that each country continues to set its own policies in relation to nonmembers. In other words, each member is free to set any tariffs, quotas, or other restrictions that it chooses for trade with countries outside the free trade area. Among such free trade areas the most notable are the European Free Trade Area (EFTA) and the North American Free Trade Agreement (NAFTA). These agreements will be discussed in detail later in the chapter.

TABLE 6.1 Forms of International Economic Integration	Abolition of Tariffs and Quotas among Members	Common Tariff and Quota System	Abolition of Restrictions on Factor Movements	Harmonization and Unification of Economic Policies and Institutions
Stage of Integration				
Free trade area	Yes	No	No	No
Customs union	Yes	Yes	No	No
Common market	Yes	Yes	Yes	No
Economic union	Yes	Yes	Yes	Yes

Source: Franklin R. Root, *International Trade and Investment,* Cincinnati, Ohio: South-Western Publishing Company, 1992, 254.

The Customs Union

The **customs union** is one step further along the spectrum of economic integration. Like members of a free trade area, members of a customs union dismantle barriers to trade in goods and services among themselves. In addition, however, the customs union establishes a common trade policy with respect to nonmembers. Typically, this takes the form of a common external tariff, whereby imports from nonmembers are subject to the same tariff when sold to any member country. Tariff revenues are then shared among members according to a prespecified formula.

The Common Market

Further still along the spectrum of economic integration is the **common market.** Like the customs union, a common market has no barriers to trade among members and has a common external trade policy. In addition, however, factors of production are also mobile among members. Factors of production include labor, capital, and technology. Thus restrictions on immigration, emigration, and cross-border investment are abolished. The importance of **factor mobility** for economic growth cannot be overstated. When factors of production are freely mobile, then capital, labor, and technology may be employed in their most productive uses. To see the importance of factor mobility, imagine the state of the U.S. economy if unemployed steelworkers in Pittsburgh were prevented from migrating to the growing Sunbelt in search of better opportunities. Alternatively, imagine that savings in New York banks could not be invested in profitable opportunities in Chicago.

Despite the obvious benefits, members of a common market must be prepared to cooperate closely in monetary, fiscal, and employment policies. Furthermore, while a common market will enhance the productivity of members in the aggregate, it is by no means clear that individual member countries will always benefit. Because of these difficulties, the goals of common markets have proved to be elusive in many areas of the world, notably Central America and Asia. However, the objective of the **Single European Act** and the 1992 process was to have a full common market in effect within the EU at the end of 1992. While many of the directives aimed at opening borders and markets were implemented on schedule, major exceptions do still exist.

The Economic Union

The creation of a true **economic union** requires integration of economic policies in addition to the free movement of goods, services, and factors of production across borders. Under an economic union, members would harmonize monetary policies, taxation, and government spending. In addition, a common currency would be used by all members. This could be accomplished de facto, or in effect, by a system of fixed exchange rates. Clearly, the formation of an economic union requires nations to surrender a large measure of their national sovereignty. Needless to say, the barriers to full economic union are quite strong. Our global political system is built on the autonomy and supreme power of the nation-state, and attempts to undermine the authority of the state will undoubtedly always encounter opposition. As a result, no true economic unions are in effect today. The European Union is committed to European unity, in name at least, through the Maastricht Treaty. The aim would be to achieve full monetary union by 1999 with a single European currency. The treaty is to be reviewed by the member states in 1996 and wide disagreement exists as to what level of integration is required.[2]

ARGUMENTS SURROUNDING ECONOMIC INTEGRATION

A number of arguments surround economic integration. They center on (1) trade creation and diversion; (2) the effects of integration on import prices, competition, economies of scale, and factor productivity; and (3) the benefits of regionalism versus nationalism.

Trade Creation and Trade Diversion

Economist Jacob Viner first formalized the economic costs and benefits of economic integration.[3] Chapter 2 illustrated that the classical theory of trade predicts a win-win result for countries participating in free trade. The question is whether similar benefits accrue when free trade is limited to one group of countries. The case examined by Viner was the customs union. The conclusion of Viner's analysis was that either negative or positive effects may result when a group of countries trade freely among themselves but maintain common barriers to trade with nonmembers.

Viner's arguments can be highlighted with a simple illustration. In 1986, Spain formally entered the European Union (EU) as a member. Prior to membership, Spain—like all nonmembers such as the United States, Canada, and Japan—traded with the EU and suffered the common external tariff. Imports of agricultural products from Spain or the United States had the same tariff applied to their products, for example, 20 percent. During this period, the United States was a lower-cost producer of wheat compared to Spain. U.S. exports to EU members may have cost $3.00 per bushel, plus a 20 percent tariff of $0.60, for a total of $3.60 per bushel. If Spain at the same time produced wheat at $3.20 per bushel, plus a 20 percent tariff of $0.64 for a total cost to EU customers of $3.84 per bushel, its wheat was more expensive and therefore less competitive.

But when Spain joined the EU as a member, its products were no longer subject to the common external tariffs; Spain had become a member of the "club" and therefore enjoyed its benefits. Spain was now the low-cost producer of wheat at $3.20 per bushel, compared to the price of $3.60 from the United States. Trade flows changed as a result. The increased export of wheat and other products by Spain to the EU as a result of its membership is termed **trade creation.** The elimination of the tariff literally created more trade between Spain and the EU. At the same time, because the United States is still outside of the EU, its products suffer the higher price as a result of tariff application. U.S. exports to the EU fall. When the source of trading competitiveness is shifted in this manner from one country to another, it is termed **trade diversion.**

Whereas trade creation is distinctly positive in moving toward freer trade, and therefore lower prices for consumers within the EU, the impact of trade diversion is negative. Trade diversion is inherently negative because the competitive advantage has shifted away from the lower-cost producer to the higher-cost producer. The benefits of Spain's membership are enjoyed by Spanish farmers (greater export sales) and EU consumers (lower prices). The two major costs are reduced tariff revenues collected and costs borne by the United States and its exports as a result of lost sales.

From the perspective of nonmembers such as the United States, the formation or expansion of a customs union is obviously negative. Most damaged will naturally be countries that may need to have trade to build their economies, such as the countries of the Third World. As Viner shows, from the perspective of members of the customs union, the formation or expansion is only beneficial if the trade creation benefits exceed trade diversion costs.

Reduced Import Prices

When a small country imposes a tariff on imports, the price of the goods will typically rise because sellers will increase prices to cover the cost of the tariff. This increase in price, in turn, will result in lower demand for the imported goods. If a bloc of countries imposes the tariff, however, the fall in demand for the imported goods will be substantial. The exporting country may then be forced to reduce the price of the goods. The possibility of lower prices for imports results from the greater market power of the bloc relative to that of a single country. The result may then be an improvement in the trade position of the bloc countries. Any gain in the trade position of bloc members, however, is offset by a deteriorating trade position for the exporting country. Again, unlike the win-win situation resulting from free trade, the scenario involving a trade bloc is instead win-lose.

Increased Competition and Economies of Scale

Integration increases market size and therefore may result in a lower degree of monopoly in the production of certain goods and services.[4] This is because a larger market will tend to increase the number of competing firms, resulting in greater efficiency and lower prices for consumers. Moreover, less energetic and productive economies may be spurred into action by competition from the more industrious bloc members.

Many industries, such as steel and automobiles, require large-scale production in order to obtain economies of scale in production. Therefore, certain industries may simply not be economically viable in smaller, trade protected countries. However, the formation of a trading bloc enlarges the market so that large-scale production is justified. The lower per-unit costs resulting from scale economies may then be obtained. These lower production costs resulting from greater production for an enlarged market are called **internal economies of scale.**

In a common market, **external economies of scale** may also be present. Because a common market allows factors of production to flow freely across borders, the firm may now have access to cheaper capital, more highly skilled labor, or superior technology. These factors will improve the quality of the firm's product or service or will lower costs or both.

Global Perspective

6.1
Labor Pains of Integration

Economic integration, despite promises of great benefits from the free flow of people, goods, services, and money, is not making everyone happy. Rich nations, such as Germany and France, fear that a deepening recession will be compounded by a hemorrhage of jobs as companies shift their operations to less prosperous regions in Europe where wages are lower. Many Europeans also complain about Britain's willingness, through various incentives, to be the "Trojan horse" that allows Europe's rivals to invade its markets.

A decision made by the U.S. vacuum cleaner maker Hoover to relocate its production facilities from France's Burgundy region to Scotland, axing 600 jobs in the process, has sparked a controversy whether the single European market will strip France of jobs. France has revived accusations that Britain is engaged in "social dumping"—eroding workers' rights in a bid to attract foreign investment. As part of the Hoover deal, the firm's Scottish work force has

agreed to accept new working practices, including limits on strike action.

Yet Hoover has done nothing wrong. To remain competitive in what is fast becoming a global business, the company believes it must concentrate vacuum cleaner production in Europe in a single plant. It also needs a flexible work force, which is a big competitive advantage in many industries. Hoover's Scottish plant employees were more willing to change their ways than their French counterparts. By shifting its production to Scotland, Hoover is estimated to cut its costs by a quarter. Part of this saving will come from economies of scale, the rest from lower wages.

Such hard-headed economics will not stop Europe's politicians from complaining when jobs are lost in their own backyard. Other companies, such as the German television maker Grundig, are considering moves. As long as politicians complain every time a company makes such a move, integration decisions are challenged.

Sources: "A Singular Market," *The Economist,* October 22, 1994, 10–16; "French Say United Europe Promotes 'Job Poaching,'" *The Washington Post,* February 10, 1993, A23, A27; "Labour Pains," *The Economist,* February 6, 1993, 71.

Higher Factor Productivity

When factors of production are freely mobile, the wealth of the common market countries, in aggregate, will likely increase. The theory behind this contention is straightforward: Factor mobility will lead to the movement of labor and capital from areas of low productivity to areas of high productivity. In addition to the economic gains from factor mobility, there are other benefits not so easily quantified. The free movement of labor fosters a higher level of communication across cultures. This, in turn, leads to a higher degree of cross-cultural understanding; as people move, their ideas, skills, and ethnicity move with them.

Again, however, factor mobility will not necessarily benefit each country in the common market. A poorer country, for example, may lose badly needed investment capital to a richer country, where opportunities are perceived to be more profitable. Another disadvantage of factor mobility that is often cited is the brain-drain phenomenon. A poorer country may lose its most talented workers when they are free to search out better opportunities.

Regionalism versus Nationalism

Economists have composed elegant and compelling arguments in favor of the various levels of economic integration. It is difficult, however, to turn these arguments into reality in the face of intense nationalism. The biggest impediment to economic integration remains in the reluctance of nations to surrender a measure of their autonomy. Integration, by its very nature, requires the surrender of national power and self-determinism. An example of this can be seen in Global Perspective 6.1.

EUROPEAN INTEGRATION

Economic Integration in Europe from 1948 to the Mid-1980s

The period of the Great Depression from the late 1920s through World War II was characterized by isolationism, protectionism, and fierce nationalism. The economic chaos and political difficulties of the period resulted in no serious attempts at economic integration until the end of the war. From the devastation of the war, however, a spirit of cooperation gradually emerged in Europe.

The first step in this regional cooperative effort was the establishment of the Organization for European Economic Cooperation (OEEC) in 1948 to administer Marshall Plan aid from the United States. Although the objective of the OEEC was limited to economic reconstruction following the war, its success set the stage for more ambitious integration programs.

In 1952, six European countries (West Germany, France, Italy, Belgium, the Netherlands, and Luxembourg) joined in establishing the European Coal and Steel Community (ECSC). The objective of the ECSC was the formation of a common market in coal, steel, and iron ore for member countries. These basic industries were rapidly revitalized into competitive and efficient producers. The stage was again set for further cooperative efforts.

In 1957, the European Economic Community (EEC) was formally established by the **Treaty of Rome.** In 1967, ECSC and EEC as well as the European Atomic Energy Community (EURATOM) were merged to form the European Community (EC). Table 6.2 shows the founding members of the community in 1957 and the members in 1995. The Treaty of Rome is a monumental document, composed of more than 200 articles. The main provisions of the treaty are summarized in Table 6.3. The document was (and is) quite ambitious. The cooperative spirit apparent throughout the treaty was based on the premise that the mobility of goods, services, labor, and capital—the "four freedoms"—was of paramount importance for the economic prosperity of the region. Founding members envisioned that the successful integration of the European economies would result in an economic power to rival that of the United States.

Some countries, however, were reluctant to embrace the ambitious integrative effort of the treaty. In 1960, a looser, less integrated philosophy was endorsed with the formation of the European Free Trade Association (EFTA) by eight countries: United Kingdom, Norway, Denmark, Sweden, Austria, Finland, Portugal, and Switzerland. Barriers to trade among member countries were dismantled, although each

TABLE 6.2 Membership of the European Union	1957	1993	1995
	France West Germany Italy Belgium Netherlands Luxembourg	+	Great Britain (1973) Ireland (1973) Denmark (1973) Greece (1981) Spain (1986) Portugal (1986)	+	Austria (1995) Finland (1995) Sweden (1995)

TABLE 6.3
Main Provisions of the
Treaty of Rome

1. Formation of a free trade area: the gradual elimination of tariffs, quotas, and other barriers to trade among members
2. Formation of a customs union: the creation of a uniform tariff schedule applicable to imports from the rest of the world
3. Formation of a common market: the removal of barriers to the movement of labor, capital, and business enterprises
4. The adoption of common agricultural policies
5. The creation of an investment fund to channel capital from the more advanced to the less developed regions of the community

country maintained its own policies with nonmember states. Since that time EFTA has lost much of its original significance due to its members joining the European Union (Denmark and the United Kingdom in 1973, Portugal in 1986, and Austria, Finland, and Sweden in 1995). EFTA countries have cooperated with the EU through bilateral free trade agreements, and, since 1994, through the European Economic Area (EEA) arrangement, which allows for free movement of people, products, services, and capital within the combined area of the EU and EFTA. Of the EFTA countries, Iceland and Liechtenstein (which joined the EEA only in May 1995) have decided not to apply for membership in the EU. Norway was to have joined in 1995, but after a referendum declined membership, as it did in 1973. Switzerland's decision to stay out of the EEA has stalled its negotiations with the EU.

Many believe that a move away from the spirit and intent of the Treaty of Rome was taken in 1966 with the passage of the Luxembourg Compromise. The Luxembourg Compromise granted member countries the right to veto any decision if they felt their "vital interests" were threatened. In fact, however, "the governments invoked 'vital interests' each time the slightest segment of their population risked a social or economic disadvantage. . . . As membership expanded it became more and more difficult to reach any decisions at all. The Luxembourg Compromise virtually paralyzed the EU."[5]

A conflict that intensified throughout the 1980s was between the richer and more industrialized countries and the poorer countries of the Mediterranean region. The power of the bloc of poorer countries was strengthened in the 1980s when Greece, Spain, and Portugal became EU members. Many argue that the dismantling of barriers between the richer and poorer countries will benefit the poorer countries by spurring them to become competitive. However, it may also be argued that the richer countries have an unfair advantage and therefore should accord protection to the poorer members before all barriers are dismantled.

Another source of difficulty that intensified in the 1980s was the administration of the community's **common agricultural policy (CAP).** Most industrialized countries, including the United States, Canada, and Japan, have adopted wide-scale government intervention and subsidization schemes for the agriculture industry. In the case of the EU, however, these policies have been implemented on a community-wide, rather than national, level. The CAP includes (1) a price-support system whereby EU agriculture officials intervene in the market to keep farm product prices within a specified range, (2) direct subsidies to farmers, and (3) rebates to farmers who export or agree to store farm products rather than sell them within the community. The implementation of these policies absorbs about two-thirds of the annual EU budget.

The CAP has caused problems both within the EU and in relationships with non-members. Within the EU, the richer, more industrialized countries resent the extensive subsidization of the more agrarian economies. Outside trading partners, especially the United States, have repeatedly charged the EU with unfair trade practices in agriculture.

The European Union Since the Mid-1980s

By the mid-1980s, a sense of "Europessimism" permeated most discussions of European integration. Although the members remained committed in principle to the "four freedoms," literally hundreds of obstacles to the free movement of goods, services, people, and capital remained. For example, there were cumbersome border restrictions on trade in many goods, and although labor was theoretically mobile, the professional certifications granted in one country were often not recognized in others.

Growing dissatisfaction with the progress of integration, as well as threats of global competition from Japan and the United States, prompted the Europeans to take action. A policy paper published in 1985 (now known as the **1992 White Paper**) exhaustively identified the remaining barriers to the four freedoms and proposed means of dismantling them.[6] It listed 282 specific measures designed to make the four freedoms a reality.

The implementation of the White Paper proposals began formally in 1987 with the passage of the Single European Act, which stated that "the community shall adopt measures with the aim of progressively establishing the internal market over a period expiring on 31 December 1992." The Single European Act envisaged a true common market where goods, people, and money move between Germany and France with the same ease that they move between Wisconsin and Illinois.

Progress toward the goal of free movement of goods has been achieved largely due to the move from a "common standards approach" to a "mutual recognition approach." Under the common standards approach, EU members were forced to negotiate the specifications for literally thousands of products, often unsuccessfully. For example, because of differences in tastes, agreement was never reached on specifications for beer, sausage, or mayonnaise. Under the mutual recognition approach, the laborious quest for common standards is in most cases no longer necessary. Instead, as long as a product meets legal and specification requirements in one member country, it may be freely exported to any other.

Less progress toward free movement of people in Europe has been made than toward free movement of goods. The primary difficulty is that EU members have been unable to agree on a common immigration policy. As long as this disagreement persists, travelers between countries must pass through border checkpoints. Some countries—notably Germany—have relatively lax immigration policies, while others—especially those with higher unemployment rates—favor strict controls on immigration. A second issue concerning the free movement of people is the acceptability of professional certifications across countries. In 1993, the largest EU member countries passed all of the professional worker directives. This means that workers' professional qualifications will be recognized throughout the EU guaranteeing them equal treatment in terms of employment, working conditions, and social protection in the host country.

Attaining free movement of capital within the EU entails several measures. First, citizens will be free to trade in EU currencies without restrictions. Second, the regulations governing banks and other financial institutions will be harmonized. In addition, mergers and acquisitions will be regulated by the EU rather than by national governments. Finally, securities will be freely tradable across countries.

A key aspect of free trade in services is the right to compete fairly to obtain government contracts. Under the 1992 guidelines, a government should not give preference to its own citizens in awarding government contracts. However, little progress has been made in this regard. Open competition in public procurement has been calculated to save $10 billion a year. And yet the nonnational share of contracts has been 5 percent since 1992. Worse still, few unsuccessful bidders complain, for fear that they would be ignored in future bids.[7]

Project 1992 has always been part of a larger plan and a process more so than a deadline.[8] Many in the EU bureaucracy argued that the 1992 campaign required a commitment to **economic and monetary union (EMU)** and subsequently to political union. These sentiments were confirmed at the Maastricht summit in December 1991, which produced various recommendations to that effect. The ratification of the **Maastricht Treaty** in late 1993 by all of the 12 member countries of the EC created the **European Union** starting January 1, 1994. The treaty calls for a commitment to economic and monetary union, with the ecu to become a common European currency by 1999. In addition, a move would be made toward political union with common foreign and security policy.[9] (The European Monetary System, its history, and future are discussed in detail in Chapter 4.)

Despite the uncertainties about the future of the EU, new countries want to join. Most EFTA countries have joined or are EU applicants in spite of the fact that the EEA treaty gives them most of the benefits of a single market. They also want to have a say in the making of EU laws and regulations. Although no timetable has been set, the EU agreed in 1994 to take steps to eventually admitting (some experts predicting a minimum of ten years) six central European nations: Bulgaria, Czech Republic, Hungary, Poland, Romania, and Slovakia. In the meanwhile, these countries will enjoy preferential trade rights through association membership with the EU. Access to EU markets is essential for growth in central Europe. The EU hopes, furthermore, that the promise of membership and access to its markets will result in greater political stability in the region.[10] The arrangement will also create investment opportunities for firms and cheaper goods for consumers in the EU. Association membership agreements were also signed in 1995 with Turkey and the Baltic Republics of Estonia, Latvia, and Lithuania. Two other countries, Cyprus and Malta, have also filed applications to join the EU, but decisions have been delayed due to political problems.

Organization of the EU

The executive body of the EU is the European Commission, headquartered in Brussels. The commission may be likened to the executive branch of the U.S. government. It is composed of 20 commissioners (two from each larger member country and one from each smaller member). The commissioners oversee 23 directorates (or departments), such as agriculture, transportation, and external relations. The commissioners are appointed by the member states, but according to the Treaty of Rome, their allegiance is to the community, not to their home country.

The Council of Ministers has the final power to decide EU actions. There are a total of 87 votes in the council. The votes are allocated to the representatives of member countries on the basis of country size. Some of the most important provisions of the Single European Act expanded the ability of the council to pass legisla-

The EU Parliament, which can veto membership applications and trade agreements with non-EU countries, is the weakest of the European Union's governing bodies. Most power is concentrated in the Council of Ministers.

Source: © St. Ellie/REA/SABA.

tion. The number of matters requiring unanimity was reduced, and countries' ability to veto legislation was weakened substantially.

The Court of Justice is somewhat analogous to the judicial branch of the U.S. government. The court is composed of 16 judges and is based in Luxembourg. The court adjudicates matters related to the European Constitution, especially trade and business disputes. Judicial proceedings may be initiated by member countries, as well as by firms and individuals.

The European Parliament is composed of 626 members elected by popular vote in member countries. The Parliament is essentially an advisory body with relatively little power. The fact that the only elected body of the EU has little policymaking power has led many to charge that the EU suffers from a "democratic deficit." In other words, decisions are made bureaucratically rather than democratically. However, the Single European Act empowered the Parliament to veto EU membership applications as well as trade agreements with non–EU countries. Many observers believe that the Parliament will gain new powers as European integration proceeds.

The entities and the process of decision making are summarized in Figure 6.1.

Implications of the Integrated European Market

Perhaps the most important implication of the four freedoms for Europe is the economic growth that is expected to result.[11] Several specific sources of increased growth have been identified. First, there will be gains from eliminating the transaction costs associated with border patrols, customs procedures, and so forth. Second, economic growth will be spurred by the economies of scale that will be achieved when production facilities become more concentrated. Third, there will be gains from more intense competition among EU companies. Firms that were monopolists in one country will now be subject to competition from firms in other EU countries. Economists have estimated that the reforms will cause an increase in European gross domestic product of about 5 percent over the medium term. In addition, perhaps 2 million new jobs will be created.

FIGURE 6.1   **Organization and Decision Making of the EU**

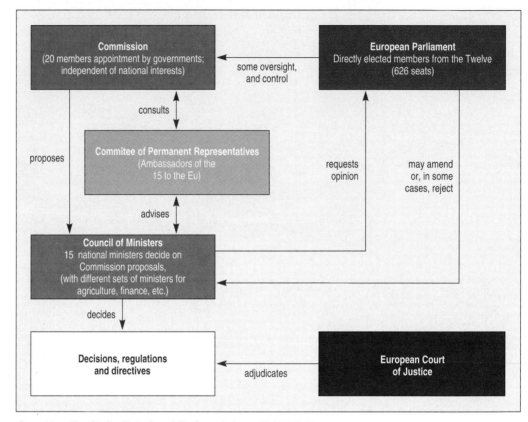

Source: Adapted from "My, How You've Grown," *The Economist,* January 25, 1992, 31–32.

The proposals have important implications for firms within and outside Europe. There will be substantial benefits for those firms already operating in Europe. Those firms will gain because their operations in one country can now be freely expanded into others, and their products may be freely sold across borders. In a borderless Europe, firms have access to many more millions of consumers. In addition, the free movement of capital will allow the firms to sell securities, raise capital, and recruit labor throughout Europe. Substantial economies of scale in production and marketing will also result. The extent of these economies of scale will depend on the ability of the managers to find panregional segments or to homogenize tastes across borders through their promotional activity.

For firms from nonmember countries, European integration presents various possibilities depending on the firm's position within the EU.[12] Table 6.4 provides four different scenarios with proposed courses of action. Well-established U.S.-based multinational marketers such as H.J. Heinz and Colgate-Palmolive will be able to take advantage of the new economies of scale. For example, 3M plants earlier turned out different versions of the company's products for various markets. Now, the 3M plant in Wales, for example, makes videotapes and videocassettes for all of Europe.[13] Colgate-Palmolive has to watch out for competitors, such as Germany's Henkel, in the brutally competitive detergent market. At the same time, large-scale retailers, such

TABLE 6.4 Proposed Company Responses to European Markets	Company Status	Challenges	Response
	Established multinational in one market/multiple markets	Exploit opportunities from improved productivity	
		Meet challenge of competitors	Pan-European strategy
		Cater to customers/ intermediaries doing same	
	Firm with one European subsidiary	Competition	Expansion
		Loss of niche	Strategic alliances
			Rationalization
			Divestment
	Exporter to Europe	Competition	European branch
		Access	Selective acquisition
			Strategic alliance
	No interest in Europe	Competition at home	Entry
		Lost opportunity	

Source: Material drawn from John F. Magee, "1992: Moves Americans Must Make," *Harvard Business Review* 67 (May–June 1989): 78–84.

as France's Carrefour and Germany's Aldi group, are undertaking their own efforts to exploit the situation with hypermarkets supplied by central warehouses with computerized inventories. Their procurement policies have to be met by companies such as Heinz. Many multinationals are developing pan-European strategies to exploit the emerging situation; that is, they are standardizing their products and processes to the greatest extent possible without compromising local input and implementation.

A company with a foothold in only one European market is faced with the danger of competitors who can use the strength of multiple markets. Furthermore, the elimination of barriers may do away with the company's competitive advantage. For example, more than half of the 45 major European food companies are in just one or two of the individual European markets and seriously lag behind broader-based U.S. and Swiss firms. Similarly, automakers PSA and Fiat are nowhere close to the cross-manufacturing presence of Ford and GM. The courses of action include expansion through acquisitions or mergers, formation of strategic alliances (for example, AT&T's joint venture with Spain's Telefonica to produce state-of-the-art microchips), rationalization by concentrating only on business segments in which the company can be a pan-European leader, and finally, divestment.

Exporters will need to worry about maintaining their competitive position and continued access to the market. Companies with a physical presence may be in a better position to assess and to take advantage of the developments. Some firms, such as Filament Fiber Technology Inc. of New Jersey, have established production units in Europe. Digital Microwave Corporation of California decided to defend its market share in Europe by joining two British communications companies and setting up a digital microwave radio and optical-fiber plant in Scotland.[14] In some industries, marketers do not see a reason either to be in Europe at all or to change from exporting to more involved modes of entry. Machinery and machine tools, for example, are in great demand in Europe, and marketers in these companies say they have little reason to manufacture there.

The term **Fortress Europe** has been used to describe the fears of many U.S. firms about a unified Europe. The concern is that while Europe dismantles internal barriers, it will raise external ones, making access to the European market difficult for U.S. and other non–EU firms. In a move designed to protect European farmers, for example, the EU has occasionally banned the import of certain agricultural goods from the United States. The EU has also called on members to limit the number of American television programs broadcast in Europe. Finally, many U.S. firms are concerned about the relatively strict domestic content rules recently passed by the EU. These rules require certain products sold in Europe to be manufactured with European inputs. One effect of the perceived threat of Fortress Europe has been increased direct investment in Europe by U.S. firms. Fears that the EU will erect barriers to U.S. exports and of the domestic content rules governing many goods have led many U.S. firms to initiate or expand European direct investment.

NORTH AMERICAN ECONOMIC INTEGRATION

Although the EU is undoubtedly the most successful and well-known integrative effort, integration efforts in North America, although only a few years old, have gained momentum and attention. What started as a trading pact between two close and economically well-developed allies has already been expanded conceptually to include Mexico, and long-term plans call for further additions. However, in North American integration the interest is purely economic; there are no constituencies for political integration.

U.S.–Canada Free Trade Agreement

After three failed tries this century, the United States and Canada signed a free trade agreement that went into effect January 1, 1989. The agreement created a $5 trillion continental economy.[15] The two countries had already had sectoral free trade arrangements; for example, one for automotive products has existed for 23 years. Even before the agreement, however, the United States and Canada were the world's largest trading partners, and there were relatively few trade barriers. The new arrangement eliminates duties selectively in three stages over the 1989–1999 period: (1) immediately, (2) five equal cuts of 20 percent beginning January 1, 1989, and (3) ten

Debate over the North American Free Trade Agreement in 1992 was complicated by difficulties associated with the existing Canadian-U.S. Free Trade Agreement. Detractors in the United States had accused Canada of subsidizing its lumber exports in order to gain an unfair advantage over the U.S. lumber industry. Disputes of this type undermine efforts toward the kind of trading partnership advocated by proponents of NAFTA.

Source: © Robert Semeniiuk/FIRST LIGHT, Toronto.

equal cuts of 10 percent beginning January 1, 1989.[16] For example, the first round eliminated a 3.9 percent tariff on U.S. computers shipped to Canada as well as 4.9–22 percent duties on trade in whiskey, skates, furs, and unprocessed fish. The sensitive sectors, such as textiles, steel, and agricultural products, will not be liberalized until the latter part of the transitionary period. Both countries see the free trade agreement as an important path to world competitiveness. Although there will be some dislocations, due to production consolidation, for example, the pact is expected to create 750,000 jobs in the United States and 150,000 in Canada. It is also expected to add as much as 1 percent in growth to both countries' economies as it takes effect in various stages. Trade between the United States and Canada hit $260 billion in 1994, up 50 percent since 1988.

North American Free Trade Agreement

Negotiations on a North American Free Trade Agreement (NAFTA) began in 1991 to create the world's largest free market, with 364 million consumers and a total output of $6 trillion.[17] The pact marked a bold departure: never before have industrialized countries created such a massive free trade area with a developing country neighbor.

Since Canada stands to gain very little from NAFTA (its trade with Mexico is 1 percent of its trade with the United States), much of the controversy has centered on the gains and losses for the United States and Mexico. Proponents have argued that the agreement will give U.S. firms access to a huge pool of relatively low-cost Mexican labor at a time when demographic trends are indicating labor shortages in many parts of the United States. At the same time, many new jobs are created in Mexico. The agreement will give firms in both countries access to millions of additional consumers, and the liberalized trade flows will result in faster economic growth in both countries. Overall, the corporate view toward NAFTA is overwhelmingly positive, as can be seen in Global Perspective 6.2. However, NAFTA suffered a serious setback due to a significant devaluation of the Mexican peso in early 1995 and the subsequent impact on trade. Critics of NAFTA argued that too much was expected too fast of a country whose political system and economy were not ready for open markets. In response, advocates of NAFTA argued that there was nothing wrong with the Mexican real economy and that the peso crisis was a political one that would be overcome with time.

Despite this, reforms have turned Mexico into an attractive market in its own right. Mexico's gross domestic product has been expanding by more than 3 percent every year since 1989, and exports to the United States have risen 72 percent since 1986. Inflation has dropped from 131 percent in 1987 to single-digit inflation in 1994. By institutionalizing the nation's turn to open markets, the free trade agreement has attracted considerable new foreign investment. The United States has benefited from Mexico's success. The U.S. trade balance with Mexico changed from a $4.9 billion deficit in 1986 to a $1.3 billion surplus in 1994 due to doubling of exports during that period. This has resulted in 264,000 jobs.[18] Among the U.S. industries to benefit are computers, autos, petrochemicals, and financial services. In 1990, Mexico opened its computer market by eliminating many burdensome licensing requirements and cutting the tariff from 50 percent to 20 percent. As a result, exports surged 23 percent in that year alone. IBM, which makes personal and mid-size computers in Mexico, anticipates sales growth to about $1 billion from that country by the mid-1990s. In Mexico's growth toward a more advanced society,

Global Perspective

6.2
NAFTA Makes Its Mark

Perhaps no sector of U.S. industry has experienced the immediate benefits of NAFTA more than the U.S. automotive industry. According to U.S. Department of Commerce statistics, in the first five months of 1994, the U.S. automotive industry exported 12,380 passenger vehicles to Mexico, a vast improvement over the 3,630 units shipped during the same period a year earlier—and already exceeding the number for the whole of 1993. Chrysler, Ford, and GM have almost completely monopolized the import boom.

In Mexico, exports are up as well as the imports for cars. Furthermore, companies not previously operating in the country have announced plans to set up manufacturing operations. The increase in exports is primarily attributed to the economic recovery, and therefore rising demand, in the United States. But the growth in exports to the United States, as well as to other countries such as Japan, is expected to continue in the long term as carmakers invested some $1.6 billion in 1994 alone to increase capacity and modernize plants. Nissan, for example, announced that it would move its entire Sentra production line from Japan to Mexico. The new plant will supply the U.S., Mexican, Japanese, Asian, and other Latin American markets.

Honda is expanding its motorcycle plant in Guadalajara to include facilities for assembling cars for the Mexican market and Latin American exports. At first, cars will be made from part kits supplied by Honda plants and con

tractors in the United States, but Mexico is expected to become an important parts center as Honda works toward its goal of production of at least 75 percent of its North American sales from plants in the continent.

Mercedes-Benz is setting up a luxury car production line at its truck plant and is building a new passenger bus factory in northern Mexico in an attempt to penetrate the U.S. market. Mercedes's main competitor in the truck and bus business, Dina, recently bought Motor Coach Industries, the U.S. market giant, and has spoken to Toyota, Hyundai, and Fiat about setting up a joint venture to expand into car production in Mexico.

Rationalization of production has also been evident as a result of NAFTA. In April 1994, Ford Motor Co. transferred the manufacture of its Thunderbird and Cougar models from its Cautitlin assembly plant in Mexico back to the United States, and began making its Contour and Mystique models solely in Cautitlin for export throughout Mexico, Canada, and the United States.

Another factor that will boost domestic sales in Mexico is the launch of the carmakers' own in-house retail credit divisions such as GMAC and Ford Credit, a by-product of the NAFTA financial service regulations. Such services were the most hard-hit by the peso devaluation in 1995, given the decline in purchasing power and purchase intentions of consumer durables in particular.

Sources: Lori Ioannou, "NAFTA's Promised Land," *International Business* (January 1995): 22–23; NAFTA Makes Its Mark," *Financial Times Survey: World Car Industry,* October 4, 1994, 9; and USA*NAFTA, *NAFTA: It's Working for America,* Washington, D.C.: USA*NAFTA, 1994.

manufacturers of consumer goods will also stand to benefit. NAFTA has already had a major impact in the emergence of new retail chains, many established to handle new products from abroad.

Free trade does produce both winners and losers. Although opponents concede that the agreement is likely to spur economic growth, they point out that segments of the U.S. economy will be harmed by the agreement. Overall wages and employment for unskilled workers in the United States will fall because of Mexico's low-cost labor pool. U.S. companies have been moving operations to Mexico since the 1960s. The door was opened when Mexico liberalized export restrictions to allow for more so-called **maquiladoras,** plants that make goods and parts or process food for export back to the United States. The supply of labor is plentiful, the pay and benefits are low, and the work regulations are lax by U.S. standards. The average maquiladora wage equals $1.73 per hour, compared with $2.17 an hour for Mexican manufacturers.[19] U.S. labor leaders also charge that Mexico's inadequate environmental and worker protections will encourage U.S. companies to move there to evade tougher standards at home. In fact, Mexican laws are just as strict as U.S. regulations, but until recently nobody enforced them. A 1993 International Trade Commission assessment estimates that while NAFTA would create a net gain of 35,000 to 93,500 U.S. jobs by 1995, it would also cause U.S. companies to shed as many as 170,000 jobs.[20] The good news is that free trade has created higher skilled and better paying jobs in the United States as a result of growth in exports. Losers have been U.S. manufacturers of auto parts, furniture, and household glass; sugar, peanut, and citrus growers; and seafood and vegetable producers. In most cases, high Mexican shipping and inventory costs will continue to make it more efficient for many U.S. industries to serve their home market from U.S. plants.

Countries dependent on trade with NAFTA countries are concerned that the agreement will divert trade and impose significant losses on their economies. Asia's continuing economic success depends largely on easy access to the North American markets, which account for more than 25 percent of annual export revenue for many Asian countries. Lower-cost producers in Asia are likely to lose some exports to the United States if they are subject to tariffs while Mexican firms are not.[21] Similarly, many in the Caribbean and Central America fear that the apparel industries of their regions will be threatened, as would much-needed investments.[22]

NAFTA may be the first step toward a hemispheric bloc, but nobody expects it to happen any time soon. It took more than three years of tough bargaining to reach an agreement between the United States and Canada, two countries with parallel economic, industrial, and social systems.[23] The challenges of expanding free trade throughout Latin America will be significant. However, many of Latin America's groupings are making provisions to join NAFTA in the 1990s. Negotiations started in 1995 to have Chile join NAFTA at the start of 1997.[24]

OTHER ECONOMIC ALLIANCES

Perhaps the world's developing countries have the most to gain from successful integrative efforts. Because many of these countries are also quite small, economic growth is difficult to generate internally. Many of these countries have adopted policies of **import substitution** to foster economic growth. With an import substitution policy, new domestic industries produce goods that were formerly imported. Many of these industries, however, can be efficient producers only with a higher level of production than can be consumed by the domestic economy. Their success, therefore, depends on accessible export markets made possible by integrative efforts.

Integration in Latin America

Before the signing of the U.S.–Canada Free Trade Agreement, all of the major trading bloc activity in the Americas had taken place in Latin America. One of the longest-lived integrative efforts among developing countries was the Latin America Free Trade Association (LAFTA), formed in 1961. As the name suggests, the primary objective of LAFTA was the elimination of trade barriers. The 1961 agreement called for trade barriers to be gradually dismantled, leading to completely free trade by 1973. By 1969, however, it was clear that a pervasive protectionist ideology would keep LAFTA from meeting this objective, and the target date was extended to 1980. In the meantime, however, the global debt crisis, the energy crisis, and the collapse of the Bretton Woods system prevented the achievement of LAFTA objectives. Dissatisfied with

LAFTA, the group made a new start as the Latin American Integration Association (LAIA) in 1980. The objective is a higher level of integration than that envisioned by LAFTA; however, the dismantling of trade barriers remains a necessary and elusive first step.

The Central American Common Market (CACM) was formed by the Treaty of Managua in 1960. The CACM has often been cited as a model integrative effort for other developing countries. By the end of the 1960s, the CACM had succeeded in eliminating restrictions on 80 percent of trade among members. A continuing source of difficulty, however, is that the benefits of integration have fallen disproportionately to the richer and more developed members. Political difficulties in the area have also hampered progress. However, the member countries renewed their commitment to integration in 1990.

Integration efforts in the Caribbean have focused on the Caribbean Community and Common Market formed in 1968. Caribbean nations (as well as Central American nations) have benefited from the **Caribbean Basin Initiative (CBI),** which, since 1983, has extended trade preferences and granted access to the markets of the United States. Under NAFTA the preferences are lost, which means that the countries have to cooperate more closely among each other. Mexico and CACM have already started planning for a free trade arrangement.

None of the activity in Latin America has been hemispheric; the Central Americans have had their structures, the Caribbean nations theirs, and the South Americans had their own different forms. However, in a dramatic transformation, these nations are now looking for free trade as a salvation from stagnation, inflation, and debt.[25] Recent foreign policy of the United States has also responded to Latin American regionalism. The **Enterprise for the Americas Initiative (EAI)** was designed to further democracy in the region by providing incentives to capitalistic development and trade liberalization. Frameworks have already been signed under the EAI. In response to the recent developments, Brazil, Argentina, Uruguay, and Paraguay set up a common market with completion by the end of 1994 called Mercosur (Mercado Común del Sur).[26] Bolivia, Colombia, Ecuador, Peru, and Venezuela have formed the Andean Common Market (ANCOM). Many Latin nations are realizing that if they do not unite, they will become decreasingly important in the global market.

The ultimate goal is a free trade zone from Point Barrow, Alaska, to Patagonia. The argument is that free trade throughout the Americas would channel investment and technology to Latin nations and give U.S. firms a head start in those markets. If Latin America grows as estimated at an average of 4 percent annually during the 1990s under trade liberalization, imports will increase by $170 billion, of which U.S. firms can capture as much as 40 percent. However, before it can become a reality, many political (such as democratization) and economic (such as market-oriented policies) changes have to take place. The first step to such a zone was taken in December 1994, when leaders of 33 countries in the Americas agreed to work toward a hemispheric trade zone by 2005.

Changes in corporate behavior have been swift. Free market reforms and economic revival have had companies ready to export and to invest in Latin America. For example, Brazil's opening of its computer market has resulted in Hewlett-Packard establishing a joint venture to produce PCs. Companies are also changing their approaches with respect to Latin America. In the past, Kodak dealt with Latin America through 11 separate country organizations. It has since streamlined its operations to five "boundariless" companies organized along product lines and, taking advantage of trade openings, created centralized distribution, thereby making deliveries more efficient and decreasing inventory-carrying costs.[27]

Integration in Asia

The development in Asia has been quite different from that in Europe and in the Americas. While European and North American arrangements have been driven by political will, market forces may compel politicians in Asia to move toward formal integration. While Japan is the dominant force in the area and might seem the choice to take leadership in such an endeavor, neither the Japanese themselves nor the other nations want Japan to do it. The concept of a "Co-Prosperity Sphere" of 50 years ago has made nations wary of Japan's influence.[28] Also, in terms of economic and political distance, the potential member countries are far from each other, especially compared to the EU. However, Asian interest in regional integration is increasing for pragmatic reasons. First, European and American markets are significant for the Asian producers and some type of organization or bloc may be needed to maintain leverage and balance against the two other blocs. Second, given that much of the growth in trade for the nations in the region is from intra-Asian trade, having a common understanding and policies will become necessary. A future arrangement will most likely be using the frame of the most established arrangement in the region, the Association of Southeast Asian Nations (ASEAN). Before late 1991, ASEAN had no real structures, and consensus was reached through information consultations. In October 1991, ASEAN members (Brunei, Indonesia, Malaysia, Philippines, Singapore, Thailand, and since July 1995, Vietnam) announced the formation of a customs union called ASEAN Free Trade Area (AFTA) with completion expected by 2003. The Malaysians have pushed for the formation of the East Asia Economic Group (EAEG), which would add Hong Kong, Japan, South Korea, and Taiwan to the list. This proposal makes sense; without Japan and the rapidly industrializing countries of the region such as South Korea and Taiwan, the effect of the arrangement would be small. Japan's reaction has been generally negative toward all types of regionalization efforts, mainly because it has had the most to gain from free trade efforts. However, part of what has been driving regionalization has been Japan's reluctance to foster some of the elements that promote free trade, such as reciprocity.[29] Should the other trading blocs turn against Japan, its only resort may be to work toward a more formal trade arrangement in Pacific Asia.

Another formal proposal for cooperation would start building bridges between two emerging trade blocs. Some individuals have publicly called for a U.S.–Japan common market. Given the differences on all fronts between the two, the proposal may be quite unrealistic at this time. Negotiated trade liberalization will not open Japanese markets due to major institutional differences, as seen in many rounds of successful negotiations but totally unsatisfactory results. The only solution for the U.S. government is to forge better cooperation between the government and the private sector to improve competitiveness.[30]

In 1988, Australia proposed the Asia Pacific Economic Cooperation (APEC) as an annual forum. The proposal called for ASEAN members to be joined by Australia, New Zealand, Japan, China, Hong Kong, Taiwan, South Korea, Canada, and the United States. It was initially modeled after the Organization for Economic Cooperation and Development (OECD), which is a center for research and high-level discussion. Since then, APEC's goals have become more ambitious. At present, APEC has 18 members with a combined GNP of $15 trillion and has the third largest economy of the world. The key objectives of APEC are to liberalize trade by 2020, to facilitate trade by harmonizing standards, and to build human capacities for realizing the region's ambitions. The trade-driven economies of the region have the world's largest pool of savings, the most advanced technologies, and fastest growing markets. Therefore, companies with interests in the region are observing APEC-related developments closely as shown in the Global Perspective 6.3.

However, the future actions of the other two blocs will determine how quickly and in what manner the Asian bloc, whatever it is, will respond. Also, the stakes are the highest for the Asian nations in the present round of GATT negotiations since their traditional export markets have been in Europe and in North America and, in this sense, very dependent on free access.

Economic integration has also taken place on the Indian subcontinent. In 1985, seven nations of the region (India, Pakistan, Bangladesh, Sri Lanka, Nepal, Bhutan, and the Maldives) launched the South Asian Association for Regional Cooperation (SAARC). Cooperation is limited to relatively noncontroversial areas, such as agriculture and regional development. Elements such as the formation of a common market have not been included.

Global Perspective

6.3
Working the New Bloc

Boeing played a major role in hosting the meeting of the Asia Pacific Economic Conference (APEC) held in Seattle in November 1993, as the airplane maker pushed for liberalized Pacific Rim trade. Aerospace already constitutes the main export to the Pacific Rim and prospects are good for its increase.

Similar to other U.S. companies, Boeing donated $50,000 to defray APEC host committee expenses. A dozen Boeing employees were assigned to help organize and operate the conference. They included Dean Thornton, president of the commercial airplane group who served as chairman of the host committee, and Ray Waldman, director of federal affairs who was the committee's executive director. Boeing provided a fleet of vans and buses and a transportation coordinator to meet APEC conference needs. The company also agreed to host 1,000 journalists who traveled to Seattle to cover APEC events.

Aerospace orders announced during the week underscored the importance of Pacific Rim trade to the United States and to Boeing specifically. United Parcel Service added ten new Boeing 757s to its order book. The $600 million purchase, including spares, will help UPS accommodate the growing international demand for its small-package delivery services. Japan Air System specified United Technologies' Pratt & Whitney 4000-series engines for its new 777 transports.

Exports to APEC countries (see accompanying table) accounted for about 31 percent of Boeing sales in 1993,

Boeing Orders in APEC Countries*

Country	Total Ordered	Total Delivered	Unfilled, Announced Orders
Australia	315	311	4
Brunei	6	6	0
Canada	201	193	8
China	167	105	62
Hong Kong	45	31	14
Indonesia	35	10	25
Japan	373	292	81
Malaysia	81	56	25
New Zealand	38	28	10
Philippines	6	4	2
Singapore	99	78	21
South Korea	88	40	48
Taiwan	43	36	7
Thailand	42	28	14
Total**	1,539	1,218	321

*Figures do not include leased aircraft, which are substantial in China and Philippines.
**Totals equal 18 percent of all Boeing transport orders, 16 percent of all deliveries, and 25 percent of all unfilled but announced orders, respectively.

compared with 3 percent in 1988. Japan has traditionally been among the top three export markets, and China, with 100 Boeing transports on order, is rapidly rising in importance.

Sources: Boeing; "Boeing Pushes Trade Issues at Asia-Pacific Conference," *Aviation Week & Space Technology* 139 (November 22, 1993): 39–40.

Integration in Africa and the Middle East

Africa's economic groupings range from currency unions among European nations and their former colonies to customs unions among neighboring states. In 1975, 16 west African nations attempted to create a megamarket large enough to interest investors from the industrialized world and reduce hardship through economic integration. The objective of the Economic Community of West African States (ECOWAS) was to form a customs union and eventual common market. Although many of its objectives have not been reached, its combined population of 160 million represents the largest economic entity in sub-Saharan Africa. Other entities in Africa include the Afro-Malagasy Economic Union, the East Africa Customs Union, the West African Economic Community, and the Maghreb Economic Community. Many of these, however, have not been successful due to the small size of the members and lack of economic infrastructure to produce goods to be traded inside the blocs.

Countries in the Arab world have made some progress in economic integration. The Gulf Cooperation Council (GCC) is one of the most powerful, economically speaking, of any trade groups. The per-capita income of its six member states (Bahrain, Kuwait, Oman, Qatar, Saudi Arabia, and the United Arab Emirates) is $7,690. The GCC was formed in 1980 mainly as a defensive measure due to the perceived threat from the Iran–Iraq war. Its aim is to achieve free trade arrangements with the EU and EFTA as well as bilateral trade agreements with western European nations.

A listing of the major regional trade agreements is provided in Table 6.5.

TABLE 6.5 **Major Regional Trade** **Associations**	**AFTA**	**ASEAN Free Trade Area** Brunei, Indonesia, Malaysia, Philippines, Singapore, Thailand, Vietnam
	ANCOM	**Andean Common Market** Bolivia, Colombia, Ecuador, Peru, Venezuela
	APEC	**Asia Pacific Economic Cooperation** Australia, Brunei, Canada, Chile, China, Hong Kong, Indonesia, Japan, Malaysia, Mexico, New Zealand, Papua New Guinea, Philippines, Singapore, South Korea, Taiwan, Thailand, United States
	CACM	**Central American Common Market** Costa Rica, El Salvador, Guatemala, Honduras, Nicaragua
	CARICOM	**Caribbean Community** Anguilla, Antigua, Bahamas, Barbados, Belize, Dominica, Grenada, Guyana, Jamaica, Montserrat, St. Kitts-Nevis, St. Lucia, St. Vincent and the Grenadines, Trinidad-Tobago
	ECOWAS	**Economic Community of West African States** Benin, Berkina Faso, Cape Verde, Gambia, Ghana, Guinea, Guinea-Bissau, Ivory Coast, Liberia, Mali, Mauritania, Niger, Nigeria, Senegal, Sierra Leone, Togo
	EU	**European Union** Austria, Belgium, Denmark, Finland, France, Germany, Greece, Ireland, Italy, Luxembourg, Netherlands, Portugal, Spain, Sweden, United Kingdom
	EFTA	**European Free Trade Association** Iceland, Liechtenstein, Norway, Switzerland
	GCC	**Gulf Cooperation Council** Bahrain, Kuwait, Oman, Qatar, Saudi Arabia, United Arab Emirates
	LAIA	**Latin American Integration Association** Argentina, Bolivia, Brazil, Chile, Colombia, Ecuador, Mexico, Paraguay, Peru, Uruguay, Venezuela
	MERCOSUR	**Southern Common Market** Argentina, Brazil, Paraguay, Uruguay
	NAFTA	**North American Free Trade Agreement** Canada, Mexico, United States

International Groupings

- OECD Organization for Economic Co-operation and Development
- OPEC Organization of the Petroleum Exporting Countries
- Commonwealth

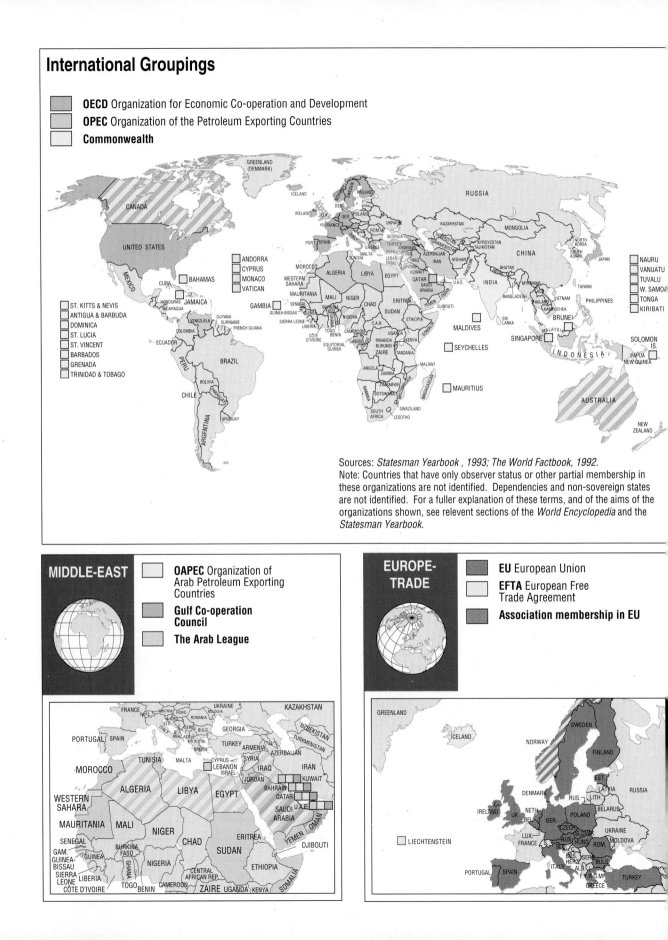

Sources: *Statesman Yearbook*, 1993; *The World Factbook, 1992.*
Note: Countries that have only observer status or other partial membership in these organizations are not identified. Dependencies and non-sovereign states are not identified. For a fuller explanation of these terms, and of the aims of the organizations shown, see relevent sections of the *World Encyclopedia* and the *Statesman Yearbook.*

MIDDLE-EAST

- OAPEC Organization of Arab Petroleum Exporting Countries
- Gulf Co-operation Council
- The Arab League

EUROPE-TRADE

- EU European Union
- EFTA European Free Trade Agreement
- Association membership in EU

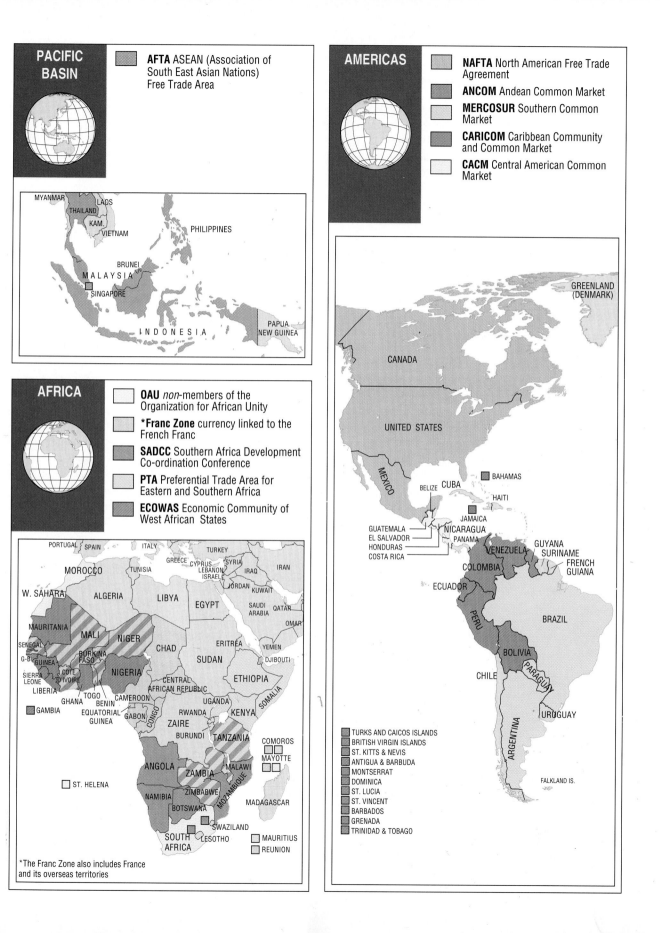

PACIFIC BASIN

- **AFTA** ASEAN (Association of South East Asian Nations) Free Trade Area

MYANMAR
LAOS
THAILAND
KAM.
VIETNAM
PHILIPPINES
MALAYSIA
BRUNEI
SINGAPORE
INDONESIA
PAPUA NEW GUINEA

AMERICAS

- **NAFTA** North American Free Trade Agreement
- **ANCOM** Andean Common Market
- **MERCOSUR** Southern Common Market
- **CARICOM** Caribbean Community and Common Market
- **CACM** Central American Common Market

GREENLAND (DENMARK)

CANADA

UNITED STATES

MEXICO
BELIZE
CUBA
BAHAMAS
HAITI
GUATEMALA
EL SALVADOR
HONDURAS
COSTA RICA
NICARAGUA
PANAMA
JAMAICA
VENEZUELA
GUYANA
SURINAME
FRENCH GUIANA
COLOMBIA
ECUADOR
PERU
BRAZIL
BOLIVIA
CHILE
PARAGUAY
URUGUAY
ARGENTINA
FALKLAND IS.

- TURKS AND CAICOS ISLANDS
- BRITISH VIRGIN ISLANDS
- ST. KITTS & NEVIS
- ANTIGUA & BARBUDA
- MONTSERRAT
- DOMINICA
- ST. LUCIA
- ST. VINCENT
- BARBADOS
- GRENADA
- TRINIDAD & TOBAGO

AFRICA

- **OAU** *non*-members of the Organization for African Unity
- ***Franc Zone** currency linked to the French Franc
- **SADCC** Southern Africa Development Co-ordination Conference
- **PTA** Preferential Trade Area for Eastern and Southern Africa
- **ECOWAS** Economic Community of West African States

PORTUGAL SPAIN ITALY TURKEY
GREECE CYPRUS SYRIA IRAN
MOROCCO TUNISIA LEBANON ISRAEL IRAQ
JORDAN KUWAIT
W. SAHARA ALGERIA LIBYA EGYPT
SAUDI ARABIA QATAR OMAR
MAURITANIA MALI NIGER CHAD SUDAN
SENEGAL ERITREA YEMEN
G-B GUINEA BURKINA FASO DJIBOUTI
SIERRA LEONE COTE D'IVOIRE NIGERIA
LIBERIA CENTRAL AFRICAN REPUBLIC ETHIOPIA
GHANA TOGO BENIN CAMEROON
GAMBIA EQUATORIAL GUINEA GABON CONGO
UGANDA KENYA SOMALIA
RWANDA
ZAIRE BURUNDI TANZANIA
COMOROS MAYOTTE
ANGOLA ZAMBIA MALAWI MOZAMBIQUE
ST. HELENA ZIMBABWE
NAMIBIA BOTSWANA MADAGASCAR
SOUTH AFRICA SWAZILAND LESOTHO
MAURITIUS REUNION

*The Franc Zone also includes France and its overseas territories

Economic Integration and the International Manager

Regional economic integration creates opportunities and challenges for the international manager. Economic integration may have an impact on a company's entry mode by favoring direct investment since one of the basic rationales for integration is to generate favorable conditions for local production and intraregional trade. By design, larger markets are created with potentially more opportunity. Harmonization efforts may result in standardized regulations, which can positively affect production and marketing efforts.

The international manager must, however, make assessments and decisions regarding integrating markets from four points of view.[31] The first task is to create a vision of the outcome of the change. Change in the competitive landscape can be dramatic if scale opportunities can be exploited in relatively homogeneous demand conditions. This could be the case, for example, for industrial goods and consumer durables, such as cameras and watches, as well as for professional services. The international manager will have to take into consideration varying degrees of change readiness within the markets themselves; that is, governments and other stakeholders, such as labor unions, may oppose the liberalization of competition in all market segments. For example, while plans have called for liberalization of air travel and automobile marketing in Europe, EU members have found loopholes to protect their own companies.

The international manager then will have to develop a strategic response to the new environment to maintain a sustainable long-term competitive advantage. Those companies already present in an integrating market should fill in gaps in product and market portfolios through acquisitions or alliances to create a balanced panregional company. Those with a weak presence, or none at all, may have to create alliances for distribution with established firms.[32] To take advantage of the new situation in Europe, James River Corporation from the United States, Nokia from Finland, and Cragnotti & Partners from Italy launched a pan–European papermaking joint venture called Jamont. Before 1992, papermaking was highly fragmented in Europe but the joint venture partners saw a chance to develop a regional manufacturing and marketing strategy. A total of 13 companies in 10 countries were acquired and production was consolidated. For example, before the new strategy, each company made deep-colored napkins; now all of Jamont's products come from one plant in Finland.[33] An additional option for the international manager is leaving the market altogether in response to the new competitive conditions or the level of investment needed to remain competitive. Bank of America sold its operations in Italy to Deutsche Bank once it determined the high cost of becoming a pan-European player.

Whatever the changes, they will call for company reorganization.[34] Structurally, authority will have to be more centralized so regional programs can be executed. In staffing, focus will have to be on individuals who understand the subtleties of consumer behavior across markets and therefore are able to evaluate the similarities and differences among cultures and markets. In developing systems for the planning and implementation of regional programs, adjustments will have to be made to incorporate views throughout the organization. If, for example, decisions on regional advertising campaigns are made at headquarters without consultation with country operations, resentment by the local staff will lead to less-than-optimal execution. Companies may even move corporate or divisional headquarters from the domestic market to be closer to the customer; AT&T estimates that several of its units may have their headquarters abroad, especially in Europe. Similarly, companies have moved their headquarters for Latin American operations from the United States to cities such as Caracas, Venezuela.

Finally, economic integration will involve various powers and procedures, such as the EU's Commission and its directives. The international manager is not powerless to influence both of them; a passive approach may result in competitors gaining an advantage or a disadvantageous situation emerging for the company. For example, it was very important for the U.S. pharmaceutical industry to obtain tight patent protection as part of the NAFTA agreement and substantial time and money was spent on lobbying both the executive and legislative branches of the U.S. government in the effort to meet its goal. Often policymakers rely heavily on the knowledge and experience of the private sector in carrying out its own work. Influencing change will therefore mean providing policymakers with industry information such as test results. Lobbying will usually have to take place at multiple levels simultaneously; within the EU, this means the European Commission in Brussels, the European Parliament in Strasbourg, or the national governments within the EU. Managers with substantial resources have established their own lobbying offices in Brussels while smaller companies get their voices heard through joint offices or their industry associations. In terms of lobbying, U.S. firms have been at an advantage given their experience in their home market; however, for many non–U.S. firms, lobbying is a new, yet necessary, skill to be acquired.

Cartels and Commodity Price Agreements

An important characteristic that distinguishes developing countries from industrialized countries is the nature of their export earnings. While industrialized countries rely heavily on the export of manufactured goods, technology, and services, the developing countries rely chiefly on the export of primary products and raw materials—for example, copper, iron ore, and agricultural products. This distinction is important for several reasons. First, the level of price competition is higher among sellers of primary products, because of the typically larger number of sellers and also because primary products are homogeneous. This can be seen by comparing the sale of computers with, for example, copper. Only three or four countries are a competitive force in the computer market, whereas at least a dozen compete in the sale of copper. Furthermore, while product differentiation and therefore brand loyalty are likely to exist in the market for computers, buyers of copper are likely to purchase on the basis of price alone. A second distinguishing factor is that supply variability will be greater in the market for primary products because production often depends on uncontrollable factors such as weather. For these reasons, market prices of primary products—and therefore developing country export earnings—are highly volatile.

Responses to this problem have included cartels and commodity price agreements. A **cartel** is an association of producers of a particular good. While a cartel may consist of an association of private firms, our interest is in the cartels formed by nations. The objective of a cartel is to suppress the market forces affecting its product in order to gain greater control over sales revenues. A cartel may accomplish this objective in several ways. First, members may engage in price fixing. This entails an agreement by producers to sell at a certain price, eliminating price competition among sellers. Second, the cartel may allocate sales territories among its members, again suppressing competition. A third tactic calls for members to agree to restrict production, and therefore supplies, resulting in artificially higher prices.

The most widely known cartel is the Organization of Petroleum Exporting Countries (OPEC). OPEC became a significant force in the world economy in the 1970s. In 1973, the Arab members of OPEC were angered by U.S. support for Israel in the war in the Mideast. In response, the Arab members declared an embargo on the shipment of oil to the United States and quadrupled the price of oil—from approximately $3 to $12 per barrel. OPEC tactics included both price fixing and production quotas. Continued price increases brought the average price per barrel to nearly $35 by 1981. The cartel experienced severe problems during the 1980s, however. First, the demand for OPEC oil declined considerably as the result of conservation, the use of alternative sources, and increased oil production by nonmembers. All of these factors also contributed to sharp declines in the price of oil. Second, the cohesiveness among members diminished. Sales often occurred at less than the agreed-upon price, and production quotas were repeatedly violated. The members of OPEC convened following the Persian Gulf war in early 1991 in an attempt to regain control over oil prices, but it remains to be seen whether OPEC will regain its influence as a major force in the world economy.

International **commodity price agreements** involve both buyers and sellers in an agreement to manage the price of a certain commodity. Often, the free market is allowed to determine the price of the commodity over a certain range. However, if demand and supply pressures cause the commodity's price to move outside that range, an elected or appointed manager will enter the market to buy or sell the commodity to bring the price back into the range. The manager controls the **buffer stock** of the commodity. If prices float downward, the manager purchases the commodity and adds to the buffer stock. Under upward pressure, the manager sells the commodity from the buffer stock. This system is somewhat analogous to a managed exchange rate system such as the EMS, in which authorities buy and sell to influence exchange rates. International commodity agreements are currently in effect for sugar, tin, rubber, cocoa, and coffee.

SUMMARY

Economic integration involves agreements among countries to establish links through the movements of goods, services, and factors of production across borders. These links may be weak or strong depending on the level of integration. Levels of integration include the free trade area, customs union, common market, and full economic union.

The benefits derived from economic integration include trade creation, economies of scale, improved terms of trade, the reduction of monopoly power, and improved cross-cultural communication. However, a number of disadvantages may also exist. Most importantly, economic integration may work to the detriment of nonmembers by causing deteriorating terms of trade and trade diversion. In addition, no guarantee exists that all members will share the gains from integration. The biggest impediment to economic integration is nationalism. There is strong resistance to surrendering autonomy and self-determinism to cooperative agreements.

The most successful example of economic integration is the European Union. The EU has succeeded in eliminating most barriers to the free flow of goods, services, and factors of production. In addition, the EU has made progress toward the evolution of a common currency and central bank, which are fundamental requirements of an economic union. In the Americas, NAFTA is paving the way for a hemispheric trade bloc.

A number of regional economic alliances exist in Africa, Latin America, and Asia, but they have achieved only low levels of integration. Political difficulties, low levels of development, and problems with cohesiveness have impeded integrative progress among many developing countries. However, many nations in these areas are seeing economic integration as the only way to prosperity in the future.

International commodity price agreements and cartels represent attempts by producers of primary products to control sales revenues and export earnings. The former involves an agreement to buy or sell a commodity to influence prices. The latter is an agreement by suppliers to fix prices, set production quotas, or allocate sales territories. OPEC had inestimable influence on the global economy during the 1970s, but its importance has since diminished.

Key Terms and Concepts

trading bloc	1992 White Paper
free trade area	Single European Act
customs union	economic and monetary union (EMU)
common market	Maastricht Treaty
factor mobility	European Union
Single European Act	Fortress Europe
economic union	maquiladoras
trade creation	import substitution
trade diversion	Caribbean Basin Initiative (CBI)
internal economies of scale	Enterprise for the Americas Initiative (EAI)
external economies of scale	cartel
Treaty of Rome	commodity price agreement
common agricultural policy (CAP)	buffer stock

Questions for Discussion

1. Explain the difference between a free trade area and a customs union. Speculate why negotiations were held for a North American Free Trade Agreement rather than for a North American Common Market.

2. What problems might a member country of a common market be concerned about?

3. Construct an example of a customs union arrangement resulting in both trade creation and trade diversion.

4. Distinguish between external and internal economies of scale resulting from economic integration.

5. What are the main provisions of the Single European Act?

6. Discuss the relationship between import substitution and economic integration among developing countries.

7. Suppose that you work for a medium-sized manufacturing firm in the Midwest. Approximately 20 percent of your sales are to European customers. What threats and opportunities does your firm face as a result of an integrated European market?

8. What type of adjustments will U.S. firms make as a result of NAFTA?

Recommended Readings

The Arthur Andersen North American Business Sourcebook. Chicago: Triumph Books, 1994.

Buiter, William, and Richard Marston. *International Economic Policy Coordination.* Cambridge, England: Cambridge University Press, 1987.

Cooper, Richard. *Economic Policy in an Interdependent World.* Cambridge, Mass.: MIT Press, 1987.

EC Commission. *Completing the Internal Market: White Paper from the Commission to the European Council.* Luxembourg: EC Commission, 1985.

Fair, D.E., and C. de Boissieu, eds. *International Monetary and Financial Integration—The European Dimension.* Norwell, Mass.: Kluwer, 1987.

Ryans, John K., Jr., and Pradeep A. Rau. *Marketing Strategies for the New Europe: A North American Perspective on 1992.* Chicago: American Marketing Association, 1990.

Sapir, André, and Alexis Jacquemin, eds. *The European Internal Market.* Oxford, England: Oxford University Press, 1990.

Schott, Jeffrey. *United States–Canada Free Trade: An Evaluation of the Agreement.* Washington, D.C.: Institute for International Economics, 1988.

Stoeckel, Andrew, David Pearce, and Gary Banks. *Western Trade Blocs.* Canberra, Australia: Centre for International Economics, 1990.

Suriyamongkol, Marjorie L. *Politics of ASEAN Economic Cooperation.* Oxford, England: Oxford University Press, 1988.

United Nations. *From the Common Market to EC92: Integration in the European Community and Transnational Corporations.* New York: United Nations Publications, 1992.

Notes

1. The discussion of economic integration is based on the pioneering work by Bela Balassa, *The Theory of Economic Integration* (Homewood, Ill.: Richard D. Irwin, 1961).

2. Europe à la Carte, *The Economist,* September 10, 1994, 14–15.

3. Jacob Viner, *The Customs Union Issue* (New York: Carnegie Endowment for International Peace, 1950).

4. J. Waelbroeck, "Measuring Degrees of Progress in Economic Integration," in *Economic Integration, Worldwide, Regional, Sectoral,* ed. F. Machlop (London: Macmillan, 1980).

5. Paul Belien, "Bitter Birthday for Europe's Common Market," *The Wall Street Journal,* March 25, 1987, 31.

6. EC Commission, *Completing the Internal Market: White Paper from the Commission to the European Council* (Luxembourg: EC Commission, 1985).

7. "A Singular Market," *The Economist,* October 22, 1994, 10–16.

8. Various aspects of the 1992 Common Market are addressed in André Sapir and Alexis Jacquemin, eds., *The European Internal Market* (Oxford, England: Oxford University Press, 1990).

9. "The Maths of Post-Maastricht Europe," *The Economist,* October 16, 1993, 51–52.

10. "Will More Be Merrier?" *The Economist,* October 17, 1992, 75.

11. Economic growth effects are discussed in Richard Baldwin, "The Growth Effects of 1992," *Economic Policy* (October 1989): 248-281; or Rudiger Dornbusch, "Europe 1992: Macroeconomic Implications," *Brookings Papers on Economic Activity* 2 (1989): 341-362.

12. John F. Magee, "1992: Moves Americans Must Make," *Harvard Business Review* 67 (May-June 1989): 72-84.

13. Richard I. Kirkland, "Outsider's Guide to Europe in 1992," *Fortune,* October 24, 1988, 121-127.

14. "Should Small U.S. Exporters Take the Plunge?" *Business Week,* November 14, 1988, 64-68.

15. "Getting Ready for the Great American Shake-out," *Business Week,* April 4, 1988, 44-46.

16. "Summary of the U.S.-Canada Free Trade Agreement," *Export Today* 4 (November-December 1988): 57-61.

17. See *The Likely Impact on the United States of a Free Trade Agreement with Mexico* (Washington, D.C.: United States International Trade Commission, 1991).

18. Ann Reilly Dowd, "Viva Free Trade with Mexico," *Fortune,* June 17, 1991, 97-100.

19. Jim Carlton, "The Lure of Cheap Labor," *The Wall Street Journal,* September 14, 1992, R16.

20. "A Noose Around NAFTA," *Business Week,* February 22, 1993, 37.

21. Andrew Stoeckel, David Pearce, and Gary Banks, *Western Trade Blocs* (Canberra, Australia: Centre for International Economics, 1990).

22. Jose De Cordoba, "Alarm Bells in the Caribbean," *The Wall Street Journal,* September 24, 1992, R8.

23. "A Giant Step Closer to North America Inc.," *Business Week,* December 5, 1988, 44-45.

24. "Next Stop South," *The Economist,* February 25, 1995, 29-30.

25. Thomas Kamm, "Latin Links," *The Wall Street Journal,* September 24, 1992, R6.

26. "The World's Newest Trading Bloc," *Business Week,* May 4, 1992, 50-51.

27. "Ripping Down the Walls Across the Americas," *Business Week,* December 26, 1994, 78-80.

28. Emily Thornton, "Will Japan Rule a New Trade Bloc?" *Fortune,* October 5, 1992, 131-132.

29. Paul Krugman, "A Global Economy Is Not the Wave of the Future," *Financial Executive* 8 (March/April 1992): 10-13.

30. Michael R. Czinkota and Masaaki Kotabe, "America's New World Trade Order," *Marketing Management* 1 (Summer 1992): 49-56.

31. Eric Friberg, Risto Perttunen, Christian Caspar, and Dan Pittard, "The Challenges of Europe 1992," *The McKinsey Quarterly* 21, 2 (1988): 3-15.

32. John A. Quelch, Robert D. Buzzell, and Eric R. Salama, *The Marketing Challenge of 1992* (Reading, Mass.: Addison-Wesley, 1990), Chapter 13.

33. "A Joint-Venture Papermaker Casts Net Across Europe," *The Wall Street Journal,* December 7, 1992, B4.

34. Gianluigi Guido, "Implementing a Pan-European Marketing Strategy," *Long Range Planning* 24, 5 (1991): 23-33.

CHAPTER 7

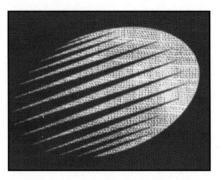

National Trade and Investment Policies

Learning Objectives

1. To see how trade and investment policies have historically been a subset of domestic policies.

2. To examine how historical attitudes toward trade and investment policies are changing.

3. To see how global linkages in trade and investment have made policymakers less able to focus solely on domestic issues.

4. To understand that nations must cooperate closely in the future to maintain a viable global trade and investment environment.

Protecting Wildlife by Restricting Trade

To demonstrate U.S. commitment to the protection of international wildlife, President Clinton announced in 1994 that trade sanctions would be imposed against Taiwan due to its continued failure to halt trade in products from endangered tigers and rhinos. According to the president, "The world's tiger and rhinoceros populations remain gravely endangered and will likely be extinct in the next two to five years if the trade in their parts and products, fueled by market demand in consuming countries, is not eliminated."

This action represents an escalation in a worldwide campaign to defend the two near-extinct mammals, and marks the first time the United States has used import prohibitions as a weapon to pressure other nations to protect endangered wildlife. The ban on wildlife imports will affect items such as handbags, shells, corals, skins, bird feathers, and eggs. Taiwanese shipments to the United States will be reduced by $20 million a year.

President Clinton acknowledged that Taiwan had taken steps to protect wildlife, but felt they were not enough. Taiwan viewed the move as deeply regrettable. Its government stated that, "We believe that dialogue and cooperation, rather than sanctions, are the best means of achieving progress towards this goal (of eradicating trade in endangered species)."

Samuel LaBudde of the Earth Island Institute said, "The White House action is perhaps the most significant event for species protection to occur in 20 years; this signals the end of an era for renegade nations who have shown only defiance and contempt for international conservation accords."

Source: Tom Kenworthy, "President Imposes Sanctions on Taiwan," *The Washington Post,* April 12, 1994, p. C1.

This chapter discusses the policy actions taken by countries. All nations have international trade and investment policies. The policies may be publicly pronounced or kept secret, they may be disjointed or coordinated, or they may be applied consciously or determined by a laissez-faire attitude. In any case, they are manifest when measures taken by governments affect the flow of trade and investment across national borders. As the opening vignette illustrates, nations can and will take actions to achieve particular policy goals. Since it often is not possible to directly interfere with a country's policies, trade measures are a frequently used vehicle to precipitate policy changes abroad.

RATIONALE AND GOALS OF TRADE AND INVESTMENT POLICIES

Government policies are designed to regulate, stimulate, direct, and protect national activities. The exercise of these policies is the result of **national sovereignty,** which provides a government with the right and burden to shape the environment of the country and its citizens. Because they are "border bound," governments focus mainly on domestic policies. Nevertheless, many policy actions have repercussions on other nations, firms, and individuals abroad and are therefore a component of a nation's trade and investment policy.

Government policy can be subdivided into two groups of policy actions that affect trade and investment. One affects trade and investment directly, the other indirectly. The domestic policy actions of most governments aim to increase the **standard of living** of the country's citizens, to improve the **quality of life,** to stimulate national development, and to achieve full employment. Clearly, all of these goals are closely intertwined. For example, an improved standard of living is likely to contribute to national development. Similarly, quality of life and standard of living are closely interlinked. Also, a high level of employment will play a major role in determining the standard of living. Yet all of these policy goals will also affect

international trade and investment indirectly. For example, if foreign industries become more competitive and rapidly increase their exports, employment in the importing countries may suffer. Likewise, if a country accumulates large quantities of debt, which at some time must be repaid, the present and future standard of living will be threatened.

In more direct ways, a country may also pursue policies of increased development that mandate either technology transfer from abroad or the exclusion of foreign industries to the benefit of domestic infant firms. Also, government officials may believe that imports threaten the culture, health, or standards of the country's citizens and thus the quality of life. As a result, officials are likely to develop regulations to protect the citizens.

Nations also institute **foreign policy** measures designed with domestic concerns in mind but explicitly aimed to exercise influence abroad. One major goal of foreign policy may be national security. For example, nations may develop alliances, coalitions, and agreements to protect their borders or their spheres of interest. Similarly, nations may take measures to enhance their national security preparedness in case of international conflict. Governments also wish to improve trade and investment opportunities and to contribute to the security and safety of their own firms abroad.

Policy aims may be approached in various ways. For example, to develop new markets abroad and to increase their sphere of influence, nations may give foreign aid to other countries. This was the case when the United States generously awarded Marshall Plan funds for the reconstruction of Europe. Governments may also feel a need to restrict or encourage trade and investment flows in order to preserve or enhance the capability of industries that are important to national security.

Each country develops its own domestic policies and therefore policy aims will vary from nation to nation. Inevitably, conflicts arise. For example, full employment policies in one country may directly affect employment policies in another. Similarly, the development aims of one country may reduce the development capability of another. Even when health issues are concerned, disputes may arise. One nation may argue that its regulations are in place to protect its citizens, whereas other nations may interpret the regulations as market barriers. An example of the latter situation is the celebrated hormone dispute between the United States and the European Union. U.S. cattle are treated with growth hormones. While the United States claims that these hormones are harmless to humans, many Europeans find them scary. Given the differences in perspectives, there is much room for conflict when it comes to trade policies, particularly when the United States wants to export more beef and the European Union attempts to restrict such beef imports.[1]

The trade disagreement between the United States and Japan in the automotive sector is another example. While the U.S. claimed that the Japanese firms prevent the importation and sale of U.S.-made auto parts, Japan's government blamed quality concerns and lack of effort by U.S. firms. As the tariff measures against Japanese luxury cars showed, such disagreements can quickly escalate into major trade conflicts.

Conflicts among nations are also likely to emerge when foreign policy goals lead to trade and investment measures. Such conflicts can even involve international aid. For example, because of its vast current account surplus, Japan is able to grant generous **developmental aid** to countries in Asia. While few governments would criticize altruistic aid, many of them dispute the use of aid funds for purposes of trade distortions. Japanese aid payments are seen as linked to the purchases of Japanese products. Even if such linkages are not overt, the simple fact that Japanese engineers and designers may assess a project and contribute to its development can have major repercussions on trade flows. The reason is that the design determines the specifications of machines, computers, and materials that will be purchased. Obviously, if influences in the design phase come from only one nation, they will provide significant direction for future purchases.

Differences among national policies have always existed and are likely to erupt into occasional conflict. Yet, the closer economic linkage among nations has made the emergence of such conflicts more frequent and the disagreements more severe. In recognition of this development, efforts have been made since 1945 to create a multilateral institutional arrangement that can help to resolve national conflicts, harmonize national policies, and facilitate increased international trade and investments.

GLOBAL TRADE REGULATION SINCE 1945

In 1945, the United States led in the belief that international trade and investment flows were a key to worldwide prosperity. Many months of international negotiations in London, Geneva, and Lake Success (New York) culminated on March 24, 1948, in Havana, Cuba, with the signing of the Havana Charter for the **International Trade Organization (ITO).** The charter represented a series of agreements among 53 countries. It was designed to cover international commercial policies, restrictive business practices, commodity agreements, employment and reconstruction, economic development and international investment, and a constitution for a new United Nations agency to administer the whole.[2]

Even though the International Trade Organization incorporated many farsighted notions, most nations refused to ratify its provisions. They feared the power and bureaucratic size of the new organization—and the consequent threats to national sovereignty. As a result, this most forward-looking approach to international trade and investment was never implemented. However, other organizations conceived at the time have made major contributions toward improving international business. An agreement was initiated for the purpose of reducing tariffs and therefore facilitating trade. In addition, international institutions such as the United Nations, the World Bank, and the International Monetary Fund were negotiated.

The **General Agreement on Tariffs and Trade (GATT)** has been called a "remarkable success story of a postwar international organization that was never intended to become one."[3] It started out in 1947 as a set of rules to ensure nondiscrimination, transparent procedures, the settlement of disputes, and the participation of the lesser-developed countries in international trade. To increase trade GATT uses tariff concessions, through which member countries agree to limit the level of tariffs they will impose on imports from other GATT members. An important tool is the **Most-Favored Nation (MFN)** clause, which calls for each member country to grant every other member country the most favorable treatment it accords to any country with respect to imports and exports.[4] MFN is in effect the equal opportunity clause of international trade.

The GATT was not originally intended to be an international organization. Rather, it was to be a multilateral treaty designed to operate under the International Trade Organization (ITO). However, because the ITO never came into being, the GATT became the governing body for settling international trade disputes. Gradually it evolved into an institution that sponsored various successful rounds of international trade negotiations. Headquartered in Geneva, Switzerland, the GATT Secretariat conducts its work as instructed by the representatives of its member nations. Even though the GATT had no independent enforcement mechanism and relied entirely on moral suasion and on frequently wavering membership adherence to its rules, it achieved major progress for world trade.

Early in its history, the GATT achieved the reduction of duties for trade in 50,000 products, amounting to two-thirds of the value of the trade among its participants.[5] In subsequent years, special GATT negotiations such as the Kennedy Round, named after John F. Kennedy, and the Tokyo Round, named after the location where the negotiations were agreed upon, further reduced trade barriers and improved dispute-settlement mechanisms. The GATT also developed better provisions for dealing with subsidies and more explicit definitions of roles for import controls. Table 7.1 provides an overview of the different GATT rounds.

The latest GATT negotiations, called the Uruguay Round, were initiated in 1987. Even though tariffs still were addressed in these negotiations, their importance had been greatly diminished due to the success of earlier agreements. The main thrust of negotiations had become the sharpening of dispute-settlement rules and the integration of the trade and investment areas that were outside of the GATT. Several key areas addressed were nontariff barriers, trade in textiles, agriculture and services, intellectual property rights, and trade-related investment measures.

After many years of often contentious negotiations, a new accord was finally ratified in early 1995. As part of this ratification, the GATT was supplanted by a new institution, the **World Trade Organization (WTO),** which now administers international trade and investment accords. The accords have brought major change to the world trade and investment environment. They will gradually reduce governmental subsidies to industries and will convert nontariff barriers into more transparent tariff barriers. The textile and clothing industries eventually will be brought into the WTO regime, resulting in decreased subsidies and fewer market restrictions. An entire new set of rules was designed to govern the service area, and agreement also was reached on new rules to encourage international investment flows.

The GATT and now the WTO have made major contributions to improved trade and investment flows around the world. The latest round alone is predicted to increase global exports by more than $755 billion by the year 2002.[6] As Global Perspective 7.1 shows, it was not just the industrialized nations that benefited from trade liberalization, but developing countries as well.

The success of the GATT and the resulting increase in welfare has refuted the old postulate that "the strong is most powerful alone." Nations have increasingly come to recognize that international trade and investment activities are important to their own economic well-being.

			Value of		Average
TABLE 7.1			**Numbers of**	**Trade**	**Average**	**Tariffs**
Negotiations in the	**Round**	**Dates**	**Countries**	**Covered**	**Tariff Cut**	**Afterward**
GATT						
	Geneva	1947	23	$10 billion	35%	n/a
	Annecy	1949	33	Unavailable		n/a
	Torquay	1950	34	Unavailable		n/a
	Geneva	1956	22	$2.5 billion		n/a
	Dillon	1960–1961	45	$4.9 billion		n/a
	Kennedy	1962–1967	48	$40 billion	35%	8.7%
	Tokyo	1973–1979	99	$155 billion	34%	4.7%
	Uruguay	1986–1994	124	$300 billion	38%	3.9%

Sources: John H. Jackson, *The World Trading System* (Cambridge, Mass.: MIT Press, 1989), and *The GATT: Uruguay Round Final Act Should Produce Overall U.S. Economic Gains,* U.S. General Accounting Office, Report to Congress, Washington, D.C., July 1994.

Global Perspective

7.1
Uruguay Round's Biggest Winners
May Be Developing Nations

On the surface, the poorer nations of the world felt side-lined and forced to accept what the rich countries dished out during the Uruguay Round GATT negotiations. But despite such early reactions, the developing countries gained a great deal.

No single group stood to lose as much if the trade round failed. The Americans and Europeans could have fallen back into their already formed regional trade blocs, and the Japanese could have concentrated on deepening Pacific trade arrangements. Countries such as India, Mauritius, or Jamaica, which don't belong to the world's economic clubs, would have been squeezed out.

The developing world could benefit most from the GATT round's least publicized accomplishment—the reduction in tariffs on a range of manufactured items such as steel, paper, and furniture. Many developing countries, particularly in East Asia, have built large manufacturing sectors. Their stake in world trade goes far beyond traditional developing-world items such as bauxite or bananas.

According to a study by economists DeAnne Julius and Richard Brown, today's 24 large, industrial economies will see manufacturing employment drop below 10 percent of their work forces during the next 30 years. Meanwhile, the developing countries will continue to increase living standards largely by dominating labor-intensive manufacturing. It is further argued that trade in manufactured goods will take on "commodity-style" characteristics, with production costs often dictating market share. The researchers' pre-dictions suggest that the developing countries will be the big beneficiaries of the manufacturing tariff reductions negotiated in Geneva.

The developing countries face improved conditions in two more traditional export areas—textiles and agriculture. "It came out pretty well for them," said Jagdish Bhagwati, a Columbia University economist and advisor to the government of India. They didn't get as much access to foreign markets as they initially sought, he said, adding, "It's still a gigantic step forward."

The eventual shrinking of export subsidies will mean that European farmers will unleash less produce on the world market, a shift that could help farmers in Africa, Latin America, and Asia. U.S. textile companies had pushed the Clinton administration to negotiate a 15-year phaseout of the current system of textile and apparel quotas, but the developing countries succeeded in getting a 10-year phaseout.

Economists agree that the GATT deal ultimately will mean most to developing countries that have built a varied manufacturing base and are less dependent on natural resources. One trouble spot is that the trade pact gives nations a fairly free hand to launch antidumping actions. Developing countries worry that the United States and Europe will use the antidumping weapon to limit incursions by low-cost competitors. Taking this worry into account, Mr. Bhagwati concluded, "The GATT deal is good, but not great."

Source: Tim Carrington, "GATT Agreement's Biggest Winners May Turn Out to Be Developing Nations," *The Wall Street Journal,* December 27, 1993, A8.

Nations also have come to accept that they must generate sufficient outgoing export and investment activities to compensate for the inflow of imports and investment taking place. In the medium and long term, the balance of payments must be maintained. For short periods of time, gold or capital transfers can be used to finance a deficit. Such financing, however, can continue only while gold and foreign assets last or while foreign countries will accept the IOUs of the deficit countries, permitting them to pile up foreign liabilities.[7] This willingness, of course, will vary. Some countries, such as the United States, can run up deficits of hundreds of billions of dollars because of political stability, acceptable rates of return, and perceived economic security. Yet, over the long term, all nations are subject to the same economic rules.

CHANGES IN THE GLOBAL POLICY ENVIRONMENT

Three major changes have occurred over time in the global policy environment: a reduction of domestic policy influence, a weakening of traditional international institutions, and a sharpening of the conflict between industrialized and developing nations. These three changes in turn have had a major effect on policy responses in the international trade and investment field.

Reduction of Domestic Policy Influences

The effects of growing global linkages on the domestic economy have been significant. Policymakers have increasingly come to recognize that it is very difficult to isolate domestic economic activity from international market events. Again and again, domestic policy measures are vetoed or counteracted by the activities of global market forces. Decisions that were once clearly in the domestic purview now have to be revised due to influences from abroad. Occasionally one can even see how international factors begin to shape or direct domestic economic policy.

Agricultural policies, for example—historically mainly a domestic issue—have been thrust into the international realm. Any time a country or a group of nations such as the European Union contemplates changes in agricultural subsidies, quantity restrictions or even quality regulations, international trade partners are quick to speak up against the resulting global effects of such changes. When countries contemplate specific industrial policies that encourage, for example, industrial innovation or collaboration, they often encounter major opposition from their trading partners who believe that their own industries are jeopardized by such policies. Those reactions and the resulting constraints are the result of growing interdependencies among nations and a closer linkage between industries around the world. The following examples highlight the penetration of U.S. society by foreign trade considerations:

- One of every four U.S. farm acres is producing for export.
- One of every six U.S. manufacturing jobs is dependent on export.
- One of every seven dollars of U.S. sales is to someone abroad.
- One of every three cars, nine of every ten television sets, two of every three suits, and every video recorder sold in the United States is imported.
- One of every four dollars' worth of U.S. bonds and notes is issued to foreigners.[8]

To some extent, the economic world as we knew it has been turned upside down. For example, trade flows used to determine currency flows and therefore the exchange rate. In the more recent past, **currency flows** have taken on a life of their own, increasing from an average daily trading volume of $18 billion in 1980 to hundreds of billions in the 1990s. As a result, they have begun to set the value of exchange rates independent of trade. These exchange rates in turn have now begun to determine the level of trade. Governments that want to counteract these developments with monetary policies find that currency flows outnumber trade flows by more than ten to one. Also, private sector financial flows vastly outnumber the financial flows that can be marshaled by governments, even when acting in concert. The interaction between global and domestic financial flows have severely limited the freedom for governmental action. For example, if the Bundesbank of Germany or the Federal Reserve of the United States changes interest rate levels, these changes will not only influence domestic activities, but also trigger international flows of capital that may reduce, enhance, or even negate the domestic effects. Similarly, constant, rapid technological change and vast advances in communication permit firms and countries to quickly emulate innovation and counteract carefully designed plans. As a result, governments are often powerless to implement effective policy measures, even when they know what to do.

Governments also find that domestic regulations often have major international repercussions. In the United States, for example, the breakup of AT&T resulted in significant changes in the purchasing practices of the newly formed Bell companies. Overnight, competitive bids became decisive in a process that previously was entirely within the firm. This change opened up the U.S. market for foreign suppliers of telecommunications equipment, with only limited commensurate market developments abroad for U.S. firms. Therefore, U.S. telecommunications firms found themselves suddenly under much greater competitive pressures than did their foreign counterparts. Trade policy changes can also assist in revitalizing industries. As Global Perspective 7.2 shows, the lessening of import restrictions in Brazil has been instrumental in the development of a competitive Brazilian automotive industry.

Global Perspective

7.2
Brazilian Policy Shifts Change the Auto Industry

Brazil's auto industry, Latin America's biggest industrial complex, was dead to the world in the 1980s. Once the symbol of the "Brazilian miracle" of the 1970s, the auto industry had become emblematic of Latin America's "lost decade" of the 1980s. A ban on imports meant that technological innovations passed the industry by, and consumers had no choices. A 1991 study by James P. Womack, of MIT, found that Brazil had "by far the oldest mix of products assembled anywhere in the world." Quality was the second worse and productivity took the prize for the lowest anywhere.

In 1994, the industry was booming. Production rose nearly 30 percent to 1.39 million units. Brazil had overtaken Italy and Mexico as the tenth largest auto producer in the world. The president of General Motors do Brasil believes the nation has the potential to crack the top five. Another industry executive envisions a car market of 5 million units by 2015, a market comparable to the United States, Europe, or Japan.

The turnaround began with President Fernando Collor de Mello, who called Brazilian-made cars "horse carts" when he replaced the ban on imports with a 35 percent duty. He also repealed the ban on imports of electronic goods, allowing cars to be equipped with such items as electronic fuel injection and digital clocks. Robots were put on some production lines.

Production is drastically changing in the wake of the country's policy shifts. General Motors do Brasil used to need about three years to develop a car. The Corsa model, launched in 1994, took 17 months. This quicker turnaround was possible in part because of trade liberalization. Previously, import restrictions forced GM to develop virtually all of the parts locally. The Corsa has only 70 percent of its parts locally made. While the earlier Chevette was made without a single robot and took 30 man-hours to assemble, the Corsa can now be made with 62 robots, imported from Japan and Sweden, and takes 22 man-hours. "The Corsa is a turning point for GM and for the industry," said an auto analyst. "It's the first car launched in Brazil almost at the same time as in the First World." There has also been a major effect on production quantity. GM has put out as many cars since 1992 as it did in the two preceding decades.

"This is a revolution; the industry is reinventing itself," said Pierre-Alain de Smedt, the president of Autolatina, the Latin American joint venture between Volkswagen AG and Ford Motor Co. But without the adjustment in the nation's trade policies, this revolution could never have developed.

Source: Thomas Kamm, "Pedal to the Metal: Brazil Swiftly Becomes Major Auto Producer As Trade Policy Shifts," *The Wall Street Journal,* April 20, 1994, A1.

Legislators around the world are confronted with such international linkages. In some countries, the implications are understood, and new legislation is devised with an understanding of its international consequences. In other nations, particularly in the United States, national sovereignty expectations often relegate international repercussions to the status of side effects that can be ignored. Yet, given the linkages among economies, this is an unwarranted and sometimes even dangerous view. It threatens to place firms at a competitive disadvantage in the international marketplace or may make it easier for foreign firms to compete in the domestic market.

Even when policymakers want to take decisive steps, they are often unable to do so. In the late 1980s, for example, the United States decided to impose **punitive tariffs** of 100 percent on selected Japanese imports to retaliate for Japanese nonadherence to a previously reached semiconductor agreement. The initial goal was clear. Yet the task became increasingly difficult as the U.S. government identified specific imports as targets. In many instances, the U.S. market was heavily dependent on the Japanese imports, which meant that U.S. manufacturers and consumers would be severely affected by punitive tariffs. As Figure 7.1 shows, many Japanese prod-

**FIGURE 7.1
Japanese Products Can
Drive U.S. Economy**

ucts are actually produced or assembled in the United States. To halt the importing of components would throw Americans out of work.

Other targeted products were not actually produced in Japan. Rather, Japanese firms had opened plants in third countries, such as Mexico. Penalizing these product imports would therefore punish Mexican workers and affect Mexican employment, an undesirable result.

More and more products were eliminated from the list before it was published. In two days of hearings, additional linkages emerged. For example, law enforcement agencies testified that if certain fingerprinting equipment from Japan were sanctioned, law enforcement efforts would suffer significantly. Of the $1.8 billion worth of products initially considered for the sanctions list, the government was barely able to scrape together $300 million worth. Figure 7.2 illustrates how far such linkages have progressed in the aircraft industry. With so many product components being sourced from different countries around the world, it becomes increasingly difficult to decide what constitutes a domestic product. In light of this uncertainty, policy actions against foreign products becomes more difficult as well.

Policymakers find themselves with increasing responsibilities, yet with fewer and less effective tools to carry them out. More segments of the domestic economy are vulnerable to international shifts at the same time that they are becoming less controllable. To regain some power to influence policies, some governments have sought to restrict the influence of world trade by erecting barriers, charging tariffs, and implementing import regulations. However, these measures too have been restrained by the existence of international agreements forged through institutions such as the WTO or bilateral negotiations. World trade has therefore changed many previously held notions about the sovereignty of nation-states and extraterritoriality. The same interdependence that made us all more affluent has left us more vulnerable.

The intense linkages among nations and the new economic environment resulting from new market entrants and the encounter of different economic systems are weakening the traditional international institutions, and are therefore affecting their roles.

The ratification of the Uruguay Round and the formation of the WTO have provided the former GATT with new impetus. However, the organization is confronted with many difficulties. One of them is the result of the organization's success. Historically, a key focus of the WTO's predecessor was on reducing tariffs. With tariff levels at an unprecedented low level, however, attention now has to rest with areas such as nontariff barriers, which are much more complex and indigenous to nations. In consequence, any emerging dispute is likely to be more heatedly contested and more difficult to resolve. A second traditional focus rested with the right to establishment in countries. Given today's technology, however, the issue has changed. Increasingly, firms will clamor for the right to operations in a country without seeking to establish themselves there. For example, given the opportunities offered by telecommunications, one can envision a bank becoming active in a country without a single office or branch.

Another key problem area results from the fact that many disagreements were set aside for the sake of concluding the negotiations. Disputes in such areas as entertainment, financial services, and intellectual property rights protection are likely to resurface in the near term and cause a series of trade conflicts among nations. If the WTO's dispute settlement mechanism is then applied to resolve the conflict, outcries in favor of national sovereignty may cause nations to withdraw from the agreement.

A final major weakness of the WTO may result from the desire of some of its members to introduce "social causes" into trade decisions. It is debated, for

FIGURE 7.2   Who Builds the Boeing 777?

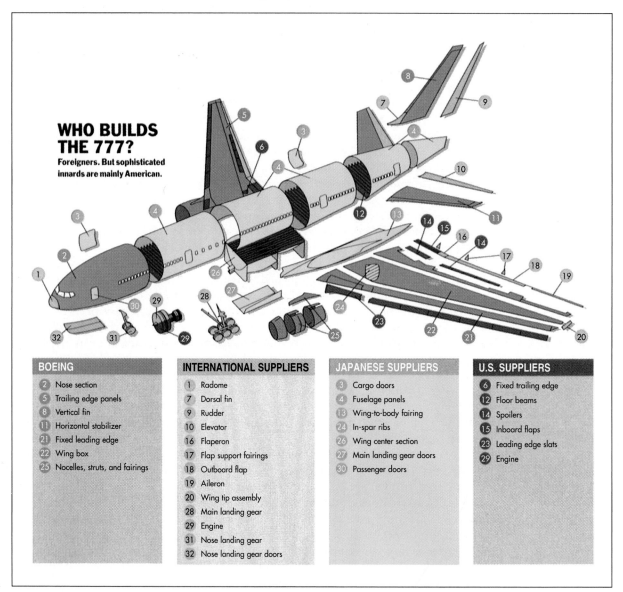

WHO BUILDS THE 777?
Foreigners. But sophisticated innards are mainly American.

BOEING
2 Nose section
5 Trailing edge panels
8 Vertical fin
11 Horizontal stabilizer
21 Fixed leading edge
22 Wing box
25 Nocelles, struts, and fairings

INTERNATIONAL SUPPLIERS
1 Radome
7 Dorsal fin
9 Rudder
10 Elevator
16 Flaperon
17 Flap support fairings
18 Outboard flap
19 Aileron
20 Wing tip assembly
28 Main landing gear
29 Engine
31 Nose landing gear
32 Nose landing gear doors

JAPANESE SUPPLIERS
3 Cargo doors
4 Fuselage panels
13 Wing-to-body fairing
24 In-spar ribs
26 Wing center section
27 Main landing gear doors
30 Passenger doors

U.S. SUPPLIERS
6 Fixed trailing edge
12 Floor beams
14 Spoilers
15 Inboard flaps
23 Leading edge slats
29 Engine

example, whether the WTO should also deal with issues such as labor laws, competition, and emigration freedoms. Other issues, such as freedom of religion, provision of health care, and the safety of animals are being raised as well. It will be very difficult to have the WTO remain a viable organization if too many nongermane issues are loaded onto the trade and investment mission. The 124 governments participating in the WTO have diverse perspectives, histories, relations, economies, and ambitions. Many of them fear that social causes can be used to devise new rules of protectionism against their exports. Then there is also the question as to how much companies—which, after all, are the ones doing the trading and investing—should be burdened with concerns outside of their scope.

To be successful, the WTO needs to be able to focus on its core mission, which deals with international trade and investment. The addition of social causes may appear politically expedient, but will be a key cause for divisiveness and dissent, and thus will inhibit progress on further liberalization of trade and investment. Failure to achieve such progress would leave the WTO without teeth and would negate much of the progress achieved in the Uruguay Round negotiations. It might be best to leave the WTO free from such pressures and look to increased economic ties to cross-pollinate cultures, values and ethics and to cause changes in the social arena.[9]

Similar problems have befallen international financial institutions. For example, although the IMF has functioned well so far, it is currently under severe challenge by the substantial financial requirements of less-developed countries and new entrants in world capital markets from the former Soviet bloc. So far, the IMF has been able to smooth over the most difficult problems, but has not found ways to solve them. For example, in the 1995 peso crisis of Mexico, the IMF was able to provide some relief through a stand-by credit. Yet, given the financial needs of many other nations such as Russia, the nations of central Europe, and many countries in Latin America, the IMF simply does not have enough funds to satisfy such needs. In case of multiple financial crises, it then is unable to provide its traditional function of calming financial markets in turmoil. Even the increase in capitalization agreed to in June of 1995 offers more of a temporary than a permanent solution.

Apart from its ability to provide funds, the IMF must also rethink its traditional rules of operations. For example, it is quite unclear whether stringent economic rules and benchmark performance measures are equally applicable to all countries seeking IMF assistance. New economic conditions that have not been experienced to date, such as the privatization of formerly centrally planned economies, may require different types of approaches. The linkage between economic and political stability also may require different considerations, possibly substantially changing the IMF's mission.

Similarly, the World Bank successfully met its goal of aiding the reconstruction of Europe but has been less successful in furthering the economic goals of the developing world and the newly emerging market economies in the former Soviet bloc. Therefore, at the same time when domestic policy measures have become less effective, international institutions that could help to develop substitute international policy measures have been weakened by new challenges to their traditional missions and insufficient resources to meet such challenges.

Sharpening of the Conflict between Industrialized and Developing Nations

In the 1960s and 1970s it was hoped that the developmental gap between industrialized nations and many countries in the less-developed world could gradually be closed. This goal was to be achieved with the transfer of technology and the infusion of major funds. Even though the 1970s saw vast quantities of petrodollars available for recycling and major growth in borrowing by some developing nations, the results have not been as expected. The Western world has recognized that the goals envisioned have not been achieved. Although several less-developed nations have gradually emerged as newly industrialized countries (NICs), even more nations are faced with grim economic futures.

In Latin America, many nations are still saddled with enormous amounts of debt, rapidly increasing populations, and very fragile economies. The newly emerging

The Global Environment: A Source of Conflict
Between Developed and Less-Developed Nations

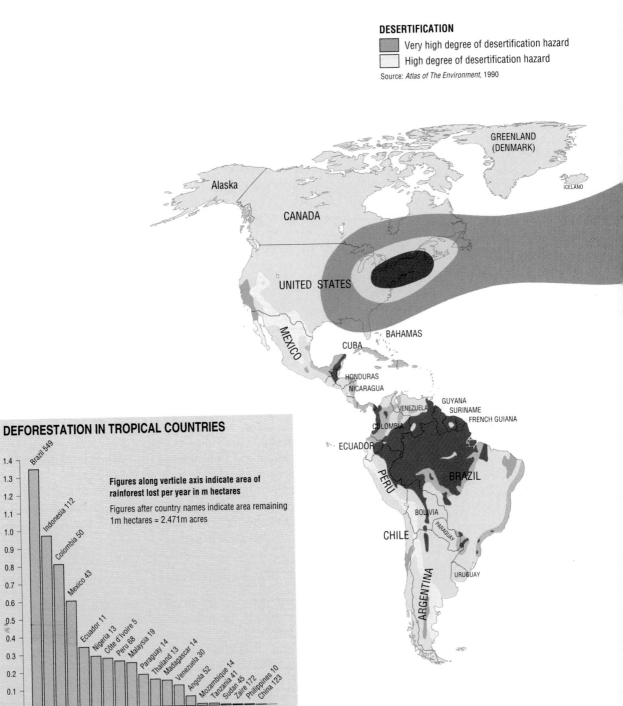

DESERTIFICATION

- Very high degree of desertification hazard
- High degree of desertification hazard

Source: *Atlas of The Environment*, 1990

GREENLAND
(DENMARK)

ICELAND

Alaska

CANADA

UNITED STATES

MEXICO

BAHAMAS

CUBA

HONDURAS
NICARAGUA

VENEZUELA

GUYANA
SURINAME
FRENCH GUIANA

COLOMBIA

ECUADOR

PERU

BRAZIL

BOLIVIA

PARAGUAY

CHILE

URUGUAY

ARGENTINA

DEFORESTATION IN TROPICAL COUNTRIES

Figures along verticle axis indicate area of rainforest lost per year in m hectares

Figures after country names indicate area remaining
1m hectares = 2.471m acres

Brazil 549
Indonesia 112
Colombia 50
Mexico 43
Ecuador 11
Nigeria 13
Côte d'Ivoire 5
Peru 68
Malaysia 19
Paraguay 14
Thailand 13
Madagascar 14
Venezuela 30
Angola 52
Mozambique 14
Tanzania 14
Sudan 41
Zaire 172
Philippines 10
China 123

Source: *The 1992 Information Please Environmental Almanac*

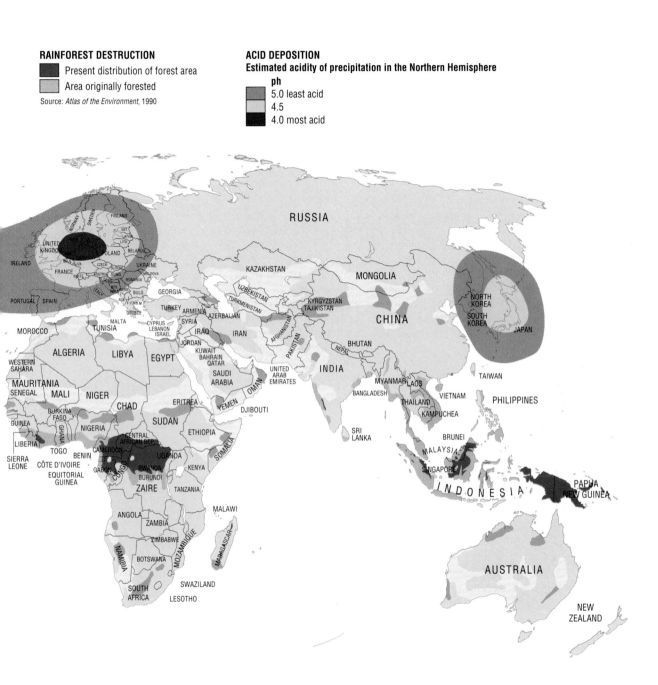

RAINFOREST DESTRUCTION

Present distribution of forest area

Area originally forested

Source: *Atlas of the Environment*, 1990

ACID DEPOSITION

Estimated acidity of precipitation in the Northern Hemisphere

ph

5.0 least acid

4.5

4.0 most acid

Source: *Atlas of the Environment*, 1990

Global Perspective

7.3
North versus South at the Earth Summit

At the Earth Summit in Rio de Janeiro, the developing world essentially wanted two things: money and technology. The industrialized nations in turn focused primarily on the environment, wanting to do something about potential threats such as global warming.

The two viewpoints often clashed. Said Jessica Ocaya-Lakidi of Uganda: "We don't yet have the big industries. We are lagging so far behind that we don't talk of industrial pollution." Maximo Kalaw, Jr., from Manila added: "The message is, if you cannot help us on debt, forget about the environmental conservation of our forests, because it is too much of a burden to handle." In essence, the developing countries are suggesting a straightforward bargain: If we get money, they say to the industrialized world, we will protect the environmental resources you claim to value so highly.

By contrast, the developed world sees a common responsibility of mankind that developing nations have to help fulfill. For example, the rosy periwinkle, a pink shrub found only in Madagascar, can be used to make drugs that have proved effective in fighting childhood leukemia and Hodgkin's disease. Plant genes found in Africa can also be used to improve varieties of wheat, corn, rice, and tomatoes. Therefore, it is important to maintain as much biodiversity as possible, a goal that requires the protection of natural resources. Some companies have already taken action to help. BankAmerica Corp., for example, forgave $6 million of its outstanding loans to Latin American countries in exchange for the debtor nations' promise to conserve ecologically critical rain forests.

In spite of the wide praise for such debt-for-nature swaps, many developing nations see them as a potential threat to their sovereignty. There is concern that these swaps are an attempt to put areas of sovereign territory somehow off-limits.

Sources: Eugene Robinson, "At Earth Summit, South Aims to Send Bill North," *The Washington Post,* June 1, 1992, A1, A14; Martha M. Hamilton, "BankAmerica to Forgive Loans in Deal to Aid Rain Forests," *The Washington Post,* June 12, 1991, C1.

democracies in central Europe and the former Soviet Union also face major debt and employment problems. In view of their shattered dreams, policymakers in these nations have become increasingly aggressive in their attempts to reshape the ground rules of the world trade and investment flows. Although many policymakers share the view that major changes are necessary to resolve the difficulties that exist, no clear-cut solutions have emerged.

Lately, an increase in environmental awareness has contributed to a further sharpening of the conflict. As Global Perspective 7.3 shows, developing countries may place different emphasis on environmental protection. If they are to take measures that will assist the industrialized nations in their environmental goals, they expect to be assisted and rewarded in these efforts. Yet, many in the industrialized world view environmental issues as "global obligation," rather than as a matter of choice, and are reluctant to pay.

POLICY RESPONSES TO CHANGING CONDITIONS

The word *policy* conjures up an image of a well-coordinated set of governmental activities. Unfortunately, in the trade and investment sector, as in most of the domestic policy areas, this is rarely the case. Policymakers need to respond too often to short-term problems, need to worry too much about what is politically salable to multiple constituencies, and in some countries, are in office too short a time to formulate a guiding set of long-term strategies. All too often, because of public and media pressures, policymakers must be concerned with current events—such as monthly trade deficit numbers and investment flow figures—that may not be very meaningful in the larger picture. In such an environment, actions may lead to extraordinarily good tactical measures but fail to achieve long-term realignments.

Policy responses in the trade and investment area tend to consist mainly of political ad hoc reactions, which over the years have changed from concern to protectionism. This is particularly true in the United States. While in the mid-1970s most lawmakers and administration officials simply regretted the poor U.S. performance in international markets, industry pressures have forced increasing action in more recent times.

Restrictions of Imports

In the United States, the Congress has increasingly focused on trade issues and provided the president with additional powers to affect trade. Unfortunately, apart from the consent to the NAFTA and WTO trade agreements, most of these new powers provide only for an increasing threat against foreign importers and investors, not for better conditions for U.S. exporters of goods, services, or capital. As a result, the power of the executive branch of government to improve international trade and investment opportunities for U.S. firms through international negotiations and the relaxation of rules, regulations, and laws has become increasingly restricted over time.

Worldwide, most countries maintain at least a surface-level conformity with international principles. However, many exert substantial restraints on free trade through import controls and barriers. Some of the more frequently encountered barriers are listed in Table 7.2. They are found particularly in countries that suffer from major trade deficits or major infrastructure problems, causing them to enter into voluntary restraint agreements with trading partners or to selectively apply trade-restricting measures such as tariffs, quotas, or nontariff barriers against trading partners.

TABLE 7.2
Trade Barriers

There are literally hundreds of ways to build a barrier. The following list provides just a few of the trade barriers that exporters face.

• Restrictive licensing	• Licenses for selected purchases
• Special import authorization	• Country quotas
• Global quotas	• Seasonal prohibitions
• Voluntary export restraints	• Health and sanitary prohibitions
• Temporary prohibitions	• Foreign exchange licensing
• Advance import deposits	• Licenses subject to barter and countertrade
• Taxes on foreign exchange deals	• Customs surcharges
• Preferential licensing applications	• Stamp taxes
• Excise duties	• Consular invoice fees
• Licensing fees	• Taxes on transport
• Statistical taxes	• Service charges
• Sales taxes	• Value-added taxes
• Consumption taxes	• Turnover taxes
• Discretionary licensing	• Internal taxes

Source: Mark Magnier, "Blockades to Food Exports Hide Behind Invisible Shields," *The Journal of Commerce* (September 18, 1989): 5A. Reprinted with permission.

Tariffs are taxes based primarily on the value of imported goods and services. **Quotas** are restrictions on the number of foreign products that can be imported. **Nontariff barriers** consist of a variety of meaures such as testing, certification, or simply bureaucratic hurdles that have the effect of restricting imports. All of these measures tend to raise the price of imported goods. They therefore constitute a transfer of funds from the buyers (or, if absorbed by them, the sellers) of imports to the government, and—if accompanied by price increases of competing domestic products—to the domestic producers of such products.

Voluntary restraint agreements are designed to help domestic industries reorganize, restructure, and recapture production prominence. Even though officially voluntary, these agreements are usually implemented through severe threats against trading partners. Due to their "voluntary" nature, the agreements are not subject to any previously negotiated bilateral or multilateral trade accords.

When nations do not resort to the subtle mechanism of voluntary agreements to affect trade flows, they often impose tariffs and quotas. For example, in 1983 the International Trade Commission imposed a five-year tariff on Japanese heavy motorcycles imported into the United States. The 49.4 percent duty was granted at the request of Harley-Davidson, which could no longer compete with the heavily discounted bikes being imported by companies such as Honda and Kawasaki. The gradually declining tariff gave Harley-Davidson the time to enact new management strategies without worrying about the pressure of the Japanese imports. Within four years, Harley-Davidson was back on its feet and again had the highest market share in the heavyweight class of bikes. In 1987, Harley-Davidson officials requested that the tariff be lifted a year early. As a result, the policy was labeled a success. However, at no time were the costs of these measures to U.S. consumers even considered.

Similarly, quotas were discussed for tuna fish packaged in water. U.S. producers complained that Japanese processors took away their market share for the product. However, U.S. firms had forced Japanese processors to concentrate on water-packed tuna by preventing them in the early 1970s from entering the U.S. market with tuna fish packed in oil. At that time, the majority of canned tuna sold in the United States was packed in oil. Only 7 percent of all canned tuna sold was water packed. Eventually the situation was reversed; most canned tuna purchased was packed in water. The Japanese firms that had been forced to concentrate on this small market niche had grown quite successful in penetrating it. They became even more successful as the niche became larger. However, the market share situation changed not because of Japanese ingenuity but because of changing consumer tastes. The Japanese adapted, whereas many U.S. firms did not.

The third major method by which imports have been restricted is nontariff barriers. These consist of buy-domestic campaigns, preferential treatment for domestic bidders compared with foreign bidders, national standards that are not comparable to international standards, and an emphasis on the design rather than the performance of products. Global Perspective 7.4 gives an example of how Japan designed new domestic regulations to reduce the import success of foreign rice. Such nontariff barriers are often the most insidious obstacles to free trade, since they are difficult to detect, hard to quantify, and demands for their removal are often blocked by references to a nation's cultural and historic heritage.

One other way in which imports are sometimes reduced is by tightening market access and entry of foreign products through involved procedures and inspections. Probably the most famous are the measures implemented by France. In order to stop or at least reduce the importation of foreign video recorders, the French gov-

Global Perspective

7.4
Can California Rice Stick in Japan?

A bad summer reduced the 1993 Japanese rice harvest, so Japan was forced to import foreign rice. Now the government wants to make sure that imports do not undermine the market for domestic rice, and that Japanese consumers will keep buying subsidized, expensive Japanese rice.

The new rice accord under GATT rules out import quotas or other barriers. Therefore, Japan's Ministry of Agriculture has designed a more subtle means to maintain control of the market. Hiding behind a superficial argument of "national equality," the ministry announced in early 1994 that no specific rice could be sold separately. All rice—domestic and imported—had to be mixed, so that the resulting rice does not have a "nationality." The directive prescribed a mix formula of 30 percent Japanese; 50 percent Californian, Chinese, and Australian combined; and 20 percent Thai rice.

Different rices have different uses. For instance, the Californian variety works well when steaming while the Chinese or Thai variety are needed for a Chinese dish and the Japanese goes very well with sushi. As no doubt was intended, the resultant nationless rice was appalling. You simply cannot steam a Californian/Thai mix.

The ministry's thinking: Given a choice, every Japanese in his right mind would buy the home-grown, nonmixed product as soon as it hit the market again. There would be no need for import quotas or other nontariff barriers. While the initial reaction to the mixed rice policy was what the ministry was looking for, it wasn't long before outrage over the restricting policies grew so strong that retailers were able to ignore the mixing directive without fearing ministry action. It had become clear that the citizens had sufficiently disliked Thai rice and had not developed a taste for Chinese rice either, thus the ministry declared that foreign rice could now be sold just by itself—with one exception. The most popular of all imports, the sticky Californian rice, still could not be sold in its pure form. It is mixed with rice from other states and sold under the name "American." The official reason for this mixing is that there is not enough Californian rice for everyone. But retailers openly admit that the rice is mixed in order to lower its quality, so that they can also sell the less popular Chinese and Thai grains.

In addition to being the object of this quality-reducing policy, the "American" mix is subject to a 580 percent tariff, which makes it exactly as expensive as medium-quality Japanese rice ($15 a pound), thereby removing any price advantage. The Japanese government is expected to take in revenues of $2.7 billion from its rice-import tariffs. The revenue is used to subsidize Japanese rice farmers and improve their irrigation systems. The idea is that as the new GATT "minimum-access rule" kicks in over a seven-year period beginning in 1995, Japanese farmers will become price competitive.

Source: Ulrike Schaede, "Japan Rice Move Leaves 'Em Steaming," *The Wall Street Journal,* June 1, 1994, A14.

ernment ruled that all of them had to be sent to the customs station at Poitiers. This customshouse was located away from major transport routes, woefully understaffed, and open only a few days each week. In addition, the few customs agents at Poitiers insisted on opening each package separately to inspect the merchandise. Within a few weeks, imports of video recorders came to a halt. Members of the French government, however, were able to point to the fact that they had not restrained trade at all; rather, they had only made some insignificant changes in the procedures of domestic governmental actions.

The discussion of import restrictions has focused thus far on merchandise trade. Similar restrictions are applicable to investment flows and, by extension, to international trade in services. In order to protect ownership, control, and development of domestic industries, many countries impose varying restrictions on investment capital flows. Most frequently, they are in the form of investment-screening agencies

that decide whether any particular foreign investment project is sufficiently merito-
rious to warrant execution. Canada, for example, has a Foreign Investment Review
Agency (FIRA) that scrutinizes foreign investments.[10] So do most developing nations,
where special government permission must be obtained for investment projects. This
permission frequently carries with it certain conditions, such as levels of ownership
permitted, levels of dividends that can be repatriated, numbers of jobs that must be
created, or the extent to which management can be carried out by individuals from
abroad.

The United States restricts foreign investment in instances where national security or related concerns are at stake. Major foreign investments may be reviewed by
the **Committee for Foreign Investments in the United States (CFIUS).** CFIUS
became active, for example, during the intended purchase of Fairchild Semiconductor
Industries by Fujitsu of Japan. The review precipitated a major national discussion
and resulted in the withdrawal of the Fujitsu purchase offer. Prior to that, national
attention was focused on investment strategies of Arab firms, governments, and individuals in the United States. The concern was that, because of their increased oil
income in the 1970s, Arab countries and nationals would be able to take over significant portions of U.S. industry and real estate. Yet the fears of being bought out
were never justified, because investor perceptions of the potential political backlash
resulted in a self-regulatory mechanism.

Foreign direct investment restrictions are often debated in many countries. Frequently, nations become concerned about levels of foreign direct investment and the
"selling out" of the patrimony. However, the bottom line is that although the restriction of investments may permit more domestic control over industries, it also
denies access to foreign capital. This in turn can result in a tightening up of credit
markets, higher interest rates, and less impetus for innovation.

The Effects of Import Restrictions   Policymakers are faced with several problems
when trying to administer import controls. First, most of the time such controls exact a huge price from domestic consumers. Import controls may mean that the most
efficient sources of supply are not available. The result is either second-best products or higher costs for restricted supplies, which in turn cause customer service
standards to drop and consumers to pay significantly higher prices. Even though
these costs may be widely distributed among many consumers and so less obvious,
the social cost of these controls may be damaging to the economy and subject to severe attack from individuals. However, these attacks are countered by pressure from
protected groups that benefit from import restrictions. For example, while citizens
of the European Union may be forced by import controls to pay an elevated price
for all the agricultural products they consume, agricultural producers in the region
benefit from higher incomes. Achieving a proper trade-off is often difficult, if not impossible, for the policymaker.

A second major problem resulting from import controls is the downstream
change in the composition of imports that may result. For example, if the importation of copper ore is restricted, through either voluntary restraints or quotas, producing countries may opt to shift their production systems and produce copper wire
instead, which they can export. As a result, initially narrowly defined protectionistic measures may snowball in order to protect one downstream industry after
another.

Another major problem that confronts the policymaker is that of efficiency. Import controls designed to provide breathing room to a domestic industry so it can
either grow or recapture its competitive position often do not work. Rather than im-

prove the productivity of an industry, such controls may provide it with a level of safety and a cushion of increased income, subsequently causing it to lag behind in technological advancements.

One must also be aware of the corporate response to import restrictions. Corporations faced with such restrictions can encourage their governments to erect similar barriers to protect them at home. The result is a gradually escalating set of trade obstacles. In addition, corporations can make strategic use of such barriers by incorporating them into their business plans and exploiting them in order to gain market share. For example, some multinational corporations have pressed governments to initiate antidumping actions against their competitors when faced with low-priced imports. In such instances, corporations may substitute adroit handling of government relations for innovation and competitiveness.

Finally, corporations also can circumvent import restrictions by shifting their activities. For example, instead of conducting trade, corporations can shift to foreign direct investment. The result may be a drop in trade inflow, yet the domestic industry may still be under strong pressure from foreign firms. The investments of Japanese car producers in the United States serve as an example. However, due to the job-creation effects of such investment, such shifts may have been the driving desire on the part of the policymakers who implemented the import controls.

Restrictions of Exports

In addition to imposing restraints on imports, nations also control their exports. The reasons are short supply, foreign policy purposes, or the desire to retain capital.

The United States, for example, regards trade as a privilege of the firm, granted by the state, rather than a right or a necessity. As will be explained in more detail in Chapter 8, U.S. legislation to control exports focuses on **national security** controls—that is, the control of weapons exports or high-technology exports that might adversely affect the safety of the nation. In addition, exports can be controlled for reasons of foreign policy and short supply. These controls restrict the international business opportunities of firms if a government believes that such a restriction would send a necessary foreign policy message to another country. Such action may be undertaken regardless of whether the message will have any impact or whether similar products can easily be supplied by companies in other nations. Although perhaps valuable as a tool of international relations, such policies give a country's firms the reputation of being unreliable suppliers and may divert orders to firms in other nations.

Many nations also restrict exports of capital, because **capital flight** is a major problem for them. Particularly in situations where countries lack necessary foreign exchange reserves, governments are likely to place restrictions on capital outflow. In essence, government has higher priorities for capital than do its citizens. They in turn, often believe that the return on investment or the safety of the capital is not sufficiently ensured in their own countries. The reason may be governmental measures or domestic economic factors such as inflation. These holders of capital want to invest abroad. By doing so, however, they deprive their domestic economy of much-needed investment funds.

Once governments impose restrictions on the export of funds, the desire to transfer capital abroad only increases. Because companies and individuals are ingenious in their efforts to achieve capital flight, governments, particularly in developing countries, continue to suffer. In addition, few new investment funds will enter the country because potential investors fear that dividends and profits will not be re-mitted easily.

Export Promotion Efforts

The desire to increase participation in international trade and investment flows has led nations to implement export promotion programs. These programs are designed primarily to help domestic firms enter and maintain their position in international markets and to match or counteract similar export promotion efforts by other nations.

Most governments supply some support to their firms participating or planning to participate in international trade. Typically, this support falls into one of four categories: export information and advice, production support, marketing support, or finance and guarantees.[11] Figure 7.3 shows an example of marketing promotion by the government of Pakistan. As Global Perspective 7.5 shows, governments often go to great lengths to assist their firms in obtaining international orders.

**FIGURE 7.3
A Marketing Promotion
Example**

Source: Newsweek, July 18, 1984.

Global Perspective

7.5
Military Exports: To Promote Or Not to Promote?

To help American defense contractors promote their products at Asian Aerospace '94 in Singapore, the Pentagon dispatched 75 U.S. military personnel and 20 top-of-the-line military aircraft. Even the aircraft carrier USS Independence was diverted so three Navy F/A-18 fighter jets could make an appearance.

Industry officials consider the strong U.S. military presence a major boost to their sales efforts in the booming Asian arms market. Joel Johnson, a vice president of the Aerospace Industries Association, said, "There's no question the services would like to be supportive. If the Malaysians are going to buy airplanes, [U.S. military officials] would rather have them be F-18s than MiG-29s. . . . The services have clearly all focused on the fact that the only thing keeping our production lines open for the next three to five years is going to be exports."

However, the Pentagon also has detractors. Some groups believe that the policy sends a wrong signal. Advocates of tighter controls on U.S. weapons exports are alarmed and say that the administration is undermining its own efforts to curb weapons exports from countries such as Russia and China while fueling a destabilizing arms race among Asian countries. "The administration sends the wrong signal to other suppliers and undercuts the prospects for controlling weapons proliferation," according to the non-profit Arms Control Association.

An administration official answered the protests by saying, "I don't think anyone is talking about creating circumstances where all of a sudden we would be selling arms to people we didn't used to because there's money to be made." A Pentagon report asserted that "demonstration of specific U.S. equipment at exhibitions such as this will in no way undermine the careful case-by-case review that the Defense and State Departments undertake before approving the sale of U.S. defense systems."

U.S. arms exports account for nearly half of all arms sales worldwide, far more than any other nation—$32.4 billion worth in 1993. One administration official said, "Whether you like it or not, weapons are a significant export earner and one area where the U.S. remains quite competitive. What should be the role, if any, of the U.S. government in promoting, encouraging, or assisting exports by U.S. defense industries, particularly during a stage when our own military procurement is shrinking? When the President of France goes overseas, he [asks his hosts], 'Why don't you buy [French-made] Mirage jets?' The question is, should the U.S. government play a more active role in doing this sort of thing?"

Source: John Lancaster, "Administration Helps Arms Makers Promote Goods at Singapore Show," *The Washington Post,* February 28, 1994, A6.

Such export promotion raises several questions. One concerns the justification of the expenditure of public funds for what is essentially an activity that should be driven by profits. It appears, however, that the start-up cost for international operations, particularly for smaller firms, may be sufficiently high to warrant some kind of government support.[12] A second question focuses on the capability of government to provide such support. Both for the selection and reach of firms as well as the distribution of support, government is not necessarily better equipped than the private sector to do a good job. A third issue concerns competitive export promotion. If countries provide such support to their firms, they may well distort the flow of trade. If other countries then increase their support of firms in order to counteract the effects, all that results is the same volume of trade activity, but at subsidized rates. It is therefore important to carefully evaluate export promotion activities as to their effectiveness and competitive impact. Perhaps such promotion is only beneficial when it addresses existing market gaps.

U.S. Export Promotion   Given the deterioration of the U.S. trade balance, U.S. government trade policy is focusing on export programs to improve the international trade performance of U.S. firms. The Department of Commerce offers information services that provide data on foreign trade and market developments. The department's Foreign Commercial Service posts hundreds of professionals around the world to gather information and to assist business executives in their activities abroad.

Another area of activity by the U.S. government is export financing. The Export-Import Bank of the United States provides U.S. firms with long-term loans and loan guarantees so that they can bid on contracts where financing is a key issue. In response to actions by foreign competitors, the bank has, on occasion also resorted to offering **mixed aid credits.** The credits, which take the form of loans composed partially of commercial interest rates and partially of highly subsidized developmental aid interest rates, result in very low interest loans to exporters.

Tax legislation that inhibited the employment of Americans by U.S. firms abroad has also been altered. In the past, U.S. nationals living abroad were, with some minor exclusions, fully subject to U.S. federal taxation. The cost of living abroad can often be quite high—for example, rent for a small apartment can approach $5,000 per month—so this tax structure often imposed a significant burden on U.S. firms and citizens abroad. As a result, companies frequently were not able to send U.S. employees to their foreign subsidiaries. However, a revision of the tax code now allows a substantial amount of income (up to $70,000) to remain tax-free. More Americans can now be posted abroad. In their work they may specify the use of U.S. products, thus enhancing the competitive position of U.S. firms.

A major U.S. export promotion effort consisted of the passage of the Export Trading Company Act of 1982. Intended to be the American response to the *sogoshosha,* the giant Japanese trading companies, this legislation permits firms to work together to form export consortia. The basic idea is to provide the foreign buyer with one-stop shopping centers in which a group of U.S. firms offers a variety of complementary and competitive products. The act exempted U.S. firms from current antitrust statutes. It also permitted banks to cooperate in the formation of the consortia through direct capital participation in the financing of trading activities. It was hoped that the legislation would enable more firms to participate in the international marketplace. Although the legislation was originally hailed as a masterstroke, so far it has not attracted a large number of successful firms. Perhaps the desire of U.S. firms to be independent is so strong that collaborative efforts are unacceptable for many companies.

Import Promotion Efforts

Some countries have also developed import promotion measures. The measures are implemented primarily by nations that have accumulated and maintained large balance of trade surpluses. They hope to allay other nations' fears of continued imbalances and to gradually redirect trade flows.

Japan, for example, has completely refurbished the operations of the Japan External Trade Organization (JETRO). This organization, which initially was formed to encourage Japanese exports, has now begun to focus on the promotion of imports to Japan. It organizes trade missions of foreign firms coming to Japan, hosts special exhibits and fairs within Japan, and provides assistance and encouragement to potential importers.

Countries such as South Korea and Taiwan sponsor buying missions to countries with which they have major trade surpluses. For example, representatives of several Korean firms, under the sponsorship of Korean government, periodically visit the United States to sign highly visible purchasing contracts. Through these measures, governments attempt to demonstrate their willingness to reduce trade imbalances.

Many countries are also implementing policy measures to attract foreign direct investment. These policies can be the result of the needs of poorer countries to attract additional foreign capital to fuel economic growth without taking out more loans that call for fixed schedules of repayment.[13] Industrialized nations also participate in these efforts since governments are under pressure to provide jobs for their citizens and have come to recognize that foreign direct investment can serve as a major means to increase employment and income. Increasingly, even state and local governments are participating in investment promotion. Some U.S. states, for example, are sending out "Invest in the USA" missions on a regular basis. Others have opened offices abroad to inform local businesses about the beneficial investment climate at home. Many countries and states also advertise widely to let the world know about the investment advantages they have to offer. Some nations highlight their willingness to assist foreign investors in order to diminish criticism of their barriers to entry. One such advertisement is reproduced as Figure 7.4.

**FIGURE 7.4
Attracting Foreign
Investors**

Incentives used by policymakers to facilitate such investments are mainly of three types: fiscal, financial, and nonfinancial. **Fiscal incentives** are specific tax measures designed to attract the foreign investor. They typically consist of special depreciation allowances, tax credits or rebates, special deductions for capital expenditures, tax holidays, and the reduction of tax burdens on the investor. **Financial incentives** offer special funding for the investor by providing, for example, land or buildings, loans, and loan guarantees. **Nonfinancial incentives** can consist of guaranteed government purchases; special protection from competition through tariffs, import quotas, and local content requirements; and investments in infrastructure facilities.

All of these incentives are designed primarily to attract more industry and therefore create more jobs. They may slightly alter the advantage of a region and therefore make it more palatable for the investor to choose to invest in that region. By themselves, they are unlikely to spur an investment decision if proper market conditions do not exist.

Investment promotion policies may succeed in luring new industries to a location and in creating new jobs, but they may also have several drawbacks. For example, when countries compete for foreign investment, several of them may offer more or less the same investment package. The slight advantage that the incentives of one country may have over another's package generally makes little difference in the investment site selected.[14] Moreover, investment policies aimed at attracting foreign direct investment may occasionally place established domestic firms at a disadvantage if they do not receive any support.

A STRATEGIC OUTLOOK FOR TRADE AND INVESTMENT POLICIES

All countries have international trade and investment policies. The importance and visibility of these policies have grown dramatically as international trade and investment flows have become more relevant to the well-being of most nations. Given the growing linkages among nations, it will be increasingly difficult to consider domestic policy without looking at international repercussions.

A U.S. Perspective

The U.S. need is for a positive trade policy rather than reactive, ad hoc responses to specific situations. Protectionistic legislation can be helpful, provided it is not enacted. Proposals in Congress, for example, can be quite useful as bargaining chips in international negotiations. If passed and signed into law, however, protectionistic legislation can result in the destruction of the international trade and investment framework.

It has been suggested that a variety of regulatory agencies could become involved in administering U.S. trade policy. Although such agencies could be useful from the standpoint of addressing narrowly defined grievances, they carry the danger that commercial policy will be determined by a new chorus of discordant voices. Shifting the power of setting trade and investment policy from the executive branch to agencies or even states could give the term *New Federalism* a quite unexpected meaning and might cause progress at the international negotiation level to grind to a halt. No U.S. negotiator can expect to retain the goodwill of foreign counterparts if he or she cannot place issues on the table that can be negotiated without constantly having to check back with various authorities.

In light of continuing large U.S. trade deficits, there is much disenchantment with past trade policies. The disappointment with past policy measures, particularly trade negotiations, is mainly the result of overblown expectations. Too often, the public has mistakenly expected successful trade negotiations to affect the domestic economy in a major way, even though the issue addressed or resolved was only of minor economic impact. Yet, in light of global changes, U.S. trade policy does need to change. Rather than treating trade policy as a strictly "foreign" phenomenon, it must be recognized that it is mainly domestic economic performance that determines global competitiveness. Therefore, trade policy must become more domestically oriented at the same time that domestic policy must become more international in vision. Such a new approach should pursue at least four key goals. First, the nation must improve the quality and amount of information government and business share to facilitate competitiveness. Second, policy must encourage collaboration among companies in such areas as product and process technologies. Third, American industry collectively must overcome its export reluctance and its short-term financial orientation. And, fourth, America must invest in its people, providing education and training suited to the competitive challenges of the next century.[15]

An International Perspective

From an international perspective, trade and investment negotiations must continue. In doing so, trade and investment policy can take either a multilateral or bilateral approach. **Bilateral negotiations** are carried out mainly between two nations, while **multilateral negotiations** are carried out among a number of nations. The approach can also be broad, covering a wide variety of products, services, or investments, or it can be narrow in that it focuses on specific problems.

In order to address narrowly defined trade issues, bilateral negotiations and a specific approach seem quite appealing. Very specific problems can be discussed and resolved expediently. However, to be successful on a global scale, negotiations need to produce winners. Narrow-based bilateral negotiations require that there be, for each issue, a clearly identified winner and loser. Therefore, such negotiations have less chance for long-term success, because no one wants to be the loser. This points toward multilateral negotiations on a broad scale, where concessions can be traded off among countries, making it possible for all participants to emerge and declare themselves as winners. The difficulty lies in devising enough incentives to bring the appropriate and desirable partners to the bargaining table.

Policymakers must be willing to trade off short-term achievements for long-term goals. All too often, measures that would be beneficial in the long term are sacrificed to short-term expediency to avoid temporary pain and the resulting political cost. Given the increasing linkages among nations and their economies, however, such adjustments are inevitable. In the recent past, trade and investment volume continued to grow for everyone. Conflicts were minimized and adjustment possibilities were increased manyfold. As trade and investment policies must be implemented in an increasingly competitive environment, however, conflicts are likely to increase significantly. Thoughtful economic coordination will therefore be required among the leading trading nations. Such coordination will result to some degree in the loss of national sovereignty.

New mechanisms to evaluate restraint measures will also need to be designed. The beneficiaries of trade and investment restraints are usually clearly defined and have much to gain, whereas the losers are much less visible, which will make coalition building a key issue. The total cost of policy measures affecting trade and investment flows must be assessed, must be communicated, and must be taken into consideration before such measures are implemented.[16]

Notes

1. Peter Passell, "Tuna and Trade: Whose Rules?" *The New York Times,* February 19, 1992, D2.

2. Michael R. Czinkota, "The World Trade Organization: Perspectives and Prospects," *Journal of International Marketing* 3, 1 (1995), 85–92.

3. Thomas R. Graham, "Global Trade: War and Peace," *Foreign Policy* 50 (Spring 1983): 124–127.

4. Edwin L. Barber III, "Investment-Trade Nexus," in *U.S. International Policy,* ed. Gary Clyde Hufbauer (Washington, D.C.: The International Law Institute, 1982), 9-4.

5. Mordechai E. Kreinin, *International Economics: A Policy Approach* (New York: Harcourt Brace Jovanovich, 1971), 12.

6. "Uruguay Round Results to Expand Trade by $755 Billion," *Focus: GATT Newsletter,* May 1994, 6.

7. Raymond J. Waldmann, *Managed Trade: The Competition between Nations* (Cambridge, Mass.: Ballinger, 1986); and *Ward's Automotive Report,* January 9, 1989.

8. Tobey, "Currency Trading," *Washington Post,* September 14, 1989, E1.

9. Michael R. Czinkota, "The World Trade Organization: Perspectives and Prospects," 85–92.

10. The U.S.–Canada Free Trade Agreement of 1988 provided for a significant downscaling of these screening activities.

11. Lisa A. Elvey, "Export Promotion and Assistance: A Comparative Analysis," in *International Perspectives on Trade Promotion and Assistance,* S.T. Cavusgil and M.R. Czinkota, eds. New York: Quorum, (1990): 133–146.

12. Masaaki Kotabe and Michael R. Czinkota, "State Government Promotion of Manufacturing Exports: A Gap Analysis," *Journal of International Business Studies* (Winter 1992): 637–658.

13. Stephen Guisinger, "Attracting and Controlling Foreign Investment," *Economic Impact* (Washington, D.C.: United States Information Agency, 1987), 18.

14. Ibid., 20.

15. Michael R. Czinkota and Masaaki Kotabe, "America's New World Trade Order," *Marketing Management* 1, 3 (1992): 46–54.

16. Michael R. Czinkota, ed., *Proceedings of the Conference on the Feasibility of a Protection Cost Index,* August 6, 1987 (Washington, D.C.: Department of Commerce, 1987), 7.

currency flows   bilateral negotiations
punitive tariff   multilateral negotiations

Questions for Discussion

1. Discuss the role of voluntary import restraints in international business.
2. What is meant by multilateral negotiations?
3. Discuss the impact of import restrictions on consumers.
4. Why would policymakers sacrifice major international progress for minor domestic policy gains?
5. Discuss the varying inputs to trade and investment restrictions by beneficiaries and by losers.
6. Why are policymakers often oriented to the short term?
7. Discuss the effect of foreign direct investment on trade.

Recommended Readings

Cavusgil, S. Tamer, and Michael R. Czinkota, eds. *International Perspectives on Trade Promotion and Assistance.* New York: Quorum, 1990.

Czinkota, Michael R., ed. *Improving U.S. Competitiveness.* Washington, D.C.: Government Printing Office, 1988.

Frazier, Michael. *Implementing State Government Export Programs.* New York: Praeger, 1992.

Guide to the Evaluation of Trade Promotion Programmes. Geneva, Switzerland: International Trade Centre, UNCTAD/GATT, 1987.

Howell, Thomas R., Alan William Wolff, Brent L. Bartlett, and R. Michael Gadbaw. *Conflict Among Nations: Trade Policies in the 1990's.* Boulder, Colo.: Westview Press, 1992.

Hufbauer, Gary Clyde, and Kimberly Ann Elliott. *Measuring the Costs of Protection in the United States.* Washington, D.C.: Institute for International Economics, 1994.

Krugman, Paul, and Alasdair Smith, eds. *Empirical Studies of Strategic Trade Policy.* Chicago: The University of Chicago Press, 1994.

McKibbin, Warwick J., and Jeffrey D. Sachs. *Global Linkages: Macroeconomic Interdependence and Cooperation in the World Economy.* Washington, D.C.: Brookings Institution, 1991.

Ramdas, Ganga Persaud. *U.S. Export Incentives and Investment Behavior.* Boulder, Colo.: Westview Press, 1991.

Schott, Jeffery J. *The Uruguay Round: An Assessment.* Washington, D.C.: Institute for International Economics, 1994.

Stern, Robert M., ed. *The Multilateral Trading System: Analysis and Options for Change.* Ann Arbor: University of Michigan Press, 1993.

Wolf, Charles, Jr. *Linking Economic Policy and Foreign Policy.* New Brunswick, N.J.: Transaction Publishers, 1991.

Notes

1. Peter Passell, "Tuna and Trade: Whose Rules?" *The New York Times,* February 19, 1992, D2.

2. Michael R. Czinkota, "The World Trade Organization: Perspectives and Prospects," *Journal of International Marketing* 3, 1 (1995), 85-92.

3. Thomas R. Graham, "Global Trade: War and Peace," *Foreign Policy* 50 (Spring 1983): 124-127.

4. Edwin L. Barber III, "Investment-Trade Nexus," in *U.S. International Policy,* ed. Gary Clyde Hufbauer (Washington, D.C.: The International Law Institute, 1982), 9-4.

5. Mordechai E. Kreinin, *International Economics: A Policy Approach* (New York: Harcourt Brace Jovanovich, 1971), 12.

6. "Uruguay Round Results to Expand Trade by $755 Billion," *Focus: GATT Newsletter,* May 1994, 6.

7. Raymond J. Waldmann, *Managed Trade: The Competition between Nations* (Cambridge, Mass.: Ballinger, 1986); and *Ward's Automotive Report,* January 9, 1989.

8. Tobey, "Currency Trading," *Washington Post,* September 14, 1989, E1.

9. Michael R. Czinkota, "The World Trade Organization: Perspectives and Prospects," 85-92.

10. The U.S.-Canada Free Trade Agreement of 1988 provided for a significant downscaling of these screening activities.

11. Lisa A. Elvey, "Export Promotion and Assistance: A Comparative Analysis," in *International Perspectives on Trade Promotion and Assistance,* S.T. Cavusgil and M.R. Czinkota, eds. New York: Quorum, (1990): 133-146.

12. Masaaki Kotabe and Michael R. Czinkota, "State Government Promotion of Manufacturing Exports: A Gap Analysis," *Journal of International Business Studies* (Winter 1992): 637-658.

13. Stephen Guisinger, "Attracting and Controlling Foreign Investment," *Economic Impact* (Washington, D.C.: United States Information Agency, 1987), 18.

14. Ibid., 20.

15. Michael R. Czinkota and Masaaki Kotabe, "America's New World Trade Order," *Marketing Management* 1, 3 (1992): 46-54.

16. Michael R. Czinkota, ed., *Proceedings of the Conference on the Feasibility of a Protection Cost Index,* August 6, 1987 (Washington, D.C.: Department of Commerce, 1987), 7.

trade negotiations, is mainly the result of overblown expectations. Too often, the public has mistakenly expected successful trade negotiations to affect the domestic economy in a major way, even though the issue addressed or resolved was only of minor economic impact. Yet, in light of global changes, U.S. trade policy does need to change. Rather than treating trade policy as a strictly "foreign" phenomenon, it must be recognized that it is mainly domestic economic performance that determines global competitiveness. Therefore, trade policy must become more domestically oriented at the same time that domestic policy must become more international in vision. Such a new approach should pursue at least four key goals. First, the nation must improve the quality and amount of information government and business share to facilitate competitiveness. Second, policy must encourage collaboration among companies in such areas as product and process technologies. Third, American industry collectively must overcome its export reluctance and its short-term financial orientation. And, fourth, America must invest in its people, providing education and training suited to the competitive challenges of the next century.[15]

An International Perspective

From an international perspective, trade and investment negotiations must continue. In doing so, trade and investment policy can take either a multilateral or bilateral approach. **Bilateral negotiations** are carried out mainly between two nations, while **multilateral negotiations** are carried out among a number of nations. The approach can also be broad, covering a wide variety of products, services, or investments, or it can be narrow in that it focuses on specific problems.

In order to address narrowly defined trade issues, bilateral negotiations and a specific approach seem quite appealing. Very specific problems can be discussed and resolved expediently. However, to be successful on a global scale, negotiations need to produce winners. Narrow-based bilateral negotiations require that there be, for each issue, a clearly identified winner and loser. Therefore, such negotiations have less chance for long-term success, because no one wants to be the loser. This points toward multilateral negotiations on a broad scale, where concessions can be traded off among countries, making it possible for all participants to emerge and declare themselves as winners. The difficulty lies in devising enough incentives to bring the appropriate and desirable partners to the bargaining table.

Policymakers must be willing to trade off short-term achievements for long-term goals. All too often, measures that would be beneficial in the long term are sacrificed to short-term expediency to avoid temporary pain and the resulting political cost. Given the increasing linkages among nations and their economies, however, such adjustments are inevitable. In the recent past, trade and investment volume continued to grow for everyone. Conflicts were minimized and adjustment possibilities were increased manyfold. As trade and investment policies must be implemented in an increasingly competitive environment, however, conflicts are likely to increase significantly. Thoughtful economic coordination will therefore be required among the leading trading nations. Such coordination will result to some degree in the loss of national sovereignty.

New mechanisms to evaluate restraint measures will also need to be designed. The beneficiaries of trade and investment restraints are usually clearly defined and have much to gain, whereas the losers are much less visible, which will make coalition building a key issue. The total cost of policy measures affecting trade and investment flows must be assessed, must be communicated, and must be taken into consideration before such measures are implemented.[16]

The affected parties need to be concerned and join forces. The voices of retailers, consumers, wholesalers, and manufacturers all need to be heard. Only then will policymakers be sufficiently responsive in setting policy objectives that increase opportunities for firms and choices for consumers.

SUMMARY

Trade and investment policies historically have been a subset of domestic policies. Domestic policies in turn have aimed primarily at maintaining and improving the standard of living, the developmental level, and the employment level within a nation. Occasionally, foreign policy concerns also played a role. Increasingly, however, this view of trade and investment policies is undergoing change. While the view was appropriate for global developments that took place following World War II, changes in the world environment require changes in policies.

Increasingly, the capability of policymakers simply to focus on domestic issues is reduced because of global linkages in trade and investment. In addition, traditional international institutions concerned with these policies have been weakened, and the developmental conflict among nations has been sharpened. As a result, there is a tendency by many nations to restrict imports either through tariff or nontariff barriers. Investment restrictions also are used to control influences from abroad. Yet, all these actions have repercussions that negatively affect industries and consumers.

Nations also undertake efforts to promote exports through information and advice, production and marketing support, and financial assistance. While helpful to the individual firm, in the aggregate such measures may only assist firms in efforts that the profit motive would encourage them to do anyway. Yet, for new entrants to the international market such assistance may be useful. Governments also promote imports and foreign direct investment in order to receive needed products or to attract economic activity.

In the future, nations must cooperate closely. They must view domestic policymaking in the global context in order to maintain a viable and growing global trade and investment environment. Policies must be long term in order to ensure the well-being of nations and individuals.

Key Terms and Concepts

national sovereignty

standard of living

quality of life

foreign policy

developmental aid

International Trade
    Organization (ITO)

General Agreement on
    Tariffs and Trade (GATT)

Most-Favored Nation (MFN)

International Monetary
    Fund (IMF)

World Bank

World Trade Organization
    (WTO)

tariffs

quotas

nontariff barriers

voluntary restraint
    agreements

Committee for Foreign
    Investments in the
    United States (CFIUS)

national security

capital flight

mixed aid credits

fiscal incentives

financial incentives

nonfinancial incentives

P A R T   2

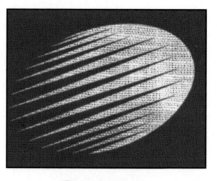

Cases

Debt-for-Nature Swaps: A Green Solution to LDC Debt

Around the world, major companies are hailing the 1990s as the "decade of the environment."[1] As concern for the environment grows from a radical idea championed by Greenpeace to a mainstream political and social reform movement, businesses are beginning to take notice. The green movement is more than a new craze. For example, in 1990 a group of environmentalists, along with institutional investors controlling $150 billion in assets, proclaimed the Valdez Principles. Crafted as a combative response to the 1989 *Valdez* oil spill in Alaska, the principles outline environmentally responsible actions and policies for corporations. The group has implied that future investments may hinge on corporations' complying with the principles. Some of the requirements specified include reducing waste and taking responsibility for past environmental harm. Shareholders at a number of large firms, including General Electric and Union Pacific, have introduced resolutions calling for the companies to subscribe to the principles.

In addition, most industrialized countries are passing more stringent environmental legislation. Some new laws hold lenders responsible for environmental damage caused by borrowers. A bank found lending to polluting borrowers can find itself in trouble. As a result, financial institutions are examining whether their loans and investments are environmentally responsible. Such examinations are known as "green audits."

Financial institutions can benefit from "green marketing"—selling their image as environmentally responsible. One form of green marketing introduced in the 1980s

Source: This case was written by Janet G. Farley and Pietra Rivoli.

[1]David Kirkpatrick, "Environmentalism: The New Crusade," *Fortune,* February 12, 1990, 44-55.

FIGURE 1

Why Is Fidelity Involved in Saving Rainforests?

In our surveys, our customers rank the environment as their highest social priority.

Traditionally, we have built Fidelity's business by giving customers access to investment diversification and professional money management. What's more, we pride ourselves on creating new and interesting opportunities for investors.

Now, Fidelity customers have an opportunity to contribute to protecting the environment through the novel debt-for-nature swap. And our customers can support a conservation effort that they may not find on their own: a rainforest protection project, sponsored by the prestigious Smithsonian Institution.

100% of the money contributed by Fidelity customers will go to the Smithsonian Rainforest Project. None of the costs of soliciting for or arranging the debt-for-nature swap comes out of your contributions to the Smithsonian, or from money invested in Fidelity funds.

Please consider this excellent opportunity to meet one of the global environment's most urgent challenges by helping to improve the future of the rainforests.

Source: "The Smithsonian Rainforest Project," *Investment Vision,* September/October 1990, 35–40.

was the debt-for-nature swap. In order to obtain desperately needed dollars to service immense debt obligations, many developing countries have witnessed the devastation of their environments in the name of progress. By using debt-for-nature swaps, indebted countries are able to cultivate their natural resources for future growth while paying off part of the billions of dollars owed to foreign lenders.

Debt-for-nature swaps work as follows: First, concerned individuals and institutions make tax deductible contributions to nonprofit organizations with a debt-for-nature swap program. Next, the nonprofit organization contacts a commercial or investment bank and buys some of the developing country's debt at a discount. For example, in early 1991, Mexico's debt was selling for approximately 47 cents per dollar of face value. Then, the developing country repays the face value of the debt in local currency. At early 1991 exchange rates, Mexico could repay one dollar (face value) in debt for about 2,500 Mexican pesos. The funds are then channeled to a local conservation organization that finances environmental projects. Because the debt is purchased at a discount, the value of the original contribution is multiplied. In one instance, a debt-for-nature swap in Ecuador increased the value of contributions eightfold. For every 12.5 cents contributed, the Ecuadoran government committed one dollar's worth of local currency to finance conservation projects.

Dr. Thomas Lovejoy, now at the Smithsonian Institution, developed the debt-for-nature swap tool in 1984. In a joint program with Fidelity Investments, Dr. Lovejoy and his team are currently working to save the Latin American rain forest (see Figure 1). Fidelity Investment customers are given the opportunity to contribute to the project without subsidizing Fidelity's management expenses. Since its inception, the program has worked in 10 countries on such projects as reforestation of buffer zones, training of conservation professionals, and preservation of one million acres of remote parklands. Fidelity's involvement in the program is a direct result of its customers' concern for the environment. Fidelity has given its customers an opportunity to contribute to global conservation efforts that they may not have had otherwise. More than just green marketing, Fidelity's program is a social response to a global concern.

The debt-for-nature swaps have reduced Third World debt by approximately $40 million while funding conservancy projects. However, total debt in these countries is well over $1,000 billion. Can debt-for-nature swaps make a dent in the Third World debt crisis? Many experts believe that the success of the swaps rests with the involvement of government and multilateral lenders such as the World Bank and the International Monetary Fund (IMF). Tax incentives that encourage institutions to swap debt for cash or equity need to be carried over to debt-for-nature swaps. IMF and World Bank endorsement will ensure debtor countries that debt-for-nature swaps are not just another form of foreign intervention, but rather a green solution to their debt problem—a solution with which the world can live.

Questions for Discussion

1. What are the benefits and costs of debt-for-nature swaps for (a) the banks and (b) the citizens of the developing countries?
2. Do you think that banks should be encouraged through tax incentives or other legislative assistance to participate in the swap programs? Why or why not?

Ownership Changes in Hollywood

During the 1980s, foreign direct investment in the United States increased by more than 250 percent. For the first time in decades, U.S. direct investment abroad fell below foreign investment in the United States. As foreign firms increased their holdings of U.S. assets, foreign direct investment in the United States became a controversial political and economic issue.

Foreign investment was particularly strong in the U.S. entertainment industry. By early 1991, foreigners had purchased four of the seven major U.S. film companies (see Table 1). In addition, foreign firms now own four of the five major U.S. record companies, several U.S. publishing companies, and several large U.S. music publishers. The entire entertainment industry is consolidating into a few large—and mostly foreign—firms. With the acquisition of MCA by Matsushita in December 1990, Americans were wondering, "Who owns Hollywood?"

The entertainment industry is becoming globally integrated. Cultural barriers have diminished and the United States—until recently the undisputed leader in the industry—no longer goes unchallenged. In addition to global competition, film studios are facing soaring production costs. The estimated industry average expenditure per film in the early 1990s was $27 million. Sheer size and financial strength will dictate whether or not a studio will survive the 1990s. Gordon Crawford, senior vice president of the Capital Research Company, notes that "global and vertical integration in the production and distribution of entertainment is a dominant theme that is going to continue."[1]

As of early 1991, Walt Disney Pictures and Paramount Pictures were the only two major movie studios that had not been acquired by another company. Walt Disney helped avoid takeover activity by generating cash through joint projects with Japanese investors. (In 1995, Disney strengthened its financial position with the purchase of Capital Cities, including ABC Broadcasting.) Industry experts believed that Paramount was a prime acquisition target, and Viacom bought it in 1994.

It was in this increasingly competitive and rapidly changing environment that MCA started to look for the capital required to compete against other industry giants. Matsushita of Japan appeared to be the perfect provider.

MCA, founded in 1923 as Music Corporation of America, owned Universal Studios, Universal Pictures, MCA Records, several theme parks, WWOR-TV, and Putnam

	Company	Owner
TABLE 1 **Ownership in the U.S.** **Movie Industry, 1990**	Columbia Pictures	Sony (Japan)
	Universal Pictures (MCA)	Matsushita (Japan)
	20th Century Fox	News Corp. (Australia)
	MGM-UA	Pathe Communications (Italy)
	Warner Brothers	Time Warner (United States)
	Walt Disney Pictures	Walt Disney Company (United States)
	Paramount Pictures	Paramount Communications (United States)

Source: The Washington Post, November 27, 1990, C1.

Source: This case was written by Janet G. Farley and Pietra Rivoli.

[1]Richard W. Stevenson, "Move Reflects a Belief in Role of Sheer Size," *The New York Times,* November 27, 1990, D7.

publishing house. In 1989, MCA's television and movie productions accounted for $1.69 billion, or half of the company's revenues. Universal Studios produced such movies as *Back to the Future* and *E.T.: The Extraterrestrial*, directed by Steven Spielberg, and the Sidney Pollack film *Out of Africa*. Universal's television production, originally specializing in one-hour television series, started to diversify into half-hour comedy shows with the TV hits "Major Dad" and "Coach."

Matsushita, a $38 billion Japanese giant, manufactures consumer electronics, including such brands as Panasonic, Quasar, and Technics. Sony, Matsushita's biggest competitor, purchased Columbia Pictures in late 1989 to protect its prominent position in consumer electronics. Hardware (television, VCR, laser disc player) superiority is partially dependent on controlling the software (movies, videos, music). Sony discovered the relationship between hardware and software the hard way: Without a library of videos in the Beta format, Sony was forced to abandon its Betamax VCR. To avoid a similar fate with its compact disc player, Sony purchased CBS Records, ensuring the CDs were available for the players. Similar logic motivated Sony's purchase of Columbia Pictures in 1989.

With the acquisition of Columbia Pictures, Sony made a strong move toward controlling emerging standards for the next generation of hardware, the high-definition television (HDTV)—a move Matsushita could not ignore. Akio Tanii, president of Matsushita, recognized that "software and hardware have been developing simultaneously. They are like wheels of the same car."[2] The company that owns movie and television production studios and therefore controls the production format will have an advantage in developing and selling the televisions and VCRs of the future.

To maintain a competitive position in consumer electronics against Sony and other Japanese manufacturers, Matsushita—in the largest purchase of a U.S. company by a Japanese firm—bought MCA on December 28, 1990, for a total of $6.13 billion in cash and $1.37 billion in shares of an MCA subsidiary for the New York area television station WWOR-TV. (Federal Communications Commission regulations prohibit foreign ownership of U.S. television networks.)

In addition to its studios and other interests, MCA owned the Yosemite Park and Curry Company, a hotel and concession business in Yosemite National Park. To appease growing public concern over a Japanese company owning an interest in one of America's national park concessions, and under increasing pressure from Secretary of the Interior Manuel Lujan, Jr., Matsushita agreed to sell the Yosemite interests to the National Park Foundation for $49.5 million, $50.5 million below their estimated $100 billion value. Under the agreement, the National Park Foundation, a nonprofit organization, would gain control of the concessions on September 30, 1993. Matsushita, under its MCA subsidiary, would continue to operate the concession and receive profits until 1993.

Many Americans voiced concern over the foreign purchases of high profile U.S. entertainment companies. Along with their resentment over American culture being "sold out" to foreign investors, many Americans feared foreign owners would influence public opinion and U.S. politics. The purchases in the entertainment industry had many Americans worried about who chooses what Americans will watch in the theaters or on television. There was also concern over the impact of FCC regulations on U.S. companies' competitiveness and over the future of proposed technology standards for such media as HDTV.

---

[2]Paul Farhi, "Matsushita Seeking Synergy," *The Washington Post*, November 28, 1990, C1.

Some observers of the film industry feared censorship by the new Japanese owners. The manipulation of Bernardo Bertolucci's movie *The Last Emperor* by a Japanese distributor was cited as an example of foreign intervention in movie content. A scene in the movie showing activities of Japanese troops in China during World War II was cut from the version shown in Japan. Only after Bertolucci protested was the scene replaced. Tanii would not guarantee that Matsushita would not interfere with the contents of MCA's movies, records, or books. However, he pointed out that this area of concern was not raised when Australian and Italian companies purchased Hollywood studios.

With or without a guarantee, Jeff Faux, president of the Economic Policy Institute, a Washington think tank, suggested that foreign ownership could lead to a change in programming through a process of self-censorship. Faux believed that "it's inevitable that producers and directors will be sensitive to Japanese interests and sensibilities, and things that criticize the Japanese may get a second look. It's simply a fact of life that he who pays the piper calls the tune."[3]

In addition to the movie industry, the U.S. television networks were also crying foul. Foreign companies do not fall under the FCC regulations prohibiting television networks from syndicating television programs both in the United States and abroad and from purchasing Hollywood studios. These FCC regulations prevented General Electric from purchasing MCA because it owns the NBC network. U.S. Representative John D. Dingell, chairman of the Energy and Commerce Committee, did not want the FCC to "protect foreign-owned companies at the expense of American enterprise."[4] The networks were using these latest Hollywood acquisitions as ammunition in their 20-year battle with the FCC to change these regulations.

The U.S. electronics industry was also unhappy with the recent purchases of movie studios by the Japanese. The future U.S. role in defining the standards for the next generation of television, HDTV, is greatly affected by who owns the companies that produce movies and television shows. As J. Richard Iverson, president of the American Electronics Association, pointed out, foreign investors were "picking up everything from womb to tomb in the communications field. If you control the production of material, the display of material, and the manufacturing of equipment, you have a significant advantage in the future information age."[5] Many worried that the United States was losing control over one more of its successful industries, an industry described as an "export powerhouse." As one electronics industry insider pointed out, "The U.S. library of motion pictures is a nonrenewable resource. It seems obvious that the value of this resource, plus the control of the studios and their production facilities, is significantly higher than the price paid by the Japanese to purchase this heritage."[6]

Despite these concerns, the United States continued to welcome foreign investment. In an increasingly global economy, the market for firms must also be global. In the case of the entertainment industry, the foreign investment brought much-

[3]Paul Farhi and John Burgess, "Buyout Expected to Get Tough Reviews in U.S.," *The Washington Post,* November 27, 1990, A6.

[4]Martin Tolchin, "Acquisition May Benefit the TV Networks," *The New York Times,* November 27, 1990, D6.

[5]Geraldine Fabrikant, "$6.13 Billion MCA Sale to Japanese," *The New York Times,* November 27, 1990, D1.

[6]Gene Parrott, "Japan's Studio Buyouts Will Hurt U.S. Long Term," *San Jose Mercury News,* December 17, 1990.

needed capital that would allow the firms to compete more effectively. In fact, if the choice is between a strong industry that is foreign owned or a weak industry owned by Americans, then perhaps there is no choice at all.

Ownership Changes

The appeal of Hollywood to Japanese corporations had faded considerably by 1995. Although MCA (Universal Pictures) was profitable in U.S. dollars, the strong yen made it an unattractive holding for Matsushita. In the summer of 1995 Seagrams spent $5.7 billion to buy out Matsushita's 80 percent share of MCA. Faced with charging off massive sums against Columbia Pictures, Sony's continued ownership of the studio was also seen by many as questionable. In financial terms, at least, the Japanese investments in the U.S. entertainment business had become box office poison.

Questions for Discussion

1. Are you concerned about foreign company purchases in the U.S. film industry? Why or why not?
2. Suppose the U.S. government prohibited foreign ownership of U.S. film companies. What would be the effect of this prohibition on the industry and the economy?

One Afternoon at the United States International Trade Commission

Chairwoman Stern: We turn now to investigation TA–201–55 regarding nonrubber footwear. Staff has assembled. Are there any questions? Vice Chairman Liebeler has a question. Please proceed.

Vice Chairman Liebeler: My questions are for the Office of Economics, Mr. Benedick. Do foreign countries have a comparative advantage in producing footwear?

Mr. Benedick: Yes, foreign producers generally have a comparative advantage vis-à-vis the domestic producers in producing footwear. Footwear production generally involves labor-intensive processes which favor the low-wage countries such as Taiwan, Korea, and Brazil, which are the three largest foreign suppliers by volume. For instance, the hourly rate for foreign footwear workers in these countries ranges from about one-twelfth to one-fourth of the rate for U.S. footwear workers.

Vice Chairman Liebeler: Is it likely that this comparative advantage will shift in favor of the domestic industries over the next several years?

Mr. Benedick: It is not very likely. There seems to be little evidence that supports this. The domestic industry's generally poor productivity performance over the last several years, which includes the period 1977 to 1981, roughly corresponding to the period of OMAs (Orderly Marketing Arrangements) for Taiwan and Korea, suggests that U.S. producers must significantly increase their modernization efforts to reduce the competitive advantage of the imported footwear.

Vice Chairman Liebeler: Have you calculated the benefits and costs of import relief using various assumptions about the responsiveness of supply and demand to changes in price?

Mr. Benedick: Yes. On the benefit side, we estimated benefits of import restrictions to U.S. producers, which included both increased domestic production and higher domestic prices. We also estimated the terms of trade benefits resulting from import restrictions. These latter benefits result from an appreciation of the U.S. dollar as a result of the import restrictions.

On the cost side, we estimated cost to consumers of the increase in average prices on total footwear purchases under the import restrictions and the consumer costs associated with the drop in total consumption due to the higher prices.

Vice Chairman Liebeler: In your work, did you take into account any retaliation by our trading partners?

Mr. Benedick: No.

Vice Chairman Liebeler: What was the 1984 level of imports?

Mr. Benedick: In 1984, imports of nonrubber footwear were approximately 726 million pairs.

Vice Chairman Liebeler: If a 600 million pair quota were imposed, what would the effect on price of domestic and foreign shoes be, and what would the market share of imports be?

Mr. Benedick: At your request, the Office of Economics estimated the effects of the 600 million pair quota. We estimate that prices of domestic footwear would increase by about 11 percent, and prices of imported footwear would increase by about 19 percent.

Source: Official Transcript Proceedings before the U.S. International Trade Commission, meeting of the Commission, June 12, 1985, Washington, D.C.

The import share, however, would drop to about 59 percent of the market in the first year of the quota.

Vice Chairman Liebeler: What would aggregate cost to consumers be of that kind of quota?

Mr. Benedick: Total consumer cost would approach 1.3 billion dollars in each year of such a quota.

Vice Chairman Liebeler: What would be the benefit to the domestic industry of this quota?

Mr. Benedick: Domestic footwear production would increase from about 299 million pairs for 1984, to about 367 million pairs, or by about 23 percent. Domestic sales would increase from about $3.8 billion to about $5.2 billion, an increase of about 37 percent.

Vice Chairman Liebeler: How many jobs would be saved?

Mr. Benedick: As a result of this quota, domestic employment would rise by about 26,000 workers over the 1984 level.

Vice Chairman Liebeler: What is the average paid to those workers?

Mr. Benedick: Based on questionnaire responses, each worker would earn approximately $11,900 per year in wages and another $2,100 in fringe benefits, for a total of about $14,000 per year.

Vice Chairman Liebeler: So what then would be the cost to consumers of each of these $14,000-a-year jobs?

Mr. Benedick: It would cost consumers approximately $49,800 annually for each of these jobs.

Vice Chairman Liebeler: Thank you very much, Mr. Benedick.

Commissioner Eckes: I have a question for the General Counsel's representative. I heard an interesting phrase a few moments ago, "comparative advantage." I don't recall seeing that phrase in Section 201. Could you tell me whether it is there and whether it is defined?

Ms. Jacobs: It is not.

Chairwoman Stern: I would like to ask about cost/benefit analysis. Perhaps the General Counsel's Office again might be the best place to direct this question. It is my understanding that the purpose of Section 201 is to determine whether a domestic industry is being injured, the requisite level for requisite reasons, imports being at least as important a cause of the serious injury as any other cause, and then to recommend a remedy which we are given kind of a short menu to select from to remedy the industry's serious injury.

Are we to take into account the impact on the consumer?

Are we to do a cost/benefit analysis when coming up with the remedy which best relieves the domestic industry's serious injury?

Ms. Jacobs: As the law currently stands, it is the responsibility of the commission to determine that relief which is a duty or import restriction which is necessary to prevent or remedy the injury that the commission has determined to exist. The president is to weigh such considerations as consumer impact, etc. The commission is not necessarily responsible for doing that. Of course, the commission may want to realize that, knowing the president is going to consider those factors, they might want to also consider them, but in fact, that it is not the responsibility of the commission. It is the responsibility of the commission only to determine that relief which is necessary to remedy the injury they have found.

Chairwoman Stern: I can understand our reporting to the president other materials which aren't part of our consideration, but nevertheless necessary for the president in his consideration, but having that information and providing it to the president is different from its being part of the commission's consideration in its recommendations.

Ms. Jacobs: That's right. Your roles are quite different in that respect.

Vice Chairman Liebeler: Nations will and should specialize in production of those commodities in which they have a comparative advantage. Fortunately, our country has a large capital stock which tends to provide labor with many productive employments. Our comparative advantage is in the production of goods that use a high ratio of capital to labor. Shoes, however, are produced with a low ratio of capital to labor.

Therefore, American footwear cannot be produced as cheaply as foreign footwear. The availability of inexpensive imports permits consumers to purchase less expensive shoes and it allows the valuable capital and labor used in this footwear industry to shift to more productive pursuits.

This situation is not unique to the footwear industry. The classic example is agriculture, where the share of the labor force engaged in farming declined from 50 percent to 3 percent over the last 100 years. This shift did not produce a 47 percent unemployment rate. It freed that labor to produce cars, housing, and computers.

The decline of the American footwear industry is part of this dynamic process. This process is sometimes very painful. Congress, by only providing for temporary relief, has recognized that our continued prosperity depends on our willingness to accept such adjustments.

The industry has sought this so-called "temporary import relief" before. The ITC has conducted approximately 170 investigations relating to this industry. This is the fourth footwear case under Section 201, and so far the industry has gotten relief twice. The 1975 petition resulted in adjustment assistance. The 1976 case resulted in orderly marketing agreements with Taiwan and Korea.

In spite of the efforts of the domestic industry to suppress imports, the industry has been shrinking. Between 1981 and 1984, 207 plants closed; 94 of these closings occurred just last year. The closing of unprofitable plants is a necessary adjustment. Import relief at this stage will retard this process and encourage entry into a dying industry.

Because there is no temporary trade restriction that would facilitate the industry's adjustment in foreign competition, I cannot recommend any import barrier.

Chairwoman Stern: The intent of the General Import Relief law is to allow a seriously injured industry to adjust to global competition. The commission must devise a remedy which corresponds to the industry and the market forces it must face.

No other manufacturing sector of our economy faces stiffer competition from abroad than the U.S. shoe industry. Imports have captured three-fourths of our market. No relief program can change the basic conditions of competition that this industry must ultimately face on its own. The best that we as a commission can do—and under Section 201 that the president can do—is to give the industry a short, predictable period of relief to allow both large and small firms to adjust, coexist, and hopefully prosper.

I am proposing to the president an overall quota on imports of 474 million pairs of shoes in the first year. Shoes with a customs value below $2.50 would not be subject to this quota. The relief would extend for a full five years.

Commissioner Lodwick: Section 201 is designed to afford the domestic industry a temporary respite in order to assist it in making an orderly adjustment to import competition. The fact that the law limits import relief to an initial period of up to five years, to be phased down after three years to the extent feasible, indicates that Congress did not intend domestic producers to find permanent shelter from import competition under the statute.

Accordingly, I intend to recommend to the president a five-year quota plan which affords the domestic nonrubber footwear industry ample opportunity to implement feasible adjustment plans which will facilitate, as the case may be, either the orderly transfer or resources to alternative uses or adjustments to new conditions of competition.

Commissioner Rohr: In making my recommendation, I emphasize the two responsibilities which are placed on the commission by statute. First, it must provide a remedy which it believes will effectively remedy the injury which is found to exist.

Secondly, Congress has stated that we, as commissioners, should attempt, to the extent possible, to develop a remedy that can be recommended to the president by a majority of the commission. I have taken seriously my obligations to attempt to fashion a remedy with which at least a majority of my colleagues can agree. Such remedy is a compromise.

I am concurring in the remedy proposal which is being presented today by a majority of the commission. This majority recommendation provides for an overall limit on imports of 474 million pairs; an exclusion from such limitation of shoes entering the United States with a value of less than $2.50 per pair; a growth in such limitation over a five-year period of 0 percent, 3 percent, and 9 percent; and the sale of import licenses through an auctioning system.

Commissioner Eckes: It is my understanding that a majority of the commission has agreed on these points. I subscribe to that and will provide a complete description of my views in my report to the president.

Questions for Discussion

1. What are your views of the ITC recommendation?
2. Should the principle of comparative advantage always dictate trade flows?
3. Why are the consumer costs of quotas so often neglected?
4. Discuss alternative solutions to the job displacement problem.
5. How would you structure a "temporary relief program"?

When "Fair Trade" Policies Backfire

In the summer of 1991, seven small American flat panel computer screen manufacturers persuaded the U.S. Department of Commerce to rule against Japanese manufacturers in an antidumping case. The American companies, calling themselves the Advanced Display Manufacturers of America, alleged that Japanese manufacturers were selling "active matrix" displays to U.S. computer manufacturers at unfairly low prices.

After investigating the allegations, the Commerce Department, in July 1991, found that foreign producers were dumping, that is, selling active matrix displays at a price far below market value in the United States. Commerce imposed a 63 percent tariff to crack down on the Japanese display makers. Although the tariff appeared to be a boon to the seven small American manufacturers hoping to compete with Japanese competitors, several large American computer manufacturers were upset because they believed prices for the displays would go up.

In August 1991, the U.S. International Trade Commission (ITC) investigated the case to determine whether U.S. firms had been injured by the dumping. The ITC ruled that U.S. industry had been materially injured by the low-priced Japanese imports. Excerpts from the hearings of the International Trade Commission appear at the end of this case.

ACTIVE MATRIX DISPLAYS

Active matrix liquid crystal displays provide sharper pictures and faster image changes than the passive liquid crystal displays that are more commonly used in laptop computers. Active displays use an electronic transistor to control each dot on the screen, whereas passive displays use a grid of wires. In the near future, the active matrix displays are destined to be crucial in aircraft cockpits, automobile dashboards, wall-sized "high-definition" television, advanced laptop computers, and potentially almost anywhere that information is electronically displayed.

Many industry experts see the new technology as a key to sustaining a healthy domestic electronics industry. "We have to do something," said Lewis Branscomb, director of the Harvard University technology policy program and the former chief scientist of IBM. "From a future trend point of view [the technology] is very important."

Considerable efforts are underway to improve and apply this emerging technology. IBM has formed a partnership with Toshiba Corp. to develop and make advanced displays in Japan. Many American universities as well as the military are also investing in the new technology. Eight major Japanese companies expect to spend about $2 billion over the next few years, in addition to participating in a cooperative research project that involves the Japanese government and 18 companies.

A U.S. Company, RCA Corp., invented the thin screen display in the 1960s using liquid crystals as an alternative to the bulky cathode ray tubes found in conventional displays. But firms in the Far East honed the technologies and invested the large sums needed to mass produce the screens. Sharp Corp. and Hosiden Corp. have led the Japanese effort to refine active matrix technology.

Source: This case was written by Mitchell J. Peyser under the supervision of Michael R. Czinkota and is based on the following articles: T. R. Reid, "In Display-Screen Case, 'Fair Trade' Policy Does Americans a Disservice," *Washington Post,* June 24, 1991, WB 18; Andrew Pollack, "Duties Sought from Japan on Some Computer Screens," *New York Times,* July 9, 1991, D1; Evelyn Richards, "A Little Guy's Fight to Regain a U.S. Edge," *Washington Post,* August 4, 1991, H1; David E. Sanger, "I.B.M. Chief Issues Threat on U.S. Tariff," *New York Times,* November 8, 1991.

U.S. PRODUCTION

As of July 1991, only one American firm, OIS Optical Imaging Systems, Inc., of Troy, Michigan, manufactured and sold the displays, mostly to the military. OIS pursued a major contract to make the displays for Apple Computer. In 1989, Apple awarded the contract to Hosiden Corporation, a Japanese supplier of the active matrix displays. OIS President Zvi Yaniv immediately suspected dumping. Yaniv banded together with six American firms that did not yet manufacture the displays on a commercial basis but were hoping to enter the market. The group, the Advanced Display Manufacturers of America, filed their claim with the Department of Commerce.

THE MANUFACTURER'S PERSPECTIVE

The Hosiden Corporation had been selling the active matrix screens in the United States at 63 percent below the production cost of domestic producers. Therefore, the Commerce Department imposed a 63 percent duty, which was designed to provide a substantial boost to domestic manufacturers capable of producing the displays. Such a boost was necessary to help the ailing domestic producers. For example, before the ruling, OIS had experienced yearly losses ranging from $2 to $9 million and had been struggling to stay in the business. The decline in U.S. military expenditures further threatened sales potential.

With the boost of the tariff, OIS hoped to make the difficult transition from the military market to the commercial market. The transition is a major one, since military orders are usually much smaller and offer higher prices than the commercial market. However, the commercial market offers a larger potential market. And with the duty to help keep prices up, other domestic firms plan to enter the market.

THE BUYER'S PERSPECTIVE

However, some major U.S. computer manufacturers were not so happy with the Commerce Department action. "We're deeply disappointed," said a spokesman for IBM. "It has the impact of increasing the cost of computers made in the U.S." The duty requires American computer companies such as IBM, Apple Computer Inc., Compaq Computer Corp., and Zenith Electronics Corp. to pay higher prices for the small computer display units they buy. Speaking in Tokyo on November 7, 1991, IBM Chairman John F. Akers said that the company might be forced to move production of some of its smallest machines out of the United States to avoid the tariff charges.

Apple Chairman John Sculley said, "The people who have lobbied Washington for protection have really misled the government people into believing they are a credible alternative. In a recession, the international market is the place computer companies are making their money. It's hard to compete if you're paying more than the other guy for displays." In fact, soon after the tariff was imposed, Apple Computer and the Toshiba Corporation had already begun to move their production of portable machines out of the United States. Computer systems that already contain the screens can be shipped to the United States without the tariff.

Excerpts from the Meeting of the U.S. International Trade Commission, Washington, D.C., August 15, 1991

Commissioner Rohr: Ms. Baker, many of the U.S. companies manufacturing flat panel displays are in the so-called developmental stage. What kind of industry performance could one expect from companies at this stage?

Ms. Baker: When an industry or company is in the developmental stage, we should recognize the product is still being brought on stream. Therefore, when we are looking at industry indicators, such as production, shipments, and employment, it is to be expected that increases might be seen in those indicators, which was characteristic of this industry.

However, another industry performance, or industry indicator of performance, financial experience, was poor.

Commissioner Rohr: Can you characterize for me the overall performance of U.S. companies making flat panel displays, including your financial investigation of financial condition?

Ms. Baker: The overall condition shows expansions in production and shipments. However, the financial experience of companies is negative.

Mr. Stewart (office of investigations): The overall financial performance of the flat panel displays industry is poor. Sales are increasing. However, operating losses are very high. And these losses are compounded by the companies' difficulty in obtaining financing to start or increase production or to produce at a level to become profitable.

Commissioner Rohr: Thank you, very much. Ms. Baker, what has happened to U.S. imports of the subject merchandise during the period of investigation?

Ms. Baker: Commissioner Rohr, subject imports of active matrix LCDs and EL displays combined from Japan increased substantially in both 1989 and 1990. Market share of subject import also increased. Trends of subject imports, active matrix LCDs, and EL displays, separately, however are confidential.

Commissioner Rohr: Thank you. Does the record show that price, that is, target prices, has a role in the decision to source from a particular supplier?

Ms. Baker: Yes, sir. The record does seem to indicate that price does have a role in the decision to source from specific suppliers. Although there are other considerations, most specifically the technical requirements of the end-user, prices also seem to have a role.

Commissioner Rohr: Thank you.

Mr. Workman, this is for you. What did our investigation discover concerning lost sales, underselling, price depression, and suppression?

Mr. Workman (office of investigations): Well, evaluation of price trends was made difficult by the fact that these are often very complex and individualized products. Nonetheless, we did get ten price series from various producers and importers. There were a couple of domestic series where the product seemed to be pretty consistent from one quarter to the next. And for the three-year period, from early 1988 on down through, it did show evidence of declining prices.

In the case of the other products, both domestic and Japanese, the series were very, very difficult to evaluate because of shifting product mix even within the category groupings that we had.

In the case of underselling, again, we had a problem in terms of our product groupings, not knowing exactly whether the products were the same or not. But in the one comparison we were able to make, it did show the Japanese—this was for the producers' and importers' questionnaire—it did show that the Japanese price was in fact lower. And there was some evidence from purchasers' questionnaires that similarly seemed to point to a somewhat lower price for imports. But this was not true in all cases.

In the lost sales, again, in discussions with purchasers and evaluating lost sales, this was a very complex process because as has been described, the process of purchasing these flat panel displays is often driven by technology—very much so, in fact, perhaps redundantly. Yet, we did find one instance where the case of a sale lost because the import was priced lower than the domestic product.

And similarly, we found one instance of lost revenue, where the imports were available, and the purchaser was able to bid down the domestic price somewhat, as a result of these lower priced imports.

Commissioner Lodwick: Mr. Bardos, does the statute authorize the International Trade Commission to consider U.S. consumer interests in making its less than fair value decisions? And if it does, how?

Mr. Bardos (office of the general counsel): The statute does not direct the commission to consider U.S. consumer interests.

Chairman Brunsdale: Mr. Workman, can you summarize how major customers of active matrix flat panel displays responded to the lost sales and lost revenue allegations?

Mr. Workman: We found a couple of instances where there were lost sales or lost revenue allegations with respect to these active matrix displays. In one case, the purchaser didn't seem to feel at all that the domestic producer was capable of supplying what they needed. So, that transaction went absolutely nowhere. And in the second case, the domestic producer had actually made a prototype sale. Its price was very high, compared to the imports. But the purchaser indicated that they felt that the main problem here was that the domestic firm would not be able to supply the amount of active matrix displays that they would need for their use. And this seemed to drive their decision to switch to the imports much more than any price consideration.

Chairman Brunsdale: We are now ready for the vote in this case. Mr. Secretary, will you please call the roll in investigation 731-TA-469 (Final) involving HIC Flat Panel Displays from Japan?

Secretary Mason: Commissioner Newquist?

Commissioner Newquist: I vote in the affirmative.

Secretary Mason: Commissioner Brunsdale.

Chairman Brunsdale: I have a short statement to read in connection with my vote. The commission has to decide in this case whether the domestic industry producing flat panel displays is materially injured, threatened with material injury, or materially retarded by reason of the dumped imports from Japan.

This case has attracted much attention and has also been discussed in the popular press as another area where Japanese firms are beating U.S. firms in a high-tech field and where competition from Japan may put U.S. firms out of business, unless the government steps in.

We at the commission cannot be swayed, and are not swayed, by the popular misconception that dumping laws are designed to bolster U.S. industries that face intense competition from abroad. An affirmative determination must be made on evidence that dumped imports cause material injury or material retardation. We cannot ask the question, would U.S. firms be better off if there were no Japanese flat panel display industry at all.

In this case, the evidence is overwhelming that the U.S. industry producing active matrix flat panel displays, used primarily in small portable computers, is not materially retarded by reason of dumped imports of flat panel displays from Japan. In the course of this investigation, major purchasers offered testimony and documentation indicating that they would not have purchased active matrix flat panel displays from U.S. producers for many reasons that had nothing to do with price.

In addition, given their relatively small market share and the low dumping margin found by the Department of Commerce, I find that the U.S. industry producing electroluminescence flat panel displays, which are used primarily in medical and control equipment, is not materially injured by reason of the dumped imports.

I will, of course, provide a complete explanation of my decisions in my written opinion. Thank you.

Secretary Mason: Commissioner Rohr.

Commissioner Rohr: The staff and the commission have worked very hard and long to get to this critical day. We have studied hundreds of pages of submissions and testimony: we created a 300-page staff report which distills this information. We have examined under a microscope a small but critical high-technology industry and then tried to understand what relationship its situation has to dumping and to the dumping law.

After many hours of study and discussion, I have come to the conclusion that the U.S. flat panel display industry is injured and there is a relationship between the dumped imports of flat panel displays and that injury. My analysis of the dynamics of the flat panel display industry leads me to believe that, while there are differences between technologies, there are enough similarities to warrant a finding of one like product consisting of all flat panel displays and that, while price may not be the single most essential factor in the decision to purchase a particular flat panel display, it is nonetheless a very important one.

The industry is made up of small companies, a number of which are still in the developmental stage. In the presence of rapidly growing dumping imports, these companies have suffered substantial negative cash flows from operations and have found themselves unable to fund research and secure the necessary physical plant to become large-scale producers.

I have heard flat panel displays characterized as the invention that got away, meaning that U.S. firms failed to turn the technology into a marketable product. But there are a few of these firms still struggling to do just that. And as they are unable to meet Japanese prices, we have seen evidence of lost sales, price suppression and depression, and certainly the inability to sustain adequate profits even in the small market niches they now occupy.

Even should this industry achieve an affirmative commission finding, I must caution that no one should view this determination as a guarantee for success in the marketplace. A commission finding will not ensure appropriate capital backing, R & D success, product innovation, manufacturing capability, or long-term viability. The antidumping law has no place in that realm. Only business savvy, hard work, imagination, and good fortune will do that.

Some have said that this case represents a manipulation and abuse of the antidumping law. Nonsense. Utter nonsense. To some extent, every industry that comes before us attempts to mold the law to the facts of the case it is trying to make. We expect that. Clearly, dumping is not the major problem this industry faces. But that is not the determination the law asks us to make. Rather, we must determine whether the dumping already found by the Commerce Department is a cause of material injury to the domestic industry.

And I am compelled to determine that it is. Whether the domestic industry can change potential investors' strategies to their benefit, whether they can develop the breakthrough to achieve color, whether they can advance to produce products even beyond what is well beyond our ability to influence. The antidumping law can only attempt to mitigate the effects of injurious dumping—no more, no less.

I therefore make an affirmative determination.

Secretary Mason: Commissioner Lodwick.

Commissioner Lodwick: Today the International Trade Commission makes a final determination in investigation number 731-TA-469, High Information Content Flat Display Panels, and Subassemblies Thereof, from Japan.

The subject imports are active matrix liquid crystal and electroluminescent high information content flat panel displays and display glass. Therefore I find that there is one domestic product like these imports, namely high information content flat panel displays and display glass. I find that the U.S. industry has been materially injured by reason of the LTFV imports from Japan.

Factors that are important in my finding include (1) the ability of the United States HIC flat panel displays industry to raise capital and invest; (2) the existing production and development efforts of the domestic industry; and (3) the rapid increase in subject imports. My complete views will be available at the conclusion of this investigation.

Secretary Mason: Madam Chairman, by a vote of three to one, we have an affirmative determination.

Chairman Brunsdale: Thank you, Mr. Secretary. Thank you very much, staff, for your particularly fine efforts in this case.

Questions for Discussion

1. How can antidumping duties be used to protect domestic manufacturers?
2. How can antidumping laws hurt consumers?
3. Evaluate the decision by the International Trade Commission.
4. Did the United States intercede on behalf of seven small companies at the expense of computer makers and their employees?
5. How important is the role of domestic consumers for ITC findings?
6. What does this case say about America's ability to compete?

Harley-Davidson (A): Protecting Hogs

On September 1, 1982, Harley-Davidson Motor Company and Harley-Davidson York, Inc., filed a petition for "relief" or protection with the U.S. International Trade Commission (ITC). The filing, a request under Section 201 of the U.S. Trade Act of 1974, was a request for escape clause relief from the damaging imports of heavyweight motorcycles into the United States. Harley-Davidson Motor Company, and more specifically its traditional large engine motorcycle, the hog,[1] was facing dwindling domestic market share. This was a last desperate act for survival.

IMPORT PENETRATION

Throughout most of the first half of the twentieth century, there were more than 150 different manufacturers of motorcycles in the United States. By 1978, however, there were only three, and only one, Harley-Davidson, was U.S.-owned. The other two U.S. manufacturers were Japanese-owned, Kawasaki and Honda America.

By the early 1980s, Harley-Davidson was in trouble. Imports held a 60 percent share of the total heavyweight motorcycle market by 1980, and they continued to grow. Harley's difficulties worsened as its products suffered increasing quality problems, with labor and management facing off against one another instead of against the competition. By the end of 1982, in a total domestic market that had seen no growth in three years, import market share rose to 69 percent.

The declining market share of domestic producers in a flat market translated into a fight of Harley against all competitors, because Harley was up against two domestic competitors who were really not domestic. Kawasaki and Honda America were producing in the United States essentially the same products as those being imported. In fact, Harley argued that the two domestic competitors were only assembling foreign-made parts in the United States and were therefore not domestic producers at all.

THE HARLEY LAW

What has become known as the "Harley Law" was the resulting finding of the ITC that imports were a contributing cause of injury to the domestic heavyweight motorcycle industry. The ITC recommended to then President Ronald Reagan that import duties be increased for a period of five years. Duties were to be raised to 45 percent the first year (1983), with the duty declining steadily over each following year until reaching 10 percent in the fifth and final year of protection (1988).

The president and his staff agreed with the finding but wanted a tariff rate quota (TRQ) instead of a straight tariff increase. A TRQ is a combination of tariffs and quotas; in this case, the increased tariff rates would be imposed only on imports (by volume) above a specific number per year. This was intended to allow specific small foreign producers to have continued access to the U.S. markets while still providing Harley with protection from the large-volume importers who were rapidly gaining domestic market share. Table 1 provides a listing of the major tariff rate quotas as specified by the ITC.

Source: This case was written by Michael H. Moffett. This case is intended for class discussion purposes only and does not represent either efficient or inefficient management practices.

[1]The motorcycles produced and sold by Harley-Davidson have traditionally been known as hogs. The nickname is primarily in reference to their traditional large size, weight, and power.

TABLE 1 Tariff Rate Quotas for Heavyweight Motorcycles	Country	Pre-1983 Share[2]	1983 Quota[1]	1983 Share	1988 Quota[3]
	West Germany	.4%	5,000	33.3%	10,000
	Japan	93.0%	6,000	40.0%	11,000
	Others	6.6%	4,000	26.7%	9,000

Notes:

[1]These quotas and tariff schedules applicable to motorcycles with engine displacement of 700 cubic centimeters and greater, only. Volume quotas are per engine.

[2]Pre-1983 shares are percentage of total imports into the United States originating from that country.

[3]All quota shares rise 1,000 units per year after 1983, with the terminal quotas of 1988 being effective only for that final year (after which there would be no further Tariff Rate Quotas).

Source: Adapted from *Trade Protection in the United States: 31 Case Studies,* Institute for International Economics, Washington, D.C., 1986, 263–264.

TABLE 2 Import and Domestic Heavyweight Motorcycle Market Shares (thousands of units)	Year	Total Sales[1]	Domestic Share (%)	Import Share (%)
	1980	326 (100%)	130 (40%)	196 (60%)
	1981	327 (100%)	125 (38%)	202 (62%)
	1982	324 (100%)	100 (31%)	224 (69%)
	1983 (TRQ)	194 (100%)	100 (52%)	94 (48%)
	1984 (TRQ)	159 (100%)	121 (76%)	38 (24%)

[1]Total sales is the sum of domestic production and imports; exports were negligible over the subject period.

Source: Adapted from *Trade Protection in the United States: 31 Case Studies,* Institute for International Economics, Washington, D.C., 1986, and various publications of the U.S. International Trade Commission.

The domestic industry that was to be protected was defined as those motorcycles "with a total piston displacement of over 700 cc."[2] This was strategic success for Harley in that most of its motorcycle sales were actually 1000 cc and higher. This meant Harley was able to hinder competitor sales in product categories other than those reflecting the head-to-head competition. Harley had also requested that the imported parts that were being used by its two domestic competitors also be subject to tariff restrictions. Harley argued that the lower-cost product that was damaging the domestic industry was composed of the same parts, whether assembled in Japan or in the United States by Kawasaki and Honda America. On this last point, however, they were unsuccessful. Domestic producers would be protected against final product sales only, and no restrictions would be placed on imported parts.

COMPETITIVE RESPONSE: COMPETITORS

TRQs were implemented for the 1983 through 1988 period. As seen in Table 2, the first two years of protection did have the desired result: import market share fell precipitously. Imports fell from a high of 69 percent in 1982 to just 24 percent in 1984. It is also interesting to note, however, that total market sales fell dramatically over this same period. After two years of significant protection, domestic production had increased only 20 percent (from 100,000 to 121,000 units per year), although the total market had fallen by 130,000 from 1982 to 1983 alone (and 1983 was a year

[2]Hufbauer, 1986, 263.

of rapid economic growth in the United States following the severe recession of 1981–1982).

The response of Harley's major competitors to the TRQs was rapid and predictable. First, the two major domestic producers, Kawasaki and Honda America, immediately stepped up production of heavyweight motorcycles within the United States. The ITC estimates that imports of parts other than engines increased 82 percent in the first year of protection (1983) and more than 200 percent in the second year (1984). The ITC also estimates that between 50 and 70 percent of the final value of the domestically produced Kawasaki and Honda America motorcycles was imported as parts. Second, the same Japanese-owned producers altered the product manufactured outside the United States, primarily in Japan, to reduce engine displacement from the designed 750 cc to between 690 and 700 cc in order to fall below the TRQ coverage. Third, the Japanese government, on behalf of its own producers, filed a complaint under Article XIII of the General Agreement on Tariffs and Trade (GATT) that the European competitors (Germany) were receiving discriminatory treatment (although filed, there were no formal findings ever made on this complaint).

COMPETITIVE RESPONSE: HARLEY

Harley-Davidson used the period of import relief to restructure, retool, and retrain. Two specific actions were taken to strengthen Harley to once again be a competitive firm.

1. **A Rededication to Quality**—Although Harley had instituted quality circles in manufacturing as early as 1976, renewed efforts in quality monitoring and labor involvement dramatically improved the quality of the product.[3] By 1988, Harley had 117 quality circles in operation with more than 50 percent of all employees involved in the improvement of their own product. The implementation of a just-in-time materials-management program, which Harley termed "materials as needed," also aided greatly in reducing costs of production.

2. **Diversification of Earnings**—In 1986, Harley purchased Holiday Rambler Corporation of Wakarusa, Indiana. Holiday Rambler is a recreational vehicle manufacturer that was expected to provide Harley with broadened earnings flows as the domestic motorcycle industry was increasingly stagnant in growth. Harley has also continued to increase production and sales of other products, such as metal bomb casings and liquid-fuel rocket engines for the U.S. Department of Defense.

Harley's measures were indeed effective in returning the company to profitability and competitiveness. In 1987, a year ahead of schedule, Harley requested that the tariff rate quotas be removed from imported motorcycles.

Questions for Discussion

1. Were the tariff rate quotas (TRQs) really effective in protecting Harley-Davidson against Japanese manufacturers' import penetration? What was the role of imported parts in this effectiveness of protection?

---

[3]When the first quality circles were created in 1976, it was estimated that the first 100 motorcycles off the production line were costing an additional $100,000 to "repair" before they were up to standards for sale. This had to change.

2. Did Harley-Davidson "adjust" to changing market conditions during the period in which the U.S. government afforded it protection from foreign competition? Do you believe it responded to the expectations of public policymakers to reclaim competitiveness on world markets?

References

Beals, Vaughn. "Harley-Davidson: An American Success Story." *Journal for Quality & Participation* 11, 2 (June 1988): A19–A23.

Gelb, Thomas. "Overhauling Corporate Engine Drives Winning Strategy." *Journal of Business Strategy* 10, 6 (November/December 1989): 8–12.

Grant, Robert M., R. Krishnan, Abraham B. Shani, and Ron Baer. "Appropriate Manufacturing Technology: A Strategic Approach." *Sloan Management Review* 33, 1 (Fall 1991): 43–54.

Hackney, Holt. "Easy Rider." *Financial World* 159, 18 (September 4, 1990): 48–49.

"How Harley Beat Back the Japanese." *Fortune,* September 25, 1989, 155–164.

Hufbauer, Gary Clyde, Diane T. Berliner, and Kimberly Ann Elliot. *Trade Protection in the United States: 31 Case Studies.* The Institute for International Economics, Washington, D.C., 1986.

"Mounting the Drive for Quality." *Manufacturing Engineering* 108, 1 (January 1992): 92, 94.

Muller, E. J. "Harley's Got the Handle on Inbound." *Distribution* 88, 3 (March 1989): 70, 74.

Pruzin, Daniel R. "Born to be Verrucht." *World Trade* 5, 4 (May 1992): 112–117.

Reid, Peter C. *Well-Made in America.* New York: McGraw-Hill, 1989.

Rudin, Brad. "Harley Revs Up Image Through Diversifying." *Pensions & Investment Age* 15, 3 (February 9, 1987): 21–23.

Sepehri, Mehran. "Manufacturing Revitalization at Harley-Davidson Motor Co." *Industrial Engineering* 19, 8 (August 1987): 86–93.

Funding from Eximbank

The Export-Import Bank of the United States (Eximbank) is an independent federal agency that provides financing support for the export sale or lease of U.S. goods and services. Its programs include:

- Loans to foreign buyers at the fixed interest rate set by the Organization for Economic Cooperation and Development (OECD). These are typically used for large export transactions of $10 million or more involving capital equipment or projects with a repayment period of seven years or more.
- Standby loans, called intermediary credits, to other lenders on export sales of less than $10 million with repayment periods of less than seven years. These are also typically used for transactions involving capital equipment or projects.
- Guarantees of repayment on medium- to long-term loans made by other lenders on export sales involving capital equipment or projects, or on U.S. bank to foreign bank credit lines for the sale of capital equipment.
- Guarantees of repayment on short-term working capital loans made by banks to U.S. exporters in support of export transactions. This program can be used in conjunction with the U.S. Small Business Administration's exporter's revolving line of credit, which has a limit of $750,000.
- Export credit insurance against commercial and specific political risks that a foreign obligor may not pay a U.S. exporter, a bank financing for an export transaction involving the sale or lease of capital equipment with a repayment period of up to five years, or the sale of services, consumables, spare parts, or raw materials with a repayment period of up to 180 days. The program is administered by Eximbank's agent, the Foreign Credit Insurance Association (FCIA).

Any responsible party (exporter, U.S. bank, foreign bank, foreign buyer) may receive a preliminary commitment from Eximbank for its support on an export transaction. All transactions must present a reasonable assurance of repayment; that is, the buyer must be creditworthy. In the case of Eximbank's working capital loan guarantee, the exporter must provide collateral for the loan. Eximbank only supports exports of products of U.S. origin. When the repayment period is short term, insurance may be used and the product must be at least 50 percent of U.S. origin, exclusive of markup. For longer repayment periods, insurance, guarantees, or loans may be used, and Eximbank will allow up to 15 percent foreign content. However, a 15 percent cash payment by the buyer is required for the longer repayment period. Guarantees and insurance make it easier for the exporter or other lenders to provide financing by protecting against credit risks. The "other" lender is often the Private Export Funding Corporation (PEFCO), which will make long-term export loans when guaranteed by Eximbank. PEFCO also purchases foreign notes when guaranteed by Eximbank. Eximbank loans are used when other lenders are unwilling to provide financing or the foreign competition is offering low-interest and/or fixed-interest rate financing supported by other export credit agencies.

Source: This case was written by Daniel V. Dowd, Export-Import Bank of the United States. Reprinted with permission.

AMERICAN DRILL

The American Drill Company provides design, assembly, and installation of irrigation well drilling rigs. It also sells parts and makes repairs. American Drill has its design and assembly operations in the United States. Repair work is done by its own personnel, sent to the site. Installation is done under the supervision of its personnel using local labor and construction materials. It sources virtually all its components in the United States, although electronic sensors are sourced in Switzerland. Due to a decline in the domestic agriculture market, it has started to pursue foreign orders, initially as a subcontractor to larger firms doing business overseas. Thus far, it has been able to get advance payments and finance its operations internally. Midwest Bank has provided financial services to American Drill in the form of working capital loans, secured by inventory, and the confirmation of foreign letters of credit. American Drill's president is anxious to expand and has been made aware of potential overseas contracts for building, repairing, and providing spare parts. The company has the personnel and expertise to fulfill such contracts; however, the overseas buyers are demanding credit and have indicated that French competitors are providing credit as part of their contract with the support of France's Export Credit Agency (COFACE).

American Drill is now faced with several problems. It will need additional working capital to acquire components if it is to expand by accepting foreign orders. Midwest is reluctant to provide additional working capital to fund an expansion based on foreign sales. The potential overseas buyers are requesting a financing proposal as part of the bid on larger contracts to build and install rigs. American Drill's personnel are neither familiar with how to structure such a proposal nor certain that the company can offer medium- or long-term financing on its own. In fact, the company's controller believes that it may even have difficulty offering short-term open account credit to potential foreign purchasers of spare parts or repair services because American Drill must pay cash to its suppliers.

Questions for Discussion

1. Should the U.S. government help American Drill to expand sales overseas?
2. Discuss the benefits and drawbacks of government involvement in competitive export financing.
3. What Eximbank programs might be of use to American Drill for the various aspects of its potential foreign sales financing needs? Who may apply?
4. How might Midwest Bank become involved in American Drill's expansion plans while minimizing its exposure to foreign credit risks?

Republica de Centroica

The Republica de Centroica (pronounced cen TRO ee ca) is a small, poor Latin American country with per capita income around $300 per year. Its transport and communications facilities are poor, and the labor force is largely semiskilled or unskilled. Only about half the people are literate at or above the sixth-grade level, and about a quarter are unemployed or underemployed.

Starting in the 1960s, the country had attempted several industrialization programs, mostly based on import substitution schemes. It had set up a number of state-owned enterprises (SOEs) to manufacture chemicals, certain metals, basic tools, and automotive equipment. However, these had proven to be politically driven, overstaffed, inefficient, and incapable of producing quality goods at competitive prices. It had also given incentives to local entrepreneurs and foreign companies to establish plants to manufacture or assemble products for the local market and, eventually, for export. These too were largely unsuccessful because their products were more expensive and lower quality than competing products available on the world market. Indeed, Centroica had to erect high tariff walls to protect these infant industries. The ventures had often caused a substantial drain of foreign exchange to pay for imports of materials and components, while producing relatively small foreign exchange savings and virtually no exports. They had created some jobs, but not as many as had originally been expected. The main beneficiaries of the industrialization program turned out to be scions of the Forty Families who had dominated Centroican government, landholdings, and banking for generations. They had been able to gain ownership interests and favored positions in most of the new industrial ventures through their wealth and political influence.

Centroica, like many countries that attempted economic development through import substitution, imposes high tariffs against many imports. Its currency is overvalued; the black market rate (pesos/$) is about double the official exchange rate. Consequently, it has had to impose exchange controls. It has enacted a minimum wage for factory workers and other urban employees that is significantly above the prevailing wages in the informal sector. In the past, in order to prevent profit abuses by foreign investors, it attempted to restrict dividend remittances to 12 percent or 15 percent of invested capital. Eventually it gave up this policy, but it restricted most foreign companies to minority ownership. (Members of the Forty Families often acquired the majority ownership holdings.) Then, in order to overcome the disincentives to investment created by these laws and policies, it enacted tax holidays and other subsidies for domestic and foreign investors. Some local companies prospered with the subsidies and protected market.

In the past, Centroica experienced frequent coups and military dictatorships. However, it conducted a relatively democratic election six years ago in which General Alberto Colon Silves was elected president. He had had a creditable military career and had earned an M.B.A. from the University of Chicago. Although descended from three of the Forty Families, he seemed to have a genuine concern for the welfare of his country and of its poorest citizens. His government has been attempting to institute pragmatic, reformist economic policies.

Source: Prepared by William A. Stoever, Keating-Crawford Professor of International Business at Seton Hall University, South Orange, New Jersey 07079. Copyright 1993 by William A. Stoever. Reprinted by permission.

The author appreciates the helpful comments of Elias Groviyannis, Chander Kant, Anthony Loviscek, Balu Swaminathan and Jason Z. Yin on this case.

Presidente Colon has noted that locales such as Hong Kong, Taiwan, Singapore, and Mexican border cities prospered in the early stages of their development by selling their most abundant asset, cheap labor. If Centroica invited in Japanese, European, and American firms to produce labor-intensive products for export, then perhaps laborers' incomes might rise more rapidly and some basic industrial skills be imparted. The average peasant in Centroica now earns less than $1 per day; he might make the equivalent of $1 an hour in a foreign-owned factory. The scheme would work only if Centroica could find some goods that it could produce efficiently and sell on world markets. Foreign technical skills, management, marketing, and capital would be essential.

Presidente Colon and his more sophisticated advisors realize that Centroica would have to liberalize some of its investment and trade restrictions to attract any significant amount of export-oriented investment. Several foreign businessmen have said they would not risk their capital in the country if they didn't exercise enough control to make their operations profitable. Thus this strategy would make his country even more dependent on the affluent industrial countries' companies and economies and might involve a significant loss of national control and autonomy. The government also realizes that labor unions and local manufacturers might object if their privileged positions were threatened.

Some of the president's advisors have noted the apparent success of export-processing zones (EPZs) in creating jobs and increasing their countries' manufactured exports in such countries as China, Taiwan, Mauritius, Indonesia, and India, and have wondered whether Centroica could establish similar zones. They argued that setting up such zones would not entail the economic disruptions and political problems that would accompany a more general economic liberalization. Other advisors noted, however, that these zones are not always successful in attracting desirable investments and at best are only a short-term, small-scale measure that avoids confronting the country's real problems.

Presidente Colon is aware that he can learn from other countries' experiences in increasing export-oriented investment and that he will need expert advice before initiating any such changes in his country.

Questions for Discussion

Suppose you were a consultant hired by the United Nations Centre on Transnational Corporations (UN-CTC) to go to Centroica and make recommendations on the following questions:

1. Should Presidente Colon try to remove his country's tariff barriers, open its economy to the world, privatize the state-owned enterprises, and shift toward a development strategy based on exports? Why or why not?

2. What problems would the Colon administration be likely to encounter if it tried to implement these changes? How should it attempt to handle these problems?

3. Should Centroica set up an Export-Processing Zone (EPZ) with improved transportation and communications infrastructures and with laws providing for 100 percent foreign ownership, tax holidays, and other incentives to attract foreign companies to set up labor-intensive export-oriented plants?

4. From another perspective, suppose you were managing a company producing microchips or inexpensive dolls in Los Angeles or Osaka. Would you consider moving your operations to Centroica? Why or why not? What risks would you worry about in making such an investment?

The War of the Bananas

The European Union (EU) is the main market in the world for bananas, constituting 37.5 percent of all world trade (see Figure 1). That is why a decision by the EU Farm Council in December of 1992 attracted attention among banana-producing nations. Up until the decision, different EU countries had different policies regarding imports of bananas. While Germany, for example, had no restrictions at all, countries such as the United Kingdom, France, and Spain restricted their imports to favor those from their current and former African, Caribbean, and Pacific (ACP) colonies. (This preferential trading agreement is known as the Lome Convention.) The decision calls for a quota of 2.1 million tons with a 20 percent tariff for all banana imports from Latin America ($126 per ton), rising to 170 percent for quantities over that limit ($1,150 per ton). Since Latin American exports to Europe were approximately 2.7 million tons in 1992, the quota would cut almost 25 percent of the countries' exports to the EU.

The main stated reason for imposing the quota and the tariffs is to protect former colonies by allowing them to enjoy preferential access to the EU market. Other reasons implied have been the $260 million in tariff revenue resulting from the measures as well as moving against the "banana dollar" (reference to the U.S. control of the Latin American banana trade through its multinationals). Belgium, Germany, and Holland objected to the measures not only because of the preference given to higher-cost, lower-quality bananas from current and former colonies, but also because of the economic impact. The Belgians estimated an immediate loss of 500 jobs in its port cities, which traditionally have handled substantial amounts of Latin American banana imports. Even in the United Kingdom, where the preferential treatment has enjoyed widespread support, there has been criticism of the decision.

Since then, the conflict has escalated and is one of the most complicated trade wars in the international trade scene. It pits EU members against one another, the United States against the EU, U.S. multinationals against European counterparts, U.S. investment interests against U.S. diplomatic concerns, Guatemala against Costa Rica, Latin American growers against Caribbean growers, and the U.S. government against four major Latin American nations.

THE LATIN AMERICAN POSITION

Bananas are the world's most-traded fruit and the $5.1 billion in banana trade makes it second only to coffee among foodstuffs. The major banana producers in the world are presented in Figure 2. For countries such as Ecuador, Costa Rica, Colombia, and Honduras the restrictions would cost $1 billion in revenues and 170,000 jobs. For countries such as Costa Rica, banana exports are vital. Bananas represent 8 percent of the country's domestic product, bring in $500 million in hard-currency earnings, and employ one-fifth of the labor force.

The presidents of Colombia, Costa Rica, Ecuador, Guatemala, Honduras, Nicaragua, Panama, and Venezuela held a summit February 11, 1993, in Ecuador and

---

Source: This case was prepared by Ilkka A. Ronkainen. It is based on "Banana Trouble," *The Washington Times,* November 6, 1994, A13–14; "Banana Regulations Split the European Community," *The Journal of Commerce* (October 22, 1993): 1; "The Banana War," *International Business Chronicle* 4 (February 1-15, 1993): 22; Organization of American States, "OAS Takes Note of Regional Statements on the Marketing of Bananas in Europe," *Report on the OAS Permanent Council Meeting,* February 24, 1993; and Joseph L. Brand, "The New World Order," *Vital Speeches of the Day* 58 (December 1991): 155-160. The help of Gladys Navarro with an earlier version of this case is appreciated.

FIGURE 1
Trade in Bananas:
EU Country Imports
by Source

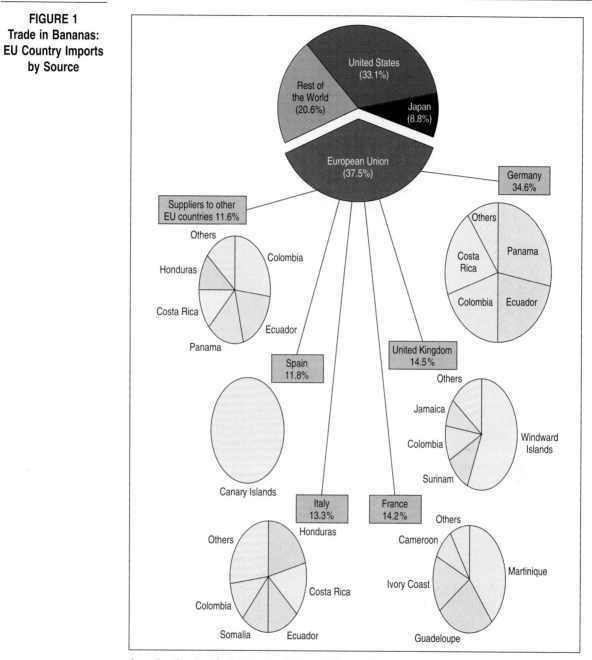

Source: Brent Borrell and Sandy Cuthbertson, *EC Banana Policy 1992*, Center for International Economics, Sydney, Australia, 1991, chart 2.1.

issued a declaration rejecting the EU banana-marketing guidelines as a violation of GATT and principles of trade liberalization. The GATT has agreed with the Latin American countries twice that tariffs and quotas were indeed harmful. Following the formal adoption of the banana decision in July 1993, the EU and four Latin American nations (Costa Rica, Colombia, Nicaragua, and Venezuela) cut a deal in March 1994. The four countries agreed to drop their GATT protest in exchange for

FIGURE 2
Leading Banana
Producers

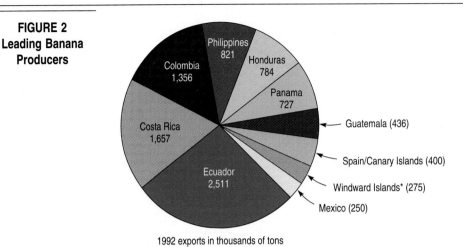

1992 exports in thousands of tons

*Includes Dominica, Grenada, Saint Lucia, Saint Vincent and Grenadines.
Source: United Nations Food and Agriculture Organization, Intergovernmental Group on Bananas.

modifications in the restrictions they face. Guatemala refused to sign the agreement, and Ecuador, Panama, and Mexico lodged protests.

The economics of production are clearly in favor of the Latin producers. The unit-cost of production in the Caribbean is nearly 2.5 times what it is for Latin American producers. For some producers, such as Matinique and Guadeloupe, the cost difference is even higher. The EU quota therefore results in major trade diversion.

The affected Latin nations have used various means at the international level to get the EU to modify its position. In addition to the summit, many are engaged in lobbying in Brussels as well as the individual EU-member capitals. They have also sought the support of the United States, given its interests both in terms of U.S. multinational corporations' involvement in the banana trade as well as its investment in encouraging economic growth in the developing democracies of Latin America.

THE U.S. POSITION

Initial U.S. reaction was that of an interested observer. The United States provided support and encouragement for the Latin Americans in their lobbying efforts in Geneva, Brussels, and the European capitals. However, in October 1994, U.S. Trade Representative Mickey Kantor announced plans to start a year-long investigation of the EU's banana restrictions, with sanctions against European imports as a possibility. This action broke new ground in trade disputes. While governments traditionally have started trade wars as a means of protecting domestic jobs and key industries, the banana dispute involves U.S. investment and overseas markets more than it does jobs at home. The probe was requested by Chiquita, the world's largest banana marketer, and the Hawaii Banana Industry Association, whose 130 small family farms constitute the entire banana-growing contingent. Although only 7,000 of the company's 45,000 employees are in the United States, Chiquita officials argued that the value added by the company's U.S. workers—marketers, shippers, and distributors—make it a major agricultural priority.

The U.S. challenge was "not politically prudent," complained Gerard Kiely, spokesperson for the EU Agricultural Commissioner, by noting that the United States does not even export bananas. However, 12 senators sent a letter to Mr. Kantor warning against the dangerous precedent if the EU banana regime went unchallenged.

THE CARIBBEAN POSITION

For many nations banana exports are the mainstay of their economies. For example, for the tiny West Indies island of St. Lucia, which sells its bananas to its former colonial master, the U.K., banana dependence is 70 percent of the national income. Furthermore, the industry employs four out of five St. Lucians.

Therefore it was not surprising that heads of government of the 13-member Caribbean Community (CARICOM) approved a resolution February 24, 1993, supporting the EU guidelines. "No one country in this hemisphere is as dependent on bananas for its economic survival as the Windward Islands," declared Ambassador Joseph Edsel Edmunds of Saint Lucia. Referring to the criticism of the EU decision by the Latin nations, he added: "Are we being told that, in the interest of free trade all past international agreements between the Caribbean and friendly nations are to be dissolved, leaving us at the mercy of Latin American states and megablocs?" He noted that Latin American banana producers command 95 percent of the world market and more than two-thirds of the EU market.

Ambassador Kingsley A. Layne of Saint Vincent and the Grenadines asserted that the issue at stake "is nothing short of a consideration of the right of small states to exist with a decent and acceptable standard of living, self-determination, and independence. The same flexibility and understanding being sought by other powerful partners in the GATT in respect of their specific national interests must also be extended to the small island developing states."

THE CORPORATE POSITION

The dispute has also pitted U.S. multinationals (Chiquita, Dole, and Del Monte) against the Europeans (Geest and Fyffes). The two European multinationals control between them virtually all of the banana shipping and marketing from such markets as Belize, Suriname, Jamaica, and the Caribbean. U.S. companies complain that the EU is arranging insider deals for Geest and Fyffes to exempt them from export licensing fees imposed by Latin American nations that have agreed with the EU, or even to secure them a slice of the export business from Latin American markets where they have no foothold at present.

Questions for Discussion

1. If you were a member of the Organization of American States (of which all of the Caribbean and Latin American countries mentioned in the case are members) and its Permanent Council (which must react to two opposing statements concerning the EU decision), with which one would you side?
2. What can the EU do to alleviate the impact of its decision on the Latin American banana producers?
3. What types of strategic moves will an international marketing manager of a Latin American banana exporter have to take in light of the quota and the tariffs?

North American Free Trade Agreement

The benefits of trade among nations are only available if countries are willing to relinquish some independence and autonomy. There are four basic levels of economic integration: the free-trade area, the customs union, the common market, and the economic union. This case, which looks at a trade pact being developed between the United States and Mexico, is an example of the first level of integration, the free trade area.

Under a free trade area, considered the least restrictive form of economic integration, all barriers to trade among members are removed. Goods and services are freely traded among members. The United States and Mexico began negotiating a free trade agreement in late 1990. The pact, the North American Free Trade Agreement, also will include Canada. The Bush administration began talks with Mexico on the belief that free trade with Mexico is crucial, and it pushed for quick approval by Congress. The fast-track approach means that when the negotiating on the agreement is done, Congress can only vote the bill up or down; it cannot amend the agreement and cannot hold it up. The negotiations are underway, and the agreement faces formidable opposition in the United States.

One concern raised by opponents is whether Mexico's lower wages will make it an unfair competitor. The worry is that Mexican goods and services will be priced much lower than those of Canada and the United States because Mexico's costs are so much lower. Lower wages also are viewed as a threat to U.S. jobs.

"If you take the United States, an average manufacturing worker earns about $10.57 an hour, thereabouts," said U.S. Sen. Donald Riegle, D-Mich. "And down in Mexico it's a tiny fraction of that, about 57 cents an hour. So I think with those huge differentials, if you have a free trade agreement, what's going to happen is the manufacturing jobs are going to run out of the United States and go down to Mexico," he said.

Former U.S. Trade Representative Carla Hills disagrees. Jobs could have tumbled down south without a free trade agreement, she counters. "What a free trade agreement will do is to reduce the barriers to our exports to Mexico."

Meanwhile, European countries are working to create economic integration through the European Community, designed to sweep away all trade barriers. Advocates of the North American Free Trade Agreement say its members, particularly the United States, need it to compete globally.

"It isn't the United States alone that's trying to produce," said U.S. Sen. John Chafee, R-R.I. "We're in a competitive position, whether we like it or not, with the European Community and with the Asian Rim countries."

According to Hills, Japan has been enormously successful in developing collaborative arrangements with lower-wage countries in east Asia. Germany has created successful collaborations with Spain and Portugal, she said. "And I can't imagine why the United States would not want to have a close, collaborative arrangement with a neighbor with whom we share a 2,000-mile border."

In addition to the wage differential, treatment of the environment along the U.S.–Mexico border is another major concern of opponents. John O'Connor of the

Source: This case was drawn from the Public Broadcasting System's television program "Adam Smith," which aired in 1991. Producer: Alvin H. Perlmutter, Inc., and David Bennett, "Trade Booming under NAFTA," *Twin Plant News/The Mexico Option,* 1995, pp. *19–22.*

National Toxics Campaign said manufacturers are "turning the border into a 2,000-mile Love Canal, the largest toxic lagoon ever known to humankind."

Treasury Secretary Lloyd Bentsen of Texas, formerly a U.S. senator and chairman of the Senate Finance Committee, said he has seen enormous improvements in the way business is conducted along the border, especially with regard to environmental protection. "I was born and reared on that Mexican border, and I have never seen the kinds of changes that are happening there, such as the privatizing of industry and the lowering of tariffs," Bentsen said. "I've seen moves made on environmental improvement that I have not seen in any other developing country." But Bentsen, who led the fight on Capitol Hill for fast-track consideration of the free trade agreement, concedes some environmental problems remain in that area.

"We've got a serious problem so far as the environment along the border," Bentsen said. "We've got a situation where in one of those towns they've been dumping 26 million gallons of raw sewage every day into the Rio Grande River. Well, that's a real problem. It creates problems of cholera and of water contamination generally. But now you're having a joint effort between the United States and Mexico to build the sewage plants, the treatment plants there. That's real progress."

Bentsen, the Democratic candidate for vice president in 1988, was asked what he says to labor unions, traditional supporters of the Democratic Party that typically oppose the free trade accord. "I stated repeatedly during these debates for the fast track that it would depend on what came back, whether I supported it or not," Bentsen said. He would support an agreement that produces a net increase in jobs on both sides. "But if we don't get that, I'll fight it just as strongly as I worked to see that we got the fast track," he said.

After the United States adopted NAFTA in 1993, new records for exports to Mexico were set. Government figures showed that in the first five months of 1994, the U.S. automobile industry exported 12,380 passenger vehicles to Mexico—nearly 4,000 more than in the comparable 1993 period, and more than the total passenger vehicles exported in 1993 (10,910). Chrysler, Ford, and GM expected to export a combined 55,000 trucks to Mexico in 1994.

At the end of 1994, however, the Mexican economy struggled with a massive devaluation of the peso and the uncertainties it meant for the near future.

Questions for Discussion

1. Compare and contrast the other three levels of economic integration with that of NAFTA.

2. What were the central arguments for and against adopting NAFTA, as outlined in the case? Were there any noneconomic arguments for or against adopting NAFTA?

3. Should the United States have adopted NAFTA? Why or why not? Be prepared to explain your position.

4. How has NAFTA developed since this video was aired? How did Bentsen's position change after he has become secretary of the Treasury?

The Tuna and the Dolphin

Marine scientists do not know why, but some kinds of dolphins swim above, or "associate with," schools of mature yellowfin, skipjack, and bigeye tuna. Thus, to catch quantities of tuna, fishermen look for the leaping dolphins and cast purse seines (nets pulled into a baglike shape to enclose fish) around both tuna and dolphins. With this method, fishermen can efficiently and reliably catch a high number of good-sized tuna. The unfortunate side effect is that the dolphins also are caught. Because they are mammals, dolphins must surface to breathe oxygen. Entangled in the net or trapped below other dolphins, some are asphyxiated.

In the late 1960s and early 1970s, the "incidental" catch of various species of dolphins by tuna fishers in the eastern tropical Pacific (the "ETP" is a major tuna-fishing area) was in the hundreds of thousands. Society's growing and vociferous concern about these senseless deaths brought about new fishing techniques to reduce dolphin mortality.

Perhaps the most important new technique is the "backdown operation." After "setting on dolphins" to catch tuna, that is, encircling both tuna and dolphins with the purse seine, the ship backs away, elongating the net, submerging the corkline in the back, and pulling the net out from under the dolphins. If the operation works correctly, and the captain and crew are willing to work with the by now sluggish and uncooperative dolphins, the tuna remain in the bottom of the net and the dolphins swim free. If, however, the operation is flawed, dolphins are injured or killed and discarded from the catch as waste.

Rather than relying on this imperfect correction of the purse seine method, some environmental groups think that entirely different methods of fishing for tuna should be employed. Alternatives could include using a pole and line or "setting" on tuna not associated with dolphins. However, according to marine scientists and fishermen, the alternative methods have serious drawbacks as well.

Some catch many sexually immature tuna, which for some reason don't associate with dolphins. Juvenile tuna often are too small to be marketed. If too many are caught, the sustainability of the population could be jeopardized. In addition, alternative methods frequently catch high numbers of other incidental species such as sharks, turtles, rays, mahi-mahi, and many kinds of noncommercial fish. Finally, all fishing methods expend energy. The practice of setting on dolphins uses the least amount of energy per volume of tuna caught.

According to many of the experts involved, including the Inter-American Tropical Tuna Commission, the U.S. National Marine Fisheries Service, and the scientific advisor to the American Tunaboat Association, the most efficient method for fishing tuna, in terms of operational cost, yield, and conservation of the tuna population, is to set on dolphins with a purse seine. From the point of view of the canning industry, only purse seine fishing provides the volume of catch necessary for growth of the industry.

Many experts also believe that with current technology, it is not possible to abandon the practice of setting on dolphins without falling into other, more grave, problems. While research to develop better techniques is now underway, positive results are not expected in the near future.

Source: This case was adapted from "The Tuna and Dolphin Controversy," by Saul Alvarez-Borrego, which was published in *UC Mexus News,* University of California Institute for Mexico and the United States 31 (Fall 1993): 8–13.

THE TRADE ASPECTS

The tuna-dolphin problem has engendered serious friction on the international level. The United States and Mexico, two countries sensitive to marine mammal protection and with solid laws in place for many years, have come head-to-head over the issue.

A U.S. trade embargo was imposed in February of 1991 on yellowfin tuna caught by Mexican fleets in the eastern tropical Pacific. This embargo resulted from violation of the Marine Mammal Act of 1972, which was amended in 1988 to prohibit the incidental kill of dolphins during commercial tuna fishing. The amendment requires the banning of tuna imports from any country that does not implement several specific measures to reduce dolphin mortality and achieve a kill-per-set rate (the number of dolphins killed in each casting of the fishing net) of no more than 1.25 times the U.S. rate.

The dolphin kill rate of Mexican tuna fishers has changed dramatically over the years. Figure 1 shows that as recently as 1986, an average of 15 dolphins were killed per set by the Mexican fleet. By 1992, the Mexican fleet had achieved an average mortality of 1.85 dolphins per set, with further reductions expected. Although the dolphin populations have not regained original numbers, they continue to increase, thanks in large part to the backdown operation. Current scientific evidence indicates that the types of dolphins chiefly targeted in tuna fishing are neither rare nor in danger of extinction and, in fact, can withstand current fishing-related mortality.

Nevertheless, because Mexico did not meet the rate of comparison with the U.S. fleet specified in the Marine Mammal Protection Act, the embargo remains in effect. Mexico believes it has been penalized unfairly, since it has dramatically reduced the dolphin mortality caused by its fleet. Data show that the average kill-per-set rate

FIGURE 1
Incidental Dolphin Mortality Rate, Mexican Tuna Fleet (set on dolphins, 1986–1993)

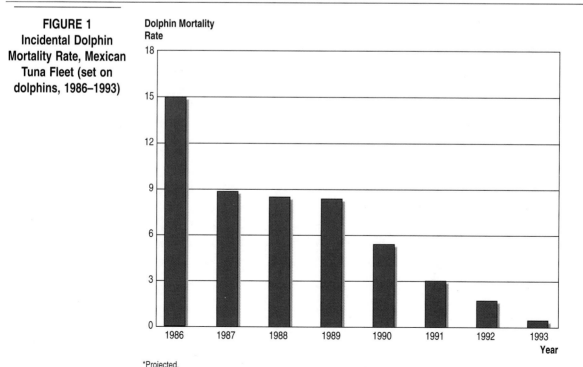

*Projected.
Source: UC Mexus News (Fall 1993): 12.

for non-U.S. fishers in the affected areas dropped rapidly from 10.9 in 1989 to 3.1 in 1991. Mexico's rates dropped far more quickly. However, since the Mexican fleet's kill-per-set rate still is not within 125 percent of the U.S. rate, the embargo continues.

Some argue that it is unfair for the United States to unilaterally impose an embargo against tuna fishers only in the ETP and to disregard how tuna is fished in other oceans. The ETP hosts the best-known and best-managed tuna fishery in the world, employing scientific data to maintain a sustainable tuna yield and putting an observer on every ship to gather accurate statistics on the dolphin kill rate. It is contended that without observer programs in other oceans it is impossible to determine the number of dolphins killed in the pursuit of tuna not currently affected by the embargo.

In spite of the political tension, the Inter-American Tropical Tuna Commission has been working toward multilateral agreements on dolphin conservation. Commitments have been made by all governments represented in the ETP to adopt 100 percent observer coverage. Since 1993, a biologist is assigned to every ship to observe fishing methods and to record dolphin mortality. The participating governments also adopted a vessel quota system in which the overall yearly quota for dolphin mortality is equally divided among the boats fishing in the region. This way, each boat is individually held responsible for its dolphin kill. Otherwise, a few careless ships could destroy the entire fishery's attempts to meet lower mortality rates for the year. In addition to these measures, the governments agreed to support a stringent program to reduce annual dolphin mortality from 19,500 in 1993 to less than 5,000 in 1999.

Currently, the total yearly mortality for each dolphin species is under 1 percent of its population, an amount that can be sustained without reducing the total number; in fact, the populations are currently increasing. Thus, most scientists now view the mortality of dolphins incidental to tuna fishing not as an environmental problem but as one of avoiding unnecessary killing. In fact, a National Marine Fisheries Service scientist has stated that if Mexico has money for research, it would be better invested on behalf of the Vaquita, a species in real danger of extinction, than in the tuna-dolphin issue, since there is no danger to the dolphin population as a whole.

Strong opposition to current practices continues to be voiced by environmentalists. States David Phillips, executive director of the Earth Island Institute: "The goal is to eliminate the killing of dolphins entirely by prohibiting the technique of setting on them to catch tuna."

Questions for Discussion

1. Why is there such a concern about dolphins?
2. What is your view of using the technologically most advanced country's performance as a benchmark for evaluating other countries' activities?
3. Is the denial of market access an appropriate tool to enforce a country's environmental standards?
4. Is a zero-dolphin-death goal realistic?

Old Ways, New Games

American business is in transition. The end of World War II witnessed the emergence of the United States as the world's only economic superpower. The defeated Axis powers, Germany and Japan, literally lay in ruins and could only look to America for the funds and assistance to pick up the pieces.

Dramatic changes have occurred over the past half-century. The defeated countries rebuilt their economies and have emerged as economic superpowers themselves, and much of their advance has come at the expense of the United States. Sadly, how this shift in economic clout came about may have as much to do with the attitude of the majority of U.S. companies as it does perseverance on the part of economic competitors.

German and Japanese companies differ in many respects from their counterparts in the United States. Japanese managers tend to take a much longer view, especially in the area of product development. Both German and Japanese companies also contrast starkly with U.S. firms when it comes to labor relations. Perhaps more importantly, German and Japanese companies seem to have devised methods that accomplish two goals: Workers have been made to feel that the company cares about them and is willing to make an investment to make them more productive and better at their jobs. This not only engenders loyalty, but raises the overall quality and productivity of the company as a whole.

We will examine some of the methods German and Japanese firms have used in rising to the status of major economic global players. But first, we should review what has been happening to two big U.S. companies over the last three decades. We'll try to discover what American businessmen overlooked as they were losing market share to the competition. Then perhaps we can figure out what they did wrong, and what methods might be helpful in making a comeback.

Perhaps no company stands as a better metaphor of the declining fortunes of U.S. business than International Business Machines. The company that once offered a de facto guarantee of lifetime employment has laid off 190,000 workers, and recently lost $13 billion over one 24-month period.

Just three decades ago profits generated by mainframe sales enabled Big Blue to dominate the computer industry. But the vast hierarchal structure that grew up at IBM hid what should have been obvious. While management rested on mainframe laurels, the computer market veered sharply in the direction of personal computers and software.

Almost before its stodgy upper managers noticed, IBM had 100,000 fast moving, technology-driven competitors. Though caught flat-footed, IBM was finally able to grind into action. The company's Boca Raton–based PC business—with the help of IBM's super-talented R&D engineers—soon developed a host of solid, technologically advanced products. But management clung to its anachronistic methods of doing things and insisted that the PC subsidiary be brought to the corporate headquarters in Armonk, New York. Very shortly the company mentality, stifling bureaucracy, and plodding-paced operations had stunted innovative thinking.

By 1991 even IBM's top brass knew the company's structure had to be altered. The decision was made to break Big Blue into 14 "baby blues." The company had finally taken a critical look at factors that made it uncompetitive. Basic decision making required time-consuming meetings, followed by orders that flowed up and down the chain of command. All too frequently, by the time new products or policy changes reached the market or the customer, they were either obsolete or had already been matched by competitors.

Perhaps more damaging, IBM managers tended to make decisions that did not consider its customer's needs. The company culture appeared finally to have achieved a fatal level of arrogance. Management acted as though customers should accept whatever products IBM offered simply because the company had once dominated the industry.

IBM was operating with a hierarchal, highly stratified structure that made fast decision making impossible. This dense bureaucracy also made it difficult to react to shifts in the market and changes in customer preferences. And that problem was exacerbated by a company culture steeped in a top-down managed, chain-of-command structure with product development far removed from the market. Without changes in each of these areas, it wasn't likely IBM would ever return to competitiveness.

Questions for Discussion

1. What are the primary reasons that large U.S. companies like IBM have lost market share to the Germans and Japanese?
2. How are IBM's problems indicative of the overall problems that have led to a decline of U.S. competitiveness?
3. IBM's new chairman Louis Gerstner, Jr. has been charged with the task of returning the company to its former glory. What strategies should he emphasize?

In many ways, the Silicon Valley represents a microcosm of the best and brightest the United States has to offer. It has long been a technological hotbed of inventions and innovations. But too often, American companies have failed to commercialize on potentially profitable ideas.

But those ideas haven't had difficulty finding a home across the Pacific in Japan. And Japanese industry takes an entirely different view of capitalizing on technology. They also have a markedly different way of treating their employees.

There are plenty of examples of how abandoned U.S. technology was taken over and exploited by Japanese industry. A talented group of RCA engineers far ahead of their time developed the first flat panel liquid crystal display. But short-sighted RCA managers feared they were facing an on-going investment black hole with an uncertain payback. They ordered the project abandoned. The Japanese had no such reservations. They patiently nurtured the technology, and today produce 98 percent of the world's flat panel displays.

As for those best and brightest Americans back in the Silicon Valley—the ones who worked for managers who focused on short-term profits—many are unemployed today. Layoffs still occur without warning, and hordes of PhDs, engineers, and other highly talented and educated people are searching for work. One industry that is thriving are self-help groups. It's at such meetings that the lament can frequently be heard that the next generation likely won't be able to live as well as this one.

During the immediate post-war period, the United States led the world in plant reinvestment, capital improvements, and R&D expenditures. That is no longer the case. And in one instance where a major U.S. car maker attempted to out-automate the Japanese, the result has been disastrous.

For two decades General Motors witnessed the steady erosion of its market share to the Japanese. And by the 1980s, chairman Roger Smith decided to do something about it.

Weary of labor difficulties and hopeful of gaining a competitive advantage over Toyota and Nissan, he oversaw the purchase of state-of-the-art plant robotics and technology. Smith's reasoning went along the lines that robots didn't require overtime pay and they didn't go out on strike. Thousands of embittered workers were laid off.

While Smith's capital improvements were taking shape at GM, Japanese automakers were employing a diametrically opposite, people-centric approach. Teamwork and kaizan worker self- and job-improvement methods were emphasized. Workers were encouraged not only to make the best product, but to become the best worker they could. And unlike their American counterparts, Japanese workers could depend on the company to either employ them for life, or find them other employment if a layoff did occur.

Workers at Mercedes Benz in Germany also are organized in self-directed work teams. Instead of the assembly-line approach used in the United States, teams complete subassembly portions of the automobile. Management vests these workers with the responsibility to accomplish their jobs well, the first time, and without oversight. Essentially, they place a great deal of faith in the individual excellence of individual workers, and their teams as a whole.

This is not the attitude GM management takes with the rank and file in U.S. auto plants. The teamwork concept is employed, but many workers claim it exists in theory but not actual practice. The element of trust is wholly lacking, and instead of delegating responsibility, finger pointing is the norm. Perhaps worst of all and reminiscent of IBM, management has insulated itself from the group it should be focused on: the customer.

Roger Smith's remake of General Motors cost a staggering $77 billion. It created plants that could mass manufacture cars around the clock. But when all the capital improvements were complete and in place, there weren't enough customers for all the cars GM was suddenly capable of producing. The state-of-art plants had to be run at 50 percent capacity, or even less. In one more parallel to another fallen industry titan IBM, General Motors assumed that if it mass produced the Chevrolet Grand Prix and Oldsmobile Cutlass as fast as it could, consumers would flock to purchase them.

They did not.

Questions for Discussion

4. What lessons could General Motors have learned from its German and Japanese counterparts that might have prevented its problems?

5. If GM were to try to emulate some of the German and Japanese management techniques, how could it ensure that the theories were actually put into practice?

6. How would you suggest that GM improve its labor relations given its dismal record?

International Business and the Nation-State

The successful international manager understands the political, legal, and cultural environments of countries in which the firm does business. Part 3 therefore begins with a discussion of the effect of politics and laws on business from the perspective of both the home country and the host country. It then outlines the agreements, treaties, and laws that govern the relationships between home and host countries.

Managing conflicts between cultures requires an understanding of cultural differences in language, religion, values, customs, and education. This knowledge is the key to developing cross-cultural competence. A chapter on culture addresses these dimensions.

Part 3 concludes with a chapter on doing business in emerging markets. Particular focus will rest with the new market orientation of nations whose economies used to be centrally planned, such as the former Soviet Union, Central and Eastern Europe, and China. In addition, the new business opportunities created by emerging nations in India, Southeast Asia, and Latin America are presented.

CHAPTER 8

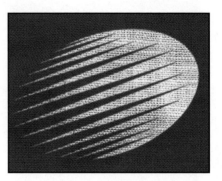

Politics and Laws

Learning Objectives

1. To understand the importance of the political and legal environments in both the home and host countries to the international business executive.

2. To learn how governments affect business through legislation and regulations.

3. To see how the political actions of countries expose firms to international risks.

4. To examine the differing laws regulating international trade found in different countries.

5. To understand how international political relations, agreements, and treaties can affect international business.

Can U.S. Firms Abroad Do Well While Doing Good?

In light of economic realities, the Clinton administration delinked China's trading status from its human rights performance. However, in conjunction with U.S. businesses, the White House has set out to produce a broad set of ethical principles for conducting business in China. At the same time, a group of government officials is looking beyond China and searching for new strategies to advance American values abroad without jeopardizing business opportunities or inciting the resentment of foreign leaders.

President Clinton wants U.S. companies to draft a "statement of principles" covering the workplace rights of their employees in China. Business representatives have provided the White House with examples of individual companies' statements such as Reebok International's "Human Rights Production Standard." It is a code addressed to Reebok's Chinese suppliers that covers fair compensation and worker health protection and forbids the use of child labor or forced labor.

Business leaders, however, worry that voluntary company-by-company statements could be transformed by Congress into legally binding requirements that would invite direct challenges by Beijing and might get them tossed out of the country. Instead, business groups hope some general statement can be worked out. "If you have a diktat from the United States that no political education of workers is permitted in U.S. plants in China, you're daring the Chinese government to do that very thing; you can be sure they will take that dare," said one business official.

In Asia, U.S. advocacy of human rights "is creating a sense of resentment and apprehension, giving ammunition to those charging we are an international nanny, if not bully," wrote Assistant Secretary of State Winston Lord. Robert A. Kapp, president of the U.S. China Business Association, has said that it is not just that the United States has lost some of the power to tell the rest of the world what to do, but "our policies [in the human rights area] may have very negative effects on us economically."

The administration must walk within the narrow lines of its human rights objectives and an economic policy that looks to expansion of U.S. business, particularly in the fast-growing markets of Asia, where resistance to a U.S. human rights agenda is strongest.

Source: Peter Behr, "Can U.S. Firms Do Well Abroad and Do Good?" *The Washington Post,* July 8, 1994, F1.

Politics and laws play a critical role in international business. Even the best plans can go awry as a result of unexpected political or legal influences, and the failure to anticipate these factors can be the undoing of an otherwise successful business venture.

Of course, a single international political and legal environment does not exist. The business executive has to be aware of political and legal factors on a variety of levels. For example, while it is useful to understand the complexities of the host country's legal system, such knowledge may not protect against sanctions imposed by the home country. The firm therefore has to be aware of conflicting expectations and demands in the international arena, and work together with governments to maintain viable international business practices, as we saw in the example that opened the chapter.

This chapter will examine politics and laws from the manager's point of view. The two subjects are considered together because laws generally are the result of political decisions. The chapter discussion will break down the study of the international political and legal environment into three segments: the politics and laws of the home country; those of the host country; and the bilateral and multilateral agreements, treaties, and laws governing the relations among host and home countries.

THE HOME-COUNTRY PERSPECTIVE

No manager can afford to ignore the rules and regulations of the country from which he or she conducts international business transactions. Many of the laws and regulations may not specifically address international business issues, yet they can have a major impact on a firm's opportunities abroad. Minimum-wage legislation, for example, has a bearing on the **international competitiveness** of a firm using production processes that are highly labor intensive. The cost of domestic safety regulations may significantly affect the pricing policies of firms. For example, U.S. legislation creating the Environmental Superfund requires payment by chemical firms based on their production volume, regardless of whether the production is sold domestically or exported. As a result, these firms are at a disadvantage internationally when exporting their commodity-type products. They are required to compete against firms that have a cost advantage because their home countries do not require payment into an environmental fund.

Other legal and regulatory measures, however, are clearly aimed at international business. Some may be designed to help firms in their international efforts. For example, governments may attempt to aid and protect the business efforts of domestic companies facing competition from abroad by setting standards for product content and quality.

The political environment in most countries tends to provide general support for the international business efforts of firms headquartered within the country. For example, a government may work to reduce trade barriers or to increase trade opportunities through bilateral and multilateral negotiations. Such actions will affect individual firms to the extent that they improve the international climate for free trade.

Often governments also have specific rules and regulations that restrict international business. Such regulations are frequently political in nature and are based on governmental objectives that override commercial concerns. The restrictions are particularly sensitive when they address activities outside the country. Such measures challenge the territorial sovereignty of other governments and raise the issue of **extraterritoriality**—meaning a nation's attempt to set policy outside its territorial limits. Yet actions implying such extraterritorial reach are common, because nations often argue that their citizens and products maintain their nationality wherever they may be, and they therefore continue to be subject to the rules and laws of their home country.

Three main areas of governmental activity are of major concern to the international business manager. They are embargoes or trade sanctions, export controls, and the regulation of international business behavior.

Embargoes and Sanctions

The terms **sanction** and **embargo** as used here refer to governmental actions that distort free flows of trade in goods, services, or ideas for decidedly adversarial and political, rather than economic, purposes. Sanctions tend to consist of specific coercive trade measures such as the cancellation of trade financing or the prohibition of high-technology trade, while embargoes are usually much broader in that they prohibit trade entirely. For example, the United States imposed sanctions against some countries by prohibiting the export of weapons to them, but it initiated an embargo against Cuba when all but humanitarian trade was banned. To understand sanctions and embargoes better, it is useful to examine the auspices and legal justifications under which they are imposed.

The United Nations' trade embargo following Iraq's invasion of Kuwait devastated Iraq's economy because most Iraqi trading partners, including many Arab nations, honored the embargo. However, the embargo did not prove effective in averting the Gulf War.

Source: © Reuters/Bettmann.

Trade embargoes have been used quite frequently and successfully in times of war or to address specific grievances. For example, in 1284, the Hansa, an association of north German merchants, believed that its members were suffering from several injustices by Norway. On learning that one of its ships had been attacked and pillaged by the Norwegians, the Hansa called an assembly of its members and resolved an economic blockade of Norway. The export of grain, flour, vegetables, and beer was prohibited on pain of fines and confiscation of the goods. The blockade was a complete success. Deprived of grain from Germany, the Norwegians were unable to obtain it from England or elsewhere. As a contemporary chronicler reports: "Then there broke out a famine so great that they were forced to make atonement." Norway was forced to pay indemnities for the financial losses that had been caused and to grant the Hansa extensive trade privileges.[1]

Over time, economic sanctions and embargoes have become a principal tool of foreign policy for many countries. Often, they are imposed unilaterally in the hope of changing a country's government or at least changing its policies. Between 1914 and 1983, there were 99 incidents in which sanctions were used to pursue political goals, 46 of which occurred after 1970.[2] Reasons for the impositions have varied, ranging from the upholding of human rights to attempts to promote nuclear nonproliferation or antiterrorism.

After World War I, the League of Nations set a precedent for the legal justification of economic sanctions by subscribing to a covenant that contained penalties or sanctions for breaching its provisions. The members of the League of Nations did not intend to use military or economic measures separately, but the success of the blockades of World War I fostered the opinion that "the economic weapon, conceived not as an instrument of war but as a means of peaceful pressure, is the greatest discovery and most precious possession of the League."[3] The basic idea was that economic sanctions could force countries to behave peacefully in the international community.

The idea of multilateral use of economic sanctions was again incorporated into international law under the charter of the United Nations, but greater emphasis was placed on the enforcement process. Sanctions decided on are mandatory, even though each permanent member of the Security Council can veto efforts to impose them. The charter also allows for sanctions as enforcement actions by regional agencies, such as the Organization of American States, the Arab League, and the Organization of African Unity, but only with the Security Council's authorization.

The apparent strength of the United Nations's enforcement system was soon revealed to be flawed. Stalemates in the Security Council and vetoes by permanent members often led to a shift of discussions to the General Assembly, where sanctions are not enforceable. Also, concepts such as "peace" and "breach of peace" were seldom perceived in the same context by all members, and thus no systematic sanctioning policy developed under the United Nations.[4]

Another problem with sanctions is that frequently their unilateral imposition has not produced the desired result. Sanctions may make the obtaining of goods more difficult or expensive for the sanctioned country, yet their purported objective is almost never achieved. In order to work, sanctions need to be imposed multilaterally—a goal that is clear, yet difficult to implement. On rare occasions, however, global cooperation can be achieved. For example, when Iraq invaded Kuwait in August of 1990, virtually all members of the United Nations condemned this hostile action and joined a trade embargo against Iraq. Typically, individual countries have different relationships with the country subject to the sanctions due to geographic or historic reasons, and therefore cannot or do not want to terminate trade relations. In this instance, however, both major and minor Iraqi trading partners—including many Arab nations—honored the United Nations trade embargo and ceased trade with Iraq in the attempt to force it to withdraw its troops from Kuwait. Agreements were made to financially compensate those countries most adversely affected by the trade measures.

This close multinational collaboration has strengthened the sanctioning mechanism of the United Nations greatly. It may well be that sanctions will reemerge as a powerful and effective international political tool in the world. When one considers that sanctions may well be the middle ground between going to war or doing nothing, their effective functioning can represent a powerful arrow in the quiver of international policy measures.

Sanctions imposed by governments usually mean significant loss of business, and the issue of compensating the domestic firms and industries affected by these sanctions is always raised. Yet, trying to impose sanctions slowly or making them less expensive to ease the burden on these firms undercuts their ultimate chance for success. The international business manager is often caught in this political web and loses business as a result. Frequently, firms try to anticipate sanctions based on their evaluations of the international political climate. Nevertheless, even when substantial precautions are taken, firms may still suffer substantial losses due to contract cancellations.

Export Controls

Many nations have **export control systems,** which are designed to deny or at least delay the acquisition of strategically important goods to adversaries. In the United States, the export control system is based on the Export Administration Act and the Munitions Control Act. These laws control all exports of goods, services, and ideas from the United States. The determinants for controls are national security, foreign policy, short supply, and nuclear nonproliferation.

For any export from the United States to take place, the exporter needs to obtain an **export license** from the Department of Commerce, which administers the Export Administration Act.[5] In consultation with other government agencies—particularly the Departments of State, Defense, and Energy—the Commerce Department has drawn up a list of commodities whose export is considered particularly sensitive. In addition, a list of countries differentiates nations according to their political

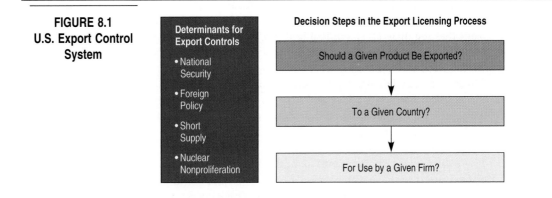

**FIGURE 8.1
U.S. Export Control
System**

Determinants for Export Controls

• National Security

• Foreign Policy

• Short Supply

• Nuclear Nonproliferation

Decision Steps in the Export Licensing Process

Should a Given Product Be Exported?

To a Given Country?

For Use by a Given Firm?

relationship with the United States. Finally, a list of individual firms that are considered to be unreliable trading partners because of past trade-diversion activities exists for each country.

After an export license application has been filed, specialists in the Department of Commerce match the commodity to be exported with the **critical commodities list,** a file containing information about products that are either particularly sensitive to national security or controlled for other purposes. The product is then matched with the country of destination and the recipient company. If no concerns regarding any of the three exist, an export license is issued. Control determinants and the steps in the decision process are summarized in Figure 8.1.

This process may sound overly cumbersome, but it does not apply in equal measure to all exports. Many international business activities can be carried out with a **general license,** which provides blanket permission to export. Under such a license, which is not even a piece of paper, exports can be freely shipped to most trading partners provided that neither the product nor the country involved is considered sensitive. However, the process becomes more complicated and cumbersome when products incorporating high-level technologies and countries not friendly to the United States are involved. The exporter must then apply for a **validated export license,** which consists of written authorization to send a product abroad.

The international business repercussions of export controls are important. It is one thing to design an export control system that is effective and that restricts those international business activities subject to important national concerns. It is, however, quite another when controls lose their effectiveness and when one country's firms are placed at a competitive disadvantage with firms in other countries whose control systems are less extensive or even nonexistent.

A Changed Environment for Export Controls

Six major changes have fundamentally altered the parameters of the traditional export control regime. The most important change has been the collapse of the Iron Curtain and the subsequent disappearance of the Soviet Union and the Eastern Bloc. As a result, both the focus and the principal objective of export controls have been altered. It makes little sense today to still speak of "Soviet adversaries," nor is the singular objective of maintaining the "strategic balance of power" still valid.

This section has been adapted from: Michael R. Czinkota and Erwin Dichtl, "Export Controls: Providing Security in a Volatile Environment," *The International Executive* 37, 5 (1995).

A second change that derives directly from the first. Nowadays, the principal focus of export controls must rest on the Third World. Quite a number of countries from this region want chemical and nuclear weapons and the technology to make use of them. For example, a country such as Libya can do little with its poison gas shells without a suitable delivery system.[6] As a result, export controls have moved from a "strategic balance" to a "tactical balance" approach. Nevertheless, even though the political hot spots addressed may be less broad in terms of their geographic expanse, the peril emanating from regional disintegration and local conflict may be just as dangerous to the world community as earlier strategic concerns with the Soviet Union.[7]

A third major change consists of the loosening of mutual bonds among allied nations. It used to be that the United States, Western Europe, and Japan, together with emerging industrialized nations, held a generally similar strategic outlook. This outlook was driven by the common desire to reduce, or at least contain, the influence of the Soviet Union. With the disappearance of the Soviet Union, however, individual national interests that had been subsumed by the overall strategic objective gained in importance. As a consequence, differences in perspectives, attitudes, and outlooks can now lead to ever-growing conflicts among the major players in the trade field.

Major change has also resulted from the increased **foreign availability** of high technology products. In the past decade, the number of participants in the international trade field has grown rapidly. In earlier decades, industrializing countries mainly participated in world trade due to wage-based competition. Today, they are increasingly focused on technology-based competition. As a result, high technology products are available worldwide from many sources. The broad availability makes any denial of such products more difficult to enforce. If a nation does control the exports of widely available products, it imposes a major competitive burden on its firms.

The speed of change and the rapid dissemination of information and innovation around the world also has shifted. For example, the current life cycle of computer chips is only 18 months. More than 70 percent of the data processing industry's sales resulted from the sale of devices that did not exist two years earlier. Experts estimate that this percentage will rise to 80 percent by 1995.[8] This enormous technical progress is accompanied by a radical change in computer architecture. Instead of having to replace a personal computer or a workstation with a new computer, it is possible now to simply exchange microprocessors or motherboards with new, more efficient ones. Furthermore, today's machines can be connected to more than one microprocessor and users can customize and update configurations almost at will. Export controls that used to be based largely on capacity criteria have become almost irrelevant because they can no longer fulfill the function assigned to them. A user simply acquires additional chips, from whomever, and uses expansion slots to enhance the capacity of his or her computer.

The question arises as to how much of the latest technology is required for a country to engage in "dangerous" activity. For example, nuclear weapons and sophisticated delivery systems were developed by the United States and the Soviet Union long before supercomputers became available. Therefore, it is reasonable to assert that researchers in countries working with equipment that is less than state of the art, or even obsolete, may well be able to achieve a threat capability that can result in major destruction and affect the world order.

From a control perspective, there is also the issue of equipment size. Due to their size, supercomputers and high technology items used to be fairly difficult to hide and any movement of such products was easily detectable. Nowadays, state-of-the-art technology has been miniaturized. Much leading-edge technological equipment is so small that it can fit into a briefcase and most equipment is no larger than the luggage compartment of a car. Given these circumstances, it has become difficult, if not impossible, to closely supervise the transfer of such equipment.

Export Control Problems and Conflicts

There are four key export control problem areas for firms and policymakers. First is the continuing debate about what constitutes military use products, civilian use products, and **dual use products** and the achievement of multilateral agreement on such classifications. Increasingly, goods are of a dual use nature. The classic example is a pesticide factory that, some years later, is revealed to be a poison gas factory.[9] It is difficult enough to clearly define weapons. It is even more problematic to achieve consensus among nations regarding dual use goods. For example, what about quite harmless screws if they are to be installed in rockets or telecommunications equipment used by the military? The problem becomes even greater with attempts to classify and list subcomponents and regulate their exportation. Individual country lists will lead to a distortion of competition if they deviate markedly from each other. The very task of drawing up any list is itself fraught with difficulty when it comes to components that are assembled. For example, the Patriot missile, which was deployed in the Persian Gulf War consists, according to German law, only of simple parts whose individual export is permissible.

Even if governments were to agree on lists and continuously updated them, the resulting control aspects would be difficult to implement. Controlling the transfer of components within and among companies across economic areas such as NAFTA or the European Union (EU) would significantly slow down business. Even more importantly, to subject only the export of physical goods to surveillance is insufficient. The transfer of knowledge and technology is of equal or greater importance. Weapons-relevant information easily can be exported via books, periodicals, and disks, therefore, their content also would have to be controlled. Foreigners would need to be prevented from gaining access to such sources during visits or from making use of data networks across borders. Attendance at conferences and symposia would have to be regulated, the flow of data across national borders would have to be controlled and today's communication systems and highways such as Internet would have to be scrutinized. These tasks would appear to be difficult if not impossible to perform.

Conflicts also result from the desire of nations to safeguard their own economic interests. Due to different industrial structures, these interests vary across nations. For example, Germany, with a strong world market position in machine tools, motors, and chemical raw materials, will think differently about controls than a country such as the United States will, which sees computers as an area of its competitive advantage. Adjustments in industrial structure add fuel to the fire. For example, as nations reduce their defense industries in size, many firms see exports as the road to survival. Yet, as Global Perspective 8.1 shows, concerns about the export of military equipment and know-how lead to disagreements between and within nations.

These problems and conflicts seem to ensure that dissent and disagreement in the export control field are unlikely to decrease, but rather will multiply in the future. As long as regulations are not harmonized internationally, firms will need to be highly sensitive to different and perhaps rapidly changing export control regimes.

Global Perspective

8.1
The Dogfight over MiG Modernization

The world obviously has changed when U.S. defense companies are wildly excited over the chance to upgrade the capabilities of the Soviet MiG-21. Firms including Martin Marietta, Honeywell, Northrop Grumman, and Litton Industries are seeking permission from federal agencies to modernize the electronics systems of 120 MiG-21s used by India's air force. The project is valued at $350 million. In addition, there is potential for billions of dollars more from similar upgradings for Poland, the Czech Republic, Romania, Egypt, and Peru.

With Pentagon cutbacks a fact of life, U.S. firms see the modernization of old MiGs as a growth market that could prevent job losses. However, the companies involved are frustrated by the delay in obtaining approval from their own government and fear this could allow foreign competitors to land the lucrative deals.

The delay stems from considerable controversy that has arisen over the deal, leading to a high-level review by the National Security Council and the State, Defense, and Commerce Departments. State Department officials fear that any U.S. industry help to the Indian military could anger Pakistan, India's rival and a U.S. ally.

Other U.S. officials express fears that the American firms would be subcontractors to Russian prime contractors on any MiG-21 upgrades. The Russians, French,

and Israelis all are bidding to be prime contractors on MiG-21 upgrades worldwide, and they would have access to the U.S. subcontractors' electronics gear. U.S. officials' fears stem from the fact that any one of the prime contractors could "reverse engineer" the gear for their own use or for sale to others. Russia is seen by some in the United States as a potential adversary to whom they don't want to give sensitive military technology. The French and Israelis are likewise viewed at times as opportunists who routinely sell high-tech military gear to rogue nations for profit.

"Some Americans may have an aversion to upgrading the equipment we spent 20 years trying to destroy. But this is perceived to be a potentially big business," said Joel Johnson, international vice president for the Aerospace Industries Association. "When U.S. firms sell the systems," he added, "the U.S. has some control over their capabilities, which we don't have when our competitors do the work."

Upgrading airplanes will become a big business as planes age and nations are unable to afford new models. If one government disallows the project, another will be quick to approve it. The bottom line is that a home government can greatly affect a firm's or an entire industry's operations on the international market.

Source: John Mintz, "U.S., Contractors in Dogfight Over MiG Modernization," *The Washington Post,* June 14, 1994, D1.

Regulating International Business Behavior

Home countries may implement special laws and regulations to ensure that the international business behavior of firms headquartered within them is conducted within moral and ethical boundaries considered appropriate. The definition of appropriateness may vary from country to country and from government to government. Therefore, the content of such regulations, their enforcement, and their impact on firms may vary substantially among nations. As a result, the international manager must walk a careful line, balancing the expectations held in different countries. Global Perspective 8.2 provides an example.

One major area in which nations attempt to govern international business activities involves **boycotts.** As an example, Arab nations developed a blacklist of companies that deal with Israel. Further, Arab customers frequently demand assurance that products they purchase are not manufactured in Israel and that the supplier

Global Perspective

8.2
Ethics in a Shrinking World

As organizations expand their relationships with other cultures, employees abroad are faced with some interesting dilemmas. One central question is whether ethics policies grounded in unique American values are exportable, or whether the attempt to apply these policies in foreign countries basically amounts to cultural imperialism.

An actual case study may be helpful. An American company executive in Tokyo has just selected a Japanese company to distribute his product in the Far East. The day before the executive leaves, the Japanese CEO presents him with a set of golf clubs and leather bag that sells for at least $2,000 in the United States and probably $4,000 in Japan. This act is in keeping with a Japanese custom of giving gifts. The American executive feigns ignorance of the custom, allowing him to avoid giving a gift, but the decision remains as to what he should do with the golf clubs.

Refusing the gift would cause the Japanese CEO to lose face in front of his employees and probably sour the relationship. Accepting the gift and then presenting the clubs to the home company seems to be a good idea, but

how does the executive do this? Should he take the tags off, scuff up the bag and club faces so they go through customs unassessed? Or should he simply pretend the whole incident never happened?

Well, eliminating this last choice is a start. Insulting the CEO isn't a wise choice either. The only viable option is the second one—presenting the clubs to the home company. The manager involved did, in fact, choose this route. One unfortunate consequence of this situation, however, is that each time the Japanese CEO visits the United States, the executive who made the deal is either sick or out of town on the day set aside to play golf.

In the rush to create ethics policies, all should be aware that their way of doing things isn't the only way and that customs of other cultures have value and validity. In the global economy, if rules of behavior are going to be written, those rules must be framed in the context of world citizenry so that employees have the ability to adapt to local customs yet comply with the values that define their corporate character.

Source: David Fagiano, "Ethics in a Shrinking World," *Business Credit,* February 1994, 48.

company does not do any business with Israel. The goal of these actions clearly is to impose a boycott on business with Israel. U.S. political ties to Israel caused the U.S. government to adopt antiboycott laws to prevent U.S. firms from complying with the boycott. The laws include a provision to deny foreign income tax benefits to companies that comply with the boycott. They also require notifying the U.S. government if boycott requests are received. U.S. firms that comply with the boycott are subject to heavy fines and to denial of export privileges.

Caught in a web of governmental activity, firms may be forced either to lose business or to pay substantial fines. This is especially true if the firm's products are competitive yet not unique, so that the supplier can opt to purchase them elsewhere. The heightening of such conflict can sometimes force companies to search for new ways to circumvent the law, which may be very risky, or to totally withdraw operations from a country.

Another area of regulatory activity affecting the international business efforts of firms is **antitrust laws.** These laws often apply to international operations as well as to domestic business. In many countries, antitrust agencies watch closely when a firm buys a company, engages in a joint venture with a foreign firm, or makes an agreement abroad with a competing firm in order to ensure that the action does not result in restraint of competition.

Given the increase in worldwide cooperation among companies, however, the wisdom of extending antitrust legislation to international activities is being questioned. Some limitations to these tough antitrust provisions were already implemented decades ago. For example, in the United States the **Webb-Pomerene Act** of 1918 excludes from antitrust prosecution firms cooperating to develop foreign markets. This law was passed as part of an effort to aid export efforts in the face of strong foreign competition by oligopolies and monopolies. The exclusion of international activities from antitrust regulation was further enhanced by the Export Trading Company Act of 1982, which ensures that cooperating firms are not exposed to the threat of treble damages. The law was designed specifically to assist small and medium-sized firms in their export efforts by permitting them to join forces. Further steps to loosen the application of antitrust laws to international business are under consideration because of increased competition from state-supported enterprises, strategic alliances, and global mega-corporations.

U.S. firms operating overseas are also affected by U.S. laws against **bribery** and **corruption.** In many countries, payments or favors are a way of life, and "a greasing of the wheels" is expected in return for government services. As a result, many companies doing business internationally routinely paid bribes or did favors for foreign officials in order to gain contracts. In the 1970s, a major national debate erupted in the United States about these business practices, led by arguments that U.S. firms have an ethical and moral leadership obligation and that contracts won through bribes do not reflect competitive market activity. As a result, the **Foreign Corrupt Practices Act** was passed in 1977, making it a crime for U.S. executives of publicly traded firms to bribe a foreign official in order to obtain business.

A number of U.S. firms have complained about the act, arguing that it hinders their efforts to compete internationally against companies whose home countries have no such antibribery laws. Global Perspective 8.3 details the problem. The problem is one of ethics versus practical needs and, to some extent, of the amounts involved. For example, it may be hard to draw the line between providing a generous tip and paying a bribe in order to speed up a business transaction. Many business executives believe that the United States should not apply its moral principles to other societies and cultures in which bribery and corruption are endemic. To compete internationally, executives argue, they must be free to use the most common methods of competition in the host country.

On the other hand, applying different standards to executives and firms based on whether they do business abroad or domestically is difficult to do. Also, bribes may open the way for shoddy performance and loose moral standards among executives and employees and may result in a spreading of general unethical business practices. Unrestricted bribery could result in firms concentrating on how to bribe best rather than on how to best produce and market their products.

The international manager must carefully distinguish between reasonable ways of doing business internationally—that is, complying with foreign expectations—and outright bribery and corruption. To assist the manager in this task, the 1988 Trade Act clarifies the applicability of the Foreign Corrupt Practices legislation. The revisions outline when a manager is expected to know about violation of the act, and they draw a distinction between the facilitation of routine governmental actions and governmental policy decisions. Routine actions concern issues such as the obtaining of permits and licenses, the processing of governmental papers (such as visas and work orders), the providing of mail and phone service, and the loading and unloading of cargo. Policy decisions refer mainly to situations in which the obtaining or retaining of a contract is at stake. While the facilitation of routine actions is not

Global Perspective

8.3
Coping in a World of Bribes

Economic growth in developing nations is fueled by many things, among them foreign aid, local resources, and political will. And then there is corruption.

With great reluctance and much sadness, development officials concede that bribes and kickbacks play a growing, crucial role in determining how and why governments spend their money. They would prefer to think that only economic reasons underlie plans to spur local growth. But all too often, they ruefully admit, payoffs have much to do with why one project or contractor is selected over another when it is time to award the work. One World Bank official who believes corruption is on the rise says, "It's not something that we . . . fully understand. We've never addressed it as a development issue, but that is changing."

Restrained by the U.S. Foreign Corrupt Practices Act, U.S. firms are at a big disadvantage to their European and Japanese rivals, who are free to bribe in countries other than their own and can claim payoffs as income tax deductions. U.S. executives often complain that they lose work for not kicking back 10 percent or 20 percent on major projects, as others do. The complaints are on the rise because many believe bribery is increasing, with recession-bound Europeans and Japanese desperate for business.

Unable to pay bribes even if they wanted to, U.S. corporations would like to restrain others as well; they talk about creating "a level playing field" and hope for effective White House diplomacy. The goal would be to convince other industrial nations to pass their own laws against bribes and end favorable tax treatment. Under intense U.S. pressure, the 25-nation Organization for Economic Cooperation and Development has recently made such a recommendation. What happens next depends on the will of member states, and whether Washington keeps pushing.

Source: Robert Keatley, "U.S. Firms Bemoan Their Disadvantage Vying for Foreign Work Without Bribes," *The Wall Street Journal,* June 10, 1994, A6.

prohibited, the illegal influencing of policy decisions can result in the imposition of severe fines and penalties.

All of these issues of governmental regulation pose difficult and complex problems, for they place managers in the position of having to choose between home-country regulations and foreign business practices. This choice is made even more difficult because diverging standards of behavior are applied to businesses in different countries.

A final, major issue that is critical for international business managers is that of general standards of behavior and ethics. Increasingly, public concerns are raised about such issues as environmental protection, global warming, pollution, and moral behavior. However, these issues are not of the same importance in every country. What may be frowned upon or even illegal in one nation may be customary or at least acceptable in others. For example, the cutting down of the Brazilian rain forest may be acceptable to the government of Brazil, but scientists and concerned consumers may object vehemently because of the effect on global warming and other climatic changes. The export of U.S. tobacco products may be legal but results in accusations of exporting death to developing nations. China may use prison labor in producing products for export, but U.S. law prohibits the importation of such products. Mexico may permit the use of low safety standards for workers, but the buyers of Mexican products may object to the resulting dangers.

International firms must understand the conflicts and should assert leadership in implementing change. Not everything that is legally possible should be exploited for profit. Although companies need to return a profit on their investments, these issues must be seen in the context of time. By acting on existing, leading-edge knowledge and standards, firms will be able to benefit in the long term through consumer goodwill and the avoidance of later recriminations.

HOST COUNTRY POLITICAL AND LEGAL ENVIRONMENT	Politics and laws of a host country affect international business operations in a variety of ways. The good manager will understand these dimensions of the countries in which the firm operates so that he or she can work within existing parameters and can anticipate and plan for changes that may occur.

Political Action and Risk

Firms usually prefer to conduct business in a country with a stable and friendly government, but such governments are not always easy to find. Managers must therefore continually monitor the government, its policies, and its stability to determine the potential for political change that could adversely affect corporate operations.

There is **political risk** in every nation, but the range of risks varies widely from country to country. In general, political risk is lowest in countries that have a history of stability and consistency. Political risk tends to be highest in nations that do not have this sort of history. In a number of countries, however, consistency and stability that were apparent on the surface have been quickly swept away by major popular movements that drew on the bottled-up frustrations of the population. Three major types of political risk can be encountered: **ownership risk,** which exposes property and life; **operating risk,** which refers to interference with the ongoing operations of a firm; and **transfer risk,** which is mainly encountered when attempts are made to shift funds between countries. Firms can be exposed to political risk due to government actions or even outside the control of governments. The type of actions and their effects are classified in Figure 8.2.

A major political risk in many countries is that of conflict and violent change. A manager will want to think twice before conducting business in a country in which the likelihood of such change is high. To begin with, if conflict breaks out, violence directed toward the firm's property and employees is a strong possibility. Guerrilla warfare, civil disturbances, and terrorism often take an anti-industry bent, making companies and their employees potential targets. International corporations are often subject to major threats, even in countries that boast of great political stability. Sometimes the sole fact that a firm is market oriented is sufficient to attract the wrath of terrorists. For example, in the spring of 1991, Detlev Rohwedder, chairman of the German Treuhand (the institution in charge of privatizing the state-owned firms of the former East Germany), was assassinated at his home in Germany by the Red Army Faction because of his "representation of capitalism."

International terrorists have frequently targeted U.S. corporate facilities, operations, and personnel abroad for attack in order to strike a blow against the United States and capitalism. U.S. firms, by their nature, cannot have the elaborate security and restricted access of U.S. diplomatic offices and military bases. As a result, United States businesses are the primary target of terrorists worldwide, and remain the most vulnerable targets in the future.[10] The methods used by terrorists against business facilities include bombing, arson, hijacking, and sabotage. To obtain funds, the terrorists resort to kidnapping executives, armed robbery, and extortion.[11]

FIGURE 8.2
Exposure to Political
Risk

Contingencies May Include:	Loss May Be the Result of:	
	The actions of legitimate government authorities	Events caused by factors outside the control of government
The involuntary loss of control over specific assets without adequate compensation	• Total or partial expropriation • Forced divestiture • Confiscation • Cancellation or unfair calling of performance bonds	• War • Revolution • Terrorism • Strikes • Extortion
A reduction in the value of a stream of benefits expected from the foreign-controlled affiliate	• Nonapplicability of "national treatment" • Restriction in access to financial, labor, or material markets • Controls on prices, outputs, or activities • Currency and remittance restrictions • Value-added and export performance requirements	• Nationalistic buyers or suppliers • Threats and disruption to operations by hostile groups • Externally induced financial constraints • Externally imposed limits on imports or exports

Source: José de la Torre and David H. Neckar, "Forecasting Political Risks for International Operations," in H. Vernon-Wortzel and L. Wortzel, *Global Strategic Management: The Essentials,* 2nd ed. (New York: John Wiley and Sons, 1990), 195.

In many countries, particularly in the developing world, **coups d'état** can result in drastic changes in government. The new government often will attack foreign firms as remnants of a Western-dominated colonial past, as has happened in Cuba, Nicaragua, and Iran. Even if such changes do not represent an immediate physical threat, they can lead to policy changes that may have a drastic effect. The past few decades have seen coups in Ghana, Ethiopia, Iraq, and Kuwait, for example, that have seriously impeded the conduct of international business.

Less drastic, but still worrisome, are changes in government policies that are not caused by changes in the government itself. These occur when, for one reason or another, a government feels pressured to change its policies toward foreign businesses. The pressure may be the result of nationalist or religious factions or widespread anti-Western feeling.

A broad range of policy changes is possible as a result of political unrest. All of the changes can affect the company's international operations, but not all of them are equal in weight. Except for extreme cases, companies do not usually have to fear violence against their employees, although violence against company property is quite common. Also common are changes in policy that result from a new government or a strong new stance that is nationalist and opposed to foreign investment. The most drastic public steps resulting from such policy changes are usually expropriation and confiscation.

Expropriation is the transfer of ownership by the host government to a domestic entity. According to the World Bank, from the early 1960s through the 1970s, a total of 1,535 firms from 22 different countries were expropriated in 511 separate actions by 76 nations.[12] Expropriation was an appealing action to many countries because it demonstrated their nationalism and transferred a certain amount of wealth and resources from foreign companies to the host country immediately. It did have costs to the host country, however, to the extent that it made other firms more hesitant to invest there. Expropriation does not relieve the host government of providing compensation to the former owners. However, these compensation negotiations are often protracted and frequently result in settlements that are unsatisfactory to the owners. For example, governments may offer compensation in the form of local, nontransferable currency or may base compensation on the book value of the firm. Even though firms that are expropriated may deplore the low levels of payment obtained, they frequently accept them in the absence of better alternatives.

The use of expropriation as a policy tool has sharply decreased over time. In the mid-1970s, more than 83 expropriations took place in a single year. By the 1980s, the annual average had declined to fewer than 3. Apparently, governments have come to recognize that the damage they inflict on themselves through expropriation exceeds the benefits they receive.[13]

Confiscation is similar to expropriation in that it results in a transfer of ownership from the firm to the host country. It differs in that it does not involve compensation for the firm. Some industries are more vulnerable than others to confiscation and expropriation because of their importance to the host country's economy and their lack of ability to shift operations. For this reason, sectors such as mining, energy, public utilities, and banking have frequently been targets of such government actions.

Confiscation and expropriation constitute major political risk for foreign investors. Other government actions, however, are equally detrimental to foreign firms. Many countries are turning from confiscation and expropriation to more subtle forms of control, such as **domestication.** The goal of domestication is the same—that is, to gain control over foreign investment—but the method is different. Through domestication, the government demands transfer of ownership and management responsibility. It can impose **local content** regulations to ensure that a large share of the product is locally produced or demand that a larger share of the profit is retained in the country. Changes in labor laws, patent protection, and tax regulations are also used for purposes of domestication.

Domestication can have profound effects on an international business operation for a number of reasons. If a firm is forced to hire nationals as managers, poor cooperation and communication can result. If domestication is imposed within a very short time span, corporate operations overseas may have to be headed by poorly trained and inexperienced local managers. Domestic content requirements may force a firm to purchase its supplies and parts locally. This can result in increased costs, higher inefficiency, and lower-quality products. Export requirements imposed on companies may create havoc for their international distribution plans and force them to change or even shut down operations in third countries. If government action consists of weakening or not enforcing **intellectual property right** protection, companies run the risk of losing their core competitive edge. Such steps may temporarily permit domestic firms to become quick imitators. Yet, in the longer term, they will not only discourage the ongoing transfer of technology and knowledge by multinational firms, but also reduce the incentive for local firms to invest in innovation and progress. Finally, domestication usually will shield an industry within one country from foreign competition. As a result, inefficiencies will be allowed to thrive due to a lack of market discipline. This will affect the long-run international competitiveness of an operation abroad and may turn into a major problem when, years later, domestication is discontinued by the government.

The Risk of Terrorist Activity: A Factor in International Business Decisions

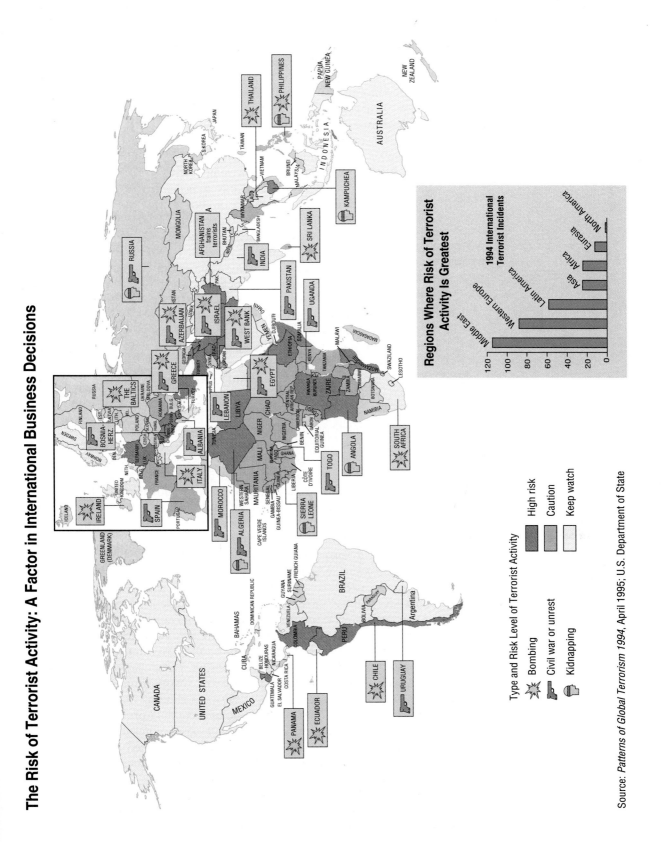

Source: *Patterns of Global Terrorism 1994*, April 1995; U.S. Department of State

Economic Risk

Most businesses operating abroad face a number of other risks that are less dangerous, but probably more common, than the drastic ones already described. A host
government's political situation or desires may lead it to impose economic regulations or laws to restrict or control the international activities of firms.

Nations that face a shortage of foreign currency sometimes will impose controls
on the movement of capital in and out of the country. Such controls may make it
difficult for a firm to remove its profits or investments from the host country. Sometimes **exchange controls** are also levied selectively against certain products or companies in an effort to reduce the importation of goods that are considered to be a
luxury or to be sufficiently available through domestic production. Such regulations
are often difficult for the international manager to deal with because they may affect the importation of parts, components, or supplies that are vital to production
operations in the country. Frequently, restrictions on such imports may force a firm
either to alter its production program or, worse yet, to shut down its entire plant.
Prolonged negotiations with government officials may be necessary to reach a compromise on what constitutes a "valid" expenditure of foreign currency resources. Because the goals of government officials and corporate managers are often quite
different, such compromises, even when they can be reached, may result in substantial damage to the international operations of the firm.

Countries may also use **tax policy** toward foreign investors in an effort to control multinational corporations and their capital. Tax increases may raise much-needed
revenue for the host country, but they can severely damage the operations of foreign investors. This damage, in turn, will frequently result in decreased income for
the host country in the long run. The raising of tax rates needs to be carefully differentiated from increased tax scrutiny of foreign investors. Many governments believe that multinational firms may be tempted to shift tax burdens to lower-tax
countries by using artificial pricing schemes between subsidiaries. In such instances,
governments are likely to take measures to obtain their fair contribution from multinational operations. In the United States, for example, increased focus on the taxation of multinational firms demanded by President Clinton has resulted in various
back-tax payments by foreign firms and the development of pricing policies jointly
with the Internal Revenue Service.[14]

The international executive also has to worry about **price controls.** In many
countries, domestic political pressures can force governments to control the prices
of imported products or services, particularly in sectors considered highly sensitive
from a political perspective, such as food or health care. A foreign firm involved in
these areas is vulnerable to price controls because the government can play on citizens' nationalistic tendencies to enforce the controls. Particularly in countries that
suffer from high inflation, frequent devaluations, or sharply rising costs, the international executive may be forced to choose between shutting down the operation
or continuing production at a loss in the hope of recouping profits when the government loosens or removes its price restrictions. Price controls can also be administered to prevent prices from being too low. As explained in more detail in
Chapter 14, governments have enacted antidumping laws, which prevent foreign
competitors from pricing their imports unfairly low in order to drive domestic competitors out of the market. Since dumping charges depend heavily on the definition
of "fair" price, a firm can sometimes become the target of such accusations quite
unexpectedly. Proving that no dumping took place can become quite onerous in
terms of time, money, and information disclosure.

Managing the Risk

Managers face the risk of confiscation, expropriation, domestication, or other government interference whenever they conduct business overseas, but ways exist to lessen the risk. Obviously, if a new government comes into power and is dedicated to the removal of all foreign influences, there is little a firm can do. In less extreme cases, however, managers can take actions that will reduce the risk, provided they understand the root causes of the host country's policies.

Adverse governmental actions are usually the result of nationalism, the desire for independence, or opposition to colonial remnants. If a host country's citizens feel exploited by foreign investors, government officials are more likely to take anti-foreign action. To reduce the risk of government intervention, the international firm needs to demonstrate that it is concerned with the host country's society and that it considers itself an integral part of the host country, rather than simply an exploitative foreign corporation. Ways of doing this include intensive local hiring and training practices, better pay, contributions to charity, and societally useful investments. In addition, the company can form joint ventures with local partners to demonstrate that it is willing to share its gains with nationals. Although such actions will not guarantee freedom from political risk, they will certainly lessen the exposure.

Another action that can be taken by corporations to protect against political risk is the close monitoring of political developments. Increasingly, private sector firms offer such monitoring assistance, permitting the overseas corporation to discover potential trouble spots as early as possible and to react quickly to prevent major losses. Figure 8.3 gives an example of such a political risk service.

Firms can also take out insurance to cover losses due to political and economic risk. Most industrialized countries offer insurance programs for their firms doing business abroad. In Germany, for example, Hermes Kreditanstalt provides exporters with insurance. In the United States, the Overseas Private Investment Corporation (OPIC)

**FIGURE 8.3
Advertisement for a
Political Risk
Advisory/Forecasting
Service**

"Politics is the key to
country risk analysis . . ."
Euromoney, September 1992

Saudi Arabia's stability not threatened by fundamentalists or financial problems . . . government spending and bloated bureaucracy undermine **Brazil's** economy . . . chaos looming in **Nigeria** . . . **China's** economy overheats, but political control is still paramount for leaders . . . serious economic reform in **Mexico** . . . multiracial regime copes with economic problems in **South Africa** . . . violence continues in **Egypt,** but Mubarak's political survival appears assured . . . business climate uncertain in **Poland** . . . new investment helps the **Philippines** . . . deteriorating conditions in **Algeria** . . . new government pushes economic reform in **Hungary** . . .

can cover three types of risk insurance: Currency inconvertibility insurance, which covers the inability to convert profits, debt service, and other remittances from local currency into U.S. dollars; Expropriation insurance, which covers the loss of an investment due to expropriation, nationalization or confiscation by a foreign government; and political violence insurance, which covers the loss of assets or income due to war, revolution, insurrection, or politically motivated civil strife, terrorism and sabotage.[15] The cost of coverage varies by country and type of activity, but it averages $0.60 for $100 of coverage per year to protect against inconvertibility, $0.60 to protect against expropriation, and $1.05 to compensate for damage to business income and assets from political violence.[16] Usually the policies do not cover commercial risks and, in the event of a claim, cover only the actual loss—not lost profits. In the event of a major political upheaval, however, risk insurance can be critical to a firm's survival.

The discussion to this point has focused primarily on the political environment. Laws have been mentioned only as they appear to be the direct result of political change. However, the laws of host countries need to be considered on their own to some extent, for the basic system of law is important to the conduct of international business.

Legal Differences and Restraints

Countries differ in their laws as well as in their use of the law. For example, over the past decade the United States has become an increasingly litigious society in which institutions and individuals are quick to initiate lawsuits. Court battles are often protracted and costly, and even the threat of a court case can reduce business opportunities. In contrast, Japan's tradition tends to minimize the role of the law and of lawyers. The country has only 15,000 fully licensed lawyers,[17] compared to over 846,000 in the United States.[18] Even if one adjusts for the multiple duties carried out by U.S. lawyers compared to the narrowly defined role of Japanese attorneys, Japan still has less than one-fifth of the lawyers in the United States.[19] Whether the number of lawyers is cause or effect, the Japanese tend not to litigate. Litigation in Japan means that the parties have failed to compromise, which is contrary to Japanese tradition and results in loss of face. A cultural predisposition therefore exists to settle conflicts outside the court system, as shown in Global Perspective 8.4.

Over the millenia of civilization, many different laws and legal systems emerged. King Hammurabi of Babylon codified a series of decisions by judges into a body of laws. Legal issues in many African tribes were settled through the verdicts of clansmen. A key legal perspective that survives today is that of theocracy. For example, Hebrew law was the result of the dictates of God. Islamic law, or the sharia, is the result of scripture, prophetic utterances and practices, and scholarly interpretations.[20] These legal systems have faith and belief as their key focus and are a mix of societal, legal, and spiritual guidelines.

While legal systems are important to society, from an international business perspective, the two major legal systems worldwide can be categorized into common law and code law. **Common law** is based on tradition and depends less on written statutes and codes than on precedent and custom. Common law originated in England and is the system of law in the United States. **Code law,** on the other hand, is based on a comprehensive set of written statutes. Countries with code law try to spell out all possible legal rules explicitly. Code law is based on Roman law and is found in the majority of the nations of the world.

Global Perspective

8.4

Two Air Disasters, Two Cultures, Two Remedies

When two jumbo jets crashed 10 days apart in Dallas and in the mountains near Tokyo, Americans and Japanese shared a common bond of shock and grief. Soon, however, all parties in Japan—from the airline to the employers of victims—moved to put the tragedy behind them. In the United States, legal tremors will continue for years.

Lawyers hustled to the scene of the Delta Air Lines accident at Dallas–Ft. Worth Airport and set up shop at an airport hotel. Proclaimed San Francisco attorney Melvin Belli: "I'm not an ambulance chaser—I get there before the ambulance." "We always file the first suit," bragged Richard Brown, a Melvin Belli associate who flew to Dallas "to get to the bottom of this and to make ourselves available." But he adds: "We never solicited anyone directly. We were called to Texas by California residents who lost their loved ones." Within 72 hours, the first suit against Delta was filed. Insurance adjusters working for Delta went quickly to work as well.

Seven thousand miles away, Japan Air Lines (JAL) President Yasumoto Takagi humbly bowed to families of the 520 victims and apologized "from the bottom of our hearts." He vowed to resign once the investigation was complete. Next of kin received "condolence payments" and negotiated settlements with the airline. Traditionally, few if any lawsuits are filed following such accidents.

Behind these differences lie standards of behavior and corporate responsibility that are worlds apart. "There is a general Japanese inclination to try to settle any disputes through negotiations between the parties before going to court," said Koichiro Fujikura, Tokyo University law professor. Added Carl Green, a Washington, D.C., attorney and specialist on Japanese law, "There is an assumption of responsibility. In our adversarial society, we don't admit responsibility. It would be admitting liability."

After a JAL jet crashed into Tokyo Bay in 1982, killing 24, JAL President Takagi visited victims' families, offered gifts, and knelt before funeral altars. JAL offered families about $2,000 each in condolence payments, then negotiated settlements reported to be worth between $166,000 and $450,000, depending on the age and earning power of each victim. Only one family sued.

Japanese legal experts expected settlements in the 1985 crash to be as high as 500 million yen—about $2.1 million—apiece. Negotiations may be prolonged. But if families believe that JAL is sincerely sorry, "I think their feelings will be soothed," predicted attorney Takeshi Odagi.

Japan's legal system encourages these traditions. "Lawyers don't descend in droves on accident scenes because they barely have enough time to handle the suits they have," says John Haley, a law professor at the University of Washington who has studied and worked in Japan. "There are fewer judges per capita than there were in 1890," Haley added. Only 500 lawyers are admitted to the bar each year.

Source: Clemens P. Work, Sarah Peterson, and Hidehiro Tanakadate, "Two Air Disasters, Two Cultures, Two Remedies," *U.S. News and World Report,* August 26, 1985, 25–26.

In general, countries with the code law system have much more rigid laws than those with the common law system. In the latter, courts adopt precedents and customs to fit cases, allowing a better idea of basic judgment likely to be rendered in new situations. The differences between code law and common law and their impact on international business, while wide in theory, are not as broad in practice. One reason is that many common law countries, including the United States, have adopted commercial codes to govern the conduct of business.

Host countries may adopt a number of laws that affect the firm's ability to do business, as discussed in Chapter 7. Tariffs and quotas, for example, can affect the entry of goods. Special licenses for foreign goods may be required.

Other laws may restrict entrepreneurial activities. In Argentina, for example, pharmacies must be owned by the pharmacist. This legislation prevents an ambitious businessperson from hiring druggists and starting a pharmacy chain. Similarly, the law prevents the addition of a drug counter to an existing business such as a supermarket and thus the broadening of the product offering to consumers.

Specific legislation may also exist regulating what does and does not constitute deceptive advertising. Many countries prohibit specific claims that compare products to the competition, or they restrict the use of promotional devices. Even when no laws exist, regulations may hamper business operations. For example, in some countries, firms are required to join the local chamber of commerce or become a member of the national trade association. These institutions in turn may have internal sets of rules that specify standards for the conduct of business that may be quite confining.

Seemingly innocuous local regulations that may easily be overlooked can have a major impact on the international firm's success. For example, Japan had an intricate process regulating the building of new department stores or supermarkets. The

Global Perspective

8.5
How Swiss Is the Swiss Army Knife?

American soldiers returning from Europe after World War II coined the phrase "Swiss Army knife" to describe the ingenious pocketknives produced in Switzerland and used by the Swiss military. Today, the knife is practically a celebrity: displayed at the New York Museum of Modern Art, sent into outer space, offered as gifts by U.S. presidents.

A federal court in Washington, D.C., has decided that the Chinese can sell cheap imitations of the famous Swiss knives—and even call them by the Swiss Army name. "It hurt," said James Kennedy, chairman of the Forschner Group in Connecticut, which has imported the Swiss-made knives since the 1950s and lost the court fight to stop the Chinese sales. Forschner had argued that the sales and reputation of the superior, original Swiss Army knife could be damaged by the inferior Chinese version. "Why don't they call it a 'Chinese Army Knife?'" asked one Swiss military official.

The Swiss-Chinese duel is part of an increasingly contentious debate in U.S. business law: Who owns geographic designations in popular product names? Is "Swiss Army knife" a generic term like Swiss cheese, Bermuda shorts, or French fries? Market research performed by University of Florida professor Joel Cohen showed that 43 percent of consumers shown the Chinese-made knife—without knowing its origin—assumed it was of high quality and Swiss origin because of its design and the "Swiss Army" name. "That's the key issue," said Cohen. "Here's the Swiss Army knife with an outstanding reputation for quality, and here's somebody who's copying their product and relying on the fact that consumers are going to make that inference about quality."

Arrow Trading Company, the seller of the Chinese-made knives and winner of the court ruling, declares that what it is selling is really not such a bad product. "It's a product that sells for a much lower price than the Swiss product sells for, and its quality is commensurate with its price," said lawyer Louis Ederer. An Arrow Trading Co. legal brief declared, "It's not false advertising to call a particular type of cheese 'Swiss cheese' even if it is made in Wisconsin."

Last year a federal judge found that the Chinese version misled the public. The judge, likening the Swiss version to a Rolls-Royce and the Chinese knife to a Yugo, ordered Arrow Trading to stop the sales. But in the most recent decision, an appeals court reversed that decision, agreeing with Arrow Trading that "Swiss Army knives" were more akin to "English muffins" or "French horns." The court did send the case back to the trial court to decide whether the "Made in China" label should be more prominent.

Source: Benjamin Weiser, "It Slices, It Dices, It Outrages the Swiss," *The Washington Post,* July 30, 1994, F1.

government's desire to protect smaller merchants brought the opening of new, large stores to a virtual standstill. As department stores and supermarkets serve as the major conduit for the sale of imported consumer products, the lack of new stores severely affected opportunities for market penetration of imported merchandise.[21] Only after intense pressure from the outside did the Japanese government decide in early 1991 to reconsider the regulations.

Finally, the interpretation and enforcement of laws and regulations may have a major effect on international business activities. As Global Perspective 8.5 shows, the interpretation given by courts to the meaning of a name can affect consumer perceptions and sales of products.

The Influencing of Politics and Laws

To succeed in a market, the international manager needs much more than business know-how. He or she must also deal with the intricacies of national politics and laws. Although to fully understand another country's legal political system will rarely be possible, the good manager will be aware of its importance and will work with people who do understand how to operate within the system.

Many areas of politics and law are not immutable. Viewpoints can be modified or even reversed, and new laws can supersede old ones. Therefore, existing political and legal restraints do not always need to be accepted. To achieve change, however, some impetus for it—such as the clamors of a constituency—must occur. Otherwise, systemic inertia is likely to allow the status quo to prevail.

The international manager has various options. One is to simply ignore prevailing rules and expect to get away with it. Pursuing this option is a high-risk strategy because the possibility of objection and even prosecution exists. A second, traditional option is to provide input to trade negotiators and expect any problem areas to be resolved in multilateral negotiations. The drawbacks to this option are, of course, the quite time-consuming process involved and the lack of control by the firm.

A third option involves the development of coalitions and constituencies that can motivate legislators and politicians to consider and ultimately implement change. This option can be pursued in various ways. First of all, direct linkages and their costs and benefits can be explained to legislators and politicians. For example, a manager can explain the employment and economic effects of certain laws and regulations and demonstrate the benefits of change. The picture can be enlarged by including indirect linkages. For example, suppliers, customers, and distributors can be asked to help explain to decision makers the benefit of change. In addition, the public at large can be involved through public statements or advertisements. Figure 8.4 provides an example of such an explanatory effort by a group of U.S. firms opposed to the World Trade Organization.

Developing such coalitions is not an easy task. Companies often seek assistance in effectively influencing the government decision-making process. Such assistance is particularly beneficial when narrow economic objectives or single-issue campaigns are involved. Typically, **lobbyists** provide this assistance. Usually, there are well-connected individuals and firms that can provide access to policymakers and legislators in order to communicate new and pertinent information.

Many U.S. firms have representatives in Washington, D.C., as well as in state capitals and are quite successful at influencing domestic policies. Often, however, they are less adept at ensuring proper representation abroad. For example, a survey of

FIGURE 8.4
A Lobbying Ad

Source: *Washington Post*, July 27, 1994, A24.

U.S. international marketing executives found that knowledge and information about foreign trade and government officials was ranked lowest among critical international business information needs. This low ranking appears to reflect the fact that many U.S. firms are far less successful in their interactions with governments abroad and far less intensive in their lobbying efforts than are foreign entities in the United States.[22]

Foreign countries and companies have been particularly effective in their lobbying in the United States. As an example, Brazil has retained nearly a dozen U.S. firms to cover and influence trade issues. Brazilian citrus exporters and computer manufacturers have hired U.S. legal and public relations firms to provide them with information on relevant U.S. legislative activity. The Banco do Brasil also successfully lobbied for the restructuring of Brazilian debt and favorable U.S. banking regulations.

Although representation of the firm's interests to government decision makers and legislators is entirely appropriate, the international manager must also consider any potential side effects. Major questions can be raised if such representation becomes very overt. Short-term gains may be far outweighed by long-term negative repercussions if the international firm is perceived as exerting too much political influence.

As Global Perspective 8.6 shows, there are major public concerns about the representation of foreign firms in Washington, D.C. Particularly the issue of representation by former government officials has come under public scrutiny, and many complaints have been voiced about the "revolving door." Legislation has therefore been passed that provides for cooling off periods during which former policymakers cannot return to their agencies and represent clients. The ethics provisions implemented by President Clinton have tightened the restrictions even more, with a focus on the representation of foreign firms. Yet, some opponents have argued that these provisions are overly harsh since they deprive former policymakers of employment, discriminate against foreign firms, and prevent individuals from seeking to serve in government.

Global Perspective

8.6
Washington: Under the Influence?

Peter Wallison, who served both the Treasury Department and the White House as legal counsel, took a lot of heat when he turned lobbyist. He was accused on the Senate floor by Sen. Donald Riegle of Michigan of serving as an intermediary between Honda Motor Co. and the U.S. Treasury Department when the U.S. Customs Service ruled that Canadian-built Honda Civic automobiles do not qualify for duty-free entry into the United States as stipulated by the free trade agreement with Canada.

Many were also unhappy when Timothy MacCarthy moved from a 16-year job at the U.S. Motor Vehicle Manufacturers Association to head Nissan North America's Washington corporate office. "I don't think I represent the Japanese company," said MacCarthy, insisting that he works for Nissan North America, a U.S. firm that employs some 6,000 workers. He sees lobbying as a corporate right in America. "If a company is not active in lobbying, that could even represent a failure to fulfill its responsibility toward its employees," said MacCarthy.

Source: Waichi Sekiguchi, "Washington: Under the Influence?" *The Nikkei Weekly,* September 12, 1992, 11.

INTERNATIONAL RELATIONS AND LAWS

In addition to understanding the politics and laws of both home and host countries, the international manager must also consider the overall international political and legal environment. This is important because policies and events occurring among countries can have a profound impact on firms trying to do business internationally.

International Politics

The effect of politics on international business is determined by both the bilateral political relations between home and host countries and by multilateral agreements governing the relations among groups of countries.

The government-to-government relationship can have a profound influence in a number of ways, particularly if it becomes hostile. Among numerous examples in recent years of the relationship between international politics and international business, perhaps the most notable involves U.S.–Iranian relations following the 1979 Iranian revolution. Although the internal political changes in the aftermath of that revolution certainly would have affected any foreign firm doing business in Iran, the deterioration in U.S.–Iranian political relations that resulted from the revolution had a significant additional impact on U.S. firms. Following the revolution, U.S. firms were injured not only by the physical damage caused by the violence, but also by the anti-American feelings of the Iranian people and their government. The resulting clashes between the two governments subsequently destroyed business relationships, regardless of corporate feelings or agreements on either side.

International political relations do not always have harmful effects. If bilateral political relations between countries improve, business can benefit. One example is the improvement in Western relations with Central Europe following the official end of the Cold War. The political warming opened the potentially lucrative former Eastern bloc markets to Western firms. Similarly, the ending of the U.S. embargo against Vietnam provided new opportunities to U.S. firms as Global Perspective 8.7 shows.

The overall international political environment has effects, whether good or bad, on international business. For this reason, the good manager will strive to remain aware of political currents and relations worldwide and will attempt to anticipate changes in the international political environment so that his or her firm can plan for them.

International Law

International law plays an important role in the conduct of international business. Although no enforceable body of international law exists, certain treaties and agreements are respected by a number of countries and profoundly influence international business operations. For example, the World Trade Organization (WTO) defines internationally acceptable economic practices for its member nations. Although it does not directly deal with individual firms, it does affect them indirectly by providing some predictability in the international environment.

International law also plays a major role in protecting intellectual property rights. Rights to intellectual property involve rights to inventions, **patents, trademarks,** and industrial designs, and copyrights for literary, musical, artistic, photographic, and cinematographic works. Currently, these types of intellectual property are not completely defined by any international treaty, and the laws differ from country to coun-

Global Perspective

8.7
Vietnam Embargo Ends, U.S. Firms Enter

One of the world's last relatively untapped opportunities for marketers from the United States has come alive with the stroke of a pen. The U.S. economic embargo that had been in place against Vietnam since 1975 was lifted by President Bill Clinton on February 3, 1994. U.S. firms moved into the market with great haste. Within two hours of the announcement, United Air Lines announced scheduled flights to Vietnam. At about the same time, Pepsi started its production line, which was fully operational within a week. Coke was not far behind, which started talk of the "new Vietnam war," Coke versus Pepsi. "There is a tremendous amount of euphoria about the prospects here," stated the president of the American Chamber of Commerce in Hong Kong.

Why so much hoopla? Vietnam has a population of 71 million and has substantial natural resources, most importantly, oil. The economy is growing at more than 7 percent per year, inflation is under control, there is 88 percent literacy, and wages are low; it is ideal for investment. The conditions sound even better considering the host nation's plans to lure $20 billion in foreign investment by decade's end.

The bad news for U.S. marketers is the fact that all these opportunities have been available for some time and have been tapped by practically all other interested nations. Non-U.S. investment in Vietnam has totaled $7.8 billion on 850 projects since 1987, with Taiwan and Hong Kong leading the way, followed closely by France and Australia. Many experts feel that Japan denied itself much of this ripe opportunity before the embargo had been lifted in order to

avoid problems with the United States. Now, however, it is expected that Japan will move forward at full speed and expand its control over strategic industries including oil and infrastructure development.

Despite their disadvantage of being late arrivals, U.S. firms are extremely optimistic—"It's going to be a scramble here. The country's so young in its economic development, there's room for everyone in every field," according to an American businessman living in Vietnam. Some of the key industries Americans expect to enter include oil exploration, construction, banking, and telecommunications. U.S. consumer goods are expected to do well because of pent-up Vietnamese demand. According to Eugene Matthews, an American private consultant in Vietnam, "particularly in consumer products and pharmaceuticals you will see the marketing muscle of American companies come into play."

"The best way to move trade is to have planes coming in and out," commented a Northwest Airlines official. Long forbidden in Vietnam, U.S. air carriers are positioning themselves for servicing the new market. All the major airlines are anxious to serve the expected flood of business travelers and the 1 million ethnic Vietnamese living in the United States. "Vietnam is one of the most promising countries in Asia," said a Continental Airlines executive.

Still to come are a bilateral trade pact and debates about mutual tariff reductions. But even in this early stage, it can be expected that U.S. firms will eventually play a large role in Vietnam's future.

Sources: John Rogers, "Firms in Place Have Advantage; Newcomers Face Uphill Climb," *The Journal of Commerce* (February 7, 1994): 6A; Susan Carey and Laurence Zuckerman, "Many Want to Fly to Vietnam, but Only Some May Land," *The Wall Street Journal,* February 7, 1994, B3; Peter Behr and Thomas Lippman, "New Market Means Prospects, Problems for American Firms," *The Washington Post,* February 4, 1994, A22; William Branigin, "Hanoi Hails Embargo End as Step to Better Ties," *The Washington Post,* February 4, 1994, A22; Urban Lehner, "U.S. Firms Head for Vietnam, but Find Asian, European Firms Already There," *The Wall Street Journal,* February 10, 1994, A14.

try on several important points. Thus the rights granted by one country's patent, trademark, or copyright may confer no protection abroad.

Some international agreements exist to ease the task of filing for intellectual property rights in those countries in which a firm wants to conduct business or ensure protection. The **Paris Convention for the Protection of Industrial Property,** to which 96 countries are party, sets minimum standards of protection and

corruption   trademark
Foreign Corrupt Practices Act   Paris Convention for the Protection of
political risk   Industrial Property
ownership risk   arbitration
operating risk

Questions for Discussion

1. Discuss this potential dilemma: "High political risk requires companies to seek a quick payback on their investments. Striving for a quick payback, however, exposes firms to charges of exploitation and results in increased political risk."

2. How appropriate is it for governments to help drum up business for their countries' companies abroad? Shouldn't commerce be completely separate from politics?

3. Discuss this statement: "The national security that our export control laws seek to protect may be threatened by the resulting lack of international competitiveness of U.S. firms."

4. Discuss the advantages and disadvantages of common law and code law.

5. Research some examples of multinational corporations that have remained untouched by waves of expropriation. What was their secret to success?

6. The United States has been described as a litigious society. How does frequent litigation affect international business?

7. After you hand your passport to the immigration officer in country X, he misplaces it. A small "donation" would certainly help him find it again. Should you give him the money? Is this a business expense to be charged to your company? Should it be tax deductible?

8. What are your views on lobbying efforts by foreign firms?

Recommended Readings

Bertsch, G.K., and S.E. Gowen, editors. *Export Controls in Transition: Perspectives, Problems, and Prospects.* Durham, N.C.: Duke University Press, 1992.

Breaking down the Barricades: Reforming Export Controls to Increase U.S. Competitiveness. Washington, D.C.: Center for Strategic and International Studies, 1994.

Choate, Pat. *Agents of Influence.* New York: Knopf, 1990.

Czinkota, Michael R., editor. *Export Controls.* New York: Praeger, 1984.

De la Torre, José, and David H. Neckar. "Forecasting Political Risks for International Operations," in *Global Strategic Management: The Essentials* 2d ed. H. Vernon-Wortzel and L. Wortzel, editors. New York: John Wiley and Sons, 1990.

Export Controls: Multilateral Efforts to Improve Enforcement. Washington, D.C.: United States General Accounting Office, GAO/NSIAD-92-167, 1992.

Hufbauer, Gary Clyde, and Jeffrey J. Schott. *Economic Sanctions Reconsidered: A History and Current Policy.* Washington, D.C.: Institute for International Economics, 1985.

The OECD Guidelines for Multinational Enterprises. Paris: Organization for Economic Cooperation and Development, 1994.

Prasad, Jyoti N. *Impact of the Foreign Corrupt Practices Act of 1977 on U.S. Exports.* New York: Garland Publishers, 1993.

SUMMARY   The political and legal environment in the home and host countries and the laws and agreements governing relationships among nations are important to the international business executive. Compliance is mandatory in order to do business successfully abroad. To avoid the problems that can result from changes in the political and legal environment, it is essential to anticipate changes and to develop strategies for coping with them. Whenever possible, the manager must avoid being taken by surprise and letting events control business decisions.

Governments affect international business through legislation and regulations, which can support or hinder business transactions. An example is when export sanctions or embargoes are imposed to enhance foreign policy objectives. Similarly, export controls are used to preserve national security. Nations also regulate the international business behavior of firms by setting standards that relate to bribery and corruption, boycotts, and restraint of competition.

Through political actions such as expropriation, confiscation, or domestication, countries expose firms to international risk. Management therefore needs to be aware of the possibility of such risk and alert to new developments. Many private sector services are available to track international risk situations. In the event of a loss, firms may rely on insurance for political risk or they may seek redress in court. International legal action, however, may be quite slow and may compensate for only part of the loss.

Managers need to be aware that different countries have different laws. One clearly pronounced difference is between code law countries, where all possible legal rules are spelled out, and common law countries such as the United States, where the law is based on tradition, precedent, and custom.

Managers must also pay attention to international political relations, agreements, and treaties. Changes in relations or rules can mean major new opportunities and occasional threats to international business.

Key Terms and Concepts

international competitiveness	transfer risk
extraterritoriality	coups d'état
sanction	expropriation
embargo	confiscation
export control system	domestication
export license	local content
critical commodities list	intellectual property rights
general license	exchange controls
validated export license	tax policy
foreign availability	price controls
dual-use products	common law
boycott	code law
antitrust laws	lobbyist
Webb-Pomerene Act	international law
bribery	patent

corruption   trademark
Foreign Corrupt Practices Act   Paris Convention for the Protection of
political risk   Industrial Property
ownership risk   arbitration
operating risk

Questions for Discussion

1. Discuss this potential dilemma: "High political risk requires companies to seek a quick payback on their investments. Striving for a quick payback, however, exposes firms to charges of exploitation and results in increased political risk."

2. How appropriate is it for governments to help drum up business for their countries' companies abroad? Shouldn't commerce be completely separate from politics?

3. Discuss this statement: "The national security that our export control laws seek to protect may be threatened by the resulting lack of international competitiveness of U.S. firms."

4. Discuss the advantages and disadvantages of common law and code law.

5. Research some examples of multinational corporations that have remained untouched by waves of expropriation. What was their secret to success?

6. The United States has been described as a litigious society. How does frequent litigation affect international business?

7. After you hand your passport to the immigration officer in country X, he misplaces it. A small "donation" would certainly help him find it again. Should you give him the money? Is this a business expense to be charged to your company? Should it be tax deductible?

8. What are your views on lobbying efforts by foreign firms?

Recommended Readings

Bertsch, G.K., and S.E. Gowen, editors. *Export Controls in Transition: Perspectives, Problems, and Prospects.* Durham, N.C.: Duke University Press, 1992.

Breaking down the Barricades: Reforming Export Controls to Increase U.S. Competitiveness. Washington, D.C.: Center for Strategic and International Studies, 1994.

Choate, Pat. *Agents of Influence.* New York: Knopf, 1990.

Czinkota, Michael R., editor. *Export Controls.* New York: Praeger, 1984.

De la Torre, José, and David H. Neckar. "Forecasting Political Risks for International Operations," in *Global Strategic Management: The Essentials* 2d ed. H. Vernon-Wortzel and L. Wortzel, editors. New York: John Wiley and Sons, 1990.

Export Controls: Multilateral Efforts to Improve Enforcement. Washington, D.C.: United States General Accounting Office, GAO/NSIAD-92-167, 1992.

Hufbauer, Gary Clyde, and Jeffrey J. Schott. *Economic Sanctions Reconsidered: A History and Current Policy.* Washington, D.C.: Institute for International Economics, 1985.

The OECD Guidelines for Multinational Enterprises. Paris: Organization for Economic Cooperation and Development, 1994.

Prasad, Jyoti N. *Impact of the Foreign Corrupt Practices Act of 1977 on U.S. Exports.* New York: Garland Publishers, 1993.

Global Perspective

8.7
Vietnam Embargo Ends, U.S. Firms Enter

One of the world's last relatively untapped opportunities for marketers from the United States has come alive with the stroke of a pen. The U.S. economic embargo that had been in place against Vietnam since 1975 was lifted by President Bill Clinton on February 3, 1994. U.S. firms moved into the market with great haste. Within two hours of the announcement, United Air Lines announced scheduled flights to Vietnam. At about the same time, Pepsi started its production line, which was fully operational within a week. Coke was not far behind, which started talk of the "new Vietnam war," Coke versus Pepsi. "There is a tremendous amount of euphoria about the prospects here," stated the president of the American Chamber of Commerce in Hong Kong.

Why so much hoopla? Vietnam has a population of 71 million and has substantial natural resources, most importantly, oil. The economy is growing at more than 7 percent per year, inflation is under control, there is 88 percent literacy, and wages are low; it is ideal for investment. The conditions sound even better considering the host nation's plans to lure $20 billion in foreign investment by decade's end.

The bad news for U.S. marketers is the fact that all these opportunities have been available for some time and have been tapped by practically all other interested nations. Non-U.S. investment in Vietnam has totaled $7.8 billion on 850 projects since 1987, with Taiwan and Hong Kong leading the way, followed closely by France and Australia. Many experts feel that Japan denied itself much of this ripe opportunity before the embargo had been lifted in order to

avoid problems with the United States. Now, however, it is expected that Japan will move forward at full speed and expand its control over strategic industries including oil and infrastructure development.

Despite their disadvantage of being late arrivals, U.S. firms are extremely optimistic—"It's going to be a scramble here. The country's so young in its economic development, there's room for everyone in every field," according to an American businessman living in Vietnam. Some of the key industries Americans expect to enter include oil exploration, construction, banking, and telecommunications. U.S. consumer goods are expected to do well because of pent-up Vietnamese demand. According to Eugene Matthews, an American private consultant in Vietnam, "particularly in consumer products and pharmaceuticals you will see the marketing muscle of American companies come into play."

"The best way to move trade is to have planes coming in and out," commented a Northwest Airlines official. Long forbidden in Vietnam, U.S. air carriers are positioning themselves for servicing the new market. All the major airlines are anxious to serve the expected flood of business travelers and the 1 million ethnic Vietnamese living in the United States. "Vietnam is one of the most promising countries in Asia," said a Continental Airlines executive.

Still to come are a bilateral trade pact and debates about mutual tariff reductions. But even in this early stage, it can be expected that U.S. firms will eventually play a large role in Vietnam's future.

Sources: John Rogers, "Firms in Place Have Advantage; Newcomers Face Uphill Climb," *The Journal of Commerce* (February 7, 1994): 6A; Susan Carey and Laurence Zuckerman, "Many Want to Fly to Vietnam, but Only Some May Land," *The Wall Street Journal,* February 7, 1994, B3; Peter Behr and Thomas Lippman, "New Market Means Prospects, Problems for American Firms," *The Washington Post,* February 4, 1994, A22; William Branigin, "Hanoi Hails Embargo End as Step to Better Ties," *The Washington Post,* February 4, 1994, A22; Urban Lehner, "U.S. Firms Head for Vietnam, but Find Asian, European Firms Already There," *The Wall Street Journal,* February 10, 1994, A14.

try on several important points. Thus the rights granted by one country's patent, trademark, or copyright may confer no protection abroad.

Some international agreements exist to ease the task of filing for intellectual property rights in those countries in which a firm wants to conduct business or ensure protection. The **Paris Convention for the Protection of Industrial Property,** to which 96 countries are party, sets minimum standards of protection and provides the right of national treatment and the right of priority. This means that members will not discriminate against foreigners and that firms have one year (six months for a design or trademark) in which to file an application.

The Patent Cooperation Treaty (PCT) provides procedures for filing one international application designating countries in which a patent is sought, which has the same effect as filing national applications in each of those countries. Similarly, the European Patent Office examines applications and issues national patents in any of its member countries. Other regional offices include the African Industrial Property Office (ARIPO), the French-speaking African Intellectual Property Organization (OAPI), and one in Saudi Arabia for six countries in the Gulf region.[23]

Much more needs to be done to protect intellectual property. Knowledge is often the firm's most precious competitive advantage, and violation of those rights can have significant financial repercussions.

International organizations such as the United Nations and the Organization for Economic Cooperation and Development have also undertaken efforts to develop codes and guidelines that affect international business. These include the Code on International Marketing of Breast-milk Substitutes, which was developed by the World Health Organization (WHO), and the UN Code of Conduct for Transnational Corporations. Even though there are 34 such codes in existence, the lack of enforcement ability hampers their full implementation.

In addition to multilateral agreements, firms are affected by bilateral treaties and conventions between the countries in which they do business. For example, a number of countries have signed bilateral Treaties of Friendship, Commerce, and Navigation (FCN). The agreements generally define the rights of firms doing business in the host country. They normally guarantee that firms will be treated by the host country in the same manner in which domestic firms are treated. While these treaties provide for some sort of stability, they can also be canceled when relations worsen.

The international legal environment also affects the manager to the extent that firms must concern themselves with jurisdictional disputes. Because no single body of international law exists, firms usually are restricted by both home and host country laws. If a conflict occurs between contracting parties in two different countries, a question arises concerning which country's laws are to be used and in which court the dispute is to be settled. Sometimes the contract will contain a jurisdictional clause, which settles the matter with little problem. If the contract does not contain such a clause, however, the parties to the dispute have a few choices. They can settle the dispute by following the laws of the country in which the agreement was made, or they can resolve it by obeying the laws of the country in which the contract will have to be fulfilled. Which laws to use and in which location to settle the dispute are two different decisions. As a result, a dispute between a U.S. exporter and a French importer could be resolved in Paris but be based on New York State law. The importance of such provisions was highlighted by the lengthy jurisdictional disputes surrounding the Bhopal incident in India.

In cases of disagreement, the parties can choose either arbitration or litigation. Litigation is usually avoided for several reasons. It often involves extensive delays and is very costly. In addition, firms may fear discrimination in foreign countries. Therefore, companies tend to prefer conciliation and **arbitration** because they result in much quicker decisions. Arbitration procedures are often spelled out in the original contract and usually provide for an intermediary who is judged to be impartial by both parties. Frequently, intermediaries will be representatives of chambers of commerce, trade associations, or third-country institutions.

Notes

1. Quoted in Philippe Dollinger, *The German Hansa* (Stanford, CA: Stanford University Press, 1970), 49.
2. Gary Clyde Hufbauer and Jeffrey J. Schott, "Economic Sanctions: An Often Used and Occasionally Effective Tool of Foreign Policy," in *Export Controls,* ed. Michael R. Czinkota (New York: Praeger, 1984), 18-33.
3. Robin Renwick, *Economic Sanctions* (Cambridge, Mass.: Harvard University Press, 1981), 11.
4. Margaret P. Doxey, *Economic Sanctions and International Enforcement* (New York: Oxford University Press, 1980), 10.
5. Robert M. Springer, Jr., "New Export Law an Aid to International Marketers," *Marketing News,* January 3, 1986, 10, 67.
6. Erwin Dichtl, "Defacto Limits of Export Controls: The Need for International Harmonization," paper presented at the 2nd Annual CiMar Conference, Rio de Janeiro, August 1994.
7. Allan S. Krass, "The Second Nuclear Era: Nuclear Weapons in a Transformed World," in *World Security: Challenges for a New Century,* 2d ed., M. Klare and D. Thomas, eds. (St. Martin's Press, 1994), 85-105.
8. Paul Freedenberg, testimony before the Subcommittee on International Finance and Monetary Policy of the Committee on Banking, Housing, and Urban Affairs, United States Senate, Washington, D.C., February 3, 1994, 2.
9. E.M. Hucko, *Aussenwirtschaftsrecht-Kriegswaffenkontrollrecht, Textsammlung mit Einführung,* 4th ed. (Cologne, 1993).
10. Michael G. Harvey, "A Survey of Corporate Programs for Managing Terrorist Threats," *Journal of International Business Studies* (Third Quarter 1993): 465-478.
11. Harvey J. Iglarsh, "Terrorism and Corporate Costs," *Terrorism* 10 (1987): 227-230.
12. Joseph V. Miscallef, "Political Risk Assessment," *Columbia Journal of World Business* 16 (January 1981): 47.
13. Michael Minor, "LDCs, TNCs, and Expropriations in the 1980s," *The CYC Reporter,* Spring 1988, 53.
14. Paul Blustein, "Kawasaki to Pay Additional Taxes to U.S.," *The Washington Post,* December 11, 1992, D1.
15. *OPIC Annual Report,* Washington, D.C., 1994, 5.
16. *Investment Insurance Handbook* (Washington, D.C.: Overseas Private Investment Corporation, 1991).
17. John Choy, *A Comprehensive Review of Japan's Legal System,* (Washington, D.C.: Japan Economic Institute, 1992).
18. Personal communication, American Bar Association, Washington, D.C., 1994.
19. Stuart M. Chemtob, Glen S. Fukushima, and Richard H. Wohl, *Practice by Foreign Lawyers in Japan* (Chicago: American Bar Association, 1989), 9.
20. Surya Prakash Sinha, *What Is Law? The Differing Theories of Jurisprudence* (New York: Paragon House, 1989).
21. Michael R. Czinkota and Jon Woronoff, *Unlocking Japan's Market* (Chicago: Probus Publishing, 1991).
22. Michael R. Czinkota, "International Information Needs for U.S. Competitiveness," *Business Horizons* 34, 6 (November/December 1991): 86-91.
23. Judy Winegar Goans, "Protecting American Intellectual Property Abroad," *Business America,* U.S. Department of Commerce, International Trade Administration, October 27, 1986, 2-7.

CHAPTER 9

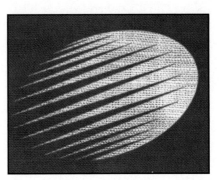

The Cultural Challenge

Learning Objectives

1. To define and demonstrate the effect of culture's various dimensions on international business.

2. To examine ways in which cultural knowledge can be acquired and individuals and organizations prepared for cross-cultural interaction.

3. To illustrate ways in which cultural risk poses a challenge to the effective conduct of business communications and transactions.

4. To suggest ways in which international businesses act as change agents in the diverse cultural environments in which they operate.

Making Culture Work for Your Success

Thousands of European and U.S. companies have entered or expanded their operations in the fastest growing region in the world, Asia. In 1993, the region outpaced the growth of the world's 24 leading industrial economies by more than six times. A total of 400 million Asian consumers have disposable incomes at least equal to the rich-world average.

Few have had as much experience—or success—as the 3M Company. The maker of everything from heart-lung machines to Scotch tape, the company's revenues for 1993 in the Far East hit $2.2 billion, having grown 40 percent over the previous year. At the root of the company's success are certain rules that allow it both to adjust to and exploit cultural differences.

• **Embrace Local Culture**—3M's new plant near Bangkok, Thailand, is one example of how the company embraces local culture. A gleaming Buddhist shrine, wreathed in flowers, pays homage to the spirits Thais believe took care of the land prior to the plant's arrival. Showing sensitivity to local customs helps sales and builds employee morale, officials say. It helps the company understand the market and keeps it from doing something inadvertently to alienate people.

• **Employ Locals to Gain Cultural Knowledge**—The best way to understand a market is to have grown up in it. Of the 7,500 3M employees in Asia, fewer than 10 are Americans. The rest are locals who know the customs and buying habits of their compatriots. 3M also makes grants of up to $50,000 available to its Asian employees to study product innovations, making them equals with their U.S. counterparts.

• **Build Relationships**—3M executives started preparing for the Chinese market soon after President Nixon's historic visit in 1972. For ten years, company officials visited Beijing and invited Chinese leaders to 3M headquarters in St. Paul, Minnesota, building contacts and trust along the way. Such efforts paid off when, in 1984, the government made 3M the first wholly owned foreign venture on Chinese soil. 3Mers call the process FIDO ("first in defeats others") which is a credo built on patience, persistence, and a long-term perspective.

• **Adapt Products to Local Markets**—Examples of how 3M adapts its products read like insightful lessons on culture. In the early 1990s, sales of 3M's famous Scotchbrite cleaning pads were languishing. Company technicians interviewed maids and housewives to determine why. The answer: Filipinos traditionally scrub floors by pushing around the rough shell of a coconut with their feet. 3M responded by making the pads brown and shaping them like a foot. In China, a big seller for 3M is a composite to fill tooth cavities. In the United States, dentists pack a soft material into the hole and blast it with a special beam of light, making it hard as enamel in five seconds. But in the People's Republic, dentists cannot afford the light. The solution is an air-drying composite that does the same thing in two minutes: it takes a little longer but is far less expensive.

• **Help Employees Understand You**—At any given time, more than 30 Asian technicians are in the United States, where they learn the latest product advances while gaining new insight into how the company works. At the same time, they are able to contribute by infusing their insights into company plans and operations.

• **Coordinate by Region**—When designers in Singapore discovered that consumers wanted to use 3M's Nomad household floor mats in their cars, they spread the word to their counterparts in Malaysia and Thailand. Today, the specially made car mats with easy-to-clean vinyl loops are big sellers across Southeast Asia. The company encourages its product managers from different Asian countries to hold regular meetings and share insights and strategies. The goal is to come up with regional programs and "Asianize" a product more quickly.

Source: John R. Engen, "Far Eastern Front," *World Trade,* December 1994, 20–24; "A Survey of Asia," *The Economist,* October 30, 1993.

As seen in the opening vignette, cultural adaptation and the use of the best from different cultures can play a significant role in a company's success. Technological innovation is bringing about the internationalization of all levels of business, and individuals at all levels of the firm are becoming involved in cross-cultural interaction. Firms expanding internationally acquire foreign clients as well as foreign personnel with whom regular communication is necessary, with the result that day-to-day operations require significant cross-cultural competence. As the distinction between domestic and international activities diminishes, cultural sensitivity in varying degrees is required from every employee.

In the past, business managers who did not want to worry about the cultural challenge could simply decide not to do so and concentrate on domestic markets. In today's business environment, a company has no choice but to face international competition. In this new environment, believing that concern about cultural elements is a waste of time often proves to be disastrous.

Cultural differences often are the subject of anecdotes, and business blunders may provide a good laugh. Cultural diversity must be recognized not simply as a fact of life but as a positive benefit; that is, differences may actually propose better solutions to challenges shared. Cultural competence must be recognized as a key management skill.[1] Adjustments will have to be made to accommodate the extraordinary variety in customer preferences and work practices by cultivating the ability to detect similarities and to allow for differences. Ideally, this means that successful ideas can be transferred across borders for efficiency and adjusted to local conditions for effectiveness. Take the case of Nestlé, for example. In one of his regular trips to company headquarters in Switzerland, the general manager of Nestlé Thailand was briefed on a summer coffee promotion from the Greek subsidiary, a cold coffee concoction called the Nescafe Shake. The Thai Group swiftly adopted and adapted the idea. It designed plastic containers to mix the drink and invented a dance, called the Shake, to popularize the activity.[2] Cultural incompetence or inflexibility, however, can easily jeopardize millions of dollars through wasted negotiations, lost purchases, sales, and contracts, and poor customer relations. Furthermore, the internal efficiency of a multinational corporation may be weakened if managers and workers are not "on the same wavelength." **Cultural risk** is just as real as political risk in the international business arena.

The intent of this chapter is to analyze the concept of culture and its various elements and then to provide suggestions for meeting the cultural challenge.

CULTURE DEFINED

Culture gives an individual an anchoring point, an identity, as well as codes of conduct. Of the more than 160 definitions of culture analyzed by Kroeber and Kluckhohn, some conceive of culture as separating humans from nonhumans, some define it as communicable knowledge, and some as the sum of historical achievements produced by man's social life.[3] All of the definitions have common elements: Culture is learned, shared, and transmitted from one generation to the next. Culture is primarily passed on from parents to their children but also transmitted by social organizations, special interest groups, the government, the schools, and churches. Common ways of thinking and behaving that are developed are then reinforced through social pressure. Hofstede calls this the "collective programming of the mind."[4] Culture is also multidimensional, consisting of a number of common elements that are interdependent. Changes occurring in one of the dimensions will affect the others as well.

For the purposes of this text, culture is defined as an integrated system of learned behavior patterns that are characteristic of the members of any given society. It includes everything that a group thinks, says, does, and makes—its customs, language, material artifacts, and shared systems of attitudes and feelings.[5] The definition, therefore, encompasses a wide variety of elements from the materialistic to the spiritual. Culture is inherently conservative, resisting change and fostering continuity. Every person is encultured into a particular culture, learning the "right way" of doing things. Problems may arise when a person encultured in one culture has to adjust to another one. The process of **acculturation**—adjusting and adapting to a specific culture other than one's own—is one of the keys to success in international operations.

Edward T. Hall, who has made some of the most valuable studies on the effects of culture on business, makes a distinction between high- and low-context cultures.[6] In **high-context cultures,** such as Japan and Saudi Arabia, context is at least as important as what is actually said. The speaker and the listener rely on a common understanding of the context. In the **low-context cultures,** however, most of the information is contained explicitly in the words. North American cultures engage in low-context communications. Unless one is aware of this basic difference, messages and intentions can easily be misunderstood. As an example, performance appraisals are typically a human resources function. If performance appraisals are to be centrally guided or conducted in a multinational corporation, those involved must be acutely aware of cultural nuances. One of the interesting differences is that the U.S. system emphasizes the individual's development, whereas the Japanese system focuses on the group within which the individual works. In the United States, criticism is more direct and recorded formally, whereas in Japan it is more subtle and verbal. What is not being said can carry more meaning than what is said.

Few cultures today are as homogeneous as those of Japan and Saudi Arabia. Elsewhere intracultural differences based on nationality, religion, race, or geographic areas have resulted in the emergence of distinct subcultures. The international manager's task is to distinguish relevant cross-cultural and intracultural differences and then to isolate potential opportunities and problems. Good examples are the Hispanic subculture in the United States and the Flemish and the Walloons in Belgium. On the other hand, borrowing and interaction among national cultures may lead to narrowing gaps between cultures. Here the international business entity will act as a **change agent** by introducing new products or ideas and practices. Although this may consist of no more than shifting consumption from one product brand to another, it may lead to massive social change in the manner of consumption, the type of products consumed, and social organization. Consider, for example, that in a 10-year period the international portion of McDonald's annual sales grew from 13 percent to 23 percent. In markets such as Taiwan, the entry of McDonald's and other fast food entities dramatically changed eating habits, especially of the younger generation.

In bringing about change or in trying to cater to increasingly homogeneous demand across markets, the international business entity may be accused of "cultural imperialism," especially if the changes brought about are dramatic or if culture-specific adaptations are not made in management or marketing programs. This is highlighted by Disney's experience in its expansion into Europe in Global Perspective 9.1. Some countries, such as Brazil, Canada, France, and Indonesia, protect their "cultural industries" (such as music and motion pictures) through restrictive rules and subsidies. The 1993 GATT agreement that allows restrictions on exports of U.S. entertainment to Europe is justified by the Europeans as a cultural safety net intended to support a desire to preserve national and regional identities.[7]

THE ELEMENTS OF CULTURE

The study of culture has led to generalizations that may apply to all cultures. Such characteristics are called **cultural universals,** which are manifestations of the total way of life of any group of people. These include such elements as bodily

Global Perspective

9.1
An American Park in Paris

EuroDisneyland, the world's biggest and splashiest theme park, opened April 12, 1992, some 20 miles east of Paris. According to Robert J. Fitzpatrick, the park's chairman, the park was supposed to "help change Europe's chemistry."

Not everyone was as excited about EuroDisneyland's prospects. Many critics in France, which is viewed as half of the theme park's market, have remained hostile. The criticisms have ranged from "not Europe's cup of tea" to a "cultural Chernobyl," a reference to the nuclear disaster in the Ukraine in 1986. Besides criticizing the cultural imperialism of the venture, many have doubted that Europeans would seek an entertainment experience in the suburbs of Paris given diversity in European tastes and the area's grim winter weather. The first year's results were not positive: Low attendance and penny-pinching guests due to Europe's recession resulted in a loss of $514 million.

Part of Disney's optimism about the park was a result of the success of Tokyo Disneyland. "Everything we imported that worked in the United States worked in Japan," said Ronald D. Pogue, managing director of Walt Disney Attractions Japan Ltd. The Europeans posed a totally different challenge, however.

European audiences tend to want more local content in their parks. While the Japanese are fond of American pop culture, Europeans are quite content with their own culture. To them, detail and craftsmanship in a theme park are more important than heart-stopping rides. While Disney's adaptation to European conditions was meticulous, some implementation issues were overlooked. "Everyone arrives at 9:30, leaves at 5:30, and wants lunch at 12:30," noted Michael Eisner, chairman of the Walt Disney Co. This resulted in huge crowds and surly patrons. The negative results in 1993 caused Disney officials to consider closing the $4 billion theme park, but a refinancing agreement saved the park.

Some are hopeful for a brighter future. The opening of the English Channel tunnel in May 1994 was hoped to bring a flood of British tourists. If forecasts for a European economic upturn become reality, the minimum attendance of 11 million for breakeven might easily be reached. At the moment, many others who had intended to develop parks in Europe are scared by the Disney experience.

Sources: "Is Disney Headed for the Euro-Trash Heap?" *Business Week*, January 24, 1994, 52; "Alarm Bells," *The Economist*, January 8, 1994, 5; David J. Jefferson, "Cheap Thrills," *The Wall Street Journal*, March 26, 1993, R11; Sara Khalili, "Is This Another Japanese 'Goofy' Investment?" *North American International Business*, February 1991, 74–75; and John Huey, "America's Hottest Export: Pop Culture," *Fortune*, December 31, 1990, 50–60.

adornment, courtship rituals, etiquette, concept of family, gestures, joking, mealtime customs, music, personal names, status differentiation, and trade customs.[8] These activities occur across cultures, but they may be uniquely manifested in a particular society, bringing about cultural diversity. Common denominators can indeed be found across cultures, but cultures may vary dramatically in how they perform the same activities.[9]

Observation of the major cultural elements summarized in Table 9.1 suggests that these elements are both material (such as tools) and abstract (such as attitudes). The sensitivity and adaptation to these elements by an international firm depends on the firm's level of involvement in the market—for example, licensing versus direct investment—and the product or service marketed. Naturally, some products and services or management practices require very little adjustment, while some have to be adapted dramatically.

Language

Language has been described as the mirror of culture. Language itself is multidimensional by nature. This is true not only of the spoken word but also of what can

TABLE 9.1 Elements of Culture	Language
	Verbal
	Nonverbal
	Religion
	Values and attitudes
	Manners and customs
	Material elements
	Aesthetics
	Education
	Social institutions

be called the nonverbal language of international business. Messages are conveyed by the words used, by how the words are spoken (for example, tone of voice), and through nonverbal means such as gestures, body position, and eye contact.

Very often mastery of the language is required before a person is accultured to a culture other than his or her own. Language mastery must go beyond technical competency because every language has words and phrases that can be readily understood only in context. Such phrases are carriers of culture; they represent special ways a culture has developed to view some aspect of human existence.

Language capability serves four distinct roles in international business.[10] Language is important in information gathering and evaluation. Rather than rely completely on the opinions of others, the manager is able to see and hear personally what is going on. People are far more comfortable speaking their own language, and this should be treated as an advantage. The best intelligence on a market is gathered by becoming part of the market rather than observing it from the outside. For example, local managers of a multinational corporation should be the firm's primary source of political information to assess potential risk. Second, language provides access to local society. Although English may be widely spoken and may even be the official company language, speaking the local language may make a dramatic difference. Third, language capability is increasingly important in company communications, whether within the corporate family or with channel members. Imagine the difficulties encountered by a country manager who must communicate with employees through an interpreter. Finally, language provides more than the ability to communicate. It extends beyond mechanics to the interpretation of contexts.

The manager's command of the national language(s) in a market must be greater than simple word recognition. Consider, for example, how dramatically different English terms can be when used in Australia, the United Kingdom, or the United States. In negotiations, U.S. delegates "tabling a proposal" mean that they want to delay a decision, while their British counterparts understand the expression to mean that immediate action is to be taken. If the British promise something "by the end of the day," this does not mean within 24 hours, but rather when they have completed the job. Additionally, they may say that negotiations "bombed," meaning that they were a success, which to an American could convey exactly the opposite message.

Difficulties with language usually arise through carelessness, which is manifested in a number of translation blunders. The old saying, "If you want to kill a message, translate it," is true. A classic example involves GM and its "Body by Fisher" theme; when translated into Flemish, this became "Corpse by Fisher." Braniff Airlines's "Fly in Leather" was translated as "Fly Naked" for the company's Latin American campaign. There is also the danger of soundalikes. For example, Chanel No. 5 would have fared poorly in Japan had it been called Chanel No. 4, because the Japanese word for four (shih) also sounds like the word for death. This is the reason the IBM's

FIGURE 9.1   **Example of Ads That Transferred Poorly**

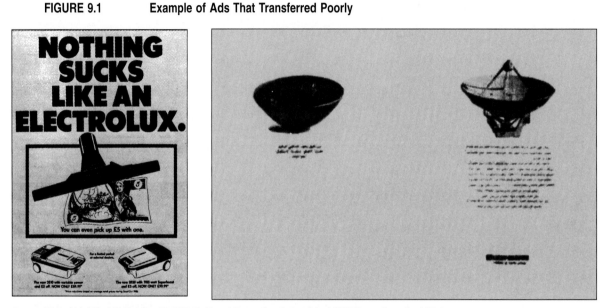

Sources: "Viewpoint," *Advertising Age,* June 29, 1987, 20; Mourad Boutros, "Lost in Translation," *M&M Europe,* September 1992, iv–v.

series 44 computers had a different number classification in Japan than in any other market. The danger of using a translingual homonym also exists; that is, an innocent English word may have strong aural resemblance to a word not used in polite company in another country. Examples in French-speaking areas include Pet milk products and a toothpaste called Cue. A French firm trying to sell pâté to a Baltimore importer experienced a problem with the brand name Tartex, which sounded like shoe polish. Kellogg renamed Bran Buds in Sweden, where the brand name translated roughly to "burned farmer."

The two advertising campaigns presented in Figure 9.1 highlight the difficulties of transferring advertising campaigns across markets. Electrolux's theme for vacuum cleaners is taken literally in the United Kingdom, but in the United States, slang implications interfere with the intended message. With Lucky Goldstar, adaptation into Arabic was carried out without considering that Arabic reads from right to left. As a result, the creative concept in this execution was destroyed.

Another consideration is the capability of language to convey different shades of meaning. As an example, a one-word equivalent to "aftertaste" does not exist in many languages and in others is far-fetched at best. To communicate the idea may require a lengthy translation of "the taste that remains in your mouth after you have finished eating or drinking." If a brand name or an advertising theme is to be extended, care has to be taken to make sure of a comfortable fit. Kellogg's Rice Krispies snap, crackle, and pop in most markets; the Japanese, who have trouble pronouncing those words, watch the caricatures "patchy, pitchy, putchy" in their commercials.

The role of language extends beyond that of a communications medium. Linguistic diversity often is an indicator of other types of diversity. In Quebec, the French language has always been a major consideration of most francophone governments, because it is one of the clear manifestations of the identity of the province vis-à-vis the English-speaking provinces. The Charter of the French Language states that the rights of the francophone collectivity are (1) the right of every person to have the civil administration, semipublic agencies, and business firms communicate with him or her in French; (2) the right of workers to carry on their activities in French; and (3) the right of consumers to be informed and served in French. The Bay, a major Quebec retailer, spends $8 million annually on its translation operations. It has even changed its name to La Baie in appropriate areas.

Dealing with the language problem invariably requires local assistance. A good local advertising agency and a good local market research firm can prevent many problems. When translation is required, as when communicating with suppliers or customers, care should be taken in selecting the translator. One of the simplest methods of control is **backtranslation**—the translating of a foreign language version back to the original language by a different person than the one who made the first translation. This approach may be able to detect only omissions and blunders, however. To assess the quality of the translation, a complete evaluation with testing of the message's impact is necessary.[11]

Nonverbal Language

Managers also must analyze and become familiar with the hidden language of foreign cultures.[12] Five key topics—time, space, material possessions, friendship patterns, and business agreements—offer a starting point from which managers can begin to acquire the understanding necessary to do business in foreign countries. In many parts of the world, time is flexible and not seen as a limited commodity; people come late to appointments or may not come at all. In Hong Kong, for example, it is futile to set exact meeting times, because getting from one place to another may take minutes or hours depending on the traffic situation. Showing indignation or impatience at such behavior would astonish an Arab, Latin American, or Asian. Understanding national and cultural differences in the concept of time is critical for the international business manager.

In some countries, extended social acquaintance and the establishment of appropriate personal rapport are essential to conducting business. The feeling is that one should know one's business partner on a personal level before transactions can occur. Therefore, rushing straight to business will not be rewarded, because deals are made on the basis of not only the best product or price but also the entity or person deemed most trustworthy. Contracts may be bound on handshakes, not lengthy and complex agreements—a fact that makes some, especially Western, businesspeople uneasy.

Individuals vary in the amount of space they want separating them from others. Arabs and Latin Americans like to stand close to people when they talk. If an American, who may not be comfortable at such close range, backs away from an Arab, this might incorrectly be taken as a negative reaction. Also, Westerners are often taken aback by the more physical nature of affection between Slavs—for example, being kissed squarely on the lips by a business partner, regardless of sex.

International body language must be included in the nonverbal language of international business. For example, an American manager may, after successful completion of negotiations, impulsively give a finger-and-thumb OK sign. In southern France, the manager would have indicated that the sale was worthless and, in Japan, that a little bribe had been requested; the gesture would be grossly insulting to Brazilians. An interesting exercise is to compare and contrast the conversation styles of different nationalities. Northern Europeans are quite reserved in using their hands and maintain a good amount of personal space, whereas southern Europeans involve their bodies to a far greater degree in making a point.

Religion

In most cultures, people find in religion a reason for being and legitimacy in the belief that they are of a larger context. To define religion requires the inclusion of the supernatural and the existence of a higher power. Religion defines the ideals for life, which in turn are reflected in the values and attitudes of societies and individuals. Such values and attitudes shape the behavior and practices of institutions and members of cultures.

Religion has an impact on international business that is seen in a culture's values and attitudes toward entrepreneurship, consumption, and social organization. The impact will vary depending on the strength of the dominant religious tenets. While religion's impact may be quite indirect in Protestant Northern Europe, its impact in countries where Islamic fundamentalism is on the rise (such as Algeria) may be profound.

Religion provides the basis for transcultural similarities under shared beliefs and behavior. The impact of these similarities will be assessed in terms of the dominant religions of the world, Christianity, Islam, Hinduism, Buddhism, and Confucianism. While some countries may officially have secularism, such as Marxism-Leninism as a state belief (for example, China, Vietnam, and Cuba), traditional religious beliefs still remain as a powerful force in shaping behavior.

International business managers must be aware of differences not only among the major religions but within those religions. The impact of the divisions may range from hostilities, as in Sri Lanka, to below-the-surface historic suspicion, as in many European countries where Protestant and Catholic are the main divisions. With some religions, such as Hinduism, people may be divided into groups and business managers need to understand the positions and the status of the groups to achieve efficient human resource management.

Christianity has the largest following among world religions, with more than 1.8 billion people.[13] While there are many significant groups within Christianity, the major ones are Catholicism and Protestantism. A prominent difference between the two is the attitude toward making money. While Catholicism has questioned it, the Protestant ethic has emphasized the importance of work and the accumulation of wealth for the glory of God. At the same time, frugality was emphasized and the residual accumulation of wealth from hard work formed the basis for investment. It has been proposed that this is the basis for the development of capitalism in the western world, and the rise of predominantly Protestant countries into world economic leadership in the twentieth century.[14]

Major holidays are often tied to religion. The holidays will be observed differently from one culture to the next, to the extent that the same holiday may have different connotations. Christian cultures observe Christmas and exchange gifts on either December 24 or December 25, with the exception of the Dutch who exchange gifts on St. Nicholas Day, December 6. Tandy Corporation, in its first year in the Netherlands, targeted its major Christmas promotion for the third week of December with less than satisfactory results. The international manager must see to it that local holidays are taken into account in the scheduling of events ranging from fact-finding missions to marketing programs and in preparing local work schedules.

Islam, which reaches from the west coast of Africa to the Philippines and across a broad band that includes Tanzania, central Asia, western China, India, and Malaysia, has more than 1 billion followers.[15] Islam is also a significant minority religion in many parts of the world, including Europe. Islam has a pervasive role in the life of its followers, referred to as Muslims, through the Sharia (law of Islam). This is most obvious in the five stated daily periods of prayer, fasting during the holy month of

Ramadan, and the pilgrimage to Mecca, Islam's holy city. While Islam is supportive of entrepreneurship, it nevertheless discourages strongly acts that may be interpreted as exploitation. Islam is also absent of discrimination, except those outside the religion. Some have argued that Islam's basic fatalism (that is, nothing happens without the will of Allah) and traditionalism have deterred economic development in countries observing the religion.

The role of women in business it tied to religion, especially in the Middle East, where they are not able to function as they would in the West. This affects the conduct of business in various ways; for example, the firm may be limited in its use of female managers or personnel in these markets as expatriates, and women's role as consumers and influencers in the consumption process may be different. Access to women in Islamic countries may only be possible through the use of female sales personnel, direct marketing, and women's specialty shops.[16] Religion impacts products and services, as well. When beef or poultry is exported to an Islamic country, the animal must be killed in the "halal" method and certified appropriately. Recognition of religious restrictions on products (for example, alcoholic beverages) can reveal opportunities, as evidenced by successful launches of several nonalcoholic beverages in the Middle East. Other restrictions may call for innovative solutions. A challenge of the Swedish firm that had the primary responsibility for building a traffic system to Mecca was that non-Muslims are not allowed access to the city. The solution was to use closed-circuit television to supervise the work. Given that Islam considers interest payments usury, bankers and Muslim scholars have worked to create an interest-free banking that relies on lease agreements, mutual funds, and other methods to avoid paying interest.[17]

Hinduism has 750 million followers, mainly in India, Nepal, Malaysia, Guyana, Suriname, and Sri Lanka. It actually is not a religion, but a way of life predicated on which caste, or class, into which one is born. While the caste system has produced social stability, its impact on business can be quite negative. For example, if one cannot rise above one's caste, individual effort is hampered. Problems in work force integration and coordination may become quite severe. Furthermore, the drive for business success may not be forthcoming because of the fact that followers place value mostly on spiritual rather than materialistic achievement.

The family is an important element of Hindu society, with extended families being a norm. The extended family structure will have an impact on the purchasing power and consumption of Hindu families and market researchers, in particular, must take this into account in assessing market potential and consumption patterns.

Buddhism, which extends its influence throughout Asia from Sri Lanka to Japan, has 334 million followers. Although it is an offspring of Hinduism, it has no caste system. Life is seen as an existence of suffering with achieving nirvana, a state marked by an absence of desire, as the solution to the suffering. The emphasis in Buddhism is on spiritual achievement rather than worldly goods.

Confucianism has 150 million followers throughout Asia, especially among the Chinese, and has been characterized as a code of conduct rather than a religion. However, its teachings that stress loyalty and relationships have been broadly adopted. Loyalty to central authority and placing the good of a group before that of the individual may explain the economic success of Japan, South Korea, Singapore, and the Republic of China. It also has led to cultural misunderstandings: in Western societies there has been a perception that the subordination of the individual to the common good has resulted in the sacrifice of human rights. The emphasis on relationships is very evident in developing business ties in Asia. The preparatory stage may take years before the needed level of understanding is reached and actual business transactions can take place.

Values and Attitudes

Values are shared beliefs or group norms that have been internalized by individuals.[18] Attitudes are evaluations of alternatives based on these values. The Japanese culture raises an almost invisible—yet often unscalable—wall against all *gaijin* (foreigners). Many middle-aged bureaucrats and company officials, for example, believe that buying foreign products is downright unpatriotic. The resistance therefore is not so much to foreign products as to those who produce and market them. Similarly, foreign-based corporations have had difficulty in hiring university graduates or mid-career personnel because of bias against foreign employers.

Even under such adverse conditions, the race can be run and won through tenacity, patience, and drive. As an example, Procter & Gamble has made impressive inroads with its products by adopting a long-term, Japanese-style view of profits. Since the mid-1970s, the company has gained some 20 percent of the detergent market and made Pampers a household word among Japanese mothers. The struggle toward such rewards can require foreign companies to take big losses for five years or more.

The more rooted that values and attitudes are in central beliefs (such as religion), the more cautiously the international business manager has to move. Attitudes toward change are basically positive in industrialized countries, whereas in more tradition-bound societies, change is viewed with great suspicion—especially when it comes from a foreign entity. Such situations call for thorough research, most likely a localized approach, and a major commitment at the top level for a considerable period of time.

Cultural differences in themselves can be a selling point suggesting luxury, prestige, or status. Sometimes U.S. companies use domestic marketing approaches when selling abroad because they believe the American look will sell the product. In Japan, Borden sells Lady Borden ice cream and Borden cheese deliberately packaged and labeled in English, exactly as they are in the United States. Similarly, in France, General Foods sells a chewing gum called Hollywood with an accompanying Pepsi-generation type of ad campaign that pictures teenagers riding bicycles on the beach.

Occasionally, U.S. firms successfully use American themes abroad that would not succeed at home. In Japan, Levi Strauss promoted its popular jeans with a television campaign featuring James Dean and Marilyn Monroe, who represent the epitome of Japanese youth's fantasy of freedom from a staid, traditional society. The commercials helped to establish Levi's as *the* prestige jeans, and status-seeking Japanese youth now willingly pay 40 percent more for them than for local brands. Their authentic Levi's, however, are designed and mostly made in Japan, where buyers like a tighter fit than do Americans.[19] At the same time, in the U.S. market many companies have been quite successful emphasizing their foreign, imported image.

Manners and Customs

Changes occurring in manners and customs must be carefully monitored, especially in cases that seem to indicate a narrowing of cultural differences among peoples. Phenomena such as McDonald's and Coke have met with success around the world, but this does not mean that the world is becoming Westernized. Modernization and Westernization are not at all the same, as can be seen in Saudi Arabia, for example.

Understanding manners and customs is especially important in negotiations, because interpretations based on one's own frame of reference may lead to a totally incorrect conclusion. Universal respect is called for in cross-cultural negotiation as seen in the Global Perspective 9.2. To negotiate effectively abroad, all types of commu-

Religions of the World: A Part of Culture

Religious beliefs among 70% or more of the population

Atheist
Buddhism
Confucian
Christian, no major sect
Christian, Lutheran
Christian, Protestant
Christian, Roman Catholic
Hindu
Indigenous
Islam
Judaism
Eastern Orthodox (all)

Source: *The World Factbook 1994.*

Global Perspective

9.2
Negotiating in Europe: Watch Out for the Differences

While the European Union is an economic dynamo with 370 million people and economic power to match any other bloc, it is also a patchwork quilt of different languages and national customs, which makes it far less homogeneous than Japan, the United States, or even Asia as a whole. All of this can make negotiating in Europe a challenge. Businesspeople tend to be relatively reserved and quite formal (especially as compared to their U.S. counterparts). One has to be prepared to wait for the work to begin and for an atmosphere of trust to be created. While any stereotyping of negotiators can be dangerous, broad characterizations do help negotiators as sensitization tools.

Even among the Europeans, if two partners have not taken the trouble to get acquainted or complete their homework, the results can be disastrous. In one case, the Italian director of a construction company went to Germany to negotiate for a project. He began the discussion with a presentation of his company that vaunted its long history and its achievements. The German managers first looked startled, then they excused themselves and walked out the door, without even listening to the offer. The explanation: Germans typically do all the necessary background research before walking in the door. They thought the Italian manager was engaged in idle boasting about his company and they found that offensive. Yet the Italian manager thought he was engaged in a vague preliminary to any real

negotiations. Real negotiating, as far as he was concerned, would not start at least for another day.

The example also illustrates the stark differences between the business styles of the northern and southern Europeans. Northern Europe, with its Protestant tradition and indoor culture, tends to emphasize the technical, the numerical, the tested. Southern Europe, on the other hand, with its Catholic background and open-air lifestyle, tends to favor personal networks, social context, innovation, and flair. Meetings in the south are often longer, but the total decision process may be faster.

The French do not neatly fit into the north-south dichotomy. In a way, the French still embrace the art of diplomatic negotiating invented in France in the fourteenth century. French managers will have carefully prepared for the negotiations, but they generally will begin with some light, logical sparring. Throughout the preliminary and middle stages of negotiating, the French manager will judge the partners carefully on their intellectual skills and their ability to reply quickly and with authority. The details come last in French negotiations, so the finalizing stage can prove to be tricky. French managers tend to slip in little extras when finalizing, like executive bonuses. It is therefore important to insist on what one wants at this stage, even if days have been spent getting to this point.

Source: Alex Blackwell, "Negotiating in Europe," *Hemispheres*, July 1994, 43–47.

nication should be read correctly. Americans often interpret inaction and silence as negative signs. As a result, Japanese executives tend to expect that their silence can get Americans to lower prices or sweeten a deal. Even a simple agreement may take days to negotiate in the Middle East because the Arab party may want to talk about unrelated issues or do something else for a while. The abrasive style of Russian negotiators and their usual last-minute change requests may cause astonishment and concern on the part of ill-prepared negotiators. As another example, consider the reaction of an American businessperson if a Finnish counterpart were to propose continuing negotiations in the sauna or if a Japanese counterpart proposed a karaoke performance be in order. Some of the potential ways in which negotiators may not be prepared include: (1) insufficient understanding of different ways of thinking; (2) insufficient attention to the necessity to save face; (3) insufficient knowledge and appreciation of the host country—its history, culture, government, and image of foreigners; (4) insufficient recognition of the decision-making process and the role of personal relations and personalities; and (5) insufficient allocation of time for negotiations.[20]

In many cultures, certain basic customs must be observed by the foreign businessperson. One of them concerns use of the right and left hands. In so-called right-hand societies, the left hand is the "toilet hand," and using it to eat, for example, is considered impolite. While many managers have caught on to cultural differences in the past decade or so, continued attention to details when approaching companies or when negotiating with their officials is necessary.

Managers must be concerned with differences in the ways products are used. Usage differences have to be translated into product form and promotional decisions. Maxwell House coffee is a worldwide brand name. It is used to sell coffee in both ground and instant form in the United States. In the United Kingdom, Maxwell House is available only in instant form. In France and Germany, it is sold in freeze-dried form only, while in the Scandinavian countries Maxwell House is positioned as the top-of-the-line entry. As a matter of fact, Maxwell House is called simply Maxwell in France and Japan, because "House" is confusing to consumers in those countries. In one South American market, a shampoo maker was concerned about poor sales of the entire product class. Research uncovered the fact that many women wash their hair with bars of soap and use shampoo only as a brief rinse or topper.

Many Western companies have stumbled in Japan because they did not learn enough about the distinctive habits of Japanese consumers. Purveyors of soup should know that the Japanese drink it mainly for breakfast. Johnson & Johnson had relatively little success in selling baby powder until research was conducted on the use conditions of the product. In their small homes, mothers fear that powder will fly around and get into their spotlessly clean kitchens. The company now sells baby powder in flat boxes with powder puffs so that mothers can apply it sparingly. Adults will not use it at all. They wash and rinse themselves before soaking in hot baths; powder would make them feel dirty again. Another classic case involves General Mills's Betty Crocker cake mix. The company designed a mix to be prepared in electric rice cookers. After the product's costly flop, the company found that the Japanese take pride in the purity of their rice, which they thought would be contaminated by cake flavors. General Mills's mistake was comparable to asking an English housewife to make coffee in her teapot.

Package sizes and labels must be adapted in many countries to suit the needs of the particular culture. In Mexico, for example, Campbell's sells soup in cans large enough to serve four or five because families are generally large. In Britain, where consumers are more accustomed to ready-to-serve soups, Campbell's prints "one can makes two" on its condensed soup labels to ensure that shoppers understand how to use it.

Managers must be careful of myths and legends. One candy company had almost decided to launch a new peanut-packed chocolate bar in Japan, aimed at giving teenagers quick energy during the cramming for exams. The company then found out about the Japanese old wives' tale that eating chocolate with peanuts can cause a nosebleed. The launch never took place. Similarly, approaches that would not be considered in the United States or Europe might be recommended in other regions; for example, when Conrad Hotels (the international division of Hilton Hotels) experienced low initial occupancy rates at its Hong Kong facility, they brought in a *fung shui* man. These traditional "consultants" are foretellers of future events and the unknown through occult means, and are used extensively by Hong Kong businesses.[21] In the Hilton's case, the *fung shui* man suggested a piece of sculpture be moved outside from the hotel's lobby because one of the characters in the statue looked like it was trying to run out of the hotel. The hotel's occupancy rate boomed.

Meticulous research plays a major role in avoiding these types of problems. Concept tests determine the potential acceptance and proper understanding of a proposed new product. **Focus groups,** each consisting of 8 to 12 consumers representative of the proposed target audience, can be interviewed and their responses used as disaster checks and to fine-tune research findings. The most sensitive types of products, such as consumer packaged goods, require consumer usage and attitude studies as well as retail distribution studies and audits to analyze the movement of the product to retailers and eventually to households.

Material Elements

Material culture refers to the results of technology and is directly related to how a society organizes its economic activity. It is manifested in the availability and adequacy of the basic economic, social, financial, and marketing infrastructure for the international business in a market. The basic **economic infrastructure** consists of transportation, energy, and communications systems. **Social infrastructure** refers to housing, health, and educational systems prevailing in the country of interest. **Financial** and **marketing infrastructures** provide the facilitating agencies for the international firm's operation in a given market—for example, banks and research firms. In some parts of the world, the international firm may have to be an integral partner in developing the various infrastructures before it can operate, whereas in others it may greatly benefit from their high level of sophistication.

The level of material culture can aid segmentation efforts if the degree of industrialization is used as a basis. For companies selling industrial goods, such as General Electric, this can provide a convenient starting point. In developing countries, demand may be highest for basic energy-generating products. In fully developed markets, time-saving home appliances may be more in demand.

Technological advances have probably been the major cause of cultural change in many countries. For example, the increase in leisure time so characteristic in Western cultures has been a direct result of technological development. With technological advancement comes also **cultural convergence.** Black and white television sets extensively penetrated U.S. households more than a decade before similar levels occurred in Europe and Japan. With color television, the lag was reduced to five years. With video cassette recorders, the difference was only three years, but this time the Europeans and Japanese led the way while the United States was concentrating on cable systems. With the compact disc, penetration rates were equal in only one year. Today, with MTV available by satellite across Europe, no lag exists.[22]

Material culture—mainly the degree to which it exists and how it is esteemed— will have an impact on business decisions. Many exporters do not understand the degree to which Americans are package conscious; for example, cans must be shiny and beautiful. In foreign markets, packaging problems may arise due to the lack of certain materials, different specifications when the material is available, and immense differences in quality and consistency of printing ink, especially in South America and the Third World. Ownership levels of television sets and radios will have an impact on the ability of media to reach target audiences.

Aesthetics

Each culture makes a clear statement concerning good taste, as expressed in the arts and in the particular symbolism of colors, form, and music. What is and what is not acceptable may vary dramatically even in otherwise highly similar markets. Sex, for example, is a big selling point in many countries. In an apparent attempt to preserve the purity of Japanese womanhood, however, advertisers frequently turn to blond, blue-eyed foreign models to make the point. In the same vein, Commodore International, the U.S.-based personal computer manufacturer, chose to sell computers in Germany by showing a naked young man in ads that ran in the German version of *Cosmopolitan.* Needless to say, approaches of this kind would not be possible in the United States because of regulations and opposition from consumer groups.

Color is often used as a mechanism for brand identification, feature reinforcement, and differentiation. In international markets, colors have more symbolic value than in domestic markets. Black, for instance, is considered the color of mourning in the United States and Europe, whereas white has the same symbolic meaning in Japan and most of the Far East. A British bank was interested in expanding its operations to Singapore and wanted to use blue and green as its identification colors. A consulting firm was quick to tell the client that green is associated with death in that country. Although the bank insisted on its original choice of colors, the green was changed to an acceptable shade.[23] Similarly, music used in broadcast advertisements is often adjusted to reflect regional differences.

International firms, such as McDonald's, have to take into consideration local tastes and concerns in designing their facilities. They may have a general policy of uniformity in building or office space design, but local tastes often warrant modifications.

Education

Education, either formal or informal, plays a major role in the passing on and sharing of culture. Educational levels of a culture can be assessed using literacy rates, enrollment in secondary education, or enrollment in higher education available from secondary data sources. International firms also need to know about the qualitative aspects of education, namely varying emphases on particular skills and the overall level of the education provided. Japan and South Korea, for example, emphasize the sciences, especially engineering, to a greater degree than do Western countries.

Educational levels will have an impact on various business functions. Training programs for a production facility will have to take the educational backgrounds of trainees into account. For example, a high level of illiteracy will suggest the use of visual aids rather than printed manuals. Local recruiting for sales jobs will be affected by the availability of suitably trained personnel. In some cases, international firms routinely send locally recruited personnel to headquarters for training.

The international manager may also have to be prepared to overcome obstacles in recruiting a suitable sales force or support personnel. For example, the Japanese culture places a premium on loyalty, and employees consider themselves members of the corporate family. If a foreign firm decides to leave Japan, its employees may find themselves stranded in mid-career, unable to find their place in the Japanese business system. Therefore, university graduates are reluctant to join any but the largest and most well known of foreign firms.[24]

If technology is marketed, the level of sophistication of the product will depend on the educational level of future users. Product adaptation decisions are often influenced by the extent to which targeted customers are able to use the product or service properly.

Social Institutions

Social institutions affect the ways people relate to each other. The family unit, which in Western industrialized countries consists of parents and children, in a number of cultures is extended to include grandparents and other relatives. This will have an impact on consumption patterns and must be taken into account, for example, when conducting market research.

The concept of kinship, or blood relations between individuals, is defined in a very broad way in societies such as those in sub-Saharan Africa. Family relations and a strong obligation to family are important factors to be considered in human resource management in those regions. Understanding tribal politics in countries such as Nigeria may help the manager avoid unnecessary complications in executing business transactions.

The division of a particular population into classes is termed **social stratification.** Stratification ranges from the situation in northern Europe, where most people are members of the middle class, to highly stratified societies in which the higher strata control most of the buying power and decision-making positions.

An important part of the socialization process of consumers worldwide is **reference groups.**[25] These groups provide the values and attitudes that influence and shape behavior. Primary reference groups include the family and coworkers and other intimate acquaintances, while secondary groups are social organizations where less-continuous interaction takes place, such as professional associations and trade organizations. In addition to providing socialization, reference groups develop a person's concept of self, which is manifested, for example, through the choice of products used. Reference groups also provide a baseline for compliance with group norms, giving the individual the option of conforming to or avoiding certain behaviors.

Social organization also determines the roles of managers and subordinates and how they relate to one another. In some cultures, managers and subordinates are separated explicitly and implicitly by various boundaries ranging from social class differences to separate office facilities. In others, cooperation is elicited through equality. For example, Nissan USA has no privileged parking spaces and no private dining rooms, everyone wears the same type of white coveralls, and the president sits in the same room with a hundred other white-collar workers.[26] The fitting of an organizational culture to the larger context of a national culture has to be executed with care. Changes that are too dramatic may cause disruption of productivity or, at the minimum, suspicion.

SOURCES OF CULTURAL KNOWLEDGE

The concept of cultural knowledge is broad and multifaceted. Cultural knowledge can be defined by the way it is acquired. Objective or factual information is obtained from others through communication, research, and education. **Experiential knowledge,** on the other hand, can be acquired only by being involved in a culture other than one's own.[27] A summary of the types of knowledge needed by the international manager is provided in Table 9.2. Both factual and experiential information can be general or country-specific. In fact, the more a manager becomes involved in the international arena, the more he or she is able to develop a metaknowledge; that is, ground rules that apply to a great extent whether in Kuala Lumpur, Malaysia, or Asunción, Paraguay. Market-specific knowledge does not necessarily travel well; the general variables on which the information is based, do.

TABLE 9.2 Types of International Information	Source of Information	Type of Information	
		General	Country Specific
	Objective	Examples: Impact of GDP Regional integration	Examples: Tariff barriers Government regulations
	Experiential	Example: Corporate adjustment to internationalization	Examples: Product acceptance Program appropriateness

TABLE 9.3 Managers' Ranking of Factors Involved in Acquiring International Expertise	Factor	Considered Critical	Considered Important
	1. Business travel	60.8%	92.0%
	2. Assignments overseas	48.8	71.2
	3. Reading/Television	16.0	63.2
	4. Training programs	6.4	28.8
	5. Precareer activities	4.0	16.0
	6. Graduate courses	2.4	15.2
	7. Nonbusiness travel	0.8	12.8
	8. Undergraduate courses	0.8	12.0

Source: Stephen J. Kobrin, International Expertise in American Business (New York: Institute of International Education, 1984), 38.

In a survey of managers on how to acquire international expertise, they ranked eight factors in terms of their importance, as shown in Table 9.3. The managers emphasized the experiential acquisition of knowledge. Written materials were indicated to play an important but supplementary role, very often providing general or country-specific information before operational decisions must be made. Interestingly, many of today's international managers have precareer experience in government, the Peace Corps, the armed forces, or missionary service. Although the survey emphasized travel, a one-time trip to London with a stay at a very large hotel and scheduled sightseeing tours does not contribute to cultural knowledge in a significant way. Travel that involves meetings with company personnel, intermediaries, facilitating agents, customers, and government officials, on the other hand, does contribute.[28]

However, from the corporate point of view, the development of a global capability requires experience acquisition in more involved ways. This translates into foreign assignments and networking across borders, for example, through the use of multicountry, multicultural teams to develop strategies and programs. At Nestlé, for example, managers move around a region (such as Asia or Latin America) at four- or five-year intervals and may have tours at headquarters for two to three years between such assignments. This allows the managers to pick up ideas and tools to be used in markets where they have not been used or where they have not been necessary before. In Thailand, where supermarkets are revolutionizing consumer-goods marketing, techniques perfected elsewhere in the Nestlé system are being put to effective use. The experiences will then, in turn, be used to develop newly emerging markets in the same region, such as Vietnam.

A variety of sources and methods are available to the manager for extending his or her knowledge of specific cultures. Most of these sources deal with factual information that provides a necessary basis for market studies. Beyond the normal business literature and its anecdotal information, specific-country studies are published by the U.S. government, private companies, and universities. The U.S. Department of Commerce's *Overseas Business Reports* cover more than 80 countries, while the Economist Intelligence Unit's *Country Reports* cover 180 countries. *Culturgrams,* which detail the customs of peoples of more than 100 countries, are published by the Center for International and Area Studies at Brigham Young University. Many facilitating agencies—such as accounting firms, advertising agencies, banks, and transportation companies—provide background information on the markets they serve for their clients. These range from the *International Business Guide* series published by Deloitte & Touche, which covers 107 countries and territories, to the Hong Kong and Shanghai Banking Corporation's *Business Profile Series* for 20 countries in the Middle East and the Far East.

Blunders in foreign markets that could have been avoided with factual information are generally inexcusable. A manager who travels to Taipei without first obtaining a visa and is therefore turned back has no one else to blame. Other oversights may lead to more costly mistakes. For example, Brazilians are several inches shorter than the average American, but this was not taken into account when Sears erected American-height shelves that block Brazilian shoppers' view of the rest of the store.

International business success requires not only comprehensive fact finding and preparation but also an ability to understand and appreciate fully the nuances of different cultural traits and patterns. Gaining this readiness requires "getting one's feet wet" over a sufficient length of time.

CULTURAL ANALYSIS

To try to understand and explain differences among cultures and subsequently in cross-cultural behavior, checklists and models showing pertinent variables and their interaction can be developed. An example of such a model is provided in Figure 9.2. Developed by Sheth and Sethi, this model is based on the premise that all international business activity should be viewed as innovation and as producing change processes.[29] After all, multinational corporations introduce management practices as well as products and services from one country to other cultures, where they are perceived to be new and different. Although many question the usefulness of such models, they do bring together, into one presentation, all or most of the relevant variables that have an impact on how consumers in different cultures may perceive, evaluate, and adopt new behaviors. However, any manager using such a tool should periodically cross-check its results with reality and experience.

The key variable of the model is propensity to change, which is a function of three constructs: (1) cultural lifestyle of individuals in terms of how deeply held their traditional beliefs and attitudes are, and also which elements of culture are dominant; (2) change agents (such as multinational corporations and their practices) and strategic-opinion leaders (for example, social elites); and (3) communication about the innovation from commercial sources, neutral sources (such as government), and social sources, such as friends and relatives.

It has been argued that differences in cultural lifestyle can be accounted for by four dimensions of culture.[30] The dimensions consist of (1) individualism ("I" consciousness versus "we" consciousness), (2) power distance (levels of equality in society), (3) uncertainty avoidance (need for formal rules and regulations), and (4) masculinity (attitude toward achievement, roles of men and women).[31] Understanding the implications of the dimensions will help prepare for international business encounters. For example, in negotiating in Germany one can expect a

FIGURE 9.2   **A Model of Cross-Cultural Behavior**

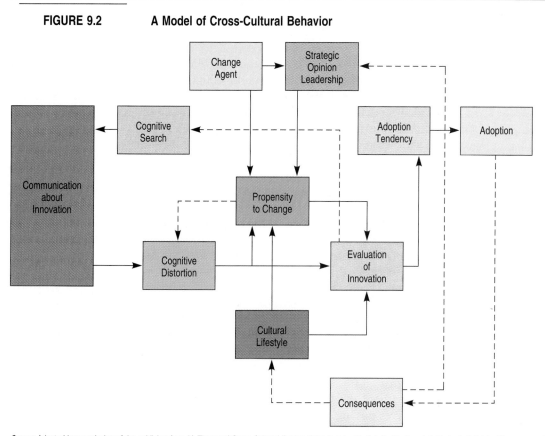

Source: Adapted by permission of the publisher from "A Theory of Cross-Cultural Buying Behavior," by Jagdish N. Sheth and S. Prakash Sethi, in *Consumer and Industrial Buyer Behavior,* eds. Arch G. Woodside, Jagdish N. Sheth, and Peter D. Bennett, 1977, 373. Copyright 1977 by Elsevier Science Publishing Co., Inc.

counterpart who is thorough, systematic, very well prepared, but also rather dogmatic and therefore lacking in flexibility and compromise. Great emphasis is placed on efficiency. In Mexico, however, the counterpart may prefer to address problems on a personal and private basis rather than on a business level. This means more emphasis on socializing and conveying one's humanity, sincerity, loyalty, and friendship. Also, the differences in pace and business practices of the region have to be accepted.[32] Boeing Airplane Company found in its annual study on world aviation safety that countries with both low individualism and substantial power distances had accident rates 2.6 times greater than at the other end of the scale. The findings naturally will have an impact on training and service operations of airlines.[33]

Communication about the innovation takes place through the physical product itself (samples) or through experiencing a new policy in the company. If a new personnel practice, such as quality circles or flextime, is in question, results may be communicated in reports or through word of mouth by the participating employees. Communication content depends on the following factors: the product's or policy's relative advantage over existing alternatives; compatibility with established behavioral patterns; complexity, or the degree to which the product or process is perceived as difficult to understand and use; trialability, or the degree to which it may be experimented with without incurring major risk; and observability, which is the extent to which the consequences of the innovation are visible.

Before the product or policy is evaluated, information about it will be compared with existing beliefs about the circumstances surrounding the situation. Distortion will occur as a result of selective attention, exposure, and retention. As examples, anything foreign may be seen in a negative light, another multinational company's efforts may have failed, or the government may implicitly discourage the proposed activity. Additional information may then be sought from any of the input sources or from opinion leaders in the market.

Adoption tendency refers to the likelihood that the product or process will be accepted. Examples are advertising in the People's Republic of China and equity joint ventures with Western participants in Russia, both of them unheard of a decade ago. If an innovation clears the hurdles, it may be adopted and slowly diffused into the entire market. An international manager has two basic choices: to adapt company offerings and methods to those in the market or to try to change market conditions to fit company programs. In Japan, a number of Western companies have run into obstructions in the Japanese distribution system, where great value is placed on established relationships; everything is done on the basis of favoring the familiar and fearing the unfamiliar. In most cases, this problem is solved by joint ventures with a major Japanese entity that has established contacts. On occasion, when the company's approach is compatible with the central beliefs of a culture, the company may be able to change existing customs rather than adjust to them. Initially, Procter & Gamble's traditional hard-selling style in television commercials jolted most Japanese viewers accustomed to more subtle approaches. Now the ads are being imitated by Japanese competitors.

Although models such as the one in Figure 9.2 may aid in strategy planning by making sure that all variables and their interlinkages are considered, any analysis is incomplete without the basic recognition of cultural differences. Adjusting to differences requires putting one's own cultural values aside. James A. Lee proposes that the natural **self-reference criterion**—the unconscious reference to one's own cultural values—is the root of most international business problems.[34] However, recognizing and admitting this are often quite difficult. The following analytical approach is recommended to reduce the influence of one's own cultural values:

1. Define the problem or goal in terms of the domestic cultural traits, habits, or norms.
2. Define the problem or goal in terms of the foreign cultural traits, habits, or norms. Make no value judgments.
3. Isolate the self-reference criterion influence in the problem, and examine it carefully to see how it complicates the problem.
4. Redefine the problem without the self-reference criterion influence, and solve for the optimum-goal situation.

This approach can be applied to product introduction. If Kellogg's wants to introduce breakfast cereals into markets where breakfast is traditionally not eaten or where consumers drink very little milk, managers must consider very carefully how to instill the new habit. The traits, habits, and norms concerning the importance of breakfast are quite different in the United States, France, and Brazil, and they have to be outlined before the product can be introduced. In France, Kellogg's commercials are aimed as much at providing nutrition lessons as they are at promoting the product. In Brazil, the company advertised on a soap opera to gain entry into the market, because Brazilians often emulate the characters of these television shows.

Analytical procedures require constant monitoring of changes caused by outside events as well as the changes caused by the business entity itself. Controlling **eth-**

nocentrism—the tendency to consider one's own culture superior to others—can be achieved only by acknowledging it and properly adjusting to its possible effects in managerial decision making. The international manager needs to be prepared and able to put that preparedness to effective use.[35]

THE TRAINING CHALLENGE

International managers face a dilemma in terms of international and intercultural competence. The lack of adequate foreign language and international business skills have cost U.S. firms lost contracts, weak negotiations, and ineffectual management. A UNESCO study of 10- to 14-year-old students in nine countries placed Americans next to last in their comprehension of foreign cultures. Even when cultural awareness is high, there is room for improvement. For example, a survey of European executives found that a shortage of international managers was considered the single most important constraint on expansion abroad.[36] The increase in the overall international activity of firms has increased the need for cultural sensitivity training at all levels of the organization. Further, today's training must take into consideration not only outsiders to the firm but interaction within the corporate family as well. However inconsequential the degree of interaction may seem, it can still cause problems if proper understanding is lacking. Consider, for example, the date 11/12/96 on a telex; a European will interpret this as the 11th of December, an American as the 12th of November.

Some companies try to avoid the training problem by hiring only nationals or well-traveled Americans for their international operations. This makes sense for the management of overseas operations but will not solve the training need, especially if transfers to a culture unfamiliar to the manager are likely. International experience may not necessarily transfer from one market to another.

To foster cultural sensitivity and acceptance of new ways of doing things within the organization, management must institute internal education programs. The programs may include (1) culture-specific information (data covering other countries, such as videopacks and culturegrams), (2) general cultural information (values, practices, and assumptions of countries other than one's own), and (3) self-specific information (identifying one's own cultural paradigm, including values, assumptions, and perceptions about others).[37] One study found that Japanese assigned to the United States get mainly language training as preparation for the task. In addition, many companies use mentoring, whereby an individual is assigned to someone who is experienced and who will spend the required time squiring and explaining. Talks given by returnees and by visiting lecturers hired specifically for the task round out the formal part of training.[38]

The objective of formal training programs is to foster the four critical characteristics of preparedness, sensitivity, patience, and flexibility in managers and other personnel. The programs vary dramatically in terms of their rigor, involvement, and, of course, cost.[39] A summary of the programs is provided in Figure 9.3.

Environmental briefings and cultural-orientation programs are types of **area studies** programs. The programs provide factual preparation for a manager to operate in, or work with people from, a particular country. Area studies should be a basic prerequisite for other types of training programs. Alone, areas studies serve little practical purpose because they do not really get the manager's feet wet. Other, more involved programs contribute the context in which to put facts so that they can be properly understood.

The **cultural assimilator** is a program in which trainees must respond to scenarios of specific situations in a particular country. The programs have been devel-

**FIGURE 9.3
Cross-Cultural Training
Methods**

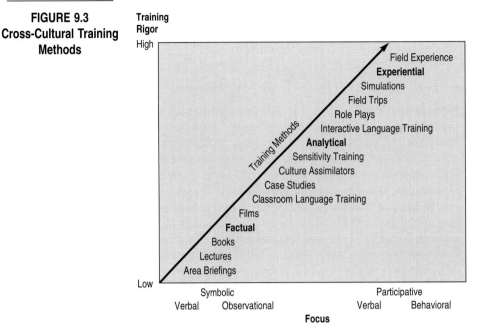

Source: J. Stewart Black and Mark Mendenhall, "A Practical but Theory-Based Framework for Selecting Cross-Cultural Training Methods," in *International Human Resource Management,* eds. Mark Mendenhall and Gary Oddou (Boston: PWS-Kent, 1991), 188.

oped for the Arab countries, Iran, Thailand, Central America, and Greece.[40] The results of the trainees' assimilator experience are evaluated by a panel of judges. This type of program has been used in particular in cases of transfers abroad on short notice.

When more time is available, managers can be trained extensively in language. This may be required if an exotic language is involved. **Sensitivity training** focuses on enhancing a manager's flexibility in situations that are quite different from those at home. The approach is based on the assumption that understanding and accepting oneself is critical to understanding a person from another culture. Finally, training may involve **field experience,** which exposes a manager to a different cultural environment for a limited amount of time. While this approach is expensive, it is used by some companies, as seen in Global Perspective 9.3.

One field experience technique that has been suggested when the training process needs to be rigorous is the host-family surrogate. This technique places a trainee (and possibly his or her family) in a domestically located family of the nationality to which they are assigned.[41]

Regardless of the degree of training, preparation, and positive personal characteristics, a manager will always remain foreign. A manager should never rely on his or her own judgment when local managers can be consulted. In many instances, a manager should have an interpreter present at negotiations, especially if the manager is not completely bilingual. Overconfidence in one's language capabilities can create problems.

SUMMARY

Culture is one of the most challenging elements of the international marketplace. This system of learned behavior patterns characteristic of the members of a given

Global Perspective

9.3
Learning the Strange Foreign Ways

Samsung, Korea's largest conglomerate, has launched an internationalization campaign. The company wants to be culturally more sensitive, and not just to avoid gaffes. It believes that learning more about foreign countries can make its products more competitive. And it is not alone in these activities. A generation of Korean managers came of age thinking that if they built it, they could sell it. Today's international competitive environment requires more.

The programs have taken various forms. At Kumho Group, the chairman has ordered all employees of the airline and tire maker to spend an hour each morning learning a language or learning more about foreign cultures. Cards taped up in bathrooms teach a phrase a day of English or Japanese. At Samsung, overseas-bound managers attend a month-long boot camp where they are awakened at 5:50 a.m. for a job, meditation, and then lessons on issues such as table manners or avoiding sexual harassment. For example, students are taught not to ask female job applicants whether they are married or when they intend to marry, or their age or religion.

Samsung is sending 400 of its brightest junior employees overseas for a year. Their mission is not 100 percent business either. "International exposure is important, but you have to develop an appreciation of the foreign en-

vironment as well. You have to goof off at the mall, watch people, and develop international tastes," say Samsung officials. The program costs about $80,000 a year per person and takes key people out of circulation. But Samsung is convinced that cultural immersion will pay off in more astute judgments about what customers want. One concrete result is that the company is tailoring more products for specific overseas markets despite resistance of engineers in Seoul. "They want one model to sell to everyone. But they are accepting the concept now," state Samsung marketers. Much of that change has been attributed to people like Park Sang Jin, who had been overseas for 15 years, mostly in the United States. "If we do not do this type of concept, we will never catch up with our competitors," he stated.

Samsung employees coming back from overseas see much work to be done. After five years in Paris, Kim Jeong Kyu recognizes that time abroad has changed him. Now back in Seoul, he is trying to change Samsung—and having problems. "Even if I have a good idea, I will not suggest it too fast," Kim said. "They will say, 'He doesn't know the Korean situation. Maybe it will work in France, but not here.'"

Source: "Sensitivity Kick," *The Wall Street Journal,* December 30, 1992, 1, 4.

society is constantly shaped by a set of dynamic variables: language, religion, values and attitudes, manners and customs, aesthetics, technology, education, and social institutions. To cope with this system, an international manager needs both factual and interpretive knowledge of culture. To some extent, the factual knowledge can be learned; its interpretation comes only through experience.

The most complicated problems in dealing with the cultural environment stem from the fact that one cannot learn culture—one has to live it. Two schools of thought exist in the business world on how to deal with cultural diversity. One is that business is business the world around, following the model of Pepsi and McDonald's. In some cases, globalization is a fact of life; however, cultural differences are still far from converging.

The other school proposes that companies must tailor business approaches to individual cultures. Setting up policies and procedures in each country has been compared to an organ transplant; the critical question centers around acceptance or rejection. The major challenge to the international manager is to make sure that rejection is not a result of cultural myopia or even blindness.

Fortune examined the international performance of a dozen large companies that earn 20 percent or more of their revenue overseas.[42] The internationally successful companies all share an important quality: patience. They have not rushed into situations but rather built their operations carefully by following the most basic business principles. These principles are to know your adversary, know your audience, and know your customer.

Key Terms and Concepts

cultural risk	social infrastructure
acculturation	financial infrastructure
high-context cultures	marketing infrastructure
low-context cultures	cultural convergence
change agent	social stratification
cultural universals	reference groups
backtranslation	experiential knowledge
Christianity	self-reference criterion
Islam	ethnocentrism
Hinduism	area studies
Buddhism	cultural assimilator
Confucianism	sensitivity training
focus groups	field experience
economic infrastructure	

Questions for Discussion

1. Comment on the assumption, "If people are serious about doing business with you, they will speak English."

2. You are on your first business visit to Germany. You feel confident about your ability to speak the language (you studied German in school and have taken a refresher course), and you decide to use it. During introductions, you want to break the ice by asking "Wie geht's?" and insisting that everyone call you by your first name. Speculate as to the reaction.

3. Q: "What do you call a person who can speak two languages?"
   A: "Bilingual."
   Q: "How about three?"
   A: "Trilingual."
   Q: "Excellent. How about one?"
   A: "Hmmmm. . . . American!"
   Is this joke malicious, or is there something to be learned from it?

4. What can be learned about a culture from reading and attending to factual materials?

5. Given the tremendous increase in international business, where will companies in a relatively early stage of the internationalization process find the personnel to handle the new challenges?

6. Management at a U.S. company trying to market tomato paste in the Middle East did not know that, translated into Arabic, "tomato paste" is "tomato glue." How could it have known in time to avoid problems?

7. Provide examples of how the self-reference criterion might manifest itself.

8. Is any international business entity not a cultural imperialist? How else could one explain the phenomenon of multinational corporations?

Recommended Readings

Axtell, Roger E. *Do's and Taboos Around the World.* New York: John Wiley & Sons, 1993.

Bache, Ellyn. *Culture Clash.* Yarmouth, Maine: Intercultural Press, 1990.

Brislin, R. W., W. J. Lonner, and R. M. Thorndike. *Cross-Cultural Research Methods.* New York: Wiley, 1973.

Catlin, Linda, and Thomas White. *Cultural Sourcebook and Case Studies.* Cincinnati: South-Western, 1994.

Copeland, Lennie, and Lewis Griggs. *Going International: How to Make Friends and Deal Effectively in the Global Marketplace.* New York: Random House, 1985.

Fisher, Glen. *International Negotiation.* Yarmouth, Maine: Intercultural Press, 1986.

Hall, Edward T., and Mildred Reed Hall. *Understanding Cultural Differences.* Yarmouth, Maine: Intercultural Press, 1990.

O'Hara-Devereaux, Mary, and Robert Johansen. *Global Work: Bridging Distance, Culture, and Time.* San Francisco: Jossey-Bass Publishers, 1994.

Storti, Craig. *The Art of Crossing Cultures.* Yarmouth, Maine: Intercultural Press, 1990.

Terpstra, Vern, and Keith David. *The Cultural Environment of International Business.* Cincinnati: South-Western, 1991.

U.S. Department of Commerce. *International Business Practices.* Washington, D.C.: U.S. Government Printing Office, 1993.

Weiss, Joseph. *Regional Cultures, Managerial Behavior, and Entrepreneurship.* Westport, Conn.: Quorum Books, 1988.

Notes

1. Mary O'Hara-Devereaux and Robert Johansen, *Global Work: Bridging Distance, Culture, and Time* (San Francisco: Jossey-Bass Publishers, 1994), 11.

2. Carla Rapoport, "Nestlé's Brand-Building Machine," *Fortune,* September 19, 1994, 147–156.

3. Alfred Kroeber and Clyde Kluckhohn, *Culture: A Critical Review of Concepts and Definitions* (New York: Random House, 1985), 11.

4. Geert Hofstede, "National Cultures Revisited," *Asia–Pacific Journal of Management* 1 (September 1984): 22–24.

5. Robert L. Kohls, *Survival Kit for Overseas Living* (Chicago: Intercultural Press, 1979), 3.

6. Edward T. Hall, *Beyond Culture* (Garden City, N.Y.: Anchor Press, 1976), 15.

7. Michael T. Malloy, "America, Go Home," *The Wall Street Journal,* March 26, 1993, R7.

8. George P. Mundak, "The Common Denominator of Cultures," in *The Science of Man in the World,* ed. Ralph Linton (New York: Columbia University Press, 1945), 123–142.

9. Philip R. Harris and Robert T. Moran, *Managing Cultural Differences* (Houston: Gulf, 1987), 201.

10. David A. Ricks, *Big Business Blunders* (Homewood, Ill.: Irwin, 1983), 4.

11. Margareta Bowen, "Business Translation," *Jerome Quarterly* (August–September 1993): 5–9.

12. Edward T. Hall, "The Silent Language of Overseas Business," *Harvard Business Review* 38 (May–June 1960): 87–96.

13. *Statistical Abstract of the United States* (Washington, D.C.: U.S. Government Printing Office, 1994): 855.

14. David McClelland, *The Achieving Society* (New York: Irvington, 1961): 90.

15. *World Almanac and the Book of Facts* (Mahwah, N.J.: Funk & Wagnalls, 1995), 734.

16. Mushtaq Luqmami, Zahir A. Quraeshi, and Linda Delene, "Marketing in Islamic Countries: A Viewpoint," *MSU Business Topics* 23 (Summer 1980): 17–24.

17. "Islamic Banking: Faith and Creativity," *New York Times,* April 8, 1994, D1, D6.

18. James F. Engel, Roger D. Blackwell, and Paul W. Miniard, *Consumer Behavior* (Hinsdale, Ill.: Dryden, 1986), 223.

19. "Learning How to Please the Baffling Japanese," *Fortune,* October 5, 1981, 122.

20. Sergey Frank, "Global Negotiations: Vive Les Differences!" *Sales and Marketing Management* 144 (May 1992): 64–69.

21. "Fung Shui Man Orders Sculpture Out of Hotel," *South China Morning Post,* July 27, 1992, 4.

22. Kenichi Ohmae, "Managing in a Borderless World," *Harvard Business Review* 67 (May–June 1989): 152–161.

23. Joe Agnew, "Cultural Differences Probed to Create Product Identity," *Marketing News,* October 24, 1986, 22.

24. Joseph A. McKinney, "Joint Ventures of United States Firms in Japan: A Survey," *Venture Japan* 1 (1988): 14–19.

25. Engel, Blackwell, and Miniard, *Consumer Behavior,* 318–324.

26. "The Difference That Japanese Management Makes," *Business Week,* July 14, 1986, 47–50.

27. James H. Sood and Patrick Adams, "Model of Management Learning Styles as a Predictor of Export Behavior and Performance," *Journal of Business Research* 12 (June 1984): 169–182.

28. Stephen J. Kobrin, *International Expertise in American Business* (New York: Institute of International Education, 1984), 36.

29. Jagdish N. Sheth and S. Prakash Sethi, "A Theory of Cross-Cultural Buying Behavior," in *Consumer and Industrial Buying Behavior,* eds. Arch G. Woodside, Jagdish N. Sheth, and Peter D. Bennett (New York: Elsevier North-Holland, 1977), 369–386.

30. Geert Hofstede, *Culture's Consequences: International Differences in Work-Related Values* (Beverly Hills, Calif.: Sage Publications, 1984), Chapter 1.

31. For applications of the framework, see Sudhir H. Kale, "Culture-Specific Marketing Communications," *International Marketing Review* 8, No. 2 (1991): 18–30; and Sudhir H. Kale, "Distribution Channel Relationships in Diverse Cultures," *International Marketing Review* 8, No. 3 (1991): 31–45.

32. Frank, "Global Negotiations: Vive Les Differences!"

33. "Building a 'Cultural Index' to World Airline Safety," *The Washington Post,* August 21, 1994, A8.

34. James A. Lee, "Cultural Analysis in Overseas Operations," *Harvard Business Review* 44 (March–April 1966): 106–114.

35. Peter D. Fitzpatrick and Alan S. Zimmerman, *Essentials of Export Marketing* (New York: American Mangement Organization, 1985), 16.

36. "Expansion Abroad: The New Direction for European Firms," *International Management* 41 (November 1986): 20–26.

37. W. Chan Kim and R. A. Mauborgne, "Cross-Cultural Strategies," *Journal of Business Strategy* 7 (Spring 1987): 28–37.

38. Mauricio Lorence, "Assignment USA: The Japanese Solution," *Sales and Marketing Management* 144 (October 1992): 60–66.

39. Rosalie Tung, "Selection and Training of Personnel for Overseas Assignments," *Columbia Journal of World Business* 16 (Spring 1981): 68–78.

40. Harris and Moran, *Managing Cultural Differences,* 267–295.

41. Simcha Ronen, "Training the International Assignee," in *Training and Career Development,* ed. I. Goldstein (San Francisco: Jossey-Bass, 1989), 426–440.

42. Kenneth Labich, "America's International Winners," *Fortune,* April 14, 1986, 34–46.

CHAPTER 10

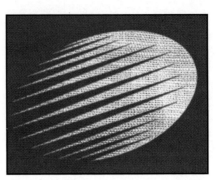

Economies in Transition

1. To understand the special concerns that must be considered by the international manager when dealing with emerging market economies.

2. To survey the vast opportunities for trade offered by emerging market economies.

3. To understand why economic change is difficult and requires much adjustment.

4. To become aware that privatization offers new opportunities for international trade and investment.

A Study of Two Transition Strategies

Both China and Russia are transforming their economies, making them more market oriented. The adjustments under way could precipitate massive changes in the global economy and are therefore watched closely by the world.

Of particular interest are the differing approaches toward market orientation used by China and Russia. Both are moving away from centrally planned, socialist systems toward capitalist, profit-driven systems. China has adopted a policy of gradualism, implementing change step-by-step, a little at a time. In contrast, the economic changes in Russia have come quickly.

So how is each country performing? Chinese industrial production was growing at 13 percent in early 1995, while Russia's economic output shrank almost 14 percent for the year. Street vendors in Beijing can be seen hawking fresh grapes in winter at affordable prices, and nearby shops sell fancy mountain bikes. The leading businesses in Moscow appear to be prostitution and casino gambling. What does all of this mean for the question of which strategy works best in developing societies? Do economic reforms work best if they are introduced in a single "Big Bang," or should they be measured out in tiny doses? From the evidence, it would appear that Chinese-style gradualism is the strategy to adopt. William Overholt, a Hong Kong–based investment banker, agrees: "The notion that one can have all good things—democracy and all forms of liberalization—instantly and simultaneously [is] a deeply held belief that has no grounding in practical historical experience." However, not everyone sees Russia's situation as definitive proof against quick and sudden change. Given the differences between the Russian and Chinese economies, some experts argue that meaningful comparisons are impossible. In a recent essay, the noted economists Jeffrey Sachs and Wing Thye

Woo stated that those wanting Russia to follow China's gradualism "might as well advise Russia to solve its agricultural problems by shifting from wheat to rice."

The "gradualists," however, stick to their proposition: Shock therapy unleashes chaos. Firms being privatized too quickly causes confusion about ownership, management responsibilities, product liability, and production strategy. Inflation is almost certain if prices are liberalized too quickly. If the central bank clamps down on the money supply to keep inflation low, unproductive enterprises will go bankrupt, workers will be stripped of their livelihoods, and social chaos will quickly follow. One Chinese leader has said that a socialist without a plan is like a bird without a cage—sure to fly away.

Once again, however, the differences between Russia's situation and China's are most important. During the early days of Chinese reform in the 1970s, 70 percent of labor was in agriculture, while less than 20 percent was in industry. The development solution was simple—do away with the agricultural collectives and turn the farmland over to the peasants. On the other hand, during Gorbachev's perestroika, more than half of Russia's labor was in industry and only 14 percent was in agriculture. The issue for Russia has therefore been how to transform a tangle of rusty, inefficient, defense-oriented heavy industries supported by cheap credit from the state into lean, self-supporting producers of consumer goods—a task much different from and more complex than China's mission.

The difference that has arisen in China, according to many experts, is that the state concerns are tiny stones that are being submerged rapidly in the rising tide of the private sector. In Russia, however, such enterprises are hulking islands that cannot be washed away easily.

Sources: Clay Chandler, "In Beijing and Moscow, Starkly Different Policies and Results," *The Washington Post,* January 30, 1994, H1, H5; "Emerging Market Indicators," *The Economist,* March 18, 1995, 110.

This chapter addresses major societal, economic, and ideological shifts that have occurred in the global economy. The focus is on the emerging democracies of central Europe and the new countries that were the former Soviet Union. In addition, economic change in large emerging markets such as China, Southeast Asia, and Latin America are presented and the role of privatization is discussed. The focus rests with the formerly centrally planned economies due to significant shifts in ideology and economic thinking that have taken place there. As this chapter's opening vignette showed, the transformations have taken on various paths and have led to important changes that have important implications for the international business manager, in terms of both opportunities and risks. Privatization is addressed because the transition of corporations from government ownership into private hands presents new opportunities for market growth and for international trade and investment.

The chapter begins with a brief description of the historical economic structures in the emerging democracies. Subsequently, we explore the realities of economic change and the challenges and opportunities facing the international manager. Joint ventures between Western firms and emerging market economies are proliferating and are therefore an important part of the future trade relationship between countries and firms. This subject will be discussed in greater detail in Chapter 13.

DOING BUSINESS WITH EMERGING MARKET ECONOMIES

The major market economies emerging out of formerly centrally planned economies are Russia and the now independent states of the former Soviet Union, East Germany (now unified with West Germany), the eastern and central European nations (Albania, Bulgaria, the Czech and Slovak Republics, Hungary, Poland, and Romania), and the People's Republic of China.

It is a common belief that business ties between the Western world and these nations are a new phenomenon. That is not the case. In the 1920s, for example, General Electric and RCA helped to develop the Soviet electrical and communications industries. Ford constructed a huge facility in Nizhni Novgorod to build Model A cars and buses. DuPont introduced its technology to Russia's chemical industry. Conversely, Tungsram in Hungary conducted research and development for General Electric. However, by the mid-1930s most American companies had withdrawn from the scene or had been forced to leave. Since then, former centrally planned economies and Western corporations engaged in international business have had rather limited contact.[1]

To a large extent, this limited contact has been the result of an ideological wariness on both sides. Socialist countries often perceived international corporations as "aggressive business organizations developed to further the imperialistic aims of Western, especially American, capitalists the world over."[2] Furthermore, many aspects of capitalism, such as the private ownership of the means of production, were seen as exploitative and antithetical to communist ideology. Western managers, in turn,

A bus shelter in Moscow's Red Square advertising foreign products is evidence of business opportunities in Russia's newly freed economy.

Source: Robert Harding Picture Library/London.

Emerging Economies of Central and Eastern Europe

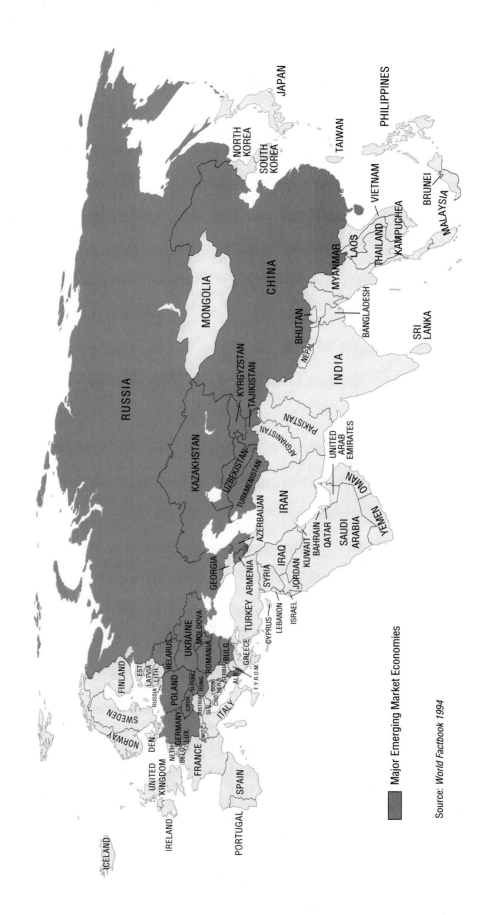

Major Emerging Market Economies

Source: *World Factbook 1994*

often saw socialism as a threat to the Western world and the capitalist system in general.

Over time, these rigid stances were modified on both sides. Decision makers in former centrally planned economies recognized the need to purchase products and technology that were unavailable domestically or that could be produced only at a substantial comparative disadvantage. They were determined to achieve economic growth and improve the very much neglected standard of living in their society, and decided that the potential benefits of cooperation in many instances outweighed the risks of decentralized economic power and reduced reliance on plans. As a result, government planners in former socialist economies began to include some market considerations in their activities and opened up their countries to Western businesses.

At the same time, the greater openness on the part of these governments resulted in more flexibility of Western government restrictions on East-West trade. The drive toward modernization of production and growing consumer demand greatly raised the attractiveness of doing business with the newly emerging democracies (NEDs). Furthermore, many Western firms experienced a need to diversify their international business activities. Faced at home with stagnant markets and increased labor costs, these firms were eager to cultivate newly arising market opportunities.[3] The large populations and pent-up demand of the NEDs offered those opportunities.

A Brief Historic Review

Due to differing politics and ideology, the trade history of socialist countries is quite different from that of the United States and the West. The former Soviet system of foreign trade dates to a decree signed by Lenin on April 22, 1918. It established that the state would have a monopoly on foreign trade and that all foreign trade operations were to be concentrated in the hands of organizations specifically authorized by the state. The organizations served as the basis for all trade, economic, scientific, and technical transactions with foreign countries.[4] This system of a state-controlled monopoly was also adopted by the East European satellites of the Soviet Union and by the People's Republic of China.

In effect, this trade structure isolated the firms and consumers in socialist economies from the West and unlinked demand from supply. Any international transaction was cumbersomely reviewed by foreign trade organizations (FTOs), ministries, and a multitude of state committees. In addition, rigid state bureaucracies regulated the entire economy. Over time, domestic economic problems emerged. In spite of some top-down and bottom-up planning interaction, the lack of attention to market forces resulted in misallocated resources, and the lack of competition promoted inefficiency. Centralized allocation prevented the emergence of effective channels of distribution. Managers of plants were more concerned with producing the quantities stipulated by a rigid **central plan** (often five-year plans, one following another) than with producing the products and the quality desired. Overfulfillment of the plan was discouraged because it would result in a quota increase for the following year. Entrepreneurship was disdained, innovation risky. Consequently, socialist economies achieved only lackluster growth, and their citizens fell far behind the West in their standard of living.

In the early 1980s, the economic orientation of centrally planned economies began to shift. Hungary and Poland started to cautiously encourage their firms to develop an export-oriented strategy. Exporting itself was nothing new, because much trade took place among the countries belonging to the communist bloc. What was new was the fact that the government policy emphasized trade with the West and increasingly exposed domestic enterprises to the pressure of international competition.[5] In addition, socialist countries began to import more equipment from the West and started to encourage direct investment from foreign firms.

In the mid-1980s, the Soviet Union developed two new political and economic programs: **perestroika** and **glasnost.** Perestroika was to fundamentally reform the Soviet economy by improving the overall technological and industrial base as well as the quality of life for Soviet citizens through increased availability of food, housing, and consumer goods. Glasnost was to complement those efforts by encouraging the free exchange of ideas and discussion of problems, pluralistic participation in decision making, and increased availability of information.[6]

The major domestic steps were followed shortly by legislative measures that thoroughly reformed the Soviet foreign-trade apparatus. In a major move away from previous trade centralization, national agencies, large enterprises, and research institutes were authorized to handle their own foreign transactions directly. A 1987 decree asserted that it was essential to develop economic ties with the capitalist world in order to use the advantages of the world division of labor, to strengthen the position of the USSR in international trade, and to introduce the achievements of world science and technology into the national economy.[7] By 1989, all Soviet enterprises that could compete in foreign markets were permitted to apply for independent trading rights.

Concurrent with the steps taken in the Soviet Union, other socialist countries also initiated major reforms affecting international business. China began to launch major programs of modernization and developed multinational corporations of its own. Virtually all socialist countries began to invite foreign investors to form joint ventures in their countries to help satisfy both domestic and international demand and started to privatize state enterprises.

THE DEMISE OF THE SOCIALIST SYSTEM

By late 1989, all the individual small shifts resulted in the emergence of a new economic and geopolitical picture. With an unexpected suddenness, the Iron Curtain disappeared, and, within less than three years, the communist empire ceased to exist. Virtually overnight, eastern Europe and the former Soviet Union, with their total population of 400 million and a combined GNP of $3 trillion,[8] shifted their political and economic orientations toward a market economy. The former socialist satellites shed their communist governments. Newly elected democratic governments decided to let market forces shape their economies. East Germany was unified with West Germany. In March 1992, Hungary was admitted as an associate member of the European Union. The Czech Republic, Slovakia, and Poland announced their desire to achieve full convertibility of their currencies and to join the GATT system. By 1992, the entire Soviet Union had disappeared. Individual regions within the Commonwealth of Independent States reasserted their independence and autonomy, resulting in a host of emerging nations, often heavily dependent on one another, but now separated by nationalistic feelings and political realities.

The political changes were accompanied by major economic action. Externally, trade flows were redirected from the former Soviet Union toward the European Union as Figure 10.1 shows. Internally, austerity programs were introduced and prices of subsidized products were adjusted upward to avoid distorted trade flows due to distorted prices. Wages were kept in check to reduce inflation. Entire industries were

**FIGURE 10.1
A Reorientation
of Trade**

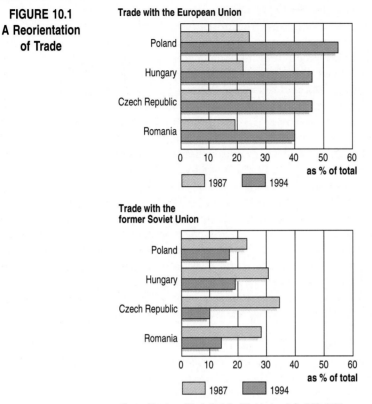

Source: Directory of Trade Statistics (Washington, D.C.: IMF), 1994.

either privatized or closed down. These steps led to a significant decrease in the standard of living of the population. Initially, the support for the internal economic transformation continued, demonstrating the great desire on the part of individuals and governments to participate in the world marketplace, and the hope that these transformations would achieve a better standard of living. Over time, however, increasing economic difficulties precipitated large levels of discontent, and, by some, a desire for a return to the old days. As a result, some countries have experienced civil and political strife, and the reemergence of political hard-liners. Economic progress will be a crucial component of democratic political stability. But these nations need to determine for themselves whether they want to continue on the arduous path toward liberalization. They will have to decide whether the pain of transition is worth the promise of democracy and free markets.[9]

Due to military intervention, China did not undergo such radical political shifts. However, its economic changes were of similar significance. New enterprise zones were opened, designed to produce products targeted for export. Foreign investors were invited. Individuals were permitted to translate their entrepreneurial skills into action and keep the profits. As Global Perspective 10.1 shows, a new perspective has permeated business and the economy.

From a Western perspective, all these changes indicated the end of the Cold War. After the ebbing of initial euphoria, it was also learned and understood that the shouts for democracy were, to a large degree, driven not only by political but also by economic desires. Freedom meant not only the right to free elections but also

Global Perspective

10.1
Private Business Clubs in China

Business club elitism seems to be an idea that goes down well in nominally socialist China where access and contacts are the keys to success. Twenty business, private, and country clubs are either open or in the works in Beijing, all vying for membership among foreign executives, Chinese tycoons, and government officials. One estimate is that there are more than 60 business and golf clubs under construction across the country.

New clubs market their prestige and facilities fiercely, advertising in print and over the radio, offering free trips and pitching enrollment in limited memberships as an investment that will pay off handsomely in the future. "I am beseiged with calls from these clubs; I refuse to speak to them anymore," said an American banking executive.

The Capital Club, perched on the fiftieth floor near a north Beijing diplomatic enclave, boasts a panoramic view of the smoggy Chinese capital. This club is the latest entry, with a mini who's who of Beijing government and business. In addition to a wood-paneled ambience and dining areas designed like boardrooms, the club also has a recreation center with a glass-domed swimming pool, bowling lanes, billiard tables, and a golf simulator. The membership fees of $7,500 for corporations and $5,000 for individuals include access to 200 associated private and country clubs in 14 countries.

"We are trying to provide better opportunities for each member to do business and for foreign and Chinese businessmen to exchange views," said Robert Dedman, chairman of Club Corp. of America, the joint venture partner of China International Trust and Investment Corporation. Other facilities in Shanghai and Guangzhou are planned. In December 1994, the Changan Club opened, with entrance fees ranging from $20,000 to $28,000. The club has private tennis courts, saunas, gymnasiums, and dining rooms and happens to be located near the walled citadel of China's Communist leadership.

Source: "New Business Clubs Prove Popular," *Financial Times,* November 7, 1994, IX.

the expectation of an increased standard of living in the form of color televisions, cars, and the many benefits of a consumer society. To sustain the drive toward democracy, these economic desires had to appear attainable. Therefore, it was in the interest of the Western world as a whole to contribute to the democratization of the former communist nations by searching for ways to bring them "the good life."

The Realities of Economic Change

For Western firms, the political and economic shifts resulted in the conversion of what had been a latent but closed market into a market offering very real and vast opportunities. Yet the shifts are only the beginning of a process. The announcement of an intention to change does not automatically result in change itself. For example, the abolition of a centrally planned economy does not create a market economy. Laws permitting the emergence of private sector entrepreneurs do not create entrepreneurship. The reduction of price controls does not immediately make goods available or affordable. Deeply ingrained systemic differences between the emerging democracies and Western firms continue. Highly prized, fully accepted fundamentals of the market economy, such as the reliance on competition, support of the profit motive, and the willingness to live with risk on a corporate and personal level, are not yet fully accepted. As Table 10.1 shows, progress towards a market economy

TABLE 10.1 Progress in Heading Toward a Market Economy	Private Sector Share of GDP, 1994, %	Score: 4 = Market Economy, 1 = Little Progress					
		Privatization		Restructuring of Companies	Prices, Competition	Trade, Foreign Exchange	Banks
		Large	Small				
Albania	50	1	3	2	3	4	2
Armenia	40	1	3	1	3	2	1
Azerbaijan	20	1	1	1	3	1	1
Belarus	15	2	2	2	2	1	1
Bulgaria	40	2	2	2	3	4	2
Croatia	40	3	4	2	3	4	3
Czech Republic	65	4	4	3	3	4	3
Estonia	55	3	4	3	3	4	3
Georgia	20	1	2	1	2	1	1
Hungary	55	3	4	3	3	4	3
Kazakhstan	20	2	2	1	2	2	1
Kirgizstan	30	3	4	2	3	3	2
Latvia	55	2	3	2	3	4	3
Lithuania	50	3	4	2	3	4	2
Macedonia	35	2	4	2	3	4	2
Moldova	20	2	2	2	3	2	2
Poland	55	3	4	3	3	4	3
Romania	35	2	3	2	3	4	2
Russia	50	3	3	2	3	3	2
Slovakia	55	3	4	3	3	4	3
Slovenia	30	2	4	3	3	4	3
Tajikistan	15	2	2	1	3	1	1
Turkmenistan	15	1	1	1	2	1	1
Ukraine	30	1	2	1	2	1	1
Uzbekistan	20	2	3	1	3	2	1

Source: The Economist, December 3, 1994, 27

has varied among the different nations, and major changes still need to take place. It is therefore useful to review the major economic and structural dimensions of the emerging democracies to identify major shortcomings and opportunities for international business.

The democratically elected governments in central Europe are a completely new phenomenon. While full of good intentions, these governments are new to the tasks of governing and have either very limited experience or none at all. At the same time, they face major legal uncertainties and old, entrenched bureaucracies, whose members are still deeply suspicious of any change and less then helpful or forthcoming. These governments have precipitated the disappearance of the previous trading system but have yet to replace the old, imperfect set of trading relationships with a new one. As a result, their ability to successfully shape the competitive environment of their nations is limited.

Many of the NEDs also face major **infrastructure shortages.** Transportation systems, particularly those leading to the West, are either nonexistent or in disrepair. The housing stock is in need of total overhaul. Communication systems will take years to improve. Market intermediaries often do not exist. Payments and funds-transfer systems are inadequate. Even though major efforts are under way to improve the infrastructure—evidenced, for example, by the former Soviet Union's desire to obtain fiber-optic telephone lines or by Hungary's success in installing a cellular telephone system—infrastructure shortcomings will inhibit economic growth for years to come.

Capital shortages are also a major constraint. Catching up with the West in virtually all industrial areas will require major capital infusions. In addition, a new environmental consciousness will require large investments in environmentally sound energy-generation and production facilities. Even though major programs are being designed to attract hidden personal savings into the economies, NEDs must rely to a large degree on attracting capital from abroad. Continued domestic uncertainties and high demand for capital around the world make this difficult.

Firms doing business with the emerging democracies encounter very interesting demand conditions. Clearly, the pent-up demand from the past bodes well for sales. Yet buyers, in many instances, have never been exposed to the problem of decision making; their preferences are vague and undefined, and they are therefore poorly trained in making market choices.[10] As a result, buyers are unlikely to demand high levels of quality or service. Rather, their demand is driven much more by product availability than by product sophistication. Yet little accurate market information is available. For example, knowledge about pricing, advertising, research, and trading is virtually nonexistent, and few institutions are able to accurately research demand and channel supply. As a result, it is quite difficult for corporations to respond to demand.

To the surprise of many investors, the emerging democracies have substantial knowledge resources to offer. For example, it is claimed that the former USSR and former eastern Europe possess about 35 to 40 percent of all researchers and engineers working in the world.[11] At the same time, however, these nations suffer from the drawback imposed by a lack of management skills. In the past, management mainly consisted of skillful maneuvering within the allocation process. Central planning, for example, required firms to request tools seven years in advance; material requirements needed to be submitted two years in advance. Ordering was done haphazardly, since requested quantities were always reduced, and surplus allocations could always be traded with other firms. The driving mechanism for management was therefore not responsiveness to existing needs, but rather plan fulfillment through the development of a finely honed **allocation mentality.**

Commitment by managers and employees to their work is difficult to find. Employees are to a large degree still caught up in old work habits, which consisted of never having to work a full shift due to other commitments and obligations. The notion that "they pretend to pay us, and we pretend to work" is still very strong. The current dismantling of the past policy of the "Iron Rice Bowl," which made layoffs virtually impossible, is further reducing rather than increasing such commitment. In addition, even on the governmental and judicial level there are significant limits to the willingness of living with the consequences of a market economy as the Global Perspective 10.2 shows.

The new environment also complicates managerial decision making. Because of the total lack of prior market orientation, even simple reforms require an almost unimaginable array of decisions about business licenses, the setting of optimal tax rates, rules of business operation, definitions of business expense for taxation purposes, safety standards, and rules concerning nondiscrimination and consumer protection.[12] All new market economies experience a gap in management skills. Closing this gap is a major challenge, for both firms and employees. Firms, whether managed by foreign investors or recently privatized, must find ways to inculcate initiative, independence, and action into their employees. Workers must overcome old

Global Perspective

10.2
Pro-Worker Bias in Russia

When two Russian women employed by the Radisson-Slavyanskaya Hotel in Moscow did not meet standards, their manager decided to do the obvious: fire the workers. The move, simple enough in the Western world's labor market, proved to be anything but that in the former USSR.

Each woman sued the partly U.S.-owned hotel for $10 million. Despite each award being reduced to only $81, the verdict was in the women's favor, setting an alarming precedent for foreign investors in Russia: the two workers kept their jobs even though their work was substandard and their contracts had run out.

Russia's labor laws have not changed their pro-worker bias since the USSR's breakup. "This just shows that the market economy isn't here yet," said the American general director of the Radisson-Slavyanskaya joint venture. "We try to bring in a new way of doing things but it's an extremely painful process."

Russian labor law all but guarantees employees their jobs once they pass a three-month probation period. Russian law views contracts with time limits as extraordinary, to be used only for executives or in cases of special "necessity," such as filling in for a worker on maternity leave. For most jobs, if an employer retains the position, he must keep the individual worker.

Most cases of worker firings in Russia have actually passed without incident, with some companies paying off fired workers to ward off legal challenges. However, the Radisson case shows how workers can and will fight back. "I don't think the business community can ignore this," said Larry Anderson, a founding member of the new American Chamber of Commerce in Russia. "Companies have been put on notice that they've got to be more careful about how they hire."

Investors had hoped that the labor code would become more employer-friendly as the Russian economy opened up, but in 1992 the former Parliament made the law even more restrictive. This court ruling only adds to the mounting fears of foreign business executives, who increasingly wonder if they are really welcome in Russia.

Source: Marya Fogel, "Pro-Worker Bias of Russian Law Fuels Foreign Worries About Doing Business," *The Wall Street Journal,* May 11, 1994, A11.

habits and find purpose in new approaches. Supervisors must learn how to develop the performance of employees even though they are ill prepared given their past economic orientation, philosophies, and practices.[13] In essence, entire societies must be retooled. Table 10.2 presents the key management skills and qualities that were found to be needed in Russia.

Implementing such attitude changes is difficult. Major cultural obstacles need to be overcome. Resistance to foreign methods needs to be reduced. Training activities must balance the communication of normative knowledge and skills with an adaption of deeply ingrained societal values. It is insufficient to simply transfer knowledge and knowledge processes—they must be cross-culturally adapted to local requirements. New approaches must also be found to ensure that knowledge communicated leads to actual changes in behavior. As a result, major emphasis needs to rest with experiential learning.

Many universities, firms, and governments have begun to offer educational programs in emerging market economies. In their work, these organizations often find that they need to learn just as much as they teach. Simply force-feeding Western management theory neglects the fact that management is largely a cultural activity.[14] Given the size and scope of the task at hand, many educational innovations should be expected to emanate from this work.

TABLE 10.2 Top Ten Management Skills and Qualities Needed in Free-Market Russia		Percentage	Frequency
	1. Connections and personal contacts	58	89
	2. Problem-solving, crisis-handling skills	53	84
	3. Marketing and sales skills	45	72
	4. Leadership and communication skills	44	70
	5. Action-oriented, willing to take risks	41	65
	6. Technical knowledge of operation and product	38	60
	7. Planning and organizing skills	37	59
	8. Financial and accounting skills	30	48
	9. Creativity and innovation	29	46
	10. Drive and persistence	22	35

Source: Clinton O. Longenecker and Serguei Popovski, "Managerial Trials of Privatization," *Business Horizons,* November-December 1994, 38.

ADJUSTING TO GLOBAL CHANGE

Both institutions and individuals tend to display some resistance to change. The resistance grows if the speed of change increases. It does not necessarily indicate a preference for the earlier conditions but rather concern about the effects of adjustment and fear of the unknown. In light of the major shifts that have occurred both politically and economically in central Europe and the former Soviet Union and the accompanying substantial dislocations, resistance should be expected. Deeply entrenched interests and traditions are not easily supplanted by the tender and shallow root of market-oriented thinking. The understanding of linkages and interactions cannot be expected to grow overnight. For example, greater financial latitude for firms also requires that inefficient firms be permitted to go into bankruptcy—a concept not cherished by many. The need for increased efficiency and productivity causes sharp reductions in employment—a painful step for the workers affected. The growing ranks of unemployed are swelled by the members of the military who have been brought home or demobilized. Concurrently, wage reforms threaten to relegate blue-collar workers, who were traditionally favored by the socialist system, to second-class status while permitting the emergence of a new entrepreneurial class of the rich, an undesirable result for those not participating in the upswing. Retail price reforms endanger the safety net of larger population segments, and widespread price changes introduce inflation. It is difficult to accept a system where there are winners and losers, particularly for those on the losing side. As a result, an increase in ambivalence and uncertainty may well produce rapid shifts in economic and political thinking, which in turn may produce another set of unexpected results.

Concurrent Shifts in Trade and Investment Flows

All these changes are accompanied by a major reorientation in global trade and investment flows triggered by the concurrent emergence of new markets particularly in Southeast Asia and Latin America. As Global Perspective 10.3 shows, the new opportunities are seen as crucial by Western corporations. For example, in the first nine months of 1994 alone, foreign investors pledged more than $57 billion worth of new investment in China. Overall, China now absorbs about half of all foreign direct investment to developing countries worldwide.[15]

In addition, many other countries are experiencing major economic growth rates and are entering the international market. For example, during the past decade, Asian

Global Perspective

10.3
China at the Top of Unilever's Wish List

Unilever's Chinese roots go way back. Starting with a Shanghai factory in the early 1920s, Unilever became China's largest maker of soap before its operations were nationalized in 1951. The company's first joint-venture since then, Shanghai Lever, was established in 1987 and brought Unilever back to the original site of its old soap factory. The location was reequipped with the most modern machinery in order to make Lux soap. The venture's product line has grown to include shampoos, shower creams, fabric softeners, and kitchen/bathroom cleaners.

Unilever has enjoyed one of the fastest growth rates of any foreign company in China. In two years, its number of employees has jumped from 700 to 2,500, of whom only 80 are expatriates. It is currently engaged in eight joint ventures, ranging from detergents and toothpaste to ice cream and tea. With $200 million of investment spent or committed, a further $100 million will be spent each year until 1999. Chinese sales are expected to rise from $200 million a year to $1.5 billion by then.

Unavoidably, however, difficulties abound in virtually all aspects of business. Local price increases have made certain imports cheaper, it can take three weeks to ship finished goods the hundreds of miles from Shanghai to Beijing, and television ads have to be produced abroad and sent to some 300 individual stations. It can take six months to get a price increase approved by officials. Distribution systems are product-specific, meaning that Unilever cannot send soap via its toothpaste distributor. In addition to all of this, reform of the government-dominated retailing system has just begun.

Despite the problems, China is at the "top of the list" of targeted emerging markets, said Unilever's Dutch cochairman, Morris Tabaksblat. The overriding importance is to be in China building experience, knowledge, brands, and business—"If you waited until the risks in China were lower, then you would simply be too late," concluded Anton Lenstra, the chairman of Unilever China.

Source: Roderick Oram, "Wait—and You'll Be Too Late," *Financial Times,* November 7, 1994, VI.

countries such as Indonesia, Malaysia, and Thailand have maintained annual growth rates exceeding 8 percent, resulting in enormous growth of their domestic markets. Vietnam has begun to participate again in world trade and investment markets and has successfully opened up to foreign investment. India has reversed some of its socialist economic policies. As a result, domestic demand and output have grown significantly, and, as Global Perspective 10.4 shows, is not just relegated to urban areas. In addition, countries in Latin America, such as Chile, Argentina, and Brazil, have become major market entrants, as has South Africa, which reentered the global trade picture after the end of Apartheid.

All the countries have major investment needs as well. For example, in South Africa the integration of society requires major investments in housing, transportation infrastructure, and manufacturing plants. In spite of the emergence of a large middle class, India still lags in basic infrastructure such as sanitation, clean water, refuse collection, and public health—as the recurrence of bubonic and pneumonic plague highlighted.[16]

The shifts also have a major impact on the established market economies of the West. Initially, the immediate changes in the West were confined to the reduction of the threat of war and a redefinition of military and political strategy. Over time, however, Western governments are discovering that the formation of new linkages and dismantling of old ones will also cause major dislocations at home. For example, the change in military threat is likely to have an effect on military budgets, which for the United States alone was $300 billion annually. Budget changes in turn will affect

Global Perspective

10.4
The Consumer Power of Rural India

The villages of India, home to 80 percent of the nation's population, still retain much of their traditional qualities. But the agrarian reforms of the last two decades, together with the migration to the cities of many villagers, has brought about a significant rise in agrarian purchasing power and a change in consumer patterns. According to India's National Council for Applied Economic Research, the importance of rural markets for manufactured consumer goods is increasing and will continue to do so as a result of the government's liberalization program.

An extensive survey conducted in 1992–1993 unveiled that 75 percent of bicycles and portable radios and 60 percent of table fans, sewing machines, and wrist watches sold in India were bought in rural areas. The survey also found that the rural share of other consumer sales has been rising in relation to sales in the cities. For instance, the percentage of color televisions that were bought in rural parts of India rose from 19 percent in 1989 to 31 percent in 1993. Perhaps the most telling statistic is that while in 1960 the average rural household spent 81 percent of its income on food, today this figure has dropped to less than 70 percent.

In recent years, a greater effort has been made to understand the particular cultural, social, and economic conditions that exist within the villages. A marketing consultant active in rural India put it this way: "Having been trained in a westernized culture, we tend to approach even the rural market with certain urban mind-sets. That doesn't always work. To effectively market a product, we have to get off our high horses and understand rural ways." Here is a historical anecdote that illustrates the concept. A few years ago, sales of a particular hair dye shot up to three bottles per consumer a month in a certain village region in India. Far from being used on the villagers' hair, the dye was being used on the local cattle. The villagers believed that the shinier the cow's coat, the better their chance of getting a good price at the local market.

Market research performed on Indian villages suggests that consumption patterns of rural consumers generally remain distinct from those of urban consumers. While many villagers are earning their wages in the towns, caste and religion continue to play a dominant role in their villages, ensuring a high degree of social conformity and respect for tradition. Status symbols remain important, as do strong personal relationships. Such factors are likely to put an increasing onus on companies developing marketing strategies that are sensitive to the peculiar needs of rural communities in India.

Source: Jimmy Burns, "Sleeping Giant Stirs," *Financial Times,* November 8, 1994, XV.

the production of military goods and the employment level in the defense sector. A declining size of armies will only reinforce the resulting employment needs.

Major changes will also result from the reorientation of trade flows. With traditional and "forced" trade relationships vanishing and the need for income from abroad increasing, many more countries exert major efforts to become partners in global trade. They attempt to export much more of their domestic production. Many of the exports will be in product categories such as agriculture, basic manufacturing, steel, aluminum, and textiles, which are precisely the economic sectors in which the industrialized nations are already experiencing surpluses. As a result, the threat of displacement will be high for traditional producers in industrialized nations.

Resistance to Change

An immediate consequence of the shifts will likely be resistance to change. Typical of such resistance is government action that attempts to contain the effect of change abroad and limit its effect at home. Such governmental restrictions of trade flows

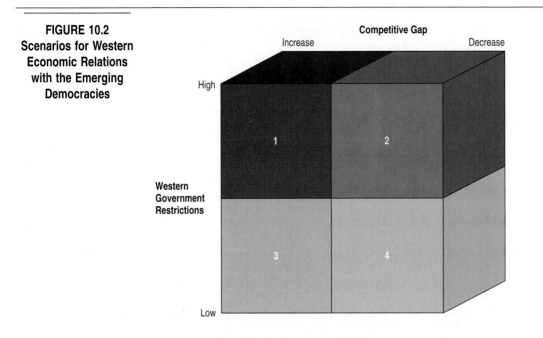

from newly emerging economies are dangerous. Figure 10.2 provides various scenarios for economic relations between industrialized nations and newly emerging markets. The two main dimensions guiding these scenarios are government restrictions of trade and the competitive gap among nations. In Scenario 1, governments attempt to reduce the inflow of trade from the newly emerging regions. Concurrently, increases in economic integration in the industrialized world, combined with the significant competitive advantages of its firms, will lead to a widening of the competitive gap. In Scenario 2, government restrictions remain high, but the competitive gap is diminished due to quick adjustments by emerging market economies and the inflow of sufficient resources to improve their competitive standing. Scenario 3 decreases government restrictions, but the competitive gap continues to increase. In Scenario 4, government restrictions decrease together with a closing of the competitive gap.

An analysis of the four possibilities shows that Scenario 1 is likely to lead to major economic and political instability in the newly emerging markets due to individual hardships and disappointed expectations. Scenario 2 is unlikely to materialize, since the investments required for a decrease in the competitive gap will not occur unless market opportunities for the exports generated by such investment exist in the industrialized nations. Scenario 3 indicates that the lowering of government restrictions is a necessary but insufficient condition for the improvement of the competitive standing of the newly emerging markets. Scenario 4 is the most desirable because it offers long-term change and economic improvement to the world. This scenario will result in the highest internal adjustment needs by industrialized nations and firms and will require significant transfers of resources to close the competitive gap. Yet, as Global Perspective 10.5 shows, strong arguments can be made in favor of coresponsibility of the West for such adjustments.

This scenario will also depend on close collaboration between the public and the private sector. Private sector investment will be required to generate the resources necessary for economic competitiveness. Even with low government restrictions, private capital flows will need encouragement. Such encouragement will, to a large degree, depend on the domestic governmental actions of the newly emerging market economies. The providing of open markets and of governmental assistance on the part of the West, however, will also be instrumental. One could argue that governmental expenditures assisting other countries should be minimized. This argument is substantially weakened if such expenditures are seen as investment or even as insurance. In light of the more than $500 billion in annual military expenses that the Western world imposed on itself during Cold War days, protection against future instability may well be worth a small percentage of the armament expenditures of the past. Yet, the transfers of governments cannot be sufficient to make a major economic difference. For example, the $2.5 billion allocated in 1994 by the United States for assistance to the former Soviet states[17] is only a drop in the bucket of the actual investment needs of the countries. Therefore, the development of an investment climate in nations that encourage private sector financial flows is imperative.

Disappointment and disenchantment in emerging markets bring the potential for social upheaval and chaos. One must recognize that economic borders can be just as divisive and perhaps even more painful than political ones.[18] Instability and confrontation result not only from tanks but also from poverty-driven countries' knowledge that the next-door neighbor lives in wealth and amplitude. To avoid conflict and increase opportunity, it is in the long-term interest of governments and citizens in industrialized nations to lower their restrictions to trade and assist in building

Global Perspective

10.5
The Coresponsibility of the West

Eastern Europe has undergone almost incomprehensible change. The Czech Republic was deeply involved in the change and its president, Vaclav Havel, has spoken very candidly about what has happened and what is at stake, for all the nations on Earth:

"The world used to be so simple: There was a single adversary who was more or less understandable, who was directed from a single center, and whose sole aim in its final years was to maintain the status quo. At the same time, the existence of this adversary drew the West together as well, because faced with this global and clearly defined danger, it could always somehow agree on a common approach. All that has vanished. The world has suddenly become unusually complex and far less intelligible. The old order has collapsed, but no one has yet created a new one.

". . . The 'postcommunist world' is constantly springing new surprises on the West: Nations hitherto unheard of are awakening and want countries of their own. Highly improbable people from God knows where are winning elections. It is not even clear whether the very people who four years ago so astonishingly roused themselves from their torpor and

overthrew communism do not actually miss that system today. . . . How much easier it must have been for Western politicians when they were faced with a homogenous Soviet mass and didn't have to worry about distinguishing one nation from another.

". . . Now that the Cold War is over, the impression is that the headaches it caused are over. But the headaches are never over. . . . Our countries must deal with their own immense problems themselves. The 'non-postcommunist West,' however, should not look on as though it were a mere visitor at a zoo or the audience at a horror movie, on edge to know how it will turn out. It should perceive these processes at the very least as something that intrinsically concerns it, and that somehow decides its own fate, that demands its own active involvement and challenges it to make sacrifices in the interests of a bearable future for us all.

". . . To make my point briefly and simply: it seems to me that the fate of the so-called West is today being decided in the so-called East. If the West does not find a key to us, who were once violently separated from the West, it will ultimately lose the key to itself."

Source: Vaclav Havel, "A Call for Sacrifice: The Coresponsibility of the West," *Foreign Affairs,* March/April 1994, 2–7.

up competitive capabilities around the world. There is an urgent need to collaborate now to encourage the formulation of joint approaches and inhibit the advancement of disjointed, incompatible policies. Such collaboration will bring painful economic shifts. Although governments and individuals may not be prepared for such pain, the burden must be borne in order to increase the likelihood of survival for market-oriented thinking and, in the longer term, to create new targets of opportunity abroad.

International Business Challenges and Opportunities

The pressure of change also presents vast opportunities for the expansion of international business activities. Large populations offer new potential consumer demand and production supply. The international manager needs to consider the current and future political environments when planning long-term business commitments. For market entry, a major challenge is the lack of information about end users. Business strives to satisfy the needs and wants of individuals and organizations. Unable to ascertain their desires directly, the international manager must use secondary information such as hearsay, educated guesses, and the opinions of intermediaries.

Another major difficulty encountered in conducting business with these countries is the frequent unavailability of convertible currency. Products, however necessary, often cannot be purchased by emerging market economies because no funds are available to pay for them. As a result, many of the countries resort to barter and countertrade. This places an additional burden on the international manager, who must not only market products to the clients but must also market the products received in return to other consumers and institutions. However, as Chapter 18 will explain, new methods of countertrade are being developed by the world business community to reduce the impact of this problem.

Problems also have arisen from the lack of protection some of the countries afford to intellectual property rights. Firms have complained about frequent illegal copying of films, books, and software, and about the counterfeiting of brand name products. Unless importers can be assured that government safeguards will protect their property, trade and technology transfer will be severely inhibited.

However, many opportunities also arise out of the enthusiasm with which a market orientation is embraced in some nations. As Global Perspective 10.6 shows, the

The fall of the Berlin Wall signaled the opening of Eastern Europe, providing vast opportunities for the expansion of international marketing activities.

Source: Filip Horvat/ISABA.

Global Perspective

10.6
Amway, the Hungarian Way

An expatriate need not feel homesick for aggressive sales pitches in Budapest. Avon Products and Mary Kay Corp. have set up shop to sell cosmetics, Herbalife International, Inc., to sell vitamins, and Tupperware to sell Tupperware. Among all direct marketers, Amway Corp. has emerged as the heavyweight champion of multilevel marketing in the Hungarian arena.

Multilevel marketers sell products to distributors, who not only sell the products but also recruit others to sell them. The distributors in Amway's structure receive benefits not only from their own sales but also from the sales of those they recruit, who in turn can recruit more distributors.

With 94,000 representatives, close to 1 percent of the country's population, Amway agents in Hungary moved $39 million of inventory in 1993. The products included soap, toiletries, knives, pots, and cosmetics. The "sales promoters," as they prefer to be called, take their jobs very seriously. They're zealous and tenacious, and consume Amway products almost religiously. They attend Amway conventions and seminars, listen to Amway motivational tapes, watch Amway videotapes, and undergo Amway's leadership training.

Western advertisements are highly visible in Budapest, where people are inundated with images of German cars, cellular phones, and Western appliances, but can only dream of buying them. Enter American multilevel marketing giants: organizations offering strong structure, corporate polish, massive motivational support, and an opportunity at residual income and relative wealth. More than 100 outfits have opened since 1991, accounting for $100 million to $150 million in annual sales. In a country where the stock exchange is valued at $1.1 billion, that's big money.

Amway's incentives for high sales bear a familiarity to times past. Where a top factory worker once was rewarded with his name in a socialist newsletter, a handsome plaque, and a holiday at one of the state's resorts, a top Amway agent now is rewarded with his or her name in *Anagram,* Amway's monthly magazine, a handsome plaque, and a holiday at one of the company's convention sites. Today, of course, a big check comes with the perks.

The real money to be made in multilevel marketing comes from recruiting others. As the lowest tier of the pyramid is constantly widening, less and less fresh ground remains to be canvassed. The result is a great deal of competition among agents to recruit people, especially in heavily populated areas of Hungary such as Budapest. In the meantime, those who have been propositioned to join, yet have declined, face the prospect of wave after wave of zealous solicitation. "This is business," said Tamas Fordos, who runs the Amway Hungary office, "so you have to be sometimes a bit pushy."

According to Klaus Tremmel, regional manager of Amway Europe, "We never advertise. This business sells itself through reference." Tremmel has opened up the company's operations in Hungary, Austria, and the Czech Republic, and was due to open the doors of Amway Slovakia in 1995. The top 325 agents in Hungary pull in at least $500 per month. With average Hungarians' salaries at $200 per month, many want to participate. But it's not easy. "The expectation of most of the people is for quick money," said Tremmel, "and that is not the case. They have to plan and they have to work."

Source: Robert Muraskin, "Workers of Hungary Unite—in Amway," *The Washington Post,* August 6, 1994, D1.

success of Amway in Hungary entirely results from the zeal of individuals wanting to be part of the market economy. Companies that are able to tap into the desire for an improved standard of living can penetrate new markets on a large scale.

Problems also can be encountered when attempting to source products from emerging market economies. Many firms have found that selling is not part of the economic culture in some of the countries. The available descriptive materials are often poorly written and devoid of useful information. Obtaining additional information about a product may be difficult and time-consuming.

Global Perspective

10.7
Russian Software Firms Look Overseas

A small but growing number of Russian software companies are bringing their ideas to the global marketplace. Russian software designers, industry insiders say, are among the world's most gifted but an undeveloped sense of what consumers want and lack of financial resources hampered such firms. Today, however, some of Russia's leading software makers are finding ways to translate their skills into commercial results.

Nikolai Lebedev, the chairman of Transas Marine, is trying to develop technology the world has never seen. The Russian company is testing a system now that allows the navigation of a virtual reality cargo ship through a three-dimensional vision of actual ports around the world. The $100,000 system, used for pilot training, combines painstakingly detailed maps with state-of-the-art graphics. The 120-person, privately owned software house expects to sell about $9 million in marine-related software in 1994, mostly overseas.

Paragraph International, another Moscow software house, already made millions of dollars by licensing technology to Apple Computer Inc. for the use of the U.S. firm's Newton MessagePad. One of several new projects is a "virtual home museum," which is touted as the photo album of the future. After transferring photos onto a personal computer, the user can arrange pictures along the walls of a gallery that can be designed on screen. Other products include a three-dimensional, medical diagnostic program and a "time travel" game that lets players interact via telephone modems in computer-generated fantasy worlds.

Russian software firms are still facing troubling barriers. Most Russian designers work with primitive equipment, forcing them to accomplish results with very little power. "We needed to be ingenious," said Arkady Moreynis, general manager of Macsimum, which develops software to run on Apple's Macintosh computers.

Despite such problems, the abundance of local talent has enticed a number of Western companies to contract out work to Russian designers. The level of skill present is portrayed in one Russian software firm named Steepler Corp. Roustem Akhiarov, a co-owner, helped create a Russian version of Nintendo after observing video-game addicts in the United States. Steepler's "Dendy," a TV video game manufactured in Taiwan, now dominates the Russian market. By the beginning of 1994, Steepler was selling 83,000 units a month for about $40 apiece.

Source: Adi Ignatius, "Russian Software Firms Look Overseas," *The Wall Street Journal,* July 8, 1994, A5.

The quality of the products obtained can also be a major problem. In spite of their great desire to participate in the global marketplace, many producers still tend to place primary emphasis on product performance and, to a large extent, to neglect style and product presentation. Therefore, the international manager needs to forge agreements that require the manufacturer to improve quality, provide for technical control, and ensure prompt delivery before sourcing products from emerging market economies.

Nevertheless, sufficient opportunities exist to make consideration of such international business activities worthwhile. Some emerging market economies have products that are unique in performance. While they were nontradable during a time of ideological conflict, they are becoming successful global products in an era of trade relations. Global Perspective 10.7 provides an example of successful Russian software exports. Other countries can offer low labor costs and, in some instances, a great availability of labor. These nations can offer consumers in industrialized nations a variety of products at lower costs.

One phenomenon that plays a major role in international business is that of the **state-owned enterprise.** Many of these firms are gradually being converted into privately owned enterprises through the privatization process. The transition also presents new opportunities for the international manager.

Reasons for the Emergence of State-Owned Enterprises

A variety of economic and noneconomic factors contributed to the existence of state-owned enterprises. Two primary ones are national security and economic security. Many countries believed that, for national security purposes, certain industrial sectors must be under state control. Typically, these sectors included telecommunications, airlines, banking, and energy.

Economic security reasons are primarily cited in countries that are heavily dependent on specific industries for their economic performance. This may be the case when countries are heavily commodity dependent. Governments frequently believe that, given such heavy national dependence on a particular industrial sector, government control is necessary to ensure national economic health.

Other reasons also contributed to the development of state-owned enterprises. On occasion, the sizable investment required for the development of an industry is too large to come from the private sector. Therefore, governments close the gap between national needs and private sector resources by developing industries themselves. In addition, governments often decided to rescue failing private enterprises by placing them in government ownership. In doing so, they fulfilled important policy objectives such as the maintenance of employment, the development of depressed areas, or the increase of exports.

Some governments also maintain that state-owned firms may be better for the country than privately held companies because they may be more societally oriented and therefore contribute more to the greater good. This was particularly the case in areas such as telecommunications and transportation, where profit maximization, at least from a governmental perspective, was not always seen as the appropriate primary objective.

The Effect of State-Owned Enterprises on International Business

Three types of activities in which the international manager is likely to encounter state-owned enterprises are market entry, the sourcing or marketing process, and international competition. On occasion, the very existence of a state-owned enterprise may inhibit or prohibit foreign market entry. For reasons of development and growth, governments frequently make market entry from the outside quite difficult so that the state-owned enterprise can perform according to plan. Even if market entry is permitted, the conditions under which a foreign firm can conduct business are often substantially less favorable than the conditions under which state-owned enterprises operate. Therefore, the international firm may be placed at a competitive disadvantage and may not be able to perform successfully even though economic factors would indicate success.

The international manager also faces a unique situation when sourcing from or marketing to state-owned enterprises. Even though the state-owned firm may appear to be simply another business partner, it is ultimately an extension of the government and its activities. Quite often this may mean that the state-owned enterprise conducts its transactions according to the overall foreign policy of the country rather than according to economic rationale. For example, political considerations can play a decisive role in purchasing decisions. Contracts may be concluded for noneconomic reasons rather than based on product offering and performance. Contract conditions may depend on foreign policy outlook, prices may be altered to reflect government displeasure, and delivery performance may change to "send a signal." Exports and imports may be delayed or encouraged depending on the current needs of government. Even though an economic rationale appears to exist within a state-owned enterprise, the interests and concerns of the owner—the state—may lead it to be driven by politics.[19]

This also holds true when the international firm encounters international competition from state-owned enterprises. Very often, the concentration of the firms is not in areas of comparative advantage, but rather in areas that at the time are most beneficial for the government owning the firm. Input costs often are much less important than policy objectives. Sometimes, state-owned enterprises may not even know the value of the products they buy and sell because prices in themselves have such a low priority. As a result, the international manager may be confronted with competition that is very tough to beat.

The Privatization Perspective

For decades, government control of enterprises grew. Beginning in the mid-1980s however, governments and citizens came to recognize the drawbacks of such control. Competition was restrained, which resulted in lower quality of goods and reduced innovation. Domestic citizens were deprived of lower prices and of choice. The international competitiveness of state-controlled enterprises was suffering, which often resulted in the need for growing government subsidies. In addition, rather than focusing on the business aspects, many government-controlled corporations had become grazing grounds for political appointees or vote winners through job allocations. As a result, many government-owned enterprises excelled in losing money.[20]

Governments began to recognize that it is possible to reduce the cost of governing by changing their role and involvement in the economy. Through **privatization,** governments were able to cut their budget costs and could still ensure that more efficient—not fewer—services were provided to their citizens. The products produced were more competitive and more innovative and the conversion of government monopolies into market-driven activities attracted foreign investment capital, bringing additional know-how and financing to enterprises. Finally, governments discovered that they could use proceeds from privatization to fund other pressing needs for which there otherwise was no budget.

As a result of these insights, governments began to develop the privatization process. Initial steps consisted of deregulation. For example, in the mid-1970s, the United States reduced government involvement in industry by deregulating domestic industries that had been tightly controlled and regulated, such as telephone service and airlines. Within a decade, deregulation spread across many industrialized and developing nations, resulting in more consumer choice and lower rates.

Britain pioneered the concept of privatization in 1979 by converting 20 state firms into privately owned companies. In the 1980s, Chile privatized 470 enterprises, which had produced 24 percent of the country's value added.[21] By the 1990s, privatization had become a key element in governmental economic strategy around the world. In addition to Asia, Africa, Latin America, and the Eastern European nations, western Europe entered the privatization field on a large scale, as Global Perspective 10.8 shows. As a result of these efforts, many new private companies that were large by global standards emerged and provided, on a local level, unprecedented lev-

Global Perspective

10.8
Privatization Sweeps the Globe

After record privatization in eastern Europe, Russia, Latin America, and Asia, privatization is now sweeping across western Europe like a tidal wave. Italy is selling off giant industries that have been part of the government since the Mussolini era. State-owned industrial conglomerates have been turned into public stock companies in fields such as oil, banking, food, power, and aerospace. France is cutting loose control over everything from computer companies to giant insurers. Even Germany is getting into the act by putting its national airline, Lufthansa, and Deutsche Bundespost Telekom on the block.

Privatization is not an easy step to take. Said Daniel Gros of the Brussels-based Center for European Policy Studies: "Some diehards don't want to sell their state firms." They give the power to government to "give people hundreds of thousands of jobs. That's where they get their power from."

Why all the privatization? First of all, state enterprises were not very successful. Under state ownership, both managers and workers have strong incentives to "decapitalize" the enterprises that employ them by extracting as much wealth as they can for themselves. They have little or no incentive to increase the value of the firm through wise investments, increasing productivity, or restraining wages and employment, because they have little chance of sharing in the firm's future prosperity. But rules in the then–European Community also helped. The rules banned billions in state subsidies that uncompetitive state firms relied on for decades to stay afloat. Finally, many countries see privatization as an opportunity to trim massive budget deficits and national debt.

Sources: Patrick Oster, "Europe Dashes to Jettison State-Owned Businesses," *The Washington Post,* July 23, 1992, D10, D14; "Owners Are the Only Answer," *The Economist,* September 21, 1991, 10.

els of innovation and quality. Figure 10.3 shows some of the large companies that originated in emerging market economies.

The methods of privatization vary from country to country. Some nations come up with a master plan for privatization, whereas others deal with it on a case-by-case basis. The Treuhandanstalt of Germany, for example, which was charged with disposing of most East German state property, aimed to sell firms but also to maximize the number of jobs retained. In other countries, ownership shares are distributed to citizens and employees. Some nations simply sell to the highest bidder in order to maximize the proceeds. For example, Mexico has used most of its privatization proceeds to amortize its internal debt, resulting in savings of nearly $1 billion a year in interest payments.

The trend toward privatization offers unique opportunities for international managers. Existing firms, both large and small, can be acquired at low cost, often with governmental support through tax exemptions, investment grants, special depreciation allowances, and low interest rate credits. The purchase of such firms enables the international firm to expand operations without having to start from scratch. In addition, since wages are often low in the countries where privatization takes place, there is a major opportunity to build low-cost manufacturing and sourcing bases. Furthermore, the international firm can also act as a catalyst by accelerating the pace of transferring business skills and technology and by boosting trade prospects. In short, the very process of change offers new opportunities to the adept manager.

FIGURE 10.3
Some Results of
Privatization

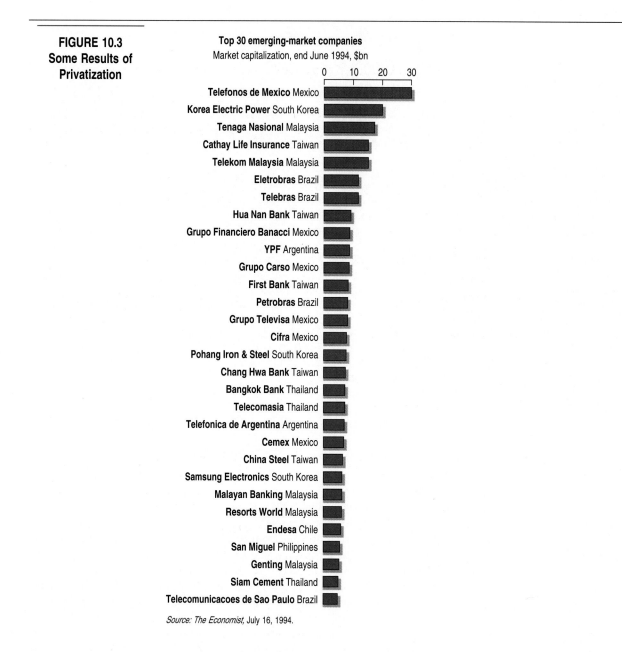

Top 30 emerging-market companies
Market capitalization, end June 1994, $bn

Source: The Economist, July 16, 1994.

SUMMARY

Special concerns must be considered by the international manager when dealing with emerging market economies. Although the former centrally planned economies offer vast opportunities for trade, business practices may be significantly different from those to which the executive is accustomed.

In the emerging market economies, the key to international business success will be an understanding of the fact that societies in transition require special adaptation of business skills and time to complete the transformation. Due to their growing degree of industrialization, other economies are also becoming part of the world trade and investment picture. It must be recognized that these global changes will, in turn, precipitate adjustments in industrialized nations, particularly in the trade sector. Adapting early to these changes can offer new opportunities to the international firm.

Often the international manager is also faced with state-owned enterprises that have been formed in noncommunist nations for reasons of national or economic security. These firms may inhibit foreign market entry, and they frequently reflect in their transactions the overall domestic and foreign policy of the country rather than any economic rationale.

The current global trend toward privatization offers new opportunities to the international firm, either through investment or by offering business skills and knowledge to assist in the success of privatization.

Key Terms and Concepts

central plan	allocation mentality
perestroika	state-owned enterprise
glasnost	privatization
infrastructure shortages	

Questions for Discussion

1. Planning is necessary, yet central planning is inefficient. Why?
2. Discuss the observation that "Russian products do what they are supposed to do—but only that."
3. How can and should the West help eastern European countries?
4. How can central European managers be trained to be market oriented?
5. Evaluate the possible dislocation effects of imports from newly emerging market economies.
6. Under what circumstances would you be in favor of state-owned enterprises?
7. Where do you see the greatest potential in future trade between emerging market economies and the West?
8. What are the benefits of privatization?

Recommended Readings

Boecker, Paul M., ed. *Latin America's Turnaround: The Paths to Privatization and Foreign Investment.* San Francisco: ICS Press, 1993.

Czinkota, Michael. "The EC '92 and Eastern Europe: Effects of Integration vs. Disintegration." *Columbia Journal of World Business* 26, 1 (1991): 20–27.

Dobek, Mariusz. *The Political Logic of Privatization: Lessons from Great Britain and Poland.* Westport, Conn.: Greenwood/Praeger, 1993.

Fogel, Daniel S. *Managing in Emerging Market Economies: Cases from the Czech and Slovak Republics.* Boulder, Colo.: Westview Press, 1994.

Gatti, Charles. "East-Central Europe: The Morning After." *Foreign Affairs* 69 (Winter 1990/91).

Goldman, Marshall. *What Went Wrong with Perestroika.* New York: W.W. Norton, 1992.

Hachette, Dominique, and Rolf Luders. *Privatization in Chile: An Economic Appraisal.* San Francisco: ICS Press, 1992.

Lardy, Nicholas R. *China in the World Economy.* Washington, D.C.: Institute for International Economics, 1994.

Puffer, Sheila M., ed. *The Russian Management Revolution.* Armonk, N.Y.: M.E. Sharpe, 1992.

Wood, Adrien. *North-South Trade, Employment and Inequality: Changing Fortunes in a Skill-Driven World.* Oxford: Oxford University Press, 1994.

Notes

1. Richard M. Hammer, "Dramatic Winds of Change," *Price Waterhouse Review* 33 (1989): 23-27.
2. Peter G. Lauter and Paul M. Dickie, "Multinational Corporations in Eastern European Socialist Economies," *Journal of Marketing* 25 (Fall 1975): 40-46.
3. Richard Ettenson, "Brand Name and Country of Origin Effects in the Emerging Market Economies of Russia, Poland, and Hungary," *International Marketing Review* (October 5, 1993): 14-36.
4. Raymond J. Waldmann, *Managed Trade: The New Competition Among Nations* (Cambridge, Mass.: Ballinger Press, 1986), 136.
5. Mihaly Simai, "Problems, Conditions, and Possibilities for an Export-Oriented Economic Policy in Hungary," in *Export Policy: A Global Assessment,* eds. M. Czinkota and G. Tesar (New York: Praeger, 1982), 20-30.
6. Eugene Theroux and Arthur L. George, *Joint Ventures in the Soviet Union: Law and Practice,* rev. ed. (Washington, D.C.: Baker & McKenzie, 1989), 1.
7. Alan B. Sherr, "Joint Ventures in the USSR: Soviet and Western Interests with Considerations for Negotiations," *Columbia Journal of World Business* 23 (Summer 1988): 27.
8. *The World Factbook 1994* (Washington, D.C.: Central Intelligence Agency, 1994).
9. Thomas Pickering, "Russia and America at Mid-Transition," *SAIS Review* (Winter/Spring 1995): 81-92.
10. Johny K. Johansson, *Marketing, Free Choice and the New International Order* (Washington, D.C.: Georgetown University, March 2, 1990), 10.
11. Mihaly Simai, *East-West Cooperation at the End of the 1980s: Global Issues, Foreign Direct Investments, and Debts* (Budapest: Hungarian Scientific Council for World Economy, 1989), 21.
12. Jerry F. Hough, *Opening Up the Soviet Economy* (Washington, D.C.: The Brookings Institution, 1988), 46.
13. Clinton O. Longenecker and Serguei Popovski, "Managerial Trials of Privatization: Retooling Russian Managers," *Business Horizons* (November/December 1994): 35-43.
14. "Educating Milos," *The Economist,* May 16, 1992, 86.
15. "Reform Momentum Slows Down," *Financial Times Survey,* November 7, 1994, I.
16. Alexander Nicoll, "Fast Start, Still Trailing," *Financial Times,* November 8, 1994, III.
17. "Money from Washington," *The Washington Post,* February 12, 1995, A36.
18. Michael R. Czinkota, "The EC '92 and Eastern Europe: Effects of Integration vs. Disintegration," *Columbia Journal of World Business* 26 (1991): 20-27.
19. Renato Mazzolini, "European Government-Controlled Enterprises: An Organizational Politics View," *Journal of International Business Studies* 11 (Spring-Summer 1980): 48-58.
20. "European Privatization: Two Half Revolutions," *The Economist,* January 22, 1994, 55, 58.
21. "Owners Are the Only Answer," *The Economist,* September 21, 1991, 10.

PART 3

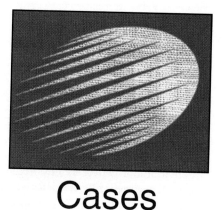

Cases

Promoting U.S. Tobacco Exports: A Conflict between Trade and Health

Tobacco and its related products have traditionally played an important role in the U.S. economy. Tobacco represents the sixth largest cash crop in the United States. Twenty-one states and more than two million people are engaged in tobacco growing, manufacturing, and marketing.

On January 11, 1964, the *Surgeon General's Report* documented the adverse health effects of smoking. Since then, the Surgeon General and other medical experts have determined that smoking can cause lung cancer and low birth weights, as well as other health problems. Concurrent with these findings, U.S. cigarette consumption, as well as other forms of tobacco use, has been gradually decreasing. While health considerations definitely played an important role in discouraging smoking, other factors such as higher cigarette prices, steeper federal and local taxes, and governmental restrictions on where smoking is permitted also contributed to the decline in U.S. cigarette consumption.

Although the use of tobacco products is no longer as socially acceptable as before, tobacco use is still tolerated and even welcomed by the government as a source of tax revenues. Apart from the desire to discourage smoking, a major rationale behind raising taxes on tobacco products continues to be the positive revenue impact

Source: This case was written by Michael R. Czinkota with the assistance of Homer Teng, using the following background material: United States General Accounting Office, "Trade and Health Issues: Dichotomy between U.S. Tobacco Export Policy and Antismoking Initiatives," May 1990; Andrew Copenhaver, statement on behalf of the United States Cigarette Export Association before the Subcommittee on Health and the Environment Committee on Energy and Commerce, United States House of Representatives, May 17, 1990; "The Tobacco Industry: Stubbed Out," *The Economist,* August 20, 1994, 26.

for the government. Even though many people have quit smoking, about 550 billion cigarettes were consumed in the United States in 1989. Consumption dropped to 468 billion by 1994. But a rising federal excise tax ensures that the amount of taxes collected is very meaningful to a deficit-constrained budget process.

THE IMPORTANCE OF EXPORTS FOR U.S. TOBACCO COMPANIES

In the face of higher domestic taxes, greater governmental restrictions on smoking in public places, and the growing unpopularity of tobacco use, U.S. tobacco companies are vigorously promoting cigarette exports overseas in order to compensate for their diminishing domestic market. Due to the high quality of American tobacco and the determination of U.S. tobacco companies to sell their products overseas, U.S. tobacco firms have been increasing their export shipments steadily since 1985.

The chief lobbyist for the tobacco industry, the United States Cigarette Export Association (USCEA), claims that the export of tobacco is beneficial to the U.S. economy. It contributes substantially to the lowering of the country's enormous trade deficit, and it generates hundreds of thousands of jobs for Americans. According to U.S. Department of Commerce statistics, U.S. net exports of unmanufactured tobacco in the first half of 1990 amounted to $362.9 million. During the same period, the trade surplus in cigarettes amounted to $2,021.3 million. More than 125,000 people were directly involved in tobacco exports in 1989, and many others were employed in the derivative areas of the tobacco industry.

U.S. TRADE POLICY

This recent boom in U.S. exports is a direct result of the opening of new overseas markets in Asia to American tobacco products. The opening was achieved due to the success of the United States Trade Representative (USTR) in negotiating the elimination of unfair trade barriers in Asia. The USTR is the governmental organization charged with the promotion of U.S. trade interests abroad. In the name of free trade, the USTR acts on behalf of U.S. companies in negotiating for the removal of unfair trade barriers and any discriminatory trade practices directed against U.S. products. Under Section 301 of the Trade Act of 1974, the United States Trade Representative is obligated to investigate cases of trade discrimination faced by U.S. companies abroad.

Throughout the 1980s, the USCEA filed several petitions under Section 301 of the Trade Act of 1974 aimed at removing unfair foreign trade barriers in Japan, South Korea, Taiwan, and Thailand, which restricted the export of American tobacco products. U.S. cigarette exporters had long been experiencing trade discrimination in these potentially lucrative Asian countries. In Thailand, for instance, more than 60 percent of the adult males smoke. According to figures from the mid-1980s, approximately 40 percent of the people of both Japan and South Korea smoke. The governments of these countries had restricted the sale of foreign tobacco products because tobacco production and manufacturing play a significant part in their national economies. For example, Japan and Taiwan are ranked eighteenth and thirty-sixth in terms of tobacco production, respectively, out of a total of 94 tobacco-growing countries worldwide. The estimated green-weight tobacco production figures are 71,000 tons for Japan and 20,100 tons for Taiwan.

Realizing the importance of tobacco to their agricultural sector and to their financial coffers, the governments of the aforementioned countries had set up monopolies to protect their tobacco industries from foreign competition. The following statement in the 1989 annual report of the Thailand Tobacco Monopoly (TTM) illustrates clearly the function of such a government-controlled monopoly.

The outcome of operation of TTM not only creates income to the government to be used to develop the country, but also benefits many tobacco ranchers in the northern and northeastern regions whose major income is derived from tobacco plantations.

Japan, Taiwan, South Korea, and Thailand traditionally blocked the import of American cigarettes by imposing high import tariffs, discriminatory taxes, and unfair marketing and distribution restrictions. These trade practices caused outrage among the U.S. tobacco companies and led to the intervention of the USTR. The following are examples of the USTR successes in opening the previously closed tobacco markets.

Following the discovery of evidence that Japan imposed high tariffs and severe restrictions on the import and manufacturing of foreign cigarettes, the president of the United States instructed the USTR to initiate a Section 301 action against the country on September 16, 1985. This led Japan to remove cigarette tariffs, as well as other discriminatory barriers directed against imported cigarettes. Similarly, on December 12, 1986, Taiwan lifted its restrictions on the distribution and sale of U.S. tobacco products following the threat of retaliatory measures from the United States. After prolonged negotiations with the USTR, the South Korean Monopoly Corporation, the government tobacco monopoly in that country, agreed to allow U.S. cigarettes to enter the Korean market without discrimination on February 16, 1988.

PROMOTION OF TOBACCO EXPORTS

Besides ensuring fair treatment for U.S. cigarettes overseas, the U.S. government actively supports the export of tobacco by funding three export-promotion programs. These are the Department of Agriculture's Cooperator Market Development Program, the Targeted Export Assistance Program, and the Export Credit Guarantee programs.

The Department of Agriculture's cooperator program aims at expanding and seeking overseas markets for U.S. agricultural products through the efforts of private, nonprofit organizations. The Department of Agriculture allocates $150,000 to Tobacco Associates, the tobacco cooperator, to promote market development activities for U.S. tobacco products.

The Targeted Export Assistance Program's purpose is to counteract the adverse effects of subsidies, import quotas, or other unfair trade practices in foreign countries on U.S. agricultural products. Again, Tobacco Associates is the private organization entrusted to carry out this endeavor. In 1990, Tobacco Associates received $5 million in U.S. government funding to provide certain countries with the technical know-how, training, and equipment to manufacture cigarettes that use U.S. flue-cured and burley tobacco products.

Finally, the Department of Agriculture's Export Credit Guarantee programs, GSM 102 and 103, help U.S. farm export sales by stimulating U.S. bank financing of foreign purchases on credit terms. The GSM 102 program guarantees the repayment of loans extended up to three years, while the GSM 103 program guarantees loans of up to ten years. During the period between October 1985 and September 1989, 66 companies received GSM guarantee credits for the sale of 127 million pounds of tobacco, which had a market value of $214 million.

CONFLICTING OBJECTIVES

The involvement of the U.S. government in furthering the export of tobacco has generated controversy within the United States. This controversy centers on the dilemma of simultaneously pursuing policies that are obviously at odds with each other.

On one hand, the U.S. government, spearheaded by the Department of Health and Human Services, has been actively discouraging smoking on the domestic scene.

Also, the United States is a strong supporter of the worldwide antismoking movement. The Department of Health and Human Services serves as a collaborating headquarters for the United Nations World Health Organization and maintains close relationships with other health organizations around the world in sharing information on the detrimental health effects of smoking. On the other hand, a different part of the government, the USTR, has been helping tobacco companies expand their export sales by opening up previously closed markets. In addition, the government is actively promoting tobacco exports overseas by funding three export market development programs. The U.S. trade policy that aims to boost the exports of tobacco products is clearly in conflict with the U.S. health policy aimed at reducing the use of tobacco.

THE CURRENT SITUATION

U.S. production of tobacco has risen because of an increase in foreign demand for high-quality U.S. tobacco leaves. The Tobacco Merchants Association concluded in a 1989 report:

> As U.S. cigarette exports gain an even greater foothold in Asia, one would expect that the foreign monopoly demand for direct burley shipments, along with high-quality U.S. flue-cured, will grow as the monopolies compete head-to-head against U.S. cigarette blends.

The economic benefits, together with the fact that Asian countries such as Japan and Thailand are permitting tobacco advertisements, lead many members of Congress, such as Rep. Thomas J. Bliley of Virginia, to support U.S. tobacco exports. However, the health and moral questions surrounding tobacco exports continue to generate congressional and public opposition to tobacco exports. A vocal opponent of tobacco exports is Rep. Henry A. Waxman, who considers U.S. tobacco export policies morally offensive and comparable to the British exports of opium to China in the nineteenth century.

Questions for Discussion

1. Should U.S. exports of tobacco products be permitted in light of the domestic campaign against smoking?
2. Should the U.S. government get involved in tearing down foreign trade barriers to U.S. tobacco?
3. Should export promotion support be provided to U.S. tobacco producers?
4. To what degree should ethics influence government policy or corporate decision making in the case of tobacco exports?
5. Will your answers change if you differentiate between the short and the long term?

Union Carbide at Bhopal

On Sunday, December 3, 1984, the peaceful life of a U.S. corporate giant was joltingly disrupted. The Union Carbide plant at Bhopal, a city less than 400 miles from New Delhi, India, had leaked poisonous gas into the air. Within one week more than 2,000 people died and more remained critically ill. More than 100,000 people were treated for nausea, blindness, and bronchial problems. It was one of history's worst industrial accidents.

Union Carbide is America's thirty-seventh largest industrial corporation, with more than 100,000 employees, and annual sales of more than $9 billion. The firm is active in petrochemicals, industrial gases, metals and carbon products, consumer products, and technology transfers.

Union Carbide operated 14 plants in India. Total Indian operations accounted for less than 2 percent of corporate sales. In spite of a policy by the Indian government to restrict foreign majority ownership of plants, Union Carbide owned 50.9 percent of the Bhopal plant. This special arrangement was granted by the government because the plant served as a major technology transfer project. In order to achieve the goal of technology transfer, management of the plant was mostly carried out by Indian nationals. General corporate safety guidelines applied to the plant, but local regulatory agencies were charged with enforcing Indian environmental laws. Only three weeks before the accident, the plant had received an "environmental clearance certificate" from the Indian State Pollution Board.

The accident resulted in wide public awareness in the United States. A poll showed that 47 percent of those questioned linked Union Carbide's name to the Bhopal disaster. The direct impact of this awareness on Union Carbide's business remains uncertain. Most U.S. consumers do not connect the Union Carbide name to its line of consumer products, which consists of brands such as Energizer, Glad, and Presto. Industrial users, on the other hand, are highly aware of Union Carbide's products. One area that could be particularly affected is that of technology transfer, which in 1983 accounted for 24 percent of Union Carbide's revenues. The firm has concentrated increasingly on that sector, selling mainly its know-how in the fields of engineering, manufacturing, and personnel training.

THE PUBLIC REACTION	Internationally, the reaction was one of widespread consumer hostility. Environmentalists demonstrated at Union Carbide plants in West Germany and Australia. Some facilities were firebombed; most were spray painted. Plans for plants in Scotland had to be frozen. The operation of a plant in France was called into question by the French government.

Major financial repercussions occurred as well. Within a week of the accident, Union Carbide stock dropped by $10, a loss in market value of nearly $900 million. A $1.2 billion line of credit was frozen. Profits of Union Carbide India Ltd., which in 1984 had been about 8.2 million rupees, or about $480,000, dropped by 1985 to |

Source: This case study was written by Michael R. Czinkota by adapting secondary source materials from: Alan Hall, "The Bhopal Tragedy Has Union Carbide Reeling," *Business Week,* December 17, 1984, 32; Clemens P. Work, "Inside Story of Union Carbide's India Nightmare," *U.S. News & World Report,* January 21, 1985, 51-52; Armin Rosencranz, "Bhopal, Transnational Corporations, and Hazardous Technologies," *Ambio* 17, no. 5 (1988): 336-341; and Sanjoy Hazarika, "Carbide Plant Closed by India Unrest," *The New York Times,* May 13, 1991, D12.

1.3 million rupees, or $78,000. By 1990, the company reported a loss of 132 million rupees, about $7.8 million.

In the ensuing debate of the Bhopal disaster, three basic issues were highlighted—responsible industrial planning, adequate industrial safety measures, and corporate accountability. In terms of industrial planning, both Union Carbide and the Indian government were said to have failed. The Indian subsidiary of Union Carbide did little to inform workers about the highly toxic methyl isocyanate (MIC) the plant was producing and the potential health threat to neighboring regions. When the accident occurred, the subsidiary's management team reportedly resisted the parent company's instructions to apply first aid to victims for fear of generating widespread panic within the corporation and the region. The Indian government, on the other hand, seemed to regard technology transfer to be a higher priority than public safety. The local government approved construction of the plant with little medical and scientific investigation into its biological effects on the environment and on people.

The second issue was the absence of a "culture of safety" among Indian technicians, engineers, and management. From the very beginning, the project lacked a team of experienced maintenance personnel who would have recognized the need for higher safety measures and, more important, a different choice of technology. When the entire Indian government wholeheartedly approved the import of the most advanced chemical production facility in any developing country without qualified personnel to handle the material and without insight into appropriate precautionary measures in case of an accident, the seeds were sown for potential disaster.

The third area of interest in the Bhopal incident is that of corporate accountability. There are three general norms of international law concerning the jurisprudence of the home government over the foreign subsidiary:

1. Both state and nonstate entities are liable to pay compensation to the victims of environmental pollution and accidents.
2. The corporation is responsible for notifying and consulting the involved officials of actual and potential harm involved in the production and transport of hazardous technologies and materials.
3. The causer or originator of environmental damage is liable to pay compensation to the victims.

These and other developing norms of international law serve to make transnational corporations more responsible for their operations.

COMPENSATION TO VICTIMS

Five days after the incident, the first damage suit, asking for $15 billion, was filed in U.S. Federal District Court. Since then, more than 130 suits were filed in the United States and more than 2,700 in India. Union Carbide offered to pay $300 million over a period of 30 years to settle the cases before the courts in the United States and India. The Indian government rejected the offer, claiming that the amount was far below its original request of $615 million. By 1986, most U.S. lawsuits had been consolidated in the New York Federal Court. In May 1986, however, the judge presiding over the collective Bhopal cases ruled that all suits arising out of the accident should be heard in the Indian judicial system, claiming that "India is where the accident occurred, and where the victims, witnesses, and documents are located." While this decision appeared to benefit Union Carbide because of lower damage awards in India, the judge explicitly stated that (1) Union Carbide (USA) and its Indian affiliate would have to submit to the jurisdiction of the Indian court system, (2) Union Carbide had to turn over all relevant documents to the plaintiffs' lawyers in India as they would have had to do if in the United States, and (3) Union Carbide had to agree to whatever judgment was rendered in India. The decision had a major effect on Union Carbide (USA) because (1) both Union Carbide (USA) and its Indian subsidiary had to answer to the Indian court and (2) the entire company's assets had become involved.

In India, the class suit traveled from the Bhopal district court to the Madhya Pradesh High Court and finally to the Indian Supreme Court, where it stood as of May 1991. Although a settlement agreement was reached between Union Carbide and the Indian government, the descendants of the 2,000 victims were not satisfied. Several victims' consumer groups and public interest lawyers filed petitions contesting the authority of the government to handle the lawsuit on behalf of the victims' descendants. The petitions claimed that the government had no right to represent the victims because governmental negligence caused the accident in the first place and the government should be as much a target as Union Carbide in the suit itself. If the Indian Supreme Court were to uphold this rationale, then the government would be unable to settle on the victims' behalf, thereby nullifying the agreed amount. As a result of the internal debate in India, the $421 million paid in settlement by Union Carbide was frozen. Instead, the Indian government itself was disbursing 200 rupees, about $10, a month to all persons who lived in the neighborhoods affected by the gas leak. The government planned to get the expenses back when the case was completed.

The lessons learned? Several chemical companies have reduced the size of their storage tanks of toxic materials while others have cut their inventories by as much as 50 percent. Many have provided information to the communities in which they manufacture. Some have even invested in risk-assessment studies of their operations of hazardous materials.

Questions for Discussion

1. How could Union Carbide have planned for an event such as Bhopal?
2. How would such planning have improved corporate response to the disaster?
3. Does it make sense to base corporate strategy on worst-case scenarios?
4. Which other firms are exposed to similar risks?
5. What are the future implications for the management of Union Carbide?
6. What are the future implications for the government of India?
7. What are your views on the delay of compensation paid to the victims?
8. In general, should joint venture partners absorb part of the blame and cost when accidents occur?

IKEA: "It's a Big Country; Someone Has to Furnish It"

IKEA, the world's largest home furnishings retail chain, was founded in Sweden in 1943 as a mail-order company and opened its first showroom 10 years later. From its headquarters in Almhult, IKEA has since expanded to worldwide sales of more than $3 billion from 121 outlets in 25 countries (see Table 1). In fact, the second store that IKEA built was in Oslo, Norway. Today, IKEA operates large warehouse showrooms in Sweden, Norway, Denmark, Holland, France, Belgium, Germany, Switzerland, Austria, Canada, the United States, Saudi Arabia, and the United Kingdom. It has smaller stores in Kuwait, Australia, Hong Kong, Singapore, the Canary Islands, and Iceland. A store near Budapest opened in 1990; today eastern/central European sales account for 1.5 percent of the total.

The international expansion of IKEA has progressed in three phases, all of them continuing at the present time: Scandinavian expansion, begun in 1963; west European expansion, begun in 1973; and North American expansion, begun in 1974. Of the individual markets, Germany is the largest, accounting for 29.7 percent of company sales. The phases of expansion are detectable in the worldwide sales shares depicted in Figure 1. "We want to bring the IKEA concept to as many people as possible," IKEA officials have said.

TABLE 1
IKEA's International Expansion

Year	Outlets[a]	Countries[a]	Coworkers[b]	Catalog Circulation[c]	Turnover in Swedish Kronor[d]
1954	1	1	15	285,000	3,000,000
1964	2	2	250	1,200,000	79,000,000
1974	10	5	1,500	13,000,000	616,000,000
1984	66	17	8,300	45,000,000	6,770,000,000
1988	75	19	13,400	50,535,000	14,500,000,000
1990	95	23	16,850	N/A	19,400,000,000
1993	121	25	24,900	N/A	27,200,000,000

[a]Stores/countries being opened by the end of 1994.

[b]24,900 coworkers are equivalent to 20,400 full-time workers.

[c]13 languages, 29 editions; exact numbers no longer made available.

[d]Corresponding to net sales of the IKEA group of companies.

Source: IKEA U.S., Inc.

Source: This case, prepared by Ilkka A. Ronkainen, is based on: Bill Saporito, "IKEA's Got 'Em Lining Up," *Fortune,* March 11, 1991, 72; Rita Martenson, "Is Standardization of Marketing Feasible in Culture-Bound Industries? A European Case Study," *International Marketing Review* 4 (Autumn 1987): 7-17; Eleanor Johnson Tracy, "Shopping Swedish Style Comes to the U.S.," *Fortune,* January 27, 1986, 63-67; Mary Krienke, "IKEA—Simple Good Taste," *Stores,* April 1986, 58; Jennifer Lin, "IKEA's U.S. Translation," *Stores,* April 1986, 63; "Furniture Chain Has a Global View," *Advertising Age,* October 26, 1987, 58; and Bill Kelley, "The New Wave from Europe," *Sales and Marketing Management,* November 1987, 46-48. Updated information provided directly by IKEA U.S., Inc.

FIGURE 1
IKEA Worldwide Sales Expressed as Percentages of Turnover

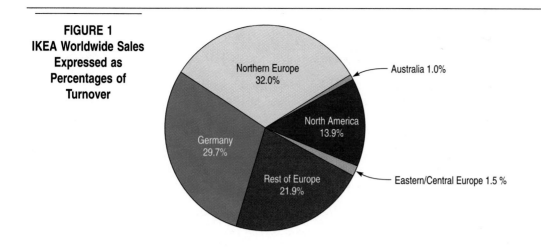

THE IKEA
CONCEPT

Ingvar Kamprad, the founder, formulated as IKEA's mission to "offer a wide range of home furnishings of good design and function at prices so low that the majority of people can afford to buy them." The principal target market of IKEA, which is similar across countries and regions in which IKEA has a presence, is composed of people who are young, highly educated, liberal in their cultural values, white-collar workers, and not especially concerned with status symbols.

IKEA follows a standardized product strategy with an identical assortment around the world. Today, IKEA carries an assortment of thousands of different home furnishings that range from plants to pots, sofas to soup spoons, and wine glasses to wallpaper. The smaller items are carried to complement the bigger ones. IKEA does not have its own manufacturing facilities but designs all of its furniture. The network of subcontracted manufacturers numbers nearly 2,300 in 70 countries. IKEA shoppers have to become "prosumers"—half producers, half consumers—because most products must be assembled.

Manufacturers are responsible for shipping the components to large warehouses, for example, to the central one in Almhult. The distribution centers (of which there are 12) then supply the various stores, which are in effect miniwarehouses. The final distribution is the customer's responsibility. IKEA does cooperate with car rental companies to offer vans and small trucks at reasonable rates for customers needing delivery service.

Although IKEA has concentrated on company-owned, larger-scale outlets, franchising has been used in areas in which the market is relatively small or where uncertainty may exist as to the response to the IKEA concept. IKEA uses mail order in Europe and Canada but has resisted expansion into it in the United States, mainly because of capacity constraints.

IKEA offers prices that are 30 to 50 percent lower than fully assembled competing products. This is a result of large-quantity purchasing, low-cost logistics, store location in suburban areas, and the do-it-yourself approach to marketing. IKEA's prices do vary from market to market, largely because of fluctuations in exchange rates and differences in taxation regimes, but price positioning is kept as standardized as possible.

TABLE 2 The IKEA Concept	Target market:	"Young people of all ages"
	Product:	IKEA offers the same products worldwide. The countries of origin of these products are: Nordic countries (33.4 percent), western Europe (29.6 percent), eastern Europe (14.3 percent), and others (22.7 percent). Most items have to be assembled by the customer. The furniture design is modern and light. Textiles and pastels.
	Distribution:	IKEA has built its own distribution network. Outlets are outside the city limits of major metropolitan areas. Products are not delivered, but IKEA cooperates with car rental companies that offer small trucks. IKEA offers mail order in Europe and Canada.
	Pricing:	The IKEA concept is based on low price. The firm tries to keep its price image constant.
	Promotion:	IKEA's promotional efforts are mainly through its catalogs. IKEA has developed a prototype communications model that must be followed by all stores. Its advertising is attention-getting and provocative. Media choices vary by market.

IKEA's promotion is centered on the catalog. The IKEA catalog is printed in 13 languages and has a worldwide circulation of well over 50 million copies. The catalogs are uniform in layout except for minor regional differences. The company's advertising goal is to generate word-of-mouth publicity through innovative approaches.

The IKEA concept is summarized in Table 2.

IKEA IN THE COMPETITIVE ENVIRONMENT

IKEA's strategic positioning is unique. As Figure 2 illustrates, few furniture retailers anywhere have engaged in long-term planning or achieved scale economies in production. European furniture retailers, especially those in Sweden, Switzerland, Germany, and Austria, are much smaller than IKEA. Even when companies have joined forces as buying groups, their heterogeneous operations have made it difficult for them to achieve the same degree of coordination and concentration as IKEA. Customers are usually content to wait for delivery of furniture, so retailers have not been forced to take purchasing risks.

The value-added dimension differentiates IKEA from its competition. IKEA offers limited customer assistance but creates opportunities for consumers to choose (for example, through informational signage), transport, and assemble units of furniture. The best summary of the competitive situation was provided by a manager at another firm: "We can't do what IKEA does, and IKEA doesn't want to do what we do."

IKEA IN THE UNITED STATES

After careful study and assessment of its Canadian experience, IKEA decided to enter the U.S. market in 1985 by establishing outlets on the East Coast and, later, one in Burbank, California. IKEA's six stores on the East Coast (Philadelphia; Woodbridge near Washington, D.C.; Baltimore; Pittsburgh; Elizabeth, New Jersey; and Hicksville, New York) generated $337 million in 1992. The overwhelming level of success in 1987 led the company to invest in a warehousing facility near Philadelphia that receives goods from Sweden as well as directly from suppliers around the world. Plans call for two to three additional stores annually over the next 25 years, concentrating on the northeastern United States and California.

**FIGURE 2
Competition in
Furniture Retailing**

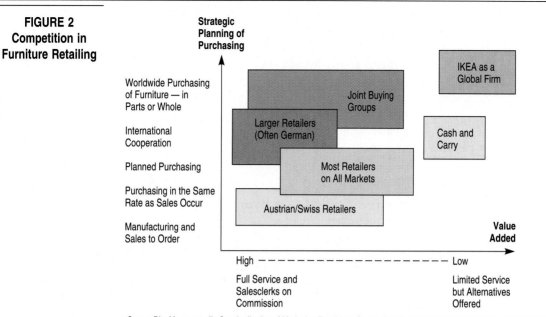

Worldwide Purchasing
of Furniture — in
Parts or Whole

International
Cooperation

Planned Purchasing

Purchasing in the Same
Rate as Sales Occur

Manufacturing and
Sales to Order

Source: Rita Martenson, "Is Standardization of Marketing Feasible in Culture-Bound Industries? A European Case Study," *International Marketing Review* 4 (Autumn 1987): *14.*

Questions for Discussion

1. What accounts for IKEA's success with a standardized product and strategy in a business that is usually described as having some of the strongest cultural influences? Consider, for example, that an American buying IKEA beds will also have to buy IKEA sheets, because the beds are in European sizes.

2. Which features of the "young people of all ages" are universal and can be exploited by a global/regional strategy?

3. Is IKEA destined to succeed everywhere it cares to establish itself?

Ecological Cooling: The Fridge from Eastern Germany

In March of 1993, mass production of the world's first refrigerator that works without damaging the earth's vital ozone layer began in Niederschmiedeberg, the hometown of a small eastern German firm. FORON Domestic Appliances GmbH offers the first "green" refrigerator, completely free of chlorofluorocarbons (CFCs). The road to this achievement, however, was not easy.

CFCs AND THE MONTREAL AGREEMENT

For decades, chlorofluorocarbons (CFCs) were the refrigerants of choice worldwide. They were nontoxic, nonflammable and energy-efficient. The price of $.57 per pound in 1980 also made CFCs quite inexpensive. Introduced in the 1930s, CFCs by 1985 represented a worldwide market of $1.5 billion a year.

Since 1974, scientists had theorized that CFCs could deplete the earth's ozone layer, which shields the earth from the sun's harmful ultraviolet rays. As a result of these implications, and due to public pressure, the U.S. government banned the use of CFCs in aerosol propellants in 1978. Due to the nonavailability of reasonable substitutes, however, the use of CFCs in refrigerators and air conditioners continued to be permitted.

After scientists observed a hole in the ozone layer over Antarctica, nations from around the world enacted the 1987 Montreal Protocol, which called for a 50 percent cut in CFC use by mid-1998. Given the growing public concern with environmental issues, the protocol was subsequently revised twice: in 1990, it was agreed that the 50 percent reduction in most CFCs was to be achieved by 1995 and the 1992 revision banned all CFC use by 1996.

The ban had a chilling effect on the producers of cooling devices since they depended heavily on CFCs. For example, to reduce energy consumption, refrigerators are insulated with polyurethane foam. During manufacture, the foam is saturated with 300 to 600 grams of CFCs. The gas remains in the foam and because it insulates better than air, the gas provides for heat insulation. The disadvantage of CFC-foamed polyurethane is that the CFCs gradually diffuse out of the foam and are replaced by air. The CFC escapes into the atmosphere and destroys the ozone layer. The energy efficiency of the refrigerators also deteriorates considerably over the years due to the CFC–air exchange.

CFCs also contribute to the actual refrigeration process. Due to their thermodynamic properties, CFCs are highly temperature responsive to compression and expansion, therefore allowing an efficient cooling process to take place. Even though hermetically sealed, a leaky pipe or uncontrolled disposal can result in the gradual release of up to 250 grams of CFCs.

dkk SCHARFENSTEIN

Deutsche Klima and Kraftmaschinen AG was founded in the German state of Saxony in 1927. The firm concentrated on producing heating and cooling devices together with compressors. In the 1950s the East German communist regime took over the firm as state property and renamed it dkk Scharfenstein. As the only firm in Eastern

Source: This case was written by Michael R. Czinkota based on discussions with Dr. Juergen Lembke, head of marketing, FORON GmbH, and reports by German and U.S. media. Financial and logistical support from the U.S. Information Agency (USIA) is gratefully acknowledged.

Europe producing both refrigerators and compressors, dkk Scharfenstein (DKK) soon achieved a leadership position in the region. By 1989, the firm's 5,200 employees produced more than 1 million refrigerators and 1.5 million compressors. Every apartment built by the East Germany regime had a refrigerator made by DKK. Ten million East German households had a DKK fridge; 80 percent of households had its freezers.

With the fall of the Berlin Wall on November 9, 1989, and the collapse of communism in Eastern Europe, DKK's markets collapsed as well. Long-term export contracts were rescinded. At the same time, domestic demand declined precipitously as stylish new products from West Germany became available. By 1992, production had declined to 200,000 refrigerators, and employment had shrunk to 1,000. In light of the continuing decline of its business, dkk Scharfenstein was taken over by Germany's Treuhandanstalt, the German government's privatization arm.

DEVELOPMENT OF THE ECO-FRIDGE

dkk Scharfenstein had been familiar with the ecological problems of CFCs since the mid-eighties. At that time, the firm had considered a switch to hydrofluorocarbon (HFC) 134a. This new chemical did not contain chlorine, but still made use of fluor, which contributes to the greenhouse effect and to global warming. However, these plans were abandoned for two reasons. First, the price of HFC 134a was far more than that of CFC. Second, unlike its Western counterparts, Scharfenstein was unable to obtain the product from Western markets due to export control regulations promulgated by the Multilateral Committee for Export Controls (COCOM). While HFC 134a was available in the Soviet Union, only very limited quantities were offered for sale.

After 1990, HFC 134a became freely available in eastern Germany. By that time, however, the Scharfenstein staff already was working on a different project. In conjunction with Professor Harry Rosin, head of the Dortmund Institute for Hygiene, Scharfenstein had focused on a mix of butane and propane gases to cool its refrigerators. The ingredients were environmentally friendly and, with newly designed compressors, the equipment operated with less electrical power.

Management presented the new product to Treuhand, in an effort to stave off the liquidation of the firm. Treuhand attempted to interest a consortium consisting of the German firms Bosch and Siemens in acquiring Scharfenstein. After a cursory review, however, both firms decided that the new technology was too radical, unproven, and flammable and withdrew from all discussions. They, like major competitors such as Whirlpool and AEG, would continue to concentrate on HFC 134a research and production. Although expensive, HFC 134a now was competitive because new taxes had increased CFC prices to more than $5 per pound. In addition, major investments had already been made into HFC production. For example, in its race against DuPont and Elf Atochem, the British firm Imperial Chemical Industries PLC alone already had invested nearly $500 million into HFC development. To ensure that retailers would share their perspective, major producers of refrigerators supplied leaflets that warned about the dangers of explosion of fridges filled with propane and butane.

Treuhand did not approve the production of the new fridge. In light of mounting losses, an additional 360 Scharfenstein employees were laid off and Treuhand announced plans to liquidate the firm.

Facing the shutdown of its operations, Scharfenstein's management decided to go public with its new product. Information on the CFC-free fridge was sent to all manufacturers of refrigeration equipment, none of whom showed any interest.

However, interest did materialize from unexpected quarters: The leadership of the Greenpeace organization. This worldwide environmental nonprofit group quickly recognized the benefits of the new fridge. It commissioned 10 prototype models to be produced, and after finding them satisfactory, mounted a $300,000 advertising campaign in favor of the production of "greenfreeze." Intense negotiations with retailers brought in orders and options for 70,000 of the refrigerators.

The future of Scharfenstein brightened immediately. The German Ministry for the Environment supported a capital infusion of $3 million into the company. Shortly thereafter, Treuhand rescinded the layoffs that had been announced. By 1993, the firm was acquired by a consortium of British, Kuwaiti, and German investors and renamed FORON Household Appliances GmbH.

Since then, FORON has received various environmental prizes and labels. The firm was awarded the government's coveted Blue Angel symbol for environmental friendliness. The German Technical Society awarded its safety seal of approval. The business magazine *DM* named the fridge its product of the year.

The giant German appliance manufacturers, which once scorned the new technology as "impossible, dangerous and too energy-consuming," now are scrambling to put out their own green refrigerators. Major efforts for CFC-free refrigerators are also being undertaken by U.S. and Japanese manufacturers. In the United States, a group of utilities offered $30 million to the manufacturer that designed the most energy efficient refrigerator without using CFCs.

FORON expects to produce more than 160,000 eco-fridges per year and actively is exploring the possibility of exports. Inquiries have been received from China, Japan, the United States, India, Australia, and New Zealand. Even though the product is priced some 5 to 10 percent more than conventional models, the firm believes that "consumers who are environmentally aware will pay the price."

Questions for Discussion

1. Why is the acceptance of innovation sometimes inhibited by established industry players?
2. Evaluate the role of Greenpeace in promoting the eco-fridge. Is such an activity appropriate for a nonprofit organization?
3. What motivated Scharfenstein's investment in environmentally friendly technology?
4. How can governments encourage the development of environmentally responsive technology?

A Taste of the West

In the mid-1980s, Mikhail Gorbachev introduced a new program called "perestroika" in the Soviet Union. Perestroika was to fundamentally reform the Soviet economy by improving the overall technological and industrial base as well as improving the quality of life for Soviet citizens through increased availability of food, housing, and consumer goods. It was hoped that this program would stimulate the entrepreneurial spirit of Soviet citizens and help the country and its government overcome crucial shortcomings. These shortcomings were the result of decades of communist orientation, which had led to significant capital and management shortages and inhibited the development of a market orientation and of consumer-oriented technology.

In subsequent years, a number of joint ventures between Western firms and Soviet institutions were either contemplated or even formed. However, many of the ventures, due to internal difficulties, met with only limited success. Nevertheless, the efforts of one firm, McDonald's—an icon of free enterprise—were hailed as a spectacular success.

The January 31, 1990, grand opening of McDonald's in the center of Moscow represented an important milestone for McDonald's Corporation and for the food-service industry in the Soviet Union. The state-of-the-art renovated building, formerly a cafe and a cultural gathering place, has indoor seating for more than 700 people, has outside seating for 200, and is fully accessible to the handicapped. It currently employs more than 1,000 people—the largest McDonald's crew in the world—and has served more than 30,000 people per day. The original plans were to serve between 10,000 and 15,000 customers per day. The Soviet Union became the fifty-second country to host the world's largest quick-service food restaurant company, and the Russian language is the twenty-eighth working language in which the company operates. McDonald's Corporation, based in Oak Brook, Illinois, serves more than 22 million people daily in 11,000 restaurants in 52 countries. The Soviet population of more than 291 million represented a major potential market of new customers for McDonald's.

THE NEGOTIATIONS

George A. Cohon, vice chairman of Moscow McDonald's and president and chief executive officer of McDonald's Restaurants of Canada, Limited, provided the leadership for the company's successful venture. His personal commitment and energy were irreplaceable during the long period of joint-venture discussions with the Soviet Union. Cohon's Canadian team spent more than 12 years negotiating the agreement for McDonald's to enter into the Soviet market. In April 1988, agreement was reached on the largest joint venture ever made between a food company and the Soviet Union. This concluded the longest new-territory negotiations by the company since it was founded in 1955.

Sources: McDonald's corporate information, 1994; "A Month Later, Moscow McDonald's Is Still Drawing Long and Hungry Lines," *Houston Post,* March 1, 1990; background information from McDonald's Restaurants of Canada, Ltd.; Jeffrey A. Tannenbaum, "Franchisers See a Future in East Bloc," *The Wall Street Journal,* June 5, 1990, B1; Kevin Maney and Diane Rinehart, "McDonald's in Moscow Opens Today," *USA Today,* January 31, 1990, B1; "McDonald's on the Volga," *Employment Review* 3 (1990); Moscow McDonald's videotape produced for Dryden Press, 1990; Oliver Wates, "Crowds Still Gather at Lenin's Tomb, but Lineups are Longer at McDonald's," *London Free Press,* June 9, 1990.

Cohon and his Canadian team had spent thousands of hours in Moscow making presentations to hundreds of senior trade officials, staff at various ministries, and countless other groups within the Soviet Union. Despite numerous setbacks and requests for endless submissions of and revisions to their proposals, Cohon persisted because many Soviets appeared to genuinely want to establish closer ties with the West. According to Cohon, McDonald's negotiations "outlived three Soviet premiers."

The historic joint-venture contract provided for an initial 20 McDonald's restaurants in Moscow and a state-of-the-art food production and distribution center to supply the restaurants. McDonald's accepts only rubles; future restaurants may accept hard currency. McDonald's Canada is managing the new venture in partnership with the Food Service Administration of the Moscow City Council in a 51 to 49 percent Soviet-Canadian partnership.

INTERNATIONAL TECHNOLOGY TRANSFER

Cohon stated that what ultimately sold the Soviets on McDonald's was the food technology it had to offer. In addition, the company's emphasis on quality, service, cleanliness, and value convinced the Moscow city officials that McDonald's could work in their city. Vladimir Malyshkov, chairman of the board of Moscow McDonald's, stated that McDonald's "created a restaurant experience like no other in the Soviet Union. It demonstrates what can be achieved when people work together."

Moscow McDonald's was clearly an international venture. McDonald's personnel from around the world helped prepare for the opening. Dutch agricultural consultants assisted in improving agricultural production. For example, they helped plant and harvest a variety of potato needed to make french fries that met McDonald's quality standards. Other international consultants assisted in negotiating contracts with farmers throughout the country to provide quality beef and other food supplies, including onions, lettuce, pickles, milk, flour, and butter. Once the Soviet farmers learned to trust the consultants, they became eager to learn about the new Western production technologies.

The technology transfer provided important long-term benefits to the Soviet citizenry. For example, through the transfer of agricultural technology and equipment, the Soviet potato farm Kishira increased its yield by 100 percent. According to the Kishira chairman, farmers from all over the Soviet Union requested technical training in production methods to increase their crop yields. Also, since the Soviet machinery lagged 15 to 20 years behind Western technology, new machinery from Holland was used to harvest the potatoes used to make french fries. However, according to a Dutch agricultural consultant, because of the McDonald's venture, it may not take the Soviets 20 years to catch up to Western production methods.

The development of a 10,000-square-meter food production and distribution center, located in the Moscow suburb of Solntsevo, was also an international effort involving equipment and furnishings from Austria, Canada, Denmark, Finland, Germany, Holland, Italy, Japan, Spain, Sweden, Switzerland, Taiwan, Turkey, the United Kingdom, the United States, and Yugoslavia. The center provides a state-of-the-art food-processing environment that meets McDonald's rigid standards.

At full capacity, the center employs more than 250 workers. Also at full capacity, the meat line produces 10,000 patties per hour from locally acquired beef. Milk delivered in McDonald's refrigerated dairy trucks from a local farm is pasteurized and processed at the center. Flour, yeast, sugar, and shortening are used to produce more than 14,000 buns per hour on the center's bakery line. Storage space at the center holds 3,000 tons of potatoes, and the pie line produces 5,000 apple pies per hour, made from fruit from local farmers.

MANAGEMENT TRAINING

Training for McDonald's crew and managers is essential to the customer service that the company provides. According to Bob Hissink, vice president of operations for Moscow McDonald's, hiring was just the beginning of assembling the largest McDonald's crew in the world. More than 25,000 applications were sorted, and 5,000 of the most qualified candidates were interviewed. Finally, the 630 new members of the first Moscow McDonald's team were selected. Initial training sessions were compressed into a four-week period with four or five shifts 12 hours a day. Seasoned McDonald's staff from around the world assisted the Soviet managers with crew training. The new crew of 353 women and 277 men was trained to work in several different capacities at the restaurant and had accumulated more than 15,000 hours of skills development by opening day. During restaurant operating hours, about 200 crew members at a time are on duty.

The training requirements were more extensive for McDonald's managers. Four Soviets selected as managers of Moscow McDonald's spent more than nine months in North American training programs that must be completed by any McDonald's manager in the world. The Soviets graduated from the Canadian Institute of Hamburgerology after completing more than 1,000 hours of training. Their studies included classroom instruction, equipment-maintenance techniques, and on-the-job restaurant management.

Their training also included a two-week, in-depth study program at Hamburger University, McDonald's international training center in Oak Brook, Illinois. With more than 200 other managers from around the world, they completed advanced restaurant operations studies in senior management techniques and operating procedures. The Soviet managers were thus qualified to manage any McDonald's restaurant in the world.

THE GRADUAL EXPANSION

Initially, McDonald's Corporation had expected a rather quick expansion of restaurants. However, political and economic difficulties slowed progress. In 1991, the Soviet Union ceased to exist. From then on, the firm had to deal with the new Russian government. But at the original McDonald's on Pushkin Square, the 27 cash registers at the 70-foot service counter kept on ringing. In spite of all the political changes, by June 1993, more than 50 million customers had been served at a rate of 40,000 to 50,000 a day. The original staff of 630 had grown to 1,500, and the initial 80 expatriates working in Moscow had dwindled to less than a dozen.

On June 1, 1993, the McDonald's office building opened in Moscow. The 12-story building had cost the equivalent of $50 million. It was the most modern office building in Moscow and had prestige tenants such as Coca-Cola, American Express, Mitsui, and the Upjohn Company. On its main floor was the second McDonald's restaurant, which was opened by Russian President Boris Yeltsin. Only one month later, the third McDonald's restaurant opened in Moscow's Arbat district. Like its predecessors, this restaurant too accepted only rubles. Ten thousand people waited in line for the opening to taste the food and see the restoration of the historic building in which the restaurant was located. By the end of the first day, this new restaurant had served 60,000 people. The day's receipts, an estimated 50 million rubles, were presented to Mrs. Yeltsin, in support of child health care.

THE LONG-TERM VISION

According to Cohon, "McDonald's is a business, but also is a responsible member of the communities it serves. The joint venture should help foster cooperation between nations and a better understanding among people. When individuals from around the world work shoulder-to-shoulder, they learn to communicate, to get along, and to be part of a team. That's what we call burger diplomacy." There is a Russian expression that says that you must eat many meals with a person before you come to know him. At 70,000 meals per day, it may not take long for the Russians to better understand the West through its corporate ambassador, McDonald's.

Questions for Discussion

1. Was Cohon's negotiation effort worth the success? Why or why not?
2. Discuss the extent of infrastructural investment necessary to start the first McDonald's restaurant in Moscow.
3. What is the effect of the "ruble only" policy?
4. How can McDonald's use the acquired rubles?

P A R T   4

International Business Preparation and Market Entry

In order to operate successfully abroad, firms must prepare for their market entry. This preparation requires substantial research to provide an understanding of country specific issues and market specific opportunities and concerns. Only after this understanding is achieved should the company enter international markets—first through exporting and international intermediaries, and later on through foreign direct investment and gradual multinational expansion.

CHAPTER 11

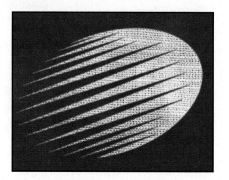

International Business Research

Learning Objectives

1. To gain an understanding of the need for research.

2. To explore the differences between domestic and international research.

3. To learn where to find and how to use sources of secondary information.

4. To gain insight into the gathering of primary data.

5. To examine the need for international management information systems.

Globalbase Has the World Covered

Information Access Company (IAC) of Foster City, California, doubled the coverage of its on-line database known as Globalbase. Approximately 350 trade journals, newspapers, and business magazines spanning 40 countries have been added, increasing Globalbase's coverage to nearly 700 titles. Ninety-five percent of these titles are published outside the United States.

Paul Owen, IAC's vice president of corporate sales and marketing, commented, "With the addition of hundreds of leading Asian and European newspapers and business journals to Globalbase, on-line users can be assured of finding unique regional, national, and international information that is indispensable to their business research."

Globalbase significantly increased its focus on Asia and Pacific Rim countries. One hundred titles from the region were added, half of which from Hong Kong and Singapore. The database also provides greater depth in its coverage of European business, with particular emphasis on the United Kingdom, France, Germany, and the Scandinavian countries. The newly improved source for international business research provides broad coverage of more than 60 major worldwide industries, and shows exceptional strength in the areas of finance, banking, and insurance.

Globalbase focuses on information relating to company activities, market data and trends, new products, and applied technologies. It also captures additional information on company spending and quarterly earnings, interim economic data, contracts, and personnel changes.

Source: "Infomat Database Renamed Globalbase, Coverage Doubled," *Information Today,* February 1994, 11.

The single most important cause for failure in international business is insufficient preparation and information. The failure of managers to comprehend cultural disparities, the failure to remember that customers differ from country to country, and the lack of investigation into whether or not a market exists prior to market entry has made international business a high-risk activity.[1] International business research is therefore instrumental to international business success since it permits the firm to take into account different environments, attitudes, and market conditions. Yet, such research has also become less complicated. As the opening vignette shows, information and research from around the globe can be obtained quite easily.

This chapter discusses data collection and provides a comprehensive overview of how to obtain general screening information on international markets, to evaluate business potential, and to assess current or potential opportunities and problems. Data sources that are low cost and that take little time to accumulate—in short, secondary data—are considered first. The balance of the chapter is devoted to more sophisticated forms of international research, including primary data collection and the development of an information system.

INTERNATIONAL AND DOMESTIC RESEARCH

The tools and techniques of international research are the same as those of domestic research. The difference is in the environment to which the tools are applied. The environment determines how well the tools, techniques, and concepts work. Although the objectives of research may be the same, the execution of international research may differ substantially from that of domestic research. The four primary reasons for this difference are new parameters, new environmental factors, an increase in the number of factors involved, and a broader definition of competition.

New Parameters   In crossing national borders, a firm encounters parameters not found in domestic business. Examples include duties, foreign currencies and changes in their value, different modes of transportation, and international documentation. New parameters also emerge because of differing modes of operating internationally. For example, the firm can export, it can license its products, it can engage in a joint venture, or it can carry out foreign direct investment. The firm that has done business only domestically will have had little or no experience with the requirements and conditions of these types of operations. Managers must therefore obtain information about them in order to make good business decisions.

New Environmental Factors   When going international, a firm is exposed to an unfamiliar environment. Many of the domestic assumptions on which the firm and its activities were founded may not hold true internationally. Management needs to learn the culture of the host country, understand its political systems and its level of stability, and comprehend the existing differences in societal structures and language. In addition, it must understand pertinent legal issues in order to avoid violating local laws. The technological level of the society must also be incorporated in the business plan. In short, all the assumptions that were formulated over the years based on domestic business activities must be reevaluated. This crucial point is often neglected because most managers are born in the environment of their domestic operations and only subconsciously learn to understand the constraints and opportunities of their business activities. The situation is analogous to learning one's native language. Even without much formal training, native speakers may use the language correctly. Only when attempting to learn a foreign language will they begin to appreciate the structure of language and the need for grammatical rules.

The Number of Factors Involved   Environmental relationships need to be relearned whenever a firm enters a new international market. The number of changing dimensions increases geometrically. Coordination of interaction among the dimensions becomes increasingly difficult because of their sheer number. The international research process can help in this undertaking.

Broader Definition of Competition   The international market exposes the firm to a much greater variety of competition than found in the home market. For example, a firm may find that ketchup competes against soy sauce. Similarly, firms that offer labor-saving devices domestically may suddenly be exposed to competition from cheap manual labor. As a result, the firms must determine the breadth of the competition, track competitive activities, and evaluate their actual and potential impact on its own operations.

RECOGNIZING THE NEED FOR INTERNATIONAL RESEARCH

Many firms do little research before they enter a foreign market. Often, decisions concerning entry and expansion in overseas markets and selection and appointment of distributors are made after a cursory, subjective assessment of the situation. The research done is often less rigorous, less formal, less quantitative than for domestic activities. Furthermore, once a firm has entered a foreign market, it is likely to discontinue researching that market. Many business executives appear to view foreign research as relatively unimportant.

A major reason why managers are reluctant to engage in international research is their lack of sensitivity to differences in culture, consumer tastes, and market demands. Often managers assume that their methods are both best and acceptable to all others. Fortunately, this is not true. What a boring place the world would be if it were!

A second reason is limited appreciation for the different environments abroad. Often firms are not prepared to accept that labor rules, distribution systems, the availability of media, or advertising regulations may be entirely different from those in the home market. Due to pressure to satisfy short-term financial goals, managers are unwilling to spend money to find out about the differences.

A third reason is lack of familiarity with national and international data sources and inability to use international data once they are obtained. As a result, the cost of conducting international research is seen as prohibitively high and therefore not a worthwhile investment relative to the benefits to be gained.[2]

Finally, firms often build their international business activities gradually, frequently based on unsolicited orders. Over time, actual business experience in a country or with a specific firm may then be used as a substitute for organized research.

Despite the reservations firms have, research is as important internationally as it is domestically. Firms must learn where the opportunities are, what customers want, why they want it, and how they satisfy their needs and wants so that the firm can serve them efficiently. Firms must obtain information about the local infrastructure, labor market, and tax rules before making a plant location decision. Doing business abroad without the benefit of research places firms, their assets, and their entire international future at risk.

Research allows management to identify and develop international strategies. The task includes the identification, evaluation, and comparison of potential foreign business opportunities and the subsequent target market selection. In addition, research is necessary for the development of a business plan that identifies all the requirements necessary for market entry, market penetration, and expansion. On a continuing basis, research provides the feedback needed to fine-tune various business activities. Finally, research can provide management with the intelligence to help anticipate events, take appropriate action, and adequately prepare for global changes.

DETERMINING RESEARCH OBJECTIVES

Before research can be undertaken, research objectives must be determined. They will vary depending on the views of management, the corporate mission of the firm, the firm's level of internationalization, and its competitive situation.

Going International—Exporting

A frequent objective of international research is that of foreign market opportunity analysis. When a firm launches its international activities, it will usually find the world to be uncharted territory. Fortunately, information can be accumulated to provide basic guidelines. The aim is not to conduct a painstaking and detailed analysis of the world on a market-by-market basis, but instead to utilize a broadbrush approach. Accomplished quickly and at low cost, this approach will narrow the possibilities for international business activities.

Such an approach should begin with a cursory analysis of general variables of a country, including total and per capita GNP, mortality rates, and population figures.

Although these factors in themselves will not provide any detailed information, they will enable the researcher to determine whether corporate objectives might be met in the market. For example, high-priced consumer products are unlikely to be successful in the People's Republic of China, as their price may be equal to a significant proportion of the annual salary of the customer, the benefit to the customer may be minimal, and the government is likely to prohibit their importation. Similarly, the offering of computer software services may be of little value in a country where there is very limited use of computers. Such a cursory evaluation will help reduce the number of markets to be considered to a more manageable number—for example, from 168 to 25.

As a next step, the researcher will require information on each individual country for a preliminary evaluation. Information typically desired will highlight the fastest growing markets, the largest markets for a particular product or service, demand trends, and business restrictions. Although precise and detailed information may not be obtainable, information is available for general product categories or service industries. Again, this overview will be cursory but will serve to quickly evaluate markets and further reduce their number.

At this stage, the researcher must select appropriate markets for in-depth evaluation. The focus will now be on opportunities for a specific type of service, product, or brand, and will include an assessment as to whether demand already exists or can be stimulated. Even though aggregate industry data have been obtained previously, this general information is insufficient to make company-specific decisions. For example, the demand for medical equipment should not be confused with the potential demand for a specific brand.[3] The research now should identify demand and supply patterns and evaluate any regulations and standards. Finally, a **competitive assessment** needs to be made, matching markets to corporate strengths and providing an analysis of the best potential for specific offerings. A summary of the various stages in the determination of market potential is provided in Figure 11.1.

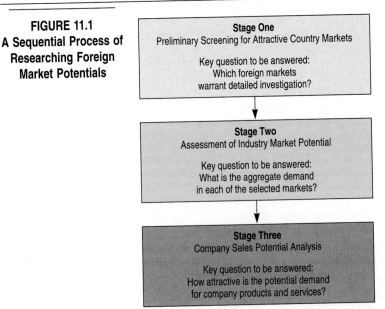

FIGURE 11.1
A Sequential Process of Researching Foreign Market Potentials

Stage One
Preliminary Screening for Attractive Country Markets

Key question to be answered:
Which foreign markets
warrant detailed investigation?

Stage Two
Assessment of Industry Market Potential

Key question to be answered:
What is the aggregate demand
in each of the selected markets?

Stage Three
Company Sales Potential Analysis

Key question to be answered:
How attractive is the potential demand
for company products and services?

Source: S. Tamer Cavusgil, "Guidelines for Export Market Research," *Business Horizons* 28 (November-December 1985): 29. Copyright 1985 by the Foundation for the School of Business at Indiana University. Reprinted by permission.

Going International—Importing

When importing, the major focus shifts from supplying to sourcing. Management must identify markets that produce supplies or materials desired or that have the potential to do so. Foreign firms must be evaluated in terms of their capabilities and competitive standing.

Just as management would want to have some details on a domestic supplier, the importer needs to know, for example, about the reliability of a foreign supplier, the consistency of its product or service quality, and the length of delivery time. Information obtained through the subsidiary office of a bank or an embassy can prove very helpful.

In addition, foreign rules must be scrutinized as to whether exportation is possible. As examples, India may set limits on the cobra handbags it allows to be exported, and laws protecting a nation's cultural heritage may prevent the exportation of pre-Columbian artifacts from Latin American countries.

The international manager must also analyze domestic restrictions and legislation that may prohibit the importation of certain goods into the home country. Even though a market may exist at home for foreign umbrella handles, for example, quotas may restrict their importation to protect domestic industries. Similarly, even though domestic demand may exist for ivory, its importation may be illegal because of legislation enacted to protect wildlife worldwide.

Market Expansion

Research objectives include obtaining more detailed information for business expansion or monitoring the political climate so that the firm successfully can maintain its international operation. Information may be needed to enable the international manager to evaluate new business partners or assess the impact of a technological breakthrough on future business operations. The better defined the research objective is, the better the researcher will be able to determine information requirements and thus conserve the time and financial resources of the firm.

CONDUCTING SECONDARY RESEARCH

Identifying Sources of Data

Typically, the information requirements of firms will cover both macro information about countries and trade, as well as micro information specific to the firm's activities. Table 11.1 provides an overview of the type of information that, according to a survey of executives, is most crucial for international business. If each firm had to go out and collect all the information needed on-site in the country under scrutiny, the task would be unwieldy and far too expensive. On many occasions, however, firms can make use of secondary data, that is, information that already has been collected by some other organization. A wide variety of sources present **secondary data.** The principal ones are governments, international institutions, service organizations, trade associations, directories, and other firms. This section provides a brief review of major data sources. Details on selected monitors of international issues are presented in Appendix 11A at the end of the chapter.

Governments   Most countries have a wide array of national and international trade data available. Typically, the information provided by governments addresses either

**TABLE 11.1
Most Critical
International
Information for
U.S. Firms**

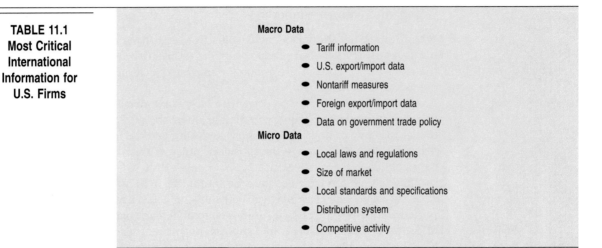

Macro Data

- Tariff information
- U.S. export/import data
- Nontariff measures
- Foreign export/import data
- Data on government trade policy

Micro Data

- Local laws and regulations
- Size of market
- Local standards and specifications
- Distribution system
- Competitive activity

Source: Michael R. Czinkota, "International Information Needs for U.S. Competitiveness," *Business Horizons* 34, 6 (November-December 1991): 86–91.

macro or micro issues or offers specific data services. Macro information includes data on population trends, general trade flows among countries, and world agricultural production. Micro information includes materials on specific industries in a country, their growth prospects, and their foreign trade activities.

Unfortunately, the data are often published only in their home countries and in their native languages. The publications mainly present numerical data, however, and so the translation task is relatively easy. In addition, the information sources are often available at embassies and consulates, whose mission includes the enhancement of trade activities. The commercial counselor or commercial attaché can provide the information available from these sources. The user should be cautioned, however, that the information is often dated and that the industry categories used abroad may not be compatible with industry categories used at home.

International Organizations Some international organizations provide useful data for the researcher. The *Statistical Yearbook* produced by the United Nations (UN) contains international trade data on products and provides information on exports and imports by country. However, because of the time needed for worldwide data collection, the information is often quite dated. Additional information is compiled and made available by specialized substructures of the United Nations. Some of these are the United Nations Conference on Trade and Development (UNCTAD), which concentrates primarily on international issues surrounding developing nations, such as debt and market access, and the United Nations Center on Transnational Corporations. The *World Atlas* published by the World Bank provides useful general data on population, growth trends, and GNP figures. The Organization for Economic Cooperation and Development (OECD) also publishes quarterly and annual trade data on its member countries. Finally, organizations such as the International Monetary Fund (IMF) and the World Bank publish summary economic data and occasional staff papers that evaluate region- or country-specific issues in depth.

Service Organizations A wide variety of service organizations that provide information include banks, accounting firms, freight forwarders, airlines, international trade consultants, research firms, and publishing houses located around the world.

Tyson Foods customizes more than 5,000 products to satisfy local taste preferences in 57 countries. Targeting research helps Tyson identify opportunities globally.

Source: Courtesy of Tyson Foods.

Frequently they are able to provide information on business practices, legislative or regulatory requirements, and political stability, as well as trade and financial data. As Figure 11.2 shows, often such service providers also can accumulate a wide variety of data from different countries and therefore offer one-stop shopping to the researcher.

Trade Associations   Associations such as world trade clubs and domestic and international chambers of commerce (such as the American Chamber of Commerce abroad) can provide good information on local markets. Often files are maintained on international trade flows and trends affecting international managers. Valuable information can also be obtained from industry associations. These groups, formed to represent entire industry segments, often collect from their members a wide variety of data that are then published in an aggregate form. Most of these associations represent the viewpoints of their member firms to the government, so they usually have one or more publicly listed representative in the capital. The information provided is often quite general, however, because of the wide variety of clientele served.

Directories and Newsletters   A large number of industry directories are available on local, national, and international levels. The directories primarily serve to identify firms and to provide very general background information, such as the name of the

Source: *Financial Times*, September 21, 1994, II (special survey).

chief executive officer, the level of capitalization of the firm, the location, the address and telephone number, and some description of the firm's products. In the past few years, a host of newsletters have sprung up discussing specific international business issues, such as international trade finance, legislative activities, countertrade, international payment flows, and customs news. Usually the newsletters cater to narrow audiences but can provide important information to the firm interested in a specific area.

Electronic Information Services   Obtaining trade information rapidly is often the key to success in the international market. With the proliferation of new technologies, such information is now more readily available than ever before. In light of the vast quantity of information available, making use of technology becomes essential. Just consider, "roughly 1,000 specialized periodicals hit the mail every year, progressively examining narrower and narrower subjects. Publishers print 1,000 new book titles each day, and the sum of printed information doubles every eight years. Currently, 40 percent of the U.S. work force helps create, process, or transmit information, and 40 percent of all business investments go into information technology."[4]

When information is needed, managers cannot spend a lot of time, energy, or money finding, sifting through, and categorizing it. Consider laboring through every copy of a trade publication to find out the latest news on how environmental concerns are affecting marketing decisions in Mexico. With electronic information services, search results can be obtained within minutes. International on-line computer database services, numbering in the thousands, can be purchased to supply information external to the firm, such as exchange rates, international news, and import restrictions. Most database hosts do not charge any sign-up fee and request payment only for actual use. The selection of initial database hosts depends on the choice of relevant databases, taking into account their product and market limitations, language used, and geographical location.

As Global Perspective 11.1 shows, databases can be scanned for specific information by entering search words, such as "China" and "foreign direct investment."

Global Perspective

11.1
Market Research On-Line

One way to get at needed information and analysis is to use market research reports, which describe the market for a given product or service and its industry, and also provide analysis, forecasts, and recommendations. Many market research reports are available in full-text on-line databases.

Euromonitor is one such source. It publishes reference and statistical sources and provides international marketing and custom reports. It has a series of published reports on the international market for a wide range of consumer products, from "In-Car Entertainment" to "Ice Cream, Yogurt, and Chilled Desserts." *Euromonitor Market Direction* is an on-line file of full-text market research reports on consumer product sectors in the United Kingdom, France, Italy, Germany, Spain, the U.S., and Japan. Examples of on-line titles include "Baby Care," "CDs, Records and Tapes," and "Health, Slimming, and Dietetic Foods." Data are collected through interviews with manufacturers in all product sectors and countries. In addition, information is taken from trade journals, manufacturer and trade associations, and Euromonitor's original market analysis and forecasts. Each report is updated twice a year.

Datamonitor is another on-line source of market reports. Instead of providing individual country reports, it takes one product and divides it into individual segments.

The on-line file contains the full text of reports that cover a wide range of products, from stockbrokerage to egg boilers. Each report analyzes major changes that occurred in the market during the previous year and provides detailed four-year market forecasts. In addition, the reports provide recent historical data on market size, segments, brand shares, advertising, trade, distribution, and consumer profiles. Data are collected through trade interviews and exclusive surveys from Gallup. Additional data are gathered from published sources, including stockbroker reports, the trade press, and government statistics. Sample Datamonitor on-line titles include "European Commercial Vehicles: Italy," "European Casualwear: Competitive Analysis," and "World Endocrine Market."

International market researchers must weigh the relative costs of purchasing an "off-the-shelf" report, one for sale to the public, with obtaining reports or parts of reports on-line. Two advantages often found with on-line reports are their lower costs and their ability to be periodically updated. If the decision is made to retrieve reports on-line, the search should be narrowed. Instead of retrieving the entire European Beer Report, a researcher should only screen for those records with information about, for instance, consumer profiles—another advantage to on-line reports.

Source: Ruth A. Pagell and Michael Halperin, *International Business Information: How to Find It, How to Use It* (Oryx Publishers, 1994), 180–182.

A list of relevant articles or reports appears within minutes. A large number of databases, developed by analysts who systematically sift through a wide range of periodicals, reports, and books in different languages, provide information on given products and markets. Many of the main news agencies now have information available through on-line databases, providing information on events that affect certain markets. Some databases cover extensive lists of companies in given countries and the products they buy and sell. A large number of databases exist that cover various categories of trade statistics. The main economic indicators of the UN, IMF, OECD, and EU are available on-line. Standards institutes in most of the G7 nations provide on-line access to their databases of technical standards and trade regulations on specific products.[5]

Compact Disk/Read-Only Memory (CD-ROM) technology allows for massive amounts of information (the equivalent of 300 books of 1,000 pages each, or 1,500 floppy disks) to be stored on a single 12-centimeter plastic disk. The disk itself is identical to the popular audio CDs. In the place of music, data are recorded. The technology increasingly is used for storing and distributing large volumes of information, such as statistical databases. Typically, the user pays no user fees but instead invests in a CD-ROM "reader" and purchases the actual CDs.

A CD-ROM service widely used in the United States is the National Trade Data Bank (NTDB), a monthly product issued by the U.S. Department of Commerce's Office of Business Analysis. The NTDB includes more than 170,000 documents, including full-text market research reports, domestic and foreign economic data, import and export statistics, trade information and country studies, all compiled from 26 government agencies.[6] The NTDB can also provide profiles of screened businesses that are interested in importing U.S. products. Figure 11.2 shows a listing of all the information available from the NTDB.

Using data services for research means that professionals do not have to leave their offices, going from library to library to locate the facts they need. Many on-line services have late-breaking information available within 24 hours to the user. These techniques of research are cost-effective as well. Stocking a company's library with all the books needed to have the same amount of data that is available on-line or with CD-ROM would be too expensive and space-consuming. After learning the methods of searching databases electronically, the ease of use also becomes an advantage. Searching on-line and CD-ROM databases provide access to a broad range of useful and timely trade information that often is not available through traditional channels. A listing of selected databases useful for international business is presented in the appendix to this chapter.

Selection of Secondary Data

Just because secondary information has been found to exist does not mean that it has to be used. Even though one key advantage of secondary data over primary research is that they are available relatively quickly and inexpensively, the researcher should still assess the effort and benefit of using them. Secondary data should be evaluated regarding the quality of their source, their recency, and their relevance to the task at hand. Clearly, since the information was collected without the current research requirements in mind, there may well be difficulties in coverage, categorization, and comparability. For example, an "engineer" in one country may differ substantially in terms of training and responsibilities from a person in another country holding the same title. It is therefore important to be careful when getting ready to interpret and analyze data.

Interpretation and Analysis of Secondary Data

Once secondary data have been obtained, the researcher must creatively convert them into information. Secondary data were originally collected to serve another purpose than the one in which the researcher is currently interested. Therefore, they can often be used only as **proxy information** in order to arrive at conclusions that address the research objectives. For example, the market penetration of television sets may be used as a proxy variable for the potential demand for video recorders. Similarly, in an industrial setting, information about plans for new port facilities may be useful in determining future containerization requirements. The researcher should proceed with caution when comparing secondary data across borders.

The researcher must use creative inferences, and such creativity brings risks. Therefore, once interpretation and analysis have taken place, a consistency check must be conducted. The researcher should always cross-check the results with other possible sources of information or with experts. Yet, if properly implemented, such creativity can open up one's eyes to new market potential, as Global Perspective 11.2 shows.

Global Perspective

11.2
Creative Research

When American entrepreneur Peter Johns went to Mexico to do business, he couldn't buy what he needed most: information. So he dug it up himself. Johns wanted to distribute mail order catalogs for upscale U.S. companies to consumers in Mexico. He thought that a large market was there just waiting to be tapped. However, when he tried to test his theory against hard data, he ran into a big blank.

Johns, who has spent 30 years in international marketing, couldn't find a useful marketing study for Mexico City. Government census reports weren't much help because they stop breaking down income levels at about $35,000, and they give ranges, rather than precise numbers, on family size.

So Johns embarked on some primary research. He went into the affluent neighborhoods and found just what he had suspected: satellite dishes, imported sports cars, and women carrying Louis Vuitton handbags. He reached his own conclusions about the target market for his catalogs. "There is no question there is a sense of consumer deprivation in the luxury market of Mexico City," said Johns.

After deciding to pursue his new enterprise, Johns reached another obstacle. His new enterprise, Choices Unlimited, had obtained rights from about 20 U.S. companies to distribute their catalogs in Mexico City. Now, he needed mailing lists, and he couldn't find them. Owners of mailing lists do not like to sell them because buyers tend to recycle the lists without authorization. Some of those that are available are expensive and may not include information such as zip codes, important barometers of household wealth.

Johns asked his local investors for membership lists of the city's exclusive golf clubs. He also obtained directories of the parents of students at some of the city's exclusive private schools. Johns received these lists for free. "That's called grass-roots marketing intelligence," said Johns.

Down the road, Johns hopes to have a Mexican customer base of 7,500 families spending an average of $600 a year on his products. By then, he should have another product to sell: his customer list.

Source: Dianna Solis, "Grass-Roots Marketing Yields Clients in Mexico City," *The Wall Street Journal,* October 24, 1991, B2.

CONDUCTING PRIMARY RESEARCH

Even though secondary data are useful to the researcher, on many occasions primary information will be required. **Primary data** are obtained by a firm to fill specific information needs. Firms specialize in primary international research, even under difficult circumstances as indicated in Figure 11.3. Although the research may not be conducted by the company with the need, the work must be carried out for a specific research purpose in order to qualify as primary research. Typically, primary research intends to answer such clear-cut questions as:

- What is our sales potential in Market X?
- How skilled is the labor force in that region?

**FIGURE 11.3
An Example of Primary Research under Difficult Conditions**

THE INTERVIEWING IS EASY...
IF THIS MAN DOESN'T SHOOT YOU FIRST

TASK :

Interview Afghans who fled across the border into Pakistan to see if they're listening to the BBC. Problem: you have to get past the local warlords who control the area.

Hand this problem to any old research company claiming to do international research, and you're in trouble. The BBC turned to Research International.

KNOWING WHAT WORKS

In today's competitive world, companies are increasingly looking toward off-shore markets. And that means good information is essential, even in developed markets.

But international research isn't just a case of taking what you do here and transplanting it there.

A national probability sample in Brazil will have you climbing a palm tree. "I will buy" on a scale in Japan doesn't mean the same thing in Spain. In tax-shy Italy, quota sampling on the basis of income won't get you very far!

**GLOBAL PERSPECTIVE
+ LOCAL INSIGHT**

We have Research International offices on the ground in 38 of the world's most important markets, from France to Argentina, the USA to Russia, London to Singapore. All our companies are leaders in their markets.

Our professional staff know their markets because they live there—not through visits or by reading the statistics.

We have conducted more than 4,000 international projects. In the last two years alone, we've worked in over 100 countries.

We know what works. And what doesn't. We know what research should cost. We know how to insure comparable high quality standards worldwide.

> **RESEARCH INTERNATIONAL
> IN NORTH AMERICA**
>
> You may be surprised to know that Research International has 6 companies and 9 offices in this region. Whether it's large scale survey work, product testing, customer satisfaction research, qualitative or observational research, we can help.
>
> We can put together an unrivaled team drawing on Research International resources in place in New York, Boston, San Francisco, Chicago, Toronto, Mexico City and in San Juan.

**COMMITMENT TO
INNOVATION WORLDWIDE**

Being on the ground all around the world also means that we have access to the best brains and the best thinking around the globe. Which means that we can offer our clients innovative, powerful techniques regardless of place of origin.

Our commitment to R. & D. runs very deep. Each year, we spend more of our own money on basic research than most of our competitors bring to the bottom line.

FREE OFFER

We've prepared a paper to help avoid some of the traps. Called "8 Common Pitfalls of International Research," it's free to marketers. Simply fax Daphne Chandler at—212-889-0487.

For specific help right now—call Daphne at 212-679-2500.

RESEARCH
INTERNATIONAL

- What will happen to demand if we raise the price by 10 percent?
- What effect will a new type of packaging have on our sales?

When extending his or her efforts abroad, the researcher must first have a clear idea of what the population under study should be and where it is located before deciding on the country or region to investigate. Conducting research in an entire country may not be necessary if, for example, only urban centers are to be penetrated. Multiple regions of a country need to be investigated, however, if a lack of homogeneity exists because of different economic, geographic, or behavioral factors. One source reports of the failure of a firm in Indonesia due to insufficient geographic dispersion of its research. The firm conducted its study only in large Indonesian cities during the height of tourism season, but projected the results to the entire population. When the company set up large production and distribution facilities to meet the expected demand, it realized only limited sales to city tourists.[7]

The discussion presented here will focus mainly on the research-specific issues. Application dimensions such as market choice and market analysis will be covered in Chapter 14.

Industrial versus Consumer Sources of Data

The researcher must decide whether research is to be conducted in the consumer or the industrial product area, which in turn determines the size of the universe and respondent accessibility. Consumers usually are a very large group, whereas the total population of industrial users may be fairly limited. Cooperation by respondents may also vary, ranging from very helpful to very limited. In the industrial setting, differentiation between users and decision makers may be important because their personalities, their outlooks, and their evaluative criteria may differ widely. Determining the proper focus of the research is therefore of major importance to its successful completion.

Determining the Research Technique

Selection of the research technique depends on a variety of factors. First, the objectivity of the data sought must be determined. Standardized techniques are more useful in the collection of objective data than of subjective data. Also, the degree of structure sought in the data collection needs to be determined. Unstructured data will require more open-ended questions and more time than structured data. Whether the data are to be collected in the real world or in a controlled environment must be determined. Finally, it must be decided whether to collect historical facts or information about future developments. This is particularly important for consumer research, because firms frequently want to determine the future intentions of consumers about buying a certain product.

Once the structure of the type of data sought is determined, the researcher must choose a research technique. As in domestic research, the types available are interviews, focus groups, observation, surveys, and experimentation. Each one provides a different depth of information and has its unique strengths and weaknesses.

Interviews   Often **interviews** with knowledgeable people can be of great value for the corporation that wants international information. Bias from the individual may be part of the findings, so the intent should be to obtain not a wide variety of data, but rather in-depth information. Particularly when specific answers are sought to very narrow questions, interviews can be most useful.

Focus Groups   **Focus groups** are a useful research tool resulting in interactive interviews. A group of knowledgeable people is gathered for a limited period of time (two to four hours). Usually, seven to ten participants is the ideal size for a focus group. A specific topic is introduced and thoroughly discussed by all group members. Because of the interaction, hidden issues are sometimes raised that would not have been detected in an individual interview. The skill of the group leader in stimulating discussion is crucial to the success of a focus group. Focus groups, like in-depth interviews, do not provide statistically significant information; however, they can be helpful in providing information about perceptions, emotions, and attitudinal factors. In addition, once individuals have been gathered, focus groups are highly efficient means of rapidly accumulating a substantial amount of information.

When planning international research using focus groups, the researcher must be aware of the importance of language and culture in the interaction process. Major differences may exist already in preparing for the focus group. In some countries, participants can simply be asked to show up at a later date at a location where they will join the focus group. In other countries, participants have to be brought into the group immediately because commitments made for a future date have little meaning. In some nations, providing a payment to participants is sufficient motivation for them to open up in discussion. In other countries, one first needs to host a luncheon or dinner for the group so that members get to know each other and are willing to interact.

Once the focus group is started, the researcher must remember that not all societies encourage frank and open exchange and disagreement among individuals. Status consciousness may result in the opinion of one participant being reflected by all others. Disagreement may be seen as impolite, or certain topics may be taboo. Unless a native focus group leader is used, it also is possible to completely misread the interactions among group participants and to miss out on nuances and constraints participants feel when commenting in the group situation. Before deciding on a focus group in an international setting, the researcher must be fully aware of these issues.

Observation   **Observation** requires the researcher to play the role of a nonparticipating observer of activity and behavior. In an international setting, observation can be extremely useful in shedding light on practices not previously encountered or understood. This aspect is especially valuable to the researcher who has no knowledge of a particular market or market situation. It can help in understanding phenomena that would have been difficult to assess with other techniques. For example, Toyota sent a group of its engineers and designers to southern California to nonchalantly observe how women get into and operate their cars. They found that women with long fingernails have trouble opening the door and operating various knobs on the dashboard. Toyota engineers and designers were able to comprehend the women's plight and redesign some of their automobile exteriors and interiors, producing more desirable cars.[8]

All the research instruments discussed so far are useful primarily for the gathering of qualitative information. The intent is not to amass data or to search for statistical significance, but rather to obtain a better understanding of given situations, behavioral patterns, or underlying dimensions. The researcher using these instruments must be cautioned that even frequent repetition of the measurements will not lead to a statistically valid result. However, statistical validity often may not be the major focus of corporate research. Rather, it may be the better understanding, description, and prediction of events that have an impact on decision making. When quantitative data are desired, surveys and experimentation are more appropriate research instruments.

Global Perspective

11.3
Market Research in Mexico

Learning which products Mexicans want is difficult because marketing research in Mexico is unpopular. Reliable information often cannot be obtained because of a lack of experience in data collection and supervision of fieldwork. In addition, Mexican consumers are not accustomed to someone calling on the phone or knocking at the door and asking for an opinion.

Market researchers must carefully consider data collection methods in order to obtain honest opinions. For instance, it is almost impossible to conduct phone surveys in Mexico. Telephone penetration in Mexico City is between 55 percent and 60 percent; in the large cities of Monterrey and Guadalajara it is less than 50 percent. In other cities, as few as 35 percent of the people have phones. Collecting data that fully represent the population is nearly impossible.

House-to-house research is believed to be the only truly reliable method in Mexico. The importance of sampling and fieldwork are crucial in this instance. Some Mexican research firms don't realize the importance of sampling. For example, when a client requires 1,000 completed interviews, many firms pick anyone from anywhere to interview and hire people to do the job as quickly as possible.

Controlling the quality of the interviewer can be difficult. When a house-to-house survey is done, usually large numbers of untrained and inexperienced interviewers are conducting it. A company representative may want to be present for the training of those who will be doing the work in order to make an evaluation.

It is possible to conduct focus groups almost anywhere in Mexico, but many major cities do not have the facilities. Sessions have to be conducted in a hotel or in a place where viewers can watch on closed-circuit TV. It is important to supervise the recruitment of participants. Many focus group facilities allow those involved to bring friends and relatives who do not meet the requirements of the screener. To avoid this problem, the facility can be asked to provide a daily progress report with the names, addresses, and phone numbers of the participants. On the day of the focus group, the moderator should reevaluate the participants before accepting them into the group.

Source: Naghi Namakforoosh, "Data Collection Methods Hold Key to Research in Mexico," *Marketing News,* August 29, 1994, 28.

Surveys   Survey research is useful in quantifying concepts. In the social sciences, it is generally accepted that the cross-cultural survey is scientifically the most powerful method of hypothesis testing.[9] **Surveys** are usually conducted via questionnaires that are administered personally, by mail, or by telephone. Use of the survey technique presupposes that the population under study is accessible and able to comprehend and respond to the question posed through the chosen medium. As Global Perspective 11.3 shows, this may not always be the case. Particularly for mail and telephone surveys, a major precondition is the feasibility of using the postal system or the widespread availability of telephones. Obviously, this is not a given in all countries. In many nations only limited records about dwellings, their location, and their occupants are available. In Venezuela, for example, most houses are not numbered but rather are given individual names such as Casa Rosa or El Retiro. In some countries, street maps are not even available. As a result, reaching respondents by mail is virtually impossible. In other countries, obtaining a correct address may be easy, but the postal system may not function well.

Telephone surveys may also be inappropriate if telephone ownership is rare. In such instances, any information obtained would be highly biased even if the researcher randomized the calls. In some cases, inadequate telephone networks and systems, frequent line congestion, and a lack of telephone directories may also the manager's decision-making process. Only rarely can corporations afford to spend large amounts of money on information that is simply "nice to know." Any information system will have to continuously address the balance to be struck between the expense of the research design and process and the value of the information to ongoing business activities. Second, the information must be *timely*. Managers derive little benefit if decision information needed today does not become available until a month from now. To be of use to the international decision maker, the system must therefore feed from a variety of international sources and be updated frequently. For multinational corporations, this means a real-time linkage between international subsidiaries and a broad-based ongoing data input operation. Third, information must be *flexible*—that is, it must be available in the form needed by management. An information system must therefore permit manipulation of the format and combination of the data. Therefore, great effort must be expended to make diverse international data compatible with and comparable to each other. Fourth, information contained in the system must be *accurate*. This is especially important in international research because information quickly becomes outdated as a result of major environmental changes. Fifth, the system's information bank must be reasonably *exhaustive*. Factors that may influence a particular decision must be appropriately represented in the information system because of the interrelationships among variables. This means that the information system must be based on a wide variety of factors. Finally, to be useful to managers, the system must be *convenient* to use. Systems that are cumbersome and time-consuming to reach and to use will not be used enough to justify corporate expenditures to build and maintain them.

To build an information system, corporations use the internal data that are available from divisions such as accounting and finance and also from various subsidiaries. In addition, many organizations put mechanisms in place to enrich the basic data flow to information systems. Three such mechanisms are environmental scanning, Delphi studies, and scenario building.

Environmental Scanning   Any changes in the business environment, whether domestic or foreign, may have serious repercussions on the activities of the firm. Corporations therefore understand the necessity for tracking new developments. Although this can be done implicitly in the domestic environment, the remoteness of international markets requires a continuous information flow. For this purpose, some large multinational organizations have formed environmental scanning groups.

Environmental scanning activities provide continuous information on political, social, and economic affairs internationally; on changes of attitudes of public institutions and private citizens; and on possible upcoming alterations. Environmental scanning models are used for a variety of purposes, some of which are:

1. The development of broad strategies and long-term policies.
2. The development of action plans and operating programs.
3. The development of a frame of reference for the annual budget.
4. The provision of a mind-stretching or educational experience for management.[13]

Obviously, the precision required for environmental scanning varies with its purpose. For example, whether information is to serve for mind stretching or for budgeting must be taken into account when constructing the framework for the scanning process. The more immediate and precise the application will be within the corporation, the greater the need for detailed information. On the other hand, heightened precision may reduce the usefulness of environmental scanning in strategic planning, which is long term.

**FIGURE 11.5
The Funny Faces Scale**

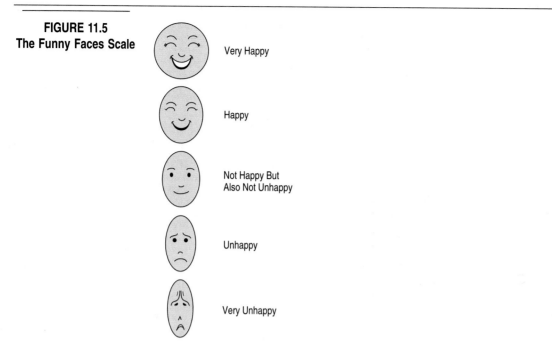

Very Happy

Happy

Not Happy But
Also Not Unhappy

Unhappy

Very Unhappy

Source: C. K. Corder, "Problems and Pitfalls in Conducting Marketing Research in Africa," in Betsy Gelb (ed.), *Marketing Expansion in a Shrinking World,* Proceedings of American Marketing Association Business Conference (Chicago: AMA, 1978), pp. 86–90.

amenable to statistical analysis. With constantly expanding technological capabilities, international researchers will be able to use this technique even more in the future.

Experimentation   Experimental techniques determine the effect of an intervening variable and help establish precise cause-and-effect relationships. However, **experimentation** is difficult to implement in international research. The researcher faces the task of designing an experiment in which most variables are held constant or are comparable across cultures. For example, an experiment to determine a causal effect within the distribution system of one country may be very difficult to transfer to another country because the distribution system may be quite different. For this reason, experimental techniques are only rarely used, even though their potential value to the international researcher is recognized.

THE INTERNATIONAL INFORMATION SYSTEM

Many organizations have data needs that go beyond specific international research projects. Most of the time, daily decisions must be made for which there is neither time nor money for special research. An information system can provide the decision maker with basic data for most ongoing decisions. Separation in time and space, as well as wide differences in culture and technological environments, makes information and data management more complex internationally than domestically.[11] The same factors, however, highlight the increased need for an international information system. Defined as "the systematic and continuous gathering, analysis, and reporting of data for decision-making purposes,"[12] such a system serves as a mechanism to coordinate the flow of information to corporate managers.

To be useful to the decision maker, the system must have certain attributes. First of all, the information must be *relevant*. The data gathered must have meaning for the manager's decision-making process. Only rarely can corporations afford to spend large amounts of money on information that is simply "nice to know." Any information system will have to continuously address the balance to be struck between the expense of the research design and process and the value of the information to ongoing business activities. Second, the information must be *timely*. Managers derive little benefit if decision information needed today does not become available until a month from now. To be of use to the international decision maker, the system must therefore feed from a variety of international sources and be updated frequently. For multinational corporations, this means a real-time linkage between international subsidiaries and a broad-based ongoing data input operation. Third, information must be *flexible*—that is, it must be available in the form needed by management. An information system must therefore permit manipulation of the format and combination of the data. Therefore, great effort must be expended to make diverse international data compatible with and comparable to each other. Fourth, information contained in the system must be *accurate*. This is especially important in international research because information quickly becomes outdated as a result of major environmental changes. Fifth, the system's information bank must be reasonably *exhaustive*. Factors that may influence a particular decision must be appropriately represented in the information system because of the interrelationships among variables. This means that the information system must be based on a wide variety of factors. Finally, to be useful to managers, the system must be *convenient* to use. Systems that are cumbersome and time-consuming to reach and to use will not be used enough to justify corporate expenditures to build and maintain them.

To build an information system, corporations use the internal data that are available from divisions such as accounting and finance and also from various subsidiaries. In addition, many organizations put mechanisms in place to enrich the basic data flow to information systems. Three such mechanisms are environmental scanning, Delphi studies, and scenario building.

Environmental Scanning   Any changes in the business environment, whether domestic or foreign, may have serious repercussions on the activities of the firm. Corporations therefore understand the necessity for tracking new developments. Although this can be done implicitly in the domestic environment, the remoteness of international markets requires a continuous information flow. For this purpose, some large multinational organizations have formed environmental scanning groups.

Environmental scanning activities provide continuous information on political, social, and economic affairs internationally; on changes of attitudes of public institutions and private citizens; and on possible upcoming alterations. Environmental scanning models are used for a variety of purposes, some of which are:

1. The development of broad strategies and long-term policies.
2. The development of action plans and operating programs.
3. The development of a frame of reference for the annual budget.
4. The provision of a mind-stretching or educational experience for management.[13]

Obviously, the precision required for environmental scanning varies with its purpose. For example, whether information is to serve for mind stretching or for budgeting must be taken into account when constructing the framework for the scanning process. The more immediate and precise the application will be within the corporation, the greater the need for detailed information. On the other hand, heightened precision may reduce the usefulness of environmental scanning in strategic planning, which is long term.

Global Perspective

11.3
Market Research in Mexico

Learning which products Mexicans want is difficult because marketing research in Mexico is unpopular. Reliable information often cannot be obtained because of a lack of experience in data collection and supervision of fieldwork. In addition, Mexican consumers are not accustomed to someone calling on the phone or knocking at the door and asking for an opinion.

Market researchers must carefully consider data collection methods in order to obtain honest opinions. For instance, it is almost impossible to conduct phone surveys in Mexico. Telephone penetration in Mexico City is between 55 percent and 60 percent; in the large cities of Monterrey and Guadalajara it is less than 50 percent. In other cities, as few as 35 percent of the people have phones. Collecting data that fully represent the population is nearly impossible.

House-to-house research is believed to be the only truly reliable method in Mexico. The importance of sampling and fieldwork are crucial in this instance. Some Mexican research firms don't realize the importance of sampling. For example, when a client requires 1,000 completed interviews, many firms pick anyone from anywhere to interview and hire people to do the job as quickly as possible.

Controlling the quality of the interviewer can be difficult. When a house-to-house survey is done, usually large numbers of untrained and inexperienced interviewers are conducting it. A company representative may want to be present for the training of those who will be doing the work in order to make an evaluation.

It is possible to conduct focus groups almost anywhere in Mexico, but many major cities do not have the facilities. Sessions have to be conducted in a hotel or in a place where viewers can watch on closed-circuit TV. It is important to supervise the recruitment of participants. Many focus group facilities allow those involved to bring friends and relatives who do not meet the requirements of the screener. To avoid this problem, the facility can be asked to provide a daily progress report with the names, addresses, and phone numbers of the participants. On the day of the focus group, the moderator should reevaluate the participants before accepting them into the group.

Source: Naghi Namakforoosh, "Data Collection Methods Hold Key to Research in Mexico," *Marketing News,* August 29, 1994, 28.

Surveys   Survey research is useful in quantifying concepts. In the social sciences, it is generally accepted that the cross-cultural survey is scientifically the most powerful method of hypothesis testing.[9] **Surveys** are usually conducted via questionnaires that are administered personally, by mail, or by telephone. Use of the survey technique presupposes that the population under study is accessible and able to comprehend and respond to the question posed through the chosen medium. As Global Perspective 11.3 shows, this may not always be the case. Particularly for mail and telephone surveys, a major precondition is the feasibility of using the postal system or the widespread availability of telephones. Obviously, this is not a given in all countries. In many nations only limited records about dwellings, their location, and their occupants are available. In Venezuela, for example, most houses are not numbered but rather are given individual names such as Casa Rosa or El Retiro. In some countries, street maps are not even available. As a result, reaching respondents by mail is virtually impossible. In other countries, obtaining a correct address may be easy, but the postal system may not function well.

Telephone surveys may also be inappropriate if telephone ownership is rare. In such instances, any information obtained would be highly biased even if the researcher randomized the calls. In some cases, inadequate telephone networks and systems, frequent line congestion, and a lack of telephone directories may also

**FIGURE 11.4
An Advertisement for
International Data
Collection**

Source: *Marketing News,* November 23, 1992.

prevent the researcher from conducting surveys. Yet, as Figure 11.4 shows, with to-day's communication capabilities, research firms are able to conduct telephone research around the world from a single location.

Since surveys deal with people, who in an international setting display major differences in culture, preference, education, and attitude, just to mention a few factors, the use of the survey technique must be carefully examined. For example, in some regions of the world, recipients of letters may be illiterate.[10] Others may be very literate, but totally unaccustomed to some of the standard research scaling techniques used in the United States and therefore may be unable to respond to the instrument. Other recipients of a survey may be reluctant to respond in writing, particularly when sensitive questions are asked. This sensitivity, of course, also varies by country. In some nations, any questions about income, even in categorical form, are considered highly proprietary; in others the purchasing behavior of individuals is not easily divulged.

The researcher needs to understand such constraints and prepare a survey that is responsive to them. For example, surveys can incorporate drawings or even cartoons to communicate better. Personal administration or collaboration with locally accepted intermediaries may improve the response rate. Indirect questions may need to substitute for direct ones in sensitive areas. Questions may have to be reworded to ensure proper communication. Figure 11.5 provides an example of a rating scale developed by researchers to work with a diverse population with relatively little education. In its use, however, it was found that the same scale aroused negative reactions among better-educated respondents, who considered the scale childish and insulting to their intelligence.

In spite of all the potential difficulties, the survey technique remains a useful one because it allows the researcher to rapidly accumulate a large quantity of data

Advances in Telephone and Data Transmission Technology Facilitate the Collection of Data for International Business Research

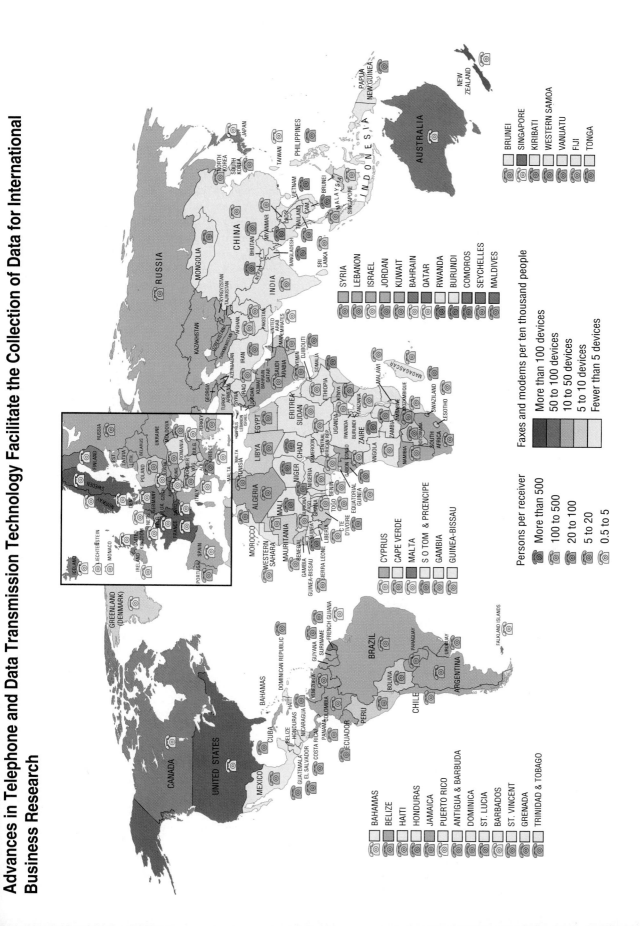

Faxes and modems per ten thousand people

More than 100 devices
50 to 100 devices
10 to 50 devices
5 to 10 devices
Fewer than 5 devices

Persons per receiver

More than 500
100 to 500
20 to 100
5 to 20
0.5 to 5

Sources: *Peters Atlas of the World, 1990; The New Book of World Rankings, 1991.*

Environmental scanning can be performed in various ways. One consists of obtaining factual input on a wide variety of demographic, social, and economic characteristics of foreign countries. Frequently, managers believe that factual data alone are insufficient for their information needs. Particularly for forecasting future developments, other methods are used to capture underlying dimensions of social change. One significant method is that of media analysis. A wide array of newspapers, magazines, and other publications are scanned worldwide in order to pinpoint over time the gradual evolution of new views or trends. Corporations also use the technique of media analysis to pinpoint upcoming changes in their line of business. For example, the Alaskan oil spill by the Exxon *Valdez* and the rash of oil spills that followed resulted in entirely new international concern about environmental protection and safety, reaching far beyond the actual incidents and participants.

With the current heightened awareness of environmental and ethical issues such as pollution, preservation of natural resources, and animal testing, firms are increasingly looking for new opportunities to expand their operations while remaining within changing moral and environmental boundaries.

Environmental scanning is conducted by a variety of groups within and outside the corporation. Quite frequently, small corporate staffs are created at headquarters to coordinate the information flow. In addition, subsidiary staff can be used to provide occasional intelligence reports. Groups of volunteers are also formed to gather and analyze information worldwide and feed their individual analyses back to corporate headquarters, where the "big picture" can then be constructed. Increasingly, large corporations also offer services in environmental scanning to outsiders. In this way, profits can be made from an in-house activity that has to be carried out anyway.

Typically, environmental scanning is designed primarily to aid the strategic planning process rather than the tactical activities of the corporation and focuses five to ten years ahead. Environmental scanning, therefore, primarily addresses the future in order to complement the continuous flow of factual data to the corporation.

Not all managers perceive environmental scanning as important to the corporate planning process. For example, researchers have noted "that in those constructs and frameworks where the environment has been given primary consideration, there has been a tendency for the approach to become so global that studies tend to become shallow and diffuse, or impractical if pursued in sufficient depth."[14] Obviously, this presents one of the major continuous challenges corporations face in their scanning activities. A trade-off exists between the breadth and depth of information. However, the continuous evolution of manipulative power through the ever-increasing capabilities of data processing may reduce at least the scope of the problem. Nevertheless, the cost of data acquisition and the issue of actual data use will continue to form major restraints on the development of environmental scanning systems.

Delphi Studies   To enrich the information obtained from factual data, corporations frequently resort to the use of creative and highly qualitative data-gathering methods. One approach is through **Delphi studies.** These studies are particularly useful in the international environment because they are "a means for aggregating the judgments of a number of . . . experts . . . who cannot come together physically."[15] This type of research clearly aims at qualitative rather than quantitative measures by aggregating the information of a group of experts. It seeks to obtain a consensus from those who know, rather than average responses from many people with only limited knowledge.

Typically, Delphi studies are carried out with groups of about 30 well-chosen participants who possess expertise in an area of concern, such as future developments of the international trade environment. The participants are asked, most frequently by mail, to identify the major issues in the given area of concern. They are also requested to rank order their statements according to importance and explain the rationale behind the order. The aggregated information and comments are then sent to all participants in the Delphi group. Group members are encouraged to agree or disagree with the various rank orders and the comments. This allows statements to be challenged. In another round, the participants respond to the challenges. Several rounds of challenges and responses result in a reasonably coherent consensus.

The Delphi technique is particularly valuable because it uses mail, facsimile, or electronic communication to bridge large distances and therefore makes experts quite accessible at a reasonable cost. It avoids the drawback of ordinary mail investigations, which lack interaction among participants. Several rounds may be required, however, so substantial time may elapse before the information is obtained. Also, a major effort must be expended in selecting the appropriate participants and in motivating them to participate in the exercise with enthusiasm and continuity. When carried out on a regular basis, Delphi studies can provide crucial augmentation of the factual data available for the information system. For example, a large portion of this book's last chapter was written based on an extensive Delphi study carried out by the authors.

Scenario Building

The information obtained through environmental scanning or Delphi studies can then be used to conduct a scenario analysis. One approach involves the development of a series of plausible scenarios that are constructed from trends observed in the environment. Another method consists of formally reviewing assumptions built into existing business plans and positions.[16] Subsequently, some of these key assumptions such as economic growth rates, import penetration, population growth, and political stability can be varied. By projecting variations for medium- to long-term periods, completely new environmental conditions can emerge. The conditions can then be analyzed for their potential domestic and international impact on corporate strategy.

The identification of crucial variables and the degree of variation are of major importance in **scenario building.** Frequently, key experts are used to gain information about potential variations and about the viability of certain scenarios. An example of input from such experts is provided in Global Perspective 11.4.

A wide variety of scenarios must be built in order to expose corporate executives to a number of potential occurrences. Ideally, even farfetched scenarios deserve some consideration, if only to address worst-case possibilities.

Scenario builders also need to recognize the nonlinearity of factors. To simply extrapolate from currently existing situations is insufficient, since extraneous factors often enter the picture with significant impact. Finally, in scenario building, the possibility of **joint occurrences** must be recognized because changes may not come about in isolated fashion but instead may spread over wide regions. For example, given large technological advances, the possibility of wholesale obsolescence of current technology must be considered. Quantum leaps in computer development and new generations of computers may render obsolete the entire technological investment of a corporation.

For scenarios to be useful, management must analyze and respond to them by formulating contingency plans. Such planning will broaden horizons and may prepare managers for unexpected situations. Through the anticipation of possible problems, managers hone their response capability and in turn shorten response times to actual problems.

Global Perspective

11.4
Advice from Kissinger Associates

Kissinger Associates is a New York-based consulting firm established in 1982 by former Secretary of State Henry Kissinger, former Undersecretary of State Lawrence S. Eagleburger, and former National Security Advisor Brent Scowcroft. For its corporate clients, the firm offers broad-brush pictures of political and economic conditions in particular countries or regions along with analyses of political and economic trends. Because none of the founders is particularly known for his business or economic expertise, an investment banker and an economist were brought on board.

Some have argued that the pointing out of political trends is an insufficient base from which to make a living. Kissinger himself stated that to provide only abstract information on the political condition in a foreign country is not fair to the client. The firm sees its primary strength to be its sensitivity to the international political situation and its continued closeness to information sources. Although Kissinger Associates offers no voluminous country reports, the principals believe that by correctly assessing, for example, the political outlook in Greece for the next five years,

they can help a client decide whether to make new investments there or preparations to leave in anticipation of a hostile socialist government. Similarly, the firm might help a U.S. oil company with limited Middle East experience in its first attempts to negotiate and work with a government in the region. Although this type of work does not involve Kissinger Associates deeply in specific business decisions, it does require a good understanding of clients' businesses and goals.

One practical reason for using high-powered consulting input was explained by a former member of Kissinger Associates: "These days, in case an investment goes sour, it is useful for [management] to be able to say, 'We got this expert advice and acted on that basis.' They have to show due diligence in exercising their fiduciary duties."

Even though client identities and fees are well-guarded secrets, congressional confirmation hearings for former employees of Kissinger Associates revealed that clients such as Union Carbide, Coca-Cola, Volvo, Fiat, and Daewoo pay between $150,000 and $400,000 per year for the firm's services.

Sources: Christopher Madison, "Kissinger Firm Hopes to Make Its Mark as Risk Advisors to Corporate Chiefs," *National Journal,* June 22, 1985, 1452–1456; and "The Out-of-Office Reign of Henry I," *U.S. News and World Report,* March 27, 1989, 10.

The development of an international information system is of major importance to the multinational corporation. It aids the ongoing decision process and becomes a vital tool in performing the strategic planning task. Only by observing global trends and changes will the firm be able to maintain and improve its competitive position. Much of the data available are quantitative in nature, but researchers must also pay attention to qualitative dimensions. Quantitative analysis will continue to improve as the ability to collect, store, analyze, and retrieve data increases as a result of computer development. Nevertheless, the qualitative dimension will remain a major component for corporate research and planning activities.

SUMMARY

Constraints of time, resources, and expertise are the major inhibitors to international research. Nevertheless, firms need to carry out planned and organized research in order to explore foreign market opportunities and challenges successfully. Such research must be linked closely to the decision-making process.

International research differs from domestic research in that the environment—which determines how well tools, techniques, and concepts apply—is different abroad. In addition, the international manager must deal with duties, exchange rates, and international documentation; a greater number of interacting factors; and a much broader definition of the concept of competition.

The research process starts by recognizing the need for research, which is often not well understood. When the firm is uninformed about international differences in consumer tastes and preferences or about foreign market environments, the need for international research is particularly great. Research objectives need to be determined based on the corporate mission, the level of international expertise, and the business plan. These objectives will enable the research to identify the information requirements.

Given the scarcity of resources, companies beginning their international effort must rely on data that have already been collected. These secondary data are available from sources such as governments, international organizations, directors, or trade associations.

To fulfill specific information requirements, the researcher may need to collect primary data. An appropriate research technique must be selected to collect the information. Sensitivity to different international environments and cultures will aid the researcher in deciding whether to use interviews, focus groups, observation, surveys, or experimentation as data-collection techniques.

To provide ongoing information to management, an information system is useful. Such a system will provide for the continuous gathering, analysis, and reporting of data for decision-making purposes. Data gathered through environmental scanning, Delphi studies, or scenario building enable management to prepare for the future and hone its decision-making abilities.

Key Terms and Concepts

competitive assessment	surveys
secondary data	experimentation
proxy information	environmental scanning
primary data	Delphi studies
interviews	scenario building
focus groups	joint occurrence
observation	

Questions for Discussion

1. What is the difference between domestic and international research?
2. How does "going international" affect the perspective of a firm?
3. You are employed by National Engineering, a firm that designs subways. Because you have had a course in international business, your boss asks you to spend the next week exploring international possibilities for the company. How will you go about this task?
4. Discuss the possible shortcomings of secondary data.
5. Why should a firm collect primary data in its international research?
6. How is international research affected by differences in language?
7. Is highly priced personalized advice from an individual really worth the money?
8. What type of data would you enter into your international information system?

Recommended Readings

Barnard, Philip. "Conducting and Co-ordinating Multicountry Quantitative Studies across Europe," in *Global Marketing Perspectives,* edited by Jagdish Sheth and Abdolreza Eshghi. Cincinnati: South-Western, 1989, 56–73.

Churchill, Gilbert A., Jr. *Marketing Research: Methodological Foundations.* 6th ed. Fort Worth, Tex.: Dryden Press, 1995.

Delphos, William S., ed. *International Direct Marketing Guide: Regional Markets and Selected Countries.* Alexandria, Va.: Braddock Communications, 1992.

Douglas, Susan P., and C. Samuel Craig. *International Marketing Research.* Englewood Cliffs, N.J.: Prentice-Hall, 1983.

Hassan, Salah S., and Roger D. Blackwell. *Global Marketing: Perspectives and Cases.* Fort Worth, Tex.: Dryden Press, 1994.

Hassan, S., and E. Kaynak, eds. *Globalization of Consumer Markets: Structures and Strategies.* Binghamton, N.Y.: The Haworth Press, 1993.

Paliwoda, Stanley J. *New Perspectives on International Marketing.* London: Routledge, 1991.

Smith, Craig N., and Paul Dainty. *The Management Research Handbook.* London: Routledge, 1991.

Notes

1. David A. Ricks, *Blunders in International Business* (Cambridge, Mass.: Blackwell, 1993).

2. Susan P. Douglas and C. Samuel Craig, *International Marketing Research* (Englewood Cliffs, N.J.: Prentice-Hall, 1983), 2.

3. S. Tamer Cavusgil, "Guidelines for Export Market Research," *Business Horizons* 28 (November–December 1985): 27–33.

4. Peter D. Moore, "Looking Ahead: The Information Age Has a Flip Side," *The Los Angeles Times,* May 2, 1990.

5. Bernard Ancel and Sonia Srivastava, "Market Information at Your Fingertips," *International Trade Forum* (April 1993): 12–17.

6. "National Trade Data Bank," Government Documents Department: Lauinger Library, Georgetown University, 1994.

7. Ricks, *Blunders in International Business,* 134.

8. Michael R. Czinkota and Masaaki Kotabe, "Product Development the Japanese Way," in M. Czinkota and I. Ronkainen, *International Marketing Strategy* (Fort Worth: Dryden Press, 1994), 285–291.

9. Lothar G. Winter and Charles R. Prohaska, "Methodological Problems in the Comparative Analysis of International Marketing Systems," *Journal of the Academy of Marketing Science* 11 (Fall 1983): 421.

10. Douglas and Craig, *International Marketing Research,* 200.

11. Sayeste Daser, "International Marketing Information Systems: A Neglected Prerequisite for Foreign Market Planning," in *International Marketing Management,* ed. E. Kaynak (New York: Praeger, 1984), 139–154.

12. Thomas C. Kinnear and James R. Taylor, *Marketing Research: An Applied approach,* 2d ed. (New York: McGraw-Hill, 1983), 120.

13. Robert N. Anthony, John Dearden, and Richard F. Vancio, *Management Control Systems,* 5th ed. (Homewood, Ill.: Richard D. Irwin, 1984).

14. Winter and Prohaska, "Methodological Problems," 429.

15. Andrel Delbecq, Andrew H. Van de Ven, and David H. Gustafson, *Group Techniques for Program Planning* (Glenview, Ill.: Scott Foresman, 1975), 83.

16. William H. Davidson, "The Role of Global Scanning in Business Planning," *Organizational Dynamics* (Winter 1991): 5–16.

Monitors of International Issues

Selected Organizations

- **American Bankers Association**
  1120 Connecticut Avenue N.W
  Washington, D.C. 20036

- **American Bar Association**
  750 N. Lake Shore Drive
  Chicago, IL 60611
  and
  1800 M Street N.W.
  Washington, D.C. 20036

- **American Management Association**
  440 First Street N.W.
  Washington, D.C. 20001

- **American Marketing Association**
  250 S. Wacker Drive Suite 200
  Chicago, IL 60606

- **American Petroleum Institute**
  1220 L Street N.W.
  Washington, D.C. 20005

- **Asian Development Bank**
  2330 Roxas Boulevard
  Pasay City, Philippines

- **Chamber of Commerce of the United States**
  1615 H Street N.W.
  Washington, D.C. 20062

- **Commission of the European Communities to the United States**
  2100 M Street N.W. Suite 707
  Washington, D.C. 20037

- **Conference Board**
  845 Third Avenue
  New York, NY 10022
  and
  1755 Massachusetts Avenue N.W. Suite 312
  Washington, D.C. 20036

- **Electronic Industries Association**
  2001 Pennsylvania Avenue N.W.
  Washington, D.C. 20004

- **European Community Information Service**
  200 Rue de la Loi
  1049 Brussels, Belgium
  and
  2100 M Street N.W. 7th Floor
  Washington, D.C. 20037

- **Export-Import Bank of the United States**
  811 Vermont Avenue N.W.
  Washington, D.C. 20571

- **Federal Reserve Bank of New York**
  33 Liberty Street
  New York, NY 10045

- **Inter-American Development Bank**
  1300 New York Avenue N.W.
  Washington, D.C. 20577

- **International Bank for Reconstruction and Development (World Bank)**
  1818 H Street N.W.
  Washington, D.C. 20433

- **International Monetary Fund**
  700 19th Street N.W.
  Washington, D.C. 20431

- **Marketing Research Society**
  111 E. Wacker Drive Suite 600
  Chicago, IL 60601

- **National Association of Manufacturers**
  1331 Pennsylvania Avenue
  Suite 1500
  Washington, D.C. 20004

- **National Federation of Independent Business**
  600 Maryland Avenue S.W.
  Suite 700
  Washington, D.C. 20024

- **Organization for Economic Cooperation and Development**
  2 rue Andre Pascal
  75775 Paris Cedex Ko, France
  and
  2001 L Street N.W. Suite 700
  Washington, D.C. 20036

- **Organization of American States**
  17th and Constitution Avenue N.W.
  Washington, D.C. 20006

- **Society for International Development**
  1401 New York Avenue N.W.
  Suite 1100
  Washington, D.C. 20005

United Nations

- **Conference of Trade and Development**
  Palais des Nations
  1211 Geneva 10
  Switzerland

- **Department of Economic and Social Affairs**
  1 United Nations Plaza
  New York, NY 10017

- **Industrial Development Organization**
  1660 L Street N.W.
  Washington, D.C. 20036
  and
  Post Office Box 300
  Vienna International Center
  A-1400 Vienna, Austria

- **UN Publications**
  Room 1194
  1 United Nations Plaza
  New York, NY 10017
- **Statistical Yearbook**
  1 United Nations Plaza
  New York, NY 10017

U.S. Government

- **Agency for International Development**
  Office of Business Relations
  Washington, D.C. 20523
- **Customs Service**
  1301 Constitution Avenue N.W.
  Washington, D.C. 20229
- **Department of Agriculture**
  12th Street and Jefferson Drive
  S.W.
  Washington, D.C. 20250
- **Department of Commerce**
  Herbert C. Hoover Building
  14th Street and Constitution
  Avenue N.W.
  Washington, D.C. 20230
- **Department of State**
  2201 C Street N.W.
  Washington, D.C. 20520
- **Department of the Treasury**
  15th Street and Pennsylvania
  Avenue N.W.
  Washington, D.C. 20220
- **Federal Trade Commission**
  6th Street and Pennsylvania
  Avenue N.W.
  Washington, D.C. 20580
- **International Trade Commission**
  500 E Street N.W.
  Washington, D.C. 20436
- **Small Business Administration**
  409 Third Street S.W.
  Washington, D.C. 20416
- **Trade Development Program**
  1621 North Kent Street
  Rosslyn, VA 22209

- **World Trade Centers Association**
  1 World Trade Center Suite 7701
  New York, NY 10048

Indexes to Literature

- **Business Periodical Index**
  H.W. Wilson Co.
  950 University Avenue
  Bronx, NY 10452
- **New York Times Index**
  University Microfilms International
  300 N. Zeeb Road
  Ann Arbor, MI 48106
- **Public Affairs Information Service Bulletin**
  11 W. 40th Street
  New York, NY 10018
- **Reader's Guide to Periodical Literature**
  H.W. Wilson Co.
  950 University Avenue
  Bronx, NY 10452
- **Wall Street Journal Index**
  University Microfilms International
  300 N. Zeeb Road
  Ann Arbor, MI 48106

Directories

- **American Register of Exporters and Importers**
  38 Park Row
  New York, NY 10038
- **Arabian Year Book**
  Dar Al-Seuassam Est. Box 42480
  Shuwahk, Kuwait
- **Directories of American Firms Operating in Foreign Countries**
  World Trade Academy Press
  Uniworld Business Publications Inc.
  50 E. 42nd Street
  New York, NY 10017

- **The Directory of International Sources of Business Information**
  Pitman
  128 Long Acre
  London, WC2E 9AN, England
- **Encyclopedia of Associations**
  Galel Research Co.
  Book Tower
  Detroit, MI 48226
- **Polk's World Bank Directory**
  R.C. Polk & Co.
  2001 Elm Hill Pike
  P.O. Box 1340
  Nashville, TN 37202
- **Verified Directory of Manufacturers' Representatives**
  MacRae's Blue Book Inc.
  817 Broadway
  New York, NY 10003
- **World Guide to Trade Associations**
  K.G. Saur & Co.
  175 Fifth Avenue
  New York, NY 10010

Encyclopedias, Handbooks, and Miscellaneous

- **A Basic Guide to Exporting**
  U.S. Government Printing Office
  Superintendent of Documents
  Washington, D.C. 20402
- **Doing business in . . . Series**
  Price Waterhouse
  1251 Avenue of the Americas
  New York, NY 10020
- **Economic Survey of Europe**
  The United Nations
  United Nations Publishing Division
  1 United Nations Plaza
  Room DC2-0853
  New York, NY 10017

- **Economic Survey of Latin America**
  United Nations
  United Nations Publishing Division
  1 United Nations Plaza
  Room DC2-0853
  New York, NY 10017

- **Encyclopedia Americana, International Edition**
  Grolier Inc.
  Danbury, CT 06816

- **Encyclopedia of Business Information Sources**
  Gale Research Co.
  Book Tower
  Detroit, MI 48226

- **Europa Year Book**
  Europa Publications Ltd.
  18 Bedford Square
  London WC1B 3JN, England

- **Export Administration Regulations**
  U.S. Government Printing Office
  Superintendent of Documents
  Washington, D.C. 20402

- **Exporters' Encyclopedia–World Marketing Guide**
  Dun's Marketing Services
  49 Old Bloomfield Rd.
  Mountain Lake, NJ 07046

- **Export-Import Bank of the United States Annual Report**
  U.S. Government Printing Office
  Superintendent of Documents
  Washington, D.C. 20402

- **Exporting for the Small Business**
  U.S. Government Printing Office
  Superintendent of Documents
  Washington, D.C. 20402

- **Exporting to the United States**
  U.S. Government Printing Office
  Superintendent of Documents
  Washington, D.C. 20402
  Export Shipping Manual

- **U.S. Government Printing Office**
  Superintendent of Documents
  Washington, D.C. 20402

- **Foreign Business Practices: Materials on Practical Aspects of Exporting, International Licensing, and Investing**
  U.S. Government Printing Office
  Superintendent of Documents
  Washington, D.C. 20402

- **A Guide to Financing Exports**
  U.S. Government Printing Office
  Superintendent of Documents
  Washington, D.C. 20402

- **Handbook of Marketing Research**
  McGraw-Hill Book Co.
  1221 Avenue of the Americas
  New York, NY 10020

Periodic Reports, Newspapers, Magazines

- **Advertising Age**
  Crain Communications Inc.
  740 N. Rush Street
  Chicago, IL 60611

- **Advertising World**
  Directories International Inc.
  150 Fifth Avenue Suite 610
  New York, NY 10011

- **Arab Report and Record**
  84 Chancery Lane
  London WC2A 1DL, England

- **Barron's**
  University Microfilms International
  300 N. Zeeb Road
  Ann Arbor, MI 48106

- **Business America**
  U.S. Department of Commerce
  14th Street and Constitution Avenue N.W.
  Washington, D.C. 20230

- **Business International**
  Business International Corp.
  One Dag Hammarskjold Plaza
  New York, NY 10017

- **Business Week**
  McGraw-Hill Publications Co.
  1221 Avenue of the Americas
  New York, NY 10020

- **Commodity Trade Statistics**
  United Nations Publications
  1 United Nations Plaza
  Room DC2-0853
  New York, NY 10017

- **Conference Board Record**
  Conference Board Inc.
  845 Third Avenue
  New York, NY 10022

- **Customs Bulletin**
  U.S. Customs Service
  1301 Constitution Avenue N.W.
  Washington, D.C. 20229

- **Dun's Business Month**
  Goldhirsh Group
  38 Commercial Wharf
  Boston, MA 02109

- **The Economist**
  Economist Newspaper Ltd.
  25 St. James Street
  London SW1A 1HG, England

- **Europe Magazine**
  2100 M Street N.W. Suite 707
  Washington, D.C. 20037

- **The Financial Times**
  Bracken House
  10 Cannon Street
  London EC4P 4BY, England

- **Forbes**
  Forbes, Inc.
  60 Fifth Avenue
  New York, NY 10011

- **Fortune**
  Time, Inc.
  Time & Life Building
  1271 Avenue of the Americas
  New York, NY 10020
- **Global Trade**
  North American Publishing Co.
  401 N. Broad Street
  Philadelphia, PA 19108
- **Industrial Marketing**
  Crain Communications, Inc.
  740 N. Rush Street
  Chicago, IL 60611
- **International Financial Statistics**
  International Monetary Fund
  Publications Unit
  700 19th Street N.W.
  Washington, D.C. 20431
- **Investor's Daily**
  Box 25970
  Los Angeles, CA 90025
  Journal of Commerce
  110 Wall Street
  New York, NY 10005
- **Sales and Marketing Management**
  Bill Communications Inc.
  633 Third Avenue
  New York, NY 10017
- **Wall Street Journal**
  Dow Jones & Company
  200 Liberty Street
  New York, NY 10281
- **World Agriculture Situation**
  U.S. Department of Agriculture
  Economics Management Staff
- **Information Division**
  1301 New York Avenue N.W.
  Washington, D.C. 20005
  World Development
- **Pergamon Press Inc.**
  Journals Division
  Maxwell House
  Fairview Park
  Elmsford, NY 10523

- **World Trade Center Association (WTCA) Directory**
  World Trade Centers Association
  1 World Trade Center
  New York, NY 10048
- **International Encyclopedia of the Social Sciences**
  Macmillan and the Free Press
  866 Third Avenue
  New York, NY 10022
- **Marketing and Communications Media Dictionary**
  Media Horizons Inc.
  50 W. 25th Street
  New York, NY 10010
- **Market Share Reports**
  U.S. Government Printing Office
  Superintendent of Documents
  Washington, D.C. 20402
- **Media Guide International: Business/Professional Publications**
  Directories International Inc.
  150 Fifth Avenue Suite 610
  New York, NY 10011
- **Overseas Business Reports**
  U.S. Government Printing Office
  Superintendent of Documents
  Washington, D.C. 20402
- **Trade Finance**
  U.S. Department of Commerce
  International Trade Administration
  Washington, D.C. 20230
- **World Economic Conditions in Relation to Agricultural Trade**
  U.S. Government Printing Office
  Superintendent of Documents
  Washington, D.C. 20402

- **Yearbook of International Trade Statistics**
  United Nations
  United Nations Publishing Division
  1 United Nations Plaza
  Room DC2-0853
  New York, NY 10017

Selected Trade Databases[1]

News agencies
Comline—Japan Newswire*
Dow Jones News
Nikkei Shimbun News Database
Omninews
Reuters Monitor
UPI

Trade publication references with bibliographic keywords
Agris*
Biocommerce Abstracts & Directory
Findex
Frost & Sullivan Market Research Reports
Marketing Surveys Index
McCarthy Press Cuttings Service
Paperchem
PTS F & S Indexes*
Trade and Industry Index*

Trade publication references with summaries
ABI/Inform*
Arab Information Bank
Asia-Pacific
BFAI
Biobusiness
CAB Abstracts*
Chemical Business Newsbase
Chemical Industry Notes
Coffeeline
Delphes
Info-South Latin American Information System*
Management Contents

---

*Available on CD-ROM as well.
[1]International Trade FORUM, International Trade Centre, UNCTAD/GATT, April 1993, 15.

NTIS Bibliographic Data Base*
Paperchem
PIRA Abstract*
PSTA
PTS Marketing & Advertising
    Reference Service
PTS Promt*
Rapra Abstracts*
Textline
Trade & Industry ASAP
World Textiles

Full text of trade publications
Datamonitor Market Reports
Dow Jones News
Euromonitor Market Direction
Federal News Service*
Financial Times Business Report
    File
Financial Times Fulltext*
Globefish
ICC Key Notes Market Research
Investext*
McCarthy Press Cuttings Service
PTS Promt*
Textline
Trade & Industry ASAP

Statistics
Agrostat (diskette only)
ARI Network/CNS
Arab Information Bank
Comext/Eurostat*
Comtrade
FAKT - German Statistics
Globefish
IMF Data
OECD Data
Piers Imports
PTS Forecasts
PTS Time Series
Reuters Monitor
Trade Statistics
Tradstat World Trade Statistics

TRAINS (CD-ROM being
    developed)
US I/E Maritime Bills of Lading
US Imports for Consumption
World Bank Statistics

Price information
ARI Network/CNS
Chemical Business Newsbase
COLEACP
Commodity Options
Commodities 2000
Market News Service of ITC
Nikkei Shimbun News Database
Reuters Monitor
UPI
US Wholesale Prices

Company registers
ABC Europe Production Europe*
Biocommerce Abstracts &
    Directory
CD-Export (CD-ROM only)
Cerved*
Company Intelligence*
D&B Dun's Market Identifiers
    (U.S.A.)
D&B European Marketing File
D&B Eastern Europe
Dun's Electronic Business
    Directory
Firmexport/Firmimport*
Hoppenstedt Austria*
Hoppenstedt Germany*
Hoppenstedt Benelux
Huco - Hungarian Companies
ICC Directory of Companies
Kompass Asia/Pacific
Kompass Europe (EKOD)*
Mexican Exporters/Importers
Piers Imports
Polu - Polish Companies
SDOE
Thomas Register*

TRAINS (CD-ROM being
    developed)
UK Importers
UK Importers (DECTA)
US Directory of Importers
US I/E Maritime Bills of Lading
World Trade Center Network

Trade opportunities, tenders
Business
Federal News Service
Huntech - Hungarian Technique
Scan-a-Bid
Tenders Electronic Daily
World Trade Center Network

Tariffs and trade regulations
Celex*
ECLAS
Justis Eastern Europe (CD-ROM
    only)
Scad*
Spearhead*
Spicers Centre for Europe
TRAINS (CD-ROM being
    developed)
US Code of Federal Regulations
US Federal Register
US Harmonized Tariff Schedule

Standards
BSI Standardline
Noriane/Perinorm*
NTIS Bibliographic Database*
Standards Infodisk ILI (CD-ROM
    only)

Shipping information
Piers Imports
Tradstat World Trade Statistics
US I/E Maritime Bills of Lading

Others
Fairbase
Ibiscus

---

*Available on CD-ROM as well.

Selected U.S. Government Publications and Services

Macrodata

World Population is issued by the U.S. Bureau of the Census, which collects and analyzes worldwide demographic data. Information is provided about total population, fertility, mortality, urban population, growth rate, and life expectancy. Also published are detailed demographic profiles, including an analysis of the labor force structure of individual countries.

Foreign Trade Highlights are annual reports published by the Department of Commerce. They provide basic data on U.S. merchandise trade with major trading partners and regions. They also contain brief analyses of recent U.S. trade developments.

Foreign Trade Report FT410 provides a monthly statistical record of shipments of all merchandise from the United States to foreign countries, including both the quantity and dollar value of exports to each country. It also contains cumulative export statistics from the first of the calendar year.

World Agriculture, a publication of the U.S. Department of Agriculture, provides production information, data, and analyses by country along with review of recent economic conditions and changes in agricultural and trade policies. Frequent supplements provide an outlook of anticipated developments for the coming year.

Country Information

National Trade Data Bank, a key product of the U.S. Department of Commerce, provides monthly CD-ROM disks that contain overseas market research, trade statistics, contact information, and other reports that may assist U.S. exporters in their international marketing efforts.

Country Marketing Plan reports on commercial activities and climate in a country and is prepared by the Foreign Commercial Service staffs abroad. It also contains an action plan for the coming year, including a list of trade events and research to be conducted.

Industry SubSector Analyses are market research reports, ranging from 5 to 20 pages, on specific product categories, for example, electromedical equipment in one country.

Overseas Business Reports (OBR) present economic and commercial profiles on specific countries and provide background statistics. Selected information on the direction and the volume and nature of U.S. foreign trade is also provided.

Background Notes, prepared by the Department of State, present a survey of a country's people, geography, economy, government, and foreign policy. The reports also include important national economic and trade information.

Foreign Economic Trends presents recent business and economic developments and the latest economic indicators of more than 100 countries.

Product Information

Export Statistics Profiles analyze exports for a single industry, product by product, country by country, over a five-year period. Data are rank-ordered by dollar value for quick identification of the leading products and industries. Tables show the sales of each product to each country as well as competitive information, growth, and future trends. Each profile also contains a narrative analysis that highlights the industry's prospects, performance, and leading products.

Export Information System Data Reports, available from the U.S. Small Business Administration, provide small businesses with a list of the 25 largest importing markets for their products and the 10 best markets for U.S. exporters of the products. Trends within those markets and the major sources of foreign competition are also discussed.

Services

Agent Distributor Service (ADS): The Foreign Commercial Service (FCS) provides a customized search for interested and qualified foreign representatives for a firm's product.

Aglink: Collaborative effort between the Foreign Agricultural Service and the Small Business Administration to match foreign buyers with U.S. agribusiness firms.

Catalog Exhibitions: The Department of Commerce organizes displays of product literature and videotape presentations overseas.

Comparison Shopping Service: The FCS provides a custom foreign market survey on a product's overall marketability, names of competitors, comparative prices, and customary business practices.

Economic Bulletin Board: The Department of Commerce provides access to the latest economic data releases, including trade opportunities, for on-line users.

Foreign Agricultural Service: Employees of the U.S. Department of Agriculture, stationed both abroad and in the United States with the mission to facilitate agricultural exports from the United States. Provides counseling, research, general market information, and market introduction services.

Foreign Buyer Program: The FCS brings foreign buyers to U.S. trade shows for industries with high export potential.

Going Global: A computerized, on-line information system that lists market opportunities, information on foreign countries, and export intermediaries. Primarily focused on agricultural firms.

Matchmaker Events: The Department of Commerce introduces U.S. companies to new markets through short visits abroad to match the U.S. firm with a representative or prospective partner.

Seminar Missions: The Department of Commerce sponsors technical seminars abroad designed to promote sales of sophisticated products and technology.

Trade Missions: Groups of U.S. business executives, led by Commerce Department staff, meet with potential foreign buyers, agents, and distributors.

Trade Opportunity Program: The FCS daily collection of trade opportunities worldwide is published and electronically distributed to subscribers.

World Traders Data Reports: The FCS publishes background research conducted by FCS officers abroad on potential trading partners, such as agents, distributors, and licensees.

CHAPTER 12

International Business Entry

Learning Objectives

1. To learn how firms gradually progress through an internationalization process.

2. To examine the differing reasons why firms internationalize.

3. To understand the strategic effects of internationalization on the firm.

4. To study the various modes of entering the international market.

5. To understand the role and functions of international intermediaries.

6. To learn about the multiple problems and challenges of export trading.

A Passionate Commitment to Exporting

A unique product and a zeal for exporting have equaled success for Mirus Industries Corporation of California. Mirus makes digital film recorders that "print" onto 35 mm film, which then can be processed into slides for color presentations. In the United States, typical users are medical researchers, college professors, business executives, and government officials. However, "in all parts of the world there is the same need to communicate ideas in an efficient and effective way," explains Mirus President Bruce MacKay.

Mirus Industries needed no coaxing into the international field of play. It knew it had a product with universal appeal and was therefore on the ball from the beginning, before it even had a single customer. In the two years since exporting became the focus, Mirus has recruited ten distributors in the Middle East, Far East, and Europe and is now exporting 60 percent of its production.

A unique feature of this successful global company is that it has a mere 13 employees. When questioned about the ability of a 13-person firm to perform internationally the way Mirus does, MacKay replies, "The answer is that you must want to export and have the courage to do it. You must approach the export market with a passionate commitment, and you must have a well-thought-out plan."

Central to Mirus's plan is the relationship with the foreign distributors. For MacKay, locating suitable distributors abroad is a "very difficult task requiring diligence, patience, and often a little luck." The often-skeptical international distributors must be made to feel comfortable and trusting. They need to know that you will be around in six months, says MacKay. He goes on to conclude that "You cannot expect instant results—you must remain patient and consistent in your dealings with distributors."

Important to Mirus is the actual travel to the foreign markets to learn about market conditions firsthand. In 18 months, MacKay has traveled to Japan four times, to Southeast Asia two times, and to Europe three times. Mirus believes that communication, quality, and collaboration are the keys to success. "You must keep in mind that international distributors are very savvy people who know what is going on in this high-tech world. Fax machines, magazines, and fast travel keep everyone up to date. Your international distributors are your local partners, and they represent your reputation. Never forget that."

Source: "Exporting Pays Off," *Business America,* August 23, 1993, 20.

International business holds out the promise of large new market areas, yet firms cannot simply jump into the international marketplace and expect to be successful. They must adjust to needs and opportunities abroad, have quality products, understand their customers, and do their homework. The must also have a major commitment to international markets, as this chapter's opening vignette shows. The rapid globalization of markets, however, reduces the time available to adjust to new market realities.

This chapter is concerned with the activities of firms preparing to enter international markets. Primary emphasis is placed on export activities. The chapter focuses on the role of management in starting up international operations and describes the basic stimuli for international activities. Entry modes for the international arena are highlighted, and the problems and benefits of each mode are discussed. Finally, the role of facilitators and intermediaries in international business is described.

THE ROLE OF MANAGEMENT

The type and quality of its management are the keys to whether or not a firm will enter the international marketplace. Researchers have found that management dynamism and commitment are crucial in the first steps toward international operations.[1] The management of firms that have been successful internationally is usually described as active rather than passive[2] or as aggressive rather than nonaggressive.[3] Conversely, the managers of firms that are unsuccessful or inactive internationally usually exhibit a lack of determination or devotion to international business. The issue of **managerial commitment** is a critical one because foreign market penetration requires a vast amount of market development activity, sensitivity toward foreign environments, research, and innovation. Regardless of what the firm produces or where it does business internationally, managerial commitment is crucial for enduring stagnation and sometimes even setbacks and failure.[4] To obtain such a commitment, it is important to involve all levels of management early on in the international planning process and to impress on all players that the effort will only succeed with a commitment that is companywide.[5]

Initiating international business activities takes the firm in an entirely new direction, quite different from adding a product line or hiring a few more people. Going international means that a fundamental strategic change is taking place. Research has shown that the decision to export, for example, usually comes from the highest levels of management. Typically, the president, chairman, or vice president of marketing is the chief decision maker.[6] A survey of the fastest growing mid-sized companies in the United States showed that for all international operations, the personal commitment and vision of the chief executive officer played a forceful role.[7]

The carrying out of the decision—that is, the initiation of international business transactions and their implementation—is then the primary responsibility of marketing personnel. It is important to establish an organizational structure in which someone has the specific responsibility for international activities. Without such a responsibility center, the focus that is necessary for success can easily be lost. Such a center need not be large. For example, just one person assigned part time to international activities can begin exploring and entering international markets. In the final decision stage of evaluating international activities, the responsibility again rests with senior management. It therefore appears that, in order to influence a firm to go international, the president first needs to be convinced. Once the decision to internationalize is made, the marketing department becomes active in international business.

The first step in developing international commitment is to become aware of international business opportunities. Management may then decide to enter the international marketplace on a limited basis and evaluate the results of the initial activities. An international business orientation develops over time.

Management in the majority of firms is much too preoccupied with short-term, immediate problems to engage in sophisticated long-run planning. As a result, most firms are simply not interested in international business. Yet certain situations may lead a manager to discover and understand the value of going international and to decide to pursue international business activities. Trigger factors frequently are foreign travel, during which new business opportunities are discovered, or the receipt of information that leads management to believe that such opportunities exist. Managers who have lived abroad and have learned foreign languages or are particularly interested in foreign cultures are more likely to investigate whether international business opportunities would be appropriate for their firms.

New management or new employees can also bring about an international orientation. For example, managers entering a firm may already have had some international business experience and may try to use this experience to further the business activities of the firm where they are currently employed.

MOTIVATIONS TO GO ABROAD

Normally, management will consider international activities only when stimulated to do so. A variety of motivations can push and pull individuals and firms along the international path. An overview of the major motivations that have been found to make firms go international is provided in Table 12.1. Proactive motivations represent stim-

TABLE 12.1 Major Motivations to Internationalize Small and Medium-Sized Firms	**Proactive**
	Profit advantage
	Unique products
	Technological advantage
	Exclusive information
	Managerial commitment
	Tax benefit
	Economies of scale
	Reactive
	Competitive pressures
	Overproduction
	Declining domestic sales
	Excess capacity
	Saturated domestic markets
	Proximity to customers and ports

uli for firm-initiated strategic change. Reactive motivations describe stimuli that result in a firm's response and adaptation to changes imposed by the outside environment. In other words, firms with proactive motivations go international because they want to; those with reactive motivations have to go international.

Proactive Motivations

Profits are the major proactive motivation for international business. Management may perceive international sales as a potential source of higher profit margins or of more added-on profits. Of course, the profitability perceived when planning to go international is often quite different from the profitability actually obtained. Recent research has indicated that, particularly in international start-up operations, initial profitability may be quite low.[8] The gap between perception and reality may be particularly large when the firm has not previously engaged in international business. Despite thorough planning, unexpected influences often shift the profit picture substantially. Shifts in exchange rates, for example, may drastically affect profit forecasts.

Unique products or a technological advantage can be another major stimulus. A firm may produce goods or services that are not widely available from international competitors. Again, real and perceived advantages must be differentiated. Many firms believe that they offer unique products or services, even though this may not be the case internationally. If products or technologies are unique, however, they certainly can provide a competitive edge. What needs to be considered is how long such an advantage will last. The length of time is a function of the product, its technology, and the creativity of competitors. In the past, a firm with a competitive edge could often count on being the sole supplier to foreign markets for years to come. This type of advantage has shrunk dramatically because of competing technologies and the frequent lack of international patent protection.

Special knowledge about foreign customers or market situations may be another proactive stimulus. Such knowledge may result from particular insights by a firm, special contacts an individual may have, in-depth research, or simply from being in the right place at the right time (for example, recognizing a good business situation during a vacation trip). Although such exclusivity can serve well as an initial stimulus for international business, it will rarely provide prolonged motivation because competitors—at least in the medium run—can be expected to catch up with the information advantage. Only if firms build up international information advantage as

Economies of scale help mass marketers such as Coca-Cola stay competitive in both domestic and international markets.

Source: © 1991 Arthur Meyerson, courtesy of Coca-Cola.

an ongoing process, through, for example, broad market scanning or assured informational exclusivity, can prolonged corporate strategy be based on this motivation.

Another motivation reflects the desire, drive, and enthusiasm of management toward international business activities. The managerial commitment can exist simply because managers like to be part of a firm that engages in international business. (It sounds impressive.) Further, such activity can often provide a good reason for international travel—for example, to call on a major customer in the Bahamas during the cold winter months. Often, however, the managerial commitment to internationalize is simply the reflection of a general entrepreneurial motivation, that is, a desire for continuous growth and market expansion.[9]

Tax benefits can also play a major motivating role. Many governments use preferential tax treatment to encourage exports. In the United States, for example, a tax mechanism called a foreign sales corporation (FSC) provides firms with certain tax deferrals and makes international business activities more profitable. (More detail on the FSC is presented in Chapter 19.) As a result of the tax benefits, firms either can offer their product at a lower cost in foreign markets or can accumulate a higher profit.

A final major proactive motivation involves economies of scale. International activities may enable the firm to increase its output and therefore climb more rapidly on the learning curve. The Boston Consulting Group has shown that the doubling of output can reduce production costs up to 30 percent. Increased production for international markets can therefore help to reduce the cost of production for domestic sales and make the firm more competitive domestically as well.[10]

Reactive Motivations

A second type of motivation, primarily characterized as reactive, influences firms to respond to environmental changes and pressures rather than to attempt to blaze trails. Competitive pressures are one example. A company may fear losing domestic market share to competing firms that have benefited from the economies of scale gained through international business activities. Further, it may fear losing foreign markets permanently to competitors that have decided to focus on these markets. Market share usually is most easily retained by firms that initially obtain it, and therefore companies frequently enter the international market head over heels. Quick entry, however, may result in similarly quick withdrawal once the firm recognizes that its preparation has been inadequate.

Similarly, overproduction can result in a major reactive motivation. During downturns in the domestic business cycle, foreign markets have historically provided an ideal outlet for excess inventories. International business expansion motivated by overproduction usually does not represent full commitment by management, but rather a safety-valve activity. As soon as domestic demand returns to previous levels, international business activities are curtailed or even terminated. Firms that have used such a strategy once may encounter difficulties when trying to employ it again because many foreign customers are not interested in temporary or sporadic business relationships.

Declining domestic sales, whether measured in sales volume or market share, have a similar motivating effect. Products marketed domestically may be at the declining stage of their product life cycle. Instead of attempting to push back the life cycle process domestically, or in addition to such an effort, firms may opt to prolong the product life cycle by expanding the market. In the past, such efforts by firms in industrialized countries often met with success because customers in less-developed countries only gradually reached the level of need and sophistication already obtained by customers in the developed countries. Increasingly, however, because of the more rapid diffusion of technology, these lags are shrinking.

Excess capacity can also be a powerful motivator. If equipment for production is not fully utilized, firms may see expansion abroad as an ideal way to achieve broader distribution of fixed costs. Alternatively, if all fixed costs are assigned to domestic production, the firm can penetrate foreign markets with a pricing scheme that focuses mainly on variable cost. Yet such a view is feasible only for market entry. A market-penetration strategy based on variable cost alone is unrealistic because, in the long run, fixed costs have to be recovered to replace production equipment.

The reactive motivation of a saturated domestic market has similar results to that of declining domestic sales. Again, firms in this situation can use the international market to prolong the life cycle of their product and even of their organization.

A final major reactive motivation is that of proximity to customers and ports. Physical and psychological closeness to the international market can often play a major role in the international business activities of the firm. For example, a firm established near a border may not even perceive itself as going abroad if it does business in the neighboring country. Except for some firms close to the Canadian or Mexican border, however, this factor is much less prevalent in the United States than in many other nations. Most European firms automatically go abroad simply because their neighbors are so close.

In general, firms that are most successful in international business are usually motivated by proactive—that is, firm internal—factors. Proactive firms are also frequently more service oriented than reactive firms. Further, proactive firms are more marketing and strategy oriented than reactive firms, which have as their major concern operational issues. The clearest differentiation between the two types of firms can probably be made ex post facto by determining how they initially entered international markets. Proactive firms are more likely to have solicited their first international order, whereas reactive firms frequently begin international activities after receiving an unsolicited order from abroad.

CONCERNS AND PROBLEMS OF GOING INTERNATIONAL

Going international presents the firm with new environments, entirely new ways of doing business, and a host of new problems. The problems have a wide range. They can consist of strategic considerations, such as service delivery and compliance with long-term government regulations, or focus on start-up issues, such as how to find and effectively communicate with customers. In addition, firms must worry about operational matters, such as information flows and the mechanics of carrying out an international business transaction. This involves a variety of new documents, including commercial invoices, bills of lading, consular invoices, inspection certificates, and shipper's export declarations. The paperwork is necessary to comply with various domestic, international, or foreign regulations. The regulations may be designed to control international business activities, to streamline the individual transaction, or, as in the case of the shipper's export declaration, to compile trade statistics. To fill out these forms, the exporter often needs to obtain specialized information—for example, the tariff schedule number for the product. The routing of the shipment must also be known in advance to provide information about the mode of transport, the point of embarkation, and the point of debarkation. Most importantly, the exporter must have full knowledge about the destination of the export. As was explained in Chapter 8, governments have an interest in ensuring that certain products are not shipped to prohibited countries and firms. Precise information about destination, intermediate recipients, and final recipients is instrumental in enforcing the export control system. By signing such forms, exporters warrant that their declarations are correct, and they can be prosecuted if that is not the case. A sample export declaration is provided in Figure 12.1.

STRATEGIC EFFECTS OF GOING INTERNATIONAL

As a firm goes international, unusual things can happen to both risk and profit. Management's perception of risk exposure grows in light of the gradual development of expertise, the many concerns about engaging in a new activity, and uncertainty about the new environment it is about to enter. Domestically, the firm has gradually learned about the market and therefore managed to decrease its risk. In the course of international expansion, the firm now encounters new and unfamiliar factors, exposing it to increased risk. At the same time, because of the investment needs required by a serious international effort, immediate profit performance may slip. In the longer term, increasing familiarity with international markets and the benefits of serving diversified markets will decrease the firm's risk below the previous "domestic only" level and increase profitability as well. In the short term, however, managers may face an unusual, and perhaps unacceptable, situation: rising risk accompanied by decreasing profitability. In light of this reality, which is depicted in Figure 12.2, many executives are tempted to either not initiate international activities or to discontinue them.[11]

Understanding the changes in risk and profitability can help management overcome the seemingly prohibitive cost of going international and shows that the negative developments may be only short term. Yet, success does require the firm to be a risk taker, and firms must realize that satisfactory international performance will take time.[12] Satisfactory performance can be achieved in three ways: effectiveness, efficiency, and competitive strength. Effectiveness is characterized by the acquisition of market share abroad and by increased sales. Efficiency is manifested later by rising profitability. Competitive strength refers to the firm's position compared to other

FIGURE 12.1   Shipper's Export Declaration

U.S. DEPARTMENT OF COMMERCE — BUREAU OF THE CENSUS — INTERNATIONAL TRADE ADMINISTRATION

FORM **7525-V** (1-1-88)   **SHIPPER'S EXPORT DECLARATION**   OMB No. 0607-0018

1a. EXPORTER (Name and address including ZIP code)

ZIP CODE   **2. DATE OF EXPORTATION**   **3. BILL OF LADING/AIR WAYBILL NO.**

b. EXPORTER'S EIN (IRS) NO.   **c. PARTIES TO TRANSACTION**   ☐ Related   ☐ Non-related

4a. ULTIMATE CONSIGNEE

b. INTERMEDIATE CONSIGNEE

5. FORWARDING AGENT

6. POINT (STATE) OF ORIGIN OR FTZ NO.   **7. COUNTRY OF ULTIMATE DESTINATION**

8. LOADING PIER (Vessel only)   **9. MODE OF TRANSPORT** (Specify)

10. EXPORTING CARRIER   **11. PORT OF EXPORT**

12. PORT OF UNLOADING (Vessel and air only)   **13. CONTAINERIZED** (Vessel only)   ☐ Yes   ☐ No

14. SCHEDULE B DESCRIPTION OF COMMODITIES.   (Use columns 17–19)

15. MARKS, NOS., AND KINDS OF PACKAGES

VALUE (U.S. dollars, omit cents) (Selling price or cost if not sold) (20)

D/F (16)	SCHEDULE B NUMBER (17)	CHECK DIGIT	QUANTITY – SCHEDULE B UNIT(S) (18)	SHIPPING WEIGHT (Kilos) (19)

21. VALIDATED LICENSE NO./GENERAL LICENSE SYMBOL   **22. ECCN** (When required)

23. Duly authorized officer or employee | The exporter authorizes the forwarder named above to act as forwarding agent for export control and customs purposes

24. I certify that all statements made and all information contained herein are true and correct and that I have read and understand the instructions for preparation of this document, set forth in the "**Correct Way to Fill Out the Shipper's Export Declaration.**" I understand that civil and criminal penalties, including forfeiture and sale, may be imposed for making false or fraudulent statements herein, failing to provide the requested information or for violation of U.S. laws on exportation (13 U.S.C. Sec. 305; 22 U.S.C. Sec. 401; 18 U.S.C. Sec. 1001; 50 U.S.C. App. 2410).

Signature

Title

Date

Confidential - For use solely for official purposes authorized by the Secretary of Commerce (13 U.S.C. 301 (g))

Export shipments are subject to inspection by U.S. Customs Service and/or Office of Export Enforcement

25. AUTHENTICATION (When required)

This form may be printed by private parties provided it conforms to the official form. For sale by the Superintendent of Documents, Government Printing Office, Washington, D.C. 20402, and local Customs District Directors. The "**Correct Way to Fill Out the Shipper's Export Declaration**" is available from the Bureau of the Census, Washington, D.C. 20233.

Source: Seaschott.

FIGURE 12.2
Profit and Risk
During Early
Internationalization

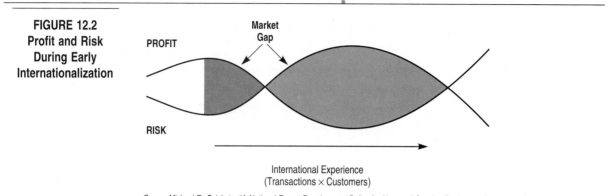

Source: Michael R. Czinkota, "A National Export Development Policy for New and Growing Businesses," *Journal of International Marketing* 2 no. 1 (1994): 95.

firms in the industry, and is, due to the benefits of international experience, likely to grow. The international executive must appreciate the time and performance dimensions associated with going abroad in order to overcome short-term setbacks for the sake of long-term success.

ALTERNATIVE ENTRY STRATEGIES

Conceivably, a new firm could create large-scale subsidiaries abroad or could even be formed for international business purposes. However, four forms of entry strategies are used by the majority of firms that initiate international business activities: indirect exporting and importing, direct exporting and importing, licensing, and franchising.[13] These alternatives are discussed in this chapter in more detail. Other modes of entry, such as direct foreign investment, management contracts, contract manufacturing, and turnkey operations, are mostly used by larger and more experienced firms and are therefore addressed in Chapter 13.

Indirect Exporting and Importing

Firms can be involved in exporting and importing in an indirect or direct way. Indirect involvement means that the firm participates in international business through an intermediary and does not deal with foreign customers or firms. Direct involvement means that the firm works with foreign customers or markets with the opportunity to develop a relationship. The end result of exporting and importing is similar whether the activities are direct or indirect. In both cases, goods and services either go abroad or come to the domestic market from abroad, and goods may have to be adapted to suit the targeted market. However, the different approaches have varying degrees of impact on the knowledge and experience levels of firms. The less direct the involvement of the firm, the less likely is the internal development of a storehouse of information and expertise on how to do business abroad, information that the firm can draw on later for further international expansion. Therefore, while indirect activities represent a form of international market entry, they are unlikely to result in growing management commitment to international markets or increased capabilities in serving them.

Many firms are indirect exporters and importers, often without their knowledge. As an example, merchandise can be sold to a domestic firm that in turn sells it abroad.

TABLE 12.2 Exporting in Your Own Backyard: A Dozen Segments of the United States for Export Markets	1. Large U.S. companies purchasing U.S. goods for their own foreign affiliates 2. Large design and construction firms purchasing U.S. goods for foreign projects awarded to them 3. U.S. branches of gigantic foreign trading companies purchasing U.S. goods for their affiliates 4. Export merchants buying for their own account 5. Large foreign companies purchasing U.S. goods through their U.S. buying office or agents 6. U.S. military purchasing for use abroad 7. U.S. exporters seeking U.S. goods to round out their own lines 8. United Nations members purchasing for development projects 9. Foreign governments purchasing U.S. goods 10. Foreign department stores purchasing U.S. goods through U.S. buying offices 11. Foreign buyers on purchasing trips 12. AID-financed transactions requiring U.S. goods

Source: Nelson Joyner, Georgetown University, teaching notes, 1995.

This is most frequently the case when smaller suppliers deliver products to large multinational corporations, which use them as input to their foreign sales.

Similarly, firms may sell products to a government agency. For example, the Department of Defense might make purchases that ultimately may be shipped to military outposts abroad. Foreign buyers may purchase products locally and then send them immediately to their home country. More examples of "exporting in your own backyard" are given in Table 12.2. While indirect exports may be the result of unwitting participation, some firms also choose this method of international entry as a strategic alternative that conserves effort and resources while still taking advantage of foreign opportunities.

At the same time, many firms that perceive themselves as buying domestically may in reality buy imported products. They may have long-standing relations with a domestic supplier who, because of cost and competitive pressures, has begun to source products from abroad rather than produce them domestically. In this case, the buyer firm has become an indirect importer.

Direct Exporting and Importing

Firms that opt to export or import directly have more opportunities ahead of them. As Global Perspective 12.1 shows, they learn more quickly the competitive advantages of their products and can therefore expand more rapidly. They also have the ability to control their international activities better and can forge relationships with their trading partners, which can lead to further international growth and success.

However, the firms also are faced with obstacles that those who access international markets indirectly avoid. These hurdles include identifying and targeting foreign suppliers and/or customers and finding retail space, processes that can be very costly and time-consuming. Some firms are overcoming such barriers through the use of mail-order catalogs ("storeless" distribution networks) or video brochures. In Japan, for example, "high-cost rents, crowded shelves, and an intricate distribution system have made launching new products via conventional methods an increasingly difficult and expensive proposition. Direct marketing via catalog short-circuits the distribution train and eliminates the need for high-priced shop space."[14] Entrepreneurs are becoming creative in other ways to avoid the high cost of land and labor in Japan. Taking advantage of the fact that the Japanese are used to vending machines

Global Perspective

12.1
No Pig in a Poke

Mike Kane, owner of Kane Manufacturing Co. of Des Moines, Iowa, manufactures products for farrow-to-finish operations in the pig industry. Products include nursery feeders for piglets, as well as other types of feeders that will handle pigs from 40 pounds to 250 pounds; baby pig waterers; and heat mats. Kane's wife, Donna, took charge of the firm's export operations four years ago and started an aggressive international program.

The export potential of their products became apparent to the Kanes when they received numerous replies to advertisements placed in the U.S. Department of Commerce catalog-magazine, *Commercial News USA,* and the magazine *Pig International.* Said Mike Kane: "The style of our feeders had never been introduced in most other countries. Our feeders are made of tough polyethylene; they don't rust, crack, break, or draw moisture. Once the pig industry overseas saw that we had something more rugged

and durable than any feeding equipment they had ever seen, we found a good demand for our product."

Initially the firm showed its products to foreign customers mainly at trade shows in the United States, starting with International Pig America in Atlanta, Georgia, and the World Pork Expo. Later on, the company also participated in overseas trade shows, including Huhn & Schwein in Hanover, Germany, and Expo Aviga in Barcelona, Spain. Explains Kane: "Distributors and other businesspeople from all over the world come to these trade shows looking for new products, and we had some that caught their eye."

In just three years, Kane's exports have increased from 10 percent of sales to 33 percent. To help fill the growing demand in Europe, the company just opened a warehouse in Germany. In addition, the firm exports to Japan, Canada, Mexico, Taiwan, Korea, New Zealand, Australia, Cyprus, and the Philippines.

Source: "Exporting Pays Off," *Business America,* June 29, 1992, 21.

(there are more than 5.4 million machines in the country), a San Diego meat-packing firm is entering the Japanese market by selling steaks in vending machines located outside train stations and convenience stores.[15]

INTERNATIONAL INTERMEDIARIES

Both direct and indirect importers and exporters frequently make use of intermediaries who can assist with troublesome yet important details such as documentation, financing, and transportation. The intermediaries also can identify foreign suppliers and customers and help the firm with long- or short-term market penetration efforts. Three major types of international intermediaries are export management companies, Webb-Pomerene associations, and trading companies. Together with export facilitators, the intermediaries can bring the global market to the domestic firm's doorstep and help overcome financial and time constraints. Global Perspective 12.2 provides examples of the efforts of international intermediaries. The extent of their involvement varies widely. Table 12.3 shows those areas in which intermediaries have been found to be particularly helpful.

It is the responsibility of the firm's management to decide how to use the intermediaries. Options range from using their help for initial market entry to developing a long-term strategic collaboration. It is the degree of corporate involvement in and control of the international effort that determines whether the firm operates as an indirect or direct internationalist.

Global Perspective

12.2
Small Firms Need Experts to Grow Foreign Business

Small businesses no longer can afford to ignore the international market. The percentage of U.S. companies that have annual revenues of less than $100 million and are exporting their products is growing rapidly. Almost half of them export. Small business owners, however, often risk losing potentially lucrative foreign contracts when they try to add export management to their heavy work load. The services of export experts are the answer for many potential exporters.

Export specialists say entrepreneurs typically underestimate the time and expertise needed to cultivate business overseas. Few realize the amount of management resources exporting will use up at the top levels of the company. Small businesses busy expanding at home seldom can spare the resources to devise exporting strategies, said Andrea Larson, an assistant business professor at the University of Virginia.

MMO Music Group Inc., of Elmsford, N.Y., is a case in point. The company's president, David Kratka, says that faxes and phone messages from Asia and Europe piled up during the 1980s while he was trying to manage the booming domestic side of his family-owned company, which produces sing-along tapes for karaoke machines. Kratka concedes he frequently ignored the export side of his business. "Many of the things were not carried out to their full potential and many of the things got started, but we never really stuck with them." Finally, the company president hired an international sales director in 1993 and foreign sales now constitute between 12 percent and 16 percent of MMO Music Group's $8 million in annual sales. This is up from about 5 percent of annual sales during most of the 1980s.

A waffle griddle and ice-cream cone maker, CoBatCo Inc., in Peoria, Ill., has managed to increase exports as a percentage of total sales to 13 percent from practically zero in 1990. In large part, the jump is attributable to help from Export Resource Associates Inc., a Minnesota consulting firm. Don Stevens, CoBatCo president, said, "I think to some extent there were some opportunities in the late eighties that could have been pursued if we had had the background to pursue them; we didn't even have knowledge of what a letter of credit was."

Meridian Group, a Los Angeles export management company, says it can handle everything from sales and distribution to credit and shipping. Its services, however, don't come cheap. Meridian Group president Charles Nevil estimated that an export manager typically charges a fee of between 10 percent and 15 percent of a shipment's wholesale value. Export managers acknowledge that they sap some control from small business owners accustomed to running the show. "The good news is that it's spoon-fed management," said Mr. Nevil, who represents about 150 small manufacturers. "The bad news is that the control of that [company's] international destiny is in the hands of someone like me."

Source: Stephanie N. Mehta, "Small Companies Look to Cultivate Foreign Business," *The Wall Street Journal,* July 7, 1994, B2.

TABLE 12.3 **How a Trade** **Intermediary Can Offer** **Assistance**	1. Knows foreign market competitive conditions 2. Has personal contacts with potential foreign buyers 3. Evaluates credit risk associated with foreign buyers 4. Has sales staff to call on current foreign customers in person 5. Assumes responsibility for physical delivery of product to foreign buyer

Source: Richard M. Castaldi, Alex F. De Noble, and Jeffrey Kantor, "The Intermediary Service Requirements of Canadian and American Exporters," *International Marketing Review* 9 no. 2 (1992): 21–40.

Export Management Companies

Firms that specialize in performing international business services as commission representatives or as distributors are known as **export management companies (EMCs).** Although few directories listing EMCs are available, more than 1,000 of these firms are estimated to be operating in the United States. A study conducted by the National Federation of Independent Businesses found that more than 20 percent of all manufactured goods exporters in the United States are EMCs.[16] Most EMCs are quite small. Many were formed by one or two principals with experience in international business or in a particular geographic area. Their expertise enables them to offer specialized services to domestic corporations.

EMCs have two primary forms of operation: They take title to goods and operate internationally on their own account, or they perform services as agents. They often serve a variety of clients, thus their mode of operation may vary from client to client and from transaction to transaction. An EMC may act as an agent for one client and as a distributor for another. It may even act as both for the same client on different occasions.

The EMC as an Agent   When working as an agent, the EMC is primarily responsible for developing foreign business and sales strategies and establishing contacts abroad. Because the EMC does not share in the profits from a sale, it depends heavily on a high sales volume, on which it charges commission. The EMC may therefore be tempted to take on as many products and as many clients as possible to obtain a high sales volume. As a result, the EMC may spread itself too thin and may be unable to adequately represent all the clients and products it carries. The risk is particularly great with small EMCs.

In addition to its international activities, this type of EMC must concentrate a substantial amount of effort on the development of domestic clients. The clients often are exactly the firms that are unwilling to commit major resources to the international business effort. They must be convinced that it is worthwhile to consider international business. To develop and expand its clientele, the EMC must divert some of its limited resources to that task.

EMCs that have specific expertise in selecting markets because of language capabilities, previous exposure, or specialized contacts appear to be the ones most successful and useful in aiding client firms in their international business efforts. For example, they can cooperate with firms that are already successful in international business but have been unable to penetrate a specific region. By sticking to their area of expertise and representing only a limited number of clients, such agents can provide quite valuable services.

The EMC as a Distributor   When operating as a distributor, the EMC purchases products from the domestic firm, takes title, and assumes the trading risk. Selling in its own name, it has the opportunity to reap greater profits than when acting as an agent. The potential for greater profit is appropriate, because the EMC has drastically reduced the risk for the domestic firm while increasing its own risk. The burden of the merchandise acquired provides a major motivation to complete an international sale successfully. The domestic firm selling to the EMC is in the comfortable position of having sold its merchandise and received its money without having to deal with the complexities of the international market. On the other hand, it is less likely to gather much international business expertise.

Compensation of EMCs

The mechanism of an EMC may be very useful to the domestic firm if such activities produce additional sales abroad. However, certain services must be performed that demand resources for which someone must pay. As an example, a firm must incur market development expenses to enter foreign markets. At the very least, products must be shown abroad, visits must be arranged, or contacts must be established. Even though it may often not be discussed, the funding for these activities must be found.

One possibility is a fee charged to the manufacturer by the EMC for market development, sometimes in the form of a retainer and often on an annual basis. The retainers vary and are dependent on the number of products represented and the difficulty of foreign market penetration. Frequently, manufacturers are also expected to pay all or part of the direct expenses associated with foreign market penetration. Some of these expenses may involve the production and translation of promotional product brochures. Others may be related to the rental of booth space at foreign trade shows, the provision of product samples, or trade advertising.[17]

Alternatively, the EMC may demand a price break for international sales. It will take on many of the business activities for the manufacturer and the EMC will want the price discounted for those activities. Therefore, sales to EMCs may occur only at a reduced price.

In one way or another, the firm that uses an EMC must pay the EMC for the international business effort. The compensation can be in the form of fees and/or cost sharing or in terms of lower prices and resulting higher profits for the EMC. Otherwise, despite promises, the EMC may simply add the firm and product in name only to its product offering and do nothing to achieve international success. Management needs to be aware of this cost and the fact that EMCs do not offer a free ride. Depending on the complexity of a product and the necessity to carry out developmental research, promotion, and services, management must be prepared to part with some portion of the potential international profitability to compensate the EMC for its efforts.

Power Conflicts between EMCs and Clients

The EMC in turn faces the continuous problem of retaining a client once foreign market penetration is achieved. Many firms use an EMC's services mainly to test the international arena, with the clear desire to become a direct participant once successful operations have been established. Of course, this is particularly true if foreign demand turns out to be strong and profit levels are high. The conflict between the EMC and its clients, with one side wanting to retain market power by not sharing too much international business information, and the other side wanting to obtain that power, often results in short-term relationships and a lack of cooperation. Since international business development is based on long-term efforts, this conflict frequently leads to a lack of success.

For the concept of an export management company to work, both parties must fully recognize the delegation of responsibilities, the costs associated with those activities, and the need for information sharing, cooperation, and mutual reliance. Use of an EMC should be viewed just like a domestic channel commitment, requiring a thorough investigation of the intermediary and the advisability of relying on its efforts, a willingness to cooperate on a relationship rather than on a transaction basis, and a willingness to properly reward its efforts. The EMC in turn must adopt a flexible approach to managing the export relationship. It must continue to upgrade the levels of services offered, constantly highlighting for the client the dimensions of post-sales service and providing in-depth information, since those are its biggest sources of differential advantage.[18] By doing so, the EMC lets the client know that the cost is worth the service and thereby reduces the desire for circumvention.

Webb-Pomerene Associations

Legislation enacted in 1918 led to **Webb-Pomerene associations** that permit firms to cooperate in terms of international sales allocation, financing, and pricing information. The associations must take care not to engage in activities that would reduce competition within the United States. To more successfully penetrate international markets, however, they can allocate markets, fix quotas, and select exclusive distributors or brokers.

In spite of this early effort to encourage joint activities by firms in the international market, the effectiveness of Webb-Pomerene associations has not been substantial. At their peak, from 1930 to 1934, 50 Webb-Pomerene associations accounted for about 12 percent of U.S. exports. By 1995 only 16 associations were active and accounted for less than 1 percent of U.S. exports.[19] In addition, it appears that most of the users of this particular form of export intermediary are not the small and medium-sized firms the act was initially intended to assist, but rather the dominant firms in their respective industries.

The lack of success of this particular intermediary has mainly been ascribed to the fact that the antitrust exemption granted was not sufficiently ironclad. Further, specialized export firms are thought to have more to offer to a domestic firm than does an association, which may be particularly true if the association is dominated by one or two major competitors in an industry. Such dominance makes joining the association undesirable for smaller firms.

Trading Companies

A third major intermediary is the trading company. The concept was originated by the European trading houses such as the Fuggers of Augsburg. Later on, monarchs chartered traders to form corporate bodies that enjoyed exclusive trading rights and protection by the naval forces in exchange for tax payments. Examples of such early trading companies are the Oost-Indische Compagnie of the Netherlands, formed in 1602, followed shortly by the British East India Company and La Compagnie des Indes chartered by France.[20] Today, the most famous trading companies are the **sogoshosha** of Japan. Names such as Mitsubishi, Mitsui, and C. Itoh have become household words around the world. The nine trading company giants of Japan act as intermediaries for about half of the country's exports and two-thirds of its imports.[21] The general trading companies play a unique role in world commerce by importing, exporting, countertrading, investing, and manufacturing. Their vast size allows them to benefit from economies of scale and perform their operations at high rates of return even though their profit margins are in the range of 2 percent.[22]

Four major reasons have been given for the success of the Japanese sogoshosha. First, by concentrating on obtaining and disseminating information about market opportunities and by investing huge funds in the development of information systems, the firms now have the mechanisms and organizations in place to gather, evaluate, and translate market information into business opportunities. Second, economies of scale permit the firms to take advantage of their vast transaction volume to obtain preferential treatment by, for example, negotiating transportation rates or even opening up new transportation routes and distribution systems. Third, the firms serve large internal markets, not only in Japan but also around the world, and can benefit from opportunities for countertrade. Finally, sogoshosha have access to vast quantities of capital, both within Japan and in the international capital markets. They can therefore carry out transactions that are too large or risky to be palatable or feasible for other firms.[23] In spite of changing trading patterns, these giants continue to succeed by shifting their strategy to expand their domestic activities in Japan, entering more newly developing markets, increasing their trading activities among third countries, and forming joint ventures with non-Japanese firms. Mitsui, for example, has more than 100 affiliated companies involved in joint ventures with local business groups in Thailand alone.[24]

Expansion of Trading Companies   For many decades, the emergence of trading companies was commonly believed to be a Japan-specific phenomenon. Particularly, Japanese cultural factors were cited as the reason that such intermediaries could operate successfully only from that country. In 1975, however, trading companies were established by government declaration in Korea. The intent was to continue Korea's export-led growth in a more efficient fashion. With the new legislation, the Korean government tied access to financing and government contracts to the formation of trading companies. Less than a decade later, the major trading companies of Korea (such as Hyundai, Samsung, and Daewoo) were handling 43 percent of Korea's total exports.[25] They were considered to be a major success. Similarly, the Turkish government devised special incentives to develop export trading firms. As a result, within a few years, such trading companies accounted for 46 percent of Turkey's exports.[26]

In the United States, **export trading company (ETC)** legislation designed to improve the export performance of small and medium-sized firms was implemented in 1982. To improve export performance, bank participation in trading companies was permitted and the antitrust threat to joint export efforts was reduced through precertification of planned activities by the U.S. Department of Commerce. Businesses were encouraged to join together to export or offer export services.

Permitting banks to participate in ETCs was intended to allow ETCs better access to capital and therefore permit more trading transactions and easier receipt of title to goods. The relaxation of antitrust provisions in turn was meant to enable firms to form joint ventures more easily. The cost of developing and penetrating international markets would then be shared, with the proportional share being, for many small and medium-sized firms, much easier to bear. As an example, in case a warehouse is needed in order to secure foreign market penetration, one firm alone does not have to bear all the costs. A consortium of firms can jointly rent a foreign warehouse. Similarly, each firm need not station a service technician abroad at substantial cost. Joint funding of a service center by several firms makes the cost less prohibitive for each one. The trading company concept also offers a one-stop shopping center for both the firm and its foreign customers. The firm can be assured that all international functions will be performed efficiently by the trading company, and at the same time, the foreign customer will have to deal with few individual firms.

The legislation permits a wide variety of possible structures for an ETC. General trading companies may handle many commodities, perform import and export services, countertrade, and work closely with foreign distributors. Regional trading companies may handle commodities produced in only one region, specializing in products in which that region possesses a comparative advantage. Product-oriented trading companies may concentrate on a limited number of products and offer their market penetration services for only these products. Trading companies may also be geographically oriented, targeting one particular foreign nation, or may be focused on certain types of projects such as turnkey operations and joint ventures with foreign investors. Finally, trading companies may develop an industry-oriented focus, handling only goods of specific industry groups, such as metals, chemicals, or pharmaceuticals.[27]

Trading Company Activities   Independent of its form of operation, an ETC can engage in a wide variety of activities. It can purchase products, act as a distributor abroad, or offer services. It can provide information on distribution costs and even handle domestic and international distribution and transportation, which can range from identifying distribution costs to booking space on ocean or air carriers and handling shipping contracts.

Although ETCs seem to offer major benefits to many U.S. firms that want to go abroad, they have not been very extensively used. By 1995 only 143 individual ETC certificates had been issued by the U.S. Department of Commerce. Since some of the certificates covered all the members of trade associations, a total of 5,000 companies were part of an ETC.[28]

This lack of acceptance requires the examination of several potential shortcomings in the export trading company concept. Banks need to consider whether the mentalities of bankers and traders can be made compatible. Traders, for example, are known for rapidly seizing the opportune moment, whereas bankers often appear to move more slowly. A key challenge will be to find ways to successfully blend business entrepreneurship with banking regulations.

Banks also need to understand the benefits they can derive from working with small or medium-sized exporters. The first impression may be that an ETC offers only added risk and cost. Yet involvement with an ETC may provide the bank with a broader client base, profitable use of its extensive international information system and network of corresponding institutions, and a stepping-stone toward the internationalization of its own banking services. Many banks have been hesitant to increase the volume of their international activities because of the international debt situation. In the long run, however, an improved understanding of this type of transaction and its profitability, plus the increasing pressures of a highly competitive deregulated home market, will lead to more international involvement by U.S. banks.

The antitrust protection offered by the ETC Act may also not be very important to many firms, particularly the small and medium-sized ones. There may even be a clash with the offered protection and the corporate goals of firms. Companies, due to reasons of independence or the fear of losing marketing information and control, may not want to band together with their competitors.

Yet, given the current market structure, in which most exporters are small and fragmented and unable to avail themselves of international markets due to a lack of resources and information, the opportunity for collaboration is still useful. However, several cautionary remarks are in order if the ETC concept is to be applied successfully.

ETC Caveats   Firms participating in trading companies by joining or forming them should be aware of the difference between product- and market-driven ETCs. Firms may have a strong tendency to use the trading company primarily to dispose of their merchandise. Successful foreign sales, however, depend on foreign demand and the foreign market. A blend of demand-driven activities and existing product lines needs to be achieved for a trading company to be successful.

The trading company itself must solicit continuous feedback on foreign market demands and changes in these demands so that its members will be able to maintain a winning international product mix. Substantial attention must be paid to gathering information on the needs and wants of foreign customers and disseminating the information to participating U.S. producers. Otherwise, lack of responsiveness to foreign market demands will constrain the ETC's effectiveness.[29] The ETC should also determine the activities on which to concentrate, basing the determination on the types of suppliers represented and the types of products exported.

Depending on whether products are differentiated or undifferentiated, the ETC should place varying degrees of emphasis on developing its capability for international promotion. At the same time, undifferentiated products require greater price competitiveness, which may be precisely the major advantage offered by an ETC as a result of economies of scale. For differentiated products, an ETC may be able to place emphasis on promotion and have greater flexibility in price determination.[30]

ETCs may still become the major vehicle for the generation of new international business entry activities by small and medium-sized firms. The concepts of synergism and cooperation certainly make sense in terms of enhancing the international competitiveness of firms. Yet the focus of ETCs should perhaps not be pure exporting. Importing and third-country trading may also generate substantial activity and profit. Through the carrying out of a wide variety of business transactions, international market knowledge is obtained. The management and consulting expertise may in itself be a salable service.

INTERNATIONAL FACILITATORS

Facilitators are entities outside the firm that assist in the process of going international by supplying knowledge and information but not participating in the transaction. Such facilitators can come both from the private and the public sector.

Private Sector Facilitators

Major encouragement and assistance can result from the statements and actions of other firms in the same industry. Information that would be considered proprietary if it involved domestic operations is often freely shared by competing firms when it concerns international business. The information not only has source credibility but is viewed with a certain amount of fear, because a too-successful competitor may eventually infringe on the firm's domestic business.

A second, quite influential group of private sector facilitators is distributors. Often a firm's distributors are engaged, through some of their business activities, in international business. To increase their international distribution volume, they encourage purely domestic firms to participate in the international market. This is true not only for exports but also for imports. For example, a major customer of a manufacturing firm may find that materials available from abroad, if used in the domestic production process, would make the product available at lower cost. In such instances, the customer may approach the supplier and strongly encourage foreign sourcing.

Banks and other service firms, such as accounting and consulting firms, can serve as major facilitators by alerting their clients to international opportunities. While these service providers historically follow their major multinational clients abroad, increasingly they are establishing a foreign presence on their own. Frequently, they

Global Perspective

12.3
Exporting with Private Sector Help

Exchange Textiles of Manchester, England, was fighting for business in a buyer's market and realized that competitors were dangerously dependent on the United Kingdom retail trade. Managing Director Richard Grubb decided that for a company to be successful in the next 10 years, it must have up to 50 percent of sales in exports. Like many smaller companies, however, Exchange Textiles had no experience at exporting. Grubb identified a possible demand for his fashionable children's underwear in the United States and Germany, but didn't know where to start.

The company was greatly helped by a Department of Trade and Industry (DTI) scheme called the Export Promoter Initiative. Under the DTI Initiative, dozens of business executives from the private sector are recruited to help the export effort. "(It) works because businessmen are working together with other businessmen, banging heads together in a way that civil servants cannot do," said Greg Shenkman, an export promoter. Each promoter adopts a

different approach in the country on which he or she focuses. Shenkman's priority is to help companies that already are trying to export to Japan to establish a more effective presence. But, like other export promoters, he also is using his knowledge of the local market to sniff out potential market opportunities for which he then seeks suppliers in the U.K.

Exchange Textiles's first contact was with promoter Andrew Garcia, who advised Grubb to send samples and a company profile to U.K. embassies in Germany. Even after the commercial secretary in Berlin put him in touch with a suitable agent, Grubb was faced with numerous questions. He had regular meetings with Garcia about the handling of foreign exchange exposure, distribution, dealing with the agent, and the exacting quality that the German market required. The effort paid off. Two years after the initial decision to export, Exchange Textiles was heading for foreign sales equal to a quarter of its total turnover.

Source: Richard Gourlay, "Sailing to New Markets," *The Financial Times,* February 1, 1994: 14.

work with domestic clients on expanding market reach in the hope that their service will be used for any international transaction that results. Given the extensive information network of many service providers—banks, for example, often have a wide variety of correspondence relationships—the role of these facilitators can be major. Like a mother hen, they can take firms under their wings and be pathfinders in foreign markets.

Chambers of commerce and other business associations that interact with firms can frequently heighten their interest in international business. Yet, in most instances, such organizations function mainly as secondary intermediaries, because true change is brought about by the presence and encouragement of other managers. Global Perspective 12.3 gives an example of such private sector assistance.

Public Sector Facilitators

Government efforts can also facilitate the international efforts of firms. In the United States, for example, the Department of Commerce provides major export assistance, as do other federal organizations such as the Small Business Administration and the Export-Import Bank. Employees of Export Assistance Centers throughout the country, with the help of voluntary groups such as export councils, visit firms and attempt to analyze their international business opportunities. Through rapid access to

Global Perspective

12.4
Matchmaking Produces Export Sales

The Small Business Administration has several initiatives to inform small companies about exporting. The export-matchmaker conferences are among the most successful.

The fourth annual export-matchmaker conference, held in 1993 in Newark, N.J., attracted more than 90 U.S. manufacturers and 66 export intermediaries. The conference provided manufacturers with an opportunity to interest export companies in taking their products to new, international markets. The export companies were just as enthusiastic about finding new, marketable products.

At such conferences, manufacturers display their products on a large exhibit floor; the goods range from seismographs, backpacks, and catheters to nail polish, software, and girdles. The 1993 conference was the first for Floyd S. Jacobs and his Jay Syrup Company. "We are still sorting out all the leads we got—about 12 viable ones," said Jacobs. Within a few weeks of the conference, Jacobs already had sent samples overseas with export companies, hoping some would agree to handle the export side of the operation.

Veteran exporters participate as well. Dallas-based Richland Beverage Corp. has been exporting for 40 years but still finds the matchmaker conference beneficial. Manny Zelzer, company president, said the matchmaker's "biggest advantage is the exposure. Hundreds of people are available in one place. We made a lot of contacts that we didn't have before. My feeling is that it certainly did accomplish what I was seeking to do."

On the other side of the equation at the matchmaker conferences are the companies in the business of helping firms export. They generally specialize in certain areas of the world and usually in certain types of products. Tamara Hoffman, president of China Information and Trade Exchange, Inc., said, "Many manufacturers are not very sure of how to use a consulting company. It will be a slow process because exporting is new to them. But we're optimistic." She, too, is developing leads based on contacts made at the conference.

The matchmaking notion seems to be gathering steam. In 1993, Halifax, Nova Scotia, hosted its first matchmaker after seeing the success of the SBA's efforts. A Montreal matchmaker took place that same year. The SBA, meanwhile, cosponsored its second Virginia conference in 1994; plans are also under way for an SBA-sponsored conference in California while Newark continues its annual program. The SBA hopes, eventually, to conduct export matchmakers in every region of the country.

Source: Roberta Maynard, "Making Overseas Connections," *Nation's Business,* January 1994: 57.

federal resources, these individuals can provide data, research reports, counseling, and financing information to firms. Government organizations can also sponsor meetings that bring interested parties together and alert them to new business opportunities abroad. Global Perspective 12.4 provides an example of such a "matchmaking" program. Key governmental facilitation also occurs when firms are abroad. By receiving information and assistance from their embassies, many business ventures abroad can be made easier. Table 12.4 shows the areas in which U.S. embassies abroad receive the most requests for assistance from companies.

Increasingly, organizations at the state and local level also are active in encouraging firms to participate in international business. Many states and provinces have formed agencies for economic development that provide information, display products abroad, conduct trade missions, and sometimes even offer financing. Similar services can also be offered by state and local port authorities and by some of the larger cities. State and local authorities can be a major factor in facilitating international activities because of their closeness to firms.

TABLE 12.4 Most Frequent Request for Business Assistance from U.S. Embassies	1. Business analysis of the foreign country 2. Introduction to local business leadership 3. Scheduling appointments with foreign government officials 4. Information about export/import regulations 5. Embassy intervention with foreign governments on contracts 6. Information about government contracts 7. Information on investment or tax incentives

Source: U.S. Department of State, Foreign Service Institute, Washington, D.C., 1993.

Educational institutions such as universities and community colleges also can be major international business facilitators. They can act as trade information clearing houses, facilitate networking opportunities, provide client counseling and technical assistance, and develop trade education programs.[31] They can also develop course projects that are useful to firms interested in international business. For example, students may visit a firm and examine its potential in the international market as a course requirement. With the skill and supervision of faculty members to help the students develop the final report, such projects can be useful to firms with scarce resources, while they expose students to real-world problems.

OTHER FORMS OF INTERNATIONAL MARKET ENTRY AND EXPANSION

Licensing and franchising are two forms of international market entry and expansion in addition to direct and indirect exporting. They are strategies that can be used by themselves or in conjunction with export activities.

Licensing

Under a **licensing agreement,** one firm permits another to use its intellectual property for compensation designated as **royalty.** The recipient firm is the licensee. The property licensed might include patents, trademarks, copyrights, technology, technical know-how, or specific business skills. For example, a firm that has developed a bag-in-the-box packaging process for milk can permit other firms abroad to use the same process. Licensing therefore amounts to exporting intangibles.

Assessment of Licensing   Licensing has intuitive appeal to many would-be international managers. As an entry strategy, it requires neither capital investment nor detailed involvement with foreign customers. By generating royalty income, licensing provides an opportunity to exploit research and development already conducted. After initial costs, the licensor can reap benefits until the end of the license contract period. Licensing also reduces the risk of expropriation because the licensee is a local company that can provide leverage against government action.

Licensing may help to avoid host-country regulations applicable to equity ventures. Licensing also may provide a means by which foreign markets can be tested without major involvement of capital or management time. Similarly, licensing can be used as a strategy to preempt a market before the entry of competition, especially if the licensor's resources permit full-scale involvement only in selected markets.

Licensing is not without disadvantages. It is the most limited form of foreign market participation and does not in any way guarantee a basis for future expansion.

As a matter of fact, quite the opposite may take place. In exchange for the royalty, the licensor may create its own competitor not only in the market for which the agreement was made but for third-country markets as well.

Licensing has also come under criticism from many governments and supranational organizations. They have alleged that licensing provides a mechanism for corporations in industrialized countries to capitalize on older technology. These accusations have been made even though licensing offers a foreign entity the opportunity for immediate market entry with a proven concept. It therefore eliminates the risk of R&D failure, the cost of designing around the licensor's patents, or the fear of patent-infringement litigation.

Some companies are increasingly hesitant to enter licensing agreements. For example, Japanese firms are delighted to sell goods to China but are unwilling to license the Chinese to produce the goods themselves. They fear that, because of the low wage structure in China, such licenses could create a powerful future competitor in markets presently held by Japan.

Principal Issues in Negotiating Licensing Agreements   The key issues in negotiating licensing agreements include the scope of the rights conveyed, compensation, licensee compliance, dispute resolution, and the term and termination of the agreement.[32] The more clearly these issues are spelled out, the more trouble free the association between the two parties can be.

The rights conveyed are product and/or patent rights. Defining their scope involves specifying the technology and know-how or show-how to be included. In addition, the transfer process must be negotiated. For example, an agreement should specify whether or not manuals will be translated into the licensee's language.

Compensation for the license is a second major issue. The licensor will want the agreement to cover (1) **transfer costs,** namely all variable costs incurred in transferring technology to a licensee and all ongoing costs of maintaining the agreement; (2) **R&D costs** incurred in developing the licensed technology; and (3) **opportunity costs** incurred in the foreclosure of other sources of profit, such as exports or direct investment. The licensor wants a share of the profits generated from the use of the license.

Licensees usually do not want to include allowances for opportunity costs and often argue that the R&D costs have already been covered by the licensor. License payments, or royalties, are therefore a function both of the licensor's minimum necessary return and the cost of the licensee's next best alternative. The methods of compensating the licensor typically take the form of running royalties—such as 5 percent of license sales—and/or up-front payments, service fees, and disclosure fees (for proprietary data).

Licensee compliance should be stipulated in the agreement. Some areas of compliance are technology transfer regulations, confidentiality of information provided, record keeping and audit provisions, and quality standards. Provisions for dispute resolution will center on the choice of law for contract interpretation and conflict resolution. Often these provisions include arbitration clauses that allow a third, neutral party to resolve any disputes that arise.

Finally, the term, termination, and survival rights of licenses must be specified. Government regulations in the licensee's market must be studied. A waiver should be applied for if the conditions are not favorable (for example, in terms of the maximum allowed duration).

A special form of licensing is **trademark licensing,** which has become a substantial source of worldwide revenue for companies that can trade on well-known names and characters. Trademark licensing permits the names or logos of designers, literary characters, sports teams, or movie stars to appear on clothing, games, foods and beverages, gift and novelties, toys, and home furnishings. Licensors can make millions of dollars with little effort, while licensees can produce a brand or product that consumers will recognize immediately. Trademark licensing is possible, however, only if the trademark name indeed conveys instant recognition. The total volume of trademark licensing amounts to more than $100 billion and is expected to grow by 8.5 percent during the 1990s.[33]

Franchising

A fourth international entry strategy, **franchising,** is the granting of the right by a parent company (the franchisor) to another, independent entity (the franchisee) to do business in a prescribed manner. The right can take the form of selling the franchisor's products; using its name, production, and marketing techniques; or using its general business approach.[34] Usually franchising involves a combination of many of those elements. The major forms of franchising are manufacturer-retailer systems (such as car dealerships), manufacturer-wholesaler systems (such as soft drink companies), and service firm–retailer systems (such as lodging services and fast-food outlets).

Typically, to be successful in international franchising, the firm must be able to offer unique products or unique selling propositions. If such uniqueness can be offered, growth can be rapid and sustained. With its uniqueness, a franchise must

Franchising is one way to expand into international markets. The Dunkin' Donuts franchise in Thailand operates some 50 stores like this one.

Source: Courtesy of Allied Lyons.

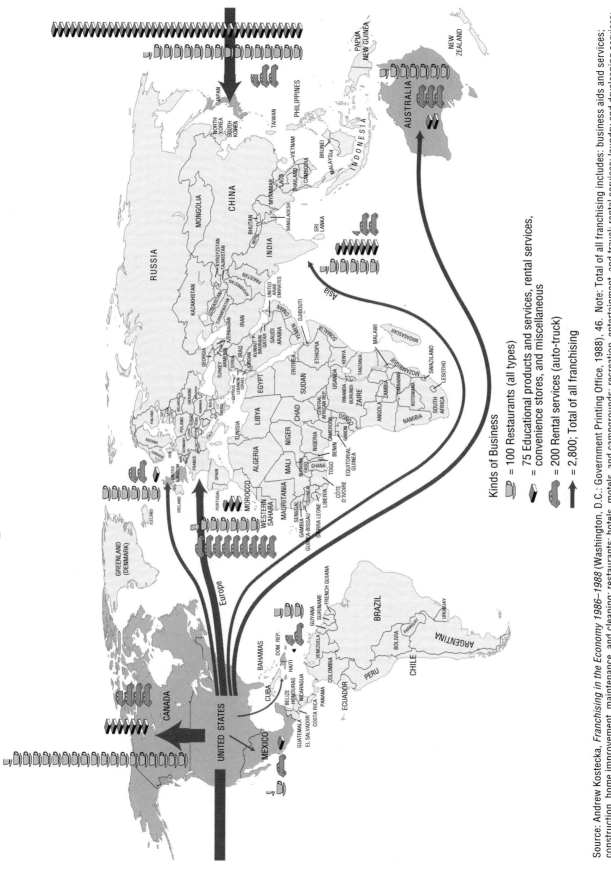

Kinds of Business

= 100 Restaurants (all types)

= 75 Educational products and services, rental services, convenience stores, and miscellaneous

= 200 Rental services (auto-truck)

= 2,800: Total of all franchising

Source: Andrew Kostecka, *Franchising in the Economy 1986–1988* (Washington, D.C.: Government Printing Office, 1988), 46. Note: Total of all franchising includes: business aids and services; construction, home improvement, maintenance, and cleaning; restaurants; hotels, motels, and campgrounds; recreation, entertainment, and travel; rental services; laundry and drycleaning services; automotive products and services; retailing (nonfood); educational products and services; rental services (equipment), convenience stores; retailing (food other than convenience stores); and miscellaneous.

Global Perspective

12.5
Taking Your Franchise Abroad

Wallace Doolin is president and CEO of TGI Friday's Inc. in Dallas, Texas. Here are his views of taking a franchise business abroad:

> While you have to modify certain strategies and procedures when you open for business abroad, you must protect the unique identity, quality of product, and standards of service that made your business a success at home.
>
> To transplant your personal identity into a foreign setting, it usually is advisable to take on a development partner—in our case, a franchisee or joint venture partner—who knows how to conduct business in whichever market you want to enter. A strong partner can help you negotiate government obstacles, labor unions, hiring practices, and other hurdles that are unique to various parts of the world.
>
> You can't overlook market research. Preliminary research might have saved us the expense of putting kimchi on the menu in South Korea. Kimchi, a kind of pickled cabbage, is a staple in Korean restaurants, and we assumed customers would look for it on our menu as well. We were wrong. It seems that customers in an American restaurant want only American food.
>
> You can't take little things for granted. In certain countries, the supplies and materials you need to run your business may be unavailable or unbelievably expensive. In Malaysia, for instance, sour cream costs $16 a pound. We found it was cheaper for us to make our own sour cream to serve with baked potatoes and potato skins.
>
> In the early years of our international expansion, one of our development partners told us we would never find the kind of outgoing, enthusiastic employees in Europe that we hire in the U.S. For example, in Britain, we were told that waiters don't

> sing "Happy Birthday" to customers. This created a dilemma. We had to ask ourselves whether we should introduce our traditional standards of customer service abroad, or adjust our standards to the local market. We decided that a restaurant without our brand of service would be a "TGI Friday's" in name only. So, with our partners, we developed a new approach to hiring that suited our style of business.
>
> When we look for employees outside the U.S., we hold auditions instead of traditional job interviews. We rent a theater or set up a stage, and ask our candidates to sing, dance, or tell a joke—anything that will show us their fun side. There are outgoing people in every culture; once we find them, we can give them the necessary job training.
>
> You can't open a restaurant in Germany or the Philippines and expect to run the place as if it were in Dallas or Detroit. Your U.S. staff can see a new operation through its start-up period, but then you must turn it over to those who truly understand the culture of the home country. Once you entrust your overseas partners and employees with your business philosophy, they must carry it forward.
>
> We seek out foreign nationals who may be on assignment or pursuing higher education in the U.S. and offer them an opportunity to return home. These individuals already understand U.S. business and service standards. But just as important, they are experts in the tradition, ethics, and ways of life of the customers we want to serve in foreign markets.
>
> Opening for business abroad requires a substantial investment—in capital and in human resources. With a knowledgeable partner and commitment to understanding your new customers, you can transcend virtually any cultural barrier.

Source: Wallace Doolin, "Taking Your Business on the Road," *The Wall Street Journal,* July 25, 1994: A14.

offer a high degree of standardization. In most cases, standardization does not require 100 percent uniformity, but rather, international recognizability. Concurrent with this recognizability, the franchisor can and should adapt to local circumstances. Food franchisors, for example, will vary the products and product lines offered depending on local market conditions and tastes. Global Perspective 12.5 provides an example of how one restaurant chain walks the fine line between adaptation and standardization.

International franchising has grown strongly in the past decade. In 1990, more than 450 franchising companies in the United States operated about 47,000 outlets in international markets.[35] Foreign franchisors are penetrating international markets as well. Examples include Holiday Rent-a-Car of Canada and Descamps, a French firm selling linens and tablecloths. Many companies can expand rapidly through franchising. Figure 12.3 provides an example of a franchising meeting, where firms buy and sell franchise opportunities.

The reasons for international expansion of franchise systems are market potential, financial gain, and saturated domestic markets. Global market demand is also very high for franchises. For example, the initial impetus for ComputerLand's expansion into the Asia/Pacific region was that "Asian entrepreneurs [were] coming knocking on our door asking for franchises."[36] From a franchisee's perspective, the franchise is beneficial because it reduces risk by implementing a proven concept. From a governmental perspective, there are also major benefits. The source country does not see a replacement of exports or export jobs. The recipient country sees franchising as requiring little outflow of foreign exchange, since the bulk of the profits generated remains within the country.[37]

Even though franchising has been growing rapidly, problems are often encountered in international markets. Some of them are summarized in Table 12.5. A major problem is foreign government intervention. In the Philippines, for example, government restrictions on franchising and royalties hindered ComputerLand's Manila store from offering a broader range of services, leading to a separation between the

**FIGURE 12.3
An Advertisement for
an International
Franchise Exposition**

Meet with Hundreds of the World's Largest Franchisors Who Are Currently Seeking International Master Licensees at the...

INTERNATIONAL Franchise Expo

"International Franchising is Wide Open Now That a Forum Exists for the Buyers and Sellers of International Master Licenses."

The biggest hurdle for the potential investor, until now, has been the expense and time involved in finding, researching and finally selecting a suitable master licensor from the many investment opportunities that exist within the franchise industry worldwide.

The INTERNATIONAL FRANCHISE EXPO addresses the needs of potential international master franchisees, giving both the sellers and buyers of master licenses a marketplace in which to evaluate each other on a grand scale.

INTERNATIONAL FRANCHISE EXPO
Washington D.C. Convention Center
April 29th, 30th, and May 1st, 1994
"The largest gathering of franchise companies in the world"

For More Information, Call or Write to:

BLENHEIM
The first name in exhibitions
1111 Louisiana Avenue, Suite 210
Winter Park, Florida 32789, USA
Phone: + 1 407 647 8521 - FAX: + 1 407 628 2042

TABLE 12.5 **Rank Order of** **Problems Encountered** **in International Markets** **by U.S. Franchise** **Systems**	1. Host government regulations and red tape 2. High import duties and taxes in foreign environment 3. Monetary uncertainties and royalty remission to franchisor 4. Logistical problems in operation of international franchise system 5. Control of franchisees 6. Location problems and real estate costs 7. Patent, trademark, and copyright protection 8. Recruitment of franchisees 9. Training of foreign franchisee personnel 10. Language and cultural barriers 11. Availability of raw materials for company product 12. Foreign ownership limitations 13. Competition in foreign market areas 14. Adaptation of franchise package to local markets

Source: Donald W. Hackett, "The International Expansion of U.S. Franchise Systems," in *Multinational Product Management,* eds. Warren Keegan and Charles Mayer (Chicago: American Marketing Association, 1979), 78.

company and its franchisee. Selection and training of franchisees represents another problem area. McDonald's lag behind Burger King in France was the result of the company's suing to revoke the license of its largest franchisee for failure to operate 14 stores according to McDonald's standards.

Many franchise systems have run into difficulty by expanding too quickly and granting franchises to unqualified entities. Although the local franchisee knows the market best, the franchisor still needs to understand the market for product adaptation and operational purposes. The franchisor, in order to remain viable in the long term, needs to coordinate the efforts of individual franchisees—for example, to share ideas and engage in joint undertakings, such as cooperative advertising.

A COMPREHENSIVE VIEW OF INTERNATIONAL EXPANSION

The central driver of internationalization is the level of managerial commitment. This commitment will grow gradually from an awareness of international potential to the adaptation of international business as a strategic business direction. It will be influenced by the information, experience, and perception of management, which in turn is shaped by motivations, concerns, and the activities of change agents.

Management's commitment and its view of the capabilities of the firm will then trigger various international business activities, which can range from indirect exporting and importing to more direct involvement in the global market. Eventually, the firm may then expand further through measures such as joint ventures, strategic alliances, or foreign direct investment. The latter activities are discussed in the next chapter.

All of the developments, processes, and factors involved in the overall process of going international are linked to each other. A comprehensive view of these linkages is presented schematically in Figure 12.4.

SUMMARY

Firms do not become experienced in international business overnight, but rather progress gradually through an internationalization process. The process is triggered by different motivations to go abroad. The motivations can be proactive or reactive.

FIGURE 12.4   A Comprehensive Model of International Entry and Expansion

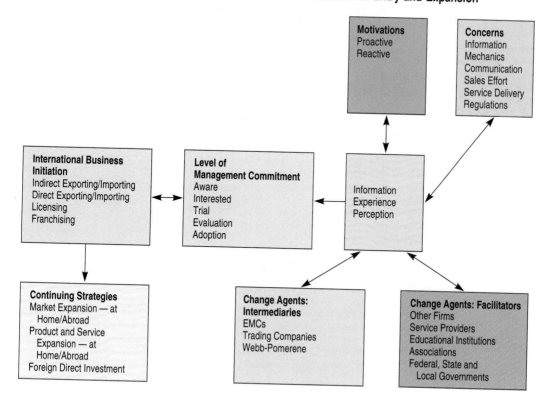

Proactive motivations are initiated by aggressive management, whereas reactive motivations are the defensive response of management to environmental changes and pressures. Firms that are primarily stimulated by proactive motivations are more likely to enter international business and succeed.

Apart from indirect and direct exporting and importing, alternatives for international business entry are licensing and franchising. The basic advantage of licensing is that it does not involve capital investment or knowledge of foreign markets. Its major disadvantage is that licensing agreements typically have time limits, are often proscribed by foreign governments, and may result in creating a competitor. The use of franchising as a means of expansion into foreign markets has increased dramatically. Franchisors must learn to strike a balance between, on the one hand, adapting to local environments and, on the other, standardizing to the degree necessary to maintain international recognizability.

In going abroad, firms encounter multiple problems and challenges, which range from a lack of information to mechanics and documentation. In order to gain assistance in its initial international experience, the firm can make use of either intermediaries or facilitators. Intermediaries are outside companies that actively participate in an international transaction. They are export management companies, Webb-Pomerene associations, or trading companies. In order for these intermediaries to perform international business functions properly, however, they must be compensated. This will result in a reduction of profits.

International facilitators do not participate in international business transactions, but they contribute knowledge and information. Increasingly, facilitating roles are played by private sector groups, such as industry associations, banks, accountants, or consultants and by universities and federal, state, and local government authorities.

Key Terms and Concepts

managerial commitment

export management
  companies (EMCs)

Webb-Pomerene association

sogoshosha

export trading company
  (ETC)

licensing agreement

royalty

transfer costs

R&D costs

opportunity costs

trademark licensing

franchising

Questions for Discussion

1. Discuss the difference between a proactive and a reactive firm, focusing your answer on international business.
2. Why is management commitment so important to export success?
3. Explain the benefits that international sales can have for domestic business activities.
4. Discuss the benefits and the drawbacks of treating international market activities as a safety-valve mechanism.
5. Give some of the reasons why distributors would want to help a firm gain a greater foothold in the international market.
6. Comment on the stance that "licensing is really not a form of international involvement because it requires no substantial additional effort on the part of the licensor."
7. Suggest reasons for the explosive international expansion of U.S.–based franchise systems.
8. What is the purpose of export intermediaries?
9. How can an export intermediary avoid circumvention by a client or customer?
10. What makes an export agent different from any other channel member?
11. Is there a need for export trading companies?
12. What makes a U.S. export trading company different from Japanese trading companies?
13. How can the discrepancy between product-driven and market-driven orientations within export trading companies be resolved?

Recommended Readings

Agmon, Tamir, and Richard Drobnick. *Small Firms in Global Competition.* New York: Oxford University Press, 1994.

Blaine, Michael James. *Co-operation in International Business: The Use of Limited Equity Arrangements.* Brookfield, Vt.: Avebury, 1994.

Contractor, Farok J. *Licensing in International Strategy: A Guide for Planning and Negotiations.* Westport, Conn.: Quorum Books, 1985.

Czinkota, Michael R. *Export Development Strategies: U.S. Promotion Policy.* New York: Praeger, 1982.

Czinkota, Michael R., Ilkka Ronkainen, and John Tarrant. *The Global Marketing Imperative.* Lincolnwood, Ill.: NTC Business Books, 1995.

Directory of Leading U.S. EMC's. 3d ed. Fairfield, Conn.: Bergano Book Co., 1991.

Eli, Max. *Japan Inc: Global Strategies of Japanese Trading Corporations.* Chicago: Probus, 1991.

———. *Investing, Licensing and Trading Conditions Abroad.* New York: Business International, 1994.

The Export Yellow Pages. Washington, D.C.: Venture Publishing, 1994.

Joyner, Nelson, and Richard G. Lurie. *How to Build an Export Business.* Washington, D.C.: U.S. Department of Commerce, Office of Minority Business Enterprise, n.d.

Perry, Anne C. *The Evolution of Selected U.S. Trade Intermediaries.* Westport, Conn.: Quorum Books, 1992.

Root, Franklin. *Entry Strategies for International Markets.* New York: Lexington Books, 1994.

Rosson, Philip J., and Stanley D. Reid. *Managing Export Entry and Expansion.* New York: Praeger, 1987.

Tomas, Michael J., and Donald G. Howard. "The Export Trading Company Act: An Update." *Journal of Marketing Channels* 2, 1 (1993): 105–119.

Yip, George S., Pierre M. Loewe, and Michael Y. Yoshino. "How to Take Your Company to the Global Market." *Columbia Journal of World Business* 23 (Winter 1988).

Notes

1. Warren J. Bilkey and George Tesar, "The Export Behavior of Smaller Sized Wisconsin Manufacturing Firms," *Journal of International Business Studies* 8 (Spring–Summer 1977): 93–98.
2. Finn Wiedersheim-Paul, H.C. Olson, and L.S. Welch, "Pre-Export Activity: The First Step in Internationalization," *Journal of International Business Studies* 9 (Spring–Summer 1978): 47–58.
3. George Tesar and Jesse S. Tarleton, "Comparison of Wisconsin and Virginia Small and Medium-Sized Exporters: Aggressive and Passive Exporters," in *Export Management,* eds. Michael R. Czinkota and George Tesar (New York: Praeger, 1982), 85–112.
4. Anthony C. Koh and James Chow, "An Empirical Investigation of the Variations in Success Factors in Exporting by Country Characteristics," *Midwest Review of International Business Research,* ed. Tom Sharkey, Vol. VII (Toledo, 1993).

5. S. Tamer Cavusgil, "Preparing for Export Marketing," *International Trade Forum* 2 (1993): 16–30.

6. Michael R. Czinkota, *Export Development Strategies* (New York: Praeger, 1982), 10.

7. *Winning in the World Market* (Washington, D.C.: American Business Conference Inc., November 1987), 20.

8. Masaaki Kotabe and Michael R. Czinkota, "State Government Promotion of Manufacturing Exports: A Gap Analysis," *Journal of International Business Studies* (Winter 1992): 637–658.

9. Yoo S. Yang, Robert P. Leone, and Dana L. Alden, "A Market Expansion Ability Approach to Identify Potential Exporters," *Journal of Marketing* 56 (January 1992): 84–96.

10. Michael R. Czinkota and Michael L. Ursic, "An Experience Curve Explanation of Export Expansion," in *International Marketing Strategy* (Fort Worth: Dryden Press, 1994), 133–141.

11. Michael R. Czinkota, "A National Export Development Policy for New and Growing Businesses," *Journal of International Marketing* 2, 1 (1994): 91–101.

12. Van Miller, Tom Becker, and Charles Crespy, "Contrasting Export Strategies: A Discriminant Analysis Study of Excellent Exporters," *The International Trade Journal* 7, 3 (1993): 321–340.

13. *Winning in the World Market,* 3–7.

14. "New 'Storeless' Market Gateways," *Focus Japan,* August 1989, 3.

15. Fred Hiatt, "Vending U.S. Steak on Japanese Corners," *International Herald Tribune,* April 5, 1990, 13.

16. Economic Consulting Services, *A Study of the Feasibility of Using Export Associations to Promote Increased Exports by Small Businesses* (Washington, D.C.: Economic Consulting Services, 1982), 29.

17. John J. Brasch, "Export Management Companies," *Journal of International Business Studies* (Spring–Summer 1978): 69.

18. Daniel C. Bello, David J. Urban, and Bronislaw J. Verhage, "Evaluating Export Middlemen in Alternative Channel Structures," *International Marketing Review* 8 (1991): 49–64.

19. Federal Trade Commission, Washington, D.C., 1994.

20. Dong-Sung Cho, *The General Trading Company: Concept and Strategy* (Lexington, Mass.: Lexington Books, 1987), 2.

21. "The Giants that Refused to Die," *Economist,* June 1, 1991: 72–73.

22. Kiyoshi Kojima and Ozawa Terutomo, *Japan's General Trading Companies: Merchants of Economic Development* (Paris: Organization for Economic Cooperation and Development, 1984), 88.

23. Yoshi Tsurumi, *Sogoshosha: Engines of Export-Based Growth* (Montreal: The Institute for Research on Public Policy, 1980).

24. Louise de Rosario, "Leaky Umbrellas," *Far Eastern Economic Review* 11 (February 1993): 48.

25. Chang-Kyun Shin, "Korean General Trading Companies: A Study of Their Development and Strategies," unpublished doctoral dissertation, George Washington University, Washington, D.C., 1984, 236.

26. Atilla Dicle and Ulku Dicle, "Effects of Government Export Policies on Turkish Export Trading Companies," *International Marketing Review* 9, no. 3 (1992): 62–76.

27. *The Export Trading Company Act of 1982* (Washington, D.C.: Chamber of Commerce of the United States of America, 1983), 4.

28. Office of Export Trading Companies, U.S. Department of Commerce, Washington, D.C., 1994.

29. Michael R. Czinkota, "The Business Response to the Export Trading Company Act of 1982," *The Columbia Journal of World Business* 19 (Fall 1984): 111.

30. Daniel C. Bello and Nicholas C. Williamson, "The American Export Trading Company, Designing a New International Marketing Institution," *Journal of Marketing* 49 (Fall 1985): 67.

31. Nancy Lloyd Pfahl, "Using a Partnership Strategy to Establish an International Trade Assistance Program," *Economic Development Review* (Winter 1994): 51–59.

32. Martin F. Connor, "International Technology Licensing" (Washington, D.C.: Seminars in International Trade, National Center for Export-Import Studies, 1985), Teaching Notes.

33. Kate Fitzgerald and Julie Liesse, "Jetsons Fly into Hot Licensing Year," *Advertising Age,* (July 16, 1990): 43.

34. Donald W. Hackett, "The International Expansion of U.S. Franchise Systems," in *Multinational Product Management,* eds. Warren J. Keegan and Charles S. Mayer (Chicago: American Marketing Association, 1979), 61–81.

35. Franchising Development Services, Norwich, U.K., 1994.

36. "ComputerLand Debugs Its Franchising Program for Asia/Pacific Region," *Business International,* September 13, 1985, 294–295.

37. Nizamettin Aydin and Madhav Kacker, "International Outlook of U.S.-Based Franchisers," *International Marketing Review* 7 (1990): 43–53.

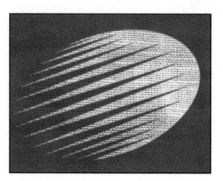

CHAPTER 13

Multinational Corporations

1. To define the concept of a multinational corporation and assess its various dimensions.

2. To compare arguments for and against foreign direct investment from the viewpoints of firms, nation-states, and other interest groups.

3. To examine the role of technology transfer in foreign direct investment and the operations of the multinational corporation.

4. To analyze the various modes of operation and cooperation available to a multinational corporation.

The Stateless Corporation

As cross-border trade and investment flows reach new heights, big global companies are effectively making decisions with little regard to national boundaries. The European, U.S., and Japanese giants heading in this direction are learning how to juggle multiple identities and multiple loyalties. Worried by the emergence of regional trading blocs in Europe, North America, and east Asia, these world corporations are building insider capabilities no matter where they operate. At the same time, factories and laboratories are moved around the world freely. Given the wave of mergers, acquisitions, and strategic alliances, the question of national control has become even more unclear. Technological change is blurring other boundaries as well. For example, fax machines allow professionals in India to perform routine architectural or audit work for clients in New York or London at sizable savings.

A fitting example of such a corporation is ABB (Asea Brown Boveri), a $28 billion electrical engineering giant. From headquarters in Zurich, Swedish, German, and Swiss managers shuffle assets around the globe, keep the books in dollars, and conduct most of their business in English. Yet the companies that make up their far-flung operations tailor ABB's turbines, transformers, robots, and high-speed trains to local markets so successfully that ABB looks like an established domestic player everywhere.

Statelessness does provide certain environmental advantages. Among the benefits are the ability to avoid trade and political problems, to sidestep regulatory hurdles, to achieve labor concessions, to balance costs, and to win technology breakthroughs.

The Canadian telecommunications giant, Northern Telecom, has moved so many of its manufacturing functions to the United States that it can win Japanese contracts on the basis of being a U.S. company. Japan favors U.S. over Canadian telecommunications companies because of the politically sensitive U.S.–Japanese trade gap.

When Germany's BASF launched biotechnology research at home, it confronted legal and political challenges from the environmentally conscious green movement. As a result, the company moved its cancer and immune-system research to Cambridge, Massachusetts, because of the availability of engineers and scientists and because the state had better resolved controversies involving safety, animal rights, and the environment.

One of the main factors that prompted U.S. pharmaceutical maker SmithKline and Britain's Beecham to merge was that they needed to guarantee that they could avoid licensing and regulatory hassles in their largest markets, western Europe and the United States. The new company can now identify itself as an inside player on both sides of the Atlantic.

When Xerox Corp. started moving copier rebuilding work to Mexico, its union in Rochester, New York, objected. The risk of job loss was clear, and the union agreed to undertake the changes in work style and productivity needed to keep the jobs.

Some world companies make almost daily decisions on where to shift production. When Dow Chemical saw European demand for a certain solvent decline recently, the company scaled back its production in Germany and shifted to producing another chemical there, one previously imported from Louisiana and Texas.

Otis Elevator Inc.'s latest product, the Elevonic 411, benefited from the company's global operations. The elevator was developed by six research centers in five countries. Otis's group in Farmington, Connecticut, handled the systems integration, Japan designed the special motor drives that make the elevators ride smoothly, France perfected the door systems, Germany handled the electronics, and Spain took care of the small-geared components. The international process saved more than $10 million in design costs and cut the development cycle from four years to two.

Multinational corporations are usually better than their more local rivals at creating, gathering and cross-fertilizing knowledge. They enjoy access to a larger pool of management talent, a wider range of skills and a greater variety of perspectives, and they are likely to know more about such things as consumer trends, technological needs and competitors' moves.

Some analysts have suggested that today's global firms will be superseded by a new form, the "relationship enterprise." These are networks of strategic alliances among big firms, spanning different industries and countries, but held together by common goals that encourage them to act almost as a single firm. For example, early in the twenty-first century, Boeing, British Airways, Siemens, TNT (an Australian parcel-delivery firm), and SNECMA (a French aircraft-engine maker) might together win a deal to build new airports in China. British Airways and TNT would receive preferential routes and landing slots, Boeing and SNECMA would win aircraft contracts, and Siemens would provide the air traffic control systems.

Sources: "Big Is Back," *The Economist,* June 24, 1995, A Survey of Multinationals, 1–24; Peter Norman, "World Economy and Finance," *Financial Times,* September 30, 1994, 1, 32; "The Global Firm: R.I.P.," *The Economist,* February 6, 1993, 69; "Cooperation Worth Copying," *The Washington Post,* December 13, 1992, H1, H6; "The Euro-Gospel According to Percy Barnevik," *Business Week,* July 23, 1990, 64–66; and "The Stateless Corporation," *Business Week,* May 14, 1990, 98–106.

Once a firm establishes a production facility abroad, its international operations take on new meaning. The firm has typically evolved to this stage through exporting and/or licensing, which by themselves no longer can satisfy its growth objectives. Many companies have found their exports dramatically curtailed because of unfavorable changes in exchange rates or trade barriers. Moreover, for firms in small domestic markets, physical presence through manufacturing is a must in the world's largest markets if the firm is to survive in the long term. Direct investment makes the firm's commitment to the international marketplace more permanent.

At the same time, the firm also becomes a corporate citizen in another nation-state, subject to its laws and regulations as well as its overall environmental influences. To remain effective and efficient as an entity, the firm has to coordinate and control its activities in multiple environments, making decisions that may not be optimal for one or more of the markets in which it operates. As a result, the firm may come under scrutiny by private and public organizations, ranging from consumer groups to supranational organizations such as the United Nations.

In today's environment—with no single country dominating the world economy or holding a monopoly on innovation—technologies, capital, and talents flow in many different directions, driving the trend toward a form of "stateless" corporation, as seen in the chapter's opening vignette.

This chapter will outline the basics of the multinational corporate phenomenon. It will compare the arguments for and against foreign direct investment from the viewpoints of firms, nation-states, and other interest groups. Further, it will analyze alternative arrangements available to multinational corporations in their operations in the world marketplace.

THE MULTINATIONAL CORPORATE PHENOMENON

Multinational entities have played a role in international trade for more than 300 years. The beginnings of these operations can be traced to the British and Dutch trading companies and, after their decline, to European overseas investments, mainly in the extractive industries. The phenomenon as it is known today is the result of the lead taken by U.S.–based companies in the post–World War II period and later followed by western European and Japanese entities.[1] By 1995 the total number of multinationals exceeded 37,000 with 206,000 affiliates around the world.[2] They are engaged in activities from the extractive to the manufacturing sectors, and they account for a significant share of the world's output. The global sales of foreign affiliates of multinationals are estimated to be $4.4 trillion, far greater than world exports at $2.5 trillion. The largest 600 multinationals are estimated to generate between one-fifth and one-fourth of the value added in the production of goods and services.[3]

The Multinational Corporation Defined

Different terms abound for the multinational corporation. They include global, world, transnational, international, supernational, and supranational corporation. The term *multinational enterprise* is used by some when referring to internationally involved entities that may not be using a corporate form. In this text, the term *multinational corporation (MNC)* will be used throughout.

Similarly, there is an abundance of definitions. The United Nations defines multinational corporations as "enterprises which own or control production or service facilities outside the country in which they are based."[4] Although this definition has been criticized as being oriented too much to the economist,[5] it nevertheless captures the quantitative and qualitative dimensions of many of the other definitions proposed.

Quantitatively, certain minimal criteria have been proposed that firms must satisfy before they can be regarded as multinational. The number of countries of operation is typically two, although the Harvard multinational enterprise project required subsidiaries in six or more nations.[6] Another measure is the proportion of overall revenue generated from foreign operations. Although no agreement exists regarding the exact percentage to be used, 25 to 30 percent is most often cited.[7] One proposal is that the degree of involvement in foreign markets has to be substantial enough to make a difference in decision making. Another study proposed that several nations should be owners of the corporation, as is the case with Royal Dutch Shell Group and Unilever or, more recently, as in the merger between Swiss Brown Boveri and Swedish Asea to form ABB.[8]

However, production abroad does not necessarily indicate a multinational corporation. Qualitatively, the behavior of the firm is the determining factor. If the firm is to be categorized as a multinational corporation, its management must consider it to be multinational and must act accordingly. In terms of management philosophies, firms can be categorized as **ethnocentric** (home-market oriented), **polycentric** (oriented toward individual foreign markets), or **regiocentric** or **geocentric** (oriented toward larger areas, even the global marketplace).[9] Even ethnocentric firms would qualify as multinational corporations if production were the sole criterion. However, the term should be reserved for firms that view their domestic operation as a part of worldwide (or regionwide) operations and direct an integrated business system. The definition excludes polycentric firms, which may be comparable to holding companies.

Both quantitative and qualitative criteria are important in the defining task. Regardless of the definition, the key criteria are that the firm controls its production facilities abroad and manages them (and its domestic operations) in an integrated fashion in pursuit of global opportunities.

The World's Multinational Corporations

Many of the world's largest corporate entities, listed in Table 13.1, are larger economically than most of their host nations. Some operate in well over 100 countries; for example, IBM has operations in 132 nations. Of the 25 firms listed, 8 are headquartered in the United States, 10 in western Europe, and 7 in east Asia. The economic power they command is enormous; according to one estimate, the 500 largest industrial corporations account for 80 percent of the world's direct investment and ownership of foreign affiliates.[10]

Although dominated by certain countries, the multinational corporate phenomenon has spread worldwide. For example, corporate headquarters for the 500 largest industrial corporations are in 32 different nations. Direct investment by firms from Africa, Asia, and Latin America has increased dramatically, especially by firms from more industrialized nations such as the Republic of Korea, Mexico, and Brazil.[11] Samsung, Korea's largest company, has assets of $16 billion and operations in 55 countries.[12]

The impact of multinationals varies by industry sector and by country. In oil, multinational corporations still command 30 percent of production, despite strong national efforts by some countries.[13] Their share in refining and marketing is still 45

| | Table 13.1 The 25 Largest Industrial Corporations Ranked by Sales: 1994 |

Rank Company	Country	Sales in ($ millions)	Foreign Revenue (% of total)	Foreign Profits (% of total)
1. General Motors	U.S.	133,621.9	28.0	91
2. Ford Motor	U.S.	108,521.0	30.3	D-P[1]
3. Exxon	U.S.	97,825.0	77.3	77
4. Royal Dutch/Shell Group	Brit./Neth.	95,134.4	N/A	N/A
5. Toyota Motor	Japan	85,283.2	26.4	N/A
6. Hitachi	Japan	68,581.8	15.0	N/A
7. Intl. Business Machines	U.S.	62,716.0	59.0	D-D[2]
8. Matsushita Electric Industrial	Japan	61,384.5	49.2	N/A
9. General Electric	U.S.	60,823.0	16.6	7.3
10. Daimler-Benz	Germany	59,102.0	60.8	N/A
11. Mobil	U.S.	56,576.0	67.5	79.8
12. Nissan Motor	Japan	53,759.8	35.7	N/A
13. British Petroleum	Britain	52,485.4	64.1	70.1
14. Samsung	South Korea	51,345.2	N/A	N/A
15. Philip Morris	U.S.	50,621.0	30.3	35.8
16. IRI	Italy	50,488.1	N/A	N/A
17. Siemens	Germany	50,381.3	N/A	N/A
18. Volkswagen	Germany	46,311.9	N/A	N/A
19. Chrysler	U.S.	43,600.0	13.2	18.5
20. Toshiba	Japan	42,917.2	30.3	N/A
21. Unilever	Brit./Neth.	41,842.6	N/A	N/A
22. Nestlé	Switzerland	38,894.5	N/A	N/A
23. Elf Aquitaine	France	37,016.3	44.0	N/A
24. Honda Motor	Japan	35,797.9	66.0	N/A
25. ENI	Italy	34,791.3	38.8	N/A

[1]D-P Deficit to Profit

[2]D-D Deficit to Deficit

Sources: "A Year for the Record Books," *Forbes,* July 18, 1994, 266–270; "The Global 500," *Fortune,* July 25, 1994, 143–147; "Everybody's Favourite Monsters," *The Economist,* March 27, 1993, 56–57; and various 1993 and 1994 annual reports.

percent. In several agribusiness sectors, such as pineapples, multinationals account for approximately 60 percent of the world output. Similarly, the contribution of multinational corporations' affiliates may account for more than one-third of the output of the marketing sector in certain countries.[14] For example, U.S. companies owned 32 percent of the paper and pulp industry, 36 percent of the mining and smelting industry, and 39 percent of manufacturing overall in Canada before the foreign direct investment climate changed in the early 1980s.[15] Despite a tightening of investment regulations, 40 percent of Canadian manufacturing was foreign owned in 1990, with U.S. firms accounting for 80 percent of that share.

The importance of the world marketplace to multinational corporations also varies. The foreign sales share of total sales for the world's largest industrial corporations has increased steadily. The percentage will naturally vary by industry (for example, oil company ratios are well over half) and by the country of origin. For many European-based companies, domestic sales may be less than 10 percent of overall sales. In 1994, for example, as a percentage of total worldwide sales, Philips's sales in Holland were 4 percent, SKF's sales in Sweden were 4 percent, and Sandoz's sales in Switzerland were a mere 2 percent. Comparable figures for U.S.-based companies, such as Johnson & Johnson and 3M, are about 50 percent.

The 1980s saw an increasing multinationalization of service companies, mainly in the finance and trade-related services, although other service MNCs such as accounting and advertising firms established considerable numbers of affiliates abroad.

FOREIGN DIRECT INVESTMENT

To understand the multinational corporate phenomenon, one must analyze the rationale for foreign direct investment. Foreign direct investment represents one component of the international business flow and includes start-ups of new operations as well as purchases of more than 10 percent of existing companies. The other component is portfolio investment—that is, the purchase of stocks and bonds internationally—which was discussed in Chapter 5.

Foreign direct investment has only recently received adequate attention. In 1974, for example, no comprehensive list of foreign firms investing in the United States was available, no one knew which firms were indeed foreign owned, and major shortcomings existed in the foreign direct investment data available.[16] In view of the fact that the U.S. data gathering system is highly sophisticated, much less information about foreign direct investment was probably available in other countries.

Recent concerted data gathering and estimation efforts by organizations such as the Organization for Economic Cooperation and Development (OECD) and the International Monetary Fund (IMF) indicate that foreign direct investments have grown tremendously. The total value of such global investment, which in 1967 was estimated at $105 billion, had climbed to an estimated $596 billion by 1984[17] and $2.125 trillion by 1993.[18] Foreign direct investment has clearly become a major avenue for foreign market entry and expansion. Foreign direct investment in the United States, for example, totaled $505 billion in 1994, up from a meager $6.9 billion in 1970.[19] Examples of this investment in terms of industries and locations are provided in Figure 13.1. At the same time, U.S. direct investment abroad totaled $607 billion.

Reasons for Foreign Direct Investment

Firms expand internationally for a variety of reasons. An overview of the major determinants of foreign direct investment is provided in Table 13.2.

Marketing Factors Marketing considerations and the corporate desire for growth are major causes of the increase in foreign direct investment. Even a sizable domestic market may present limitations to growth. Firms therefore need to seek wider market access in order to maintain and increase their sales. Laidlaw Transportation Ltd., the biggest school bus operator in Canada, moved south of the border, where it saw considerably more room to grow. Business has quadrupled, and the company now draws 60 percent of its revenue from the United States.[20] Some firms make investments in order to be closer to and better serve some of their major clients, such as Siemens with its $4.3 billion investment in the U.S. market. The growth objective can be achieved most quickly through the acquisition of foreign firms. In 1994, the value of cross-border deals was $239 billion with U.S. firms leading in the efforts by buying 1,173 companies abroad and selling 668 companies to non-U.S. entities.[21] One of the companies that has made the largest acquisitions in the U.S. market in recent years is Nestlé, which has acquired companies such as Carnation and Alcon Laboratories. Other reasons for foreign direct investment include the desire to gain know-how and the need to add to existing sales force strength.

FIGURE 13.1   A Sampler of Foreign Investment in the United States

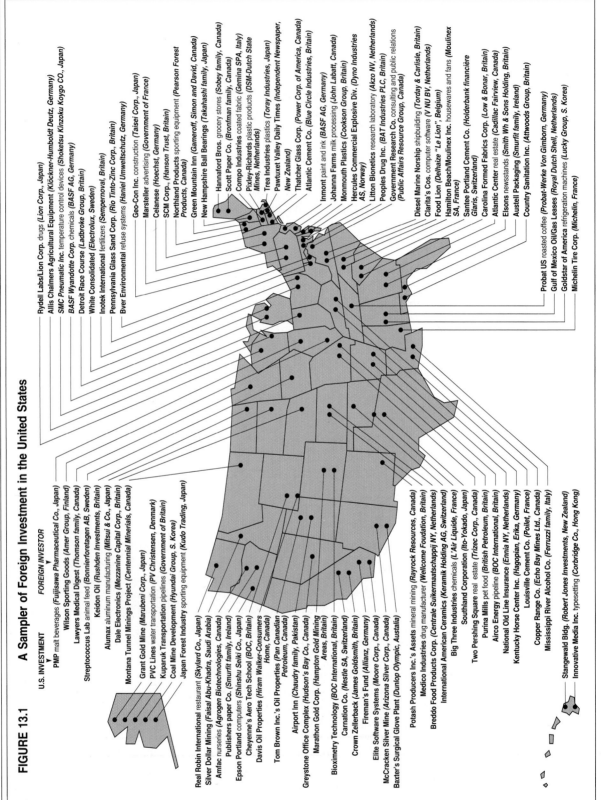

U.S. INVESTMENT **FOREIGN INVESTOR**

PMP malt beverages (Fujisawa Pharmaceutical Co., Japan)
Wilson Sporting Goods (Amer Group, Finland)
Lawyers Medical Digest (Thomson family, Canada)
Streptococcus Lab animal feed (Bonnierföretagen AB, Sweden)
Keidon Oil (Rushden Investments, Britain)
Alumax aluminum manufacturing (Mitsui & Co., Japan)
Dale Electronics (Mezzanine Capital Corp., Britain)
Montana Tunnel Minings Project (Centennial Minerials, Canada)

Real Robin International restaurant (Skylard Co., Japan)
Silver Dollar Mining (Faisal Abu-Khadra, Saudi Arabia)
Amfac nurseries (Agrogen Biotechnologies, Canada)
Publishers paper Co. (Smurfit family, Ireland)
Epson Portland computers (Shinshu Seiki Co., Japan)
Cheyenne's Aero Tech School (BOC, Britain)
Davis Oil Properties (Hiram Walker-Consumers Home, Canada)
Tom Brown Inc.'s Oil Properties (Pan Canadian Petroleum, Canada)
Airport Inn (Chaudry family, Pakistan)
Greystone Office Complex (Hudson's Bay Co., Canada)
Marathon Gold Corp. (Hampton Gold Mining Areas, Britain)
Bioximetry Technology (BOC International, Britain)
Carnation Co. (Nestle SA, Switzerland)
Crown Zellerback (James Goldsmith, Britain)
Fireman's Fund (Allianz, Germany)
Elite Software Systems (Moore Corp., Canada)
McCracken Silver Mine (Arizona Silver Corp., Canada)
Baxter's Surgical Glove Plant (Dunlop Olympic, Austalia)

Potash Producers Inc.'s Assets mineral mining (Rayrock Resources, Canada)
Medico Industries drug manufacturer (Wellcome Foudation, Britain)
Breddo Food Products Corp. (Centrale Suikermaatschappij NV, Netherlands)
International American Ceramics (Keramik Holding AG, Switzerland)
Big Three Industries chemicals (L'Air Liquide, France)
Southland Corporation (Ito-Yokado, Japan)
Two Pershing Square real estate (Trizec Corp., Canada)
Purina Mills pet food (British Petroleum, Britain)
Airco Energy pipeline (BOC International, Britain)
National Old Line Insurance (Ennia NV, Netherlands)
Kentucky Horse Center Inc. (Hagopian, Erika, Germany)
Louisville Cement Co. (Poilet, France)

Copper Range Co. (Echo Bay Mines Ltd., Canada)
Mississippi River Alcohol Co. (Ferruzzi family, Italy)

Stangewald Bldg. (Robert Jones Investments, New Zealand)
Innovative Media Inc. typesetting (Corbridge Co., Hong Kong)

Rydell Labs/Lion Corp. drugs (Lion Corp., Japan)
Allis Chalmers Agricultural Equipment (Klöckner-Humboldt Deutz, Germany)
SMC Pneumatic Inc. temperature control devices (Shoketsu Kinzoku Koygo CO., Japan)
BASF Wyandotte Corp. chemicals (BASF AG, Germany)
Detroit Race Course (Ladbroke Group, Britain)
White Consolidated (Electrolux, Sweden)
Inotek International fertilizers (Sempernoval, Britain)
Pennsylvania Glass Sand Corp. (Rio Tinto-Zinc Corp., Britain)
Bver Environmental refuse systems (Haniel Umweltschutz, Germany)

Geo-Con Inc. construction (Taisei Corp., Japan)
Marsteller advertising (Government of France)
Celanese (Hoechst, Germany)
SCM Corp. (Hanson Trust, Britain)
Northland Products sporting equipment (Pearson Forest Products, Canada)
Green Mountain Inn (Gameroff, Simon and David, Canada)
New Hampshire Ball Bearings (Takahashi family, Japan)

Hannaford Bros. grocery stores (Sobey family, Canada)
Scott Paper Co. (Bronfman family, Canada)
Compo Industries coated fabric (Gemina SPA, Italy)
Pixley-Richards plastic products (DSM-Dutch State Mines, Netherlands)
Trea Industries plastics (Toray Industries, Japan)
Pawtuxet Valley Daily Times (Independent Newspaper, New Zealand)
Thatcher Glass Corp. (Power Corp. of America, Canada)
Atlantic Cement Co. (Blue Circle Industries, Britain)

Inmont paint and ink (BASF AG, Germany)
Johanna Farms milk processing (John Labatt, Canada)
Monmouth Plastics (Cookson Group, Britain)
Hercules Commercial Explosive Div. (Dyno Industries AS, Norway)
Litton Bionetics research laboratory (Akzo NV, Netherlands)
Peoples Drug Inc. (BAT Industries PLC, Britain)
Government Research Co. consulting and public relations (Public Affairs Resource Group, Canada)

Diesel Marine Norship shipbuilding (Torday & Carlisle, Britain)
Clarita's Cos. computer software (V NU BV, Netherlands)
Food Lion (Delhaize "Le Lion", Belgium)
Hamilton Beach/Moulinex Inc. housewares and fans (Moulinex SA, France)
Santee Portland Cement Co. (Holderbank financière Glaris, Switzerland)
Carolina Formed Fabrics Corp. (Low & Bonar, Britain)
Atlantic Center real estate (Cadillac Fairview, Canada)
Elsons newstands (Smith Wh & Sons Holding, Britain)
Austell Packaging (Smurfit family, Ireland)
Country Sanitation Inc. (Attwoods Group, Britain)

Probat US roasted coffee (Probat-Werke Von Gimborn, Germany)
Gulf of Mexico Oil/Gas Leases (Royal Dutch Shell, Netherlands)
Goldstar of America refigeration machines (Lucky Group, S. Korea)
Michelin Tire Corp. (Michelin, France)

Source: Jaclyn Fierman, "The Selling Off of America," *Fortune*, December 22, 1986, 46–47. ©1986 Time Inc. All rights reserved. Reprinted with permission. Updated from "Fewer Deals, Less Investment," *Forbes*, July 20, 1992, 290–292.

**Table 13.2
Major Determinants of
Direct Foreign
Investment**

Marketing Factors
1. Size of market
2. Market growth
3. Desire to maintain share of market
4. Desire to advance exports of parent company
5. Need to maintain close customer contact
6. Dissatisfaction with existing market arrangements
7. Export base
8. Desire to follow customers
9. Desire to follow competition

Barriers to Trade
1. Government-erected barriers to trade
2. Preference of local customers for local products

Cost Factors
1. Desire to be near source of supply
2. Availability of labor
3. Availability of raw materials
4. Availability of capital/technology
5. Lower labor costs
6. Lower other production costs
7. Lower transport costs
8. Financial (and other) inducements by government
9. More favorable cost levels

Investment Climate
1. General attitude toward foreign investment
2. Political stability
3. Limitation on ownership
4. Currency exchange regulations
5. Stability of foreign exchange
6. Tax structure
7. Familiarity with country

General
1. Expected higher profits
2. Other

Source: Adapted from Organization for Economic Cooperation and Development, *International Investment and Multinational Enterprises* (Paris: OECD, 1983), 41.

A major cause for the recent growth in foreign direct investment is derived demand. Often, as large multinational firms move abroad, they are quite interested in maintaining their established business relationships with other firms. Therefore, they frequently encourage their suppliers to follow them and continue to supply them from the new foreign location. For example, advertising agencies often move abroad in order to service foreign affiliates of their domestic clients. Similarly, engineering firms, insurance companies, and law firms often are invited to provide their services abroad. Yet not all of these developments come about from co-optation by client firms. Often firms invest abroad for defensive reasons, out of fear that their clients may find other sources abroad, which also eventually might jeopardize their status even in the domestic market. To preserve quality, Japanese automakers have urged more than 40 of their suppliers from Japan to establish production in the United States.[22]

For similar reasons, firms follow their competitors abroad. Competitive firms influence not only their engaging in foreign direct investment, but even where the investments are made.[23] Many firms have found that even their competitive position at home is affected by their ability to effectively compete in foreign markets.

Barriers to Trade   Foreign direct investment permits firms to circumvent barriers to trade and operate abroad as domestic firms, unaffected by duties, tariffs, or other import restrictions. The enormous amount of U.S. investment would not have been attracted to Canada had it not been for the barriers to trade erected by the Canadian government to support domestic industry.

In addition to government-erected barriers, barriers may also be imposed by customers through their insistence on domestic goods and services, either as a result of nationalistic tendencies or as a function of cultural differences. Furthermore, local buyers may want to buy from sources that they perceive to be reliable in their supply, which means buying from local producers. For some products, country-of-origin effects may force a firm to establish a plant in a country that has a built-in positive stereotype for product quality.[24]

Cost Factors   Servicing markets at sizable geographic distances and with sizable tariff barriers has made many exporters' offerings in foreign markets prohibitively expensive. Many manufacturing multinationals have established plants overseas to gain cost advantages in terms of labor and raw materials. For example, many of the border plants in Mexico provide their U.S. parents with low-cost inputs and components through the maquiladora program.

Foreign direct investment occurs not only horizontally, by firms acquiring or establishing similar firms abroad, but also vertically. Some firms engage in foreign direct investment to secure their sources of supply for raw materials and other intermediary goods. This usually secures supply and may provide it at a lower cost as well.

All in all, cost factors are not necessarily the primary attraction for manufacturers to make foreign direct investments, as seen in Global Perspective 13.1. The need for highly skilled labor and developed communication, transportation, and institutional infrastructures has increased.[25] The emergence of manufacturing technologies such as flexible manufacturing systems and total quality management have increased the importance of worker education and skill. Just-in-time logistics systems increase dependence on suppliers and the reliability of the transportation infrastructure. While manufacturing sites may be chosen due to proximity to technological resources, such as Motorola's decision to produce cellular phones in the "Silicon Glen" area of Scotland, choosing a site for a distribution center in integrated markets will be influenced by the countries' logistics platforms (as seen in Chapter 16). For example, Bausch & Lomb's European distribution center is located at Schipol Airport in Amsterdam, Holland, due not only to its central geographic location but also to the excellent logistics network.

Investment Climate   Foreign direct investment by definition implies a degree of control over the enterprise.[26] Yet this may be unavailable because of environmental constraints, even if the firm owns 100 percent of the subsidiary. The general attitude toward foreign investment and its development over time may be indicative of the long-term prospects for investment. For example, if asked to choose, 48 percent of Americans would discourage Japanese investment and only 18 percent would encourage it.[27] In many countries, foreign direct investment tends to arouse nationalistic feelings. Political risk has to be defined broadly to include not only the threat of political upheaval but also the likelihood of arbitrary or discriminatory government action that will result in financial loss. This could take the form of tax increases, price controls, or measures directed specifically at foreign firms such as partial divestment of ownership, local-content requirements, remittance restrictions, export

Global Perspective

13.1
Making It Close to Customers

A study by Ernst & Young finds that only one-third of 650 projects announced by U.S. public companies during 1991 went to countries with low-cost labor and that the majority were placed in targeted industrialized markets. Getting as close as possible to customers now outweighs all other variables. Although producing close to customers is not new, it has taken on added significance as competitive pressures have escalated and manufacturing processes constantly have changed.

Just two of the ten countries that attracted the most U.S. investments, Mexico and the former Soviet Union, have cheap labor (defined by the U.S. Labor Department as less than 25 percent of U.S. wages). Altogether, only 196 new projects (30 percent) were destined for low-cost-labor nations. The most popular sites for new projects were Canada, the United Kingdom, Germany, and France.

The main reasons U.S. manufacturers locate overseas is to gain footholds in prime markets. Many U.S. companies are looking to build market share in industrialized countries by gaining access to customers, technology, and skills, as opposed to choosing a country due to the availability of cheap labor. Other important factors, particularly for first-time investors, are financial incentives and low corporate tax rates. The importance of labor costs naturally is affected by the type of business. Labor-intensive industries such as textiles are still looking for cheap employment. But even those industries will think first about producing in countries that have both low labor costs and big markets.

Europe, mainly the EU, was the most popular site for U.S. investment (357 projects). Asia attracted 20 percent of all the projects, and four-fifths of the projects in Asia were joint ventures. Only 22 projects were announced for South America and the Caribbean, 6 for the Middle East, and only 1 for Africa.

Top U.S. Investment Locations

Country*	Number of Projects
Canada	84
United Kingdom	72
Germany	60
France	59
MEXICO	56
Japan	43
RUSSIA	20
Australia	17
Italy	17
Netherlands	16
Spain	16
Ireland	15
CHINA	14
HUNGARY	14
POLAND	12
INDIA	11
Belgium	10
South Korea	10
Brazil	8
INDONESIA	8

*Uppercase indicates countries with low rates for hourly labor.

Source: Carla Kruytbosch, "Where in the World to Make It," *International Business,* February 1994, 53–76; and Gregory Sandler, "NAFTA Aims Spotlight at Border Site," *Export Today* 8 (November/December 1992): 19.

requirements, and limits on expatriate employment.[28] The investment climate is also measured in terms of foreign currency risk. The evaluations will typically focus on possible accounting translation exposure levels and cashflows in foreign currency.

In a survey of 108 U.S.–based multinational corporations, foreign direct investment was found to be profit and growth driven.[29] The influence of the other variables will vary depending on the characteristics of the firm and its management, on its objectives, and on external conditions. Firms can be divided into three categories according to their orientations: resource seekers, market seekers, and efficiency seekers.[30]

Resource seekers are after either natural or human resources. Natural resources are typically based on mineral, agricultural, or oceanographic advantages and result in firms locating in areas where they are available. The availability of choices is therefore tied to the availability of the resources sought. If human resources are sought for reasons of cost or skill level, the decision can be altered over time if the labor advantage or environmental conditions change. Firms primarily in search of better opportunities to enter and expand within markets are **market seekers.** Particularly when markets are closed or access is restricted, firms have a major incentive to locate in them. **Efficiency seekers,** for their part, attempt to obtain the most economical sources of production. They frequently have affiliates in various markets that are highly specialized in product lines or components and engage in major intrafirm transfers in order to maximize the benefits to the entire firm.

The Host-Country Perspective

The host government is caught in a love–hate relationship with foreign direct investment.[31] On the one hand, the host country has to appreciate the various contributions, especially economic, that the foreign direct investment will make. On the other hand, fears of dominance, interference, and dependence are often voiced and acted on. The major positive and negative impacts are summarized in Table 13.3.

The Positive Impact   Foreign direct investment has contributed greatly to world development in the past 40 years. Said Lord Lever, a British businessman who served in the cabinets of Harold Wilson and James Callaghan, "Europe got 20 times more out of American investment after the war than the multinationals did; every country gains by productive investment.[32]

Capital flows are especially beneficial to countries with limited domestic sources and restricted opportunities to raise funds in the world's capital markets. In addition, foreign direct investment may attract local capital to a project for which local capital alone would not have sufficed.

The role of foreign direct investment has been seen as that of **technology transfer.**[33] Technology transfer includes the introduction of not only new hardware to the market but also the techniques and skills to operate it. In industries where the role of intellectual property is substantial, such as pharmaceuticals or software de-

Table 13.3 Positive and Negative Impacts of Foreign Direct Investment on Host Countries	**Positive Impact** 1. Capital formation 2. Technology and management skills transfer 3. Regional and sectoral development 4. Internal competition and entrepreneurship 5. Favorable effect on balance of payments 6. Increased employment **Negative Impact** 1. Industrial dominance 2. Technological dependence 3. Disturbance of economic plans 4. Cultural change 5. Interference by home government of multinational corporation

Sources: Jack N. Behrman, *National Interests and the Multinational Enterprise* (Englewood Cliffs, N.J.: Prentice-Hall, 1970), Chapters 2 through 5; Jack N. Behrman, *Industrial Policies: International Restructuring and Transnationals* (Lexington, Mass.: Lexington Books, 1984), Chapter 5; and Christopher M. Korth, *International Business* (Englewood Cliffs, N.J.: Prentice-Hall, 1985), Chapters 12 and 13.

velopment, access to parent companies' research and development provides benefits that may be far greater than those gained through infusion of capital. This explains the interest that many governments have expressed in having multinational corporations establish R&D facilities in their countries.

An integral part of technology transfer is managerial skills, which are the most significant labor component of foreign direct investment. With the growth of the service sector, many economies need skills rather than expatriate personnel to perform the tasks.

Foreign direct investment can be used effectively in developing a geographical region or a particular industry sector. Foreign direct investment is one of the most expedient ways in which unemployment can be reduced in chosen regions of a country. Furthermore, the costs of establishing an industry are often too prohibitive and the time needed too excessive for the domestic industry, even with governmental help, to try it on its own. In many developing countries, foreign direct investment may be a way to diversify the industrial base and thereby reduce the country's dependence on one or a few sectors.

At the company level, foreign direct investment may intensify competition and result in benefits to the economy as a whole as well as to consumers through increased productivity and possibly lower prices. Competition typically introduces new techniques, products and services, and ideas to the markets. It may improve existing patterns of how business is done.

The major impact of foreign direct investment on the balance of payments is long term. Import substitution, export earnings, and subsidized imports of technology and management all assist the host nation on the trade account side of the balance of payments. Not only may a new production facility substantially decrease the need to import the type of products manufactured, but it may start earning export revenue as well. Several countries, such as Brazil, have imposed export requirements as a precondition for foreign direct investment. On the capital account side, foreign direct investment may have short-term impact in lowering a deficit as well as long-term impact in keeping capital at home that otherwise could have been invested or transferred abroad. However, measurement is difficult because significant portions of the flows may miss—or evade—the usual government reporting channels. In 1990, more than half of foreign investment was "unidentified," in that experts could not figure out what type it was or where it came from.[34]

Jobs are often the most obvious reason to cheer about foreign direct investment. Foreign companies directly employ three million Americans, or about 3 percent of the workforce, and indirectly create opportunities for millions more. The benefits reach far beyond mere employment. Salaries paid by multinational corporations are usually higher than those paid by domestic firms. The creation of jobs translates also into the training and development of a skilled work force. Consider, for example, the situation of many Caribbean states that are dependent on tourism for their well-being. In most cases, multinational hotel chains have been instrumental in establishing a pool of trained hospitality workers and managers.

All of the benefits discussed are indeed possible advantages of foreign direct investment. Their combined effect can lead to an overall enhancement in the standard of living in the market as well as an increase in the host country's access to the world market and its international competitiveness. It is equally possible, however, that the impact can be negative rather than positive.

The Negative Impact   In 1971, Herb Gray attributed Canada's economic plight largely to the extensive foreign ownership of its industries. Gray in 1980 was industry minister in Pierre Trudeau's cabinet, which cracked down on foreign—especially

U.S.—investment. Canada had a branch-plant economy, the characteristics of which included stunted economic development and low levels of research and development. Gray argued that foreign-owned companies did not provide their host countries with benefits equal to those provided by indigenous companies.[35]

Although some of the threats posed by multinational corporations and foreign direct investment are exaggerated, in many countries some industrial sectors are dominated by foreign-owned entities. In France, for example, three-fourths of the computer and data-processing equipment sector was dominated by foreign affiliates in the 1980s.[36] In Belgium, oil refining (78 percent) and electrical engineering (87 percent) showed the highest rates of foreign participation.[37]

Foreign direct investment most often is concentrated in technology-intensive industries, therefore, research and development is another area of tension. Multinational corporations usually want to concentrate their R&D efforts, especially their basic research. With its technology transfer, the multinational corporation can assist the host country's economic development, but it may leave the host country dependent on flows of new and updated technology. Furthermore, the multinational firm may contribute to the **brain drain** by attracting scientists from host countries to its central research facility. Many countries have demanded and received research facilities on their soil, the results of which they can control to a better extent. Many countries are weary of the technological dominance of the United States and Japan and view it as a long-term threat. Western European nations, for example, are joining forces in basic research and development under the auspices of the so-called EUREKA project, which is a pan-European pooling of resources to develop new technologies with both governmental and private sector help.

Many of the economic benefits of foreign direct investment are controversial as well. Capital inflows may be accompanied by outflows in a higher degree and over a longer term than is satisfactory to the host government. For example, many of the hotels built in the Caribbean by multinational chains were unable to find local suppliers and had to import supplies and thus spend much-needed foreign currency. Many officials also complain that the promised training of local personnel, especially for management positions, has never taken place. Rather than stimulate local competition and encourage entrepreneurship, multinationals with their often superior product offering and marketing skills have stifled competition. Many countries, including the United States, have found that multinational companies do not necessarily want to rely on local suppliers but rather bring along their own from their domestic market.

Many governments see multinationals as a disturbance to their economic planning. Decisions are made concerning their economy over which they have little or no control. Host countries do not look favorably on a multinational that may want to keep the import content of a product high, especially when local suppliers may be available.

Multinational companies are, by definition, change agents. They bring about change not only in the way business may be conducted but also, through the products and services they generate and the way they are marketed, cause change in the life-styles of the consumers in the market. The extent to which this is welcomed or accepted varies by country. For example, the introduction of fast-food restaurants to Taiwan dramatically altered eating patterns, especially of teenagers, who made these outlets extremely popular and profitable. Concern has been expressed about the apparent change in eating patterns and the higher relative cost of eating in such establishments.

The multinational corporation will also have an impact on business practices. Although multinationals usually pay a higher salary, they may also engage in prac-

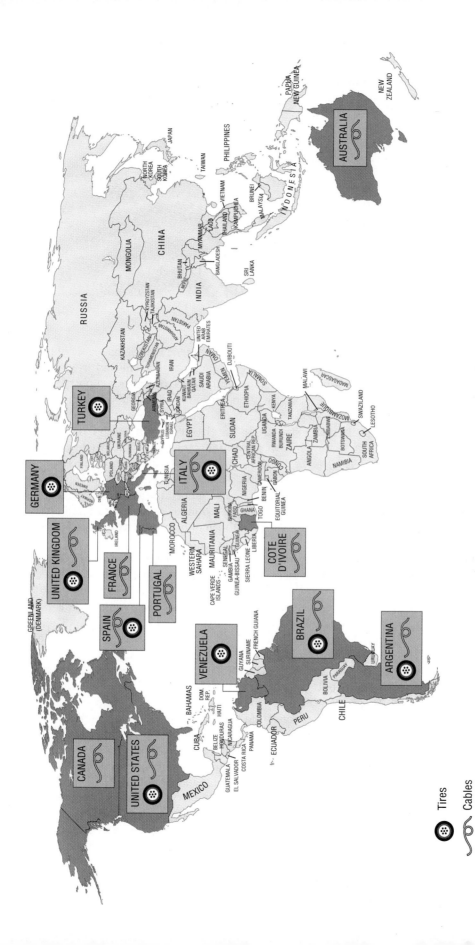

Tires

Cables

Source: Pirelli Group

Foreign direct investment creates jobs. Even developed nations such as the United States benefit from additional employment opportunities provided by foreign investment in production facilities such as the Toyota-GM plant in California.

Source: Courtesy of New United Motor Manufacturing, Inc.

tices that are alien to the local work force, such as greater flexibility in work rules. Older operators in Japan, for example, may be removed from production lines to make room for more productive employees. In another country where the Japanese firm establishes a plant, tradition and union rules may prevent this.[38]

Some host nations have expressed concern over the possibility of interference, economically and politically, by the home government of the multinational corporation; that is, they fear that the multinational may be used as an instrument of influence.[39] The United States has used U.S.-based corporations to extend its foreign policy in areas of capital flows, technology controls, and competition. Foreign direct investment regulations were introduced in the United States in the 1960s to diminish capital outflows from the country and thus to strengthen the country's balance of payment situation. If the actions of affiliates of U.S.-based companies are seen to have a negative impact on competition in the U.S. market, antitrust decrees may be used to change the situation. Increasingly, major foreign direct investments are screened by the Committee for Foreign Investments in the United States (CFIUS). Concerns have been raised mainly in terms of national security and the large numbers of investors from a particular country; for example, in the 1970s, Arabs were perceived by some as wielding too much influence through their investments in the United States and, in the late 1980s, there was the same perception about the Japanese.

Of course, the multinational is available not only to the home government as a political or economic instrument but to the host government and other groups as well. Fixed investments by multinationals can be held hostage by a host country in trying to win concessions from other governments. In an increasing number of cases, host governments insist on quid pro quo deals in which foreign direct investment is contingent on adherence to specified requirements, such as export targets. Many United Nations sanctions, although approved by governments, have to be carried out through the compliance of multinational companies, as was the case with the divestment that took place to force the South African government to abandon the policy of apartheid.

Countries engage in formal evaluation of foreign direct investment, both outbound and inbound. Canada, for example, uses the Foreign Investment Review Agency to determine whether foreign-owned companies are good corporate citizens. Sweden reviews outbound foreign direct investment in terms of its impact on the home country, especially employment.

The Home-Country Perspective

Most of the aspects of foreign direct investment that concern host countries apply to the home country as well. Foreign direct investment means addition to the home country's gross national product from profits, royalties, and fees remitted by affiliates.[40] In many cases, intracompany transfers bring about additional export possibilities.[40] Many countries, in promoting foreign direct investment, see it as a means to stimulate economic growth—an end that would expand export markets and serve other goals, such as political motives, as well. For example, the **Overseas Private Investment Corporation** provides insurance for new U.S. foreign direct investment in friendly developing countries against currency inconvertibility, expropriation, and political violence.[41] Some countries, such as Japan, have tried to gain preferential access to raw materials through firms that owned the deposits. Other factors of production can be obtained through foreign direct investment as well. Companies today may not have the luxury of establishing R&D facilities wherever they choose but must locate them where human power is available. This explains, for example, why Northern Telecom, the Canadian telecommunications giant, has more than 500 of its roughly 2,000 R&D people based in the United States, mostly in California.

The major negative issue centers on employment. Many unions point not only to outright job loss but also to the effect on imports and exports. The most controversial have been investments in plants in developing countries that export back to the home countries. Multinationals such as electronics manufacturers, who have moved plants to southeast Asia and Mexico, have justified this as a necessary cost-cutting competitive measure.

Another critical issue is that of technological advantage. Some critics state that, by establishing plants abroad or forming joint ventures with foreign entities, the country may be giving away its competitive position in the world marketplace. This is especially true when the recipients may be able to avoid the time and expense involved in developing new technologies.

The U.S. government has also taken a position on the behavior of U.S.-based firms overseas. The Foreign Corrupt Practices Act was passed in 1977, and a section of it deals with bribery. It is a form of the extraterritoriality concept discussed earlier; in this case, the concern is the ethics of business practices. Although clear-cut bribery of elected officials is universally banned, the United States is the only country in the world that has legislation as extensive as the Foreign Corrupt Practices Act guiding the conduct of its firms. Many firms have indeed complained about the negative impact that compliance has in some markets of the world where facilitating payments are common.[42]

Management of the Relationship

Arguments for and against foreign direct investment are endless. Costs and benefits must be weighed. Only the multinational corporation itself can assess expected gains against perceived risks in its overseas commitments. At the same time, only the host and home countries can assess benefits realized against costs in terms of their national priorities. If these entities cannot agree on objectives because their most basic interests are in conflict, they cannot agree on the means either. In most cases, the relationship between the parties is not necessarily based on logic, fairness, or equity, but on the relative bargaining power of each.[43] Furthermore, political changes may cause rapid changes in host government–MNC relations, as seen in Global Perspective 13.2.

Global Perspective

13.2
Giving Up on Russia?

Businesspeople from around the world have flocked to Moscow since 1986 when Soviet President Mikhail Gorbachev encouraged them to seek joint ventures with Soviet partners. Gorbachev's strategy was to revitalize the Soviet economy by introducing modern technology and Western business methods. The foreign companies were attracted by the huge untapped markets. After the breakup of the Soviet Union in December 1991, most of the interest focused on Russia as the largest of the new states.

By early 1995, there were 18,000 joint ventures in Russia and more than $10 billion in foreign direct investment. Companies from United States had the largest number of joint ventures in Russia, followed by Germany, Finland, and Austria. Large U.S. industrials are there, including IBM, GE, Kodak, Playtex, and AT&T. In 1993, PepsiCo. signed a $3 billion multiyear trade pact, and in 1989–1990 McDonald's invested $50 million in a food-processing plant in Moscow. Thousands of small and mid-sized ventures also have arrived. Most of the joint ventures have been in software, tourism, and heavy industrial production. Significant growth has occurred in research and development. Companies such as Bell Labs are working with Russian scientists to study space, electronics, optics, lasers, and nuclear energy.

Some estimate that only 8 percent of the joint ventures have been successful due to conflicts with partners, capitalization problems, and clashes with bureaucracy. Once in Russia, a company has to live with a bewildering array of legal, economic, and political uncertainties. The struggle to introduce capitalism has produced a hodgepodge of commercial laws and regulations that are often vague, bizarre, or contradictory. Rules may change overnight. And it is frequently impossible to know which official is responsible for what decision. Companies may have to face more or less independent "substates" that decide which federal laws are accepted and which are not. One U.S. company spent several months preparing bids for a project after it had been assured that foreign bids would be considered. When the time came for the authorities to make the decision, however, they reversed themselves and allowed only Russian companies to bid.

Among the biggest pitfalls is the uncertainty over property rights. Power struggles as to who controls physical assets may leave the Western entity in limbo. Otis Elevator Company, which has formed four joint ventures in Russia, obtains written statements from the highest public officials possible and then hopes for the best. "If a company needs a cast-iron guarantee that everything is in compliance with all laws and regulations, it will be very difficult to get things done," one company executive noted.

Other Western investors cut through legal tangles by persuading political leaders to issue decrees on their behalf. For example, a decree from Boris Yeltsin helped France's Elf Aquitane set up an oil exploration venture in Russia. Forming strong personal connections with regional leaders also will help. A high level of involvement will help convince the leaders and their constituents that the company's intent is not only to profit from Russia, but also to improve life in the community. In establishing an operation in Moscow, Coca-Cola shipped $650,000 of medical supplies for a local hospital. In some cases, only tougher measures will help. When a $5 per barrel surcharge was imposed on Conoco after a deal was signed to develop pipeline and infrastructure projects in three Russian oil and gas regions, the company was able to get an exemption from the surcharge by threatening to cancel its plans to develop another field.

Despite the concerns, many are convinced that no one or nothing can lead Russia astray from the road to market-oriented reforms, for the simple reason that there is no other path. Says Jim Tilley, head of Conoco's Moscow office, "There will be ups and downs; it is just a matter of how far those downs go." Michael Adams, CEO of Young & Rubicam/Sovero, an advertising joint venture, said, "This is a lousy business environment, but there is great growth potential. Right now, most people are happy if they aren't bleeding to death." Many have concluded that not investing poses the greater risk.

Sources: "Russian Investment Dilemma," Harvard Business Review 72 (May–June 1994): 35–44; Vladimir Kvint, "Don't Give Up on Russia," Harvard Business Review 72 (March–April 1994): 62–74; and Paul Hofheinz, "Russia 1993: Europe's Timebomb," Fortune, January 25, 1993, 106–108.

**Figure 13.2
Bargaining Position of
Multinational
Corporation (MNC) and
Host Country**

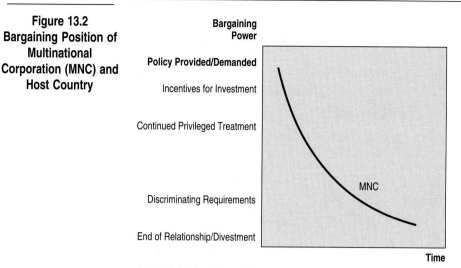

Bargaining
Power

Policy Provided/Demanded

Incentives for Investment

Continued Privileged Treatment

Discriminating Requirements

End of Relationship/Divestment

MNC

Time

Sources: Christopher M. Korth, *International Business* (Englewood Cliffs, N.J.: Prentice-Hall, 1985), 350; and Thomas A. Poynter, "Managing Government Intervention: A Strategy for Defending the Subsidy," *Columbia Journal of World Business* 21 (Winter 1986): 55–65.

The bargaining positions of the multinational corporation and the host country change over time. The course of these changes is summarized in Figure 13.2. The multinational wields its greatest power before the investment is actually made; in the negotiation period, it can require a number of incentives over a period of time. Whether or not the full cycle of events takes place depends on developments in the market as well as the continued bargaining strength of the multinational.

The multinational corporation can maintain its bargaining strength by developing a local support system through local financing, procurement, and business contacts as well as by maintaining control over access to technology and markets. The first approach attempts to gain support from local market entities if discriminating actions by the government take place. The second approach aims to make the operation of the affiliate impossible without the contribution of the parent.

Host countries, on the other hand, try to enhance their role by instituting control policies and performance requirements. Governments attempt to prevent the integration of activities among affiliates and control by the parent. In this effort, they exclude or limit foreign participation in certain sectors of the economy and require local participation in the ownership and management of the entities established. The extent of this participation will vary by industry, depending on how much the investment is needed by the host economy. Performance requirements typically are programs aimed at established foreign investors in an economy. These often are such discriminatory policies as local content requirements, export requirements, limits on foreign payments (especially profit repatriation), and demands concerning the type of technology transferred or the sophistication and level of operation engaged in. In some cases, demands of this type have led to firms' packing their bags. For example, Coca-Cola left India when the government demanded access to what the firm considered to be confidential intellectual property. Only India's free-market reforms have brought Coca-Cola amongst many other investors back to the country. Cadbury Schweppes sold its plant in Kenya because price controls made its operation unprofitable.[44] On their part, governments can, as a last resort, expropriate the affiliate, especially if they see that the benefits are greater than the cost.[45]

**Figure 13.3
Developing a
Local Image**

The approaches and procedures that have been discussed are quite negative by nature. However, relations between the firm and its host country, or the home country for that matter, by no means need to be adversarial. The multinational corporation can satisfy its own objectives and find local acceptability by implementing activities that contribute to the following six goals: (1) efficiency, by applying appropriate technologies to different markets; (2) equity, by reinvesting earnings; (3) participation, by establishing local training programs; (4) creativity, by introducing indigenous R&D capabilities in local affiliates; (5) stability, by consistently and openly explaining behavior; and (6) diversity, by developing product lines specifically for local demand.[46] Communication of the goals to various constituents can take place through advertising. The approaches taken by ABB and Siemens are provided in Figure 13.3.

Environmental concerns are emerging as an important part of a multinational's normal business operations. Multinationals have extensive involvement in many pollution-intensive industries and have, by definition, mobility to seek attractive locations for production sites. However, multinationals give rise to higher expectations and often are expected to assume leadership roles in environmental protection due to their financial, managerial, and technological strength. Studies have found that although multinationals may have adopted lower environmental standards in their operations in developing countries, overall they maintain a better record than their local counterparts.[47]

A number of efforts have been made in the past 25 years to establish guidelines for the conduct of multinational corporations. The major ones are those drafted by the Organization of Economic Cooperation and Development and by the United

Nations. Most multinationals have drafted their own versions of codes of conduct as well as value systems.[48]

Dealing with Other Constituents

Multinational corporations also have to manage their relations with various other constituencies. This is crucial because even small, organized groups of stockholders may influence control of the firm, particularly if the ownership base is wide. Companies must, therefore, adopt policies that will allow them to effectively respond to pressure and criticism, which will continue to surface. Oliver Williams suggested that these policies have the following traits: (1) openness about corporate activities with a focus on how the activities enhance social and economic performance; (2) preparedness to utilize the tremendous power of the multinational corporation in a responsible manner and, in the case of pressure, to counter criticisms swiftly; (3) integrity, which very often means that the corporation must avoid not only actual wrongdoing but the mere appearance of it; and (4) clarity, because it will help ameliorate hostility if a common language is used with those pressuring the corporation.[49] He proposed that the corporation's role is one of enlightened self-interest: Reasonable critics understand that the business cannot compromise the bottom line.

Complicating the situation often is the fact that groups in one market criticize what the marketer is doing in another market. For example, the Interfaith Center on Corporate Responsibility urged Colgate-Palmolive to stop marketing Darkie toothpaste under that brand name in Asia because of the term's offensiveness elsewhere in the world. Darkie toothpaste was sold in Thailand, Hong Kong, Singapore, Malaysia, and Taiwan, packaged in a box that features a likeness of Al Jolson in blackface.[50]

TRANSFER OF TECHNOLOGY

To a great extent, the role of foreign direct investment is that of technology transfer. Technology transfer is the transfer of systematic knowledge for the manufacture of a product, for the application of a process, or for the rendering of a service and does not extend to the mere sale or lease of goods.[51] Multinational corporations are one of the major vehicles for channeling technology to other countries.

The Basics of Technology Transfer

The essential requirements for the transfer of technology are: (1) the availability of suitable technology, (2) social and economic conditions favoring transfer, and (3) the willingness and ability of the receiving party to use and adapt the technology. In industrialized countries, sophisticated processes can be applied economically, with specialists available to solve problems and develop techniques. The problems arise in smaller developing countries with little industrial experience. Production facilities must be scaled down for small series; machinery and procedures must be simplified to cope with the lack of skill and training. Yet, in most cases, the quality has yet to meet worldwide standards. To overcome these kinds of problems, the Dutch electronics giant Philips created a special pilot plant. The plant sees to it that the many elements constituting an industrial activity are properly adapted to local circumstances and that the necessary know-how and other elements are transferred to developing countries. The elements of the transfer are summarized in Table 13.4. Through people and capital, the necessary personnel, software, and hardware are

Table 13.4 Elements of Technology Transfer	Personnel	Software	Hardware
	Product know-how	Manuals	Buildings
	Manufacturing know-how	Procedures	Assembly lines
	Equipment know-how	Documentation	Equipment
	Training	Information	Tools
			Components
			Raw materials

Source: J. C. Ramaer and P. H. Pijs, "Adapting Technology," undated working paper, Utrecht, The Netherlands: Philips.

combined for the transfer of appropriate manufacturing technology. The transfer cannot be accomplished by sending machinery and manuals; it is achieved as technicians show the recipients what should be done and how.

Technology transfer can occur both formally and informally. Formal channels include licensing, foreign direct investment, and joint ventures. Informal channels include reverse engineering, diversions, and industrial espionage. Most of the technology trade has traditionally taken place among developed countries. A significant proportion of the trade has also occurred through traditional equity interactions (subsidiaries or joint ventures) and nonequity interactions, such as licensing agreements between nonaffiliated entities.[52] The informal channels' share of the market, although difficult to determine, is of concern to both the governments and the entities generating technology.

Technology transfer is likely to increase considerably with increased industrialization, which will generate not only new technological needs but also more sophisticated processes and technologies in existing sectors. Many countries no longer are satisfied to receive as much know-how as possible as quickly as possible; they want to possess technology themselves and to generate technology indigenously.

Adapting Technology to Local Conditions

Technology has to be adapted to factors that are often contradictory. For example, three standards for color television are in use in the world: NTSC in the Americas (except for Brazil) and Japan; PAL in Europe, British Commonwealth Countries, the Middle East, and Brazil; and SECAM in France, former French colonies, and eastern and central Europe. The standards differ from each other in terms of the numbers of fields and lines in the picture. Videotapes from the NTSC, PAL, or SECAM standards cannot be played on the others' machines. In some cases, performance requirements at the transfer location may even be more challenging; for example, machinery may have to be operated in a facility where it is not completely protected from the elements. If the multinational corporation has multiple production bases, technology may have to be adjusted at each one and still meet worldwide quality standards. Often the quantities to be produced are a factor in technology transfer. For example, producing 7,000 sets in Thailand is considerably different from producing 700,000 in Holland.

Of critical concern in preparing the transfer are the strengths and weaknesses of the people who will be involved in production, including their practical knowledge, experience, abilities, and attitudes. Machinery may need to be simplified and on-site maintenance may need to be provided. Moreover, technology from countries such as the United States and Japan may be inappropriate if the recipient wants labor-intensive technology to create employment and income-earning opportunities. In such cases, the adjustment may consist of backward invention whereby a technically simplified version of the product is developed. Technology transfer also involves providing management and staff with advance information about conditions they will find in the transfer location. Costs of the various input elements for the production process such as labor, energy, materials, and components will vary from one market to the next and thus call for differing specifications in the technology transferred.

The quality of the infrastructure requires special attention. For example, frequent power outages may be characteristic of the area in which machinery is to be used; this would indicate the need for features in the technology to avoid variations in output and quality. Some industries, such as home electronics, spend as much as 50 percent of each dollar earned on the purchase of component parts. Yet, in smaller developing countries, the few existing suppliers may need extensive technical assistance to produce what is needed. The designs for components often must be simplified to allow for local production. The assistance may be critical because of government regulation of component imports. Other government policies may affect payment for technology, types of technology that can be transferred, and foreign involvement in the process through, for example, work permits for foreigners.

MODES OF OPERATION

In carrying out its foreign direct investment, a multinational corporation has a variety of ownership choices, ranging from 100 percent ownership to a minority interest. With international competition intensifying, risks in market entry and product development escalating, and the need for global strategy increasing, many companies rely on interfirm cooperation as a means of survival. When the investment alternative is not attractive or feasible, management contracts provide a mode of foreign market participation.

Full Ownership

For many firms, the foreign direct investment decision is, initially at least, considered in the context of 100 percent ownership. The reason may have an ethnocentric basis; that is, management may believe that no outside entity should have an impact on corporate decision making. Alternatively, it may be based on financial concerns. For example, the management of IBM until very recently held the belief that by relinquishing a portion of its ownership abroad, it would be setting a precedent for shared control with local partners that would cost more than that which could possibly be gained.[53] In some cases, IBM withdrew operations from countries rather than agree to government demands for local ownership.

In order to make a rational decision about the extent of ownership, management must evaluate the extent to which total control is important to the success of its international marketing activities. Often full ownership may be a desirable, but not a necessary, prerequisite for international success. At other times it may be essential, particularly when strong linkages exist within the corporation. Interdependencies between and among local operations and headquarters may be so strong that nothing short of total coordination will result in an acceptable benefit to the firm as a whole.[54]

Increasingly, however, the international environment is hostile to full ownership by multinational firms. Government action through outright legal restrictions or discriminatory actions is making the option less attractive. The choice is either to abide by existing restraints and accept a reduction in control or to lose the opportunity to operate in the country. In addition to formal action by the government, the general conditions in the market may make it advisable for the firm to join forces with local entities.

Interfirm Cooperation

The world is too large and the competition too strong for even the largest multinational corporations to do everything independently. Technologies are converging and markets becoming integrated, thus making the costs and risks of both product and market development ever greater. Partly as a reaction to and partly to exploit the developments, management in multinational corporations has become more pragmatic about what it takes to be successful in global markets.[55] The result has been the formation of **strategic alliances** with suppliers, customers, competitors, and companies in other industries to achieve multiple goals.

A strategic alliance (or partnership) is an informal or formal arrangement between two or more companies with a common business objective. It is something more than the traditional customer-vendor relationship but something less than an outright acquisition. The alliances can take forms ranging from informal cooperation to joint ownership of worldwide operations. For example, Texas Instruments has reported agreements with companies such as IBM, Hyundai, Fujitsu, Alcatel, and L. M. Ericsson using such terms as "joint development agreement," "cooperative technical effort," "joint program for development," "alternative sourcing agreement," and "design/exchange agreement for cooperative product development and exchange of technical data."[56]

Reasons for Interfirm Cooperation

Strategic alliances are being used for many different purposes by the partners involved. Market development is one common focus. Penetrating foreign markets is a primary objective of many companies. In Japan, Motorola is sharing chip designs and manufacturing facilities with Toshiba to gain greater access to the Japanese market. Some alliances are aimed at defending home markets. With no orders coming in for nuclear power plants, Bechtel Group has teamed up with Germany's Siemens to service existing U.S. plants.[57] Another focus is the spreading of the cost and risk inherent in production and development efforts. Texas Instruments and Hitachi have teamed up to develop the next generation of memory chips. The costs of developing new jet engines are so vast that they force aerospace companies into collaboration; one such consortium was formed by United Technologies' Pratt & Whitney division, Britain's Rolls-Royce, Motoren-und-Turbinen Union from Germany, Fiat of Italy, and Japanese Aero Engines (made up of Ishikawajima Heavy Industries and Kawasaki Heavy Industries).[58] Some alliances are formed to block and co-opt competitors.[59] For example, Caterpillar formed a heavy equipment joint venture with Mitsubishi in Japan to strike back at its main global rival, Komatsu, in its home market. In the case of new technologies, companies have joined forces to win over markets to their operating standard. Toshiba and Time-Warner jointly developed the DVD (double-sided, digital videodisc) to compete against another format developed by Sony and Philips in an effort to establish the world standard for interactive compact discs.[60]

The most successful alliances are those that match the complementary strengths of partners to satisfy a joint objective. Often the partners have different product,

Global Perspective

13.3
Outsourcing: Just Do It!

Nike, the footwear company based in Beaverton, Oregon, is expanding in international markets in both sales and production. While international sales currently account for one-third of Nike's total, 100 percent of its footwear is produced by subcontractors, most of them outside the United States. Nike's own people focus on the services part of the production process, including design, product development, marketing, and distribution. For example, through its "Futures" inventory control system, Nike knows exactly what it needs to order early enough to plan production accordingly. This avoids excess inventory and assures better prices from its subcontractors.

To achieve both stability and flexibility in its supplier relationships, Nike has three distinct groups of subcontractors in its network:

- Developed partners, the most important group, participate in joint product development and concentrate on the production of the newest designs. Traditionally, they have been located in the People's Republic of China and Republic of China but, given rising labor costs, some of the more labor-intensive activities have been moved

out. The developed partners typically have worked exclusively for Nike on a minimum monthly order basis.

- The second group of Nike's suppliers are called developing sources and offer low labor costs and the opportunity for Nike to diversify assembly sites. Currently, they are located in the People's Republic of China, Indonesia, and Thailand. Nearly all are exclusive suppliers to Nike and as such receive considerable assistance from the company with a view of upgrading their production. They will be the next generation of developed partners for Nike.

- The third group, volume producers, are large-scale factories serving a number of other independent buyers. They generally manufacture a specific product for Nike, but they are not involved in any new product because of fears they could leak proprietary information to competitors. Orders from Nike for suppliers in this group fluctuate, with variations of 50 percent between monthly orders.

Source: "Can Nike Just Do It? *Business Week,* April 18, 1994, 86–90; and United Nations, *World Investment Report 1994: An Executive Summary* (New York: United Nations, 1994), 15.

In some parts of the world and in certain industries, governments insist on complete or majority ownership of firms, which has caused multinational companies to turn to an alternative method of enlarging their overseas business.[66] The alternative is a **management contract,** in which the firm sells its expertise in running a company while avoiding the risk or benefit of ownership. Depending on the extensiveness of the contract, it may even permit some measure of control. As an example, the manufacturing process may have to be relinquished to foreign firms, yet international distribution may be required for the product. A management contract could serve to maintain a strong hold on the operation by ensuring that all distribution channels remain firmly controlled.

Management contracts may be more than a defensive measure. Although they are used to protect existing investment interests when they have been partly expropriated by the local government, an increasing number of companies are using them as a profitable opportunity to sell valuable skills and resources. For example, companies in the service sector often have independent entities with the sole task of seeking out opportunities and operating management contracts.[67]

**Figure 13.5
Forms of Interfirm
Cooperation**

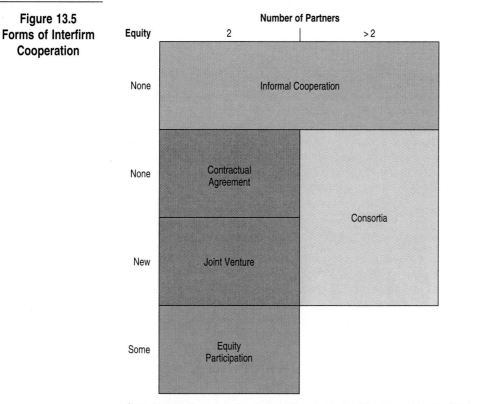

Source: Adapted with permission from Bernard L. Simonin, *Transfer of Knowledge of International Strategic Alliances: A Structural Approach,* unpublished dissertation, the University of Michigan, Ann Arbor, 1991.

lines have started to share hubs, coordinate schedules, and simplify ticketing. SAS has entered into joint marketing deals with All Nippon Airways, Lan-Chile, and Canadian Airlines International to provide links to routes and hubs in Tokyo, Latin America, and Toronto.[65]

Contractual agreements also exist for outsourcing; for example, General Motors buys cars and components from South Korea's Daewoo, and Siemens buys computers from Fujitsu. As corporations look for ways to simultaneously grow and maintain their competitive advantage, outsourcing has become a powerful new tool for achieving those goals. **Contract manufacturing** allows the corporation to separate the physical production of goods from the research and development and marketing stages, especially if the latter are the core competencies of the firm. Such contracting is popular in the footwear and garment industries as seen in the Global Perspective 13.3. The benefits of such contracting are to improve company focus on higher value added activities, to gain access to world-class capabilities, and to reduce operating costs. Contract manufacturing has been criticized because of the pressure it puts on the contractors to cut prices and thereby labor costs. However, such work does provide many companies, especially in developing countries, the opportunity to gain the necessary experience in product design and manufacturing technology to allow them to function in world markets. Some have even voiced concerns that the experience eventually may make them competitors of their former developed-country partners.

Global Perspective

13.3
Outsourcing: Just Do It!

Nike, the footwear company based in Beaverton, Oregon, is expanding in international markets in both sales and production. While international sales currently account for one-third of Nike's total, 100 percent of its footwear is produced by subcontractors, most of them outside the United States. Nike's own people focus on the services part of the production process, including design, product development, marketing, and distribution. For example, through its "Futures" inventory control system, Nike knows exactly what it needs to order early enough to plan production accordingly. This avoids excess inventory and assures better prices from its subcontractors.

To achieve both stability and flexibility in its supplier relationships, Nike has three distinct groups of subcontractors in its network:

- Developed partners, the most important group, participate in joint product development and concentrate on the production of the newest designs. Traditionally, they have been located in the People's Republic of China and Republic of China but, given rising labor costs, some of the more labor-intensive activities have been moved

out. The developed partners typically have worked exclusively for Nike on a minimum monthly order basis.

- The second group of Nike's suppliers are called developing sources and offer low labor costs and the opportunity for Nike to diversify assembly sites. Currently, they are located in the People's Republic of China, Indonesia, and Thailand. Nearly all are exclusive suppliers to Nike and as such receive considerable assistance from the company with a view of upgrading their production. They will be the next generation of developed partners for Nike.

- The third group, volume producers, are large-scale factories serving a number of other independent buyers. They generally manufacture a specific product for Nike, but they are not involved in any new product because of fears they could leak proprietary information to competitors. Orders from Nike for suppliers in this group fluctuate, with variations of 50 percent between monthly orders.

Source: "Can Nike Just Do It? *Business Week,* April 18, 1994, 86–90; and United Nations, *World Investment Report 1994: An Executive Summary* (New York: United Nations, 1994), 15.

In some parts of the world and in certain industries, governments insist on complete or majority ownership of firms, which has caused multinational companies to turn to an alternative method of enlarging their overseas business.[66] The alternative is a **management contract,** in which the firm sells its expertise in running a company while avoiding the risk or benefit of ownership. Depending on the extensiveness of the contract, it may even permit some measure of control. As an example, the manufacturing process may have to be relinquished to foreign firms, yet international distribution may be required for the product. A management contract could serve to maintain a strong hold on the operation by ensuring that all distribution channels remain firmly controlled.

Management contracts may be more than a defensive measure. Although they are used to protect existing investment interests when they have been partly expropriated by the local government, an increasing number of companies are using them as a profitable opportunity to sell valuable skills and resources. For example, companies in the service sector often have independent entities with the sole task of seeking out opportunities and operating management contracts.[67]

criminatory actions is making the option less attractive. The choice is either to abide by existing restraints and accept a reduction in control or to lose the opportunity to operate in the country. In addition to formal action by the government, the general conditions in the market may make it advisable for the firm to join forces with local entities.

Interfirm Cooperation

The world is too large and the competition too strong for even the largest multinational corporations to do everything independently. Technologies are converging and markets becoming integrated, thus making the costs and risks of both product and market development ever greater. Partly as a reaction to and partly to exploit the developments, management in multinational corporations has become more pragmatic about what it takes to be successful in global markets.[55] The result has been the formation of **strategic alliances** with suppliers, customers, competitors, and companies in other industries to achieve multiple goals.

A strategic alliance (or partnership) is an informal or formal arrangement between two or more companies with a common business objective. It is something more than the traditional customer-vendor relationship but something less than an outright acquisition. The alliances can take forms ranging from informal cooperation to joint ownership of worldwide operations. For example, Texas Instruments has reported agreements with companies such as IBM, Hyundai, Fujitsu, Alcatel, and L. M. Ericsson using such terms as "joint development agreement," "cooperative technical effort," "joint program for development," "alternative sourcing agreement," and "design/exchange agreement for cooperative product development and exchange of technical data."[56]

Reasons for Interfirm Cooperation

Strategic alliances are being used for many different purposes by the partners involved. Market development is one common focus. Penetrating foreign markets is a primary objective of many companies. In Japan, Motorola is sharing chip designs and manufacturing facilities with Toshiba to gain greater access to the Japanese market. Some alliances are aimed at defending home markets. With no orders coming in for nuclear power plants, Bechtel Group has teamed up with Germany's Siemens to service existing U.S. plants.[57] Another focus is the spreading of the cost and risk inherent in production and development efforts. Texas Instruments and Hitachi have teamed up to develop the next generation of memory chips. The costs of developing new jet engines are so vast that they force aerospace companies into collaboration; one such consortium was formed by United Technologies' Pratt & Whitney division, Britain's Rolls-Royce, Motoren-und-Turbinen Union from Germany, Fiat of Italy, and Japanese Aero Engines (made up of Ishikawa-jima Heavy Industries and Kawasaki Heavy Industries).[58] Some alliances are formed to block and co-opt competitors.[59] For example, Caterpillar formed a heavy equipment joint venture with Mitsubishi in Japan to strike back at its main global rival, Komatsu, in its home market. In the case of new technologies, companies have joined forces to win over markets to their operating standard. Toshiba and Time-Warner jointly developed the DVD (double-sided, digital videodisc) to compete against another format developed by Sony and Philips in an effort to establish the world standard for interactive compact discs.[60]

The most successful alliances are those that match the complementary strengths of partners to satisfy a joint objective. Often the partners have different product, geographic, or functional strengths that the partners build on, rather than use to fill gaps.[61] Some of the major alliances created on this basis are provided in Figure 13.4.

Types of Interfirm Cooperation Each form of alliance is distinct in terms of the amount of commitment required and the degree of control each partner has. The equity alliances—minority ownership, joint ventures, and consortia—feature the most extensive commitment and shared control. The types of strategic alliances are summarized in Figure 13.5, using the extent of equity involved and the number of partners in the endeavor as defining characteristics. More detailed discussion of the various alliances follows.

Informal Cooperation In informal cooperative deals, partners work together without a binding agreement. This arrangement often takes the form of visits to exchange information about new products, processes, and technologies or may take the more formal form of the exchange of personnel for limited amounts of time. Often such partners are of no real threat in each other's markets and of modest size in comparision to the competition, making collaboration necessary.[62] The relationships are based on mutual trust and friendship, and they may lead to more formal arrangements, such as contractual agreements or joint projects.

Contractual Agreements Strategic alliance partners may join forces for joint R&D, joint marketing, or joint production. Similarly, their joint efforts might include licensing, cross-licensing, or cross-marketing activities. Nestlé and General Mills have signed an agreement whereby Honey Nut Cheerios and Golden Grahams are made in General Mills's U.S. plants, shipped in bulk to Europe for packaging at a Nestlé plant, and then marketed in France, Spain, and Portugal by Nestlé.[63] This arrangement—complementary marketing (also known as piggybacking)—allows firms to reach objectives that they cannot reach efficiently by themselves.[64] Firms also can have a reciprocal arrangement whereby each partner provides the other access to its markets for a product. AT&T and Olivetti have had such a cross-marketing agreement covering the United States and Europe. In the service sector, international air-

Figure 13.4 Complementary Strengths Create Value	Partner *Strength...*	+ Partner *Strength...*	= Joint Objective
	Pepsico *marketing clout for canned beverages*	**Lipton** *recognized tea brand and customer franchise*	*To sell canned iced tea beverages jointly*
	Coca-Cola *marketing clout for canned beverages*	**Nestle** *recognized tea brand and customer franchise*	*To sell canned iced tea beverages jointly*
	KFC *established brand and store format, and operations skills*	**Mitsubishi** *real estate and site-selection skills in Japan*	*To establish a KFC chain in Japan*
	Siemens *presence in range of telecommunications markets worldwide and cable-manufacturing technology*	**Corning** *technological strength in optical fibers and glass*	*To create a fiber-optic-cable business*
	Ericsson *technological strength in public telecommunications networks*	**Hewlett-Packard** *computers, software, and access to electronics-channels*	*To create and market network management systems*

Source: Joel Bleeke and David Ernst, "Is Your Strategic Alliance Really a Sale?" *Harvard Business Review* 73 (January–February 1995): 97–105; and Melanie Wells, "Coca-Cola Proclaims Nestea Time for CAA," *Advertising Age,* January 30, 1995, 2.

Often a management contract is the critical element in the success of a project. For example, financial institutions may gain confidence in a project because of the existence of a management contract and may sometimes even make it a precondition for funding.[68]

One specialized form of management contract is the **turnkey operation.** Here, the arrangement permits a client to acquire a complete international system, together with skills investment sufficient to allow unassisted maintenance and operation of the system following its completion.[69] The client need not search for individual contractors or subcontractors or deal with scheduling conflicts or with difficulties in assigning responsibilities or blame. Instead, a package arrangement permits the accumulation of responsibility in one entity, thus greatly easing the negotiation and supervision requirements and subsequent accountability. When the project is going, the system will be totally owned, controlled, and operated by the customer. An example of such an arrangement is the Kama River truck plant in Russia, built mainly by U.S. firms.

Management contracts have clear benefits for the client. They provide organizational skills not available locally, expertise that is immediately available rather than built up, and management assistance in the form of support services that would be difficult and costly to replicate locally. For example, hotels managed by the Sheraton Corporation have access to Sheraton's worldwide reservation system. Management contracts today typically involve training locals to take over the operation after a given period.

Similar advantages exist for the supplier. The risk of participating in an international venture is substantially lowered, while significant amounts of control are still exercised. Existing know-how that has been built up through substantial investment can be commercialized, and frequently the impact of fluctuations in business volume can be reduced by making use of experienced personnel who otherwise would have to be laid off. In industrialized countries such as the United States, with economies that are increasingly service based, accumulated service knowledge and comparative advantage should be used internationally. Management contracts permit firms to do so.

Management contracts require an attitude change on two accounts: Control must be shared, and the time involvement may be limited. Establishing a working relationship with the owner in which both understand and respect their roles is essential. Even though the management contractor may be training local personnel to eventually take over, this by no means signifies the end of the relationship. For example, the hotel once managed by Sheraton may well remain in the system to buy reservation services, thus providing Sheraton with additional revenue.

From the client's perspective, the main drawbacks to consider are overdependence and potential loss of some essential control. For example, if the management contractor maintains all of the international relationships, little if any experience may be passed on to the local operation. Instead of a gradual transfer of skills leading to increasing independence, the client may have to rely more and more on the performance of the contractor.

Equity Participation Many multinational corporations have acquired minority ownerships in companies that have strategic importance for them to ensure supplier viability and build formal and informal working relationships. An example of this is Ford Motor Company's 25 percent share of Mazda. The partners continue operating as distinctly separate entities, but each enjoys the strengths the other partner provides. For example, thanks to Mazda, Ford has excellent support in the design and manufacture of subcompact cars, while Mazda has improved access to the global marketplace. The recipient of the investment will benefit as well. GM's purchase of 50 percent of Saab helped Saab not only to become profitable but also enhanced its competitiveness through sharing parts with other GM models. Without GM's resources, Saab also could not have afforded the development of new models.[70]

Another significant reason for equity ownership is market entry and support of global operations. Telefonica de Espana has acquired varying stakes in Latin American telecommunications systems—a market that is the fastest growing region of the world after Asia.[71]

Joint Ventures   A joint venture can be defined as the participation of two or more companies in an enterprise in which each party contributes assets, owns the entity to some degree, and shares risk.[72] The venture is also considered long term.[73] The reasons for establishing a joint venture can be divided into three groups: (1) government suasion or legislation, (2) one partner's needs for other partners' skills, and (3) one partner's needs for other partners' attributes or assets.[74] Equality of the partners is not necessary. In some joint ventures, each partner holds an equal share; in others, one partner has the majority of shares. The partners' contributions—typically consisting of funds, technology, plant, or labor—also vary.

The key to a joint venture is the sharing of a common business objective, which makes the arrangement more than a customer-vendor relationship but less than an outright acquisition. The partners' rationales for entering into the arrangement may vary. An example is New United Motor Manufacturing Inc. (NUMMI), the joint venture between Toyota and GM. Toyota needed direct access to the U.S. market, while GM benefited from the technology and management approaches provided by its Japanese partner.

Joint ventures may be the only way in which a firm can profitably participate in a particular market. For example, India restricts equity participation in local operations by foreigners to 40 percent. Other entry modes may limit the scale of operation substantially; for example, exports may be restricted because of tariff barriers. Many Western firms are using joint ventures to gain access to eastern and central European markets.

Joint ventures are valuable when the pooling of resources results in a better outcome for each partner than if each were to conduct its activities individually. This is particularly the case when each partner has a specialized advantage in areas that benefit the venture. For example, a firm may have new technology yet lack sufficient capital to carry out foreign direct investment on its own. Through a joint venture, the technology can be used more quickly and market penetration achieved more easily. Similarly, one of the partners may have a distribution system already established or have better access to local suppliers, either of which permits a greater volume of sales in a shorter period of time.

Joint ventures also permit better relationships with local government and other organizations such as labor unions. Government-related reasons are the major rationale for joint ventures in less-developed countries four times more frequently than in developed countries.[75] Particularly if the local partner is the government, or the local partner is politically influential, the new venture may be eligible for tax incentives, grants, and government support. Negotiations for certifications or licenses may be easier because authorities may not perceive themselves as dealing with a foreign firm. Relationships between the local partner and the local financial establishment may enable the joint venture to tap local capital markets. The greater experience

A joint venture with Sterch Controls enabled Honeywell to enter the potentially vast markets of central Europe and the former Soviet Union.

Source: © Jim Sims for Honeywell.

(and therefore greater familiarity) with the local culture and environment of the local partner may enable the joint venture to benefit from greater insights into changing market conditions and needs.

A final major commercial reason to participate in joint ventures is the desire to minimize the risk of exposing long-term investment capital, while at the same time maximizing the leverage on the capital that is invested.[76] Economic and political conditions in many countries are increasingly volatile. At the same time, corporations tend to shorten their investment planning time span more and more. This financial rationale therefore takes on more importance.

Seven out of ten joint ventures have been found to fall short of expectations and/or are disbanded.[77] The reasons typically relate to conflicts of interest, problems with disclosure of sensitive information, and disagreement over how profits are to be shared—in general—to lack of communication before, during, and after formation of the venture. In some cases, managers have been more interested in the launching of the venture than the actual running of the enterprise. Many of the problems stem from a lack of careful consideration in advance of how to manage the new endeavor. A partnership works on the basis of trust and commitment or not at all. Actually, if either or both partners insist on voting on critical matters, the venture has already failed.

Typical disagreements cover the whole range of business decisions, including strategy, management style, accounting and control, marketing policies and strategies, research and development, and personnel. The joint venture may, for example, identify a particular market as a target only to find that one of the partners already has individual plans for it. U.S. partners have frequently complained that their Japanese counterparts do not send their most competent personnel to the joint venture; instead, because of their lifetime employment practice, they get rid of less competent managers by sending them to the new entities.

Similarly, the issue of profit accumulation and distribution may cause discontent. If one partner supplies the joint venture with a product, the partner will prefer that any profits accumulate at headquarters and accrue 100 percent to one firm rather than at the joint venture, where profits are divided according to equity participation. Such a decision may not be greeted with enthusiasm by the other partner. Further, once profits are accumulated, their distribution may lead to dispute. For example, one partner may insist on a high payout of dividends because of financial needs, whereas the other may prefer the reinvestment of profits into a growing operation.

Consortia A new drug can cost $200 million to develop and bring to market; a mainframe computer or a telecommunications switch can require $1 billion. Some $4 billion will go into creating the generation of computer chips due out in the early 1990s; up to $7 billion will be needed to develop the next generation. To combat the high costs and risks of research and development, research consortia have emerged in the United States, Japan, and Europe. For example, IBM, Siemens and Toshiba—three of the world's largest electronics companies—have teamed up to develop 256-megabite memory chips.[78] Since the passage of the **Joint Research and Development Act** of 1984 (which allows both domestic and foreign firms to participate in joint basic research efforts without the fear of antitrust action), well over 100 consortia have been registered in the United States. The consortia pool their resources for research into technologies ranging from artificial intelligence to those needed to overtake the Japanese lead in semiconductor manufacturing. (The major consortia in those fields are MCC and Sematech.)[79] The Europeans have five mega-projects to develop new technologies registered under the names EUREKA, ESPRIT,

BRITE, RACE, and COMET. The Japanese consortia have worked on producing the world's highest-capacity memory chip and advanced computer technologies. On the manufacturing side, the formation of Airbus Industrie secured European production of commercial jets. The consortium, backed by France's Aerospatiale, German's Messerschmitt Boklow Blohm, British Aerospace, and Spain's Construcciones Aeronauticas, has become a prime global competitor.

Managerial Considerations   The first requirement of interfirm cooperation is to find the right partner. Partners should have an orientation and goals in common and should bring complementary and relevant benefits to the endeavor. The venture makes little sense if the expertise of both partners is in the same area; for example, if both have production expertise but neither has distribution know-how. Patience should be exercised; a deal should not be rushed into, nor should the partners expect immediate results. Learning should be paramount in the endeavor while, at the same time, partners must try not to give away core secrets to each other.[80]

Second, the more formal the arrangement, the greater care that needs to be taken in negotiating the agreement. In joint venture negotiations, for example, extensive provisions must be made for contingencies. The points to be explored should include, depending on the partner and the venture: (1) a clear definition of the venture and its duration; (2) ownership, control, and management; (3) financial structure and policies; (4) taxation and fiscal obligation; (5) employment and training; (6) production; (7) government assistance; (8) transfer of technology; (9) marketing arrangements; (10) environmental protection; (11) record keeping and inspection; and (12) settlement of disputes.[81] The issues have to be addressed before the formation of the venture; otherwise, they eventually will surface as points of contention. A joint venture agreement, although comparable to a marriage agreement, should contain the elements of a divorce contract. In case the joint venture cannot be maintained to the satisfaction of partners, plans must exist for the dissolution of the agreement and for the allocation of profits and costs. Typically, however, one of the partners buys out the other partner(s) when partners decide to part ways.

A strategic alliance, by definition, also means a joining of two corporate cultures, which can often be quite different. To meet this challenge, partners must have frequent communication and interaction at three levels of the organization: the top management, operational leaders, and work force levels. Trust and relinquishing control are difficult not only at the top but also at levels where the future of the venture is determined. A dominant partner may determine the corporate culture, but even then the other partners should be consulted.

Strategic alliances operate in a dynamic business environment and must therefore adjust to changing market conditions. The agreement between partners should provide for changes in the original concept so that the venture can flourish and grow. The trick is to have an a priori understanding as to which party will take care of which pains and problems so that a common goal is reached.

Government attitudes and policies have to be part of the environmental considerations of corporate decision makers. While some alliances may be seen as a threat to the long-term economic security of a nation, such as the planned equity investment by Taiwan Aerospace in McDonnell-Douglas's commercial airframe operation, in some cases links with foreign operators may be encouraged. For example, the U.S. government urged major U.S. airlines to form alliances with foreign carriers to gain access to emerging world markets, partly in response to the failure to achieve free access to all markets for U.S. airlines through so-called "open-skies" agreements.[82]

SUMMARY

Multinational corporations are probably among the most powerful economic institutions of all time. They not only have production facilities in multiple countries but also look beyond their own domestic markets for opportunities. They scan the globe to expand their operations. Multinational corporations are no longer the monopoly of the United States, western Europe, and Japan; many developing countries have a growing amount of foreign direct investment.

Foreign direct investment is sought by nations and firms alike. Nations are looking to foreign direct investment for economic development and employment, firms for new markets, resources, and increased efficiency. The relationships among the entities involved—the firm, the host government, and the home government—have to be managed to make each benefit. The critical role of foreign direct investment is technology transfer, which means the transfer of a combination of hardware, software, and skills for production processes.

Different operational modes are possible for the multinational corporation. Full ownership is becoming more unlikely in many markets as well as industries, and the firm has to look at alternative approaches. The main alternative is interfirm cooperation, in which the firm joins forces with other business entities, possibly even a foreign government. In some cases, when the firm may not want to make a direct investment, it will offer its management expertise for sale in the form of management contracts.

Key Terms and Concepts

ethnocentric

polycentric

regiocentric

geocentric

resource seekers

market seekers

efficiency seekers

technology transfer

brain drain

Overseas Private Investment Corporation

strategic alliances

contract manufacturing

management contract

turnkey operation

Joint Research and Development Act

Questions for Discussion

1. Of the quantitative and qualitative criteria that a firm has to satisfy to be considered a multinational corporation, which should be the major determinants?

2. Foreigners claim 5 percent of corporate earnings in the United States, yet there is concern about the selling off of corporate America. Is it justified?

3. Should every country have guidelines or a code of behavior for foreign companies to follow if they want to be viewed as good corporate citizens?

4. The Middle East is an attractive market for technology transfer. How would Saudi Arabia, Egypt, and Iran differ in the type of technology they seek?

5. Discuss possible reasons why IBM withdrew from India's computer market rather than share ownership, yet Burroughs and International Computer entered the market at the same time as minority owners.

6. The rate of expropriation has been 10 times greater for a joint venture with the host government than for a 100 percent U.S.-owned subsidiary, according to a study on expropriation since 1960. Is this not contrary to logic?
7. Comment on the observation that "a joint venture may be a combination of Leonardo da Vinci's brain and Carl Lewis's legs; one wants to fly, the other insists on running."
8. Why would an internationalizing company opt for a management contract over other modes of operation? Relate your answer especially to the case of hospitality companies such as Hyatt, Marriott, and Sheraton.

Recommended Readings

Badaracoo, Joseph L. *The Knowledge Link: Competing Through Strategic Alliances.* Boston: Harvard Business School Press, 1991.

Barnet, Richard J., and John Cavanagh. *Global Dreams: Imperial Corporations and the New World Order.* New York: Simon & Schuster, 1994.

Bleeke, Joel, and David Ernst. *Using Strategic Alliances and Acquisitions in the Global Marketplace.* New York: John Wiley, 1993.

Culpan, Refik, ed. *Multinational Strategic Alliances.* Binghamton, N.Y.: International Business Press, 1993.

Dunning, John H. *Multinational Enterprises and the Global Economy.* Wokingham, England: Addison Wesley, 1994.

Dunning, John H., ed. *The United Nations Library on Transnational Corporations.* Volumes 1–20. New York: Routledge, 1993.

Lewis, Jordan D. *Partnerships for Profit: Structuring and Managing Strategic Alliances.* New York: The Free Press, 1990.

Luostarinen, Reijo, and Lawrence Welch. *International Business Operations.* Helsinki, Finland: Kyriiri Oy, 1990.

Prahalad, C. K. *The Multinational Mission: Balancing Local and Global Vision.* New York: The Free Press, 1987.

Robinson, Richard D. *The International Transfer of Technology: Theory, Issues, and Practice.* Cambridge, Mass.: Ballinger, 1988.

Strafford, David C., and Richard H. A. Purkis. *Director of Multinationals.* New York: Stockton Press, 1989.

Tolchin, Martin, and Susan Tolchin. *Buying into America.* New York: Times Books, 1988.

Walmsley, John. *The Development of International Markets.* Higham, Mass.: Graham & Trotman, 1990.

Notes

1. Mark Casson, *Alternatives to the Multinational Enterprise* (London: Macmillan, 1979), 1.
2. United Nations, *World Investment Report: 1994* (New York: United Nations, 1994), 1.
3. United Nations, *Transnational Corporations in World Development* (New York: United Nations, 1988), 16.

4. United Nations, *Multinational Corporation in World Development* (New York: United Nations, 1973), 23.

5. Alan M. Rugman, *Inside the Multinationals* (London: Croom Helm, 1981), 31.

6. Raymond Vernon, *Sovereignty at Bay: The Multinational Spread of United States Enterprises* (New York: Basic Books, 1971), 11.

7. Alan M. Rugman, "Risk Reduction by International Diversification," *Journal of International Business Studies* 7 (Fall 1976): 75-80.

8. Donald Kircher, "Now the Transnational Enterprise," *Harvard Business Review* 42 (March-April 1964): 6-10, 172-176.

9. Howard V. Perlmutter, "The Tortuous Evolution of the Multinational Corporation," *Columbia Journal of World Business* 4 (January-February 1969): 9-18; Howard V. Perlmutter and David A. Heenan, "How Multinational Should Your Top Managers Be?" *Harvard Business Review* 52 (November-December 1974): 121-132; and Yoram Wind, Susan P. Douglas, and Howard V. Perlmutter, "Guidelines for Developing International Marketing Strategies," *Journal of Marketing* 37 (April 1973): 14-23.

10. John M. Stopford, *The World Directory of Multinational Enterprises* (London: Macmillan, 1982), xii.

11. Krishna Kumar and Maxwell G. McLeod, *Multinationals from Developing Countries* (Lexington, Mass.: Lexington Books, 1981), xv-xxv.

12. "Korea's Biggest Firm Teaches Junior Execs Strange Foreign Ways," *The Wall Street Journal,* December 30, 1992, 1.

13. George Chandler, "The Innocence of Oil Companies," *Foreign Policy* 27 (Summer 1977), 60.

14. United Nations Economic and Social Council, *Transnational Corporations in World Development: A Re-Examination* (New York: United Nations, 1978), 13.

15. Herbert E. Meyer, "Trudeau's War on U.S. Business," *Fortune,* April 6, 1981, 74-82.

16. Jeffrey Arpan and David A. Ricks, "Foreign Direct Investments in the U.S. and Some Attendant Research Problems," *Journal of International Business Studies* 5 (Spring 1974): 1-7.

17. Harvey A. Poniachek, *Direct Foreign Investment in the United States* (Lexington, Mass.: Lexington Books, 1986), 2.

18. United Nations, *World Investment Report 1994* (New York: United Nations, 1994), 19.

19. U.S. Department of Commerce, Bureau of Economic Analysis, *Survey of Current Business,* August 1995.

20. Jaclyn Fierman, "The Selling Off of America," *Fortune,* December 22, 1986, 34-43.

21. "The Global Deal Mill," *Business Week,* February 13, 1995, 8.

22. "The Difference Japanese Management Makes," *Business Week,* July 14, 1986, 47-50.

23. Edward B. Flowers, "Oligopolistic Reactions in European and Canadian Direct Investment in the United States," *Journal of International Business Studies* 7 (Fall-Winter 1976): 43-55.

24. Philip D. White and Edward W. Cundiff, "Assessing the Quality of Industrial Products," *Journal of Marketing* 42 (January 1978): 80-86.

25. Alan D. MacCormack, Lawrence J. Newman III, and Donald B. Rosenfeld, "The New Dynamics of Global Manufacturing Site Location," *Sloan Management Review* 36 (Summer 1994): 69-80.

26. Frank G. Vukmanic, Michael R. Czinkota, and David A. Ricks, "National and International Data Problems and Solutions in the Empirical Analysis of Intra-Industry Direct Foreign Investment," ed. A. Erdilek, *Multinationals as Mutual Invaders: Intra-Industry Direct Foreign Investment* (Beckenham, Kent: Croom Helm Ltd., 1985), 160-184.

27. "Japan, U.S.A.," *Business Week,* July 14, 1986, 45-46.

28. Stephen Kobrin, "Assessing Political Risk Overseas," *The Wharton Magazine* 6 (No. 2, 1981): 6-14.

29. Marie E. Wicks Kelly and George C. Philippatos, "Comparative Analysis of the Foreign Investment Evaluation Practices by U.S.-Based Manufacturing Multinational Companies," *Journal of International Business Studies* 13 (Winter 1982): 19-42.

30. Jack N. Behrman, "Transnational Corporations in the New International Economic Order," *Journal of International Business Studies* 12 (Spring-Summer 1981): 29-42.

31. Jack N. Behrman, *National Interests and the Multinational Enterprise* (Englewood Cliffs, N.J.: Prentice-Hall, 1970), 7.

32. Fierman, "The Selling Off of America," 35.

33. Casson, *Alternatives to the Multinational Enterprise,* 4.

34. Vivian Brownstein, "The Credit Crunch Myth," *Fortune,* December 17, 1990, 59-69.

35. Meyer, "Trudeau's War on U.S. Business," 76.

36. Charles Albert Michalet and Therese Chevallier, "France," in *Multinational Enterprises, Economic Structure and International Competitiveness,* ed. John H. Dunning (Chichester, England: Wiley, 1985), 91-125.

37. Daniel Van Den Bulcke, "Belgium," in *Multinational Enterprise, Economic Structure and International Competitiveness,* ed. John H. Dunning (Chichester, England: Wiley, 1985), 249-280.

38. "At Sanyo's Arkansas Plant the Magic Isn't Working," *Business Week,* July 14, 1986, 51-52.

39. Joseph S. Nye, "Multinational Corporations in World Politics," *Foreign Affairs* 53 (October 1974): 153-175.

40. Lawrence Franko, "Foreign Direct Investment in Less Developed Countries: Impact on Home Countries," *Journal of International Business Studies* 9 (Winter 1978): 55-65.

41. Paul S. Haar, "U.S. Government Political Risk Insurance Program" (Paper delivered at International Insurance and Political Risk Seminar, March 25, 1985, Washington, D.C.), 2.

42. Michael G. Harvey and Ilkka A. Ronkainen, "The Three Faces of the Foreign Corrupt Practices Act," *1984 AMA Educators' Proceedings* (Chicago: American Marketing Association, 1984), 230-235.

43. Peter P. Gabriel, "MNCs in the Third World: Is Conflict Unavoidable?" *Harvard Business Review* 50 (July-August 1972): 91-102.

44. Victor H. Frank, "Living with Price Control Abroad," *Harvard Business Review* 62 (March-April 1984): 137-142.

45. Thomas W. Shreeve, "Be Prepared for Political Changes Abroad," *Harvard Business Review* 62 (July-August 1984): 111-118.

46. Jack N. Behrman, *Industrial Policies: International Restructuring and Transnationals* (Lexington, Mass.: Lexington Books, 1984), 114-115.

47. William C. Frederick, "The Moral Authority of Transnational Corporations," *Journal of Business Ethics* 10 (March 1991): 165-178; and United Nations, *World Investment Report: An Executive Summary* (New York: United Nations, 1993), 11-12.

48. John M. Kline, *International Codes and Multinational Business: Setting Guidelines for International Business Operations* (Westport, Conn.: Quorum Books, 1985), Chapter 1.

49. Oliver Williams, "Who Cast the First Stone?" *Harvard Business Review* 62 (September-October 1984): 151-160.

50. "Church Group Gnashes Colgate-Palmolive," *Advertising Age,* March 24, 1986, 46.

51. United Nations, *Draft International Code of Conduct on the Transfer of Technology* (New York: United Nations, 1981), 3.

52. Asim Erdilek, "International Technology Transfer in the Middle East," in *International Business with the Middle East,* ed. Erdener Kaynak (New York: Praeger, 1984), 85-99.

53. Dennis J. Encarnation and Sushil Vachani, "Foreign Ownership: When Hosts Change the Rules," *Harvard Business Review* 63 (September-October 1985): 152-160.

54. Richard H. Holton, "Making International Joint Ventures Work" (Paper presented at the seminar on the Management of Headquarters/Subsidiary Relationships in Transnational Corporations, Stockholm School of Economics, June 2-4, 1980), 4.

55. *Collaborative Ventures: An Emerging Phenomenon in the Information Industry* (New York: Coopers & Lybrand, 1984), 3.

56. Thomas Gross and John Neuman, "Strategic Alliances Vital in Global Marketing," *Marketing News,* June 19, 1989, 1-2.

57. Louis Kraar, "Your Rivals Can Be Your Allies," *Fortune,* March 27, 1989, 66-76.

58. "MD-90 Airliner Unveiled by McDonnell Douglas," *The Washington Post,* February 14, 1993, A4.

59. Jordan D. Lewis, *Partnerships for Profit: Structuring and Managing Strategic Alliances* (New York: The Free Press, 1990), 85-87.

60. "Video Warfare: How Toshiba Took the High Ground," *Business Week,* February 20, 1995, 64-65; and Nikhil Hutheesing, "Betamax Versus VHS All Over Again?" *Forbes,* January 3, 1994, 88-89.

61. Joel Bleeke and David Ernst, "Is Your Strategic Alliance Really a Sale?" *Harvard Business Review* 73 (January-February 1995): 97-105.

62. Gary Hamel, Yves L. Doz, and C. K. Prahalad, "Collaborate with Your Competitors—and Win," *Harvard Business Review* 67 (January-February 1989): 133-139.

63. Richard Gibson, "Cereal Venture Is Planning Honey of a Battle in Europe," *The Wall Street Journal,* November 14, 1990, B1, B8.

64. Vern Terpstra and Chwo-Ming J. Yu, "Piggybacking: A Quick Road to Internationalization," *International Marketing Review* 7 (Number 4, 1990): 52–63.

65. "Can SAS Keep Flying with the Big Birds?" *Business Week,* November 27, 1989, 142–146.

66. Lawrence S. Welch and Anubis Pacifico, "Management Contracts: A Role in Internationalization?" *International Marketing Review* 7 (Number 4, 1990): 64–74.

67. Richard Ellison, "An Alternative to Direct Investment Abroad," *International Management* 31 (June 1976): 25–27.

68. Michael Z. Brooke, *Selling Management Services Contracts in International Business* (London: Holt, Rinehart and Winston, 1985), 7.

69. Richard W. Wright and Colin S. Russel, "Joint Ventures in Developing Countries: Realities and Responses," *Columbia Journal of World Business* 10 (Spring 1975): 74–80.

70. "Saab and GM Prove a Good Match," *Business Week,* February 20, 1995, 48.

71. "Spain's Phone Giant has Latin America Buzzing," *Business Week,* September 12, 1994, 92.

72. Kathryn Rudie Harrigan, "Joint Ventures and Global Strategies," *Columbia Journal of World Business* 19 (Summer 1984): 7–16.

73. W. G. Friedman and G. Kalmanoff, *Joint International Business Ventures* (New York: Columbia University Press, 1961), 5.

74. J. Peter Killing, *Strategies for Joint Venture Success* (New York: Praeger, 1983), 11–12.

75. Paul W. Beamish, "The Characteristics of Joint Ventures in Developed and Developing Countries," *Columbia Journal of World Business* 20 (Fall 1985), 13–19.

76. Charles Oman, *New Forms of International Investment in Developing Countries* (Paris: Organization for Economic Cooperation and Development, 1984), 79.

77. Yankelovich, Skelly and White, Inc., *Collaborative Ventures: A Pragmatic Approach to Business Expansion in the Eighties* (New York: Coopers and Lybrand, 1984), 10.

78. "What's the Word in the Lab? Collaborate," *Business Week,* June 27, 1994, 78–80.

79. Lee Smith, "Can Consortiums Defeat Japan?" *Fortune,* June 5, 1989, 245–254.

80. Jeremy Main, "Making Global Alliances Work," *Fortune,* December 17, 1990, 121–126.

81. United Nations, *Guidelines for Foreign Direct Investment* (New York: United Nations, 1975), 65–76.

82. "Airlines Urged to Link with Foreign Carriers," *The Washington Post,* November 2, 1994, F1, F3.

P A R T 4

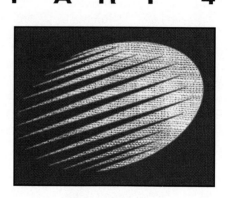

Cases

Damar International

Damar International, a fledgling firm importing handicrafts of chiefly Indonesian origin, was established in January 1984 in Burke, Virginia, a suburb of Washington, D.C. Organized as a general partnership, the firm is owned entirely by Dewi Soemantoro, its president, and Ronald I. Asche, its vice president. Their part-time, unsalaried efforts and those of Soemantoro's relatives in Indonesia constitute the entire labor base of the firm. Outside financing has been limited to borrowing from friends and relatives of the partners in Indonesia and the United States.

Damar International imported its first shipment of handicrafts in April 1984 and estimates that its current annual sales revenues are between $20,000 and $30,000. Although the firm has yet to reach the break-even point, its sales revenues and customer base have expanded more rapidly than anticipated in Damar's original business plan. The partners are generally satisfied with results to date and plan to continue to broaden their operations.

Damar International was established to capitalize on Soemantoro's international experience and contacts. The daughter of an Indonesian Foreign Service officer, Soemantoro spent most of her youth and early adulthood in western Europe and has for the past 18 years resided in the United States. Her immediate family, including her mother, now resides in Indonesia. In addition to English and Malay, Soemantoro speaks French, German, and Italian. Although she has spent the past four years working in information management in the Washington area, first for MCI and currently for Records Management Inc., her interest in importing derives from about six years she previously spent as a management consultant. In this capacity, she was frequently called on to advise clients about importing clothing, furniture, and decorative items

Source: This case was prepared by Michael R. Czinkota and Laura M. Gould.

from Indonesia. At the urging of family and friends, she decided to start her own business. While Soemantoro handles the purchasing and administrative aspects of the business, Asche is responsible for marketing and sales.

Damar International currently imports clothing, high-quality brassware, batik accessories, wood carvings, and furnishings from Indonesia. All of these items are handcrafted by village artisans working on a cottage-industry basis. Damar International estimates that 30 percent of its revenues from the sale of Indonesian imports are derived from clothing, 30 percent from batik accessories, and 30 percent from wood carvings, with the remainder divided equally between brassware and furnishings. In addition, Damar markets in the eastern United States comparable Thai and Philippine handcrafted items imported by a small California firm. This firm in turn markets some of Damar's Indonesian imports on the West Coast.

Most of Damar's buyers are small shops and boutiques. Damar does not supply large department stores or retail chain outlets. By participating in gift shows, trade fairs, and handicraft exhibitions, the firm has expanded its customer base from the Washington area to many locations in the eastern United States.

In supplying small retail outlets with handcrafted Indonesian artifacts, Damar is pursuing a niche strategy. Although numerous importers market similar mass-produced, manufactured Indonesian items chiefly to department stores and chain retailers, Damar knows of no competitors that supply handcrafted artifacts to boutiques. Small retailers find it difficult to purchase in sufficient volume to order directly from large-scale importers of mass-produced items. More important, it is difficult to organize Indonesian artisans to produce handcrafted goods in sufficient quantity to supply the needs of large retailers.

Damar's policy is to carry little if any inventory. Orders from buyers are transmitted by Soemantoro to her family in Indonesia, who contract production to artisans in the rural villages of Java and Bali. Within broad parameters, buyers can specify modifications of traditional Indonesian wares. Frequently, Soemantoro cooperates with her mother in creating designs that adapt traditional products to American tastes and to the specifications of U.S. buyers. Soemantoro is in contact with her family in Indonesia at least once a week by telex or phone to report new orders and check on the progress of previous orders. In addition, Soemantoro makes an annual visit to Indonesia to coordinate policy with her family and maintain contacts with artisans.

Damar also fills orders placed by Soemantoro's family in Indonesia. The firm therefore in essence acts as both an importer and an exporter despite its extremely limited personnel base. In this, as well as in its source of financing, Damar is highly atypical. The firm's great strength, which allows it to fill a virtually vacant market niche with extremely limited capital and labor resources, is clearly the Soemantoro family's nexus of personal connections. Without the use of middlemen, this single bicultural family is capable of linking U.S. retailers and Indonesian village artisans and supplying products which, while unique and nonstandardized, are specifically oriented to the U.S. market.

Damar's principal weakness is its financing structure. There are obvious limits to the amount of money that can be borrowed from family and friends for such an enterprise. Working capital is necessary because the Indonesian artisans must be paid before full payment is received from U.S. buyers. Although a 10 percent deposit is required from buyers when an order is placed, the remaining 90 percent is not due until 30 days from the date of shipment F.O.B. Washington, D.C. However, the simplicity of Damar's financing structure has advantages: To date, it has been able to operate without letters of credit and their concomitant paperwork burdens.

One major importing problem to date has been the paperwork and red tape involved in U.S. customs and quota regulations. Satisfying these regulations has occasionally delayed fulfillment of orders. Furthermore, because the Indonesian trade office in the United States is located in New York rather than Washington, assistance from the Indonesian government in expediting such problems has at times been difficult to obtain with Damar's limited personnel. For example, an order was once delayed in U.S. customs because of confusion between the U.S. Department of Commerce and Indonesian export authorities concerning import stamping and labeling. Several weeks were required to resolve the difficulty.

Although Damar received regulatory information directly from the U.S. Department of Commerce when it began importing, its routine contact with the government is minimal because regulatory paperwork is contracted to customs brokers.

One of the most important lessons that the firm has learned is the critical role of participating in gift shows, trade fairs, and craft exhibitions. Soemantoro believes that the firm's greatest mistake to date was not attending a trade show in New York. In connecting with potential buyers, both through trade shows and "walk-in scouting" of boutiques, Damar has benefited greatly from helpful references from existing customers. Buyers have been particularly helpful in identifying trade fairs that would be useful for Damar to attend. Here too, the importance of Damar's cultivation of personal contacts is apparent.

Similarly, personal contacts offer Damar the possibility of diversifying into new import lines. Through a contact established by a friend in France, Soemantoro is currently planning to import handmade French porcelain and silk blouses.

Damar is worried about sustained expansion of its Indonesian handicraft import business because the firm does not currently have the resources to organize large-scale cottage-industry production in Indonesia. Other major concerns are potential shipping delays and exchange rate fluctuations.

Questions for Discussion

1. Evaluate alternative expansion strategies for Damar International in the United States.
2. Discuss Damar's expansion alternatives in Indonesia and France and their implications for the U.S. market.
3. How can Damar protect itself against exchange rate fluctuations?
4. What are the likely effects of shipment delays on Damar? How can these effects be overcome?

Tollens N.V.—Holland Surfstone

SURFSTONE

Peering out into the Amsterdam skyline, Kees van der Maas contemplates the result of the board meeting. Flat European sales have caused a great deal of concern for this Dutch maker of surfacing materials. Intense competition, difficulty of signing new distributors, and increasing cost of raw materials converged to create a somewhat pessimistic perspective for Surfstone in Europe. To maintain the healthy growth trend of the last eight years, a major shift in the strategic orientation of the company was required. Except for Mr. Rosier, the comptroller, the board in its majority concurred with this assessment. Part of the strategic change was to develop new markets for Surfstone. The most logical target, for its population size and per-capita income, is the United States. Kees, the idea champion, was given the charge of developing an entry strategy proposal for the United States. This was the first time the company would attempt to sell outside of Europe.

THE COMPANY

The company, Tollens N.V., was established in 1953 by its founder, master cabinetmaker Alex Tollens. Mr. Tollens saw a market for high-quality kitchen furnishings as the buying power of war-torn Holland increased. The company grew at a healthy pace throughout the 1950s and 1960s, expanding into neighboring Germany and Belgium.

During this period, the company expanded through the excellent reputation of its kitchen furnishings. The marketing effort was concentrated on creating and maintaining a close relationship with distributors based on commitment, honesty, and reliability. The company was not seen as an aggressive player in the industry; however, the loyalty of its distributor/fabricator organization was unbeatable in Northern Europe.

In the early 1970s, in reaction to the general economic contraction, the company engaged in an aggressive market expansion program. The results of the efforts became evident after 1977 when sales doubled 1971 revenues. In the period 1972 to 1977, Surfstone entered and developed a position in France, Switzerland, Italy, and the United Kingdom. Later expansions led to a broad coverage of Europe by 1990 (see Table 1). Also, at the urging of its distributors, Tollens expanded its product line to include furnishings for the bathroom.

Mr. Tollens died in 1982 and control of the company was passed to his three sons. After two months of indecision, the brothers decided to discard their father's strategy of relying solely upon their distributors to promote the product. They hired several experienced marketing managers to lead a Europewide marketing campaign; Kees van der Maas was one of the managers. The marketing effort increased sales by 90 percent over the next seven years. Competition in the industry began to stiffen during the late 1980s as new entrants from Europe and overseas challenged the

Source: This case was written by John M. Zerio, Ph.D., associate professor of marketing and Nittaya Wongtada, Ph.D., assistant professor of marketing, Thunderbird-American Graduate School of International Management. This case was prepared as the basis for class discussion rather than to illustrate either effective or ineffective handling of an administrative situation. The assistance of Fred Rodkey (Thunderbird '90) is gratefully acknowledged.

TABLE 1
Sales Distribution—Surfstone, 1990

Country	Sales Percentage	Number of Distributors	Number of Fabricators	Number of Warehouses
Holland	41	22	172	1
Belgium	19	12	102	2
Germany	14	13	33	2
Italy	7	1	78	1
U.K.	6	7	53	2
France	9	17	18	1
Spain	1	4	12	0
Others	3	12	23	1
Total	100	88	491	10

established companies. One of Tollens's most successful products, the Surfstone line of solid surface material, had won 17 percent of the European market for solid surface materials.

Kees van der Maas was appointed director of sales in September of 1986. The boom of the 1980s gave him an opportunity to demonstrate his superb acumen for planning and managing of a complex web of salespeople, distributors, dealers, and fabricators. However, despite his skills, the increasing presence of foreign competitors in its major markets, coupled with a trend toward consolidation of distributors and fast growth of construction supply store chains, were rapidly compressing Tollen's margins. Even though Tollens's total sales in 1989 has risen to $435 million, margins had shrunk to 3.3 percent from a 1984 high of 4.2 percent. Indeed, were these trends to continue or accelerate, the attractiveness of the solid surface materials business would be highly questionable.

Tollens's expansion formula was based on a skillful association of its expertise in cabinetmaking with the manufacturing of countertops. Recognizing the importance of local tastes and traditions, Tollens decided to concentrate its resources on the manufacturing of solid surface material sheets and develop a wide network of certified fabricators of countertops. Within five years, Tollens had trained personnel of more than 350 fabricators. In addition, it strongly emphasized on-site training seminars for distributors' sales personnel. The importance of training in Tollens's success cannot be overemphasized.

At the heart of Tollens's competitive posture in Europe was the quality of its relationship with distributors. Trust and commitment were hallmarks of Tollens. More than 60 percent of Tollens's distributors had been with the company for ten years or more. Relationships were very personalized. Tollens's regional managers had built over the years strong personal links with distributors, fabricators, architects, and interior designers. Regional managers were indeed the glue and blood of Tollens's international distribution system. They were active in the recruiting, hiring, and training of fabricators, in recruiting and developing distributors, and were extensively involved in the continuous training of distributors' sales personnel.

They had become particularly valuable to the firm for their ability to develop sales leads and opportunities that were quickly routed to distributors. Tollens's managers were very well positioned socially and professionally in the construction circles. They were particularly well connected with architects and interior design associations. In a business environment where personal connections are essential, they excelled in the use of their network.

Training was an essential element of Tollens's differentiation strategy until 1986 when other competitors introduced their own massive certification programs. Training courses were offered on a regular basis in Amsterdam, and twice a year in every major European capital. A small team of highly trained instructors, former fabricators, or interior designers conducted the programs. Tollens's distinctiveness in the eyes of major channel intermediaries rapidly blurred. Although their image of top quality was not tarnished, the new competitive dynamics enormously raised end-users' price sensitivity.

Tollens's distinctive reputation was in great part based on its obsession with order fulfillment. Its ability to fill 92 percent of approved orders in five working days became a source of pride and an essential tool for maintaining an edge over competitors. Tollens maintained a number of warehouses strategically located near every major market (see Table 1) and a very efficient electronic order-processing system. Each warehouse operated with a small fleet of medium-size trucks sufficient to serve a clientele within a 300-mile radius. In addition, a transportation agreement (piggyback) was established with a large continental supplier of clay pipe and pipe connections for the servicing of clients outside of the warehouse radius. Only sporadically did Tollens have to hire the services of transportation companies.

THE PRODUCT

Solid surface materials are primarily used for countertops, although the product is becoming increasingly popular for molded items, for example, integrated countertop-sinks and integrated and separate lavatories. Although nearly three times more expensive, solid surface materials offer many advantages over laminated countertops. They are more durable than laminates and are easily repaired. Scratches may be removed by lightly sanding the damaged area. Chips and dents may be fixed by applying a repair compound and sanding after it has dried. The solid surface materials use a seamless installation technique that enhances the appearance of the product. In addition to the benefits of durability, the material may be finished using common woodworking tools. This significantly increases the attractiveness of the material, since installation and customizing do not require special tools or techniques. The solid surface material may also be used in powdered form for molding into desired shapes.

Surfstone is a polymer-based solid surface material. It is sold in several standard thicknesses and in 15 colors. Of these colors, eight are bright pastels and seven are granites. Surfstone offers standard sheets and a collection of molded parts, including a variety of integrated countertop-sinks and lavatories.

THE U.S. MARKET ENTRY

Kees had developed an affinity for the United States during a six-month college exchange student program, but he knew that marketing a product in the United States was a much greater challenge. Even though he relished the challenge of introducing the product in the American market, he was conscious of his limitations and of the need to obtain professional marketing assistance. Through a friend associated with the U.S. Kitchen and Bath Association, a consulting contract was negotiated with Jonathan Butler, a marketing consultant with more than 20 years of experience in the industry. Mr. Butler's assignment included three major areas: the size and structure of the American market for solid surface materials; an analysis of the major end-users, their purchasing criteria, and their purchasing decision-making process; and a profile of the major solid surface manufacturers. Given this information, Kees felt he would be able to structure a comprehensive market-entry program for presentation to the board of directors. Six weeks later, a Federal Express courier delivered the following report to Kees, with a greeting card from Jonathan Butler and an invoice for $17,350.

**REPORT:
THE AMERICAN
SOLID SURFACE
MATERIALS
MARKET[1]**

The American Market

In 1990, the American market for solid surface materials is estimated to be $600 million. Of this amount, approximately 33 percent, or $198 million, is used in the construction industry. This can be further broken down into 16 percent used by the hospital/laboratory industry and 17 percent used by a variety of sectors including restaurants and schools. The remaining 67 percent of the solid surface market is used by the residential home construction and renovation market. Kitchen renovation projects represent approximately 40 percent of the solid surface market, or $240 million.

The Major End-Users

The Hospital Industry   According to Moody's, prospects for certain sectors of the medical facilities are positive, but the outlook for 1991 remains unfavorable. Inadequate reimbursement under Medicare and Medicaid programs, intensified competition, and rising operating costs all are contributing to the industry's troubles. The 1983 implementation of Medicare's prospective payment system (PPS) initiated a revolutionary change in the nation's health-care delivery system. PPS reimburses hospitals according to a fixed schedule of fees based on some 470 illness categories, or diagnostic related groups (DRGs). This more restrictive reimbursement environment had an immediate impact on the industry. Hospitals were forced to cut costs, curtail services, and otherwise increase efficiency to operate profitably with DRG constraints. As a result, admissions, average lengths of stay, occupancy rates, and other measures of inpatient utilization began a long, steady slide in 1984. Conversely, outpatient utilization has shown strong growth over the past five years, largely at the expense of inpatient business, and managed-care plans such as health maintenance organizations (HMOs) have gained popularity. Finally, the more strenuous operating environment has led to a fair amount of consolidation and corporate restructuring, especially within the investor-owned segment of the business.

   New health-care-facility construction is expected to slow, but the renovation of existing facilities is expected to grow. The typical hospital now renovates every five years to keep up with technology and maintain the aesthetics of the facility. Solid surface materials are not widely used yet in hospitals because of the high cost. The areas of installation are generally in those with high public traffic, rest rooms for example, where durability and an aseptic appearance are prized.

The Laboratory Industry   The growth in the laboratory industry is expected to be slow but steady. Intense competition is causing the labs to become very cost-conscious. Most of the construction in the industry is expected to come from the ren-

---

Prepared by Butler Consultants for Kees van der Maas of Tollens N.V.

ovation/replacement of existing facilities. Solid surfaces are very important to the laboratory industry: their nonpermeable surface discourages the growth of germs and mildew. The seamless construction of solid surface materials also increases the aseptic quality. These are advantages which laminates cannot offer. The labs typically remodel every one to five years, depending upon their industrial sector. Most labs remodel due to technological improvements, state regulations, or for the maintenance of sterilization standards. As an example, public labs must change solid surfaces every year to comply with health and safety standards.

The Home Construction/Renovation Industry   According to Moody's Industry Surveys, the home-building industry is in the doldrums. Housing starts were down marginally. Estimates indicate housing starts for the full year 1991 at 1,410,000, down 5.7 percent from the 1989 level.

A major cause of these prospects resides in negative demographics. The primary problem is the aging of the baby-boom generation and the arrival of the baby-bust generation. The transition quite simply means fewer household formations. In the 1970s, household formations averaged around 1.7 million per year. Not surprisingly, there were housing booms in several of those years. In the 1980s, the rate of formations slipped to about 1.5 million per year. In contrast, the demographics of the baby-bust generation point to housing formations of only about 1.2 million per year during the 1990s.

The lower numbers of household formations will affect two major markets, the market for first time homebuyers and the rental market for apartments. Small starter homes and apartments are generally where young individuals and couples enter the housing market.

There is one positive trend in the demographics of the 1990s: The aging of the baby-boom generation means that the market for larger homes should remain strong, as homeowners trade up to more spacious dwellings.

The renovation of existing homes is expected to continue its strong growth of the past several years. This growth in renovation is driven by do-it-yourselfers who are cutting costs and adding value to their properties. The primary areas of use for solid surface materials are in bathrooms and kitchens. There is also a strong trend toward more attractive, open, and brighter kitchens. Tables 2 and 3 and Figures 1 and 2 provide an overview of the kitchen color and countertop material preferences in the United States, and general information about the housing industry. Table 4 estimates the potential for solid surface sales in the kitchen industry.

TABLE 2 Kitchen Colors and Material Often Used	Kitchen Colors Most Frequently Requested	Percentage	Kitchen Countertop Material Often Used	Percentage
	White	41	Laminate	63
	Almond	25	Solid Surface	25
	Wood Tones	19	Tile	5
	Pastels	6	Granite	1
	Gray	5	Marble	1
	Other	3	Cult. Marble	1
			Other	4

Source: National Kitchen and Bath Association Survey.

TABLE 3
Kitchen Countertop Material Used by Region

Region	Laminate (%)	SS (%)	Tile (%)	Granite (%)
Northeast	62	36	2	—
Mideast	80	18	2	—
Southeast	76	21	2	1
Midwest	70	22	8	—
Southwest	52	48	—	—
West	32	30	30	8

Source: National Kitchen and Bath Association Survey, 1989.

TABLE 4
Solid Surface Market Potential Estimate of Kitchen Industry

Kitchen jobs performed in 1990	5.5 Million
Estimated growth (conservative 7%)	10%
Kitchen jobs that install new countertops	60%
Kitchen jobs that use solid surface countertops	25%
Cost per kitchen job	$3,000–$4,000
Therefore the calculation:	
Growth in kitchen jobs	5,500,000 × 1.07
	5,885,000
Kitchen jobs with new countertops	5,885,000 × .60
	3,531,000
Of these with solid surface countertops	3,531,000 × .25
	882,800
Total industry	882,800 × $3,500
	3,089,625,000
Total industry including labor	**$3,089,625,000**

Source: National Kitchen and Bath Association Survey, 1989.

FIGURE 1
Change in Total Households, Forecasted Change (%), 1987–1992

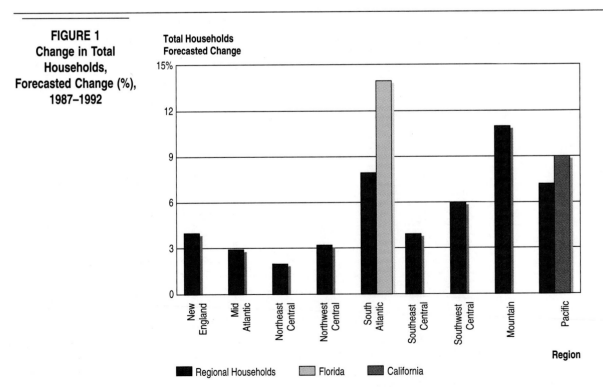

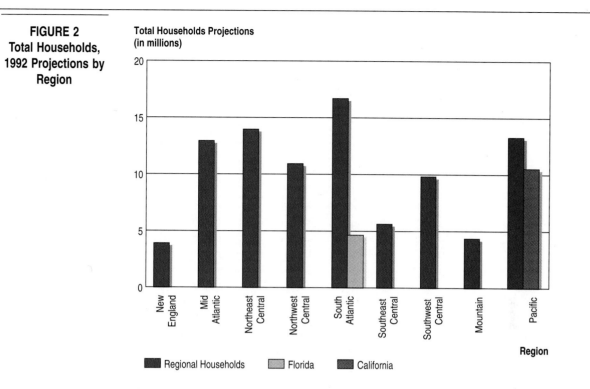

FIGURE 2
Total Households, 1992 Projections by Region

Total Households Projections (in millions)

Regions: New England, Mid Atlantic, Northeast Central, Northwest Central, South Atlantic, Southeast Central, Southwest Central, Mountain, Pacific

Legend: Regional Households, Florida, California

The Purchase Decision-Making Process

Each of the above-mentioned industries has a particular decision process and specific participants with different roles and levels of influence.

The Hospital Industry   In the case of hospitals, architects make the decision to use solid surface materials. The subcontractor/fabricator may choose the brand if the architect has not specified one. The hospital administrators have final budgetary control. In times of tight budgets, the relatively expensive solid surface materials may be one of the first items to be slashed. In this purchasing process, price sensitivity is high since the solid surface materials are viewed as a luxury.

The Laboratory Industry   The laboratory industry may be broken down into four subgroupings for further analysis of the purchasing decision process. These are the private labs, corporate labs, government labs, and academic labs.

Private labs are usually small and major construction material decisions are made by the owner/operator. The owner/operator usually makes the remodeling decisions. In the case of new construction, the architect decides on the use of solid surface materials. The owner/operator may request a specific brand. If neither of these decision makers has specified a brand, the subcontractor/fabricator will decide. Since these labs are for-profit operations, cost is a major consideration.

Corporate labs use a centralized or a regional buying procedure. The local lab releases a request and specifications for a solid surface material. They may request a specific brand. The regional purchasing office solicits bids from suppliers and issues the purchase order. Depending on the local lab/purchasing office relationship, the office may have veto rights over the local lab specification of a specific brand, especially if a large price disparity exists. Price and supplier location are the most important considerations.

Government labs utilize a complex purchasing process. If the cost of the work exceeds $500, the order must be placed through the local government purchasing office. The office matches the specifications of the request against the authorized list and solicits bids from the appropriate suppliers. The winning supplier must install the material. Cost is of the greatest importance with warranty and supplier location being secondary.

Academic labs specify a purchase to their physical plant office. It is then the responsibility of the office to locate potential suppliers, solicit bids, order, and install the material. As in the case of the corporate lab, the lab director may specify the brand, depending upon his influence on the physical plant purchaser. Price, reputation, and location are of major importance to the physical plant purchasers.

Kitchen Renovation and Design   The purchasing decision-making process for this market is very complex, with many players involved. The distributors of solid surface materials are licensed by the manufacturer of the material and carry a line of brands. Certified Kitchen Designers (CKD) are often hired by home owners to help make the decisions regarding kitchen renovation. The CKD may be following the materials choice of the customer, with budget being the only other factor, or the CKD may be acting as a "lifestyle counselor," given the charge of selecting the appropriate material for the customer's needs. In this case, the home owner will approve the choice of certain colors/materials. The CKD may also play a role in the distribution chain, often being the licensed distributor/dealer for at least one solid surface material. Fabricators may serve an important role in the decision-making process and may be dealers themselves. They have hands-on experience and are consulted by other decision makers for expert product advice. Fabricators are often certified by more than one solid surface company. A fabricator may be the licensed dealer and the distributor for the products it installs.

Residential Home Construction   The architect decides on the specifications and passes them on to the builder. The purchasing agent solicits bids on a variety of materials available. The vice president of sales/marketing reviews the available suppliers and determines the options to be offered. The kitchen countertop plan will offer a number of color and material options from which the customer can choose. Once the material has been selected, the subcontractor (who may also be the dealer and fabricator) will make the decision as to which material to use based on financial constraints, ease of fabrication, and safety factors involved. Safety concerns arise from the dust and fumes created when working with the material; it is a major concern for the fabricators.

The American Competition

Butler Consultants commissioned an independent laboratory test of Surfstone in comparison with the four main American competitors. The results showed that Surfstone was the least porous (therefore most hygienic) and proved the most resistant to chemicals. In addition, Surfstone produced the least amount of dust and fumes when cut.

Corian   The major competition in the United States comes from the giant Du Pont Co. concern and its Corian brand of solid surface materials. Corian was the original solid surface countertop, introduced in 1972. This material was unchallenged in the market for 13 years and now holds a commanding 85 percent of the market. The Corian product line includes sheets, integral and separate lavatories, and integral and separate kitchen and bar sinks. In addition, Corian offers prefabricated shower-surround and tub-surround kits. Ten colors are available. Sheets are offered in the standard $1/2''$ and $3/4''$ thicknesses, and are also available in a $1/4''$ sheet. The sheets come in a variety of lengths and widths. Du Pont offers a ten-year limited warranty against defects, which has become the industry standard. Du Pont also offers courses in the proper installation of Corian and certifies fabricators.

Du Pont's marketing strategy for Corian consists of a sophisticated network of elements that interact to produce brand awareness and an image of Corian as the premium brand of solid surface materials. Du Pont uses print advertisement as a primary means of building brand awareness and recognition of the product's qualities and uses in various sectors of the distribution channel. Print ads appear in 19 trade publications that reach architects, interior designers, engineers, contractors, kitchen and bath designers, and end-users.

Other niche players have appeared over the past four years, three of which have captured approximately 3 percent of the market each.

Fountainhead

The manufacturer of Fountainhead is the Nevamar Corporation, Maryland, an experienced manufacturer of laminated countertops for 40 years. It has been producing the Fountainhead line of solid surface materials for two years. Fountainhead is a blend of polyester and acrylic in combination with an alumina trihydrate filler. This blend is considered superior to polyester in durability and workability. The Fountainhead line offers sheets and lavatory bowls available in nine colors. Like Corian, the sheets are offered in $1/4''$, $1/2''$, and $3/4''$ thicknesses, and in a variety of lengths and widths. A ten-year warranty covers the material against defects. Classes are held for the fabricators, although a formal certification is not given. There are approximately 80 Nevamar distributors scattered throughout the United States. Most of these distributors are wholly owned subsidiaries and can buy at cost from each other. In 1990, Nevamar had sales of $140 million.

Avonite

Avonite was the second entrant into the solid surface market, having entered four years ago. The product consists of a blend of polyester alloys and fillers. It has created a niche by offering a wide variety of color combinations and designs, positioning itself as the "Decorative Surface Material."

The sheets are available in 20 colors, including 13 granites and 7 agates (marble). The colors may be matched to any type of color for custom applications. They come in only one standard sheet size, available in $1/2''$ and $3/4''$ thicknesses. Custom sizes are available and a $1/8''$ thick sheet may be special ordered. Avonite recently experienced an interruption in production due to the transfer of its manufacturing facilities from California to New Mexico, causing some damage to its market share. A new manufacturing facility will open in Vancouver to produce shaped products. It plans to produce undermount and surface mount vanities, kitchen sinks, tubs, and pedestal vanities. It has just introduced a new product, Inlays, which is a sheet having two different colors in a Southwest pattern. Avonite, like the other manufacturers, carries a ten-year warranty, yet only if installed by a certified fabricator. The company conducts certification seminars.

Surrel/2000X

Manufactured by the well-known surfacing company Formica, Surrel complements a line of laminates and surface materials for walls and cabinets. Surrel is a fully densified polyester resin compound with fillers. It is available in sheets, vanity tops, shower walls, bath walls, tubs, and integral and separate lavatory bowls. Surrel is available in six colors, generally a pale pastel, although three granite colors will be available soon. The sheets come in $1/4"$, $1/2"$, and $3/4"$ thicknesses and in a variety of sizes. Expansion of its manufacturing capacity is expected soon. Surrel was the last of the above-mentioned to enter the market and owes much of its current success to its inclusion in the Formica line of products. Surrel carries the industry-standard warranty of ten years and provides a 32-page pictorial instruction book for the installers.

Until 1985, Formica was a division of Cyanamid. It was sold to its long-time top executives in a leveraged buyout for $200 million. In 1987, the company was taken public in an offering designed to lighten the company's debt load. Formica's management has taken harsh measures to make the company more competitive. In the United States, its market share (30 percent) is second to Ralph Wilson Plastics (35 percent). Formica sales in 1986 reached $378 million, 92 percent of which corresponded to sales of its high-pressure decorative laminates.

Other Entrants Other companies have entered the market with products that are not significantly different from the above products. One significant new entrant is the Gardsman Company with its Solidex brand. It is just arriving in the market and little data are available. The product has been successfully marketed in Canada. It is a polyester resin and is available in molded shapes in eight colors. Solidex is offered with a 12-year warranty, the only solid surface manufacturer offering this guarantee. The product is expected to be priced competitively.

Price

A manufacturer price comparison of $1/2"$ thick, $30" \times 145"$, for these leading brands is used as an illustration. Prices vary with thickness, size, and color.

	New York	Los Angeles
Corian	$284	$295
Fountainhead	280	293
Avonite		
Standard	387	375
Inlays	514	487
Surrel	332	332
Surfstone	245*	266*

*DDP-delivered duties paid

DECIDING A STRATEGY

Kees was pleased with the report, but his presentation to the board is in just five days. He is expected to present an evaluation of the marketing opportunity presented by each market/industry and recommend a market for the initial introduction of Surfstone.

Undoubtedly, the board will be highly concerned with gaining a solid initial presence in the market, for it will surely determine the long-term prospects of the company. Kees is aware that the key to Tollens's success lies in a solid, yet aggressive, competitive positioning of company operations in the market. The ability to offer a high level of service, undoubtedly, is conditioned by the selection of the market and type of entry strategy adopted. Should one of the European export models be transplanted to the United States, or would a nontraditional approach be more appropriate? In Italy, the strategy of exporting to a full-service master distributor has been very profitable. Equally attractive is the Belgian option of shipping directly to 12 regional distributors under the supervision of a Belgian sales manager. What is the best route to compete in the United States?

Even though other issues are highly critical, such as media selection, logistics, and pricing, they are not to be addressed at this stage.

Spectrum Color Systems Inc.

Anthony Cordera, executive vice president of Spectrum Color Systems, sighed as he hung up the phone. The conversation still raced through his mind as he surveyed the fall foliage outside his office window. Cordera went over every nuance of the telephone conversation he had just completed with Roberto Cortez, vice president of European operations at BASF International. BASF had been a good customer for Spectrum, but today Cortez spoke with disdain, accusing Spectrum of questionable practices in its dealings with BASF. Cordera hated to see such a profitable relationship sour, but he saw no solution. As he turned back toward his desk, he wondered whether Spectrum might soon face similar sentiment from other large multinational clients. At the same time, he wondered how to address the issue at the upcoming board meeting without alarming the company president and the board of directors.

HISTORY

Spectrum Color Systems is a medium-sized industrial firm with headquarters in the eastern United States. The firm was founded in 1952 when Daniel Clark, a government scientist working on techniques to measure aspects of color and appearance, was approached by Procter and Gamble (P&G).

Procter and Gamble recognized that customers held a perception of quality related to the color of its products. To offer consistency to its customers and as part of its quality-control program, P&G sought a process to help it standardize the color and appearance of the products it manufactured. Clark balked at the request to work for P&G, building a machine that could quantify aspects of color, but as he recognized widespread commercial applications of such a machine, Clark went into business for himself. Spectrum Color Systems started with the simple philosophy of providing solutions to customers' problems relating to measurement and control of color and appearance attributes. The first machines were developed under contract with P&G. As the quality-control movement developed throughout the industrialized world, the demand for Spectrum's products grew.

Spectrum Color Systems remains privately held; majority ownership and controlling voting rights remain in the Clark family. In 1990 Daniel Clark died. His son Paul is CEO and president; he runs domestic sales, finance, and human resources. Anthony Cordera joined Spectrum in 1985. As executive vice president, he is responsible for manufacturing, engineering, international sales, shipping, and receiving. He reports directly to Paul Clark.

The Clark family retains approximately 55 percent of company stock, including all voting stock. The executive and associate staff participate in an employee stock ownership plan and together own the remaining 45 percent of shares.

PRODUCT LINE

Spectrum Color Systems manufactures and sells an extensive array of colorimeters and spectrophotometers. These machines quantify aspects of color and appearance. As Appendix A discusses, such measurements are important, but no easy task. A colorimeter is the most basic instrument, with some models starting at $2,000. Most

Source: This case study was developed by Professor Michael R. Czinkota and MBA candidate Marc S. Gross. Funding support by the U.S. Department of Education is gratefully acknowledged. Some names have been disguised to protect proprietary interests.

large manufacturers choose spectrophotometers, which are more exacting in their measurement ability, providing better performance and more options. These are generally integrated systems that can cost as much as $150,000.

Spectrum offers both on-line products and lab products. On-line products are designed for use on a production line, where products run under the instrument, which continuously monitors the product's appearance. These systems are manufactured in batch operations and customized to meet customer specifications. Typically, custom features are oriented to specific user applications and include hardware components such as moving optical scanners that measure lateral color variance as well as software components designed to meet the needs of specific industries. The first instruments built in the 1950s provided users with numerical values via a primitive screen and tape printer system with a 15- to 30-second lag between measurement and numerical output. Today, all of Spectrum's products are driven by user-friendly software that monitors color trends throughout a production run with real time output. Lab products are used when a customer takes a sample from a production line and brings it to the instrument for measurement.

Spectrum instruments are used in a wide variety of industries. Large food product companies measure the color of their products as well as packaging to ensure consistency. Paint companies purchase instruments to match colors and lease the machinery to paint stores. Automobile companies use Spectrum products to ensure that the color of interior cloth material, plastic molding, and exterior paint match. Some companies have forced suppliers to provide color-variance data sheets with all shipments. Spectrum recently supplied several instruments to a large bakery that produces buns for McDonald's. McDonald's had stipulated in its contract that buns be produced not only on time, but within certain color specifications. The bakery approached Spectrum to help meet the color standards.

A major manufacturer and supplier of denim uses Spectrum's "Color-Probe" spectrophotometer in its dye house to measure and grade the color of every strand of denim it produces. Color determines the value of the denim; it has a tremendous impact when millions of yards of denim are produced and the price fluctuates significantly depending on color.

THE COMPETITION

The color- and appearance-measurement market is considered a niche market with approximately $130 million to $140 million in annual sales worldwide. Spectrum has averaged $20 million annually in both retail and wholesale sales revenue over the past three years, placing it second in terms of market share. The industry became concentrated in 1990 when Color Value, a Swiss company with $5 million to $10 million in annual sales revenue, decided to dominate the color business. Color Value International, owned by a large Swiss brewery, purchased two competitors: Color Systems (CS), based in the United States and representing $35 million in annual sales, and International Color, based in the United Kingdom and representing $20 million in annual sales. Two smaller companies occupy third and fourth market share position; Speare accounts for approximately $12 million a year in sales, and Scientific Color generates about $9 million a year in sales (see Figure 1).

Although Color Value International holds almost 50 percent of world market share, Cordera believes that Spectrum now has a unique window of opportunity. The confusion associated with integrating three companies and the loss of goodwill caused by changing CS's company name, a well-established and respected brand, to Color Value International gave Spectrum a sales advantage. In addition Spectrum entered the color matching and formulation market, one of Color Value's most

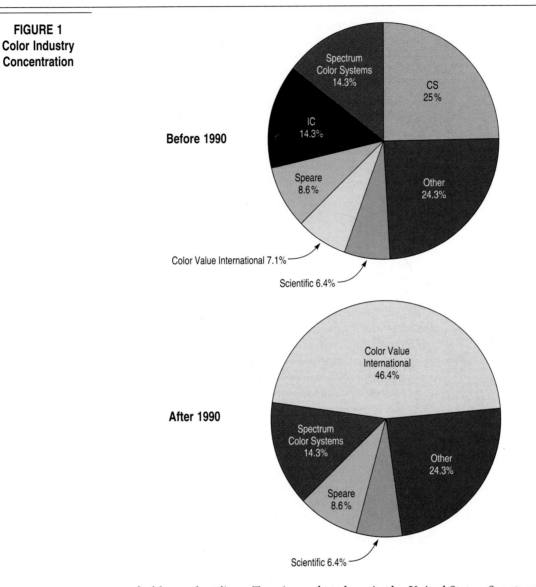

FIGURE 1
Color Industry
Concentration

profitable product lines. To gain market share in the United States, Spectrum's management decided to become the low-cost vendor and offered its new machines and color-matching software at prices of about one-half of that of the competition. Whereas the typical color-matching spectrophotometer by Color Value International was priced at $50,000, Spectrum offered a simpler $25,000 machine. To compete, Color Value International was forced to drastically reduce its prices to meet those of Spectrum, thus cutting deeply into profits.

INTERNATIONAL EXPANSION

In the 1950s and 1960s, Spectrum's management spent most of its time building the instruments and getting them out the door to meet the demand rather than developing a strategy to expand the company domestically or internationally. Spectrum's expansion into international markets succeeded despite its lack of strategic planning.

In the early days, Spectrum simply responded to requests from large companies such as Procter and Gamble to provide instruments to overseas subsidiaries. As the

Clarks became more comfortable with this process, they decided to begin selling actively in Europe. By 1984, international sales comprised about one-fourth of total corporate sales. By 1992, the share had grown to more than one-third.

SALES FORCE

Spectrum Color Systems used independent sales agents domestically from its inception until 1986, when it developed an internal sales force. Cordera, drawing on his experience in marketing, set up the domestic sales force to provide more direct control over the marketing and sales strategies. After touring a number of agent offices, Cordera began to calculate the real cost of such a sales relationship. Working closely with Bob Holland, Spectrum's chief financial officer, Cordera tried to quantify some of the intangible and hidden costs of the agent relationship. Spectrum spent significant resources lobbying for agents' time and attention to sales of Spectrum products and provided all the technical support since few of the agents had technical expertise. Additionally, although Spectrum was responsible for billing customers and paid 15 percent of the sales price to the agent as commission, it had no access to lists of end users and decision makers within the client's organization. Spectrum is an application-oriented company, thus access to decision makers and end users within client organizations provides valuable information for product development and sales of transferable applications to current and future clients. A detailed financial analysis compared the true cost of using sales agents to the anticipated cost of an internal sales force. The analysis indicated that Spectrum could increase sales, reduce cost, and increase its control by developing its own sales force.

Internationally, Spectrum still relied mainly on independent distributors for its sales. The firm sold instruments outright to distributors at wholesale price and billed the distributors with terms of 30 days net. Spectrum provided its distributors sales brochures and manuals in English. Distributors then translated the brochures as needed.

In the early days, distributors were selected largely through happenstance. Distributors of other products would hear about Spectrum and write a letter to the Clarks expressing interest in the distribution of their instruments. The Clarks would invite the distributor to the United States to see the products and get trained in their operation and thus become a Spectrum distributor. Spectrum now has distributors all over the world with extensive market penetration in Europe and the Far East. Although the company has encountered a steady international demand for its products, it continues to encounter problems with international distributors.

In 1984, Spectrum's sole French distributor, Gerard Bieux, abruptly closed his operation for medical reasons. Bieux had kept his sales operation close to his vest and thus maintained no customer lists or sales records. There was no one who could fill the void Bieux left, and Spectrum's management was forced to start over again building up its French distribution.

Cordera spent a great deal of time locating another French distributor and developing a profitable relationship. The relationship served Spectrum well until 1990, when a major competitor purchased the distributor. Again Cordera was left without a French representative for Spectrum instruments.

Cordera realized that the distributor-selection process was critical to Spectrum's international expansion and decided to become more proactive in selecting distributors. He worked closely with Holland to establish selection criteria for distributors based on financial stability, formal training programs, and financial goals. Additionally, Spectrum insisted that all distributors have service technicians trained at its U.S. facility. The distributor was responsible for paying the airfare for the technician, and

Spectrum supplied food, lodging, and training. This strategy was not pursued so much for financial reasons, but to force the distributor to make both a financial and emotional investment in selling Spectrum products.

With the domestic direct sales force up and running, Cordera decided that if he was going to put the effort into forging an international presence, Spectrum should move toward an international direct sales force. In 1991, Spectrum opened its first European sales office in Paris. It opened an office in Germany in 1992.

DEVELOPMENT OF AN INTERNATIONAL DIRECT SALES FORCE

In spite of the detailed planning, financial budgeting, and strategy analysis that preceded the opening of both European offices, each showed a net loss in its first year of operation. Cordera consulted with large accounting firms in both France and Germany to gain insight into European business law and to develop first-year budget projections. In addition, Spectrum management solicited information from its state Department of Economic Development on issues of taxation, international shipping, work permits, and visa restrictions for U.S. nationals working abroad. Despite such efforts, the combination of operating costs, which exceeded Spectrum's estimates, and slow sales associated with a European recession resulted in first-year losses in both France and Germany.

Cultural differences contributed to rising costs. Unlike the U.S. sales force where the majority of a sales representative's compensation consists of commission, European sales representatives are traditionally paid high salaries and relatively low commissions. In addition, employees are paid an annual salary bonus equivalent to one month's salary regardless of performance. Terminated employees can receive up to one year of severance pay based on the longevity of their relationship and position with the company. Middle managers and above expect to be provided with company cars, which was particularly difficult for Spectrum management to swallow since neither Cordera nor Clark was provided with a company car. Despite his uneasiness, Cordera agreed to provide the benefits since he believed it important to attract high-quality employees for the new offices. All of the benefits were stipulated in the long-term employment contracts required in Europe.

Difficulties soon became apparent with Spectrum's sales representative in Paris. In staffing the Paris office, Cordera, largely out of a desire to get someone out on the road in France, settled for an individual who, although the most qualified of the candidates, lacked the aggressiveness, sales orientation, and technical competence for the position. Cordera was disappointed by the sales representative's performance but found the process of terminating the employee a long and arduous one. Spectrum began working with an attorney in Paris, providing the employee with written documentation detailing the reasons for dissatisfaction, as well as sales goals that were to be met in order to retain the position. In the end, Spectrum was forced to negotiate an expensive severance package.

But now, the international activities seem to be on track. Spectrum has two international offices abroad. The Paris office consists of the international sales director, one sales representative, one service technician, and two secretaries. From that office, Spectrum conducts marketing activities, sales, installation, and service for France. The German office employs two sales representatives, one secretary, and one service technician covering the German market.

To avoid future hiring difficulties, Cordera instituted a program that brings key individuals from European operations to its headquarters facility. The mission of this program is to integrate those individuals into Spectrum's corporate culture and create a team environment. On this point, Cordera remarked, "The fax machine and telephone are great pieces of equipment, but nothing beats a face-to-face dinner or lunch where we can sit down and talk to each other."

COMMITMENT TO EUROPEAN CUSTOMERS

Spectrum management had historically marketed the same products throughout the world. Over time Spectrum recognized that the European market and the U.S. market had different needs and preferences in both hardware and software. For example, Spectrum sales representatives frequently found their sales efforts focusing on the software that accompanies the instruments, since that is the part the customer sees and touches.

To achieve market success, Spectrum management believed it had to design products to meet the needs of the European customers. There were two choices. The first was to translate existing software and then add the nuances the Europeans wanted. This proposition promised to be time-consuming and very costly. The second option was to acquire a software company abroad.

In 1991, Cordera located a small software company in Switzerland that already had software written in German, French, Italian, and Spanish that was very applicable to the Spectrum system. Spectrum purchased the company for $275,000. Along with the company's assets and software copyrights, Spectrum also acquired the services of the company founder. This proved invaluable as he speaks five languages and can adapt Spectrum's software products to meet the needs of the European market.

Spectrum Color Systems paid for its acquisition out of the cash it had generated from operations. Spectrum management historically has taken a conservative view of financing. The focus is on cash management, trying to generate enough cash to finance any expansion. In fact, Spectrum would not have made the purchase unless it had the cash.

Spectrum does maintain a line of credit, but as yet it has not used loans to finance expansion. Occasionally, management borrows $500,000 on its credit line, invests in short-term CDs and repays the loan early just to show activity on its account.

DECISION SITUATION

In all remaining international markets, Spectrum still uses distributors. Recently this has resulted in significant problems. When BASF International in Germany purchased an instrument from Spectrum's German operation, it recommended that the BASF subsidiary in Spain buy the same instrument. When BASF received the invoice from Spectrum's Spanish distributor, the price was more than 50 percent higher than that paid in Germany. Cortez naturally felt that BASF was somehow being taken advantage of in Spain. However, there is little Spectrum can do about such disparities, since, pursuant to the distributor agreements, distributors purchase Spectrum products outright and determine the markup themselves. In addition, European Community antitrust regulations prevent Spectrum from setting a standardized price for its distributors.

This distributor arrangement is particularly advantageous in Italy and Spain. Given Spectrum's focus on cash management, the firm is leery about setting up direct operations in these countries. Cordera believes it is difficult to manage cash effectively in Italy and Spain, where vendors can wait six months to a year to receive payment from customers. There is an advantage to selling through distributors because Spectrum can collect cash on the sale in 30 or 45 days and the distributor has to wait for payment.

German Luxury Cars: Made in the U.S.A.

Two southern U.S. states, South Carolina and Alabama, received what many view as just rewards for their hospitality, generosity, and pro-business environment. The rewards came in the form of multimillion-dollar investments for new automobile plants. The German luxury car legends BMW and Mercedes-Benz both chose to invest in new production sites in the southern United States. For BMW, the search ended in the summer of 1992, when management decided to locate its plant in the Greenville-Spartanburg area of South Carolina. Mercedes concluded its closely watched search in the fall of 1993, choosing tiny Vance, Alabama, as home for its new plant.

The German investments represent two key facets of a very competitive industry: the need to cut costs and easy access to target markets. U.S. wages are, on average, 60 percent lower than in Germany. Both German car makers are competing head-to-head with Japanese producers that are already well-ensconced on the U.S. production scene.

Both South Carolina and Alabama are celebrating the hard-fought battle that won them thousands of future jobs, potential financial returns in the billions, and the prestige of having landed such world-class companies. These developments are also expected to make other potential investors take a long, hard look at the two states as well.

Each investment decision was based on different details; however, the underlying case of trying to land a world-class investor at seemingly whatever means possible is present in both examples. A closer look at the two foreign direct investments provides the opportunity to view some of the different details and circumstances, as well as the similarities, that exist in luring desirable investment.

THE BMW DECISION

When BMW chose to locate in South Carolina, it was joining a group of European firms (BASF Corp., Rieter Corp., Marzoli International Inc., and Michelin Tire Corp.) that had already discovered the comparatively cheaper and competent work force as well as a hospitable, pro-business atmosphere. BMW planned to begin production in 1995 of a new, more affordable model that will be aimed at the American market, specifically, graying baby boomers. Over three years, the auto maker looked at 250 locations in 10 countries. When it was clear that BMW planned on producing the new model in the United States, a race ensued among competing states to win the cherished investment. In the end, the choice came down to Nebraska and South Carolina.

South Carolina Governor Carroll Campbell put up a strong recruiting effort, visiting BMW in Germany and making offers that were hard to refuse. To obtain the $640-million plant and the expected 6,000 new state jobs, a bit of Southern finesse was added. For instance, the site most desired by BMW had 134 separate landowners. In order to ease land acquisition problems, Gov. Campbell secured a $25-million appropriation from the state legislature to buy the property. He personally tele-

Sources: This case was written by Michael R. Czinkota and Peter Fitzmaurice based on the following sources: "Why Mercedes Is Alabama Bound," *Business Week,* October 11, 1993, 138–139; "Alabama Steers Mercedes South," *ENR,* October 11, 1993, 6–7; "Mercedes-Benz Parks $300 Million Plant in Alabama," *Site Selection,* December 1993; "Europe Loves Dixie," *Europe,* October 1992, 30–36; "The Beemer Spotlight Falls on Spartanburg, USA," *Business Week,* July 6, 1992, 38; "The Boom Belt," *Business Week,* September 27, 1993, 98–104.

**Figure 2
The Three-Dimensional
Color-Coordinate
System**

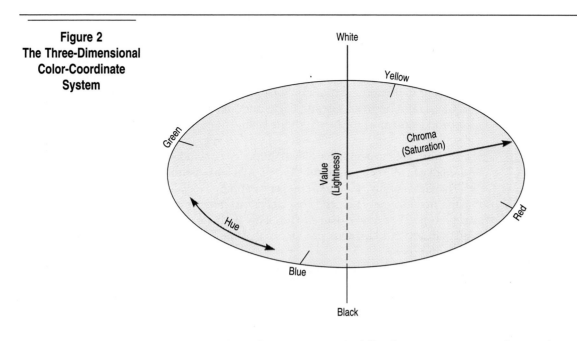

Appearance characteristics are difficult to communicate objectively. Certainly a sample of the product could be sent to another person, but what is "close enough" when deciding if a match exists?

The Language of Color

Color is a three-dimensional characteristic of appearance consisting of a lightness attribute, often called "value," and two chromatic attributes, called "hue" and "chroma." Colors can be distinguished from one another by specifying these three visual attributes. Figure 2 shows a common arrangement of these three attributes often termed "color solid" or "color space."

Hue   Hue is often the first attribute of color that is mentioned. Consider the school bus. The most obvious thing about it is that it is a shade of yellow rather than blue or green. Hue is the attribute of color perception by which an object is judged to be red, yellow, green, blue, and so forth.

Chroma   A color specification requires more than just a designation of hue. How concentrated is the yellow? That is, how much color does there appear to be? Words such as depth, vividness, purity, and saturation have been used to convey how different the color is from gray. Chroma is the more accepted term and is used to specify the position of the color between gray and the pure hue.

Value   A third dimension is necessary to complete our specification. This is a luminous or lightness attribute, which distinguishes "light" colors from "dark" colors. Value is the term commonly used to express this attribute and is shown as the vertical axis in Figure 2.

German Luxury Cars: Made in the U.S.A.

Two southern U.S. states, South Carolina and Alabama, received what many view as just rewards for their hospitality, generosity, and pro-business environment. The rewards came in the form of multimillion-dollar investments for new automobile plants. The German luxury car legends BMW and Mercedes-Benz both chose to invest in new production sites in the southern United States. For BMW, the search ended in the summer of 1992, when management decided to locate its plant in the Greenville-Spartanburg area of South Carolina. Mercedes concluded its closely watched search in the fall of 1993, choosing tiny Vance, Alabama, as home for its new plant.

The German investments represent two key facets of a very competitive industry: the need to cut costs and easy access to target markets. U.S. wages are, on average, 60 percent lower than in Germany. Both German car makers are competing head-to-head with Japanese producers that are already well-ensconced on the U.S. production scene.

Both South Carolina and Alabama are celebrating the hard-fought battle that won them thousands of future jobs, potential financial returns in the billions, and the prestige of having landed such world-class companies. These developments are also expected to make other potential investors take a long, hard look at the two states as well.

Each investment decision was based on different details; however, the underlying case of trying to land a world-class investor at seemingly whatever means possible is present in both examples. A closer look at the two foreign direct investments provides the opportunity to view some of the different details and circumstances, as well as the similarities, that exist in luring desirable investment.

THE BMW DECISION

When BMW chose to locate in South Carolina, it was joining a group of European firms (BASF Corp., Rieter Corp., Marzoli International Inc., and Michelin Tire Corp.) that had already discovered the comparatively cheaper and competent work force as well as a hospitable, pro-business atmosphere. BMW planned to begin production in 1995 of a new, more affordable model that will be aimed at the American market, specifically, graying baby boomers. Over three years, the auto maker looked at 250 locations in 10 countries. When it was clear that BMW planned on producing the new model in the United States, a race ensued among competing states to win the cherished investment. In the end, the choice came down to Nebraska and South Carolina.

South Carolina Governor Carroll Campbell put up a strong recruiting effort, visiting BMW in Germany and making offers that were hard to refuse. To obtain the $640-million plant and the expected 6,000 new state jobs, a bit of Southern finesse was added. For instance, the site most desired by BMW had 134 separate landowners. In order to ease land acquisition problems, Gov. Campbell secured a $25-million appropriation from the state legislature to buy the property. He personally tele-

Sources: This case was written by Michael R. Czinkota and Peter Fitzmaurice based on the following sources: "Why Mercedes Is Alabama Bound," *Business Week,* October 11, 1993, 138–139; "Alabama Steers Mercedes South," *ENR,* October 11, 1993, 6–7; "Mercedes-Benz Parks $300 Million Plant in Alabama," *Site Selection,* December 1993; "Europe Loves Dixie," *Europe,* October 1992, 30–36; "The Beemer Spotlight Falls on Spartanburg, USA," *Business Week,* July 6, 1992, 38; "The Boom Belt," *Business Week,* September 27, 1993, 98–104.

ate a team environment. On this point, Cordera remarked, "The fax machine and telephone are great pieces of equipment, but nothing beats a face-to-face dinner or lunch where we can sit down and talk to each other."

COMMITMENT TO EUROPEAN CUSTOMERS

Spectrum management had historically marketed the same products throughout the world. Over time Spectrum recognized that the European market and the U.S. market had different needs and preferences in both hardware and software. For example, Spectrum sales representatives frequently found their sales efforts focusing on the software that accompanies the instruments, since that is the part the customer sees and touches.

To achieve market success, Spectrum management believed it had to design products to meet the needs of the European customers. There were two choices. The first was to translate existing software and then add the nuances the Europeans wanted. This proposition promised to be time-consuming and very costly. The second option was to acquire a software company abroad.

In 1991, Cordera located a small software company in Switzerland that already had software written in German, French, Italian, and Spanish that was very applicable to the Spectrum system. Spectrum purchased the company for $275,000. Along with the company's assets and software copyrights, Spectrum also acquired the services of the company founder. This proved invaluable as he speaks five languages and can adapt Spectrum's software products to meet the needs of the European market.

Spectrum Color Systems paid for its acquisition out of the cash it had generated from operations. Spectrum management historically has taken a conservative view of financing. The focus is on cash management, trying to generate enough cash to finance any expansion. In fact, Spectrum would not have made the purchase unless it had the cash.

Spectrum does maintain a line of credit, but as yet it has not used loans to finance expansion. Occasionally, management borrows $500,000 on its credit line, invests in short-term CDs and repays the loan early just to show activity on its account.

DECISION SITUATION

In all remaining international markets, Spectrum still uses distributors. Recently this has resulted in significant problems. When BASF International in Germany purchased an instrument from Spectrum's German operation, it recommended that the BASF subsidiary in Spain buy the same instrument. When BASF received the invoice from Spectrum's Spanish distributor, the price was more than 50 percent higher than that paid in Germany. Cortez naturally felt that BASF was somehow being taken advantage of in Spain. However, there is little Spectrum can do about such disparities, since, pursuant to the distributor agreements, distributors purchase Spectrum products outright and determine the markup themselves. In addition, European Community antitrust regulations prevent Spectrum from setting a standardized price for its distributors.

This distributor arrangement is particularly advantageous in Italy and Spain. Given Spectrum's focus on cash management, the firm is leery about setting up direct operations in these countries. Cordera believes it is difficult to manage cash effectively in Italy and Spain, where vendors can wait six months to a year to receive payment from customers. There is an advantage to selling through distributors because Spectrum can collect cash on the sale in 30 or 45 days and the distributor has to wait for payment.

FUTURE STRATEGIES

By 1993, both European sales offices had become profitable. The emergence of the European Union could allow Spectrum to use its French and German operations as a base to expand into other countries without duplicating tasks. For example, the firm could place direct sales representatives throughout Europe with support provided by central office service technicians who would cross borders to perform installations and service. Yet Cordera still considered direct offices to be an expensive and somewhat risky proposition. His experience indicated that direct sales offices would not become self-sufficient for at least one year, and these types of financial losses caused friction with Spectrum's president and board of directors. Therefore, Cordera was not prepared for direct confrontation with distributors over markup. He dreaded the thought of being prematurely forced into opening other direct sales offices and repeating or even compounding the problems Spectrum had already endured.

In addition, recent changes in the exchange rates between the U.S. dollar and European currencies had tightened margins on export sales and decreased available cash. This pinch threatened to delay Cordera's planned expansion in the Far East.

Currently, Spectrum sells through distributors in the Pacific Rim and China, but Cordera was in the process of negotiating a joint venture in China. Cordera thought that for Spectrum to continue its growth throughout the world and especially in the Pacific Rim, it should establish a joint operation. The cultural differences in the Pacific Rim seemed too great for Spectrum to overcome alone, so Cordera sought to marry Spectrum's technology and sales distribution with a company that had manufacturing capabilities similar to Spectrum's.

Questions for Discussion

1. Are current EU regulations beneficial or detrimental to Spectrum Color System's European operations in terms of distributor pricing and direct company sales?
2. How do fluctuations in the currency exchange rates affect Spectrum's revenues? Do you think Spectrum management would prefer to see a strong or weak dollar? Why?
3. How should Spectrum management respond to the BASF situation?
4. What has Spectrum done to meet the different needs of international customers? What more could be done to accommodate them?

APPENDIX A

The Basics of Color and Appearance

What words would you use to describe a school bus? Yellow or slightly reddish yellow or perhaps orange? You might add the word shiny or maybe even glossy. But could the person on the other end of a telephone be expected to make a gallon of paint for touch up based on those words? Most likely not.

To further complicate matters, is your color vision the same as the person's making the paint? What about the lighting under which you made the initial judgment of color? Have you ever noticed how some colors appear quite different under the lamps used in your home or office compared to the outdoors?

phoned reluctant sellers and within 14 weeks, the state and local governments had spent $36.6 million to buy every single property—including a home that one family had just finished building two weeks before they were approached. To sweeten the deal, new roads and site improvements were included, and the runway at the local airport was to be extended to accommodate BMW's cargo planes. The state also offered a $41-million property tax break to BMW. Furthermore, the local airport's free trade zone status was extended to include the 900-acre plant site, meaning BMW will not have to pay duties on parts imported from Germany or elsewhere until cars actually leave the plant for sale in the United States.

One of the big determinants for BMW was South Carolina's excellent technical school system. Under the investment agreement, the state customizes its training program for the company, even sending instructors to Munich to study the equipment that will be used. In all, the state has promised to spend $3 million to train workers for BMW alone, a considerable sum when one takes into account that in 1992 South Carolina spent $5.8 million on technical training for the entire state. In addition, local businesses offered to pay up to $3 million for additional training.

The constant stream of amenities and special treatment that South Carolina extended to BMW was especially critical to completing this deal, according to industry analysts, given the fact that BMW is considered to be a conservative corporation not prone to bold moves. The firm does not just want to be accepted, it wants to be welcomed. Stated Carl Flescher, a vice president with BMW North America: "I've only been down there for about 10 or 15 days and I am very impressed. The embracing of this whole thing is incredible. You go to the Holiday Inn and there is a sign that says 'Welcome BMW.' You pull up to the Hertz rental car and they know who you are. People are genuinely friendly, open, and elated." Gov. Campbell sums up the whole mission best: "The name BMW is generally associated with excellence and quality and that by itself is a benefit. Other companies will say, 'Well, wait a minute, BMW is rated as one of the best, and they chose South Carolina. So, they must be doing something right.'"

THE MERCEDES INVESTMENT

Mercedes offered the prospects of a $300-million plant and 1,500 new jobs. Initially, the firm's search included 170 sites in 30 states. Alabama knew that to win the investment, its offer to Mercedes would have to be outstanding. One state official recalls the message from a Mercedes consulting firm representative: "Everyone knows what South Carolina gave BMW. My client feels they are better than BMW!"

So the race was on and in the end, Alabama won the "industrial crown jewel," as Governor Jim Folsom, Jr., refers to it. The German company was impressed by the entrepreneurial, nonbureaucratic attitude of Alabama's state government. The firm also liked the access to interstate highways, railroads, and ports, adequate available labor, proximity to schools, quality of life, and, of course, a lucrative package of financial incentives. Here is a partial list of those incentives: $92.2 million to buy and develop the site, create a foreign trade zone, and build an employee training center; $77.5 million to extend water, gas, and sewer lines along with other infrastructure; $60 million in government funds to train Mercedes employees, suppliers, and workers in related industries, enriched by $15 million from the private sector; $8.7 million in tax breaks; in all, a total of more than $253 million.

The plant will make a sport utility vehicle costing between $20,000 and $30,000. About half of the annual output of 60,000 vehicles will be exported to Europe and other continents. Mercedes will ship engines and transmissions for the vehicle from

Germany, but it expects to purchase most other parts from U.S. suppliers. Construction of the facility began in 1994, with production scheduled to start in 1997.

Alabama believes it invested wisely. One study found that the $253 million used to lure the German investment will yield shining returns of $365 million during the first year and $7.3 billion over the next 20 years.

But there are limits to the lure of state incentives. One state official commented: "Ultimately it comes down to the company's personal choice." Said Mercedes project leader Andreas Renschler: "Whether you get $10 million more or less in one state doesn't make any difference. We sensed a much higher dedication to our project."

A competing participant in the race to capture the Mercedes plant was North Carolina. The state's governor, Jim Hunt, criticized parts of Alabama's incentives package saying, "We do not need to risk the future of the franchise to recruit star players." In particular, Hunt pointed to what some refer to as the "Benz Bill," passed by the Alabama legislature during a special session. It allows 5 percent of corporate income tax from the plant and 5 percent of the plant's employees' taxes to be used to retire debt.

Critics are contending that states are "buying" industry at too steep a price. The financial incentives necessary to land the BMW plant—including a $1-a-year lease on the 900 acres—will cost South Carolina taxpayers $130 million over 30 years, although most of the incentives are in the first year.

North Carolina may be correct in denouncing certain types of tactics to lure investment. However, the attitude of not giving away "the franchise" is increasingly being seen as detrimental. A report by an international site-selection consultant, commissioned by North Carolina after losing the chance to land BMW, read that the state "is increasingly seen as a nonparticipant in incentive practices at a time when incentives are growing in importance." So the question, "How much is too much?" is complicated by the fact that growing expectations and necessities may warrant the types of grandiose offers that are portrayed in the Mercedes and BMW cases.

Questions for Discussion

1. Do you believe that states should encourage foreign direct investment? Why or why not?

2. Do incentives determine whether or not a company will invest in the United States?

3. How should a state government determine the upper limit of its investment support?

4. Do FDI incentives place local established firms at a disadvantage?

Lakewood Forest Products

Since the 1970s the United States has had a merchandise trade deficit with the rest of the world. Up to 1982, this deficit mattered little because it was relatively small. As of 1983, however, the trade deficit increased rapidly and became, due to its size and future implications, an issue of major national concern. Suddenly, trade moved to the forefront of national debate. Concurrently, a debate ensued on the issue of the international competitiveness of U.S. firms. The onerous question here was whether U.S. firms could and would achieve sufficient improvements in areas such as productivity, quality, and price to remain long-term successful international marketing players.

U.S.–Japanese trade relations took on particular significance, because it was between those two countries that the largest bilateral trade deficit existed. In spite of trade negotiations, market-opening measures, trade legislation, and other governmental efforts, it was clear that the impetus for a reversal of the deficit through more U.S. exports to Japan had to come from the private sector. Therefore, the activities of any U.S. firm that appeared successful in penetrating the Japanese market were widely hailed. One company whose effort to market in Japan aroused particular interest was Lakewood Forest Products, of Hibbing, Minnesota.

In 1983, Ian J. Ward was an export merchant in difficulty. Throughout the 1970s his company, Ward, Bedas Canadian Ltd., had successfully sold Canadian lumber and salmon to countries in the Persian Gulf. Over time, the company had opened four offices worldwide. However, when the Iran–Iraq war erupted, most of Ward's long-term trading relationships disappeared within a matter of months. In addition, the international lumber market began to collapse. As a result, Ward, Bedas Canadian Ltd. went into a survivalist mode and sent employees all over the world to look for new markets and business opportunities. Late that year, the company received an interesting order. A firm in Korea urgently needed to purchase lumber for the production of chopsticks.

Learning about the Chopstick Market

In discussing the wood deal with the Koreans, Ward learned that in order to produce good chopsticks more than 60 percent of the wood fiber would be wasted. Given the high transportation cost involved, the large degree of wasted materials, and his need for new business, Ward decided to explore the Korean and Japanese chopstick industry in more detail.

He quickly determined that chopstick making in the Far East is a fragmented industry, working with old technology and suffering from a lack of natural resources. In Asia, chopsticks are produced in very small quantities, often by family organizations.

Source: This case was written by Michael R. Czinkota based on the following sources: Mark Clayton, "Minnesota Chopstick Maker Finds Japanese Eager to Import His Quality Waribashi," *The Christian Science Monitor,* October 16, 1987, 11; Roger Worthington, "Improbable Chopstick Capitol of the World," *Chicago Tribune,* June 5, 1988, 39; Mark Gill, "The Great American Chopstick Master," *American Way,* August 1, 1987, 34, 78–79; "Perpich of Croatia," *The Economist,* April 20, 1991, 27; and personal interview with Ian J. Ward, president, Lakewood Forest Products.

Even the largest of the 450 chopstick factories in Japan turns out only 5 million chopsticks a month. This compares to an overall market size of 130 million pairs of disposable chopsticks a day. In addition, chopsticks represent a growing market. With increased wealth in Asia, people eat out more often and therefore have a greater demand for disposable chopsticks. The fear of communicable diseases has greatly reduced the use of reusable chopsticks. Renewable plastic chopsticks have been attacked by many groups as too newfangled and as causing future ecological problems.

From his research, Ward concluded that a competitive niche existed in the world chopstick market. He believed that, if he could use low-cost raw materials and ensure that the labor cost component would remain small, he could successfully compete in the world market.

The Founding of Lakewood Forest Products

In exploring opportunities afforded by the newly identified international marketing niche for chopsticks, Ward set four criteria for plant location:

1. Access to suitable raw materials
2. Proximity of other wood product users who could make use of the 60 percent waste for their production purposes
3. Proximity to a port that would facilitate shipment to the Far East
4. Availability of labor

In addition, Ward was aware of the importance of product quality. People use chopsticks on a daily basis and are accustomed to products that are visually inspected one by one, so he would have to live up to high quality expectations to compete successfully. Chopsticks could not be bowed or misshapen, have blemishes in the wood, or splinter.

Ward needed financing to implement his plan. Private lenders were skeptical and slow to provide funds. The skepticism resulted from the unusual direction of Ward's proposal. Far Eastern companies have generally held the cost advantage in a variety of industries, especially those as labor intensive as chopstick manufacturing. U.S. companies rarely have an advantage in producing low-cost items. Further, only a very small domestic market exists for chopsticks.

However, Ward found that the state of Minnesota was willing to participate in his new venture. Since the decline of the mining industry, regional unemployment had been rising rapidly in the state. In 1983, unemployment in Minnesota's Iron Range peaked at 22 percent. Therefore, state and local officials were anxious to attract new industries that would be independent of mining activities. Of particular help was the enthusiasm of Governor Rudy Perpich. The governor had been boosting Minnesota business on the international scene by traveling abroad and receiving many foreign visitors. He was excited about Ward's plans, which called for the creation of more than 100 new jobs within a year.

Hibbing, Minnesota, turned out to be an ideal location for Ward's project. The area had an abundant supply of aspen wood, which, because it grows in clay soil, tends to be unmarred. The fact that Hibbing was the hometown of the governor also did not hurt. In addition, Hibbing boasted an excellent labor pool, and both the city and the state were willing to make loans totaling $500,000. Further, the Iron Range Resources Rehabilitation Board was willing to sell $3.4 million in industrial revenue bonds for the project. Together with jobs and training wage subsidies, enterprise zone credits, and tax increment financing benefits, the initial public support of the project added up to about 30 percent of its start-up costs. The potential benefit of the new venture to the region was quite clear. When Lakewood Forest Products advertised its first 30 jobs, more than 3,000 people showed up to apply.

THE PRODUCTION AND SALE OF CHOPSTICKS

Ward insisted that to truly penetrate the international market, he would need to keep his labor cost low. As a result, he decided to automate as much of the production as possible. However, no equipment was readily available to produce chopsticks, because no one had automated the process before.

After much searching, Ward identified a European equipment manufacturer who produced machinery for making popsicle sticks. He purchased equipment from the Danish firm to better carry out the sorting and finishing processes. However, because aspen wood was quite different from the wood for which the machine was designed, as was the final product, substantial design adjustments had to be made. Sophisticated equipment was also purchased to strip the bark from the wood and peel it into long, thin sheets. Finally, a computer vision system was acquired to detect defects in the chopsticks. The system rejected more than 20 percent of the production, and yet some of the chopsticks that passed inspection were splintering. However, Ward firmly believed that further fine-tuning of the equipment and training of the new work force would gradually take care of the problem.

Given this fully automated process, Lakewood Forest Products was able to develop capacity for up to 7 million chopsticks a day. With a unit manufacturing cost of $0.03 and an anticipated unit selling price of $0.057, Ward expected to earn a pretax profit of $4.7 million in 1988.

Due to intense marketing efforts in Japan and the fact that Japanese customers were struggling to obtain sufficient supplies of disposable chopsticks, Ward was able to presell the first five years of production quite quickly. By late 1987, Lakewood Forest Products was ready to enter the international market. With an ample supply of raw materials and an almost totally automated plant, Lakewood was positioned as the world's largest and least labor-intensive manufacturer of chopsticks. The first shipment of six containers with a load of 12 million pairs of chopsticks to Japan was made in October 1987.

Questions for Discussion

1. What are the future implications of continuing large U.S. trade deficits?
2. What are the important variables for the international marketing success of chopsticks?
3. Rank the variables in Question 2 according to the priority you believe they have for foreign customers.
4. Why haven't Japanese firms thought of automating the chopstick production process?
5. How long will Lakewood Forest Products be able to maintain its competitive advantage?

ESPRIT

"Europe now has a position in technologies where we are no longer in danger of losing the pace." This statement by a European executive underlines the fact that Europe's experiment in cooperative research and development (R&D) is paying off. Since the mid-1980s, companies and research institutes from Denmark to Spain have pooled their resources in megaprojects ranging from genetic engineering to thermonuclear fusion. One of the most ambitious efforts is ESPRIT (European Strategic Programs for Research in Information Technologies). In the first period of ESPRIT (ESPRIT 1), 1984–1989, a total of 1.5 billion ECU ($2 billion) were spent; in the second period (ESPRIT 2), 1987–1991, an additional 3.2 billion ECU ($4.4 billion) was made available, and for ESPRIT 3, which ended in 1994, another 2.7 billion ECU ($3.7 billion) was allocated. ESPRIT 4, which started January 1, 1995, and will have a duration of four years, already has had 1.9 billion ($2.5 billion) proposed for its projects to "contribute toward the construction of a European information infrastructure in order to ensure the future competitiveness of all European industry and to improve the quality of life."

BACKGROUND

The history of intra-European cooperation had a shaky beginning at best. The rising costs of research in aerospace, electronics, and chemicals, as well as the substantial technological gap between European and U.S. firms in the 1960s, provided the impetus for greater intra-European collaboration. In April 1970, the European Commission proposed the creation of an EC office to coordinate development contracts in advanced technology. Although the number of mergers did rise in the 1970s, the decade was marked by a series of failures in intra-European cooperation. Most prominent was the failure of UNIDATA, a computing resource venture by Bull, Philips, and Siemens.

In 1980, Étienne Daignon, then Commissioner of Industry in the EC, invited 12 of Europe's largest information technology firms (Siemens, AEG, and Nixdorf of Germany; Plessey, GEC, and STC of the United Kingdom; CGE, Thomson, and Bull of France; Philips of the Netherlands; and Olivetti and Stet of Italy) to help create a cooperative work program for their industry to be called ESPRIT. The objectives of the effort were (1) to promote intra-European industrial cooperation, (2) to furnish European industry with the basic technologies that it would need to bolster its competitiveness over the next five to ten years, and (3) to develop European norms and standards. Five major themes were agreed upon: advanced micro electronics, software technology, advanced information processing, office systems, and computer in-

Source: This case was compiled by Ilkka A. Ronkainen. It is based on "Screened Out," *The Economist,* September 24, 1994, 66; Marc Van Wegberg, Arjen Van Witteloostuijn, and Michiel Roscam Abbing, "Multimarket and Multiproject Collusion," *De Economist* 142 (Number 3, 1994): 253–285; Willem A. Ledeboer and Tjerk R. Gorter, "ESPRIT: Successful Industrial R&D Cooperation in Europe," *International Journal of Technology Management* 8 (Numbers 6, 7, 8, 1993): 528–543; "Do Not Adjust Your Set Yet," *The Economist,* February 27, 1993, 65–66; "Sematech Claims Major Advance by Halving Size of Chip Circuits," *The Wall Street Journal,* January 22, 1992, B5; Louis Kraar, "Your Rivals Can Be Your Allies," *Fortune,* March 27, 1989, 63–76; Les Smith, "Can Consortiums Defeat Japan?" *Fortune,* June 5, 1989, 215–254; Jonathan B. Levine, "Hanging Tough by Teaming Up," *Business Week,* October 22, 1990, 121; and Jeremy Main, "Making Global Alliances Work," *Fortune,* December 17, 1990, 121–126. Thanks to Boyd J. Miller for his assistance with an earlier version of this case.

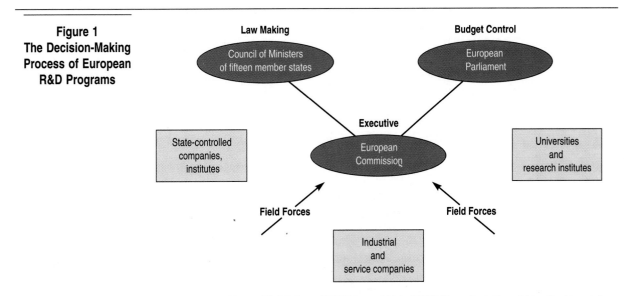

Figure 1
The Decision-Making Process of European R&D Programs

Source: Willem A. Ledeboer and Tjerk R. Gorter, "ESPRIT: Successful Industrial R&D Cooperation in Europe," *International Journal of Technology Management* 8, 6, 7, 8 (1993): 530.

tegrated manufacture. The European Commission wanted to make clear from the beginning that ESPRIT was not meant as an industrial policy on a regional level, but rather a technology policy that had the task of identifying key areas of technology. ESPRIT launched a pilot program in 1983 and began full-scale operations a year later.

The involved parties and the influences in the decision-making process of European R&D projects are summarized in Figure 1. Industry specifies the subject areas and priorities, while the European Commission makes a coherent work plan, acts as a program director and contract manager, and makes the selection of projects and monitors their progress. The Commission is obligated to report to the Council of Ministers, the European Parliament, and the Economic and Social Committee.

Today, roughly half of ESPRIT's budget is paid for by the EU. The other half is provided by the participating companies. Specific measures, such as actions to encourage standardization and measures to provide general service tools to research centers and universities, may qualify for an EU contribution of up to 100 percent of total costs. ESPRIT's project rules require that at least two firms located in two different EU countries be represented. This rule ensures that ESPRIT is an intercontinental program. Initially, the vast majority of programs included the Big-12 firms. Over time, smaller firms, research institutes, and universities have become significant contributors. Since a significant amount of financing comes from taxpayers, officials must disperse funds equitably rather than to the strongest competitors. This has allowed smaller firms, such as IMEC, to collaborate with multinational giants such as Philips. The results are discussed and exhibited annually during "ESPRIT Week" in Brussels.

ESPRIT plays different roles for the participating entities. For firms already engaged in alliances, ESPRIT has helped complement them. Commitment levels to R&D and to individual projects have also improved. For example, European information technology companies increased their R&D and capital spending by 5 percent in the four years ended in 1990, to 19.2 percent of revenues from 14.5 percent, nearly matching the level of U.S. companies. Furthermore, ESPRIT has allowed participants to work together in the development of new European standards of technology to ensure, for example, that computer systems are able to work together.

By subsidizing the costs of R&D, facilitating the emergence of complementary technologies between firms, and promoting standardization, the ESPRIT program enhances interfirm cooperation without requiring explicit, formal, long-term contractual arrangements. A total of 1,027 projects have been started under ESPRIT's auspices: 241 with ESPRIT 1, 433 with ESPRIT 2, and 353 with ESPRIT 3 (many of which are still under execution). Fewer than 5 percent have been terminated because of poor results or trouble within the consortium.

INDUSTRY CHALLENGES

Both the computer and telecommunications industries suffer from rising R&D costs, relatively short product life cycles, rapid product obsolescence, and extensive capital requirements. As product development costs soar, small and medium-sized firms especially come under considerable financial pressure to keep up with technological developments.

It is estimated that it takes nearly $1 billion to develop a new telecommunications switching system or a new generation of semiconductor. For this investment to be profitable, markets of nearly $14 billion are needed. New production lines also require considerable capital investment. In semiconductors, for example, the minimum investment for a new microelectronics production line is approaching the total value of annual output for that plant.

With rising R&D costs and shortened product life cycles, competition has intensified, and firms see little future in becoming national monopolies. Securing access to foreign markets and reducing costs and risks are essential to long-term survival in the industry.

COOPERATIVE EFFORTS IN JAPAN AND THE UNITED STATES

The success of the Ministry of International Trade and Industry (MITI) in Japan in including the private sector in public planning decisions was the inspiration for ESPRIT. In the late 1970s, a consortium of six companies, including NTT, Mitsubishi, and Matsushita, that was designed to overtake the United States in producing very large scale integrated (VLSI) circuits—high-powered memories-on-a-chip—functioned so well that the U.S. government pressured the Japanese government to stop giving the consortium money. It was too late: by the mid-1980s, Japanese companies dominated the market. Since then, the Japanese have launched other consortia. One of them consists of nine companies (including Hitachi, Toshiba, and NEC) whose mission is to develop advanced computer technologies such as artificial intelligence and parallel processing.

Activities are organized under three headings: (1) underpinning technologies: software technologies, technologies for components and subsystems (e.g., semiconductors, microsystems, and peripherals), and multimedia; (2) long-term research to ensure potential for next-generation solutions; and (3) focused research on projects such as high-performance computing and networking and integration in manufacturing.

In the United States, well over 100 R&D consortia have registered with the Justice Department to pool their resources for research into technologies ranging from artificial intelligence to those needed to overtake the Japanese lead in semiconductor manufacturing. The major consortia are MCC (Microelectronics and Computer Technology Corp.) and Sematech, which boast as members the largest U.S. companies such as AT&T, GE, IBM, Motorola, and 3M. Sematech, founded in 1988, was formed to rescue an ailing U.S. computer chip industry. Funded jointly by the U.S. government and member companies, the consortium is credited with slowing the market-share drop of U.S. chip-equipment makers, who now control 53 percent of a $10 billion world market, up from less than 40 percent five years earlier. Although in theory most consortia have no real limitations on membership, barriers may exist. Sematech, for example, refuses to accept foreign firms, worrying that if Europeans were allowed to join, there would be no way to keep out the Japanese.

The race for developing the standard for high-definition television (HDTV) in the United States created interesting alliances. The government entity involved, the Federal Communications Commission (FCC), did not finance or participate actively in the choice of the standard; it formed a private sector advisory committee to pick the technically best system in an open contest. One team formed for this contest included the U.S. subsidiaries of France's Thomson and Holland's Philips (backed by the EU to develop Europe's standard) as well as NBC, one of the major U.S. broadcast networks. The other two teams included Zenith and AT&T in one and General Instrument (a maker of cable TV gear) and the Massachusetts Institute of Technology in the other one. In the spring of 1993, the FCC was encouraging all three teams to form a "grand alliance," combining all systems for a final round of testing. In late May of 1993, the three teams decided to join forces in a single approach, a move that was strongly supported by top federal officials. While many expected the agreement to hasten the introduction of HDTV (because it reduces the likelihood of protracted disputes and litigation and represents a broad technical consensus for the next generation of television sets), it has been delayed because of the reluctance of television networks to re-equip their studios and the forecast that consumers would not switch to HDTV until set prices would drop to around $500—an impossibility with today's technology.

MANAGEMENT OF COLLABORATIVE EFFORTS

Three factors have been shown to make collaborative efforts succeed: leaders who are inspired, angry, or even scared; goals that are limited and well defined; and a dependable source of revenue. Some never overcome inherent problems. As cooperative ventures, they are intrinsically anticompetitive, so they risk becoming sluggish and stifling.

The broader and more formal the collaborative effort, the greater the hazard that it will get bogged down in bureaucracy. Management by committee could be a problem if it results in a lack of responsiveness to the marketplace. Some also decry the participation of governments in these efforts, pointing to possible meddling in the choice of programs and the way they are run.

Culture clash can also threaten collaborative efforts, since the efforts are often staffed at least partly by people on the payrolls of their members. Mixing corporate cultures may result in conflict. "Consortia are the wave of the future, but they sure are hard to manage," said a former consortium chief operating officer. Furthermore, if dominant companies refuse to join in an effort, and those participating remain aloof and suspicious of each other, the effort will not succeed.

The bottom line is that entities participating in collaborative efforts have to be as attentive to executing and maintaining them as they are to initiating them. Since working with former competitors is frequently a new experience, it requires new ground rules: from domestic market to a global economic and cultural perspective, from blanket secrecy and suspicion to judicious trust and openness, and from win-lose to win-win relationships.

Questions for Discussion

1. Can collaborative efforts, such as ESPRIT, really do things no single company could—or would—undertake?

2. What additional challenges are introduced when R&D collaboration is across national borders; i.e., will ESPRIT prove to be more problematic than Sematech (which does not allow non-U.S. members)?

3. How will ESPRIT's development of pan-European standards help Europe and European companies?

4. Will small and medium-sized firms benefit more from their participation in projects such as ESPRIT than the large, multinational corporation?

P A R T   5

International Business Strategy and Operations

Now that the firm has entered and established itself in international markets, it is important to devise and implement strategies which will help provide a competitively advantageous position. Part 5 presents such strategies by focusing on important overarching dimensions such as services, logistics, and countertrade—as well as on the traditional functional areas of marketing, finance, accounting, taxation, human resources, and management.

Each one of the chapters in Part 5 is structured to differentiate between smaller firms and multinational corporations (MNCs). At the beginning of Part 5, low cost and low resource approaches are presented for firms with little international experience. Subsequent chapters assume a globally oriented perspective with a major focus on MNC. Part 5 concludes with a chapter covering the newest developments, knowledge, and speculations about international business as well as information about professional and employment options in the international business field.

CHAPTER 14

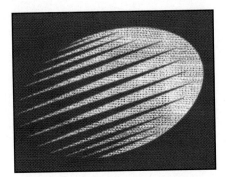

International Marketing

Learning Objectives

1. To suggest how markets for international expansion can be selected, their demand assessed, and appropriate strategies for their development devised.

2. To describe how environmental differences generate new challenges for the international marketing manager.

3. To compare and contrast the merits of standardization versus localization strategies for country markets and of regional versus global marketing efforts.

4. To discuss market-specific and global challenges within each of the marketing functions: product, price, distribution, and promotion.

Thinking Globally, Acting Locally

Automakers around the world are trying to figure out what automotive customers in 200 countries want—and to beat their competitors to the punch. However, they are faced by the most fundamental global marketing challenge in their quest: while the customer's desire for cost savings drives the automakers' idea for global automobiles, the danger is that the resulting vehicles will be too compromised to appeal to specific markets.

Ignoring local marketing input is a sure way to imperil a marketer's international aspirations. For example, Germany's Volkswagen AG operated for years with the philosophy that only one car was good enough for all of the world. VW marketing executives in the United States tried in vain to include items such as cupholders and American-style seatback release levers in cars destined for the U.S. market. VW is now rethinking this strategy, as are many of its competitors that have seen their sales and profitability slip as a result of not paying enough attention to what its customers want.

Nissan determined that it cannot afford to build, design, and market completely distinct models, such as the Infiniti Q45 and J30, just for the U.S. market. Instead, future Infiniti models will be variations of cars designed for affluent Japanese customers as well as U.S. buyers. Nissan strategists look at the marketing requirements of Japan, the United States, and Europe to determine which customer preferences overlap.

Then Nissan's export, research and development, and accounting departments decide which car model to manufacture for each market. There is still a strong economic need to manufacture similar products even when working in different markets, of course.

France's Renault has taken the middle road between developing a world car and one for a single market. More than 90 percent of the company's sales are generated in Europe. Minor alterations—such as better air conditioning in southern markets and stronger heaters in the Nordic countries—are made, but the body, engine, transmission, and chassis are identical for each model.

Ford's approach is best seen in its introduction of the Mondeo in Europe and its sister cars, the Ford Contour and Mercury Mystique, in the North American market. The Mondeo varies slightly for the different European markets; for example, for some markets a sun roof is standard, while for others an air conditioner may be included. The Mondeo's image will vary from market to market, since the economies of scale do not carry over to positioning. In Italy, where the Mondeo competes against Fiat, the Mondeo is not seen as an upmarket car. But in Germany, where the Mondeo competes with Mercedes and BMW, Ford advertises with quotations from car industry publications to make the Mondeo appear more upscale.

Source: Ray Serafin, "Auto Marketers Gas Up for World Car Drive," *Advertising Age,* January 16, 1995, I–16; "Another New Model . . ." *The Economist,* January 7, 1995, 52–53; and Alex Taylor III, "New Ideas from Europe's Automakers," *Fortune,* December 12, 1994, 159–172.

Marketing is the process of planning and executing the conception, pricing, promotion, and distribution of ideas, goods, and services to create exchanges that satisfy individual and organizational objectives.[1] The concepts of satisfaction and exchange are at the core of marketing. For an exchange to take place, two or more parties have to come together physically, through the mails, or through technology, and they must communicate and deliver things of perceived value. Customers should be perceived as information seekers who evaluate marketers' offerings in terms of their own drives and needs. When the offering is consistent with their needs, they tend to choose the product or service; if it is not, other alternatives are chosen. A key task of the marketer is to recognize the ever-changing nature of needs and wants. Marketing techniques apply not only to products but to ideas and services as well. Further, well over 50 percent of all marketing activities are business marketing—directed at other businesses, governmental entities, and various types of institutions.

The marketing manager's task is to plan and execute programs that will ensure a long-term competitive advantage for the company. This task has two integral parts: (1) the determining of specific target markets and (2) marketing management, which consists of manipulating marketing mix elements to best satisfy the needs of the individual target markets. Regardless of geographic markets, the basic tasks do not vary; they have been called the technical universals of marketing.[2]

This chapter will focus on the formulation of marketing strategy for international operations. The first section describes target market selection and how to identify pertinent characteristics of the various markets. The balance of the chapter is devoted to adjusting the elements of the marketing program to a particular market for maximum effectiveness and efficiency, while attempting to exploit global and regional similarities. The attempt to produce globally but market locally in the automobile industry is described in the opening vignette.

TARGET MARKET SELECTION

The process of target market selection involves narrowing down potential country markets to a feasible number of countries and market segments within them. Rather than try to appeal to everyone, firms best utilize their resources by (1) identifying potential markets for entry and (2) expanding selectively over time to those deemed attractive.

Identification and Screening

A four-stage process for screening and analyzing foreign markets is presented in Figure 14.1. It begins with very general criteria and ends with product-specific market analyses. The data and the methods needed for decision making change from secondary to primary as the steps are taken in sequence. Although presented here as a screening process for choosing target markets, the process is also applicable to change of entry mode or even divestment.

If markets were similar in their characteristics, the international marketer could enter any one of the potential markets. However, differences among markets exist in three dimensions: physical, psychic, and economic.[3] Physical distance is the geographic distance between home and target countries; its impact has decreased as a result of recent technological developments. Psychic, or cultural, distance refers to differences in language, tradition, and customs between two countries. Economic distance is created by differences in the economic environments of the host country and the target market. Generally, the greater the overall distance—or difference—between the two countries, the less knowledge the marketer has about the target market. The amount of information that is available varies dramatically. For example, although the marketer can easily learn about the economic environment from secondary sources, invaluable interpretive information may not be available until the firm actually operates in the market. In the early stages of the assessment, international marketers can be assisted by numerous on-line and CD-ROM-based data sources as shown in Chapter 11.

The four stages in the screening process are: preliminary screening, estimation of market potential, estimation of sales potential, and identification of segments.[4] Each stage should be given careful attention. The first stage, for example, should not merely reduce the number of alternatives to a manageable few for the sake of reduction, even though the expense of analyzing markets in depth is great. Unless care is taken, attractive alternatives may be eliminated.

Preliminary Screening   The preliminary screening process must rely chiefly on secondary data for country-specific factors as well as product- and industry-specific fac-

FIGURE 14.1
The Screening Process
in Target Market Choice

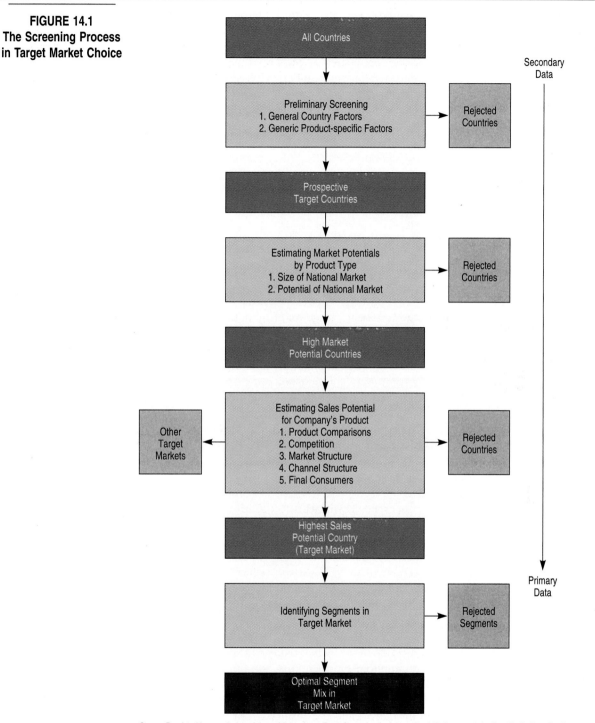

Source: Reprinted by permission of the publisher from *Entry Strategies for International Markets,* p. 56, by Franklin R. Root (Lexington, Mass.: Lexington Books, D.C. Heath & Co., Copyright 1994, D. C. Heath & Co.).

tors. Country-specific factors typically include those that would indicate the market's overall buying power; for example, population, gross national product in total and per capita, total exports and imports, and production of cement, electricity, and steel.[5] Product-specific factors narrow the analysis to the firm's specific areas of operation. A company such as Motorola, manufacturing for the automotive aftermarket, is interested in the number of passenger cars, trucks, and buses in use. The statistical analyses must be accompanied by qualitative assessments of the impact of cultural elements and the overall climate for foreign firms and products. A market that satisfies the levels set becomes a prospective target country.

Estimating Market Potential   Total market potential is the sales, in physical or monetary units, that might be available to all firms in an industry during a given period under a given level of industry marketing effort and given environmental conditions.[6] The international marketer needs to assess the size of existing markets and forecast the size of future markets.

Because of the lack of resources, and frequently the lack of data, market potentials are often estimated using analytical techniques based on secondary data.[7] The techniques focus on or utilize demand patterns, income elasticity measurements, multiple-factor indexes, estimation by analogy, and input-output analysis.

Demand pattern analysis indicates typical patterns of growth and decline in manufacturing. At early stages of growth, for example, manufacturing is concentrated in food, beverage, and textile industries, and some light industry. An awareness of trends in manufacturing will enable the marketer to estimate potential markets for input, such as raw materials or machinery. **Income elasticity of demand** describes the relationship between demand and economic progress as indicated by growth in income. The share of income spent on necessities will provide both an estimate of the market's level of development and an approximation of how much money is left for other purchases.

Multiple-factor indexes measure market potential indirectly by using proxy variables that have been shown (either through research or intuition) to correlate closely with the demand for the particular product. An index for consumer goods might involve population, disposable personal income, and retail sales in the market or area concerned. **Estimation by analogy** is used when data for a particular market do not exist. The market size for a product in country A is estimated by comparing a ratio for an available indicator (such as disposable income) for country A and country B, and using this ratio in conjunction with detailed market data available for country B. Few statistics serve as better indicators of future economic prospects or consumer demand than working-age population.

Finally, **input-output analysis** provides a method of estimating market potentials, especially in the industrial sector. Input-output tables provide a summary of the structure of an economy by showing the impact of changes in the demand for one industry's products on other industries' products. Using the tables and combining them with economic projections, the international marketer can estimate the volume demanded by the various sectors of the economy.

Despite the valuable insight generated through the techniques, caution should be used in interpreting the results. All of the quantitative techniques are based on historical data that may be obsolete or inapplicable because of differences in cultural and geographic traits of the market. Further, with today's technological developments, lags between markets are no longer at a level that would make all of the measurements valid. Moreover, the measurements look at a market as an aggregate; that

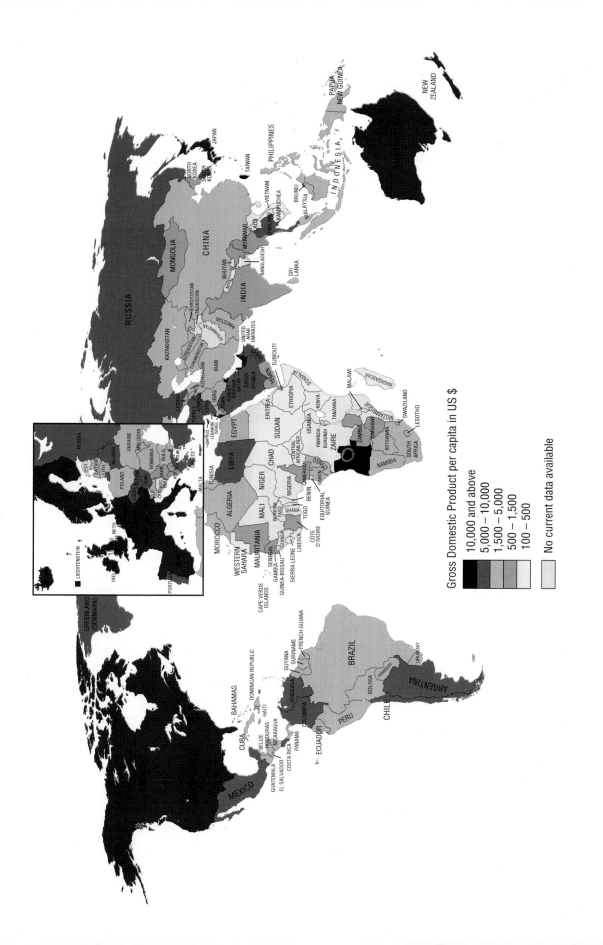

Gross Domestic Product per capita in US $

- 10,000 and above
- 5,000 – 10,000
- 1,500 – 5,000
- 500 – 1,500
- 100 – 500
- No current data available

Source: *The World Factbook 1994.*

is, no regional differences are taken into account. In industrialized countries, the richest 10 percent of the population consume 20 percent of all goods and services whereas the respective figure for the developing countries may be as high as 47 percent.[8] Therefore, even in the developing countries with low GNP figures, segments exist with buying power rivaled only in the richest developed countries.

In addition to these quantitative techniques that rely on secondary data, international marketers can use various survey techniques. They are especially useful when marketing new technologies. A survey of end-user interest and responses may provide a relatively clear picture of the possibilities in a new market.

Comparing figures for market potential with actual sales will provide the international marketer with further understanding of his or her firm's chances in the market. If the difference between potential and reality is substantial, the reasons can be evaluated using **gap analysis.** The differences can be the result of usage, distribution, or product line gaps.[9] If the firm is already in the market, part of the difference between its sales and the market potential can be explained through the competitive gap. Usage gaps indicate that not all potential users are using the product or that those using it are not using as much as they could, which suggests mainly a promotional task. Distribution gaps indicate coverage problems, which may be vertical (not enough regions) or horizontal (if the product is not marketed as well as it could be). Product line gaps typically suggest latent demand. An emerging trend in which Japanese consumers want to acquire an American look will help drive sales for companies like Ralph Lauren, L. L. Bean, and Northeastern Log Homes.

Estimating Sales Potential   Even when the international marketer has gained an understanding of markets with the greatest overall promise, the firm's own possibilities in those markets are still not known. Sales potential is the share of the market potential that the firm can reasonably expect to get over the longer term. To arrive at an estimate, the marketer needs to collect product- and market-specific data. The data will have to do with:

1. Competition—strength, likely reaction to entry.
2. Market—strength of barriers.
3. Consumers—ability and willingness to buy.
4. Product—degree of relative advantage, compatibility, complexity, trialability, and communicability.
5. Channel structure—access to retail level.

The marketer's questions can never be fully answered until the firm has made a commitment to enter the market and is operational. The mode of entry has special significance in determining the firm's sales potential.[10]

Identifying Segments   Within the markets selected, individuals and organizations will vary in their wants, resources, geographical locations, buying attitudes, and buying practices. Initially, the firm may cater to one or only a few segments and later expand to others, especially if the product is innovative. Segmentation is indicated when segments are indeed different enough to warrant individualized attention, are large enough for profit potential, and can be reached through the methods that the international marketer wants to use.

Once the process is complete for a market or group of markets, the international marketer may begin again for another one. When growth potential is no longer in market development, the firm may opt for market penetration.

Concentration versus Diversification

Choosing a market expansion policy involves the allocation of effort among various markets. The major alternatives are **concentration** on a small number of markets or **diversification,** which is characterized by growth in a relatively large number of markets in the early stages of international market expansion.[11]

Expansion Alternatives   Either concentration or diversification is applicable to market segments or to total markets, depending on the resource commitment the international marketer is willing and able to make. One option is a dual-concentration strategy, in which efforts are focused on a few segments in a limited number of countries. Another is a dual-diversification strategy, in which entry is to most segments in most available markets. The first is a likely strategy for small firms or firms that market specialized products to clearly definable markets, for example, ocean-capable sailing boats. The second is typical for large consumer-oriented companies that have sufficient resources for broad coverage. Market concentration/segment diversification opts for a limited number of markets but for wide coverage within them, putting emphasis on company acceptance. Market diversification/segment concentration usually involves the identification of a segment, possibly worldwide, to which the company can market without major changes in its marketing mix.

Factors Affecting Expansion Strategy   Expansion strategy is determined by the factors relating to market, mix, and company that are listed in Table 14.1. In most cases, the factors are interrelated.

Market-Related Factors   These factors are the ones that were influential in determining the attractiveness of the market in the first place. In the choice of expansion strategy, demand for the firm's products is a critical factor. With high and stable growth rates in certain markets, the firm will most likely opt for a concentration strategy. If the demand is strong worldwide, diversification may be attractive.

A forecast of the sales response function can be used to predict sales at various levels of marketing expenditure. Two general response functions exist: concave and S curve. When the function is concave, sales will increase at a decreasing rate because of competition and a lowering adoption rate. The function might involve a unique, innovative product or marketing program. An S-curve function assumes that viable market share can be achieved only through sizable marketing efforts. This is typical for new entrants to well-established markets.

TABLE 14.1 **Factors Affecting the Choice between Concentration and Diversification Strategies**		

Factor	Diversification	Concentration
Market growth rate	Low	High
Sales stability	Low	High
Sales response function	Concave	S curve
Competitive lead time	Short	Long
Spillover effects	High	Low
Need for product adaptation	Low	High
Need for communication adaption	Low	High
Economics of scale in distribution	Low	High
Extent of constraints	Low	High
Program control requirements	Low	High

Source: Igal Ayal and Jehiel Zif, "Marketing Expansion Strategies in Multinational Marketing," *Journal of Marketing* 43 (Spring 1979): 89.

The uniqueness of the firm's offering with respect to competition is also a factor in the expansion strategy. If lead time over competition is considerable, the decision to diversify may not seem urgent. Complacency can be a mistake in today's competitive environment; competitors can rush new products into the market in a matter of days.

In many product categories marketers will be, knowingly or unknowingly, affected by spillover effects. Consider, for example, the impact that satellite channels have had on advertising in Europe, where ads for a product now reach most of the European market. Where geographic (and psychic) distances are short, spillover is likely, and marketers are most likely to diversify.

Government constraints—or the threat of them—can be a powerful motivator in a firm's expansion. While government barriers may naturally prevent new-market entry, marketers may seek access through new entry modes, adjusting marketing programs, or getting into a market before entry barriers are erected.

Global Perspective

14.1
Born Global

Exports account for 95 percent of Cochlear's sales, which were $40 million after a real annual compounded rate of 25 percent throughout the 1990s. Cochlear is a company specializing in the production of implants for the profoundly deaf. Based in Australia, it maintains a global technological lead through its strong links with hospitals and research units and through its collaborative research with a network of institutions around the world.

Cochlear is a prime example of the small to medium-sized firms that are remaking the global corporation of the 1990s. Sheer size is no longer a buffer against competition in markets where customers are demanding specialized and customized products. With the advent of electronic process technology, these marketers are able to compete on price and quality—often with greater flexibility. By taking advantage of today's more open trading regions, they can serve the world from a handful of manufacturing bases, sparing them from the necessity of building a plant in every country. Developments in information technology have enabled them both to gain access to data throughout most of the world and to run inexpensive and responsive sales and service operations across languages and time zones.

Their smaller bureaucracies allow them to move swiftly in seizing new markets and developing new products, typically in focused markets. In many cases, the new markets have been developed by the companies themselves. For example, Symbol Technologies Inc., of Bohemia, New York, invented hand-held laser scanners and now dominates the field. Cisco Systems Inc. of Menlo Park, California, claims 50 percent of the world market for gear that connects networks of computers, a field that did not even exist in 1988. The key, according to Perkin-Elmer Corp. CEO Riccardo Pigliucci, is to "Do what you know how to do. Do it right. And do it everywhere." That philosophy helps companies grow without diversifying too far afield, which could make them vulnerable to multinational marketers.

The lessons from these new-generation global players are (1) keep focused and concentrate on being first or second in a technology niche; (2) stay lean by having small headquarters to save on costs and to accelerate decision making; (3) take ideas and technologies to and from wherever they can be found; (4) encourage employees to globalize their thinking, regardless of nationality; and (5) solve customers' problems by involving them rather than pushing standardized solutions on them.

Sources: Julian Weiss, "The Global Office: When the Traveling Trader Stays Home," *Export Today* 10 (October/November 1994): 48–50; Michael W. Rennie, "Born Global," *The McKinsey Quarterly,* (Number 4, 1993): 45–52; and "Mininationals Are Making Maximum Impact," *Business Week,* September 6, 1993, 66–69.

Mix-Related Factors   These factors relate to the degree to which marketing mix elements—primarily product, promotion, and distribution—can be standardized. The more that standardization is possible, the more diversification is indicated. Overall savings through economies of scale can then be utilized in marketing efforts.

Depending on the product, each market will have its own challenges. Whether constraints are apparent (such as tariffs) or hidden (such as tests or standards), they will complicate all of the other factors. Nevertheless, regional integration has allowed many marketers to diversify their efforts.

Company-Related Factors   These include the objectives set by the company for its international operations and the policies it adopts in those markets. As an example, the firm may require—either by stated policy or because of its products—extensive interaction with intermediaries and clients. When this is the case, the firm's efforts will likely be concentrated because of resource constraints.

The opportunity to take advantage of diversification is available for all types of companies, not only the large ones. The identification of unique worldwide segments for which a customized marketing mix is provided has proven to be successful for many small and medium-sized companies and is highlighted in Global Perspective 14.1.

MARKETING MANAGEMENT

After target markets are selected, the next step is the determination of marketing efforts at appropriate levels. A key question in international marketing concerns the extent to which the elements of the marketing mix—product, price, place, and distribution—should be standardized. The marketer also faces the specific challenges of adjusting each of the mix elements in the international marketplace.

Standardization versus Adaptation

The international marketer must first decide what modifications in the mix policy are needed or warranted. Three basic alternatives in approaching international markets are available:

1. Make no special provisions for the international marketplace but, rather, identify potential target markets and then choose products that can easily be marketed with little or no modification.
2. Adapt to local conditions in each and every target market (the multidomestic approach).
3. Incorporate differences into a regional or global strategy that will allow for local differences in implementation (globalization approach).

In today's environment, standardization usually means cross-national strategies rather than a policy of viewing foreign markets as secondary and therefore not important enough to have products adapted for them. Ideally, the international marketer should think globally and act locally,[12] focusing on neither extreme: full standardization or full localization. Global thinking requires flexibility in exploiting good ideas and products on a worldwide basis.

The question of whether to standardize or to tailor marketing programs in each country has continued to trouble practitioners and academics alike and has produced many and varied opinions. In the 1960s, Robert Buzzell stated that it depends on the strengths of the barriers to standardization, such as national differences in consumer preferences and legal restrictions, and on the potential payoffs of standardizing

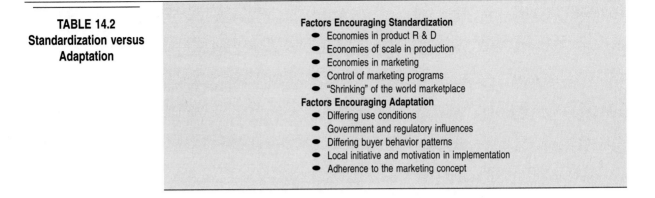

TABLE 14.2
Standardization versus Adaptation

Factors Encouraging Standardization
- Economies in product R & D
- Economies of scale in production
- Economies in marketing
- Control of marketing programs
- "Shrinking" of the world marketplace

Factors Encouraging Adaptation
- Differing use conditions
- Government and regulatory influences
- Differing buyer behavior patterns
- Local initiative and motivation in implementation
- Adherence to the marketing concept

marketing strategy.[13] Studies on how firms view standardization have found that arguments in favor of standardizing whenever possible fall into two categories: better marketing performance and lower marketing cost.[14] Factors that encourage standardization or adaptation are summarized in Table 14.2.

The World Customer Controversy The world customer[15] identified by Ernest Dichter more than 20 years ago has gained new meaning with Theodore Levitt's suggestion that inexpensive air travel and new technologies have led consumers the world over increasingly to think and shop alike.[16] In addition, Kenichi Ohmae has identified a new group of consumers that is emerging in a triad composed of the United States, Japan, and western Europe. Marketers can treat the triad as a single market with the same spending habits.[17] Approximately 600 million in number, the consumers have similar educational backgrounds, income levels, lifestyles, use of leisure time, and aspirations. One reason given for the similarities in their consumer demand is a level of purchasing power that is ten times greater than that of less developed countries (LDCs) or newly industrialized countries (NICs). This translates into higher diffusion rates for certain products. Another reason is that developed infrastructures—ownership of telephones and an abundance of paved roads—lead to attractive markets for other products. Products can be designed to meet similar demand conditions throughout the triad. Whirlpool, after conducting consumer research throughout Europe, entered the fast-growing microwave market with a product that offered various product features with different appeal in different countries clearly targeted at the Euroconsumer.[18]

Even companies that are famous for following the same methods worldwide that they follow domestically have made numerous changes in their marketing programs. For instance, McDonald's serves abroad the same menu of hamburgers, soft drinks, and other foods that it does in the United States, and the restaurants look the same. But in Japan, Ronald McDonald is called Donald McDonald because it is easier to pronounce. Menu adjustments include beer in Germany and wine in France. Of course, similar situations may occur in domestic markets; for example, U.S. fast-food restaurants in the South offer iced tea, but those in the Northeast do not.

Globalization Globalization is a business initiative based on the belief that the world is becoming more homogenous; further, distinctions among national markets are not only fading but, for some products, will eventually disappear. As a result, companies need to globalize their international strategy by formulating it across country markets to take advantage of underlying market, cost, environmental, and competitive factors.[19]

<table>
<tr><td rowspan="2">**TABLE 14.3**
Globalization of the
Marketing Mix by Two
Multinational
Companies—Coca-Cola
and Nestlé</td></tr>
</table>

Marketing Mix Elements	Adaptation		Standardization	
	Full	Partial	Partial	Full
Product design			N	C
Brand name			N	C
Product positioning		N		C
Packaging			C/N	
Advertising theme		N		C
Pricing		N	C	
Advertising copy	N			C
Distribution	N	C		
Sales promotion	N	C		
Customer service	N	C		

Key: C = Coca-Cola; N = Nestlé

Source: John A. Quelch and Edward J. Hoff, "Customizing Global Marketing," *Harvard Business Review,* May–June 1986 (Boston: Harvard Business School Publishing Division), 61.

About 20 percent of large U.S. corporations now consider themselves global marketers.[20] Companies such as Coca-Cola and Levi Strauss have proven that universal appeal exists. Coke's "one sight, one sound, one sell" approach is a legend among global marketers. Other companies have some "world products" and some products that are not. If cultural and competitive differences are less important than similarities, a single advertising approach can exploit the similarities to stimulate sales everywhere. This can be done at far lower cost than if campaigns were developed for each market.

Globalization differs from the multidomestic approach in three basic ways:

1. The global approach looks for similarities among markets. The multidomestic approach ignores similarities.

2. The global approach actively seeks homogeneity in products, image, marketing, and advertising message. The multidomestic approach results in unnecessary differences from market to market.

3. The global approach asks, "Is this product or process suitable for world consumption?" The multidomestic approach, relying solely on local autonomy, never asks the question.[21]

In a globalization strategy, marketing is typically the most "localized" of the business functions. Even within marketing, however, differences exist in mix elements and between companies. Elements that are strategic—such as positioning—are more easily globalized, while tactical elements—such as sales promotions—are typically determined locally. A comparison of the marketing mix elements of two multinational companies is given in Table 14.3. Notice that adaptation is present even at Coca-Cola, which is acknowledged to be one of the world's most global marketers. The key is the worldwide use of good ideas rather than absolute standardization of all facets of the marketing programs, as seen in Global Perspective 14.2.

Globalization, by definition, means the centralization of decision making. Changes in philosophy concerning local autonomy are delicate issues, and the "not invented here" syndrome may become a problem. It can be solved by utilizing various motivational policies:

1. Encourage local managers to generate ideas.

2. Ensure that local managers participate in the development of marketing strategies and programs for global brands.

3. Maintain a product portfolio that includes local as well as regional and global brands.

4. Allow local managers control over their marketing budgets so they can respond to local consumer needs and counter local competition.[22]

Finding the balance between overglobalizing and underglobalizing is indeed difficult. While the benefits of cost reduction and improved quality and competitiveness of products and programs are attractive, there are pitfalls that can leave the marketing effort catering to no one.[23] For example, Lego A/S, the Danish toy manufacturer, tried American-style consumer promotions, which had proven highly suc-

Global Perspective

14.2
It Played in Phon Phaeng . . . and Peoria, Too

Executing an advertising campaign in multiple markets requires a balance between conveying the message and allowing for local nuances. The localization of global ideas can be achieved by using a modular approach, localizing international symbols, and using international advertising agencies.

In 1989, McCann-Erickson Worldwide developed a dozen global ads, of which half were adapted for domestic TV. An estimated two billion people in nearly 100 nations saw the ads. To adapt the global ads to the U.S. market, some shots of bottles (which are more popular overseas) were replaced by shots of cans. And "Coke," the name the original formula carries in most countries, was changed to "Coke Classic."

Language differences present a challenge to global campaigns. Translation is rarely used; what copywriters in individual markets try to do is convey the common idea in the message. The worldwide theme, "Can't Beat the Feeling," was "I Feel Coke," in Japan, "Unique Sensation," in Italy, and "Feeling of Life" in Chile. In Germany, where no translation really worked, the original English-language theme was used.

Blueprint advertising, which uses the same theme throughout the world but adjusts to local variations, is a major factor in global advertising strategy. The frames displayed are from a set of 14 developed by McCann for its client. The U.S. set featured former Pittsburgh Steeler "Mean Joe" Greene, while local sports celebrities were used

elsewhere. They included soccer stars Niwat in Thailand (shown) and Diego Maradona in many Latin American markets.

Sources: Maj-Lis Tanner, "Pan-Eurooppalainen Mainonta Lisaantyy," Optio, March 26, 1992; "Coke Spins the Same Sell All Around the World," USA Today, December 29, 1988; "Global Marketing Campaigns with a Local Touch," Business International, July 4, 1988, 205–210; and Anne B. Fisher, "The Ad Biz Gloms onto 'Global,'" Fortune, November 12, 1984, 77. Photos courtesy of The Coca-Cola Company/McCann-Erickson Worldwide.

cessful in North America, unaltered in Japan. Subsequent research showed that Japanese consumers considered them wasteful, expensive, and not very appealing.

Some firms approach markets regionally, and some have bridged local and global strategies through a regionalization policy.[24] As an example, Colgate-Palmolive considered using a "one sight, one sound" approach and hiring one advertising agency for all brands. Eventually management settled on a regional approach, with one agency in Europe, another in Asia, and another for Latin America.

Factors Affecting Adaptation   Even when marketing programs are based on highly standardized ideas and strategies, they depend on three sets of variables: (1) the market(s) targeted, (2) the product and its characteristics, and (3) company characteristics, including factors such as resources and policy.[25]

Questions of adaptation have no easy answers. Marketers in many firms rely on decision-support systems to aid in program adaptation, while others consider every situation independently. All products must, of course, conform to environmental conditions over which the marketer has no control. Further, the international marketer may use adaptation to enhance its competitiveness in the marketplace.

Product Policy

Products or services form the core of the firm's international operations. Its success depends on how well products satisfy needs and wants and how well they are differentiated from those of the competition. This section focuses on product and product-line adaptation to foreign markets as well as product counterfeiting as a current problem facing international marketers.

Factors in Product Adaptation   Factors affecting product adaptation to foreign market conditions are summarized in Figure 14.2. The changes vary from minor ones,

---

FIGURE 14.2   **Factors Affecting Product Adaptation Decisions**

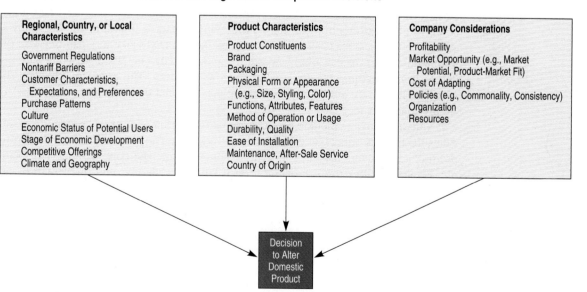

Source: V. Yorio, *Adapting Products for Export* (New York: The Conference Board, 1983), 7.

such as translation of a user's manual, to major ones, such as a more economical version of the product. Many of the factors have an impact on product selection as well as product adaptation for a given market.

A detailed examination of 174 consumer packaged goods destined for developing countries showed that, on the average, 4.1 changes per product were made in terms of brand name, packaging, measurement units, labeling, constituents, product features, and usage instructions. Only one out of ten products was transferred without modification. Some of the changes were mandatory, some discretionary.[26]

Regional, Country, or Local Characteristics   Typically, the market environment mandates the majority of product modifications. However, the most stringent requirements often result from government regulations. Some of the requirements may serve no purpose other than a political one (such as protection of domestic industry or response to political pressures). Because of the sovereignty of nations, individual firms must comply, but they can influence the situation by lobbying directly or through industry associations to have the issue raised during trade negotiations. Government regulations may be spelled out, but firms need to be ever vigilant for changes and exceptions. The 18 member countries of the European Economic Area are imposing standards in more than 10,000 product categories ranging from toys to tractor seats. While companies such as Murray Manufacturing have had to change their products to comply with the standards (in Murray's case, making its lawnmowers quieter), they will be able to produce one European product in the future. Overall, U.S. producers may be forced to improve quality of all their products because some product rules require adoption of an overall system approved by the International Standards Organization (ISO).[27]

Product decisions made by marketers of consumer products are especially affected by local behavior, tastes, attitudes, and traditions—all reflecting the marketer's need to gain the customer's approval. A knowledge of cultural and psychological differences may be the key to success. For example, Brazilians rarely eat breakfast; therefore, Dunkin' Donuts markets doughnuts as snacks, as dessert, and for parties. To further appeal to Brazilians, doughnuts are made with local fruit fillings such as papaya and guava.

Often no concrete product changes are needed, only a change in the product's **positioning.** Positioning is the perception by consumers of the firm's brand in relation to competitor's brands; that is, the mental image a brand, or the company as a whole, evokes. Coca-Cola took a risk in marketing Diet Coke in Japan because the population is not overweight by Western standards. Further, Japanese women do not like to drink anything clearly labeled as a diet product. The company changed the name to Coke Light and subtly shifted the promotional theme from "weight loss" to "figure maintenance."

Nontariff barriers include product standards, testing or approval procedures, subsidies for local products, and bureaucratic red tape. The nontariff barriers affecting product adjustments usually concern elements outside the core product. For example, France requires the use of the French language "in any offer, presentation, advertisement, written or spoken, instructions for use, specification or guarantee terms for goods or services, as well as for invoices and receipts." Because nontariff barriers are usually in place to keep foreign products out or to protect domestic producers, getting around them may be the single toughest problem for the international marketer.

The monitoring of competitors' product features, as well as determining what has to be done to meet and beat them, is critical to product-adaptation decisions.

Competitive offerings may provide a baseline against which resources can be measured—for example, they may help to determine what it takes to reach a critical market share in a given competitive situation. American Hospital Supply, a Chicago-based producer of medical equipment, adjusts its product in a preemptive way by making products that are hard to duplicate. As a result, the firm increased sales and earnings in Japan about 40 percent a year over a 10-year period.

Product decisions are affected by cultural variables discussed in Chapter 9. Reflecting the social, political, and religious heritage of the country, culture often presents the most difficult variable for any company to change. For example, Chinese and Western consumers share similar standards when it comes to evaluating brand names. Both appreciate a brand name that is catchy, memorable, distinct, and says something indicative of the product. But, because of cultural and linguistic factors, Chinese consumers expect more in terms of how the names are spelled, written, and styled, and whether they are considered lucky. In 1994, PepsiCo, Inc., introduced Cheetos in the Chinese market under a Chinese name, *qi duo,* roughly pronounced "chee-do," that translates as "many surprises."[28]

Management must take into account the stage of economic development of the overseas market. As a country's economy advances, buyers are in a better position to buy and to demand more sophisticated products and product versions. On the other hand, the situation in some developing markets may require **backward innovation;** that is, the market may require a drastically simplified version of the firm's product because of lack of purchasing power or of usage conditions. Economic conditions may affect packaging decisions. For example, Pillsbury packages its products in six- and eight-serving sizes for developing-country markets, while the most popular size in the North American market is two servings.[29]

The target market's physical separation from the host country and its climatic conditions will usually have an effect on the total product offering: the core product; tangible elements, mainly packaging; and the augmented features. The international marketer must consider two sometimes contradictory aspects of packaging. On the one hand, the product itself has to be protected against longer transit times and possibly longer shelf life. On the other hand, care has to be taken not to use proscribed preservatives. Initial attempts to sell Colombian guava paste in the United States were not successful because the original packaging could not withstand the longer distribution channels and the longer time required for distribution.

Product Characteristics   Product characteristics are the inherent features of the product offering, whether actual or perceived. The inherent characteristics of products, and the benefits they provide to consumers in the various markets in which they are marketed, make certain products good candidates for standardization—and others not.

The international marketer has to make sure that products do not contain ingredients that might violate legal requirements or religious or social customs. DEP Corporation, a Los Angeles manufacturer with $19 million in annual sales of hair and skin products, takes particular pains to make sure that no Japan-bound products contain formaldehyde, an ingredient commonly used in the United States, but illegal in Japan.[30] Where religion or custom determines consumption, ingredients may have to be replaced for the product to be acceptable. In Islamic countries, for example, vegetable shortening has to be substituted for animal fats.

Packaging is an area where firms generally do make modifications.[31] Due to the longer time that products spend in channels of distribution, international companies, especially those marketing food products, have used more expensive packaging materials and/or more expensive transportation modes for export shipments. Food processors have solved the problem by using airtight, reclosable containers that seal out moisture and other contaminants.

The promotional aspect of packaging relates primarily to labeling. The major adjustments concern legally required bilinguality, as in Canada (French and English), Belgium (French and Flemish), and Finland (Finnish and Swedish). Other governmental requirements include more informative labeling of products for consumer protection and education. Inadequate identification, failure to use the required languages, or inadequate or incorrect descriptions printed on the labels all may cause problems. Increasingly, environmental concerns are having an impact on packaging decisions. On the one hand, governments want to reduce the amount of packaging waste by encouraging marketers to adopt the four environmentally correct Rs: redesign, reduce, reuse, and recycle. On the other hand, many markets have sizable segments of consumers who are concerned enough about protecting the environment to change their consumption patterns, which has resulted in product modifications such as the introduction of recyclable yogurt containers from marketers such as Dany and Danone in Europe.

Brand names convey the image of the product or service. Offhand, brands may seem to be one of the most standardizable items in the product offering. However, the establishment of worldwide brands is difficult; how can a marketer of consumer products establish world brands when the firm sells 800 products in more than 200 countries and most of them under different names? This is the situation of Gillette. A typical example is Silkience hair conditioner, which is sold as Soyance in France, Sientel in Italy, and Silkience in Germany. Standardizing the name to reap promotional benefits is difficult because names have become established in each market, and the action would lead to objections from local managers. In some markets, brand name changes are required by the government. In Korea, unnecessary foreign words are barred from use; for example, Sprite has been renamed Kin.

Adjustments in product styling, color, size, and other appearance features are more common in consumer marketing than in industrial marketing. Color plays an important role in how consumers perceive a product, and marketers must be aware of what signal their product's color is sending. Color can be used for brand identification—for example, the yellow of Hertz or red of Avis. It can be used for feature reinforcement; for example, Rolls-Royce uses a dazzling silver paint that spells luxury. Colors communicate in a subtle way in developed societies, whereas they have direct meaning in more traditional societies.

The product offered in the domestic market may not be operable in the foreign market. One of the major differences faced by appliance manufacturers is electrical power systems. In some cases, variations may exist within a country, such as Brazil. Some companies have adjusted their products to operate in different systems; for example, VCR equipment can be adjusted to record and play back on different color systems.

When a product that is sold internationally requires repairs, parts, or service, the problems of obtaining, training, and holding a sophisticated engineering or repair staff are not easy to solve. If the product breaks down and the repair arrangements are not up to standard, the product image will suffer. In some cases, products abroad may not even be used for their intended purpose and thus may require not only modifications in product configuration but also in service frequency. For instance, snowplows exported from the United States are used to remove sand from driveways in Saudi Arabia.

The country of origin of a product, typically communicated by the phrase "made in (country)," has considerable influence on quality perceptions. The perception of products manufactured in certain countries is affected by a built-in positive or negative assumption about quality. One study of machine tool buyers found that the United States and Germany were rated higher than Japan, with Brazil rated below all three of them.[32] These types of findings indicate that steps must be taken by the international marketer to overcome or at least neutralize biases. The issue is especially important to developing countries, which need to increase exports, and for importers who source products from countries different from where they are sold.[33]

Company Considerations Company policy will often determine the presence and degree of adaptation. Discussions of product adaptation often end with the question, "Is it worth it?" The answer depends on the company's ability to control costs, to correctly estimate market potential and, finally, to secure profitability. The decision to adapt should be preceded by a thorough analysis of the market. Formal market research with primary data collection and/or testing is warranted. From the financial standpoint, some companies have specific return on investment levels (for example, 25 percent) to be satisfied before adaptation. Others let the requirement vary as a function of the market considered and also the time in the market—that is, profitability may be initially compromised for proper market entry.

Most companies aim for consistency in their market efforts. This means that all products must fit in terms of quality, price, and user perceptions. Consistency may be difficult to attain in, for example, the area of warranties. Warranties can be uniform only if use conditions do not vary drastically and if the company is able to deliver equally on its promise anywhere it has a presence.

Product Line Management
International marketers' product lines consist of local, regional, and global brands. In a given market, an exporter's product line, typically shorter than domestically, concentrates on the most profitable products. Product lines may vary dramatically from one market to another depending on the extent of the firm's operations. Some firms at first cater only to a particular market segment and eventually expand to cover an entire market. For example, Japanese auto manufacturers moved into the highly profitable luxury car segment after establishing a strong position in the world small-car segment.[34]

The domestic market is not the only source of new-product ideas for the international marketer, nor is it the only place where they are developed.[35] Some products may be developed elsewhere for worldwide consumption because of an advantage in skills, for example. Mazda, which is 25 percent owned by Ford, has designed and engineered cars to be produced by others in the Ford empire. Ford Motor Co. of Australia Ltd. developed a two-seater, sports-style specialty car because of its expertise in low-volume production.[36] In fact, many firms have benefited greatly from subsidiaries' local or regional product lines when demand conditions changed in the domestic market to favor new product characteristics. U.S. car manufacturers, for example, have used products from their European operations to compete in the small-sized and sports-style segments.

Sensitivity to local tastes also has to be reflected in the company's product line. In Brazil, Levi Strauss developed the Femina line of jeans exclusively for women there, who prefer ultratight jeans. However, what is learned in one market can often be adopted in another. Levi's line of chino pants and casual wear originated in the company's Argentine unit and was applied to loosely cut pants by its Japanese subsidiary. The company's U.S. operation adopted both in 1986, and the line generated $550 million in North American revenues in 1990.[37]

Product Counterfeiting   About $20 billion in domestic and export sales are estimated to be lost by U.S. companies annually because of product counterfeiting and trademark patent infringement of consumer and industrial products. Counterfeit goods are any goods bearing an unauthorized representation of a trademark, patented invention, or copyrighted work that is legally protected in the country where it is marketed.

The practice of product counterfeiting has spread to high technology and services from the traditionally counterfeited products: high-visibility, strong brand name consumer goods. In addition, a new dimension has emerged to complicate the situation. Previously, the only concern was whether a firm's product was being counterfeited; now, management has to worry about whether raw materials and components purchased for production are themselves real.[38]

Four types of action against counterfeiting are legislative action, bilateral and multilateral negotiations, joint private sector action, and measures taken by individual firms. Governments have enacted special legislation and set country-specific negotiation objectives for reciprocity and retaliatory options for intellectual property protection.

In today's environment, firms are taking more aggressive steps to protect themselves. Victimized firms not only are losing sales but also goodwill in the longer term if customers, believing they are getting the real product, unknowingly end up with a copy of inferior quality. In addition to the normal measures of registering trademarks and copyrights, firms are taking steps in product development to prevent copying of trademarked goods. For example, new authentication materials in labeling are virtually impossible to duplicate. Jointly, companies have formed organizations to lobby for legislation and to act as information clearinghouses.

Pricing Policy

Pricing is the only element in the marketing mix that is revenue generating; all of the others are costs. It should therefore be used as an active instrument of strategy in the major areas of marketing decision making. Pricing in the international environment is more complicated than in the domestic market, however, because of such factors as government influence, different currencies, and additional costs. International pricing situations can be divided into three general categories: export pricing, foreign market pricing, and intracompany, or transfer, pricing.[39]

Export Pricing   Three general price-setting strategies in international marketing are a standard worldwide price; dual pricing, which differentiates between domestic and export prices; and market-differentiated pricing.[40] The first two are cost-oriented pricing methods that are relatively simple to establish, easy to understand, and cover all of the necessary costs. **Standard worldwide pricing** is based on average unit costs of fixed, variable, and export-related costs.

In **dual pricing,** the export price is often based on marginal cost pricing, resulting in a lower export price than the domestic price. This method, based on incremental costs, considers the direct costs of producing and selling products for export as the floor beneath which prices cannot be set, while the firm considers other fixed costs (such as basic R&D) to have been recaptured by domestic operations. This may open the company to dumping charges, because determination of dumping has generally been based on average total costs, which can be considerably higher. Lower export prices are common, especially among western European companies, which have a heavier tax burden (value-added tax) on their domestically sold products than on exported products because the tax is refunded for exported products. Cost-oriented pricing creates some major problems because it (1) is based on arbitrary cost allocations, (2) does not take into consideration highly differing market conditions, and (3) is subject to differing internal conditions in the various markets, such as entry mode and stage of the product's life cycle in the respective markets.

On the other hand, **market-differentiated pricing** is based on a demand-oriented strategy and is thus more consistent with the marketing concept. This method also allows consideration of competitive forces in setting export price. The major problem is the exporter's perennial dilemma: lack of information. Therefore, in most cases, marginal costs provide a basis for competitive comparisons, on which the export price is set.

In preparing a quotation, the exporter must be careful to take into account unique export-related costs and, if possible, include them. They are in addition to the normal costs shared with the domestic side. They include:

1. The cost incurred in modifying the product for foreign markets.
2. Operational costs of the export operation. Examples are personnel, market research, additional shipping and insurance costs, communications costs with foreign customers, and overseas promotional costs.
3. Costs incurred in entering foreign markets. These include tariffs and taxes; risks associated with a buyer in a different market (mainly commercial credit risks and political risks); and dealing in other than the exporter's domestic currency—that is, foreign exchange risk.

The combined effect of both clear-cut and hidden costs results in export prices far in excess of domestic prices. This is called **price escalation.**

Export credit and terms add another dimension to the profitability of an export transaction. Before the transaction, the exporter has in all likelihood formulated a credit policy that determines the degree of risk the firm is willing to assume and the preferred selling terms. The main objective is to meet the importer's requirements without jeopardizing the firm's financial goals. The exporter will be concerned about being paid for the goods shipped and will, therefore, consider the following factors in negotiating terms of payment: (1) the amount of payment and the need for protection, (2) terms offered by competitors, (3) practices in the industry, (4) capacity for financing international transactions, and (5) relative strength of the parties involved.[41] If the exporter is well established in the market with a unique product and accompanying service, price and terms of trade can be set according to the exporter's preferences. If, on the other hand, the exporter is breaking into a new market, or if competitive pressures exist, pricing and selling terms should be used as major competitive tools.

Inexpensive imports often trigger accusations of **dumping**—that is, selling goods overseas for less than in the exporter's home market, or at a price below the cost of production, or both. Cases that have been reported include charges by Florida tomato growers that Mexican vegetables were being dumped across the border and the ruling of the Canadian Anti-Dumping Tribunal that U.S. firms were dumping radioactive diagnostic reagents in Canada.[42]

Dumping ranges from predatory to unintentional. Predatory dumping is the tactic of a foreign firm that intentionally sells at a loss in another country to increase its market share at the expense of domestic producers. This amounts to an international price war. Unintentional dumping is the result of time lags between the date of sales transactions, shipment, and arrival. Prices, including exchange rates, can change in such a way that the final sales price is below the cost of production or below the price prevailing in the exporter's home market.

In the United States, domestic producers may petition the government to impose antidumping duties on imports alleged to be dumped. The remedy is a duty equal to the dumping margin. International agreements and U.S. law provide for countervailing duties. They may be imposed on imports that are found to be subsidized by foreign governments. They are designed to offset the advantages imports would otherwise receive from the subsidy.

Foreign Market Pricing   Pricing within the individual markets in which the firm operates is determined by (1) corporate objectives, (2) costs, (3) customer behavior and market conditions, (4) market structure, and (5) environmental constraints. All of these factors vary from country to country, and pricing policies of the multinational corporation must vary as well. Despite arguments in favor of uniform pricing in multinational markets, price discrimination is an essential characteristic of the pricing policies of firms conducting business in differing markets.[43] In a study of 42 U.S.–based multinational corporations, the major problem areas they reported in making pricing decisions were meeting competition, cost, lack of competitive information, distribution and channel factors, and governmental barriers.[44]

The issue of standard worldwide pricing may be mostly a theoretical one because of the influence of a variety of factors. However, coordination of the pricing function is necessary, especially in larger, regional markets such as the European Union. Standardization efforts usually address price levels and the use of pricing as a positioning tool.

Of great importance to multinational corporations is the control and coordination of pricing to intermediaries. When discrepancies in currency exchange rates widen, **gray markets** emerge. The term refers to brand name imports that enter a country legally but outside regular, authorized distribution channels. The gray market is fueled by companies that sell goods in foreign markets at prices that are far lower than prices charged to, for example, U.S. distributors, and by one strong currency, such as the dollar or the yen. The gray market in the United States has flourished in cars, watches, and even baby powder, cameras, and chewing gum. The retail value of gray markets in the United States has been estimated at $6 billion to $10 billion. This phenomenon not only harms the company financially but also may harm its reputation, because authorized distributors often refuse to honor warranties on items bought through the gray market. Cars bought through the gray market, for example, may not pass EPA inspections and thus may cause major expense to the unsuspecting buyer.[45]

The proponents of gray marketing argue for their right to "free trade" by pointing to manufacturers who are both overproducing and overpricing in some markets. The main beneficiaries are consumers, who benefit from lower prices, and discount distributors, who now have access to the product.

Transfer Pricing Transfer, or intracompany, pricing is the pricing of sales to members of the corporate family. The overall competitive and financial position of the firm forms the basis of any pricing policy. In this, transfer pricing plays a key role. Intracorporate sales can easily change consolidated global results because they often are one of the most important ongoing decision areas in a company. Transfer prices are usually set by the firm's major financial officer—the financial vice president or comptroller—and parent company executives are uniformly unwilling to allow much participation by other departments or subsidiary executives.[46]

Four main transfer-pricing possibilities have merged over time: (1) transfer at direct cost, (2) transfer at direct cost plus additional expenses, (3) transfer at a price derived from end-market prices, and (4) transfer at an **arm's length price,** or the price that unrelated parties would have reached on the same transaction. Doing business overseas requires coping with complexities of environmental peculiarities, the effect of which can be alleviated by manipulating transfer prices. Factors that call for adjustments include taxes, import duties, inflationary tendencies, unstable governments, and other regulations.[47] For example, high transfer prices on goods shipped to a subsidiary and low ones on goods imported from it will result in minimizing the tax liability of a subsidiary operating in a country with a high income tax. Tax liability thus results not only from the absolute tax rate but also from differences in how income is computed. On the other hand, a higher transfer price may have an effect on the import duty, especially if it is assessed on an ad valorem basis. Exceeding a certain threshold may boost the duty substantially and thus have a negative impact on the subsidiary's posture.

The main concerns with transfer pricing are both internal and external to the multinational corporation. Manipulating intracorporate prices complicates internal control measures and, without proper documentation, will cause major problems. If the firm operates on a profit-center basis, some consideration must be given to the effect of transfer pricing on the subsidiary's apparent profit and its actual performance. To judge a subsidiary's profit performance as not satisfactory when it was targeted to be a net source of funds can easily create morale problems. The situation may be further complicated by cultural differences among subsidiaries, especially if the need to subsidize less-efficient members of the corporate family is not made clear. An adjustment in the control mechanism is called for to give appropriate credit to the divisions for their actual contributions. The method called for may range from dual bookkeeping to compensation in budgets and profit plans. Regardless of the method, proper organizational communication is required to avoid unnecessary conflict between subsidiaries and headquarters.

Transfer prices will by definition involve tax and regulatory jurisdiction of the countries in which the company does business. Sales and transfers of tangible properties and transfers of intangibles such as patent rights and manufacturing know-how are subject to close review and to determinations about the adequacy of compensation received. Typically, authorities try to establish or approximate an arm's length level. Quite often the multinational corporation is put in a difficult position. U.S. authorities may think the transfer price is too low, whereas the foreign entity (especially a less-developed country) may perceive it to be too high.

In the host environments, the concern of the multinational corporation is to maintain its status as a good corporate citizen. Many corporations, in drafting multinational codes of conduct, have specified that intracorporate pricing will follow the arm's length principle. Multinationals have also been found to closely abide by tax regulations governing transfer pricing.[48]

Global Perspective

14.3
Different Ways of Getting the Job Done

Changing market conditions from the Rio Grande to Tierra del Fuego are making U.S., European, and Japanese companies reassess their distribution strategies in South and Central America. Regional trade pacts and free trade are enabling companies to consider entry and to reformulate their strategies in the region. In the past, the infrastructure for effective and efficient distribution was largely missing. For example, in the past, underdeveloped and monopolistic distributor networks saw their primary job as distributing sales literature, cutting through red tape and charging invariably high fees.

Times are changing for the intermediaries, however. The agent of that change is competition. Outside competition has forced distributors to add value to what they do, either by carrying inventory, providing specialized packaging, participating in the logistics infrastructure, or otherwise serving the customers' needs. And if locals do not measure up, companies are willing to look for other solutions, such as using outside captive distribution systems or putting their people in place.

There are no standard answers as to distribution system design. In many cases, companies have found that a mix of techniques yields the best results and allows greater responsiveness to customer requests, as shown by the following three examples.

- **Motorola in Brazil**—Motorola's subsidiary combines in-house systems with an independent distributor network. It uses an in-house sales force to service large manufacturing clients and major end users of its line of imported and domestic semiconductors, portable radios, and cellular telephones. Other customers are served through four large distribution firms. Subrepresentatives are contracted by distributors to provide coverage in areas where they do not have a direct presence. The company has determined that

sales made via a distributor at this level are cheaper than direct sales. Distributors can offer fast delivery because in-house inventories are maintained.
- **ICI in Mexico**—ICI markets agrochemicals, explosives, paints, specialty chemicals, and dyes and chooses a distribution approach based on the size of sales and need for technical assistance. The company prefers to sell industrial products directly when possible due to the technical service they require. For example, the firm trains mining clients in explosives and provides on-site studies to determine appropriate blasting methods. The paint business in Mexico City is handled by in-house sales representatives that sell directly to retail stores. ICI products are oriented toward the high-quality, high-price market. Management takes pains to ensure the quality of retail service, with sales representatives monitoring outlets. Even when independents handle products, the company's sales department continuously assesses the performance of the distribution chain.
- **Eveready in Argentina**—Battery makers sell a large share of their production through small retailers. In Argentina, where kiosks are one of the most important outlets and product turnover is high, Eveready reaches thousands of kiosks by selling to some 600 independent distributors throughout the country. Distributors are attracted to the firm because of the high product turnover rate and its strong name recognition. Eveready reaches distributors through a national shipping company that carries products to remote markets.

Sources: Joseph V. Barks, "Penetrating Latin America," *International Business,* February 1994, 76–80; "Choosing the Right System: Direct Sales vs. Independents," *Business International,* January 13, 1992, 12; and "Winning Approaches to Distribution in LA," *Business International,* January 13, 1992, 12–13.

Distribution Policy

Channels of distribution provide the essential linkages that connect producers and customers. The channel decision is the longest term of the marketing mix decisions in that it cannot be readily changed. In addition, it involves relinquishing some of the control the firm has over the marketing of its products. The two factors make choosing the right channel structure a crucial decision. Properly structured and staffed, the distribution system will function more as one rather than as a collection of often quite different units.

Channel Design   The term *channel design* refers to the length and width of the channel employed. **Channel design** is determined by factors that can be summarized as the 11 Cs: customer, culture, competition, company, character, capital, cost, coverage, control, continuity, and communication. While there are no standard answers to channel design as shown in Global Perspective 14.3, the international marketer can use the 11 Cs as a checklist to determine the proper approach to reach target audiences before selecting channel members to fill the roles. The first three factors are givens in that the company must adjust its approach to the existing structures. The other eight are controllable to a certain extent by the marketer.

The demographic and psychographic characteristics of targeted *customers* will form the basis for channel-design decisions. Answers to questions such as what customers need as well as why, when, and how they buy are used to determine ways in which products should be made available to generate a competitive advantage. Anheuser-Busch's success in Japan began in 1981, for example, when Suntory, one of the country's largest liquor distillers, acquired the importing rights. One important aspect of Suntory's marketing plan was to stress distribution of Budweiser in discos, pubs, and other night spots where Japan's affluent, well-traveled youth gather. Young people in Japan are influenced by American culture and adapt more readily to new products than do older Japanese. Taking advantage of this fact, Suntory concentrated its efforts on one generation. The result was that on-premise sales led to major off-premise (retail outlet) sales as well.

Customer characteristics may cause one product to be distributed through two different types of channels. All sales of Caterpillar's earthmoving equipment are handled by independent dealers, except for sales to the U.S. government and the People's Republic of China, which are direct.

The marketer must analyze existing channel structures, or what might be called the distribution *culture* of a market. For example, the general nature of the Japanese distribution system presents one of the major reasons for the apparent failure of foreign companies to penetrate the market.[49] In most cases, the international marketer must adjust to existing structures. In Finland, for example, 92 percent of all distribution of nondurable consumer goods is through four wholesale chains. In the United Kingdom, major retail chains control markets. Without their support, no significant penetration of the market is possible.

Foreign legislation affecting distributors and agents is an essential part of the distribution culture of a market. For example, legislation may require foreign companies to be represented only by firms that are 100 percent locally owned. Some countries have prohibited the use of dealers so as to protect consumers from abuses in which intermediaries have engaged.

Channels used by *competitors* form another basis for plans. First, channels utilized by the competition may make up the only distribution system that is accepted both by the trade and by consumers. In this case, the international marketer's task is to use the structure more effectively and efficiently. An alternate strategy is to use a totally different distribution approach from the competition and hope to develop a competitive advantage in that manner. A new approach will have to be carefully analyzed and tested against the cultural, political, and legal environments in which it is to be introduced. In some cases, all feasible channels may be blocked by domestic competitors through contractual agreements or other means.

No channel of distribution can be properly selected unless it meets the requirements set by overall *company objectives* for market share and profitability. Sometimes management may simply want to use a particular channel of distribution, even though no sound business basis exists for the decision. Some management goals may have conflicting results. When investment in the restaurant business in Japan was liberalized, a number of U.S. fast-food chains rushed in to capitalize on the development. The companies attempted to establish mass sales as soon as possible by opening numerous restaurants in the busiest sections of several Japanese cities. Unfortunately, control proved to be quite difficult because of the sheer number of openings over a relatively short period of time. The individual stores changed the product as they grew, ruining the major asset—standardization—that the U.S. companies were advocating.[50]

The *character* of the product will have an impact on the design of the channel. Generally, the more specialized, expensive, bulky, or perishable the product and the more it may require after-sale service, the more likely the channel is to be relatively short. Staple items, such as soap, tend to have longer channels. The type of channel chosen has to match the overall positioning of the product in the market. Changes in overall market conditions, such as currency fluctuations, may require changes in distribution as well. An increase in the value of the dollar may cause a repositioning of the marketed product as a luxury item, necessitating an appropriate channel (such as an upscale department store) for its distribution.

The term *capital* is used to describe the financial requirements in setting up a channel system. The international marketer's financial strength will determine the type of channel and the basis on which channel relationships will be built. The stronger the marketer's finances, the more able the firm is to establish channels it either owns or controls. Intermediaries' requirements for beginning inventories, selling on a consignment basis, preferential loans, and need for training all will have an impact on the type of approach chosen by the international marketer.

Closely related to the capital dimension is *cost*—that is, the expenditure incurred in maintaining a channel once it is established. Costs will naturally vary over the life cycle of the relationship as well as over the life cycle of the products marketed. An example of the costs involved is promotional monies spent by a distributor for the marketer's product. Costs may also be incurred in protecting the company's distributors against adverse market conditions. A number of U.S. manufacturers helped their distributors maintain competitive prices through subsidies when the exchange rate for the U.S. dollar caused pricing problems.

The term *coverage* is used to describe both the number of areas in which the marketer's products are represented and the quality of that representation. Coverage, therefore, is two dimensional in that horizontal and vertical coverage need to be considered in channel design. The number of areas to be covered depends on the dispersion of demand in the market and also the time elapsed since the product's introduction to the market. A company typically enters a market with one local distributor, but, as volume expands, the distribution base often has to be adjusted.

The use of intermediaries will automatically lead to loss of some *control* over the marketing of the firm's products. The looser the relationship is between the marketer and the intermediaries, the less control can be exerted. The longer the channel, the more difficult it becomes for the marketer to have a final say over pricing, promotion, and the types of outlets in which the product will be made available.

Nurturing *continuity* rests heavily on the marketer because foreign distributors may have a more short-term view of the relationship. For example, Japanese wholesalers believe that it is important for manufacturers to follow up initial success with continuous improvement of the product. If such improvements are not forthcoming, competitors are likely to enter the market with similar, but lower priced, products and the wholesalers of the imported product will turn to the Japanese suppliers.[51]

Communication provides the exchange of information that is essential to the functioning of the channel. Proper communication will perform important roles for the international marketer. It will help convey the marketer's goals to the distributors, help solve conflict situations, and aid in the overall marketing of the product. Communication is a two-way process that does not permit the marketer to dictate to intermediaries. Sometimes the planned program may not work because of a lack of communication. Prices may not be competitive; promotional materials may be obsolete or inaccurate and not well received overall.[52]

Selection and Screening of Intermediaries   Once the basic design of the channel has been determined, the international marketer must begin a search to fill the defined roles with the best available candidates. Choices will have to be made within the framework of the company's overall philosophy on distributors versus agents, as well as whether the company will use an indirect or direct approach to foreign markets.

Firms that have successful international distribution attest to the importance of finding top representatives. The undertaking should be held in the same regard as recruiting and hiring within the company because "an ineffective foreign distributor can set you back years; it is almost better to have no distributor than a bad one in a major market."[53]

Various sources exist to assist the marketer in locating intermediary candidates. One of the easiest and most economical ways is to use the services of governmental agencies. The U.S. Department of Commerce has various services that can assist firms in identifying suitable representatives abroad; some have been designed specifically for that purpose. A number of private sources are also available to the international marketer. Trade directories, many of them published by Dun & Bradstreet, usually list foreign representatives geographically and by product classification. Telephone directories, especially the yellow page sections or editions, can provide distributor lists. Although not detailed, the listings will give addresses and an indication of the products sold. The firm can solicit the support of some of its facilitating agencies, such as banks, advertising agencies, shipping lines, and airlines. The marketer can take an even more direct approach by buying advertising space to solicit representation. The advertisements typically indicate the type of support the marketer will be able to give to its distributor.

Intermediaries can be screened on their performance and professionalism. An intermediary's performance can be evaluated on the basis of financial standing and sales as well as the likely fit it would provide in terms of its existing product lines

TABLE 14.4 Managing Relations with Overseas Distributors	High Export Performance Inhibitors ———→	Bring ———————→	Remedy Lies In
	Separate ownership	• Divided loyalties • Seller-buyer atmosphere • Unclear future intentions	Offering good incentives, helpful support schemes, discussing plans frankly, and interacting in a mutually beneficial way
	Geographic and cultural separation	• Communication blocks • Negative attitudes toward foreigners • Physical distribution strains	Making judicious use of two-way visits, establishing a well-managed communication program
	Different rules of law	• Vertical trading restrictions • Dismissal difficulties	Complying fully with the law, drafting a strong distributor agreement

Source: Philip J. Rosson, "Source Factors in Manufacture–Overseas Distributor Relationships in International Marketing," in *International Marketing Management,* ed. Erdener Kaynak (New York: Praeger, 1984), 95.

and coverage. Professionalism can be assessed through reputation and overall standing in the business community.

Managing the Channel Relationship   A channel relationship can be likened to a marriage in that it brings together two independent entities that have shared goals. For the relationship to work, each party has to be open about its expectations and openly communicate changes perceived in the other's behavior that might be contrary to the agreement. An excellent framework for managing channel relationships is provided in Table 14.4.

The complicating factors that separate the two parties fall into three categories: ownership, geographic and cultural distance, and different rules of law. Rather than lament heir existence, both parties must take strong action to remedy them. Often the first major step is for both parties to acknowledge that differences exist.

Promotional Policy

The international marketer must choose a proper combination of the various promotional tools—advertising, personal selling, sales promotion, and publicity—to create images among the intended target audience. The choice will depend on the target audience, company objectives, the product or service marketed, the resources available for the endeavor, and the availability of the tool in a particular market.

Advertising   The key decision-making areas in advertising are (1) media strategy, (2) the promotional message, and (3) the organization of the promotional program.

Media strategy is applied to the selection of media vehicles and the development of a media schedule. In some cases, the international marketer may find that the choice is limited by regulations that vary dramatically. Even within the EU there is no uniform legal standard. For example, the J. Walter Thompson advertising agency has estimated that advertising expenditures on western European television would be $2.4 to $3.3 billion more if regulations were completely eased.[54] Some of the regulations include limits on the amount of time available for advertisements; in Italy, for example, the state channels allow a maximum of 12 percent advertising per hour and 4 percent over a week, and commercial stations allow 18 percent per hour and 15 percent per week. Furthermore, the leading Italian stations do not guarantee audience delivery when spots are bought. Strict separation between programs and commercials is almost a universal requirement, preventing U.S.-style sponsored programs. Restrictions on items such as comparative claims and gender stereotypes are prevalent; for example, Germany prohibits the use of superlatives such as "best."

Consumer protection dominated the regulatory scene of the 1980s and is expected to continue in the 1990s.[55] Tobacco products and alcoholic beverages are the most heavily regulated products in terms of promotion; however, the manufacturers of these products have not abandoned their promotional efforts. Philip Morris engages in corporate image advertising via its cowboy spokesperson. John Player sponsors sports events, especially Formula-One car racing. What is and is not allowable is very much a reflection of the country imposing the rules.

Some media vehicles have been developed that have target audiences on at least three continents and for which the media buying takes place through a centralized office. Global media have traditionally been publications that, in addition to the worldwide edition, have provided advertisers the option of using regional editions. For example, *Time* provides 133 editions, enabling advertising to reach a particular country, continent, or the world. Other global publications include *The International Herald Tribune, The Wall Street Journal,* and *National Geographic.*

In broadcast media, panregional radio stations have been joined in Europe by television as a result of satellite technology. By the end of the 1990s, approximately half of the households in Europe will have access to additional television broadcasts either through cable or direct satellite, and television will no longer be restricted by national boundaries. As a result, marketers need to make sure that advertising works not only within markets but across countries as well.[56]

Developing the **promotional message** is referred to as creative strategy. The marketer must determine what the consumer is really buying—that is, the consumer's motivations. They will vary, depending on:

1. The diffusion of the product into the market. For example, to penetrate Third World markets with business computers is difficult when potential customers may not be able to type.
2. The criteria on which the consumer will evaluate the product. For example, in traditional societies, the time-saving qualities of a product may not be the best ones to feature, as Campbell Soup learned in Italy and in Brazil, where housewives felt inadequate as homemakers if they did not make soups from scratch.
3. The product's positioning. For example, Parker Pen's upscale image around the world may not be profitable enough in a market that is more or less a commodity business. The solution is to create an image for a commodity product and make the public pay for it—for example, the positioning of Perrier in the United States as a premium mineral water.

The ideal situation in developing message strategy is to have a world brand—a product that is manufactured, packaged, and positioned the same around the world. However, a number of factors will force companies to abandon identical campaigns in favor of recognizable campaigns. The factors are culture, of which language is the main manifestation, economic development, and life-styles. Consider, for example, the campaign for Compaq Computer presented in Figure 14.3. While the ads share

FIGURE 14.3
A Campaign Adapted to
Local Conditions

Source: Lloyd Dobyns; "Selling to the World," *Trade & Culture,* no. 2 (1993), 37.

common graphic elements (photo on left and bold-lettered text on the right), each European subsidiary enjoys freedom of creativity. For example, the ad with a man biting a carrot appears in German but ran in Northern Europe as well, with appropriate translations. The approach was chosen because it marks Compaq as environmentally friendly. In Italy, where environmental issues are not nearly as important, more dramatic poses with other messages—such as the one stressing compatibility—are popular.[57]

Many multinational corporations are staffed and equipped to perform the full range of promotional activities. In most cases, however, they rely on the outside expertise of advertising agencies and other promotions-related companies such as media-buying companies and specialty marketing firms. According to a Grey Advertising survey of 50 multinational marketers, 76 percent believe the ideal situation is to use the same agency worldwide, with some local deviation as necessary. The same percentage believes an ad agency should be centrally run, and 72 percent believe in using the same advertising strategy worldwide.[58] Local agencies will survive, however, because of governmental regulations. In Peru, for example, a law mandates that any commercial aired on Peruvian television must be 100 percent nationally produced. Local agencies tend to forge ties with foreign ad agencies for better coverage and customer service and thus become part of the general globalization effort.

Personal Selling   Although advertising is often equated with the promotional effort, in many cases promotional efforts consist of personal selling. In the early stages of internationalization, exporters rely heavily on personal contact. The marketing of industrial goods, especially of high-priced items, requires strong personal selling efforts. In some cases, personal selling may be truly international; for example, Boeing or Northrop salespeople engage in sales efforts around the world. However, in most cases, personal selling takes place at the local level. The best interests of any company in the industrial area lie in establishing a solid base of dealerships staffed by local people. Personal selling efforts can be developed in the same fashion as advertising. For the multinational company, the primary goal again is the enhancement and standardization of personal selling efforts, especially if the product offering is standardized.

As an example, Eastman Kodak has developed a line-of-business approach to allow for standardized strategy throughout a region.[59] In Europe, one person is placed in charge of the entire copier-duplicator program in each country. That person is responsible for all sales and service teams within the country. Typically, each customer is served by three representatives, each with a different responsibility. Sales representatives maintain ultimate responsibility for the account; they conduct demonstrations, analyze customer requirements, determine the right type of equipment for each installation, and obtain orders. Service representatives install and maintain the equipment and retrofit new-product improvements to existing equipment. Customer service representatives are the liaison between sales and service. They provide operator training on a continuing basis and handle routine questions and complaints. Each team is positioned to respond to any European customer within four hours.

Sales Promotion   Sales promotion has been used as the catchall term for promotion that is not advertising, personal selling, or publicity. Sales promotion directed at consumers involves such activities as couponing, sampling, premiums, consumer education and demonstration activities, cents-off packages, point-of-purchase materials, and direct mail. The success in Latin America of Tang, General Foods's–presweetened powder juice substitute, is for the most part traceable to successful sales promotion efforts. One promotion involved trading Tang pouches for free popsicles from Kibon (General Foods's Brazilian subsidiary). Kibon also placed coupons for free groceries in Tang pouches. In Puerto Rico, General Foods ran Tang sweepstakes. In Argentina, in-store sampling featured Tang poured from Tang pitchers by girls in orange Tang dresses. Decorative Tang pitchers were a hit throughout Latin America.

For sales promotion to work, the campaigns planned by manufacturers or their agencies have to gain the support of the local retailer population. As an example, retailers must redeem coupons presented by consumers and forward them to the manufacturer or to the company handling the promotion. A. C. Nielsen tried to introduce cents-off coupons in Chile and ran into trouble with the nation's supermarket union, which notified its members that it opposed the project and recommended that coupons not be accepted. The main complaint was that an intermediary, such

Global Perspective

14.4
Expanding the Social Vision: Global Community Relations

At a time when many companies are making more money overseas than in their home countries, executives are realizing that they should devote substantial attention to community relations. The attention should not be developed only as a reaction to a crisis, nor should it be a fuzzy, piecemeal effort; corporations should have a social vision and a planned, long-term social policy.

IBM's policy of good corporate citizenship means accepting responsibility as a participant in community and national affairs and striving to be among the most admired companies in its host countries. In 1989, IBM introduced Worldwide Initiatives in Volunteerism, a $1-million-plus program to fund projects worldwide and promote employee volunteerism. In Thailand, for example, IBM provides equipment and personnel to universities and donates money to the nation's wildlife fund and environmental protection agency. In 1986, the firm became one of only two companies with a U.S.–based parent to win the Garuda Award, which recognizes significant contributions to Thailand's social and economic development. As part of its long-term strategy for growth in Latin America, IBM is investing millions of dollars in an initiative that brings the latest technology to local schools. IBM does not donate the computers (those are bought by governments, institutions, and other private firms), but it does provide the needed teacher training and technological support. By 1993, some 800,000 children and 10,000 teachers in 10 countries had benefited from the program. IBM Latin America's technology-in-education initiative is a creative combination of marketing, social responsibility, and long-term relationship building that

fits in with the company's goal of becoming a "national asset" in Latin American countries.

Increased privatization and government cutbacks in social services in many countries offer numerous opportunities for companies to make substantive contributions to solving various global, regional, and local problems. Conservative governments in Europe are welcoming private sector programs to provide job training for inner city youth, to meet the needs of immigrants, and to solve massive pollution problems. And, in eastern and central Europe, where the lines between the private and public sectors just now are being drawn, corporations have a unique opportunity to take a leadership role in shaping new societies.

Corporate support can also be of assistance after natural disasters. Following the deadly earthquake in Kobe, Japan, numerous multinationals launched programs to help the victims. Northwest Airlines drummed up support during Superbowl XIX by purchasing four spots asking for donations. The carrier also delivered donations, such as clothing (Lands' End), batteries (Duracell), bandages (J&J), and even prefabricated houses (Sprung Instant Structures).

James Parkel, director of IBM's Office of Corporate Support Programs, summarizes the new expectations in the following way: "Employees don't want to work for companies that have no social conscience, customers don't want to do business with companies that pollute the environment or are notorious for shoddy products and practices, and communities don't welcome companies that aren't good corporate citizens. Many shareholder issues are socially driven."

Sources: "Multinationals Pouring Earthquake Aid into Japan," *Advertising Age,* January 30, 1995, 34; "IBM Promotes Education," *Business Latin America,* May 24, 1993, 6–7; "Corporate Generosity Is Greatly Appreciated," *Business Week,* November 2, 1992, 118–120; "Achieving Success in Asia: IBM Sees 'Localization' As a Critical Element," *Business International,* November 11, 1991, 379–383; "Global Community Relations: Expanding the Social Vision," *Business International,* September 16, 1991, 313–314; and "How Corporate Activism Can Spread Your Message," *Business International,* June 10, 1991, 199.

as Nielsen, would unnecessarily raise costs and thus the prices to be charged to consumers. Also, some critics felt that coupons would limit individual negotiations, because Chileans often bargain for their purchases.

Sales promotion directed at intermediaries, also known as trade promotion, includes activities such as trade shows and exhibits, trade discounts, and cooperative advertising. For example, attendance at an appropriate trade show is one of the best ways to make contacts with government officials and decision makers, work with present intermediaries, or attract new ones.

Public Relations Public relations is the marketing communications function charged with executing programs to earn public understanding and acceptance, which means both internal and external communication. Internal communication is important, especially in multinational companies, to create an appropriate corporate culture. External campaigns can be achieved through the use of corporate symbols, corporate advertising, customer relations programs, and the generation of publicity. Some material on the firm is produced for special audiences to assist in personal selling.

A significant part of public relations activity focuses on portraying multinational corporations as good citizens of their host markets. Examples of these "social investments" are provided in Global Perspective 14.4.

Public relations activity includes anticipating and countering criticism. The criticisms range from general ones against all multinational corporations to specific complaints. They may be based on a market; for example, a company's presence in China. They may concern a product; for example, Nestlé's practices in advertising and promoting infant formula in developing countries where infant mortality is unacceptably high. They may center on the company's conduct in a given situation; for example, Union Carbide's perceived lack of response in the Bhopal disaster. If not addressed, such criticisms can lead to more significant problems, such as an internationally orchestrated boycott of products. The six-year boycott of Nestlé did not so much harm earnings as it harmed image and employee morale.

SUMMARY

The task of the international marketer is to seek new opportunities in the world marketplace and satisfy emerging needs through creative management of the firm's product, pricing, distribution, and promotional policies. By its very nature, marketing is the most sensitive of business functions to environmental effects and influences.

The analysis of target markets is the first of the international marketer's challenges. Potential and existing markets need to be evaluated and priorities established for each, ranging from rejection to a temporary holding position to entry. Decisions at the level of the overall marketing effort must be made with respect to the selected markets, and a plan for future expansion must be formulated. The closer that potential target markets are in terms of their geographical, cultural, and economic distance, the more attractive they typically are to the international marketer.

A critical decision in international marketing concerns the degree to which the overall marketing program should be standardized or localized. The ideal is to standardize as much as possible without compromising the basic task of marketing: satisfying the needs and wants of the target market. Many multinational marketers are adopting globalization strategies that involve the standardization of good ideas, while leaving the implementation to local entities.

The technical side of marketing management is universal, but environments require adaptation within all of the mix elements. The degree of adaptation will vary by market, product, or service marketed, and overall company objectives.

Key Terms and Concepts

demand pattern analysis	standard worldwide pricing
income elasticity of demand	dual pricing
multiple-factor indexes	market-differentiated pricing
estimation by analogy	price escalation
input-output analysis	dumping
gap analysis	gray markets
concentration	arm's length price
diversification	channel design
positioning	media strategy
backward innovation	promotional message

Questions for Discussion

1. Many rational reasons exist for rejecting a particular market in the early stages of screening. Such decisions are made by humans, thus some irrational reasons must exist as well. Suggest some.

2. If, indeed, the three dimensions of distance are valid, to which countries would U.S. companies initially expand? Consider the interrelationships of the distance concepts.

3. Is globalization ever a serious possibility, or is the regional approach the closest the international marketer can ever hope to get to standardization?

4. Is a "world car" a possibility?

5. What are the possible exporter reactions to extreme foreign exchange rate fluctuations?

6. Argue for and against gray marketing.

7. What courses of action are open to an international marketer who finds all attractive intermediaries already under contract to competitors?

8. You are planning a pan-European advertising campaign with a back-to-school theme for calculators. The guideline specifies illustrating the various models sold in the market along the margins of the advertisement and using a title that suggests calculators help students to do better in school and college. What type of local adjustments do you expect to make to the campaign?

Recommended Readings

Czinkota, Michael R., and Ilkka A. Ronkainen. *Global Marketing Imperative: Positioning Your Company for the New World of Business.* Lincolnwood, Ill.: NTC, 1995.

Czinkota, Michael R., and Ilkka A. Ronkainen. *International Marketing.* Ft. Worth, Texas: Dryden, 1995.

Czinkota, Michael R., and Jon Woronoff. *Unlocking Japan's Market.* Chicago: Probus Publishers, 1991.

Douglas, Susan P., and C. Samuel Craig. *International Marketing Research.* Englewood Cliffs, N.J.: Prentice-Hall, 1983.

Leo Burnett. *Worldwide Advertising and Media Fact Book.* Chicago, IL: Triumph Books, 1994.

Ohmae, Kenichi. *Triad Power: The Coming Shape of Global Competition.* New York: The Free Press, 1985.

Root, Franklin. *Entry Strategies for International Markets.* Lexington, Mass.: Lexington Books, 1990.

Smith, N. Craig, and John A. Quelch. *Ethics in Marketing.* Homewood, Ill.: Irwin, 1993.

U.S. Department of Commerce. *A Basic Guide to Exporting.* Washington, D.C.: U.S. Government Printing Office, 1989.

Walmsley, James. *The Development of International Markets.* Hingham, Mass.: Graham & Trotman, 1990.

Yip, George S. *Total Global Strategy.* Englewood Cliffs, N.J.: Prentice-Hall, 1992.

Notes

1. "AMA Board Approves New Marketing Definition," *Marketing News,* March 1, 1985, 1.
2. Robert Bartels, "Are Domestic and International Marketing Dissimilar?" *Journal of Marketing* 36 (July 1968): 56–61.
3. Reijo Luostarinen, *Internationalization of the Firm* (Helsinki, Finland: The Helsinki School of Economics, 1979), 124–133.
4. Franklin R. Root, *Entry Strategies for Foreign Markets: From Domestic to International Business* (Lexington, Mass.: Lexington Books, 1990), 15–20.
5. For one of the best summaries, see Business International, *Indicators of Market Size for 117 Countries* (New York: Business International, 1992).
6. Philip Kotler, *Marketing Management: Analysis, Planning and Control* (Englewood Cliffs, N.J.: Prentice-Hall, 1984), 234.
7. Reed Moyer, "International Market Analysis," *Journal of Marketing Research* 16 (November 1968): 353–360.
8. The World Bank, *World Development Report 1993* (New York: Oxford University Press, 1993), 296.

9. J. A. Weber, "Comparing Growth Opportunities in the International Marketplace," *Management International Review* 19 (Winter 1979): 47–54.
10. Root, *Entry Strategies for Foreign Markets,* 19.
11. Igal Ayal and Jehiel Zif, "Marketing Expansion Strategies in Multinational Marketing," *Journal of Marketing* 43 (Spring 1979): 84–94.
12. Alice Rudolph, "Standardization Not Standard for Global Marketers," *Marketing News,* September 27, 1985, 3–4.
13. Robert Buzzell, "Can You Standardize Multinational Marketing?" *Journal of Marketing* 46 (November–December 1968): 98–104.
14. Ralph Z. Sorenson and Ulrich E. Wiechmann, "How Multinationals View Marketing Standardization," *Harvard Business Review* 53 (May–June 1975): 38–56.
15. Ernest Dichter, "The World Customer," *Harvard Business Review* 40 (July–August 1962): 113–122.
16. Theodore Levitt, *The Marketing Imagination* (New York: The Free Press, 1983), 20–49.
17. Kenichi Ohmae, *Triad Power: The Coming Shape of Global Competition* (New York: The Free Press, 1985), 22–27.

18. Warren Strugatch, "Make Way for the Euroconsumer," *World Trade*, February 1993, 46-50.

19. George Yip, "Global Strategy . . . In a World of Nations," *Sloan Management Review* 31 (Fall 1989): 29-41.

20. Anne B. Fisher, "The Ad Biz Gloms onto 'Global,'" *Fortune*, November 12, 1984, 77-80.

21. Laurence Farley, "Going Global: Choices and Challenges" (paper presented at the American Management Association Conference, Chicago, Ill., June 10, 1985).

22. John A. Quelch and Edward J. Hoff, "Customizing Global Marketing," *Harvard Business Review* 64 (May-June 1986): 59-68.

23. Kamran Kashani, "Beware the Pitfalls of Global Marketing," *Harvard Business Review* 67 (September-October 1989): 91-98.

24. John Daniels, "Bridging National and Global Marketing Strategies through Regional Operations," *International Marketing Review* 4 (Autumn 1987): 29-44.

25. V. Yorio, *Adapting Products for Export* (New York: The Conference Board, 1983), 1.

26. John S. Hill and Richard R. Still, "Adapting Products to LDC Tastes," *Harvard Business Review* 62 (March-April 1984): 92-101.

27. Cyndee Miller, "U.S. Firms Lag in Meeting Global Quality Standards," *Marketing News*, February 15, 1993, 1, 6; and "Europe's Standards Blitz Has Firms Scrambling," *The Washington Post*, October 18, 1992, H1, H4.

28. "The Puff, the Magic, the Dragon," *The Washington Post*, September 2, 1994, B1, B3; and "Big Names Draw Fine Line on Logo Imagery," *South China Morning Post*, July 7, 1994, 3.

29. Hill and Still, "Adapting Products to LDC Tastes," 92-101.

30. "Going through Customs," *Inc.*, December 1984, 180-184.

31. Bruce Seifert and John Ford, "Are Exporting Firms Modifying Their Product, Pricing and Promotion Policies?" *International Marketing Review* 6 (Number 6, 1989): 53-68.

32. Phillip D. White and Edward W. Cundiff, "Assessing the Quality of Industrial Products," *Journal of Marketing* 42 (January 1978): 80-86.

33. Warren J. Bilkey and Erik Nes, "Country-of-Origin Effects on Product Evaluations," *Journal of International Business Studies* 13 (Spring-Summer 1982): 89-99.

34. "Detroit Beware: Japan Is Ready to Sell Luxury," *Business Week*, December 9, 1985, 114-118.

35. Ilkka A. Ronkainen, "Product Development in the Multinational Firm," *International Marketing Review* 1 (Winter 1983): 24-30.

36. "Can Ford Stay on Top?" *Business Week*, September 28, 1987, 78-88.

37. "For Levi's, a Flattering Fit Overseas," *Business Week*, November 5, 1990, 76-77.

38. Michael G. Harvey and Ilkka A. Ronkainen, "International Counterfeiters: Marketing Success without the Cost or Risk," *Columbia Journal of World Business* 20 (Fall 1985): 37-46.

39. Helmut Becker, "Pricing: An International Marketing Challenge," in *International Marketing Strategy*, eds. Hans Thorelli and Helmut Becker (New York: Pergamon Press, 1980), 201-215.

40. Richard D. Robinson, *Internationalization of Business: An Introduction* (Hinsdale, Ill.: Dryden, 1984), 49-54.

41. Chase Manhattan Bank, *Dynamics of Trade Finance* (New York: Chase Manhattan Bank, 1984), 10-11.

42. Steven Plaut, "Why Dumping Is Good for Us," *Fortune*, May 5, 1980, 212-222.

43. Peter Kessler, "Is Uniform Pricing Desirable in Multinational Markets?" *Akron Business and Economic Review* 2 (Winter 1971): 3-8.

44. James C. Baker and John K. Ryans, "Some Aspects of International Pricing: A Neglected Area of Management Policy," *Management Decisions* (Summer 1973): 177-182.

45. Ilkka A. Ronkainen and Linda Van de Gucht, "Making a Case for Gray Markets," *Journal of Commerce*, January 6, 1987, 13A.

46. Jeffrey Arpan, "Multinational Firm Pricing in International Markets," *Sloan Management Review* 15 (Winter 1973): 1-9.

47. James Shulman, "When the Price is Wrong—By Design," *Columbia Journal of World Business* 4 (May-June 1967): 69-76.

48. Mohammad F. Al-Eryani, Pervaiz Alam, and Syed H. Akhter, "Transfer Pricing Determinants of U.S. Multinationals," *Journal of International Business Studies* 21 (Fall 1990): 409-425.

49. Randolph Ross, "Understanding the Japanese Distribution System: An Explanatory Framework," *European Journal of Marketing* 17 (Winter 1983): 5-15.

50. Robert H. Luke, "Successful Marketing in Japan: Guidelines and Recommendations," in *Contemporary Perspectives in International Business,* eds. Harold W. Berkman and Ivan R. Vernon (Chicago, Ill.: Rand McNally, 1979), 307-315.

51. Michael R. Czinkota, "Distribution of Consumer Products in Japan," *International Marketing Review* 2 (Autumn 1985): 39-51.

52. Philip J. Rosson, "Success Factors in Manufacturer-Overseas Distributor Relationships in International Marketing," in *International Marketing Management,* ed. Erdener Kaynak (New York: Praeger, 1984), 91-107.

53. "How to Evaluate Foreign Distributors: A *BI* Checklist," *Business International,* May 10, 1985, 145-149.

54. D. Pridgen, "Satellite Television Advertising and Regulatory Conflict in Western Europe," *Journal of Advertising* 14 (Winter 1985): 23-29.

55. Jean J. Boddewyn, "Advertising Regulation in the 1980s," *Journal of Marketing* 46 (Winter 1982): 22-28.

56. John Clemens, "Television Advertising in Europe," *Columbia Journal of World Business* 22 (Fall 1987): 35-41.

57. Lloyd Dobyns, "Selling to the World," *Trade & Culture* 1 (Number 2, 1993): 32-41.

58. Dennis Chase, "Global Marketing: The New Wave," *Advertising Age,* June 25, 1984, 49, 74.

59. Joseph A. Lawton, "Kodak Penetrates the European Copier Market with Customized Marketing Strategy and Product Changes," *Marketing News,* August 3, 1984, 1, 6.

CHAPTER 15

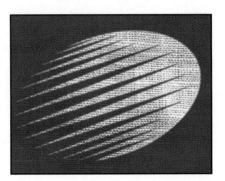

International Services

Learning Objectives

1. To examine the increasingly important role of services in international business.

2. To understand why international trade in services is more complex than international trade in goods.

3. To appreciate the heightened sensitivity required for international service success.

4. To learn that stand-alone services are becoming more important to world trade.

5. To examine the competitive advantage of firms in service sectors.

The Global Service of Plastic Money

Visa International, MasterCard International, and American Express Co. are carrying to foreign shores their fierce fight to sign up as many banks, shops, and consumers as possible. Much is at stake. Over $1 trillion was spent globally via plastic cards in 1993 and estimates call for the global card market to hit at least $2 trillion by the year 2000.

Visa holds the lead in the global card war with 323.3 million cards worldwide and more than a 50 percent share of card volume. MasterCard, with 204 million cards outstanding, is second but catching up. American Express has targeted a more limited but affluent market, with 35.4 million cards.

In such efforts to go global, the big card concerns face an array of problems. Lawyers have to pore over regulations to determine what various governments will and won't allow. Technicians seek ways to shuttle vast amounts of data over sometimes-primitive electronics and telecommunications networks, and develop equipment to detect or prevent fraud or other misuse. Marketers must figure out what makes the consumer in a given country tick. Adjusting to diverse cultural values is at the heart of every card issuer's strategy.

Seizing foreign markets is never a simple task. Americans have long been enthusiastic about charging purchases. But to many European consumers taking out a loan to pay for anything is anathema. Germans especially are reluctant to buy on credit. Italy has a sophisticated credit and banking system well suited to handling credit and debit cards, but Italians prefer to carry cash, often huge wads of it. An Italian banking official has noted, "It's as if we'd built a perfectly modern highway system, but people continued using country roads instead."

Japanese consumers are especially vexing to the card issuers. Most Japanese have a credit card but card purchases amount to less than 1 percent of all consumer transactions. "They have them, they pay the membership fees, but they never use them," said the president of a New York consulting firm. Japan has the potential to be a high growth area for any issuer. The challenge is to persuade the Japanese to use their plastic at home. Currently, most spending on credit is done when traveling abroad, to avoid carrying cash.

The real growth in plastic cards will come increasingly from newly industrialized nations, such as Taiwan. Card usage by Taiwanese consumers skyrocketed once credit and foreign exchange controls were lifted in 1990. In the following 18 months, the number of cards outstanding soared to 1.3 million from just 50,000. Visa is so widely accepted in Taiwan that one of the country's top vocalists hit the top of the charts with the song "Do You Love Me or Your Visa Card More?"

Looking to the future, the vast market in China beckons. Spending per card is higher in China than in almost any other country. This can be explained because almost all of the cards issued are solely for business use. Businesses find cards particularly appealing since China doesn't have an efficient means of transferring money or paying bills. Few consumers have cards, and the major card issuers are moving cautiously in China, at least in part because of ambiguous laws governing payment collection. Visa's CEO Carl Pascarella explained, "There's a great mass of people, but cards haven't been mass issued."

Source: Steven Lipin, Brian Coleman, and Jeremy Mark, "Pick A Card: Visa, American Express, and MasterCard Vie in Overseas Strategies," *The Wall Street Journal,* Feb. 15, 1994: A1.

International services are a major component of world trade. To reflect this situation, this chapter will highlight business dimensions that are specific to services, with particular attention given to their international aspects. A definition of services will be provided, and trade in services and in products will be differentiated. The role of services in the world economy will then be explained. The chapter will discuss the opportunities and new problems that have arisen because of increasing service trade, with particular focus on the worldwide transformations of industries as a result of profound changes in the environment and in technology. The strategic responses to the transformations by both governments and firms will be explained. Finally, the chapter will outline the initial steps that firms need to undertake to offer services internationally and will look at the future of international service trade.

DIFFERENCES BETWEEN SERVICES AND PRODUCTS

We rarely contemplate or analyze the precise role of services in our lives. Services often accompany products, but they are also, by themselves, an increasingly important part of the economy. One author has contrasted services and products by stating that "a good is an object, a device, a thing; a service is a deed, a performance, an effort."[1] The definition, although quite general, captures the essence of the difference between products and services. Services tend to be more intangible, personalized, and custom-made than products. In addition, services are the fastest growing sector in world trade. The major differences bring with them the need for a major differentiation because they add dimensions to services that are not present in products.

Linkage between Services and Products

Services may complement products; at other times, products may complement services. The offering of products that are in need of substantial technological support and maintenance may be useless if no proper assurance for service can be provided. For this reason, the initial contract of sale often includes the service dimension. This practice is frequent in aircraft sales. When an aircraft is purchased, the buyer contracts not only for the physical product—namely, the plane—but often for the training of personnel, maintenance service, and the promise of continuous technological updates. Similarly, the sale of computer hardware depends on the availability of proper servicing and software. In an international setting, the proper service support can often be crucial. Particularly for newly opening markets or for products new to market, the provision of the product alone may be insufficient. The buyer wants to be convinced that proper service backup will be provided for the product before making a commitment. In addition, communication services need to be used to inform the new market about the availability and performance of the product.

The linkage between products and services often brings a new dimension to international business efforts. A foreign buyer, for example, may want to purchase helicopters and contract for service support over a period of 10 years. If the sale involves a U.S. firm, both the product and the service sale will require an export license. Such licenses, however, are issued only for an immediate sale. Therefore, over the 10 years, the seller will have to apply for an export license each time service is to be provided. The issuance of a license is often dependent on the political climate, therefore, the buyer and the seller are haunted by uncertainty. As a result, sales may be lost to firms in countries that can unconditionally guarantee the long-term supply of product-supporting services.

Services can be just as dependent on products. For example, an airline that prides itself on providing an efficient reservation system and excellent linkups with rental cars and hotel reservations could not survive if it were not for its airplanes. As a result, many offerings in the marketplace consist of a combination of products and services. A graphic illustration of the tangible and intangible elements in the market offering of an airline is provided in Figure 15.1.

The simple knowledge that services and products interact, however, is not enough. Successful managers must recognize that different customer groups will frequently view the service–product combination differently. The type of use and the usage conditions will also affect evaluations of the market offering. For example, the intangible dimension of "on-time arrival" by airlines may be valued differently by college students than by business executives. Similarly, a 20-minute delay will be judged

FIGURE 15.1
Tangible and Intangible Offerings of Airlines

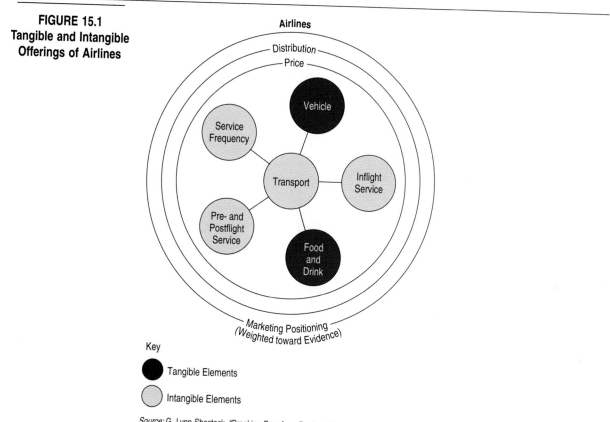

Source: G. Lynn Shostack, "Breaking Free from Product Marketing," in *Services Marketing: Text, Cases, and Readings*, ed. Christopher H. Lovelock (Englewood Cliffs, N.J.: Prentice-Hall, Inc., 1984), 40.

differently by a passenger arriving at his or her final destination than by one who has just missed an overseas connection. As a result, adjustment possibilities in both the service and the product areas emerge that can be used as a strategic tool to stimulate demand and increase profitability. As Figure 15.2 shows, service and product elements may vary substantially. The manager must identify the role of each and adjust all of them to meet the desires of the target customer group. By rating the offerings on a scale ranging from dominant tangibility to dominant intangibility, the manager can compare offerings and also generate information for subsequent market positioning strategies.

Stand-Alone Services

Services do not have to come in unison with products. They can compete against products and become an alternative offering. For example, rather than buy an in-house computer, the business executive can contract computing work to a local or foreign service firm. Similarly, the purchase of a car (a product) can be converted into the purchase of a service by leasing the car from an agency.

Services by themselves can satisfy needs and wants of customers. For example, as this chapter's opening vignette showed, financial services facilitate the purchasing activities of customers. Entertainment services such as movies or music offer

FIGURE 15.2
Scale of Elemental
Dominance

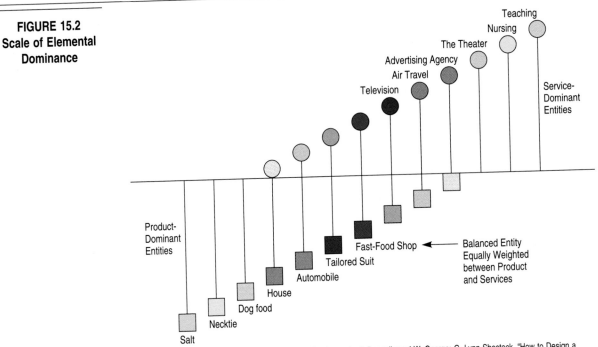

Source: Reprinted with permission from *Marketing of Services*, eds. J. Donnelly and W. George; G. Lynn Shostack, "How to Design a Service," 1981, p. 222, published by the American Marketing Association, Chicago, IL 60606.

leisure time enjoyment. Insurance services can protect people from financial ruin in case of a calamity.

Services may also compete against one another. As an example, a store may have the option of offering full service to customers or of converting to the self-service format. The store may provide only checkout services, with customers engaging in other activities such as selection, transportation, and sometimes even packaging and pricing.

Services differ from products most strongly in their **intangibility:** They are frequently consumed rather than possessed. Though the intangibility of services is a primary differentiating criterion, it is not always present. For example, publishing services ultimately result in a tangible product—namely, a book or a computer disk. Similarly, construction services eventually result in a building, a subway, or a bridge. Even in those instances, however, the intangible component that leads to the final product is of major concern to both the producer of the service and the recipient of the ultimate output, because it brings with it major considerations that are nontraditional to products.

Another major difference concerns the storing of services. Due to their nature, services are difficult to inventory. If they are not used, the "brown around the edges" syndrome tends to result in high **perishability.** Unused capacity in the form of an empty seat on an airplane, for example, becomes nonsalable quickly. Once the plane has taken off, selling an empty seat is virtually impossible—except for an in-flight upgrade from coach to first class—and the capacity cannot be stored for future use. Similarly, the difficulty of inventorying services makes it troublesome to provide service backup for peak demand. To maintain **service capacity** constantly at levels necessary to satisfy peak demand would be very expensive. The business manager must therefore attempt to smooth out demand levels in order to optimize overall use of capacity.

For the services offering, the time of production is usually very close to or even simultaneous with the time of consumption. This often means close **customer involvement** in the production of services. Customers frequently either service themselves or cooperate in the delivery of services. As a result, the service provider may need to be physically present when the service is delivered. This physical presence creates both problems and opportunities, and introduces a new constraint that is seldom present in the marketing of products. For example, close interaction with the customer requires a much greater understanding of and emphasis on the cultural dimension of each market. A good service delivered in a culturally unacceptable fashion is doomed to failure as Figure 15.3 shows. A common pattern of internationalization for service businesses is therefore to develop stand-alone business systems in each country.[2]

The close interaction with customers also points to the fact that services often are custom-made. This contradicts the desire of the firm to standardize its offering; yet at the same time, it offers the service provider an opportunity to differentiate the service. The concomitant problem is that, in order to fulfill customer expectations, **service consistency** is required. For anything offered on-line, however, consistency is difficult to maintain over the long run. Therefore, the human element in the service offering takes on a much greater role than in the product offering. Errors may enter the system, and unpredictable individual influences may affect the outcome of the service delivery. The issue of quality control affects the provider as well as the recipient of services because efforts to increase control through uniform service may sometimes be perceived by customers as the limiting of options. It may therefore have a negative market effect.[3]

Buyers have more difficulty observing and evaluating services than products. This is particularly true when the shopper tries to choose intelligently among service providers. Even when sellers of services are willing and able to provide more **market transparency,** the buyer's problem is complicated: Customers receiving the same service may use it differently. This aspect of service heterogeneity results in services that may never be the same from one delivery to another. For example, the counseling by a teacher, even if it is provided on the same day by the same person, may vary substantially depending on the student. But over time, even for the same student, the counseling may change. As a result, service offerings are not directly comparable, which makes quality measurements quite challenging. Therefore, service quality may vary for each delivery. The reputation of the service provider plays an overwhelming role in the customer's choice process.

Services often require entirely new forms of distribution. Traditional channels frequently are multitiered and long and therefore slow. They often cannot be used at all because of the perishability of services. A weather news service, for example, either reaches its audience quickly or rapidly loses value. As a result, direct delivery and short distribution channels are required for international services. When they do not exist, service providers need to be distribution innovators to reach their market.

Increasingly, many services are "footloose," in that they are not tied to any specific location. Advances in technology make it possible for firms to separate production and consumption of services. As a result, labor-intensive service performance can be moved anywhere around the world where qualified, low-cost labor is plentiful. As Global Perspective 15.1 shows, already services such as hotel reservations

**FIGURE 15.3
The Benefit of
International Service
Experience**

"The blonde on the Harley worked great in Peoria."
"Why don't we run it in Japan?"

-"International Planning Meeting," Multinational, U.S.A.

Your head office calls it global vision. Your Japanese Marketing Department, with a collective roll of the eyes, calls it multi-national madness. Your job, now that you decided to accept it, is to keep both parties happy, to create substantial growth, to plan for the future, and at the same time, to keep building brands on a solid day to day level.

Welcome to Japan!

Now the good news. An American cowboy, fine tuned for local sensitivities, sells a lot of cigarettes here. A Green Giant, refined for local tastes, drives a lot of sales. So does a Florida Orange, a French Cognac, the Union Jack on a sports shoe and an Armenian hair stylist.

The advertising agency that helped turn these diverse and perplexing international symbols into some of Japan's most valuable advertising properties is called Leo Burnett-Kyodo. Quite intentionally, we're a peculiar mix too.

Our President is American, our Chief Creative Officer is Japanese, our Director of Business Development is British. We've got a Kiwi on computers, an Aussie in print production and even a Greek Finance chief. (Mind you, that's a half page all of its own.) They along with our 20 other gaijins, are here because they bring a global perspective to the task of building brands.

But, and here's the key to our success, driving the heart of the agency are 257 of the most committed Japanese Creative Directors, Account Directors, Researchers, Copy Writers, Art Directors, Designers, Interpreters, T.V. Producers, Sales Promotion, Media and Direct Marketing experts you'll ever find under one roof.

A team which, for the last 17 years, has offered our clients that highly sought after advertising asset: the ability to utilize global strategies in arriving at uniquely potent, local advertising solutions.

We believe we've got just what it takes to turn your brand's global stature into hard, healthy Japanese sales.

For proof, call Bill Smith, our President or Mitsuhiko Sasao, our Chief Creative Officer, on 03-3584-2331. Naturally, they'll be pleased to talk to you in any language: advertising, brand management, research, distribution, media, sales promotion, etc., etc.

Leo Burnett-Kyodo. Our belief is that the only vision everyone in your organization can really share, is the sight of a growing brand.

 **LEO BURNETT-KYODO CO., LTD.
ADVERTISING**
Akasaka Twin Tower, 2-17-22, Akasaka, Minato-ku,
Tokyo 107, Japan Tel: 03-3584-2331 Fax: 03-3584-2330

Our Clients: Goodyear, Jas. Hennessy & Co., Jardine Wines & Spirits, Kirin/Tropicana, Max Factor, Meiji-McVitie, Philip Morris, Pillsbury/Green Giant, Procter & Gamble, Reebok, United Distillers

Source: Tokyo Business Today, June 1994, p. 23.

or insurance claim processing are performed with great ease far from the customer. As communication technology further improves, other services such as teaching, medical diagnosis, or bank account management can originate from any point in the world that offers the most cost-efficient service production location and reach customers in many countries.

Global Perspective

15.1
White-Collar Jobs Move Abroad

If you dial the toll-free reservation number for Jamaica's Wexford Court Hotel, you'll find yourself speaking to an agent with a Jamaican accent. Your call will have automatically become an international one, because the hotel's booking office for American guests is located on Jamaica, and calls are routed there by satellite. Previously, the work had been done by a Miami reservation center.

Tom Kelly, who heads a $70 million Eastman Kodak research laboratory, can see Mount Fuji from the lab. He works in Yokohama, where his job requires him to hire Japanese researchers to develop new technology for Kodak. According to Kelly, "If you're serious about staying competitive globally, you've got to be on the ground [in Japan]."

If the buzzword in the 1980s was the "global factory," with U.S.–owned factories operating in lower-cost nations, the more current trend is the "global office." Thanks to advances in communications technology and a more sophisticated work force in many countries, white-collar jobs are increasingly moving around the world.

Companies in many industries have taken advantage of the global office. Cigna Corporation, the huge insurer, plans to open in the Irish town of Loughrea a $5 million center for processing medical claims. A software development facility set up by Texas Instruments in Bangalore, India, is linked by satellite to TI's Dallas headquarters. Editors in Barbados prepare manuscripts for Chicago publisher R. R. Donnelley & Sons to print in the United States. And many companies, including Texas Instruments, Dow Corning, and IBM, have set up research laboratories in Japan.

In response to the exodus of blue-collar jobs to low-wage countries, many economists downplayed the importance of manufacturing to the U.S. economy's long-term vitality. The enormous growth in the service sector, they say, is more than adequate to make up the difference. However, as white-collar jobs move overseas, they seem a less dependable part of America's economic future.

Many developing countries are offering tax incentives and start-up assistance to woo service companies to their shores. In addition, workers in these countries earn only one-third the rate paid to comparable U.S. workers. With these advantages, businesses in developing countries are hopeful that they will be able to handle such operations as software development, telemarketing, and data entry.

The trend has caused some concern among U.S. labor unions. According to Dennis Chamot, who works for the AFL-CIO's department for professional employees, "As office work becomes more electronic, it becomes easier to move."

Sources: John Burgess, "Global Offices on Rise as Firms Shift Service Jobs Abroad," *The Washington Post,* April 20, 1990, E1; and Susan Moffat, "Picking Japan's Research Brains," *Fortune,* March 25, 1991, 84–86.

The unique dimensions of services exist in both international and domestic settings, but their impact has greater importance for the international manager. For example, the perishability of a service, which may be a mere obstacle in domestic business, may become a major barrier internationally because of the longer distances involved. Similarly, quality control for international services may be much more difficult because of different service uses, changing expectations, and varying national regulations.

Services are delivered directly to the user and are therefore frequently much more sensitive to cultural factors than are products. Their influence on the individual abroad may be welcomed or greeted with hostility. For example, Walt Disney, the first studio guaranteed a time slot on Polish television, began broadcasting Disney animated shows and live-action features in September 1990.[4] On the other hand, countries that place a strong emphasis on cultural identity have set barriers inhibit-

**FIGURE 15.4
Employment in
Industrial Sectors as a
Percentage of the Total
Labor Force**

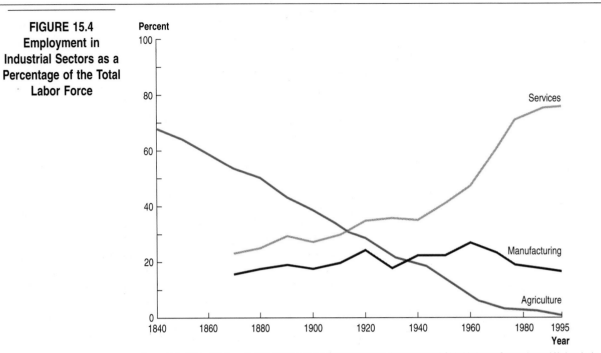

Source: J. B. Quinn, "The Impacts of Technology on the Services Sector," *Technology and Global Industry: Companies and Nations in the World Economy* (Washington, D.C.: National Academy of Sciences, 1987).

ing market penetration by foreign films. For instance, France is leading a major effort within the European Union to cap the volume of U.S.–produced films to obtain more playing time for French movies.

THE ROLE OF SERVICES IN THE GLOBAL ECONOMY

Since the last century, industrialized nations have seen themselves as primary international competitors in the production of goods. In the past few decades, however, most of these countries have developed very large service sectors. Figure 15.4 shows the changes in employment in different industrial sectors of the United States, where in 1994 the service sector produced 74 percent of GDP and employed 79 percent of the work force.[5] Between 1959 and 1990, employment in the U.S. business and personal services sector almost tripled, while employment in the goods-producing industries increased by only 22 percent.[6]

The major segments that compose the service sector are communications, transportation, public utilities, finance, insurance and real estate, wholesale and retail businesses, government, and a diverse category of other services, including business services, personal services, and professional and health services. Of course, only a limited segment of the total range of services is traded internationally. Federal, state, and local government employees, for example, sell few of their services to foreigners. Laundries and restaurants only occasionally service foreign tourists. Many service industries that do sell abroad often have at their disposal large organizations, specialized technology, or advanced professional expertise. Strength in these characteristics has enabled the United States to become the world's largest exporter of services. Total U.S. services exported grew from $6 billion in 1958 to about $190 billion in 1994, nearly doubling within only five years.[7]

Global Perspective

15.2
Indian Exports: Not Just Carpets but Software

Tata Consultancy Services, the leading software maker in India, sold in just one year 11,000 copies of a $140 accounting program for personal computers. That is remarkable because it shows that the world's second most populous nation may be beginning to build a viable domestic software market. Such a development may well put India in a position to compete in global software markets.

India's domestic software market grew by 45 percent in 1992. This growth is helping the 500 local software houses to hone their development and marketing skills at home so they can sell abroad. Software exports jumped by 67 percent, to $144 million. If the growth keeps up, it will mean that India's 2.5 million computer and software professionals can advance their careers without relocating abroad.

In 1991, the World Bank surveyed 150 prominent U.S. and European hardware and software manufacturers. The respondents ranked India's programmers first out of eight countries for both on-site and offshore software development, ahead of Ireland, Israel, Mexico, and Singapore. With average annual programmer salaries of about $3,000, quality software production in India costs much less than what it would cost in the United States.

Source: Sunita Wadekar Bhargava, "Software from India? Yes, it's for Real," *Business Week,* January 18, 1993, p. 77.

International service trade has had very beneficial results for many firms. Citibank, for example, receives 65 percent of its total revenues from non–U.S. operations; the world's top 10 advertising agencies obtain most of their gross revenue from abroad. The top 10 U.S. construction contractors derive more than 40 percent of their revenues from overseas. Table 15.1 demonstrates that many international service firms have become truly formidable in size.

Competition in international services is rising rapidly at all levels. Hong Kong, Singapore, and western Europe are increasingly active in service industries such as banking, insurance, and advertising. Years ago, U.S. construction firms could count on a virtual monopoly on large-scale construction projects. Today, firms from South Korea, Italy, and other countries are taking a major share of the international construction business. The result of these developments is that the U.S. share of international service trade is estimated to have declined in relative terms—from 25 to 20 percent of the world market—within a decade.

At the present time, services trade is taking place mainly among the industrialized countries. However, the trend appears to be changing. The economies of developing countries have traditionally first established a strong agricultural and then a manufacturing sector to meet basic needs such as food and shelter before venturing into the services sector. Some countries, such as Mexico, Singapore, Hong Kong, Bermuda, and the Bahamas, are steering away from the traditional economic development pattern and are concentrating on developing strong service sectors.[8] The reasons vary from a lack of natural resources with which to develop agricultural and/or manufacturing sectors to recognition of the strong global demand for services and the ability to provide them through a willing, skilled, and inexpensive labor force. Global Perspective 15.2 provides an example. It is anticipated that services trade will continue to grow. However, as more countries enter the sector, the international services business will become more competitive.

TABLE 15.1
The 50 Largest Diversified Service Companies

Rank by Sales 1993	Company (Major Industry)	Country	Sales ($ millions)	Profits ($ millions)	Rank	Assets ($ millions)	Rank	Stockholders' Equity ($ millions)	Rank
1	Mitsui (trading)	Japan	163,453.2	142.0	26	72,180.6	3	5,643.5	9
2	Mitsubishi (trading)	Japan	160,109.4	170.4	24	85,327.4	2	6,824.6	6
3	Sumitomo (trading)	Japan	157,551.2	67.7	45	48,922.3	7	6,885.7	5
4	Itochu (trading)	Japan	155,161.8	(130.9)	92	62,980.2	5	4,543.9	14
5	Marubeni (trading)	Japan	144,502.6	50.9	51	68,939.3	4	4,285.3	17
6	Nissho Iwai (trading)	Japan	95,462.9	99.5	34	45,879.4	8	2,356.6	34
7	American Telephone & Telegraph (telecomm.)	U.S.	67,156.0	(3,794.0)	100	60,766.0	6	13,850.0	2
8	Tomen (trading)	Japan	64,631.2	14.6	72	21,799.9	19	1,132.2	52
9	Nippon Telegraph & Telephone (telecomm.)	Japan	61,651.2	462.4	7	119,381.7	1	42,196.5	1
10	Nichimen (trading)	Japan	53,482.7	35.2	60	21,534.5	20	1,429.6	44
11	Kanematsu (trading)	Japan	52,746.7	(59.9)	87	16,460.2	23	938.3	63
12	Veba Group (trading)	Germany	37,064.5	498.9	5	31,929.2	14	8,673.2	3
13	RWE Group (energy)	Germany	28,786.4	562.1	4	34,767.5	12	4,507.7	15
14	CIE Générale Des Eaux (construction)	France	25,573.3	565.8	3	35,292.7	11	5,340.9	10
15	Shimizu (engineering, construction)	Japan	21,359.1	405.0	11	29,147.8	16	3,621.2	23
16	Taisei (construction, engineering)	Japan	21,125.9	234.8	19	31,752.4	15	3,845.2	21
17	Kajima (construction, engineering)	Japan	18,299.9	11.3	74	32,151.0	13	3,694.4	22
18	BCE (telecommunications)	Canada	16,255.6	(508.4)	97	27,693.7	17	8,240.7	4
19	Supervalu (wholesale)	U.S.	15,936.9	185.3	22	4,042.4	70	1,275.5	48
20	Toyota Tsusho (trading)	Japan	15,756.6	20.3	68	7,262.7	51	1,287.4	47
21	Takenaka (construction)	Japan	15,665.0	195.7	21	15,359.5	26	2,560.0	33
22	Obayashi (engineering, construction)	Japan	15,317.5	92.9	37	24,354.4	18	2,775.3	29
23	Franz Haniel (wholesale)	Germany	14,771.0	88.6	40	5,839.0	57	844.2	66
24	Hyundai (trading)	South Korea	13,738.7	6.8	78	387.6	100	88.3	97
25	Kawasho (trading)	Japan	13,302.5	9.6	76	7,756.2	47	456.1	81
26	Sinochem (trading)	China	13,241.0	90.3	38	42,517.0	9	N.A.	
27	Fleming (wholesale)	U.S.	13,092.1	35.2	61	3,102.6	80	1,060.4	55
28	McKesson (wholesale)	U.S.	12,428.2	136.2	27	3,192.7	79	678.6	71
29	Mitsui Fudosan (construction)	Japan	12,065.4	94.4	36	35,902.3	10	5,899.3	8
30	MCI Communications (telecomm.)	U.S.	11,921.0	582.0	2	11,276.0	34	4,713.0	13
31	SHV Holdings (trading)	Netherlands Antilles	11,897.2	178.6	23	6,495.6	55	1,536.6	40
32	Sekisui House (homebuilder)	Japan	11,756.3	366.0	13	14,029.7	30	5,900.6	7
33	Sprint (telecommunications)	U.S.	11,367.8	54.9	47	14,148.9	29	3,918.3	20
34	Neste (petroleum)	Finland	11,026.5	(265.0)	96	7,802.8	46	562.4	76
35	Dentsu (marketing)	Japan	10,990.1	22.9	67	5,724.4	59	1,475.6	43
36	Bouygues (construction, engineering)	France	10,801.3	82.8	43	10,686.6	35	1,615.8	39
37	Columbia/HCA Healthcare (health care)	U.S.	10,775.0	50.7	52	10,216.0	37	3,471.0	26
38	Sysco (wholesale)	U.S.	10,021.5	201.8	20	2,530.0	87	1,137.2	50
39	Nittetsu Shoji (trading)	Japan	10,014.0	(99.2)	91	8,308.9	43	66.6	98
40	Sumikin Bussan (trading)	Japan	9,954.4	0.6	83	5,141.3	63	127.2	95
41	George Weston (food service)	Canada	9,247.4	44.2	56	3,364.0	76	972.5	61
42	WMX Technologies (waste management)	U.S.	9,135.6	452.8	9	16,264.5	25	4,159.5	19
43	Inchcape (trading)	Britain	8,825.5	264.8	18	4,665.9	65	1,135.9	51
44	Daiwa House Industry (homebuilder)	Japan	8,741.0	371.3	12	11,437.3	33	4,160.6	18
45	Thyssen Handelsunion (trading)	Germany	8,698.2	23.8	65	3,263.2	78	350.9	86
46	Kumagai Gumi (construction)	Japan	8,612.1	(60.3)	88	18,328.9	21	3,157.8	28
47	Walt Disney (theme parks)	U.S.	8,529.2	299.8	17	11,751.1	31	5,030.5	12
48	Electronic Data Systems (computing)	U.S.	8,507.3	724.0	1	6,942.1	54	3,617.4	24
49	Jardine Matheson (trading)	Hong Kong	8,424.5	424.0	10	9,798.9	38	2,720.4	30
50	Edeka Zentrale (wholesale)	Germany	8,196.6	13.8	73	2,029.9	90	146.7	93

Source: Fortune, August 22, 1994, p. 182.

Global Perspective

15.3
Europe Speeds Phone Competition

In 1984, the British government opened the U.K. phone market to competition and privatized British Telecommunications PLC. By 1987, the EU Commission issued its first proposals advocating the end of all state monopolies on telecommunications equipment and selected services. The proposals were adopted a year later by the EU Council. By 1990, the Commission issued its Services Directive ordering the opening of EU markets for data communications and other "value-added" communications services. In 1993, the EU Council set January 1, 1998, as the deadline for all remaining state monopolies on voice-telephone services to end. But Europe's telecommunications D day is coming a lot sooner.

The politics of liberalization are changing so fast that the debate in the industry is when the market will open, not on how much it will open. Four main forces in Europe traditionally have kept markets under state monopoly: the state phone companies themselves, their unionized workers, their political masters at communications ministries, and bureaucratic inertia. The last force remains a formidable obstacle. All the other promonopoly forces, however, are weakening. Many governments, in dire need of cash, now view phone monopolies as assets to sell rather than industries to control. Share sales have taken place in Britain, the Netherlands, and Denmark; they are planned or considered likely for Germany, Italy, Greece, Portugal,

Spain, Belgium, and possibly France. In some countries, generous pension and job-security offers have placated phone company unions.

Phone company managers are moving rapidly to position themselves for liberalization. Unisource NV, a joint venture of the Dutch, Swedish, and Swiss phone companies, is joining AT&T's global WorldPartners Association of international telephone companies. The president of AT&T's European division noted, "1998 is here and now." British Telecommunications PLC has agreed to buy 20 percent of MCI and Deutsche Telekom and France Telecom have agreed jointly to buy 20 percent of Sprint. Other companies, such as Germany's Viag, aren't waiting for 1998 either. In 1995, Viag will offer phone service to big German companies over a fiber optic network in one of the first real alternatives to state run Deutsche Telekom. Viag is setting a goal for telecommunications revenue by 1998 of as much as one billion marks a year (about $620 million).

The state phone companies still have an advantage in that only they have the right to own the basic wires and switches over which most services travel. Any new competitor must, therefore, lease most of its wires—its raw materials—from a state phone company. Many are hoping the EU Commission will come out with a policy endorsing "alternative infrastructures," such as wires already laid privately by electricity companies.

Source: Richard L. Hudson, "European Companies Speed Shift to Phone Competition," *The Wall Street Journal*, June 24, 1994, p. B4.

GLOBAL TRANSFORMATIONS IN THE SERVICES SECTOR

Two major factors, environmental and technological change, account for the dramatic rise in services trade. One key environmental change has been the reduction of government regulation of service industries. In the early 1980s, many governments adopted the view that reduced government interference in the marketplace would enhance competition. As a result, new players have entered the marketplace. Some service sectors have benefited and others have suffered from this withdrawal of government intervention. Regulatory changes were initially thought to have primarily domestic effects, but they have rapidly spread internationally. For example, the 1984 **deregulation** of the U.S. telecommunication giant AT&T has given rise to competition not only in the United States. Japan's telecommunication monopoly, NT&T, was deregulated in 1985. Today, domestic and international competition in the telecommunications sector has increased dramatically as Global Perspective 15.3 shows.

Istanbul, Turkey, at the crossroads of Europe and Asia, is served by a Motorola digital cellular telephone system. Motorola has more than 30 contracts worldwide for GSM systems. (Global System for Mobile Communications).

Source: Courtesy of Motorola, Inc.

Similarly, deregulatory efforts in the transportation sector have had international repercussions. New air carriers have entered the market to compete against established trunk carriers and have done so successfully by pricing their services differently both nationally and internationally. Deregulatory efforts therefore have also affected international regulations, such as **conference pricing,** and have caused a global movement toward deregulation. Obviously, a British airline can count only to a limited extent on government support to remain competitive with new, low-priced fares offered by other carriers also serving the British market. The deregulatory movement has fostered new competition and new competitive practices. Many of these changes resulted in lower prices, stimulating demand and leading to a rise in the volume of international services trade.

Another major environmental change has been the decreased regulation of service industries by their service groups. For example, business practices in fields such as health care, law, and accounting are becoming increasingly competitive and aggressive. New economic realities require firms in these industries to search for new ways to attract market share and expand their markets. International markets are one frequently untapped possibility for market expansion and have therefore become a prime target for such firms.

Technological advancement is the second major change that has taken place. Increasingly, progress in technology is offering new ways of doing business and is permitting businesses to expand their horizons internationally. Through computerization, for instance, service exchanges that previously would have been prohibitively expensive are now feasible. As an example, Ford Motor Company uses one major computer system to carry out new car designs simultaneously in the United States and Europe. This practice not only lowers expenditures on hardware and permits better utilization of existing equipment but also allows design teams based in different countries to interact closely and produce a car that can be successful in multiple markets. Of course, this development could take place only after advances in data transmission procedures. Similarly, more rapid data transmission also has enabled financial institutions to expand their service delivery through a worldwide network.

Another result of technological advancement is that service industry expansion is not confined to those services that are labor intensive and therefore better performed in areas of the world where labor possesses a comparative advantage. Rather, technology-intensive services are becoming the sunrise industries of the next century.

PROBLEMS IN INTERNATIONAL SERVICE TRADE

Together with the increase in the importance of service trade, new problems have emerged in the service sector. Many of these problems have been characterized as affecting mainly the negotiations between nations, but they are of sufficient importance to firms engaged in international activities to merit a brief review.

Data Collection Problems

The data collected on service trade are often sketchy. Service transactions are often invisible statistically as well as physically. For example, the trip abroad of a consultant for business purposes may be hard to track and measure. The fact that governments have precise data on the number of trucks exported down to the last bolt but little information on reinsurance flows reflects past governmental inattention to services. Only recently has it been recognized that the income generated and the jobs created through the sale of services abroad are just as important as income and jobs resulting from the production and exportation of goods. In spite of increased attention paid to the issue, official government sources have stated that "we don't really know how much is being earned from service exports, but we do know that service exports are growing substantially."[9] Consequently, estimates of services trade vary widely. Total actual volume of services trade may actually be much larger than the amount shown by official statistics.

When considering the dimension of the problem of data collection on services in industrialized countries, with their sophisticated data gathering and information systems, it is easy to imagine how many more problems are encountered in countries lacking such elaborate systems and unwilling to allocate funds for them. The gathering of information is made substantially more difficult because services are intangible and more difficult to measure and to trace than products. Insufficient knowledge and information have led to a lack of transparency, making it difficult for nations either to gauge or to influence services trade. As a result, regulations are often put into place without precise information as to their repercussions on actual trade performance.

U.S. Disincentives to the Offering of International Services

Despite its commitment to free trade, the United States has erected and maintained major barriers to international services. These disincentives affect both inbound and outbound services. Barriers to services destined for the U.S. market result mainly from regulatory practices. The fields of banking, insurance, and accounting provide some examples. These industries are regulated at both federal and state levels, and the regulations often pose a formidable barrier to potential entrants from abroad.

The chief complaint of foreign countries is not that the United States discriminates against foreign service providers, but rather that the United States places more

Services as a Portion of Gross Domestic Product

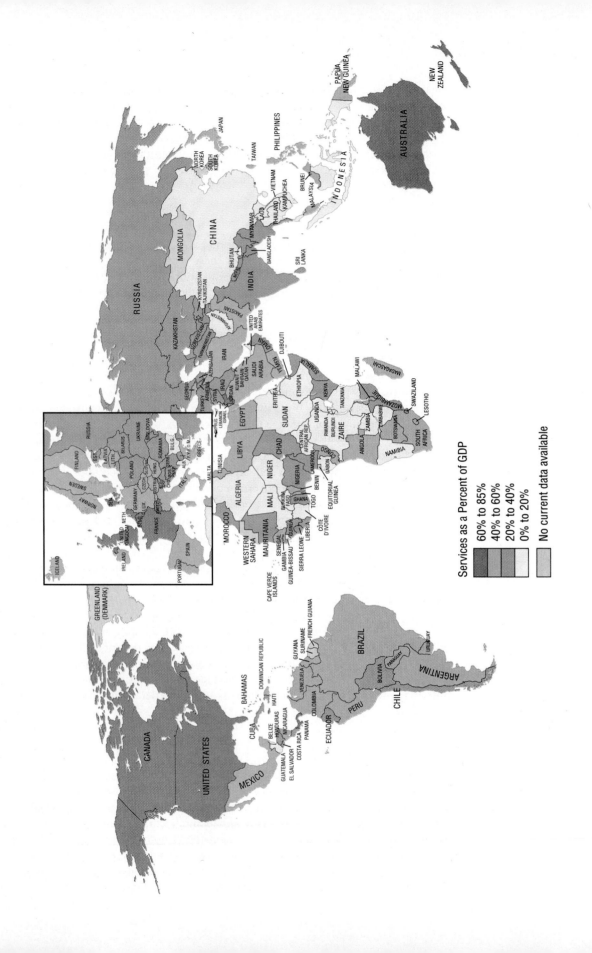

Services as a Percent of GDP

60% to 85%
40% to 60%
20% to 40%
0% to 20%

No current data available

severe restrictions on them than do foreign countries. In addition, the entire U.S. regulatory process gives little weight to international policy issues and often operates in isolation from executive branch direction.[10] The barriers are, of course, a reflection of the decision-making process within the U.S. domestic economy and are unlikely to change in the near future. A coherent approach toward international commerce in services is hardly likely to emerge from the disparate decisions of agencies such as the Interstate Commerce Commission (ICC), the Federal Communications Commission (FCC), the Securities and Exchange Commission (SEC), and the many licensing agencies at the state level.

Various domestic laws and regulations also often impede the export of U.S. services. One disincentive frequently mentioned in the past is the Foreign Corrupt Practices Act, which arguably discourages U.S. businesses and particularly service industries from competing overseas. Similarly, export-control legislation increasingly has been extended to the services sector and limits the possibility of services exports.

Global Regulations of Services

Global obstacles to service trade can be categorized into two major types: barriers to entry and problems in performing services abroad.

Barriers to entry are often justified by reference to "national security" and "economic security." For example, the impact of banking on domestic economic activity is given as a reason why banking should be carried out only by nationals or indeed should be operated entirely under government control. Sometimes the protection of service users is cited, particularly of bank depositors and insurance policyholders. Another justification for barriers is the frequently used infant-industry argument: "With sufficient time to develop on our own, we can compete in world markets." Often, however, this argument is used simply to prolong the ample licensing profits generated by restricted entry. Yet, defining a barrier to services is not always easy. For example, Taiwan gives an extensive written examination to prospective accountants (as do most countries) to ensure that licensed accountants are qualified to practice. Naturally, the examination is given in Chinese. The fact that few German accountants, for example, read and write Chinese and hence are unable to pass the examination does not necessarily constitute a barrier to trade in accountancy services.[11]

Even if barriers to entry are nonexistent or can be overcome, service companies have difficulty performing abroad effectively once they have achieved access to the local market. One reason is that rules and regulations based on tradition may inhibit innovation. A more important reason is that governments pursue social objectives through national regulations. The distinction between discriminatory and nondiscriminatory regulations is of primary importance here. Regulations that impose larger operating costs on foreign service providers than on the local competitors, that provide subsidies to local firms only, or that deny competitive opportunities to foreign suppliers are a proper cause for international concern. The problem of discrimination becomes even more acute when foreign firms face competition from government-owned or government-controlled enterprises. On the other hand, nondiscriminatory regulations may be inconvenient and may hamper business operations, but they offer less cause for international criticism. Yet, such national regulations can be key inhibitors for service innovations. For example, in Japan, pharmaceuticals cannot be sold outside of a licensed pharmacy. Similarly, travel arrangements can only be made within a registered travel office and banking can only be done during banking hours. As a result, multimedia innovations offered by today's communications technology cannot be brought to bear in these industries.[12]

All of these regulations make it difficult for international services to penetrate world markets. At the governmental level, services frequently are not recognized as a major facet of world trade or are viewed with suspicion because of a lack of understanding, and barriers to entry often result. To make progress in tearing them down, much educational work needs to be done.

An early postwar multilateral effort to liberalize international trade in services was the OECD code on invisible transactions, which in the 1950s removed some barriers to service trade. Within the GATT, the United States attempted in the late 1970s, near the end of the **Tokyo Round,** to add service issues to the agenda. However, this move was greeted with international suspicion because the United States has the largest service economy and the most service exports, and other nations suspected that any liberalization would principally benefit the United States. Moreover, some of the negotiating partners were as lacking in knowledge about services trade as U.S. negotiators had been a few years earlier. As a result, services were addressed only to a very limited extent in the Tokyo Round.

Services were therefore covered in the international trade framework only by the **Government Procurement Code** and the **Subsidies and Countervailing Measures Code.** The former covers services only to the extent that they are ancillary to purchases of goods and do not exceed the goods in value. The latter is restricted to services that are ancillary to trade in goods.

In a major breakthrough in Punta del Este in 1986, the major GATT participants agreed to conduct services trade negotiations parallel with product negotiations in the Uruguay Round. The negotiations resulted in the forging of a **General Agreement on Trade in Services (GATS),** the first multilateral, legally enforceable agreement covering trade and investment in the services sector. Similar to earlier agreements in the product sector, GATS provides for most-favored-nation treatment, national treatment, transparency in rule making, and the free flow of payments and transfers. Market-access provisions restrict the ability of governments to limit competition and new-market entry. In addition, sectoral agreements were made for the movement of personnel, telecommunications, and aviation. However, in several sectors, such as financial services and entertainment, no agreement was obtained. In addition, many provisions, due to their newness, are very narrow. Therefore, future negotiations have been agreed upon, which, at five-year intervals, will attempt to improve free trade in services.[13]

The new GATS signifies major progress in recognizing the importance of trade in services. However, it can be expected that substantial improvements still will be necessary to allow services to be truly uninhibited internationally.

CORPORATE INVOLVEMENT IN INTERNATIONAL SERVICE TRADE

Typical International Services

Although many firms are active in the international service arena, others do not perceive their existing competitive advantage. Numerous services that are efficiently performed in the home market may have great potential for internationalization.

U.S. financial institutions, for example, are very competitive internationally in providing **banking services.** In particular, they possess an advantage in the areas of mergers and acquisitions, credit card operations, customer service, and collection management. In the general area of international finance, however, the leadership role has been taken by banks in Japan and Europe, which are boosted by large assets, as seen in Table 15.2.

TABLE 15.2
The 50 Largest Commercial Banking Companies

Rank by Sales 1993	Commercial Banking Company	Country	Assets ($ millions)	Deposits ($ millions)	Rank	Loans ($ millions)	Rank	Profits ($ millions)	Rank	Stockholders' Equity ($ millions)	Rank
1	Fuji Bank	Japan	538,243.2	381,655.7	6	332,580.7	5	305.3	47	19,545.5	4
2	Dai-Ichi Kangyo Bank	Japan	535,356.5	435,460.6	2	352,046.2	2	107.9	77	19,399.7	5
3	Sumitomo Bank	Japan	531,835.3	435,419.8	3	346,544.0	4	329.7	40	21,931.4	2
4	Sanwa Bank	Japan	525,126.8	435,256.7	4	348,053.1	3	423.3	35	19,813.9	3
5	Sakura Bank	Japan	523,730.6	436,639.6	1	359,071.5	1	211.8	57	17,842.9	8
6	Mitsubishi Bank	Japan	487,547.2	399,404.6	5	315,966.7	6	440.4	33	17,887.3	7
7	Norinchukin Bank	Japan	435,599.1	311,082.6	8	180,398.6	16	439.5	34	3,391.9	77
8	Industrial Bank of Japan	Japan	414,925.5	330,974.2	7	243,677.4	9	202.9	59	13,659.0	13
9	Crédit Lyonnais	France	337,503.0	143,237.5	33	163,823.1	19	(1,124.2)	100	10,839.0	19
10	Bank of China	China	334,752.7	147,044.4	29	121,724.1	31	2,133.5	3	12,871.6	14
11	Mitsubishi Trust & Banking	Japan	330,478.7	297,572.0	9	140,070.6	22	137.5	69	7,960.4	30
12	Tokai Bank	Japan	328,685.4	253,874.7	14	198,069.7	13	314.1	45	10,982.5	17
13	Deutsche Bank	Germany	319,997.7	283,085.4	10	247,576.3	8	1,311.0	9	11,321.6	15
14	Long-Term Credit Bank of Japan	Japan	315,026.1	259,770.8	13	199,835.1	12	315.4	43	10,949.7	18
15	Sumitomo Trust & Banking	Japan	305,347.4	277,509.4	11	133,347.2	27	132.4	70	7,708.7	34
16	HSBC Holdings	Britain	304,521.3	231,226.4	16	248,519.5	7	2,712.1	1	13,791.4	12
17	Mitsui Trust & Banking	Japan	296,910.5	269,561.4	12	118,269.1	32	101.4	79	6,330.4	40
18	Crédit Agricole	France	281,787.3	208,481.2	20	171,143.8	18	972.4	13	18,415.3	6
19	Asahi Bank	Japan	277,688.1	235,635.9	15	202,080.2	10	190.2	62	10,468.6	20
20	Bank of Tokyo	Japan	273,884.3	205,521.9	22	139,023.8	23	469.2	32	10,238.2	22
21	Daiwa Bank	Japan	262,567.4	227,258.8	17	118,098.3	33	120.9	73	5,842.5	44
22	Société Générale	France	259,128.7	212,760.8	19	173,512.1	17	637.3	22	7,800.8	33
23	Abn Amro Holding	Netherlands	252,167.7	133,229.3	37	137,738.8	24	1,089.5	11	10,366.7	21
24	Banque Nationale de Paris	France	249,110.3	198,559.4	23	192,720.7	14	179.8	63	7,147.0	35
25	Barclays Bank	Britain	245,283.7	206,250.0	21	201,948.9	11	470.0	31	7,848.7	32
26	Yasuda Trust & Banking	Japan	235,527.6	215,418.8	18	97,715.8	40	90.0	82	50,445.4	1
27	Cie Financière de Paribas	France	229,025.0	126,731.5	39	93,726.6	42	255.8	52	6,538.3	38
28	National Westminster Bank	Britain	225,859.9	186,866.1	25	181,783.4	15	926.6	15	8,460.4	28
29	Dresdner Bank	Germany	218,887.9	198,241.5	24	153,724.6	20	620.5	23	6,782.2	37
30	Citicorp	U.S.	216,574.0	145,089.0	32	134,588.0	25	2,219.0	2	13,953.0	11
31	Union Bank of Switzerland	Switzerland	209,176.7	120,309.8	41	105,821.2	38	1,534.5	7	14,596.8	10
32	Toyo Trust & Banking	Japan	204,003.1	181,575.0	26	82,589.1	51	65.1	87	4,317.8	61
33	Westdeutsche Landesbank	Germany	191,213.2	170,787.1	27	141,109.7	21	263.4	51	N.A.	
34	Bankamerica Corp.	U.S.	186,933.0	141,618.0	35	122,871.0	30	1,954.0	4	17,144.0	9
35	Nippon Credit Bank	Japan	168,052.4	146,651.6	31	108,671.7	37	158.5	68	5,528.9	46
36	Bayerische Vereinsbank	Germany	166,261.6	158,100.6	28	133,846.5	26	321.7	41	4,148.4	66
37	Commerzbank	Germany	164,057.5	113,888.5	43	104,236.8	39	379.1	38	4,536.9	55
38	Shoko Chukin Bank	Japan	160,861.1	147,008.2	30	117,731.0	34	101.6	78	4,530.9	57
39	Nationsbank Corp.	U.S.	157,686.0	91,113.0	52	89,838.0	44	1,501.0	8	9,979.0	23
40	Crédit Suisse	Switzerland	156,042.3	136,842.7	36	83,282.9	50	824.1	18	9,317.9	25
41	Groupe des Caisses d'Épargne	France	155,972.3	17,638.1	99	50,008.4	74	300.1	48	9,173.8	26
42	Bayerische Hypotheken & Wechsel	Germany	152,656.5	141,641.6	34	130,488.1	28	315.1	44	4,234.4	64
43	Chemical Banking Corp.	U.S.	149,888.0	98,277.0	48	72,361.0	55	1,604.0	5	11,164.0	16
44	Bayerische Landesbank	Germany	149,590.6	132,463.6	38	116,311.4	35	178.1	64	5,157.6	50
45	Istituto Banc. San Paolo di Torino	Italy	145,915.6	126,233.7	40	113,383.6	36	64.6	88	4,628.3	53
46	Banca di Roma	Italy	141,760.9	79,298.6	57	68,162.5	57	127.1	72	4,291.9	63
47	Swiss Bank Corp.	Switzerland	139,091.4	97,659.3	49	126,030.2	29	923.5	16	8,823.3	27
48	Zenshinren Bank	Japan	137,430.9	101,458.8	46	54,035.8	70	129.9	71	2,491.5	86
49	J.P. Morgan & Co.	U.S.	133,888.0	40,402.0	91	23,223.0	98	1,586.0	6	9,859.0	24
50	Rabobank	Netherlands	130,049.3	73,606.7	61	84,366.3	48	604.5	24	7,886.2	31

Source: Fortune, August 22, 1994.

Construction, design, and **engineering services** also have great international potential. Providers of these services can achieve economies of scale not only for machinery and material but also in areas such as personnel management and the overall management of projects. Particularly for international projects that are large scale and long term, the experience advantage weighs heavily in favor of international firms.

Insurance services can be sold internationally by firms knowledgeable about underwriting, risk evaluation, and operations. Firms offering legal and accounting services can aid their clients abroad through support activities; they can also help foreign firms and countries improve business and governmental operations. Knowledge of computer operations, data manipulations, data transmission, and data analysis is insufficiently exploited internationally by many small and medium-sized firms.

FIGURE 15.5
An Advertisement for an International Communications Service

Source: Courtesy of AT&T.

Similarly, **communication services** have substantial future international opportunities. For example, firms experienced in the areas of videotext, home banking, and home shopping can find international success, particularly where geographic obstacles make the establishment of retail outlets cumbersome and expensive. Alternatively, global communication services, as shown in Figure 15.5, can greatly expand the reach of corporations.

Many institutions in the educational and the corporate sectors have developed expertise in **teaching services.** They are very knowledgeable in training and motivation as well as the teaching of operational, managerial, and theoretical issues, yet have largely concentrated their work in their domestic markets. It is time to take education global! Too much good and important knowledge is not made available to broad audiences. More knowledge must be communicated, be it through distance learning, study and teaching abroad, or attracting foreign students into the domestic market. The latter option can spur a service industry in itself, as Global Perspective 15.4 shows. The performance of such teaching services, however, should not consist of simply using the standard approach developed at home for domestic audiences. Rather, just like for any other service, adaptation and cultural sensitivity are key ingredients for success.

In the same vein, management **consulting services** can be provided by firms and individuals to the many countries and corporations in need of them. Of particular value could be management expertise in areas where many developing economies need most help, such as transportation and logistics. Major opportunities also exist for industries that deal with societal problems. For example, firms that develop environmentally safe products or produce pollution-control equipment may be able to exploit new markets as nations around the world increase their awareness of and concern about the environment and tighten their laws. Similarly, advances in health care or new knowledge in combating AIDS will offer major opportunities for global service success.

It should also be remembered that **tourism** represents a major service export. Every time foreign citizens come to a country and spend their funds, the current account effect is that of an export. Measured in current dollars, worldwide tourism receipts have tripled in the past 10 years, making this particular service one of the most important ones in the world.[14] Global Perspective 15.5 provides more examples about the worldwide significance of tourism.

An attractive international service mix might also be achieved by pairing the strengths of different partners. For example, information technology from one country could be combined with the financial resources of other countries. The strengths of the partners can then be used to offer maximum benefits to the international community.

Combining international advantages in services may ultimately result in the development of an even more drastic comparative lead. For example, the United States has an international head start in such areas as high technology, information gathering, information processing, information analysis, and teaching. Ultimately, the major thrust of U.S. international services might not be to provide these service components individually but rather to ensure that, based on a combination of competitive resources, better decisions are made. If better decision making is transferable to a wide variety of international situations, this in itself might become the overriding future comparative advantage of the United States in the international market.

Global Perspective

15.4
A Service for Students Abroad

The number of Japanese studying in the United States rose from 18,050 in 1987 to 42,840 in 1992. With this growing number of young Japanese men and women leaving home and coming to the U.S., there's a simultaneous increase in fearful Japanese parents. Thoughts run through the parents' minds of the 1992 shooting death of a Japanese student in Louisiana who knocked on the wrong door while looking for a party.

A Japanese-American named Ron Hasegawa has built a business around such circumstances. The firm is based in Santa Monica, California, and offers a package deal to Japanese parents who have said good-bye to their son or daughter as he or she heads for the United States. Intersec will monitor and counsel Japanese exchange students and report back to their anxious parents, all for an annual rate of $3,000, plus any expenses. It is a business built on the premise that when two very different cultures meet, opportunities exist for entrepreneurs who can smooth out the rough spots.

Hasegawa has lived in the U.S. since 1969 and admits that the fears that are stoked by certain events can help his business. Without advertising, he and his Tokyo partner signed up almost two dozen clients in the first five months of operation. Newly arrived students get an eight-hour orientation by Hasegawa that covers topics ranging from AIDS to drunken-driving laws. Intersec's four full-time staffers and its handful of support volunteers in several states then call the students weekly and visit them every other month to make sure they are getting good grades, going to class, and not hanging out with the wrong crowd. The parents get regular written reports.

While tapping into perceptions of America as a dark and dangerous place may play well in Japan, Intersec's approach has raised eyebrows in the U.S. The students who are being "watched" are some of the biggest critics. Complaints of lack of freedom are common. One student said, "I don't like the idea that my parents will be told how I'm doing in school. But I really don't have a choice." Others active in the field of advising Japanese exchange students criticize Intersec's use of scare tactics. Mr. Hasegawa states that his firm is just trying to help.

Most agree that many Japanese parents have good reason to worry. Although diligent students continue to flood in from Japan, so do those that are only avoiding the competitive college entrance exam system in that country. "Many students misunderstand the meaning of freedom in the U.S.," says Grace Kikuchi, of the Los Angeles office of the Center for International Cultural Studies and Education. "They think they can do whatever they want."

Source: Sarah Lubman, "Firm Taps Into Japanese Parents' Fears," *The Wall Street Journal,* September 1, 1994: B1.

Starting to Offer Services Internationally

For services that are delivered mainly in support of or in conjunction with products, the most sensible approach for the international novice is to follow the path of the product. For years, many large accounting and banking firms have done this by determining where their major multinational clients have set up new operations and then following them. Smaller service providers who supply manufacturing firms can determine where the manufacturing firms are operating internationally. Ideally, of course, it would be possible to follow clusters of manufacturers abroad to obtain economies of scale internationally while simultaneously looking for entirely new client groups.

Service providers whose activities are independent from products need a different strategy. These individuals and firms must search for market situations abroad that are similar to the domestic market. Such a search should be concentrated in their area of expertise. For example, a design firm learning about construction projects abroad can investigate the possibility of rendering its design services. Similarly,

Global Perspective

15.5
Tourism: The Global Growth Industry

As a contributor to the global economy, tourism has no equal. Expectations for growth in global tourism in the coming years are around 6 percent, substantially exceeding the growth of overall world trade. Between 1990 and 1993, travel and tourism employment grew 50 percent faster than world employment. The World Travel and Tourism Council forecasts travel and tourism will create 144 million jobs worldwide between now and the year 2005, with an estimated 112 million in the booming Asia-Pacific region.

To obtain a true understanding of global tourism's scope, consider the following:

- It employs 204 million people worldwide, or 1 in every 9 workers, 10.6 percent of the global work force.

- It is the world's leading economic contributor, producing an incredible 10.2 percent of the world's gross national product.
- It is the leading producer of tax revenues at $655 billion.
- It is the world's largest industry in terms of gross output, approaching $3.4 trillion.
- It accounts for 10.9 percent of all consumer spending, 10.7 percent of all capital investment, and 6.9 percent of all government spending.

Source: John Naisbitt, "Unraveling the Global Paradox," *Director,* March 1994, p. 13.

a management consultant learning about the plans of a country or firm to computerize its operations can explore the possibility of overseeing a smooth transition from manual to computerized activities. What is required is the understanding that similar problems are likely to occur in similar situations.

Another opportunity consists of identifying and understanding points of transition abroad. If, for example, new transportation services are introduced in a country, an expert in containerization may wish to consider whether to offer his or her service to improve the efficiency of the new system.

Leads for international service opportunities can also be gained by keeping informed about international projects sponsored by domestic organizations such as the U.S. Agency for International Development or the Trade Development Program, as well as international organizations such as the United Nations, the International Finance Corporation, or the World Bank. Frequently, such projects are in need of support through services. Overall, the international service provider needs to search for similar situations, similar problems, or scenarios requiring similar solutions to formulate an effective international expansion strategy.

Strategic Indications

To be successful in the international service offering, the manager must first determine the nature and the aim of the services-offering core—that is, whether the service will be aimed at people or at things and whether the service act in itself will result in tangible or intangible actions. Table 15.3 provides examples of such a classification strategy that will help the manager to better determine the position of the services effort.

TABLE 15.3 Understanding the Nature of the Service Act	Direct Recipient of the Service	
Nature of the Service Act	**People**	**Things**
Tangible Actions	**Services directed at people's bodies:**	**Services directed at goods and other physical possessions:**
	Health care	Freight transportation
	Passenger transportation	Industrial equipment repair and maintenance
	Beauty salons	Janitorial services
	Exercise clinics	Laundry and dry cleaning services
	Restaurants	Landscaping/lawn care
	Haircutting	Veterinary care
Intangible Actions	**Services directed at people's minds:**	**Services directed at intangible assets:**
	Education	Banking
	Broadcasting	Legal services
	Information services	Accounting
	Theaters	Securities
	Museums	Insurance

Source: Christopher H. Lovelock, *Managing Services: Marketing, Operations, and Human Resources* (Englewood Cliffs, N.J.: Prentice-Hall, Inc., 1988), 47.

During this determination, the manager must consider other tactical variables that have an impact on the preparation of the service offering. For example, in conducting research for services, the measurement of capacity and delivery efficiency often remains highly qualitative rather than quantitative. In communication and promotional efforts, the intangibility of the service reduces the manager's ability to provide samples. This makes communicating the service offered much more difficult than communicating a product offer. Brochures or catalogs explaining services often must show a proxy for the service to provide the prospective customer with tangible clues. A cleaning service, for instance, can show a picture of an individual removing trash or cleaning a window. However, the picture will not fully communicate the performance of the service. Due to the different needs and requirements of individual consumers, the manager must also pay attention to the two-way flow of communication. In the service area, mass communication often must be supported by intimate one-on-one follow-up.

The role of personnel deserves special consideration in international service delivery. The customer interface is intense, therefore, proper provisions need to be made for training of personnel both domestically and internationally. Major emphasis must be placed on appearance. Most of the time the person delivering the service—rather than the service itself—will communicate the spirit, value, and attitudes of the service corporation.

This close interaction with the consumer will also have organizational implications. While tight control over personnel may be desired, the individual interaction that is required points toward the need for an international decentralization of service delivery. This, in turn, requires delegation of large amounts of responsibility to individuals and service "subsidiaries" and requires a great deal of trust in all organizational units. This trust, of course, can be greatly enhanced through proper methods of training and supervision. Sole ownership also helps strengthen this trust. Research has shown that service firms, in their international expansion, tend to greatly prefer the establishment of full-control ventures. Only when costs escalate and the company-specific advantage diminishes will service firms seek out shared-control ventures.[15]

The areas of pricing and financing require special attention. Because services cannot be stored, much greater responsiveness to demand fluctuation must exist, and therefore greater pricing flexibility must be maintained. At the same time, flexibility is countered by the desire to provide transparency for both the seller and the buyer of services in order to foster an ongoing relationship. The intangibility of services also makes financing more difficult. Frequently, even financial institutions with large amounts of international experience are less willing to provide financial support for international services than for products. The reasons are that the value of services is more difficult to assess, service performance is more difficult to monitor, and services are difficult to repossess. Therefore, customer complaints and difficulties in receiving payments are much more troublesome for a lender to evaluate in the area of services than for products.

Finally, the distribution implications of international services must be considered. Usually, short and direct channels are required. Within these channels, closeness to the customer is of overriding importance to understand what the customer really wants, to trace the use of the service, and to aid the customer in obtaining a truly tailor-made service.

SUMMARY

Services are taking on an increasing importance in international trade. They need to be considered separately from trade in merchandise because they no longer simply complement products. Often, products complement services or are in competition with them. Service attributes such as their intangibility, their perishability, their custom design, and their cultural sensitivity, frequently make international trade in services more complex than trade in goods.

Services play an increasing role in the global economy. International growth and competition in this sector have begun to outstrip that of merchandise trade and are likely to intensify in the future. Even though services are unlikely to replace production, the sector will account for the shaping of new competitive advantages internationally.

The many service firms now operating only domestically need to investigate the possibility of going global. Historical patterns of service providers following manufacturers abroad have become partially obsolete as stand-alone services become more important to world trade. Management must therefore assess its vulnerability to service competition from abroad and explore opportunities to provide its services internationally.

Key Terms and Concepts

intangibility	deregulation
perishability	conference pricing
service capacity	Tokyo Round
customer involvement	Government Procurement Code
service consistency	Subsidies and Countervailing Measures Code
market transparency	General Agreement on Trade in Services (GATS)

Questions for Discussion

1. Discuss the major reasons for the growth of international services.
2. Why has the U.S. world market share in trade in services declined?
3. Do specific countries have a comparative advantage in services sectors?
4. How does the international sale of services differ from the sale of goods?
5. What are some of the international business implications of service intangibility?
6. What are some ways for a firm to expand its services internationally?
7. Some predict that "the main future U.S. international service will be to offer better decisions." Do you agree? Why or why not?
8. How can a firm in a developing country participate in the international services boom?
9. Which services would you expect to migrate abroad in the next decade? Why?

Recommended Readings

Aharoni, Yair. *Coalitions and Competition: The Globalization of Professional Business Services.* London and New York: Routledge, 1993.

Bateson, John E. G. *Managing Services Marketing* 3rd ed. Fort Worth, Tex.: Dryden Press, 1995.

Berry, Leonard L., David R. Bennett, and Carter W. Brown. *Service Quality.* Homewood, Ill.: Dow Jones-Irwin, 1989.

Feketekuty, Geza. *International Trade in Services.* Cambridge, Mass.: Ballinger, 1988.

Hoekman, Bernard M. *Liberalizing Trade in Services.* Washington, D.C.: The World Bank, 1994.

Lanvin, Bruno. *Trading in a New World Order: The Impact of Telecommunications and Data Services on International Trade in Services.* Boulder and Oxford: Westview Press, 1993.

Lovelock, Christopher H. *Services Marketing.* 2nd ed. Englewood Cliffs, N.J.: Prentice-Hall, 1991.

McKee, David L., and Don E. Garner. *Accounting Services, The International Economy and Third World Development.* New York: Praeger, 1992.

United States Congress. *International Competition in Services.* Washington, D.C.: Congress of the United States, Office of Technology Assessment, undated.

Notes

1. Leonard L. Berry, "Services Marketing Is Different," in *Services Marketing,* ed. Christopher H. Lovelock (Englewood Cliffs, N.J.: Prentice-Hall, 1984), 30.
2. *Winning in the World Market* (Washington, D.C.: American Business Conference, November 1987), 17.
3. G. Lynn Shostack, "Service Positioning through Structural Change," *Journal of Marketing* 51 (January 1987): 38.
4. "Mickey and Co. Go to Poland," *Journal of Commerce* (July 20, 1990): 5A.
5. *Fortune,* June 27, 1994: 49.

6. Jack E. Triplett, "Economic Concepts for Economic Classification—Changes for the Future," *The Service Economy,* vol. 7, no. 4, 1993: 1-6.

7. U.S. Department of Commerce, *U.S. Industrial Outlook 1994* (Washington, D.C.: Government Printing Office, 1994), 1.

8. Allen Sinai and Zaharo Sofianou, "Service Sectors in Developing Countries: Some Exceptions to the Rule," *The Service Economy,* July 1990, 13.

9. *Current Developments in the U.S. International Service Industries* (Washington, D.C.: U.S. Department of Commerce, March 1980).

10. Gary C. Hufbauer, remarks, seminar on Services in the World Economy, organized by the United States Council of the International Chamber of Commerce, New York, May 5, 1980, 3.

11. Dorothy I. Riddle, *Key LDCs: Trade in Services,* American Graduate School of International Studies, Glendale, Ariz., March 1987, 346-347.

12. Masao Yukawa, *The Information Superhighway and Multimedia: Dreams and Realities in Japan,* American Chamber of Commerce in Japan, Tokyo, October 12, 1994.

13. Letter from President Clinton to Speaker of the House Tom Foley, Washington, D.C., December 15, 1993.

14. *Tourism Policy and International Tourism in OECD Countries* (Paris: Organisation for Economic Co-Operation and Development, 1994).

15. M. Krishna Erramilli and C. P. Rao, "Service Firms' International Entry-Mode Choice: A Modified Transaction-Cost Analysis Approach," *Journal of Marketing* 57 (July 1993): 19-38.

CHAPTER 16

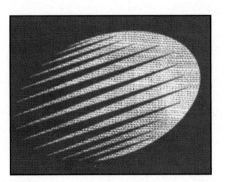

International Logistics

Learning Objectives

1. To understand the escalating importance of international logistics as competitiveness becomes increasingly dependent on cost efficiency.

2. To learn about materials management and physical distribution, both part of international logistics.

3. To learn why international logistics is more complex than domestic logistics.

4. To see how the transportation infrastructure in host countries often dictates the options open to the international manager.

5. To learn why inventory management is crucial for international success.

African Trade Depends on Logistics

Africa jumped into the global perishable market when world prices for its traditional foreign currency earners (such as cocoa, coffee, tea, and tobacco) began to decline. Now, African countries are becoming major exporters of fresh fruit, vegetables, and flowers. Yet shipments of these perishable goods are getting locked out of the U.S. market for lack of adequate transportation.

"There's no transportation from Africa for fresh fruit. I don't think you're going to find anything of importance in fruit from Africa for a long time," said Peter Kopke, president of Kopke Inc., an importer of fresh fruit and vegetables based in Lake Success, New York.

The biggest buyers of African fruits, vegetables, and flowers are in Europe, the Middle East, and Japan. Kenya is now the world's fourth-largest exporter of flowers—particularly carnations, roses, and orchids—but sells barely $300,000 worth of flowers in the United States each year.

"It's simply a matter of logistics. Freight economics do not permit [perishables] being brought into the United States from Africa," said Larry Ladutko, Miami's First Flower Corp. president.

"I'm sure those who do export to Europe have looked at the U.S. market," said Phillip Michelini, who tracks U.S. commercial relations with a number of West African countries for the Commerce Department. "But so far, there's no produce sold to the United States in any quantity. There's a basic problem of keeping such perishables as bananas and pineapples refrigerated."

Whether African producers will begin to rival Latin American, European, and Asian suppliers in the U.S. perishable market depends on whether they can solve the problem of cold storage facilities and air cargo space.

African exporters depend on national airlines. According to most U.S. and European cargo carriers and charter operators, there is still not enough African trade to fill flights.

Source: Rosalind Rachid, "African Exporters Find U.S. Tough," *The Journal of Commerce* (September 21, 1990): 1A. Reprinted with permission.

For the international firm, customer locations and sourcing opportunities are widely dispersed. The physical distribution and logistics aspects of international business therefore have great importance. To obtain and maintain favorable results from the complex international environment, the international manager must coordinate activities globally both within and outside of the firm. The firm can attain a strategically advantageous position only if system synergism exists. Neglect of logistics issues brings not only higher costs but also the risk of eventual noncompetitiveness, due to diminished market share, more expensive supplies, or lower profits. As discussed in the opening vignette, logistics problems can prevent exporters from fully exploiting a potentially profitable market overseas. Worse yet, different logistics regulations based on environmental concerns may even preclude any market participation.

This chapter will focus on international logistics activities. Primary areas of concern are transportation, inventory, packaging, storage, and logistics management. The logistics problems and opportunities that are peculiar to international business will also be highlighted.

THE FIELD OF INTERNATIONAL LOGISTICS

The concept of business logistics as part of academic discussion is relatively new. Although some aspects were discussed as early as 1951, John F. Magee is generally credited with publishing the first article on logistics theory in 1960.[1] The theoretical development of international logistics is even more recent, probably originating in a 1966 article by Robert E. McGarrah on "Logistics for the International Manufacturer.[2]

The importance of international logistics has quickly been recognized by practitioners of international business. Managers realize that "competition is the name of the game" in international business and that logistics "is key to making—and keeping—customers."[3] They also believe that future sales growth in the international market will come mainly from the development of wider and better logistics systems.[4]

A Definition of International Logistics

International logistics is defined as the designing and managing of a system that controls the flow of materials into, through, and out of the international corporation. It encompasses the total movement concept by covering the entire range of operations concerned with product movement, including therefore both exports and imports simultaneously. By taking a systems approach, the firm explicitly recognizes the linkages among the traditionally separate logistics components within the corporation. By recognizing the logistics interaction with outside organizations and individuals such as suppliers and customers, the firm is enabled to build on jointness of purpose by all partners in the areas of performance, quality, and timing. As a result of implementing these systems considerations successfully, the firm can develop just-in-time (JIT) delivery for lower inventory cost, electronic data interchange (EDI) for more efficient order processing, and early supplier involvement (ESI) for better planning of product movement. The use of such strategic tools in the international arena can then assist the firm in developing key competitive advantages. An overview of the logistics function is provided in Figure 16.1.

Two major phases in the movement of materials are of logistical importance. The first phase is **materials management,** or the timely movement of raw materials, parts, and supplies into and through the firm. The second phase is **physical distribution,** which involves the movement of the firm's finished product to its

FIGURE 16.1   The Logistics Function

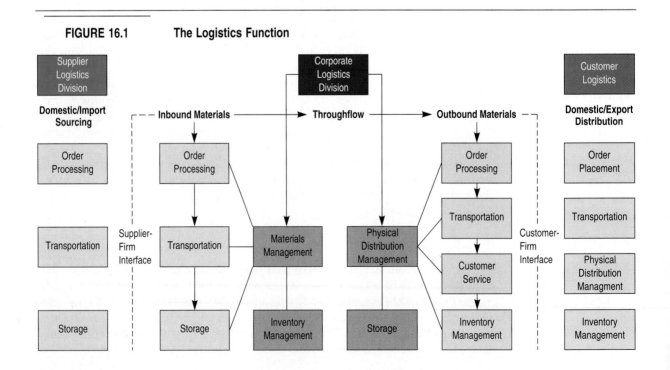

customers. In both phases, movement is seen within the context of the entire process. Stationary periods (storage and inventory) are therefore included. The basic goal of logistics management is the effective coordination of both phases and their various components to result in maximum cost effectiveness while maintaining service goals and requirements. In the words of the director of international logistics operations of General Motors Corporation, the purpose of international logistics is "to plan cost-effective systems for future use, attempt to eliminate duplication of effort, and determine where distribution policy is lacking or inappropriate. Emphasis is placed on consolidating existing movements, planning new systems, identifying useful ideas, techniques, or experiences, and working with various divisions toward implementation of beneficial changes."[5]

The growth of logistics as a field has brought to the forefront three major new concepts: the systems concept, the total cost concept, and the trade-off concept. The **systems concept** is based on the notion that materials-flow activities within and outside of the firm are so extensive and complex that they can be considered only in the context of their interaction. Instead of each corporate function, supplier, and customer operating with the goal of individual optimization, the systems concept stipulates that some components may have to work suboptimally to maximize the benefits of the system as a whole. The systems concept intends to provide the firm, its suppliers, and its customers, both domestic and foreign, with the benefits of synergism expected from the coordinated application of size.

A logical outgrowth of the systems concept is the development of the **total cost concept.** To evaluate and optimize logistical activities, cost is used as a basis for measurement. The purpose of the total cost concept is to minimize the firm's overall logistics cost by implementing the systems concept appropriately. Increasingly, however, the total cost concept is being partially supplanted by **a total after-tax profit concept.** This takes into account the impact of national tax policies on the logistics function and has the objective of maximizing after-tax profits rather than minimizing total cost. Tax variations in the international arena often have major consequences, therefore, the focus appears quite appropriate.[6]

The **trade-off concept,** finally, recognizes the linkages within logistics systems that result from the interaction of their components. For example, locating a warehouse near the customer may reduce the cost of transportation. However, additional costs are associated with new warehouses. Similarly, a reduction of inventories will save money but may increase the need for costly emergency shipments. Managers can maximize performance of logistics systems only by formulating decisions based on the recognition and analysis of such trade-offs.

The Impact of International Logistics

Logistics cost comprise between 10 and 25 percent of the total landed cost of an international order. International firms already have achieved many of the cost reductions that are possible in financing and production, and they now are beginning to look at international logistics as a competitive tool. Research shows that the environment facing logistics managers in the next 10 years will be dynamic and explosive. Technological advances and progress in communication systems and information-processing capabilities will be particularly significant in the design and management of logistics systems.

For example, close collaboration with suppliers is required to develop a just-in-time inventory system, which in turn may be crucial to maintaining manufacturing costs at globally competitive levels. Yet, without electronic data interchange, such collaborations or alliances are severely handicapped. While most industrialized countries can offer the technological infrastructure for such computer-to-computer exchange of business information, the application of such a system in the global environment often is severely restricted. It may not be just the lack of technology that forms the key obstacle to modern logistics management, but rather the entire business infrastructure, ranging from ways of doing business in fields such as accounting and inventory tracking, to the willingness of businesses to collaborate with each other. A contrast between the United States and Russia is useful here.

In the United States, 40 percent of shipments are under a just-in-time/quick response regime. For the U.S. economy, the total cost of distribution in 1995 is close to 11 percent of GNP. By contrast, Russia only now is beginning to learn about the rhythm of demand and the need to bring supply in line. The country is battling space constraints, poor lines of supply, nonexistent distribution and service centers, limited rolling stock, and inadequate transportation systems. Producers are uninformed about issues such as inventory carrying costs, store assortment efficiencies, and replenishment techniques. The need for information development and exchange systems, for integrated supplier–distributor alliances, and for efficient communication systems is only poorly understood. As a result, distribution costs remain at well above 30 percent of GNP, holding back the domestic economy and severely restricting its international competitiveness. Unless substantial improvements are made, major participation by Russian producers in world trade will be unlikely,[7] since the high logistics and transaction costs let Western buyers encounter high "frictional resistance" in their procurement process.[8]

Logistics may well become the key dimension by which firms distinguish themselves internationally. Given the speed of technological change and the efficiency demands placed on business, competitiveness, international sales growth and international marketing success increasingly will depend on the logistics function.[9]

Differences between Domestic and International Logistics

In domestic operations, logistics decisions are guided by the experience of the manager, possible industry comparisons, an intimate knowledge of trends, and discovered heuristics—or rules of thumb. The logistics manager in the international firm, on the other hand, frequently has to depend on educated guesses to determine the steps required to obtain a desired service level. Variations in locale mean variations in environment. Lack of familiarity with such variations leads to uncertainty in the decision-making process. By applying decision rules based only on the environment encountered at home, the firm will be unable to adapt well to new circumstances and the result will be inadequate profit performance. The long-term survival of international activities depends on an understanding of the differences inherent in the international logistics field. The variations can be classified as basic differences and country-specific differences.[10]

Basic Differences Basic differences in international logistics emerge because the corporation is active in more than one country. One example of a basic difference is distance. International business activities frequently require goods to be shipped farther to reach final customers. These distances in turn result in longer lead times, more opportunities for things to go wrong, more inventories—in short, greater complexity. Currency variation is a second basic difference in international logistics. The corporation must adjust its planning to incorporate the existence of different currencies and changes in exchange rates. The border-crossing process brings with it the need for conformity with national regulations, an inspection at customs, and proper documentation. As a result, additional intermediaries participate in the international logistics process. They include freight forwarders, customs agents, customs brokers, banks, and other financial intermediaries. Finally, the **transportation modes** may also be different. Most domestic transportation is either by truck or by rail, whereas the multinational corporation quite frequently ships its products by air or by sea. Airfreight and ocean freight have their own stipulations and rules that require new knowledge and skills.

Country-Specific Differences Within each country, the firm faces specific logistical attributes that may be quite different from those experienced at home. Transportation systems and intermediaries may vary. The computation of freight rates may be unfamiliar. Packaging and labeling requirements differ from country to country. Management must consider all of these factors to develop an efficient international logistics operation.

| INTERNATIONAL TRANSPORTATION ISSUES | International transportation is of major concern to the international firm because transportation determines how and when goods will be received. The transportation issue can be divided into three components: infrastructure, the availability of modes, and the choice of modes among the given alternatives. |

Transportation Infrastructure

In industrialized countries, firms can count on an established transportation network. Around the globe, however, major infrastructural variations will be encountered. Some countries may have excellent inbound and outbound transportation systems but weak internal transportation links. This is particularly true in former colonies, where the original transportation systems were designed to maximize the extractive potential of the countries. In such instances, shipping to the market may be easy, but distribution within the market may represent a very difficult and time-consuming task. Infrastructure problems can also be found in countries where most transportation networks were established between major ports and cities in past centuries. The areas lying outside the major transportation networks will encounter problems in bringing their goods to market. Global Perspective 16.1 shows what a difference a new transportation linkage can make.

Due to the political changes that have occurred in the recent past, new routes of commerce have also opened up, particularly between the former East and West political blocs. Yet, without the proper infrastructure the opening of markets is mainly accompanied by major new bottlenecks. On the part of the firm, it is crucial to have wide market access to be able to appeal to sufficient customers. The firm's **logistics platform,** which is determined by a location's ease and convenience of market reach under favorable cost circumstances, is a key component of a firm's competitive position. Since different countries and regions may offer alternative logistics platforms, the firm must recognize that such alternatives can be the difference between success and failure.

The logistics manager must therefore learn about existing and planned infrastructures abroad and at home and factor them into the firm's strategy. In some coun-

Global Perspective

16.1
The Logistics Effects of the Channel Tunnel

The opening of the 32-mile English Channel tunnel connecting the United Kingdom with mainland Europe offers the prospect of vastly improved distribution links between the two land masses. Ten thousand miles of British railway will be directly joined to the mainland European network of 150,000 miles. Intermodal transport through the tunnel should avoid traffic jams, ferry cancellations in rough weather, and continental bans on long-distance truck journeys on weekends and public holidays. Railfreight Distribution, the British Railways freight subsidiary responsible for container shipments to the Continent, calculates that the opening of the tunnel will increase rail-freight volumes from 2 million tons a year to 6.5 million tons within two years. It expects freight shipments to reach 9 million tons by about the year 2000. Rail-borne freight currently accounts for just 7 percent of cross-Channel shipments by container and other similar methods.

The environmental benefits of a shift to rail are attractive to politicians and the general public. In addition to the long-distance freight services that will use the tunnel, truckers will be able to place their rig on Eurotunnel's freight shuttles running between Folkestone, England, and Calais, France.

If the tunnel can provide regular, reliable service, guaranteed delivery times could prove invaluable to companies supplying customers or field engineers with components from a central European warehouse. Companies could push back the cutoff point for orders of next-day delivery of spare parts from, say, 4 p.m. to 5 p.m. and still get the order there on time.

Food retailers shipping chilled foods through the tunnel by a combination of road and rail could gain an extra 12 to 48 hours longer on the supermarket shelf, said Pat Lee of Wincanton, a food distribution specialist. "The speed of movement will allow an honest claim that the fruit, say, was only picked the day before," he added.

Source: Charles Batchelor, "It's Still Early Days," *The Financial Times*, September 21, 1994: Survey on Logistics, p. II.

tries, for example, railroads may be an excellent transportation mode, far surpassing the performance of trucking, while in others the use of railroads for freight distribution may be a gamble at best. The future routing of pipelines must be determined before any major commitments are made to a particular location if the product is amenable to pipeline transportation. The transportation methods used to carry cargo to seaports or airports must be investigated. Mistakes in the evaluation of transportation options can prove to be very costly. One researcher reported the case of a food processing firm that built a pineapple cannery at the delta of a river in Mexico. Since the pineapple plantation was located upstream, the company planned to float the ripe fruit down to the cannery on barges. To its dismay, however, the firm soon discovered that at harvest time the river current was far too strong for barge traffic. Since no other feasible alternative method of transportation existed, the plant was closed and the new equipment was sold for a fraction of its original cost.[11]

Extreme variations also exist in the frequency of transportation services. For example, a particular port may not be visited by a ship for weeks or even months. Sometimes only carriers with particular characteristics, such as small size, will serve a given location.

All of these infrastructural concerns must be taken into account in the planning of the firm's location and transportation framework. The opportunity of a highly competitive logistics platform may be decisive for the firm's investment decision, since it forms a key component of the cost advantages sought by multinational corporations as was explained in Chapter 13. If a location loses its logistics benefits, due to, for example, a deterioration of the railroad system, a firm may well decide to move on to another, more favorable locale. Business strategist Michael Porter addressed the importance of infrastructure as a determinant of national competitive advantage and highlighted the capability of governmental efforts to influence this critical issue.[12] Governments must keep the transportation dimension in mind when attempting to attract new industries or trying to retain existing firms. Global Perspective 16.2 shows how a strategic location combined with efficient transportation operations can help create a hub of economic activity.

Availability of Modes

International transportation frequently requires ocean or airfreight modes, which many corporations only rarely use domestically. In addition, combinations such as **land bridges** or **sea bridges** may permit the transfer of freight among various modes of transportation, resulting in **intermodal movements.** The international logistics manager must understand the specific properties of the different modes to be able to use them intelligently.

Ocean Shipping   Water transportation is a key mode for international freight movement.[13] Three types of vessels operating in **ocean shipping** can be distinguished

Global Perspective

16.2
Germany: Gateway to Central Europe

Of interest to shippers is not only Germany the potential export market, but also Germany the strategically located logistics powerhouse that provides exporters with an entry to the emerging market economies of Central Europe.

Dryvit Systems, Inc., a Rhode Island manufacturer of an acrylic polymer exterior wall covering, has been exporting to Central Europe since 1992. Getting the firm's products to Poland, Hungary, and the Czech Republic begins by sending the cargo by ocean carrier to the port of Bremerhaven in Germany. The ports of Bremen and Bremerhaven are the key logistical links in Germany for getting cargo to Central Europe. "We surveyed every major port in Europe and found that, while each has its strengths, Bremerhaven was the only one that met all of our requirements," said Thomas O'Rourke, Dryvit's director of international logistics.

For O'Rourke and Dryvit, the top features of Bremerhaven are the door-to-door service by ocean carriers to points in Hungary and the Czech Republic, great feeder

service to the port of Gdynia in Poland, and the cooperation of BLG, the port of Bremerhaven's operating company.

"There is truck service to Hungary and the Czech Republic from Bremen and Bremerhaven," explained Bernd Homann, a representative of the ports. There is also daily train service from the ports to Prague, Budapest, and Sopron, Hungary. There are feeder services from Bremerhaven to Finland, from which cargo is trucked to the Baltic States and the Russian interior. The cargo is routed through Finland to avoid the congestion at the port of St. Petersburg. "These days, only cargo destined for St. Petersburg itself is routed to that port," said Homann. BLG runs several different distribution centers in the port areas. In addition, there are a number of smaller local warehouses. Considering the growing international trade activity in Central Europe and the geographic complexity that logistics managers face, the port of Bremerhaven can expect to be busy for a long time to come.

Source: Peter Buxbaum, "Destinations: Germany," *Distribution,* May 1994: 68.

by their service: liner service, bulk service, and tramp or charter service. **Liner service** offers regularly scheduled passage on established routes. **Bulk service** mainly provides contractual services for individual voyages or for prolonged periods of time. **Tramp service** is available for irregular routes and scheduled only on demand.

In addition to the services offered by ocean carriers, the type of cargo a vessel can carry is also important. Most common are conventional (break bulk) cargo vessels, container ships, and roll-on-roll-off vessels. Conventional cargo vessels are useful for oversized and unusual cargoes but may be less efficient in their port operations. **Container ships** carry standardized containers that greatly facilitate the loading and unloading of cargo and intermodal transfers. As a result, the time the ship has to spend in port is reduced. **Roll-on-roll-off (RORO)** vessels are essentially ocean-going ferries. Trucks can drive onto built-in ramps and roll off at the destination. Another vessel similar to the RORO vessel is the LASH (lighter aboard ship) vessel. LASH vessels consist of barges stored on the ship and lowered at the point of destination. The individual barges can then operate on inland waterways, a feature that is particularly useful in shallow water.

The availability of a certain type of vessel, however, does not automatically mean that it can be used. The greatest constraint in international ocean shipping is the lack of ports and port services. For example, modern container ships cannot serve some ports because the local equipment cannot handle the resulting traffic. The problem is often found in developing countries, where local authorities lack the funds to develop facilities. In some instances, nations may purposely limit the development of **ports** to impede the inflow of imports. Increasingly, however, governments have begun to recognize the importance of an appropriate port facility structure and are developing such facilities in spite of the large investments necessary. If such investments are accompanied by concurrent changes in the overall infrastructure, transportation efficiency should, in the long run, more than recoup the original investment. The investment may be even more profitable if ports of neighboring countries are not adequate. Merchants may opt to use those ports with facilities that are up to their standards and then transport the goods over land to their final destination.

Large investments in infrastructure are always necessary to produce results. Selective allocation of funds to transportation usually results only in the shifting of bottlenecks to some other point in the infrastructure. If the bottlenecks are not removed, the consequences may be felt in the overall economic performance of the nation.

Air Shipping   To and from most countries, **airfreight** is available. This includes the developing world, where it is often a matter of national prestige to operate a national airline. The tremendous growth in international airfreight over past decades is shown in Figure 16.2. The total volume of airfreight in relation to total shipping volume in international business remains quite small. It accounts for less than 1 percent of the total volume of international shipments, although it often represents more than 20 percent of the value shipped by industrialized countries.[14] Clearly, high-value items are more likely to be shipped by air, particularly if they have a high **density,** that is, a high weight-to-volume ratio.

Over the years, airlines have made major efforts to increase the volume of airfreight. Many of these activities have concentrated on developing better, more efficient ground facilities, automating air waybills, introducing airfreight containers, and providing and marketing a wide variety of special services to shippers. In addition, some airfreight companies and ports have specialized and become partners in the international logistics effort.

Changes have also taken place within the aircraft. As an example, 30 years ago, the holds of large propeller aircraft could take only about 10 tons of cargo. Today's jumbo jets can hold more than 92 tons and can therefore transport bulky products, as Figure 16.3 shows. In addition, aircraft manufacturers have responded to in-

**FIGURE 16.2
International Airfreight,
1960–1994[a]**

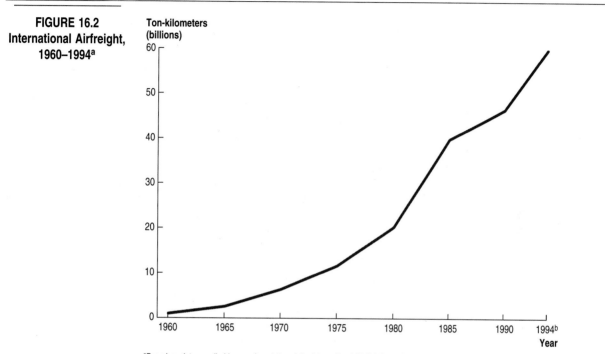

[a]Based on data supplied by member states of the International Civil Aviation Organization (ICAO). As the number of member states increased from 116 in 1970 to 150 in 1983, there is some upward bias in the data, particularly from 1970 on, when data for the USSR were included for the first time.
[b]Preliminary figure.
Source: Civil Aviation Statistics of the World (Montreal: ICAO, 1995).

**FIGURE 16.3
Loading a Train on a
Plane**

Source: Printed in the *Journal of Commerce,* August 29, 1994.

dustry demands by developing both jumbo cargo planes and combination passenger and cargo aircraft. The latter carry passengers in one section of the main deck and freight in another. These hybrids can be used by carriers on routes that would be uneconomical for passengers or freight alone.

From the shipper's perspective, the products involved must be appropriate for air shipment in terms of their size. In addition, the market situation for any given product must be evaluated. Airfreight may be needed if a product is perishable or if, for other reasons, it requires a short transit time. The level of customer service needs and expectations can also play a decisive role. For example, the shipment of an industrial product that is vital to the ongoing operations of a customer is usually much more urgent than the shipment of most consumer products.

Choice of Modes

The international logistics manager must make the appropriate selection from the available modes of transportation. The decision will be heavily influenced by the needs of the firm and its customers. The manager must consider the performance of each mode on four dimensions: transit time, predictability, cost, and noneconomic factors.

Transit Time The period between departure and arrival of the carrier varies significantly between ocean freight and airfreight. For example, the 45-day **transit time** of an ocean shipment can be reduced to 24 hours if the firm chooses airfreight. The length of transit time can have a major impact on the overall operations of the firm. As an example, a short transit time may reduce or even eliminate the need for an overseas depot. Also, inventories can be significantly reduced if they are replenished frequently. As a result, capital can be freed up and used to finance other corporate opportunities. Transit time can also play a major role in emergency situations. For example, if the shipper is about to miss an important delivery date because of production delays, a shipment normally made by ocean freight can be made by air.

Perishable products require shorter transit times. Transporting them rapidly prolongs the shelf life in the foreign market. As shown in Figure 16.4, air delivery may be the only way to successfully enter foreign markets with products that have a short life span. International sales of cut flowers have reached their current volume only as a result of airfreight.

The interaction among selling price, market distance, and form of transportation is not new. Centuries ago, Johann von Thünen, a noted German economist, developed models for the market reach of agricultural products that incorporated these factors. Yet, given the forms of transportation available today, the factors no longer pose the rigid constraints postulated by von Thünen, but rather offer new opportunities in international business.

Predictability Providers of both ocean freight and airfreight service wrestle with the issue of reliability. Both modes are subject to the vagaries of nature, which may impose delays. Yet, because **reliability** is a relative measure, the delay of one day for airfreight tends to be seen as much more severe and "unreliable" than the same delay for ocean freight. However, delays tend to be shorter in absolute time for air shipments. As a result, arrival time via air is more predictable. This attribute has a major influence on corporate strategy. For example, because of the higher predictability of airfreight, inventory safety stock can be kept at lower levels. Greater

**FIGURE 16.4
An Advertisement for
Cut Flowers**

How to ship tulips by air and come up smelling like a rose.

Cut flowers are almost as ephemeral as dreams. Beautiful, fragile, fragrant, they have a life span of mere days under the best of circumstances. So the challenge of shipping tulips from a field in Holland to a table in Ohio, still in their glorious prime, is a major one.

That's why so many tulip growers in Holland choose The New York & New Jersey Air Cargo Center through which to ship their flowers. Last year, more than $55 million worth of tulips were shipped through our airports.

The Dutch shippers know that time, coordination and connections are of the essence. They know that our Federal inspectors and import brokers are available when needed to meet their shipments as they arrive and to help expedite the flowers through the airport and on their way to market. And, they know we have the best air and surface connections to protect their flowers' freshness in transport and to meet tight delivery schedules.

We really care about the life of your product. We want you to come up smelling like a rose, whatever you ship.

Whether it's tulips or tubas, if it's going through the NY/NJ Air Cargo System, we'll get it there fast, fresh and—if it began that way—still fragrant.

For more information on air cargo services at the New York/New Jersey Airports, write to:

Manager, Air Cargo Market Development
Port Authority of New York and New Jersey
One World Trade Center, Suite 64N
New York, NY 10048

NEW YORK/NEW JERSEY AIRPORTS
Kennedy Newark LaGuardia

THE PORT AUTHORITY OF NY & NJ

Source: Courtesy of Customer and Marketing Services Division, Aviation Department, Port Authority of New York and New Jersey.

predictability also can serve as a useful sales tool for foreign distributors, which can make more precise delivery promises to their customers. If inadequate port facilities exist, airfreight may again be the better alternative. Unloading operations for oceangoing vessels are more cumbersome and time-consuming than for planes. Merchandise shipped via air is likely to suffer less loss and damage from exposure of the cargo to movement. Therefore, once the merchandise arrives, it is more likely to be ready for immediate delivery—a facet that also enhances predictability.

An important aspect of predictability is also the capability of a shipper to track goods at any point during the shipment. *Tracking* becomes particularly important as corporations increasingly obtain products from and send them to multiple locations around the world. Being able to coordinate the smooth flow of a multitude of interdependent shipments can make a vast difference in a corporation's performance.[15] Tracking allows the shipper to check on the supply chain and to take remedial action if problems occur. Cargo also can be redirected if sudden demand surges so require. However, such enhanced corporate response to the predictability issue is only possible if an appropriate information system is developed by the shipper and the carrier.

Cost of Transportation   A major consideration in choosing international transportation modes is the cost factor. International transportation services are usually priced on the basis of both cost of the service provided and value of the service to the shipper. Due to the high value of the products shipped by air, airfreight is often priced according to the value of the service. In this instance, of course, price becomes a function of market demand and the monopolistic power of the carrier.

The manager must decide whether the clearly higher cost of airfreight can be justified. In part, this will depend on the cargo's properties. For example, the physical density and the value of the cargo will affect the decision. Bulky products may be too expensive to ship by air, whereas very compact products may be more appropriate for airfreight transportation. High-priced items can absorb transportation costs more easily than low-priced goods because the cost of transportation as a percentage of total product cost will be lower. As a result, sending diamonds by airfreight is easier to justify than sending coal. Alternatively, a shipper can decide to mix modes of transportation in order to reduce overall cost and time delays. For example, part of the shipment route can be covered by air, while another portion can be covered by truck or ship. Global Perspective 16.3 gives an example of such intermodal shipments.

Most important, however, are the overall logistical considerations of the firm. The manager must determine how important it is for merchandise to arrive on time. The need to reduce or increase international inventory must be carefully measured. Related to these considerations are the effect of transportation cost on price and the need for product availability abroad. For example, some firms may want to use airfreight as a new tool for aggressive market expansion. Airfreight may also be considered a good way to begin operations in new markets without making sizable investments for warehouses and distribution centers.

Although costs are the major consideration in modal choice, the overall strategic perspective must be explored. Simply comparing transportation modes on the basis of price alone is insufficient. The manager must factor in all corporate activities that are affected by the modal choice and explore the total cost effects of each alternative.

Noneconomic Factors   Often noneconomic dimensions will enter into the selection process for a proper form of transportation. The transportation sector, nationally and internationally, both benefits and suffers from government involvement. Even though transportation carriers are one prime target in the sweep of privatization around the globe, many carriers are still owned or heavily subsidized by governments. As a result, governmental pressure is exerted on shippers to use national carriers, even if more economical alternatives exist. Such **preferential policies** are most often enforced when government cargo is being transported. Restrictions are not limited to developing countries. For example, in the United States, the federal government requires that all travelers on government business use national flag carriers when available.

For balance of payments reasons, international quota systems of transportation have been proposed. The United Nations Conference on Trade and Development

Global Perspective

16.3
Sea-Air: The Best of Both Worlds

In a global economy, the need for timely and predictable transport of products and production materials is vital. Without a doubt, air transport is the quickest and most reliable mode. However, sea transport often qualifies as the cheapest mode. Customers love speedy delivery, yet the need to keep transportation costs low is equally vital. A real problem for the logistics manager is the dilemma of one mode being absolutely too expensive and the other absolutely too slow.

Ask shippers nowadays how they cope with the problem and they'll give you a strange response: They use both! It's called "sea-air" transport and literally a ship and plane are used together to avoid the two extremes of high cost and long shipping delays. For example, many Japanese shippers will send Europe-bound cargo by ship to the U.S. west coast. From there, the cargo is flown to its final destination in Europe. By combining the two modes, the entire trip will last about two weeks, as opposed to four or five weeks with an all-water route and the cost will be about half of an all-air route.

A growing practice among Japanese and European shippers sending goods to South America is to sail to U.S. ports and then fly south from there. Ocean carriers from Japan will unload at the port of Los Angeles and either fly on from there or truck the cargo to Miami. From the grow-

ing sea-air port of Miami, the cargo proceeds by air to destinations such as Brazil. An all-water route from Japan to South America can take a month, while sea-air takes a week and a half. Certain types of cargo, such as perishables and bulky items, will have to be shipped solely one way or the other, so sea-air isn't for everyone. But for cargo that fits the bill, it can be the best of both worlds!

The key to the entire process is the transfer point. Specific capabilities are required at the port to justify sea-air activity. At this time, only three ports worldwide (Seattle, Singapore, and Dubai) have come close to perfecting the "switch." First of all, a short and easy commute is needed between dock and airport. The largest sea-air hub in the world, Seattle's ocean port, is just 13 miles from its airport. Second is the ability to quickly off-load from one mode, transport, and on-load to the second mode as smoothly as possible. A third vital feature is committed port authorities who will aid in the minimization of customs, paperwork, and other red tape that goes along with international transportation. Crucial to successful sea-air transport is also the willingness of local transportation providers to prioritize designated sea-air cargo. When all of these features are brought together, the utilization of sea and air make for a happy ending.

Source: "Sea-Air: Cheap and Fast," *Global Trade,* Feb. 1992, 16–18.

(UNCTAD), for example, has recommended that 40 percent of the traffic between two nations be allocated to vessels of the exporting country, 40 percent to vessels of the importing country, and 20 percent to third-country vessels. However, stiff international competition among carriers and the price sensitivity of customers frequently render such proposals ineffective, particularly for trade between industrialized countries.

Although many justifications are possible for such national policies, ranging from prestige to national security, they distort the economic choices of the international corporation. Yet, these policies are a reflection of the international environment within which the firm must operate. Proper adaptation is necessary.

Export Documentation

A firm must deal with numerous forms and documents when exporting to ensure that all goods meet local and foreign laws and regulations.

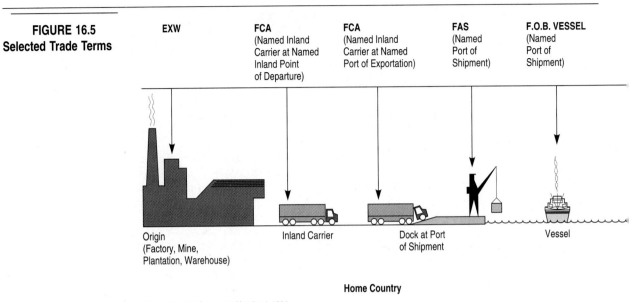

FIGURE 16.5
Selected Trade Terms

EXW

FCA (Named Inland Carrier at Named Inland Point of Departure)

FCA (Named Inland Carrier at Named Port of Exportation)

FAS (Named Port of Shipment)

F.O.B. VESSEL (Named Port of Shipment)

Origin (Factory, Mine, Plantation, Warehouse)

Inland Carrier

Dock at Port of Shipment

Vessel

Home Country

Source: *Foreign Commerce Handbook*, 1994.

A **bill of lading** is a contract between the exporter and the carrier indicating that the carrier has accepted responsibility for the goods and will provide transportation in return for payment. The bill of lading can also be used as a receipt and to prove ownership of the merchandise. There are two types of bills, negotiable and nonnegotiable. **Straight bills of lading** are nonnegotiable and are typically used in prepaid transactions. The goods are delivered to a specific individual or company. **Shipper's order** bills of lading are negotiable; they can be bought, sold, or traded while the goods are still in transit and are used for letter of credit transactions. The customer usually needs the original or a copy of the bill of lading as proof of ownership to take possession of the goods.

A **commercial invoice** is a bill for the goods stating basic information about the transaction, including a description of the merchandise, total cost of the goods sold, addresses of the shipper and seller, and delivery and payment terms. The buyer needs the invoice to prove ownership and to arrange payment. Some governments use the commercial invoice to assess customs duties.

Other export documents that may be required include export licenses, consular invoices (used to control and identify goods, they are obtained from the country to which the goods are being shipped), certificates of origin, inspection certification, dock and/or warehouse receipts, destination control statements (serve to notify the carrier and all foreign parties that the item may only be exported to certain destinations), insurance certificates, shipper's export declarations (used to control exports and compile trade statistics), and export packaging lists.[16]

The documentation required depends on the merchandise in the shipment and its destination. The number of documents required can be quite cumbersome and costly, creating a deterrent to trade. For example, before the introduction of document simplification, it was estimated that the border-related red tape and controls within the then-European Community cost European companies $9.2 billion in extra administrative costs and delays annually.[17] To eliminate the barriers posed by all this required documentation, the EC introduced the Single Administrative Document (SAD) in 1988. The SAD led to the elimination of nearly 200 customs forms required of truckers throughout the EC when traveling from one member country to another.

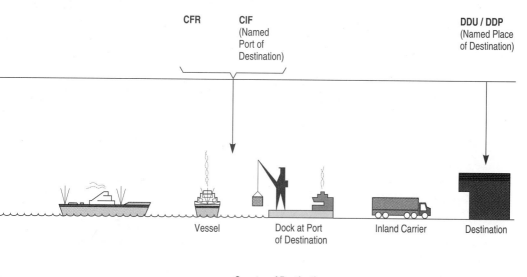

CFR

CIF
(Named
Port of
Destination)

DDU / DDP
(Named Place
of Destination)

Vessel

Dock at Port
of Destination

Inland Carrier

Destination

Country of Destination

To ensure that all documentation required is accurately completed and to minimize potential problems, firms just entering the international market should consider using **freight forwarders,** who specialize in handling export documentation.

Terms of Shipment and Sale   The responsibilities of the buyer and the seller should be spelled out as they relate to what is and what is not included in the price quotation and when ownership of goods passes from seller to buyer. **Incoterms** are the internationally accepted standard definitions for terms of sale by the International Chamber of Commerce (ICC). Although the same terms may be used in domestic transactions, they gain new meaning in the international arena. The most common Incoterms used in international business are summarized in Figure 16.5.

Prices quoted **ex-works (EXW)** apply only at the point of origin, and the seller agrees to place the goods at the disposal of the buyer at the specified place on the date or within the fixed period. All other charges are for the account of the buyer.

Free carrier (FCA) applies only at a designated inland shipping point. The seller is responsible for loading goods into the means of transportation; the buyer is responsible for all subsequent expenses. If a port of exportation is named, the costs of transporting the goods to the named port are included in the price.

Free alongside ship (FAS) at a named port of export means that the exporter quotes a price for the goods, including charges for delivery of the goods alongside a vessel at the port. The seller handles the cost of unloading and wharfage; loading, ocean transportation, and insurance are left to the buyer.

Free on board (FOB) applies only to vessel shipments. The seller quotes a price covering all expenses up to and including delivery of goods on an overseas vessel provided by or for the buyer.

Under **cost and freight (CFR)** to a named overseas port of import, the seller quotes a price for the goods, including the cost of transportation to the named port of debarkation. The cost of insurance and the choice of insurer are left to the buyer.

With **cost, insurance, and freight (CIF)** to a named overseas port of import, the seller quotes a price including insurance, all transportation, and miscellaneous charges to the point of debarkation from the vessel or aircraft. Items that may enter into the calculation of the CIF cost are (1) port charges: unloading, wharfage (terminal use) handling, storage, cartage, heavy lift, and demurrage; (2) documentation charges: certification of invoice, certificate of origin, weight certificate, and consular forms; and (3) other charges, such as fees of the freight forwarder and freight (inland and ocean) insurance premiums (marine, war, credit).

With **delivery duty paid (DDP),** the seller delivers the goods, with import duties paid, including inland transportation from import point to the buyer's premises. With **delivered duty unpaid (DDU),** only the destination customs duty and taxes are paid by the consignee. When comparing the different terms it becomes evident that ex-works signifies the maximum obligation for the buyer; delivered duty paid puts the maximum burden on the seller.

The careful determination and clear understanding of terms used and their acceptance by the parties involved are vital if subsequent misunderstandings and disputes are to be avoided.

The terms are also powerful competitive tools. The exporter should therefore learn what importers usually prefer in the particular market and what the specific transaction may require. An exporter should quote CIF whenever possible because it clearly shows the buyer the cost to get the product to a nearby port.

An inexperienced importer might be discouraged from further action by a quote such as ex-plant Jessup, Maryland, whereas CIF Kotka will enable the Finnish importer to handle the remaining costs because they are incurred at home.

INTERNATIONAL INVENTORY ISSUES

Inventories tie up a major portion of corporate funds. Capital used for inventory is not available for other corporate opportunities. Annual **inventory carrying costs** (the expense of maintaining inventories) can easily account for 25 percent or more of the value of the inventories themselves.[18] Therefore, proper inventory policies should be of major concern to the international logistician. In addition, **just-in-time inventory** policies are increasingly being adopted by multinational manufacturers and distributors. The policies minimize the volume of inventory by making it available only when it is needed. Firms using such a policy will choose suppliers on the basis of their delivery and inventory performance. Proper inventory management may therefore become a determining variable in obtaining a sale.

Although inventories are closely monitored domestically, this is often not the case internationally. This lack of preoccupation, however, does not reduce the importance of the issue. In its international inventory management, the multinational corporation is faced not only with new situations that affect inventories negatively but also with new opportunities and alternatives.

The purpose of establishing **inventory** systems—to maintain product movement in the delivery pipeline and to have a cushion to absorb demand fluctuations—is the same for domestic and international operations. The international environment, however, includes unique factors such as currency exchange rates, greater distances, and duties. At the same time, international operations provide the corporation with an opportunity to explore alternatives not available in a domestic setting, such as new sourcing or location alternatives. In international operations, the firm can make use of currency fluctuations by placing varying degrees of emphasis on inventory operations, depending on the stability of the currency of a specific country. Entire operations can be shifted to different nations to take advantage of new opportunities. International inventory management can therefore be much more flexible in its response to environmental changes.

In deciding the level of inventory to be maintained, the international manager must consider three factors: the order cycle time, desired customer service levels, and use of inventories as a strategic tool.

Order Cycle Time

The total time that passes between the placement of an order and the receipt of the merchandise is referred to as **order cycle time.** Two dimensions are of major importance to inventory management: the length of the total order cycle and its consistency. In international business, the order cycle is frequently longer than in domestic business. It comprises the time involved in order transmission, order filling, packing and preparation for shipment, and transportation. Order transmission time varies greatly internationally depending on whether electronic data interchange (EDI), facsimile, telex, telephone, or mail is used in communicating. The order-filling time may also be increased because lack of familiarity with a foreign market makes the anticipation of new orders more difficult. Packing and shipment preparation require more detailed attention. Finally, of course, transportation time increases with the distances involved. As a result, total order cycle time can approach 100 days or more. Larger inventories may have to be maintained both domestically and internationally to bridge the time gaps.

Consistency, the second dimension of order cycle time, is also more difficult to maintain in international business. Depending on the choice of transportation mode, delivery times may vary considerably from shipment to shipment. The variation requires the maintenance of larger safety stocks to be able to fill demand in periods when delays occur.

The international inventory manager should attempt to reduce order cycle time and increase its consistency without an increase in total costs. This can be accomplished by altering methods of transportation, changing inventory locations, or improving any of the other components of the order cycle time, such as the way orders are transmitted. Shifting order placement from a mail to a facsimile system can significantly reduce the order cycle time. Yet, because such a shift is likely to increase the cost of order transmittal, offsetting savings in other inventory areas must be achieved.

Customer Service Levels

The level of **customer service** denotes the responsiveness that inventory policies permit for any given situation. A customer service level of 100 percent would be defined as the ability to fill all orders within a set time—for example, three days. If, within the same three days, only 70 percent of the orders can be filled, the customer service level is 70 percent. The choice of customer service level for the firm has a major impact on the inventories needed. In highly industrialized nations, firms frequently are expected to adhere to very high levels of customer service. For example, in the European Union, actual performance measures for on-time delivery are 92 percent, for order accuracy 93 percent, and for damage-free delivery 95 percent.[19] Corporations are often tempted to design international customer service standards to similar levels.

Many managers do not realize that standards determined heuristically and based on competitive activity in the home market may be inappropriate abroad. Different locales have country-specific customer service needs and requirements. Service levels should not be oriented primarily around cost or customary domestic standards. Rather, the level chosen for use internationally should be based on expectations encountered in each market. The expectations are dependent on past performance, product desirability, customer sophistication, and the competitive status of the firm.

Because high customer service levels are costly, the goal should not be the highest customer service level possible, but rather an acceptable level. If, for example, foreign customers expect to receive their merchandise within 30 days, for the international corporation to promise delivery within 10 or 15 days does not make sense. Customers may not demand or expect such quick delivery. Indeed, such delivery may result in storage problems. In addition, the higher prices associated with higher customer service levels may reduce the competitiveness of a firm's product.

Inventory as a Strategic Tool   Inventories can be used by the international corporation as a strategic tool in dealing with currency valuation changes or to hedge against inflation. By increasing inventories before an imminent devaluation of a currency instead of holding cash, the corporation may reduce its exposure to devaluation losses. Similarly, in the case of high inflation, large inventories can provide an important inflation hedge. In such circumstances, the international inventory manager must balance the cost of maintaining high levels of inventories with the benefits accruing to the firm from hedging against inflation or devaluation. Many countries, for example, charge a property tax on stored goods. If the increase in tax payments outweighs the hedging benefits to the corporation, it would be unwise to increase inventories before a devaluation.

Despite the benefits of reducing the firm's financial risk, inventory management must still fall in line with the overall corporate market strategy. Only by recognizing the trade-offs, which may result in less than optimal inventory policies, can the overall benefit to the corporation be maximized. Operations research models can be very helpful in modeling such trade-offs.

INTERNATIONAL PACKAGING ISSUES

Packaging is of particular importance in international logistics because it is instrumental in getting the merchandise to the ultimate destination in a safe, maintainable, and presentable condition. Packaging that is adequate for domestic shipping may be inadequate for international transportation because the shipment will be subject to the motions of the vessel on which it is carried. Added stress in international shipping also arises from the transfer of goods among different modes of transportation. Figure 16.6 provides examples of some sources of stress in intermodal movement that are most frequently found in international transportation.

The responsibility for appropriate packaging rests with the shipper of goods. The U.S. Carriage of Goods by Sea Act of 1936 states: "Neither the carrier nor the ship shall be responsible for loss or damage arising or resulting from insufficiency of packing." The shipper must therefore ensure that the goods are prepared appropriately for international shipping. This is important because it has been found that "the losses that occur as a result of breakage, pilferage, and theft exceed the losses caused by major maritime casualties, which include fires, sinkings, and collision of vessels. Thus the largest of these losses is a preventable loss."[20]

Packaging decisions must also take into account differences in environmental conditions—for example, climate. When the ultimate destination is very humid or particularly cold, special provisions must be made to prevent damage to the product. The task becomes even more challenging when one considers that, in the course of long-distance transportation, dramatic changes in climate can take place. Still famous is the case of a firm in Taiwan that shipped drinking glasses to the Middle East. The company used wooden crates and padded the glasses with hay. Most of the glasses, however, were broken by the time they reached their destination. As the crates traveled into the drier Middle East, the moisture content of the hay had dropped. By the time the crates were delivered, the thin straw offered almost no protection.[21]

FIGURE 16.6   **Stresses in Intermodal Movement**

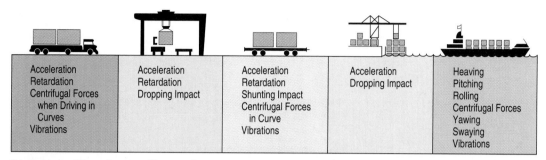

| Acceleration Retardation Centrifugal Forces when Driving in Curves Vibrations | Acceleration Retardation Dropping Impact | Acceleration Retardation Shunting Impact Centrifugal Forces in Curve Vibrations | Acceleration Dropping Impact | Heaving Pitching Rolling Centrifugal Forces Yawing Swaying Vibrations |

Note: Each transportation mode exerts a different set of stresses and strains on containerized cargoes. The most commonly overlooked are those associated with ocean transport.

Source: David Greenfield, "Perfect Packing for Export," from *Handling and Shipping Management,* September 1980 (Cleveland, Ohio: Penton Publishing), 47.

The weight of packaging must also be considered, particularly when airfreight is used, as the cost of shipping is often based on weight. At the same time, packaging material must be sufficiently strong to permit stacking in international transportation. Another consideration is that, in some countries, duties are assessed according to the gross weight of shipments, which includes the weight of packaging. Obviously, the heavier the packaging, the higher the duty will be.

The shipper must pay sufficient attention to instructions provided by the customer for packaging. For example, requests by the customer that the weight of any one package should not exceed a certain limit or that specific package dimensions should be adhered to, usually are made for a reason. Often they reflect limitations in transportation or handling facilities at the point of destination.

Although the packaging of a product is often used as a form of display abroad, international packaging can rarely serve the dual purpose of protection and display. Therefore double packaging may be necessary. The display package is for future use at the point of destination; another package surrounds it for protective purposes.

One solution to the packaging problem in international logistics has been the development of intermodal containers—large metal boxes that fit on trucks, ships, railroad cars, and airplanes and ease the frequent transfer of goods in international shipments. Developed in different forms for both sea and air transportation, containers also offer better utilization of carrier space because of standardization of size. The shipper therefore may benefit from lower transportation rates. In addition, containers can offer greater safety from pilferage and damage. Of course, at the same time, the use of containers allows thieves to abscond with an entire shipment rather than just parts of it. On some routes in Russia, for example, theft and pilferage of cargo are so common that liability insurers will not insure container haulers in the region.[22]

Container traffic is heavily dependent on the existence of appropriate handling facilities, both domestically and internationally. In addition, the quality of inland transportation must be considered. If transportation for containers is not available and the merchandise must be removed, the expected cost reductions may not materialize.

In some countries, rules for the handling of containers may be designed to maintain employment. For example, U.S. union rules obligate shippers to withhold containers from firms that do not employ members of the International Longshoremen's

Trade and Travel Networks

Civilization depends on trade for growth and travel makes this possible. Shipping is the most important method of world transport but economic progress and mobility are constantly being improved by the development of new routes and new methods of transport.

Road and Rail

Integrated road and rail networks are the basis of industrial society. Containerization and the extension of modern highway systems have increased flexibility and reduced the emphasis on railways transporting freight.

Roads

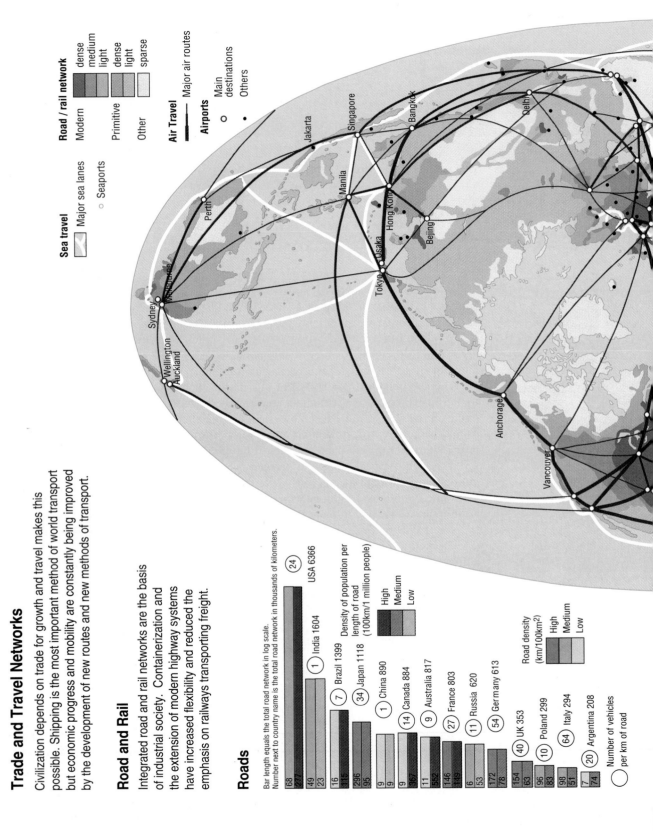

Bar length equals the total road network in log scale.
Number next to country name is the total road network in thousands of kilometers.

68 277	(24)	USA 6366	
49 23	(1)	India 1604	
16 116	(7)	Brazil 1399	
296 95	(34)	Japan 1118	
9 9	(1)	China 890	
9 357	(14)	Canada 884	
11 552	(9)	Australia 817	
146 149	(27)	France 803	
6 53	(11)	Russia 620	
172 78	(54)	Germany 613	
154 63	(40)	UK 353	
96 83	(10)	Poland 299	
98 51	(64)	Italy 294	
7 74	(20)	Argentina 208	

Density of population per length of road (100km/1 million people)

High	Medium	Low

Road density (km/100km²)

High	Medium	Low

( ) Number of vehicles per km of road

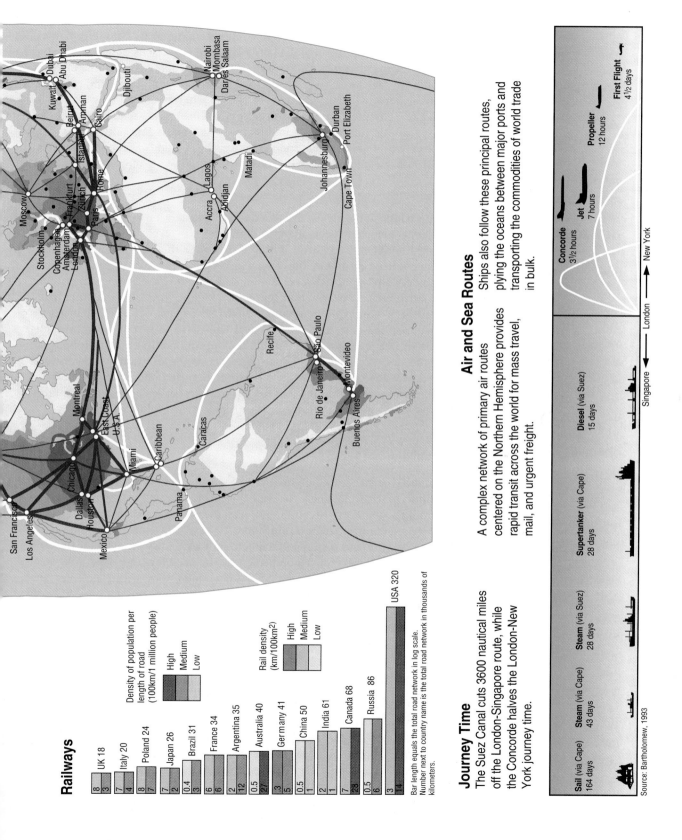

Railways

Density of population per length of road
(100km/1 million people)

High
Medium
Low

Rail density
(km/100km²)

High
Medium
Low

UK 18	8 / 3
Italy 20	7 / 4
Poland 24	8 / 7
Japan 26	7 / 2
Brazil 31	0.4 / 3
France 34	6 / 6
Argentina 35	2 / 12
Australia 40	0.5 / 27
Germany 41	3 / 5
China 50	0.5 / 1
India 61	2 / 1
Canada 68	7 / 28
Russia 86	0.5 / 6
USA 320	3 / 14

Bar length equals the total road network in log scale.
Number next to country name is the total road network in thousands of kilometers.

Air and Sea Routes

A complex network of primary air routes centered on the Northern Hemisphere provides rapid transit across the world for mass travel, mail, and urgent freight.

Ships also follow these principal routes, plying the oceans between major ports and transporting the commodities of world trade in bulk.

Journey Time

The Suez Canal cuts 3600 nautical miles off the London-Singapore route, while the Concorde halves the London-New York journey time.

Singapore — London — New York

Sail (via Cape) 164 days	Steam (via Cape) 43 days	Steam (via Suez) 28 days	Supertanker (via Cape) 28 days	Diesel (via Suez) 15 days

Concorde 3½ hours	Jet 7 hours	Propeller 12 hours	First Flight 4½ days

Source: Bartholomew, 1993

Association for the loading or unloading of containers within a 50-mile radius of Atlantic or Gulf ports. Such restrictions can result in an onerous cost burden. Packaging issues also need to be closely linked to overall strategic plans. The international logistician should focus on the total delivery picture to ensure customer satisfaction. The type of packaging, method of transportation, route, country of destination, port facilities, customs procedures, identification markings, final destination, and customer specifications all need to be taken into consideration when packing goods for export.

Overall, close attention must be paid to international packaging. The customer who ordered and paid for the merchandise expects it to arrive on time and in good condition. Even with replacements and insurance, the customer will not be satisfied if there are delays. Dissatisfaction will usually translate directly into lost sales.

INTERNATIONAL STORAGE ISSUES

Although international logistics is discussed as a movement or flow of goods, a stationary period is involved when merchandise becomes inventory stored in warehouses. Heated arguments can arise within a firm over the need for and utility of warehousing internationally. On the one hand, customers may expect quick responses to orders and rapid delivery. Accommodating the customer's expectations may require locating many distribution centers around the world. On the other hand, warehouse space is expensive. In addition, the larger volume of inventory increases the inventory carrying cost. The international logistician must consider the trade-offs between service and cost to determine the appropriate levels of warehousing. Other trade-offs also exist within the logistics function. As an example, fewer warehouses will allow for consolidation of transportation and therefore lower transportation rates to the warehouse. However, if the warehouses are located far from customers, the cost of outgoing transportation from them will increase.

Storage Facilities

The international logistician is faced with the **location decision** of how many distribution centers to have and where to locate them. The availability of facilities abroad will differ from the domestic situation. For example, while public storage is widely available in some countries, such facilities may be scarce or entirely lacking in others. Also, the standards and quality of facilities can vary widely. As a result, the storage decision of the firm is often accompanied by the need for large-scale, long-term investments. An example of the possible costs encountered by a firm seeking warehouse space internationally is given in Global Perspective 16.4. Despite the high cost, international storage facilities should be established if they support the overall logistics effort. In many markets, adequate storage facilities are imperative to satisfy customer demands and to compete successfully. For example, since the establishment of a warehouse connotes a visible presence, in doing so a firm can convince local distributors and customers of its commitment to remain in the market for the long term.

Once the decision is made to use storage facilities abroad, the warehouses must be carefully analyzed. As an example, in some countries warehouses have low ceilings. Packaging developed for the high stacking of products is therefore unnecessary or even counterproductive. In other countries, automated warehousing is available. Proper bar coding of products and the use of package dimensions acceptable to the warehousing system are basic requirements. In contrast, in warehouses still stocked manually, weight limitations will be of major concern. And, if no forklift trucks are available, palletized delivery is of little use.

Global Perspective

16.4
The Cost of Warehousing in Japan

One of the major shortcomings of the Japanese distribution system is its lack of warehousing facilities. Even though the Japanese government has begun to introduce change by making warehousing facilities more widely available and by legislating the building of distribution centers, the cost of storage space is quite high. In order to obtain space in an existing distribution center, tenants often must pay a number of charges. Some of these are:

- Construction contribution fund: Participation in this fund consists of a one-time payment, which is refundable only after 10 years, with no interest payment.

- Security deposit: This deposit is refundable only at the end of the lease, with no interest payment.
- Monthly rent.
- Administrative charges: These charges are paid for administrative support that is rendered by the management of the distribution center.

Leases typically need to be signed for a minimum of 10 years. Despite the substantial costs, vacancy rates at existing distribution centers are extremely low, with outside turnover often lower than 2 percent.

Sources: Michael R. Czinkota and Jon Woronoff, *Unlocking Japan's Market* (Chicago: Probus Publishing, 1991), 90; and John Fahy and Fuyuki Taguchi, "Reassessing the Japanese Distribution System," *Sloan Management Review,* Winter 1995, 49–61.

To optimize the logistics system, the logistician should analyze international product sales and then rank order products according to warehousing needs. Products that are most sensitive to delivery time might be classified as "A" products. "A" products would be stocked in all distribution centers, and safety stock levels would be kept high. Alternatively, the storage of products can be more selective, if quick delivery by air can be guaranteed. Products for which immediate delivery is not urgent could be classified as "B" products. They would be stored only at selected distribution centers around the world. Finally, products for which there is little demand would be stocked only at headquarters. Should an urgent need for delivery arise, airfreight could again assure rapid shipment. Classifying products enables the international logistician to substantially reduce total international warehousing requirements and still maintain acceptable service levels.

However, at all times the logistician must take into account the service requirements and sensitivities of the customer. When equipment downtime runs $100,000 an hour, delivery of a part within 24 or 48 hours is simply not acceptable. In such instances, strategically placed depots in a region must ensure that instantaneous response becomes possible. For example, Storage Technologies, a maker of storage devices for mainframe computers, keeps parts at seven of its European subsidiary offices so that in an emergency it can reach any continental customer within four hours.[23]

Special Trade Zones

Areas where foreign goods may be held or processed and then reexported without incurring duties are called **foreign trade zones.** The zones can be found at major ports of entry and also at inland locations near major production facilities. For example, Kansas City, Missouri, has one of the largest foreign trade zones in the United States.

The existence of trade zones can be quite useful to the international firm. For example, in a particular country, the benefits derived from lower labor costs may be offset by high duties and tariffs. As a result, location of manufacturing and storage facilities in that country may prove uneconomical. Foreign trade zones are designed to exclude the impact of duties from the location decision. This is done by exempting merchandise in the foreign trade zone from duty payment. The international firm can therefore import merchandise; store it in the foreign trade zone; and process, alter, test, or demonstrate it—all without paying duties. If the merchandise is subsequently shipped abroad (that is, reexported), no duty payments are ever due. Duty payments become due only if the merchandise is shipped into the country from the foreign trade zone.

Trade zones can also be useful as transshipment points to reduce logistics cost and redesign marketing approaches. For example, Audiovox was shipping small quantities of car alarms from a Taiwanese contract manufacturer directly to distributors in Chile. The shipments were costly and the marketing strategy of requiring high minimum orders stopped distributors from buying. The firm resolved the dilemma by using a Miami trade zone to ship the alarms from Taiwan and consolidate the goods with other shipments to Chile. The savings in freight costs allowed the Chilean distributors to order whatever quantity they wanted and allowed the company to quote lower prices. As a result, sales improved markedly.[24]

All parties to the arrangement benefit from foreign trade zones. The government maintaining the trade zone achieves increased employment and investment. The firm using the trade zone obtains a spearhead in the foreign market without incurring all of the costs customarily associated with such an activity. As a result, goods can be reassembled, and large shipments can be broken down into smaller units. Also, goods can be repackaged when packaging weight becomes part of the duty assessment. Finally, goods can be given domestic "made-in" status if assembled in the foreign trade zone. Thus, duties may be payable only on the imported materials and component parts rather than on the labor that is used to finish the product.

In addition to foreign trade zones, governments also have established export processing zones and special economic areas. The common dimensions for all the zones are that special rules apply to them when compared with other regions of the country, and that the purpose of these special rules lies in the government's desire to stimulate the economy, particularly the export side of international trade.

Export processing zones usually provide tax- and duty-free treatment for production facilities whose output is destined abroad. The **maquiladoras** of Mexico are one example of a program that permits firms to take advantage of sharp differentials in labor costs. Firms can carry out the labor-intensive part of their operations in Mexico, while sourcing raw materials or component parts from other nations. Even though the eventual tariff reductions that will result from the signing of the North American Free Trade Agreement (NAFTA) will reduce some benefits of the maquiladora program, low Mexican labor costs will continue to attract labor-intensive industries.

One country that has used trade zones very successfully for its own economic development is China. Through the creation of *special economic zones,* in which there are no tariffs, substantial tax incentives, and low prices for land and labor, the government has attracted many foreign investors bringing in billions of dollars. The investors have brought new equipment, technology, and managerial know-how and have substantially increased the local economic prosperity. For example, the job generation effect has been so strong that the central Chinese government has expressed concern about the overheating of the economy and the inequities between regions with and without trade zones.[25]

For the logistician, the decision whether to use such zones mainly is framed by the overall benefit for the logistics system. Clearly, additional transport and retransport are required, warehousing facilities need to be constructed, and material handling frequency will increase. However, the costs may well be balanced by the preferential government treatment or by lower labor costs.

MANAGEMENT OF INTERNATIONAL LOGISTICS

The very purpose of a multinational firm is to benefit from system synergism and a persuasive argument can be made for the coordination of international logistics at corporate headquarters. Without coordination, subsidiaries will tend to optimize their individual efficiency but jeopardize the efficiency of the overall performance of the firm.

Centralized Logistics Management

A significant characteristic of the centralized approach to international logistics is the existence of headquarters staff that retains decision-making power over logistics activities affecting international subsidiaries. If headquarters exerts control, it must also take the primary responsibility for its decisions. Clearly, ill will may arise if local managers are appraised and rewarded on the basis of a performance they do not control. This may be particularly problematic if headquarters staff suffers from a lack of information or expertise.

To avoid internal problems, both headquarters staff and local management should report to one person. This person, whether the vice president for international logistics or the president of the firm, can then become the final arbiter to decide the firm's priorities. Of course, the individual should also be in charge of determining appropriate rewards for managers, both at headquarters and abroad, so that corporate decisions that alter a manager's performance level will not affect the manager's appraisal and evaluation. Further, the individual can contribute an objective view when inevitable conflicts arise in international logistics coordination. The internationally centralized decision-making process leads to an overall logistics management perspective that can dramatically improve profitability.

Decentralized Logistics Management

An alternative to the centralized international logistics system is the "decentralized full profit center model."[26] The main rationale for such decentralization is the fact that "when an organization attempts to deal with markets on a global scale, there are problems of coordination."[27] Particularly when the firm serves many international markets that are diverse in nature, total centralization would leave the firm unresponsive to local adaptation needs.

If each subsidiary is made a profit center in itself, each one carries the full responsibility for its performance, which can lead to greater local management satisfaction and to better adaptation to local market conditions. Yet often such decentralization deprives the logistics function of the benefits of coordination. For example, while headquarters, referring to its large volume of overall international shipments, may be able to extract bottom rates from transportation firms, individual subsidiaries by themselves may not have similar bargaining power.

Once products are within a specific market, however, increased input from local logistics operations should be expected and encouraged. At the very least, local managers should be able to provide input into the logistics decisions generated by headquarters. Ideally, within a frequent planning cycle, local managers can identify the logistics benefits and constraints existing in their particular market and communicate them to headquarters. Headquarters can then either adjust its international logistics strategy accordingly or explain to the manager why system optimization requires actions different from the ones recommended. Such a justification process will help greatly in reducing the potential for animosity between local and headquarters operations.

Outsourcing Logistics Services

A third option, used by some corporations, is the systematic outsourcing of logistics capabilities. By collaborating with transportation firms, private warehouses, or other

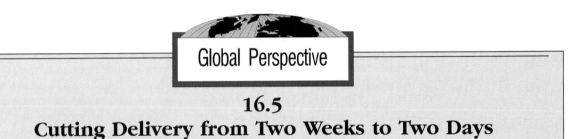

Global Perspective

16.5
Cutting Delivery from Two Weeks to Two Days

Today information moves around the world in the blink of an eye. Semiconductors are instrumental in making this happen. Increasingly producers of semiconductors recognize that their products need to move from producer to customer nearly as fast.

One company that attempts to do just that is National Semiconductor Corporation (NSC) located in California. The firm realized that to allow greater speed of delivery, it needed to overhaul its global supply network. The old logistical network of decentralized control was a tangle of unnecessary interchanges, propped up by 44 different international freight forwarders and 18 different air carriers. "The complexity of it all wasn't allowing consistent service," commented Kelvin Phillips, NSC director of worldwide logistics.

National Semiconductor wanted to change its 5- to 18-day delivery time and offer a 2-day delivery guarantee. The key factor in the strategy was the recruitment of a third party logistics firm to provide valuable expertise as well as needed infrastructure. NSC turned to Federal Express's Business Logistics Services (BLS) as a partner. Explained Phillips, "Our company competes on technology; we cannot compete on logistics. Federal's core competency is delivery. It can do what we can't." BLS was able to provide National Semiconductor with a formidable logistics network

by granting access to 420 aircraft, 1,869 worldwide facilities, more than 100,000 computer terminals, 31,211 surface vehicles, and an infrastructure with more than 90,000 employees. Phillips views Federal as "using the experts who spend billions on logistics."

Five Asian NSC plants produce 95 percent of its product. In the past, an unconsolidated system of distribution existed where each plant optimized its own business performance by individually holding an inventory, performing pick and pack, and directing shipments to the main distribution centers in Scotland and California. With the help of BLS, product pickups are now made at each of the plants and funneled to a centralized distribution center in Singapore. At this point, orders are consolidated for more cost-effective routing and deliveries are made directly from Singapore within two business days. An additional advantage of using BLS is the availability of dedicated freighter capacity, something in short supply in this market during certain seasons.

The undertaking was of no small scale and as Phillips noted, "When people have been doing things one way for 20 years, the switch is difficult." However, the cost of change is worth the savings gained from a more efficient and sensible global delivery system.

Source: "Macro Logistics for Microprocessors," *Distribution,* April 1993: 66–72.

specialists, corporate resources can be concentrated on the firm's core product. Global Perspective 16.5 provides an example. While the cost savings and specialization benefits of such a strategy seem clear, one must also consider the loss of control both for the firm and its customers that may result from such outsourcing. Yet, contract logistics does not and should not require the handing over of control. Rather, it offers concentration on one's specialization—a division of labor. The control and responsibility toward the customer remain with the firm, even though operations may move to a highly trained outside organization.

LOGISTICS AND THE ENVIRONMENT

Apart from the structure of the logistics function, major changes are also occurring in the strategic orientation of the field. The logistician plays an increasingly important role in allowing the firm to operate in an environmentally conscious way. Environmental laws, expectations, and self-imposed goals set by firms are difficult to adhere to without a logistics orientation that systematically takes such concerns into account. Since laws and regulations differ across the world, the firm's efforts need to be responsive to a wide variety of requirements. One new logistics orientation that has grown in importance due to environmental concerns is the development of **reverse distribution** systems. Such systems are instrumental in ensuring that the firm not only delivers the product to the market, but also can retrieve it from the market for subsequent use, recycling, or disposal. As Global Perspective 16.6 shows, to a growing degree the ability to develop such reverse logistics is a key determinant for market acceptance and profitability.

Society is also beginning to recognize that retrieval should not be restricted to short-term consumer goods, such as bottles. Rather, it may be even more important to devise systems that enable the retrieval and disposal of long-term capital goods, such as cars, refrigerators, air conditioners, and industrial goods, with the least possible burden on the environment. In Germany, for example, since January 1, 1995,

Global Perspective

16.6
Environmental Impact on Logistics

Increasingly, countries pass laws that create environmental standards. A recent German law regulates packaging, a U.S. law levies taxes on certain chemicals destined for toxic waste dumps, a law in Denmark requires that drinks be sold in refillable bottles, and a Canadian regulation requires deposits on beer bottles.

On the surface, it appears that these laws are a necessary and appropriate response to growing world concerns about the environment. Yet, the environmental standards may have been motivated at least in part by protectionistic reasons. For example, a provision of Germany's packaging law requires that at most, 28 percent of all beer and soft-drink containers can be "one-trip" (disposable). Importers suspect the provision was designed to benefit small German brewers who will find it easier to collect and refill the empties. Packagers also dislike the law's insistence that companies collect their used packaging for recycling. The fact that this will be easier for local manufacturers may prejudice retailers in favor of domestically produced goods.

Sources: "Free Trade's Green Hurdle," *Economist,* June 15, 1991, 61–62; and "Should Trade Go Green?" *Economist,* January 26, 1991, 13–14.

car manufacturers have been required to take back their used vehicles for dismantling and recycling purposes. The design of such long-term systems across the world may well be one of the key challenges and opportunities for the logistician and will require close collaboration with all other functions in the firm, such as design, production, and marketing.

On the transportation side, logistics managers will need to expand their involvement in carrier and routing selection. For example, shippers of oil or other potentially hazardous materials increasingly will be expected to ensure that the carriers used have excellent safety records and use only double-hulled ships. Society may even expect corporate involvement in choosing the route that the shipment will travel, preferring routes that are far from ecologically important and sensitive zones.

The logistician also will need to consider trade-offs between firm-specific performance and the resulting environmental burden. For example, even though a just-in-time inventory system may connote highly desirable inventory savings, the resulting cost of frequent delivery, additional highway congestion, and incremental air pollution also need to be factored into the planning horizon. Despite the difficulty, firms will need to assert leadership in such trade-off considerations to provide society with a better quality of life.

SUMMARY

As competitiveness is becoming increasingly dependent on cost efficiency, the field of international logistics is emerging as one of major importance because international distribution accounts for between 10 and 25 percent of the total landed cost of an international order.

International logistics is concerned with the flow of materials into, through, and out of the international corporation and therefore includes materials management as well as physical distribution. The logistician must recognize the total systems demands on the firm, its suppliers, and customers to develop trade-offs between various logistics components.

International logistics differs from domestic activities in that it deals with greater distances, new variables, and greater complexity because of national differences. One major factor to consider is transportation. The international manager needs to understand transportation infrastructures in other countries and modes of transportation such as ocean shipping and airfreight. The choice among these modes will depend on the customer's demands and the firm's transit time, predictability, and cost requirements. In addition, noneconomic factors such as government regulations weigh heavily in this decision.

Inventory management is another major consideration. Inventories abroad are expensive to maintain yet often crucial for international success. The logistician must evaluate requirements for order cycle times and customer service levels to develop an international inventory policy that can also serve as a strategic management tool.

International packaging is important because it ensures arrival of the merchandise at the ultimate destination in safe condition. In developing packaging, environmental conditions such as climate and handling conditions must be considered.

The logistics manager must also deal with international storage issues and determine where to locate inventories. International warehouse space will have to be leased or purchased and decisions will have to be made about utilizing foreign trade zones.

International logistics management is increasing in importance. Connecting the logistics function with overall corporate strategic concerns and environmental demands will increasingly be a requirement for successful global competitiveness.

Key Terms and Concepts

materials management	bill of lading
physical distribution	straight bill of lading
systems concept	shipper's order
total cost concept	commercial invoice
total after-tax profit concept	freight forwarders
trade-off concept	Incoterms
transportation modes	ex-works (EXW)
logistics platform	free carrier (FCA)
land bridges	free alongside ship (FAS)
sea bridges	free on board (FOB)
intermodal movements	cost and freight (CFR)
ocean shipping	cost, insurance, and freight (CIF)
liner service	delivery duty paid (DDP)
bulk service	delivery duty unpaid (DDU)
tramp service	inventory carrying costs
container ships	just-in-time inventory
roll-on-roll-off (RORO)	inventory
ports	order cycle time
airfreight	customer service
density	location decision
transit time	foreign trade zones
reliability	maquiladora
preferential policies	reverse distribution

Questions for Discussion

1. Why do international firms pay so little attention to international logistics issues?
2. Contrast the use of ocean shipping and airfreight.
3. Explain the meaning and impact of transit time in international logistics.
4. How and why do governments interfere in "rational" freight carrier selection?
5. What is your view of the 40/40/20 freight allocation rule of the United Nations Conference on Trade and Development?
6. How can an international firm reduce its order cycle time?
7. Why should customer service levels differ internationally? Is it, for example, ethical to offer a lower customer service level in developing countries than in industrialized countries?
8. What role can the international logistician play in improving the environmental friendliness of the firm?

Recommended Readings

Ballou, Ronald H. *Business Logistics Management.* Englewood Cliffs, N.J.: Prentice-Hall, 1992.

Banister, David, and Joseph Berechman, eds. *Transport in a Unified Europe: Policies and Challenges*. Amsterdam: North Holland, 1993.

Christopher, Martin. *Logistics: The Strategic Issues*. New York: Chapman & Hall, 1992.

Ewert, Donald E. *Export Shipping*. Cincinnati: International Business Publications, 1992.

Kotabe, Masaaki. *Global Sourcing Strategy: R&D, Manufacturing and Marketing Interfaces*. New York: Quorum Books, 1992.

LaLonde, Bernard, Martha Cooper, and Thomas Noordewier. *Customer Service: A Third Party Perspective*. Oakbrook, Ill.: Council of Logistics Management, 1989.

McConville, J. *Shipping Business and Maritime Economics: An Annotated International Bibliography*. London: Mansell, 1995.

O'Laughlin, Kevin A., James Cooper, and Eric Cabocel. *Reconfiguring European Logistics Systems*. Oak Brook, Ill.: Council of Logistics Management, 1993.

Polak, Jacob, and Arnold Heertje, eds. *European Transport Economics*. Cambridge: Blackwell Publishers, 1993.

Wood, Donald F., ed. *International Logistics*. New York: Chapman & Hall, 1994.

Notes

1. John F. Magee, "The Logistics of Distribution," *Harvard Business Review* 38 (July–August 1960).

2. Robert E. McGarrah, "Logistics for the International Manufacturer," *Harvard Business Review* 44 (March–April 1966).

3. Dennis Davis, "New Involvement in the Orient," *Distribution* 78 (October 1979).

4. U.S. Department of Commerce, *Survey of Export Management Companies on the Export Trading Company Concept* (Washington, D.C.: Government Printing Office, 1977).

5. Rex R. Williams, "International Physical Distribution Management," in *Contemporary Physical Distribution and Logistics*, 4th ed., ed. James C. Johnson and Donald F. Wood (Tulsa, Okla.: Penwell Books, 1981), 150.

6. Paul T. Nelson and Gadi Toledano, "Challenges for International Logistics Management," *Journal of Business Logistics* 1, 2 (1979): 7.

7. Michael R. Czinkota, "Global Neighbors, Poor Relations," *Marketing Management* 3, 1 (1994): 46–52.

8. Hans-Christian Pfohl and Rudolf Lange, "Sourcing from Central and Eastern Europe: Conditions and Implementation," *International Journal of Physical Distribution and Logistics Management* 23, 8 (1993): 5–15.

9. James H. Perry, "Emerging Economic and Technological Futures: Implications for Design and Management of Logistics Systems in the 1990's," *Journal of Business Logistics* 12 (1991): 1–16.

10. Nelson and Toledano, "Challenges for International Logistics Management," 2.

11. David A. Ricks, *Blunders in International Business* (Cambridge: Blackwell Publishers, 1993), 16.

12. Michael E. Porter, *The Competitive Advantage of Nations* (New York: The Free Press, 1990).

13. Paul R. Murphy, Douglas R. Dalenberg, and James M. Daley, "Analyzing International Water Transportation: The Perspectives of Large U.S. Industrial Corporations," *Journal of Business Logistics* 12 (1991): 169–190.

14. Gunnar K. Sletmo and Jacques Picard, "International Distribution Policies and the Role of Air Freight," *Journal of Business Logistics* 6 (No. 1, 1984): 35–52.

15. Peter Buxbaum, "Timberland's New Spin on Global Logistics," *Distribution* (May 1994): 32–36.

16. *A Basic Guide to Exporting* (Lincolnwood, Ill.: NTC Publishers, 1989).

17. Julie Wolf, "Help for Distribution in Europe," *Northeast International Business,* January 1989, 52.

18. Bernard J. LaLonde and Paul H. Zinszer, *Customer Service: Meaning and Measurement* (Chicago: National Council of Physical Distribution Management, 1976).

19. Patrick M. Byrne, Johan C. Aurik, and Jan Van der Oord, "New Priorities for Logistics Services in Europe," *Transportation and Distribution* (February 1994): 43–48.

20. Charles A. Taft, *Management of Physical Distribution and Transportation,* 7th ed. (Homewood, Ill.: Irwin, 1984), 324.

21. Ricks, *Blunders in International Business,* 27.

22. Elizabeth Canna, "Russian Supply Chains," *American Shipper,* June 1994, 49–53.

23. Gregory L. Miles, "Have Spares, Will Travel," *International Business* (December 1994): 26–27.

24. Marita von Oldenborgh, "Power Logistics," *International Business* (October 1994): 32–34.

25. Li Rongxia, "Free Trade Zones in China," *Beijing Review,* August 2–8, 1993, 14–21.

26. Jacques Picard, "Physical Distribution Organization in Multinationals: The Position of Authority," *International Journal of Physical Distribution and Materials Management* 13, 2 (1983): 24.

27. Philip B. Schary, *Logistics Decisions* (Hinsdale, Ill.: Dryden, 1984), 407.

CHAPTER 17

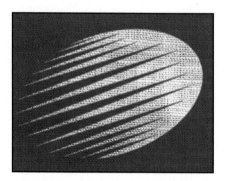

International Financial Management

Learning Objectives

1. To understand how international business and investment activity alters the traditional financial management activities of the firm.

2. To explore how the very value of all firms, even those with no direct international business activity, changes with exchange rate movements.

3. To examine the three exposures of multinational firms to exchange rate changes over time.

4. To understand which strategies and financial techniques are used to manage the currency risks of the modern multinational firm.

Chinese Banks Holding Up Payments
On Delivered Goods

HONG KONG - Some foreign exporters say they are being forced to wait as long as six months for payment on goods delivered to customers in China. And the culprits are cash-strapped Chinese banks, according to analysts and company executives in Hong Kong.

Under a system that foreign companies and U.S. trade negotiators have long decried, any foreign enterprise exporting goods to China must sell through a state-owned import-export company. Customers, from retailers to factories, must pay this middleman in renminbi for the goods. The import-export company's bank then remits the money to the foreign supplier in foreign exchange.

While extricating money from Chinese banks has never been easy, the delays have lengthened in recent months. Ultronics International Holdings, Ltd., a Hong Kong medical equipment distributor that relies on China for 90 percent of its sales, has faced increasing delays in payments since the end of last year. The wait used to be one or two months, now it is as long as six months, said Leo Lam, the company's financial controller.

There are ways for companies to cushion themselves. Goldlion Holdings Ltd., which has close to 70 percent of its sales in China, insists on letters of credit for almost all of its transactions on the mainland. Under this system, when Goldlion delivers its goods—men's ties, leather goods and accessories—it receives a letter of credit, which it then presents to the customer's bank. That bank must transfer money to Goldlion within a set time, which can range from several days to several weeks, said Louis Lau, Goldlion's financial controller. "With a letter of credit, the risk is basically none," Lau said.

However, both men concede that it can be difficult to negotiate such payment terms with customers and remain competitive. And others scoff at the idea that China's banks will honor a letter of credit more readily than another contract. "Getting a letter of credit in China is practically useless," said a Hong Kong exporter whose company rarely uses them. "Under international practice, banks are supposed to pay (when a letter of credit is presented). But in China, they can refuse payment if they don't have the money."

Source: Extracted from Leslie Chang, "Exporters Say Struggling Chinese Banks Hold Up Payments on Delivered Goods," *The Wall Street Journal,* November 22, 1994, A17.

Financial management is a broad term that covers all the business decisions of the firm that involve cash flows. The cash flows may be simply getting paid for products sold (as in collecting on exports to China described in the opening vignette), the funding of the firm (raising capital on domestic and international financial markets), or the management of the exchange rate and interest rate risks that all firms face when operating in the multinational market.

OVERVIEW OF INTERNATIONAL FINANCIAL MANAGEMENT

International financial management is not a separate set of issues from domestic or traditional financial management, but the additional levels of risk and complexity introduced by the conduct of business across borders. Business across borders introduces different laws, different methods, different markets, different interest rates, and most of all, different currencies.

The many dimensions of international financial management are most easily explained in the context of a firm's financial decision-making process in evaluating a potential foreign investment. Such an evaluation includes:

- Capital budgeting, which is the process of evaluating the financial feasibility of an individual investment, whether it be the purchase of a stock, real estate, or a firm.

- Capital structure, which is the determination of the relative quantities of debt capital and equity capital that will constitute the funding of the investment.

- Raising long-term capital, which is the acquisition of equity or debt for the investment. It requires the selection of the exact form of capital, its maturity, its reward or repayment structure, its currency of denomination, and its source.

- Working capital and cash flow management, which is the management of operating and financial cash flows passing in and out of a specific investment project.

International financial management means that all the above financial activities will be complicated by the differences in markets, laws, and especially currencies. This is the field of financial risk management. Firms may intentionally borrow foreign currencies, buy forward contracts, or price their products in different currencies to manage their cash flows that are denominated in foreign currencies.

Changes in interest and exchange rates will affect each of the above steps in the international investment process. All firms, no matter how "domestic" they may seem in structure, are influenced by exchange rate changes. The financial managers of a firm that has any dimension of international activity, imports or exports, foreign subsidiaries or affiliates, must pay special attention to these issues if the firm is to succeed in its international endeavors. The discussion begins with the difficulties of simply getting paid for international sales, import/export financing.

IMPORT/EXPORT TRADE FINANCING

Unlike most domestic business, international business often occurs between two parties that do not know each other very well. Yet, in order to conduct business, a large degree of financial trust must exist. This financial trust is basically the trust that the buyer of a product will actually pay for it on or after delivery. For example, if a furniture manufacturer in South Carolina receives an order from a distributor located in Cleveland, Ohio, the furniture maker will ordinarily fill the order, ship the furniture, and await payment. Payment terms are usually 30 to 60 days. This is trade on an "open account basis." The furniture manufacturer has placed a considerable amount of financial trust in the buyer but normally is paid with little problem.

Internationally, however, financial trust is pushed to its limit. An order from a foreign buyer may constitute a degree of credit risk (the risk of not being repaid) that the producer (the exporter) cannot afford to take. The exporter needs some guarantee that the importer will pay for the goods. Other factors that tend to intensify this problem include the increased lag times necessary for international shipments and the potential risks of payments in different currencies. For this reason, arrangements that provide guarantees for exports are important to countries and companies wanting to expand international sales. This can be accomplished through a sequence of documents surrounding the letter of credit.

Trade Financing Using a Letter of Credit (L/C)

A lumber manufacturer in the Pacific Northwest of the United States, Vanport, receives a large order from a Japanese construction company, Endaka, for a shipment of old-growth pine lumber. Vanport has not worked with Endaka before and there-

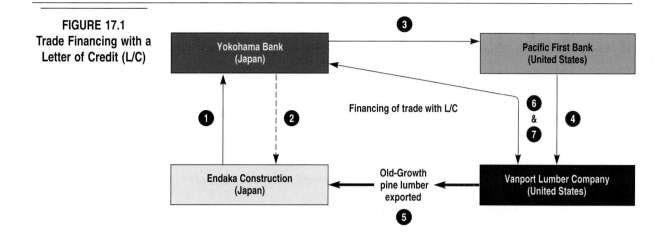

FIGURE 17.1
Trade Financing with a Letter of Credit (L/C)

fore seeks some assurance that payment for the lumber will actually be made. Vanport ordinarily does not require any assurance of the buyer's ability to pay (sometimes a small down payment or deposit is made as a sign of good faith), but an international sale of this size is too large a risk. If Endaka could not or would not pay, the cost of returning the lumber products to the United States would be prohibitive. Figure 17.1 illustrates the following sequence of events that will complete the transaction.

1. Endaka Construction (JAP) requests a letter of credit (L/C) to be issued by its bank, Yokohama Bank.

2. Yokohama Bank will determine whether Endaka is financially sound and capable of making the payments as required. This is a very important step because Yokohama Bank simply wants to guarantee the payment, not make the payment.

3. Yokohama Bank, once satisfied with Endaka's application, issues the L/C to a representative in the United States or to the exporter's bank, Pacific First Bank. The L/C guarantees payment for the merchandise if the goods are shipped as stipulated in accompanying documents. Customary documents include the commercial invoice, customs clearance and invoice, the packing list, certification of insurance, and a bill of lading.

4. The exporter's bank, Pacific First, assures Vanport that payment will be made after evaluating the letter of credit. At this point the credit standing of Yokohama Bank has been substituted for the credit standing of the importer itself, Endaka Construction.

5. When the lumber order is ready, it is loaded on-board the shipper (called a common carrier). When the exporter signs a contract with a shipper, the signed contract serves as the receipt that the common carrier has received the goods, and it is termed the **bill of lading.**

6. Vanport draws a draft against Yokohama Bank for payment. The draft is the document used in international trade to effect payment and explicitly requests payment for the merchandise, which is now shown to be shipped and insured consistent with all requirements of the previously issued L/C. (If the draft is issued to the bank issuing the L/C, Yokohama Bank, it is termed a **bank draft.** If the draft is issued against the importer, Endaka

Construction, it is a **trade draft.**) The draft, L/C, and other appropriate documents are presented to Pacific First Bank for payment.

7. If Pacific First Bank (US) had confirmed the letter of credit from Yokohama Bank, it would immediately pay Vanport for the lumber and then collect from the issuing bank, Yokohama. If Pacific First Bank had not confirmed the letter of credit, it only passes the documents to Yokohama Bank for payment (to Vanport). The confirmed, as opposed to unconfirmed, letter of credit obviously speeds up payment to the exporter.

Regardless, with the letter of credit as the financial assurance, the exporter or the exporter's bank is collecting payment from the importer's bank, not from the importer itself. It is up to the specific arrangements between the importer (Endaka) and the importer's bank (Yokohama) to arrange the final settlement at that end of the purchase.

If the trade relationship continues over time, both parties will gain faith and confidence in the other. With this strengthening of financial trust, the trade financing relationship will loosen. Sustained buyer-seller relations across borders eventually end up operating on an open account basis similar to domestic commerce.

INTERNATIONAL CAPITAL BUDGETING

Any investment, whether it be the purchase of stock, the acquisition of real estate, or the construction of a manufacturing facility in another country, is financially justified if the present value of expected cash inflows is greater than the present value of expected cash outflows, in other words, if it has a positive **net present value (NPV).** The construction of a **capital budget** is the process of projecting the net operating cash flows of the potential investment to determine if it is indeed a good investment.

Capital Budget Components and Decision Criteria

All capital budgets, domestic and international, are only as good as the accuracy of the cost and revenue assumptions. Adequately anticipating all of the incremental expenses that the individual project imposes on the firm is critical to a proper analysis. The critical term here is incremental. If the undertaking of a new project in a foreign country requires the parent firm to establish a new office to handle personnel and shipments of materials, this needs to be added to the incremental cash flows of the project. Only after all such values are estimated for the entire life span of the investment would the necessary information exist for financial analysis.

A capital budget is composed of three primary cash flow components:

1. **Initial Expenses and Capital Outlays.** The initial capital outlays are normally the largest net cash outflow occurring over the life of a proposed investment. Because the cash flows occur up front, they have a substantial impact on the net present value of the project.

2. **Operating Cash Flows.** The operating cash flows are the net cash flows the project is expected to yield once production is under way. The primary positive net cash flows of the project are realized in this stage; net operating cash flows will determine the success or failure of the proposed investment.

3. **Terminal Cash Flows.** The final component of the capital budget is composed of the salvage value or resale value of the project at its end. The terminal value will include whatever working capital balances can be recaptured once the project is no longer in operation (at least by this owner).

The financial decision criterion for an individual investment is whether the net present value of the project is positive or negative.[1] The net cash flows in the future are discounted by the average cost of capital for the firm (the average of debt and equity costs). The purpose of discounting is to capture the fact that the firm has acquired investment capital at a cost (interest). The same capital could have been used for other projects or other investments. It is therefore necessary to discount the future cash flows to account for this foregone income of the capital, its opportunity cost. If NPV is positive, then the project is an acceptable investment. If the project's NPV is negative, then the cash flows expected to result from the investment are insufficient to provide an acceptable rate of return, and the project should be rejected.

A Proposed Project Evaluation

The capital budget for a manufacturing plant in Singapore serves as a basic example. ACME, a U.S. manufacturer of household consumer products, is considering the construction of a plant in Singapore in 1996. It would cost US$1,660,000 to build and would be ready for operation on January 1, 1997. ACME would operate the plant for three years and then would sell the plant to the Singapore government.

To analyze the proposed investment, ACME must estimate what the sales revenues would be per year, the costs of production, the overhead expenses of operating the plant per year, the depreciation allowances for the new plant and equipment, and the Singapore tax rate on corporate income. The estimation of all net operating cash flows is very important to the analysis of the project. Often the entire acceptability of a foreign investment may depend on the sales forecast for the foreign project.

But ACME needs U.S. dollars, not Singapore dollars. The only way the stockholders of ACME would be willing to undertake the investment is if it would be profitable in terms of their own currency, the U.S. dollar. This is the primary theoretical distinction between a domestic capital budget and a multinational capital budget. The evaluation of the project in the viewpoint of the parent will focus on whatever cash flows, either operational or financial, will find their way back to the parent firm in U.S. dollars.

ACME must therefore forecast the movement of the Singapore dollar (S$) over the four-year period as well. The spot rate on January 1, 1996, is S$1.6600/US$. ACME concludes that the rate of inflation will be roughly 5 percent higher per year in Singapore than in the United States. If the theory of purchasing power parity holds, as described in Chapter 5, it should take roughly 5 percent more Singapore dollars to buy a U.S. dollar per year. Using this assumption, ACME forecasts the exchange rate from 1996 to 1999.

After considerable study and analysis, ACME estimates that the net cash flows of the Singapore project, in Singapore dollars, would be those on line 1 in Table 17.1. Line 2 lists the expected exchange rate between Singapore dollars and U.S. dollars over the four-year period, assuming it takes 5 percent more Singapore dollars per U.S. dollar each year (the Singapore dollar is therefore expected to depreciate versus

TABLE 17.1	Line #	Description	1996	1997	1998	1999
Multinational	1	Net cash flow in S$	(1,660,000)	300,000	600,000	1,500,000
Capital Budget:	2	Exchange rate, S$/US$	1.6600	1.7430	1.8302	1.9217
Singapore	3	Net cash flow in US$	(1,000,000)	172,117	327,833	780,559
Manufacturing Facility	4	Present value factor	1.0000	0.8621	0.7432	0.6407
	5	Present value in US$	(1,000,000)	148,377	243,633	500,071
	6	Net present value in US$	(107,919)			
	7	Net present value in S$	5,505			

Notes:

a. The spot exchange rate of S$1.6600/US$ is assumed to change by 5 percent per year, 1.6600 × 1.05 = 1.7430.

b. The present value factor assumes a weighted average cost of capital, the discount rate, of 16 percent. The present value factor then is found using the standard formula of $1/(1 + .16)^t$, where t is the number of years in the future (1, 2, or 3).

the U.S. dollar). Combining the net cash flow forecast in Singapore dollars with the expected exchange rates, ACME can now calculate the net cash flow per year in U.S. dollars. ACME notes that although the initial expense is sizable, S$1,660,000 or US$1,000,000, the project produces positive net cash flows in its very first year of operations (1997) of US$172,117, and remains positive every year after.

ACME estimates that its cost of capital, both debt and equity combined (the weighted average cost of capital), is about 16 percent per year. Using this as the rate of discount, the discount factor for each of the future years is found. Finally, the net cash flow in U.S. dollars multiplied by the present value factor yields the present values of each net cash flow. The net present value of the Singapore project is a negative US$107,919; ACME may now decide not to proceed with the project since it is financially unacceptable.

Risks in International Investments

How is the ACME capital budget different from a similar project constructed in Phoenix, Arizona? It is riskier, at least from the standpoint of cross-border risk. The higher risk of an international investment arises from the different countries, their laws, regulations, potential for interference with the normal operations of the investment project, and obviously currencies, all of which are unique to international investment.

The risk of international investment is considered greater because the proposed investment will be within the jurisdiction of a different government. Governments have the ability to pass new laws, including the potential nationalization of the entire project. The typical problems that may arise from operating in a different country are changes in foreign tax laws, restrictions placed on when or how much in profits may be repatriated to the parent company, and other types of restrictions that hinder the free movement of merchandise and capital among the proposed project, the parent, and any other country relevant to its material inputs or sales.

The other major distinction between a domestic investment and a foreign investment is that the viewpoint or perspective of the parent and the project are no longer the same. The two perspectives differ because the parent only values cash flows it derives from the project. So, for example, in Table 17.1 the project generates sufficient net cash flows in Singapore dollars that the project is acceptable from the project's viewpoint, but not from the parent's viewpoint. Assuming the same 16% discount rate, the NPV in Singapore dollars is +S$5,505, while the NPV to the U.S. parent was –US$107,919 as noted previously. But what if the exchange rate

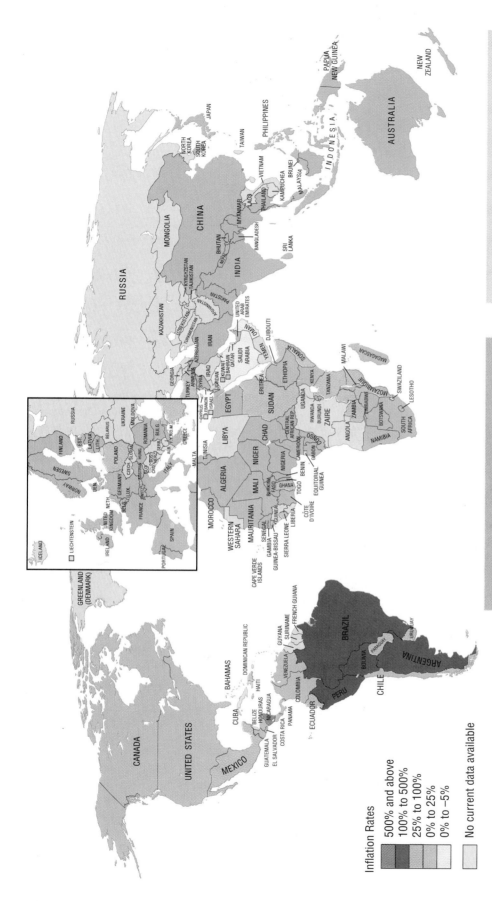

Inflation Rates

- 500% and above
- 100% to 500%
- 25% to 100%
- 0% to 25%
- 0% to –5%
- No current data available

Top 15 Inflation Rates

Nicaragua	656.2	Mexico	62.4
Argentina	402.3	Sierra Leone	60.8
Brazil	370.2	Guinea-Bissau	59.3
Peru	311.7	Turkey	46.3
Bolivia	220.9	Ecuador	39.5
Israel	78.9	Ghana	38.7
Poland	67.9	Mozambique	38.0
Uruguay	66.2		

Top 15 Lending Rates

Peru	173.8	Colombia	37.3
Uruguay	117.8	Uganda	34.4
Bulgaria	64.1	Venezuela	33.9
Sierra Leone	62.8	Hungary	30.0
Ecuador	60.2	Greece	28.7
Guinea-Bissau	50.3	Costa Rica	28.5
Bolivia	45.5	Thailand	25.0
Poland	39.0		

Source: *World Development Report, 1994*

Although projects may be similar, the capital budgeting process must include an assessment of the higher risks associated with international projects, such as Mobil Corporation's expanded oil production platforms in the British sector of the North Sea.
Source: © Larry Lee 1992.

were not to change at all—remain *fixed* for the 1996–1999 period? The NPV would then be positive from both viewpoints (project NPV remains +S$5,505, parent's NPV is now US$3,316). Or what if the Singapore government were to restrict the payment of dividends back to the U.S. parent firm, or somehow prohibit the Singapore subsidiary from exchanging Singapore dollars for U.S. dollars (capital controls)? Without cash flows in U.S. dollars, the parent would have no way of justifying the investment. And all of this could occur while the project itself is sufficiently profitable when measured in local currency (Singapore dollars). This split between project and parent viewpoint is a critical difference in international investment analysis. Any individual investment can be judged only on the basis of the future cash flows that it will generate in the investor's own currency.

CAPITAL STRUCTURE: INTERNATIONAL DIMENSIONS

The choice of how to fund the firm is called capital structure. Capital is needed to open a factory, build an amusement park, or even start a hot dog stand. If capital is provided by owners of the firm, it is called equity. If capital is obtained by borrowing from others, such as commercial banking institutions, it is termed debt. Debt must be repaid with interest over some specified schedule. Equity capital, however, is kept in the firm. Owners are risking their own capital in the enterprise; they are entitled to a proportion of the profits.

The Capital Structure of the Firm

The trade-offs between debt and equity are easily seen by looking at extreme examples of capital structures. If a firm had no debt, all capital would have to come from the owners. This may limit the size of the firm, as the owners do not have bottomless pockets. The primary benefit is that all net operating revenues are kept. There are no principal or interest payments to make. A firm with a large debt (highly leveraged), however, would have the capital of others with which to work. The scale of the firm could be larger, and all net profits would still accrue to the equity holders alone. The primary disadvantage of debt is the increasing expense of making principal and interest payments. At the extreme, this could prove to be an ever-increasing proportion of net cash flows.

Any firm's ability to grow and expand is dependent on its ability to acquire additional capital as it grows. The net profits generated over previous periods may be valuable but are rarely enough to provide needed capital expansion. Firms therefore need access to capital markets, both debt and equity. Chapter 5 provided an overview of the major debt and equity markets available internationally, but it is important to remember that the firm must have access to the markets to enjoy their fruits. Smaller firms operating in the smaller markets are generally unable to tap the larger international capital markets, which still are the domains of the multinational firms, the behemoths of multinational business.

The Capital Structure of Foreign Subsidiaries

The choice of what proportions of debt and equity to use in international investments is usually dictated by either the debt-equity structure of the parent firm or the debt-equity structure of the competitive firms in the country where the investment is to be made. The parent firm sees equity investment as capital at risk; it, therefore, would usually prefer to provide as little equity capital as possible. Although funding the foreign subsidiary primarily with debt would still put the parent's capital at risk, debt service provides a strict schedule for cash flow repatriation to the lender—regular principal and interest payments according to the debt agreement. Equity capital's return, dividends from profits, depends on managerial discretion. It is this discretion, the proportion of profits returned to the parent versus profits retained and reinvested in the project or firm, that often leads to conflict between host-country authorities and the multinational firm.

The sources of debt for a foreign subsidiary theoretically are quite large, but in reality they often are quite limited. The alternatives listed in Table 17.2 are often reduced radically in practice because many countries have relatively small capital markets. These countries often either officially restrict the borrowing by foreign-owned firms in their countries or simply do not have affordable capital available for the foreign firm's use. The parent firm is then often forced to provide not only the equity but also a large proportion of the debt to its foreign subsidiaries. If the project or subsidiary is a new project, it has no existing line of business or credit standing. The parent must then represent the subsidiary's credit worth, and provide the debt capital at least until the project is operating and showing (it is hoped) positive net cash flows.

The larger firms internationally will often have their own financial subsidiaries, companies purely for the purpose of acquiring the capital needed for the entire

TABLE 17.2 **Financing Alternatives** **for Foreign Affiliates**	Foreign Affiliate Can Raise Equity Capital:	Foreign Affiliate Can Raise Debt Capital:
	1. From the parent	1. From the parent
	2. From a joint-venture partner in the parent's country, a joint-venture partner in the host country, or a share issue in the host country	2. From a bank loan or bond issue in the host country or the parent firm's home country
	3. From a third-country market such as a share issue in the Euro-equity market	3. From a third-country bank loan, bond issue, Euro-syndicated credit, or Euro-bond issue

company's continuing growth needs. The financial subsidiaries will often be the actual unit extending the debt or equity capital to the foreign project or subsidiary. The hope is that, with time and success, the foreign investment will grow sufficiently to establish its own credit standing and acquire more and more of its capital needs from the local markets in which it operates, or even from the international markets which become aware of its growth.

INTERNATIONAL WORKING CAPITAL AND CASH FLOW MANAGEMENT

Working capital management is the financing of short-term or current assets, but the term is used here to describe all short-term financing and financial management of the firm. Even a small multinational firm will have a number of different cash flows moving throughout its system at one time. The maintenance of proper liquidity, the monitoring of payments, and the acquisition of additional capital when needed—all of these require a great degree of organization and planning in international operations.

Operating Cash Flows and Financing Cash Flows

Firms possess both operating cash flows and financing cash flows. **Operating cash flows** arise from the everyday business activities of the firm such as paying for materials or resources (accounts payable) or receiving payments for items sold (accounts receivable). In addition to the direct cost and revenue cash flows from operations, there are a number of indirect cash flows. The indirect cash flows are primarily license fees paid to the owners of particular technological processes and royalties to the holders of patents or copyrights.

Financing cash flows arise from the funding activities of the firm. The servicing of existing funding sources, interest on existing debt, and dividend payments to shareholders constitute potentially large and frequent cash flows. Periodic additions to debt or equity through new bank loans, new bond issuances, or supplemental stock sales may also add to the volume of financing cash flows in the multinational firm.

A Sample Cash Flow Mapping

Figure 17.2 provides an overview of how operational and financial cash flows may appear for a U.S.-based multinational firm. In addition to having some export sales in Canada, it may import some materials from Mexico. The firm has gained access to several different European markets by first selling its product to its German subsidiary, which then provides the final touches necessary for sales in Germany, France, and Switzerland. Sales and purchases by the parent with Canada and Mexico give rise to a continuing series of accounts receivables and accounts payable which may be denominated in Canadian dollars, Mexican pesos, or U.S. dollars.

Intrafirm Cash Flows and Transfer Prices

Cash flows between the U.S. parent and the German subsidiary will be both operational and financial in nature. The sale of the major product line to the German subsidiary creates intrafirm account receivables and payables. The payments may be denominated in either U.S. dollars or German marks. The intrafirm sales may, in fact,

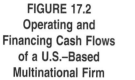

**FIGURE 17.2
Operating and
Financing Cash Flows
of a U.S.–Based
Multinational Firm**

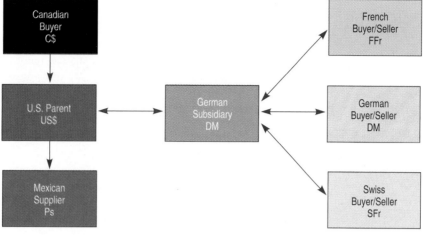

be two-way if the German subsidiary is actually producing a form of the product not made in the United States but needed there.

One of the most difficult pricing decisions many multinational firms must make concerns the price at which they sell their products to their own subsidiaries and affiliates. These prices, called **transfer prices,** theoretically are equivalent to what the same product would cost if purchased on the open market. However, it is often impossible to find such a product on the open market; if may be unique to the firm and its product line. The result is a price that is set internally and may result in the subsidiary being more or less profitable. This, in turn, has impacts on taxes paid in host countries. (See Chapter 15 for a more detailed discussion of transfer pricing.)

The foreign subsidiary may also be using techniques, machinery, or processes that are owned or patented by the parent firm and so must pay royalties and license fees. The cash flows are usually calculated as a percentage of the sales price in Germany. Many multinational firms also spread the overhead and management expenses incurred at the parent over their foreign affiliates and subsidiaries that are using the parent's administrative services.

There are also a number of financing cash flows between the U.S. parent and the German subsidiary. If the subsidiary is partially financed by loans extended by the parent, the subsidiary needs to make regular principal and interest payments to the parent. If the German subsidiary is successful in its operations and generates a profit, that portion of the profits not reinvested in the subsidiary will need to be sent back to the parent as dividends. If, at some point, the German subsidiary needs more capital than what it can retain from its own profits, it may need additional debt or equity capital (from any of the potential sources listed in Table 17.2). These obviously would add to the potential financial cash flow volume.

The subsidiary, in turn, is dependent on its sales in Germany (German mark revenues), France (French franc revenues), and Switzerland (Swiss franc revenues) to generate the needed cash flows for paying everyone else. This "map" of operating and financing cash flows does not even attempt to describe the frequency of the various foreign currency cash flows, or to assign the responsibility for managing the currency risks. The management of cash flows in a larger multinational firm, one with possibly 10 or 20 subsidiaries, is obviously complex. The proper management of the cash flows is, however, critical to the success of the multinational business.

Cash Flow Management

The structure of the firm dictates how cash flows and financial resources can be managed. The trend in the past decade has been for the increasing centralization of most financial and treasury operations. The centralized treasury often is responsible for both funding operations and cash flow management. The centralized treasury often may enjoy significant economies of scale, offering more services and expertise to the various units of the firm worldwide than the individual units themselves could support. However, regardless of whether the firm follows a centralized or decentralized approach, there are a number of operating structures that help the multinational firm manage its cash flows.

Netting   Figure 17.3 expands our firm to two European subsidiaries, one in Germany and one in France. The figure illustrates how many of the cash flows between units of a multinational firm are two-way and may result in unneeded transfer costs and transaction expenses. Coordination between units simply requires planning and budgeting of intrafirm cash flows so that two-way flows are "netted" against one another, with only one smaller cash flow as opposed to two having to be undertaken.

   Netting can occur between each subsidiary and the parent, and between the subsidiaries themselves (it is often forgotten that many of the activities in a multinational firm occur between subsidiaries, and not just between individual subsidiaries and the parent). Netting is particularly helpful if the two-way flow is in two different currencies, as each would be suffering currency exchange charges for intrafirm transfers.

Cash Pooling   A large firm with a number of units operating both within an individual country and across countries may be able to economize on the amount of firm assets needed in cash if one central pool is used for **cash pooling.** With one pool of capital and up-to-date information on the cash flows in and out of the various units, the firm spends much less in terms of foregone interest on cash balances, which are held in safekeeping against unforeseen cash flow shortfalls.

   For example, for the firm described in Figure 17.3, the parent and German and French subsidiaries may be able to consolidate all cash management and resources in one place—for example, New York (associated with the U.S. parent). One cash manager for all units would be in a better position for planning intercompany payments, including controlling the currency exposures of the individual units. A single large pool also may allow the firm to negotiate better financial service rates with banking institutions for cash-clearing purposes. In the event that the cash manager would need to be closer to the individual units (both proximity and time zone), the two European units could combine to run cash from one or the other for both.

**FIGURE 17.3
Netting and Cash
Pooling of Cash
Flows in the
Multinational Firm**

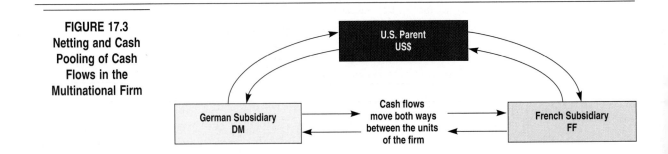

Leads and Lags   The timing of payments between units of a multinational is somewhat flexible. Again, this allows the management of payments between the French and German subsidiaries and between the parent and the subsidiaries to be much more flexible, letting the firm not only to position cash flows where they are needed most, but also to help manage currency risk. A foreign subsidiary that is expecting its local currency to fall in value relative to the U.S. dollar may try to speed-up or **lead** its payments to the parent. Similarly, if the local currency is expected to rise versus the dollar, the subsidiary may want to wait, or **lag,** payments until exchange rates are more favorable.

Reinvoicing   Multinational firms with a variety of manufacturing and distribution subsidiaries scattered over a number of countries within a region may often find it more economical to have one office or subsidiary taking ownership of all invoices and payments between units.

For example, Figure 17.4 illustrates how our sample firm could be restructured to incorporate a **reinvoicing** center. The site for the reinvoicing center in this case is Luxembourg, a country that is known to have low taxes and few restrictions on income earned from international business operations. The Luxembourg subsidiary literally buys from one unit and sells to a second unit, therefore taking ownership of the goods and reinvoicing the sale to the next unit. Once ownership is taken, the sale/purchase can be redenominated in a different currency, netted against other payments, hedged against specific currency exposures, or repriced in accordance with potential tax benefits of the reinvoicing center's host country. The additional flexibility achievable in cash flow management, product pricing, and profit placement may be substantial.

Internal Banks   Some multinational firms have found that their financial resources and needs are becoming either too large or too sophisticated for the financial services that are available in many of their local subsidiary markets. One solution to this has been the establishment of an **internal bank** within the firm. The internal bank actually buys and sells payables and receivables from the various units, which frees the units of the firm from struggling for continual working capital financing and lets them focus on their primary business activities.

All of these structures and management techniques often are combined in different ways to fit the needs of the individual multinational firm. Some techniques

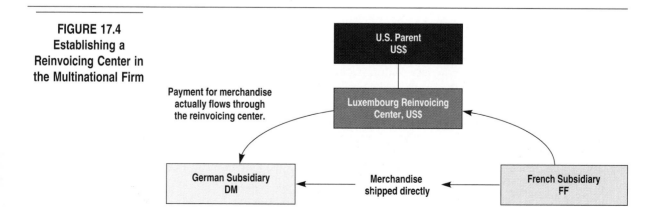

FIGURE 17.4
Establishing a
Reinvoicing Center in
the Multinational Firm

are encouraged or prohibited by laws and regulations (for example, many countries limit the ability to lead and lag payments), depending on the host-country's government and stage of capital market liberalization. It is not uncommon to find one type of system at work in one hemisphere of firm operations, with a very different system in use in the other hemisphere. Multinational cash flow management requires flexibility in thinking—artistry in some cases—as much as technique on the part of managers.

FINANCIAL RISK MANAGEMENT

All firms are in some way influenced by three financial prices; exchange rates, interest rates, and commodity prices. The management of these prices—these risks— is termed **financial risk management.** Interest rates have always received, deservedly, much of management's attention in business; it is only recently that many firms have chosen to acknowledge their financial health is also affected by exchange rates and commodity prices. The following analysis focuses on the exchange rate risks suffered by firms operating internationally.

Financial Price Risk and Firm Value

Risk is a word that deserves more respect than it is commonly afforded. Most dictionaries will refer to risk as the possibility of suffering harm or loss; danger; or a factor or element involving uncertain hazards. The definitions are negative. Yet in the field of finance, the word risk has a neutral definition: a value or result that is at present unknown. This means that the impact of risk can be either positive or negative.

There are three categories of financial price risk: interest rate risk, exchange rate risk, and commodity price risk. Each can have potentially positive or negative impacts on the profitability or value of the firm. For example, a U.S. exporter such as Eastman Kodak pays specific attention to the value of the U.S. dollar. If the dollar were to appreciate against other major currencies such as the Japanese yen, Kodak's products would be more expensive to foreign buyers, and it could lose market share to foreign competitors (like Fuji).

The negative relationship between Kodak's firm value and the yen–dollar exchange rate is illustrated in Figure 17.5. As the dollar appreciates versus the yen (for example, if the spot rate moved from ¥125/$ to ¥140/$), Kodak would suffer falling sales in Japan, and possibly also in the United States, because Fuji's comparable products would be relatively cheaper. The result is a fall in the value of Kodak. Corporate management expects financial managers to control such risks and protect the firm against exchange rate risks as best they can.

The same firm-value sensitivity also exists for interest rates and commodity prices. Most firms are at least partially financed with short-term floating rate debt. Therefore, whenever interest rates rise, the firms suffer higher financing costs, reducing the value of the firms.

Similarly, an increase in the price of commodities such as oil or coal, which are inputs into the production processes of many firms, will also reduce the value of those firms. But it does vary across firms. For example, a company such as Kidder Peabody, which mines coal, will see rising profits and firm value when coal prices rise. Each firm is different. It simply depends on the markets and makeup of each company. Although the following sections will focus on the measurement and management of exchange rate risk, it is important to remember that other financial price

**FIGURE 17.5
Financial Price Risks
and the Value of
the Firm**

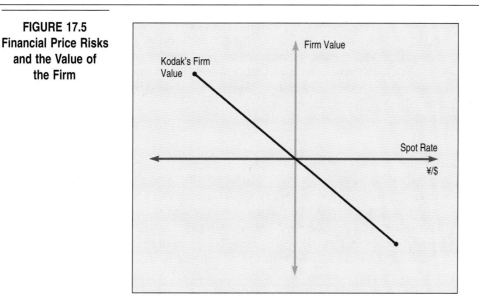

risks such as those of interest rates and commodity prices are fundamentally the same. They too can be measured and managed by firms.

Classification of Foreign Currency Exposures

Companies today know the risks of international operations. They are aware of the substantial risks to balance sheet values and annual earnings that interest rates and exchange rates may inflict on any firm at any time. And as is the case with most potential risks or problems to the firm, senior management expects junior management to do something about it. Financial managers, international treasurers, and financial officers of all kinds are expected to protect the firm from such risks. But before risk can be managed, it must be measured. Firms have, in varying degrees, three types of foreign currency exposure:

1. **Transaction exposure.** This is the risk associated with a contractual payment of foreign currency. For example, a U.S. firm that exports products to France will receive a guaranteed (by contract) payment in French francs in the future. Firms that buy or sell internationally have **transaction exposure** if any of the cash flows are denominated in foreign currency.

2. **Economic exposure.** This is the risk to the firm that its long-term cash flows will be affected, positively or negatively, by unexpected future exchange rate changes. Although many firms that consider themselves to be purely domestic may not realize it, all firms have some degree of **economic exposure.**

3. **Translation exposure.** This risk arises from the legal requirement that all firms consolidate their financial statements (balance sheets and income statements) of all worldwide operations annually. Therefore, any firm with operations outside its home country, operations that will be either earning foreign currency or valued in foreign currency, has **translation exposure.**

Transaction exposure and economic exposure are "true exposures" in the financial sense. This means they both present potential threats to the value of a firm's cash flows over time. The third exposure, translation, is a problem that arises from accounting. Under the present accounting principles in practice across most of the world's industrialized countries, translation exposure is not the problem it once was. For the most part, few real cash resources should be devoted to a purely accounting-based event.

TRANSACTION EXPOSURE

Transaction exposure is the most commonly observed type of exchange rate risk. Only two conditions are necessary for a transaction exposure to exist: (1) a cash flow that is denominated in a foreign currency, and (2) the cash flow will occur at a future date. Any contract, agreement, purchase, or sale that is denominated in a foreign currency that will be settled in the future constitutes a transaction exposure.[2]

The risk of a transaction exposure is that the exchange rate might change between the present date and the settlement date. The change may be for the better or for the worse. For example, suppose that an American firm signs a contract to purchase heavy rolled-steel pipe from a South Korean steel producer for 21,000,000 Korean won. The payment is due in 30 days upon delivery. The 30-day account payable, so typical of international trade and commerce, is a transaction exposure for the U.S. firm. If the spot exchange rate on the date the contract is signed is Won 700/$, the U.S. firm would expect to pay

$$\frac{\text{Won } 21,000,000}{\text{Won } 700/\$} = \$30,000$$

But the firm is not assured of what the exchange rate will be in 30 days. If the spot rate at the end of 30 days is Won 720/$, the U.S. firm would actually pay less. The payment would then be $29,167. If, however, the exchange rate changed in the opposite direction, for example to Won 650/$, the payment could just as easily increase to $32,308. This type of price risk, transaction exposure, is a major problem for international commerce.

Transaction Exposure Management

Management of transaction exposures usually is accomplished by either **natural hedging** or **contractual hedging.** Natural hedging is the term used to describe how a firm might arrange to have foreign currency cash flows coming in and going out at roughly the same times and same amounts. This is referred to as natural hedging because the management or hedging of the exposure is accomplished by matching offsetting foreign currency cash flows and therefore does not require the firm to undertake unusual financial contracts or activities to manage the exposure. For example, a Canadian firm that generates a significant portion of its total sales in U.S. dollars may acquire U.S. dollar debt. The U.S. dollar earnings from sales could then be used to service the dollar debt as needed. In this way, regardless of whether the C$/US$ exchange rate goes up or down, the firm would be naturally hedged against the movement. If the U.S. dollar went up in value against the Canadian dollar, the U.S. dollars needed for debt service would be generated automatically by the export sales to the United States. U.S. dollar cash inflows would match U.S. dollar cash outflows.

Contractual hedging is when the firm uses financial contracts to hedge the transaction exposure. The most common foreign currency contractual hedge is the **for-**

Global Perspective

17.1
"Lost in a Maze of Hedges"

Volatile exchange rates in recent weeks have sent many a nervous boss scurrying to his finance department to check up on its currency hedging strategy. Few of them will emerge much the wiser, for the typical multinational's strategy can seem impenetrable.

Hedging is simple enough in theory. Just doing business exposes many firms to foreign exchange risk: if an exchange rate moves the wrong way, profit or the balance sheet suffers. Suppose a British exporter sells goods that will be paid for in dollars three months later. If the dollar weakens against the pound, the exporter will get less in sterling than it expected. Hedging lets firms reduce or eliminate this risk by using a financial instrument that moves in the opposite way when exchange rates change. For the British exporter, that means one that is worth more pounds as the dollar falls.

The best way to hedge is to do it "naturally." Firms can design their trading, borrowing, and investment strategies to match their sales and assets in a particular currency with their purchases and liabilities in it. If, say, a British firm owns an asset valued in dollars, it can hedge by borrowing in dollars. No matter what happens to the pound–dollar exchange rate, there will be no net effect on the firm's balance sheet.

Few firms can hedge all, or even most, of their risk naturally. So many hedge actively in the financial markets, mainly using forward contracts and options. Forward contracts, agreements to buy or sell a given amount of a currency at an agreed exchange rate on a particular date, get

rid of all exchange rate risk, and are often thought of as the perfect hedge. If the British exporter is going to be paid $1m in three months, it can make a forward contract to sell the $1m on that date and know exactly how many pounds it will get in return even if exchange rates fluctuate in the spot market.

The trouble with forward contracts is that they are irrevocable. If the dollar strengthens against sterling, the British exporter with a forward contract is worse off than it would have been with no hedge at all. Options, which give firms the right, but not the obligation, to use a particular forward contract, are more flexible. Imagine that the British exporter buys an option to sell dollars in three months at the forward rate. If the exchange rate moves against the firm, it can use its option and limit the damage; if the rate goes in its favor, it can let the option lapse and enjoy the windfall.

Firms seem to use forward contracts at least twice as often as options. One reason is cost. Forward contracts are no dearer than an ordinary trade in the spot market. Options, by contrast, are expensive and must be paid for whether or not they are used. Option prices can jump about wildly, depending on which currencies are involved and how volatile the market is. Prices have gone through the roof recently: on September 29 Swiss Bank Corporation priced a three-month option to sell dollars at 2.7 percent of the contract, a hefty $27,000 for a British exporter wanting to hedge $1 million.

Source: Abstracted from "Lost in a Maze of Hedges," *The Economist,* October 3, 1992, p. 84. Copyright © 1992, The Economist, Ltd. Distributed by The New York Times/Special Features.

ward contract, although other financial instruments and derivatives, such as currency futures and options, are also used. The forward contract (see Chapter 5) would allow the firm to be assured a fixed rate of exchange between the desired two currencies at the precise future date. The forward contract would also be for the exact amount of the exposure. Both natural hedging and contractual hedging are discussed in Global Perspective 17.1.

Before proceeding further into financial and currency risk management, it is important to be precise regarding the definition of hedging. A **hedge** is an asset or a position whose value moves in the equal but opposite direction of the exposure. This means that if an exposure experienced a loss in value of $50, the hedge asset would offset the loss with a gain in value of $50. The total value of the position would not change. This would be termed a perfect hedge.

But perfect hedges are hard to find. And many people would not use them if they were readily available. Why? The presence of a perfect hedge eliminates all down-side risk, but also eliminates all up-side potential. Many businesses accept this two-sided risk as part of doing business. However, it is generally best to accept risk in the line of business, not in the cash-payment process of settling the business. By hedging the value of the currency, the total value of the position will be protected against either good or bad exchange rate changes.

Risk Management versus Speculation

The distinction between managing currency cash flows and speculating with currency cash flows is sometimes lost among those responsible for the safekeeping of the firm's treasury. If the previous description of currency hedging is followed closely (the selection of assets or positions only to counteract potential losses on existing exposures), few problems should arise. Problems arise when currency positions or financial instruments are purchased (or sold) with the expectation that a specific currency movement will result in a profit.

There are a number of major multinational firms that treat their international treasury centers as "service centers," but rarely do they consider financial management a "profit center." One of the most visible examples of what can go wrong when currency speculation is undertaken for corporate profit occurred in Great Britain in 1991. A large British food conglomerate, Allied-Lyons, suffered losses of £158 million ($268 million) on currency speculation after members of its international treasury staff suffered losses on currency positions at the start of the Persian Gulf War and then doubled-up on their positions in the following weeks in an attempt to recover previous losses. They lost even more.[3]

Transaction Exposure Case: Lufthansa (1985)

In January 1985, the German airline Lufthansa purchased 20 Boeing 737 jet aircraft. The jets would be delivered to Lufthansa in one year, in January 1986. Upon delivery of the aircraft, Lufthansa would pay Boeing (U.S.) $500 million. This constituted a huge transaction exposure for Lufthansa. (Note that the exposure falls on Lufthansa, not Boeing. If the purchase agreement had been stated in deutschemarks, the transaction exposure would have been transferred to Boeing.)

The Exposure   The spot exchange rate in January 1985, when Lufthansa signed the agreement, was DM 3.2/$. The expected cost of the aircraft to Lufthansa was then

$$\$500,000,000 \times DM3.2/\$ = DM1,600,000,000.$$

Figure 17.6 illustrates how the expected total cost of $500 million changes to Lufthansa with the spot exchange rate. If the deutschemark continued to fall against the U.S. dollar as it had been doing for more than four years, the cost to Lufthansa of the Boeing jets could skyrocket easily to more than DM 2 billion.

But the most important word here is expected. There was no guarantee that the spot exchange rate in effect in January of the following year would be DM 3.2/$. The U.S. dollar had been appreciating against the deutschemark for more than four years at this point. Senior management of Lufthansa was afraid the appreciating dollar trend might continue. For example, if the U.S. dollar appreciated over the coming year from DM 3.2/$ to DM 3.4/$, the cost of the aircraft purchased from Boeing would rise by DM 100 million. Figure 17.7 shows how the DM/$ exchange rate had

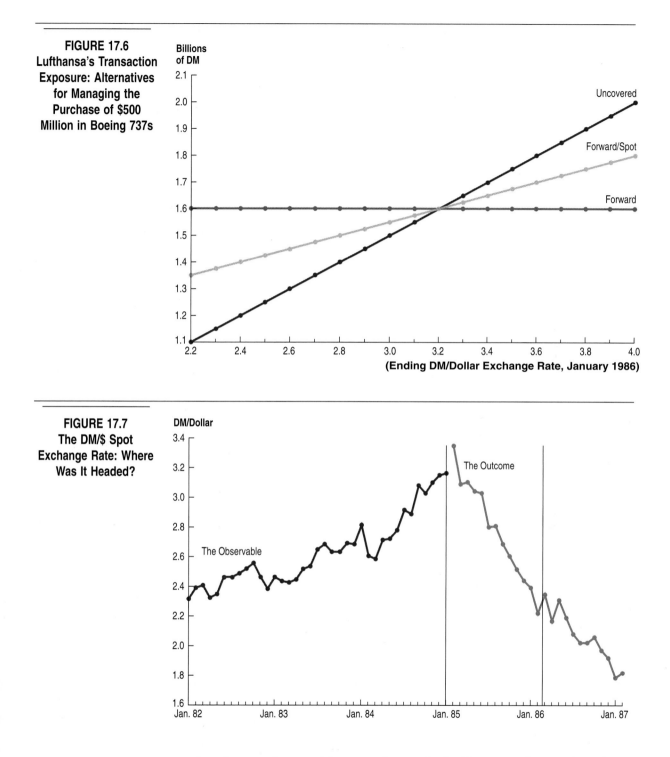

FIGURE 17.6
Lufthansa's Transaction
Exposure: Alternatives
for Managing the
Purchase of $500
Million in Boeing 737s

Billions of DM

Uncovered

Forward/Spot

Forward

(Ending DM/Dollar Exchange Rate, January 1986)

FIGURE 17.7
The DM/$ Spot
Exchange Rate: Where
Was It Headed?

DM/Dollar

The Outcome

The Observable

continued to trend upward for several years. By looking at graphics such as this, it was hard to believe that the U.S. dollar would do anything but continue to rise. It takes the truly brave to buck the trend.

But at the same time many senior members of Lufthansa's management believed that the U.S. dollar had risen as far as it would go. They argued that the dollar would fall over the coming year against the deutschemark (see Figure 17.7). If, for example, the spot rate fell to DM 3.0/$ by January 1986, Lufthansa would pay only DM 1,500 million, a savings of DM 100 million. This was true currency risk, in every sense of the word.

The Management Strategy   After much debate, Lufthansa's management decided to use forward contracts to hedge one-half of the $500 million exposure. This was obviously a compromise. First, because the exposure was a single large foreign currency payment, to occur one time only, natural hedging was not a realistic alternative. Second, although management believed the dollar would fall, the risk was too large to ignore. It was thought that by covering one-half of the exposure, Lufthansa would be protected against the U.S. dollar appreciating, yet still allow Lufthansa some opportunity to benefit from a fall in the dollar. Lufthansa signed a one-year forward contract (sold $250 million forward) at a forward rate of DM 3.2/$. The remaining $250 million owed Boeing was left unhedged.

The Outcome   By January 1986, the U.S. dollar not only fell, it plummeted versus the deutschemark. The spot rate fell from DM 3.2/$ in January 1985 to DM 2.3/$ in January 1986. Lufthansa had therefore benefited from leaving half the transaction exposure uncovered. But this meant that the half that was covered with forward contracts "cost" the firm DM 225 million!

The total cost to Lufthansa of delivering $250 million at the forward rate of DM 3.2/$ and $250 million at the ending spot rate of DM 2.3/$ was

$$[\$250{,}000{,}000 \times DM3.2/\$] + [\$250{,}000{,}000 \times DM2.3/\$] = DM\ 1{,}375{,}000{,}000.$$

Although this was DM 225 million less than the expected purchase price when the contract was signed in January 1985, Lufthansa's management was heavily criticized for covering any of the exposure. If the entire transaction exposure had been left uncovered, the final cost would have been only DM 1,150 million. The critics, of course, had perfect hindsight.

Currency Risk Sharing

Firms that import and export on a continuing basis have constant transaction exposures. If a firm is interested in maintaining a good business relationship with one of its suppliers, it must work with that supplier to assure it that it will not force all currency risk or exposure off on the other party on a continual basis. Exchange rate movements are inherently random; therefore some type of risk-sharing arrangement may prove useful.

If Ford (U.S.) imports automotive parts from Mazda (Japan) every month, year after year, major swings in exchange rates can benefit one party at the expense of the other. One solution would be for Ford and Mazda to agree that all purchases by Ford will be made in Japanese yen as long as the spot rate on the payment date is between ¥120/$ and ¥130/$. If the exchange rate is between these values on the payment dates, Ford agrees to accept whatever transaction exposure exists (because it is paying in a foreign currency). If, however, the exchange rate falls outside of this range on the payment date, Ford and Mazda will "share" the difference. If the spot rate on settlement date is ¥110/$, the Japanese yen would have appreciated versus the dollar, causing Ford's costs of purchasing automotive parts to rise. Since this rate falls outside the contractual range, Mazda would agree to accept a total payment in Japanese yen that would result from a "shared" difference of ¥10. Thus, Ford's total payment in Japanese yen would be calculated using an exchange rate of ¥115/$.

Risk-sharing agreements like these have been in use for nearly 50 years on world markets. They became something of a rarity during the 1950s and 1960s, when exchange rates were relatively stable (under the Bretton Woods Agreement). But with the return to floating exchange rates in the 1970s, firms with long-term customer-supplier relationships across borders returned to some old ways of keeping old friends. And sometimes old ways work very well.

ECONOMIC EXPOSURE

Economic exposure, also called operating exposure, is the change in the value of a firm arising from unexpected changes in exchange rates. Economic exposure emphasizes that there is a limit to a firm's ability to predict either cash flows or exchange rate changes in the medium to long term. All firms, either directly or indirectly, have economic exposure.

It is customary to think of only firms that actively trade internationally as having any type of currency exposure (such as Lufthansa or Eastman Kodak described previously). But actually all firms that operate in economies affected by international financial events such as exchange rate changes are affected. A barber in Ottumwa, Iowa, seemingly isolated from exchange rate chaos, still is affected when the dollar rises as it did in the early 1980s. U.S. products become increasingly expensive to foreign buyers, American manufacturers such as John Deere & Co. in Iowa are forced to cut back production and lay off workers, and businesses of all types decline. Even the business of barbers. The impacts are real, and they affect all firms, domestic and international alike.

How exposed is an individual firm in terms of economic exposure? It is impossible to say. Measuring economic exposure is subjective, and for the most part it is dependent on the degree of internationalization present in the firm's cost and revenue structure, as well as potential changes over the long run. But simply because it is difficult to measure does not mean that management cannot take some steps to prepare the firm for the unexpected.

Impact of Economic Exposure

The impacts of economic exposure are as diverse as are firms in their international structure. Take the case of a U.S. corporation with a successful British subsidiary. The British subsidiary manufactured and then distributed the firm's products in Great Britain, Germany, and France. The profits of the British subsidiary are paid out annually to the American parent corporation. What would be the impact on the profitability of the British subsidiary and the entire U.S. firm if the British pound suddenly fell in value against all other major currencies (as it did in September and October 1992)?

If the British firm had been facing competition in Germany, France, and its own home market from firms from those other two continental countries, it would now be more competitive. If the British pound is cheaper, so are the products sold internationally by British-based firms. The British subsidiary of the American firm would, in all likelihood, see rising profits from increased sales.

But what of the value of the British subsidiary to the U.S. parent corporation? The same fall in the British pound that allowed the British subsidiary to gain profits would also result in substantially fewer U.S. dollars when the British pound earnings are converted to U.S. dollars at the end of the year. It seems that it is nearly impossible to win in this situation. Actually, from the perspective of economic exposure management, the fact that the firm's total value, subsidiary and parent together, is

U.S. companies are establishing manufacturing operations in foreign countries. This is part of the global strategy at Corning Incorporated. One of the beneficial outcomes is that this tends to insulate such companies against market fluctuations. Here a Japanese worker applies his skills at the Corning Japan K.K. plant in Shizuoka, Japan.

Source: Courtesy of Corning Incorporated.

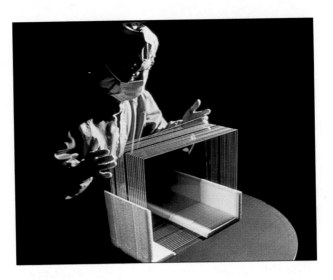

roughly a wash as a result of the exchange rate change is desirable. Sound financial management assumes that a firm will profit and bear risk in its line of business, not in the process of settling payments on business already completed.

Economic Exposure Management

Management of economic exposure is being prepared for the unexpected. A firm such as Hewlett Packard (HP), which is highly dependent on its ability to remain cost competitive in markets both at home and abroad, may choose to take actions now that would allow it to passively withstand any sudden unexpected rise of the dollar. This could be accomplished through diversification: diversification of operations and diversification of financing.

Diversification of operations would allow the firm to be desensitized to the impacts of any one pair of exchange rate changes. For example, a multinational firm such as Hewlett Packard may produce the same product in manufacturing facilities in Singapore, the United States, Puerto Rico, and Europe. If a sudden and prolonged rise in the dollar made production in the United States prohibitively expensive and uncompetitive, HP is already positioned to shift production to a relatively cheaper currency environment. Although firms rarely diversify production location for the sole purpose of currency diversification, it is a substantial additional benefit from such global expansion. Global Perspective 17.2 demonstrates how Mexican automakers have "diversified."

Diversification of financing serves to hedge economic exposure much in the same way as it did with transaction exposures. A firm with debt denominated in many different currencies is sensitive to many different interest rates. If one country or currency experiences rapidly rising inflation rates and interest rates, a firm with diversified debt will not be subject to the full impact of such movements. Purely domestic firms, however, are actually somewhat captive to the local conditions and are unable to ride out such interest rate storms as easily.

It should be noted that, in both cases, diversification is a passive solution to the exposure problem. This means that without knowing when or where or what the problem may be, the firm simply spreads its operations and financial structure out over a variety of countries and currencies to be prepared.

Global Perspective

17.2
Economic Exposure:
Foreign Automakers in Mexico

Foreign automakers in Mexico enjoyed double-digit sales growth throughout 1993 and 1994, in the transition years of the North American Free Trade Agreement (NAFTA). Volkswagen (Germany), Chrysler (USA), Nissan (Japan), and Ford (USA), just to name a few, all saw record sales in the rapidly expanded deregulated Mexican consumer market. Then, in December 1994, the peso fell.

The peso crisis immediately sent much of the domestic market down. Increasingly tight monetary policies, cuts in government spending, and emergency measures to shore up the falling peso all contributed to a sudden and drastic drop in domestic automobile sales. Within the first two weeks of 1995, the automakers shifted the focus of their sales from domestic to export. The devalued peso made exported automobiles attractive to buyers worldwide, and increasing exports was a commercial policy definitely supported by the anxiety-ridden Mexican government.

TRANSLATION EXPOSURE

Translation or accounting exposure results from the conversion or translation of foreign currency denominated financial statements of foreign subsidiaries and affiliates into the home currency of the parent. This is necessary to prepare consolidated financial statements for all firms as country-law requires. The purpose is to have all operations worldwide stated in the same currency terms for comparison purposes. Management often uses the translated statements to judge the performance of foreign affiliates and their personnel on the same currency terms as the parent itself.

The problem, however, arises from the translation of balance sheets in foreign currencies into the domestic currency. Which assets and liabilities are to be translated at current exchange rates (at the current balance sheet date) versus historical rates (those in effect on the date of the initial investment)? Or should all assets and liabilities be translated at the same rate? The answer is somewhere in between, and the process of translation is dictated by financial accounting standards.

The Current Rate Method

At present in the United States, the proper method for translating foreign financial statements is given in Financial Accounting Standards Board statement No. 52 (FASB 52). According to FASB 52, if a foreign subsidiary is operating in a foreign currency functional environment,[4] most assets, liabilities, and income statement items of foreign affiliates are translated using current exchange rates (the exchange rate in effect on the balance sheet date). For this reason, it is often referred to as the current rate method. Table 17.3 provides an example of how this translation process might work.

A U.S. firm, Moab, established a Canadian subsidiary two years ago. The subsidiary, Moab-Can, is wholly owned and operated by Moab. The balance sheet of

TABLE 17.3 Translation of Foreign Affiliate's Balance Sheet: Canadian Subsidiary of a U.S. Firm	(1) Canadian Dollars (thousands)	(2) Current Rate C$/$	(3) U.S. Dollars (thousands)
Assets			
Cash	120	1.20	100
Accounts payable	240	1.20	200
Inventory	120	1.20	100
Net plant and equipment	480	1.20	400
Total	C$ 960		$ 800
Liabilities and Net Worth			
Accounts payable	120	1.20	100
Short-term debt	120	1.20	100
Long-term debt	240	1.20	200
Equity capital	480	1.10	436
Cumulative Translation Adjustment			(36)
Total	C$ 960		$ 800

Moab-Can on December 31, 1992, is shown in Canadian dollars in Column (1) of Table 17.3. To construct a consolidated financial statement, all Moab-Can's assets and liabilities must be translated into U.S. dollars at the end-of-year exchange rate. This rate is C$1.20/$. All assets and liabilities are translated at the current rate except for equity capital, which is translated at the exchange rate in effect at the time of the Canadian subsidiary's establishment, C$1.10/$. The exchange rates used to translate each individual asset and liability of the Canadian subsidiary are listed in Column (2).

The U.S.–dollar value of all translated assets and liabilities is shown in Column (3). An imbalance results because all assets and liabilities, except equity capital, were translated at the current rate. A new account must be created for the translated balance sheet to balance. The new account, the cumulative translation adjustment or CTA, takes on a gain or loss value necessary to maintain a balanced translation. Moab-Can, because the equity capital was invested when the Canadian dollar was stronger, now represents a CTA translation loss of US$36,000 to the parent company.

What does this translation loss mean to the company? The CTA account is an accounting construction. It is created to produce a consolidated balance sheet. Neither the Canadian subsidiary nor the U.S. parent experiences any cash flow impact as a result of the translation gain or loss. It is quite possible that consolidation in the following year or years could result in CTA translation gains that could reduce or even cancel this year's loss.

The translation of the income statement of Moab-Can offers no such problems under FASB 52, so that consolidated reporting results in no other surprises or problems. The CTA account remains a "paper fiction" until the time the Canadian subsidiary is either sold or liquidated. On the sale or liquidation of the Canadian subsidiary, the CTA gains or losses attributed to Moab-Can must be realized by the parent company. The result is that the gains or losses are included with other current income of the parent for that period.[5]

Translation Exposure Management

Translation exposure under FASB 52 results in no cash flow impacts under normal circumstances. Although consolidated accounting does result in CTA translation losses or gains on the parent's consolidated balance sheet, the accounting entries are not ordinarily realized. Unless liquidation or sale of the subsidiary is anticipated, neither the subsidiary nor the parent firm should expend real resources on the management of an accounting convention.

In the event that the realization of the CTA translation gain or loss is imminent, traditional currency hedging instruments can be used. If Moab planned on liquidating Moab-Can this year, Moab could use a forward contract hedge to protect the firm's income for the period. The value of the forward contract would make up for part of the expected loss if the firm believed the Canadian dollar would be lower than C$1.10/$ by the end of the year. Firms that are more concerned with their CTA position will structure their foreign subsidiaries to reduce the degree of net translation exposure. The primary method for this is the holding of some assets that are not denominated in the functional currency. For example, in the previous Moab-Can balance sheet shown in Table 17.3, if some portion of cash or accounts payable had been denominated in U.S. dollars rather than Canadian dollars, Moab-Can's net exposure, its translation loss in this case, would have been less. Such restructuring of the foreign subsidiary's balance sheet is termed a balance sheet hedge. Although this will protect the parent against translation losses or gains, it is often difficult or costly to achieve in practice.

INTEREST RATE AND CURRENCY SWAPS

One of the most significant developments in international finance in the 1980s was the development of the interest rate and currency swap markets. Although markets of all kinds (goods, services, labor, and capital) have continued to open up across the world in the past two decades, there are still "paper walls" between many capital markets. Firms operating in their home markets are both helped and hindered; they are well known in their own capital markets but still may not be recognized in other potentially larger capital markets. The interest rate and currency swap markets have allowed firms to arbitrage the differences between markets, using their comparative advantage of borrowing in their home market and swapping for interest rates or currencies that are not as readily accessible.

Interest Rate Swaps

Firms that are considered to be better borrowers in financial markets borrow at lower rates. The lower rates may be lower fixed rates or lower spreads over floating rate bases. In fact, lower quality borrowers often are limited in their choices to floating rates in many markets. The **interest rate swap,** often called the "plain vanilla swap," allows one firm to use its good credit standing to borrow capital at low fixed rates and exchange its interest payments with a slightly lower credit-rated borrower who has debt service payments at floating rates. Each borrower ends up making net interest payments at rates below those it could have achieved on its own.

If Firm Alpha is considered an extremely sound borrower, it can borrow capital at lower interest rates, probably fixed rates, than a second firm, Zeta. Zeta, although profitable and sound, is simply not rated as highly as a borrower in the eyes of the financial markets, and it must borrow at higher rates, often only at floating rates. If each firm were to borrow where it is "well received," using its comparative advantages, they may then swap or exchange their debt service payments. Alpha, which has taken on fixed rate debt service payments, will exchange these payments for Zeta's floating rate payments. Both companies end up paying less interest in the form

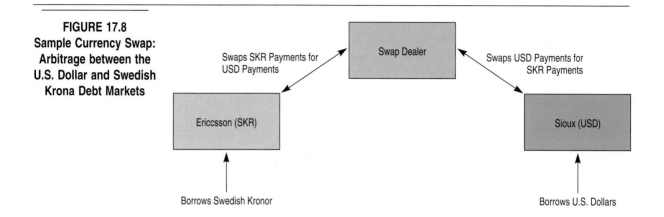

FIGURE 17.8
Sample Currency Swap:
Arbitrage between the
U.S. Dollar and Swedish
Krona Debt Markets

that they desired by negotiating rates between themselves that are better than what the markets had offered directly.

Currency Swaps

The **currency swap** is the equivalent of the interest rate swap, only the currency of denomination of the debt is different. Many international and multinational firms need capital denominated in different currencies for international investments or even for the purpose of risk management (for natural hedging, as described previously). Foreign firms often find themselves at a disadvantage, however, when trying to enter new markets. The interest rates available to them in the necessary currencies simply may not be affordable.

Figure 17.8 illustrates how a currency swap arrangement would work for a Swedish firm desiring U.S. dollar debt, and a U.S. firm desiring Swedish krona debt. The mechanics of the swap are actually quite simple. The Swedish firm, Ericsson, borrows capital in its home market, where it is well known and can obtain capital at attractive interest rates. The U.S. firm, Sioux, also acquires local debt in its own advantaged-access market. Then, working through a swap dealer, each firm exchanges the debt service payment schedule on its own debt for the debt service payment schedule of the other firm's debt. The principal amounts borrowed must be equal at current exchange rates for the swap to be made. The U.S. firm, Sioux, now agrees to make interest payments in Swedish kronor, and the Swedish firm, Ericsson, agrees to make U.S. dollar interest payments. The two firms have swapped payment schedules.

But what of the risk of nonpayment? If one of the swap parties does not make its agreed-upon payments, who is responsible for meeting the obligations of the original debt agreement? The answer is that the initial borrower is responsible for covering any shortfall or nonpayment by the swap party. This risk, termed counterparty risk, is an increasing concern in the interest rate and currency swap markets as more and more firms utilize the markets to manage their debt structures.

The currency swap market allows any firm to exchange its own comparative advantage in acquiring capital for the advantaged access of another firm in the foreign currency market. Both parties benefit from the free exchange of their comparative advantages. Although the swap market is not a source of capital, it is an important way to change the characteristics of capital.

623

The swap markets have grown rapidly over the past decade as more firms have sought to diversify their operations and their financing. In the early days of the market (early 1980s), most swaps were literally matched pairs of firms and debt issues as described above. The market has since grown and matured to the stage that most firms can now simply contact the swap desk of major international banks and arrange a swap directly with the bank. The bank is able to find the counterparty for the transaction on its own without involving the other firm. As more firms attempt to expand internationally, the swap market is expected to grow in significance as a means of managing the international financial risks and exposures of the firm.

SUMMARY

International financial management is both complex and critical to the multinational firm. All traditional functional areas of financial management are affected by the internationalization of the firm. Capital budgeting, firm financing, capital structure, and working capital and cash flow management, all traditional functions, are made more difficult by business activities that cross borders and oceans, not to mention currencies and markets.

In addition to the traditional areas of financial management, international financial management must deal with the three types of currency exposure: (1) transaction exposure, (2) economic exposure, and (3) translation exposure. Each type of currency risk confronts a firm with serious choices regarding its exposure analysis and its degree of willingness to manage the inherent risks.

This chapter described not only the basic types of risk, but also outlined a number of the basic strategies employed in the management of the exposures. Some of the solutions available today have only arisen with the development of new types of international financial markets and instruments, such as the currency swap. Others, such as currency risk-sharing agreements, are as old as exchange rates themselves.

Key Terms and Concepts

net present value (NPV)	reinvoicing
capital budget	internal bank
bill of lading	financial risk management
bank draft	transaction exposure
trade draft	economic exposure
working capital management	translation exposure
operating cash flows	natural hedging
financing cash flows	contractual hedging
transfer prices	forward contract
netting	hedge
cash pooling	interest rate swap
leads	currency swap
lags	

Questions for Discussion

1. Why is it important to identify the cash flows of a foreign investment from the perspective of the parent rather than from just the project?

2. Is currency risk unique to international firms? Is currency risk good or bad for the potential profitability of the multinational?

3. Which type of currency risk is the least important to the multinational firm? Should resources be spent to manage this risk?

4. Are firms with no direct international business (imports and exports) subject to economic exposure?

5. What would you have recommended that Lufthansa do to manage its transaction exposure if you had been the airline's chief financial officer in January 1985?

6. Why do you think Lufthansa and Boeing did not use some form of "currency risk sharing" in their 1985–1986 transaction?

7. Which type of firm do you believe is more "naturally hedged" against exchange rate exposure, the purely domestic firm (the barber) or the multinational firm (subsidiaries all over the world)?

8. Why have the currency and interest rate swap markets grown so rapidly in the past decade?

Recommended Readings

Ahn, Mark J., and William D. Falloon. *Strategic Risk Management: How Global Corporations Manage Financial Risk for Competitive Advantage.* Chicago: Probus Publishing, 1991.

Brigham, Eugene F., and Louis C. Gapenski. *Intermediate Financial Management.* Fort Worth, Tex.: Dryden, 1993.

Eiteman, David K., Arthur I. Stonehill, and Michael H. Moffett. *Multinational Business Finance,* seventh edition. Reading, Mass.: Addison-Wesley Publishing, 1995.

Giddy, Ian H. *Global Financial Markets.* Lexington, Mass.: Elsevier, 1994.

Grabbe, J. Orlin. *International Financial Markets,* second edition. Lexington, Mass.: Elsevier, 1992.

Howcroft, Barry, and Christopher Storey. *Management and Control of Currency and Interest Rate Risk.* Chicago: Probus Publishing, 1989.

Shapiro, Alan C. *Multinational Financial Management,* fourth edition. Allyn & Bacon, 1992.

Smith, Clifford W., Charles W. Smithson, and D. Sykes Wilford. *Managing Financial Risk,* The Institutional Investor Series in Finance. New York: Harper Business, 1990.

Smith, Roy C., and Ingo Walter. *Global Financial Services.* New York: Harper & Row Publishers, 1990.

Wunnicke, Diane B., David R. Wilson, and Brooke Wunnicke. *Corporate Financial Risk Management.* New York: John Wiley & Sons, 1992.

Notes

1. There are, of course, other traditional decision criteria used in capital budgeting, such as the internal rate of return, modified internal rate of return, payback period, and so forth. For the sake of simplicity, NPV is used throughout the analysis in this chapter. Under most conditions, NPV is also the most consistent criterion for selecting good projects, as well as selecting among projects.

2. Many firms only acknowledge the existence of a transaction exposure when they "book" the receivable, when they ship the order to the customer and issue the account receivable. In fact, whether they realize it or not, when they accepted the order at a fixed price in terms of foreign currency, they gave birth to a transaction exposure.

3. A note of particular irony in this case was that the chief currency trader for Allied-Lyons had authored an article in the British trade journal *The Treasurer* only a few months before. The article had described the proper methods and strategies for careful corporate foreign currency risk management. He had concluded with the caution to never confuse "good luck with skillful trading."

4. The distinction as to what the "functional currency" of a foreign subsidiary or affiliate operation is depends on a number of factors, including the currency that dominates expenses and revenues. If the foreign subsidiary's dominant currency is the local currency, the current rate method of translation is used. If, however, the functional currency of the foreign subsidiary is identified as the currency of the parent, the U.S. dollar in the example, the temporal method of translation is used. The temporal method is the procedure that was used in the United States from 1975 to 1981 under FASB 8.

5. Prior to the passage of FASB 52, FASB 8 had been the primary directive on translation in the United States. FASB 8, often termed the monetary/nonmonetary method, differed from FASB 52 in two important ways. First, it applied historical exchange rates to several of the long-term asset categories, usually resulting in a lower net exposed asset position. Second, all translation gains and losses were passed through the parent's consolidated income for the current period. This resulted in volatile swings in the critical earnings per share (EPS) reported by multinational firms. Although this was still only an accounting convention, the volatility introduced to EPS caused much concern among firms.

CHAPTER 18

Countertrade

Learning Objectives

1. To understand why countertrade transactions are becoming increasingly common.

2. To see how countertrade transactions are becoming more sophisticated and creative.

3. To discover some of the problems and dislocations caused by countertrade.

4. To understand that corporations increasingly use countertrade as a competitive tool to maintain or increase market share.

5. To learn about the new intermediaries that have emerged to facilitate countertrade transactions.

Implementing International Countertrade

Despite political and economic reforms in the Eastern bloc and in many developing countries, countertrade promises to be a significant tool for consummating international transactions. It is unlikely that these countries will find all the foreign exchange they need to finance their restructuring programs. Thus, international managers need to develop a countertrade plan within their overall international marketing plan. A method to identify and take advantage of countertrade opportunities also needs to be developed.

There are many facets to establishing a countertrade strategy. One of the perplexing problems is that countertrade takes on so many forms. Despite the potential confusion, the clear evidence that countertrade arrangements are growing means that they can be more innovative. Managers can develop new types of countertrade arrangements to fit the particular deal being negotiated. Any previously developed typology should not constrain the executor of countertrade.

Firms have a considerable choice of countertrade intermediaries including specialized countertrading companies, switch traders, or barter merchants. Specialized countertrading companies can put together countertrade transactions for their clients and use the leverage of a trading company for clients. Switch traders facilitate countertrade transactions by identifying and bringing parties together. Barter merchants buy goods from corporations for trade credits rather than cash.

An information system that gathers data pertinent to countertrade transactions is necessary for firms that are active countertraders. It is necessary to know which firms or countries have goods to sell or buy. Also, the motives and policies of countertrade participants need to be continuously monitored.

Countertraders need to consider the product, promotion, pricing, and distribution tactics necessary to support the deal. For instance, what level of product quality is acceptable to the firm?

A firm that believes countertrade is an opportunity to increase profits or obtain astronomical returns on investment may be disappointed. Countertrade deals are difficult to measure using traditional indicators of success for two reasons. First, countertrade typically involves a long time frame and, therefore, does not lend itself to typical yearly determinations of performance. Second, countertrade transactions can strain company resources. Tremendous negotiations and cost can be involved in switching products, transportation, and storage of products, not to mention the possibility of unsold goods.

Source: Sam C. Okoroafa, "Implementing International Countertrade: A Dyadic Approach," *Industrial Marketing Management,* July 1994: 229–234.

General Motors exchanged automobiles for a trainload of strawberries. Control Data swapped a computer for a package of Polish furniture, Hungarian carpet backing, and Russian greeting cards. Ford traded cars for sheepskins from Uruguay, potatoes from Spain, toilet seats from Finland, cranes from Norway, and coffee from Colombia.[1] Usbekistan, one of the new countries of the former Soviet Union, is offering crude venom of vipers, toads, scorpions, black widows, and tarantulas, as well as growth-controlling substances from snakes and lizards, in countertrade.[2] These are all examples of countertrade activities carried out around the world. As noted in the chapter's opening vignette, countertrade is growing in volume as well as in complexity.

This chapter will focus on the ancient, yet new, forms of barter and countertrade that are reemerging in world trade. The types of countertrade that currently exist and the reasons why these types of transactions are reemerging will be discussed. Policy issues associated with countertrade will be explored by examining the attitudes held toward countertrade by both national governments and international bodies such as the GATT, the OECD, and the U.N. Corporate countertrade practices will be reviewed as we examine what firms do and why they do it. Finally, information will be provided on how to organize for countertrade, how to cope with potential problems, and how countertrade can be used as an effective international business tool.

A DEFINITION OF COUNTERTRADE

Countertrade is a sale that encompasses more than an exchange of goods, services, or ideas for money. In the international market, countertrade transactions "are those transactions which have as a basic characteristic a linkage, legal or otherwise, between exports and imports of goods or services in addition to, or in place of, financial settlements."[3] Historically, countertrade was mainly conducted in the form of **barter,** which is a direct exchange of goods of approximately equal value between parties, with no money involved. Such transactions were the very essence of business at times during which no money—that is, no common medium of exchange—existed or was available. Over time, money emerged as a convenient medium that unlinked transactions from individual parties and their joint timing and therefore permitted greater flexibility in trading activities. Repeatedly, however, we can see returns to the barter system as a result of environmental circumstances. For example, because of the tight financial constraints of both students and the institution, Georgetown University during its initial years of operation after 1789 charged part of its tuition in foodstuffs and required students to participate in the construction of university buildings. During periods of high inflation in Europe in the 1920s, goods such as bread, meat, and gold were seen as much more useful and secure than paper money, which decreased in real value by the minute. In the late 1940s, American cigarettes were an acceptable medium of exchange in most European countries, much more so than any particular currency except for the dollar.

Countertrade transactions have therefore always arisen when economic circumstances made it more acceptable to exchange goods directly rather than to use money as an intermediary. Conditions that encourage such business activities are lack of money, lack of value of or faith in money, lack of acceptability of money as an exchange medium, or greater ease of transaction by using goods.

The same reasons prevail in today's resurgence of countertrade. Beginning in the 1950s, countertrade and barter transactions were mainly carried out with Eastern bloc countries. The currencies of these countries were not acceptable elsewhere, because they were not freely convertible. At the same time, the countries did not want their currencies distributed outside of their economic bloc. They did not possess sufficient foreign "hard" currency to make purchases of crucial goods that were not available within COMECON countries. To some extent, the countries solved their currency problem by depleting their gold reserves—which, because of the world market price for gold, was an indirect financial transaction. However, many Eastern bloc countries also insisted in their dealings with Western nations that the goods they produced be taken in exchange for imports so as to reduce their need for foreign currencies.

Throughout the decades, the official use of countertrade steadily increased. In 1972, countertrade was in regular use by only 15 countries. By 1983, the countries conducting countertrade transactions numbered 88, and by 1995, the number was 105. Figure 18.1 lists the countries that currently request countertrade transactions from their trading partners. Estimates as to the total volume of global countertrade vary widely. A consensus of experts has put the percentage of world trade financed through countertrade transactions between 15 and 20 percent.[4] Such an estimate conflicts with IMF figures, which attribute only a very small percentage of world trade to countertrade. Yet, if all business transactions in which countertrade plays some kind of role are considered, the estimate could be reasonable.

Increasingly, countries and companies are deciding that countertrade transactions are more beneficial to them than transactions based on financial exchange alone. One reason is that the world debt crisis has made ordinary trade financing very risky.

**FIGURE 18.1
Countries Requesting
Countertrade**

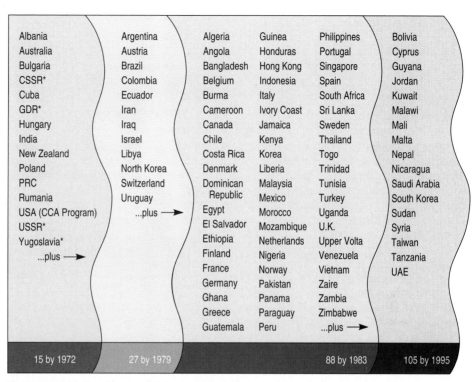

Albania	Argentina	Algeria	Guinea	Philippines	Bolivia
Australia	Austria	Angola	Honduras	Portugal	Cyprus
Bulgaria	Brazil	Bangladesh	Hong Kong	Singapore	Guyana
CSSR*	Colombia	Belgium	Indonesia	Spain	Jordan
Cuba	Ecuador	Burma	Italy	South Africa	Kuwait
GDR*	Iran	Cameroon	Ivory Coast	Sri Lanka	Malawi
Hungary	Iraq	Canada	Jamaica	Sweden	Mali
India	Israel	Chile	Kenya	Thailand	Malta
New Zealand	Libya	Costa Rica	Korea	Togo	Nepal
Poland	North Korea	Denmark	Liberia	Trinidad	Nicaragua
PRC	Switzerland	Dominican	Malaysia	Tunisia	Saudi Arabia
Rumania	Uruguay	Republic	Mexico	Turkey	South Korea
USA (CCA Program)	...plus →	Egypt	Morocco	Uganda	Sudan
USSR*		El Salvador	Mozambique	U.K.	Syria
Yugoslavia*		Ethiopia	Netherlands	Upper Volta	Taiwan
...plus →		Finland	Nigeria	Venezuela	Tanzania
		France	Norway	Vietnam	UAE
		Germany	Pakistan	Zaire	
		Ghana	Panama	Zambia	
		Greece	Paraguay	Zimbabwe	
		Guatemala	Peru	...plus →	
15 by 1972	27 by 1979			88 by 1983	105 by 1995

*Denotes countries that have been reconstituted
Source: Pompiliu Verzariu, Office of Barter and Countertrade, U.S. Department of Commerce, January 1995.

Many countries, particularly in the developing world, simply cannot obtain the trade credit or financial assistance necessary to pay for desired imports. Heavily indebted countries, faced with the possibility of not being able to afford imports at all, hasten to use countertrade to maintain at least some product inflow. However, it should be recognized that countertrade does not reduce commercial risk. Countertrade transactions will therefore be encouraged by stability and economic progress. Research has shown that countertrade appears to increase with a country's creditworthiness, since good credit encourages traders to participate in unconventional trading practices.[5]

The use of countertrade permits the covert reduction of prices and therefore allows the circumvention of price and exchange controls.[6] Particularly in commodity markets with operative cartel arrangements, such as oil or agriculture, this benefit may be very useful to a producer. For example, by using oil as a countertraded product for industrial equipment, a surreptitious discount (by using a higher price for the acquired products) may expand market share.

Another reason for the increase in countertrade is that many countries are again responding favorably to the notion of bilateralism. Thinking along the lines of "you scratch my back and I'll scratch yours," they prefer to exchange goods with countries that are their major business partners. At an extreme level, nations can build their entire trading system on such reciprocity. Global Perspective 18.1 explains how Turkmenistan has implemented such an approach.

Countertrade is also often viewed by firms and nations alike as an excellent mechanism to gain entry into new markets. When a producer believes that marketing is not its strong suit, particularly in product areas that face strong international

Global Perspective

18.1
Turkmenistan Embraces Countertrade

Turkmenistan is the first of the former Soviet republics to adopt a foreign trade system that is based solely on reciprocal trade, balancing each import with an equivalent value of exported raw materials. The government no longer makes available hard currency for imports, under the terms of an executive decree. Imports are authorized only from countries that are prepared to purchase an equivalent value of Turkmen products. Should traders from the supplying country not find the products in Turkmenistan that they need at home, they can enter triangular deals to liquidate their counterpurchases from Turkmenistan.

The basis of the newly mandated countertrade import regime is the allocation of quotas of raw materials among individual ministries. Each ministry is expected to exchange its share of allocated raw materials for the imports needed by the economic and industrial sectors for which it is responsible. This replaces a previous policy that permitted imported goods to be paid for with hard currency purchased from a state bank. The state banks obtained their hard currency from auctions held each Saturday in Ashgabad. Proposed countertrade deals had to be presented in hard currency terms before they could obtain official authorization. This was part of a liberalized international commercial environment adopted by the Turkmen government after the dissolution of the USSR. Since early 1993, however, the foreign trade system of Turkmenistan again has become increasingly regulated.

The government justifies the introduction of its new import regime on the grounds that the country still lacks the institutional framework for liberalized foreign trade. Considering that Turkmenistan imports 70 percent of its manufactures, including consumer goods, the government is not prepared to surrender its control over foreign trade and flows of hard currency.

Turkmenistan supplies Russia, its largest trading partner, with cotton below the world market price in exchange for crude oil and oil products. The trade with Russia is regulated by a bilateral trade agreement, with a ruble clearing account based in Moscow. Similar clearing arrangements have been established with the central banks of Armenia, Azerbaijan, Georgia, Kazakstan, Tajikistan, Ukraine, and Uzbekistan. Turkmenistan supplies each with natural gas in exchange for a variety of raw materials, industrial equipment, and consumer goods. Should one of the clearing partners fail to pay for the gas deliveries, the Turkmen government simply closes the valve. This already has happened in the case of four of the countries. Since it became independent, Turkmenistan has had a positive trade balance, amounting to US$910 million in 1993. The surplus includes all forms of trade including conventional and countertrade.

Source: "Turkmenistan Adopts CT-Based Trade System," *Countertrade Outlook,* DP Publications Co., Vol. XII, No. 7, April 11, 1994: 1–2.

competition, it often sees countertrade as useful. The producer often hopes that the party receiving the goods will serve as a new distributor, opening up new international marketing channels and ultimately expanding the original market. For example, countertrade transactions agreed to between the Japanese firm NEC and the government of Egypt have resulted in a major increase of Japanese tourism to Egypt.[7]

Conversely, because countertrade is highly sought after in many enormous, but hard-currency poor emerging market economies such as China, the CIS, and the former Eastern bloc countries, as well as in other cash-strapped countries in South America and the Third World, engaging in such transactions can provide major growth opportunities for firms. In increasingly competitive world markets, countertrade can be a good way to attract new buyers. By providing countertrade services, the seller is in effect differentiating its product from those of its competitors.[8]

Countertrade also can provide stability for long-term sales. For example, if a firm is tied to a countertrade agreement, it will need to source the product from a particular supplier, whether or not it wants to do so. This stability is often valued very highly because it eliminates, or at least reduces, vast swings in demand and thus allows for better planning. Countertrade, therefore, can serve as a major mechanism to shift risk from the producer to another party. In that sense, one can argue that countertrade offers a substitute for missing forward markets.[9] Finally, under certain conditions, countertrade can ensure the quality of an international transaction. In instances where the seller of technology is paid in output produced by the technology delivered, the seller's revenue depends on the success of the technology transfer and maintenance services in production. Therefore, the seller is more likely to be concerned about the provision of services, maintenance, and general technology transfer.[10]

In spite of all the apparent benefits of countertrade, there are strong economic arguments against the activity. The arguments are based mainly on efficiency grounds. As Samuelson stated, "Instead of there being a double coincidence of wants, there is likely to be a want of coincidence; so that, unless a hungry tailor happens to find an undraped farmer, who has both food and a desire for a pair of pants, neither can make a trade."[11] Clearly, countertrade ensures that instead of balances being settled on a multilateral basis, with surpluses from one country being balanced by deficits with another, accounts must now be settled on a country-by-country or even transaction-by-transaction basis. Trade then results only from the ability of two parties or countries to purchase specified goods from one another rather than from competition. As a result, uncompetitive goods may be traded. In consequence, the ability of countries and their industries to adjust structurally to more efficient production may be restricted. Countertrade can therefore be seen as eroding the quality and efficiency of production and as lowering world consumption.

These economic arguments notwithstanding, however, countries and companies increasingly see countertrade as an alternative that may be flawed but worthwhile to undertake. As the accompanying map shows, both industrialized and developing countries exchange a wide variety of goods via countertrade.

TYPES OF COUNTERTRADE

Under the traditional types of barter arrangements, goods are exchanged directly for other goods of approximately equal value. As Table 18.1 shows, such transactions can encompass the exchange of a wide variety of goods—for example, an airplane for mango juice—and are carried out both in developing and industrialized countries. However, such straightforward barter transactions, which were quite frequent in the 1950s, are used less often today "because it is difficult to find two parties prepared to make a simultaneous or near-simultaneous exchange of goods of equivalent value."[12]

Increasingly, participants in countertrade have resorted to more sophisticated versions of exchanging goods that often also include some use of money. Figure 18.2 provides an overview of the different forms of countertrade. One such refinement of simple barter is the **counterpurchase,** or **parallel barter,** agreement. To unlink the timing of contract performance, the participating parties sign two separate contracts that specify the goods and services to be exchanged. In this way, one transaction can go forward even though the second transaction needs more time. Such an arrangement can be particularly advantageous if delivery performance is dependent on a future event—for example, the harvest. Frequently, the exchange is not of precisely equal value; therefore some amount of cash will be involved. However, despite the lack of linkage in terms of timing, an exchange of goods for goods does take place. A special case of parallel barter is that of reverse reciprocity, "whereby

Preferred Items for Export in Countertrade Transactions

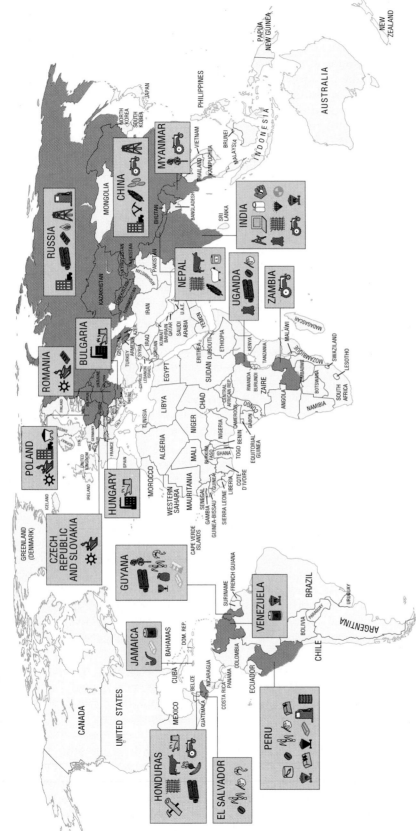

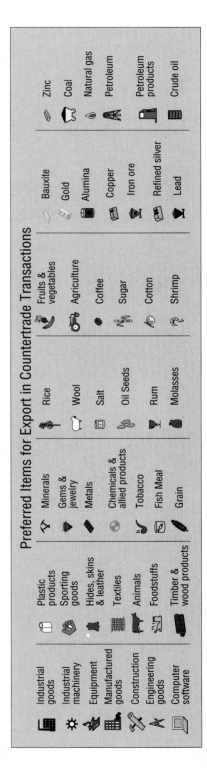

Preferred Items for Export in Countertrade Transactions

Industrial goods		Minerals		Fruits & vegetables	
Industrial machinery		Gems & jewelry		Agriculture	
Equipment		Metals		Coffee	
Manufactured goods		Chemicals & allied products		Sugar	
Construction		Animals		Cotton	
Engineering goods		Foodstuffs		Shrimp	
Computer software		Timber & wood products			

Plastic products		Rice		Bauxite		Zinc
Sporting goods		Wool		Gold		Coal
Hides, skins & leather		Salt		Alumina		Natural gas
Textiles		Oil Seeds		Copper		Petroleum
		Rum		Iron ore		Petroleum products
		Fish Meal		Refined silver		Crude oil
		Molasses		Lead		
		Grain				

**TABLE 18.1
A Sample of Barter
Agreements**

Country		Exported Commodity	
A	**B**	**A**	**B**
Poland	Ukraine	coal	iron ore, other metallurgical products
Switzerland	Russia	$22 million water works facility	40% hard currency plus diesel engines, saw timber, lacquers, paints/enamels, wrist watches, and cables
Japan	Vietnam	motor bikes	rice
India	Vietnam	locomotives, textile machinery, other manufacturers	rice
Malaysia	Myanmar	$96 million investment in infrastructure development	exclusive rights to joint ventures, rice, timber, and gold
Iraq	Czech Republic	oil ($800 million)	petrochemicals and farm equipment
China	Russia	212 railway trucks of mango juice	passenger jet
Indonesia	Uzbekistan	Indian tea, Vietnamese rice, miscellaneous Indonesian products	150,000 tons of cotton over three years
Hungary	Ukraine	food stuffs, tinned foods, pharmaceuticals	timber

Sources: Countertrade Outlook, DP Publications Co.: June 27, 1994, April 25, 1994, August 15, 1994; *Trade Finance,* January 1992, April 1992, July 1992, December 1992, and June 1993.

parallel contracts are signed, granting each party access to needed resources (for example, oil in exchange for nuclear power plants)."[13] Such contracts are useful when long-term exchange relationships are desired.

Another common form of countertrade is the **buy-back,** or **compensation arrangement.** One party agrees to supply technology or equipment that enables the other party to produce goods with which the price of the supplied products or technology is repaid. The arrangements often "include larger amounts of time, money, and products than straight barter arrangements."[14] They originally evolved in response to the reluctance of communist countries to permit ownership of productive resources by the private sector thus restricting foreign direct investment.[15] One example of such a buy-back arrangement is an agreement entered into by Levi Strauss and Hungary. The company transferred know-how and the Levi's trademark to Hungary. A Hungarian firm began to produce Levi's products. Some of the output was sold domestically and the rest was marketed in western Europe by Levi Strauss, in compensation for the know-how. In the past decade, buy-back arrangements have been extended to encompass many developing and newly industrialized nations.

Another form of more refined barter, which tries to reduce the effect of bilateralism and the immediacy of the transaction, is called **clearing account barter.** Here, clearing accounts are established to track debits and credits of trades. The entries merely represent purchasing power, however, and are not directly withdrawable in cash. As a result, each party can agree in a single contract to purchase goods or services of a specified value. Although the account may be out of balance on a transaction-by-transaction basis, the agreement stipulates that over the long term a balance in the account will be restored. Frequently, the goods available for purchase with clearing account funds are tightly stipulated. In fact, funds have on occasion been labeled "apple clearing dollars" or "horseradish clearing funds." Sometimes, additional flexibility is given to the clearing account by permitting **switch-trading,** in which credits in the account can be sold or transferred to a third party. Doing so

FIGURE 18.2   **Classification of Forms of Countertrade**

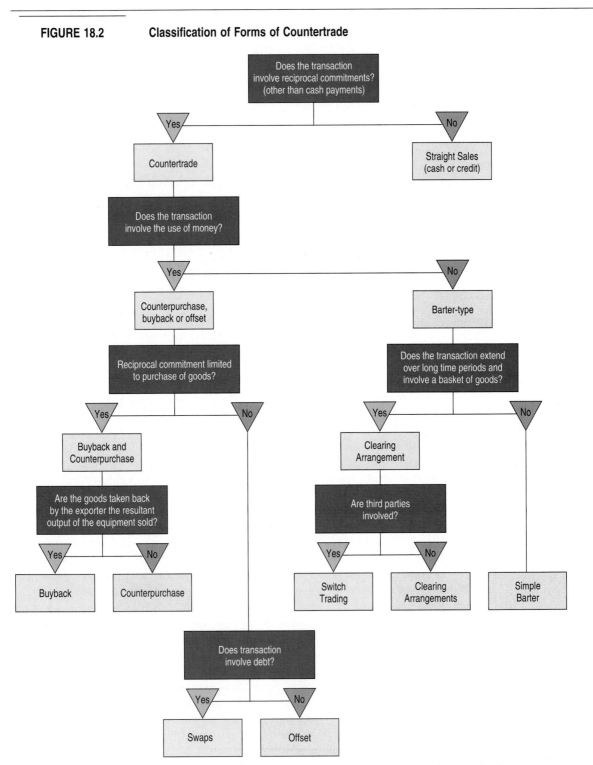

Source: Adapted from Jean-François Hennart, "Some Empirical Dimensions of Countertrade," *Journal of International Business Studies* 21, 2 (1990): 245.

can provide creative intermediaries with opportunities for deal making by identifying clearing account relationships with major imbalances and structuring business transactions to reduce them.

Another major form of countertrade arrangement is called **offset.** These arrangements are most frequently found in the defense-related sector and in sales of large-scale, high-priced items such as aircraft. Offset arrangements are designed to "offset" the negative effects of large purchases from abroad on the current account of a country. For example, a country purchasing aircraft from the United States might require that certain portions of the aircraft be produced and assembled in the purchasing country. Such a requirement is often a condition for awarding the contract or is used as a determining factor in contract decisions. Offset arrangements can take on many forms, such as coproduction, licensing, subcontracting, or joint ventures; they typically are long term. Table 18.2 provides an overview of some key offset practices. In Global Perspective 18.2 an example of governmental offset activities is provided and the risks associated with that practice are explained.

A final form of countertrade, chiefly used as a financial tool, consists of **debt swaps.** These swaps are carried out particularly with less-developed countries in which both the government and the private sector face large debt burdens. The debtors are unable to repay the debt anytime soon, therefore, debt holders have grown increasingly amenable to exchange of the debt for something else. Five types of swaps are most prevalent: debt-for-debt swaps, debt-for-equity swaps, debt-for-product swaps, debt-for-nature swaps, and debt-for-education swaps.

TABLE 18.2 A Sample of Direct and Indirect Offset Practices	Type	Description
	Direct Offsets	
	Coproduction	Overseas production based on government-to-government or producer agreements that permit a foreign government to acquire the technical information and tooling to manufacture all or part of a defense article.
	Directed Subcontracting	The procurement of domestic-made components for incorporation or installation in the items sold to that same nation under direct commercial contracts.
	Concessions	Commercial compensation practices whereby capabilities and items are given free of charge to the buyer.
	Technology transfers/ Licensed production	Helping countries establish defense industry capabilities by providing valuable technology and manufacturing know-how.
	Investments in defense firms	Capital invested to establish or expand a company in the purchasing country.
	Indirect Offsets	
	Procurements	Purchases of parts/components from the purchasing country which are unrelated to the military system being acquired.
	Investments in nondefense firms	Establishing corporations in the purchasing countries to invest capital in the nations' companies.
	Trading of commodities	Using brokers to link buyers with commodities sellers in the purchasing country.
	Foreign defense-related projects	Assisting the recipient country's military services.

Source: United States General Accounting Office, *Report to Congressional Requesters, Military Exports: Concerns Over Offsets Generated With U.S. Foreign Military Financing Program Funds*, June 1994: 18–19.

Global Perspective

18.2
When Governments Do Offset Deals

An unfulfilled offset contract between France and Greece has soured relations between the two countries and resulted in a major policy turnabout by the French Ministry of Defense. No longer will the French ministry become directly involved in offset performance.

It all began in 1985 when the French firm Dessault won a contract to supply Mirage fighter planes worth 8 billion French francs to the Greek Air Force. The French government accepted a 60 percent offset commitment on the total value of the contract, to be fulfilled in 10 to 15 years. The French Defense Ministry decided to play a direct role and assumed 20 percent of the offset liability, believing it not to be too onerous a chore. As the fulfillment deadline approaches, the Ministry concedes that it has not even begun to perform its obligation.

A Ministry official explained that it's not very easy to find good deals. There have been efforts to identify offset opportunities. For example, the Ministry has considered purchasing motor cars and ammunition for military use, but without success.

Dessault, the prime contractor, has delivered all of the fighters and performed its own portion of the offset obligations according to the schedule fixed by Greece. The offsets included investments in the industrial and agricultural sectors and the counterpurchase of products from Greek industries.

An unnamed Defense Ministry official had this to say about the deal, "This has shown to the French public that its administration is often tempted to interfere, but it is not an administration's job to deal directly in offsets. A Minister . . . is not a manufacturer . . . and this is a good example of what they should not do."

Source: "French Government Eschews Future Role in Offset Fulfillment," *Countertrade Outlook,* April 25, 1994: 5.

A **debt-for-debt swap** takes place when a loan held by one creditor is simply exchanged for a loan held by another creditor. For example, a U.S. bank may swap Argentine debt for Chilean debt with a German bank. Through this mechanism, debt holders are able to consolidate their outstanding loans and concentrate on particular countries or regions.

Debt-for-equity swaps arise when debt is converted into foreign equity in a domestic firm. The swap therefore serves as the vehicle for foreign direct investment. Although the equity itself is denominated in local currency, the terms of the conversion may allow the investor future access to foreign exchange for dividend remittances and capital repatriation.[16] In some countries, the debt-for-equity swaps have been very successful. For example, within a few years, investments in Chile retired about $13 billion of the country's external debt.[17]

A third form of debt swap consists of **debt-for-product swaps.** Here, debt is exchanged for products. Usually, the transactions require that an additional cash payment be made for the product. For example, First Interstate Bank of California concluded an arrangement with Peruvian authorities whereby a commitment was made to purchase $3 worth of Peruvian products for every $1 of products paid for by Peru against debt.[18]

An emerging form of debt swap with major environmental implications is that of the **debt-for-nature swap.** Firms or entities buy what are otherwise considered to be nonperforming loans at substantial discounts and return the debt to the country in exchange for the preservation of natural resources. The banks like these deals because they recoup some of the money they had written off; some countries like them, as they are able to retire debt, but others do not because they believe they are selling their natural resources. However, pressing environmental concerns can be addressed by applying debt-for-nature swaps. As an example, Conservation International, an American environmental group, paid Citicorp $100,000 for $650,000 of Bolivian debt, then returned the debt to Bolivia in exchange for an agreement to turn a 4-million-acre stretch of the Amazon Basin into a wildlife sanctuary and pay for its upkeep.[19] Growing environmental concerns combined with ongoing difficulties of debt repayment are likely to increase the swaps of debt for social causes.

Debt-for-education swaps have been suggested in the U.S. government by one of the authors as a means to reduce debt burdens and to enable more students to study abroad. This approach could greatly enhance the international orientation, foreign language training, and cultural sensitivity of an educational system.[20] As Global Perspective 18.3 shows, some universities already are taking advantage of this form of countertrade.

With the increasing sophistication of countertrade, the original form of straight barter is less used today. Most frequently used is the counterpurchase agreement. Due to high military expenditures, offsets are the second most frequently used form. Figure 18.3 presents the results of a survey of U.S. firms that showed the relatively

Global Perspective

18.3
Debt Funds Study Abroad

Harvard University recently agreed to extend a helping hand to the debt-burdened government of Ecuador in South America. In an unprecedented agreement, the university will help convert a portion of Ecuador's $11 billion debt into scholarships for Ecuadorean students to attend Harvard.

The debt-for-scholarship agreement exchanges foreign debt for educational opportunities. Ecuador has passed special legislation making the agreement possible. "Harvard is putting up the original money to purchase the debt, and then the Ecuadorean government is basically financing the rest through the debt swap," said Ned Strong, area director of the Harvard-based Latin American Scholarship Program of American Universities (LASPAU). Harvard will buy $5 million in Ecuadorean debt at the market price. The current rate is 15 percent of face value; therefore, the school will invest $750,000.

That debt will be given to the Fundacion Capacitar, an educational foundation in Ecuador that will exchange the debt for Ecuadorean government bonds worth 50 percent of the debt's face value, or $2.5 million.

"The national government obviously much prefers to have half as much debt outstanding," says Robert Scott, vice president for finance at Harvard.

The government bonds, issued in *sucres,* the local currency, will be sold in Ecuador by the foundation. Income from the sale will be converted to dollars and invested in the United States to create an endowment providing scholarship funds for the Ecuadorean students.

The arrangement also provides funds for Harvard students and professors to conduct research and internships in Ecuador. For the Ecuadoreans, the debt-reduction agreement is simply a mechanism to bring educational opportunities to their citizens. "The main purpose is the capacity for studying at Harvard," said Miguel Falconi, president of Fundacion Capacitar.

"It's definitely a two-way street," said Strong of LASPAU. The foreign student gets advanced training and enriches the university community, he says.

**FIGURE 18.3
Countertrade Usage—
by Types**

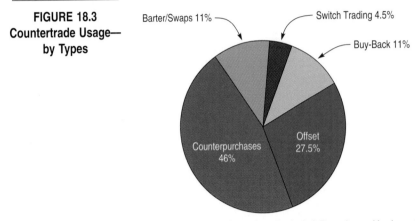

Source: Laura B. Forker, *Countertrade: Purchasing's Perceptions and Involvement* (Tempe: Center for Advanced Purchasing Studies, Arizona State University, 1991), 29.

low use of barter, findings confirmed by other research.[21] Investigations in other countries have shown that compensation or buy-back arrangements are on the rise.[22]

OFFICIAL ATTITUDES TOWARD COUNTERTRADE

A U.S. Policy Perspective

When trying to ascertain government policy, one must investigate the various departments within the executive, legislative, and judicial branches. On occasion, a coherent policy view can be identified. More often than not, discrepancies among the different groups become visible because they have different outlooks and serve different constituencies. Such discrepancies are particularly obvious when looking at the issue of countertrade.

A government report on U.S. competitiveness made a strong statement against countertrade by concluding "that the transactions are purely bilateral in nature and are not competitive since they squeeze out competition from a third market or specify the export market. Trade is formulated on the basis of the willingness to countertrade and not on economic considerations."[23]

The Department of the Treasury stated that "offset and coproduction agreements mandated by governments [do not] promote . . . economic . . . efficiency. They may constitute implicit subsidies to the industry of the purchasing countries. They may result in diversion of business away from efficient U.S. producers . . . thus causing economic inefficiency and dislocations. . . . Since these practices appear to involve spillover effects on nondefense production and trade, they may have adverse effects on future U.S. production, trade, employment, and tax revenue."[24]

The Office of the U.S. Trade Representative, which is the chief U.S. trade negotiator, is somewhat more flexible. "Our position is that countertrade is a second-best option for international trade transactions. It represents a distortion of international trade and is contrary to an open, free trading system. It is not in the long-run interest of the United States or the U.S. business community. Nevertheless, as a matter of policy, the U.S. government does not oppose U.S. companies' participating in countertrade arrangements unless such actions could have a negative impact on national security. If a company believes a countertrade transaction is in its interest, the company is in a better position than we are to make that business decision."[25]

The Department of Defense is concerned with enhancing its principles of RSI—rationalization, standardization, and interoperability. This means that the department strongly encourages other nations allied with the United States to use similar equipment that can be interchanged in case of an armed conflict. For this reason, the Department of Defense tries to encourage foreign acquisitions of U.S. military hardware. Such acquisition is likely to come about only through promises of offsets and co-production, thus the department tends to display a policy of "positive neutrality" toward the countertrade methods.

This attitude makes sense from the perspective of production cost. Given the economies of scale and the learning curve effects inherent in the manufacture of arms, more international sales result in longer production runs, which in turn permit weapons manufacturers to offer their products at a lower price. If the Department of Defense can encourage more international sales, it can either buy a given number of products for less money or purchase more products with a given budget. From that perspective, one could argue that countertrade transactions contribute to U.S. national security.

The Department of Commerce displays the most supportive view of countertrade in the official community. Given its mandate to help U.S. firms compete internationally, the department has its own Office of Barter and Countertrade, which provides advice to firms interested in such transactions. However, this office was established only after significant congressional pressure.

While all these different views exist within the departments of the administration, Congress repeatedly has passed bills that permit or even encourage countertrade transactions. The legislation primarily has focused on barter possibilities for U.S. agricultural commodities or stockpiling purposes. As a result, the Commodities Credit Corporation and the General Services Administration have been carrying out countertrade transactions for years. An example is the swap of U.S. agricultural commodities for Jamaican bauxite. The large-scale transaction was designed to reduce the U.S. surplus of agricultural products while increasing national stockpiles of a strategic material.

In the judicial branch, countertrade involvement stems mostly from the enforcement activities of the Internal Revenue Service. The IRS is, of course, primarily concerned with the accounting and taxation issues presented in the next chapter. In the countertrade context, this concern refers to the valuation of countertrade transactions and with ensuring that proper tax payments are made. A proper

The Department of Defense encourages nations allied with the United States to use similar equipment to facilitate repairs in the event of an armed conflict. Here, a Luftwaffe flight-test team checks a Hughes-built radar on a German F-4F aircraft.

Source: Courtesy of Hughes Aircraft Company.

Global Perspective

18.4
Coping with Offsets

Many governments of countries that experience trade deficits view imports as a problem. As a result, they may limit imports through the use of tariffs, quotas, or other non-tariff barriers. A small but growing number of governments restrict imports, and simultaneously encourage exports, by requiring firms to offset import sales with export spending. The rationale behind such actions is to restrict imports, increase exports, and create jobs.

One way governments offset a negative impact on the trade or current account is through offset purchasing. This means that a company that desires to import products must prove to the government that it is purchasing an agreed-upon percentage of the imports in local goods or services, which in turn are exported. The thought is that if the importer purchases local products for export, local companies will be strengthened and export volume will grow.

The Business Development Group at a U.S. computer firm faces offset regulations every day. In its drive to open new markets around the globe, the firm is increasingly confronted with government demands to offset the trade balance effect of its computer imports. The Business Development Group works with the Procurement Group, third-party suppliers, and governments to comply with offset regulations. For example, the Business Development Group will attempt to source components that are required to build computers, printers, and peripherals from firms in

those countries to which computers are exported. Often, the goals of the Business Development Group and the procurement organization within the firm tend to clash. Procurement favors suppliers that offer the best combination of cost, quality, and delivery. Business Development, in turn, prefers sourcing from those suppliers that enable the company to fulfill offset requirements, since doing so will increase sales volume abroad. Unfortunately, the suppliers often do not offer lowest cost, highest quality, or fastest delivery. To reduce the intraorganizational conflict, Business Development has begun to work with foreign suppliers to give them the tools necessary to compete with other suppliers. As a result, technology transfer, training, and quality instructions are often provided abroad.

One concurrent problem faced by the Business Development Group is the fact that it is very difficult to count the dollar volume of purchases from countries. Today, international trade is so complex that it is difficult to tell from which country a good or service originated. Goods are often transshipped before arriving at their final destination. Distributors often do not know from where a certain shipment came. Goods and services often have component parts from a number of countries. In consequence, the Business Development Group is in the process of revamping the firm's entire sourcing system in order to track country of origin more carefully.

Source: Scott Ciener, Georgetown University.

pricing flexibility. Yet, as Global Perspective 18.4 shows, the development of such a new corporate direction is not without its problems.

Particularly for longer range countertrade transactions, executives may not be as risk averse as for shorter range transactions. By the time the countertrade requirements fall due, which may be five to ten years in the future, they may not be around to take the blame if problems arise because they may have been promoted, changed positions, or retired. On the other hand, for these long-term risks, many companies make it clear that the preferred compensation is cash, and that any kind of countertrade transaction is not acceptable. However, the number of stalwart opponents of all countertrade deals is decreasing.

Companies and countries imposing countertrade requirements believe that there are more merits to the transactions than purely conserving foreign currency. For example, the countertrade partner can be used as a marketing arm to explore new markets. Long-term countertrade requirements can ensure markets for future output;

FIGURE 18.5
An Advertisement
for a Countertrade
Database

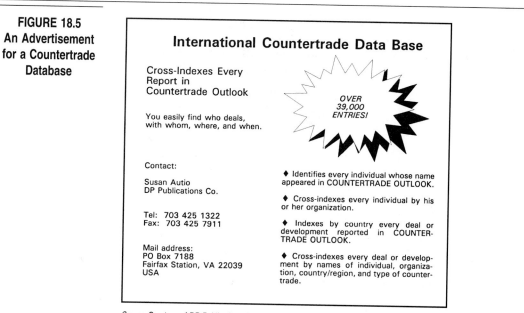

International Countertrade Data Base

Cross-Indexes Every Report in Countertrade Outlook

You easily find who deals, with whom, where, and when.

OVER 39,000 ENTRIES!

Contact:

Susan Autio
DP Publications Co.

Tel: 703 425 1322
Fax: 703 425 7911

Mail address:
PO Box 7188
Fairfax Station, VA 22039
USA

◆ Identifies every individual whose name appeared in COUNTERTRADE OUTLOOK.

◆ Cross-indexes every individual by his or her organization.

◆ Indexes by country every deal or development reported in COUNTER-TRADE OUTLOOK.

◆ Cross-indexes every deal or development by names of individual, organization, country/region, and type of counter-trade.

Source: Courtesy of DP Publications Company.

Countertrade intermediaries need not be large. Smaller firms can successfully compete with a niche strategy. By exploiting specialized geographic or product knowledge and developing countertrade transactions that may be too small for the multinational firm, an entrepreneur can conduct trades with little capital, yet receive sound profit margins.

Another new type of intermediary, mostly smaller, is represented by counter-trade information service providers. They provide data bases on countertrade products and countertrade regulations in various countries, which subscribers may tap. They are beginning also to provide computerized matchmaking services between companies in debit to some country's counterpurchase system and those in credit, or those willing to buy counterpurchase items.[34] Figure 18.5 provides an example of such a data base service.

PREPARING FOR COUNTERTRADE

The majority of countertrade transactions in the United States are consummated by countertrade specialists who are outside the corporation, as Figure 18.6 shows. However, increasingly companies consider carrying out countertrade transactions in-house. If this can be done, the need for steep discounts may decrease and the profitability of countertrade may improve.

Developing an in-house capability for handling countertrade should be done with great caution. First, the company should determine the import priorities of its products to the country or firm to which it is trying to sell. Goods that are highly desirable and/or necessary for a country mandating countertrade are less likely to be subject to countertrade requirements or may be subject to less stringent requirements than goods considered luxurious and unnecessary. Next, the firm needs to

**FIGURE 18.6
Countertrade Services
Employed by U.S. Firms**

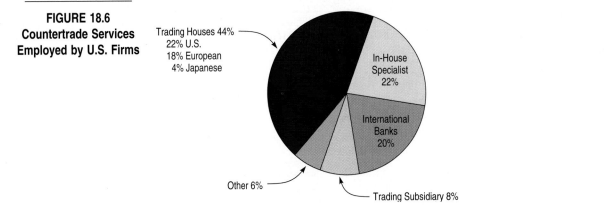

Trading Houses 44%
22% U.S.
18% European
4% Japanese

In-House Specialist 22%

International Banks 20%

Other 6%

Trading Subsidiary 8%

Source: Willis A. Bussard, "An Overview of Countertrade Practices of Corporations and Individual Nations," in *International Countertrade,* ed. C. Korth (Westwood, Conn.: Quorum Books, a division of Greenwood Press, Inc., 1987), 21.

identify the countertrade arrangements and regulations that exist in the country to which it exports. An awareness of the alternatives available and of the various countertrade percentages demanded will strengthen the company's bargaining position at the precontract stage. Obtaining the information is also important to incorporate possible countertrade costs early into the pricing scheme. Once a "cash deal" price has been quoted, increasing the price is difficult if a subsequent countertrade demand is made.

At this stage, the most favored countertrade arrangement from the buyer's perspective should be identified. The company should find out why this particular arrangement is the most favored one and explore whether other forms of transactions would similarly meet the objectives of the countertrading partner. To do this, the goals and objectives of the countertrading parties need to be determined. As discussed earlier, they can consist of investment or import substitution, a preservation of hard currency, export promotion, and so on.

The next step is to match the strengths of the firm with current and potential countertrade situations. This requires an assessment of corporate capabilities and resources. Any internal sourcing needs that might be used to fulfill a countertrade contract should be determined—that is, raw materials or intermediate products that could be obtained from the countertrade partner rather than current suppliers. However, this assessment should not be restricted to the internal corporate use of a countertraded product. The company should also determine whether it can use, for example, its distribution capabilities or its contacts with other customers and suppliers to help in its countertrade transactions.

At this point, the company can decide whether it should engage in countertrade transactions. The accounting and taxation aspects of the countertrade transactions should be considered, because they are often quite different from usual procedures. The use of an accounting or tax professional is essential to compliance with difficult and obscure tax regulations in this area.

Next, all of the risks involved in countertrade must be considered. This means that the goods to be obtained need to be specified, that the delivery time for the goods needs to be determined, and that the reliability of the supplier and the quality and consistency of the goods need to be assessed. It is also useful to explore the impact of countertrade on future prices, both for the specific goods obtained and

FIGURE 18.4   Advertisement Offering Countertrade Services

these are particularly important to producers in industries highly sensitive to capacity utilization. Security and stability of purchasing and sales arrangements can also play a major role. Some countries also see counterpurchases as a major way of ensuring that technology transfer is carried out as promised, because the transferor will have to take back the product produced and will therefore ensure that the repayment will be of high quality.

Other reasons for engaging in countertrade can be more effective introduction of new products, the desire to more easily enter new markets, and the goal of expanding the company's market share. Countertrade has been found to provide "outlets for integrative growth in addition to market penetration and development."[32] Finally, countertrade can provide markets and open up new trade channels for surplus products that could not be sold otherwise.[33] Particularly in instances when a world market glut exists for commodities that are in ample supply in some countries yet scarce in others, countertrade transactions may be an appealing trade mechanism.

THE EMERGENCE OF NEW INTERMEDIARIES

The rise in countertrade transactions has resulted in the emergence of new specialists to handle such transactions. The intermediaries can be either in-house or outside the corporation. Some companies have been founded to facilitate countertrade transactions for other firms. By purchasing unwanted inventories from companies at a steep discount, sometimes very high profit margins can be obtained. For example, Fred Tarter of Deerfield Communications founded his company on this principle and made $17 million when he sold it in 1984 to Integrated Barter International of New York. He took on inventory from companies and paid for it in cash or advertising time or both. When he paid in advertising, he exchanged bartered goods for other bartered commodities that were more desirable.

Other intermediaries that have benefited from the rise of countertrade are trading companies or trading houses that frequently act as third-party intermediaries. Some of them are subsidiaries of large corporations that seek to supplement the trading volume generated by their corporation with business from other firms. An example of such multinational activity is provided in Figure 18.4. Due to their widespread connections around the world, trading companies or trading houses can dispose of countertraded goods more easily than can corporations that only infrequently consummate countertrade transactions. They are also more capable of evaluating the risks of such transactions and can benefit from both the discount and the markup portion of the exchange.

Firms that deal with trading houses to receive assistance in their countertrade transactions need to be aware that the fees charged are often quite steep and may increase cumulatively. For example, there may be an initial consulting fee when the transaction is contemplated, a fee for the consummation of the acquisition, and a subsequent steep discount for the disposal of the acquired products. Also, the trading houses frequently refuse to take countertraded goods on a nonrecourse basis, which means that the company that has obtained countertraded goods still shares some of the risks inherent in their disposal.

International banks also have some involvement in countertrade to serve their clients better and to increase their own profitability. Banks may be able to use their experience in international trade finance and apply it to the financial aspects of countertrade transactions. Banks may also have a comparative advantage over trading firms by having more knowledge and expertise about financial risk management and more information about and contacts with the global market.

Global Perspective

18.4
Coping with Offsets

Many governments of countries that experience trade deficits view imports as a problem. As a result, they may limit imports through the use of tariffs, quotas, or other non-tariff barriers. A small but growing number of governments restrict imports, and simultaneously encourage exports, by requiring firms to offset import sales with export spending. The rationale behind such actions is to restrict imports, increase exports, and create jobs.

One way governments offset a negative impact on the trade or current account is through offset purchasing. This means that a company that desires to import products must prove to the government that it is purchasing an agreed-upon percentage of the imports in local goods or services, which in turn are exported. The thought is that if the importer purchases local products for export, local companies will be strengthened and export volume will grow.

The Business Development Group at a U.S. computer firm faces offset regulations every day. In its drive to open new markets around the globe, the firm is increasingly confronted with government demands to offset the trade balance effect of its computer imports. The Business Development Group works with the Procurement Group, third-party suppliers, and governments to comply with off-set regulations. For example, the Business Development Group will attempt to source components that are required to build computers, printers, and peripherals from firms in those countries to which computers are exported. Often, the goals of the Business Development Group and the procurement organization within the firm tend to clash. Procurement favors suppliers that offer the best combination of cost, quality, and delivery. Business Development, in turn, prefers sourcing from those suppliers that enable the company to fulfill offset requirements, since doing so will increase sales volume abroad. Unfortunately, the suppliers often do not offer lowest cost, highest quality, or fastest delivery. To reduce the intraorganizational conflict, Business Development has begun to work with foreign suppliers to give them the tools necessary to compete with other suppliers. As a result, technology transfer, training, and quality instructions are often provided abroad.

One concurrent problem faced by the Business Development Group is the fact that it is very difficult to count the dollar volume of purchases from countries. Today, international trade is so complex that it is difficult to tell from which country a good or service originated. Goods are often transshipped before arriving at their final destination. Distributors often do not know from where a certain shipment came. Goods and services often have component parts from a number of countries. In consequence, the Business Development Group is in the process of revamping the firm's entire sourcing system in order to track country of origin more carefully.

Source: Scott Ciener, Georgetown University.

pricing flexibility. Yet, as Global Perspective 18.4 shows, the development of such a new corporate direction is not without its problems.

Particularly for longer range countertrade transactions, executives may not be as risk averse as for shorter range transactions. By the time the countertrade requirements fall due, which may be five to ten years in the future, they may not be around to take the blame if problems arise because they may have been promoted, changed positions, or retired. On the other hand, for these long-term risks, many companies make it clear that the preferred compensation is cash, and that any kind of countertrade transaction is not acceptable. However, the number of stalwart opponents of all countertrade deals is decreasing.

Companies and countries imposing countertrade requirements believe that there are more merits to the transactions than purely conserving foreign currency. For example, the countertrade partner can be used as a marketing arm to explore new markets. Long-term countertrade requirements can ensure markets for future output;

The international organization most neutral toward countertrade is the United Nations. A report of the secretary general stated only that there appeared to be some economic and financial problems with countertrade transactions and that any global, uniform regulation of countertrade might be difficult to implement because of the complexity and variety of transactions. The report lacks any kind of general conclusion, because such conclusions "may be somewhat hazardous in the absence of a sufficient volume of contracts that are easily available."[29]

The United Nations statement highlights one of the major problems faced by policymakers interested in countertrade. Corporations and executives consider the subject of countertrade to be sensitive, because public discussion of such practices could imply that a product line may be difficult to sell or indicate that the corporation is willing to conduct countertrade. Such knowledge would result in a weakening of the corporation's international negotiation position, thus executives are usually tight-lipped about their firm's countertrade transactions.[30] At the same time, rumors about countertrade deals are often rampant, even though many of the transactions gossiped about may never materialize. To some extent, therefore, the public view of countertrade may represent an inverted iceberg: Much more is on the surface than below. Policymakers therefore are uncertain about the precise volume and impact of countertrade, a fact that makes taking proper policy actions all the more difficult.

Countertrade does appear to be on the increase. The main reason for that conclusion is the fact that countertrade may perhaps be the only practical solution to the fundamental difficulties in the world economy, of which it is a symptom. Access to developed markets for the less-developed countries has become increasingly limited. Balance of payment crises, debt problems, and other financial difficulties have hurt their ability to import needed products. In the face of limited trade and investment opportunities, both less-developed countries and industrialized nations appear to regard countertrade as an alternative solution to no trade at all.[31]

THE CORPORATE SITUATION

A few years ago, most executives claimed both in public and in private that countertrade was a hindrance to international business and was avoided by their firms. More recently, however, changes in corporate thinking have taken place. Even though companies may not like countertrade transactions, a refusal may mean business lost to foreign rivals who are willing to participate in countertrade. Increasingly, companies are altering their perspective from a reactive to a proactive one. In the past, U.S. corporations frequently resorted to countertrade only because they were compelled by circumstances to do so. Today, however, companies have begun to use countertrade as a tool to improve their market position. Rockwell International Corporation, for example, uses its own internal barter capabilities through its trading subsidiary. As a result, Rockwell's products have a special appeal abroad because of the company's willingness to engage in countertrade. Similarly, Daimler-Benz has established a countertrade subsidiary that has swapped warning triangles, screwdrivers, jacks, and even bananas for Mercedes trucks.

Increasingly, companies are formulating international business strategies and are planning to acquire market share from their competition by seeking out countertrade opportunities, provided they lead to an expansion of their own product sales. The companies go beyond the traditional view that some sales, even those subject to countertrade, are better than no sales. They are using countertrade systematically as a strategic tool that brings with it favorable government consideration and greater

The Department of Defense is concerned with enhancing its principles of RSI—rationalization, standardization, and interoperability. This means that the department strongly encourages other nations allied with the United States to use similar equipment that can be interchanged in case of an armed conflict. For this reason, the Department of Defense tries to encourage foreign acquisitions of U.S. military hardware. Such acquisition is likely to come about only through promises of offsets and coproduction, thus the department tends to display a policy of "positive neutrality" toward the countertrade methods.

This attitude makes sense from the perspective of production cost. Given the economies of scale and the learning curve effects inherent in the manufacture of arms, more international sales result in longer production runs, which in turn permit weapons manufacturers to offer their products at a lower price. If the Department of Defense can encourage more international sales, it can either buy a given number of products for less money or purchase more products with a given budget. From that perspective, one could argue that countertrade transactions contribute to U.S. national security.

The Department of Commerce displays the most supportive view of countertrade in the official community. Given its mandate to help U.S. firms compete internationally, the department has its own Office of Barter and Countertrade, which provides advice to firms interested in such transactions. However, this office was established only after significant congressional pressure.

While all these different views exist within the departments of the administration, Congress repeatedly has passed bills that permit or even encourage countertrade transactions. The legislation primarily has focused on barter possibilities for U.S. agricultural commodities or stockpiling purposes. As a result, the Commodities Credit Corporation and the General Services Administration have been carrying out countertrade transactions for years. An example is the swap of U.S. agricultural commodities for Jamaican bauxite. The large-scale transaction was designed to reduce the U.S. surplus of agricultural products while increasing national stockpiles of a strategic material.

In the judicial branch, countertrade involvement stems mostly from the enforcement activities of the Internal Revenue Service. The IRS is, of course, primarily concerned with the accounting and taxation issues presented in the next chapter. In the countertrade context, this concern refers to the valuation of countertrade transactions and with ensuring that proper tax payments are made. A proper

The Department of Defense encourages nations allied with the United States to use similar equipment to facilitate repairs in the event of an armed conflict. Here, a Luftwaffe flight-test team checks a Hughes-built radar on a German F-4F aircraft.

Source: Courtesy of Hughes Aircraft Company.

assessment of taxes, however, usually requires a painstaking determination of all facets of the transaction. Difficulties are often encountered in ascertaining the exact value of the countertraded goods, the time when the income has been received, and the profitability of the entire transaction. As a result of these problems, tax authorities are not in favor of countertrade. Other judicial activities are mainly concerned with valuation issues for import purposes. One major issue is the threat of dumping, whereby goods obtained through countertrade transactions may be disposed of cheaply in the domestic market and therefore harm domestic competitors, who do not benefit from the sales end of a countertrade transaction.

The differing views within the administration and in the legislative and the judicial branches indicate that countertrade is partially encouraged, as long as no major negative effects on nonparticipants are visible within the domestic economy.

Other Government Views

Most industrialized countries, including western European countries, Japan, New Zealand, and Australia, have participated actively in the growing countertrade phenomenon. Frequently, they are catalysts for countertrade transactions. The emerging market economies have continued to favor countertrade. Countries in the developing world have taken varied positions. Indonesia, for example, cited two choices it faced as its export revenues declined dramatically: One was to drastically limit its imports, the other was to liberalize its trade with alternative measures such as countertrade. As a result, the government officially instituted a mandatory countertrade requirement for any transaction exceeding a value of $500,000.

Other developing countries have more subtle policies but are implementing and supporting countertrade nonetheless. Brazil, for example, keeps quite a low profile. Although the country "has issued no countertrade regulations and does not officially sanction its practice, . . . awards of import licenses and export performance are linked at the level of the firm."[26] This is a position taken more and more frequently by less-developed countries. Although officially they abhor the use of countertrade, unofficially they have made it clear that, in order to do business, countertrade transactions are mandatory.

Attitudes of International Organizations

International organizations almost uniformly condemn countertrade. Public statements by both the IMF and the WTO indicate that their opposition is based on broad considerations of macroeconomic efficiency. The authorities complain that instead of a rational system of exchange, based on product quality and price, countertrade introduces extraneous elements into the sales equation. Countertrade is viewed as being inconsistent with an open, free trading system and not in the best long-term interest of the contracting parties.[27] The WTO, for example, sees dangers to the principle of nondiscrimination and warns of the politicization of international trade.

Officials from the OECD (Organization for Economic Cooperation and Development) also deplore countertrade arrangements. They think that such arrangements would lead to an increase in trade conflicts as competitive suppliers, unwilling to undertake countertrade arrangements, are displaced by less competitive suppliers who are willing to do so.[28]

TABLE 18.3 Organizing for Countertrade: In-House versus Third Parties	Advantages	Disadvantages
	In-House	
	• Lower costs	• Less expertise
	• Customer contact	• Reselling problems
	• More control	• Recruitment and training costs
	• More flexibility	• Less objectivity
	• More learning	• Problems coordinating interfunctional staff
	• More confidentiality	
	Third Parties	
	• Expert specialists	• May be costly
	• Customer contacts	• Distanced from customer
	• Reselling contacts	• Less flexibility
	• Legal acumen	• Less confidentiality
	• More objectivity	• Less learning

Source: Charles W. Neale, David D. Shipley, and J. Colin Dodds, "The Countertrading Experience of British and Canadian Firms," *Management International Review,* 31 no. 1 (1991): 33.

for the world market price for the category of goods. For example, a countertrade transaction may appear to be quite profitable at the time of agreement. Several months or even years may pass before the transaction is actually consummated, however, thus a change in world market prices may severely affect the transaction's profitability. The effect of a countertrade transaction on the world market price should also be considered. In cases of large-volume transactions, the established price may be affected because of a glut of supply. Such a situation may not only affect the profitability of a transaction but can also result in possible legal actions by other suppliers of similar products.

In conjunction with the evaluation of the countertraded products, which as a general requirement should be specified in as much detail as possible rather than left open, the corporation needs to explore the market for the products. This includes forecasting future market developments, paying particular attention to competitive reaction and price fluctuations. It is also useful at this stage to determine the impact of the countertraded products on the sales and profits of other complementary product lines currently marketed by the firm. Possible repercussions from outside groups should be investigated. Such repercussions may consist of antidumping actions brought about by competitors or reactions from totally unsuspected quarters. For example, McDonnell-Douglas ran into strong opposition when it used bartered Yugoslavian ham in its employees' cafeteria and as Christmas gifts. The local meat-packers' union complained vociferously that McDonnell-Douglas was threatening the jobs of its members.

Using all the information obtained, the company can finally evaluate the length of the intended relationship with the countertrading partner and the importance of the relationship for its future plans and goals. The parameters will be decisive for the final action, because they may form constraints overriding short-term economic effects. Management also can then make the final decision as to whether the transaction should be handled within or outside of the firm. Table 18.3 summarizes the advantages and disadvantages of such organizational alternatives. Overall, management needs to remember that, in most instances, a countertrade transaction should remain a means for successful international business and not become an end in itself.

SUMMARY

Countertrades are business transactions in which the sale of goods is linked to other goods or performance rather than only to money. In spite of their economic inefficiency, such transactions are emerging with increasing frequency in many nations around the world.

Concurrent with their increased use, countertrade transactions also have become more sophisticated. Rather than exchange goods for goods in a straight barter deal, companies and countries now structure counterpurchase agreements, compensation arrangements, clearing accounts, offset agreements, and debt swaps to promote their industrial policies and encourage development.

Governments and international organizations are concerned about the trend toward countertrade, yet in light of existing competition and the need to find creative ways of financing trade, they exercise very little interference with countertrade.

Corporations are increasingly using countertrade as a competitive tool to maintain or increase market share. The complexity of the transactions requires careful planning in order to avoid major corporate losses. Management must consider how the acquired merchandise will be disposed of, what the potential for market disruptions is, and to what extent countertraded goods fit in with the corporate mission.

New intermediaries have emerged to facilitate countertrade transactions, yet their services can be very expensive. However, they can enable firms without countertrade experience to participate in this growing business practice. In addition, the development of intermediary skills may offer profitable opportunities for small business entrepreneurs.

Key Terms and Concepts

barter

counterpurchase

parallel barter

buy-back

compensation arrangement

clearing account barter

switch-trading

offset

debt swaps

debt-for-debt swap

debt-for-equity swap

debt-for-product swap

debt-for-nature swap

debt-for-education swap

assessment of taxes

Questions for Discussion

1. What are some of the major causes for the resurgence of countertrade?
2. What forms of countertrade exist and how do they differ?
3. Discuss the advantages and drawbacks of countertrade.
4. How would you characterize the government's position toward countertrade?
5. How consistent is countertrade with the international trade framework?
6. Why would a firm take goods rather than cash?
7. Why would a buyer insist on countertrade transactions?

8. What particular benefits can an outside countertrade intermediary offer to a firm engaged in such transactions?

9. How would you prepare your firm for countertrade?

10. Develop a corporate goals statement that uses countertrade as a proactive tool for international expansion.

11. Explain why countertrade may be encouraged by the increasing technology transfer taking place.

12. What are some of the dangers of using countertraded goods in-house?

Recommended Readings

Alexandrides, C.G., and B.L. Bowers. *Countertrade.* New York: Wiley, 1987.

Countertrade Outlook, published by DP Publications Co.

Directory of Organizations Providing Countertrade Services. Fairfax Station, Va.: DP Publications Co., 1994.

International Buy-Back Contracts. New York: United Nations, 1991.

Kopinski, Thaddeus C. *Negotiating Countertrade and Offsets: Avoiding Legal and Contractual Pitfalls.* Arlington, Va.: Asian Press, 1987.

Korth, Christopher M., ed. *International Countertrade.* Westport, Conn.: Quorum Books, 1987.

Mohring, Wolfgang. *Gegengeschaefte: Analyse einer Handelsform.* Frankfurt: M.P. Lang, 1991.

Schaffer, Matt. *Winning the Countertrade War: New Export Strategies for America.* New York: Wiley, 1989.

UNCITRAL Legal Guide on International Countertrade Transactions. New York: United Nations, 1993.

Verzariu, Pompiliu. *International Countertrade, A Guide for Managers and Executives.* Washington, D.C.: U.S. Department of Commerce, 1992.

Verzariu, Pompiliu, and Paula Mitchell. *International Countertrade, Individual Country Practices.* Washington, D.C.: U.S. Department of Commerce, 1992.

Zurawicki, Leon, and Louis Suichmezian. *Global Countertrade, An Annotated Bibliography.* New York: Garland Publishers, 1991.

Notes

1. Raj Aggarwal, "International Business through Barter and Countertrade," *Long Range Planning,* June 1989, 75–81.

2. *Trade Finance,* May 1992, 13.

3. "Current Activities of International Organizations in the Field of Barter and Barter-Like Transactions," *Report of the Secretary General,* United Nations, General Assembly, 1984, 4.

4. Jean-François Hennart and Erin Anderson, "Countertrade and the Minimization of Transaction Costs: An Empirical Examination," *The Journal of Law, Economics, and Organization,* September 2, 1993, 290–313.

5. Ibid., 307.

6. Jean-François Hennart, "Some Empirical Dimensions of Countertrade," *Journal of International Business Studies,* 21(2) (Second Quarter, 1990): 243–270.

7. Abla M. Abdel-Latif and Jeffrey B. Nugent, "Countertrade as Trade Creation and Trade Diversion," *Contemporary Economic Policy,* 12, January 1994, 1–10.

8. Jong H. Park, "Is Countertrade Merely a Passing Phenomenon? Some Public Policy Implications," in *Proceedings of the 1988 Conference,* ed. R. King (Charleston, S.C.: Academy of International Business, Southeast Region, 1988), 67–71.

9. Hennart, "Some Empirical Dimensions of Countertrade."

10. Rolf Mirus and Bernard Yeung, "Why Countertrade? An Economic Perspective," *The International Trade Journal* 7, 4 (1993): 409–433.

11. Paul Samuelson, *Economics,* 11th ed. (New York: McGraw Hill, 1980), 260.

12. "Current Activities of International Organizations," 4.

13. Christopher M. Korth, "The Promotion of Exports with Barter," in *Export Promotion,* ed. M. Czinkota (New York: Praeger, 1983), 42.

14. Donna U. Vogt, *U.S. Government International Barter;* Congressional Research Service, Report No. 83-211ENR (Washington, D.C.: Government Printing Office, 1983), 65.

15. Korth, "The Promotion of Exports with Barter," 42.

16. Richard A. Debts, David L. Roberts, and Eli M. Remolona, *Finance for Developing Countries* (New York: Group of 30, 1987), 18.

17. Rudolph Mye, U.S. Department of Commerce, Chilean Desk, October 1991.

18. Pompiliu Verzariu, "An Overview of Nontraditional Finance Techniques in International Commerce," in *Trade Finance: Current Issues and Developments* (Washington, D.C.: Government Printing Office, 1988), 50.

19. "Greensback-Debt," *The Economist,* August 6, 1988, 62–63.

20. Michael R. Czinkota and Martin J. Kohn, *A Report to the Secretary of Commerce: Improving U.S. Competitiveness—Swapping Debt for Education* (Washington, D.C.: Government Printing Office, 1988).

21. Donald J. Lecraw, "The Management of Countertrade: Factors Influencing Success," *Journal of International Business Studies* 20 (Spring 1989): 41–59.

22. Aspy P. Palia and Oded Shenkar, "Countertrade Practices in China," *Industrial Marketing Management* 20, 1991, 57–65.

23. *Report of the President on U.S. Competitiveness* (transmitted to Congress in September, 1980), V–45.

24. John D. Lange, Jr., Director, Office of Trade Finance, U.S. Department of the Treasury, testimony before the House Economic Stabilization Subcommittee, Committee on Banking, Finance, and Urban Affairs, 97th Congress, 1st session, September 24, 1981.

25. Donald W. Eiss, statement before the Subcommittee on Arms Control, International Security and Science and the Subcommittee on International Economic Policy and Trade, Committee on Foreign Affairs, U.S. House of Representatives, July 1, 1987, 4–5.

26. Steven M. Rubin, "Countertrade Controversies Stirring Global Economy," *The Journal of Commerce,* September 24, 1984, 14.

27. Patricia Daily and S. M. Ghazanfar, "Countertrade: Help or Hindrance to Less-Developed Countries," *The Journal of Social, Political and Economic Studies* 18 no. 1 (1993): 61–76.

28. Jacques de Miramon, "Countertrade: A Modern Form of Barter," *OECD Observer,* January 1982, 12.

29. "Current Activities of International Organizations," 5.

30. Michael R. Czinkota, "New Challenges in U.S.–Soviet Trade," *Journal of the Academy of Marketing Science* 5 (Special Issue, Summer 1977): 17–20.

31. Michael R. Czinkota and Anne Talbot, "Countertrade and GATT: Prospects for Regulation," *International Trade Journal* 1 (Fall 1986): 173.

32. Sandra M. Huszagh and Hiram C. Barksdale, "International Barter and Countertrade: An Exploratory Study," *Journal of the Academy of Marketing Science* 14 (Spring 1986): 21–28.

33. Lynn G. Reiling, "Countertrade Revives 'Dead Goods,'" *Marketing News,* August 29, 1986, 1, 22.

34. Kate Mortimer, "Countertrade in Western Europe," in *International Countertrade,* ed. Christopher M. Korth (Westport, Conn.: Quorum Books, 1987), 41.

CHAPTER 19

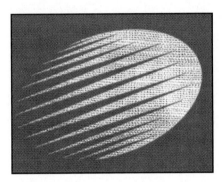

International Accounting and Taxation

1. To understand how accounting practices differ across countries, and how these differences may alter the competitiveness of firms in international markets.

2. To isolate which accounting practices are likely to constitute much of the competitiveness debate in the coming decade.

3. To examine the two basic philosophies of international taxation as practiced by governments, and how they in turn deal with foreign firms in their home markets and domestic firms in foreign markets.

4. To understand how the degree of ownership and control of a foreign enterprise alters the taxable income of a foreign enterprise in the eyes of U.S. tax authorities.

5. To understand the problems faced by many U.S.-based multinational firms in paying taxes both in foreign countries and in the United States.

U.S. Accounting Practices Would Halve EPS

Under U.S. accounting practices for goodwill, earnings at Attwoods, the U.K. waste services group, would be more than halved. That was one of the main points stressed in the offer document for the group published by Browning-Ferris Industries (BFI), the Texas-based waste management group, shortly after it launched a hostile £364m bid for Attwoods.

BFI offered 109p cash for each ordinary share—just above the year's low of 105p. But using U.S. accounting methods, estimated 1994 earnings would be cut from 5.3p to 2.5p, the document said. In the U.S., goodwill is written off through the

profit and loss account over up to 40 years. In the U.K., it is taken through the balance sheet. At the end of July 1993, Attwoods had £179.1m of goodwill written off.

BFI, which attacked Attwoods's financial record as "dismal," said that since the company makes 65 percent of its operating profits in the U.S., a proper comparison with other U.S. waste companies should reflect U.S. accounting standards. "All we are trying to do is compare apples with apples," said Greg Muldoon, senior vice president at BFI. "Attwoods earnings are inflated by U.S. standards."

Source: Adapted from David Blackwell, "BFI Says U.S. Practices Would Cut Attwoods' EPS," *Financial Times,* October 4, 1994, 27.

The methods used in the measurement of company operations, accounting principles and practices, vary across countries. The methods have a very large impact on how firms operate, how they compare against domestic and international competitors, and how governments view their respective place in society. Accounting principles are, however, moving toward more standardization across countries.

Taxation and accounting are fundamentally related. The principles by which a firm measures its sales and expenses, its assets and liabilities, all go into the formulation of profits, which are subject to taxation. The tax policies of more and more governments, in conjunction with accounting principles, are also becoming increasingly similar. Many of the tax issues of specific interest to officials, such as the avoidance of taxes in high-tax countries or the shielding of income from taxation by holding profits in so-called tax havens, are slowly being eliminated by increasing cooperation between governments. Like the old expression of "death and taxes," they are today, more than ever, inevitable.

This chapter provides an overview of the major differences between accounting practices and corporate taxation philosophies among major industrial countries. Although the average business manager cannot be expected to have a detailed understanding (or recall) of the multitudes of tax laws and accounting principles across countries, a basic understanding of many of these issues aid in the understanding of why "certain things are done certain ways" in international business.

ACCOUNTING DIVERSITY

The fact that accounting principles differ across countries is not, by itself, a problem. The primary problem is that real economic decisions by lenders, investors, or government policymakers may be distorted by the differences. Table 19.1 provides a simple example of the potential problems that may arise if two identical firms were operating in similar or dissimilar economic and accounting environments.

First, if two identical firms (in terms of structure, products, and strategies) are operating in similar economic situations and are subject to similar accounting treatment (cell A), a comparison of their performance will be logical in practice and

TABLE 19.1 Accounting Diversity and Economic Environments	Accounting Treatment	Economic Situation of Two Identical Firms	
		Similar	**Dissimilar**
	Similar	Logical practice A Results are comparable	May/may not be logical B Results may/may not be comparable
	Dissimilar	Illogical practice C Results are not comparable	Logical practice D Results may not be comparable

Source: "International Accounting Diversity and Capital Market Decisions," Frederick D.S. Choi and Richard Levich, in *The Handbook of International Accounting,* Frederick D.S. Choi, ed., 1992.

easily interpreted. The results of a competitive comparison or even an accounting audit (measurement and monitoring of their accounting practices) will lead to results that make sense. The two same firms operating in dissimilar economic situations will, when subject to the same accounting treatment, potentially look very different. And it may be that they should appear different if they are operating in totally different environments.

For example, one airline may depreciate its aircraft over five years, while another airline may depreciate over 10 years. Is this justified? It is if the two identical air carriers are in fundamentally different economic situations. If the first airline flies predominantly short commuter routes, which require thousands of takeoffs and landings, and the second airline flies only long intercontinental flights, which require far fewer takeoffs and landings, the first may be justified in depreciating its fixed assets much faster. The airline with more frequent takeoffs and landings will wear out its aircraft more quickly, which is what the accounting principle of depreciation is attempting to capture.[1] The economic situations are different.

The most blatantly obvious mismatch of economic environments and accounting treatments is probably that of cell C. Two identical firms operating within the same economic environment that receive different accounting treatment are not comparable. The same firms, if placed in the same environment, would appear differently, with one potentially gaining competitive advantage over the other simply because of accounting treatment. This is inconsistent with most of the private and public goals of accounting in all countries.

Finally, cell D offers the mismatch of different environments and different accounting treatments. Although logical in premise, the results are most likely incomparable in outcome. Identical firms in differing economic environments require differing approaches to financial measurement. But the fact that the results of financial comparison may not be usable is not an error; it is simply a fact of the differing markets in which the firms operate. As firms expand internationally, as markets expand across borders, as businesses diversify across currencies, cultures, and economies, the movement toward cell A continues from market forces rather than from government intention.

PRINCIPAL ACCOUNTING DIFFERENCES ACROSS COUNTRIES

International **accounting diversity** can lead to any of the following problems in international business conducted with the use of financial statements: (1) poor or improper business decision making; (2) hinder the ability of a firm or enterprise to raise capital in different or foreign markets; and (3) hinder or prevent a firm from monitoring competitive factors across firms, industries, and countries. Examples of these problems abound in international business literature. For example, it is widely believed that much of the recent trend of British firms acquiring U.S. companies is primarily a result of their ability to completely expense "goodwill" (the added cost of a firm purchased over and above the fair market value of its constituent components).

Origins of Differences

Accounting standards and practices are in many ways no different from any other legislative or regulatory statutes in their origins. Laws reflect the people, places, and events of their time (see Global Perspective 19.1). Most accounting practices and laws are linked to the objectives of the parties who will use the financial information, including investors, lenders, and governments.

National accounting principles are also frequently affected by other environmental factors, such as the dominance of one country's trade and financial activity over the trade and financial activity of another country. Although there are substantial differences between U.S. and Canadian accounting practices, many of the recent changes forced on Canadian firms have their origins in U.S. practice. Global Perspective 19.2 discusses an evolving accounting challenge.

Global Perspective

19.1
The Father of Accounting: Luca Pacioli Who?

Doctors have Hippocrates and philosophers have Plato. But who is the father of accounting? Knowing that accountants have long had inferiority complexes, two Seattle University professors have decided that the profession should have a father and that he should be Luca Pacioli.

But their anointing of the Renaissance scholar occasions an identity crisis. Hardly anyone—accountants included—has ever heard of Pacioli (pronounced pot-CHEE-oh-lee).

Five centuries ago, Pacioli published *"Summa de Arithmetica, Geometria, Proportioni et Proportionalita."* It contained a slender tract for merchants on double-entry bookkeeping, which had been in wide use in Venice for years. Due to that, some accounting historians including Professors Weis and Tinius credit Pacioli with codifying accounting principles for the first time. That would seem to establish paternity.

Professor Vangermeersch, of the University of Rhode Island, says the origins of double-entry bookkeeping are open to question. "If you're crediting people of past centuries for contributions to accounting, you should include Leonardo of Pisa, who brought Arabic numerals to the West; James Peele, who initiated journal-entry systems; and Emile Garcke and J.M. Fells, who applied accounting to factory use," he said. All the men have another thing in common, he added: They are just as obscure as Luca Pacioli.

Even in literature, says Vangermeersch, the only famous accountant was Daniel Defoe, who wrote *Robinson Crusoe.* Unfortunately, Defoe was a terrible businessman and failed in a series of ventures, the professor observed. "Even as a dissenter and pamphleteer, he was tarred and feathered by the public."

Global Perspective

19.2
Countertrade Accountants in the Dark

For the exporter contemplating countertrade, there is more to the decision process than a simple yes or no. Key to a company's ability to perform countertrade in-house is its accounting capabilities. This facet of operations at first may seem of secondary consideration, but it is in fact a major problem spot for many countertraders. Along with such aspects as pricing and foreign regulations, accounting is a key consideration in developing an in-house system of countertrade.

Countertrade poses unique and difficult situations for accountants mainly due to the partial or total absence of currency as a base for accounting practices. In addition, relevant guidelines for nonmonetary transactions are practically nonexistent. There is no mention of nonmonetary transactions in the Generally Accepted Accounting Principles. The one statement made by the Financial Accounting Standards Board concerning nonmonetary transactions was promulgated back when they were far more simple. Today's countertrade arrangements can contain such complexities as multiyear contracts and the risk of noncompliance or substandard goods. Accountants responsible for dealing with these situations have very little upon which to draw.

A whole array of problematic situations can confront accountants in a countertrading company. The first point of contention may very well be whether a sale or a purchase has occurred. In a goods-for-cash transaction, it is obvious whether you bought or you sold; the accountant has no problem making the correct entry. With countertrade, however, determining which action to record is a bit more nebulous. There are even those who believe that countertrade transactions should be viewed as both a purchase and a sale. An eighteenth century textbook author once stated that, "The exchange of goods for goods is nothing else but buying and selling blended together." The implications of not being able to distinguish between sales and purchases can only be imagined.

Problems also abound concerning the valuation of nontraditional goods, goods that will be received in the future, and goods that will be surrendered in the future, all under the agreed-to provisions. In many cases, the market value will fluctuate. Regardless, many accountants value the future obligations at current fair market value. Beyond this, questions exist as to when a transaction should be reported on a multiyear contract now, because it is inevitable, or later, once it is realized.

Other uncertainties surround the timing and amounts for gains and losses, revenue recognition, countertrade fees and incidental expenses, and disclosure of increased risks. Until further pronouncements are made, accountants involved with countertrade will remain in the dark, and countertrade transactions will have to be scrutinized quite closely to determine their value.

Source: "Are We Ignoring Countertrade?" *Management Accounting* (December 1992): 43–47.

Classification Systems

There are several ways to classify and group national accounting systems and practices. Figure 19.1 illustrates one such classification based on a statistically based clustering of practices across countries by C. W. Nobes. The systems are first subdivided into micro-based (characteristics of the firms and industries) and macro-uniform (following fundamental government or economic factors per country). The micro-based national accounting systems are then broken down into those that follow a theoretical principle or pragmatic concerns. The latter category includes the national accounting systems of countries as diverse as the United States, Canada, Japan, the United Kingdom, and Mexico.

The macro-uniform systems, according to Nobes, are primarily used in European countries. The continental Europeans are typified by accounting systems that are for-

FIGURE 19.1 Nobes Classification of National Accounting Systems

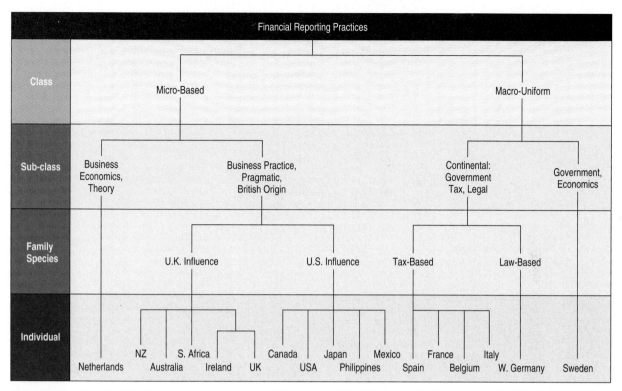

Source: C.W. Nobes, "International Classification of Accounting Systems," unpublished paper, April 1980, Table C, as cited in *International Accounting,* 2d ed., Frederick D.S. Choi and Gerhard G. Mueller, Prentice-Hall, Englewood Cliffs, N.J., 1992, p. 34.

mulated in secondary importance to legal organizational forms (Germany) or for the apportionment and application of national tax laws (France, Spain, Italy), or the more pure forms of government and economic models (Sweden). An alternative approach to those in the European classification would be those such as Sweden and Germany, which have pushed their firms to adopt more widespread uniform standards. However, as with all classification systems, the subtle differences across countries can quickly make such classifications useless in practice. As the following sections will illustrate, slight differences can also yield significant competitive advantages or disadvantages to companies organized and measured under different financial reporting systems.

Principal Differences: The Issues

The resulting impact of accounting differences is to separate or segment international markets for investors and firms alike. Communicating the financial results of a foreign company operating in a foreign country and foreign currency is often a task that must be undertaken completely separately from the accounting duties of the firm. Actually, financial results must often be reinterpreted and presented in other markets as illustrated in Figure 19.2, in which Cathay Pacific, a Hong Kong-based

FIGURE 19.2
Cathay Pacific Airways:
Communicating
Financial Results

The Swire Group

Cathay Pacific Airways Limited

1992 Interim Results – Highlights

Consolidated results — unaudited:

	Six months ended 30 June	
	1992 US$M	1991 US$M
Turnover	1,420	1,262
Operating profit	201	174
Net finance charges	29	15
Net operating profit	172	159
Associated companies	15	10
Profit before taxation	187	169
Taxation	23	25
Profit after taxation	164	144
Minority interest	1	1
Profit attributable to shareholders	163	143
Dividend	39	39
Retained profit	124	104
Earnings per share	US5.7¢	US5.0¢
Interim dividend per share	US1.3¢	US1.3¢

	12 months ended	
	30/6/92	30/6/91
Available tonne kilometres (millions)	5,963	5,525	+7.9%

Note: The results of the Company have been translated from Hong Kong dollars, its currency of account, into United States dollars at an exchange rate of HK$7.731 = US$1, the approximate free rate of exchange at 30th June 1992.

Prospects
The passenger revenue forecast for the full year suggests that the passenger load factor should exceed the 1991 level but there are concerns about yields caused by widespread fare wars. On the cargo front, Hong Kong revenue is expected to recover and there are encouraging signs for the new freighter service to Los Angeles.
On the cost side, inflation is still the prime concern. The persistently high rate of inflation in Hong Kong, compared with major economies, continues to erode the competitive advantages of Hong Kong. "Operation Better Shape", which was introduced in 1991 to improve productivity, continues to be the main focus to mitigate the effects of rising costs.
Provided that there is no worsening of an already difficult operating environment, we are looking for improved results for the full year.

Interim Dividend
The interim dividend will be paid on 2nd October 1992 to shareholders registered at the close of business on 25th September 1992. The share register will be closed from 21st September 1992 to 25th September 1992, both dates inclusive.

P D A Sutch
Chairman

Hong Kong, 26th August 1992

CATHAY PACIFIC

Source: The Economist, September 5, 1992, 22.

firm, must have its financial results presented in terms that are known to the larger U.S. dollar markets through a marketing presentation. As long as significant accounting practices differ across countries, markets will continue to be segmented (and accountants may be required to be interpreters and marketers as much as bookkeepers).

Table 19.2 provides an overview of nine major areas of significant differences in accounting practices across countries.[2] There are, of course, many more hundreds of differences, but the nine serve to highlight some of the fundamental philosophical differences across countries. Accounting differences are real and persistent, and there is still substantial question of competitive advantages and informational deficiencies that may result from these continuing differences across countries.

Accounting for Research and Development Expenses
Are research and development expenses capitalized or expensed as costs are incurred? Those who argue that

TABLE 19.2 Summary of Principal Accounting Differences around the World

Accounting Principle	United States	Japan	United Kingdom	France	Germany	Netherlands	Switzerland	Canada	Italy	Brazil
1. Capitalization of R&D costs	Not allowed	Allowed in certain cases	Allowed in certain cases	Allowed in certain cases	Not allowed	Allowed in certain cases	Allowed in certain cases	Allowed in certain cases	Allowed in certain cases	Allowed in certain cases
2. Fixed asset revaluations stated at amount in excess of cost	Not allowed	Not allowed	Allowed	Allowed	Not allowed	Allowed in certain cases	Not allowed	Not allowed	Allowed in certain cases	Allowed
3. Inventory valuation using LIFO	Allowed	Allowed	Allowed but rarely done	Not allowed	Allowed in certain cases	Allowed	Allowed	Allowed	Allowed	Allowed but rarely done
4. Finance leases capitalized	Required	Allowed in certain cases	Required	Not allowed	Allowed in certain cases	Required	Allowed	Required	Not allowed	Not allowed
5. Pension expense accrued during period of service	Required	Allowed	Required	Allowed	Required	Required	Allowed	Required	Allowed	Allowed
6. Book and tax timing differences on balance sheet as deferred tax	Required	Allowed in certain cases	Allowed	Allowed in certain cases	Allowed but rarely done	Required	Allowed	Allowed	Allowed but rarely done	Allowed
7. Current rate method of currency translation	Required	Allowed in certain cases	Required	Allowed	Allowed	Required	Required	Allowed in certain cases	Required	Required
8. Pooling method used for mergers	Required in certain cases	Allowed in certain cases	Allowed in certain cases	Not allowed	Allowed in certain cases	Allowed but rarely done	Allowed but rarely done	Allowed but rarely done	Not allowed	Allowed but rarely done
9. Equity method used for 20–50% ownership	Required	Required	Required	Allowed in certain cases	Allowed	Required	Required	Required	Allowed	Required

Source: Adapted from "A Summary of Accounting Principle Differences Around the World," Philip R. Peller and Frank J. Schwitter, 1991, p. 4.3.

there is no certainty that the R&D expenditures will lead to benefits in future periods would require immediate recognition of all expenses as in typical conservative practice. Alternatively, if R&D expenditures do lead to future benefits and revenues, the matching of expenses and revenues would be better served if the R&D expenditures were capitalized, and expenses therefore spread out over the future benefit periods.

Accounting for Fixed Assets How are fixed assets (land, buildings, machinery, equipment) to be expensed and carried? The assets constitute large outlays of capital, result in assets that are held by the firm for many years, and yield benefits for many future years. All countries require companies to capitalize these fixed assets, so that they are depreciated over their future economic lives (once again spreading the costs out over periods roughly matching the revenue-earning useful life). There are, however, significant differences in depreciation methods used (straight-line, sum-of-years-digits, accelerated methods of cost recovery, and so forth), resulting in very different expensing schedules across countries.

The primary issue related to the accounting of fixed assets is whether they are to be carried on company financial statements at historical cost or current value. The conservative approach, used, for example, in the United States, is to carry the fixed assets at historical cost and allow analysts to use their own methods and additional financial statement notes to ascertain current values of individual fixed assets. The alternative is to allow the values of fixed assets to be periodically revalued, up or down, depending on the latest appraised value. Countries such as the Netherlands argue that this is more appropriate, given that the balance sheet of a firm should present the present fair market value of all assets. There is no doubt, however, that with more flexibility in the valuation of fixed assets there is also more opportunity for abuse of the valuation methods, potentially giving firms the ability to manipulate the values of fixed assets carried on the balance sheet.

Inventory Accounting Treatment   How are inventories to be valued? For many companies inventories are the single largest asset. Therefore, the reconciliation of how goods are valued as sold (on the income statement) and valued as carried in inventory unsold (on the balance sheet) is important. The three typical inventory-valuation principles are last-in-first-out, **LIFO,** the **average cost method,** and first-in-first-out, **FIFO.**

The LIFO method assumes that the last goods purchased by the firm (last-in) are the first ones sold (first-out). This is considered conservative by accounting standards in that the remaining inventory goods were the first ones purchased. The resulting expenses of cost of goods sold is therefore higher. The only country listed in Table 19.2 that does not allow the use of LIFO is France, although Germany only allows its use in specific cases, making it rarely used. The use of FIFO is thought to be more consistent theoretically with the matching of costs and revenues of actual inventory

Differences in depreciation methods used in accounting for fixed assets, such as this Arco chemical plant under construction in Marseille, France, result in different expensing schedules across countries.

flows. The use of FIFO is generally regarded as creating a more accurately measured balance sheet as inventory is stated at the most recent prices.

Capitalizing or Expensing Leases

Are financing leases to be capitalized? The recent growth in popularity of leasing for its financial and tax flexibility has created a substantial amount of accounting discussion across countries. The primary question is whether a leased item should actually be carried on the balance sheet of the firm at all, since a lease is essentially the purchase of an asset only for a specified period of time. If not carried on the books, should the lease payments be expenses paid as if a rent payment?

Some argue that the lease results in the transfer of all risks and benefits of ownership to the firm (from the lessor to the lessee) and the lease contract should be accounted for as the purchase of an asset. This would be a capital lease, and if the lessee borrowed money in order to acquire the asset, the lease payments of principal and interest should be accounted for in the same manner as the purchase of any other capital asset. The Netherlands, the United Kingdom, Switzerland, the United States, and other countries require capital lease payment if certain criteria are met.

The alternative is that the lessee has simply acquired the rental use of the services of the asset for a specified period of time, and payments on this **operating lease** should be treated only as rent. In this case the asset would remain on the books of the lessor. France, Italy, and Brazil require all leases to be treated as operating leases.

Pension Plan Accounting

The accounting treatment of private pension plans is one of the most recent and significant accounting developments. A private pension plan is the promise by an employer to provide a continuing income stream to employees after their retirement from the firm. The critical accounting question is whether the pension promise should be expensed and carried at the time the employee is working for the firm (providing a service to the firm that will not be fully paid for by the firm until all pension payments are completed) or expensed only as pension payments are made after retirement.

The primary problem with expensing the pension as services are provided is that the firm does not know the exact amount or timing of the eventual pension payments. If it is assumed that these eventual pension payments can be reasonably approximated, the conservative approach is to account for the expenses as employee services are provided and carry the **pension liabilities** on the books of the firm. In some countries if it is believed that these pension liabilities cannot be accurately estimated, they will be expensed only as they are incurred on payment.

Accounting for Income Taxes

All countries require the payment of income taxes on earnings, however, the definition and timing of earnings can constitute a problem. In many countries the definition of earnings for financial accounting purposes differs from earnings for tax purposes. The question then focuses on whether the tax effect should be recognized during the period in which the item appears on the income statement or during the period in which the item appears on the tax return.

If the expense is recognized during the period in which the item appears on the income statement, the tax gives rise to an associated asset or liability referred to as deferred tax. Some countries do not suffer the debate of whether the deferred tax should actually appear on the balance sheet of the firm by having all financial reporting follow tax rules. Examples include Germany, France, and Japan. However, most countries must deal with the timing mismatch of the deferred tax.

Foreign Currency Translation   As discussed in Chapter 17, corporations that operate in more than one country and one currency must periodically *translate* and *consolidate* all financial statements for home-country reporting purposes. The primary issues in foreign currency translation are which exchange rates should be used in the translation of currencies (historical or current rates) and how gains or losses resulting from the translation should be handled in the consolidation. The critical handling issue is whether the gains or losses are recognized in current income or carried on the consolidated balance sheet as an item under equity capital.

The first method used is the **current rate method,** which translates assets and liabilities at the exchange rate in effect on the balance sheet date, with adjustments charged or credited to the equity account. Equity and income statement items are translated at a weighted average exchange rate, which results in translation gains and losses that are carried as a direct adjustment to equity and avoids altering current net income. This is particularly attractive given the movement of exchange rates are clearly outside the control of the firm, and the gains and losses are resulting not from

**FIGURE 19.3
United States
Translation Procedure
Flow Chart**

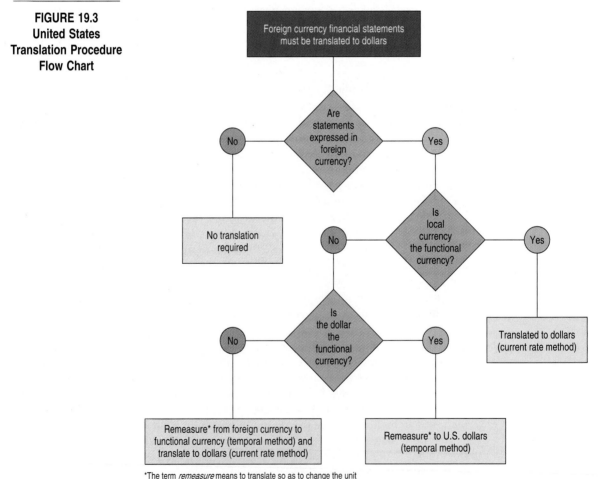

*The term *remeasure* means to translate so as to change the unit of measure from a foreign currency to the functional currency.

Source: International Accounting, 2d ed., Frederick D.S. Choi and Gerhard G. Mueller, Prentice-Hall, Englewood Cliffs, N.J., 1992, p. 169.

real cash flows but only from consolidation of foreign operations for reporting purposes.

The second translation method is the **temporal method.** This method translates assets and liabilities at the current exchange rate, with all fixed assets and common stock translated at historical exchange rates. The method is more consistent with the principle of how the company's balance sheet would have looked if the original assets and liabilities and continuing operations had all occurred in the one currency of the parent corporation. The primary disadvantage is that remaining gains and losses from the translation process under the temporal method are typically included within current income and may result in substantial earnings volatility caused by exchange rates. Countries that encourage the use of the temporal method include Canada and France.

Figure 19.3 provides a simple decision tree approach to translation of foreign affiliates for U.S. corporations. The mechanical details of the translation of foreign affiliate balance sheets are covered in Chapter 17.

Accounting for Mergers and Acquisitions

This is a relatively new issue in international accounting, given the sudden and rapid growth of merger and acquisition activity beginning in the United States and the United Kingdom in the 1980s. The primary accounting question is whether the assets and liabilities acquired should be carried at their original historic value or at the value at acquisition? In certain cases, however, it is believed that the shareholders of the acquired company end up owning shares of the acquirer, and accountants argue that their assets and liabilities should not be revalued, but simply merged or pooled. Accounting principles in the countries experiencing most mergers and acquisitions, the United States, the United Kingdom, Germany, and Japan, allow the use of pooling or merger accounting when certain criteria are met.

A second accounting issue of some concern is that often in the case of acquisitions, the price paid exceeds the fair value of the assets acquired. This is termed "goodwill" and constitutes a significant accounting problem. Many accountants argue that this is a true value that is purchased, and would not have been paid for if it did not exist. Even if goodwill is accepted as a legitimate economic value, the question remains as to how it is to be carried on the firm's balance sheet, as shown in the chapter's opening vignette. The United States, Japan, France, Canada, and Brazil all require that goodwill be accounted for as an asset, with amortization occurring over a maximum of anywhere from 5 to 40 years.

In other countries, accountants do not believe that goodwill is a real asset and therefore should not be carried on the books of the firm. In this case, such as in the United Kingdom, the firm is allowed to write off the entire amount against equity in the year of acquisition. It is also argued that this gives British firms a distinct advantage in their ability to make acquisitions and not suffer income statement dilution impacts in the years following as the asset is amortized in the countries that capitalize goodwill. This is a classic example of the potential competitive benefits of a similar activity receiving dissimilar accounting treatment discussed at the beginning of this chapter and presented in Table 19.1.

Consolidation of Equity Securities Holdings

When one company purchases and holds an investment in another company, the question arises as to how to account for the holdings. There are two major methods of consolidation of equity holdings, the equity method and the consolidation method. The equity method requires that

Global Perspective

19.3
How Green Is My Balance Sheet?

When it comes to environmental accounting, many companies have yet to come clean. Those that publish green accounts usually offer a few charts (printed, of course, on recycled and unbleached paper) showing trends in their output of waste. But the gases and gunk are measured in kilos or tonnes, not pounds or dollars. Few companies convert such data into figures that can appear in financial accounts (which are usually printed on unrecycled, chlorine-bleached paper).

The task is easier in America than elsewhere, if only because U.S. accounting rules force companies to include detailed data on known environmental liabilities in their accounts. But in Europe, where no such rules exist, information is much more patchy. Some firms, such as British Coal and Thorn EMI, publish figures on environmental liabilities. But Roger Adams, of Britain's Chartered Association of Certified Accountants, wishes that more would follow their lead. For the past four years, his institute has run a competition for the best corporate environmental accounts in Britain; this year, it is inviting entries from companies in other parts of Europe, too.

It might help if companies had a blueprint to follow. In fact, there are several different guidelines on corporate environmental reporting, including ones from the International Chamber of Commerce and from Japan's employers' association. Most favor reporting a firm's energy consumption and impact on the environment, but none tell green bean-counters how to translate this into monetary values in firms' accounts.

A few have tried anyway. One is BSO/Origin, a Dutch information-technology firm in which Philips, an electronics firm, has a 40 percent stake. It has recently published its fourth annual attempt to value the natural resources it uses and the environmental damage it does. In 1993, its environmental costs totalled 3.7m guilders ($2m), from which the company subtracted 450,000 guilders of "environmental expenditure"—taxes on fuel and waste collection—to arrive at a total of 3.3m guilders of "net value extracted." Eckhart Wintzen, BSO's president, wishes that companies were taxed on this figure. BSO/Origin's big shareholders, a less environmentally sensitive bunch, disagree.

Source: Abstracted from "How Green Is My Balance Sheet?" *The Economist,* September 3, 1994, 75.

the holder list the security holdings as a line item on the firm's balance sheet. This is generally required when the firm holds substantial interest in the other firm, typically 20 to 50 percent of outstanding voting shares, such that it can exert substantial influence over the other firm but not necessarily dictate management or policy. The equity method is required in many countries, including the United States, Japan, Switzerland, Canada, and Brazil.

The second method of equity holdings, the consolidation method, requires the addition of all of the investee's individual assets and liabilities to the company's assets and liabilities. A minority interest is then subtracted out for all assets for the percentage of the net asset not owned. When an investor has controlling interest in the other firm, most countries require the use of the consolidation method. The remaining accounting debates focus on whether the individual assets and liabilities should be consolidated when the subsidiaries are very dissimilar, even if controlling interest is held. Countries such as Italy and the United Kingdom believe that consolidation of dissimilar firms results in misleading information regarding the true financial status of the firms.

THE PROCESS OF ACCOUNTING STANDARDIZATION

One of the best indications as to the degree of success that has been achieved in international accounting standards is that there is still some conflict over the terminology of harmonization, standardization, or promulgation of uniform standards. As early as 1966, an Accountants International Study Group was formed by professional institutes in Canada, the United States, and the United Kingdom to begin the study of significant accounting differences across countries, but primarily only to aid in the understanding of foreign practices, not to form guidelines for more consistent or harmonious policies.

The establishment of the International Accounting Standards Committee (IASC) in 1973 was the first strong movement toward the establishment of international accounting standards. In the latter half of the 1970s, other international institutions such as the United Nations, the Organization for Economic Cooperation and Development (OECD), and the European Union also began forming study groups and analyzing specific issues of confusion, such as corporate organization and varying degrees of disclosure required across countries.[3] The efforts of the European Union to harmonize standards between countries, not standardize, is particularly important in understanding how accounting principles and practices may be reformed to allow individual country differences but at the same time minimize the economic distortions. The recent completion of much of the Internal Financial Market of the Single European Program known as 1992 Europe has seen much progress along this harmonization front.

Two other recent developments concerning international standardization merit special note. In 1985, the General Electric Company became the first major U.S. corporation to acknowledge that the accounting principles underlying its 1984 financial statements "are generally accepted in the United States and are consistent with standards issued by the International Accounting Standards Committee."[4] Second, the Financial Accounting Standards Board (FASB), the organization in the United States charged with setting most standards for corporate accounting practices, committed itself to the full consideration of "an international perspective" to all its work in the future. And as other issues of international consequence arise—even environmentalism—accounting questions arise, as shown in Global Perspective 19.3.

INTERNATIONAL TAXATION

Governments alone have the power to tax. Each government wants to tax all companies within its jurisdiction without placing burdens on domestic or foreign companies that would restrain trade. Each country will state its jurisdictional approach formally in the tax treaties that it signs with other countries. One of the primary purposes of tax treaties is to establish the bounds of each country's jurisdiction to prevent double taxation of international income. Global Perspective 19.4 shows the effect of taxes on one firm by its own government.

Tax Jurisdictions

Nations usually follow one of two basic approaches to international taxation: a residential approach or a territorial or source approach. The residential approach to international taxation taxes the international income of its residents without regard to

Global Perspective

19.4
Did Stolichnaya Taxes
Put Vodka on the Rocks?

MOSCOW—Ask the makers of Russia's most famous vodka, Stolichnaya, about their major competition. Absolut? Nope. Smirnoff? Wrong. "It's the Russian government," said Sergei Nikultsev, deputy director of Kristall, the factory that produces Stolichnaya and about 70 other brands of liquor.

A strange answer, considering that the state is the majority partner in Kristall. But since the government declared Kristall insolvent last week, citing more than $3 million in debts, relations between the Kremlin and Russia's foremost vodka producer have been on the rocks. Kristall complained that it was being crushed by taxes amounting to 92 percent of the factory's sales. The government lowered taxes a little, but not enough, Kristall managers said.

Kristall is becoming a test case of the government's determination to force "red directors," as they are known, to run their plants in a new way for Russia: profitably and efficiently. "We're not acting as police, and it's not our aim to sack the director," said Nodor Sarkisian, of the bankruptcy office. "But they have got to restructure." Sarkisian,

34, is typical of the young reformers who staff the bankruptcy office, a bastion of free market thinking. A former mathematician and engineering professor, he is convinced that bloated enterprises such as Kristall, whose managers for years have done as they pleased with no regard for the bottom line, must begin behaving with the discipline and rationality of capitalists.

Vodka production, which remains a government monopoly, always has had a privileged position in Russia. It is a guaranteed money-maker for czars and commissars alike. So popular is vodka in these times of financial hardship that it often serves as an alternate currency. Short on cash? Pay the plumber with a couple of bottles of vodka.

"The government created conditions that left us like an athlete stuck in the starting blocks," said Nikultsev. "The state should be proud to have such famous brands of vodka as those we make—famous all over the world. In the West, the state would never impose such taxes or try to strangle a business like ours."

Source: Adapted from Lee Hockstader, "Did Stolichnaya Taxes Put Vodka on Rocks?" *International Herald Tribune,* August 25, 1994, 13.

where the income is earned. The territorial approach to transnational income taxes all parties, regardless of country of residency, within its territorial jurisdiction.

Most countries in practice must combine the two approaches to tax foreign and domestic firms equally. For example, the United States and Japan both apply the residential approach to their own resident corporations and the territorial approach to income earned by nonresidents within their territorial jurisdictions. Other countries, such as Germany, apply the territorial approach to dividends paid to domestic firms from their foreign subsidiaries; such dividends are assumed taxed abroad and are exempt from further taxation.

Within the territorial jurisdiction of tax authorities, a foreign corporation is typically defined as any business that earns income within the host country's borders but is incorporated under the laws of another country. The foreign corporation usually must surpass some minimum level of activity (gross income) before the host country assumes primary tax jurisdiction. However, if the foreign corporation owns income-producing assets or a permanent establishment, the threshold is automatically surpassed.

Accounting practices for the costs of environmental contamination treatment and restoration, such as Amoco Corporation's reclamation of the dunes of Coatham Sands, Great Britain, is an evolving issue in international business.
Source: Courtesy of Amoco Corporation.

Tax Types

Taxes are generally classified as direct and indirect. **Direct taxes** are calculated on actual income, either individual or firm income. **Indirect taxes,** such as sales taxes, severance taxes, tariffs, and value-added taxes, are applied to purchase prices, material costs, quantities of natural resources mined, and so forth. Although most countries still rely on income taxes as the primary method of raising revenue, tax structures vary widely across countries.

The **value-added tax (VAT)** is the primary revenue source for the European Union. A value-added tax is applied to the amount of product value added by the production process. The tax is calculated as a percentage of the product price less the cost of materials and inputs used in its manufacture, which have been taxed previously. Through this process, tax revenues are collected literally on the value added by that specific stage of the production process. Under the existing General Agreement on Tariffs and Trade (GATT), the legal framework under which international trade operates, value-added taxes may be levied on imports into a country or group of countries (such as the European Union) in order to treat foreign producers entering the domestic markets equally with firms within the country paying the VAT. Similarly, the VAT may be refunded on export sales or sales to tourists who purchase products for consumption outside the country or community. For example, an American tourist leaving London may collect a refund on all value-added taxes paid on goods purchased within the United Kingdom. The refunding usually requires documentation of the actual purchase price and the amount of tax paid.

Income Categories and Taxation

There are three primary methods used for the transfer of funds across tax jurisdictions: royalties, interest, and dividends. Royalties are under license for the use of intangible assets such as patents, designs, trademarks, techniques, or copyrights. Interest is the payment for the use of capital lent for the financing of normal business activity. Dividends are income paid or deemed paid to the shareholders of the corporation from the residual earnings of operations. When a corporation declares the percentage of residual earnings that is to go to shareholders, the dividend is declared and distributed.

TABLE 19.3
Comparison of
Corporate Tax Rates:
Japan, Germany, and
the United States

Taxable Income Category	Japan	Germany	United States
Corporate income tax rates:			
Profits distributed to stockholders	37.5%	36%	35%
Undistributed profits	37.5%	47.75%	35%
Branches of foreign corporations	37.5%	43.93%	35%
Withholding taxes on dividends (portfolio):			
with Japan	—	15/25%	15%
with Germany	15%	—	15%
with United States	15%	5/10%	—
Withholding taxes on dividends (substantial holdings):			
with Japan	—	15%	10%
with Germany	10%	—	5%
with United States	10%	10%	—
Withholding taxes on interest:			
with Japan	—	10%	10%
with Germany	10%	—	0%
with United States	10%	0%	—
Withholding taxes on royalties:			
with Japan	—	10%	10%
with Germany	10%	—	0%
with United States	10%	0%	—

Source: Corporate Taxes: A Worldwide Summary. Price Waterhouse, 1993.

Taxation of corporate income differs substantially across countries. Table 19.3 provides a summary comparison for Japan, Germany, and the United States. In some countries, for example the United States and Japan, there is one **corporate income tax** rate applied to all residual earnings, regardless of what is retained versus what is distributed as dividends. In other countries, for example Germany, separate tax rates apply to **distributed** and **undistributed earnings.** (Note that Germany lists a specific corporate income tax rate for the branches of foreign corporations operating within Germany.)

Royalty and interest payments to nonresidents are normally subject to **withholding taxes.** Corporate profits are typically double taxed in most countries, through corporate and personal taxes. Corporate income is first taxed at the business level with corporate taxes, then a second time when the income of distributed earnings is taxed through personal income taxes. Withholding tax rates also differ by the degree of ownership that the corporation possesses in the foreign corporation. Minor ownership is termed portfolio, while major or controlling influence is categorized as substantial holdings. In the case of dividends, interest, or royalties paid to nonresidents, governments routinely apply withholding taxes to their payment in the reasonable expectation that the nonresidents will not report and declare such income with the host-country tax authorities. Withholding taxes are specified by income category in all bilateral tax treaties. Notice in Table 19.3 the differentials in withholding taxes across countries by bilateral tax treaties. The U.S. tax treaty with Germany results in a 0 percent withholding of interest or royalty payments earned by German corporations operating in the United States.

U.S. TAXATION OF FOREIGN OPERATIONS

The United States exercises its rights to tax U.S. residents' incomes regardless of where the income is earned. The two major categories for U.S. taxation of foreign-source income are foreign branches of U.S. corporations and foreign subsidiaries of U.S. corporations.

Taxation of Foreign Branches of U.S. Corporations

The income of a foreign branch of a U.S. corporation is treated the same as if the income was derived from sources within the United States. Since a foreign branch is an extension of the U.S. corporation and not independently capitalized and established, its profits are taxed with those of the parent whether actually remitted to the parent or not. Similarly, losses suffered by foreign branches of U.S. corporations are also fully and immediately deductible against U.S. taxable income.

As always, however, the U.S. tax authorities want to prevent double taxation. The United States grants primary tax authority to the country in which the income is derived. If taxes are paid by the foreign branch to host-country tax authorities, the tax payments may be claimed as a tax credit toward U.S. tax liabilities on the same income.

Taxation of Foreign Subsidiaries of U.S. Corporations

Just as the United States taxes corporations from other countries operating within its borders, foreign countries tax the operations of U.S. corporations within their jurisdiction. Corporations operating in more than one country are therefore subject to double taxation. Double taxation could hinder the ability of U.S. corporations to operate and compete effectively abroad. The U.S. tax code removes the burden by reducing the U.S. taxes due on the foreign-source income by the amount of foreign taxes deemed paid.

FIGURE 19.4 Classification of U.S. Ownership of Foreign Corporations for Tax Uses

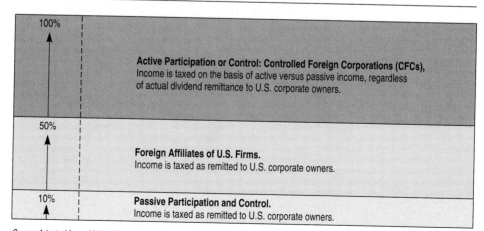

Source: Adapted from *Multinational Business Finance*, 7th ed., Eiteman, Stonehill, and Moffett, Addison-Wesley, Reading, 1995, Chapter 21.

Corporate Tax Rates Around the World

Source: *1993 International Tax Summaries: A Guide for Planning and Decisions*
Note: Tax rates listed are statutory rates for general manufacturing firms incorporated in the host country listed. Rates may not apply to firms operating in industries or areas under specific provisions or development programs of the host country.

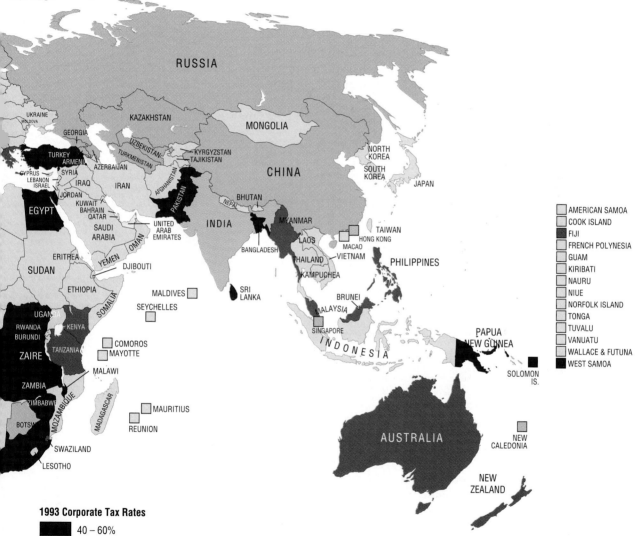

RUSSIA

UKRAINE
MOLDOVA

KAZAKHSTAN

MONGOLIA

GEORGIA

UZBEKISTAN

KYRGYZSTAN

TURKMENISTAN

TAJIKISTAN

NORTH
KOREA

TURKEY
ARMENIA

AZERBAIJAN

CHINA

SOUTH
KOREA

JAPAN

CYPRUS
LEBANON
ISRAEL

SYRIA

IRAQ

IRAN

AFGHANISTAN

BHUTAN

JORDAN

KUWAIT
BAHRAIN
QATAR

PAKISTAN

NEPAL

TAIWAN

EGYPT

SAUDI
ARABIA

UNITED
ARAB
EMIRATES

INDIA

MYANMAR

LAOS

HONG KONG

MACAO

OMAN

THAILAND

VIETNAM

PHILIPPINES

ERITREA

YEMEN

BANGLADESH

SUDAN

DJIBOUTI

KAMPUCHEA

ETHIOPIA

MALDIVES

SRI
LANKA

SOMALIA

SEYCHELLES

BRUNEI

UGANDA

KENYA

MALAYSIA

RWANDA
BURUNDI

ZAIRE

TANZANIA

COMOROS

MAYOTTE

SINGAPORE

INDONESIA

PAPUA
NEW GUINEA

AMERICAN SAMOA

COOK ISLAND

FIJI

FRENCH POLYNESIA

GUAM

KIRIBATI

NAURU

NIUE

NORFOLK ISLAND

TONGA

TUVALU

VANUATU

WALLACE & FUTUNA

WEST SAMOA

ZAMBIA

MALAWI

SOLOMON
IS.

ZIMBABWE

MOZAMBIQUE

MADAGASCAR

BOTSW.

MAURITIUS

REUNION

AUSTRALIA

NEW
CALEDONIA

SWAZILAND

LESOTHO

NEW
ZEALAND

1993 Corporate Tax Rates

40 – 60%

35 – 40%

30 – 35%

1 – 30%

0%

No current data available

The calculation of the foreign income taxes deemed paid and the additional U.S. taxes due, if any, involves the interaction of the following four components.

- **Degree of Ownership and Control.** The degree of ownership and control of the foreign corporation has a significant impact on the calculation of U.S. taxes payable on the foreign-source income. There are three basic ownership ranges applicable to taxation: (1) less than 10 percent; (2) 10 to 50 percent; and (3) more than 50 percent. Figure 19.4 illustrates the three ownership classes under U.S. tax law. If the U.S. corporation owns more than 50 percent of the voting shares in the foreign corporation, the foreign corporation is classified as a Controlled Foreign Corporation (CFC).[5]

- **Proportion of Income Distributed.** The proportion of after-tax income that is distributed as profits to stockholders as dividends is also important to the calculation of U.S. tax liability. Income that is retained by the foreign corporation and not distributed to shareholders, U.S. or other, will have the result, in certain cases, of reducing the U.S. tax liability on the foreign corporation's income.

TABLE 19.4
U.S. Taxation of Foreign-Source Income (thousands of U.S. dollars)

	Case 1	Case 2	Case 3	Case 4
Baseline Values				
a. Foreign corporate income tax rate	40%	20%	20%	20%
b. U.S. corporate income tax rate	35%	35%	35%	35%
c. Foreign dividend withholding tax rate	10%	10%	10%	10%
d. Proportional ownership held by U.S. corporation in foreign corporation	30%	30%	30%	100%
e. Payout rate (proportion of after-tax income declared as dividends)	100%	100%	50%	100%
Foreign Affiliate Tax Computation				
1. Taxable income of foreign affiliate	$2,000	$2,000	$2,000	$2,000
2. Foreign corporate income taxes (@ rate a above)	(800)	(400)	(400)	(400)
3. Net income available for profit distribution	$1,200	$1,600	$1,600	$1,600
4. Retained earnings (1 − rate e above × line 3)	—	—	800	—
5. Distributed earnings (rate e above × line 3)	$1,200	$1,600	$ 800	$1,600
6. Distributed earnings to U.S. corporation (rate d × line 5)	$ 360	$ 480	$ 240	$1,600
7. Withholding taxes on dividends to nonresidents (rate c × line 6)	(36)	(48)	(24)	(160)
8. Remittance of foreign income to U.S. corporation	$ 324	$ 432	$ 216	$1,440
U.S. Corporate Tax Computation on Foreign-Source Income				
9. Grossed-up U.S. income (rate d × rate e × line 1)	$ 600	$ 600	$ 300	$2,000
10. Tentative (theoretical) U.S. tax liability (rate b × line 9)	− 210	− 210	− 105	− 700
11. Foreign tax credit (rate d × rate e × line 2 + line 7)	276	168	84	560
12. Additional U.S. taxes due on foreign-source income (line 10 + line 11; if 11 > 10, U.S. tax liability is 0)	0	− 42	− 21	− 140
13. After-tax dividends received by U.S. corporation (line 8 + line 12)	$ 324	$ 390	$ 195	$1,300
Worldwide Tax Burden				
14. Total worldwide taxes paid (line 10 or line 11, whichever is greater)	276	210	105	700
15. Effective tax rate on foreign income (line 14/line 9)	46.0%	35.0%	35.0%	35.0%

Note: When proportional ownership of the foreign corporation exceeds 50%, U.S. tax authorities classify it as a Controlled Foreign Corporation (CFC) and all passive income earned is taxed regardless of the payout rate or actual remittance to the U.S. corporation.

- **Active versus Passive Income.** If a foreign subsidiary generates income through its own actions or activities (e.g., producing a product, selling a product, providing a service), the income is classified as *active*. If, however, the foreign subsidiary or affiliate earns income through its ownership in another firm, or by acting as a creditor to another firm and earning interest income, the income is classified as *passive*. It is quite common for a foreign subsidiary to have both active and passive income. Each is then treated separately for tax purposes.
- **Relative Corporate Income Taxes.** Whether foreign corporate income taxes are higher or lower than similar U.S. corporate income taxes will largely determine whether the U.S. shareholders will owe additional taxes in the United States on the foreign-source income, or whether the foreign tax credit will completely cover U.S. tax liabilities. If withholding taxes were applied to dividends paid to nonresidents (the U.S. corporation owner), this also would affect the U.S. tax liability.

Calculation of U.S. Taxes on Foreign-Source Earnings

Table 19.4 illustrates the complete calculation of foreign taxes, U.S. tax credits, additional U.S. taxes due on foreign income, and total worldwide tax burdens for four different potential cases. Each of the four cases is structured to highlight the different combinations of the three components, relative corporate income taxes (lines a, b, and c), degree of control or ownership of the U.S. corporation in the foreign corporation (line d), and the proportion of available income distributed to stockholders as dividends (line e).

Case 1: Foreign Affiliate of a U.S. Corporation in a High-Tax Environment

This is a very common case. A U.S. corporation earns income in the form of distributed earnings (100 percent payout of available earnings to stockholders) from a foreign corporation in which it holds substantial interest (more than 10 percent) but does not control (less than 50 percent). The foreign corporate income tax rate (40 percent) is higher than the U.S. rate (35 percent). The foreign corporation has total taxable income of $2,000 (thousands of dollars), pays a 40 percent corporate income tax in the host country of $800, and distributes the entire after-tax income to stockholders. Total distributed earnings are therefore $1,200.

The foreign country imposes a 10 percent withholding tax on dividends paid to nonresidents. The U.S. corporation therefore receives its proportion of earnings (its 30 percent ownership entitles it to 30 percent of all dividends paid out) less the amount of the withholding taxes, $360 − $36, or $324. This is the net cash remittance actually received by the U.S. corporation on foreign earnings.

The calculation of U.S. taxes on foreign-source income requires first that the income be "grossed up," or reinflated to the amount of income the U.S. corporation has rights to prior to taxation by the foreign government. This is simply the percentage of ownership (30 percent) times the payout rate (100 percent) times the gross taxable income of the foreign affiliate ($2,000), or $600. A theoretical or **"tentative U.S. tax"** is calculated on this income to estimate U.S. tax payments that would be due on this income if it had been earned in the United States (or simply not taxed at all in the foreign country). U.S. taxes of 35 percent yield a tentative tax liability of $210.

Since taxes were paid abroad, however, U.S. tax law allows U.S. tax liabilities to be reduced by the amount of the **foreign tax credit.** The foreign tax credit is the proportion of foreign taxes deemed paid attributable to its ownership (30 percent ownership times the 100 percent payout rate of the foreign taxes paid, $800, plus the amount of withholding taxes imposed on the distributed dividends to the U.S. corporation, $36). The total foreign tax credit is then $240 + $36, or $276. Since the foreign tax credit exceeds the total tentative U.S. tax liability, no additional taxes are due the U.S. tax authorities on this foreign-source income. Special note should be made that the foreign tax credit may exceed the U.S. tax liabilities, but any excess cannot be applied toward other U.S. tax liabilities in the current period (it can be carried forward or back against this foreign-source income, however).

Finally, an additional calculation allows the estimation of the total taxes paid, both abroad and in the United States, on this income. In this first case, the $276 of total tax on gross income of $600 is an **effective tax rate** of 46 percent.

Case 2: Foreign Affiliate of a U.S. Corporation in a Low-Tax Environment

This case is exactly the same as the previous example, with the sole exception that the foreign tax rate (20 percent) is lower than the U.S. corporate tax rate (35 percent). All earnings, tax calculations, and dividends distributions are the same as before.

With lower foreign corporate income taxes, there is obviously more profit to be distributed, more income to the U.S. corporation's 30 percent share, and more withholding taxes to be paid on the larger dividends distributed. Yet the grossed-up income of the foreign-source income is the same as in the previous case, because grossed-up income is proportional ownership and distribution in the absence of taxes.

With lower foreign taxes, the foreign tax credit is significantly lower and is no longer sufficient to cover fully the tentative U.S. tax liability. The U.S. corporation will have an additional $42 due in taxes on the foreign-source income. After-tax dividends in total are still higher, however, rising to $390 from $324. Total worldwide taxes paid are now significantly less, $210 rather than $276.

Cases 1 and 2 point out the single most significant feature of the U.S. tax code's impact on foreign operations of U.S. corporations: The effective tax rate may be higher on foreign-source income but will never drop lower than the basic corporate income tax rate in effect in the United States (35 percent).

Case 3: Foreign Affiliate of a U.S. Corporation in a Low-Tax Environment, 50 Percent Payout

The third case changes only one of the baseline values of the previous case, the proportion of income available for dividends that is paid out to stockholders. All distributed earnings and withholding taxes are therefore half what they were previously, as is grossed-up income and the additional U.S. tax liability (because the foreign tax credit has also been cut in half).

This third case illustrates that a reduced income distribution by the foreign subsidiary does reduce income received and taxes due in the United States on the foreign income. The effective tax rate is again at the minimum achievable, the rate of taxation that would be in effect if the income had been earned within the United States. As will be shown in the fourth and final case, this third case's results rely partially on the fact that the foreign corporation is only an affiliate (less than 50 percent ownership) of the U.S. corporation and is not controlled by the U.S. corporation.

Case 4: Foreign Subsidiary of a U.S. Corporation Is a CFC in a Low-Tax Environment

This final case highlights one of the critical components of U.S. taxation of foreign subsidiary earnings. If the foreign corporation is effectively controlled by the U.S. corporation, as indicated by its greater than 50 percent ownership, and all income is passive income, U.S. tax authorities calculate U.S. tax liabilities on the foreign income as if the entire income available for distribution to shareholders were remitted to the U.S. parent, regardless of what the actual payout rate is.

This tax policy, a result of the 1962 tax reform act, is referred to as Subpart F income. Subpart F income taxation is a reflection of the control component; it is assumed that the U.S. corporation exercises sufficient control over the management of the foreign subsidiary to determine the payout rate. If the subsidiary has chosen not to pay out all passive earnings, it is taken as a choice of the U.S. corporation and is deemed to be an effort at postponing U.S. tax liabilities on the income.

The 1962 tax act was largely aimed at eliminating the abuses of foreign affiliates of U.S. corporations paying dividends and other passive income flows out to subsidiaries in various tax havens (such as Bermuda, the Bahamas, Panama, Luxembourg, and the Cayman Islands), and not remitting the income back to the U.S. corporation. By placing the passive income in the tax havens, they effectively were postponing and evading taxation by the U.S. government.

Concluding Remarks Regarding U.S. Taxation of Foreign Income

The previous series of sample tax calculations highlights the interplay of ownership, distribution, and relative tax rates between countries in determining the tax liabilities of income earned by U.S. interests abroad. In many ways, the case with the most long-term strategic significance was the first, the high-tax foreign environment. U.S. corporate income tax rates are among the lowest in the world. The usual result is the accumulation of substantial foreign tax credits by U.S. corporate interests, credits that increasingly cannot be applied to U.S. tax liabilities. The result is, as in Case 1, an effective tax rate that is significantly higher than if the income had been generated in the United States.

Recent accounting and tax rule changes may actually result in worsening this effective tax rate and excess foreign tax credit problem for U.S. corporations. Recent rule changes now require U.S. corporations to spread increasing amounts of parent-supplied overhead expenses to their foreign affiliates and subsidiaries, charging them for services provided. This results in increased costs for the foreign subsidiaries, reducing their profitability, reducing their taxable gross income, and subsequently reducing the foreign taxes, and tax credits, deemed paid. This is likely to increase the proportion of total taxes that are paid in the United States on the foreign-source income. Unfortunately, many of the overhead distributions are not recognized as a legitimate expense by many other governments (differing accounting practices in action), and the foreign units are paying a charge to the U.S. corporation that they are unable to expense against their local earnings. Recent concerns over the use of intrafirm sales (so-called transfer prices; see Chapter 15) to manipulate the profitability of foreign firms operating in the United States also has added fuel to the fires of governments and their individual shares of the world "tax pie." With that, the subject of accounting and taxation of international operations has completed a full circle.

SUMMARY   Accounting practices differ substantially across countries. The efforts of a number of international associates and agencies in the past two decades have, however, led to increasing cooperation and agreement among national accounting authorities. Real accounting differences remain, and many of these differences still contribute to the advantaged competitive position of some countries' firms over international competitors.

International taxation is a subject close to the pocketbook of every multinational firm. Although the tax policies of most countries are theoretically designed to not change or influence financial and business decision making by firms, they often do. Global Perspective 19.5, for example, shows how taxes can actually cause an industry to literally fly away.

The taxation of the foreign operations of U.S. multinational firms involves the elaborate process of crediting U.S. corporations for taxes paid to foreign governments. The combined influence of different corporate tax rates across countries, the degree of ownership and control a multinational may have or exercise in a foreign affiliate, and the proportion of profits distributed to stockholders at home and abroad combine to determine the size of the parent's tax bill. As governments worldwide search for new ways to close their fiscal deficits and tax shortfalls, the pressures on international taxation and the reporting of foreign-source income will only increase.

Global Perspective

19.5
Taxing Lessons from Albania

TIRANA—Albania, Europe's poorest country, seems jinxed in its dealings with foreign investors. The latest mishap is the collapse of the national flag-carrier, Albanian Airlines, a joint venture between the state-owned Albtransport and Austria's Tyrolean Airlines, which was launched with much fanfare last year.

The prospects for yet another airline serving Tirana (a city where the average monthly salary is around $40 a month) were never great, but the government was determined to have the status symbol of a national carrier. Now, thanks to its habit of passing retrospective financial legislation, it seems to have killed it.

Earlier this year the government required all carriers with their own branch offices in Tirana to pay a tax of 15 percent on net ticket revenues, backdated to March 1993.

Instead of filling the government's empty coffers, this provoked a revolt by the foreign airlines, which include giants such as Swissair and Alitalia, as well as Albanian Airlines and a tiny local French carrier, ADA Air. Several—including Swissair which faced an unexpected bill for more than $1m—threatened to suspend flights to Tirana.

Tyrolean Airlines, which supplied the Albanian Airlines aircraft, decided to pull the plug on what was already a loss-making business. Albania's government hastily offered to exempt Albanian Airlines from the tax, a move which caused fury amongst other airlines without persuading the Austrians to change their decision. Albanian Airlines offices are now open intermittently for refund inquiries. The government, which has dropped the entire tax scheme, is looking for a new foreign partner.

Source: "Lessons from Albania (part 97)," *The Economist,* September 17, 1994, 79.

Key Terms and Concepts

accounting diversity	indirect taxes
LIFO	value-added tax (VAT)
average cost method	corporate income tax
FIFO	distributed earnings
operating or service lease	undistributed earnings
pension liabilities	withholding taxes
current rate method	"tentative U.S. tax"
temporal method	foreign tax credit
direct taxes	effective tax rate

Questions for Discussion

1. Do you think all firms, in all economic environments, should operate under the same set of accounting principles?

2. What is the nature of the purported benefit that accounting principles provide British firms over American firms in the competition for mergers and acquisitions?

3. Why do most U.S. corporations prefer the current rate method of translation over the temporal method? How does each method affect reported earnings per share per period?

4. Name two major indications that progress is being made toward standardizing accounting principles across countries.

5. What is the distinction between harmonizing accounting rules and standardizing accounting procedures and practices across countries?

6. Why are foreign subsidiaries in which U.S. corporations hold more than 50 percent voting power classified and treated differently for U.S. tax purposes?

7. Why do the U.S. tax authorities want U.S. corporations to charge their foreign subsidiaries for general and administrative services? What does this mean for the creation of excess foreign tax credits by U.S. corporations with foreign operations?

8. What would be the tax implications of combining Cases 1 and 4 in the U.S. taxation of foreign-source income, a U.S. Controlled Foreign Corporation (CFC) that is operating in a high-tax environment?

9. Why does countertrade pose special problems for accountants?

Recommended Readings

Alhashim, Dhia D., and Jeffrey S. Arpan. *International Dimensions of Accounting.* 3d ed. Boston: PWS-Kent Publishing Company, 1992.

Arpan, Jeffrey S., and Lee H. Radebaugh. *International Accounting and Multinational Enterprises.* New York: John Wiley & Sons, 1985.

BenDaniel, David J., and Arthur H. Rosenbloom. *The Handbook of International Mergers and Acquisitions.* Englewood Cliffs, N.J.: Prentice-Hall, 1990.

Bodner, Paul M. "International Taxation," in *The Handbook of International Accounting,* Frederick D.S. Choi, ed. New York: John Wiley & Sons, 1992.

Choi, Frederick D.S., ed. *The Handbook of International Accounting.* New York: John Wiley & Sons, 1991.

Choi, Frederick D.S., and Richard Levich. "International Accounting Diversity and Capital Market Decisions," in *The Handbook of International Accounting,* Frederick D.S. Choi, ed. New York: John Wiley & Sons, 1992.

Choi, Frederick D.S., and Gerhard G. Mueller. *International Accounting.* 2d ed. Englewood Cliffs, N.J.: Prentice-Hall, 1992.

Coopers & Lybrand, *International Accounting Summaries.* 2d ed. New York: John Wiley & Sons, 1993.

Eiteman, David K., Arthur I. Stonehill, and Michael H. Moffett. *Multinational Business Finance.* 7th ed. Reading, Mass.: Addison-Wesley Publishing, 1995.

Goeltz, Richard K. "International Accounting Harmonization: The Impossible (and Unnecessary?) Dream," *Accounting Horizons,* March 1991, 85–88.

Haskins, M., K. Ferris, and T. Selling. *International Financial Reporting and Analysis.* R.D. Irwin, 1995

Hosseini, Ahmad, and Raj Aggarwal. "Evaluating Foreign Affiliates: The Impact of Alternative Foreign Currency Translation Methods." *International Journal of Accounting* (Fall 1983): 65–87.

Neuhausen, Benjamin. "Consolidated Financial Statements and Joint Venture Accounting," in *The Handbook of International Accounting,* Frederick D.S. Choi, ed. New York: John Wiley & Sons, 1992.

Nobes, Christopher, and Robert Parker. *Comparative International Accounting.* 3d ed. London: Prentice Hall International, Ltd., 1991.

Price Waterhouse. *Corporate Taxes: A Worldwide Summary.* 1994 International edition. New York, 1994.

Notes

1. This example is borrowed from "International Accounting Diversity and Capital Market Decisions," by Choi and Levich, 1992.

2. This table and the following associated discussion draws heavily on the recent excellent study of this subject by Philip R. Peller and Frank J. Schwitter of Arthur Andersen & Company, "A Summary of Accounting Principle Differences Around the World," in *The Handbook of International Accounting,* Frederick D.S. Choi, ed., 1992, Chapter 4.

3. Disclosure has continued to be one of the largest sources of frustration between countries. The disclosure requirements of the Securities and Exchange Commission (SEC) in the United States for firms—foreign or domestic—in order to issue publicly traded securities are some of the strictest in the world. Many experts in the field have long been convinced that the depth of U.S. disclosure requirements has prevented many foreign firms from issuing securities in the United States. The SEC's approval of Rule 144A, selective secondary market trading of private placements, is an attempt to alleviate some of the pressure on foreign firms from U.S. disclosure.

4. Frederick D.S. Choi and Gerhard G. Mueller, *International Accounting,* 2d ed. (Englewood Cliffs, N.J.: Prentice-Hall, 1992), 262.

5. A U.S. shareholder is a U.S. person (a citizen or resident of the United States, domestic partnership, domestic corporation, or any nonforeign trust or estate) owning 10 percent or more of the voting power of a controlled foreign corporation. A controlled foreign corporation (CFC) is any foreign corporation in which U.S. shareholders, including corporate parents, own more than 50 percent of the combined voting power or total value. The percentages are calculated on a constructive ownership basis, in which an individual is considered to own shares registered in the name of other family members, members of a trust, or any other related group.

CHAPTER 20

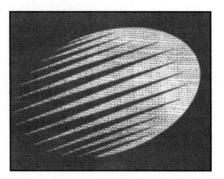

International Human Resource Management*

*This chapter was contributed by Susan C. Ronkainen.

Learning Objectives

1. To describe the challenges of managing managers and labor personnel both in individual international markets and in worldwide operations.

2. To examine the sources, qualifications, and compensation of international managers.

3. To assess the effects of culture on managers and management policies.

4. To illustrate the different roles of labor in international markets, especially that of labor participation in management.

Global Talent Search

Many corporate decision makers have realized that human resources play at least as significant a role as advanced technology and economies of scale when it comes to competing successfully in the new global world order.

According to a 1994 *International Business* survey of 1,200 mid-size U.S. multinationals with annual sales of $1 billion or less, senior executives seek managers who are culturally diverse but responsive to the direction of headquarters. Most U.S.–based companies try to fill senior positions abroad with locals, using expatriates only for such specific projects as technology transfer. However, the same companies send their U.S. middle managers the clear message that overseas operations are so important to corporate welfare that solid international experience is needed for advancement.

While major markets in Europe and Asia possess deeper pools of managerial talent than ever before, many of the nationals prefer to work for domestic rather than foreign firms. In particularly short supply are marketing managers and it is especially hard to find people who have the cross-cultural experience to make good regional managers.

Very few global leaders are born that way; that is, with an international childhood, command of several languages, and an education from an institution with an international focus. In most cases, they have to be trained and nurtured carefully. To achieve this goal, companies are using various approaches.

Gaynor Kelley, chairman, and Riccardo Pigliucci, president and COO, of Perkin-Elmer Corp., which makes analytical instruments, frequently attend monthly meetings of senior executives held at production and sales locations around the world. The meetings permit the two men to assess the performance of company managers—be they nationals or expatriates. Pigliucci is a prime example of Perkin-Elmer's desire to breed global managers. He joined the company as a chemist from the University of Milan, and served stints in product development and sales and marketing in Europe and North America.

NetFRAME Systems Inc., a maker of networking computers, gathers its expatriate and non–U.S. managers at its California headquarters every quarter. The idea is to encourage joint planning and problem solving on a global basis. By building cross-border employee cooperatives, companies not only can design solutions to better meet the needs of various customer constituencies, they can develop organizations where the sun never sets on innovation.

Some companies take what can be called the "Dutch uncle" approach. They pair a key overseas manager with one at headquarters. This helps top management to keep tabs on the manager's progress and helps the manager stay in tune with what is going on back at the source of power. Such mentoring can also provide vital input into management succession strategizing.

Companies spending time and money creating and training global talent naturally want to retain it for as long as possible. Loctite Corp., maker of industrial adhesives, offers global opportunity, professional challenge, and a competitive compensation package to keep its rising stars. Of the three approaches, claims the company, compensation is the least important to the managers.

Sources: "Globe Trotter: If It's 5:30, This Must Be Tel-Aviv," *Business Week,* October 17, 1994, 102; and Lori Ioannou, "It's a Small World After All," *International Business,* February 1994, 82–88.

Organizations have two general human resource objectives.[1] The first is the recruitment and retention of a work force made up of the best people available for the jobs to be done. The recruiter in international operations will need to keep in mind both cross-cultural and cross-national differences in productivity and expectations when selecting employees. Once they are hired, the firm's best interest lies in maintaining a stable and experienced work force.

The second objective is to increase the effectiveness of the work force. This depends to a great extent on achieving the first objective. Competent managers or workers are likely to perform at a more effective level if proper attention is given to factors that motivate them.

To attain the two major objectives, the activities and skills needed include:

1. Personnel planning and staffing, the assessment of personnel needs, and recruitment.
2. Personnel training to achieve a perfect fit between the employee and the assignment.
3. Compensation of employees according to their effectiveness.
4. An understanding of labor–management relations in terms of how the two groups view each other and how their respective power positions are established.

This chapter will examine the management of human resources in international business from two points of view, first that of managers and then that of labor.

MANAGING MANAGERS

The importance of the quality of the work force in international business cannot be overemphasized, regardless of the stage of internationalization of the firm. As seen in the chapter's opening vignette, international business systems are complex and dynamic and require competent people to develop and direct them.

Early Stages of Internationalization

The marketing or sales manager of the firm typically is responsible for beginning export activities. As foreign sales increase, an export manager will be appointed and given the responsibility for developing and maintaining customers, interacting with the firm's intermediaries, and planning for overall market expansion. The export manager also must champion the international effort within the company because the general attitude among employees may be to view the domestic market as more important. Another critical function is the supervision of export transactions, particularly documentation. The requirements are quite different for international transactions than for domestic ones, and sales or profits may be lost if documentation is not properly handled. The first task of the new export manager, in fact, often is to hire a staff to handle paperwork that typically had previously been done by a facilitating agent, such as a freight forwarder.

The firm starting international operations will usually hire an export manager from outside rather than promote from within. The reason is that knowledge of the product or industry is less important than international experience. The cost of learning through experience to manage an export department is simply too great from the firm's standpoint. Further, the inexperienced manager would be put in the position of having to demonstrate his or her effectiveness almost at once.

The manager who is hired will have obtained experience through Foreign Service duty or with another corporation. In the early stages, a highly entrepreneurial spirit with a heavy dose of trader mentality is required. Even then, management should not expect the new export department to earn a profit for the first year or so.

Advanced Stages of Internationalization

As the firm progresses from exporting to an international division to foreign direct involvement, manpower-planning activities will initially focus on need vis-à-vis various markets and functions. Existing personnel can be assessed and plans made to recruit, select, and train employees for positions that cannot be filled internally. The four major categories of overseas assignments are: (1) CEO, to oversee and direct the entire operation; (2) functional head, to establish and maintain departments and ensure their proper performance; (3) troubleshooters, who are utilized for their special expertise in analyzing, and thereby preventing or solving, particular problems; and (4) white- or blue-collar workers.[2] International oil companies typically assign many employees overseas when the available pool is small, such as in Saudi Arabia.

One of the major sources of competitive advantage of global corporations is their ability to attract talent around the world. The corporations need systematic management-development systems, with the objective of creating and carefully allocating management personnel. An example of this is provided in Figure 20.1. Increasingly, plans call for international experience as a prerequisite for advancement; for example, at Ford, the goal is to have 100 percent of the top managers with international work experience with the company.[3]

In global corporations, there is no such thing as a universal global manager, but a network of global specialists in four general groups of managers has to work together.[4] Global business (product) managers have the task to further the company's global-scale efficiency and competitiveness. Country managers have to be sensitive and responsive to local market needs and demands but, at the same time, be aware of global implications. Functional managers have to make sure that the corporation's capabilities in technical, manufacturing, marketing, human resource, and financial expertise are linked and can benefit from each other. Corporate executives at headquarters have to manage interactions among the three groups of managers as well as identify and develop the talent to fill the positions.

As an example of manpower planning, a management review of human resources is conducted twice a year with each general manager of Heineken operating companies, which are located in such countries as Canada, France, Ireland, and Spain. The meeting is attended by the general manager, the personnel manager, the regional coordinating director in whose region the operating company is located, and the corporate director of management development. Special attention is given to managers "in the fast lane," the extent to which they are mobile, what might be done to foster their development, and where they fit into succession planning.[5] Of course, any gaps must be filled by recruitment efforts.

International companies should show clear career paths for managers assigned overseas and develop the systems and the organization for promotion. This approach serves to eliminate many of the perceived problems and thus motivates managers to seek out foreign assignments. Foreign assignments can occur at various stages of the manager's tenure. In the early stages, assignments may be short-term, such as a membership in an international task force or six to twelve months at headquarters in a staff function. Later, an individual may serve as a business-unit manager overseas. Many companies use cross-postings to other countries or across product lines to further an individual's acculturation to the corporation.[6] A period in a head office department or a subsidiary will not only provide an understanding of different national cultures and attitudes but also improve an individual's "know-who" and therefore establish unity and common sense of purpose necessary for the proper implementation of global programs.

Interfirm Cooperative Ventures

Global competition is forging new cooperative ties between firms from different countries, thereby adding a new management challenge for the firms involved. Although many of the reasons cited for these alliances (described in Chapter 13) are competitive and strategic, the human resource function is critical to their implementation. As a matter of fact, some of the basic reasons so many of these ventures fail relate to human resource management; for example, managers from disparate venture partners cannot work together, or managers within the venture cannot work with the owners' managers.[7] These challenges are highlighted in Global Perspective 20.1.

While the ingredients for success of the human resource function will differ with the type of cooperative venture, two basic types of tasks are needed.[8] The first task is to assign and motivate people in appropriate ways so that the venture will fulfill its set strategic tasks. This requires particular attention to such issues as job skills and compatibility of communication and other work styles. For example, some cooperative ventures have failed due to one of the partners' assigning relatively weak management resources to the venture or due to managers' finding themselves with conflicting loyalties to the parent organization and the cooperative venture organization. The second task is the strategic management of the human resources, that is, the appropriate use of managerial capabilities not only in the cooperative venture but in other later contexts, possibly back in the parent organization. An individual manager needs to see that an assignment in a cooperative venture is part of his or her overall career development.

FIGURE 20.1   **An Example of an International Management Development System**

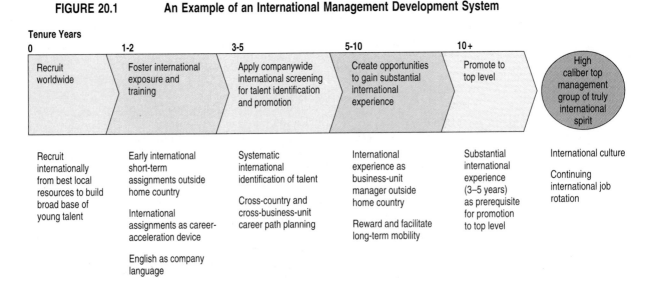

Tenure Years					
0	1-2	3-5	5-10	10+	
Recruit worldwide	Foster international exposure and training	Apply companywide international screening for talent identification and promotion	Create opportunities to gain substantial international experience	Promote to top level	High caliber top management group of truly international spirit
Recruit internationally from best local resources to build broad base of young talent	Early international short-term assignments outside home country	Systematic international identification of talent	International experience as business-unit manager outside home country	Substantial international experience (3–5 years) as prerequisite for promotion to top level	International culture
	International assignments as career-acceleration device	Cross-country and cross-business-unit career path planning	Reward and facilitate long-term mobility		Continuing international job rotation
	English as company language				

Source: Ingo Theuerkauf, "Reshaping the Global Organization," *McKinsey Quarterly* 3 (1991): 103–119.

Global Perspective

20.1
The Challenge of How to Best Manage Together

For many Western companies, a joint venture with a local company is the only sensible way to enter the Chinese market; some 7,500 U.S. companies are following that route. However, more than half fail or are dissolved. In many joint ventures between Chinese and Western companies, senior managers selected to run them regularly misunderstand each other, sometimes so profoundly that they are unable to continue working together. One of the major contributing factors is the Chinese emphasis on the concept of *guanxi,* or relationships. While Western business practice has developed impersonal structures for channeling power and influence through reliance on law and contracts, the Chinese emphasize getting on the good side of someone and storing up political capital with them. Things can get done without *guanxi* only if one invests enormous personal energy, is willing to offend even close friends and trusted associates, and is prepared to see such victories melt away while one is off on a business trip or on home leave.

Many of the areas of potential conflict to watch out for are in the daily management of the joint venture:

- **Hiring of Staff**—Westerners prefer objective hiring; using newspaper advertisements and other public means to solicit candidates, followed by interviews, testing, and picking the most qualified person. The Chinese side wants to hire people who are "known," preferably through trusted friends.

- **Application of Rules and Regulations**—Westerners tend to view company rules and regulations as more important than the relationship of any one person with another. The Chinese managers will respect rules but never view them as more important than *guanxi.*

- **Accountability**—Westerners view managers at every level directly responsible for the discipline and performance of their immediate subordinates. Chinese managers feel responsible to communicate rules and work targets, but workers themselves should be the only ones accountable

for what they do. This can lead to Chinese managers spending more time at the desk than Western managers think they should.

- **Horizontal Communication**—In the West, direct horizontal communication is considered positive since it increases efficiency. In China, however, horizontal communication is awkward because it cuts through *guanxi* networks. The preferred method is to communicate upward to your patron and let him communicate over and down to another patron.

- **Budgets and Business Plans**—While Western managers tend to regard a budget or other formal plan as critical to navigating through the year, Chinese managers shy away from plans. The most frequent objection is, "You never know what will happen, so it is better not to tie yourself down."

Newly arrived senior managers in China may feel pressure to justify their presence (especially when his/her salaries are 100 times greater than their Chinese counterparts') and resort to what has worked for them in the past, such as wanting to look at accounts, assess budgets, or talk with those working on plans. Chinese colleagues want managers to ask to meet contacts in government, industry, banks, and suppliers. They invite managers to dinners, but during them the managers may ask very direct questions such as, "Why is our export license taking so long?" Managers are expected to take advantage of their enviable positions to create goodwill as managers of prestigious joint ventures. In the end, managers may feel powerless and frustrated, unable to get things done, sometimes convinced that the Chinese managers have deliberately turned them into "foreign window dressing" for basically a Chinese firm. Chinese colleagues, on the other hand, are amazed that the Westerners consistently pass up the opportunities they provide to enter into their *guanxi* network and really be effective.

Sources: John R. Engen, "Getting Your Chinese Work Force Up to Speed," *International Business,* August 1994, 44–48; and Peter MacInnis, "*Guanxi* or Contract: A Way to Understand and Predict Conflict Between Chinese and Western Senior Managers in China-Based Joint Ventures," in Daniel E. McCarthy and Stanley J. Hille, eds., *Research on Multinational Business Management and Internationalization of Business Enterprises* (Nanjing, China: Nanjing University Press, 1993), 345–351.

TABLE 20.1 Factors Determining the Choice between Local and Expatriate Managers	• Availability of Managers
	• Competence
	    Market
	    Technical
		• Corporate objectives
		  Control
		  Management development
		  Corporate citizenship
			• Cost
			• Environment
			  Legal
			  Cultural
			  Economic

Sources for Management Recruitment

The location and the nationality of candidates for a particular job are the key issues in recruitment. A decision will have to be made to recruit from within the company or, in the case of larger corporations, within other product or regional groups, or to rely on external talent. Similarly, decisions will have to be made whether to hire or promote locally or use **expatriates;** that is, home-country nationals or third-country nationals (citizens of countries other than the home or host country). The factors that influence this choice process are summarized in Table 20.1. They fall into three general categories: (1) the availability and quality of the talent pool, (2) corporate policies and their cost, and (3) environmental constraints.

Firms use a similar pattern of recruitment during the internationalization process.[9] During the export stage, outside expertise is sought at first, but the firm then begins to develop its own personnel for international operations. With expanded and more involved foreign operations, the firm's reliance on home-country personnel will be reduced as host-country nationals are prepared for management positions. The use of home-country and third-country nationals may be directed at special assignments, such as transfer of technology or expertise. The use of expatriates will continue as a matter of corporate policy to internationalize management and to foster the infusion of particular corporate culture into operations around the world.

When international operations are expanded, a management development dilemma may result. Through internal recruitment, young managers will be offered interesting new opportunities. However, some senior managers may object to the constant drain of young talent from their units. Selective recruitment from the outside will help to maintain a desirable combination of inside talent and fresh blood. Furthermore, with dynamic market changes or new markets and new business development, outside recruitment may be the only available approach. Even in Japan, the taboo against hiring executives from other companies is breaking down. The practice of hiring from the top universities can no longer be depended on to provide the right people in all circumstances.[10]

Currently, most managers in subsidiaries are host-country nationals, as shown in the survey results of 1,200 U.S. multinational corporations (see Figure 20.2). The reasons include an increase in availability of local talent, corporate relations in the particular market, and the economies realized by not having to maintain a corps of managers overseas. Local managers are generally more familiar with environmental conditions and how they should be interpreted. By employing local management, the multinational is responding to host-country demands for increased localization and providing advancement as an incentive to local managers. In this respect, however, localization can be carried too far. If the firm does not subscribe to a global philosophy, the manager's development is tied to the local operation or to a particular level of management in that operation. This has been an issue of contention, especially with Japanese employers in the United States. As a result, managers who

FIGURE 20.2
Staffing Abroad

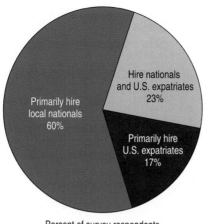

Hire nationals
and U.S. expatriates
23%

Primarily hire
local nationals
60%

Primarily hire
U.S. expatriates
17%

Percent of survey respondents

Source: Lori Ioannou, "It's a Small World After All," *International Business*, February 1994, 84.

outgrow the local operation may have nowhere to go except to another company.[11] Although the Japanese continue to express frustration in what they perceive to be disloyalty and opportunism on the part of U.S. employees, they are starting to change their practices so that they can retain talented U.S. nationals.[12]

Local managers, if not properly trained and indoctrinated, may see things differently from the way they are viewed at headquarters. As a result, both control and the overall coordination of programs may be jeopardized. For the corporation to work effectively, of course, employees must first of all understand each other. Most corporations have adopted a common corporate language, with English as the **lingua franca;** that is, the language habitually used among people of diverse speech to facilitate communication. At Olivetti, all top-level meetings are conducted in English.[13] In some companies, two languages are officially in use; for example, at Nestlé both English and French are corporate languages. A second goal is to avoid overemphasis on localization, which would prevent the development of an internationalized group of managers with a proper understanding of the impact of the environment on operations. To develop language skills and promote an international outlook in their management pools, multinational corporations are increasingly recruiting among foreign students at business schools in the United States, western Europe, and the Far East. When these young managers return home, following an initial assignment at corporate headquarters, they will have a command of the basic philosophies of multinational operations.

Cultural differences that shape managerial attitudes must be considered when developing multinational management programs. For example, British managers place more emphasis than most other nationals on individual achievement and autonomy. French managers, however, value competent supervision, sound company policies, fringe benefits, security, and comfortable working conditions.[14]

The decision as to whether to use home-country nationals in a particular operation depends on such factors as the type of industry, the life cycle stage of the product, the availability of managers from other sources, and the functional areas involved. The number of home-country managers is typically higher in the service sector than in the industrial sector. However, some overseas assignments, particularly in the service sector, may be quite short term. For example, many international hotel chains have established management contracts in the People's Republic of China with the understanding that home-country managers will train local successors within three to five years. In the start-up phase of an endeavor, headquarters involvement is generally substantial. This applies to all functions, including personnel. Especially if no significant pool of local managers is available or their competence levels are not satisfactory, home-country nationals may be used. For control and communication reasons, some companies always maintain a home-country national as manager in certain functional areas, such as accounting or finance.

The number of home-country nationals in an overseas operation rarely rises above 10 percent of the work force and is typically only 1 percent. The reasons are both internal and external. In addition to the substantial cost of transfer, a manager may not fully adjust to foreign working and living conditions. Good corporate citizenship today requires multinational companies to develop the host country's work force at the management level. Legal impediments to manager transfers may exist, or other difficulties may be encountered. Many U.S.–based hotel corporations, for example, have complained about delays in obtaining visas to the United States not only for managers but also for management trainees.

The use of third-country nationals is most often seen in large multinational companies that have adopted a global philosophy. The practice of some companies, such as the Dutch electronics giant N. V. Philips, is to employ third-country nationals as managing directors in subsidiaries. An advantage is that third-country nationals may contribute to the firm's overall international expertise. However, many third-country nationals are career international managers, and they may become targets for raids by competitors looking for high levels of talent. They may be a considerable asset in regional expansion; for example, established subsidiary managers in Singapore might be used to start up a subsidiary in Malaysia. On the other hand, some transfers may be inadvisable for cultural or historical reasons, with transfers between Turkey and Greece as an example.

The ability to recruit for international assignments is determined by the value an individual company places on international operations and the experience gained in working in them. Based on a survey of 1,500 senior executives around the world, U.S. executives still place less emphasis on international dimensions than their Japanese, western European, and Latin American counterparts. While most executives agree that an international outlook is essential for future executives, 70 percent of

In Tokyo, Merck representative Satomi Tomihari confers with Yasumasa Nakamura, M.D. Tomihari is one of twenty-five women recruited by Merck affiliate, Banyu Pharmaceutical, Ltd.

Source: Griffiths, photographer for Magnum Photo. Courtesy of Merck & Co., Inc.

	Competence	Adaptability	Personal Characteristics
TABLE 20.2 **Criteria for Selecting Managers for Overseas Assignment**	Technical knowledge Leadership ability Experience, past performance Area expertise Language	Interest in overseas work Relational abilities Cultural empathy Appreciation of new management styles Appreciation of environmental constraints Adaptability of family	Age Education Sex Health Marital relations Social acceptability

foreign executives think that experience outside one's home country is important, compared with only 35 percent of U.S. executives, and foreign language capability was seen as important by only 19 percent of U.S. respondents, compared with 64 percent of non–U.S. executives.[15]

In an era of regional integration, many companies are facing a severe shortage of managers who can think and operate regionally or even globally. Very few companies—even those characterizing themselves as global—have systematically developed international managers by rotating young executives through a series of assignments in different parts of the world.[16] To help find the best cross-border talent, executive search firms, such as A. T. Kearney and Heidrick & Struggles, can be used.

Selection Criteria for Overseas Assignments

The traits that have been suggested as necessary for the international manager range from the ideal to the real. One characterization describes "a flexible personality, with broad intellectual horizons, attitudinal values of cultural empathy, general friendliness, patience and prudence, impeccable educational and professional (or technical) credentials—all topped off with immaculate health, creative resourcefulness, and respect of peers. If the family is equally well endowed, all the better."[17] Although this would seem to describe a supermanager, a number of companies believe that the qualities that make a successful international manager are increasingly the traits needed at headquarters.[18] Traits typically mentioned in the choosing of managers for overseas assignments are listed in Table 20.2. Their relative importance may vary dramatically, of course, depending on the firm and the situation.

Competence Factors An expatriate manager usually has far more responsibility than a manager in a comparable domestic position and must be far more self-sufficient in making decisions and conducting daily business. To be selected in the first place, the manager's technical competence level has to be superior to that of local candidates'; otherwise, the firm would in most cases have chosen a local person. The manager's ability to do the job in the technical sense is one of the main determinants of ultimate success or failure in an overseas assignment.[19] However, management skills will not transfer from one culture to another without some degree of adaptation. This means that, regardless of the level of technical skills, the new environment still requires the ability to adapt the skills to local conditions. Technical competence must also be accompanied by the ability to lead subordinates in any situation or under any conditions.

Especially in global-minded enterprises, managers are selected for overseas assignments on the basis of solid experience and past performance. Many firms use

the foreign tour as a step toward top management. By sending abroad internally recruited, experienced managers, the firm also ensures the continuation of corporate
culture—a set of shared values, norms, and beliefs and an emphasis on a particular
facet of performance. Two examples are IBM's concern with customer service and
3M's concentration on innovation.[20]

The role of **factual cultural knowledge** in the selection process has been widely
debated. **Area expertise** includes a knowledge of the basic systems in the region
or market for which the manager will be responsible—such as the roles of various
ministries in international business, the significance of holidays, and the general way
of doing business. None of these variables is as important as language, although language skill is not always highly ranked by firms themselves.[21] A manager who does
not know the language of the country may get by with the help of associates and
interpreters but is not in a position to assess the situation fully. Of the Japanese representing their companies in the United States, for example, almost all speak English. Of the Americans representing U.S. companies in Japan, however, few speak
Japanese well.[22] Some companies place language skills or aptitude in a larger context; they see a strong correlation between language skill and adaptability. Another
reason to look for language competence in managers considered for assignments
overseas is that all managers spend most of their time communicating.

Adaptability Factors   The manager's own motivation to a great extent determines
the viability of an overseas assignment and consequently its success. The manager's
interest in the foreign culture must go well beyond that of the average tourist if he
or she is to understand what an assignment abroad involves. In most cases, the manager will need counseling and training to comprehend the true nature of the undertaking.

Adaptability means a positive and flexible attitude toward change. The manager
assigned overseas must progress from factual knowledge of culture to **interpretive
cultural knowledge,** trying as much as possible to become part of the new scene,
which may be quite different from the one at home. The work habits of middle-level
managers may be more lax, productivity and attention to detail less, and overall environmental restrictions far greater. The manager on a foreign assignment is part of
a multicultural team, in which both internal and external interactions determine the
future of the firm's operations. For example, a manager from the United States may
be used to an informal, democratic type of leadership that may not be applicable
in countries such as Mexico or Japan, where employees expect more authoritarian
leadership.[23]

Adaptability does not depend solely on the manager. Firms look carefully at the
family situation because a foreign assignment often puts more strain on other family members than on the manager. As an example, a U.S. engineering firm had problems in Italy that were traced to the inability of one executive's wife to adapt. She
complained to other wives, who began to feel that they too suffered hardships and
then complained to their husbands. Morale became so low that the company, after
missing important deadlines, replaced most of the Americans on the job.[24] This extreme case shows that spouses need to participate throughout the decision process.

The characteristics of the family as a whole are important. Screeners look for
family cohesiveness and check for marital instability or for behavioral difficulties in
children. Abroad, the need to work together as a family often makes strong marriages
stronger and causes the downfall of weak ones. Further, commitments or interests
beyond the nuclear family affect the adjustment of family members to a new envi-

ronment. Some firms use earlier transfers within the home country as an indicator of how a family will handle transfer abroad. With the dramatic increase in two-career households, foreign assignments usually call for one of the spouses to sacrifice a career or, at best, to put it on hold. As a result, a group of 38 corporations have formed a consortium to try to tackle this problem. Members of the group interview accompanying spouses and try to find them positions with other member companies.[25]

Personal Characteristics   Despite all of the efforts made by multinational companies to recruit the best person available, demographics still play a role in the selection process. Due to either a minimum age requirement or the level of experience needed, many foreign assignments go to managers in their mid-30s or older. Normally, companies do not recruit candidates from graduating classes for immediate assignment overseas. They want their international people first to become experienced and familiar with the corporate culture, and this can best be done at the headquarters location.

Although the number of women in overseas assignments is only 12 percent according to one count, women are as interested as men are in the assignments.[26] Corporate hiring practices may be based on the myth that women will not be accepted in the host countries. Many of the relatively few women managers report being treated as foreign business people and not singled out as women.[27] These issues are highlighted in Global Perspective 20.2.

In the selection process, firms are concerned about the health of the people they may send abroad. Some assignments are in host countries with dramatically different environmental conditions from the home country, and they may aggravate existing health problems. Moreover, if the candidate selected is not properly prepared, foreign assignments may increase stress levels and contribute to the development of peptic ulcers, colitis, or other problems.

When candidates are screened, being married is usually considered a plus. Marriage brings stability and an inherent support system, provided family relations are in order. It may also facilitate adaptation to the local culture by increasing the number of social functions to which the manager is invited.

Social acceptability varies from one culture to another and can be a function of any of the other personal characteristics. Background, religion, race, and sex usually become critical only in extreme cases in which a host environment would clearly reject a candidate based on one or more of these variables. The Arab boycott of the state of Israel, for example, puts constraints on the use of managers of Jewish and Arab origin. Women cannot negotiate contracts in many Middle Eastern countries. This would hold true even if the woman were president of the company.

The Selection and Orientation Challenge   Due to the cost of transferring a manager overseas, many firms go beyond standard selection procedures and use **adaptability screening** as an integral part of the process. During the screening phase, the method most often used involves interviewing the candidate and the family. The interviews are conducted by senior executives, human relations specialists within the firm, or outside firms. Interviewers ask the candidate and the family to consider the personal issues involved in the transfer; for example, what each will miss the most. In some cases, candidates themselves will refuse an assignment. In others, the firm will withhold the assignment on the basis of interviews that clearly show a degree of risk.

Global Perspective

20.2
Women's Global Career Ladder

There is growing evidence to suggest that women are making greater strides on the international front than ever before. The 1994 Global Relocation Survey, conducted by Windham International and the National Foreign Trade Council, provides various measures of this trend. A full 12 percent of American corporate expatriates are women, up from 5 percent in 1992. The figure is expected to reach 20 percent by the year 2000. Nearly three-fourths of U.S. companies expect the number of female expatriates to increase by 1995, while only 9 percent expect the number to fall. *Fortune* magazine summarized it by stating, "The best reason for believing that more women will be in charge before long is that in a ferociously competitive global economy, no company can afford to waste valuable brainpower simply because it's wearing a skirt."

Some argue that the numbers are relatively small due to commonly held myths about women in international business. The first is that women do not want to be international managers, and the second is that foreigners' prejudice against them renders them ineffective, whether they are nationals or not.

In a study of more than 1,000 graduating MBAs from schools in North America and Europe, females and males displayed equal interest in pursuing international careers. They did also agree that firms offer fewer opportunities to women pursuing international careers than to those pursuing domestic ones. Women expatriate managers agree that convincing superiors to let them go called for patience and persistence.

Expatriate women have generally reported numerous professional advantages to being female. Being highly visible (both internally and externally) has often been quoted as an advantage given that many women expatriates are "firsts" for their companies. Foreign clients are curious about them, want to meet them, and remember them after the first encounter. Emanuel Monogenis, a managing partner at the international search firm of Heidrick & Struggles, observed, "My clients now see women as equals in top global searches. In fact, more and more executives are saying they prefer women because they feel they are willing to work harder and take less for granted than male counterparts. Many also believe women have more of a sensibility and insight into human behavior and relationships than their male counterparts, and this is highly valued in culturally diverse workforces."

No person will be chosen for an assignment abroad without having the necessary technical and professional qualifications. The most successful approach for female managers is to be gently persistent in "educating" one's employer and constituents around the world to be open to the possibility of sending women abroad and granting them the same status and support accorded to male peers. One female expatriate summarized her experiences in this way, "Although I am viewed as a foreigner, I still have to cope with some chauvinism, but after I prove I have a brain, it is business as usual."

Sources: Lori Ioannou, "Women's Global Career Ladder," *International Business,* December 1994, 57–60; Nancy J. Adler and Dafna N. Izraeli, eds., *Competitive Frontiers: Women Managers in a Global Economy* (Cambridge, Mass.: Blackwell Business, 1994): Chapters 1 and 2; Diana Kunde, "Management Opportunities for Women Brighten," *The Washington Post,* December 19, 1993, H2; and Anne B. Fisher, "When Will Women Get to the Top?" *Fortune,* September 21, 1992, 44–56.

The candidate selected will participate in an **orientation program** on internal and external aspects of the assignment. Internal aspects include issues such as compensation and reporting. External aspects are concerned with what to expect at the destination in terms of customs and culture. The extent and level of the programs will vary; for example, in a survey of 120 U.S. companies, 42 percent reported having no cultural preparation training for their executives. As shown in Figure 20.3, most programs offered extend the orientation to the spouse or the entire family. If

FIGURE 20.3
Companies Offering
Cultural Training

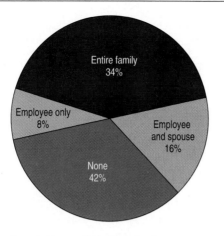

Source: Lori Ioannou, "Cultivating the New Expatriate Executive," *International Business,* July 1994, 46.

the company is still in the export stage, the emphasis in this training will be on interpersonal skills and local culture. With expatriates, the focus will be on both training and interacting with host-country nationals. Actual methods vary from area studies to sensitivity training. For a discussion of these methods, see Chapter 9.

The attrition rate in overseas assignments averages 40 percent among companies with neither adaptability screening nor orientation programs, 25 percent among companies with cultural orientation programs, and 5 to 10 percent among companies that use both kinds of programs.[28] Considering the cost of a transfer, catching even one potentially disastrous situation pays for the program for a full year. Most companies have no program at all, however, and others provide them for higher level management positions only. Companies that have the lowest failure rates typically employ a four-tiered approach to expatriate use: (1) clearly stated criteria, (2) rigorous procedures to determine the suitability of an individual across the criteria, (3) appropriate orientation, and (4) constant evaluation of the effectiveness of the procedures.[29]

Culture Shock

The effectiveness of orientation procedures can be measured only after managers are overseas. A unique phenomenon they face is **culture shock.** Although they all feel it, individuals differ widely in how they allow themselves to be affected by it.

Causes and Remedies   Culture shock is the term used for the more pronounced reactions to the psychological disorientation that most people experience when they move for an extended period of time into a culture markedly different from their own.[30] Culture shock and its severity may be a function of the individual's lack of adaptability but may equally be a result of the firm's lack of understanding of the situation into which the manager was sent. Often goals set for a subsidiary or a project may be unrealistic or the means by which they are to be reached may be totally inadequate. All of these lead to external manifestations of culture shock, such as bit-

FIGURE 20.4
Culture Shock Cycle for
an Overseas
Assignment

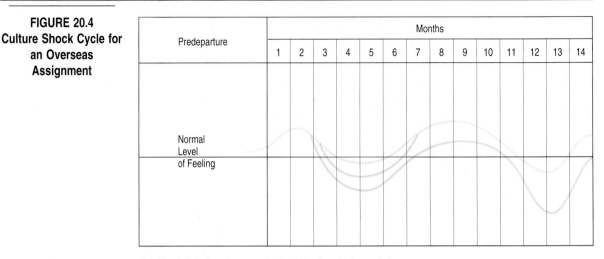

Note: Lines indicate the extreme severity with which culture shock may attack.
Source: L. Robert Kohls, *Survival Kit for Overseas Living* (Yarmouth, Maine: Intercultural Press, 1984), 68.

terness and even physical illness. In extreme cases, they can lead to hostility toward anything in the host environment.

The culture shock cycle for an overseas assignment is presented in Figure 20.4. Four distinct stages of adjustment exist during a foreign assignment. The length of the stages is highly individual. The four stages are:

1. **Initial Euphoria:** Enjoying the novelty, largely from the perspective of a spectator.
2. **Irritation and Hostility:** Experiencing cultural differences, such as the concept of time, through increased participation.
3. **Adjustment:** Adapting to the situation, which in some cases leads to biculturalism and even accusations from corporate headquarters of "going native."
4. **Reentry:** Returning home to face a possibly changed home environment.

The manager may fare better at the second stage than other members of the family, especially if their opportunities for work and other activities are severely restricted. The fourth stage may actually cause a reverse culture shock when the adjustment phase has been highly successful and the return home is not desired.

Firms themselves must take responsibility for easing one of the causes of culture shock: isolation. By maintaining contact with the manager beyond business-related communication, some of the shock may be alleviated. Exxon, for example, assigns each expatriate a contact person at headquarters to share general information.

Terrorism: Tangible Culture Shock   International terrorists have frequently targeted for attack U.S. corporate facilities, operations, and personnel abroad.[31] Of the 120 incidents against U.S. interests abroad in 1994, 43 were attacks on businesses.[32] Corporate reactions have ranged from letting terrorism have little effect on operations to abandoning certain markets. Some companies try to protect their managers in various ways by fortifying their homes and using local-sounding names to do business in troubled parts of the world.[33] Of course, insurance is available to cover key executives; the cost ranges from a few thousand dollars to hundreds of thousands a year depending on the extent and location of the company's operations. Leading insurers include American International Underwriters, Chubb & Son, and Lloyd's of London.[34] The threat of terrorist activity may have an effect on the company's operations beyond the immediate geographic area of concern. For example, when hostilities between Iraq and the United States started in early 1991, many multinational companies restricted or completely banned foreign travel.

Repatriation

Returning home may evoke mixed feelings on the part of the expatriate and the family. Their concerns are both professional and personal. Even in two years, dramatic changes may have occurred not only at home but also in the way the individual and the family perceive the foreign environment. At worst, reverse culture shock may emerge.

The most important professional issue is finding a proper place in the corporate hierarchy. If no provisions have been made, a returning manager may be caught in a holding pattern for an intolerable length of time. For this reason, Dow Chemical, for example, provides each manager embarking on an overseas assignment with a letter that promises a job at least equal in responsibility upon return. Furthermore, because of their isolation, assignments abroad mean greater autonomy and authority than similar domestic positions. Both financially and psychologically, many expatriates find the overseas position difficult to give up. Many executive perks, such as club memberships, will not be funded at home. Financial reasons, for example, make many officers of the U.S. and Foreign Commercial Service dread a summons for a two-year tour in the United States.

The family, too, may be reluctant to give up their special status. In India, for example, expatriate families have servants for most of the tasks they perform themselves at home. Many longer-term expatriates are shocked by increases in the prices of housing and education at home. For the many managers who want to stay abroad, this may mean a change of company or even career—from employee to independent business person. According to one study, 20 percent of the employees who complete overseas assignments want to leave the company upon their return.[35]

This alternative is not an attractive one for the company, which stands to lose valuable individuals who could become members of an international corps of managers. Therefore, planning for repatriation is necessary.[36] A four-step process can be used for this purpose. The first step involves an assessment of foreign assignments in terms of environmental constraints and corporate objectives, making sure that the latter are realistically defined. The second stage is preparation of the individual for an overseas assignment, which should include a clear understanding of when and how repatriation takes place. During the actual tour, the manager should be kept abreast of developments at headquarters, especially in terms of career paths. Finally, during the actual reentry, the manager should receive intensive organizational reorientation, reasonable professional adjustment time, and counseling for the entire family on matters of, for example, finance. A program of this type allows the expatriate to feel a close bond with headquarters regardless of geographical distance.

Compensation

A Japanese executive's salary in cash is quite modest by U.S. standards, but he is comfortable in the knowledge that the company will take care of him. Compensation is paternalistic; for example, a manager with two children in college and a sizable mortgage would be paid more than a childless manager in a comparable job. As this example suggests, Japanese compensation issues go beyond salary comparisons. They include exchange rates, local taxes, and what the money will buy in different countries. Many compensation packages include elements other than cash.[37]

A firm's international compensation program has to be effective in (1) providing an incentive to leave the home country on a foreign assignment, (2) maintaining a given standard of living, (3) taking into consideration career and family needs, and (4) facilitating reentry into the home country.[38] To achieve these objectives, firms pay a high premium beyond base salaries to induce managers to accept overseas assignments. The costs to the firm are 2 to 2.5 times the cost of maintaining a manager in a comparable position at home. For example, the average compensation package of a U.S. manager in Hong Kong is $225,500 (base salary is 47 percent of this figure) and for the British manager $170,500 (57 percent). U.S. firms traditionally offer their employees more high-value perks, such as bigger apartments.[39]

The compensation of the manager overseas can be divided into two general categories: (1) base salary and salary-related allowances and (2) nonsalary-related allowances. Although incentives to leave home are justifiable in both categories, they create administrative complications for the personnel department in tying them to packages at home and elsewhere. As the number of transfers increases, firms develop general policies for compensating the manager rather than negotiate individually on every aspect of the arrangement.

Base Salary and Salary-Related Allowances   A manager's **base salary** depends on qualifications, responsibilities, and duties, just as it would for a domestic position. Furthermore, criteria applying to merit increases, promotions, and other increases are administered as they are domestically. Equity and comparability with domestic positions are important, especially in ensuring that repatriation will not cause cuts in base pay.[40] For administrative and control purposes, the compensation and benefits function in multinational corporations is most often centralized.[41]

The cost of living varies considerably around the world, as can be seen in Global Perspective 20.3. The purpose of the **cost of living allowance (COLA)** is to enable the manager to maintain as closely as possible the same standard of living that he or she would have at home. COLA is calculated by determining a percentage of base salary that would be spent on goods and services at the foreign location. (Figures around 50 percent are typical.) The ratios will naturally vary as a function of income and family size. COLA tables for various U.S. cities (of which Washington, D.C., is the most often used) and locations worldwide are available through the U.S. State Department Allowances Staff and various consulting firms, such as Business International Corporation. Fluctuating exchange rates will of course have an effect on the COLA as well, and changes will call for reviews of the allowance. As an example, assume that living in Helsinki costs the manager 71 percent more than living in Washington, D.C. The manager's monthly pay is $4,000, and for his family of four, the disposable income is $2,150 (53.75 percent). Further assume that the dollar weakens from 5.5 Fmks to 4.7 Fmks. The COLA would be:

$$\$2,150 \times 171/100 \times 5.5/4.7 = \$4,302.$$

Global Perspective

20.3
How Far Will Your Salary Go?

Living cost comparisons for Americans residing in foreign areas are developed four times a year by the U.S. Department of State Allowances Staff. For each post, two measures are computed: (1) a government index to establish post allowances for U.S. government employees and (2) a local index for use by private organizations. The government index takes into consideration prices of goods imported to posts and price advantages available only to U.S. government employees.

The local index is used by many business firms and private organizations to determine the cost of living al-

lowance for their American employees assigned abroad. Local index measures for 12 key areas around the world are shown in the accompanying table. Maximum housing allowances, calculated separately, are also given.

The reports are issued four times annually under the title *U.S. Department of State Indexes of Living Costs Abroad, Quarters Allowances, and Hardship Differentials* by the U.S. Department of Labor.

Location	Cost of Living Index[a] (Washington, D.C. = 100)		Maximum Annual Housing Allowance[b]		
	Survey Date	Index	Effective Date	Family of 2	Family of 3–4
Buenos Aires, Argentina	Dec. 1993	155	NA	NA	NA
Canberra, Australia	Nov. 1993	112	NA	NA	NA
Brussels, Belgium	Oct. 1992	166	July 1994	$27,900	$30,690
Rio de Janeiro, Brazil	Mar. 1994	112	NA	NA	NA
Paris, France	Mar. 1994	161	July 1994	$31,700	$34,870
Frankfurt, Germany	Oct. 1992	156	July 1994	$21,900	$24,090
Hong Kong	Apr. 1993	130	NA	NA	NA
Tokyo, Japan	Oct. 1993	205	July 1994	$85,900	$94,490
Mexico City	Mar. 1993	112	June 1993	$37,500	$41,250
The Hague, Netherlands	Feb. 1994	138	July 1994	$32,300	$35,530
Geneva, Switzerland	May 1993	165	July 1994	$44,600	$49,060
London, U.K.	Apr. 1994	139	July 1994	$30,200	$33,220

[a]Excluding housing and education.
[b]For a family of three to four members with an annual income of $55,000 and over. Allowances are computed and paid in U.S. dollars.
NA = not available.

Similarly, if the local currency depreciated, the COLA would be less. When the cost of living is less than in the United States, no COLA is determined.

The **foreign service premium** is actually a bribe to encourage a manager to leave familiar conditions and adapt to new surroundings. Although the methods of paying the premium vary, as do its percentages, most firms pay it as a percentage of the base salary. The percentages range from 10 to 25 percent of base salary. One variation of the straightforward percentage is a sliding scale by amount—15 percent of the first $20,000, then 10 percent, and sometimes a ceiling beyond which a premium is not paid. Another variation is by duration, with the percentages decreasing with every year the manager spends abroad. Despite the controversial nature of foreign service premiums paid at some locations, they are a generally accepted competitive practice.

The environments in which a manager will work and the family will live vary dramatically. For example, consider being assigned to London or Brisbane versus Dar es Salaam or Port Moresby or even Bogota or Buenos Aires. Some locations may require little, if any, adjustment. Some call for major adaptation because of climatic differences; political instability; inadequacies in housing, education, shopping, or recreation; or overall isolation. For example, a family assigned to Beijing may find that schooling is difficult to arrange, with the result that younger children go to school in Tokyo and the older ones in the United States. To compensate for this type of expense and adjustment, firms pay **hardship allowances.** The allowances are based on U.S. State Department Foreign Post Differentials. The percentages vary from zero (for example, the manager in Helsinki) to 50 percent (as in Monrovia). The higher allowances typically include a danger pay extra added to any hardship allowance.[42]

Housing costs and related expenses are typically the largest expenditure in the expatriate manager's budget. Firms usually provide a **housing allowance** commensurate with the manager's salary level and position. When the expatriate is the country manager for the firm, the housing allowance will provide for suitable quarters in which to receive business associates. In most cases, firms set a range within which the manager must find housing. For common utilities, firms either provide an allowance or pay the costs outright.

One of the major determinants of the manager's lifestyle abroad is taxes. A U.S. manager earning $100,000 in Canada would pay nearly $40,000 in taxes—in excess of $10,000 more than in the United States. For this reason, 90 percent of U.S. multinational corporations have **tax-equalization** plans. When a manager's overseas taxes are higher than at home, the firm will make up the difference. However, in countries with a lower rate of taxation, the company simply keeps the difference. The firms' rationalization is that "it does not make any sense for the manager in Hong Kong to make more money than the guy who happened to land in Singapore."[43] Tax equalization is usually handled by accounting firms that make the needed calculations and prepare the proper forms. Managers can exclude a portion of their expatriate salary from U.S. tax; in 1995 the amount was $70,000, with the figure having steadily declined in the 1980s.

Nonsalary-Related Allowances   Other types of allowances are made available to ease the transition into the period of service abroad.[44] Typical allowances during the transition stage include (1) a relocation allowance to compensate for the additional expense of a move, such as purchase of electric converters; (2) a mobility allowance as an incentive to managers to go overseas, usually paid in a lump sum and as a substitute for the foreign service premium (some companies pay 50 percent at transfer, 50 percent at repatriation); (3) allowances related to housing, such as home sale or rental protection, shipment and storage of household goods, or provision of household furnishings in overseas locations; (4) automobile protection in terms of covering possible losses on the sale of a car or cars at transfer and having to buy others overseas, usually at a higher cost; (5) travel expenses, using economy-class transportation except for long flights (for example, from Washington to Taipei); and (6) temporary living expenses, which may become substantial if housing is not immediately available—as for the expatriate family that had to spend a year at a hotel in Beijing, for example.

Education for children is one of the major concerns of expatriate families. Free public schooling may not be available and the private alternatives expensive. In many cases, children may have to go to school in a different country. Firms will typically reimburse for such expenses in the form of an **education allowance.** In the case of college education, firms reimburse for one round-trip airfare every year, leaving tuition expenses to the family.

Finally, firms provide support for medical expenses, especially to provide medical services at a level comparable to the expatriate's home country. In some cases, this means traveling to another country for care; for example, from Malaysia to Singapore, where the medical system is the most advanced in southeast Asia.

Other issues should be covered by a clearly stated policy. Home leave is provided every year, typically after 11 months overseas, although some companies require a longer period. Home leaves are usually accompanied by consultation and training sessions at headquarters. Some hardship posts, such as Port Moresby, include rest and relaxation leaves to maintain morale. At some posts, club memberships are necessary because (1) the status of the manager requires them and (2) they provide family members with access to the type of recreation they are used to in the home environment. Because they are extremely expensive—for example, a "mandatory" golf club membership in Tokyo might cost thousands of dollars—the firm's assistance is needed.

Method of Payment   The method of payment, especially in terms of currency, is determined by a number of factors. The most common method is to pay part of the salary in the local currency and part in the currency of the manager's home country. Host-country regulations, ranging for taxation to the availability of foreign currency, will influence the decision. Firms themselves look at the situation from the accounting and administrative point of view and would like, in most cases, to pay in local currencies to avoid burdening the subsidiary. The expatriate naturally will want to have some of the compensation in his or her own currency for various reasons; for example, if exchange controls are in effect, to get savings out of the country upon repatriation may be very difficult.

Compensation of Host-Country Nationals   The compensation packages paid to local managers—cash, benefits, and privileges—are largely determined as a function of internal equity and external competitiveness. Internal equity may be complicated because of cultural differences in compensation; for example, in Japan a year-end bonus of an additional month's salary is common. On the other hand, some incentive programs to increase productivity may be unknown to some nationals. Furthermore, in many countries, the state provides benefits that may be provided by the firm elsewhere. Since the firm and its employees contribute to the programs by law, the services need not be duplicated.

External competitiveness depends on the market price of trained individuals and their attraction to the firm. External competitiveness is best assessed through surveys of compensation and benefits levels for a particular market. The firm must keep its local managers informed of the survey results to help them realize the value of their compensation packages.

MANAGING LABOR PERSONNEL

None of the firm's objectives can be realized without a labor force, which can become one of the firm's major assets or one of its major problems depending on the relationship that is established. Because of local patterns and legislation, headquarters' role in shaping the relations is mainly advisory, limited to setting the overall tone for the interaction. However, many of the practices adopted in one market or

Team building at Avery Label Systems in the United Kingdom, a division of Avery Dennison Corporation, has created "work cell teams" that have full product responsibility throughout the production process. Each team member can perform every other team member's job.

Source: Courtesy of Avery Dennison Corporation.

region may easily come under discussion in another, making it necessary for multinational corporations to set general policies concerning labor relations. Often multinational corporations have been instrumental in bringing about changes in the overall work environment in a country. And as decisions are made where to locate and how to streamline operations, education and training become important criteria for both countries and companies as seen in Global Perspective 20.4.

Labor strategy can be viewed from three perspectives: (1) the participation of labor in the affairs of the firm, especially as it affects performance and well-being; (2) the role and impact of unions in the relationship; and (3) specific human resource policies in terms of recruitment, training, and compensation.

Labor Participation in Management

Over the past quarter century, many changes have occurred in the traditional labor–management relationship as a result of dramatic changes in the economic environment and the actions of both firms and the labor force. The role of the worker is changing both at the level of the job performed and in terms of participation in the decision-making process. To enhance workers' role in decision making, various techniques have emerged: self-management, codetermination, minority board membership, and work councils. In striving for improvements in quality of work life, programs that have been initiated include flextime, quality circles, and work-flow reorganization. Furthermore, employee ownership has moved into the mainstream.

Labor Participation in Decision Making   The degree to which workers around the world can participate in corporate decision making varies considerably. Rights of information, consultation, and codetermination develop on three levels:

1. The shop-floor level, or direct involvement; for example, the right to be consulted in advance concerning transfers.
2. The management level, or through representative bodies; for example, work council participation in setting of new policies or changing of existing ones.
3. The board level; for example, labor membership on the board of directors.[45]

20.4
Workers of the World: Get Training!

Around the world, steps are being taken to break up often hierarchical business cultures. From its use of high-speed networking to its flexible management, Bangalore (India)-based Infosys resembles California rivals more than India's traditional hierarchical giants. In southern Italy, auto maker Fiat opened a $2.9 billion plant in an ambitious attempts to shake off hidebound work practices. Fiat spent $64 million training workers and engineers to operate in independent, multiskilled teams. Factory workers and office staff now work under the same roof.

The spread of information technology, moves to flatten hierarchies and empower workers, and rising global competition have begun to force a rethinking of work worldwide. Decisions such as facility location and how to provide more value to customers than competitors are will be influenced by education and training.

If change is coming, where will workers be best prepared? One key component will be education and training, increasingly seen by developed and developing countries alike as crucial to creating adaptable labor forces. In a ranking combining quality of public education, levels of secondary schooling and on-the-job training, computer literacy, and worker motivation, the twenty countries listed below were the highest ranked.

Training is especially needed as low-level jobs are lost to technology and the remaining jobs require higher skills. Even factory work will require more education.

Many Asian countries look best prepared. Beyond schools, Asian employers typically add considerable job training, creating a broad, technically literate labor pool. Governments across Latin America are waking to the need to follow Asia's lead. In Mexico, for example, fears about losing unskilled jobs to even cheaper Chinese or Indian workers have brought calls to improve education and training, particularly for the 40 percent of students who do not finish school.

At many companies, educational programs are a means of leveraging valuable company resources. Kodak has established eight training "centers of excellence" with functional specializations (for example, technical training and general business education). At AT&T, the number of customers who are students is rising. In China, AT&T has provided customized technical training to the government workers who will run the AT&T-supplied telecommunications networks.

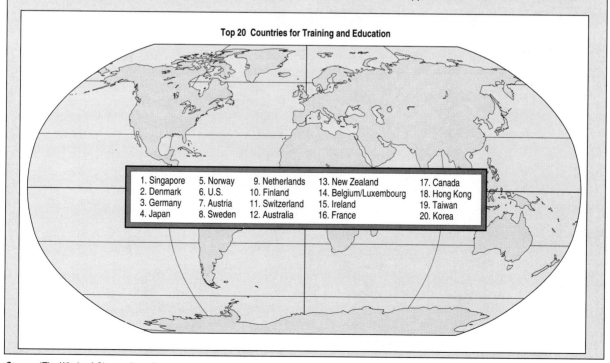

Top 20 Countries for Training and Education

1. Singapore	5. Norway	9. Netherlands	13. New Zealand	17. Canada
2. Denmark	6. U.S.	10. Finland	14. Belgium/Luxembourg	18. Hong Kong
3. Germany	7. Austria	11. Switzerland	15. Ireland	19. Taiwan
4. Japan	8. Sweden	12. Australia	16. France	20. Korea

Sources: "The Winds of Change Blow Everywhere," *Business Week,* October 17, 1994; and "School Days at Work: Firms See Training as Key to Empowerment," *Crossborder Monitor,* August 3, 1994, 1, 7.

Organized Labor as a Percentage of the Labor Force

Organized Labor

- 60% to 100%
- 40% to 60%
- 20% to 40%
- 0% to 20%

No current data available

Source: *The World Factbook, 1992*

	Direct Involvement of Workers[a]	Involvement of Representative Bodies[a]	Board Representation Standing[b]	Overall Standing[c]
Germany	3	1	1	A
Sweden	4	2	1	A
Norway	1	10	1	B
Netherlands	9	4	2	C
France	7	3	2	C
Belgium	5	6	3	D
Finland	2	9	3	D
Denmark	8	7	1	D
Israel	11	5	3	D
Italy	6	8	3	E
Great Britain	10	11	3	E

TABLE 20.3
Degree of Worker Involvement in Decision Making of Firms

[a]Involvement is rated on an 11-point scale, where 1 stands for the greatest degree of involvement and 11 for almost no involvement.
[b]All cases without any kind of board participation are coded 3; the right to appoint two or more members, 1; the in-between category, 2.
[c]Rankings are from high (A) to low (E).
Source: Industrial Democracy in Europe International Research Group, *Industrial Democracy in Europe* (Oxford, England: Clarendon Press,

The extent of worker participation in decision making in 11 countries is summarized in Table 20.3. Yugoslavia, before its breakup, used to have the highest amount of worker participation in any country; **self-management** was standard through workers' councils, which decided all major issues including the choice of managing director and supervisory board.[46]

In some countries, employees are represented on the supervisory boards to facilitate communication between management and labor by giving labor a clearer picture of the financial limits of management and by providing management with new awareness of labor's point of view. The process is called **codetermination.** In Germany, companies have a two-tiered management system with a supervisory board and the board of managers, which actually runs the firm. In a firm with 20,000 employees, for example, labor would have 10 of the 20 supervisory board slots divided in the following way: three places for union officials and the balance to be elected from the work force. At least one member must be a white-collar employee and one a managerial employee.[47] The supervisory board is legally responsible for the managing board. Reactions to codetermination vary. Six European nations—Sweden, the Netherlands, Norway, Luxembourg, Denmark, and France—have introduced their own versions and report lower levels of labor strife.[48] In some countries, labor has **minority participation.** In the Netherlands, for example, work councils can nominate (not appoint) board members and can veto the appointment of new members appointed by others. In other countries, such as the United States, codetermination has been opposed by unions as an undesirable means of cooperation, especially when management–labor relations are confrontational.

A tradition in labor relations, especially in Britain, is **work councils.** They provide labor a say in corporate decision making through a representative body, which may consist entirely of workers or of a combination of managers and workers. The councils participate in decisions on overall working conditions, training, transfers, work allocation, and compensation. In some countries, such as Finland and Belgium, workers' rights to direct involvement, especially as it involves their positions, are quite strong.

The countries described are unique in the world. In many countries and regions, workers have few, if any, of these rights. The result is long-term potential for labor strife in those countries and possible negative publicity elsewhere. In addition to labor groups and the media, investors and shareholders also are scrutinizing multinationals' track records on labor practices. As a result, a company investing in foreign countries should hold to international standards of safety and health, not simply local standards. This can be achieved, for example, through the use of modern equipment and training. Local labor also should be paid adequately. This increases the price of labor, yet ensures the best available talent and helps avoid charges of exploitation.[49] Companies subcontracting work to local or joint-venture factories need to evaluate industrial relations throughout the system not only to avoid lost production due to disruptions such as strikes, but to ensure that no exploitation exists at the facilities. Several large firms, such as Nike and Reebok, require subcontractors to sign agreements saying they will abide by minimum wage standards.[50]

Improvement of Quality of Work Life   The term **quality of work life** has come to encompass various efforts in the areas of personal and professional development. Its two clear objectives are to increase productivity and to increase the satisfaction of employees. Of course, programs leading to increased participation in corporate decision making are part of the programs; however, this section concentrates on individual job-related programs: work redesign, team building, and work scheduling.[51]

By adding both horizontal and vertical dimensions to the work, **work redesign programs** attack undesirable features of jobs. Horizontally, task complexity is added by incorporating work stages normally done before and after the stage being redesigned. Vertically, each employee is given more responsibility for making the decisions that affect how the work is done.[52] Japanese car manufacturers have changed some of the work routines in their plants in the United States. For example, at Honda's unit in Marysville, Ohio, workers have reacted favorably to the responsibilities they have been given, such as inspecting their own work and instructing others.[53] On the other hand, work redesign may have significant costs attached, including wage increases, facility change costs, and training costs.

Closely related to work redesign are efforts aimed at **team building.** For example, at Volvo's Kalmar plant in Sweden, work is organized so that groups are responsible for a particular, identifiable portion of the car, such as interiors. Each group has its own areas in which to pace itself and to organize the work. The group must take responsibility for the work, including inspections, whether it is performed individually or in groups. The group is informed about its performance through a computer system.[54] The team-building effort includes job rotation to enable workers to understand all facets of their jobs. Visiting American autoworkers were impressed with Volvo's physical working conditions, but they believed that teamwork would become tedious. Despite claims for increased worker participation, Americans expressed a preference for the more grass-roots unionism of the United States and its well-tested grievance procedure.[55] Another approach to team building makes use of **quality circles,** in which groups of workers regularly meet to discuss issues relating to their productivity. Pioneered in Japan, quality circles began to appear in U.S. industry in the mid-1970s.

Flexibility in **work scheduling** has led to changes in when and how long workers are at the workplace. **Flextime** allows workers to determine their starting and ending hours in a given workday; for example, they might arrive between 7:00 and 9:30 A.M. and leave between 3:00 and 5:30 P.M. The idea spread from Germany, where it originated in 1967, to the European Union and to other countries such as Switzerland, Japan, New Zealand, and the United States. Despite its advantages in reducing absenteeism, flextime is not applicable to industries using assembly lines. Flexible work scheduling has also led to compressed workweeks—for example, the four-day week—and job sharing, which allows a position to be filled by more than one person.

Firms around the world also have other programs for personal and professional development, such as career counseling and health counseling. All of them are dependent on various factors external and internal to the firm. Of the external factors, the most important are the overall characteristics of the economy and the labor force. Internally, either the programs must fit into existing organizational structures or management must be inclined toward change. In many cases, labor unions have been one of the major resisting forces. Their view is that firms are trying to prevent workers from organizing by allowing them to participate in decision making and management.

The Role of Labor Unions

When two of the world's largest producers of electrotechnology, Swedish Asea and Switzerland's Brown Boveri, merged to remain internationally competitive in a market dominated by a few companies such as General Electric, Siemens, Hitachi, and Toshiba, not everyone reacted positively to the alliance. For tax reasons, headquarters would not be located in Sweden, and this caused the four main Swedish labor unions to oppose the merger. They demanded that the Swedish government exercise its right to veto the undertaking because Swedish workers would no longer have a say in their company's affairs if it were headquartered elsewhere. Furthermore, Swedes objected to Brown Boveri's four subsidiaries in South Africa.[56]

The incident is an example of the role labor unions play in the operation of a multinational corporation. It also points up the concerns of local labor unions when they must deal with organizations directed from outside their national borders.

The role of labor unions varies from country to country, often because of local traditions in management–labor relations. The variations include the extent of union power in negotiations and the activities of unions in general. In Europe, especially in the northern European countries, collective bargaining takes place between an employers' association and an umbrella organization of unions, on either a national or a regional basis, establishing the conditions for an entire industry. On the other end of the spectrum, negotiations in Japan are on the company level, and the role of larger scale unions is usually consultative. Another striking difference emerges in terms of the objectives of unions and the means by which they attempt to attain them. In the United Kingdom, for example, union activity tends to be politically motivated and identified with political ideology. In the United States, the emphasis has always been on improving workers' overall quality of life.

Internationalization of business has created a number of challenges for labor unions. The main concerns that have been voiced are: (1) the power of the firm to move production from one country to another if attractive terms are not reached in a particular market; (2) the availability of data, especially financial information, to support unions' bargaining positions; (3) insufficient attention to local issues and problems while focusing on global optimization; and (4) difficulty in being heard by those who eventually make the decisions.[57]

Although the concerns are valid, all of the problems anticipated may not develop. For example, transferring production from one country to another in the short term may be impossible, and labor strife in the long term may well influence such moves. To maintain participation in corporate decision making, unions are taking

Global Perspective

20.5
Cooperation Worth Copying

The southern shore of Lake Ontario seems an unlikely spot to fight a border war with Mexico. But it is here that Xerox Corp. and its union, the Amalgamated Clothing and Textile Workers Union of America (ACTWU), have fought the Mexicans to a standoff for more than a decade. Three times since 1982, the 200 workers who put together the wire harnesses for Xerox copiers have been forced to boost quality and cut costs to keep their jobs from going to Mexico, where wage rates are less than $1 an hour.

The result has been an alliance between labor and management that is an experiment in how to continue to provide well-paying factory jobs in the United States in the face of global competition. Working with its union, Xerox is developing what it sees as the factory of the future, the "focus factory," with equipment on wheels so that it can literally be rearranged over the weekend to deliver new products quickly and cheaper than its competitors without sacrificing quality.

By 1982, just before the ACTWU and Xerox began to explore seriously the idea of plant-floor cooperation, Xerox found that it could move the operation to an industrial park near Mexico City and eliminate further jobs in addition to cost savings and meet the competition presented by the Japanese Canon and Ricoh. The union went to Xerox management and insisted that if employee involvement was to be a reality, the workers should be given a chance to develop a plan to squeeze enough costs (approximately $3 million) out of the operation to make it competitive with Mexico and save the jobs. This was accomplished. Furthermore, the workers argued that while their costs would be higher, the quality of their products was much higher.

The search for cost cuts continues. In late 1989, the company and the union formed the first of what they dubbed the "A-Delta-T" teams to study the actual performance of each work process to try to identify the best possible way that work can be performed in terms of cost. The work-study teams are trying to reduce inventories and streamline production for the just-in-time manufacturing process. The goal is to produce a quality product quicker and cheaper than anyone else in the world in a continuous effort to keep the manufacturing operation in the United States. So far it has been working well. While the efficiencies require fewer people to perform the job, expanding markets for the Xerox products have actually created new jobs.

Source: "Cooperation Worth Copying?" *The Washington Post,* December 13, 1992, H1, H6.

action individually and across national boundaries as seen in Global Perspective 20.5. Individual unions refer to contracts signed elsewhere when setting the agenda for their own negotiations. Supranational organizations such as the International Trade Secretariats and industry-specific organizations such as the International Metal Workers' Federation exchange information and discuss bargaining tactics. The goal is also to coordinate bargaining with multinational corporations across national boundaries. The International Labor Organization, a specialized agency of the United Nations, has an information bank on multinational corporations' policies concerning wage structures, benefits packages, and overall working conditions.

Human Resource Policies

The objectives of a human resource policy pertaining to workers are the same as for management: to anticipate the demand for various skills and to have in place programs that will ensure the availability of employees when needed. For workers, however, the firm faces the problem on a larger scale and does not have, in most cases, an expatriate alternative. This means that, among other things, when technology is transferred for a plant, it has to be adapted to the local work force.

Although most countries have legislation and restrictions concerning the hiring of expatriates, many of them—for example some of the EU countries and some oil-rich Middle Eastern countries—have offset labor shortages by importing large numbers of workers from countries such as Turkey and Jordan. The EU by design allows free movement of labor. A mixture of backgrounds in the available labor pool can put a strain on personnel development. As an example, the firm may incur considerable expense to provide language training to employees. In Sweden, a certain minimum amount of language training must be provided for all "guest workers" at the firm's expense.

Bringing a local labor force to the level of competency desired by the firm may also call for changes. As an example, managers at Honda's plant in Ohio encountered a number of problems: Labor costs were 50 percent higher and productivity 10 percent lower than in Japan. Automobiles produced there cost $500 more than the same models made in Japan and then delivered to the United States. Before Honda began to produce the Accord in the United States, it flew 200 workers representing all areas of the factory to Japan to learn to build Hondas the Sayama way and then to teach their coworkers the skills.[58]

Compensation of the work force is a controversial issue. Payroll expenses must be controlled for the firm to remain competitive; on the other hand, the firm must attract in appropriate numbers the type of workers it needs. The compensation packages of U.S.–based multinational companies have come under criticism, especially when their level of compensation is lower in developing countries than in the United States. Criticism has occurred even when the salaries or wages paid were substantially higher than the local average.[59]

Comparisons of compensation packages are difficult because of differences in the packages that are shaped by culture, legislation, collective bargaining, taxation, and individual characteristics of the job. In northern Europe, for example, new fathers can accompany their wives on a two-week paternity leave at the employer's expense.

SUMMARY

A business organization is the sum of its human resources. To recruit and retain a pool of effective people for each of its operations requires (1) personnel planning and staffing, (2) training activities, (3) compensation decisions, and (4) attention to labor–management relations.

Firms attract international managers from a number of sources, both internal and external. In the earlier stages of internationalization, recruitment must be external. Later, an internal pool often provides candidates for transfer. The decision then becomes whether to use home-country, host-country, or third-country nationals. If expatriate managers are used, selection policies should focus on competence, adaptability, and personal traits. Policies should also be set for the compensation and career progression of candidates selected for out-of-country assignments. At the same time, the firm must be attentive to the needs of local managers for training and development.

Labor can no longer be considered as simply services to be bought. Increasingly, workers are taking an active role in the decision making of the firm and in issues related to their own welfare. Various programs are causing dramatic organizational change, not only by enhancing the position of workers but by increasing the productivity of the work force as well. Workers employed by the firm usually are local, as are the unions that represent them. Their primary concerns in working for a multinational firm are job security and benefits. Unions therefore are cooperating across national boundaries to equalize benefits for workers employed by the same firm in different countries.

Key Terms and Concepts

lingua franca

factual cultural knowledge

area expertise

interpretive cultural
  knowledge

adaptability screening

orientation program

culture shock

expatriate

base salary

cost of living allowance
  (COLA)

foreign service premium

hardship allowance

housing allowance

tax equalization

education allowance

self-management

codetermination

minority participation

work councils

quality of work life

work redesign programs

team building

quality circles

work scheduling

flextime

Questions for Discussion

1. Is a "supranational executive corps," consisting of cosmopolitan individuals of multiple nationalities who would be an asset wherever utilized, a possibility for any corporation?

2. Comment on this statement by Lee Iacocca: "If a guy wants to be a chief executive 25 or 50 years from now, he will have to be well rounded. There will be no more of 'Is he a good lawyer, is he a good marketing guy, is he a good finance guy?' His education and his experience will make him a total entrepreneur in a world that has really turned into one huge market. He better speak Japanese or German, he better understand the history of both of those countries and how they got to where they are, and he better know their economics pretty cold."

3. What additional benefit is brought into the expatriate selection and training process by adaptability screening?

4. Develop general principles that firms could use in dealing with terrorism, apart from pulling out of a given market.

5. A manager with a current base salary of $100,000 is being assigned to Lagos, Nigeria. Assuming that you are that manager, develop a compensation and benefits package for yourself in terms of both salary-related and nonsalary-related items.

6. What accounts for the success of Japanese companies with both American unions and the more ferocious British unions? In terms of the changes that have come about, are there winners or losers among management and workers? Could both have gained?

7. How transferable are quality-of-work-life programs from one market to another? What internal and external variables determine their level of acceptance and success?

8. Develop general policies that the multinational corporation should follow in dealing (or choosing not to deal) with a local labor union.

Recommended Readings

Adler, Nancy J., and Dafna N. Izraeli, eds. *Competitive Frontiers: Women Managers in a Global Economy.* Cambridge, Mass.: Blackwell Business, 1994.

Austin, James. *Managing in Developing Countries.* New York: Free Press, 1990.

Bamber, Greg J., and Russell D. Lansbury, eds. *International and Comparative Industrial Relations.* London, England: Allen & Unwin, 1989.

Black, J. Stewart, Hal B. Gregsen, and Mark E. Mendenhall. *Global Assignments.* San Francisco, Calif.: Jossey-Bass Publishers, 1992.

Casse, Pierre. *Training for the Multicultural Manager.* Washington, D.C.: SIETAR, 1987.

Dowling, Peter J., and Randall S. Schuler. *International Dimensions of Human Resource Management.* Boston: PWS–Kent, 1990.

Harris, Philip, and Robert T. Moran. *Managing Cultural Differences.* Houston, Tex.: Gulf, 1990.

Hodgetts, Richard, and Fred Luthans. *International Management.* New York: McGraw-Hill, 1994.

Holley, William H., and Kenneth M. Jennings. *The Labor Relations Process.* Fort Worth, Tex.: Dryden Press, 1994.

Lewis, Tom, and Robert Jungman, eds. *On Being Foreign: Culture Shock in Short Fiction.* Yarmouth, Maine: Intercultural Press, 1986.

Marquardt, Michael J., and Dean W. Engel. *Global Resource Development.* Englewood Cliffs, N.J.: Prentice-Hall, 1993.

Mendenhall, Mark, and Gary Oddou. *International Human Resource Management.* Boston: PWS–Kent, 1991.

Pucik, Vladimir, Noel M. Tichy, and Carole K. Barnett. *Globalizing Management: Creating and Leading the Competitive Organization.* New York: John Wiley, 1992.

Notes

1. Herbert G. Heneman and Donald P. Schwab, "Overview of the Personnel/Human Resource Function," in *Perspectives on Personnel/Human Resource Management,* eds. Herbert G. Heneman and Donald P. Schwab (Homewood, Ill.: Irwin, 1986), 3–11.

2. Richard D. Hays, "Expatriate Selection: Insuring Success and Avoiding Failure," *Journal of International Business Studies* 5 (Summer 1974): 25–37.

3. "Ford's Brave New World," *The Washington Post,* October 16, 1994, H1, H4.

4. Christopher A. Bartlett and Sumantra Ghoshal, "What Is a Global Manager?" *Harvard Business Review* 70 (September–October 1992): 124–132.

5. Jan van Rosmalen, "Internationalising Heineken: Human Resource Policy in a Growing International Company," *International Management Development* (Summer 1985): 11–13.

6. Floris Majlers, "Inside Unilever: The Evolving Transnational Company," *Harvard Business Review* 70 (September–October 1992): 46–52.

7. Randall S. Schuler, Susan E. Jackson, Peter J. Dowling, and Denice E. Welch, "The Formation of an International Joint Venture: Davidson Instrument Panel," in *International Human Resource Management,* eds. Mark Mendenhall and Gary Oddou (Boston: PWS–Kent, 1991), 83–96.

8. Peter Lorange, "Human Resource Management in Multinational Cooperative Ventures," *Human Resources Management* 25 (Winter 1986): 133–148.

9. Lawrence G. Franko, "Who Manages Multinational Enterprises?" *Columbia Journal of World Business* 8 (Summer 1973): 30–42.

10. Carla Rapoport, "The Switch Is On in Japan," *Fortune,* May 21, 1990, 144.

11. Anders Edström and Peter Lorange, "Matching Strategy and Human Resources in Multinational Corporations," *Journal of International Business Studies* 16 (Fall 1985): 125–137.

12. Elizabeth Klein, "The U.S./Japanese HR Culture Clash," *Personnel Journal* 71 (November 1992): 30–38.

13. "How Business Is Creating Europe Inc.," *Business Week,* September 7, 1987, 40–41.

14. Rabindra Kanungo and Richard W. Wright, "A Cross-Cultural Comparative Study of Managerial Job Attitudes," *Journal of International Business Studies* 14 (Fall 1983): 115–129.

15. Lester B. Korn, "How the Next CEO Will Be Different," *Fortune,* May 22, 1990, 157–161.

16. "The Elusive Euromanager," *The Economist,* November 7, 1993, 83.

17. Jean E. Heller, "Criteria for Selecting an International Manager," *Personnel* (May–June 1980): 18–22.

18. Walter Kiechel, "Our Person in Pomparippu," *Fortune,* October 17, 1983, 213–218.

19. Richard D. Hays, "Ascribed Behavioral Determinants of Success-Failure among U.S. Expatriate Managers," *Journal of International Business Studies* 2 (Summer 1971): 40–46.

20. Richard Pascale, "Fitting New Employees into the Corporate Culture," *Fortune,* May 28, 1984, 28–40.

21. *Compensating International Executives* (New York: Business International, 1970), 35.

22. Lennie Copeland, "Training Americans to Do Business Overseas," *Training,* July 1984, 22–33.

23. Lee Smith, "Japan's Autocratic Managers," *Fortune,* January 7, 1985, 14–23.

24. "Gauging a Family's Suitability for a Stint Overseas," *Business Week,* April 16, 1979, 127–130.

25. "Global Managing," *The Wall Street Journal Europe,* January 10–11, 1992, 1, 20.

26. Nancy J. Adler, "Expecting International Success: Female Managers Overseas," *Columbia Journal of World Business* 19 (Fall 1984): 79–85.

27. Nancy J. Adler, "Pacific Basin Managers: A Gaijin, Not a Woman," *Human Resource Management* 26 (Summer 1987): 169–191.

28. "Gauging a Family's Suitability for a Stint Overseas."

29. Rosalie Tung, "Selection and Training of Personnel for Overseas Assignments," *Columbia Journal of World Business* 16 (Spring 1981): 68–78.

30. L. Robert Kohls, *Survival Kit for Overseas Living* (Yarmouth, Maine: Intercultural Press, 1979), 62–68.

31. Harvey Iglarsh, "Terrorism and Corporate Costs," *Terrorism* 10 (Fall 1987): 22–25.

32. Data provided by Pinkerton Risk Assessment Services, May 19, 1995.

33. Michael J. Harvey, "A Survey of Corporate Programs for Managing Terrorist Threats," *Journal of International Business Studies* 24 (number 3, 1993): 465–478.

34. Mary Helen Frederick, "Keeping Safe," *International Business,* October, 1992, 68–69.

35. Nancy J. Adler, *International Dimensions of Organizational Behavior* (Boston: PWS–Kent, 1990), Chapter 4.

36. Michael G. Harvey, "The Other Side of Foreign Assignments: Dealing with the Repatriation Dilemma," *Columbia Journal of World Business* 16 (Spring 1981): 79–85.

37. Lisa Miller Mesdag, "Are You Underpaid?" *Fortune,* March 19, 1984, 20–25.

38. Raymond J. Stone, "Compensation: Pay and Perks for Overseas Executives," *Personnel Journal* (January 1986): 64–69.

39. "Americans Lead the HK Perks Race," *Sunday Morning Post,* July 12, 1992, 14.

40. *1987 Professional Development Seminar: International Compensation* (Phoenix, Ariz.: American Compensation Association, 1987), module 1.

41. Brian Toyne and Robert J. Kuhne, "The Management of the International Executive Compensation and Benefits Process," *Journal of International Business Studies* 14 (Winter 1983): 37–49.

42. U.S. Department of State, *Indexes of Living Costs Abroad, Quarters Allowances, and Hardship Differentials,* January 1995, Table 1.

43. "How to Make a Foreign Job Pay," *Business Week,* December 23, 1985, 84–85.

44. *1987 Professional Development Seminar: International Compensation,* modules 4 and 5.

45. Industrial Democracy in Europe International Research Group, *Industrial Democracy in Europe* (Oxford, England: Clarendon Press, 1981), Chapter 14.

46. Osmo A. Wiio, *Yritysdemokratia ja Muuttuva Yhteiskunta* (Tapiola, Finland: Weilin + Goos, 1970), Chapter 13.

47. E. B. Hoffman, "The German Way of Industrial Relations—Could We, Should We, Import It?" *Across the Board,* October 1977, 38–47.

48. Richard D. Robinson, *Internationalization of Business* (Hinsdale, Ill.: Dryden, 1986), Chapter 3.

49. "MNCs Under Fire to Link Trade with Global Labor Rights," *Crossborder Monitor,* May 25, 1994, 1.

50. "Labor Strife in Indonesia Spotlights Development Challenge," *Crossborder Monitor,* May 25, 1994, 7.

51. Herman Gadon, "Making Sense of Quality of Work Life Programs," *Business Horizons* 27 (January–February 1984): 42–46.

52. Antone Alber, "The Costs of Job Enrichment," *Business Horizons* 22 (February 1984): 60–72.

53. Faye Rice, "America's New No. 4 Automaker—Honda," *Fortune,* October 28, 1985, 26–29.

54. Pehr G. Gyllenhammar, "How Volvo Adapts Work to People," *Harvard Business Review* 55 (July–August 1977): 24–28.

55. Joe Kelly and Kamran Khozan, "Participative Management: Can It Work?" *Business Horizons* 23 (August 1980): 74–79.

56. "Asean Ammattiliitot Vaativat Suuryhtyman Paapaikkaa Ruotsiin," *Helsingin Sanomat,* September 16, 1987, 34.

57. S. B. Prasad and Y. Krishna Shetty, *An Introduction to Multinational Management* (Englewood Cliffs, N.J.: Prentice-Hall, 1976), Appendix 8-A.

58. Rice, "America's New No. 4 Automaker—Honda."

59. Oliver Williams, "Who Cast the First Stone?" *Harvard Business Review* 62 (September–October 1984): 151–160.

CHAPTER 21

Organization and Control in International Operations

Borderless Management

Ford Motor Co. has been an international enterprise from the days of Henry Ford selling the Model A. Five years after its founding in 1903, it set up its first overseas sales branch in France and by 1911 it was making cars in Britain. But more than 80 years and dozens of overseas endeavors later, Ford still is trying to figure out what it means to be a global company.

The latest reorganization at Ford in April of 1994 was dramatic: Ford merged its large and culturally distinct European and North American auto operations and plans later to fold in its Latin American and Asia-Pacific operations. The rationale, according to Ford's Chairman Alexander J. Trotman, is to make more efficient use of its engineering and product development resources against rapidly globalizing rivals in the "all out global car race." The potential advantages are considerable. If resources can be pooled and turf wars between national entities eliminated, Ford estimates that its savings can reach $3 billion a year. Planning and implementation have to work, however. When a company such as Ford centralizes all product development, a mistake that would have been confined to one country in the former organizational structure could become a global disaster. "If you misjudge the market, you are wrong in 15 countries rather than only one," said one European executive.

Ford's move makes one thing clear: With world markets rapidly merging and converging, companies that have been slow to globalize their operations will now have to scramble to catch up. In May, 1994, IBM reorganized its marketing and sales organizations into 14 worldwide industry groups, such as banking, retail, and insurance. In moving away from an organization based on geography, IBM hoped to enhance its responsiveness to customers, many of which themselves are global operators. Soon after IBM's announcement, drug giant Bristol-Myers Squibb Co. revamped its consumer business by installing a new chief responsible for its worldwide consumer medicines such as Excedrin and Bufferin. A new unit was also formed to have worldwide responsibility for its Clairol and other hair-care products.

Globalization is not taking any one form. Indeed, most companies have adopted mixed organizational formats. Unilever plc uses a classic regional structure with local managers in three areas of the world: Africa/Middle East, Latin America, and East Asia/Pacific. But in Europe and North America, where consumer preferences are more similar, the structure is different. The president of Lever Brothers Co. in New York, for example, reports to the Unilever worldwide detergents-products coordinator in London.

Simply redrawing lines on an organization chart will not make a company global. Building trust and creating a common vision among the entities that will now cooperate rather than work independently is the critical task. The effort will focus on eliminating headquarters myopia and use of cross-cultural teams to foster a one-company culture.

Source: "Borderless Management: Companies Strive to Become Truly Stateless," *Business Week,* May 23, 1994, 24–25; "IBM Revamps Sales Teams," *Advertising Age,* May 9, 1994, 2; Regina Fazio Maruca, "The Right Way to Go Global: An Interview with Whirlpool CEO David Whitwam," *Harvard Business Review* 72 (March–April 1994): 134–145; and "The Global Firm: R.I.P.," *The Economist,* February 6, 1993, 69.

As companies evolve from purely domestic to multinational, their organizational structure and control systems must change to reflect new strategies. With growth comes diversity in terms of products and services, geographic markets, and people in the company itself, bringing along a set of challenges for the company. Two critical issues are basic to all of these challenges: (1) the type of organization that provides the best framework for developing worldwide strategies and maintaining flexibility with respect to individual markets and operations, and (2) the type and degree of control to be exercised from headquarters to maximize total effort. Organizational structures and control systems have to be adjusted as market conditions change, as seen in the chapter's opening vignette.

This chapter will focus on the advantages and disadvantages of various organizational structures, as well as their appropriateness at different stages of internationalization. A determining factor is where decision-making authority within the organizational structure will be placed. Also, the roles of the different entities that make up the organization need to be defined. The chapter will also outline the need for devising a control system to oversee the international operations of the company, emphasizing the additional control instruments needed beyond those used in domestic business and the control strategies of multinational corporations. The appropriateness and eventual cost of the various control approaches will vary as the firm expands its international operations. The overall objective of the chapter is to study the intraorganizational relationships critical to the firm's attempt to optimize its competitiveness.

ORGANIZATIONAL STRUCTURE

The basic functions of an organization are to provide (1) a route and locus of decision making and coordination and (2) a system for reporting and communications. Authority and communication networks are typically depicted in the organizational chart.

Organizational Designs

The basic configurations of international organizations correspond to those of purely domestic ones; the greater the degree of internationalization, the more complex the structures can become. The types of structures that companies use to manage foreign activities can be divided into three categories, based on the degree of internationalization:

1. Little or no formal organizational recognition of international activities of the firm. This category ranges from domestic operations handling an occasional international transaction on an ad hoc basis to firms with separate export departments.
2. International division. Firms in this category recognize the ever-growing importance of the international involvement.
3. Global organizations. These can be structured by product, area, function, process, or customer, but ignore the traditional domestic-international split.

Hybrid structures may exist as well, in which one market may be structured by product, another by areas. Matrix organizations have merged in large multinational corporations to combine product-specific, regional, and functional expertise. As worldwide competition has increased dramatically in many industries, the latest organizational response is networked global organizations in which heavy flows of hardware, software, and personnel take place between strategically interdependent units to establish greater global integration.

Little or No Formal Organization   In the very early stages of international involvement, domestic operations assume responsibility for international activities. The role of international activities in the sales and profits of the corporation is initially so minor that no organizational adjustment takes place. No consolidation of information or authority over international sales is undertaken or is necessary. Transactions are conducted on a case-by-case basis, either by the resident expert or quite often with the help of facilitating agents, such as freight forwarders.

As demand from the international marketplace grows and interest within the firm expands, the organizational structure will reflect it. As shown in Figure 21.1, an export department appears as a separate entity. This may be an outside export

FIGURE 21.1   The Export Department Structure

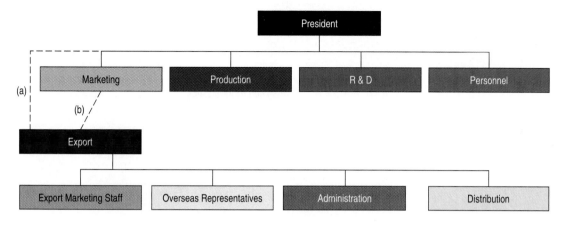

management company—that is, an independent company that becomes the de facto export department of the firm. This is an indirect approach to international involvement in that very little experience is accumulated within the firm itself. Alternatively, a firm may establish its own export department, hiring a few seasoned individuals to take responsibility for international activities. Organizationally, the department may be a subdepartment of marketing (alternative b in Figure 21.1) or may have equal ranking with the various functional departments (alternative a). The choice will depend on the importance assigned to overseas activities by the firm. The export department is the first real step toward internationalizing the organizational structures; it should be a full-fledged marketing organization and not merely a sales organization.

Licensing as an international entry mode may be assigned to the R&D function despite its importance to the overall international strategy of the firm. A formal liaison among the export, marketing, production, and R&D functions has to be formed for the maximum utilization of licensing.[1] If licensing indeed becomes a major activity for the firm, a separate manager should be appointed.

The more the firm becomes involved in foreign markets, the more quickly the export department structure will become obsolete. For example, the firm may undertake joint ventures or direct foreign investment, which require those involved to have functional experience. The firm therefore typically establishes an international division.

Some firms that acquire foreign production facilities pass through an additional stage in which foreign subsidiaries report directly to the president or to a manager specifically assigned the duty.[2] However, the amount of coordination and control that are required quickly establish the need for a more formal international organization in the firm.

The International Division   The international division centralizes in one entity, with or without separate incorporation, all of the responsibility for international activities, as illustrated in Figure 21.2. The approach aims to eliminate a possible bias against international operations that may exist if domestic divisions are allowed to serve international customers independently. In some cases, international markets

FIGURE 21.2   **The International Division Structure**

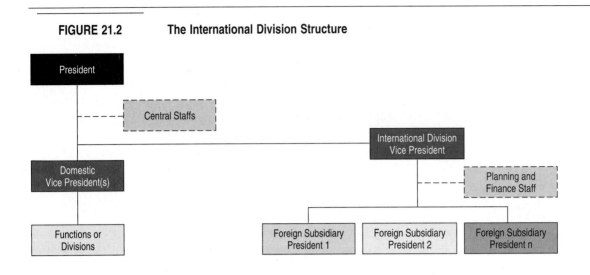

have been treated as secondary to domestic markets. The international division concentrates international expertise, information flows concerning foreign market opportunities, and authority over international activities. However, manufacturing and other related functions remain with the domestic divisions to take advantage of economies of scale.

To avoid putting the international division at a disadvantage in competing for products, personnel, and corporate services, coordination between domestic and international operations is necessary. Coordination can be achieved through a joint staff or by requiring domestic and international divisions to interact in strategic planning and to submit the plans to headquarters. Further, many corporations require and encourage frequent interaction between domestic and international personnel to discuss common problems in areas such as product planning. At Loctite Corporation, for example, coordination is also important because domestic operations are typically organized along product or functional lines, whereas international divisions are geographically oriented.

International divisions best serve firms with few products that do not vary significantly in terms of their environmental sensitivity and with international sales and profits that are still quite insignificant compared with those of the domestic divisions.[3] Companies may outgrow their international divisions as their international sales grow in significance, diversity, and complexity. A number of U.S.–based companies in the 1970s started the shift from a traditional organizational structure with an independent international division to entities built around worldwide or global structures with no differentiation between "domestic" and "international" operations.[4]

Size in itself is not a limitation on the use of the international division structure. Some of the world's largest corporations rely on international divisions.[5] The management of these companies believes that specialization is needed, primarily in terms of the environment.

Global Organizational Structures   Global structures have grown out of competitive necessity. In many industries, competition is on a global basis, with a result that companies must have a high degree of reactive capability. European firms have traditionally had a global structure because of the relatively small size of their domestic markets. N.V. Philips, Nestlé, or Nokia, for example, never could have grown to their current status by relying only on their home markets.

Six basic types of global structures are available:

1. Global product structure, in which product divisions are responsible for all manufacture and marketing worldwide.
2. Global area structure, in which geographic divisions are responsible for all manufacture and marketing in their respective areas.
3. Global functional structures, in which functional areas (such as production, marketing, finance, and personnel) are responsible for the worldwide operations of their own functional area.
4. Global customer structures, in which operations are structured based on distinct worldwide customer groups.
5. Mixed—or hybrid—structures, which may combine the other alternatives.
6. Matrix structures, in which operations have reporting responsibility to more than one group (typically, product, functions, or area).

Product Structure The **product structure** is the form most often used by multinational corporations.[6] The approach gives worldwide responsibility to strategic business units for the marketing of their product lines, as shown in Figure 21.3. Most consumer-product firms use some form of this approach, mainly because of the diversity of their products. One of the major benefits of the approach is improved cost efficiency through centralization of manufacturing facilities. This is crucial in industries in which competitive position is determined by world market share, which in

FIGURE 21.3   **The Global Product Structure**

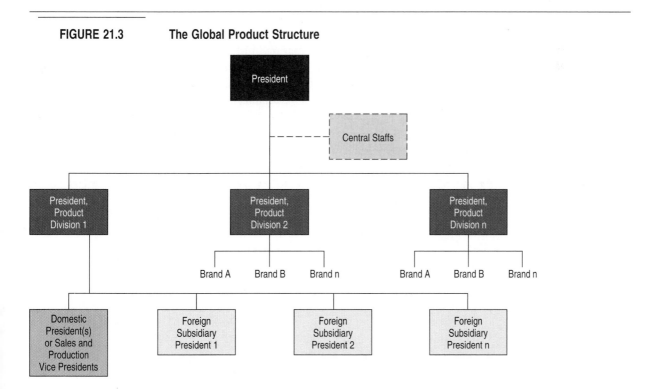

A truckload of tires from Vienna arrives in Budapest, site of Goodyear's first sales office in central Europe.
Source: Peter Korniss/Black Star.

turn is often determined by the degree to which manufacturing is rationalized.[7] Adaptation to this approach may cause problems because it is usually accompanied by consolidation of operations and plant closings. A good example is Black & Decker, which in the mid-1980s rationalized many of its operations in its worldwide competitive effort against Makita, the Japanese power tool manufacturer. Similarly, Goodyear reorganized itself in 1988 into a single global organization with a complete business-team approach for tires and general products. The move was largely prompted by tightening worldwide competition.[8]

Other benefits of the product structure are the ability to balance the functional inputs needed for a product and the ability to react quickly to product-specific problems in the marketplace. Even smaller brands receive individual attention. Product-specific attention is important because products vary in terms of the adaptation they need for different foreign markets. All in all, the product approach is ideally suited to the development of a global strategic focus in response to global competition.

At the same time, the product structure fragments international expertise within the firm because a central pool of international experience no longer exists. The structure assumes that managers will have adequate regional experience or advice to allow them to make balanced decisions. Coordination of activities among the various product groups operating in the same markets is crucial to avoid unnecessary duplication of basic tasks. For some of these tasks, such as market research, special staff functions may be created and then filled by the product divisions when needed. If they lack an appreciation for the international dimension, product managers may focus their attention only on the larger markets or only on the domestic, and fail to take the long-term view.

Area Structure   The second most used approach is the **area structure,** illustrated in Figure 21.4. Such firms are organized on the basis of geographical areas; for example, operations may be divided into those dealing with North America, the Far East, Latin America, and Europe. Ideally, no special preference is given to the region in which the headquarters is located—for example, North America or Europe. Central staffs are responsible for providing coordination support for worldwide planning and control activities performed at headquarters.

Regional integration is playing a major role in area structuring; for example, many multinational corporations have located their European headquarters in Brussels,

FIGURE 21.4   The Global Area Structure

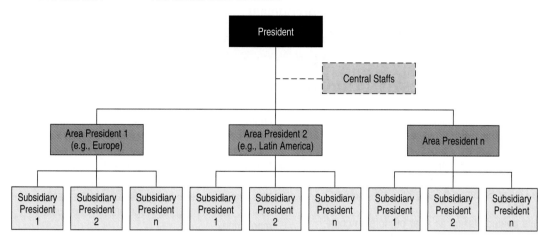

where the EU has its headquarters. Procter & Gamble's Latin American subsidiaries report to the Latin American headquarters in Caracas, Venezuela, rather than to Cincinnati where headquarters for the operations used to exist.[9] Organizational changes made at 3M Company as a result of NAFTA are recounted in the Global Perspective 21.1.

The area approach follows the marketing concept most closely because individual areas and markets are given concentrated attention. If market conditions with respect to product acceptance and operating conditions vary dramatically, the area approach is the one to choose. Companies opting for this alternative typically have relatively narrow product lines with similar end uses and end users. However, expertise is needed in adapting the product and its marketing to local market conditions. Once again, to avoid duplication of effort in product management and in functional areas, staff specialists—for product categories, for example—may be used.

Without appropriate coordination from the staff, essential information and experience may not be transferred from one regional entity to another. Also, if the company expands its product lines and if end markets begin to diversify, the area structure may become inappropriate.

Functional Structure   Of all the approaches, the **functional structure** is the simplest from the administrative viewpoint because it emphasizes the basic tasks of the firm—for example, manufacturing, sales, and research and development. The approach, illustrated in Figure 21.5, works best when both products and customers are relatively few and similar in nature. Coordination is typically the key problem, therefore, staff functions have been created to interact between the functional areas. Otherwise, the company's marketing and regional expertise may not be exploited to the fullest extent possible.

A variation of the functional approach is one that uses processes as a basis for structure. The **process structure** is common in the energy and mining industries, where one corporate entity may be in charge of exploration worldwide and another may be responsible for the actual mining operations.

Customer Structure   Firms may also organize their operations using the **customer structure,** especially if the customer groups they serve are dramatically different—

FIGURE 21.6   **The Global Mixed Structure**

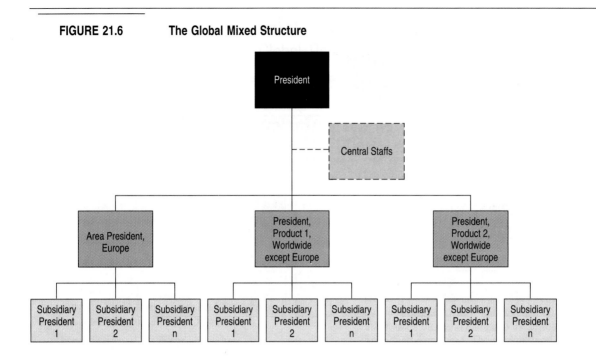

Organizational matrices integrate the various approaches already discussed, as the N.V. Philips example in Figure 21.7 illustrates. The eight product divisions (which are then divided into 60 product groups) have rationalized manufacturing to provide products for continentwide markets rather than lines of products for individual markets. Philips has three general types of country organizations. In "key" markets, such as the United States, France, and Japan, product divisions manage their own marketing as well as manufacturing. In "local business" countries, such as Nigeria and Peru, the organizations function as importers from product divisions and if manufacturing occurs it is purely for the local market. In "large" markets, such as Brazil, Spain, and Taiwan, a hybrid arrangement is used, depending on the size and situation. The product divisions and the national subsidiaries interact in a matrixlike configuration, with the product divisions responsible for the globalization dimension and the national subsidiaries responsible for local representation and coordination of common areas of interest, such as recruiting.

Matrices vary in terms of their number of dimensions. For example, Dow Chemical's three-dimensional matrix consists of five geographic areas, three major functions (marketing, manufacturing, and research), and more than 70 products. The matrix approach helps cut through enormous organizational complexities in making business managers, functional managers, and strategy managers cooperate. However, the matrix requires sensitive, well-trained middle managers who can cope with problems that arise from reporting to two bosses—for example, a product-line manager and an area manager. At 3M, for example, every management unit has a multidimensional reporting relationship, which may cross functional, regional, or operational lines. For example, on a regional basis, group managers in Europe report administratively to a vice president of operations for Europe, but report functionally to group vice presidents at headquarters in Minneapolis-St. Paul.[14]

Most companies have found the matrix arrangement problematic.[15] The dual reporting channel easily causes conflict, complex issues are forced into a two-dimen-

FIGURE 21.5   The Global Function Structure

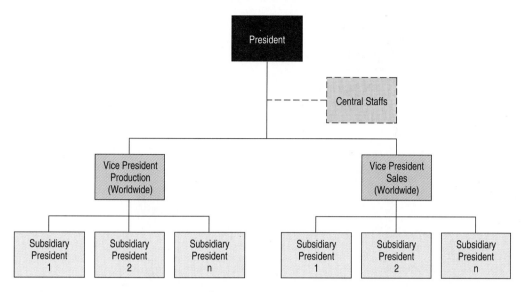

Mixed Structure   In some cases, mixed, or hybrid, organizations exist. A **mixed structure,** such as the one shown in Figure 21.6, combines two or more organizational dimensions simultaneously. It permits adequate attention to product, area, or functional needs as is needed by the company. The approach may only be a result of a transitional period after a merger or an acquisition, or it may come about due to unique market characteristics or product line. It may also provide a useful structure before the implementation of a worldwide matrix structure.[10] At Procter & Gamble, for example, U.S.–based operations are organized along product lines, whereas international operations are by area through four continental groups. The area organizations are divided further, for example, European operations into Northern Europe, Central Europe, Southern Europe, and Africa/Middle East. For Disposables and Beverages, the profit-and-loss responsibility has been established on a pan-European basis. As a consequence of the Richardson-Vicks acquisition, there still are two separate sets of European operations. Given environmental trends, P&G eventually may move from an area emphasis to more of a product focus.[11]

    Naturally, organizational structures are never as clear-cut and simple as presented here. Whatever the basic format, product, functional, and area inputs are needed. Alternatives could include an initial product structure that would subsequently have regional groupings or an initial regional structure with subsequent product groupings. However, in the long term, coordination and control across such structures become tedious.

Matrix Structure   Many multinational corporations, in an attempt to facilitate planning for, organizing, and controlling interdependent businesses, critical resources, strategies, and geographic regions, have adopted the **matrix structure.**[12] Eastman Kodak shifted from a functional organization to a matrix system based on business units. Business is driven by a worldwide business unit (for example, photographic products or commercial and information systems) and implemented by a geographic unit (for example, Europe or Latin America). The geographical units, as well as their country subsidiaries, serve as the "glue" between autonomous product operations.[13]

FIGURE 21.6   The Global Mixed Structure

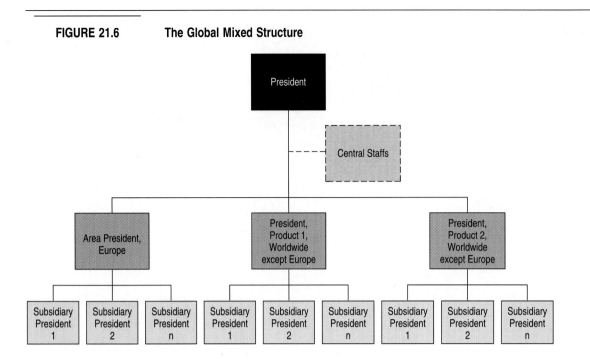

Organizational matrices integrate the various approaches already discussed, as the N.V. Philips example in Figure 21.7 illustrates. The eight product divisions (which are then divided into 60 product groups) have rationalized manufacturing to provide products for continentwide markets rather than lines of products for individual markets. Philips has three general types of country organizations. In "key" markets, such as the United States, France, and Japan, product divisions manage their own marketing as well as manufacturing. In "local business" countries, such as Nigeria and Peru, the organizations function as importers from product divisions and if manufacturing occurs it is purely for the local market. In "large" markets, such as Brazil, Spain, and Taiwan, a hybrid arrangement is used, depending on the size and situation. The product divisions and the national subsidiaries interact in a matrixlike configuration, with the product divisions responsible for the globalization dimension and the national subsidiaries responsible for local representation and coordination of common areas of interest, such as recruiting.

Matrices vary in terms of their number of dimensions. For example, Dow Chemical's three-dimensional matrix consists of five geographic areas, three major functions (marketing, manufacturing, and research), and more than 70 products. The matrix approach helps cut through enormous organizational complexities in making business managers, functional managers, and strategy managers cooperate. However, the matrix requires sensitive, well-trained middle managers who can cope with problems that arise from reporting to two bosses—for example, a product-line manager and an area manager. At 3M, for example, every management unit has a multidimensional reporting relationship, which may cross functional, regional, or operational lines. For example, on a regional basis, group managers in Europe report administratively to a vice president of operations for Europe, but report functionally to group vice presidents at headquarters in Minneapolis-St. Paul.[14]

Most companies have found the matrix arrangement problematic.[15] The dual reporting channel easily causes conflict, complex issues are forced into a two-dimen-

FIGURE 21.4   **The Global Area Structure**

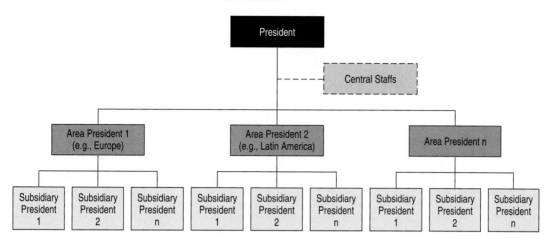

where the EU has its headquarters. Procter & Gamble's Latin American subsidiaries report to the Latin American headquarters in Caracas, Venezuela, rather than to Cincinnati where headquarters for the operations used to exist.[9] Organizational changes made at 3M Company as a result of NAFTA are recounted in the Global Perspective 21.1.

The area approach follows the marketing concept most closely because individual areas and markets are given concentrated attention. If market conditions with respect to product acceptance and operating conditions vary dramatically, the area approach is the one to choose. Companies opting for this alternative typically have relatively narrow product lines with similar end uses and end users. However, expertise is needed in adapting the product and its marketing to local market conditions. Once again, to avoid duplication of effort in product management and in functional areas, staff specialists—for product categories, for example—may be used.

Without appropriate coordination from the staff, essential information and experience may not be transferred from one regional entity to another. Also, if the company expands its product lines and if end markets begin to diversify, the area structure may become inappropriate.

Functional Structure   Of all the approaches, the **functional structure** is the simplest from the administrative viewpoint because it emphasizes the basic tasks of the firm—for example, manufacturing, sales, and research and development. The approach, illustrated in Figure 21.5, works best when both products and customers are relatively few and similar in nature. Coordination is typically the key problem, therefore, staff functions have been created to interact between the functional areas. Otherwise, the company's marketing and regional expertise may not be exploited to the fullest extent possible.

A variation of the functional approach is one that uses processes as a basis for structure. The **process structure** is common in the energy and mining industries, where one corporate entity may be in charge of exploration worldwide and another may be responsible for the actual mining operations.

Customer Structure   Firms may also organize their operations using the **customer structure,** especially if the customer groups they serve are dramatically different—

Global Perspective

21.1
Restructuring for NAFTA

A number of businesses are adopting strategic plans to take full advantage of the trilateral free trade pact of NAFTA. 3M's North American operational plan centers on organizational restructuring based on three concepts: simplification, linkage, and empowerment. The plan was fully implemented in the United States and Canada in 1992; Mexico was added in 1994.

"We always treated Mexico as a far off, foreign country," said David Olsen, 3M's manager of customs and chairman of the company's task force on NAFTA. Now, the company intends to manage by area rather than by country. Key goals of the operational plan are:

- Eliminate the role of 3M International Operations in cross-border activities within North America. All business units in Canada and Mexico will deal directly with 3M's divisions in the United States.
- Redefine management functions. Each general sales and marketing manager in Canada and Mexico will have a new title—business manager—and will serve as the key link between local customers and the corresponding U.S. general managers. The business managers also will be members of 3M U.S.'s planning, pricing, and operating committees, will participate in the early stages of the global business planning, and will execute the global strategy in Canada and Mexico.
- Coordinate functions and share resources among the three countries, especially in marketing, advertising, and sales. New-product launches will be synchronized throughout North America, with standardized sizing and part numbers wherever possible. Distribution strategies and agreements will be

coordinated. Sales literature, packaging, and labeling will be uniform and written in the appropriate local language.
- Establish North American tactical teams. Members of the groups will be drawn from all three countries and will work on projects such as market research, new-product development, and competitor monitoring.
- Set up centers of excellence. To maximize efficiency and to avoid duplication of effort, each country will specialize in the function or process that it does best and eliminate those that can be performed elsewhere. The centers may be built around manufacturing of a product or product line, market niches, customer service, or technical skills.
- Modify performance-measurement criteria. North American performance will be gauged by North American—not U.S., Canadian, or Mexican—market share, earnings growth, and income.

At 3M Canada, major changes have taken place. Layers of management have been trimmed, communication and coordination have been enhanced, and the requirement to go through the international division removed. Incorporating Mexico into the plan has presented some unique challenges, however. For 3M U.S. headquarters, meeting or communicating electronically with Canadian counterparts is far easier than doing the same with Mexico. Language and cultural barriers also present potential challenges. Given that only products—not people—are free to cross borders, sales personnel cannot solicit business across borders and direct cross-border reporting may not be possible.

Source: "3M Restructuring for NAFTA," *Business Latin America*, July 19, 1993, 6–7.

for example, consumers and businesses and governments. Catering to such diverse groups may require concentrating specialists in particular divisions. The product may be the same, but the buying processes of the various customer groups may differ. Governmental buying is characterized by bidding, in which price plays a larger role than when businesses are the buyers.

FIGURE 21.7   **The Global Matrix Structure at N.V. Philips**

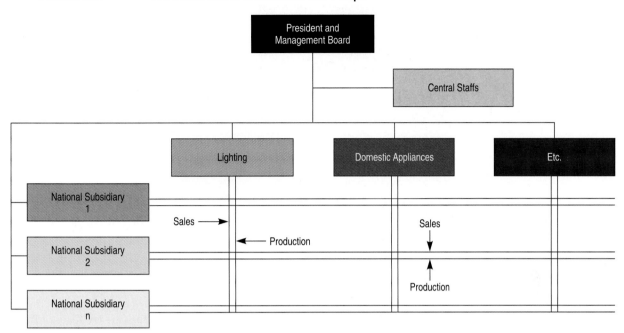

sional decision framework, and even minor issues may have to be solved through committee discussion. Ideally, managers should solve the problems themselves through formal and informal communication; however, physical and psychic distance often make that impossible. The matrix structure, with its inherent complexity, may actually increase the reaction time of a company, a potentially serious problem when competitive conditions require quick responses. As a result, the authority has started to shift in many organizations from area to product, although the matrix still may officially be used.

Evolution of Organizational Structures   Companies have been shown to develop new structures in a pattern of stages as their products diversify and share of foreign sales increases.[16] At the first stage are autonomous subsidiaries reporting directly to top management; the establishment of an international division follows. As product diversity and the importance of the foreign marketplace increase, companies develop global structures to coordinate subsidiary operations and rationalize worldwide production. As multinational corporations have been faced with simultaneous pressures to adapt to local market conditions and to rationalize production and globalize competitive reactions, many have opted for the matrix structure.[17] The matrix structure probably allows a corporation to best meet the challenges of global markets (to be global and local, big and small, decentralized with centralized reporting) by allowing the optimizing of businesses globally and maximizing performance in every country of operation.[18] The evolutionary process is summarized in Figure 21.8.

Locus of Decision Making

Organizational structures themselves do not indicate where the authority for decision making and control rests within the organization. If subsidiaries are granted a

**FIGURE 21.8
Evolution of
International Structures**

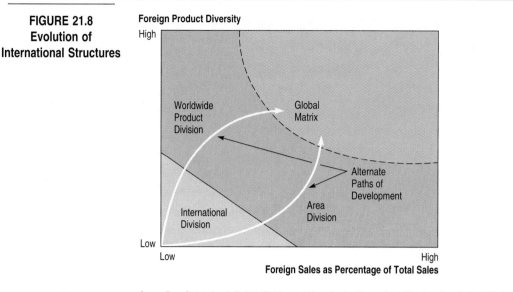

Source: From Christopher A. Bartlett, "Building and Managing the Transnational: The New Organizational Challenge," in *Competition in Global Industries*, ed. Michael E. Porter (Boston: Harvard Business School Press, 1986), 368.

high degree of autonomy, the system is called **decentralization.** In decentralized systems, controls are relatively loose and simple, and the flows between headquarters and subsidiaries are mainly financial; that is, each subsidiary operates as a profit center. On the other hand, if controls are tight and the strategic decision making is concentrated at headquarters, the system is described as **centralization.** Firms are typically neither completely centralized nor decentralized; for example, some functions of the firm—such as finance—lend themselves to more centralized decision making; others—such as promotional decisions—do so far less. Research and development in organizations is typically centralized, especially in cases of basic research work. Some companies have, partly due to governmental pressures, added R&D functions on a regional or local basis. In many cases, however, variations are product and market based; for example, Corning Glass Work's TV tube marketing strategy requires global decision making for pricing and local decision making for service and delivery.

The basic advantage of allowing maximum flexibility at the subsidiary level is that subsidiary management knows its market and can react to changes more quickly. Problems of motivation and acceptance are avoided when decision makers are also the implementors of the strategy. On the other hand, many multinationals faced with global competitive threats and opportunities have adopted global strategy formulation, which by definition requires a higher degree of centralization. What has emerged as a result can be called **coordinated decentralization.** This means that overall corporate strategy is provided from headquarters, while subsidiaries are free to implement it within the range agreed on in consultation with headquarters.

Factors Affecting Structure and Decision Making

The organizational structure and locus of decision making in a multinational corporation are determined by a number of factors, such as (1) its degree of involvement in international operations, (2) the products the firm markets, (3) the size and importance of the firm's markets, and (4) the human resource capability of the firm.[19]

The effect of the degree of involvement on structure and decision making was discussed earlier in the chapter. With low degrees of involvement, subsidiaries can enjoy high degrees of autonomy as long as they meet their profit targets. The same situation can occur even with the most globally oriented companies, but within a different framework. Consider, for example, the North American Philips Corporation, a separate entity from the Dutch Philips, which enjoys independent status in terms of local policy setting and managerial practices but is still, nevertheless, within the parent company's planning and control system.

The firm's country of origin and the political history of the area can also affect organizational structure and decision making. For example, Swiss-based Nestlé, with only 3 to 4 percent of its sales from its small domestic market, has traditionally had a highly decentralized organization. Moreover, European history for the past 80 years—particularly the two world wars—has often forced subsidiaries of European-based companies to act independently to survive.

The type and variety of products marketed will affect organizational decisions. Companies that market consumer products typically have product organizations with high degrees of decentralization, allowing for maximum local flexibility. On the other hand, companies that market technologically sophisticated products—such as GE, which markets turbines—display centralized organizations with worldwide product responsibilities. Even within matrix organizations, one of the dimensions may be granted more say in decisions; for example, at Dow Chemical, geographical managers have been granted more authority than other managers.

Going global has recently meant transferring world headquarters of important business units abroad. For example, Hyundai Electronics Industries moved its personal computer division to San Jose, California, from Seoul, South Korea, to better compete in that industry's biggest market.[20] The unit has complete autonomy in setting strategies and managing day-to-day operations, quite necessary if the unit is to respond to rapid changes in the U.S. market. In some cases, however, the difficulty of overseeing units based thousands of miles away has led corporations to reassess a move. Cadbury Schweppes moved the global headquarters of its beverage division back to London from Stamford, Connecticut, to enhance interaction between unit managers and corporate managers.

The human factor in any organization is critical. Management personnel both at headquarters and in the subsidiaries have to bridge the physical and psychic distances separating them. If subsidiaries have competent management that does not have to rely on headquarters consultation to solve the majority of its problems, they may be granted high degrees of autonomy. In the case of global organizations, subsidiary management has to understand the corporate culture of the firm to be an efficient part of the corporation, especially when decisions are called for that are not optimum for the local market but meet the long-term objectives of the firm as a whole.

The Networked Global Organization

There seems to be no ideal international structure, and some have challenged the wisdom of even looking for one. They have recommended attention to new processes that would, in a given structure, help to develop new perspectives and attitudes that reflect and respond to the complex, opposing demands of global integration and local responsiveness.[21] The question thus changes from which structural alternative is best to how the different perspectives of various corporate entities can better be taken into account when making decisions. In structural terms, nothing may change. As a matter of fact, Philips has not changed its basic matrix structure, although it

FIGURE 21.9
The Networked Global
Organization

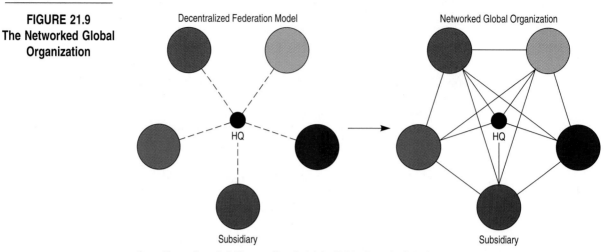

Source: Thomas Gross, Ernie Turner, and Lars Cederholm, "Building Teams for Global Operations," Management Review, June 1987 (New York: American Management Association), 34.

has made major changes in how it conducts its internal relations.[22] It went from a decentralized federation model to a networked global organization, the effects of which are depicted in Figure 21.9. The term **glocal** has been coined to describe this approach.[23]

Companies that have adopted the approach have incorporated the following three dimensions into their organizations: (1) the development and communication of a clear corporate vision, (2) the effective management of human resource tools to broaden individual perspectives and develop identification with corporate goals, and (3) the integration of individual thinking and activities into the broad corporate agenda.[24] The first dimension relates to a clear and consistent long-term corporate mission that guides individuals wherever they work in the organization. Examples of this are Johnson & Johnson's corporate credo of customer focus and NEC's C&C (computers and communications). The second relates both to the development of global managers who can find opportunities in spite of environmental challenges as well as creating a global perspective among country managers. The last dimension relates to the development of a cooperative mind-set among country organizations to ensure effective implementation of global strategies. Managers may believe that global strategies are intrusions on their operations if they do not have an understanding of the corporate vision, if they have not contributed to the global corporate agenda, or if they are not given direct responsibility for its implementation. Defensive, territorial attitudes can lead to the emergence of the **not-invented-here syndrome;** i.e., country organizations objecting to or rejecting an otherwise sound strategy.

The network avoids the problems of effort duplication, inefficiency of operations, and nonacceptance of ideas developed elsewhere by giving subsidiaries the latitude, encouragement, and tools to pursue local business development within the framework of the global strategy. Headquarters considers each unit a source of ideas, skills, capabilities, and knowledge that can be utilized for the benefit of the entire organization. This means that subsidiaries must be upgraded from mere implementors and adaptors to contributors and partners in the development and execution of worldwide strategies. Efficient plants may be converted into international production centers, innovative R&D units converted into centers of excellence (and thus role models), and leading subsidiary groups given the leadership role in developing new strategies for the entire corporation. At Ford Motor Company, development of a specific car or component is centralized in whichever Ford technical center worldwide has the greatest expertise in that product.

The main tool of implementation used in this approach is international teams of managers who meet regularly to develop strategy. While final direction may come from headquarters, it has been informed of local conditions, and implementation of the strategy is enhanced since local-country managers were involved in its development. The approach has worked even in cases involving seemingly impossible market differences. Both Procter & Gamble and Henkel have successfully introduced pan-European brands for which strategy was developed by European teams. The teams consisted of country managers and staff personnel to smooth eventual implementation and to avoid unnecessarily long and disruptive discussions about the fit of a new product to individual markets.

As can be seen from the discussion, the networked approach is not a structural adaptation but a procedural one, calling for a change in management mentality. It requires adjustment mainly in the coordination and control functions of the firm. And while there is still considerable disagreement as to which of the approaches work, some measures have been shown to correlate with success as seen in Global Perspective 21.2.

The Role of Country Organizations

Country organizations should be treated as a source of supply as much as a source of demand. Quite often, however, headquarters managers see their role as the coordinators of key decisions and controllers of resources and perceive subsidiaries as implementors and adaptors of global strategy in their respective local markets. Furthermore, they may see all country organizations as the same. This view severely limits utilization of the firm's resources and deprives country managers of the opportunity to exercise their creativity.[25]

The role that a particular country organization can play naturally depends on that market's overall strategic importance as well as its organizational competence. Using these criteria, four different roles emerge, as shown in Figure 21.10.

The role of a **strategic leader** can be played by a highly competent national subsidiary located in a strategically critical market. Such a country organization serves as a partner of headquarters in developing and implementing strategy. Procter & Gamble's Eurobrand teams, which analyze opportunities for greater product and marketing program standardization, are chaired by a brand manager from a "lead country."[26]

A **contributor** is a country organization with a distinctive competence, such as product development. Increasingly, country organizations are the source of new products. These range from IBM's recent breakthrough in superconductivity research, generated in its Zurich lab, to low-end innovations such as Procter & Gamble's liquid Tide, made with a fabric-softening compound developed in Europe.[27] Similarly, country organizations may be designated as worldwide centers of excellence for a particular product category, such as ABB Strömberg in Finland for electric drives, a category for which it is a recognized world leader.[28]

Implementors provide the critical mass for the international marketing effort. These country organizations may exist in smaller, less-developed countries in which there is less corporate commitment for market development. Although most entities

Global Perspective

21.2
Characteristics of Success

A survey of chief executive officers of 43 leading U.S. consumer companies by McKinsey & Co. sheds light on organizational features that distinguish internationally successful companies. Companies were classified as more or less successful compared to their specific industry average, using international sales and profit growth over the 1986–1991 period as the most important indicators of success.

The survey results indicate 11 distinctive traits that are correlated with high performance in international markets. The following are moves that companies can make to enhance prospects for international success:

- Take a different approach to international decision making.
- Differentiate treatment of international subsidiaries.
- Let product managers in subsidiaries report to the country general manager.
- Have a worldwide management development program.

- Make international experience a condition for promotion to top management.
- Have a more multinational management group.
- Support international managers with global electronic networking capabilities.
- Manage cross-border acquisitions particularly well.
- Have overseas R & D centers.
- Focus on international.
- Remain open to organizational change and continuous self-renewal.

In general, successful companies coordinate their international decision making globally, with more central direction than less successful competitors as seen in the accompanying exhibit. The difference is most marked in brand positioning, designing packaging, and setting prices. The one notable exception is an increasing tendency to decentralize product development.

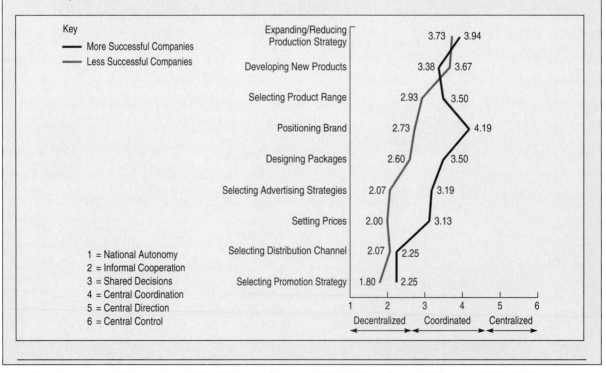

Key
— More Successful Companies
— Less Successful Companies

1 = National Autonomy
2 = Informal Cooperation
3 = Shared Decisions
4 = Central Coordination
5 = Central Direction
6 = Central Control

	More Successful	Less Successful
Expanding/Reducing Production Strategy	3.94	3.73
Developing New Products	3.38	3.67
Selecting Product Range	3.50	2.93
Positioning Brand	4.19	2.73
Designing Packages	3.50	2.60
Selecting Advertising Strategies	3.19	2.07
Setting Prices	3.13	2.00
Selecting Distribution Channel	2.25	2.07
Selecting Promotion Strategy	2.25	1.80

1   2   3   4   5   6
Decentralized   Coordinated   Centralized

Source: Ingo Theuerkauf, David Ernst, and Amir Mahini, "Think Local, Organize . . .?" *The McKinsey Quarterly* 30 (Number 1, 1993): 107–114.

**FIGURE 21.10
Roles for Country
Organizations**

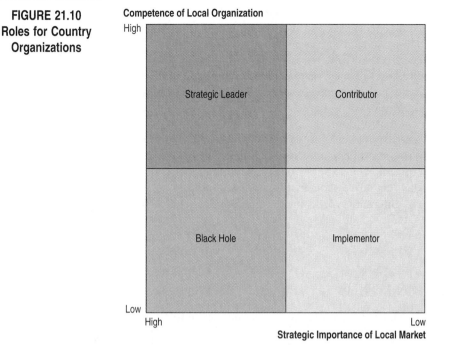

Competence of Local Organization

Strategic Leader

Contributor

Black Hole

Implementor

Strategic Importance of Local Market

Source: Christopher Bartlett and Sumantra Ghoshal, "Tap Your Subsidiaries for Global Reach," *Harvard Business Review* 64, November–December 1986 (Boston: Harvard Business School Publishing Division), 87–94.

are given this role, it should not be slighted, since the implementors provide the opportunity to capture economies of scale and scope that are the basis of a global strategy.

The **black hole** situation is one in which the international marketer has a low-competence country organization—or no organization at all—in a highly strategic market. In strategically important markets such as the European Union, a local presence is necessary to maintain the company's global position and, in some cases, to protect others. One of the major ways of remedying the black hole situation is to enter into strategic alliances. In the 1980s, AT&T, which had long restricted itself to its domestic market, needed to go global fast. Some of the alliances it formed were with Philips in telecommunications and Olivetti in computers and office automation.[29] In some cases, firms may use their presence in a major market as an observation post to keep up with developments before a major thrust for entry is executed.

Depending on the role of the country organization, its relationship with headquarters will vary from loose control based mostly on support to tighter control to ensure that strategies get implemented appropriately. Yet, in each of these cases, it is imperative that country organizations have enough operating independence to cater to local needs and to provide motivation to country managers. For example, an implementor's ideas concerning the development of a regional or global strategy or program should be heard. Strategy formulators should make sure that appropriate implementation can be achieved at the country level.

CONTROLS

The function of the organizational structure is to provide a framework in which objectives can be met. A set of instruments and processes is needed, however, to influence the performance of organizational members so as to meet the goals. Controls focus on means to verify and correct actions that differ from established plans.

Compliance needs to be secured from subordinates through different means of co-ordinating specialized and interdependent parts of the organization.[30] Within an organization, control serves as an integrating mechanism. Controls are designed to reduce uncertainty, increase predictability, and ensure that behaviors originating in separate parts of the organization are compatible and in support of common organizational goals despite physical, psychic, and temporal distances.[31]

The critical issue here is the same as with organizational structure: What is the ideal amount of control? On the one hand, headquarters needs controls to ensure that international activities contribute the greatest benefit to the overall organization. On the other hand, they should not be construed as a code of laws and subsequently allowed to stifle local initiative.

This section will focus on the design and functions of control instruments available for international business operations, along with an assessment of their appropriateness. Emphasis will be placed on the degree of formality of controls used by firms.

Types of Controls

Most organizations display some administrative flexibility, as demonstrated by variations in how they apply management directives, corporate objectives, or measurement systems. A distinction should be made, however, between variations that have emerged by design and those that are the result of autonomy. The first are the result of a management decision, whereas the second typically have grown without central direction and are based on emerging practices. In both instances, some type of control will be exercised. Controls that result from headquarters initiative rather than those that are the consequences of tolerated practices will be discussed here. Firms that wait for self-emerging controls often experience rapid international growth but subsequent problems in product-line performance, program coordination, and strategic planning.[32]

Not all control systems evolve in the way originally envisioned. For example, shifts may be triggered by changes over time in the relative importance of headquarters when compared to the volume of international activity. Such a change was experienced by the Hoover Corporation in its European operations. Initially, the U.S. headquarters control capability was strong; over time, however, the European operations asserted an increasing role in overall corporate planning and control as they grew in importance.

In the design of the control systems, a major decision concerns the object of control. Two major objects are typically identified: output and behavior.[33] Output controls include balance sheets, sales data, production data, product-line growth, and performance reviews of personnel. Measures of output are accumulated at regular intervals and forwarded from the foreign locale to headquarters, where they are evaluated and critiqued based on comparisons to the plan or budget. Behavioral controls require the exertion of influence over behavior after—or, ideally, before—it leads to action. Behavioral controls can be achieved through the preparation of manuals on such topics as sales techniques to be made available to subsidiary personnel, or through efforts to fit new employees into the corporate culture.

To institute either of these measures, instruments of control have to be decided upon. The general alternatives are either bureaucratic/formalized control or cultural control.[34] Bureaucratic controls consist of a limited and explicit set of regulations and rules that outline the desired levels of performance. Cultural controls, on the

	Type of Control	
TABLE 21.1 Comparison of Bureaucratic and Cultural Control Mechanisms	**Object of Control**	**Pure Bureaucratic/Formalized Control**	**Pure Cultural Control**
	Output	Formal performance reports	Shared norms of performance
	Behavior	Company policies, manuals	Shared philosophy of management

Source: B.R. Baliga and Alfred M. Jaeger, "Multinational Corporations: Control Systems and Delegation Issues," *Journal of International Business Studies* 15 (Fall 1984): 25–40.

other hand, are much less formal and are the result of shared beliefs and expectations among the members of an organization. Table 21.1 provides a schematic explanation of the types of controls and their objectives.

Bureaucratic/Formalized Control   The elements of a bureaucratic/formalized control system are (1) an international budget and planning system, (2) the functional reporting system, and (3) policy manuals used to direct functional performance.

Budgets refers to shorter term guidelines regarding investment, cash, and personnel policies, while *plans* refers to formalized plans with more than a one-year horizon. The budget and planning process is the major control instrument in headquarters-subsidiary relationships. Although systems and their execution vary, the objective is to achieve as good a fit as possible with the objectives and characteristics of the firm and its environment.

The budgetary period is typically one year, since it is tied to the accounting systems of the multinational. The budget system is used for four main purposes: (1) allocation of funds among subsidiaries, (2) planning and coordination of global production capacity and supplies, (3) evaluation of subsidiary performance, and (4) communication and information exchange among subsidiaries, product organizations, and corporate headquarters.[35] Long-range plans vary dramatically, ranging from two years to ten years in length, and are more qualitative and judgmental in nature. However, shorter periods such as two years are the norm, considering the added uncertainty of diverse foreign environments.

Although firms strive for uniformity, achieving it may be as difficult as trying to design a suit to fit the average person. The processes themselves are very formalized in terms of the schedules to be followed.

Functional reports are another control instrument used by headquarters in managing subsidiary relations. These vary in number, complexity, and frequency. Table 21.2 summarizes the various types of functional reports used in a total of 117 multinational corporations in the United States, Germany, and Japan. The structure and elements of the reports are typically highly standardized to allow for consolidation in the headquarters level.

Since the frequency of reports required from subsidiaries is likely to increase due to globalization, it is essential that subsidiaries see the rationale for the often time-consuming exercise. Two approaches, used in tandem, can facilitate the process: participation and feedback. The first refers to avoiding the perception at subsidiary levels that reports are "art for art's sake" by involving the preparers in the actual use of the reports. When this is not possible, feedback about their consequences is warranted. Through this process, communication is enhanced as well.

On the behavioral front, headquarters may want to guide the way in which subsidiaries make decisions and implement agreed-upon strategies. U.S.-based multinationals tend to be far more formalized than their Japanese and European counterparts, with a heavy reliance on manuals for all major functions.[36] The manuals discuss such

TABLE 21.2
Types of Functional
Reports in Multinational
Corporations

Type of Report	U.S. MNCs (33)	German MNCs (44)	Japanese MNCs (40)
Balance sheet	97	49	42
Profit and loss statements	91	49	42
Production output	94	50	47
Market share	70	48	31
Cash and credit statement	100	41	39
Inventory levels	88	46	38
Sales per product	88	37	44
Performance review of personnel	9	15	2
Report on local economic and political conditions	33	32	12

Source: Anant R. Negandhi and Martin Welge, *Beyond Theory Z* (Greenwich, Conn.: JAI, 1984): 18.

items as recruitment, training, motivation, and dismissal policies. The use of manuals is in direct correlation with the required level of reports from subsidiaries, discussed in the previous section.

Cultural Control   As seen from the country comparisons, less emphasis is placed outside the United States on formal controls, as they are viewed as too rigid and too quantitatively oriented. Rather, MNCs in other countries emphasize corporate values and culture, and evaluations are based on the extent to which an individual or entity fits in with the norms. Cultural controls require an extensive socialization process to which informal, personal interaction is central. Substantial resources have to be spent to train the individual to share the corporate cultures, or "the way things are done at the company."[37] To build common vision and values, managers spend a substantial share of their first months at Matsushita in what the company calls "cultural and spiritual training." They study the company credo, the "Seven Spirits of Matsushita," and the philosophy of the founder, Konosuke Matsushita and learn how to translate the internalized lessons into daily behavior and operational decisions. Although more prevalent in Japanese organizations, many Western entities have similar programs, such as Philips's "organization cohesion training" and Unilever's "indoctrination."[38]

The primary instruments of cultural control are the careful selection and training of corporate personnel and the institution of self-control. The choice of cultural controls can be justified if the company enjoys a low turnover rate; they are thus applied when companies can offer and expect lifetime or long-term employment, as many firms do in Japan.

In selecting home-country nationals and, to some extent, third-country nationals, MNCs are exercising cultural control. The assumption is that the managers have already internalized the norms and values of the company. For example, only 4 of 3M's 53 managing directors of overseas subsidiaries are local nationals. The company's experience is that nonnationals tend to run a country organization with a more global view. In some cases, the use of headquarters personnel to ensure uniformity in decision making may be advisable; for example, Volvo uses a home-country national for the position of chief financial officer. Expatriates are used in subsidiaries not only for control purposes but also to effect change processes. Companies control the efforts of management specifically through compensation and promotion policies, as well as through policies concerning replacement.

When the expatriate corps is small, headquarters can still exercise its control through other means. Management training programs for overseas managers as well as time at headquarters will indoctrinate individuals as to the company's ways of doing things. For instance, a Chinese executive selected to run Loctite's new operation in China spent two years at the company's headquarters before taking over in Beijing.[39] Similarly, formal visits by headquarters teams (for example, for a strategy audit) or informal visits (perhaps to launch a new product) will enhance the feeling of belonging to the same corporate family.

Corporations rarely use one pure control mechanism. Rather, most use both quantitative and qualitative measures. Corporations are likely, however, to place different levels of emphasis on different types of performance measures and on how they are derived.

Exercising Controls

Within most corporations, different functional areas are subject to different guidelines because they are subject to different constraints. For example, the marketing function has traditionally been seen as incorporating many more behavioral dimensions than manufacturing or finance. As a result, many multinational corporations employ control systems that are responsive to the needs of the function. Yet such differentiation is sometimes based less on appropriateness than on personalities. It has been hypothesized that manufacturing subsidiaries are controlled more intensively than sales subsidiaries because production more readily lends itself to centralized direction, and technicians and engineers adhere more firmly to standards and regulations than do salespeople.[40] This trend is causing a significant change in the role of the country general manager as seen in Global Perspective 21.3. Despite increasing integration, country managers will retain an important role in staying close to local customers, competitors, and policymakers in host governments.

In their international operations, U.S.–based multinationals place major emphasis on obtaining quantitative data. Although this allows for good centralized comparisons against standards and benchmarks or cross-comparisons among different corporate units, it entails several drawbacks. In the international environment, new dimensions—such as inflation, differing rates of taxation, and exchange rate fluctuations—may distort the performance evaluation of any given individual or organizational unit. For the global corporation, measurement of whether a business unit in a particular country is earning a superior return on investment relative to risk may be irrelevant to the contribution an investment may make worldwide or to the long-term results of the firm. In the short term, the return may even be negative.[41] Therefore, the control mechanism may quite inappropriately indicate reward or punishment. Standardizing the information received may be difficult if the various environments involved fluctuate and require frequent and major adaptations. Further complicating the issue is the fact that although quantitative information may be collected monthly, or at least quarterly, environmental data may be acquired annually or "now and then," especially when a crisis seems to loom on the horizon. To design a control system that is acceptable not only to headquarters but also to the organization and individuals abroad, great care must be taken to use only relevant data. Major concerns, therefore, are the data collection process and the analysis and utilization of data. Evaluators need management information systems that provide for greater comparability and equity in administering controls. The more behaviorally based and culture-oriented controls are, the more care needs to be taken.[42]

In designing a control system, management must consider the costs of establishing and maintaining it versus the benefits to be gained. Any control system will require investment in a management structure and in systems design. Consider, for example, costs associated with cultural controls: Personal interaction, use of expatriates, and training programs are all quite expensive. Yet these expenses may be justified by cost savings through lower employee turnover, an extensive worldwide

Global Perspective

21.3
The Country Manager of the 1990s

Organizationally, the forces of globalization are changing the country manager's role significantly. With profit and loss responsibility, oversight of multiple functions, and the benefit of distance from headquarters, the country operations enjoyed considerable decision-making autonomy as well as entrepreneurial initiative. Today, however, multinational companies have to emphasize the product dimension of the product-geography matrix, which means that power has to shift at least to some extent from country managers to worldwide strategic business unit and product-line managers. Many of the previously local decisions are subordinated to global strategic moves.

The changing task mix toward more implementation calls for action on the part of the multinational companies to retain the entrepreneurial drive needed at the country level. A sample of 50 country managers in Asian, European, and North American multinationals resulted in recommendations of the following skills and attitudes for future operations:

1. **External Focus.** Country managers will have to spend less time on internal functions, such as manufacturing, and more time in the front office dealing with local customers, monitoring marketing initiatives by local and global competitors, and cultivating relations with trade, industry associations and the government.

2. **Government Relations.** Country managers will have to make sure that local governments see the subsidiary as a good corporate citizen of its host environment through contributions to the economy and to the local communities.

3. **Corporate Perspective.** Country managers will be asked to seek and identify similarities across national markets, to encourage the export and import of good ideas among subsidiaries, and to gather intelligence useful to others in the organization.

4. **Team Player.** Country managers will have to derive satisfaction not only from enhancing the performance and capabilities of their subsidiaries, but also from influencing results beyond the boundaries of their own domains.

5. **Multiple Roles.** For efficiency reasons, country managers may have to wear many hats. A country manager for Spain or Finland, for example, might also have to oversee a subregion such as Iberia or the Baltics, be the strategic director for a product line throughout southern or northern Europe, and oversee a function such as manufacturing on a panregional basis.

Source: John A. Quelch, "The New Country Managers" *The McKinsey Quarterly* 29 (Number 4, 1992): 155–165.

information system, and an improved control system.[43] Moreover, the impact goes beyond the administrative component. If controls are misguided or too time-consuming, they can slow or undermine the strategy implementation process and thus the overall capability of the firm. The result will be lost opportunities or, worse yet, increased threats. In addition, time spent on reporting takes time from everything else, and if the exercise is seen as mundane, results in lowered motivation. A parsimonious design is therefore imperative. The control system should collect all the information required and trigger all the intervention necessary; however, it should not lead to the pulling of strings by a puppeteer.

The impact of the environment has to be taken into account as well, in two ways. First, the control system must measure only those dimensions over which the organization has actual control. Rewards or sanctions make little sense if they are based on dimensions that may be relevant to overall corporate performance but over which no influence can be exerted, such as price controls. Neglecting the factor of

The European Union: An Example of Area Structure

ICELAND

SWEDEN

FINLAND

RUSSIA

NORWAY

ESTONIA

LATVIA

DENMARK

LITHUANIA

RUSSIA

BELARUS

IRELAND

UNITED KINGDOM

NETH.

GERMANY

POLAND

The European Commission

Brussels ★

BELGIUM

Luxembourg

UKRAINE

LUX.

The European Court of Justice

CZECH

SLOVAKIA

MOLDOVA

Strasbourg 🏛

AUSTRIA

HUNGARY

The European Parliment

SWITZ.

SLOVENIA

ROMANIA

FRANCE

CROATIA

BOSNIA-HERCEGOVINA

FORMER YUGOSLAVIA

BULGARIA

ITALY

MACEDONIA

PORTUGAL

ANDORRA

ALBANIA

GREECE

TURKEY

SPAIN

CYPRUS

MOROCCO

ALGERIA

TUNISIA

EGYPT

LIBYA

Source: *Atlas of the New Europe*, 1992 and *The World Factbook 1994*.

individual performance capability would send wrong signals and severely harm motivation. Second, control systems have to be in harmony with local regulations and customs. In some cases, however, corporate behavioral controls have to be exercised against local customs even though overall operations may be affected negatively. This type of situation occurs, for example, when a subsidiary operates in markets in which unauthorized facilitating payments are a common business practice.

Corporations are faced with major challenges in appropriate and adequate control systems in today's business environment. Given increased local government demands for a share in companies established, controls can become tedious, especially if the MNC is a minority partner. Even if the new entity is a result of two companies' joining forces through a merger—such as the one between ASEA and Brown Boveri—or two companies' joining forces to form a new entity—such as NUMMI, established by Toyota and GM—the backgrounds of the partners may be different enough to cause problems in devising the required controls.

SUMMARY

This chapter discussed the structures and control mechanisms needed to operate in the international business field. The elements define relationships between the entities of the firm and provide the channels through which the relationships develop.

International firms can choose from a variety of organizational structures, ranging from a domestic organization that handles ad hoc export orders to a full-fledged global organization. The choice will depend heavily on the degree of internationalization of the firm, the diversity of international activities, and the relative importance of product, area, function, and customer variables in the process. A determining factor is also the degree to which headquarters wants to decide important issues concerning the whole corporation and the individual subsidiaries. Organizations that function effectively still need to be revisited periodically to ensure that they remain responsive to a changing environment. Some of the responsiveness is showing up not as structural changes, but rather in how the entities conduct their internal business.

In addition to organization, the control function takes on major importance for multinationals, due to the high variability in performance resulting from divergent local environments and the need to reconcile local objectives with the corporate goal of synergism. While it is important to grant autonomy to country organizations so that they can be responsive to local market needs, it is of equal importance to ensure close cooperation among units to optimize corporate effectiveness.

Control can be exercised through bureaucratic means, which emphasize formal reporting and evaluation of benchmark data or through cultural means, in which norms and values are understood by the individuals and entities that make up the corporation. U.S. firms typically rely more on bureaucratic controls, while MNCs from other countries frequently run operations abroad through informal means and rely less on stringent measures.

The implementation of controls requires great sensitivity to behavioral dimensions and the environment. The measurements used must be appropriate and reflective of actual performance rather than marketplace vagaries. Similarly, entities should be judged only on factors over which they have some degree of control.

Table 21.3 shows how some of the world's most successful multinational corporations deal with the organizational and control issues discussed in this chapter. As can be seen in the table, they use widely varying approaches to achieve an overall balance between control and attention to local conditions.

TABLE 21.3   **Organizational and Control Characteristics of Selected Multinational Corporations**

Company	Dominant Organizational Concept	Planning and Control	Research and/or Product Development	Handling of U.S. Business
Ciba-Geigy Corporation (Switzerland)	Product divisions with global responsibility.	Moderate reliance on strategic planning by global product divisions: gradual buildup of the role of key regional companies in the planning process; operational plans and capital budgets by country organizations and their product divisions, with the latter playing the more active role.	Research and product development activities carried out by domestic product divisions and certain product divisions by key geographic areas.	Dual reporting relationship with U.S. company reporting directly to headquarters and its local divisions also reporting to their counterpart domestic divisions.
Imperial Chemical Industries (U.K.)	Strategic business units with global responsibility supported by limited regional organization, especially in developing markets.	Strategic and operational planning at the strategic business level with portfolio, financial, and other performance monitoring tightly controlled by headquarters.	Research and product/process development driven by the business units sometimes using shared regional facilities. A network of technical staff provides custodianship of identified technological areas of core competence.	U.S. board sets local policies and standards for U.S. units, which operate within the strategies agreed on for the international strategic businesses.
Philips Electronics N.V. (The Netherlands)	Product divisions with global responsibility.	Moderate to heavy reliance on strategic planning by product divisions, selected national organizations, and Central Planning Department; operational plans by division and national organizations, with initiative from the former; monthly review of performance.	Highly centralized research, but with product development by product divisions; research centers located in U.S. plus other key countries.	Philips Electronics North America Corporation, New York, reports to parent and coordinates corporate services for domestic product divisions. Certain U.S. product divisions operate research, design, and manufacturing centers abroad. U.S. divisions also export, particularly components.

(CONTINUED)

Key Terms and Concepts

product structure

area structure

functional structure

process structure

customer structure

mixed structure

matrix structure

decentralization

centralization

coordinated decentralization

glocal

not-invented-here syndrome

strategic leader

contributor

implementor

black hole

TABLE 21.3   **Organizational and Control Characteristics of Selected Multinational Corporations**

Company	Dominant Organizational Concept	Planning and Control	Research and/or Product Development	Handling of U.S. Business
Rhône-Poulenc S.A. (France)	Product divisions with global responsibility, but special status business enterprises responsible for operations in geographical zones: North America, Europe, Latin America and Asia/Pacific.	Strategic planning responsibility resides with business leaders. Each business has leader in one of the four zones designated to provide strategic leadership to worldwide business.	Research and product development activities carried out by product divisions, several large centers, each focusing on different specializations.	Special reporting relationship directly to headquarters. U.S. company coordinates activities with product divisions at headquarters.
Solvay S.A. (Belgium)	Management of product sectors have primary responsibility for strategic direction of business activities (with functional support from regional organizations). Delegation of authority and responsibility as much as possible to create a lean, participative, and entrepreneurial organization that is highly responsive to the market.	Overall strategy and budgets are defined by sector by the senior management of the parent company, in consultation with regional organizations.	A central research and product development activity, with major national organizations also carrying out product development (main research centers: USA—Houston, Tex.; Minneapolis, Minn.; Atlanta, Ga.; Elkhart, Ind.; Europe—Belgium, the Netherlands, Germany, France, Italy, the United Kingdom; Asia—Tokyo; South America—Brazil.	U.S. holding company and its subsidiaries are legal entities. Holding company oversees activities of subsidiaries, which are responsible for conducting operations within strategic guidelines set by sector management at European parent.

Source: Company data collected by interview, January 1995. Original chart appears in Drake Rodman and Lee M. Caudill, "Management of the Large Multinational: Trends and Future Challenges," *Business Horizons* 24 (May–June 1981): 88–90.

Questions for Discussion

1. Firms differ, often substantially, in their organizational structures even within the same industry. What accounts for the differences in their approaches?
2. Discuss the benefits gained in adopting a matrix form of organizational structure.
3. What changes in the firm and/or in the environment might cause a firm to abandon the functional approach?
4. Is there more to the not-invented-here syndrome than simply hurt feelings on the part of those who believe they are being dictated to by headquarters?
5. If the purposes of the budget are in conflict, as is sometimes argued, what can be done about it?
6. Performance reviews of subsidiary managers and personnel are required rarely, if at all, by headquarters. Why?
7. Why do European-based multinational corporations differ from U.S.-based corporations in the instruments they choose for exerting control?
8. One of the most efficient means of control is self-control. What type of program would you prepare for an incoming employee?

Recommended Readings

Bartlett, Christopher, and Sumantra Ghoshal. *Managing Across Borders.* Cambridge, Mass.: Harvard Business Press, 1989.

Davidson, William H., and José de la Torre. *Managing the Global Corporation.* New York: McGraw-Hill, 1989.

Hedlung, Gunar, and Per Aman. *Managing Relationships with Foreign Subsidiaries.* Stockholm, Sweden: Mekan, 1984.

Humes, Samuel. *Managing the Multinational: Confronting the Global-Local Dilemma.* London, England: Prentice-Hall, 1993.

Moran, Robert T., Philip R. Harris, and William G. Strip. *Developing the Global Organization.* Houston, TX: Gulf Publishing Co., 1993.

Negandhi, Anant, and Martin Welge. *Beyond Theory Z.* Greenwich, Conn.: JAI Press, 1984.

Otterback, Lars, ed. *The Management of Headquarters-Subsidiary Relationships in Multinational Corporations.* Aldershot, England: Gower Publishing Company, 1981.

Porter, Michael E., ed. *Competition in Global Industries.* Boston: Harvard Business School Press, 1986.

Stopford, John M., and Louis T. Wells. *Managing the Multinational Enterprise: Organization of the Firm and Ownership of the Subsidiary.* New York: Basic Books, 1972.

Notes

1. Michael Z. Brooke, *International Management: A Review of Strategies and Operations* (London: Hutchinson, 1986), 173-174.
2. Stefan Robock and Kenneth Simmonds, *International Business and Multinational Enterprises* (Homewood, Ill.: Richard D. Irwin, 1973), 429.
3. Richard D. Robinson, *Internationalization of Business: An Introduction* (Hinsdale, Ill.: The Dryden Press, 1984).
4. William H. Davidson and Philippe Haspeslagh, "Shaping a Global Product Organization," *Harvard Business Review* 59 (March/April 1982): 69-76.
5. L. S. Walsh, *International Marketing* (Plymouth, England: MacDonald and Evans, 1981), 161.
6. See Joan P. Curhan, William H. Davidson, and Suri Rajan, *Tracing the Multinationals* (Cambridge, Mass.: Ballinger, 1977); M.E. Wicks, *A Comparative Analysis of the Foreign Investment Evaluation Practices of U.S.-based Multinational Corporations* (New York: McKinsey & Co., 1980); and Lawrence G. Franko, "Organizational Structures and Multinational Strategies of Continental European Enterprises," in *European Research in International Business,* eds. Michel Ghertman and James Leontiades (Amsterdam, Holland: North Holland Publishing Co., 1977).
7. Davidson and Haspeslagh, "Shaping a Global Product Organization."
8. "How Goodyear Sharpened Organization and Production for a Tough World Market," *Business International,* January 16, 1989, 11-14.
9. "Integration for Profit," *Business Latin America,* July 5, 1993, 6-7.
10. Daniel Robey, *Designing Organizations: A Macro Perspective* (Homewood, Ill.: Richard D. Irwin, 1982), 327.
11. Samuel Humes, *Managing the Multinational* (London, England: Prentice-Hall, 1993), 143.
12. Thomas H. Naylor, "International Strategy Matrix," *Columbia Journal of World Business* 20 (Summer 1985): 11-19.
13. "Kodak's Matrix System Focuses on Product Business Units," *Business International,* July 18, 1988, 221-223.
14. "How 3M Develops Managers to Meet Global Strategic Objectives," *Business International,* March 21, 1988, 81-82.
15. Thomas J. Peters, "Beyond the Matrix Organization," *Business Horizons* 22 (October 1979): 15-27.
16. See John M. Stopford and Louis T. Wells, *Managing the Multinational Enterprise* (New York: Basic Books, 1972); also A. D. Chandler, *Strategy and Structure* (Cambridge, Mass.: MIT Press, 1962); and B. R. Scott, *Stages of Corporate Development* (Boston: ICCH, 1971).
17. Stanley M. Davis, "Trends in the Organization of Multinational Corporations," *Columbia Journal of World Business* 11 (Summer 1976): 59-71.
18. William Taylor, "The Logic of Global Business," *Harvard Business Review* 68 (March-April 1990): 91-105.
19. Rodman Drake and Lee M. Caudill, "Management of the Large Multinational: Trends and Future Challenges," *Business Horizons* 24 (May-June 1981): 83-91.
20. "So Big," *Across the Board,* 30 (January/February 1993): 16-21.
21. Christopher Bartlett, "MNCs: Get Off the Reorganization Merry-Go-Round," *Harvard Business Review* 60 (March/April 1983): 138-146.
22. Cheryll Barron, "Format Fears at Philips," *Management Today,* August 1978, 35-41, 101-102.
23. Thomas Gross, Ernie Turner, and Lars Cederholm, "Building Teams for Global Operations" *Management Review,* June 1987, 32-36.
24. Christopher A. Bartlett and Sumantra Ghoshal, "Matrix Management: Not a Structure, a Frame of Mind," *Harvard Business Review* 68 (July-August 1990): 138-145.
25. Christopher A. Bartlett and Sumantra Ghoshal, "Tap Your Subsidiaries for Global Reach," *Harvard Business Review* 64 (November-December 1986): 87-94.
26. John A. Quelch and Edward J. Hoff, "Customizing Global Marketing," *Harvard Business Review* 64 (May-June 1986): 59-68.
27. Richard I. Kirkland, Jr., "Entering a New World of Boundless Competition," *Fortune,* March 14, 1988, 18-22.
28. "Percy Barnevik's Global Crusade," *Business Week Enterprise 1993,* 204-211.
29. Louis Kraar, "Your Rivals Can Be Your Allies," *Fortune,* March 27, 1989, 66-76.
30. Amitai Etzioni, *A Comparative Analysis of Complex Organizations* (Glencoe, England: Free Press, 1961).

31. William G. Egelhoff, "Patterns of Control in U.S., U.K., and European Multinational Corporations," *Journal of International Business Studies* 15 (Fall 1984): 73–83.

32. William H. Davidson, "Administrative Orientation and International Performance," *Journal of International Business Studies* 15 (Fall 1984): 11–23.

33. William G. Ouchi, "The Relationship between Organizational Structure and Organizational Control," *Administrative Science Quarterly* 22 (March 1977): 95–112.

34. B. R. Baliga and Alfred M. Jaeger, "Multinational Corporations: Control Systems and Delegation Issues," *Journal of International Business Studies* 15 (Fall 1984): 25–40.

35. Laurent Leksell, *Headquarters-Subsidiary Relationships in Multinational Corporations* (Stockholm, Sweden: Stockholm School of Economics, 1981), Chapter 5.

36. Anant R. Negandhi and Martin Welge, *Beyond Theory Z* (Greenwich, Conn.: JAI Press, 1984), 16.

37. Richard Pascale, "Fitting New Employees into the Company Culture," *Fortune,* May 28, 1984, 28–40.

38. Bartlett and Ghoshal, "Matrix Management: Not a Structure, A Frame of Mind."

39. Nathaniel Gilbert, "How Middle-Sized Corporations Manage Global Operations," *Management Review,* October 1988, 46–50.

40. R. J. Alsegg, *Control Relationships between American Corporations and Their European Subsidiaries,* AMA Research Study No. 107 (New York: American Management Association, 1971), 7.

41. John J. Dyment, "Strategies and Management Controls for Global Corporations," *Journal of Business Strategy* 7 (Spring 1987): 20–26.

42. Hans Schoellhammer, "Decision-Making and Intraorganizational Conflicts in Multinational Companies," presentation at the Symposium on Management of Headquarter-Subsidiary Relationships in Transnational Corporations, Stockholm School of Economics, June 2–4, 1980.

43. Alfred M. Jaeger, "The Transfer of Organizational Culture Overseas: An Approach to Control in the Multinational Corporation," *Journal of International Business Studies* 14 (Fall 1983): 91–106.

CHAPTER 22

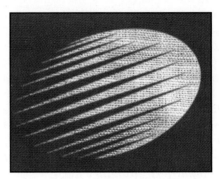

The Future

Learning Objectives

1. To understand the many changing dimensions that shape international business.

2. To learn about and evaluate the international business forecasts made by a panel of experts.

3. To be informed about different career opportunities in international business.

The Demise of the Global Firm?

Cyrus Freidheim, vice chairman of the consulting firm Booz, Allen & Hamilton, has a provocative perspective of the global firm. He predicts that current economic and political developments mean that global firms will be superseded by the "relationship-enterprise," a network of strategic alliances among big firms, spanning different industries and countries, but held together by common goals that encourage them to act almost as a single firm. He envisions the enterprises to be corporate juggernauts, with total revenues approaching $1 trillion by early next century, larger than all but the world's six biggest economies.

He suggests that early in the twenty-first century, Boeing, British Airways, Siemens, TNT (an Australian parcel delivery firm), and SNECMA (a French aero-engine maker) might together win a deal to build ten new airports in China. As part of the deal, British Airways and TNT would receive preferential routes and landing slots, the Chinese government would buy all state aircraft from Boeing-SNECMA, and Siemens would provide the air traffic control systems for all ten airports.

While this may sound farfetched, consider that Boeing, members of the airbus consortium, McDonnell Douglas, Mitsubishi, Kawasaki, and Fuji already are talking about jointly developing a new super-jumbo jet. Mitsubishi and Daimler-Benz already share engineers. General Motors and Toyota are discussing the possibility of Toyota's building light trucks in a GM plant.

According to Freidheim, the conventional model of the global firm is flawed. Most so-called global companies are still perceived as having a home base. For example, in 1991, only 2 percent of the board members of big American companies were foreigners. In Japanese companies, foreign directors are as rare as British sumo wrestlers. Firms therefore have a natural home-country bias, with the big decisions kept firmly at home.

This bias, together with various other constraints, hinders companies' efforts to become truly global. For instance, when capital is limited, firms tend to protect their home market at the expense of developing untapped markets overseas. Second, antitrust laws limit the ability of global firms to expand through takeovers. But most important of all is the problem of nationalism. No country likes foreigners controlling its industries. By contrast, a relationship enterprise can sidestep these constraints. Such an alliance can draw on lots of money; it can dodge antitrust barriers; and with home bases in all the main markets, it has the political advantage of being a local firm almost everywhere.

Source: "The Global Firm: R.I.P." *The Economist,* February 6, 1993, 69.

All international businesses face constantly changing world economic conditions. This is not a new situation nor one to be feared, because change provides the opportunity for new market positions to emerge and for managerial talent to improve the competitive position of the firm. Recognizing the importance of change and adapting creatively to new situations are the most important tasks of the international business executive.

Recently, changes are occurring more frequently, more rapidly, and have a more severe impact. The past has lost much of its value as a predictor of the future. What occurs today may not only be altered in short order but be completely overturned or reversed. For example, some countries find their major exports, which have increased steadily over decades, shrinking markedly in a brief period. Political stability can be completely disrupted over the course of a few months. Countries that have been considered enemies for decades, and with which no executive would dream of doing business, become close allies and offer a wealth of business opportunities. A major, sudden decline in world stock markets leaves corporations, investors, and consumers with strong feelings of uncertainty. An overnight currency decline of 40 percent results in an entirely new business climate for international suppliers and their customers. In all, international business managers today face complex and rapidly changing economic and political conditions.

This chapter will discuss possible future developments in the international business environment, highlight the implications of the changes for international business management, and offer suggestions for a creative response to the changes. The chapter also will explore the meaning of strategic changes as they relate to career choice and career path alternatives in international business.

THE INTERNATIONAL BUSINESS ENVIRONMENT

This section analyzes the international business environment by looking at political, financial, societal, and technological conditions of change and providing a glimpse of possible future developments as envisioned by an international panel of experts.* The impact of these factors on doing business abroad, on international trade relations, and on government policy is of particular interest to the international manager.

The Political Environment

The international political environment is undergoing a substantial transformation characterized by the reshaping of existing political blocs, the formation of new groupings, and the breakup of old coalitions.

The East-West Relationship   From 1945 to 1985, the adverse relationship between the dominant powers in the East and West changed little. Within a few years, however, the relationship was transformed. The communist empire briefly reshaped itself into a socialist league, only to emerge shortly thereafter as individual, distinct entities. The former eastern European satellite nations of the Soviet Union reasserted their independence and implemented market-oriented economies. The Soviet Union itself has been replaced by a loose confederation of independent states. Politically and economically, the repercussions of the changes have been far reaching. The key collaborative military mechanism in the East—the Warsaw Pact—ceased to exist. The economic agreement among the socialist countries—the Council for Mutual Economic Assistance (CMEA or COMECON)—has been disbanded.

Such rapid transformations cause major internal adjustments and economic dislocations, which in turn have political repercussions. A rapid rise of inflation in these nations is accompanied by deepening individual dissatisfaction due to unmet expectations of economic progress. Employment, domestic markets, and trade volumes are shrinking due to necessary adjustments in production capabilities based on market forces. Both the countries and companies involved suffer from deteriorating liquidity positions and a growing number of insolvencies.

The raising of the Iron Curtain has brought two separate economic and business systems closer together. A reduction of export controls, direct linkages with economic blocs, and the West's desire to help are transforming the business relations of the past.

As a result of easing political tensions, firms are presented with new opportunities. Demand—particularly for consumer products, which had been repressed in the past—now can be met with goods from the West. Yet, due to very limited consumer choice skills and knowledge levels, firms entering the new markets need to develop demand from the ground up—a difficult task.

Concurrently, central Europe emerges as a significant source of products and services destined for export. An increase in the formation of international joint ventures

*The information presented here is based largely on an original Delphi study by Michael R. Czinkota and Ilkka A. Ronkainen utilizing an international panel of experts.

and cooperative alliances is taking place. Yet many Western nations still are unprepared to accept an inflow of goods from a new source of competition. The inflow could throw carefully balanced trade relationships out of kilter and results in heated political discussions. To protect themselves against an avalanche of supplies from new quarters, governments frequently slow down the dismantling of old trade barriers, and sometimes even erect new ones. In doing so, they inhibit the development of a market orientation in the nations in transition by robbing them of incentive for change.[1]

Overall, many business activities will be subject to regional economic and political instability, increasing the risk of foreign business partners. Progress toward the institution of market-based economies may be halted or even reversed as large population segments are exposed to growing hardship during the transformation process. Still, large pools of untapped potential customers and production opportunities that are enhanced by the availability of a relatively cheap and well-trained labor force, may help offset the risk. To manage risks and operations, it will be crucial for corporations to find capable executives who can organize operations in these countries. As Global Perspective 22.1 shows, finding such executives is not easy, but the fact that they are needed is an incentive for new talent to adopt a global vision.

The North-South Relationship   The distinction between developed and less-developed countries (LDCs) is unlikely to change. Some theoreticians argue that the economic gap between the two groups will diminish, whereas others hold that the gap will increase. Both arguments lead to the conclusion that a gap will endure for some time. The ongoing disparity between developed and developing nations is likely to be based, in part, on continuing debt burdens and problems with satisfying basic needs. As a result, political uncertainty may well result in increased polarization between the haves and have-nots, with growing potential for political and economic conflict. Demands for political solutions to economic and financial problems are likely to increase. Some countries may consider migration as a key solution to population-growth problems, yet many emigrants may encounter government barriers to their migration. As a result, there may well be more investment flows by firms bringing their labor and skill-intensive manufacturing operations to these countries.[2] In addition, new approaches to international development taken by multilateral institutions may be effective in strengthening the grass roots of developing economies. Global Perspective 22.2 provides an example.

The issue of environmental protection will also be a major force shaping the relationship between the developed and the developing world. In light of the need and desire to grow their economies, however, there may be much disagreement on the part of the industrializing nations as to what approaches to take. Three possible scenarios emerge.

One scenario is that of continued international cooperation. The developed countries could relinquish part of their economic power to less-developed ones, thus contributing actively to their economic growth through a sharing of resources and technology. Although such cross-subsidization will be useful and necessary for the development of LDCs, it may reduce the rate of growth of the standard of living in the more developed countries. It would, however, increase trade flows between developed and less developed countries and precipitate the emergence of new international business opportunities.

A second scenario is that of confrontation. Due to an unwillingness to share resources and technology sufficiently (or excessively, depending on the point of view), the developing and the developed areas of the world may become increasingly hostile toward one another. As a result, the volume of international business, both by

Global Perspective

22.1
The Struggle to Fill Positions in China

With demand for executives outstripping supply, salary levels and job-hopping are spiraling out of control in China. Few local managers in that land of 1.2 billion boast Western business experience. Expatriates, wary about harsh living conditions in parts of China, seek lavish compensation packages.

Five U.S. executive search firms recently have opened offices in China. Executive Access Ltd. in Hong Kong, one of Asia's largest search firms, expects to conduct about 120 China assignments for corporate clients in 1994. But the task is not easy. Ranjan Marwah, chief executive, spent seven fruitless months seeking a $100,000-a-year agricultural manager in China for a major U.S. food producer. The candidate had to speak English and Mandarin, have business experience in China, and be able to negotiate with farmers and government officials. "Such a collection of experience doesn't exist at this point," said Marwah.

A senior U.S. executive relocating to China can command an expatriate package that typically includes a hardship allowance ranging between 20 percent and 35 percent of base salary, free housing, frequent "rest and relaxation" trips to Hong Kong, and a chauffeur-driven car.

The hottest candidates for China assignments are "bicultural" Asian managers, typically born outside the mainland but with both Western and Asian work experience. Certain bicultural executives can even get a dual-housing

benefit—living in China during the week and rejoining families on the weekend in Hong Kong.

Local managers who have international experience are valuable to companies. Indigenous managers provide contacts and knowledge of the Chinese market, and also cost companies only one tenth of the salary of expatriates. A mid-level government functionary recently agreed to run a big Canadian company's office in Beijing for a pay package that totaled 200,000 Hong Kong dollars (about US$26,000). The sum was one-tenth the size of a package rejected by an American expatriate with three other job offers. But the former bureaucrat now earns about 27 times what he had made working for the government.

The intense demand for talent in China has provoked considerable job-hopping by both local and foreign managers. Francis Kwong, a Hong Kong native, has worked for AT&T in China for less than a year. He previously worked for IBM in Hong Kong and Beijing. Several search firms approached him before he accepted AT&T's bid. Headhunters still call at least once a month.

Avon tends to lose locally hired Chinese managers to the lure of doubled salaries, free housing, promotions, training, and travel offered by U.S. consumer product makers. "These people are in a race to better their lives," said one Avon executive.

Source: Joann S. Lublin and Craig S. Smith, "U.S. Companies Struggle With Scarcity of Executives to Run Outposts in China," *The Wall Street Journal,* August 23, 1994, B1.

mandate of governments and by choice of the private sector, could be severely reduced.

A third scenario is that of isolation. Although there may be some cooperation between them, both groups, in order to achieve their domestic and international goals, may choose to remain economically isolated. This alternative may be particularly attractive if each region believes that it faces unique problems and therefore must seek their own solutions.

Emergence of New Economic Blocs   Some foresee the realignment of global strategic power through the emergence of new economic blocs. One such bloc would consist of a reshaped Europe, which would include political and economic membership of the 15 European Union nations, the central European nations, and possibly even some of the former Soviet republics. A second bloc would be led by Japan

Global Perspective

22.2
Lenders Target Women in the Developing World

The developing world's women are gaining a measure of economic autonomy as perceptions of them and their role in developing economies change. Even the big development agencies and multilateral banks are increasingly funding women-led small businesses and farming projects based on an assumption that women, more than men, are the critical players in the fight to relieve poverty. Agencies such as the World Bank, Agency for International Development, and Inter-American Development Bank say women are usually better at repaying their loans and less prone to waste or loot development money.

The motivation to target women has less to do with sexual politics than with the economic reality that women do much of the work in developing countries. "All over the developing world, in rural areas, the women are the mainstay of the local economy," said Gustave Speth, administrator of the United Nations Development Programme. A recent World Bank study found that women head half the households in sub-Saharan Africa. A study of village life in Cameroon found that women work an average of 64 hours a week, compared with 32 for men. And women's earnings are more likely to be used for the health and education of the next generation.

The focus on women's economic activities coincides with a growing interest in financing the thousands of tiny businesses that make up the developing world's vast "informal sector." Many of these so-called microenterprises, ranging from food sellers on street corners to one-person apparel makers, are run by women. Though statistics are shaky, it is estimated that informal-sector businesses make up as much as half of all economic activity in many devel

oping countries. Yet, until recently, the international institutions have funneled nearly all development funds to governments and state enterprises for projects that often did little for the poorest population segments.

In the Dominican Republic, the marriage between the large international agencies and grass roots groups is helping to get money into the hands of more poor women running businesses. To some extent, the small Caribbean state is seen as a model for others working on programs to lend to the poor. Within a year, development experts from Botswana, Brazil, Colombia, Jamaica, Mexico, and Senegal visited and studied how Dominican lenders extend credit to the poorest segments of society but still cover costs and stay afloat. Pedro Jimenez, the executive director of the largest small-enterprise lender in the Dominican Republic, argued that bankers to the poor have to avoid a "charity window" mentality. To stay in business, he says, lenders must charge real interest rates, usually about 30 percent, that cover the lenders' costs plus any inflation risk. Jimenez's bank grants loans for an average amount of $800 and has a 98.6 percent repayment rate.

In Niger, CARE is helping establish women's savings groups in about 45 villages. "They haven't had access to banking systems anywhere," said Ann Duval, the program's overseer. About 35 women contribute 50 cents per week. Two-week loans are made, with an interest rate of about 10 percent. Periodically the women liquidate their banks and distribute the money for certain needs. But the banks always start up again. Once they have had a bank, the women don't want to go without one.

Source: Tim Carrington, "Gender Economics: In Developing World, International Lenders Are Targeting Women," *The Wall Street Journal,* June 22, 1994, A1.

and would be mainly trade based; members would come mainly from the Pacific Rim. A third bloc could emerge in the Western Hemisphere, led by the United States and including Canada, Mexico, and several Central and South American nations. Such a bloc would be primarily trade based, but could eventually also incorporate political dimensions.

The bloc formations could result in heightened business stability and cooperation within each arrangement. Yet a concurrent danger might be the emergence of bloc-based competition and protectionism. Such a development could force global firms to choose a "home bloc" and could introduce new inefficiencies into global trade relations. On the positive side, however, due to their relative equality of power, the blocs could also be the precursors of global cooperation, resulting in an even more open and free global business environment.

A Divergence of Values   It might well be that different nations or cultures become increasingly disparate in terms of values and priorities. For example, in some countries, the aim for financial progress and an improved quantitative standard of living may well give way to priorities based on religion or the environment. Even if nations share similar values, their priorities among these values may differ strongly. For example, within a market-oriented system, some countries may prioritize profits and efficiency, while others may place social harmony first, even at the cost of maintaining inefficient industries.

Such a divergence of values will require a major readjustment of the activities of the international corporation. A continuous scanning of newly emerging national values thus becomes imperative for the international executive.

The International Financial Environment

Even though the international debt problem of the developing world appears temporarily subdued, it will remain a major international trade and business issue into the 2000s. Debt constraints and low commodity prices create slow growth prospects for many developing countries. They will be forced to reduce their levels of imports and to exert more pressure on industrialized nations to open up their markets. Even if the markets are opened, however, demand for most primary products will be far lower than supply. Ensuing competition for market share will therefore continue to depress prices.

Developed nations have a strong incentive to help the debtor nations. The incentive consists of the market opportunities that economically healthy developing countries can offer and of national security concerns. As a result, industrialized nations may very well be in a situation in which a funds transfer to debtor nations, accompanied by debt-relief measures such as debt forgiveness, are necessary to achieve economic stimulation at home.

The dollar will remain one of the major international currencies with little probability of gold returning to its former status in the near future. However, international transactions in both trade and finance are increasingly likely to be denominated in nondollar terms, using regional currencies such as the European Currency Unit (ECU). The system of floating currencies will likely continue, with occasional attempts by nations to manage exchange rate relationships or at least reduce the volatility of swings in currency values. However, given the vast flows of financial resources across borders, it would appear that market forces rather than government action will be the key determinant of a currency's value. Factors such as investor trust, economic conditions, earnings perceptions, and political stability are therefore likely to have a much greater effect on the international value of currencies than domestic monetary and fiscal experimentation.

Given the close linkages among financial markets, shocks in one market will quickly translate into rapid shifts in others and easily overpower the financial resources of individual governments. Even if there should be a decision by governments to pursue closely coordinated fiscal and monetary policies, they are unlikely to be able to negate long-term market effects in response to changes in economic fundamentals.

A looming concern in the international financial environment will be the **international debt load** of the United States. Both domestically and internationally, the United States is incurring debt that would have been inconceivable only a few decades ago. For example, in the 1970s the accumulation of financial resources by the Arab nations was of major concern in the United States. Congressional hearings focused on whether Arab money was "buying out America." At that time, however, Arab holdings in the United States were $10 billion to $20 billion. Today the accumulation of dollar holding inside and outside of the United States has led to much more significant shifts in foreign holdings.

In 1985, the United States became a net negative investor internationally. The United States entered the 1990s with an international debt burden of more than $800 billion, making it the largest debtor nation in the world, owing more to other nations than all the developing countries combined. Mitigating this burden are the facts that most of the debts are denominated in U.S. dollars and that, even at such a large debt volume, U.S. debt-service requirements are only a small portion of GNP. Yet this accumulation of foreign debt may very well introduce entirely new dimensions into the international business relationships of individuals and nations. Once debt has reached a certain level, the creditor as well as the debtor is hostage to the loans.

Since foreign creditors expect a return on their investment, a substantial portion of future U.S. international trade activity will have to be devoted to generating sufficient funds for such repayment. For example, at an assumed interest rate or rate of return of 10 percent, the international U.S. debt level—without any growth—would require the annual payment of $80 billion, which amounts to about 10 percent of current U.S. exports. Therefore, it seems highly likely that international business will become a greater priority than it is today and will serve as a source of major economic growth for firms in the United States.

To some degree, foreign holders of dollars may also choose to convert their financial holdings into real property and investments in the United States. This will result in an entirely new pluralism in U.S. society. It will become increasingly difficult and, perhaps, even unnecessary to distinguish between domestic and foreign products—as is already the case with Hondas made in Ohio. Senators and members of Congress, governors, municipalities, and unions will gradually be faced with conflicting concerns in trying to develop a national consensus on international trade and investment. National security issues may also be raised as major industries become majority owned by foreign firms.

At the same time, U.S. international debt will, among other things, contribute to an increasingly tight money supply around the world. When combined with the financial needs of the emerging central and eastern European market economies, the fund flows to the former Soviet Union, and the aid requirements of many developing nations, a more heated competition for capital is likely to emerge, with continuing scarcity leading to relatively high real interest rates worldwide. Industrialized countries are likely to attempt to narrow the domestic gap between savings and investments through fiscal policies. Without concurrent restrictions on international capital flows, such policies are likely to meet with only limited success. Lending institutions can be expected to become more conservative in their financing, a move that may hit smaller firms and developing countries the hardest. Comparatively easier access to better financial resources will become a key competitive determinant and perhaps even be critical to the survival of many companies. At the same time, firms must strive to become best in their class. Given the increasing competition worldwide, products and services that only offer me-too features and capabilities will be hard pressed to stay in the market.

The Effects of Population Shifts

The population discrepancy between less-developed nations and the industrialized countries will continue to increase. In the industrialized world, an increase in **population growth** will become a national priority, given the fact that in many countries, particularly in Western Europe, the population is shrinking rather than increasing. The shrinkage may lead to labor shortages and to major societal difficulties in providing for a growing elderly population.

In the developing world, the reduction of population growth will continue to be one of the major challenges of governmental policy. In spite of well-intentioned economic planning, continued rapid increases in population will make it more difficult to ensure that the pace of economic development exceeds population growth. If the standard of living of a nation is determined by dividing the GNP by its population, any increase in the denominator will require equal increases in the numerator to maintain the standard of living. Therefore, if the population's rate of growth continues at its current pace, even greater efforts must be made to increase the economic activity within these nations. With an annual increase in the world population of 100 million people, the task is daunting. It becomes even more complex when one considers that within countries with high population increases, large migration flows take place from rural to urban areas. As a result, by the end of this decade, most of the world's 10 largest metropolitan areas will be in the developing world.[3]

The Technological Environment

The concept of the global village is commonly accepted today and indicates the importance of communication in the technological environment. Satellite dishes can be built out of easily obtainable components. The rapidly expanding use of fax machines, portable telephones, and personal communication devices points to the evolution of unrestricted information flows. The importance of these technologies is driven home when one considers that, since 1991, the fax traffic between the United States and Europe has exceeded voice traffic.[4] Concurrently, the availability of information to be communicated has increased dramatically. Since all this information includes details about lifestyles, opportunities, and aspirations, international communication will be a great equalizer in the future.

Changes in other technologies will be equally rapid and will have a major effect on business in general. For example, the appearance of superconductive materials and composite materials has made possible the development of new systems in fields such as transportation and electric power, pushing the frontiers of human activity into as yet unexplored areas such as outer space and the depths of the oceans. The development of biotechnology is already leading to revolutionary progress not only in agriculture, medicine, and chemistry but also in manufacturing systems within industry.[5]

High technology is expected to become one of the more volatile areas of economic activity. Order of magnitude changes in technology can totally wipe out private and public national investment in a high-technology sector. In the hard-hitting race toward technological primacy, some nations will inevitably fall behind and others will be able to catch up only with extreme difficulty.

Even firms and countries that are at the leading edge of technology will find it increasingly difficult to marshal the funds necessary for further advancements. For example, investments in semiconductor technology are measured in billions rather than millions of dollars and do not bring any assurance of success. Not to engage in the race, however, will mean falling behind quickly in all areas of manufacturing when virtually every industrial and consumer product is "smart" due to its chip technology.

As this chapter's opening vignette showed, it is likely that firms will join forces through cooperative agreements, joint ventures, and strategic partnerings to compete for major projects, spread the necessary financial commitments, and reduce the risk of technology development. Concurrently, governments will increase their spending on research and development in order to further "techno-nationalism" through the creation of more sources of technological innovation within their boundaries. Government-sponsored collaborative research ventures are likely to increase across industries and country groupings. However, difficulties may emerge when global firms threaten to rapidly internationalize any gains from such regionalized research ventures.

CHANGES IN TRADE RELATIONS	The formation of the World Trade Organization (WTO) has brought to conclusion a lengthy and sometimes acrimonious round of global trade negotiations. However, key disagreements among major trading partners are likely to persist, particularly in the areas of financial and information services. Ongoing major imbalances in trade flows will tempt nations to apply their own national trade remedies, particularly in the antidumping field. Even though WTO rules permit for a retaliation against unfair trade practices, such actions would only result in an ever-increasing spiral of adverse trade relations.

A key question will be whether nations are willing to abrogate some of their sovereignty even during difficult economic times. An affirmative answer will strengthen the multilateral trade system and enhance the flow of trade. However, if key trading nations resort to the development of insidious nontariff barriers, unilateral actions, and bilateral negotiations, protectionism will increase on a global scale and the volume of international trade is likely to decline.

International trade relations also will be shaped by new participants whose market entry will restructure the composition of global trade. For example, new players with exceptionally large productive potential, such as the People's Republic of China and Central Europe will substantially alter world trade flows. And while both governments and firms will be required to change many trading policies and practices as a result, they will also benefit in terms of market opportunities and sourcing alternatives.

Finally, the efforts of governments to achieve self-sufficiency in economic sectors, particularly in agriculture and heavy industries, have ensured the creation of long-term, worldwide oversupply of some commodities and products, many of which historically had been traded widely. As a result, after some period of intense market share competition aided by subsidies and governmental support, a gradual and painful restructuring of these economic sectors will have to take place. This will be particularly true for agricultural cash crops such as wheat, corn, and dairy products and industrial products such as steel, chemicals, and automobiles.

GOVERNMENTAL POLICY

International trade activity now affects domestic policy more than ever. For example, trade flows can cause major structural shifts in employment. Linkages between industries spread these effects throughout the economy. Fewer domestically produced automobiles will affect the activities of the steel industry. Shifts in the sourcing of textiles will affect the cotton industry. Global productivity gains and competitive pressures will force many industries to restructure their activities. In such circumstances, industries are likely to ask their governments to help in their restructuring efforts. Often, such assistance includes a built-in tendency toward protectionist action.

Such restructuring is not necessarily negative. For example, since the turn of the century, farm employment in the United States has dropped from more than 40 percent of the population to less than 3 percent. Yet today, the farm industry feeds 270 million people in the United States and still produces large surpluses. A restructuring of industries can greatly increase productivity and provide the opportunity for resource allocation to emerging sectors of an economy.

Governments cannot be expected, for the sake of the theoretical ideal of "free trade," to sit back and watch the effects of deindustrialization on their countries. The most that can be expected is that they will permit an open-market orientation subject to the needs of domestic policy. Even an open-market orientation is maintainable only if governments can provide reasonable assurances to their own firms and citizens that the openness applies to foreign markets as well. Therefore, unfair trade practices such as governmental subsidization, dumping, and industrial targeting will be examined more closely, and retaliation for such activities is likely to be swift and harsh.

Increasingly, governments will need to coordinate policies that affect the international business environment. The development of international indexes and **trigger mechanisms,** which precipitate government action at predetermined intervention points, will be a useful step in that direction. Yet, for them to be effective, governments will need to muster the political fortitude to implement the policies necessary for cooperation. For example, international monetary cooperation will work in the long term only if domestic fiscal policies are responsive to the achievement of the coordinated goals.

At the same time as the need for collaboration among governments grows, it will become more difficult to achieve a consensus. In the Western world, the time from 1945 through 1990 was characterized by a commonality of purpose. The common defense against the communist enemy remanded trade relations to second place, and provided a bond that encouraged collaboration. With the common threat gone, however, the bonds have been diminished—if not dissolved—and the priority of economic performance has increased. Unless a new key jointness of purpose can be found by governments, collaborative approaches will become increasingly difficult.[6]

Governmental policymakers must take into account the international repercussions of domestic legislation. For example, in imposing a special surcharge tax on the chemical industry designed to provide for the cleanup of toxic waste products, they need to consider its repercussions on the international competitiveness of the chemical industry. Similarly, current laws such as antitrust legislation need to be reviewed if the laws hinder the international competitiveness of domestic firms.

Policymakers also need a better understanding of the nature of the international trade issues confronting them. Most countries today face both short-term and long-term trade problems. Trade balance issues, for example, are short term in nature, while competitiveness issues are much more long term. All too often, however, short-term issues are attacked with long-term **trade policy mechanisms,** and vice versa. In the United States, for example, the desire to "level the international playing field" with mechanisms such as vigorous implementation of import restrictions or voluntary restraint agreements may serve long-term competitiveness well, but it does little to alleviate the publicly perceived problem of the trade deficit. Similarly, a further opening of Japan's market to foreign corporations will have only a minor immediate effect on that country's trade surplus or the trading partners' deficit. Yet it is the expectation and hope of many in both the public and the private sectors that such instant changes will occur. For the sake of the credibility of policymakers, it therefore becomes imperative to precisely identify the nature of the problem and to design and use policy measures that are appropriate for its resolution.

In the years to come, governments will be faced with an accelerating technological race and with emerging problems that seem insurmountable by individual firms alone, such as pollution of the environment and global warming. As market gaps emerge and time becomes crucial, both governments and the private sector will find that even if the private sector knows that a lighthouse is needed, it may still be difficult, time-consuming, and maybe even impossible to build one with private funds alone. As a result, it seems likely that the concepts of administrative guidance and government–corporate collaboration will increasingly become part of the policy behavior of governments. The international manager in turn will have to spend more time and effort dealing with governments and with macro rather than micro issues.

THE FUTURE OF INTERNATIONAL BUSINESS MANAGEMENT

Global change results in an increase in risk. One shortsighted alternative for risk-averse managers would be the termination of international activities altogether. However, businesses will not achieve long-run success by engaging only in risk-free actions. Further, other factors make the pursuit of international business mandatory.

International markets remain a source of high profits, as a quick look at a list of multinational firms would show.[7] International activities help cushion slack in domestic sales resulting from recessionary or adverse domestic conditions and may be crucial to the very survival of the firm. International markets also provide firms with foreign experience that helps them compete more successfully with foreign firms in the domestic market.

International Planning and Research

Firms must continue to serve customers well to be active participants in the international marketplace. One major change that will come about is that the international manager will need to respond to general governmental concerns to a greater degree when planning a business strategy. Further, societal concern about macro problems needs to be taken into account directly and quickly because societies have come to expect more social responsibility from corporations. Taking on a leadership role regarding social causes may also benefit corporations' bottom lines, since consumers appear more willing than ever to act as significant pressure points for policy changes and to pay for their social concerns.

Another trend consists of increased competition in international markets. The trend will create a need for more niches in which firms can create a distinct international competence. As a result, increased specialization and segmentation will let firms fill very narrow and specific demands or resolve very specific problems for

Ford Motor Co. currently sponsers "Ocean Planet," an exhibition focusing on ocean conservation. This exhibit opened in Washington, D.C. and will travel to 11 cities before the year 2000. The motivation prompting its creation is to create awareness now, through education, regarding ocean conservation before this issue becomes "the rain forest" of the '90s.

Source: Courtesy Ford Motor Co.

CARS AREN'T THE ONLY BODIES WE'RE CONCERNED ABOUT.

That's why Ford Motor Company is proud to be a sponsor of Ocean Planet. Glorious in scope, the Smithsonian Institution's traveling exhibition dramatically illustrates how all life is affected by the health of the ocean and highlights the urgent need for ocean conservation. Our support of Ocean Planet underscores an ongoing commitment to ENVIRONMENTAL concerns. Back in 1903 Henry Ford himself designed suppliers' shipping crates so they could be dismantled and used as running boards and wooden trim, reducing packing waste. Since then our engineers have continued to create INNOVATIVE ways of protecting our environment such as recycling and reducing harmful emissions, as well as developing cars that run on electricity and NATURAL gas. We're honored to be a part of Ocean Planet, and we urge everyone to visit the exhibition and learn what we can do to assure our world's survival. A topic that's a concern to us all.

QUALITY IS JOB 1

their international customers.[8] Identifying and filling the niches will be easier in the future because of the greater availability of international research tools and information. The key challenge to global firms will be to build and manage decision-making processes that allow quick responses to multiple changing environmental demands. This capability is important since firms face a growing need for worldwide coordination and integration of internal activities, such as logistics and operations, while being confronted with the need for greater national differentiation and responsiveness at the customer level.[9]

In spite of the frequent short-term orientation by corporations and investors, companies will need to learn to prepare for long-term horizons. Particularly in an environment of heated competition and technological battles, of large projects and slow payoffs, companies, their stakeholders, and governments will need to find avenues that not only permit but encourage the development of strategic perspectives. Figure 22.1 provides an example of such a long-term view.

Governments both at home and abroad will demand that private business practices not increase public costs and that businesses serve customers equally and nondiscriminately.[10] The concept directly counters the desire to serve first the markets that are most profitable and least costly. International executives will therefore be torn in two directions and, to provide results that are acceptable both to customers and to the societies they serve, they must walk a fine line, balancing the public and the private good.

International Product Policy

Two major trends are emerging in the product policies of multinational corporations. On one hand, automation and the search for increasing economies of scale demand that firms serve more markets. Even large domestic markets such as the United States

---

FIGURE 22.1   Long-Term Planning

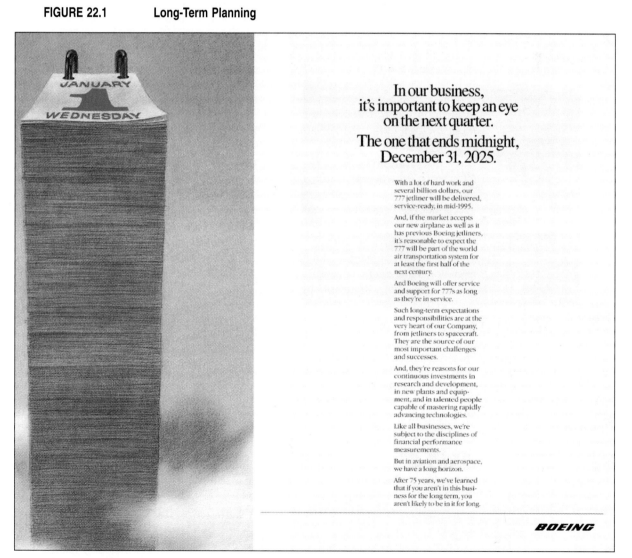

Source: *The Economist*, October 24, 1992, 29.

or Japan may be "too small to absorb the output of the world-class automated plants needed for economies of scale in many product areas."[11] Europe, Japan, and the United States harbor the greatest buying power and concentration of demand in the world for many products. For example, the three regions account for nearly 85 percent of the world's demand for consumer electronic goods; they also consumed 85 percent of the computers and 70 percent of the machine tools produced in the world.[12] According to these facts, production should be concentrated in one of the regions and output widely distributed.

Although this trend would argue for greater exports and greater standardization of products, a counterargument holds that, because of increasing protectionist policies and the desire of nations to obtain and develop their own technology, foreign direct investment and multiple plant locations will replace exports.[13] As long as firms have the flexibility of choice of location, managers will have substantial leverage over domestic legislation and regulations that would affect their international effort. Governments will run the risk of unemployment growth if domestic firms, because of an unsatisfactory **competitive platform,** move their operations abroad.

Regardless of which avenue firms use to take their products and services abroad, it appears certain that worldwide introduction of products will occur much more rapidly in the future. As a result of the ever-quickening pace of technological change, the life cycles of most products will be greatly shortened. To stay ahead of the competition, firms will need to constantly adapt, adjust, and incrementally improve their products.[14] As a result, new products will be developed based on a system-oriented integration within the firm, where management, marketing, research, and development are joint rather than separate activities. Due to a more rapid commercialization of new technology, firms will have to develop more efficient, faster, and better targeted marketing strategies around the world, accompanied by better and shorter distribution channels. The homogenization of patterns of consumption will assist these efforts through the emergence of global or regional consumer segments, which will accelerate the penetration of global brands. Overall, product introduction will grow more complex, more expensive, and riskier, and the rewards to be reaped from a successful product will need to be accumulated more quickly.

Factor endowment advantages have a significant impact on the decisions of international managers. Given the acceleration of product life cycles, nations with low production costs will be able to develop and offer products more cheaply. Countries such as India, Israel, or the Philippines offer large pools of skilled people at labor rates much lower than in Europe, Japan, or the United States. For example, India has the third largest number of engineers after the United States and the CIS. All this talent also results in a much wider dissemination of technological creativity, a factor that will affect the innovative capability of firms. For example, in 1994, 43 percent of all the patents in the United States were granted to foreign inventors. Table 22.1 shows the countries of origin of patent recipients in 1994.

Firms need to make global knowledge and advantages part of their production strategies—or they need to develop consistent comparative advantages in production technology—to stay ahead of the game. Similarly, workers engaged in the productive process must attempt, through training and skill enhancement, to stay ahead of foreign workers who are willing to charge less for their time. The need to stay ahead highlights the importance, for governments, companies, and workers alike, to invest in human capital so that the interest from such investment can be drawn on for competitive success.

Firms also will need to evaluate the formation of collaborative arrangements between nominally competing companies and search for complementary strengths, be

TABLE 22.1
U.S. Patents Granted to Foreign Inventors in 1994

Country	Patents	Country	Patents
Antigua	1	Luxembourg	41
Argentina	27	Malaysia	16
Australia	533	Malta	1
Austria	337	Mauritius	1
Belgium	410	Mexico	56
Bermuda	2	Monaco	6
Brazil	57	Netherlands	944
British Virgin Islands	2	New Zealand	51
Bulgaria	2	Norway	128
Canada	2,275	Pakistan	1
Cayman Islands	2	Peru	2
Chile	6	Philippines	1
China (Mainland)	41	Poland	6
Colombia	7	Portugal	6
Costa Rica	7	Romania	1
Croatia	3	Russian Federation	22
Cuba	9	Saudi Arabia	9
Cyprus	2	San Marino	1
Czechoslovakia	20	Singapore	58
Denmark	260	Slovenia	10
Dominican Republic	1	South Africa	99
Ecuador	3	Soviet Union	63
Egypt	4	Spain	131
Faroe Islands	1	St. Vincent/The Grenadas	1
Finland	387	Sweden	754
France	3,051	Switzerland	1,225
Germany	7,024	Taiwan	1,709
Greece	16	Thailand	13
Guadeloupe	1	Trinidad & Tobago	2
Guatemala	2	Tunisia	1
Hong Kong	200	Turkey	1
Hungary	50	Uganda	3
Iceland	6	Ukraine	5
India	33	United Arab Emirates	1
Indonesia	9	United Kingdom	2,424
Iran	1	Uzbekistan	1
Ireland	53	Venezuela	31
Israel	354	Yemen	1
Italy	1,376	Yugoslavia	19
Japan	23,764	Zimbabwe	4
Korea, Dem. Republic of	1	Total patents issued in U.S., 1994	113,268
Korea, Republic of	947	Total patents issued to U.S. inventors	64,119
Kuwait	1	Total patents issued to foreign inventors	49,149
Lebanon	1	Foreign patents as percentage of total	43%
Liechtenstein	11		

Source: Patents Issued to Residents of the United States and Patents Issued to Residents of Foreign Countries, United States Department of Commerce, Patent and Trademark Office, January 1995.

they in personnel availability, specialized skills, access to capital markets, or technical know-how. The partners do not need to be large to make a major contribution. Depending on the type of product, very small firms can serve as coordinating subcontractors and collaborate in product and service development and production and distribution. For example, in Belgium, in the center of Europe, sits European Telecom, a company that allows customers to dial their international calls by remote control by way of California, using American carriers. The service saves customers one-third in comparison to the stiff European rates. European Telecom has only three employees and only $50,000 worth of equipment."[15]

International Communications

The advances made in international communications will also have a profound impact on international management. Entire industries are becoming more footloose in their operations; that is, they are less tied to their current location in their interaction with markets. For example, Best Western Hotels in the United States has channeled its entire reservation system through a toll-free number that is being serviced out of the prison system in Utah. Companies could even concentrate their communications activities in other countries. Communications for worldwide operations, for example, could easily be located in Africa or Asia without impairing international corporate activities.

Staff in different countries can not only talk together but can also share pictures and data on their computer screens. Worldwide rapid product development has therefore become feasible. Technology also makes it possible to merge the capabilities of computers, televisions, and telecommunications. Communication costs are decreasing significantly at the same time that the capabilities of communication tools increase. As a result, firms have the opportunity for worldwide data exchange and benefit from virtually unlimited availability of detailed market and customer data. The challenge is to see who can use and apply information technology best.

Distribution Strategies

Worldwide distribution systems are assisting global business development. Integrated systems, labeled sea bridges or land bridges, already are operational. Major trading routes that offer substantial distribution economies of scale are being developed. The international manager will experience relative ease in planning distribution as long as he or she stays within established routes but will encounter difficulties when attempting to deviate from them. Customers who are on the routes benefit from the low cost of distribution and see a widening in their choice of products. Off-route customers have fewer product choices and pay increased prices for foreign products. Market access is also a crucial component in determining a firm's capability to develop new products since lack of customers will sharply reduce the economic benefits derived from new products. Therefore, the distribution systems may often become the deciding factor in whether markets can be served and whether industry will develop. Communications advances will ensure that the customers in different markets are informed about product availability, making distribution limitations even more painful.

More sophisticated distribution systems will also offer new management opportunities to firms but, at the same time, will introduce new uncertainties and fragilities into corporate planning. For example, the development of just-in-time delivery systems makes firms more efficient yet, on an international basis, also exposes them to more risk due to distribution interruptions. A strike in a faraway country may therefore be newly significant for a company that depends on the timely delivery of supplies.

Advances in telecommunications allow staff in different countries to talk together and share pictures and data on their computer screens. In the state-of-the-art video conference center at Hoffmann-LaRoche's U.S. headquarters in Nutley, N.J., scientists discuss research goals and results with Roche colleagues in Basel, Switzerland.

Source: Courtesy of Hoffmann-LaRoche, Inc.

International Pricing

International pricing competition will become increasingly heated. As their distribution spreads throughout the world, many products will take on commodity characteristics, as semiconductors did in the 1980s. Therefore, price differentials of one cent per unit may become crucial in making an international sale. However, since many new products and technologies will address completely new needs, forward pricing will become increasingly difficult and controversial as demand levels are impossible to predict with any kind of accuracy.

Even for consumer products, price competition will be substantial. Because of the increased dissemination of technology, the firm that introduces a product will no longer be able to justify higher prices for long; domestically produced products will soon be of similar quality. As a result, exchange rate movements may play more significant roles in maintaining the competitiveness of the international firm. Firms can be expected to prevail on their government to manage the country's currency to maintain a favorable exchange rate.

Through subsidization, targeting, government contracts, or other hidden forms of support, nations will attempt to stimulate their international competitiveness. Due to the price sensitivity of many products, the international manager will be forced to identify such unfair practices quickly, communicate them to his or her government, and insist on either similar benefits or government action to create an internationally level playing field.

At the same time, many firms will work hard to reduce the price sensitivity of their customers. By developing relationships with their markets rather than just carrying out transactions, other dimensions such as loyalty, consistency, the cost of shifting suppliers, and responsiveness to client needs may become much more important than price in future competition.

CAREERS IN INTERNATIONAL BUSINESS

By studying this book you have learned about the intricacies, complexities, and thrills of international business. Of course, a career in international business is more than jet-set travel between New Delhi, Tokyo, Frankfurt, and New York. It is hard work and requires knowledge and expertise. Yet, in spite of the difficulties, international business allows an individual to break away from set patterns and offers new horizons, new experiences, and new opportunities for growth, as Global Perspective 22.3 shows.

To prepare, you should be well versed in a specific functional business area and take summer internships abroad. You should take language courses and travel, not simply for pleasure but to observe business operations abroad and gain a greater appreciation of different peoples and cultures. The following pages provide an overview of principal further training and employment opportunities in the international business field.

Further Training

One option for the student on the road to more international involvement is to obtain further in-depth training by enrolling in graduate business school programs that specialize in international business education. Even though the international orientation of U.S. universities is relatively recent, a substantial number of schools have de-

Global Perspective

22.3
Japanese Women Make Career Moves

To get the job they want, a growing number of determined Japanese career women are leaving Japan. "I can be powerful," said a 28-year-old Japanese sales executive at the Hong Kong branch of a Japanese furniture company. Back home, she said, she never would have obtained such a career-track position: "It's the businessmen who have the power. . . . Women are just part of the machine."

While women always have faced discrimination in Japan's male-oriented corporate culture, the situation worsened dramatically with Japan's economic slump. It has become so bad that a growing number of women are leaving Japan for the work opportunities and more-equal environments of North American, European, and other Asian countries. Hong Kong, not exactly a bastion of feminism, is in fact the biggest draw. The number of Japanese women in Hong Kong jumped by nearly 25 percent between 1991 and 1993, to 7,381. "They came to Hong Kong, not like before for sightseeing and shopping, but only to look for jobs," said the director of an employment agency. Demand is snowballing for qualified staff, particularly among the growing number of Japanese companies setting up shop there. Good opportunities exist in fields such as sales, finance, and translation services. Midori Wantanabe, 24, took a $5,020 pay cut to leave her job in Japan and relocate to

Hong Kong. "I had no chance to become an officer [in Japan]—there was nothing more I could do there," she said. Faced with a limited number of qualified applicants in a thriving economy, most companies can't afford to be picky about gender.

Japan has no effective legal barriers to intrusive—or potentially sexist—questions in employment interviews. One Japanese woman, searching for a job, was told her legs were too fat and another was asked whether she was a virgin. Japan's equal employment opportunity law, which bars sex discrimination, carries no penalty. Despite all of this, Japan's first female Supreme Court judge, Hisako Takahashi, exclaimed, "We have a saying in Japan: However dark the night, there is no night that does not end." She calls on men and women to work together to educate Japanese society about women's true abilities.

"It's not my job" to change Japanese society, said one female investment analyst at a securities firm. She moved to Hong Kong and has no plans to return. "In Japan, if you go to a sales meeting, you are the only female." In Hong Kong, close to half the fund managers she meets are women. "Japanese women can come here and be themselves."

Source: Jennifer Cody, "To Forge Ahead, Career Women Are Venturing Out of Japan," *The Wall Street Journal,* August 29, 1994, B1.

veloped specific international programs. Many universities around the world also specialize in training international managers. A review of college catalogues and of materials from groups such as the Academy of International Business will be useful here.

In addition, as the world becomes more global, many organizations are able to assist students interested in studying abroad or in gathering foreign work experience. Over time, an increasing number of scholarships and exchange programs have become available. Table 22.2 lists some key international exchange and training programs and the eligible participants.

For those ready to enter or rejoin the "real world," different employment opportunities need to be evaluated.

Employment with a Large Firm

One career alternative in international business is to work for a large multinational corporation. These firms constantly search for personnel to help them in their international operations. For example, a Procter & Gamble recruiting advertisement published in a university's student newspaper is reproduced in Figure 22.2.

Many multinational firms, while seeking specialized knowledge such as languages, expect employees to be firmly grounded in the practice and management of business. Rarely, if ever, will a firm hire a new employee at the starting level and immediately place him or her in a position of international responsibility. Usually, a new employee is expected to become thoroughly familiar with the company's internal operations before being considered for an international position. Reasons a manager is sent abroad include that the company expects him or her to reflect the corporate spirit, to be tightly wed to the corporate cultures, and to be able to communicate well with both local and corporate management personnel. In this liaison position, the manager will have to be exceptionally sensitive to both headquarters and local operations. As an intermediary, the expatriate must be empathetic, understanding, and yet fully prepared to implement the goals set by headquarters.

It is very expensive for companies to send an employee overseas. As this chapter's map shows, the annual cost of maintaining a manager overseas is often a multiple of the cost of hiring a local manager. Companies want to be sure that the expenditure is worth the benefit they will receive. Failure not only affects individual careers, but also sets back the business operations of the firm. Therefore, firms increasingly develop training programs for employees destined to go abroad. Global Perspective 22.4 provides insights into the rationale and activities of such training programs.

Even if a position opens up in international operations, there is some truth in the saying that the best place to be in international business is on the same floor as the chief executive at headquarters. Employees of firms that have taken the international route often come back to headquarters to find only a few positions available for them. After spending time in foreign operations, where independence is often high and authority significant, a return to a regular job at home, which sometimes may not even call on the many skills acquired abroad, may turn out to be a difficult and deflating experience. Such encounters lead to some disenchantment with international activities as well as to financial pressures and family problems, all of which may add up to significant executive stress during reentry.[16] Although many firms depend on their international operations for a substantial amount of sales volume and profits, reentry programs are often viewed as an unnecessary expense. The decision is difficult for the internationalist who wants to go abroad, make his or her mark, and return home to an equivalent or even better position. However, as

TABLE 22.2
U.S.-Funded International Exchange and Training Programs

Agency and Name of Program	Under-graduate Students	Eligible Participants					
		Graduate Students	Other Students	Teachers	Professors	Researchers	Post doctorate Scholars
Agency for International Development							
Thomas Jefferson Fellowship Program	X	X		X	X	X	X
Participant Training Program Europe	X	X		X	X	X	X
Regional Human Resources Program	X	X		X			
Department of Agriculture							
Research and Scientific Exchange Program		X		X	X	X	X
Department of Commerce							
Exchange Visitor Program						X	
Special American Business Internship Training Program							
Department of Defense							
International Military Education and Training Program		X		X	X		
National Security Education Program	X	X					X
Navy Exchange Scientist Program							
Professional Military Education Exchanges							
U.S. Military Academies Exchanges	X						
Department of Education							
Foreign Language and Area Studies Fellowship Program		X					
Fulbright-Hays Group Projects Abroad	X	X		X	X		
Fulbright-Hays Doctoral Dissertation Research Abroad		X					
Fulbright-Hays Faculty Research Abroad					X	X	X
Fulbright-Hays Seminars Abroad				X	X		
Department of Health and Human Services							
International Research Fellowships						X	
Senior International Fellowships					X	X	
Scholars in Residence					X	X	
National Research Service Awards							
Visitor and Training Program							
Individual Health Scientist Exchanges and							
Biomedical Research Exchange Programs					X	X	
Visiting Program						X	
National Institutes of Health-French Postdoctoral Fellowship					X	X	
Inter-American Foundation							
Academic Fellowship Program		X					
Department of the Interior							
U.S.–Russia Environmental Agreement						X	
U.S.–China Nature Conservation Protocol						X	
Japan–U.S. Friendship Commission							
Japan–U.S. Friendship Commission Grants		X		X	X	X	
Department of Labor							
International Visitors Labor Studies							
National Endowment for the Arts							
U.S. Artists at International Festivals and Exhibitions							
U.S.–Japan Artist Exchanges							
International Projects Initiative							
Travel Grants Program							
U.S.–Mexico Artist Residencies							
British America Arts Association Fellowships							
National Endowment for the Humanities							
Elementary and Secondary Education in the Humanities				X			
Higher Education in the Humanities					X		
NEH Teachers-Scholars				X	X		
Foreign Language Education				X	X		
Travel to Collections					X		X

Agency and Name of Program	Under-graduate Students	Eligible Participants					
		Graduate Students	Other Students	Teachers	Professors	Researchers	Post doctorate Scholars
Interpretive Research					X	X	X
Summer Seminars for School Teachers				X			
International Research							X
Summer Stipends				X	X		X
Humanities Projects in Museums and Historical Organizations						X	
Summer Seminars for College Teachers					X	X	X
Fellowship for College Teachers and Independent Scholars				X	X	X	X
Humanities Projects in Media					X	X	
Public Humanities Projects					X	X	
Centers for Advanced Study							X
Fellowship for University Teachers				X	X		X
Humanities Projects in Libraries and Archives						X	
National Science Foundation							
Summer Institute in Japan		X					
U.S.–India Exchange of Scientists					X	X	X
Smithsonian Institution							
Bureau Appointments	X	X					X
Wildlife Conservation and Management Training	X	X		X	X	X	X
Department of State							
Russian, Eurasian, and Eastern European Studies Program		X			X	X	X
U.S. Information Agency							
Fulbright Academic Program	X	X		X	X	X	X
International Visitors Program					X		
Citizens Exchanges	X	X		X	X		
Hubert H. Humphrey Fellowship							
Youth Programs	X		X				
University Affiliations Program					X	X	X
Performing Arts Exchanges							
Study of the United States				X	X		
Academic Specialist Program					X		
U.S. Speakers					X	X	
Media Training Program							
Arts America Program							
Fulbright Teacher Exchange				X			
Library Fellows Program							
English Teaching Fellow				X			
American Cultural Specialists							
Artistic Ambassadors							
Arts America Speakers							

Source: U.S. General Accounting Office, *Exchange Programs: Inventory of International Educational, Cultural and Training Programs,* Washington, D.C., June 1993.

firms begin to recognize the importance of international operations, more efforts toward proper personnel management are likely to be made. Eventually, most firms will make international experience a requirement for further moves upon the corporate ladder.

Employment with a Small or Medium-Sized Firm

A second alternative is to begin work in a small or medium-sized firm. Very often, such firms have only recently developed an international outlook, and the new

The Cost of Living in the World's Major Business Cities

(in U.S. dollars)

Legend:
- Public Transportation
- Food Prices
- Prices including Rent by City
- Apartment Rents

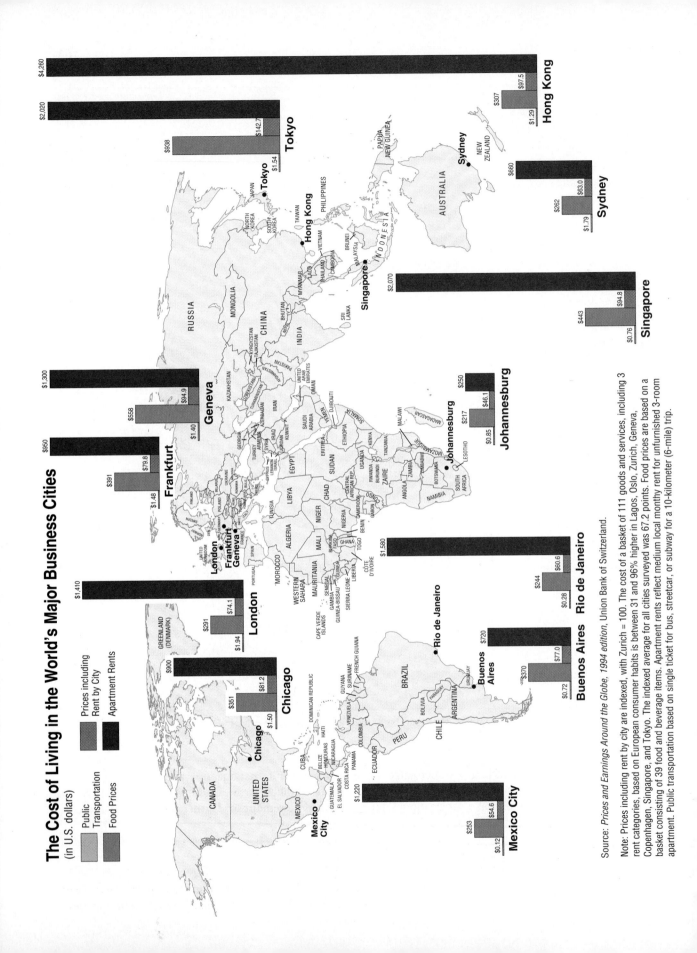

Hong Kong — $4,260; $307; $97.5; $1.29

Tokyo — $2,020; $938; $142.7; $1.54

Sydney — $660; $262; $63.0; $1.79

Singapore — $2,070; $443; $94.8; $0.76

Geneva — $1,300; $558; $94.9; $1.40

Frankfurt — $950; $391; $79.8; $1.48

London — $1,410; $291; $74.1; $1.94

Chicago — $900; $351; $81.2; $1.50

Johannesburg — $250; $217; $46.1; $0.85

Rio de Janeiro — $1,580; $244; $60.6; $0.28

Buenos Aires — $720; $370; $77.0; $0.72

Mexico City — $1,220; $253; $54.6; $0.12

Source: *Prices and Earnings Around the Globe, 1994 edition*, Union Bank of Switzerland.

Note: Prices including rent by city are indexed, with Zurich = 100. The cost of a basket of 111 goods and services, including 3 rent categories, based on European consumer habits is between 31 and 96% higher in Lagos, Oslo, Zurich, Geneva, Copenhagen, Singapore, and Tokyo. The indexed average for all cities surveyed was 67.2 points. Food prices are based on a basket consisting of 39 food and beverage items. Apartment rents reflect medium local monthy rent for unfurnished 3-room apartment. Public transportation based on single ticket for bus, streetcar, or subway for a 10-kilometer (6-mile) trip.

EN BUSCA DE SU TALENTO

Procter & Gamble
División de Peru/Latino America

¤ Más de 40 productos de consumo en Latino America como Pampers, Ace, Ariel, Crest, Head & Shoulders, Camay y Vicks.

¤El area tiene el mayor volumen de ventas entre todas las divisiones Internacionales de P&G.

¤Oportunidades de desarrollar una carrera profesional en areas como Mercadeo, Finanzas, Computación, Ventas, etc.

Buscamos individuos con Talento, Empuje, Liderazgo, y continuo afán de superación para posiciones permanentes o practicas de verano en Peru, Puerto Rico, México, Colombia, Venezuela, Brazil, Chile, etc.

Es muy importante que envies tu RESUME pronto ya que estaremos visitando tu Universidad en la primera semana de Noviembre.

¿QUE DEBES HACER?
Envia tu resume tan pronto como sea posible a la atencion de Ms. Cynthia Huddleston (MBA Career Services) antes del 18 de Octubre.

Source: *The Hoya,* Georgetown University, October 6, 1989, 2.

employee will arrive on the "ground floor." Initial involvement will normally be in the export field—evaluating potential foreign customers, preparing quotes, and dealing with activities such as shipping and transportation. With a very limited budget, the export manager will only occasionally visit foreign markets to discuss business

Global Perspective

22.4
Preparing for an International Assignment

Up to 40 percent of expatriate managers terminate their assignments early, costing their companies between $50,000 and $150,000 and derailing their careers. Moreover, 50 percent of those who do not terminate their assignments early function at a low level of effectiveness.

Many expatriates fail primarily because they neglect to prepare for such assignments. Prospective expatriates can better the chances of success if they determine whether an overseas assignment is really for them. After a short period of entrancement by the new culture and the excitement of traveling, a period of disillusionment develops during which the expatriate no longer finds it romantic to converse with a limited vocabulary or navigate around a new city without proper directions. After three to six months, expatriates either have terminated the assignment or have begun to adjust to life in the host country. Research indicates that individuals with such personal characteristics as adaptability, flexibility, and tolerance for ambiguity are more likely to pass through the stage of disillusionment and successfully complete the assignment. They must be able to recognize and accept societal and business norms that may seem alien.

Since experts and support systems usually available to managers often are not present at foreign locations, expatriates often must have all the technical skills necessary to complete the assignment by themselves. Further, expatriate managers are usually their own bosses, having to make decisions that at home typically would be made by their supervisors. Therefore, expatriate managers must be able to complete their assignments with little or no help from above or below in the organizational hierarchy.

An understanding of nonverbal communications will help to avoid costly errors and assist in the analysis of business transactions. For example, in the United States the spoken word is heavily relied upon, while in Japan, China, and the Middle East, the external environment, the situation, and nonverbal behavior are crucial to accurate communication. A knowledge of business etiquette helps avoid problems. Although the Germans, French, British, and Italians will discuss the general details of business over lunch, the Swiss instead use the time to strengthen relationships and do not discuss business. Before departing on an international assignment, a basic knowledge is needed in such things as acceptable greetings, the proper use of business cards, the country's dress code, the concept of time, proper dining manners, gift-giving protocol, and religious and political taboos.

Expatriates need to discard the myth that says, "If you're effective in New York, you'll be effective in Hong Kong." Simulation training can help trainees; presented with a number of vignettes about international situations and judged by a panel of experts, they learn to interact with people of other cultures and are provided with models of appropriate and inappropriate behaviors.

Courses that provide information about a particular country are also available. Some of the programs begin with a training exercise called BaFa BaFa. In the exercise, two teams try to trade with each other without knowing the negotiation rules. Most participants in the exercise make inaccurate assumptions about the other team's behaviors and motives. The exercise encourages trainees to reserve judgment about other cultures until they have more information.

Source: Howard Tu and Sherry E. Sullivan, "Preparing Yourself for an International Assignment," *Business Horizons,* January–February 1994, 67.

strategies with foreign distributors. Most of the work will be done by mail, via telex, by fax, or by telephone. The hours are often long because of the need, for example, to reach a contact during business hours in Hong Kong. Yet the possibilities for implementing creative business transactions are virtually limitless. It is also gratifying and often rewarding that one's successful contribution will be visible directly through the firm's growing export volume.

Alternatively, international work in a small firm may involve importing; that is, finding low-cost sources that can be substituted for domestically sourced products. Decisions often must be based on limited information, and the manager is faced with many uncertainties. Often things do not work out as planned. Shipments are delayed, letters of credit are canceled, and products almost never arrive in exactly the form and shape anticipated. Yet the problems are always new and offer an ongoing challenge.

As a training ground for international activities, there probably is no better starting place than a small or medium-sized firm. Later on, the person with some experience may find work with an export-trading or export-management company, resolving other people's problems and concentrating almost exclusively on the international arena.

Self-Employment

A third alternative is to hang up a consultant's shingle or to establish a trading firm. Many companies are in need of help for their international business efforts and are prepared to part with a portion of their profits in order to receive it. Yet it requires in-depth knowledge and broad experience to make a major contribution from the outside or to successfully run a trading firm.

Specialized services that might be offered by a consultant include international market research, international strategic planning, or, particularly desirable, beginning-to-end assistance for international entry or international negotiations. For an international business expert, the hourly billable rate typically is as high as $250 for principals and $100 for staff. Whenever international travel is required, overseas activities are often billed at the daily rate of $2,000 plus expenses. Even at such high rates, solid groundwork must be completed before all the overhead is paid. The advantage of this career option is the opportunity to become a true international entrepreneur. Consultants and those who conduct their own export-import or foreign direct investment activities work at a higher degree of risk than those who are not self-employed, but they have an opportunity for higher rewards.

SUMMARY

This final chapter has provided an overview of the environmental changes facing international managers and alternative managerial response to the changes. International business is a complex and difficult activity, yet it affords many opportunities and challenges. Observing changes and analyzing how to best incorporate them in the international business mission is the most important task of the international manager. If the international environment were constant, there would be little challenge to international business. The frequent changes are precisely what make international business so fascinating and often highly profitable for those who are active in the field.

Key Terms and Concepts

international debt load

population growth

trigger mechanisms

trade policy mechanisms

competitive platform

Questions for Discussion

1. For many developing countries, debt repayment and trade are closely linked. What does protectionism mean to them?

2. Should one worry about the fact that the United States is a debtor nation?

3. How can a firm in a developed country compete in light of low wages paid to workers abroad?

4. Is international segmentation ethical if it deprives poor countries of products?

5. How would our lives and our society change if imports were banned?

Recommended Readings

Adler, Nancy J., and Dafna N. Izraeli, eds. *Competitive Frontiers: Women Managers in a Global Economy.* Cambridge, Mass.: Blackwell, 1994.

Czinkota, Michael R., and Ilkka Ronkainen. "Global Marketing 2000: A Marketing Survival Guide." *Marketing Management.* Winter 1992: 36-45.

de Vries, Andre. *The Directory of Jobs and Careers Abroad.* Oxford: Gresham Press, 1993.

Kocher, Eric. *International Jobs: Where They Are and How to Get Them.* Reading, Mass.: Addison-Wesley, 1993.

Naisbitt, John. *Global Paradox.* New York: Morrow and Co., 1994.

Phillips, Nicola. *Managing International Teams.* Burr Ridge, Ill.: Irwin, 1994.

Pinto Carland, Maria, and Daniel H. Spatz. *Careers in International Affairs.* Washington, D.C.: School of Foreign Service, Georgetown University, 1991.

Rossman, Marlene L. *The International Businesswoman of the 1990's: A Guide to Success in the Global Marketplace.* New York: Praeger, 1990.

Work Study Travel Abroad 1992-1993. 11th ed. New York: St. Martins Press, 1992.

Notes

1. Michael R. Czinkota, Ilkka Ronkainen, and John Tarrant, *The Global Marketing Imperative* (Lincolnwood, Ill: NTC Publishing, 1995), 9.

2. William B. Johnston, "Global Workforce 2000: The New World Labor Market," *Harvard Business Review* (March–April 1991): 115-127.

3. *State of World Population* London: United Nations Population Fund, 1993.

4. John Naisbitt, *Global Paradox* (New York: Morrow and Co., 1994), 97.

5. Shinji Fukukawa, *The Future of U.S.-Japan Relationship and Its Contribution to New Globalism* (Tokyo: Ministry of International Trade and Industry, 1989), 10-11.

6. Michael R. Czinkota, "Rich Neighbors, Poor Relations," *Marketing Management* (Spring 1994): 46-52.

7. *U.S. Manufacturers in the Global Marketplace* (New York: The Conference Board, 1994).

8. Sudhir H. Kale and D. Sudharshan, "A Strategic Approach to International Segmentation," *International Marketing Review* 4 (Summer 1987): 60.

9. Benn R. Konsynski and Jahangir Karimi, "On the Design of Global Information Systems," in eds. S. Bradley, J. Hausman, and R. Nolan, *Globalization, Technology, and Competition: The Fusion of Computers and Telecommunications in the 1990s* (Boston: 1993), 81-108.

10. Robert Bartels, *Global Development and Marketing* (Columbus, Ohio: Grid, 1981), 111.

11. Kenichi Ohmae, "Only Triad Insiders Will Succeed," *The New York Times,* November 2, 1984, 2f.

12. Ibid.

13. Bartels, *Global Development and Marketing,* 112.

14. Michael R. Czinkota and Masaaki Kotabe, "Product Development the Japanese Way," in eds. M. Czinkota and I. Ronkainen, *International Marketing Strategy* (Fort Worth, Tex.: The Dryden Press, 1994), 285-291.

15. Naisbitt, *Global Paradox,* 18.

16. Michael G. Harvey, "Repatriation of Corporate Executives: An Empirical Study," *Journal of International Business Studies* 20 (Spring 1989): 131-144.

Cases

Harley-Davidson (B) Hedging Hogs

Harley-Davidson's competitive comeback in the late 1980s is one of the few protectionist success stories. It is the story of a firm that used government protection to adjust to a changing competitive global market. But Harley's success in the late 1980s brought along new problems that threatened to undermine much of the progress already attained. Harley's primary problem was the same problem faced by many undiversified international firms: it produced its motorcycles, hogs,[1] in only one country and exported its product to all foreign markets. But exchange rates change, and prices and earnings originally denominated in foreign currencies end up being worth very different amounts when finding their way back home to the

EXPORTING HOGS   Harley's sales in 1990 were more than $864 million. Of total sales, $268 million, or 31 percent, were international sales. Harley had been exporting for a very long time: for 50 years to Japan and more than 80 years to Germany. New markets were growing in countries such as Greece, Argentina, Brazil, and even the Virgin Islands. Although international sales were obviously very important to Harley's present profitability, they also represented its future. The domestic market in the United

Source: This case was written by Michael H. Moffett, the University of Michigan, March 1993. The case is intended for class discussion purposes only and does not represent either efficient or inefficient financial management practices. Do not quote without prior permission.

[1]The motorcycles produced and sold by Harley-Davidson have traditionally been known as hogs. The nickname is primarily in reference to their traditional large size, weight, and power.

[2]This case draws upon several articles including "Harley Uses 'Risk Sharing' To Hedge Foreign Currencies," by Lawrence R. Quinn, *Business International Money Report,* March 16, 1992, 105–106; and "Harley: Wheeling and Dealing," by Lawrence Quinn, *Corporate Finance,* April 1992, 29–30.

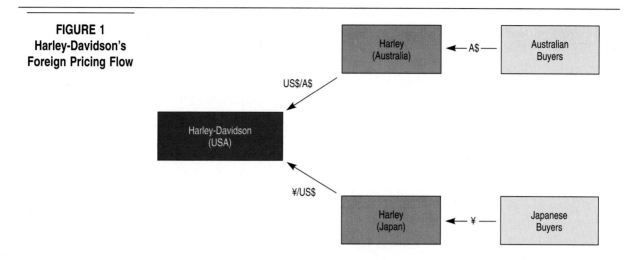

FIGURE 1
Harley-Davidson's
Foreign Pricing Flow

States for motorcycles—any firm's motorcycles—was beginning to decline. This was generally thought to be a result of changing consumer profiles and tastes. International market potential for Harley looked quite promising, but Harley had only 15 percent of the world market. It needed to do better, much better.

Harley's problem was that foreign distributors and dealers needed two things for continued growth and market share expansion: (1) local currency prices, and (2) stable prices. First, local currency pricing, whether it be Japanese yen, German marks, Australian dollars, or Canadian dollars, would allow the foreign dealers to compete on price in same currency terms with all competitors. And this competition would not be hindered by the dealers and distributors adding currency surcharges to sticker prices as a result of their own need to cover currency exposure.[3] Harley needed to sell its hogs to foreign dealers and distributorships in local currency, but that would not really solve the problems. First, Harley itself would now be responsible for managing the currency exposure. Second, it still did not assure the foreign dealers of stable prices, not unless Harley intended to absorb all exchange rate changes itself.

Figure 1 illustrates the foreign currency pricing issue for sales of Harleys in Australia and Japan. Australian consumers shop, compare, and purchase in Australian dollars. Starting at the opposite end, however, is the fact that Harley hogs are produced and initially priced in U.S. dollars. Someone must bear the risk of currency exchange, either the parent, the distributor, or the consumer; it rarely will be the consumer.

CURRENCY RISK SHARING AT HARLEY

John Hevey, manager of international finance, instituted a system that Harley calls "risk sharing." The idea is not new, but it has not been fashionable for some time. The idea is fairly simple: as long as the spot exchange rate does not move a great distance from the rate in effect when Harley quotes foreign currency prices to its foreign dealers, Harley will maintain that single price. This allows the foreign

---

[3]For example, an independent Australian dealer who sells and earns Australian dollar revenues but must pay for the Harley hogs shipped from the United States in U.S. dollars will be accepting currency risk. If the Australian dealer then adds a margin to the hog price to cover currency-hedging costs, the product is less competitive.

FIGURE 2
Currency Risk Sharing

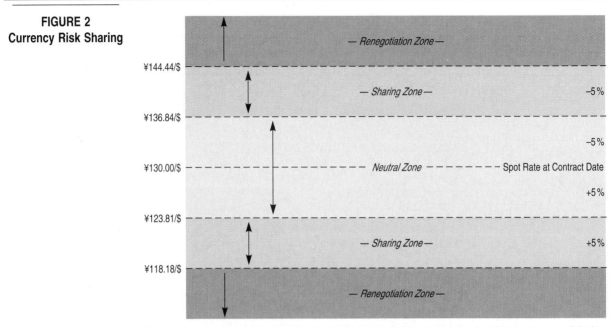

Note: Percentage changes are in the value of the Japanese yen versus U.S. dollar. For example, a "+ 5%" is a 5 percent appreciation in the value of the yen, from ¥130.00/$ to ¥123.81/$.

dealers and distributors, both those owned and not owned by Harley, to be assured of predictable and stable prices. The stable prices needed to be denominated in the currency of the foreign dealer and distributor's operations. Harley would then be responsible for managing the currency exposures.

A typical currency risk-sharing arrangement specifies three bands or zones of exchanges: (1) neutral zone, (2) sharing zone, and (3) renegotiation zone. Figure 2 provides an example of how the currency zones may be constructed between a U.S. parent firm and its Japanese dealers or distributors. The neutral zone in Figure 2 is constructed as a band of $+/-5$ percent change about the central rate specified in the contract, ¥130.00/$. The central rate can be determined a number of ways, for example, the spot rate in effect on the date of the contract's consummation, the average rate for the past three-month period, or a moving average of monthly rates. In this case, the neutral zone's boundaries are ¥136.84/$ and ¥123.81/$.[4] As long as the spot exchange rate between the yen and dollar remains within this neutral zone, the U.S. parent assures the Japanese dealers of a constant price in yen. If a particular product line was priced in the United States at $4,000, the yen-denominated price

---

[4]The upper and lower exchange rates of the band are calculated as:

$$\frac{¥130.00/\$ - ¥136.84/\$}{¥136.84/\$} \times 100 = -5.0\%.$$

and

$$\frac{¥130.00/\$ - ¥123.81/\$}{¥123.81/\$} \times 100 = +5.0\%.$$

would be ¥520,000. This assures the Japanese dealers a constant supply price in their own currency terms. The predictability of costs reduces the currency risks of the Japanese dealers and allows them to pass on the more predictable local currency prices to their customers.

If, however, the spot rate moves out of the neutral zone into the sharing zone, the U.S. parent and the Japanese dealer will share the costs or benefits of the margin beyond the neutral zone rate. For example, if the Japanese yen depreciated against the dollar to ¥140.00/$, the spot rate will have moved into the upper sharing zone. If the contract specified that the sharing would be a 50/50 split, the new price to the Japanese dealer would be

$$\$4,000 \times \left[¥130.00/\$ + \frac{¥140.00/\$ - ¥136.84/\$}{2} \right] = \$4,000 \times ¥131.58/\$ = ¥526,320.$$

Although the supply costs have indeed risen to the Japanese dealers, from ¥520,000 to ¥526,320, the percentage increase is significantly less than the percentage change in the exchange rate.[5] The Japanese dealer is insulated against the constant fluctuations of the exchange rate and subsequent fluctuations on supply costs.

Finally, if the spot rate were to move drastically from the neutral zone into the renegotiation zone, the risk-sharing agreement calls for a renegotiation of the price to bring it more in line with current exchange rates and the economic and competitive realities of the market.

CURRENCY MANAGEMENT AT HARLEY

Harley's risk-sharing program has allowed the firm to increase the stability of prices in foreign markets. But this stability has come about by the parent firm's accepting a larger proportion of the exchange rate risk. Harley's approach to currency management is conservative, both in what it hedges and how it hedges.

The "what," the exposures that Harley actually manages, are primarily its sales, which are denominated in foreign currencies. Although Harley does import some inputs, the volume of imports denominated in foreign currencies (accounts payable) are relatively small compared to the export sales (the accounts receivable). Harley is a bit more aggressive in its exposure time frame than many other firms, however. Harley will hedge sales that will be made in the near future, anticipated sales, extending about 12 months out. The ability of the firm to hedge sales that have not yet been "booked" is a result of the firm's consistency and predictability of sales in the various markets. Like most firms that hedge future sales, however, Harley will intentionally leave itself a margin of error, therefore hedging less than 100 percent of the expected exposures.

Presently Harley is rather conservative in the "how," the instruments and methods used for currency hedging. Harley uses currency forward contracts for all hedging. Harley will estimate the amount of the various foreign currency payments to be received per period and sell those foreign currency quantities forward (less the percentage margin for error). Like many other firms expanding international operations, Harley is now studying the use of additional currency management approaches, such

---

[5]The yen price has risen only 1.22 percent while the Japanese yen has depreciated 7.14 percent versus the U.S. dollar.

as the use of foreign currency options. At present, however, Harley executives are satisfied with their currency management program.

FINANCIAL MANAGEMENT'S GROWING RESPONSIBILITIES

A third dimension of the new financial/currency management program at Harley is the increased role of financial management with sales. The finance staff keeps in touch with the sales and marketing staffs to work toward the most competitive combinations and packages of pricing. Financial staff also attempts to keep information lines open between its foreign dealers and distributors to help them maintain price competitiveness.

Harley-Davidson is a firm that continues to be unique in many ways. Not only is it one of the true "success stories" for American protectionism, but it has continued to work to improve its international competitiveness by responding to the needs of not only its customers, but also its distributors and dealers.

Questions for Discussion

1. Why is it so important for Harley-Davidson to both price in foreign currencies in foreign markets and provide stable prices?
2. How effective will "risk sharing" be in actually achieving Harley's stated goals? Is there a better solution?
3. Who is bearing the brunt of the costs of the financial risk management program?

References

Hufbauer, Gary Clyde, Diane T. Berliner, and Kimberly Ann Elliot. *Trade Protection in the United States: 31 Case Studies.* Washington, D.C.: The Institute for International Economics, 1986.

Pruzin, Daniel R. "Born to be Verrucht." *World Trade* 5, Issue 4, May 1992, 112–117.

Quinn, Lawrence R. "Harley Uses 'Risk Sharing' to Hedge Foreign Currencies." *Business International Money Report,* March 16, 1992, 105–106.

———, "Harley: Wheeling and Dealing." *Corporate Finance,* April 1992, 29–30.

Establishing an Overseas Law Office

Stuffim & Bacom is a 20-year-old, 125-member law firm based in St. Paul, Minnesota. Aside from its home office, the firm maintains offices in Washington, D.C.; Denver, Colorado; and Paris, France. As in any major firm, there are many areas of practice, but the firm's fastest growing section is its international business department. This department is headed by the firm's principal rainmaker and senior Washington partner, Harley Hambone, assisted by an aggressive junior partner, Sylvester Soupspoon, also based in Washington.

Stuffim & Bacom has just begun to acquire business on the African continent. Its biggest client, Safari Air Lines (SAL), is an international airfreight company with corporate headquarters in Abidjan, Ivory Coast. Last year, SAL was the major airfreight carrier for all of east, central, and west Africa. Recently, Hambone, an international finance expert and master salesman, persuaded SAL to drop the law firm of Bend, Spindell & Mutilate, an old-line New York City firm, as the company's U.S. counsel and transfer all of SAL's business to the Stuffim firm. SAL is now almost a $1 million per year account for Stuffim & Bacom, which includes work with airline regulatory agencies in the United States, as well as general advice regarding international aviation matters.

In addition, Soupspoon, a transportation attorney, recently brought in as a new client Livingstone Tours Inc., a small but burgeoning U.S.–based travel agency specializing in three-month African safaris. Livingstone maintains its only overseas office in Nairobi, Kenya. Stuffim bills Livingstone less than $500,000 per year, mainly for preparing and negotiating agreements with international charter airlines and local tour operators serving east Africa.

Due to their already substantial client obligations, as well as the sudden, unexpected growth in their business on the African continent and the impracticality of handling the work out of their Washington, D.C., office, Hambone and Soupspoon have decided to propose that the firm open an office in Africa to cover its growing client needs in that part of the world. This would not only enable the firm to better serve SAL and Livingstone Tours, but it would also help the firm garner more African business.

SAL and Livingstone Tours are each pressing Stuffim & Bacom to set up an African office as soon as possible, preferably close to their respective African operations. That would require the firm to invest $250,000 to start up an office, as well as yearly expenditures (including related overhead) of $125,000 per U.S. attorney and $75,000 per local attorney to staff it with qualified lawyers.

Establishing a foreign office is nothing new to Stuffim & Bacom. For almost 10 years, the firm has maintained an office in Paris, France. As with many foreign branches of U.S. law firms, the Paris office generates very little profit and is regarded by the firm as something of a prestigious "foreign outpost." The firm continues to maintain the Paris office at a break-even level, mainly for the benefit of one major client, Ali Nord, an Arab- and French-owned freight forwarding company with extensive business in the United States, Central America, and the Middle East.

Source: This case was written by William E. Casselman II, managing partner in the law firm of Casselman and Associates (Washington office). Reprinted with permission. It is intended only to describe fictional business situations, and any resemblance to real individuals or business organizations is purely coincidental. The various economic, legal, political, and cultural conditions described in the case are for illustration only and do not necessarily reflect the actual conditions prevailing within the regions or countries mentioned.

The Paris office's only attorney, Sylvia Souffle, a senior partner and member of the Colorado bar, is qualified under French law to advise clients, such as Ali Nord, on questions of foreign and international law but may not appear in French courts or advise clients regarding French law. After 10 years of general corporate practice in France, she has recently indicated her desire to leave the Paris office and head the proposed office in the Ivory Coast, a former French colony in West Africa. Souffle has many contacts in the Ivory Coast, where French is the official language.

The firm has also opened two other offices abroad, neither of which succeeded. The first office was opened six years ago in Saudi Arabia to represent U.S. engineering and construction firms doing business there. The branch closed after one year due to a lack of business stemming from a decline in the price of oil and threats from Middle East terrorists, who were upset over Stuffim's representation of Ali Nord, which they wrongly believed to be a CIA front. More recently, a heretofore unknown terrorist group announced in the Middle East that it would "go to the ends of the earth" to wreak revenge upon Ali Nord and its "yellow running dog lackeys of Yankee imperialism," including the Stuffim firm.

The second office was opened three years ago in Bangkok, Thailand, to service Torch & Glow Industries, a Colorado corporation and major provider of fire-resistant tiling and roofing materials. Torch & Glow had experienced an unanticipated boom in business in Southeast Asia. Therefore, Stuffim & Bacom opened a regional office in Bangkok with special permission of the Thai government to represent Torch & Glow in Thailand, and then only on matters not requiring appearances in the courts of Thailand. Unfortunately, a massive class action suit was brought against Torch & Glow in both the United States and Thailand for damages caused by the unexplained flammability of the company's products when used in tropical climates. As a result, Torch & Glow recently went out of business, as did Stuffim's office in Bangkok. Both of these failures cost the firm a great deal of money in lost start-up expense and attorney and employee severance payments, and the firm's partners swore never again to open another overseas office.

Undaunted by these past failures, Hambone and Soupspoon want to pursue the concept of a Stuffim & Bacom office in Africa. They have several options, which include, but are not limited to, the following: First, they could send a contingent of at least three Stuffim lawyers, possibly led by Souffle, to establish an Abidjan office. Unfortunately, none of the firm's current attorneys, other than Souffle, speaks adequate French. Second, they could recruit a group of SAL's in-house Ivory Coast lawyers from its headquarters in Abidjan, make them special partners in the Stuffim firm, and have them run Stuffim's office. Third, they could send one or more lawyers to open an office in Kenya, an English-speaking nation and former British colony, to work principally on the Livingstone account and secondarily on the SAL account. Fourth, they could form a joint venture with a Kenyan law firm to staff and run the Nairobi office.

Soupspoon, aware that Livingstone already employs a local law firm, Amen & Hadafly, to handle some of its legal needs in Kenya, approached that firm about its willingness to form a joint venture with Stuffim to run the Nairobi office. However, Amen & Hadafly, although personal friends of Soupspoon, would agree only on the condition that they received full partnership status, not just a share of the local office profits to which special partners are entitled. In view of this demand, as well as Amen & Hadafly's somewhat questionable reputation in the Kenyan legal community, Hambone was reluctant to accept the offer. On the other hand, because Amen & Hadafly is well connected in the local legal establishment, it is unlikely that any other local firm would agree to such a joint venture. There are no joint venture possibilities in the Ivory Coast, owing to SAL's having its own in-house attorneys and preferring to work only with the Stuffim firm because of its expertise in international transportation law.

In addition to the differences in legal systems and languages, Kenya and the Ivory Coast also have different infrastructure conditions. For example, Nairobi has good telecommunications but a shortage of available office space. Abidjan is known for its modern office buildings but lacks the more up-to-date communications facilities found in Nairobi. Both countries enjoy roughly the same political and economic stability and have a generally favorable attitude toward foreign investment.

Further complicating matters, the laws of both the Ivory Coast and Kenya place serious restrictions on foreign law firms establishing local offices with foreign lawyers, requiring any foreign law firm to employ a majority of local lawyers or to ensure that their local office is managed by a local lawyer. Moreover, any foreign lawyer who wants to practice before the courts of either country has to be certified by the local bar association as being competent to do so (and no Stuffim lawyers are so certified in either the Ivory Coast or Kenya). There is one exception—any lawyer qualified in a comparable legal system can practice without satisfying the formal requirements. The United States common law system has not been recognized in the Ivory Coast, but, because of the Ivory Coast's close ties to France, the French code system has. Conversely, the Kenyan bar recognizes the English and U.S. systems, but not the French system. Of course, it might be possible to persuade either government to create an exception for a single Stuffim & Bacom client, as was done in Thailand for Torch & Glow.

Even if Hambone and Soupspoon could persuade the governments involved to permit them to practice locally without meeting local requirements, they would still have to persuade the rest of Stuffim & Bacom's partners that an African office is a good idea. In light of the two recent overseas office failures, the remaining partners, most of whom are in the St. Paul office, are not expected to enthusiastically embrace Hambone and Soupspoon's idea for an office in Africa.

The time has come for Hambone and Soupspoon to lay their idea on the line. Hambone has arranged meetings with government officials in the Ivory Coast and Kenya to negotiate an office in one of the two countries. Soupspoon must persuade the Stuffim & Bacom partners of the merits of establishing an African office in the country selected by Hambone. You have been asked by Hambone and Soupspoon to prepare them for these crucial meetings.

Questions for Discussion

1. Advise Hambone of the various business, legal, political, and cultural obstacles standing in the way of opening an office in each country and how he can best overcome them. Also make a recommendation as to where you think the office should be located and how (and by whom) it should be staffed and operated.

2. Advise Soupspoon as to how he can convince his fellow partners that an African office will be profitable for the firm, if not in the short term, then in the long term. This would include the type of representation arrangements that the Stuffim firm should make with its clients in Africa to minimize its financial risk.

3. How do you believe Stuffim & Bacom, as a growing international law firm, should respond to terrorist threats?

Aston Systems Corporation

Gail Hartley, international regional manager of Aston Systems Corporation, briskly thumbed through the pile of fax transmittals on her desk as she finished her phone conversation and hung up. "I'm going to have to cut this meeting short," she said as she glanced across her office apologetically. "Our attorney is going out of town tonight, and I will be in Europe all next week. It's important that I meet with him to discuss the pending litigation."

As her coworkers left the room, Hartley began to reflect on the recent problems she had faced at Aston. Realizing this wasn't the time for reflection, she gathered her papers and rushed out to make her appointment.

HISTORY

Aston Systems Corporation is a medium-sized computer software company with headquarters located in the eastern United States. The firm was founded in 1983 by a young software engineer named Roger McGuire and his wife, Cynthia Drake. The company's original focus was on marketing software that McGuire had developed to monitor and manage the performance of the IBM mainframe operating system. The initial product was the industry's first complete performance-management system running in CICS,[1] one of IBM's smaller operating systems. By 1986, the company had branched out, developing software that managed a diverse group of larger operating system platforms and subsystems.

Drake made the first sales, but within the first year, Aston hired Jeff Black as vice president of domestic sales. Black began hiring a sales force to meet the growing demand. By 1992, Aston had 230 employees, 95 percent of whom were based at its headquarters, with the other 5 percent based in its California sales office. From its headquarters, Aston's management oversaw domestic and international sales as well as product development and acquisition of other products and companies.

Aston experienced remarkable growth, with gross revenues climbing from $56,000 in 1983 to more than $50 million in 1992 (see Figure 1). Aston management expected revenues to reach $100 million by 1994. To reach this goal, Aston initiated an aggressive program to acquire complementary products and companies and planned to utilize its established distribution network to add value and thus increase profit.

PRODUCTS

Aston sells system software tools for IBM mainframe computer users. The software packages operate in a number of IBM operating environments, including CICS, MVS, DB2, and VTAM. All Aston software products are easily integrated, menu driven, and share a common architecture and format. This means that once a customer has mastered the commands for an Aston software package, the same commands apply to all other Aston software. The user-friendly attributes encourage the purchase of multiple products.

Aston's complete performance-management software systems are designed to monitor IBM mainframe performance and diagnose information system problems

Source: This case was developed by Professor Michael R. Czinkota and MBA candidate Marc S. Gross. Funding support by the U.S. Department of Education is gratefully acknowledged. Names have been disguised to protect proprietary interests.

[1]CICS stands for Customer Information Control System, which acts as transaction processing software. CICS is one of many operating systems for IBM mainframe computer systems.

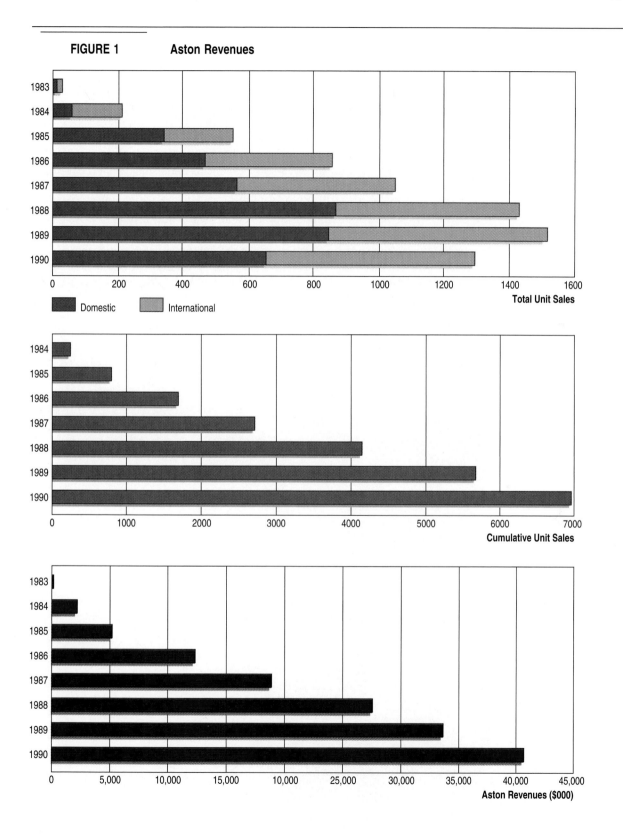

FIGURE 1   Aston Revenues

quickly, before they affect the user through costly system downtime. The performance-monitoring tools provide users with critical information about memory allocation, bottlenecks, and file utilization through full color charts, graphs, and real-time access. In addition, the tools provide upper management with an overview of the information system, its response times, number of tasks, and program and transaction codes. This helps users to optimize existing computer resources and plan for hardware upgrades.

The main Aston products as percent of sales both in units and revenues for the first half of 1992 were as follows: Monitor for CICS—45 percent of units sold, 49 percent of revenues; Monitor for MVS—17 percent of units sold, 23 percent of revenues; Monitor for DB2—14 percent of units sold, 17 percent of revenues; Monitor for VTAM—2 percent of units sold, 1 percent of revenues (see Figure 2). The monitor for the VTAM network communication systems was a new product that had been acquired from Cashwell Research, Inc., in 1990 and introduced only recently.

In addition to the software itself, much of the customer value came from Aston's after-sales service and support. Furthermore, Aston offered the finest in English-language brochures and reference manuals as part of the software package.

FIGURE 2
Aston: Percent of Units Sold First Half of 1992
Aston: Percent of Revenues First Half of 1992

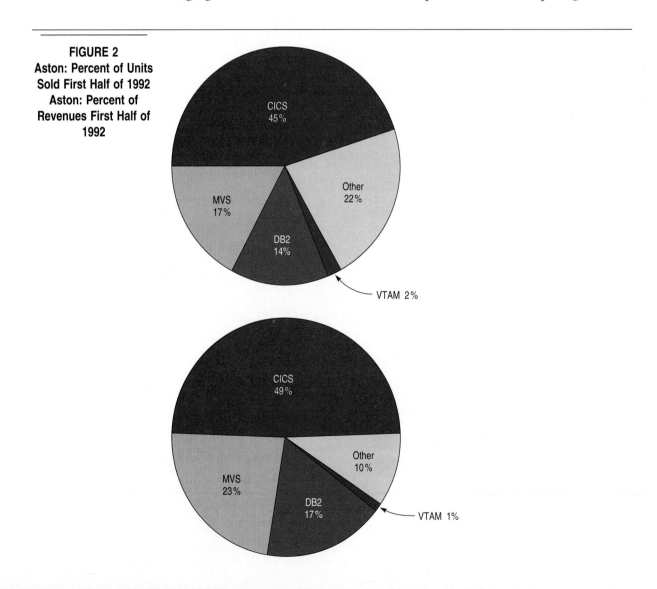

INTERNATIONAL EXPANSION

Aston was unique in its international expansion. Contrary to the normal patterns of expanding into international markets after establishing domestic sales, Aston had made its first sale to a company in the Netherlands. In 1983, Drake was attending a user group meeting for Oxford Software Company in Holland. At that meeting, she was introduced to Alex Nagle, one of Oxford's marketing representatives. As Drake told Nagle about Aston's product, he became increasingly enthusiastic about its market potential in Europe. Aston gave Nagle the opportunity to distribute the product, a relationship that proved to be long and prosperous.

As European sales grew, Aston authorized Nagle to establish agent relationships on its behalf. He then established distributorships in Sweden, Switzerland, the United Kingdom, France, Holland, and Germany. All distributors initially reported to Nagle, who maintained records and reported to Aston management.

In the software-production process at Aston, software engineers wrote commands to a master tape. To reduce overhead and administrative costs, Aston shipped master tapes directly to distributors and granted exclusive rights to reproduce and distribute the software and license to end users. End users received the software on floppy disks, which could be installed directly into their computer systems. In addition, the user received numerous English-language brochures and reference manuals.

Sixty percent of sales revenue went to the distributor, who incurred production and marketing costs. Nagle received the remaining 40 percent, retaining 10 percent of gross sales revenue as a fee for managing the relationship with distributors and sending the remaining 30 percent to Aston.

For example, if a German distributor sold an Aston software package for DM 20,000, she would retain DM 12,000 to cover overhead expenses and sales commission. Nagle would receive DM 8,000, of which he would retain DM 2,000 for his management services and forward the dollar equivalent of the remaining DM 6,000 to Aston. Since Aston's distributors set prices in local currency, the dollar value of the revenue Aston received from its 30 percent margin varied as exchange rates fluctuated.

In 1989, a rapid increase in European sales caused Aston management to reconsider its relationship with Nagle. Aston management believed it had enough people employed in its headquarters to effectively manage distributors and wanted higher margins to continue its expansion. At the same time, Nagle no longer wanted to manage the effort, and Aston bought out the remainder of his contract. Aston retained all of its distributors and established direct communication and reporting channels and new contractual distributor agreements to replace the agreements distributors had with Nagle. The agreements granted distributors exclusive geographical marketing rights and provided them the same 60 percent of sales revenue. The remaining 40 percent went to Aston.

The nature of the distribution agreement provided Aston a built-in reporting system as a safeguard against unreported sales. Pursuant to the agreement, Aston provided sales support in terms of seminars, marketing materials and on-site client visits, as well as in-depth research support directly to clients. Most clients will at one time or another have a problem requiring direct contact with Aston technical support staff. Having an unreported customer contact Aston for technical support could be very embarrassing and ultimately devastating for a distributor. Although Aston responded to both distributor and end-user inquiries from around the globe, there was no formal means of responding to inquiries made in languages other than English.

Currently, Aston has 21 international distributors marketing in more than 70 countries. International sales account for 51 percent of the total. In 1992, Aston's

12 largest distributors in Europe represented more than 60 percent of international income; Japan represented another 16 percent.

In late 1992, Hartley was in the process of finalizing an agreement to establish Aston's first subsidiary in the United Kingdom. Aston had recently acquired Integrated Software Group (ISG), which had developed a software product for the widely used UNIX operating platform. The subsidiary consisted of one full-time sales employee, formerly with ISG, a car, and a cellular telephone. Although Aston management was focused on minimization of overhead, it planned to launch the initial marketing phase of the product through this subsidiary. Although it had not yet been decided how to appoint distributors for the new product, Hartley did not plan to offer distributors exclusive marketing rights to the product as had been the case with other Aston products.

DISTRIBUTOR SELECTION

In selecting new distributors, Hartley relies heavily on referrals. She contacts current distributors for referrals as well as a variety of other vendors to find out whom they are using and if a candidate's performance has been satisfactory. After making contact with the prospective distributor, Hartley begins a formal interview process, much like that of hiring someone for a job within the company. Hartley looks to a distributor's financial backing, debt/equity structure, and business history, ensuring that there are sufficient assets to continue operations and sufficient business experience to minimize the risk of dissolution. In essence, Aston is looking to establish a long-term relationship with its distributors. On the administrative side, Aston analyzes credit reports provided by Dunn and Bradstreet to ensure that prospective distributors are paying creditors on time. In the final analysis, Hartley relies on her gut feeling of whether or not the distributor is hungry to get its hands on the product and sell it. Hartley travels abroad approximately two weeks out of each month to monitor distributor operations, interview potential distributors, and meet with large clients.

DECISION SITUATION

Despite Aston's rigorous screening process, the firm has encountered problems with distributors. In 1990, Aston's Spanish distributor, Francisco Del Mar, decided to dissolve his company and establish a new company to sell a different range of products. Unbeknownst to Aston, Del Mar, who was based in the Netherlands Antilles, viewed his Spanish operation simply as a tax haven. Del Mar did not provide any advance notice of his intentions and left Aston without representation in Spain.

Recently, Hartley had also encountered problems with the Spanish distributor who replaced Del Mar. The individuals running the company had excellent backgrounds and credentials. They were former Anderson Consulting partners who had been in management consulting for a long time. Despite having met all of Aston's rigorous selection criteria, the company overextended itself, hiring too large a staff too rapidly. After starting with only two employees, the company hired more than 150 within nine months. When the firm encountered difficulties in meeting overhead expense, it began using Aston's royalty share to finance other ventures and pay salaries. Aston had always been willing to work with distributors through legitimate short-term cash flow problems. Normally Aston received payment in full within 30 days of a sale, as was stipulated in the distributor agreement, but it had occasionally extended the payment period. In this case, however, the problem seemed to go beyond the short term. Aston was in the process of terminating the distributor and as yet had no replacement.

ADDITIONAL UNCERTAINTIES

In addition to the uncertainties with the current Spanish distributor, the challenges associated with the launch of a foreign subsidiary and major exchange rate fluctuation significantly threaten revenues at Aston. Furthermore, a deepening global recession could severely impact cash flow and jeopardize Aston's stated goals of rapid expansion and product acquisition.

Questions for Discussion

1. How are Aston's revenues affected by fluctuations in currency exchange rates? Which is better for Aston, a strong or weak dollar? Why?
2. With such a large portion of revenues generated internationally, how should Aston handle inquiries and service requests made from abroad?
3. Should Aston actively pursue recovery of its money from its Spanish distributor?
4. How can Aston avoid distributor problems in the future without placing unreasonable constraints on distributors and market growth? How does the subsidiary relationship fit into Aston's stated long-term goals?

Hathaway Electronics: The Foreign Assignment

Charlie Dixon stared at the columns of figures on the page of the report in front of him without really seeing them. He took another gulp from his coffee mug and untangled a pile of paper clips on his desk, but he still couldn't concentrate on those numbers. He tried staring out the window of his fifth floor office, watched the small human figures strolling along the plaza-like area in front of the Hathaway Electronics Company building, and wondered why he felt uneasy. Things seemed to be going pretty well. He had started with Hathaway nine years ago, right out of college. His salary had increased satisfactorily each year. He'd had three different job assignments, starting in one of the branch plants as a cost analyst, then on to a departmental supervisory job here at headquarters, and now was an assistant controller with his name on the door, a rug on the floor, and his own secretary.

The phone interrupted his idle study of the patterns of the moving humanity below. It was his boss's secretary. "Mr. Wilbur would like to see you in his office at eleven." That was all. Charlie asked what the subject of the meeting was, who else was invited, what should he bring, but got zero answers. He swung around to the window again, staring at the people below. He chanced to gaze at a rather heavyset man, bustling toward the front entrance of the building. Even from his vantage point, Charles recognized the rumpled suit, vest unbuttoned, cigarette dangling from the lips, and the bulging, somewhat tattered briefcase under the arm. It was Frank Miller, the American who was the head of Hathaway's French subsidiary.

Hathaway Electronics generated about 20 percent of its sales overseas. The company sold its products through an export sales department that had eight sales offices located in major cities in Europe, South America, and the Far East. Overseas manufacturing activities were a more recent part of the company's strategy. First there was a joint venture with a Brazilian electrical firm. Then Hathaway formed a wholly owned subsidiary to manufacture components in Taiwan for shipment and ultimate incorporation into the products made in the U.S. plants. Encouraged by the success of the two foreign operations, the company looked for a way to establish a stronger position for its products in the larger market potential of Europe. The subsequent strategy was to buy majority control of an existing French company that made a few electronic components but less than half of the items in Hathaway's line. It was also believed by the Hathaway top management that their own products were technologically quite superior to French ones and that the French company's sales could be increased substantially by transfusions of the Hathaway "know-how" and research capabilities. Charlie didn't have very much responsibility for or contact with the foreign activities. However, one of his major tasks was to review requests for capital from all parts of the Hathaway organization.

That chance spotting of Frank Miller, striding across the elegant entranceway to the building, gave Charlie a jolt. Last week a very large request for capital had come to his desk from the French subsidiary. Charlie had given it careful study since it was for an amount well into the board-approval category, and he had then written a strong letter recommending rejection of the proposal. The request was for virtually a complete replacement of the French company's manufacturing equipment line. Charlie's

Source: This case is adapted from the book, *Hathaway Electronics* by Julian Allen and Gerald Parkhouse. For further information contact Gerald Parkhouse at Elmira College, Elmira, New York.

recommendation faulted the absence of supporting data to justify the vastly increased sales projections. He had found arithmetic errors in the calculations of reduced costs. The French writer of the proposal had not handled depreciation costs as prescribed in the controller's procedures, and the savings claimed had overlooked taxes on the increased profits. Finally, the whole project had not been included in the subsidiary's capital budget for the year, and there was no explanation of changed circumstances to warrant such a deviation from plan. In summary, it was one of the poorest requests Charlie had ever seen. He had sent out his expressive recommendations on Wednesday of last week, addressing his memo to the controller, Bob Wilbur, the financial vice president, Frank Miller, and the vice president of international operations. Now, on Thursday, eight days later, he suddenly realized he had had absolutely no response to his written outburst. Now Charlie realized why he had been uneasy. The strange summons to an 11 a.m. meeting and the sight of Frank Miller striding (angrily?) into the building increased his anxiety. He went off to face the music.

The controller's secretary looked up and said, "Go right in. Mr. Wilbur is waiting for you."

Wilbur was standing, looking out of a window. He turned as Charlie came in. "Hi, Charlie. Close the door and have a chair."

"Did you want to discuss my recommendation on the French capital request?"

"No. I haven't read it yet."

A long pause followed. Wilbur resumed his study of the scene outside the window. Finally he said, "Have you ever been to France, Charlie?"

"No."

"Your personnel file says you're fluent in French."

"I had five years of it between high school and college. Tried it once outside the classroom on a visit to Quebec. Why?"

"International wants you to go to France."

Charlie frowned, "To check out that crazy capital request?"

"No. Transfer. To be the subsidiary's controller." He paused for about three seconds. "And vice president."

"Why me? Because I'm supposedly fluent in French? It's been ten years since I studied or used French. I don't think the French would consider me fluent."

Wilbur finally moved to his desk chair, leaned back, adjusted his shirt sleeves. "They've got a lot of problems over there. We've poured buckets of money into that outfit the last three years and sent over some top engineering talent, but we don't seem to get any results. They haven't gained market share, their costs have gone up, not down. Their financial statements don't come in on time. They don't seem to be able to explain the figures when we do get them. Last week Pierre Lanson, their controller, resigned. Miller told us he wanted an American this time. Someone who understood the figures and could explain them. Someone who understood what the top brass back here wanted, and someone who could speak French so he'd know what they're talking about."

Now Charlie was on the edge of his chair. Questions were flitting about in his mind faster than he could articulate them. Move to France? For how long? Where would they live? What would his wife think? What would the salary be? Should he take the eight-month-old car? School, my God, what about the kids' school? What kind of guy would Miller be to work for? Suppose the whole subsidiary goes in the red, how long would the board hang on to it? What about his house, only three years into his 25-year mortgage?

Suddenly Charlie realized that Wilbur was still talking . . . "and you've probably got a lot of questions. Here's what I want you to do now. Frank Miller's in the next office waiting to meet with you. Now don't let him scare you. He's sort of gruff; he's personally sloppy—gets cigarette ashes all over his shirt all the time—and he gets very impatient with people he calls 'lousy bureaucrats.' But he's an absolute mechanical and electronic genius. Talk to Frank as long as you want, but don't give him an answer yet. I want you to also talk with two others. Go see Bill Bradshaw over in Personnel. He can answer a lot of the compensation questions that Miller can't. Then there's a man in the Marketing group on the second floor. I want you to see him. He'll be expecting you. His name is Ted Martin and he's rather new with us, but he lived in Europe for ten years working for two different American companies, and he can give you an unbiased rundown on what it's like to be an American working in a foreign country. Then, of course, talk it over at home."

"How soon does the company need my answer?"

"Well, Miller is going back on a Friday night flight, so we ought to know by tomorrow noon. If your answer is no, Miller will have to stay over and talk with someone else. So on your way and I'll see you tomorrow."

Charlie's meeting with Frank Miller was not what he expected. First, Miller apologized for not being able to have lunch with Charlie, then spent only ten minutes with him before dashing off. Speaking very rapidly he outlined the job, indicating that in addition to the responsibilities the departing French controller had had, Miller wanted Charlie to take over all the "office functions" covering purchasing, production planning and scheduling, the treasury function, and the Personnel Department (except for labor relations). His purpose in the reorganizing was to relieve himself (Miller) of all that "paper shoveling stuff" so he could concentrate all his time on engineering and manufacturing problems. In addition, he expected Charlie to handle most of the contacts with the U.S. headquarters. "Keep those guys out of my way. Handle it so there aren't any more memos like the one you just wrote about our expansion request. And design all the accounting and budget reports so both the French managers and the top management at home can use and understand the same figures. I gotta go. I'll see you tomorrow. Your salary will be increased 20 percent and there are some overseas fringe benefits that Bradshaw in Personnel will explain."

Frank Miller got up abruptly and left the office leaving a trail of cigarette ashes. Charlie sat still for a minute or two then decided to go back to his own office and try to reach Bradshaw. There he found Bradshaw reading *The Wall Street Journal*, sitting in Charlie's own chair, feet up on the desk. Seeing Charlie come in, he stood up, shook hands, and settled into another chair.

"I figured you'd be a bit late," Bradshaw explained, "so I've taken the liberty of having some sandwiches and coffee sent here so we can discuss your opportunity. Where shall we start?"

"He said you would explain the fringe benefits."

"That's the easy part. All the overseas benefits are based on your base salary. The new one, not your present salary. And all the overseas fringes apply only to the time you are actually overseas, and cease when you return to the U.S. First, there is an overseas salary premium—an extra amount theoretically based on the hardship of living in a foreign country. For France, it's 10 percent. Second, there's a housing allowance since living in the Paris area will cost more—whether you rent or buy—than in this area. It's not designed to cover your entire housing cost, but the assumed extra cost over what housing costs are—on the average—for someone in your salary grade living here. Of course, just as with a domestic transfer, the company will pay all your moving costs. Both ways, unless you should resign while over there."

"A subtle disincentive?"

"Sure. Next is a little complicated. While you're living in France, you'll have to pay some French taxes. There's a tax that is something like our Social Security tax that is deducted from your pay. It covers certain medical costs and provides, theoretically, for a retirement income. Since this is a payroll deduction some of your salary will be paid to you over there in France; the balance will be sent to your bank here in dollars. Since you are a U.S. citizen, you will still have deductions out of your check for Social Security and U.S. income taxes."

"How about French income taxes?"

"You'll owe those, too, but they don't have payroll withholding. Also, the U.S. in effect gives you credit for your French income taxes, so you don't pay twice on the same income. But you must file with both governments. The company will provide you with tax accounting to do this."

"What about schools?"

"Good question. You have two options, either send your kids to a French school or to the American School of Paris. It's a private school, K through 12th grade, standard American curriculum and activities. No football, though, nobody to play against. If you choose the American school, the company pays the tuition."

"Do they teach French?"

"I forgot to mention that. French classes are required at all grade levels."

Charlie sat reflecting on all this for a moment or two, then asked, "How long do you think the assignment would be?"

"There's no way to predict that. It could be a year, it could be ten years. I suppose in our history, the average overseas stint has been four to five years. Look, we do want you to talk to Ted Martin. He's on the third floor and he's expecting you."

Ted Martin was indeed expecting him. After appropriate self-introductions, Martin settled comfortably back in his chair and began what was essentially a monologue.

"I have some idea of what's going through your mind right now, so maybe I can help. You have the chance to take a new assignment that can either be the most exciting, challenging, and broadening experience in your life or it could be the most frustrating, discouraging, and seemingly unending assignment you've ever had. Probably the most important factor in determining which it will be both for you and your family is your own attitude about living in a foreign country. If you—or your family—approach the move as a rare chance to learn new things, meet new and different people, gain a new perspective on history (including the history of the U.S.), find that other cultures have different ways of looking at life, then you'll think it was the best thing that ever happened. But if you have what I call the 'peanut-butter syndrome,' you'll be miserable."

"What's the peanut-butter syndrome?"

"In many foreign countries you can't find peanut butter in the local markets. Or Post's 40 percent Raisin Bran Flakes or your particular brand of shampoo. If you miss these things, if you can't stand not watching Tom Brokaw every night or seeing three or four NFL games every weekend, you could be miserable. It's not the same as being a tourist, when you know that after seeing a certain number of cathedrals and museums and chateaux you'll be back in your own home. But if it's going to finally get to you to put up with door handles that don't work the way they do in the U.S. and tiny refrigerators and exasperating telephone service—then don't go. A tourist is only concerned about understanding the money and how good his hotel room is and what time the plane leaves for Rome. But an expatriate has a whole set of different problems. He has to get 'papers' from the government to have permission to live there, another set to have permission to work there. The whole business of home finding and the relationship between landlord and tenant is completely different from our practices."

"How do you find out things like that?"

"Generally the hard way—by doing it the wrong way first. Now all these things that are different lead many Americans to compare on a judgmental basis. The French way is better on this custom but the American way is better on that situation. The better or worse approach is self-defeating. Just think of it as different."

"I think I see your point," Charlie said. "Do you think it's possible for Americans and French to work together in the same organization?"

"Sure, but it's not easy. Imagine how you'd feel if a Japanese or a Saudi Arabian firm bought control of Hathaway and the new owners sent over their executives to take over Hathaway's top jobs. Then these new top people talked to each other in their own language, introduced different strategies for running the business, imposed a new and different accounting system, judged your performance in their home-country's currency, ignoring the differences in the accounting treatment of the two countries involved and also ignoring the fluctuations in the currency exchange rates."

"Wow! I see your point. Do we look that bad to the French?"

"Well, the term, 'The Ugly American' is more than just a book title. Working in the international arena of business does require a heightened degree of sensitivity to the other guy's viewpoint and some diplomatic skills as well. And mentioning the word diplomacy reminds me of another problem you might have to face. Sooner or later some issue will come up where the corporate made-in-the-U.S.A. policy or strategy will be in conflict with your host nation's policy. Another problem you might have to handle could come up where there is a conflict between the governmental policies of France and the United States."

"I'd expect that kind of problem would be handled by top management here."

"Sure, but you might be the one who identifies such a problem and presents it along with local French lawyers' opinions on the subject."

"Well, I'd just have to face those kinds of problems when and if they arise. But you can help me with a more immediate problem. Bradshaw told me my kids could go either to the French public schools or, at company expense, to the American school. Which would you advise?"

"Since I don't know your kids, I can't really advise you, but I can tell you about the experience of other Americans. The French schools are very good. Longer days, more hours per week, more homework. They have far more emphasis on languages, literature, history, philosophy—much less of the typical American emphasis on 'let's all learn to get along with each other!' If the child starts out in the French system at a very young age, he can do very well, mastering the new language in very short order. But the older child will find it far more difficult at first to learn both French and the material being taught at the same time. How old are your kids?"

"Five and eight."

"That's a tough call. Good luck. Any other questions?"

"I'll think of dozens as soon as I get home."

"OK. Give me a call at home tonight if I can help with anything else. If you take the job it will change your life and your family's lives to a far greater degree than any domestic move could. Most of those changes will be on the plus side. But there is one minus you should factor in. An overseas experience will increase your managerial ability significantly. You'll find ways to cope with problems that nobody here has ever experienced. You'll gain maturity and wisdom and perspective faster than if you remain on a U.S. assignment. But the fly in the ointment is that your career progress up the managerial ladder could be slower!"

"That doesn't make sense."

"It doesn't necessarily happen this way, but it does happen more often than it should. Let's say you stay in France for five years. You do a bang up job. You've achieved the goals set out for you. But except for the few people back here who have had international experience themselves, most of the top managers in the company have no appreciation of the magnitude of the problems you had to deal with or the progress you made in solving these problems. They will remember you the way you are today."

"Is there a solution to that problem?"

"Maybe not a solution, but a reduction of the possible magnitude of the problem. Undoubtedly your job in France will require your coming back here several times a year. These visits should be scheduled for long enough to allow time to get around and see everybody you can. Keep in touch with the changes going on here. Mend fences and so on. Don't let people forget who you are and what you're doing."

Charlie drifted through a meeting that had been scheduled for four o'clock. When it eventually ended he headed for the parking lot without his normal last check in at his own office. As he started his car for the 15-minute drive to his home, he grappled with the problem of how to introduce the unexpected turn of events to his family.

Questions for Discussion

1. Do you think the combination of Charlie Dixon with the current American general manager in France will be effective?

2. What should Charlie do if he suspects that he might suffer from the "peanut-butter syndrome"?

3. If you were Charlie, would you take the job?

McDonnell Douglas: The F-18 Hornet Offset

In May of 1992, the Finnish government's selection of the F/A-18 Hornet over the Swedish JAS-39 Gripen, the French Mirage 2000-5, and fellow American F-16 to modernize the fighter fleet of its air force was a major boost to McDonnell Douglas (MDC) in an otherwise quiet market. The deal would involve the sale of 57 F/A-18 Cs and 7 F/A-18 Ds at a cost of FIM 9.5 billion (approximately $2 billion). Deliveries would take place between 1995 and 2000.

Winning the contract was critical since MDC had been on the losing side of two major aircraft competitions in the United States in 1991. In addition, one of its major projects with the U.S. Navy had been terminated (the A-12), and the government of the Republic of Korea had changed its mind to buy F-16 aircraft after it already had an agreement with MDC for F/A-18 Hornets.

However, the $2 billion will not be earned without strings attached. Contractually, McDonnell Douglas and its main subcontractors (Northrop Grumman, General Electric, and General Motors's subsidiary Hughes), the "F-18 Team," are obligated to facilitate an equivalent amount of business for Finnish industry over a ten-year period (1992–2002) using various offset arrangements.

OFFSETS

Offsets are various forms of industrial and business activities required as a condition of purchase. They are an obligation imposed on the seller in major (most often military hardware) purchases by or for foreign governments to minimize any trade imbalance or other adverse economic impact caused by the outflow of currency required to pay for such purchases. In wealthier countries, it is often used for establishing infrastructure. Two basic types of offset arrangements exist: direct and indirect (as seen in Figure 1). Although offsets have long been associated only with the defense sector, there are now increasing demands for offsets in commercial sales in which the government is the purchaser or user.

Direct offset consists of product-related manufacturing or assembly either for the purposes of the project in question only or for a longer-term partnership. The purchase, therefore, enables the purchaser to be involved in the manufacturing process. Various Spanish companies produce dorsal covers, rudders, aft fuselage panels, and speed brakes for the F/A-18s designated for the Spanish Air Force. In addition to co-production arrangements, licensed production is prominent. Examples include Egypt producing U.S. M1-A1 tanks, China producing MDC's MD-82 aircraft, and Korea assembling the F-16 fighter. An integral part of the arrangements is the training of the local employees. Training is not only for production/assembly purposes but also for maintenance and overhaul of the equipment in the longer term. Some offsets have buy-back provisions; that is, the seller is obligated to purchase output from the facility or operations it has set up or licensed. For example, Westland takes up an agreed level of parts and components from the Korean plant that produces Lynx Helicopters under license. In practice, therefore, direct offsets amount to technology transfer.

Source: This case study was written by Ilkka A. Ronkainen and funded in part by a grant from the Business and International Education Program of the U.S. Department of Education. The assistance of the various organizations cited in the case is appreciated. Special thanks to David Danjczek of Western Atlas, Inc.

FIGURE 1
The Offset Process

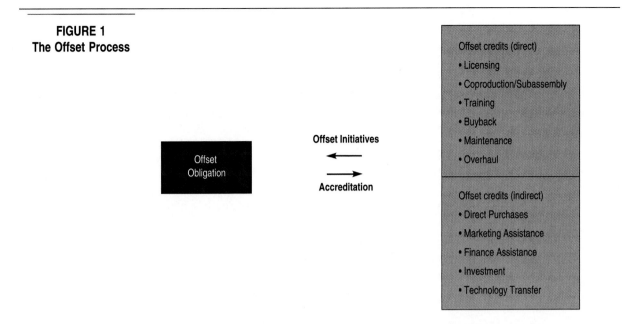

Indirect offsets are deals that involve products, investments, and so forth which are not to be used in the original sales contract but that will satisfy part of the seller's "local" obligation. Direct purchases of raw materials, equipment, or supplies by the seller or its suppliers from the offset customer country present the clearest case of indirect offsets. The offset arrangements are analogous to counterpurchases and switch trading. Sellers faced with offset obligations work closely with their supplier base, some having goals of increasing supplier participation in excess of 50 percent. Teamwork does make the process more effective and efficient. There are various business activities taking place and procurement decisions being made by one of the sellers or its suppliers without offset needs that others may be able to use as offset credit to satisfy an indirect obligation.

Many governments see offsets as a mechanism to develop their indigenous business and industrial sectors. Training in management techniques may be attractive to both parties. The upgrading of personnel may be seen by the government as more critical for improving international competitiveness than efforts focused only on hardware. For the seller, training is relatively inexpensive, but it provides good credits because of its political benefit.

An important dimension of the developmental effort will relate to exports. This may involve the analysis of business sectors showing the greatest foreign market potential, improving organizational and product readiness, conducting market research (e.g., estimating demand or assessing competition), identifying buyers or partners for foreign market development, or assisting in the export process (e.g., company visits, support in negotiations and reaching a final agreement, facilitating trial/sample shipments, handling documentation needs).

Sales are often won or lost on the availability of financing and favorable credit terms to the buyer. Financing packages put together by one of the seller's entities, if it is critical in winning the bid, will earn offset credits.

Buyer nations focusing on industrial development and technology transfer have negotiated contracts that call for offsetting the cost of their purchases through investments. Saudi Arabian purchases of military technology have recently been tied to sellers' willingness to invest in manufacturing plants, defense-related industries, or special-interest projects in the country. British Aerospace, for example, has agreed to invest in factories for the production of farm feed and sanitary ware.

Most often, the final offset deal includes a combination of activities, both direct and indirect vis-à-vis the sale, and no two offset deals are alike. With increasing frequency, governments may require "pre-deal counterpurchases" as a sign of commitment and ability to deliver should they be awarded the contract. Some companies, such as United Technologies, argue that there is limited advantage in carrying out offset activities in advance of the contract, unless the buyer agrees to a firm commitment. While none of the bidders may like it, buyer's market conditions give them very little room to argue. Even if a bidder loses the deal, it can always attempt to sell its offset credits to the winner or use the credits in conjunction with other sales that one of its divisions may have. Some of the companies involved in the bidding in Finland maintain offset accounts with the Finnish government.

FIGURE 2
F/A-18 Hornet Strike Fighter

Prime contractor	McDonnell Douglas
	Principal subcontractor
Northrop Corporation	
Type	Single- (C) and two-seat (D), twin-turbofan for fighter and attack missions
Powerplant	Two General Electric F404-GE-402 (enhanced performance engine)
Thrust	4800 kp each (opprox.)
Afterburning thrust	8000 kp each (approx.)
Dimensions	
Length	1 7.07 m
Span	11.43 m
Wing area	37.16 m^2
Height	4.66 m
Weights	
Empty	10 455 kg
	Normal takeoff16 650 kg
Maximum takeoff	22 328 kg
Wing loading	450 kg/m^2
Fuel (internal)	6 435 litre (4925 kg)
Fuel (with external tanks)	7 687 litre
Armament	
Cannon	One General Electric M61A-1 Vulcan
	rotary-barrel 20-mm
Missiles	Six AIM-9 Sidewinder air-to-air
	Four AIM-7 Sparrow
	Six AIM-120 AMRAAM
Radar	AN/APG-73 multi-mode air-to-air and air-to-surface
Performance	
Takeoff distance	430 m
Landing distance	850 m
Fighter-mission radius	> 740 km
Maximum speed	1.8 Mach (1 915 km/h)at high altitude
	1.0 Mach at intermediate power
Service ceiling	15 240 m
Payload	7 710 kg
Used since	1983
Expected manufacturing lifetime	2000+
Users	USA, Australia, Canada, Spain, and Kuwait
Ordered quantity	1,168

McDonnell's Deal with the Finnish Air Force

The F/A-18 Hornet is a twin-engine, twin-tail, multimission tactical aircraft that can be operated from aircraft carriers or from land bases (see Figure 2). It is both a fighter (air-to-air) and an attack (air-to-ground) aircraft. McDonnell Aircraft Company, a division of MDC, is the prime contractor for the F/A-18. Subcontractors include General Electric for the Hornet's smokeless F404 low-bypass turbofan engines, Hughes Aircraft Company for the APG-73 radar, and Northrop Grumman for the airframe. Approximately 1,100 F/A-18s have been delivered worldwide. Although it had been in use by the United States since 1983, it had been (and can continue to be) upgraded during its operational lifetime. Furthermore, it had proven its combat readiness in the Persian Gulf War.

Only since June of 1990 has the F/A-18 been available to countries that are not members of the North Atlantic Treaty Organization (NATO). The change in U.S. government position resulted from the rapidly changed East–West political situation. The attractive deals available in neutral countries such as Switzerland and Finland helped push the government as well. When the Finnish Air Force initiated its program in 1986, MDC was not invited to (and would not have been able to) offer a bid because of U.S. government restrictions.

THE FINNISH GOVERNMENT POSITION	The Finnish government's role in the deal had two critical dimensions: one related to the choice of the aircraft, the other related to managing the offset agreement in a fashion to maximize the benefit to the country's industry for the long term.

Selecting the Fighter

In 1986, the Finnish Air Force (FAF) decided to replace its aging Swedish-made Drakens and Soviet-made MIG-21s, which made up three fighter squadrons. At that time, the remaining service life of the aircraft was estimated to be 15 years, calling for the new squadrons to be operational by the year 2000 and to be up-to-date even in 2025. Finland, due to its strategic geographic location, has always needed a reliable air defense system. The position of neutrality adopted by Finland had favored split procurement between Eastern and Western suppliers until the December 1991 collapse of the Soviet Union made it politically possible to purchase fighters from a single Western supplier.

The first significant contacts with potential bidders were made in 1988 and in February 1990, the FAF requested proposals from the French Dassault-Breguet, Sweden's Industrigruppen JAS, and General Dynamics in the United States for 40 fighters and trainer aircraft. In January 1991, the bid was amended to 60 fighters and 7 trainers. Three months later, MDC joined the bidding, and by July 1991, binding bids were received from all of the four manufacturers.

During the evaluative period, the four bidders tried to gain favor for their alternative. One approach was the provision of deals for Finnish companies as "pre-deal counterpurchases." For example, General Dynamics negotiated for Vaisala (a major Finnish electronics firm) to become a subcontractor of specialty sensors for the F-16. Before the final decision, the Swedish bidder had arranged for deals worth $250 million for Finnish companies, the French for more than $100 million, and General Dynamics for $40 million. MDC, due to its later start, had none to speak of. Other tactics were used as well. The Swedes pointed out the long ties that the countries have had, and especially the possibilities to develop them further on the economic front. As a matter of fact, offsets were the main appeal of the Swedish bid since the aircraft itself was facing development cost overruns and delays. The French reminded the Finnish government that choosing a European fighter might help in Finland's bid to join the European Union (EU) in 1995. Since the FAF preferred the U.S. AMRAAM missile system for its new fighters, the U.S. government cautioned that its availability depended on the choice of the fighter. The companies themselves also worked on making their bid sweeter: Just before the official announcement, General Dynamics improved its offer to include 67 aircraft for the budgeted sum and a guarantee of 125 percent offsets; that is, the amount of in-country participation would be 125 percent of the sale price paid by the Finnish government for the aircraft.

After extensive flight testing, both in the producers' countries and in Finland (especially for winter conditions), the Hornet was chosen as the winner. Despite the high absolute cost of the aircraft (only 57 will be bought versus 60), the Hornet's cost-effectiveness relative to performance was high. The other alternatives were perceived to have problems: The JAS-39 Gripen had the teething problems of a brand-new aircraft, the Mirage's model 2000-5 had not yet been produced, and the F-16 may be coming to the end of its product life cycle. The MIG-29 from the Soviet Union/Russia was never seriously in the running due to the political turmoil in that country. Some did propose purchasing the needed three squadrons from the stockpiles of the defunct East Germany (and they could have been had quite economically), but the uncertainties were too great for a strategically important product.

Working Out the Offsets

Typically, a specific committee is set up by the government to evaluate which arrangements qualify as part of the offset. In Finland's case, the Finnish Offset Committee (FOC) consists of five members with Ministries of Defense, Foreign Affairs, and Industry and Trade represented. Its task is to provide recommendations as to which export contracts qualify and which do not. The Technical Working Group was set up to support its decision making, especially in cases concerning technology transfer. From 1977 to 1991, the procedures and final decisions were made by the Ministry of Defense; since then, the responsibility has been transferred to the Ministry of Trade and Industry (see Figure 3). The transfer was logical given the increased demands and expectations on the trade and technology fronts of the F/A-18 deal.

When the committee was established in 1977 in conjunction with a major military purchase, almost all contracts qualified until an export developmental role for offsets was outlined. The Finnish exporter is required to show that the offset agreement played a pivotal role in securing its particular contract.

Two different approaches are taken by the government to attain its developmental objective. First, the government will not make available (or give offset credit) for counterpurchasing goods that already have established market positions unless the counterpurchaser can show that the particular sale would not have materialized without its support (for example, through distribution or financing). Second, the government is using compensation "multipliers" for the first time. While previous deals were executed on a one-on-one basis, the government now wants, through the use of multipliers, to direct purchases to certain industries or types of companies. For example, in the case of small- or medium-sized companies, a multiplier of two may be used; that is, a purchase of $500,000 from such a firm will satisfy a $1-million share of the counterpurchaser's requirement. Attractive multipliers also may be used that may generate long-term export opportunities or support Finland's in-

FIGURE 3
Offset: Finnish Industry
Input

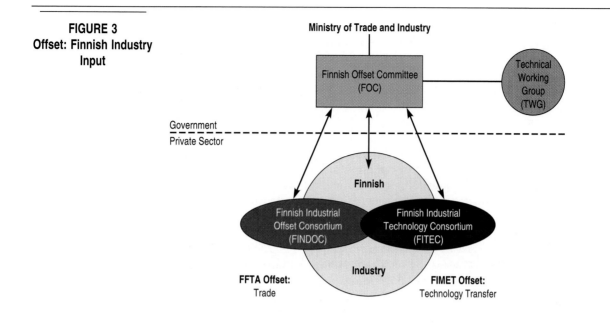

digenous arms or other targeted industry. Similarly, the seller may also insist on the use of multipliers. In the case of technology transfer, the seller may request a high multiplier because of the high initial cost of research and development that may have gone into the technology licensed or provided to the joint venture as well as its relative importance to the recipient country's economic development.

Finnish industry is working closely with the government on two fronts. The Finnish Industrial Offset Consortium (FINDOC) was established to collaborate with the Finnish Foreign Trade Association (a quasi-governmental organization) on trade development. FINDOC's 21 members represent 15 main business areas (e.g., aircraft, shipbuilding, pulp and paper machinery, and metal and engineering) and are among the main Finnish exporters. Their consortium was set up to take advantage of offset opportunities more efficiently and to provide a focal point for the F-18 Team's efforts. For example, MDC and FINDOC arranged for a familiarization trip to the United States for interested Finnish businesses in the fall of 1992. For those companies not in FINDOC, it is the task of the FFTA to provide information on possibilities to benefit from the deal. The Finnish Industrial Technology Consortium (FITEC) was established to facilitate technology transfer to and from the Finnish metal, engineering, and electrotechnical industries.

THE F-18 TEAM'S
POSITION

The monies related to offset management and associated development are not generally allowed as a separate cost in the sales contract. Profit margins for aircraft sales are narrow, and any additional costs must be watched closely. Extraordinary demands by the buyer make bidding more challenging and time-consuming. For example, the customer may want extensive changes in the product without changes in the final price. Switzerland wanted major alterations made to the airframe and additional equipment that made its total cost per plane higher than the price in Finland. In the experience of high-tech firms, the add-on for direct offsets ranges from 3 to 8 percent, which has to be incorporated into the feasibility plans. Offsets have to make good business sense and, once agreed to, successfully executed.

Competing for the Deal

In accepting the offer to bid for the FAF deal, the F-18 team believed it had only a 5 percent chance to win the deal but, given its size, decided to go ahead. From the time it received a request to bid from the FAF, MDC had three months to prepare its proposal. The only main negative factor from the short preparation time was MDC's inability to arrange for "prepurchase" deals and generate goodwill with the constituents.

After two fact-finding missions to Finland, MDC established an office in Helsinki in August 1991. The decision to have a full-time office in Finland (compared to the competitors whose representatives were in Helsinki two days a week on the average) was made based on the experiences from Korea and Switzerland. MDC's approach was to be ready and able to help the customer in terms of information and be involved with all the constituents of the process, such as the testing groups of the FAF, the Ministry of Defense (owners of the program), and the Parliament (supporters of the program).

Beyond the technical merits of the Hornet, MDC's capabilities in meeting the pending offset obligations were a critical factor in winning the deal. MDC had by 1992 a total of 100 offset programs in 25 countries with a value of $8 billion, and its track record in administering them was excellent. Another factor in MDC's favor was its long-term relation with Finnair, the national airline. Finnair's aircraft have predominantly come from MDC, starting with the DC-2 in 1941 to the MD-11 aircraft delivered in 1991.

Satisfying the Offset Obligation

Offset deals are not barter where the seller and the buyer swap products of equal value over a relatively short time period. The F-18 team members have to complete the offset program by the year 2002 through a number of different elements including marketing assistance, export development, technology transfer, team purchases, and investment financing. One of the major beneficiaries of the offset arrangement is Valmet, the only major aircraft manufacturer in Finland. Valmet will assemble the 57 C-versions in Finland and is also counting on the F-18 team's connections to open markets for its Redigo trainer aircraft. The F-18 team works with Finnish companies to develop exports for their products and services by identifying potential buyers and introducing the two parties to each other. For example, Global Connection, a Los Angeles–based consulting firm, will be preparing small and medium-sized Finnish firms to start export operations into the United States through the use of seminars and workshops. Expenses will be paid by Northrop Grumman. Purchases can come from within the contractor companies, suppliers to the F-18 contractors, and third parties. The motivation for completing offset projects is financial penalties for the prime team members if they do not meet contract deadlines.

However, no one in the F-18 team or among its suppliers is obligated to engage in a given transaction just because Finland purchased fighters from McDonnell Douglas. The key point is that products must meet specifications, delivery dates, and price criteria to be successfully sold in any market. After an appropriate purchase has taken place, the F-18 team receives offset credit based on the Finnish-manufactured content of the transaction value as approved by the Finnish Offset Committee. For example, when Finnyards won the bid to build a passenger ferry for the Danish Stena Line, Northrop Grumman received offset credits due to its role in financing Finnyard's bid.

The offset obligations are not limited to the United States. The team has offset partners all over the world because the members operate worldwide. Furthermore, given the long time frame involved, there are no pressing time constraints on the members to earn offset credits.

Since 1992, the MDC office in Helsinki has had two officers: one in charge of the aircraft, the other focused on offsets. Due to the worst recession in recent Finnish history, the response to the offset program has been unprecedented, and the office has been inundated with requests for information. By the end of 1994, deals worth $883 million satisfying offset criteria had been completed. Of these, $249 million were direct offset and $634 million were indirect. The share of small and medium-sized businesses was 13 percent.

ONE COMPANY'S EXPERIENCE

Hackman, one of Finland's leading exporters in the metal sector, started its cooperation with McDonnell Douglas by putting together a portfolio of Hackman products that offer the best offset potential. The proposal ended up covering a wide range of products ranging from tableware to turnkey cheese plants. Disinfecting machines and food processors created the most interest because of McDonnell Douglas's contracts in the hospital and construction sectors.

The first project identification came in July 1992 when word came from Mc-Donnell Douglas that a $187-million hotel being planned for Denver, Colorado, was a potential offset target. The contractor was seeking export financing (for example, through GE Finance) in exchange for sourcing products through offset from Finland for which offset credits could be used by MDC. Ideally, the contractor would get attractive financing, the F-18 team would get offset credits, and Finnish participants would get a shot at a huge deal worth up to $40 million in total.

Questions for Discussion

1. Why would the members of the F-18 team, McDonnell Douglas, Northrop Grumman, General Electric, and Hughes agree to such a deal rather than insist on a money-based transaction?

2. After the deal was signed, many Finnish companies expected that contracts and money would start rolling in by merely calling up McDonnell Douglas. What are the fundamental flaws in this thinking?

3. Why do Western governments typically take an unsupportive stance on countertrade arrangements?

4. Comment on this statement: "Offset arrangements involving overseas production that permits a foreign government or producer to acquire the technical information to manufacture all or part of a U.S.-origin article trade short-term sales for long-term loss of market position."

References

"Countertrade's Growth Continues." *BarterNews* 27 (1993): 54–55.

"Investing, Licensing, and Trading Conditions Abroad: Saudi Arabia." *Business International,* May 15, 1990, 5.

Matthews, Ron. "Countering or Countenancing Countertrade." *Management Accounting* 53 (October 1991): 42–44.

"Offsets in the Aerospace Industry." *BarterNews* 27 (1993): 56-57.

Saastamoinen, Jukka. "Jaita Vastakauppiaan Hattuun." *Optio,* May 21, 1992, 26-28.

Silverang, Keith. "Behind the Myth of Offset." *Style & Steel* 2 (Spring 1992): 28-29.

Verzariu, Pompiliu, and Paula Mitchell. *International Countertrade: Individual Country Practices.* Washington, D.C.: U.S. Department of Commerce, Part 1, 1992.

Charting a Course in a Global Economy

The goal in the world of private, for-profit industry is simple: maximizing shareholder wealth. But some believe private businesses have other responsibilities as well, including the duty to be a good corporate citizen. After all, businesses do not exist in a vacuum, some argue. They are part of a larger community and draw from the resources of that community to exist and succeed. Therefore, they should act responsibly.

Assume that your organization decides to adopt an ethical approach to business, what then? Who is to say what is ethical in any given situation? Whose ethics? The dilemma becomes more complicated if your business is global in nature. What if your foreign customers and competitors have a different set of moral bearings? Consider the case of human resource management in an international setting where cultural differences can complicate decision making.

A group from the Columbia University Business School was asked the following: What would you do if you were responsible for appointing a new director for your company's Asian office? The position is a key step on the fast track, and the most qualified candidate is a woman. However, you know that several important customers in the region will refuse to deal with a woman. You also expect some friction from the local staff. Do you go ahead with the appointment anyway?

Jennifer McVea is a manager in the international advertising group at AT&T. She is in Columbia's MBA program for mid-career executives. "I can speak from personal experience on this, having done business in the Far East," she said. "I think it would be difficult, especially in some countries perhaps more than others, to be in a leadership role as a woman. Some other cultures, and especially some Asian cultures, have not necessarily accepted women in that role yet. And while we Americans have, and perhaps as an American company operating in an Asian country, I don't believe that we can necessarily force our values on another culture."

McVea was then asked how she would respond if her company appointed her director of Asian affairs.

"I think if a company made the decision that it was going to offer the job to a woman, I would just hope that it would have taken into account, first of all, the cultural shock for the woman in terms that she may not get, will not get, the same level of acceptance that a man would," McVea said. "But also the possible business repercussions, in terms of other people either in that office, if they are nationals, who may not even be used to working for an American, let alone an American woman."

But given that condition, perhaps American companies should consider whether they have a role in influencing change in that condition, McVea was told.

Steve Markscheid, a vice president at First Chicago Bank and also a student in Columbia's executive MBA program, has some dealings with China through his work. Markscheid disagreed with McVea.

"I think we're working for American companies, and we have American values. And we don't let those fall by the wayside when we do our business overseas," recognizing, of course, that there could be a cost involved, he said.

The panel was asked what would happen if a woman who got the Asian appointment didn't do well on the job because she could not hurdle the cultural barriers.

Eric Guthrie, a law student who is studying ethics at the business school, replied. "I think Asian companies have to realize that the women in the corporations today

Source: This case was drawn from the Public Broadcasting System's television program "Adam Smith," which aired on Oct. 5, 1990. Producer: Alvin H. Perlmutter, Inc.

are playing a major role. If they want to expand to the [West] and all around the globe, they have to consider that the woman is going to play a major part in the corporation," he said.

The panel was asked to consider the fact that competitors to the company might not have women in such roles and might thus find it easier to conduct business.

James Kuhn is a professor at Columbia who runs the school's teaching program in business ethics. "If you stop at women, where do we stop?" he asked. "Because we have blacks, we have Hispanics, we have Filipinos. I don't think this country can afford to give up on that kind of value."

Markscheid added: "What sort of message are we sending to the people who work in our company back home, as well as to our customers? That we discriminate internally to take advantage of transient commercial opportunities overseas?"

Boors Yavitz, a former dean, also teaches in the Columbia business school. "I think that's an easy one," he said. "Assuming that the company has thought through and said, 'This is the right person,' and I assume they're not novices and they know the difficulties a woman will have, I think you clearly have to stick to your guns. Not only is it the right thing, but I think this is an interesting reversal of the Europeans, the Asians always preaching to us to be sensitive to their cultural differences. We have to make it clear to our Asian customers that we operate in an American environment where this is not acceptable."

What do you do after a year if your company is losing ground, the panel was asked.

"Well, there is the short term and the long term," replied Guthrie. "And maybe in the short term you will lose some ground, but the adversity in the long term is very profitable. It will pay off in the long run, and the corporations that do practice those stringent procedures will eventually turn around—at least I would hope so," he said.

"We've got to be true to whatever our culture is, and its basic values—and we're talking about a very basic value here—and on this, I think we may be leaders in the world," said Kuhn. "If we pay a cost for that, then I think it is a short-term cost that will have a very high payoff in the long term."

Global standards are changing, are beginning to become more homogenized, said Yavitz. "I think they're moving to the more enlightened, liberal kind of view of life. Part of that is simply the sunlight, the fact that more and more is known, more and more is publicized. And my sense is that if we as American companies push our set of values and keep emphasizing those, that they do rub off, that you do get a change in the way global business is done."

Questions for Discussion

1. If U.S. companies can transmit their values abroad, should foreign firms be allowed to apply theirs in the United States?

2. Should personal characteristics, such as gender, nationality, or age, for example, be taken into consideration when selecting managers for overseas assignments? Why or why not? What could be the outcome of considering, or not considering, personal characteristics?

3. Other than personal characteristics, what are other selection criteria for overseas managers? Provide examples of each. Which are the most important criteria? Why?

4. Define culture shock. What are its four stages? What can be done to alleviate it?

TROLL–AEG[1]

It was late afternoon of January 21, 1992, and Miguel Tey Feliu de la Peña, managing director of J. Feliu de la Peña, S.A., a Spanish manufacturer of lighting elements known for its modern designs marketed under the TROLL brand, was reflecting on the reciprocal commercial distribution contracts which were to be signed the next day with the managers of AEG's Technical Lighting Business Area (AEG Aktiengesellschaft Fachbereich Lichttechnik, or AEG-LT), from Germany.

Basically, these were two "mirror" contracts by which, in one of them, J. Feliu de la Peña, S.A. (JFP) granted AEG a non-exclusive[2] right to distribute its products in Germany while, by virtue of the second contract, AEG granted JFP and its subsidiary TROLL–France a non-exclusive right to distribute its products in Spain and France, respectively. See Exhibit 1 for further information on these contracts.

The simultaneous signature of both contracts, scheduled for the next day, would be marked by a certain degree of solemnity as it would be presided by the Right Honourable Mr. Antoni Subirà i Claus, Councillor for Industry and Energy of the Government of the Generalitat of Catalonia.

Miguel Tey did not doubt that the contracts would be signed. But, reflecting on the matter, several questions came to his mind:

> "First, when I review the decisions that have been taken up to this point in time, I wonder if we are doing the right thing in entering into this type of agreement or whether it would have been better to continue following our own fully autonomous growth path, as we have done until now. At the same time, I wonder whether AEG is the best partner for us. Also, when I reread the two contracts, I wonder if something is missing or should not be there, or whether any of the sections should be reworded.
>
> "Second, if we accept everything done until now and do sign the contracts, then there are two major questions with regard to our immediate future that must be answered: What must we decide and do to ensure that this new reciprocal relationship between TROLL and AEG works, and works well? And finally, how will all this end up? In other words, where will our company be three, five or ten years from now? Will these agreements still be in full force?"

No doubt because of the obvious difference in size between JFP and AEG, someone had recently said, only half joking, "In no time at all, we'll all be wearing AEG T-shirts. . . ."

Source: This case won first prize in the "Joint Ventures and Strategic Alliances" category in the 1995 EFMD European Case Competition Contest, organized by the European Foundation for Management Development.

[1]Case of the Research Department at IESE. Prepared by Javier Sarda, MED-1992, under the supervision of Francesc Parés, Lecturer, and Professor Lluís G. Renart, October 1992. Copyright ©1992, by IESE. No part of this publication may be reproduced without the written permission of IESE.

As any reader will easily realize, this case was written on the basis of data and interviews granted by managers of JFP, S.A. Therefore, the TROLL-AEG alliance is presented here from the point of view of the Spanish partner.

[2]Even though the contracts were formally "non-exclusive" both parties had agreed that, in essence, the spirit of both contracts was of full exclusivity. It is a well known fact that, in case of termination, dissolving exclusive contracts is very difficult and cumbersome.

EXHIBIT 1
The Reciprocal
Distribution Contracts

These were two "mirror" contracts. In one of these, JFP granted AEG a nonexclusive right to distribute certain products in Germany. In the other, AEG Aktiengesellschaft granted JFP a nonexclusive right to distribute certain products in Spain and France. In both cases, the products included were specified in an attachment and the possibility of including new products in the future was left open.

Both contracts specified, in an identical and reciprocal fashion for both companies, a series of rights and obligations. In the opinion of the casewriter, the most important were the following:

The importer should have a sales organization able to satisfactorily sell the other party's products.

The marketing costs would be borne by the importer-distributor, including the obligation to hold sufficient stock to supply its customers and to have a spare parts stock and aftersales service.

In the event of faulty products, the seller would pay the importer 70 percent of the cost of correcting such faults.

The importer would "effectively advertise" the products imported, using the documentation provided by the supplier.

Each party would help the other to sell its products and, after prior agreement, could send specialists to support the importer's sales team, advise its customers or carry out market research. Unless agreed otherwise, the specialist's travelling and living expenses would be paid for by the exporter.

Both parties undertook: to inform the other party in the event that one of them should decide to represent other companies; to keep secret any information it might have received on the other party; to inform the other party on developments in its company and the status of the market and sales; to buy and sell in accordance with the prices included as an attachment to the contract.

The contract's duration would be from the date the contract was signed to December 31, 1993. It could be renewed for successive calendar years, unless one of the parties announced its intention to terminate the contract with a minimum of six months notice.

Both contracts could also be considered terminated in the event of serious breach of the conditions agreed, in the event that the sales targets were not reached, in the event of changes in the other company's ownership or management team, or if either of the two declared themselves to be insolvent or suspended payments.

Finally, a series of articles provided for the steps that would be taken if the contract were to be terminated (return of documents, disposal of stocks, discontinuation in the use of brandnames and marks,. . .) and an article according to which any possible disputes would be submitted to arbitration, following the Rules of the International Chamber of Commerce.

However, in the casewriter's opinion, there were a few points or details in which the contracts were not exactly symmetrical or "mirror-like":

Brand names: JFP undertook to sell AEG-LT's products in Spain and France under the "AEG" brand while JFP's products sold by AEG-LT in Germany would also be labelled "AEG," although the sales leaflets would also include the indication "designed by TROLL."

The sales targets for products manufactured by JFP and sold by AEG-LT in Germany were more ambitious (approximately 1.6 times higher) than the sum of the sales targets for AEG products in Spain and France together, as shown in the following table in Deutschmarks (accompanied by their exchange rates in the original contracts):

	1992	1993	1994
AEG purchases	DM2,200,000	DM4,500,000	DM7,300,000
JFP purchases			
In Spain	DM800,000	DM1,800,000	DM2,800,000
In France	DM500,000	DM1,100,000	DM1,800,000
Total JFP purchases to AEG	DM1,300,000	DM2,900,000	DM4,600,000

BACKGROUND OF J. FELIU DE LA PEÑA, S.A. (JFP)

Mr. Julio Feliu de la Peña, grandfather of the brothers Xavier and Miguel Tey Feliu de la Peña, started manufacturing "classic" design lamps back in 1929, in Barcelona.[3]

Miguel joined the company as an apprentice in 1960, when he was 15 years old. However, one year later, he was already managing the business. Meanwhile, his elder brother, Xavier, continued his university studies, eventually obtaining a doctorate in industrial engineering.

In 1974, when Miguel was 29 years old, they became owners of the business, which at that time operated from a ground floor premises in Bruc Street, on the corner of Valencia Street, that is, very close to the center of Barcelona, and it was legally incorporated as a stock company ("Sociedad Anónima").

> "The company was completely outmoded," said Miguel. "It had 15 very old employees, who basically carried out assembly tasks. We were not experts in anything and sold classic design lamps through salesmen who were paid a fixed salary plus commission. Although it was small, the company had a reputation for being reliable and serious. In addition to making its own lamps, the company also had exclusive distribution agreements with other lamp manufacturers. It had one sales outlet for both wholesale and retail sales."

In the same year, 1974, Nordart Industria, S.A. offered them the possibility of selling its products, which were marketed under the TROLL brand. It was a new lighting system made up by spot projectors, power tracks and adapters (the adapter being the part linking the spot projector to the power carrying track). Miguel saw that the product had a modern design and was very well presented and offered to buy their entire output if he was given exclusive sales rights for Spain. Nordart Industria, S.A. was a small factory without any salesforce and had also been badly stung when a distributor had copied their product and left them in the lurch. Joaquim Masó, the company's owner, accepted to appoint JFP its sole agent after establishing that JFP would operate with a gross margin of 30 percent.

In the remaining six months of 1974, they sold about 16 million pesetas worth of TROLL products. In 1975, sales rose to about 32 million pesetas. In 1976, sales ran at almost 60 million pesetas and by 1977, their TROLL sales had increased to 130 million pesetas. Miguel realised that "the future was TROLL."

In 1978, Joaquim Masó and the Tey brothers agreed to merge both companies with each partner owning one-third of the resulting company, which continued to be called J. Feliu de la Peña, S.A.[4]

> "The next decade, 1978–1988, was a period of strong growth for JFP. It stopped manufacturing its classic lamps to manufacture only TROLL lighting elements. After 1981, our products were spotlights, built-in downlights and self-connecting space frames in decorative fluorescence."

During this decade, the company's sales grew at a compound annual rate of slightly more than 50 percent. The workforce increased from 25 to 100 employees and the company became market leader in Spain in this type of accent lighting elements.

---

[3]Throughout this case, the words "lamp" or "lighting elements" are used to refer to the lampholder which holds the light source(s), and does not mean the light bulbs or other light sources. "Spot" lights or "accent" lighting elements create a fairly specific field of light, while leaving the surrounding area in comparative darkness.

[4]In early 1992, they still had the same shareholding positions.

JFP's success can be attributed basically to the combination of two success factors: the changes in the distribution channel and the continuous improvement and redesign of its products.

Regarding changes in its distribution policy, JFP ceased selling through traditional (normally classic design) lamp retailers and pioneered the sale of spotlights and downlights through electrical goods wholesalers/stockists.[5]

Miguel Tey considered that this change of distribution policy had only been partly successful as he soon realised that his negotiating power with these wholesalers was very limited:

> "I was the 'fellow selling spots,' in other words, a rather unwelcome visitor who was attempting to sell them a very limited range of products, which was relatively new or unusual in their stores and which accounted for only a minute fraction of their total sales. No doubt that was the reason why most often I only got to speak with one of the electrical goods store's sales assistants."

In order to counteract this situation, Miguel sought to create an alliance with other companies who manufactured products that were not directly competitive with each other but which were sold through the same electrical goods stores. Finally, he managed to persuade the general managers of a wire company, a transformer company and a cable fastener company to join forces with him in such an alliance.

The agreement consisted of organizing a network of self-employed representatives who would sell the products of all four manufacturers.

The first of these representatives was appointed in 1978, in Madrid. The following working procedure was established with this representative: all four manufacturers would place their products on consignment in the representative's warehouse. The representative would then sell and deliver the goods, sending the delivery note to each manufacturer. The manufacturers would then issue the invoice, give credit if applicable and collect payment on the invoice. Should the customer default on payment, the representative would personally assist them in collecting payment.

In exchange for these functions, the representative received a commission that was agreed upon separately with each one of the four manufacturing companies.

Once the Madrid representative was working satisfactorily, the same procedure was followed in Barcelona, appointing a previous TROLL representative. Next came the turn of Palma de Mallorca and when all three were seen to be operating successfully, the process was continued, establishing a total of 13 joint "branches" covering practically the entire Spanish market.

> "And all that with just paying a commission, that is, a variable cost, and with a minimum investment in stock in all thirteen warehouses. An important point to remember is that thanks to our pioneering role in selling accent lighting elements in Spain, JFP's margins were very high. Our sale price to the electrical goods store was between 2.5 and 3 times our manufacturing cost!"

Initially the least well-known of the four allied companies, J. Feliu de la Peña, S.A. exploited the new situation to the maximum. The higher pooled sales turnover

---

[5]In Spain, this kind of wholesalers/stockists sell mostly to contractors specialising in electrical installations either in new buildings or in building refurbishing jobs. Most of their sales were "counter" sales, made on the spot to contractors who came to their outlet with a list of their immediate needs. Most of them would take the goods with them.

enabled the companies to recruit better representatives and to increase their negotiating power with the electrical goods stores. With the passing of time, JFP became the unofficial leader of the network as the representatives mainly followed Miguel Tey's lead. JFP's young general manager had managed to win them over through a combination of an extremely cordial personal relationship, an excellent service from his company, a product range with skyrocketing sales and a 10 percent commission, compared with the 5 percent commission or less given to them by the other three companies.

CHANGES IN THE PRODUCT RANGE

The other part of Miguel's enormous success during those years was due to the changes made to the products' design which, in turn, considerably improved the level of service given to the representatives. Until then, each lamp model, of which there were about 50, was manufactured in sixteen colors and consisted of several parts that were specific to each model, plus their variants. In total, there were about 3,200 different stock keeping units (sku's).

Miguel reduced the color range from 16 to 4 (white, black, gold, and stainless steel). The slower-moving designs were dropped from the collection. But the most important change was in the design of the lamp parts, when a new system of universal connector was introduced which allowed all parts to be easily interconnected by simple pressure plus a security screw. This innovation made the four basic parts of the lighting systems manufactured fully interchangeable. This enabled him to cut down the number of sku's to less than 200, leading to a dramatic increase in turnover in all the warehouses in the logistics chain, including, of course, of its immediate customers, that is, the electrical goods stores.

Miguel also implemented major changes in the design process of its lighting elements. Indeed, in the early days, Miguel himself had designed the lighting elements, drawing his inspiration from the designs he saw at the international fairs he attended as a mere visitor. By 1985, Miguel decided that he needed to create an aesthetic consistency and identifying style in his lighting element designs and started to commission original designs from two free lance industrial designers. Miguel wanted his lighting elements to be immediately recognisable:

> "I wanted people to say, when they saw one of our lamps: 'That's TROLL,' without having to read the brandname. Braun was my guiding light in design. I wanted to be 'the Braun of lighting.'" For that and other reasons, in 1987 the two designers were recruited to the company as full-time, salaried employees."

Thus, the combination of having pioneered accent lighting in Spain (with downlights, spots and tracks), the network of "branches" made up of the 13 independent representatives, a reasonably well-designed product range, and very ample margins turned the company into one of the most profitable in this industry in Spain. Forecast sales for 1988 were estimated at about 1.5 billion pesetas, with a net income of about 400 million pesetas, and a market share between 25 percent and 30 percent in this kind of product, that is, indoor accent lighting elements.

As Exhibit 2 shows, the company had taken a few tentative steps in exporting, with the recruitment of Josep Sala in 1984. The new factory located in Canovelles, near Granollers (province of Barcelona) was opened in 1985 as described in Exhibit 3. With an initial floor area of 5,000 square meters, it was subsequently expanded to 10,000 square meters.

EXHIBIT 2
J. Feliu de la Peña, S.A.

	Exports Made in the Year					
To	**1986¹**	**1987**	**1988**	**1989**	**1990**	**1991**
Portugal	72% = 10.8 M̄	44% = 9.2 M̄	5.9% = 3.4 M̄	14% = 12.6 M̄	*	*
United States	12% = 1.8 M̄	*	*	*	*	*
France	7% = 1.1 M̄	18% = 3.8 M̄	80.3% = 46.3 M̄	45% = 40.5 M̄	28.9% = 48.9 M̄	29.6% = 68.1 M̄
Saudi Arabia	6% = 0.9 M̄	5% = 1.1 M̄	*	*	*	*
Belgium-Luxembourg	* (²)	19% = 4.0 M̄	*	*	*	*
United Kingdom	*	*	*	15% = 13.5 M̄	14.9% = 25.3 M̄	*
Greece	*	*	*	7% = 6.3 M̄	*	*
UEBL	*	*	8.1% = 4.6 M̄	*	*	*
Switzerland	*	*	3.3% = 1.9 M̄	*	*	*
West Germany	*	*	*	*	15.2% = 25.8 M̄	25.9% = 59.6 M̄
Italy	*	*	*	*	9.8% = 16.6 M̄	*
U.A.E.	*	*	*	*	*	7.0% = 16.1 M̄
Holland	*	*	*	*	*	12.8% = 29.4 M̄
Other countries	3% = 0.4 M̄	14% = 2.9 M̄	2.4% = 1.4 M̄	19% = 17.1 M̄	31.2% = 53 M̄	24.7% = 56.8 M̄
Total exports each year	100% = 15 M̄	100% = 21 M̄	100% = 57.6 M̄	100% = 90 M̄	100% = 169.6 M̄	100% = 230 M̄
Total JFP, S.A. sales (³)	N.A.	1,000 M̄	1,541 M̄	1,541 M̄	1,470 M̄	1,615 M̄

[1]The "Official Census of Spanish Exporters—1987," which publishes data on export activity during 1986, indicates that between 1985 and 1986, J. Feliu de la Peña, S.A.'s exports grew 154%. This seems to indicate that exports in 1985 must have amounted to about 6 million pesetas. The 1986 Census did not publish any data on the company, no doubt because the amount of 5,000,000 pesetas was too small and J.F. de la Peña, S.A. was not included in the Census.

[2]An asterisk indicates that in the year in question, we do not know whether or not the company exported to that country, as the Census only gives data on exports to the company's top four importing countries.

In the event that the company had exported to a country marked with an asterisk, this would be included in the line "Other countries" and the amount exported would always be less than that exported to the fourth highest importing country.

For example, if the company exported to the United Kingdom in 1986, it did not export more than the 900,000 pesetas indicated for Saudi Arabia in that year.

1988: RECRUITMENT OF JAVIER ROCASALBAS AND THE GROWTH OF THE COMPANY WITHIN SPAIN	Faced with a strong increase in demand, the company no longer had sufficient capacity to supply all the orders. Furthermore, Miguel was in serious danger of being overwhelmed by the increasing complexity of the company's management. Consequently, he decided to recruit Javier Rocasalbas as general manager, while he became managing director and his brother Xavier became president.

In 1988, Javier Rocasalbas was 40 years old. Having initially graduated as an industrial engineer, his early work experience was centered in the engineering-production area, first in a factory making fuel pumps for diesel motors and later in a hydraulic pump manufacturer. Before joining JFP, he had worked in a plastics factory, where, for the first time, his duties had gone beyond the strictly technical.

Javier summarised the company's situation when he joined it in late May, 1989, as follows:

"J. Feliu de la Peña, S.A. was the typical family business where the management style was heavily influenced by the owner's personality. The chief problem was purely industrial. On the one hand, on occasion the lead-times quoted to the customers were very long. Furthermore, there was a clear lack of internal organization in production, even though

**EXHIBIT 3
A Visit to the Barcelona
Branch**

J. Feliu de la Peña, S.A.'s Barcelona branch was located at No. 68, Numancia Street, relatively near the center of the city. The TROLL logo prominently displayed above the door and a sign with smaller type with the words "Catalonia Branch. Showroom and Projects" clearly stated its identity and purpose.

Any visitor could go there and ask them to draw up a lighting project for a house or apartment, a shop or an industrial premises or an office. This service was free of charge.

From the entrance door, the visitor entered a reception area. Behind the reception, there was a door that gave onto a large room measuring about 100 square meters, divided into various sectors or settings: part of the room portrayed a garden setting; another part represented a stretch of supermarket shelving; another simulated a restaurant table; another, part of an office; two of the walls looked like an art gallery or museum; and another part had a clearly commercial setting, with a large display window with two dummies and some sports accessories, complemented with four display cases measuring 70 by 70 centimeters similar to those that can be found in some jewelers' shops.

Also, in the same room, there was a "lighting robot," a temperature cabinet and a tiny conference area, equipped with about ten or twelve chairs, a projection screen and a lectern.

Each one of the sectors or settings was equipped with different types of lights. The TROLL technician accompanying the visitor could place him in front of a certain setting (for example, the supermarket) and turn on and off different types of lights, equipped with different types of bulbs (incandescent, halogen, dichromatic, fluorescent, etc.) to show the visitor the different lighting effects that could be obtained with the TROLL lighting elements.

Xavier Lopez and Manuel Santos accompanied the casewriter. In the course of the visit, they commented, "Our aim is to show the shopowners that good lighting is good business and profitable, because it helps them to sell more. The products are more attractive and the colors are more vivid and realistic."

The so-called "lighting robot" was not a robot as such. It was a facility consisting basically of an H-shaped metal stand on rails that allowed it to be moved towards and away from a vertical wall.

Different types of lighting elements could be fitted on the stand, each one of them with different types of bulbs, focusing them onto the wall vertically or at an angle. The stand was also fitted with a device for measuring light intensity, which could be read in digital form on a small screen.

The measuring device's cells or sensors were located on the vertical wall in front of the stand. The wall was squared and there was a cell or sensor on each intersection of the grid. Each cell or sensor could be turned on or off individually by switches on the stand.

The "robot" enabled numerical readings of the light intensity impinging on any point of the wall to be obtained each time any of the variables were changed: lamp type, bulb type and wattage, distance from the wall, the light rays' angle of incidence on the wall, etc.

The color temperature cabinet was fitted with a series of windows. Each window had strips of cardboard painted with the main colors from red to violet. All the windows had exactly the same palette of colors and hues. However, the palette in each window was lit by a different type of bulb, which enabled the visitor to clearly see how his or her perception of the colors changed when using one bulb or another.

On his way out, the casewriter walked through a small warehouse also measuring about 100 square meters, which was not open to the public, from which the branch supplied the orders received from the specialty retail stores or distributors.

JFP was (and still is in 1992) basically a design and assembly company.[6] My first actions were therefore eminently industrial in nature, and included computerising the production process."

Upon turning his attention to design, Rocasalbas realised that the products' aesthetic quality was excellent but the technical quality was poor: the electromechanical aspects had been neglected to a considerable extent, which led to difficulties when attempting to assemble the lighting elements on an industrial scale.

---

[6]In addition to design and assembly, the company confined itself to carrying out by itself some metal forming work (pressing and cutting) and certain painting and surface finishing tasks. It usually bought or subcontracted to outside suppliers the following: small electrical or electronic items, plastic injection, aluminum injection or extrusion, glass fittings, minor mechanical parts (screws, connectors, etc.) and certain surface finishes other than painting (chrome plating, gold plating, etc.).

Therefore, in 1989, Rocasalbas increased the design team by recruiting Carlos Galán, an industrial engineer and electromechanical designer as its manager. A designer specialised in mechanical functions and a draftsman were also recruited to the team. By the end of 1991, the design and quality department was composed of 12 to 14 people including Galán.

This team was responsible not only for ensuring that the products performed their function properly as lighting elements but also that they complied with electrical safety standards and that their aesthetic quality made the grade both as individual items and as integral parts of the entire collection. Finally, under Rocasalbas and Galán's management, the company completed the transition from a design process in which the cost price would be known at the end, as a result, to a process in which a cost price was set before starting the design work, as a goal to be achieved, carrying out value analysis processes along the way.

The star products at that time (1988) were the fixed, low-voltage built-in downlight in black or white and the swivelling ball-spot. In total, the company handled less than 300 stock keeping units.

They were relatively simple products to design, manufacture, assemble and install in the point of use. In fact, they could be considered standard products of average quality and were usually bought by electricians or electrical contractors for installing, without any technical complications, in private homes, shops, offices, etc.

The branches, that is, the 13 sales representatives with their own warehouse, sold indiscriminately and massively, without distinguishing between different types of customers. JFP published a single price list, which carried a discount that was the same for all JFP's customers, namely, about 45 percent.

THE MODEL STARTS TO SUFFER SOME TENSIONS

However, from 1988 onwards, this strategy started to encounter increasing difficulties.

On the one hand, competition in Spain became a lot fiercer. A large number of lamp manufacturers sprung up, flooding the market with lighting elements which had designs very similar to those of TROLL, even to the point, in some cases, of using TROLL products to take the photographs for some competitor's catalog. By the end of 1991, Javier Rocasalbas estimated that between 25 and 30 Spanish lamp manufacturers offered virtually identical, standard accent lighting elements.

The resulting price war quickly and severely eroded sales margins, which fell from about 30 percent in 1988 to about 15 percent in 1991.

At the same time, in 1988, Miguel decided that if TROLL products sold well in Spain, they should also be able to attain success in France, which had accounted for almost 4 million pesetas of the company's exports in 1987. Always impulsive and quick off the bat, Miguel went to Lyon and bought an old building near the high-speed train (TGV) station. Although requiring a certain degree of restoration, it had an area of 300 square meters each in a basement, ground floor and first floor. The operation seemed to be a good buy from the real estate viewpoint as it seemed that the zoning regulations would allow them to build up several additional floors.

Miguel recruited Josep Sitjà as general manager of TROLL–France. A Catalan by birth, he had worked until that time as an electrical contractor in Marseille. As can be seen in Exhibit 2, by 1988, JFP was exporting products to the tune of 46 million pesetas to France.

However, things were not going so smoothly as this might make one believe. On the one hand, part of this export figure included the necessary start-up stock of finished product shipped to Lyon. It also soon became clear that the standard product offered by the company was encountering serious difficulties in being accepted on the French market. The quality was not right, the price was not right and it was not certified as conforming with the French NF standards. However, on the positive side, they found out that the design's aesthetic aspects were very well accepted and could become the major factor differentiating TROLL lamps, in spite of the lack of electromechanical quality at that time.

In addition to showing them the French market's perception of their products' quality, the experience in France also opened JFP's managers' eyes to another important issue: it was very difficult to achieve a significant level of sales in France without offering an integral, complete and coherent product range. In other words, the TROLL range was composed solely of interior accent lighting elements, that is, tracks and spots, downlights and suspended fluorescent lights self-connected by jacks.

However, they had no built-in fluorescent panels (used mainly in offices), industrial lights (for lighting factories), or any type of lighting elements for installation and use outdoors, to light public highways, parks and gardens, tunnels, sports facilities, etc.

THE REACTION

Miguel and Javier's reaction to this setback was to ratify their firm resolve to gain a presence on the European market. They therefore ruled out the option of withdrawing and confining themselves back to the Spanish market.

Therefore, in late 1988 to early 1989, they decided to initiate as soon as possible a change in the composition of their product range, consisting of slowly phasing out their standard products and starting to design, manufacture and sell technical architectural lighting elements, able to offer special lighting applications in accordance with defined specifications to satisfy the final customer's lighting requirements.

> "We considered that the more sophisticated features of the new generation of lighting elements we wanted to design and launch onto the market would be more difficult for our direct competitors to imitate, most of which were small companies. We were up against companies who were not only limited by their technical skills but also by their financial possibilities, as an 'architectural' lighting element of this type may mean investing about 20 million pesetas in design, tooling, molds, etc.," said Rocasalbas.

> "It was rather an intuitive change; I don't think we really knew what we were letting ourselves in for. Or, at least, at that time, we were not aware that the change in focus of the product range would also necessarily involve a drastic change in the type of final customer, in distribution channels and in the marketing resources to be used to promote our products."

Indeed, when they started to launch the first new-generation lighting elements on the market (see Exhibit 4), they realised that the electrical goods wholesaler/stockist neither bought nor distributed technical architectural lighting products. These were too sophisticated, designed for specific applications, slow-selling, and their installation required a prior analysis to ensure their match with certain specific lighting needs, circumstances or environments.

In a manner slightly analogous to medicines sold under prescription, technical architectural lighting elements had to be promoted by persuading the prescribers to use them. Within the field of technical lighting, a prescriber could be an architect, an interior decorator, a shop window designer, an engineer or technician specialised in lighting, an engineering firm, etc.

EXHIBIT 4
The Launching of the New Generation of Technical Architectural Lighting Elements

The first model of this new product policy, focused towards technical architectural lighting elements was the so-called "model 699." It was first introduced on the occasion of the Hannover trade fair, in April 1989.

Model 699 was composed of a certain number of basic bodies, equipped or not with a transformer. Different heads and accessories (such as reflectors, filters, filter holders or barndoors) could be adapted to the different bodies to obtain different lighting results. This combination of bodies and heads and accessories was done in a way similar to how a professional photographer may use different lenses with different camera bodies.

Soon after that, in 1990, the company redesigned their system of spatial self-connecting lighting structures. Patents were obtained for this so-called "Jack System," composed of different prewired elements and its many accessories.

Further, two more families of versatile projectors were designed and developed: "Vector" and "Delta." Also the "Compact" product range was created, which could be used both as a downlight or as a projector.

The latter three models or families received the "IF" awards, yearly granted by a prestigious international jury on the occasion of the Industrie Forum event in Hannover.

Sometime later, towards the end of 1991, JFP launched a very complete collection of 20 models of professional downlights.

Finally, the latest development had been the "Gallery" model, made up of a family of projectors offering different lighting solutions, expected to be attractive to art galleries, musea, etc.

When faced with certain lighting requirements (a hotel, a stadium, a modern shop, a hospital, etc.), the prescriber studied the lighting needs (light intensity, colorimetry, possible combinations within the surroundings, etc.) and diagnosed the type, quantity, characteristics and location of each lighting point to be installed in order to obtain the desired decorative and lighting results. In the case of new buildings, it was vital to incline the prescriber in favor of a certain light brand and model while the architectural design was still on the drawing-board.

"The prescriber was a new factor to be reckoned with during the sales process carried out by JFP," said Rocasalbas.

"Until then, we had not taken any steps to influence their decisions because, given the relative simplicity of our products, it was simply not necessary.

"We realised that the image they had of us—if they had any at all—would be something like that of SEAT when it was manufacturing the 600, while now we had decided to make Mercedes Benz!

"Perhaps at that time we might have given other strategic responses to our competitors, such as trying to cut them short by lowering prices or creating a second 'fighting' brand name but the fact is we consciously didn't. This does not mean, however, that we did not fight hard to defend our position in the standard product market, as we were fully aware that the bulk of our sales were precisely composed—and, at the close of 1991, they still are—of these standard products."

Although the need for a change in the sales organization was clearly seen, curiously enough, the first move was made by the Madrid and Barcelona representatives. Apparently, these had secretly come to an agreement in 1988 to propose a change in their manner of functioning, consisting of acting as fully independent and exclusive distributors in their geographical area, buying set quantities and reselling the product on their own account, thus earning a margin instead of a commission.

The proposal had a mixed reception from the four manufacturers in the alliance. The transformer manufacturer accepted the proposed change. However, the cable manufacturer not only rejected the proposal but cancelled the agency agreement with them. Rocasalbas' reaction was more cool-headed: he too turned down the proposal but continued to work with them, trying to get them to start promoting to prescribers too, while continuing to sell the standard lighting elements.

In order to help them in this, in mid-1990, JFP took on four middle-aged, well-groomed women (two in Madrid and two in Barcelona). These women would start to contact prescribers, introducing them to the company and telling them that JFP was entering the technical architectural lighting market.

"We were not yet out 'project hunting,'" said Rocasalbas. "But we soon realised that 'good grooming' was not enough. We had to be able to solve the prescriber's problem or at least to be able to provide them with all the necessary means for them to solve it themselves. This included providing prescribers with all the necessary technical data, free product samples and to have a showroom where they could handle the lights and test lighting effects.

"We soon found out that the selling process was very complex because the final decision on the light brand and model to be installed not only depends on the prescriber but also on the contractor installing the entire electrical and lighting system and, in the final analysis, on the building's owner, as the person footing the bill.

"Later on, we began to notice certain strange behaviors. In some cases, a certain lighting installation was literally 'auctioned off' to see which manufacturer finally offered the best price. Sometimes, we have suspected that some manufacturers, particularly foreign manufacturers eager to get a foothold in the Spanish market, seemed to be prepared to quote at cost price or even below cost price in order to be able to install its lighting elements in a particularly unique or emblematic building and thus be able to use it as an example and show it. In other cases, a customer's association with a certain corporation tips the balance in favor of a manufacturer of lighting elements who happens to be linked with the same corporation.

"In short, the sale of lighting projects is neither as easy nor as clearcut nor as technically aseptic as we originally, and perhaps rather naively, thought."

Thus, they managed to slowly penetrate the technical architectural lighting market, selling by promoting and carrying out projects for the prescriber. However, in 1990, this market segment only accounted for about 5 percent of JFP's total sales. Quite on the contrary, marketing and sales costs increased substantially.

In an attempt to speed up the change process, in April 1991 they decided to terminate their relationship with the Barcelona representative and open a sales office of their own, complete with a showroom. In December 1991, they did the same thing in Madrid with the result that, by the end of the year, JFP had two branches of its own and eleven independent representatives.

In their Barcelona branch, which was responsible for promotion and sales throughout Catalonia, two sales teams had been created. One team consisted of three full-time employed salesmen who covered the electrical goods wholesalers/stockists and the lamp specialty retailers, mainly selling them the more "standard" product range. At the end of 1991, the other Barcelona-Catalonia sales team targeted the prescription market and was composed of three salaried salesmen who visited prospective customers and another person, who drew up the design projects on the branch's design table.[7]

The first team was much more profitable than the second as, at the end of 1991, sales of standard products continued to account for about 80 percent of the company's total sales.

There was a possibility that, in the future, JFP would open similar fully owned branches in other major Spanish cities, although the decision would depend on two distinct factors: first, the degree of sales and financial success achieved by the two

---

[7]The yearly cost of each one of these salesmen could be estimated to be about 6.7 million pesetas (including social security), plus another million pesetas spent in travel and miscellaneous expenses.

JFP branches already operating (Barcelona and Madrid); second, on the current "old" representatives' attitude and behavior, as they had to show their willingness and effectiveness in promoting the new generation of architectural technical lighting products.

At the end of 1991, Javier Rocasalbas said,

"Perhaps I'm wrong, but I think that even the minimally observant person had realised that lighting in houses and apartments, offices, shops, public areas, etc. had become increasingly sophisticated. Indeed, lighting was becoming an increasingly important part of the building or premise's aesthetics. The challenge for us, then, is to give TROLL lamps the technical capacity to contribute lighting solutions, on the one hand, and to be able to integrate themselves aesthetically with their surroundings, on the other hand. But we also have to explain this to prescribers, without forgetting to 'close the loop,' that is, acting actively and positively on the contractor and on the building's owner or his purchasing manager. Any one of these people, at any particular time, can act for or against a type, brand or model of lamp. It is crucial to identify new projects at an early stage, in order to mature the final decision in our favor. This selling and 'maturing' process can take several months, with a significant investment in time. And even with all that, we only manage to get one out of every ten projects we bid for!

"To put it another way, when we 'mature' a project, we are not selling 'lighting elements.' We are selling 'a particular lighting solution.'"

In 1991 the company had spent a total of about 100 million pesetas in advertising expenses, brochures and product catalogs, and attending trade fairs. This amount includes the cost of these expenses by TROLL–France, S.A.

THE INTERNATIONAL-IZATION PROCESS

As has already been mentioned, Josep Sala joined the company in 1984 to create the export department. The result of his efforts over time is shown in Exhibit 2.

TROLL–France S.A., created in Lyon in 1988 was initially under Josep Sitjá as General Manager. Sitjà organized a sales team whose members were independent sales reps on commission, working for several principals. This was similar to the sales organization in Spain. Quite on the contrary, however, these French reps did not do any warehousing. The only warehouse under the control of the company was that of TROLL–France, S.A., located in Lyon.

Towards the end of 1989, Sitjà opened an office in Paris, in a rented space.

In mid-1990, a new General Manager was hired. Philippe Martínez, of Spanish descent, was very knowledgeable about the lighting element market in France. He was a well organised manager, with clear ideas about marketing plans and policies (see Exhibit 5).

When he was designated general manager of TROLL–France, S.A., Martínez made a proposal to change the sales organisation. He set up a team of salaried sales reps, exclusively selling TROLL products. This new team would carry out a double selling task: on the one hand, they would sell to electrical goods wholesalers-stockists ("sell in"). On the other hand, the same sales team would carry out promotional tasks to prescribers, with the purpose of selling lighting projects. If they succeeded in "selling" the idea to a prescriber of using TROLL lighting elements in a certain project, they would "transfer" the order to a wholesaler-stockist for him to supply and invoice the goods. In a similar way as in Spain, TROLL–France never sold directly to contractors or to end customers. At the beginning of 1992, TROLL–France, S.A. had six full time sales reps in its payroll.

In spite of substantial subsidies that had been granted to JFP by ICEX and COPCA (two state and regional agencies devoted to promoting Spanish exports),

EXHIBIT 5 Price Lists, Discounts and Gross Margins	

JFP, S.A., as a privately held company, did not publish its yearly accounts. However, the following figures might be derived from their usual way of operating:

1. Sales in Spain

1.1. Sales of TROLL products

Published price list of prices to be charged to final buyers/consumers	100
Discount made in the invoice[1]	− 50
Net price invoiced by JFP, S.A. to wholesalers	50
Selling and marketing costs of JFP, S.A.[2]	− 11
Gross margin of JFP, S.A.[3]	39

1.2. Sales of AEG products

Managers of JFP, S.A. had not yet made a final decision regarding the gross margin they would charge to AEG products imported into and sold in Spain (and France) by JFP. However, they were aware of the fact that other independent importer-distributors in the same trade or industry and performing similar sales and marketing functions (purchasing, holding stocks, promotion sales, advertising, after-sales service, etc.) usually charged margins around 30 percent on sales. That means that the difference between the net paid cost to a foreign supplier such as AEG, and the net price collected from wholesalers (that is, after discount in invoice), was about 30 percent of the latter net price collected.

2. Exports to AEG or to other countries with an importer-distributor

Net export price invoiced by JFP, S.A.[4]	40
Export sales and marketing costs[5]	− 4
Gross margin of JFP, S.A.[6]	36

3. Exports to TROLL–France, S.A. (own subsidiary)

Net export price invoiced by JFP, S.A. to TROLL–France, S.A.[7]	36
Export sales and marketing costs[8]	− 3.4
Gross margin of JFP, S.A. (in Spain)[9]	32.6

[1]The total amount of this discount could somehow be shared between the wholesaler-stockist, the contractor, maybe a retailer, if there was one in the channel, and even the final buyer-consumer, if the latter succeeded in negotiating a price which was lower than the official list price as published by JFP, S.A.

[2]Sales and marketing costs of JFP, S.A. would include commissions paid (both to independent reps with warehouse and to salaried reps in the payroll of JFP, S.A., located in Madrid and Barcelona branches); transportation and warehousing; advertising; attending trade shows and organising sales meetings; sales training and seminars; salaries and social security; and travel and accommodation expenses of sales and marketing employees.

[3]Obviously out of this gross margin many other deductions had to be subsequently made, such as cost of goods sold; general overhead and administration costs; financial expenses; etc.

[4]This means that the net selling price collected from foreign importer-distributors (40), was approximately 80% of the net selling price collected from wholesalers in Spain (50, as per point 1.1 above).

[5]Advertising, transportation and warehousing in Spain.

[6]Even though the gross margin of JFP, S.A. when selling to AEG or to other foreign importer-distributors was only 36, that is, somewhat lower than the 39 generated when selling to wholesalers-stockists in Spain, managers of JFP, S.A. pointed out that this difference was likely to be partially or fully compensated by the manufacturing economies of scale derived from the fact that orders received from foreign importers-distributors were substantially larger.

[7]This net invoiced price was, in fact, a transfer price between headquarters and its fully owned subsidiary. It may have been unusually low, up to 1991, to help finance the French subsidiary.

[8]These sales and marketing costs included: advertising expenses paid by headquarters; trade show attendance costs; sales seminars and sales training costs; warehousing in Spain.

[9]TROLL–France, S.A., in turn, operated under the following set of figures:

Published price list by TROLL–France to final buyers/consumers	120
Discount made in the invoice	− 60
Net price invoiced by TROLL–France to wholesalers	60
Cost of goods sold, as paid by TROLL–France to JFP, S.A. (Spain)	− 36
Gross margin by TROLL–France S.A. (*)	24

(*)Out of this gross margin, TROLL–France S.A. had to pay for the following: transportation costs from Canovelles to Lyon, and from Lyon to wholesalers all over France; all of its sales and marketing expenses; all of its overhead, general and administrative costs, including rent of the Paris office; and, of course, including all salaries, wages and social security costs and travel expenses of all of its employees, including sales reps.

TROLL–France, S.A. had had important losses from the time of its setting up. These losses had amounted to a total of over 120 million pesetas in the period 1988–1991 (four years). Managers of JFF expected TROLL–France, S.A. to reach its break-even point in 1992.

Towards the end of 1991, Miguel Tey and Javier Rocasalbas had had a long conversation. They had tried to share their points of view, and to evaluate all they had done in France up to that point in time.

They were aware of the fact that TROLL–France, S.A., had spent about 250 million Spanish pesetas in start up funds. Some of these funds had been used to buy and decorate the Lyon building, to the financing of stocks, accounts receivable, etc.

Rocasalbas thought that if the subsidiary had not been set up, this amount of cash would be available in the balance sheet of JFP, S.A., or the level of indebtedness of the company would be so much lower than it was now. This is why he said to Miguel: "From a strictly economical point of view, the economic effort undertaken in France would be highly questionable."

But Miguel retorted:

"First of all, we have to take into account the investment made in the Lyon building, to the amount of some 30 million Spanish pesetas. We have had contacts with prospective buyers of this building, which have led me to estimate its present market value to be around 100 million Spanish pesetas. This would mean that we have potential profits of about 70 million pesetas in that building.

"Furthermore, we have to take into account the fact that we are entering a market which is twice as large as the Spanish market. Our factory will not need any major enlargement, and we shall be able to vastly increase our sales volume. We must see this in a longer time horizon. A businessman cannot evaluate his decisions on purely economic terms. One must also take into account the spirit, the fact of creating and consolidating a new and competitive business venture, the cost of opening up a new market, the amount of shareholder value created as good will, the improved corporate image, etc.

"We must not only maintain Lyon. I have the purpose of changing our Paris Office and turn it into a large showroom.

"If we had not made the good (even if expensive) decision to go out of Spain at the time when the Spanish economy was buoyant, we would find ourselves in a difficult position today, when the Spanish market is stagnant. We would not be able to grow in Spain because the competition in our domestic market is increasing. Quite the contrary, we can now continue growing up."

In other countries, JFP sold to importers-distributors, among which we may mention Ulrich Sattler, in Germany, as we will see further on.

The company regularly attended the Hannover trade fair, which was without doubt the most important fair in the lighting industry. Attendance at this fair provided confirmation of the lessons learnt in France, namely that the European market demanded more quality (look, engineering, certifications, packaging, technical specifications) and that it was easier to sell if a company offered the most comprehensive product range possible, covering all the categories of lighting products.

The growing international presence of JFP on the market and at the trade fairs attracted the attention of several European companies.

CONTACTS WITH OTHER EUROPEAN MANUFACTURERS OF LIGHTING ELEMENTS

Between 1990 and 1991, four European multinational companies approached JFP with the intention of buying or associating with the Catalan company. These companies were one from Austria, one from Belgium, one from Holland, and AEG (Germany).

Curiously enough, all four companies were after virtually the same goal, although by different means: gain access to TROLL products in order to enhance their respective indoor accent lighting lamp collections and thereby to be able to offer the market a more complete product range.

"The first thing that caught our eye was that these four big European companies seemed to want to come to an agreement with TROLL because they did not think that they had neither the economic capacity nor the time nor the human resources required to create their own indoor accent lighting lamp collection," said Rocasalbas.

"This gave us a lot of food for thought because we needed to go the opposite way, that is, with a collection or range of accent lighting elements as our starting point, in order to be able to compete in Europe we would have had to develop the other types of lighting elements that at that time JFP did not manufacture: fluorescent lamp holders, outdoor lighting elements for gardens, sports stadiums, etc.

"Our thoughts were: if they, who are much bigger than us, do not dare to do it, we would neither be able to follow the same business development path the other way around. This made us much more open to listening carefully to their proposals."

CONTACTS WITH THE AUSTRIAN COMPANY

In late 1990, they had contacts with the owner of a large Austrian company. At the beginning of 1991, JFP's managers visited his factory in Austria and were very impressed by what they interpreted as Far East luxury. The Austrian expressed an interest in buying 30 percent of JFP in order to turn TROLL into its technical indoor decorative lighting division. The owners of the Spanish company did not feel inclined to lose their independence in exchange for a minority holding, so their answer was, "Buy all or nothing."

Contacts were broken off because JFP's shareholders were not interested in selling unless it was for a very high premium.

CONTACTS WITH THE DUTCH COMPANY

The first contacts were made at the 1990 Hannover trade fair. The Dutch multinational was interested in turning JFP into its workshop, that is, a supplier of accent lighting elements which would then be sold by the Dutch company's marketing organization under its own brand.

The Dutch already had a limited range of indoor accent lighting elements and wanted to expand it.

Although an agreement of this type could generate significant sales for JFP, the managers of the Catalan company did not feel very happy about the loss of identity this could involve. Also, they feared that they might become too dependent on this kind of sales.

Finally, an agreement was reached by which JFP would manufacture a JFP-designed adaptor and a transformer for the Dutch.

This relationship was still in force in early 1992, although it only accounted for a relatively small part of JFP's sales. The managers of the Catalan company did not plan to increase its scope or sales volume:

"Our priority objective is to build and strengthen the TROLL brand. This does not mean that we won't accept manufacturing for another company under their brand but, obviously, it is not our greatest priority," said Rocasalbas.

"For the same reason, we are not actively looking for other customers like the Dutch."

THE BELGIAN COMPANY

This Belgian company was one of the largest, if not *the* largest, classic lamp manufacturers in Europe. The first contacts with JFP took place at the end of 1991, that is, when negotiations with AEG were already at a fairly advanced stage.

Their proposal was to form an alliance to sell TROLL lamps in the Benelux countries, subsequently expanding the distribution area in gradual stages.

In the end, the conversations with the Belgians were dropped, possibly for two reasons: on the one hand, JFP's managers observed that there were major differences in "lighting culture" between them, as the Belgians had a classic lamp manufacturer mentality. Furthermore, contacts with AEG were already in an advanced stage and JFP's managers felt more in tune with them than with the Belgian managers. Although, as will be explained further on, the agreement with AEG presumably would only cover the German market, neither Miguel Tey nor Javier Rocasalbas felt that it was coherent or desirable to sign two different agreements with two different partners to cover different countries.

THE CONTACTS AND THE NEGOTIATION PROCESS WITH AEG

AEG was a company belonging to the Daimler-Benz Group, which, in turn, was linked with the Deutsche Bank. The Daimler-Benz Group was composed of several companies, including the well-known automobile manufacturer Mercedes-Benz, Deutsche Aerospace A.G., AEG Aktiengesellschaft, etc.

In 1990, AEG Aktiengesellschaft had almost 80,000 employees worldwide. Its sales turnover by divisions was: office and communication techniques, 8 percent; railway systems, 6 percent; automation techniques, 22 percent; electronic equipment and components, 35 percent; microelectronics, 9 percent; and household appliances, 20 percent.

AEG's technical lighting business area (AEG Aktiengesellschaft Fachbereich Lichttechnik) specialised in the manufacture of various types of lighting elements, particularly fluorescent strip lighting. AEG-LT's product range included products in all categories of technical lighting elements, for indoor or for outdoors, with the only exception of elements of accent lighting. It included, for instance, several models for outdoor street lighting, parks, roads and highways, airports, stadiums, etc. Also, for interior lighting, they had lighting elements for offices (inset and suspended fluorescent lighting elements), for factories, warehouses, supermarkets, etc. Its sales amounted to 23 billion pesetas in 1990, of which about two-thirds corresponded to indoor lighting elements and the remaining third, to outdoor lighting elements.

Contacts with JFP were started by Dr. Kappler in April, 1990.

Right from the start, his proposal was crystal-clear in that he was offering JFP a double contract of reciprocal distribution, and that it was not his intention to buy JFP but only to reach a commercial agreement. AEG-LT did not have a range of technical decorative indoor accent lighting elements. Its present customers in Germany were asking for this type of lighting element, but they did not want to develop this new line themselves as the investment required would be too large. They preferred to come to an agreement with a company like JFP that had already developed such a product line.

The German company's managers had been watching the development of JFP since 1987, mainly at the international trade fairs, and considered that the company was following a line which could be interesting for them.

Initially, JFP's management, especially Miguel, was very wary of starting conversations. The early contacts were fairly informal: visits to each other's factory, lunches together, etc.

However, they picked up pace and consolidated significantly when Dr. Kappler was transferred to another area and Dr. Herbert Willmy became the Business Area's new president. Until then, Dr. Willmy had been the area's marketing and sales director (for Germany and foreign markets) and had been involved in the negotiations in that capacity.

"Willmy is overwhelmingly straightforward and clear. He is a person who immediately wins you over with his humanity and honesty," said Rocasalbas.

The negotiator for AEG was Willmy in person. The negotiators for JFP were Miguel Tey and Javier Rocasalbas.

"The negotiation was very much based on the human relationship between both parties and was by no means plain sailing because Miguel had difficulties in following the English," explained Rocasalbas.

Apparently, AEG-LT's managers had been attracted by the following features of JFP: an advanced and original design; a good industrial production capacity, both in-house and subcontracted; good prices; a good range of indoor accent lighting elements; and all this in a company that was effectively managed and economically sound.

"I think that they were aware that JFP was only 'an embryo' AEG distributor in Spain and France. However, even so, we were perhaps the best distributor available to them," commented Rocasalbas.

"Sometimes, the negotiations were even fun. For example, sometimes we were wary and even expressed fears that, should we sign an agreement with AEG-LT, somehow we would be putting ourselves in their power and that 'if they sneezed, we could catch a double pneumonia.'

"On these occasions, in order to get the negotiations out of the rut, Willmy suggested that we do a kind of role-playing, challenging us to put ourselves in his place, as if Miguel or I were the managers of the AEG-LT business area, and try to identify decisions or actions that could harm JFP. As soon as we said something, each time Willmy would come up with the defensive or protective countermeasure that JFP could take, thus effectively knocking down all our objections.

"Willmy caught on very quickly to JFP's way of being and doing business."

For JFP, the single factor that worked most in favor of reaching an agreement with AEG-LT was the possibility of obtaining a high-volume and almost instantaneous distribution of TROLL lighting elements in Germany, through AEG-LT's sales network, composed of about 70 sales engineers; also, the link with the Daimler-Benz Group and the Deutsche Bank could perhaps lead to a certain volume of "captive" or induced sales, thanks to the purchasing priority presumably given to AEG-LT by the other companies in the group. They also hoped that their association with AEG-LT would be a decisive factor in helping them to rapidly obtain the VDE certifications in Germany for their lighting elements.

Another positive factor was the understanding that, wherever AEG had a subsidiary in Europe, JFP could sell through them their accent lighting elements. However, if JFP managers considered that some or any of AEG's subsidiaries were not adequate for this task, they could freely choose any other distributor or marketing channel.

Aside from this, JFP also saw major advantages in distributing AEG-LT's products in Spain and France.

"Obviously, the AEG brand, and its German origin, count for a lot. We realised that AEG-LT's products would be positioned in the high-quality, high-price segment in Spain, so perhaps we might not achieve high sales volumes or high margins for JFP as importers-distributors. However, it was clear to us that the 'partnership' with AEG-LT would give prestige to JFP in Spain and would help us consolidate the image of the TROLL products and our image as a company. This would help us to gain easier access to prescribers.

"Also, it would obviously help us complete the product range we could offer in France and Spain. Now, we would be able to quote virtually all the lighting elements needed for an entire new building or for a complete architectural project. In other words, we would have a complete product range, and we could suggest a solution for any technical lighting need, in the broadest sense."

Rocasalbas expected that distributing AEG-LT lighting elements in Spain and France would not require additional salesmen. Quite on the contrary, he expected to have higher financial expenses due to higher stocks, and higher needs for physical space in their warehouse.

However, negotiating the specific clauses of the contracts had not been without its problems and there had even been moments when it seemed that negotiations would be broken off.

One of those moments was when it came to setting each company's sales targets and purchase commitments for the other company's products.

Another significant difficulty appeared when Miguel Tey said that he was not prepared to stop supplying TROLL lamps to Ulrich Sattler. Ulrich owned an electrical contracting company and a retail store in Stuttgart. He had been JFP's importer-distributor since 1989. In 1991, he had bought about one million deutsche marks.[8] Miguel did not want to lose this sales volume. Also, he thought it would be wise to keep Sattler on, just in case the agreement with AEG did not materialize or work out properly.

In the face of Miguel's adamance, it was finally agreed that Ulrich Sattler would continue to sell the less sophisticated part of JFP's lamp collection under the TROLL brand name, while AEG-LT would concentrate on selling the more sophisticated products—namely, architectural lighting—as AEG products, even though brochures and catalogs would carry the caption: "AEG, designed by TROLL."

Rocasalbas said on that occasion:

"I think we are making a strategic mistake, which will be very difficult to correct. Why don't we impose to Ulrich Sattler that he sell JFP supplied lighting elements under another new brand which isn't TROLL?"

The fact of the matter was that the contract was to be signed with AEG stating that the products sold by AEG-LT in Germany would be labelled "AEG," although sales leaflets would say "AEG, designed by TROLL."

REFLECTIONS IN THE LATE AFTERNOON OF JANUARY 21, 1992

Everything seemed to have been taken care of but there were still a number of points that worried Miguel. On the one hand, there was the "big guy will eat the little guy" complex. He felt that if AEG's purchases were to attain very high volumes, the Germans would have too much power over the Catalans and would end up taking them over. Was this a real danger? How could he prevent it? Another point was that he did not know to what extent he should commit himself to this alliance. Should it be a purely commercial alliance or should it include other aspects? How could they get maximum benefit from the alliance? What other synergies were there that might be as yet untapped? He also wondered what he should do with Sattler, the German distributor, and whether AEG had any kind of hidden agenda. With these thoughts running through his mind, Miguel got up, went to his desk and started to read, once again, the contracts that had to be signed the next day.

---

[8]One deutsche mark was approximately equivalent to 63 Spanish pesetas in 1991.

By way of final reflection, it seemed to him that for both companies, the "Spain sells to Germany" flow or relationship was much more important than the "Germany sells to Spain and France" relationship. Out of a hypothetical and speculative total value or sum of both flows or relationships, Miguel would have estimated the weighting of the former as 90 and that of the latter at perhaps only 10.

Otjiwarongo Crocodile Ranch

In the hot and humid hatchery of his crocodile ranch in the small Namibian town of Otjiwarongo, Mr. van Dyk was worriedly stacking the plastic crates containing 1,350 newly laid crocodile eggs into the limited space. It was December 10, 1993 and he knew that he had to expand the hatching and nursing facilities of his crocodile ranch before January 1996 in order to provide the necessary space to accommodate twice the present production of eggs expected in the 1996 breeding season.

To finance this expansion, Mr. van Dyk hoped to enter a stable and regular market for his supply of crocodile skins. With his limited experience in marketing, he was not sure as to how and where to start exporting.

Mr. van Dyk was also considering the option of exporting processed crocodile skin products, like handbags, shoes and belts. Without the resources to construct his own tannery, he would have to find processing and manufacturing facilities. There was the possibility to send the skins to South Africa for processing into finished products before exporting them. Thinking about options to finance the expansion, Mr. van Dyk also remembered the proposal for a partnership he had received from an investor in Europe who could process the skins into quality products: during a visit in September 1993, a German tourist had expressed interest in investing in Mr. van Dyk's crocodile ranch.

Stepping out of the hatchery into the equally hot, but less humid, nursery where he raised the young crocodiles, Mr. van Dyk knew he had to take some action well before the 1996 breeding season.

BACKGROUND

Mr. van Dyk started the Otjiwarongo Crocodile Ranch in 1986. Prior to this, he had his own motor service station and a bakery in Khorixas, a town in the far north of Namibia. He had also farmed with cattle and sheep, but due to droughts and a high theft rate, he abandoned his farming operations. He sold his business and made the decision to start up a crocodile ranch because he considered himself to be a farmer at heart and also because he was very interested in tourism. He visited various crocodile farms in South Africa and Botswana, where he made a thorough study of crocodile farming during 1985.

Mr. van Dyk chose Otjiwarongo as the ideal location for his business. The climate of Otjiwarongo—hot during summer months and warm in winter—was favourable for crocodile farming. It was on the main tourism route of Namibia, and he could find a regular supply of meat to feed the crocodiles as the Otjiwarongo abattoir was prepared to supply him with unborn calves.

Breeding crocodiles was a capital intensive venture. A hatchery and nursery were built next to the breeding yard to ensure that the eggs could be hatched and the crocodiles raised in ideal conditions. The buildings on Mr. van Dyk's property were valued at N$800,000 in 1988. The planned expansion was expected to cost about N$600,000 (US$1.00 = N$3.60).

Mr. van Dyk had also built a curio shop which served as entrance to the ranch. In the curio shop, he kept various crocodile products like eggshells, skulls and skele-

This case was written by Daan Strauss, Coordinator, Small Enterprise Development, Institute for Management and Leadership Training (IMLT), Namibia, under the ITC/PRODEC Project for Improving International Business Training at selected African Institutions. The case is intended for use in training programmes and is not meant to illustrate correct or incorrect handling of business situations. 1995.

Source: African Cases in International Business, International Trade Centre and PRODEC, Geneva 1995.

tons, along with a few crocodile skin products made from skins he had sent to South Africa to be manufactured into shoes and belts. Mr. van Dyk and his wife regretted the fact that they could not stock the shop with more products, but supplies had to be kept at a minimum due to the lack of funds.

Ever since they started the crocodile ranch, Mr. van Dyk and his wife had been inviting tourists to visit the ranch in Otjiwarongo, in the Northern highlands of central Namibia. The crocodile ranch received an average of 1,000 tourists per month. The visitors' entry fees represented a substantial means of income before exports of crocodile skins started in 1991. In 1993, tourists still contributed N$6,000 per month to Mr. van Dyk's income, although exporting crocodile skins had become the main source of income.

Additional income for the crocodile ranch was earned by selling crocodile meat to interested restaurants in Namibian towns. During 1993, Mr. van Dyk sold 1,100kg of crocodile meat. He planned to slaughter 600 crocodiles in 1994, which would mean that he could sell 15,000kg of meat. There was a possibility for exporting crocodile meat to Singapore, but the dealer he spoke to in Singapore wanted at least four tons of meat at a time. This meant that Mr. van Dyk would have had to slaughter at least 1,500 crocodiles at a time to be able to fill up a container for exporting purposes, which was not possible for him in 1993. He planned to start exporting meat by 1998.

Mr. van Dyk was a member of the Transvaal Crocodile Breeders' Association in Pretoria, South Africa. In 1991, he obtained his license to trade in endangered species from CITES (Convention on International Trade in Endangered Species of Wild Fauna and Flora) in Lausanne, Switzerland, which had a membership of 112 countries worldwide. Membership of CITES was a condition for exporting crocodile skins, as most crocodilians were on the endangered species list of the CITES.

According to an article published in the "Industrie du cuir" in Paris in February 1992, raising was considered a good method of preserving those species which had become rare while continuing trading in their skins. Two types of "farming" crocodilians had been developed:

- "Ranches," particularly in Southern Africa (notably Zimbabwe), which tended to concentrate on Nile crocodiles. Eggs were taken from the wild and the young were raised in captivity until the commercial length of 1.5m to 2m was attained, when they were slaughtered.
- "Farms," which, in general, handled the whole reproduction cycle. There were numerous "farms" in Thailand and the United States.

The article assumed that 80 percent of the current world supply of crocodile skins, estimated at around 400,000 per annum, were sourced from farms. Ten years earlier, before legislation on the protection of endangered species had been passed in many countries, the figure of world supply had been around 2 million skins per year.

CROCODILE BREEDING

Mr. van Dyk bought his original breeding stock of 49 adult Nile crocodiles from a farmer in Botswana in 1986 for N$220,000. The hatchlings from the first eggs were kept and after spending four years in the nursery, these 58 female crocodiles were housed in a second breeding yard that Mr. van Dyk had been developing since 1987. These females were expected to start producing in the 1996 breeding season.

Having adapted to their new environment, the production of eggs by the adult crocodiles increased steadily. Mr. van Dyk managed to successfully hatch crocodile eggs as follows:

1986	58 hatchlings out of	71 eggs
1987	364 hatchlings out of	408 eggs
1988	488 hatchlings out of	530 eggs
1989	540 hatchlings out of	630 eggs
1990	630 hatchlings out of	714 eggs
1991	705 hatchlings out of	838 eggs
1992	936 hatchlings out of	1,273 eggs
1993	1,050 hatchlings out of	1,356 eggs

During the mating season, outside temperatures influenced the fertility rate of the eggs. In 1993, 12 percent of the eggs were unfertilized, while the figure for 1992 was 23 percent.

The amount of eggs laid by a female crocodile depended on her age. The younger ones laid on average 21 per breeding season and the mature ones could lay up to 75. This gave an average of 48 eggs per female. As soon as the female crocodiles laid their eggs, they were packed into crates and taken to the hatchery. To further ensure successful hatching of the eggs, they had to be stacked into the crates in exactly the same position as they had been laid.

To maximize profits, Mr. van Dyk had to ensure that he produced first-grade skins. The newly hatched crocodiles were kept in a nursery for two and a half years, at which age they were about 1.4m long and provided skins of 35cm wide, fetching the best price. The nursery was free of stones to avoid scratches on the crocodiles' skins. Maintenance of high humidity and ideal temperatures, a regular supply of vitamins to the young crocodiles, and clean and hygienic conditions were necessary to keep the young crocodiles healthy, which in turn meant a more favourable environment to ensure first-grade skins.

At the slaughter-age of two and a half years, the crocodiles would normally start to fight among each other, resulting in skins being scratched or damaged, and thus reducing their value. This was also the age at which they became dangerous and would attack workers cleaning the nursery.

Being extremely sensitive creatures, the young crocodiles could easily be upset by loud noise, sudden movements, light and vibrations. Because of the influence tourists had on the crocodiles, Mr. van Dyk kept only 10 percent of the young crocodiles on view for visiting purposes, and the tourists were always requested to keep their voices low and move slowly.

COSTS AND REVENUES

Mr. van Dyk raised start-up capital for the crocodile ranch through a commercial bank and through a development corporation in Namibia. In 1993, he was still indebted to both institutions for loans taken in 1988, payable over a 5- and 13-year period respectively.

Mr. van Dyk's monthly expenses in the last quarter of 1993 were as follows:

Water and electricity:	N$2,200
Crocodile feeding:	N$4,000
Wages:	N$2,000
Veterinarian costs:	N$ 150
Administrative costs:	N$ 100
Other (including his salary):	N$5,000
Installments and interest:	N$5,000

For December 1993, Mr. van Dyk expected the following revenues:

Export of 150 skins: N$30,000
Sales of meat: N$ 8,000
Tourists' entry fees: N$ 6,000

December 1993 was, however, an exceptional month because of a planned initial export of 150 skins to Germany, an order which had not yet been confirmed. The average monthly income was N$20,000.

MARKETING

The constitution of the Transvaal Crocodile Breeders' Association stipulated that each individual breeder was responsible for the marketing of his own products. This left the responsibility for marketing and selling with Mr. van Dyk, who did not have much experience in this field.

Although the Otjiwarongo Crocodile Ranch was the only one of its kind in Namibia, it faced worldwide competition for exports of crocodile skins. Crocodilians, including caimans and gharials, alligators and crocodiles, were to be found all around the world: caimans in Central and South America, alligators in the south east of the United States and in China. The more than 20 different species of crocodiles were scattered far more widely: North of Australia, Africa, South-East Asia, India, Central and South America and the West Indies. Size of the crocodilians varied with the species, from 1.5m to 2m in dwarf species, such as the dwarf crocodile and Schneider's caiman, up to 5m to 7m for the Nile and Indopacific crocodiles. In Southern Africa alone there were 23 competitors breeding crocodiles, most of them in the province of Natal, South Africa, but also in Zimbabwe, Zambia, Botswana, Malawi and Mozambique. Zimbabwe was the leading exporter of Nile Crocodile skins in Southern Africa and was the second largest producer after the United States of America.

Other exotic hides, like ostrich and buffalo skins formed part of the competition Mr. van Dyk faced. The trade in exotic skins was subject to fashion trends. Mr. van Dyk considered this to be one reason for the fluctuating prices, which ranged from US$9.00 per centimeter in 1991 to US$3.00 in 1993 for first-grade skins of 30cm wide.

Because of his limited funds, Mr. van Dyk did not advertise. "I have to first look after my crocodiles before I can find the money to advertise," he stated.

Mr. van Dyk had started exporting crocodile skins in December 1991. Quantities and destinations of exports were as follows:

1991	163 skins to Spain	(Direct transaction)
1992	250 skins to Spain	(Direct transaction)
1993	100 skins to Singapore	(Direct transaction)
1993	150 skins to Singapore	(Through a South African agent)

In November 1993, he managed to secure an order from a German buyer for an initial 150 skins followed by 50 skins per month through an agent in South Africa. The German buyer indicated that he would be in South Africa by the beginning of December 1993, but failed to turn up. This left Mr. van Dyk quite unsure as to whether the deal would go through.

The few times that he had exported skins, he contacted embassies in Windhoek for addresses of potential buyers, or alternatively was contacted by buyers who had come to know about him.

The most recent order from Germany in November 1993 quoted the following prices per centimeter for first-grade skins:

20–24 cm: US$1.80
25–29 cm: US$2.80
30–34 cm: US$3.50
35 cm + 1 :   US$5.00

Prices for second grade skins were 25 percent less, while third grade skins were not accepted on the market.

For international business, Mr. van Dyk preferred to deal with German buyers. As Namibia had historical links with Germany, most of the tourists visiting the crocodile ranch were German speaking. Mr. van Dyk also communicated well in German and found direct communication with other countries difficult. If he were to enter into a partnership, he would prefer a German or Swiss partner. This preference, however, did not prevent him from selling to non-German buyers.

To do business with buyers abroad, Mr. van Dyk would either deal with them directly, through an agent or eventually through a prospective foreign partner. However, both Mr. van Dyk and his wife were very reluctant to enter into a partnership because of a previous unpleasant incident with a partner abroad, who became disinterested when revenues were not as quickly forthcoming as he thought they would. While still considering this as an alternative, the van Dyks were not sure whether the advantages outweighed the disadvantages. The potential German investor had indicated that he would visit them in January 1994 to take up further discussions, and Mr. and Mrs. van Dyk were thinking about the terms and conditions they should propose for an eventual partnership. Mr. van Dyk hoped to enter into an agreement where the partner would be responsible for all marketing activities, while he himself would see to the smooth running of the ranch and the visiting tourists.

Because of the pressing need for funds to finance expansion, Mr. van Dyk also thought about the possibility of exporting processed crocodile skin products. This could be done through a tannery in South Africa, but he knew that this would be expensive because of the time-span between sending of the skins for processing and eventual sales of the finished products. He would have to carry the costs for the tanning and manufacturing of the products in the meantime. In 1993, the cost of tanning alone was N$2.50 per centimeter, amounting to approximately N$75.00 per skin. He also considered selling the products in his curio shop at the ranch, but these up-market products did not sell fast enough in Otjiwarongo. It was only the occasional well-off tourist that would buy some of the products, but it was a possible source of income nonetheless. The other option was to have the skins processed through the intended partner in Europe, so that the finished products would be nearer to the user.

There was another possibility to do business with an Italian buyer who had announced his visit to the ranch for January 1994. This was not definite as yet and Mr. van Dyk was worried about dealings with buyers who did not seem to be reliable. However, he had got some information on the Italian market (see appendix) and was ready to explore any business opportunities.

In December 1993, Mr. van Dyk had 600 crocodiles ready for the market out of the 2,100 growing young crocodiles in the nursery. He forecasted a production of 2,000 hatchlings for 1994 and 3,000 hatchlings for 1995. As from 1996 he could double this production, when the females in the second breeding yard started producing. This implied that he would have to find a way to build the second hatchery and nursery before 1996. His average monthly income was only adequate to ensure the smooth running of the ranch. His forecasts for 1996 onwards promised enough income for expansion, but if the necessary facilities were not ready before 1996, he would not be in a position to cater to the increased production.

Being the only crocodile farmer in Namibia and responsible for his own marketing, Mr. van Dyk wondered what action he should take to ensure the necessary expansion of his operations before 1996.

Questions for Discussion

1. What are the advantages and disadvantages of options open to Mr. van Dyk?
2. Which criteria should Mr. van Dyk use in selecting his market(s)?
3. Depending on the suggested selection criteria, what additional information would Mr. van Dyk need to formulate his marketing strategy?
4. What should be the most urgent steps in Mr. van Dyk's export marketing action plan?

APPENDIX: International Trade in Nile Crocodile Skins

THE CROCODILE SKIN MARKETS IN ITALY AND FRANCE*

Overview

World prices for Nile crocodile skins dropped tremendously since the late 1980s and demand was steeply going down. Changes in fashion trends and consumer tastes as well as the world recession had greatly contributed to this decline in demand for farmed skins of the crocodylus niloticus (the Nile crocodile from Africa).

Competition in the supply of wet-salted Nile crocodile skin was reported to come from Zimbabwe, Zambia, Malawi, Botswana and Mozambique and also from Ethiopia, Kenya, Madagascar and Tanzania who had a reservation on the species and therefore traded under a specified annual export quota system. As indicated in the table below, Zimbabwe was the leading exporter of Nile crocodile skins and the second largest producer of crocodile or alligator skins after the United States.

Exports of African Countries (in number of skins)

Country	1986	1987	1988	1989
Zimbabwe	7,216	7,924	11,609	10,647
Malawi	684	1,173	1,329	2,104
Tanzania	763	1,724	2,311	1,715
South Africa	87	758	1,905	4,326
Madagascar	673	4,338	3,177	4,543
Kenya	—	150	1,400	2,499
Mozambique	—	529	795	1,554
Botswana	10	65	69	204
Zambia	3,117	3,235	3,738	2,389

Source: CITES Annual Returns.

Since the 1990s, competition from the United States was increasing, flooding the market with cheaper skins from its farms. South America was also providing large quantities of wild skins of the caiman crocodiles.

Skins from the United States were cheaper than African skins, with an average price of about US$3.00/cm in the early 1990s, while skins from South America were larger and therefore preferred for the production of handbags which required skins of more than 35cm across the belly.

*Excerpts from the PRODEC Market Research Report No. 12/91 by Ms. Queen Sachile "The markets for Zambian wet-salted crocodile skins in Italy and France," Helsinki 1991. Published by the Programme for Development Cooperation at the Helsinki School of Economics (PRODEC), Töölönkatu 11A, 00100 Helsinki, Finland.

World Imports of Nile Crocodile Skins (in number of skins)	Year	World Imports
	1986	18,753
	1987	24,147
	1988	29,524
	1989	35,515

Source: CITES Annual Returns.

The Italian Market

The report stated that Italy imported crocodile skins from various sources around the globe, and indicated the origin of imports as shown in the table below.

According to the views of the tanners interviewed for the report, the erratic import figures were a reflection of limited availability from the supplying countries which forced the tanners to buy the maximum of available quantities from whatever source as the demand for the commodity was very high at the time.

All the interviewed tanners said they were currently operating about 50 percent below capacity due to declining demand, and were getting most of their raw skins from South America and the United States which were cheaper sources. In addition, skins from South America were also larger. None of the interviewed processors was interested in a joint venture for the production of crocodylus niloticus skins.

Most crocodile skins were imported into Italy by tanneries who processed the skins and treated them into different colours as specified by manufacturers of crocodile items. Items included belts, handbags, wallets and shoes for sale either in the local market or for export.

The majority of Italian tanners imported directly from farmers in the export countries. The import of raw skins did not attract any duty regardless of source of supply. Skins were airfreighted into Italy packed in double jute bags with labels indicating the number of skins and the weight.

The average CIF price indicated by CITES in 1990 for different types of skins were:

Nile crocodile	US$12–14/cm
Porosus	US$12–14/cm
Caiman crocodile	US$45–48/per sq.ft
Mississippi alligator	US$6–8/cm

CITES estimated that these prices had fallen by 50 percent in 1991.

Crocodylus Niloticus Imports in Italy (in number of skins)	Country of origin	1985	1986	1987	1988	1989
	Kenya	—	—	2	600	—
	Madagascar	—	92	100	100	—
	Malawi	—	181	—	766	700
	South Africa	—	—	—	570	—
	Sudan	108	289	1,251	—	—
	Tanzania	—	3	—	1	—
	Zambia	3	4	256	566	—
	Zimbabwe	1	—	—	1,937	—
	Total	112	569	1,609	4,540	700

Source: CITES Annual Returns.

The French Market

Due to the oversupply of the French market with farmed skins from the United States at a lower price than that offered by African farmers, a competitive factor had been introduced which hitherto had been totally absent. African farmers faced a steadily increasing price competition among different African countries producing crocodylus niloticus skins, as well as the strong price competition from the United States.

Most French tanners were buying from the United States not only for the lower prices but also because of the assured United States market for the processed skins and items. French importers sourced their skins directly from farmers by air. Companies interviewed for the report were interested in importing farmed skins from Africa in future, but at a price lower than US$5.00/cm. In 1991, skins from the United States were sourced in France at US$2.50/cm for skin sizes 18-24cm, US$4.50/cm for skin sizes 25-35cm and US$10.00/cm for skins above 35cm.

With respect to joint ventures in Africa, French companies felt that market requirements with respect to delivery time, quality and colour specifications of crocodile items would make a tanning operation located in Africa difficult to manage. Their position was that they would get in touch with African farmers when the demand situation in Europe improved.

Crocodylus Niloticus Imports in France (in number of skins)	Country of origin	1986	1987	1988	1989
	Botswana	—	60	66	193
	Kenya	—	150	551	2,184
	Madagascar	418	4,231	3,074	4,525
	Malawi	403	572	507	741
	Congo	332	649	150	150
	Mozambique	—	529	795	1,554
	South Africa	40	757	633	3,612
	Sudan	2,650	2,499	1,500	54
	Zambia	2,082	1,552	2,692	2,385
	Zimbabwe	4,714	7,159	6,042	10,237
	Total	10,639	18,158	16,010	25,635

Source: CITES Annual Returns.

IMPORTS OF CROCODYLUS NILOTICUS SKINS*

Germany

Country of origin	1986	1987	1988	1989	1990	1991	1992
Unknown	427	322	371	863	1,900	1,075	266
Botswana			1	601			1
Côte d'Ivoire						3	
Mozambique						1	
Sudan				2			
Zambia		1					
Zimbabwe							299
Total	427	323	372	1,466	1,900	1,079	566

Italy

Country of origin	1986	1987	1988	1989	1990	1991	1992
Unknown	280	709	4,544	3,543	1,931	1,380	578
Botswana				200			
Kenya						1,310	
Madagascar				1			
Sudan	870	906			41		
South Africa						320	
Zimbabwe				4	1	1,338	257
Total	1,150	1,615	4,544	3,748	1,973	4,348	1,095

France

Country of origin	1986	1987	1988	1989	1990	1991	1992
Unknown	11,879	20,117	18,613	28,797	18,661	29,737	9,500
Botswana				890	554		
Kenya				2	10	401	
Tanzania				5			682
South Africa					5	122	
Zambia					1		
Zimbabwe			100	88	10	1,138	186
Total	11,879	20,117	18,713	29,782	19,241	31,276	10,490

Other Major Importing Countries

Country	1990	1991	1992	Total
Belgium	3,945	3	4	3,951
Egypt	900		7,900	8,800
Japan	12,979	7,075	11,693	31,747
Singapore	1	7,010	32,946	39,958
Switzerland	342	1,401	407	2,150

Source: *World Conservation Monitoring Centre, Cambridge, United Kingdom.

The Culture of Commerce

The world has always been a diverse place. So it's no surprise that each country has its own way of doing business. That's particularly true of the capitalistic global giants Germany, Japan and the United States.

In the Japanese culture, employees enter what has customarily been regarded as a lifetime agreement. They pledge their best efforts, and are loyal to their companies almost as though a familial bond existed. This sentiment endures because company objectives are regarded as morally correct. Often, ceremonies play an important part in reinforcing these ties. The company's side of the bargain is fulfilled by a defacto guarantee of lifetime employment. Recently, this implied contract has been tested. Difficult economic times have made employee cutbacks unavoidable. But most workers who were laid off saw their companies honor the spirit of this agreement. Instead of offering severance pay or job counseling, many companies actually found their workers new positions.

Hard economic times have also come to Germany. But in Germany's capitalistic system, government and private industries work in close cooperation. The law requires companies to come up with written plans detailing how layoffs can be minimized, if not avoided completely. And within the companies themselves, labor and management also closely coordinate activities. Generally, all parties—government, industry, and labor—give input on how best to keep workers employed.

The approach of U.S. companies to layoffs is quite different. Workers are often given only two weeks notice—some are shown the door without even being allowed to clean out their desks—once the company no longer needs them. Retraining and job placement help is spotty. Management focuses instead on daily stock prices and quarterly profits.

Three cultures, all capitalistic, but with very different value systems and approaches to dealing with employees. A closer look inside some actual companies can shed even more light on the issue.

The midsized German steelmaker, VSG, is a recent example of the cooperation between the government and private industry. The company had to cut costs to stay competitive. But simply turning the workers out on the street was not considered an option. Instead, a joint group of company managers and state officials retrained the workers who would have been laid off. In Germany, this is viewed as managing structural changes in the economy.

The German approach contrasts sharply with how things are done in the U.S. steel industry. Take the Monongahela Valley Works Steel Co. in Pittsburgh. It spent $250 million in capital improvements for the specific purpose of cutting labor costs. US Steel put off similar reinvestment in automation so long that it was forced to lay off huge numbers of workers when the plan was finally implemented. Many steelworkers have been unemployed as long as two years, and it's estimated that as many as 80 percent have left the region for good. Those that remain have often had to take a two-thirds cut in pay for the work they can find.

US Steel CEO Tom Usher's view of the company's responsibilities to terminated workers offers insight into the U.S. mentality. Essentially, he thinks economic fluctuations that put people out of work are simply the reality of capitalism. Finding another job is the worker's own problem. And if they require retraining, the company has no obligation to offer assistance. According to Usher, management's primary responsibility is to maximize returns to shareholders.

Questions for Discussion

1. Would the German model of cooperation between government and industry work in the United States? Why or why not?

2. What long-term repercussions, if any, do U.S. companies face as a result of their hard-line approach to layoffs?

3. Who should management feel primarily responsible to: the work force or the stockholders?

The way things work at Daimler Benz in Germany would probably give a U.S. executive like Usher heartburn. The automaker's board is divided evenly between owners and representatives for the company's 360,000 employees. The work force is the nation's highest paid, and it also has the most benefits. Cooperation between labor and management is smooth and fluid. Work councils determine the best and most efficient method of getting work done. Strikes are extremely rare. The system is known as codetermination.

The actual way power is shared at Daimler Benz might well give Usher a heart attack. Labor can veto the appointment of any top executive, including the CEO. Not surprisingly, this set-up has led to fair and evenhanded dealings between the company's top brass and the rank and file. Power sharing also has led to strong alliances between executives and labor representatives. It helps that most German companies, including Daimler Benz, don't focus on the short term, but instead have business plans that stretch as long as seven years.

Again, things are different in the United States, and a couple of companies graphically illustrate this fact. Probably nowhere else in the world are labor-management relations as poisoned as at Caterpillar Inc. In 1992, CEO Don Fites, arguing that labor costs had to be reduced or the company could not compete in the world market, effectively declared war on labor. The bitterness that ensued is unmatched in anything seen since the early 1900s. Many union workers are back on the job, but they are resentful of the company and most put forth only the minimum level of effort.

Recent problems at General Motors can be attributed in large part to a compliant board of directors. This hand-picked group of cronies failed in their function as overseers under the assumption that CEO Roger Smith knew how to run the business. But Smith spent $77 billion in capital improvements that made the auto maker inflexible and inefficient because of overcapacity. As for employees, GM management doesn't have any labor representatives on the board. Most executives never even see actual workers.

The Mitsubishi company is a good example of why multinationals from anywhere else in the world find it tough to crack the Japanese market. Mitsubishi literally has millions of products and processes. But the major difference between Mitsubishi and its overseas competitors is this: its executives will seldom do business with any company not underneath their corporate umbrella. These groups, called keiretsus, work together and provide complimentary services, including manufacturing processes, marketing, distribution, and the like. Often, banks are part of the process as well. And when governmental assistance is also thrown in, a formidable entity is created. Few outside companies can effectively compete.

Capitalistic purists may scream foul, but the governments of many countries now actively support their private industries. A while back, and much to the chagrin of the Boeing Corporation and other U.S. aircraft manufacturers, the governments of France, Germany, Britain, and Spain cooperated on the development of the Airbus.

They soon captured nearly a third of the world market. They eclipsed McDonnell Douglas and were closing in on Boeing, both of which were still smarting from Defense Department contract cutbacks.

Boeing counterpunched with its 777 aircraft. The plane represented a leap forward for the company. The old-line approach was scrapped, and the plane was largely designed by computer. Teams of engineers, factory hands, marketing personnel, and even financial people all assisted. And in the biggest break with tradition, Boeing permitted eight other airline manufacturers to offer input on how best to create the jet.

Top executives came away from the experience convinced that a cooperative effort between government and industry is the only way to keep the playing field level and to give United States a chance to be competitive in world markets.

Even a quick overview of various economies and companies leaves little doubt that capitalistic systems differ greatly. Culture and customs are huge factors in how capitalism evolves. But some fundamentals can be pinned down. Just as companies must stay close to their customer base, so too must they stay close to their employees. U.S. management and labor may never develop the rapport that exists in Japan or Germany, but it certainly would appear they could benefit from a closer relationship than now exists.

Questions for Discussion

4. List what you think are the three primary strengths of the Japanese and German systems. What are the principal shortcomings?

5. If you were a U.S. executive, what approach would you take to out-maneuver the keiretsu groups and crack the Japanese market?

6. What are the biggest differences in the way Boeing designed and built the 777 from the traditional design and manufacturing process?

Glossary

absolute advantage   The ability to produce a good or service more cheaply than it can be produced elsewhere.

accounting diversity   The range of differences in national accounting practices.

acculturation   The process of adjusting and adapting to a specific culture other than one's own.

adaptability screening   A selection procedure that usually involves interviewing both the candidate for an overseas assignment and his or her family members to determine how well they are likely to adapt to another culture.

airfreight   Transport of goods by air; accounts for less than one percent of the total volume of international shipments, but more than 20 percent of value.

allocation mentality   The tradition of acquiring resources based not on what is needed but on what is available.

American terms   Quoting a currency rate as the U.S. dollar against a country's currency (e.g., U.S. dollars/yen).

antitrust laws   Laws that prohibit monopolies, restraint of trade, and conspiracies to inhibit competition.

arbitration   The procedure for settling a dispute in which an objective third party hears both sides and makes a decision; a procedure for resolving conflict in the international business arena through the use of intermediaries such as representatives of chambers of commerce, trade associations, or third-country institutions.

area expertise   A knowledge of the basic systems in a particular region or market.

area structure   An organizational structure in which geographic divisions are responsible for all manufacturing and marketing in their respective areas.

area studies   Training programs that provide factual preparation prior to an overseas assignment.

arm's length price   A price that unrelated parties would have reached.

assessment of taxes   The valuation of property or transactions for purposes of taxation; in countertrade, based on the exact value of the goods exchanged, the time when income was received, and the profitability of the transaction.

autarky   A country that is not participating in international trade.

average cost method   An accounting principle by which the value of inventory is estimated as the average cost of the items in inventory.

backtranslation   The retranslation of text to the original language by a different person than the one who made the first translation.

backward innovation   The development of a drastically simplified version of a product.

Balance of Payments (BOP)   A statement of all transactions between one country and the rest of the world during a given period; a record of flows of goods, services, and investments across borders.

balance sheet hedge   The counterbalance of exposed assets with exposed liabilities to reduce translation or transaction exposure.

bank draft   A withdrawal document drawn against a bank.

barter   A direct exchange of goods of approximately equal value, with no money involved.

base salary   Salary not including special payments such as allowances paid during overseas assignments.

basic balance   A summary measure of a country's Balance of Payments which is the sum of the current account and the long-term capital account.

bearer bond   A bond owned officially by whoever is holding it.

bilateral negotiations   Negotiations carried out between two nations focusing only on their interests.

bill of lading   A contract between an exporter and a carrier indicating that the carrier has accepted responsibility for the goods and will provide transportation in return for payment.

black hole   The situation that arises when an international marketer has a low-competence subsidiary—or none at all—in a highly strategic market.

boycott   An organized effort to refrain from conducting business with a particular seller of goods or services; used in the international arena for political or economic reasons.

brain drain   A migration of professional people from one country to another, usually for the purpose of improving their incomes or living conditions.

Bretton Woods Agreement   An agreement reached in 1944 among finance ministers of 45 Western nations to establish a system of fixed exchange rates.

bribery   The use of payments or favors to obtain some right or benefit to which the briber has no legal right; a criminal offense in the United States but a way of life in many countries.

Buddhism   A religion that extends through Asia from Sri Lanka to Japan and has 334 million followers, emphasizing spiritual attainment rather than worldly goods.

buffer stock   Stock of a commodity kept on hand to prevent a shortage in times of unexpectedly great demand; under international commodity and price agreements, the stock controlled by an elected or appointed manager for the purpose of managing the price of the commodity.

bulk service   Ocean shipping provided on contract either for individual voyages or for prolonged periods of time.

bureaucratic controls   A limited and explicit set of regulations and rules that outline desired levels of performance.

buy-back   A refinement of simple barter with one party supplying technology or equipment that enables the other party to produce goods, which are then used to pay for the technology or equipment that was supplied.

capital account   An account in the BOP statement that records transactions involving borrowing, lending, and investing across borders.

capital budget   The financial evaluation of a proposed investment to determine whether the expected returns are sufficient to justify the investment expenses.

capital flight   The flow of private funds abroad because investors believe that the return on investment or the safety of capital is not sufficiently ensured in their own countries.

capital or financial lease   A lease that transfers all substantial benefits and costs inherent in the ownership of the property to the lessee. The lessee accounts for the lease as if it is an acquisition of an asset or incurrence of a liability.

capital structure   The mix of debt and equity used in a corporation.

capitalizing The accounting practice of charging a portion of the cost of a capital equipment purchase over a number of years, thus depreciating its useful life out over time.

Caribbean Basin Initiative (CBI) Extended trade preferences to Caribbean countries and granted them special access to the markets of the United States.

cartel An association of producers of a particular good, consisting either of private firms or of nations, formed for the purpose of suppressing the market forces affecting prices.

cash pooling Pooling cash by a multinational firm so that individual units' cash flows are centralized, resulting in less spending on foregone interest on unnecessary cash balances.

central plan The economic plan for the nation devised by the government of a socialist state; often a five-year plan that stipulated the quantities of industrial goods to be produced.

centralization The concentrating of control and strategic decision making at headquarters.

change agent A person or institution who facilitates change in a firm or in a host country.

channel design The length and width of the distribution channel.

Christianity The largest world religion with 1.8 billion followers; Protestantism encourages work and accumulation of wealth.

clearing account barter A refinement of simple barter in which clearing accounts are established to track debits and credits. CAB permits barter transactions to take place over longer time periods.

code law Law based on a comprehensive set of written statutes.

codetermination A management approach in which employees are represented on supervisory boards to facilitate communication and collaboration between management and labor.

commercial invoice A bill for transported goods that describes the merchandise and its total cost and lists the addresses of the shipper and seller and delivery and payment terms.

Committee for Foreign Investments in the United States (CFIUS) A federal committee, chaired by the U.S. Treasury, with the responsibility for reviewing major foreign investments to determine whether national security or related concerns are at stake.

commodity price agreement An agreement involving both buyers and sellers to manage the price of a particular commodity, but often only when the price moves outside a predetermined range.

common agricultural policy (CAP) An integrated system of subsidies and rebates applied to agricultural interests in the European Union.

common law Law based on tradition and depending less on written statutes and codes than on precedent and custom—used in the United States.

common market A group of countries that agree to remove all barriers to trade among members, to establish a common trade policy with respect to nonmembers, and also to allow mobility for factors of production—for example, labor, capital, and technology.

comparative advantage The ability to produce a good or service more cheaply, relative to other goods and services, than is possible in other countries.

compensation arrangement Another term for buyback.

competitive advantage The ability to produce a good or service more cheaply than other countries due to favorable factor conditions and demand conditions, strong related and supporting industries, and favorable firm strategy, structure, and rivalry conditions.

competitive assessment A research process that consists of matching markets to corporate strengths and providing an analysis of the best potential for specific offerings.

competitive devaluation Reducing the value of one nation's currency in terms of other currencies to stimulate exports.

competitive platform The business environment provided by a nation to its firms which affects their international competitiveness.

composition of trade The ratio of primary commodities to manufactured goods in a country's trade.

concentration The market expansion policy that involves concentrating on a small number of markets.

conference pricing The establishment of prices by a cartel; used in shipping.

confirmed letter of credit A letter of credit confirmed by the recipient's bank.

confiscation The forceful government seizure of a company without compensation for the assets seized.

confucianism A code of conduct with 150 million followers throughout Asia, stressing loyalty and relationships.

container ships Ships designed to carry standardized containers, which greatly facilitate loading and unloading as well as intermodal transfers.

contract manufacturing Outsourcing the actual production of goods so that the corporation can focus on research, development, and marketing.

contractual hedging A multinational firm's use of contracts to minimize its transaction exposure.

contributor A national subsidiary with a distinctive competence, such as product development.

convertibility The ability to exchange a currency for any other currency without being subject to government restrictions, approvals, or government specified rates of exchange.

coordinated decentralization The providing of overall corporate strategy by headquarters while granting subsidiaries the freedom to implement it within established ranges.

Coordinating Committee for Multilateral Export Controls (COCOM) A body formed by NATO countries (including Japan, but not Iceland) to continually define those items for which exports need to be controlled, or decontrolled, and to structure national policies to result in a unified and effective export control system; abolished in 1994.

corporate income tax A tax applied to all residual earnings, regardless of what is retained or what is distributed as dividends.

corruption Payments or favors made to officials in return for services.

correspondent banks Banks located in different countries and unrelated by ownership that have a reciprocal agreement to provide services to each other's customers.

cost and freight (CFR) Seller quotes a price for the goods, including the cost of transportation to the named port of debarkation. Cost and choice of insurance are left to the buyer.

cost, insurance, and freight (CIF) Seller quotes a price including insurance, all transportation, and miscellaneous charges to the point of debarkation from the vessel or aircraft.

cost of living allowance (COLA) An allowance paid during assignment overseas to enable the employee to maintain the same standard of living as at home.

counterpurchase A refinement of simple barter that unlinks the timing of the two transactions.

coups d'etat A forced change in a country's government, often resulting in the new government's attacking foreign firms and policy changes.

critical commodities list   A U.S. Department of Commerce file containing information about products that are either particularly sensitive to national security or controlled for other purposes.

cross rates   Exchange rate quotations which do not include the U.S. dollar as one of the two currencies quoted.

cultural assimilator   A program in which trainees for overseas assignments must respond to scenarios of specific situations in a particular country.

cultural convergence   Exposure to foreign cultures accelerated by technological advances.

cultural risk   The risk of business blunders, poor customer relations, and wasted negotiations that results when firms fail to understand and adapt to the cultural differences between their own and host countries' cultures.

cultural universals   Manifestations of the total way of life of any group of people.

culture shock   The more pronounced reactions to the psychological disorientation that most people feel when they move for an extended period of time in a markedly different culture.

currency flows   The flows of currency from nation to nation, which in turn determine exchange rates.

currency swap   An agreement by which a firm exchanges or swaps its debt service payments in one currency for debt service payments in a different currency. The equivalent of the interest rate swap, only the currency of denomination of the debt is different.

current account   An account in the BOP statement that records the results of transactions involving merchandise, services, and unilateral transfers between countries.

current rate method   A method for translating financial statements of a foreign subsidiary from the functional currency into the parent's reporting currency.

customer involvement   The active participation of customers; a characteristic of services in that customers often are actively involved in the provision of services they consume.

customer service   A total corporate effort aimed at customer satisfaction; customer service levels in terms of responsiveness that inventory policies permit for a given situation.

customer structure   An organizational structure in which divisions are formed on the basis of customer groups.

customs union   A union among trading countries in which members dismantle barriers to trade in goods and services and also establish a common trade policy with respect to nonmembers.

debt-for-debt swap   The exchange of a loan held by one creditor for a loan held by another creditor; allows debt holders to consolidate outstanding loans.

debt-for-education swap   The exchange of debt for educational opportunities in a foreign country.

debt-for-equity swap   An exchange of developing country debts for equity investments in the countries.

debt-for-nature swap   The purchase of nonperforming loans at substantial discounts and their subsequent return to the debtor country in exchange for the preservation of natural resources.

debt-for-product swap   An exchange of debt for products, often requiring an additional cash payment for the product.

debt swaps   An emerging form of countertrade in which debt holders exchange the debt of a less-developed country for some other good or service or financial instru-ment.

decentralization   The granting of a high degree of autonomy to subsidiaries.

delivery duty paid (DDP)   Seller delivers the goods, with import duties paid, including inland transportation from import point to the buyer's premises.

delivery duty unpaid (DDU)   Only the destination customs duty and taxes are paid by the consignee.

Delphi studies   A research tool using a group of participants with expertise in the area of concern to state and rank major issues.

demand pattern analysis   Analysis that indicates typical patterns of growth and decline in manufacturing.

density   Weight-to-volume ratio; often used to determine shipping rates.

deregulation   Removal of government regulation.

developmental aid   International aid to developing countries.

direct investment   An account in the BOP statement that records investments with an expected maturity of more than one year and an investor's ownership position of at least 10 percent.

direct quotation   A foreign exchange quotation that specifies the amount of home country currency needed to purchase one unit of foreign currency.

direct taxes   Taxes applied directly to income.

distributed earnings   The proportion of a firm's net income after taxes which is paid out or distributed to the stockholders of the firm.

diversification   A market expansion policy characterized by growth in a relatively large number of markets or market segments.

division of labor   The premise of modern industrial production where each stage in the production of a good is performed by one individual separately, rather than one individual being responsible for the entire production of the good.

domestication   Government demand for partial transfer of ownership and management responsibility from a foreign company to local entities, with or without compensation.

double-entry bookkeeping   Accounting methodology where each transaction gives rise to both a debit and a credit of the same currency amount. It is used in the construction of the Balance of Payments.

double taxation   Taxing of the same income twice; taxing of multinational corporations by the home country and the host country.

dual pricing   Price-setting strategy in which the export price may be based on marginal cost pricing, resulting in a lower export price than domestic price; may open the company to dumping charges.

dumping   Selling goods overseas at a price lower than in the exporter's home market, or at a price below the cost of production, or both.

economic and monetary union (EMU)   The ideal among European leaders that economic integration should move beyond the four freedoms; specifically, it entails (1) closer coordination of economic policies to promote exchange rate stability and convergence of inflation rates and growth rates, (2) creation of a European central bank called the Eurofed, and (3) replacement of national monetary authorities by the Eurofed and adoption of the ECU as the European currency.

economic exposure   The potential for long-term effects on a firm's value as the result of changing currency values.

economic infrastructure   The transportation, energy, and communication systems in a country.

economic union   A union among trading countries that would have the characteristics of a common market and would also harmonize monetary policies, taxation, and government spending and use a common currency; none exists currently.

economies of scale   Production economies made possible by operating on a large scale.

education allowance   Reimbursement by the company for dependent educational expenses incurred while a parent is assigned overseas.

effective tax rate   Actual total tax burden after including all applicable tax liabilities and credits.

efficiency seekers   Firms attempting to obtain the most economical sources of production.

embargo   A governmental action, usually prohibiting trade entirely, for a decidedly adversarial or political rather than economic purpose.

Enterprise for the Americas Initiative (EAI)   An attempt by the United States to further democracy in Latin America by providing incentives for market development and trade liberalization.

environmental scanning   Obtaining ongoing data about an environment.

equity method   An accounting method used for investments; a method used when a U.S. firm owns a substantial amount of voting stock in a foreign company, meaning more than 10 percent but less than 50 percent.

estimation by analogy   A method for estimating market potential when data for the particular market do not exist.

ethics   The local morality that global companies need to recognize as a rule in conducting business.

ethnocentric   Tending to regard one's own culture as superior; tending to be home-market oriented.

ethnocentrism   The regarding of one's own culture as superior to others'.

Eurobanks   Large international banks comprising the most active participants in the Eurocurrency markets.

Eurobond   A bond that is denominated in a currency other than the currency of the country in which the bond is sold.

Euro-commercial paper (ELP)   A short-term debt instrument, typically 30, 60, 90, or 180 days in maturity, sold in the Eurocurrency markets.

Eurocurrency   A bank deposit in a currency other than the currency of the country where the bank is located; not confined to banks in Europe.

Eurocurrency interest rates   Loan or deposit rates of interest on foreign currency denominated deposits.

Eurodollars   U.S. dollars deposited in banks outside the United States; not confined to banks in Europe.

Euromarkets   Money and capital markets in which transactions are denominated in a currency other than that of the place of the transaction; not confined to Europe.

Euronote   A short to medium-term debt instrument sold in the Eurocurrency markets. The three major classes of Euronotes are Euro-commercial paper, Euro-medium-term notes, and Euronotes.

European Monetary System (EMS)   An organization formed in 1979 by eight EC members committed to maintaining the values of their currencies within a 2 1/4 percent of each other's.

European terms   Quoting a currency rate as a country's currency against the U.S. dollar (e.g., yen/U.S. dollars).

European Union   The January 1, 1994 organization created by the 12 member countries of the European Community (now 15 members).

exchange controls   Controls on the movement of capital in and out of a country, sometimes imposed when the country faces a shortage of foreign currency.

exchange rate mechanism (ERM)   The acceptance of responsibility by a European Monetary System member to actively maintain its own currency within agreed-upon limits versus other member currencies established by the European Monetary System.

expatriate   One living in a foreign land; a corporate manager assigned to an overseas location.

expensing   The accounting practice of claiming the entire cost of a purchase as a deductible expense from current income entirely in the present period.

experiential knowledge   Knowledge acquired through involvement (as opposed to information, which is obtained through communication, research, and education).

experimentation   A research tool to determine the effects of a variable on an operation.

export-control system   A system designed to deny or at least delay the acquisition of strategically important goods to adversaries; in the United States, based on the Export Administration Act and the Munitions Control Act.

export license   A license obtainable from the U.S. Department of Commerce Bureau of Export Administration, which is responsible for administering the Export Administration Act.

export management companies (EMCs)   Domestic firms that specialize in performing international business services as commission representatives or as distributors.

export trading company (ETC)   The result of 1982 legislation to improve the export performance of small and medium-sized firms, the export trading company allows businesses to band together to export or offer export services. Additionally, the law permits bank participation in trading companies and relaxes antitrust provisions.

expropriation   The government takeover of a company with compensation frequently at a level lower than the investment value of the company's assets.

external economies of scale   Lower production costs resulting from the free mobility of factors of production in a common market.

extraterritoriality   An exemption from rules and regulations of one country that may challenge the national sovereignty of another. The application of one country's rules and regulations abroad.

ex-works (EXW)   Price quotes that apply only at the point of origin; the seller agrees to place the goods at the disposal of the buyer at the specified place on the date or within the fixed period.

factor intensities   The proportion of capital input to labor input used in the production of a good.

factor mobility   The ability to freely move factors of production across borders, as among common market countries.

factor proportions theory   Systematic explanation of the source of comparative advantage.

factors of production   All inputs into the production process, including capital, labor, land, and technology.

factual cultural knowledge   Knowledge obtainable from specific country studies published by governments, private companies, and universities and also available in the form of background information from facilitating agencies such as banks, advertising agencies, and transportation companies.

field experience   Experience acquired in actual rather than laboratory settings; training that exposes a corporate manager to a different cultural environment for a limited amount of time.

FIFO   Method of valuation of inventories for accounting purposes, meaning First-In-First-Out. The principle rests on the assumption that costs should be charged against revenue in the order in which they occur.

Financial Accounting Standards Board Statement No. 52 (FASB 52)   A 1982 ruling governing accounting for international transactions and operations.

financial incentives   Monetary offers intended to motivate; special funding designed to attract foreign direct investosors that may take the form of land or building, loans, or loan guarantees.

financial infrastructure   Facilitating financial agencies in a country; for example, banks.

financial risk management   The management of a firm's cash flows associated with the three basic financial dimensions of interest rates, exchange rates, and commodity prices.

financing cash flows   The cash flows arising from the firms funding activities.

fiscal incentives   Incentives used to attract foreign direct investment that provide specific tax measures to attract the investor.

flextime   A modification of work scheduling that allows workers to determine their own starting and ending times within a broad range of available hours.

focus group   A research technique in which representatives of a proposed target audience contribute to market research by participating in an unstructured discussion.

foreign bond   Bonds that are issued by a country's borrowers in other countries, subject to the same restrictions as bonds issued by domestic borrowers.

Foreign Corrupt Practices Act   A 1977 act making it a crime for U.S. executives of publicly traded firms to bribe a foreign official in order to obtain business.

foreign direct investment   The establishment or expansion of operations of a firm in a foreign country. Like all investments, it assumes a transfer of capital.

foreign policy   The area of public policy concerned with relationships with other countries.

foreign service premium   A financial incentive to accept an assignment overseas, usually paid as a percentage of the base salary.

foreign tax credit   Credit applied to home-country tax payments due for taxes paid abroad.

foreign trade organizations (FTOs)   Organizations authorized to make purchases and sales internationally as specified by the government; in the past, prevalent in the Soviet Union, Eastern Europe, and China.

foreign trade zones   Special areas where foreign goods may be held or processed without incurring duties and taxes.

Fortress Europe   Suspicion raised by trading partners of Western Europe, claiming that the integration of the European Union may result in increased restrictions on trade and investment by outsiders.

forward contracts   Agreements between firms and banks which permit the firm to either sell or buy a specific foreign currency at a future date at a known price.

forward rates   Contracts that provide for two parties to exchange currencies on a future date at an agreed-upon exchange rate.

franchising   A form of licensing that allows a distributor or retailer exclusive rights to sell a product or service in a specified area.

free alongside ship (FAS)   Exporter quotes a price for the goods, including charges for delivery of the goods alongside a vessel at a U.S. port. Seller handles cost of unloading and wharfage; loading, ocean transportation, and insurance are left to the buyer.

free carrier (FCA)   Applies only at a designated inland shipping point. Seller is responsible for loading goods into the means of transportation; buyer is responsible for all subsequent expenses.

free on board (FOB)   Applies only to vessel shipments. Seller quotes a price covering all expenses up to and including delivery of goods on an overseas vessel provided by or for the buyer.

free trade area   An area in which all barriers to trade among member countries are removed, although sometimes only for certain goods or services.

freight forwarders   Specialists in handling international transportation by contracting with carriers on behalf of shippers.

functional structure   An organizational structure in which departments are formed on the basis of functional areas such as production, marketing, and finance.

fundamental disequilibrium   A term commonly understood to mean persistent BOP imbalances that are unlikely to correct themselves.

gap analysis   Analysis of the difference between market potential and actual sales.

General Agreement on Tariffs and Trade (GATT)   An international code of tariffs and trade rules signed by 23 nations in 1947; headquartered in Geneva, Switzerland; 124 members currently; now part of the World Trade Organization.

General Agreement on Trade in Services (GATS)   A legally enforceable pact among GATT participants that covers trade and investments in the services sector.

general license   An export license that provides blanket permission to ship nonsensitive products to most trading partners.

geocentric   Tending to take a world view; tending to be oriented toward the global marketplace.

glasnost   The Soviet policy of encouraging the free exchange of ideas and discussion of problems, pluralistic participation in decision making, and increased availability of information.

global linkages   Worldwide interdependencies of financial markets, technology, and living standards.

globalization   Awareness, understanding, and response to global developments as they affect a company.

glocal   A term coined to describe the networked global organization approach to an organizational structure.

gold standard   A standard for international currencies in which currency values were stated in terms of gold.

Government Procurement Code   A 1979 agreement among trading nations that opened government contracts to competitive bids from firms in other nations that were party to the agreement.

gray market   A market entered in a way not intended by the manufacturer of the goods.

Group of Five   The United States, Great Britain, Germany, France, and Japan.

Group of Seven   The United States, Great Britain, Germany, France, Japan, Italy, and Canada. The meeting of finance ministers of these seven countries in Jamaica in 1976 resulted in an agreement to allow their currencies to continue to float.

Group of Ten   The United States, Great Britain, Germany, France, Japan, Italy, Canada, Sweden, Netherlands, and Belgium.

hardship allowance   An allowance paid during an assignment to an overseas area that requires major adaptation.

hedge   To counterbalance a present sale or purchase with a sale or purchase for future delivery as a way to minimize loss due to price fluctuations; to make counterbalancing sales or purchases in the international market as protection against adverse movements in the exchange rate.

high-context cultures   Cultures in which behavioral and environmental nuances are an important means of conveying information.

Hinduism   With 750 million followers, a way of life rather than a religion, with economic and other attainment dictated by the caste into which its followers are born.

housing allowance   An allowance paid during assignment overseas to provide living quarters.

implementor   The typical subsidiary role, which involves implementing strategy that originates with headquarters.

import substitution   A policy for economic growth adopted by many developing countries that involves the systematic encouragement of domestic production of goods formerly imported.

income elasticity of demand   A means of describing change in demand in relative response to a change in income.

incoterms   International Commerce Terms. Widely accepted terms used in quoting export prices.

indirect quotation   Foreign exchange quotation that specifies the units of foreign currency that could be purchased with one unit of the home currency.

indirect taxes   Taxes applied to non-income items, such as value-added taxes, excise taxes, tariffs, and so on.

industrial policy   Official planning for industry as a whole or for a particular industry; in the United States, occurs only indirectly.

infrastructure shortages   Problems in a country's underlying physical structure, such as transportation, utilities, and so on.

input-output analysis   A method for estimating market activities and potential that measures the factor inflows into production and the resultant outflow of products.

intangibility   The inability to be seen, tasted, or touched in a conventional sense; the characteristic of services that most strongly differentiates them from products.

intellectual property rights   Protects the technology and knowledge of multinational firms.

Interbank interest rates   The interest rate charged by banks to banks in the major international financial centers.

interest rate swap   A firm uses its credit standing to borrow capital at low fixed rates and exchange its interest payments with a slightly lower credit-rated borrower who has debt-service payments at floating rates.

intermodal movements   The transfer of freight from one mode or type of transportation to another.

internal bank   A multinational firm's financial management tool that actually acts as a bank to coordinate finances among its units.

internal economies of scale   Lower production costs resulting from greater production for an enlarged market.

internalization   Occurs when a firm establishes its own multinational operation, keeping information that is at the core of its competitiveness within the firm.

International Bank for Reconstruction and Development (World Bank)   An institution established in 1945 to make loans for reconstruction of war-ravaged countries; now focused on making loans to developing countries.

International Banking Act of 1978   An act that established a comprehensive federal government role in the regulation of foreign bank operations in the United States.

International Banking Facility (IBF)   Operations established by U.S. international banks that are free from a number of regulations restraining domestic banks, including deposit insurance and reserve requirements.

international bond   Bond issued in domestic capital markets by foreign borrowers (foreign bonds) or issued in the Eurocurrency markets in currency different from that of the home currency of the borrower (Eurobonds).

international competitiveness   The ability of a firm, an industry, or a country to compete in the international marketplace at a stable or rising standard of living.

international debt load   Total accumulated negative net investment of a nation.

international investment   Investment by companies in one country in enterprises in other countries.

international law   The body of rules governing relationships between sovereign states; also certain treaties and agreements respected by a number of countries.

International Monetary Fund (IMF)   A specialized agency of the United Nations established in 1944. An international financial institution for dealing with Balance of Payment problems; the first international monetary authority with at least some degree of power over national authorities.

international monetary system   The set of rules or procedures in place for making and receiving international payments.

International Trade Organization (ITO)   A forwardlooking approach to international trade and investment embodied in the 1948 Havana Charter; due to disagreements among sponsoring nations, its provisions were never ratified.

interpretive cultural knowledge   An acquired ability to understand and fully appreciate the nuances of foreign cultural traits and patterns.

interviews   A face-to-face research tool to obtain in-depth information.

intrafirm transfers   The sale of goods or services between units of the same firm. For example, the sale of an unfinished product by the U.S. parent firm to its foreign subsidiary in the United Kingdom.

Intraindustry trade   The simultaneous export and import of the same good by a country. It is of interest due to the traditional theory that a country will either export or import a good, but not do both at the same time.

inventory   Materials on hand for use in the production process; also finished goods on hand.

inventory carrying costs   The expense of maintaining inventories.

investment income   The proportion of net income that is paid back to a parent company.

Islam   A religion that has over 1 billion followers from the west coast of Africa to the Phillipines, as well as in the rest of the world and is supportive of entrepreneurism but not of exploitation.

Jamaica Agreement   An agreement reached in 1976 by the Group of Seven to continue to allow their currencies to float in response to market pressures.

joint occurrence   Occurrence of a phenomenon affecting the business environment in several locations simultaneously.

Joint Research and Development Act   A 1984 act that allows both domestic and foreign firms to participate in joint basic-research efforts without fear of U.S. antitrust action.

just-in-time inventory   Materials scheduled to arrive precisely when they are needed on a production line.

lags   Paying a debt late to take advantage of exchange rates.

land bridge   Transfer of ocean freight on land among various modes of transportation.

Law of One Price   The theory that the relative prices of any single good between countries, expressed in each country's currency, is representative of the proper or appropriate exchange rate value.

Leads   Paying a debt early to take advantage of exchange rates.

Leontief Paradox   Wassily Leontief's studies of U.S. trade indicated that the United States was a labor-abundant country, exporting labor-intensive products. This was a paradox because of the general belief that the United States was a capital-abundant country which should be exporting capital-intensive products.

letter of credit   Document issued by a bank promising to pay a specified amount of money to an exporter; the most common mechanism for financing international trade.

LIBOR   The London InterBank Offer Rate. The rate of interest charged by top-quality international banks on loans to similar quality banks in London. This interest rate is often used in both domestic and international markets as the rate of interest on loans and other financial agreements.

licensing agreement   An agreement in which one firm permits another to use its intellectual property for compensation.

LIFO   Method of valuation of inventories for accounting purposes, meaning Last-In-First-Out. The principle rests on the practice of recording inventory by "layer" of the cost at which it was incurred.

liner service   Ocean shipping characterized by regularly scheduled passage on established routes.

lingua franca   The language habitually used among people of diverse speech to facilitate communication.

lobbyist   Typically, a well-connected person or firm that is hired by a business to influence the decision making of policymakers and legislators.

local content   Regulations to gain control over foreign investment by ensuring that a large share of the product is locally produced or a larger share of the profit is retained in the country.

location decision   A decision concerning the number of facilities to establish and where they should be situated.

logistics platform   Vital to a firm's competitive position, it is determined by a location's ease and convenience of market reach under favorable cost circumstances.

London Interbank Offer Rate (LIBOR)   The rate at which large London banks will lend funds to each other in Eurodollars.

Louvre Accord   Another name for the Paris Pact.

low-context cultures   Cultures in which most information is conveyed explicitly rather than through behavioral and environmental nuances.

Maastricht Treaty   The agreement signed in December 1991 in Maastricht, the Netherlands, in which European Community members agreed to a specific timetable and set of necessary conditions to create a single currency for the EU countries by the end of this century.

macroeconomic approach   An approach concerned with total output, income, and employment; an approach to accounting that gives government officials the information they need to take an active role in managing the economy, as occurs in centrally planned economies.

macroeconomic level   Level at which trading relationships affect individual markets.

management contract   An international business alternative in which the firm sells its expertise in running a company while avoiding the risk or benefit of ownership.

managerial commitment   The desire and drive on the part of management to act on an idea and to support it in the long run.

maquiladoras   Mexican border plants that make goods and parts or process food for export back to the United States. They benefit from lower labor costs.

market-differentiated pricing   Price-setting strategy based on demand rather than cost.

market imperfections   Depart from the strict assumptions of competitive economic theory; rationale for government intervention; for example, market gaps in long-term, high-volume export financing.

market seekers   Firms basing their growth strategy on better opportunities in foreign markets.

market transparency   Availability of full disclosure and information about key market factors such as supply, demand, quality, service, and prices.

marketing infrastructure   Facilitating marketing agencies in a country; for example, market research firms, channel members.

materials management   The timely movement of raw materials, parts, and supplies into and through the firm.

matrix structure   An organizational structure that uses functional and divisional structures simultaneously.

media strategy   Strategy applied to the selection of media vehicles and the development of a media schedule.

mercantilism   Political and economic policy in the 17th and early 18th centuries aimed at increasing a nation's wealth and power by encouraging the export of goods in return for gold.

merchandise trade   An account of the BOP statement that records funds used for merchandise imports and funds obtained from merchandise exports.

microeconomic level   Level of business concerns that affect an individual firm or industry.

minority participation   Participation by a group having less than the number of votes necessary for control.

mixed aid credits   Credits at rates composed partially of commercial interest rates and partially of highly subsidized developmental aid interest rates.

mixed structure   An organizational structure that combines two or more organizational dimensions; for example, products, areas, or functions.

money market hedge   The international equivalent of selling accounts receivable. A firm may wish to avoid currency risk by selling at a discount the foreign currency denominated receivable today to obtain the money now, eliminating the exposure.

Most-Favored Nation (MFN)   A term describing a GATT clause that calls for member countries to grant other member countries the most favorable treatment they accord any country concerning imports and exports.

multilateral negotiations   Negotiations carried out among a number of countries.

multilateral netting   The process of settling only the net difference in payments between units of a multinational firm.

multilateral trade negotiations   Trade negotiations among more than two parties; the intricate relationships among trading countries.

multinational corporations   Companies that invest in countries around the globe.

multiple factor indexes   Indexes that measure market potential indirectly by using proxy variables.

national security   The ability of a nation to protect its internal values from external threats.

national sovereignty   The supreme right of nations to determine national policies; freedom from external control.

natural hedging   The structuring of a firm's operations so that cash flows by currency, inflows against outflows, are matched.

net present value (NPV)   The sum of the present values of all cash inflows and outflows from an investment project discounted at the cost of capital.

netting   Cash flow coordination between a corporation's global units so that only one smaller cash transfer must be made.

1992 White Paper   A key document developed by the EC Commission to outline the further requirements necessary for a successful integration of the European Union.

nonfinancial incentives   Nonmonetary offers intended to motivate; special offers designed to attract foreign direct investors that may take the form of guaranteed government purchases, special protection from competition, or improved infrastructure facilities.

nontariff barriers   Barriers to trade, other than tariffs. Examples include buy-domestic campaigns, preferential treatment for domestic bidders, and restrictions on market entry of foreign products such as involved inspection procedures.

not-invented-here syndrome   A defensive, territorial attitude that, if held by managers, can frustrate effective implementation of global strategies.

observation   A research tool where the subjects' activity and behavior is observed.

ocean shipping   The forwarding of freight by ocean carrier.

official reserves account   An account in the BOP statement that shows (1) the change in the amount of funds immediately available to a country for making international payments and (2) the borrowing and lending that has taken place between the monetary authorities of different countries either directly or through the International Monetary Fund.

official settlements balance   A summary measure of a country's Balance of Payments which is the sum of the current account, long-term and short-term capital accounts, and the net balance on errors and omissions.

offset   A form of barter arrangement designed to reduce the Balance of Payment effect of an international transaction. Usually calls for portions of a purchased product to be produced or assembled in the purchasing country; may take the form of coproduction, licensing, subcontracting, or joint venture; mostly used in the context of military sales.

offshore banking   The use of banks or bank branches located in low-tax countries, often Caribbean islands, to raise and hold capital for multinational operations.

open account   A type of trade credit that allows buyers to purchase goods or services and pay for them within a specified period of time without charges or interest.

operating cash flows   The cash flows arising from the firm's everyday business activities.

operating or service lease   A lease that transfers most but not all benefits and costs inherent in the ownership of the property to the lessee. Payments do not fully cover the cost of purchasing the asset or incurring the liability.

operating risk   The danger of interference by governments or other groups in one's corporate operations abroad.

opportunity cost   Cost incurred by a firm as the result of foreclosure of other sources of profit; for example, for the licenser in a licensing agreement, the cost of for going alternatives such as exports or direct investment.

order cycle time   The total time that passes between the placement of an order and the receipt of the merchandise.

orientation program   A program that familiarizes new workers with their roles; the preparation of employees for assignment overseas.

Overseas Private Investment Corporation   A federal agency that provides insurance to U.S. direct foreign investors.

ownership risk   The risk inherent in maintaining ownership of property abroad. The exposure of foreign owned assets to governmental intervention.

par value   The face value of a financial instrument.

parallel barter   Another term for counterpurchase.

Paris Convention for the Protection of Industrial Property   An agreement among 96 countries to set minimum standards of protection for patents, designs, and trademarks.

Paris Pact   Agreements reached in 1987 by the Group of Five plus Canada to cooperate closely to foster stability of exchange rates.

patent   A government grant to an inventor providing an exclusive right to the invention for 17 years.

pax Americana   An American peace between 1945 through 1990 that led to increased international business transactions.

pax Romana   Two relatively peaceful centuries in the Roman Empire.

pegging   Establishing and maintaining a par value for a currency; usually by linking its value to another currency.

pension liabilities   The accumulating obligations of employers to fund the retirement or pension plans of employees.

perestroika   A movement to fundamentally reform the Soviet economy by improving the overall technological and industrial base and the quality of life for Soviet citizens through increased availability of food, housing, and consumer goods.

perishability   Susceptibility to deterioration; the characteristic of services that makes them difficult to inventory.

physical distribution   The movement of finished products to customers.

Plaza Agreement   An accord reached in 1985 by the Group of Five that held that the major nations should join in a coordinated effort to bring down the value of the U.S. dollar.

political risk   The risk of loss by an international corporation of assets, earning power, or managerial control as a result of political actions by the host country.

polycentric   Tending to regard each culture as a separate entity; tending to be oriented toward individual foreign markets.

population growth   The effect of changes in countries' populations on economic matters.

portfolio investment   An account in the BOP statement that records investments in assets with an original maturity of more than one year and where an investor's ownership position is less than 10 percent.

ports   Harbor towns or cities where ships may take on or discharge cargo; the lack of ports and port services is the greatest constraint in ocean shipping.

positioning   The perception by consumers of a firm's product in relation to competitors' products.

preferential policies   Government policies that favor certain (usually domestic) firms; for example, the use of national carriers for the transport of government freight even when more economical alternatives exist.

price controls   Government regulation of the prices of goods and services; control of the prices of imported goods or services as a result of domestic political pressures.

price escalation   The establishing of export prices far in excess of domestic prices—often due to a long distribution channel and frequent markups.

primary data   Data obtained directly for a specific research purpose through interviews, focus groups, surveys, observation, or experimentation.

private placement   The sale of debt securities to private or institutional investors without going through a public issuance like that of a bond issue or equity issue.

privatization   A policy of shifting operation of government operations to privately owned enterprises to cut budget costs and ensure more efficient services.

process structure   A variation of the functional structure in which departments are formed on the basis of production processes.

product cycle theory   A theory that views products as passing through four stages: introduction, growth, maturity, decline; during which the location of production moves from industrialized to lower-cost developing nations.

product differentiation   The effort to build unique differences or improvements into products.

product structure   An organizational structure in which product divisions are responsible for all manufacturing and marketing.

production possibilities frontier   A theoretical method of representing the total productive capabilities of a nation used in the formulation of classical and modern trade theory.

promotional message   The content of an advertisement or a publicity release.

proxy information   Data used as a substitute for more desirable data that are unobtainable.

punitive tariff   A tax on an imported good or service intended to punish a trading partner.

purchasing power parity (PPP)   A theory that the prices of tradable goods will tend to equalize across countries.

quality circles   Groups of workers who meet regularly to discuss issues related to productivity.

quality of life   The standard of living combined with environmental factors, it determines the level of well-being of individuals.

quality of work life   Various corporate efforts in the areas of personal and professional development undertaken with the objectives of increasing employee satisfaction and increasing productivity.

quotas   Legal restrictions on the import quantity of particular goods, imposed by governments as barriers to trade.

R&D cost   Research and development cost; the costs incurred in developing technology.

real returns   The rate of return after adjusting for inflation.

reciprocity provisions   Provisions for the purchase of goods on a preferential basis with the expectation that the seller will in turn buy on a preferential basis.

recognizability   The characteristic of appearing to be previously known; the ability of a product to be recognized even though it has been adapted to local market conditions.

reference groups   Groups such as the family, coworkers, and professional and trade associations that provide the values and attitudes that influence and shape behavior, including consumer behavior.

reference zone   Another name for a managed float.

regiocentric   Tending to be oriented toward regions larger than individual countries as markets.

reinvoicing   The policy of buying goods from one unit and selling them to a second unit and reinvoicing the sale to the next unit, to take advantage of favorable exchange rates.

reliability   Dependability; the predictability of the outcome of an action. For example, the reliability of arrival time for ocean freight or airfreight.

representative office   An office of an international bank established in a foreign country to serve the bank's customers in the area in an advisory capacity; does not take deposits or make loans.

resource seekers   Firms looking for either natural or human resources.

reverse distribution   A system responding to environmental concerns that ensures a firm can retrieve a product from the market for subsequent use, recycling, or disposal.

roll-on-roll-off (RORO)   Transportation vessels built to accommodate trucks, which can drive on in one port and drive off at their destinations.

royalty   The compensation paid by one firm to another under an agreement.

rules of the game   An expression symbolizing the unwritten rules of the gold standard—a country will allow gold to flow in and out in order to preserve currency values versus gold.

safe haven   The role played by the U.S. dollar as a currency which international investors may flock to during times of international crisis. The Japanese yen, however, is increasingly replacing the U.S. dollar as a safe haven.

sanction   A governmental action, usually consisting of a specific coercive trade measure, that distorts the free flow of trade for an adversarial or political purpose rather than an economic one.

scenario building   The identification of crucial variables and determining their effects on different cases or approaches.

sea bridge   The transfer of freight among various modes of transportation at sea.

secondary data   Data originally collected to serve another purpose than the one in which the researcher is currently interested.

securitization   The conversion of developing country bank debt into tradable securities.

self-management   Independent decision making; a high degree of worker involvement in corporate decision making.

self-reference criterion   The unconscious reference to one's own cultural values.

selling forward   A market transaction in which the seller promises to sell currency at a certain future date at a prespecified price.

sensitivity training   Training in human relations that focuses on personal and interpersonal interactions; training that focuses on enhancing an expatriate's flexibility in situations quite different from those at home.

service capacity   The maximum level at which a service provider is able to provide services to customers.

service consistency   Uniform quality of service.

service trade   The international exchange of personal or professional services, such as financial and banking services, construction, and tourism.

shipper's order   A negotiable bill of lading that can be bought, sold, or traded while the subject goods are still in transit and that is used for letter of credit transactions.

Single Europe Act   The legislative basis for the European Integration.

Smithsonian Agreement   An agreement reached by the Group of Ten in 1971 concerning changes in the Bretton Woods Agreement on currency values.

Smoot-Hawley Act   A 1930 act that raised import duties to the highest rates ever imposed by the United States; designed to promote domestic production, it resulted in the downfall of the world trading system.

social infrastructure   The housing, health, educational, and other social systems in a country.

social stratification   The division of a particular population into classes.

sogoshosha   A large Japanese general trading company.

Special Drawing Right (SDR)   International reserves created by the IMF to support growth in international trade and investment; essentially, a currency used only in transactions among central banks.

specie   Gold and silver.

spot rates   Contracts that provide for two parties to exchange currencies with delivery in two business days.

spread   The difference between two amounts; a bank's profit on foreign exchange trading.

standard of living   The level of material affluence of a group or nation, measured as a composite of quantities and qualities of goods.

standard worldwide pricing   Price-setting strategy based on average unit costs of fixed, variable, and export-related costs.

state-owned enterprise   A corporate form that has emerged in non-Communist countries, primarily for reasons of national security and economic security.

straight bill of lading   A nonnegotiable bill of lading usually used in prepaid transactions in which the transported goods involved are delivered to a specific individual or company.

strategic alliances   A new term for collaboration among firms, often similar to joint ventures.

strategic leader   A highly competent firm located in a strategically critical market.

Subpart F income   Passive income as defined by the Tax Reform Act of 1986.

Subsidies and Countervailing Measures Code   An agreement reached during the Tokyo Round of negotiations that seeks to reduce the distortive effects of export subsidies on world trade.

surveys   Typically, the use of questionnaires to quantify concepts.

switch-trading   A refinement of clearing account barter in which credits and debits can be sold or transferred to a third party.

syndicated loan   A loan which is arranged and managed by a small group of 2 to 5 banks and then sold in pieces to other banking institutions worldwide.

systems concept   A concept of logistics based on the notion that materials-flow activities are so complex that they can be considered only in the context of their interaction.

tariffs   Taxes on imported goods and services, instituted by governments as a means to raise revenue and as barriers to trade.

tax equalization   Reimbursement by the company when an employee in an overseas assignment pays taxes at a higher rate than if he or she were at home.

tax policy   A means by which countries may control foreign investors.

team building   A process that enhances the cohesiveness of a department or group by helping members learn how to organize their work and assume responsibility for it.

technology transfer   The transfer of systematic knowledge for the manufacture of a product, the application of a process, or the rendering of a service.

temporal method   A method for translating the financial statements of a foreign subsidiary from the host country's currency to the functional currency.

"Tentative U.S. tax"   The calculation of U.S. taxes on foreign source incomes to estimate U.S. tax payments.

Tokyo Round   One of a series of trade conferences sponsored by the General Agreement on Tariffs and Trade.

total after-tax profit concept   A decision concept that takes into account the impact of national tax policies on the logistics function.

total cost concept   A decision concept that uses cost as a basis for measurement in order to evaluate and optimize logistical activities.

Trade Act of 1974   An act that, among other provisions, expanded the definition of international trade to include trade in services.

trade creation   A benefit of economic integration; the benefit to a particular country when a group of countries trade a product freely among themselves but maintain common barriers to trade with nonmembers.

trade diversion   A cost of economic integration; the cost to a particular country when a group of countries trade a product freely among themselves but maintain common barriers to trade with nonmembers.

trade draft   A withdrawal document drawn against a company.

trade-off concept   A decision concept that recognizes linkages within the decision system.

trade policy mechanisms   Measures used to influence and alter trade relationships.

trademark   The distinctive identification of a product or service in the form of a name, symbol, letter, picture, or other device to distinguish it from similar offerings.

trademark licensing   A special form of licensing that permits the names or logos of recognizable individuals or groups to be used on products.

trading blocks   Formed by agreements among countries to establish links through movement of goods, services, capital, and labor across borders.

tramp service   Ocean shipping via irregular routes, scheduled only on demand.

transaction exposure   The potential for losses or gains when a firm is engaged in a transaction denominated in a foreign currency.

transfer cost   All variable costs incurred in transferring technology to a licensee and all ongoing costs of maintaining the licensing agreement.

transfer prices   The prices at which a firm sells its products to its own subsidiaries and affiliates.

transfer risk   The danger of having one's ability to transfer profits or products in and out of a country inhibited by governmental rules and regulations.

transit time   The period between departure and arrival of a carrier.

translation exposure   The potential effect on a firm's financial statements of a change in currency values.

transportation modes   Forms of transportation.

Treaty of Rome   The original agreement that established the foundation for the formation of the European Economic Community.

triangular arbitrage   The exchange of one currency for a second currency, the second for a third, and the third for the first in order to make a profit.

trigger mechanisms   Specific acts or stimuli that set off reactions.

tunnel   A term describing the 1971 Smithsonian Agreement's allowance of a 2 1/4 percent variation from par value for currency exchange rates.

turnkey operation   A specialized form of management contract between a customer and an organization to provide a complete operational system together with the skills investment needed for unassisted maintenance and operation.

undistributed earnings   The proportion of a firm's net income after taxes which is retained within the firm for internal purposes.

uniform accounting   A system of accounting that follows uniform standards prescribed by law, as in Germany and France.

unilateral transfer   A current account on the Balance of Payments statement that records gifts from the residents of one country to the residents of another.

United States Trade Representative   A U.S. cabinet position responsible for the area of trade negotiations, as designated in the Trade Act of 1979.

validated export license   An export license from the Department of Commerce that authorizes shipment of a high-technology product.

value-added tax (VAT)   A tax on the value added at each stage of the production and distribution process; a tax assessed in most European countries and also common among Latin American countries.

voluntary agreements   Trade-restraint agreements resulting in self-imposed restrictions not covered by the GATT rules; used to manage or distort trade flows. For example, Japanese restraints on the export of cars to the United States.

Webb-Pomerene Act   A 1918 statute that excludes from antitrust prosecution U.S. firms cooperating to develop foreign markets.

Webb-Pomerene association   A group of U.S. firms cooperating to develop foreign markets, as permitted by the Webb-Pomerene Act.

withholding taxes   Taxes applied to the payment of dividends, interest, or royalties by firms.

work councils   Councils that provide labor a say in corporate decision making through a representative body that may consist entirely of workers or of a combination of managers and workers.

work redesign programs   Programs that alter jobs to increase both the quality of the work experience and productivity.

work scheduling   Preparing schedules of when and how long workers are at the workplace.

working capital management   The management of a firm's current assets (cash, accounts receivable, inventories) and current liabilities (accounts payable, short-term debt).

World Bank   An international financial institution created to facilitate trade.

World Trade Organization   The institution that supplanted GATT in 1995 to administer international trade and investment accords.

Name Index

Subject Index